Introduction To Paralegal Studies and the Law:
A Practical Approach

The West Legal Studies Series

Your options keep growing with West Legal Studies
Each year our list continues to offer you more options for every area of the law to meet your course or on-the-job reference requirements. We now have over 140 titles from which to choose in the following areas:

Administrative Law	Family Law
Alternative Dispute Resolution	Federal Taxation
Bankruptcy	Intellectual Property
Business Organizations/Corporations	Introduction to Law
Civil Litigation and Procedure	Introduction to Paralegalism
CLA Exam Preparation	Law Office Management
Client Accounting	Law Office Procedures
Computer in the Law Office	Legal Research, Writing, and Analysis
Constitutional Law	Legal Terminology
Contract Law	Paralegal Employment
Criminal Law and Procedure	Real Estate Law
Document Preparation	Reference Materials
Environmental Law	Torts and Personal Injury Law
Ethics	Will, Trusts, and Estate Administration

You will find unparalleled, practical support
Each book is augmented by instructor and student supplements to ensure the best learning experience possible. We also offer custom publishing and other benefits such as West's Student Achievement Award. In addition, our sales representatives are ready to provide you with dependable service.

We want to hear from you
Our best contributions for improving the quality of our books and instructional materials is feedback from the people who use them. If you have a question, concern, or observation about any of our materials, or you have a product proposal or manuscript, we want to hear from you. Please contact your local representative or write us at the following address:

West Legal Studies, 3 Columbia Circle, P.O. Box 15015, Albany, NY 12212-5015

For additional information point your browser at
www.westlegalstudies.com

WEST
THOMSON LEARNING

Introduction To Paralegal Studies and the Law:
A Practical Approach

Linda L. Edwards, J.D., Ph.D.

J. Stanley Edwards, J.D.

WEST

THOMSON LEARNING

Australia Canada Mexico Singapore Spain United Kingdom United States

WEST

THOMSON LEARNING

WEST LEGAL STUDIES

Introduction to Paralegal Studies and the Law: A Practical Approach
by Linda L. Edwards and J. Stanley Edwards

Business Unit Director:
Susan L. Simpfenderfer

Executive Editor:
Marlene McHugh Pratt

Acquisitions Editor:
Joan M. Gill

Developmental Editor:
Rhonda Dearborn

Editorial Assistant:
Lisa Flatley

Executive Production Manager:
Wendy A. Troeger

Production Manager:
Carolyn Miller

Cover Image:
©1999 COMSTOCK, Inc.

Executive Marketing Manager:
Donna J. Lewis

Channel Manager:
Nigar Hale

Library of Congress Cataloging-in-Publication Data

Edwards, Linda L.
    Introduction to paralegal studies and law: a
practical approach / Linda L. Edwards, J. Stanley
Edwards.
        p. cm.
    "West Legal Studies series."
    Includes bibliographical references and index.
    ISBN 0-7668-3589-8
    1. Legal assistants—United States.
    2. Law—Vocational guidance—United States.
    I. Title: Paralegal studies and the law. II. Edwards,
J. Stanley. III. Title.

KF320.L4E39 2001
340'.023'73—dc21   2001026527

NOTICE TO THE READER

*We dedicate this book to all the students we have had in
our Introduction to Law classes and, in particular, to one
of our most memorable classes: the Introduction to Law class
in the fall semester of 1989. They were bright, personable, dedicated,
diligent, fun, and funny. Wherever you are and whatever you are
doing, we salute you. Mary, Vicky, Faye, Gunn, Burt, and
everyone else: Thanks for the memories!*

Contents

2 Developing the Case 49

RECESS 72

RECESS   149

4   Initiating a Case   203

RECESS   *226*

5   Discovery and Motion Practice   275

RECESS　　　　　　　　　　　　　　　　　　　　　*298*

7 Criminal Law and Procedure 405

RECESS 427

8   Alternative Dispute Resolution (ADR), Tribal Court Advocacy and Administrative Law   473

RECESS 491

9 Business Law 525

RECESS	**552**

10   Family Law

RECESS   *613*

11   Real Estate and Probate Law   639

RECESS

Table of Cases

PURPOSE OF TEXT

No text is better than the extent to which it is read. It can have all of the pedagogical "bells and whistles," be astutely researched, and steeped in academic traditions, but if students are not motivated to read it, all of its attributes are for naught.

With that in mind, this book is intended to be—first and foremost—a book that students will find stimulating to read, that will draw them into the content, and that will excite them about the paralegal career they have chosen to explore. Toward that end, a story line, written in the form of a mini-novel, winds through each chapter, serving as the connecting thread that links each concept to the next. In the style of the "cliffhangers" characteristic of televised series, each chapter ends with unanswered questions that prompt the reader to move to the next chapter to find resolution. Although numerous texts use hypotheticals to illustrate concepts and even carry those hypos from chapter to chapter, this text is unique in that the characters are fleshed out with personalities and desires that make them real.

A second purpose of the book is to provide students with practical information and guidance. More attention is given to discussion of the procedural aspects of paralegal practice than is typically offered in introductory texts. The authors deliberately emphasize the "how-to"s of paralegal practice as a result of over twenty years of teaching experience. During this time, they discovered that students who are well-versed in the mechanics of the legal profession fare better in the work world than those whose knowledge is primarily theoretical. While legal terminology is emphasized and fundamental academic concepts are introduced, students are given considerable information about specific skills, such as calculating deadlines, finding public records, preparing complaints and answers, interviewing, drafting motions and memoranda, digesting depositions, and billing. Students who read this text should come away with a clear idea of many of the tasks they will be expected to perform as paralegals.

A third purpose of this text is to introduce students to fundamental concepts in substantive law. Tort law is introduced in the context of the story line that runs through chapters 1 through 6. A domestic relations situation, which involved one of the key characters, serves as the context for ADR (Chapter 8), family law (Chapter 10), real estate law (Chapter 11), and probate (Chapter 11). A separate business law problem is used to introduce contract law and the law of business organizations (Chapter 9). To help students better understand the differences between the civil and criminal systems, criminal law is presented from the viewpoint of one of the lead characters. While most texts portray the criminal justice process from an impersonal, clinical perspective, having a former defendant relate his experiences personalizes the process and helps students appreciate the purpose and significance of criminal procedures and constitutional safeguards. Administrative law (Chapter 8) also relates to the criminal law problem. Although none of these tangential story lines is as fully developed as the primary plot that drives Chapters 1 through 6, they continue to serve as the unifying thread that connects the substantive law principles and concepts in each chapter.

A fourth function of this book is to give students an opportunity to put into practice the major concepts to which they have been exposed. Accordingly, exercises are included throughout the text and at the end of each chapter. Some of the exercises merely prompt students to become actively engaged in what they are reading; others stimulate critical thought. A fundamental philosophy of the authors in their own teaching is that students must be challenged and guided to do more than simply regurgitate factual data. This text reflects that philosophy in its inclusion of both concepts and pedagogy that require comparison, application of information, and critical analysis.

A final function this book serves is providing technologically relevant information. Internet links to relevant Web sites are included throughout the text, encouraging students to find additional information. Some of these sites will provide students with information not included in the text, and others will familiarize them with organizations (such as NALA and NFPA) and associations (such as their local and state bar associations) and assist them in doing research projects in the future. At the end of each chapter are exercises that require students to use the Internet.

ORGANIZATION OF TEXT

The most unique and powerful aspect of this book is its story-line format. Many books use hypotheticals to illustrate concepts and some books even have an ongoing hypothetical that weaves throughout the presentation of content, but this book is (to our knowledge) one of a kind in that it *organizes the content around the story line*. To accommodate this story line, the organization of information is somewhat atypical, but it follows a logical progression. In fact, faculty who choose to ignore the story can use the content outline as a basis for organizing their lectures.

The story itself is compelling to read because it involves a dramatic unfolding of events: the campus shooting of a high school football hero for mysterious reasons. The legal questions that arise out of this shooting are intriguing and as yet unresolved by the courts, making the debate about how they should be answered more interesting to students.

We believe that this story-telling approach to conveying legal information is more effective than the more conventional and pedantic style found in other texts. What is the basis for this belief?

Pedagogical theory tells us that people learn by connecting what they do not know to what they already know. This is why analogies are such powerful teaching tools. When people are given a context (e.g., a story) in which to assimilate and organize information, they find it easier to incorporate new ideas than when these ideas are presented in a purely abstract format. The intense media coverage of the electoral battle for the White House in 2000 is a prime example. Having an almost voyeuristic perspective of the Florida circuit trials and the Florida and United States Supreme Courts oral arguments undoubtedly gave students studying judicial discretion, the court system, and the appellate process a more visceral and realistic understanding than those students who dutifully committed these concepts to memory after reading them in a textbook.

Stories are a traditional way of passing on information from one generation to another. In thinking back to the teachers who most inspired and motivated us, many of us will remember those teachers who regaled us with stories. Certainly, every culture's tradition of myths, parables, and fairy tales point to the power of teaching within the context of stories.

People learn best when they are motivated to learn. Stories, especially those that are plausible and that grab us at some emotional level, motivate us to read on. Like the proverbial candy-coated medicine, stories help students digest information they might otherwise find unpalatable.

Many of today's students have grown up in a media-rich environment that revolves around the telling of stories, and they respond favorably to any presentation that is entertaining. Although some students may never be enraptured with reading, they are more likely to endure the rigors of reading a textbook if they find it entertaining.

Another consideration that guides the organization of this text is its inherently practical approach to presenting information. Concepts are introduced as they would be presented to someone apprenticing in a law office. The reader is taken from the introduction of the client to the final collection of the judgment in the chronology that would normally occur in litigation. Along the way, all of the practical tasks requisite to legal practice—such as docketing timelines, office politics, setting up and organizing files, timekeeping, and asset assessment—are considered. Strategic decisions are also explored as they arise naturally before suit is filed, in the discovery process, motion practice, trial, judgment collection, and the appeal process.

FEATURES OF TEXT

This is a student-friendly text. Pedagogical tools abound to assist the student in acquiring information and in carrying out continual self-assessments. Several features are included in each chapter that are designed to assist students in fully and easily assimilating concepts and to facilitate faculty in clearly and imaginatively presenting information.

NET NEWS

These links to a wide variety of Web sites are liberally sprinkled throughout the text. Some of these links acquaint students with the more commonly used sites, such as *findlaw.com* and the Legal Information Institute (*www.law.cornell.edu*); some provide sample documents and explain procedures; others provide links to federal or state agencies; still others give students an opportunity to have incredible virtual experiences (such as taking a tour of the U.S. Supreme Court).

INTERNET WARNING:

Please remember that Web addresses change frequently, Web sites can undergo construction, and Web pages can simply disappear. For these reasons, the links that are valid at the time of publication may not be valid by the time they are visited by students. If students find a Web address that appears to have changed, they can try shortening the Web address by deleting everything after the last slash mark. For example, they can take

www.law.cornell.edu/uniform.probate.html and shorten it to *www.law.cornell.edu/uniform/*.

If they still get an error message, they can shorten it again to *www.law.cornell.edu.*

This will take them to the home page unless the site has gone down or moved. If the site has moved, they might still be able to find it by running a search under the site's name (in this case, Legal Information Institute).

PUTTING IT INTO PRACTICE EXERCISES

These exercises are interspersed throughout the chapters. They require students to interact with the text by immediately thinking about and applying the information they have just read. Students who use these exercises cannot be passive readers. Suggested responses are included in the Appendix so that students get immediate feedback.

LOCAL LINKS

These prompt students and faculty to consider the rules and practices unique to their jurisdiction. While the text is necessarily generic, these inquiries allow faculty to explain the procedures and terms used in their locale. Space is provided to record this important data so students can easily refer to it in the future.

BONUS POINTERS

Additional information is provided for those students and faculty who want that little bit of additional knowledge. Faculty can instruct students to omit any and all Bonus Pointers they consider superfluous or irrelevant. Questions in the Practice Exam that come from the Bonus Pointers are starred so that they can be omitted if desired.

ETHICAL ETIQUETTE

Ethical issues are discussed in the context in which they normally occur rather than segregated in a separate chapter. These highlighted sections allow faculty to emphasize important ethical rules as they arise in the story line.

TIM'S TECHNO TIPS

Computer literacy is a must for today's paralegal. A separate section at the end of each chapter addresses key technological developments apropos to the subject matter in that chapter. The discussion is basic and designed to familiarize students with fundamental terminology, hardware, and software. At the end of each tip is a section entitled "Techno Trip" that contains questions that require students to either apply what they have just read or search for additional information. Several of these exercises require use of the Internet.

CASE LAW

In each of the chapters discussing substantive law (as well as the research chapter), an edited case is included that illustrates one of the concepts presented in that section. The questions that follow each case are designed to lead students step-by-step through the case, prompting them to recognize the most important details and helping them to analyze the case.

PRACTICE EXAM, REVIEW QUESTIONS, CHAPTER SUMMARY, AND KEY TERMS

Each chapter is divided in half. The chapters are organized in relation to broad topics in the law, requiring them to be fairly long. Because some faculty and students prefer dealing with material in smaller chunks, a "recess" has been instituted halfway through each chapter. At this "recess," those who choose to can use a practice test, a list of key terms, a chapter summary, and some overview questions

to review the material that has been covered up to this point. While these features cover only those concepts covered in half of the chapter, the features described below cover all of the concepts and vocabulary used in the entire chapter. Answers to the Practice Exams are included in the Appendix so that students can check their own answers.

INTERNET INQUIRIES

Searching the Internet is the best way to build confidence and become familiar with what is available. These exercises provide some structure to that search. Some of these exercises are fairly structured means of familiarizing students with particular Web sites, whereas other exercises are more exploratory in nature, encouraging students to discover and report what they find. Students are encouraged to put their answers in the book. This way they have a permanent record of Web sites they have found and the steps they followed in finding those Web sites.

LEGAL LINGO

Mastery of legal terminology is a goal of any introductory course. Students are given an opportunity to practice the appropriate use of vocabulary using game formats, such as crossword puzzles and word scrambles. These games not only provide an interesting way to utilize newly acquired vocabulary skills, but also emphasize proper spelling.

LEGAL LOGISTICS

This section includes questions that require students to assimilate information they have learned throughout the chapter (sometimes incorporating concepts discussed in previous chapters). These questions are more provocative than those in the Practice Exams and necessitate integration of knowledge. They could easily serve as the basis for class discussion.

A TRIP TO THE MOVIES

Because many of today's students have grown up on television, videos, and movies, they are accustomed to processing information visually. Furthermore, the media have created stories that have become common ground for peoples of all generations, backgrounds, and experiences. Movies form a natural vehicle for the transmission of ideas that transcend what can be captured in the print media.

This section uses movies as a means of putting basic concepts into practice. A variety of movies, ranging from the traditional (*To Kill a Mockingbird*) to the contemporary (*The Insider, A Civil Action,* and *Erin Brockovich*), paint the legal profession in contrasting colors. Having students either watch these movies on video or showing them in class allows them not only to put what they have learned into a realistic context and to implement their recently acquired knowledge, but can also provoke an animated discussion about the legal profession in general.

COURSE OBJECTIVES

Objectives are outlined at the beginning of the chapter to alert the student to the basic coverage of that chapter.

VOCABULARY TERMS IN MARGINS

When terms are first introduced, they are defined in the margins.

HOW TO USE THIS BOOK

Instructors may or may not want to incorporate the story line into their classroom presentations. If the choice is made to follow the story, the dialogue and situations arising out of the story will provide a stimulus for classroom discussion. Is the situation presented in the story and the response of the characters realistic? Would this procedure be followed in your jurisdiction? Of course, the story can also be embellished and further examples can be offered.

Alternatively, an instructor may choose to ignore the story line for purposes of classroom instruction and simply focus on the content in each chapter. No matter which approach is selected, several instructional tools will facilitate content presentation.

The "Local Links" interspersed throughout the chapter alert the instructor to content that is jurisdiction-specific. The text provides information that is generally true (or that is applicable in Arizona, where the story takes place); the instructor can then choose to give students the information that is apropos for their state or region or can assign them to find the information themselves.

"Putting It Into Practice" questions can be assigned or can form the focus of discussion in class. (The answers to these questions are provided in the Appendix so that students can receive immediate feedback as they are reading to see if they are on the right track.)

Assignments or questions can also be generated using the "Net News" sections that indicate Web sites relevant to the content being presented in the chapter. Or the instructor may decide to assign the "Internet Inquiries" at the end of the chapter, which are designed to familiarize students with commonly used law-related Internet sites.

The films mentioned in "A Trip to the Movies" are also likely to generate lively in-class discussion, especially if students are assigned to watch these films outside of class. (Encouraging them to do this as a group will create the side benefit of creating friendships and community that might not otherwise occur naturally.)

The questions posed in the "Legal Logistics" are designed to stimulate students to integrate and apply concepts and go beyond rote memorization. These problems can be assigned for either individual completion or as part of a group project.

Other suggestions for classroom activities can be found in the Instructor's Manual.

ANCILLARY MATERIALS

The Instructor's Manual contains the following.

- ◆ a test bank, based on the questions in the Practice Exams in each chapter
- ◆ answers to Review Questions, Legal Lingo, Legal Logistics, A Trip to the Movies, and Internet Inquiries
- ◆ transparency masters that correlate with the chapters
- ◆ suggested classroom activities
- ◆ lecture outlines

Computerized Test Bank—The Test Bank found in the *Instructor's Manual* is also available in a computerized format on CD-ROM. The platforms supported include Windows 3.1, Windows 95, Windows NT, and Macintosh. Features include:

Multiple methods of question selection
Multiple outputs – that is print, ASCII, RTF
Graphic support (black and white)
Random questioning output
Special character support

Westlaw®—West's online computerized legal-research system offers students "hands-on" experience with a system commonly used in law offices. Qualified adopters can receive ten free hours of Westlaw®. Westlaw® can be accessed with Macintosh and IBM PCs and compatibles. A modem is required.

Citation-At-a-Glance—This handy reference card provides a quick, portable reference to the basic rules of citation for the most commonly cited legal sources, including judicial opinions, statues, and secondary sources. *Citation-At-a-Glance* uses the rules set forth in *The Bluebook: A Uniform System of Citation*. A free copy of this valuable supplement is included with every student text.

Strategies and Tips for Paralegal Educators—Written by Anita Tebbe of Johnson County Community College, provides teaching strategies specifically designed for paralegal educators. A copy of this pamphlet is available to each adopter. Quantities for distribution to adjunct instructors are available for purchase at a minimal price. A coupon in the pamphlet provides ordering information.

Survival Guide for Paralegal Students—Written by Kathleen Mercer and Bradene Moore covers practical and basic information to help students make the most of their paralegal courses. Topics covered include choosing courses of study and note-taking skills.

West's Paralegal Video Library includes:
The following videos are available at no charge to qualified adopters.

The Drama of the Law II: Paralegal Issues Video
I Never Said I Was a Lawyer: Paralegal Issues Video
The Making of a Case: Video
Mock Trials Videos—Anatomy of a Trial: A Contracts Case (Business Litigation)
Mock Trials Videos—Trial Techniques: A Products Liability Case

Court TV Videos—West Legal Studies is pleased to offer the following videos from Court TV. Available for a minimal fee:

New York v. Ferguson–Murder on the 5:33: The Trial of Colin Ferguson
Ohio v. Alfieri–Road Rage
Flynn v. Goldman Sachs–Fired on Wall Street: A Case of Sex Discrimination?
Dodd v. Dodd: Religion and Child Custody in Conflict
Fentress v. Eli Lilly & Co., et al.–Prozac on Trial
In RE Custody of Baby Girl Clausen–Child of Mine: The Fight of Baby Jessica
Garcia v. Garcia
Northside Partners v. Page and New Kids on the Block (Intellectual Property)
Maglica v. Maglica (Contract Law)
Hall v. Hall (Family Law)
Berring Legal Research Videos

ACKNOWLEDGEMENTS

Any understanding we have of the learning process we owe to the thousands of students who have taught us over the years. To them, we extend our heartfelt thanks. We also offer this text as evidence of what we gleaned from their teachings.

We are deeply grateful to Joan Gill, our developmental and acquisitions editor, who has supported us in taking what we know to be a leap of faith. She has believed in us and our academic mission even when we wavered, and has supported us fully every step of the way. We also want to thank her assistant, Lisa Flatley, for her reliable guidance, her willingness to persist until she gets an answer, and her unflappable courtesy. Finally, a special thanks to Carolyn Miller, our production manager, and Mary Jo Graham, our production editor, who have patiently and competently guided us through the final stages of this creative process.

The reviewers for this book have been especially helpful, offering suggestions and prompting us with questions that motivated us to continue revising and seeking better ways to convey ideas. They were invaluable in finding errors and in detecting ambiguities that, left uncorrected, would have detracted from the quality of this text. To them we are very appreciative.

Anthony Piazza
David N. Myers College, OH

Rene Denham
William Rainey Harper College, MD

Catherine Stevens
Charles County Community College, MD

Sharon Lynch Norton
St. John's University, NY

Les Sturdivant Ennis
Cumberland School of Law, AL

Sybil Taylor Aytch
The Weinberger Law Firm, AZ

Brian McCully
Fresno City College, CA

Julia Tryk
Cuyahoga Community College, OH

Wendy Edson
Hilbert College, NY

Nicholas Riggs
Sullivan College, KY

Holly Enterline
State Technical Institute at Memphis, TN

Linda Murphy
Cuyahoga Community College, OH

Stonewall Van Wie
Del Mar College, TX

Chris Whaley
Roane State Community College, TN

Nancy Blazek
Attorney at Law, NY

FEEDBACK

We would very much like to receive your comments, questions, and suggestions in reference to this text, especially in regard to its unique features and approach to presenting the material. Please feel free to contact us at linda.edwards@azbar.org.

ABOUT THE AUTHORS

LINDA L. EDWARDS, J.D., Ph.D.

Presently, Dr. Edwards is an attorney in Springerville, Arizona. Recently retired from teaching, Linda was an instructor in the Justice and Legal Studies Department at Phoenix College for over 24 years. She has served as both program director of the Legal Assisting Program and department chairperson. As program director, she was actively involved in getting the Legal Assisting Program approved by the American Bar Association. During her tenure, Linda has created dozens of new classes in both legal assisting and criminal justice and is well-known for her innovations in the field of education. An individual of many interests, Linda's B.S. is in Chemistry, her M.S. in Criminal Justice, and her Ph.D. in Holistic Healing; she is also a certified homeopath, Bowen therapist, and Edu-K practitioner. Linda and Stan have also just created one of the first, accredited, fully online legal assisting programs. The program's first host is Arizona's Northland Pioneer College. Linda is author of five other books, *Tort Law for Legal Assistants, 2E, Practical Case Analysis, Civil Procedure and Litigation: A Practical Approach, Guide to Factual Investigations* and *Introduction to Paralegal Studies: A Practical Approach.*

J. STANLEY EDWARDS, J.D.

Stan Edwards has been a sole practitioner for over 22 years after a brief stint as associate patent counsel for Honeywell, Inc. He has offices in Cave Creek and Springerville, Arizona. Stan's initial career was as a digital design engineer with a bachelors degree in electrical engineering. He has a general litigation practice and has tried numerous cases to juries. Stan is a *judge pro tempore* for the Maricopa County Superior Court and a certified arbitrator for the U.S. District Court for Arizona. Stan has twice been named volunteer lawyer of the month by the Maricopa County Bar Association. Stan is co-author with Linda of *Tort Law for Legal Assistants, 2E, Civil Procedure and Litigation: A Practical Approach, Guide to Factual Investigations,* and *Introduction to Paralegal Studies: A Practical Approach.*

1

Introduction to Paralegalism
As a Profession

OBJECTIVES: _____

In this chapter you will learn:

- ◆ what a paralegal is
- ◆ how paralegals are employed
- ◆ what paralegal associations support paralegals
- ◆ what types of paralegal education are available
- ◆ the steps to be taken in getting a paralegal job
- ◆ the difference between certification and licensure
- ◆ what constitutes the unauthorized practice of law

- ◆ the qualities of a successful paralegal
- ◆ how law offices are organized
- ◆ what ethical codes govern attorneys and affect paralegals
- ◆ the ethical rules regarding solicitation and advertising

"Is This What Being a Paralegal Boils Down To?"

Words of protest rose up in Martha's throat, but she choked them back. "No problem, Ms. Copple. I'll get those copies made right away." But inwardly, she complained, "I can't endure this another day. If I have to spend one more hour in front of that blasted copy machine, I think I'll lose my mind." Resolutely, she planted herself in front of her nemesis and braced herself for hours of monotony. "So this is what I endured four years of night school for, " she muttered to herself. "Is this what being a paralegal boils down to? Am I nothing but a glorified copy girl?"

DEFINITIONS OF PARALEGAL

paralegal or legal assistants
a paraprofessional who is qualified by education, training, or experience to do work of a legal nature under the supervision of an attorney. The terms *paralegal* and *legal assistant* are synonymous; we have chosen to use the word *paralegal* throughout this text for the sake of consistency.

The American Bar Association (ABA) defines **paralegals** or **legal assistants** as persons qualified by education, training or work experience who are employed or retained by a lawyer, law office, corporation, governmental agency or other entity who perform specifically designated substantive legal work for which a lawyer is responsible.

Paralegal professional associations, such as the National Association of Legal Assistants (NALA) and the National Federation of Paralegal Associations (NFPA), which will be discussed later in this chapter, take exception to parts of the above definition and have developed their own (see Figure 1-1 for their definitions).

Generally speaking, someone becomes a paralegal by experience or training. Because no law yet defines what a paralegal is or sets forth any licensing requirements, individuals can theoretically become paralegals simply by declaring themselves so. In reality, however, employers seek out paralegals who are appropriately educated and trained.

Although several definitions of paralegal exist, all describe paralegals as those who perform the same tasks carried out by attorneys, but who do so under the supervision of an attorney. Paralegals are not authorized to practice law in that they cannot give legal opinions, prepare legal documents (unless supervised by

---

NET NEWS

To see NALA's definition, go to *www.nalanet.org* and click on "What Is a Paralegal?" Look under the opening section "Background and Definition," and click on the link entitled "Summary of Definitions of Terms 'Paralegal' and 'Legal Assistant'." This article will introduce you to not only NALA's definition of *paralegal,* but to the definitions developed in various states and by a number of courts. For another review of how some legislatures and bar associations have defined *paralegal,* go to NFPA's Web page (*www.paralegals.org/reporter*), go to the "1998 Year-End Edition," and click on the article "Who Are You?" You will find NFPA's, NALA's, and ABA's definitions of *paralegal* and *legal assistant* in the section "One Side Makes You Taller."

---

legal technicians   a layperson who provides legal services directly to the public. Some use this term to indicate an independent paralegal, that is, someone who is trained to be a paralegal but who works independently.

lay advocates   a layperson who represents individuals at administrative hearings in administrative agencies that permit lay representation.

◆ **LOCAL LINKS** ◆

What position do the local and state bar associations in your jurisdiction take on the use of the terms *paralegal* and *legal assistant?*

---

attorney), represent clients in most judicial proceedings (an exception exists for certain types of administrative hearings), set fees, create attorney-client relationships, or perform any number of other legal functions. Paralegals should be distinguished from legal technicians and lay advocates, both of whom work without the supervision of an attorney. **Legal technicians** provide legal services directly to the public. Because they do so without being under an attorney's supervision, they are frequently the butt of unauthorized practice of law allegations. **Lay advocates** represent individuals at administrative hearings and are limited to working within the procedural confines of an administrative agency that permits lay representation. Legal services may also be provided by a secretarial service that prepares standardized legal documents for people representing themselves in court. These service providers are less likely than legal technicians to be accused of practicing law without a license because they provide typing services only.

Paralegals are relatively new to the legal profession. They were first utilized in the 1960s in the War on Poverty to provide low-cost legal services so that a larger sector of the population could have access to legal advice and representation. They were, nevertheless, virtually unheard of before the 1970s. The utilization of paralegals increased as paralegal associations organized and began to raise awareness in the legal system as to how paralegals could serve the legal profession. Today many law offices employ at least one. The strongest incentives to the hiring of paralegals have been the savings they bring to clients and their ability to generate income for law firms. Furthermore, paralegals enhance the efficiency of law firms because they can perform many tasks that can be effectively delegated to non-lawyers, thereby freeing lawyers to address matters requiring their expertise.

"A Silly Mistake Can Be a Disaster When the Attorney Shows Up In Court."

"I find it helps to pass the time if you skim over the documents before you copy them. That way you get a sense of the information they contain. It gives you something to do and definitely gives you a heads-up when it comes time to begin working the case." Andrew's voice startled Martha, but when the words registered she realized with some humiliation that Andrew spoke the truth.

The rising pink in Martha's cheeks telegraphed her embarrassment. Andrew graciously pointed out that he had required some enlightening himself before he had adopted this practice. "I learned this from Suzanne, you know. Before she said anything, I used to hate copywork. Once she explained how important it was to make sure that copies were made correctly, that papers didn't stick together, and that no pages were missed in the copying, I began to pay more attention to what I was doing. I realized that a silly oversight could be a disaster when the attorney showed up in court."

Martha did not know Suzanne, but had heard tales of her brilliance. She was one of the first paralegals the firm had ever hired and had set the standard for all the paralegals that had followed in her wake. Suzanne was now a successful freelance paralegal.

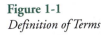

Figure 1-1
Definition of Terms

Term	Definition
Paralegals	American Bar Association (ABA)
	Persons qualified by education, training or work experience who are employed or retained by a lawyer, law office, corporation, governmental agency or other entity who perform specifically designated substantive legal work for which a lawyer is responsible.
	National Association of Legal Assistants (NALA)
	A distinguishable group of persons who assist attorneys in the delivery of legal services. Through formal education, training, and experience, they have knowledge and expertise regarding the legal system and substantive and procedural law which qualify them to do work of a legal nature under the supervision of an attorney.
	National Federation of Paralegal Associations (NFPA)
	Persons qualified through education, training or work experience to perform substantive legal work that requires knowledge of legal concepts and is customarily, but not exclusively, performed by a lawyer. These people may be retained or employed by a lawyer, law office, governmental agency or other entity or may be authorized by administrative, statutory or court authority to perform this work.
Legal Technicians	Those who provide legal services directly to the public and who do not work under the supervision of an attorney.
Lay Advocates	Those who represent individuals at administrative hearings in administrative agencies that permit Lay representation.
Freelance Paralegals	Self-employed paralegals who works as independent contractors for attorneys on special projects.
Independent Paralegals	Some use this term synonymously with freelance paralegals; others use it synonymously with legal technicians.

AREAS OF PARALEGAL EMPLOYMENT

Paralegals typically find work in several areas.

1. *Law firms*—These are traditional forms of legal practice in which income is generated from the fees of individual clients.
2. *Legal clinics*—These are nontraditional private firms that usually charge lower fees and rely on a high volume of cases. They are more likely to advertise and to rely on extensive use of paralegals than the more traditional law firms.
3. *Government agencies*—These include the civil service departments of federal and state agencies. Examples of agencies that hire paralegals are the attorney general, legislature, U.S. Department of Justice, U.S. Equal Employment Opportunity Commission, and the civil rights division of government agencies.
4. *Criminal law offices*—These are governmental agencies such as the prosecutor's, district attorney's or public defender's office as well as private defense counsel.
5. *In-house legal departments*—These are law departments within businesses or corporations.
6. *Legal aid or legal service clinics*—These are community legal service offices that provide legal services to the poor.
7. *Special interest groups*—These include environmental protection groups, consumer protection groups, unions, trade associations, and other such

---

NET NEWS

For more information about freelancing, go to *www.paralegals.org/reporter,* click on "Summer 2000," and read the article "Freelancing Paralegal Services to Small Firms and Solos."

---

freelance paralegals a self-employed paralegal who works as an independent contractor for attorneys on special projects. They are sometimes referred to as *independent paralegals* or *contract paralegals*. Others use the terms *independent paralegal* or *legal technician* to refer to a paralegal who works directly with the public and is not supervised by an attorney.

groups that monitor legislation, lobby, and provide legal services for the organization.

8. **Freelance paralegals**—These are independent paralegals who work as independent contractors for attorneys on special projects, but who are supervised in this work by an attorney; they are sometimes referred to as *independent paralegals.*

Within the wide variety of areas of employment in which paralegals may specialize, some possible areas of specialization include the following.

1. *Administrative law*—Paralegals represent citizens and the government before some administrative agencies. They do legal research, assist in preparing for administrative hearings, conduct investigations, draft documents for hearings and for proposed regulations, conduct interviews, and attend rule-making hearings.
2. *Bankruptcy law*—Paralegals help clients assemble documents and fill out forms, conduct investigations, prepare documentation, draft bankruptcy petitions, prepare status reports and asset inventories, and coordinate with creditors and bankruptcy trustees.
3. *Collections practice*—Paralegals prepare inventories, draft pleadings, conduct investigations, file documents, and assist in collecting judgments and settling claims.
4. *Contract law*—Paralegals review contracts, prepare forms, do legal research, and conduct investigations.
5. *Corporate law*—Paralegals draft a number of forms and reports (including minutes, bylaws, annual reports, and resolutions), record documents, conduct research, and file documents.
6. *Criminal law*—Paralegals conduct legal research, serve as a liaison with other agencies, conduct witness interviews, prepare documents, conduct investigations, and assist in trial preparation.
7. *Environmental law*—Paralegals conduct legal and factual research, draft documents, assist in trial preparation, and assist in the preparation of legal briefs.
8. *Family law*—Paralegals communicate with clients, prepare and file documents, conduct interviews, draft pleadings and motions, assist in gathering and analyzing financial information, and help prepare for hearings.
9. *Intellectual property law*—Paralegals conduct investigations, collect data, help prepare contracts, assist clients in applying for copyrights and patents, conduct patent searches, conduct research, and file applications.
10. *Labor law*—Paralegals conduct investigations, assist companies in designing policies, and assist in litigation.
11. *Litigation*—Paralegals prepare and organize files, conduct investigations, research records, conduct investigations, file documents, assist in discovery

and in trial preparation, serve as liaison with clients and witnesses, conduct legal research, draft pleadings, and assist in obtaining experts.

12. *Probate law*—Paralegals collect data, draft documents (such as wills and trusts), perform investment analysis, manage accounting of trusts and estates, file documents, assist in valuation of assets, organize financial data, conduct factual and legal research, draft documents, and assist in litigation.

13. *Real estate law*—Paralegals prepare drafts of contracts, research regulations, perform title searches, collect data necessary for closing, prepare and organize documents, record and file documents, assist in closing, prepare a number of forms (such as UCC-1 financing statements), and assist with sale documents.

14. *Water law*—Paralegals conduct legal and factual research, communicate with agencies, prepare documents and reports, prepare historic use affidavits, and perform title searches.

A quick review of the foregoing specialties reveals that, despite all of the possible variations, certain basic functions are performed by most paralegals. They include:

- ◆ performing factual investigations
- ◆ performing basic legal research
- ◆ drafting documents
- ◆ serving and filing documents
- ◆ reviewing records
- ◆ conducting interviews
- ◆ preparing for trials and hearings

Putting It Into Practice 1.1:

Which of these areas of law are of greatest interest to you? Find out more about those areas by using the Internet. Keep in mind that additional areas of law practice not mentioned in the abbreviated list above are also available. They include animal law, elder law, entertainment law, insurance law, international law, public health law, social security law, tax law, tribal law, welfare law, and worker's compensation law. If any of these areas sound intriguing, include them in your Internet search.

HOW PARALEGALS ARE UTILIZED

In 1998, the American Bar Association published the results of a comprehensive survey of its members engaged in private practice. The survey, which examined the utilization of legal assistants (the term used in this survey rather than *paralegal*), revealed the following.

- ◆ Almost two-thirds of the lawyers who responded to the survey employed legal assistants.
- ◆ Large firms are more likely to employ legal assistants than small firms.
- ◆ Lawyers in smaller firms delegate more tasks, such as drafting correspondence and legal documents, interviewing clients, and serving as a liaison with clients, to legal assistants than those in large firms.

NET NEWS

To get more information about some of the specialties that are available to paralegals, go to the Web page for NFPA (*www.paralegals.org/reporter*) and click on the editions indicated in Table 1-1. These articles were written by paralegals working in a variety of capacities. Another site that lists tasks by legal specialty is *www.lawcost.com/paras.htm.*

TABLE 1-1

Specialties Available to Paralegals

Specialty	Edition	Name of Article
Alternative Dispute Resolution	Fall 1997	Paralegal Roles and Responsibilities
Banking	Fall 1998	Are You a Paralegal or a Banker? Paralegal Roles and Responsibilities
Corporate	Summer 1999	A Different Road to Success
Criminal	Summer 1999	Life as an Oregon DOJ At the City Attorney's Office Paralegal Roles and Responsibilities
	1999 Year-End	Paralegal Roles and Responsibilities
Immigration	Spring 2000	Immigration Law and Practice Paralegal Roles and Responsibilities
Intellectual Property	1998 Year-End	Paralegal Roles and Responsibilities
Litigation	Spring 1998	Paralegal Roles and Responsibilities
Medical Malpractice	Winter 1998	Three Important Qualities of a Medical Malpractice Paralegal Paralegal Roles and Responsibilities
Military	Fall 1997 Winter 1997	Reaching for the Sky: Paralegals in the Air Force Air National Guard Paralegals: Strength Through Support
Probate	Summer 1998	Probate: An Overview Paralegal Roles and Responsibilities
Products Liability	Winter 1998 Winter 1999	Product Liability: An In-house Perspective Paralegal Roles in Products Liability Cases
Real Estate	Summer 1997 Spring 1999	So You Want to Work in Real Estate Paralegal Roles and Responsibilities

◆ Almost half the respondents utilized legal assistants for research, preparing pleadings and discovery responses, and deposition outlines.
◆ About two-thirds of the responding firms required either an associate's or a bachelor's degree.

The survey also revealed the most common tasks assigned to legal assistants. (Results are given in percentages.)

Maintain client files	73.7%
Draft correspondence	72.4%

Perform factual research	70.9%
Monitor deadline dates	69.9%
Conduct factual investigations	67.6%
File documents	65.3%
Draft legal documents	61.5%
Maintain liaison with clients	60.8%
Proofread legal documents	58.0%
Maintain liaison with opposing firm	45.1%
Meet with clients	41.0%
Maintain liaison with courts	36.5%
Perform legal research	34.2%
Calculate and process invoices, fees, and taxes	33.2%
Interview clients	31.1%
Serve legal documents	24.8%
Assist in firm's pro bono work	23.0%
Appear before administrative agencies	2.3%

Paralegals can perform many more tasks than those listed above, however. To understand the broad spectrum of skills a paralegal must possess, consider the following list of tasks that can be assigned to paralegals in the criminal, domestic relations, environmental, and estate areas of practice. (The lists are extracted from the article "Paralegals: Changing the Practice of Law" by Jacqueline Rasmussen and Paul Sedlacek, which appeared in the 1999 *South Dakota Law Review*.) Many of the terms used below will be unfamiliar to you at this time. They are included only for the purpose of giving you a sense of the broad scope of tasks assigned to paralegals. For now, simply skim over this list; then, after you have read the entire text, come back to this section and read the list more carefully to get a clearer picture of what paralegals are asked to do.

Criminal Defense
1. Gather initial information from the client.
2. Assist the attorney in the bail process, the preliminary hearing, and the trial and appeal processes.
3. Obtain information with regard to the charge.
4. Research possible defenses.
5. Obtain copies of related court documents and records.
6. Locate evidence and obtain exhibits.
7. Investigate the crime scene.
8. Locate and interview witnesses.
9. Locate expert witnesses.
10. Review the State's evidence with the attorney.
11. Maintain a tickler with regard to dates and deadlines.
12. Prepare legal research for pretrial motions and trial.
13. Assist in the development of defenses, theories of the case, and trial strategy.
14. Draft pretrial motions and supporting documents.
15. Obtain, list, and mark exhibits.
16. Organize and index files.
17. Prepare subpoenas and arrange for service.
18. Review the jury list.
19. Draft voir dire examination questions.

20. Assist in preparation of direct and cross-examination questions for clients and witnesses.
21. Assist in preparation of clients and witnesses.
22. Draft the jury instructions.
23. Schedule the witnesses' times for testimony.
24. Arrange for travel and accommodations for witnesses.
25. Prepare trial notebooks.
26. Prepare exhibits and visual aids.
27. Prepare trial briefs.
28. Assist in the trial.
29. Assist in the preparation of post-trial motions and other proceedings.
30. Assist in the preparation for sentencing hearing.
31. Draft the notice of appeal.
32. Research and draft the appellate briefs.

Domestic Relations

1. Conduct the initial interviews of prospective clients.
2. Maintain files on resource materials for clients.
3. Draft the commencement pleadings including the summons, complaint, affidavits, admissions of service, and protection orders.
4. Draft correspondence to clients, courts, and attorneys.
5. Arrange for service of process.
6. Investigate the facts.
7. Develop forms for gathering information from clients.
8. Conduct client interviews.
9. Conduct witness interviews.
10. Collect documents.
11. Set hearing dates and arrange for notice.
12. Assist in settlement negotiations.
13. Draft stipulations for temporary orders.
14. Draft subpoenas and arrange for service.
15. Prepare financial affidavits.
16. Analyze income and expense information.
17. Work with accountants, financial advisors, and other experts.
18. Retain appraisers for real estate, business, and personal property.
19. Prepare child support worksheets.
20. Work with clients and child support agencies in compiling information for determining child support.
21. Draft discovery requests.
22. Assist clients in gathering documents and data to respond to discovery requests.
23. Prepare responses to discovery requests.
24. Organize, index, and summarize discovered and produced materials.
25. Prepare for and assist at depositions.
26. Develop and maintain databases for indexing and tracking discovered and produced materials.
27. Maintain files on mediation professionals.
28. Assist in scheduling mediation sessions with clients and opposing counsel.
29. Assist in preparing clients for mediation.
30. Communicate settlement proposals and counteroffers to the client and opposing counsel.
31. Assist the attorney in an analysis of proposed settlements.

32. Research legal questions and assist in drafting correspondence, briefs, and memoranda.
33. Maintain files on current case law.
34. Maintain files on stipulation provisions.
35. Assist in drafting stipulations.
36. Prepare decrees, affidavits, and orders.
37. Prepare motions and supporting documents.
38. Prepare trial notebooks and trial exhibits.
39. Prepare pretrial conference checklists.
40. Maintain files on experts in various fields.
41. Arrange for expert witnesses and assist in preparing witnesses and clients for trial.
42. Assist at trial.
43. Prepare findings and conclusions, final orders, and notices of entry of judgment.
44. Prepare documents for a transfer of assets.
45. Arrange for filing and recording of transfer documents.
46. Review bills for tax-deductible fees.
47. Prepare post-trial and execution documents.
48. Draft pleadings for withdrawal from case.
49. Prepare the notice of appeal.
50. Research and draft an appellate brief.

Environmental Law

1. Research questions pertaining to environmental law.
2. Maintain files on pertinent state and federal statutes.
3. Maintain files on pertinent case law.
4. Maintain files on state and federal regulations.
5. Maintain files on pertinent secondary materials for a broad information base.
6. Gather and examine information from various governmental agencies.
7. Review abstracts of title.
8. Correspond with government officials for data and answers to questions.
9. Draft memoranda.
10. Draft instruments such as deeds and assignments.
11. Draft pleadings.
12. Maintain indexing and inventory systems for documents.
13. Review county records.
14. Prepare affidavits.
15. Investigate the facts.
16. Interview clients and other persons.
17. Prepare information summaries.
18. Prepare necessary reports.
19. Develop and maintain research notebooks for future reference.
20. Prepare bibliographies on environmental topics.
21. Draft memoranda regarding pertinent issues or public policy developments.
22. Research the history of the legislation.
23. Assist in preparation of environmental assessments.
24. Assist in preparation of environmental impact statements.
25. Prepare briefs and other memoranda.
26. Locate and schedule witnesses for hearings.
27. Assist in preparation for hearings.

28. Prepare property exhibits.
29. Assist at hearings.

Estate Administration

1. Locate the original will and file it with the court.
2. Assist with client interviews and obtain information.
3. Inventory decedent's residence and review decedent's papers for pertinent asset information.
4. Conduct preliminary valuation of estate assets.
5. Draft and file all necessary court documents to probate will and/or commence administration.
6. Prepare ticklers and progress charts for dates and deadlines.
7. Prepare and mail a notice to known creditors and publish a notice to any unknown creditors in an appropriate newspaper.
8. Deliver the notice and proof of publication to court.
9. Mail or deliver information and notices to any interested parties.
10. Establish estate bank accounts and maintain or monitor all estate records.
11. Correspond with banks, businesses, insurance companies, brokerage firms, employers, accountants, creditors, debtors, and others to collect asset and debt information and other pertinent information.
12. Arrange for and attend the inventory of a safe deposit box.
13. Arrange for appraisals and correspond with professionals to obtain financial information.
14. Review and study financial information.
15. Draft interim court papers such as inventories and petitions.
16. Draft requests for exempt property and family allowances.
17. Correspond with court personnel regarding estate administration.
18. Assist in processing medical claims.
19. Prepare and file claims for life insurance proceeds and health benefits.
20. Assist the client with address changes, notifying the Social Security Administration, canceling credit cards and subscriptions, and requesting refunds.
21. Check for any special insurance requirements.
22. Monitor the specific bequests for timely distributions.
23. Determine, at the end of the creditors' period, if any claims have been filed against the estate.
24. Prepare disallowance of claims and documents for sale of assets.
25. Draft papers for the distribution of assets.
26. Prepare accountings.
27. Research issues that arise.
28. Assist with post-mortem tax planning options.
29. Provide the attorney with information necessary to choose the estate's taxable year.
30. Request the decedent's income tax returns.
31. Prepare the federal gift and estate tax returns, state inheritance tax returns, decedent's final income tax return, and fiduciary income tax returns.
32. Prepare other IRS forms.
33. Prepare applications for extension of time to file or pay taxes, if necessary.
34. Prepare correspondence with tax authorities.
35. Prepare all affidavits, declarations, or statements requested by the tax authorities.

NET NEWS

For additional information about the specific types of tasks paralegals perform, go to 'Lectric Law Library (*www.lectlaw.com*) and click on "Rotunda," on "Legal Professionals' Lounge," and then on "Paralegals." Go to the article entitled "A Lengthy List of Activities Performed by Paralegals."

36. Prepare all pleadings to close the estate.
37. Assist in the final conference with the client.

For more detailed information about the types of work paralegals engage in, refer to William Statsky's *Introduction to Paralegalism: Perspectives, Problems and Skills* (West Publishing, 5th edition, 1997).

BONUS POINTERS:

COMPENSATION

According to the Center for Legal Studies in Golden, Colorado, the paralegal profession was ranked as one of the top growth professions for 1999 and into the current millennium because of the rise of lawsuits and the increased complexity of the laws. Paralegal salaries vary greatly by location and specialty. Salary data is outdated as soon as it appears in print, but the following statistics are included here to give you a ballpark figure for salary ranges. NFPA conducts a compensation and benefits survey every two years. Its 1999 survey revealed an average salary of $38,085 (compared to an average salary of $29,607 in 1991). To order a copy of NFPA's most recent survey, go to *www.paralegals.org/Publications;* to read an executive summary of the most recent salary survey, go to *www.paralegals.org,* click on "What's New" and then on the most recent "Compensation and Benefits Report"; or call NFPA at (816) 941-4000.

A 1998 National Compensation Survey conducted by the Legal Assistant Management Association (LAMA) of Atlanta, Georgia, represented a cross section of legal assistants in terms of responsibility and background. Nearly half of the respondents, however, worked in firms of more than 200 lawyers. The survey revealed the following.

1. Compensation increases with the number of years in the profession. The highest percentage of change in compensation (30.0%) was evident in the 6-to-10- and 11-to-15-year ranges, while the second major increase occurred between 0 to 2 and 3 to 5 years. But most respondents actually saw a decrease in average base salary once they had been with their firms 16 to 20 or more years.

2. Only 24% of respondents said their firm required certification as a condition of employment, while 75% said their organizations provided no additional compensation for those with a certificate.

3. Firms in the Pacific region (Alaska, California, Hawaii, Idaho, Montana, Nevada, Oregon, Utah, and Washington state) offer, on average, the highest base salaries ($36,780). Those in the Northeast (Connecticut, Delaware, Maine, Massachusetts, New Hampshire, New Jersey, New York, Pennsylvania, Rhode Island, Vermont) offer the lowest base salaries ($30,770).

4. The average billable hours amount to approximately 1,500 to 1,600 per year. Interestingly, respondents reported that billing more does not necessarily mean a larger base salary. Overtime pay, however, makes up for the gap. Eighty percent of respondents receive time-and-a-half for overtime versus other methods, such as fluctuating work weeks, incentive bonuses, and flex time.

5. More than half of those surveyed specialized in litigation, while the second most significant number specialized in corporate. Litigation, however, was among the lowest paying practice areas represented in the data. Those who did trusts and estates work earned far more than their peers: $38,406 in average base salary.

The following tables are taken from the LAMA survey and represent average base salaries in relationship to location, billable hours, and specialization.

TABLE 1-2

Legal Assistant/Paralegal Salaries in 12 Cities

Key City	Average Base Salary
Atlanta	$40,452
Boston	39,270
Chicago	27,205
Cincinnati/Cleveland/Columbus	34,483
Dallas	35,279
Houston	46,112
Los Angeles	41,132
Minneapolis/St. Paul	36,450
New York City	30,448
Philadelphia	29,187
Portland, Ore./Seattle	36,323
Richmond	30,448
San Francisco	27,563
Washington, D.C.	37,143

TABLE 1-3

Legal Assistant/Paralegal Salaries by Billable Hours

Billable Hours	Average Base Salary
0 to 500	$32,687
501 to 750	33,542
751 to 1,000	33,083
1,001 to 1,250	33,441
1,251 to 1,500	33,695
1,501 to 1,750	32,905
1,751 to 2,000	31,606
More than 2,000	29,977

TABLE 1-4

Legal Assistant/Paralegal Salaries by Specialization

Specialization	Average Base Salary
Bankruptcy	$32,420
Corporate	34,389
Environment	32,177
Intellectual property, patents, and trademarks	36,311
Litigation	31,782
Real estate	36,269
Trusts and estates	38,406
No specialty/generalist	37,960
Other	31,779

◆ **LOCAL LINKS** ◆

Have any salary surveys for paralegals been conducted in your state/city? What were the results of those surveys? What is the employment picture for paralegals where you live?

TABLE 1-5

Percentage of Legal Assistants in Major Cities Receiving These Base Salaries

City	$45,000 or More	$40,000 to $44,999	$35,000 to $39,999	$30,000 to $34,999
Atlanta	18.6%	17.4%	29.1%	18.6%
Boston	28.6	15.6	23.4	13.0
Chicago	30.1	9.1	17.2	23.4
Dallas	19.8	15.3	32.8	19.8
Denver	17.4	21.7	23.9	13.0
Detroit	7.3	18.2	18.2	27.3
Houston	23.0	16.4	26.2	24.6
Los Angeles	54.4	20.3	11.2	7.5
Miami	25.0	41.7	25.0	6.9
Minneapolis/St. Paul	12.9	20.4	18.9	18.4
New York City	32.7	8.6	14.2	15.4
Portland, Ore.	4.5	15.9	38.6	27.3
San Francisco	39.7	15.5	22.4	14.7
Seattle	31.7	12.2	22.0	13.4
Washington, D.C.	22.4	12.8	13.2	14.3
Percentage	27.7	15.3	18.5	16.0

BONUS POINTERS:

EMPLOYMENT

The U.S. Department of Labor found 113,000 paralegals working in the U.S. in 1996. The U.S. Bureau of Labor Statistics predicts 74,000 paralegal job openings in the next eight years and an average salary of $45,000 by 2005. The 58 percent projected growth rate through 2005 for paralegals places them among the twenty fastest-growing occupations of the more than 500 studied. Despite this rosy picture, however, the caveat is that the competition for these new jobs will remain keen as the number of people pursuing paralegal positions keeps pace with the increasing availability of jobs.

At this point, the majority of paralegals (about 87 percent) work for private law firms or in-house corporate law offices with the number of paralegals in corporate environments increasing. In fact, corporate legal departments are hiring paralegals at a faster rate than law firms, and in the next few years may be hiring more paralegals than lawyers because of the cost-effectiveness of paralegals and because of the desire to maintain more in-house control of legal work. While private law firms will probably continue to be the largest employers of paralegals, other organizations, such as insurance companies, banks and real estate and title insurance firms, will also be hiring. One of the changes fueling the job growth for paralegals is that more work is being done with computerization and access to the Internet—the kinds of tasks at which paralegals excel.

It appears that, in the future, paralegals will be required more and more to specialize. Although the law is by nature cyclical (based largely on changes in the economy), the that are "hot" today are real estate, environmental law, probate and estate work, intellectual property law, corporate law, and employee benefits.

"Don't Underestimate the Value of Your Life Experiences."

"Your point is well taken," responded Martha graciously. "I was so busy feeling sorry for myself I forgot how important all these documents can be. I just get so tired of doing all this copying day in and day out. I've been here for almost six months and I'm still doing grunt work. I'm beginning to wonder if I'm ever going to be given an opportunity to advance to something a little more challenging."

"I hear you," chuckled Andrew. "I went through the same thing when I first started here. Maybe they do it intentionally just to test us."

"Well, this job for Ms. Copple may just push me over the edge," Martha laughed.

"If you'd like to talk about how to move ahead in this firm, I'd be glad to give you some pointers." Andrew had been with the firm for five years and was highly respected by all of the attorneys with whom he had worked. Martha had had little contact with him because they worked in different departments, but she was well aware of Andrew's reputation. She jumped at the chance to get some advice.

"That would be great. Just let me know when would be a good time for you."

"How about a late lunch today—around 1:00?" suggested Andrew pleasantly.

"You bet—my treat!" exclaimed Martha.

"All right, I'll drop by your office at 1:00." Andrew began to walk away and then turned back. "I almost forgot why I came by to see you. I'm supposed to do a little bio on you for our local paralegal association newsletter. We like to introduce our new members to the rest of the membership. Could you type up a brief summary of your work experiences, educational background, professional accomplishments, and personal interests and get it to me by the first of next week?"

"Sure. But this is only my second real paralegal job so I don't have a lot to say," confessed Martha.

"You're a mother, aren't you?" challenged Andrew. "I'd say that's a 'real' job. Don't underestimate the value of your life experiences. They're probably what helped you get hired here. Just because you started a family before you started a career doesn't mean we value your experiences any less. Be proud of what you've accomplished as a wife, mother, and community member."

"Boy, I should have you as my agent. But I get your point. Thanks for the pep talk," acknowledged Martha appreciatively.

PARALEGAL ASSOCIATIONS

The National Association of Legal Assistants (NALA) is an association of paralegals that has been active in the political and educational arenas relating to the promotion of paralegalism. Individuals can join NALA or one of the numerous state and local paralegal organizations affiliated with it. NALA has created an entry-level certification exam, known as the CLA or Certified Legal Assistant exam, for those who are interested in earning the designation CLA (Certified Legal Assistant).

The National Federation of Paralegal Associations (NFPA) is an association of state and local paralegal associations; individual paralegals can belong to NFPA through their local associations. Like NALA, NFPA is involved in continuing legal education and political action. Unlike NALA, NFPA does not support certification for entry-level paralegals but has created a certification exam for advanced paralegals called PACE (Paralegal Advanced Competency Exam). Successful completion of this exam results in one's becoming a registered paralegal.

Although NALA and NFPA have contrasting viewpoints about certification, licensure, the relationship between paralegals and bar associations, and other issues, they both have issued a set of ethical guidelines that their members agree to follow. They also do their best to monitor those activities of the legislature, courts, and bar associations that potentially affect their membership.

Paralegals are allowed to become associate members of the American Bar Association (ABA), which is a voluntary association of attorneys. The ABA has a special committee called the Standing Committee on Legal Assistants, which was formed

---

◆ **LOCAL LINKS** ◆

What kinds of local paralegal organizations exist where you live? Do the state and local bar associations in your jurisdiction allow paralegals to become members?

NET NEWS

To learn more about NALA and the benefits of membership, go to *www.nalanet.org* and click on "Association Information."

To learn more about NFPA and the benefits of membership, go to *www.paralegals.org* and click on "Membership Information."

To read NALA's Model Guidelines, go to *www.nalanet.org* and click on "Paralegal Profession" then click on "Professional Standards." To read NFPA's guidelines, go to *www.paralegals.org* and click on "Professional Development" and then on "Model Code of Ethics and Professional Responsibility and Guidelines for Enforcement."

To find out more about the purpose and goals of the ABA Standing Committee on Legal Assistants, go to *www.abanet.org/legalassts/approval.html.*

Figure 1-2
Differences Between NALA and NFPA

	NALA	**NFPA**
Terminology	Limited definition Uses legal assistant and paralegal interchangeably	Expansive definition Prefers term paralegal
Certification	CLA exam Entry level paralegals	PACE Exam Paralegals with Experience only
Designation of Achievement	Certified Legal Assistant	Registered Paralegal
Licensure	Opposes licensure	Supports licensure

to study how attorneys could most effectively use nonlawyers in their practice and meet the committee's goal of providing affordable legal services to the public. Some local and state bar associations have followed the ABA's lead in allowing paralegals to become associate members. Additionally, state, regional, and city paralegal associations, some of which are associated with either NALA or NFPA and some of which are associated with neither, also exist.

Putting It Into Practice 1.2:

Why might it be to your advantage to join a professional organization as a student?

Heeding Andrew's advice, Martha quickly scanned each paper before copying it and began to better understand the issue being litigated. The more involved she became in the case, the less aware she was of the passage of time. It was almost 1:00 p.m. when she glanced up at the clock. As she combed her hair and touched up her make-up, she reflected on the serendipitous events that had led to her employment with White and Treadwell.

Even her decision to attend paralegal school had been a fluke. She had intended to enroll in a pre-nursing program, but all of the classes had been full. Her advisor suggested she take some general education classes, which included a pre-law class that met the social science requirement. She had been so enamored with the subject matter and the zest with which the instructor presented the material that she decided to change majors. The program was rigorous and stimulating, and she had been frustrated that her need to work full-time prevented her from taking more than a few classes each semester. Although she had questioned the relevance of some of the information she was required to learn, she had, for the most part, been a veritable sponge, soaking up all the information that came her way. Anxious to put what she had mastered into practice, she had been ecstatic when she was able to rearrange her work schedule at the bank so she could take an internship.

EDUCATIONAL PROGRAMS

Although no formal requirements exist to be a paralegal, most attorneys look for experience or participation in a formal education process. Most paralegals have received training in one of the more than 800 paralegal programs currently available. In the early 1970s, community colleges and proprietary schools around the country began offering paralegal programs. Today, several four-year baccalaureate and post-baccalaureate programs exist as well.

Although the content and quality of programs vary, most institutions provide students with a knowledge of basic legal terminology, procedural law, substantive law (usually in torts, contracts, probate, family, and corporate law), legal research and writing, and legal ethics. In addition to learning basic legal concepts, students are challenged to think logically and analytically and to express themselves clearly and concisely, both verbally and in writing.

To help rectify the lack of consistency among paralegal schools, the American Bar Association adopted a set of standards in 1973 for granting ABA approval to paralegal programs. Over one-fourth of the existing programs have received ABA approval. The remaining programs either do not meet the ABA's standards or have opted for philosophic or economic reasons to forego the demanding and time-consuming approval process. Programs that have not applied for ABA approval but do appear to meet those standards are referred to as being in "substantial compliance."

Another effort to improve the quality of paralegal education came in 1981 in the formation of the American Association for Paralegal Education (AAfPE). This organization has members from colleges and universities around the country. It serves as a forum for discussion and vehicle for dissemination of information in reference to the paralegal profession and paralegal education. Voting members of AAfPE must work for institutions that are ABA approved or that are in "substantial compliance" with ABA standards.

NET NEWS

To get NFPA's perspective on how to choose a quality paralegal educational program, go to *www.paralegals.org* and click on "Getting Started." For guidance from the American Association for Paralegal Education (a national organization of paralegal educators), go to *www.aafpe.org* and click on "How Do I Choose a Paralegal Educational Program?"

During the internship seminar, which was required of students doing the internship, Martha learned about the importance of networking, prepared a sample resume, attended a mock interview, and essentially learned how to "sell" herself to potential employers.

GETTING A JOB

Getting a job typically requires advance planning. Begin now, in your first semester, taking steps so that when you graduate you are prepared to actively seek employment.

Self-Assessment

Begin by assessing your current job skills. What have you done in the past that would be valuable to future employers? Do you have office skills? Have you been

Figure 1-3
Getting a Job

	Self-Assessment	
Resumes		Interviewing
	GETTING A JOB	
Writing Samples		Networking
	Want Ads Selling Yourself	

responsible for a budget? Have you had experience in managing or training others? Have you been responsible for planning activities? Have you been in positions requiring others to depend on you? Have you received any recognition or been promoted because of what you have accomplished? Do you speak any languages other than English? Have you traveled extensively? Do you have expertise in any particular field or do you have a hobby that requires special skills?

In doing this assessment include volunteer work, school activities, and parental responsibilities. Include anything you have done that demonstrates your ability to show initiative and be responsible, timely, dependable, competent, and creative. Remember that everyone has to get that first job in the legal field. Most employers do not expect everyone they hire to have years of legal experience. But you will have to convince them you have the potential to be an employee they can rely on to perform every task to the best of your ability, to ask questions when you do not understand, to take directions, to be punctual, to be self-reliant and thorough, and to take criticism graciously.

Once you have assessed your current bank of skills, have a paralegal instructor, someone employed in the legal field, or a college career counselor evaluate them. Ask this individual to assess your strengths and weaknesses and recommend actions you might take to remedy any deficiencies. If, for example, your computer skills need improvement, you should certainly take classes now to become proficient. Almost all paralegals work on the computer daily, so most law firms will not even consider your application if you do not have basic skills. By the same token, consider expanding whatever computer skills you currently have. Even those attorneys who are marginally computer literate themselves are acutely aware of the value that computers bring to the legal process and actively recruit paralegals who can perform essential computer tasks. (We will discuss specific computer software with which you should be familiar in a subsequent section of this chapter, "Tim's Techno Tips.")

Putting It Into Practice 1.3:

Use the following questions to help you assess your current computer skills.

1. Can you type? How many words per minute?
2. Are you proficient in using a computer keyboard?
3. Are you proficient with a word processor? If so, which one and which version?
4. Are you accustomed to using a MacIntosh or a PC?
5. With what operating system are you most familiar?
6. Do you know how to use a scanner?

7. Are you familiar with any optical character recognition (OCR) programs? If so, which ones?
8. Can you create a table of cases with your word processor?
9. Are you familiar with the search and replace functions?
10. Are you familiar with any of the following software programs?
    (a) Summation
    (b) TimeSlips
    (c) Abacus
    (d) Excel
    If not, are you familiar with any other timekeeping, document management, database management, spreadsheet, or accounting programs?

Communication skills are also essential in the legal arena. If your written or oral communication skills are somewhat shaky, use the time you are in school to rebuild or expand these skills. Paralegals with excellent writing skills invariably progress faster and further than those with marginal skills. Paralegals who are verbally articulate almost always stand out in the minds of their supervising attorneys, especially because many attorneys have carefully polished their own verbal skills. Instead of avoiding classes that require writing, verbal presentations, and independent thinking, seek them out.

Finally, if you have not had any experience working in an office setting, consider taking business classes that teach the basic elements of telephone etiquette and professionalism. Knowing how to function in a business environment is not an innate skill and must be acquired through training or experience. Once you have reviewed your skills and visited with an advisor, prepare a resume and update it each semester. This will give you a baseline from which to expand your skills.

Putting It Into Practice 1.4:

Assess your current skills. What are your strengths? In what areas do you need some practice or skill-building? How might you improve these skills?

Experience

Experience is that all-important ingredient that employers seek and that students usually lack. So how do you go about getting that experience? If at all possible, get a part-time job in a legal setting, perhaps as a receptionist or a typist. The ideal job is in a law firm or government agency that employs paralegals. This kind of job allows you to see the practice of law firsthand, to gain exposure to the day-to-day realities of legal procedures, to have contact with attorneys and other legal personnel who can later write letters of recommendation, and to learn how to perform tasks that will obviate the need for training when you are hired.

But what if that ideal job is not available? Alternatively, look for work as a **runner** (someone who hand-delivers documents to law firms, agencies, the courts, and other entities) or as a **process server** (someone who personally serves subpoenas and summonses—although age requirements and the necessity of being bonded restrict eligibility for this sometimes dangerous job). While these individuals do not have the privilege of working within the confines of an office, they do have the opportunity to observe a wide variety of players in the legal field and to make contact with individuals who can later offer them assistance when it comes time to get a job. Even this brief exposure to legal personnel can clue you in as to which legal environments look appealing and which ones do not.

runner   an individual who hand-delivers documents to law firms, agencies, the courts, and other entities

process server   an individual who personally serves subpoenas and summonses

public interest law firms
law firm dedicated to dealing with issues in the public interest, such as environmental and civil rights issues

If getting a job is out of the question, consider doing volunteer work a few hours each week in a law office or law-related field. Legal service clinics and **public interest law firms** are good places to begin looking because they are usually understaffed and working on a shoestring budget. Most schools offer an internship program; some even require their students to complete an internship. If such a program is available at your school, do your best to take advantage of it. An internship gives you the requisite experience and allows you to earn credit at the same time.

Putting It Into Practice 1.5:

How do you plan to get experience? If you do not plan to get experience, how will you address your lack of experience when you meet with potential employers?

Resumes

Just as you need to begin reflecting on and expanding your experiences now, so do you need to begin thinking now about preparing your resume. Be aware that there is no one "right" way to develop a resume. Start now collecting sample resumes (from form books, for example) and getting feedback from people in the legal field who review resumes to determine what kinds of resumes they prefer and what sorts of information they seek. How long should the resume be? What are the most common errors made in resumes? What should the cover letter say? In what order should the information in the resume be presented? How detailed should it be? How can you make your non-legal experiences relevant to the legal job you are seeking?

Be sure to write down the responses to these questions so you have them when it comes time to draft your resume. Begin a draft now and keep revising it as you receive additional information. Books are available to assist you in preparing a resume; they contain sample resumes for you to review and blank worksheets you can use to build your resume. (See, for example, *How to Land Your First Paralegal Job* by Andrea Wagner.)

NET NEWS

For more information about writing resumes, go to *www.paralegals.org/reporter,* click on "Fall 1996," and go to the article entitled "Writing a Winning Resume." An online resume bank is available at LawMatch (*www.lawmatch.com*).

Writing Samples

Begin collecting writing samples now. Many employers want to see samples of what you are capable of producing. Being able to show your writing ability is especially important when you are getting that first job.

Ideal writing samples are research memoranda, motions, complaints, wills, contracts, or extensive reports. Make sure whatever you submit is typewritten, has no spelling or grammatical errors, is well-organized, and looks professional. Have someone you know to be a good writer evaluate it to ensure that it is a high-quality product worthy of representing your abilities.

Networking

Make as many contacts in the legal profession as you can as soon as you can. Attend meetings of your local paralegal association (which usually have reduced student fees), join NALA- or NFPA-associated organizations, and subscribe to paralegal newsletters and publications. (NALA publishes *Facts and Findings* and NFPA publishes the *National Paralegal Reporter.*) Paralegal associations provide networking opportunities with working paralegals, have job bank services, and usually list local job openings. If you find someone in one of these organizations who is willing to mentor you, avail yourself of this person's generosity. Ask if you can "shadow" them at the office for a day or more to get an idea of what a typical day at the office is like.

One way to get information about specific areas of practice is to conduct informational interviews in which you ask the attorney or paralegal about what they do. This is not a job interview (and should not be turned into one), but is rather a means of learning about a particular type of law practice, discerning what a typical day in the office is like, what kinds of tasks the individual performs, what the most challenging and frustrating aspects of the job are, how one might best prepare to work in this area of law, and other questions of interest to you.

NET NEWS

The NFPA Web site posts job listings on its World Wide Paralegal Resume Service, which you can access by going to *www. paralegals.org* and clicking on "Career Center." On the NALA Web page (*www.nalanet.org*), click on "CareerNet" to connect with "LawMatch," which facilitates connections between employers and those seeking employment. Another site that will facilitate your job search through the newspapers is CareerBuilder—*www.careerpath.com.*

Want Ads

You may not be graduating for another few years, but begin reading the want ads in your local newspaper now to get a sense of the employment opportunities in your area. If you want to peruse the national picture, consult the *National Law Journal* or the *American Lawyer.* On the Internet, you can locate want ads from all over the United States and post your resume as well.

Mock Interviews

The ability to interview well is a critical skill. Some students with superior skills and wonderful attitudes do not always get the best jobs because they have not mastered the art of interviewing. Find out where you can participate in mock interviews. Then ask to be videotaped so you can see yourself and appreciate how others see you. Observe your body language, your tone of voice, your speech, your mannerisms, and your visual reactions to certain questions. You may learn a lot about yourself you did not know. With those insights, you can change those things that may improve your chances of successfully landing the job of your choice.

Many schools have placement offices or career centers that discuss the interviewing process and provide mock interviews. You can learn what types of questions to anticipate, the purpose of these questions, suggested ways to respond, and the types of questions that are illegal. Take advantage of these services and practice, practice, practice!

NET NEWS

For more information about interviewing, read the article "Interviewing with Success," which can be found by going to *www.paralegals.org/reporter* and clicking on "Spring 1999." The article is continued in the "Summer 1999" edition.

To get an idea about hiring trends for paralegals nationally, go to *www.paralegals.org/reporter,* click on "Summer 1997," and then on the article "Hiring Trends." To find out the extent to which paralegals are satisfied with their career choice, consider the article "Are You Getting What You Were Promised from Your Career?" (found at the same site in the "Fall 1997" edition).

Selling Yourself

Getting a job often involves learning to sell yourself: to convince employers they are making a good investment in hiring and training you and that you are a better choice than your competitors. Doing this takes courage, initiative, and creativity.

Consider one of our former students who placed an ad in the local legal newsletter after having completed one year of community college classes. In the ad, he described in detail his legal knowledge, his attributes as an individual, and what he would bring to a law office. He received so many replies that he ended up connecting his fellow students with some of the attorneys who responded. Not only did he get a job immediately, but he employed several of his friends as well!

Putting It Into Practice 1.6:

Ask yourself, "Why should an attorney hire me?" Be as objective as you can about yourself. What are your best selling points? What aspects of you could stand to be improved? If you were an agent for yourself, how would you go about promoting you? Beginning now, what do you need to do to support this promotion?

Martha's internship with the county attorney's office was the highlight of her educational experience. She was allowed to work in several divisions, sit in on some trials, witness interviews, prepare documents, and follow several cases as they were carried through the criminal justice process. She also had to do menial tasks that many interns complained reduced them to some kind of slave labor. Martha accepted this work as part of the learning process and tried to learn whatever she could from every assignment she was given. Her pleasant disposition and eagerness to do whatever was asked of her made her a favorite with the attorneys and paralegal supervisors. They were delighted to recommend her when the time came for her to seek employment.

Some suggested, however, that she seek certification before trying to get a job. They reasoned that she would be better able to prepare to take the Certified Legal Assistant (CLA) exam while the knowledge she had gained from her college program was still fresh in her mind. In her enthusiasm to begin working in the field, she decided to postpone taking the CLA exam until after she had acquired some practical experience. She believed the fact that she had graduated from an ABA-approved program would enhance her chances of getting employment even though she was not a CLA.

Putting It Into Practice 1.7:

Does your institution offer some kind of internship? If so, consider now what you need to do to avail yourself of this opportunity. If no such internship is available, consider what you might do to create a type of internship for yourself.

RECESS

SUMMARY – PART A

A paralegal (also known as a legal assistant) is someone who, through formal education, training, or experience, has the knowledge and expertise of the legal system and of substantive and procedural law to perform legal work under the supervision of an attorney. Paralegals should be distinguished from legal technicians and lay advocates, who do not work under the supervision of an attorney. Successful paralegals are detail-oriented, well-organized, analytical, logical, proficient with a computer, effective communicators, resilient, well-prepared, and generally able to use good professional judgment.

Two professional paralegal organizations, NALA and NFPA, are involved in paralegal education and political action activities. Through NALA, entry-level paralegals can become certified by taking a CLA exam, and through NFPA, more advanced paralegals can receive certification by taking PACE.

Those interested in obtaining a paralegal job should begin by assessing their skills and determining the areas in which they need remediation. They should focus particularly on improving their computer and communication skills and getting experience working or volunteering in some kind of legal capacity. They should also network, look over the want ads periodically, begin preparing a resume, collect writing samples, participate in mock interviews, and consider what they can do to best sell themselves to future employers.

KEY TERMS

Freelance paralegals
Process server

Lay advocates
Public interest law firms

Legal technicians
Runner

Paralegal/legal assistant

REVIEW QUESTIONS – PART A

1. Compare a paralegal with a legal assistant, a legal technician, and a lay advocate.
2. In what types of offices can paralegals be employed?
3. What are some of the most common tasks performed by paralegals?
4. What are the two major national paralegal associations and how do they compare?
5. What efforts have been made to improve the quality of paralegal education in the United States?
6. What are the steps a student should take in preparing to find a paralegal job?

PRACTICE EXAM – PART A

MULTIPLE CHOICE

1. A paralegal is
   a. the same as a legal technician
   b. someone who can do legal work under the supervision of an attorney
   c. different from a legal assistant
   d. a lay advocate
2. Paralegals cannot
   a. give legal advice
   b. prepare legal documents
   c. represent clients at certain types of administrative hearings
   d. do any of the above
3. Paralegals are
   a. relatively new to the legal profession
   b. in greater use today than 30 years ago in part because of the work of paralegal organizations
   c. used today by most law offices
   d. all of the above

4. Paralegals
   a. enhance the efficiency but not the productivity of lawyers
   b. bring savings to law firms
   c. cannot perform any of the tasks performed by lawyers
   d. are not utilized as much today as they were 10 years ago
5. Paralegals doing copywork should skim over the documents before they copy them because
   a. it gives them something constructive to do
   b. it gives them some insights when it comes time to work the case
   c. it allows them to know what information the documents contain
   d. all of the above
6. NALA and NFPA have both
   a. agreed that paralegals should be licensed
   b. created entry-level certification exams
   c. created ethical guidelines for paralegals
   d. done all of the above
7. An educational paralegal program
   a. that is not ABA approved is by definition sub-standard
   b. that is ABA approved has met the standards set forth by NALA
   c. may be in "substantial compliance" with ABA standards even if it has not applied for ABA approval
   d. none of the above
8. AAfPE
   a. is a national organization of paralegals
   b. disseminates information about paralegal education
   c. is an organization that certifies paralegals
   d. was designed to advocate on behalf of paralegals in the legislature
9. The skills that are required of a paralegal include
   a. computer skills
   b. communication skills
   c. organizational skills
   d. all of the above
10. In order to get experience
    a. a part-time job is useful as long as it does not involve being a runner or a process server
    b. get a job in a law office but avoid jobs in legal service clinics or public interest law firms
    c. do an internship
    d. all of the above
11. As a student
    a. it is helpful to attend local paralegal association meetings but not necessary to join NALA or NFPA until you are employed
    b. try to find someone you can "shadow"
    c. begin interviewing for jobs immediately
    d. wait to go on informational interviews until you are ready to graduate
12. To assist you in getting a job, you should
    a. assess your current skills
    b. prepare writing samples
    c. take classes that develop your communication, writing, and analytical skills
    d. all of the above

FILL IN THE BLANK

13. A legal assistant must be distinguished from a _____ , who performs legal work but not under the supervision of an attorney.
14. A _____ is someone who represents clients at administrative hearings in agencies that permit lay representation.
15. A _____ paralegal is a self-employed paralegal who works on special projects for attorneys.
16. _____ are nontraditional firms that rely extensively on paralegals, charge lower fees than traditional law firms, and work on a high volume of cases.
17. An _____ law office is a law department within a corporation, whereas a _____ is an office that provides legal services to the poor. A _____ law firm is dedicated to working with public interest issues, such as environmental and civil rights issues.
18. The _____ is a national organization that paralegals can join individually or in affiliation with local organizations; this organization has created an entry-level exam known as the _____ exam.
19. The _____ is a national organization that is affiliated with numerous state and local organizations; it has created a certification exam for advanced paralegals called the _____ exam.
20. Two jobs that allow one to be in contact with law offices are _____ (someone who hand delivers documents) and _____ (someone who serves subpoenas and summonses).

TRUE OR FALSE

_____ 21. Several different definitions of paralegal exist.

_____ 22. Someone can become a paralegal only through training or experience.

_____ 23. The terms *legal assistant* and *paralegal* are synonymous.

_____ 24. Legal technicians are less likely than secretarial services (which prepare standardized legal documents) to be accused of being engaged in the unauthorized practice of law.

_____ 25. Paralegals have been in practice since the early 1900s.

_____ 26. Small firms are more likely than large firms to employ paralegals, but are less likely to delegate tasks to paralegals.

_____ 27. Most paralegals have either an associate's or bachelor's degree.

_____ 28. One of the most common tasks performed by a paralegal is the maintenance of client files.

_____ *29. The paralegal profession is ranked as one of the top growth professions for the current millenium.

_____ *30. Paralegal salaries vary greatly by location and specialty.

_____ *31. Paralegal salaries increase the most the first five years and after 20 years of employment.

_____ *32. Most firms require their paralegals to be certified.

_____ *33. A larger number of billable hours directly correlates with a larger base salary.

_____ *34. One of the highest paying areas of paralegal work is litigation.

_____ *35. Houston has one of the highest average base salaries for paralegals while Chicago has one of the lowest.

_____ *36. Because of the increasing availability of paralegal jobs, the competition for paralegal jobs will decrease in the current millenium.

_____ *37. The majority of paralegals work for private firms or in-house corporate law offices.

_____ *38. In the future, paralegals will be required to specialize more and more.

_____ 39. Paralegals are not allowed to become associate members of the American Bar Association.

_____ 40. No formal educational requirements exist to be a paralegal.

_____ 41. Life experiences such as doing volunteer work and carrying out parental responsibilities have no importance when it comes to getting a job as a paralegal.

_____ 42. Preparing resumes can be left until it is time to get a job because resumes are so standardized.

_____ 43. Writing samples can be helpful in showing attorneys what the paralegal is capable of producing.

_____ 44. It is wise to begin reading the want ads when you are still a student.

_____ 45. Participating in mock interviews is an important part of the job-hunting process.

_____ 46. Getting a job requires selling yourself, which entails both courage and creativity.

*Questions taken from Bonus Pointers

PART B

CERTIFICATION AND LICENSURE

certification a voluntary process that recognizes those individuals who have met specified qualifications set forth by NALA, NFPA, and other state organizations

Certification is a voluntary process undertaken by two national organizations (NALA and NFPA) and four state organizations to recognize those individuals who have met specified qualifications set forth by those organizations. NALA has established the Certified Legal Assistant (CLA) exam, which can be taken by anyone regardless of whether they have paralegal experience. NFPA has established the Paralegal Advanced Competency Exam (PACE), which requires a minimum of two years of paralegal experience, a bachelor's degree, and completion of a paralegal program at an accredited school. NALA also offers a Certified Legal Assistant Specialist (CLAS) certification in one of the following areas: bankruptcy, civil litigation, corporate law, criminal law, intellectual property, probate, or real estate law. Only CLAs are qualified to sit for the CLAS exam. Some states, such as California, Florida, Louisiana, and Texas, have state-specific certification exams.

NET NEWS

For more information about the CLA exam, go to *www.nalanet.org* and click on "Certification." To find out more about the PACE exam, go to *www.paralegals.org* and click on "PACE."

licensure mandatory regulation by the government in which a government agency grants individuals permission to engage in a profession

While certification comes from a non-governmental organization, **licensure** comes from the government. At this point, paralegals are not subject to any kind of licensing, but the issue itself is very controversial. In 1986, an ABA Committee on Professionalism suggested limited licensing of paralegals to perform such specific functions as drafting simple wills, doing real estate closings, and handling certain kinds of tax matters. In 1995, the ABA established a Commission on Non-lawyer Practice, which conducted hearings around the country regarding the issue of nonlawyer practice and its effects on society and the legal system. In its final report, the Commission recommended the expansion of the paralegal role and suggested that each state decide for itself whether it wanted to adopt limited licensing for paralegals.

In assessing the wisdom of licensing paralegals, the states have had to consider the serious problem of the unavailability of legal representation for the poor and many of the middle class. Many people cannot afford to hire an attorney even to handle relatively straightforward matters. These cases are not economical for attorneys to handle and can be easily handled by paralegals. On the other hand, serious ramifications can result from a paralegal's providing inadequate legal services. Another reason some question the wisdom of licensing paralegals is that consumers may find it difficult to assess when it is appropriate for a paralegal rather than an attorney to do the work. Furthermore, the cost of establishing a licensing scheme intricate enough to address such concerns may outweigh any advantages gained by creating licensed paralegals. Several states have considered limited licensing proposals, but none have adopted them to date.

◆ **LOCAL LINKS** ◆

Are paralegals encouraged to take the CLA or PACE exams in your area?

If so, what reasons are given for taking either of these exams?

When is it suggested you take them?

Does your state have a state-specific certification exam or is one being considered?

If your state has such a program, what are the specifics of that program?

NALA and NFPA have taken opposing positions in reference to licensing. While NFPA has drafted a Model Act for Paralegal Licensure and has proposed the creation of a State Board of Paralegal Practice to regulate paralegal practice, NALA has opposed attempts to license independent paralegals. NALA is concerned that the licensing of independent paralegals could lead to licensing of traditional paralegals and that such licensure could lead to direct confrontation with attorneys.

Even those who agree that licensing is commendable question the nature of the standards that should be set. For example, what kind of degree, if any, should be required? What kind of accreditation should be required of the educational institution granting the degree? How much specialized education should be required? Some differences exist in regard to what agency or institution should be responsible for administering paralegal licensure. Should it fall within the purview of the courts or should an independent licensing agency be established? What kind of licensing test should be used? Who should develop it? Who should grade it? These administrative issues further complicate the licensing issue.

BONUS POINTERS: ## THE NEW JERSEY EXPERIENCE

New Jersey's recent consideration of licensing requirements for paralegals illustrates the arguments made on both sides of this issue. Paralegals, attorneys, and court systems around the country watched the developments in New Jersey closely because it was the most wide-ranging licensing plan yet proposed by any state. In addition to licensure, the proposal included establishing a code of conduct for licensed paralegals, imposing mandatory educational requirements, and creating an Administrative Office of the Courts (AOC) to oversee the regulation of paralegals. The New Jersey Supreme Court studied the plan for five years before publishing the so-called Kestin Report (named after its chairman, Appellate Judge Howard Kestin).

The ABA opposed the plan, arguing that it provided no tangible benefits to the public or the profession and predicting that it would hinder the public's access to affordable legal services if the proposal resulted in limiting entry into the paralegal profession. But paralegal organizations maintained that standards for education, licensing, and conduct would enhance their profession, especially since there were more job openings in New Jersey than qualified paralegals to fill them. Critics responded that licensing was unnecessary because competition in the marketplace dictated that paralegals maintain the highest standards possible. Furthermore, they argued that establishing another level of bureaucracy for licensing and oversight by the AOC would be expensive. Although the Kestin Report indicated that the AOC would be "self-funding," most questioned the feasibility of that and argued that, without state support or assistance from some other outside source, paralegals would not be able to support this agency. The three paralegal associations in the state overwhelmingly approved the licensure and regulation of paralegals, but expressed some concern about the Kestin Report's requirement that educational programs be ABA-approved.

The New Jersey Supreme Court rejected the recommendations in the Kestin Report, thereby bringing closure to the impassioned six-year debate that had attracted so much attention nationwide. The court said that supervision of legal assistants was best left to attorneys, but did direct one of its panels to develop guidelines to be followed by lawyers in supervising paralegals. Although rejecting outright licensure, the justices did encourage developing a "credentialing system" to recognize qualified paralegals.

NET NEWS

To get more in-depth information about NFPA's position on licensing and its reaction to the New Jersey proposal, go to *www.paralegals.org*, click on "Professional Development," and then on "Regulations" and also on "Unauthorized Practice of Law." For NALA's position on these issues, go to *www.nala.org*, click on "Information and Articles," and then on "Professional Issues."

Figure 1-4
Licensure Issues

Pros and Cons of Licensure

Pros
Need for legal representation by middle class and poor
Ability of paralegals to provide legal services economically

Cons
Serious ramifications for providing poor legal services
Clients may not be able to assess when they need attorney
Cost of setting up licensing scheme

Questions Raised by Licensure

What kinds of degrees should be required?
What kind of accreditation should be required of institutions
Granting degrees?
What kind of licensing test should be used?
Who should develop licensing test?
Who should administer and grade licensing exam?
How much specialized education should be required?

When she began sending out resumes and going to interviews, Martha was thankful she had opted to participate in an internship. The single most frequently asked question was about her experience. Without the internship, she would have been hard pressed to come up with any legal experience. As it was, she could say she had done everything from drafting complaints to helping prepare trial notebooks, and she had at least six attorneys who were willing to vouch for her competence and zeal.

Because of her former experience as a real estate agent, she thought she was best suited to work in the field of real estate law and accepted a position with a sole practitioner who specialized in that area of law. After a month in the office with little or no supervision, however, she realized the attorney assumed she could do a lot more than she was capable of at that point. When she asked for more guidance, the attorney assured her (as she went zipping out the door) that she had the utmost confidence in her abilities and that she would review her work when she returned. Upon learning that the attorney did not review her work before sending it out, Martha could see a **malpractice** suit in the making and decided to quit before one of them committed a grievous error.

malpractice failure to conform to the reasonable standard of care expected of a professional

Putting It Into Practice 1.8:

Based on what you know at this point, do you plan to take the CLA or PACE exam? If so, when do you plan to take it?

Putting It Into Practice 1.9:

Is Martha justified in quitting because of the real estate attorney's lack of supervision?

ETHICAL ETIQUETTE

UNAUTHORIZED PRACTICE OF LAW

Paralegals are prohibited from engaging in the unauthorized practice of law, and, if they do so, can be fined or even imprisoned. The purpose of this prohibition is presumably to protect consumers from being advised by unqualified individuals. The courts are also concerned about lay people engaging in legal practices when they are not governed by the same ethical restraints that apply to attorneys. Some, however, believe that the true purpose of this prohibition is to protect attorneys from competition by lay people who can provide comparable services for less money.

The state statutes prohibiting nonlawyers from practicing law do not clearly define "practice of law." The Model Code (see below) defines it as any activity that calls for the exercise of professional judgment, which is defined as "the educated ability to relate the general body and philosophy of law to a specific legal problem of a client." (EC 3-5) The courts have struggled with the ambiguity of these definitions and have concluded that certain tasks are prohibited. Paralegals cannot, for example, appear in court to present cases or argue motions. They can, however, represent clients at certain administrative hearings, such as those at the Immigration and Naturalization Service, the Social Security Administration, the Interstate Commerce Commission, and the Patent Office.

They also cannot give legal advice, although what constitutes legal advice is not always clear. Generally speaking, any advice about how to achieve a particular legal result or how to resolve a specific legal problem is giving legal advice. In other words, paralegals can provide information of a factual nature but cannot offer information wide-involving subjective judgments. They can respond to questions such as "What happens now that we have filed a complaint?" by talking about the timelines that must be adhered to, the court papers the defendant must file, the options available to the defendant, and so on. They are not permitted to respond to a question such as "What do you think our chances of prevailing in this lawsuit are?" other than suggesting that the individual contact the attorney assigned to the case. In small offices, in particular, paralegals are often tempted to walk the edge of law practice by clients who want them to give information, make projections, and discuss strategies. Clients turn to paralegals because they cannot get what they want from attorneys who are either unavailable or unwilling to speculate. But paralegals must resist the temptation to inappropriately advise clients, even when they are desperate for information.

Paralegals can draft legal documents, but these documents must be reviewed by an attorney before they can be seen by anyone outside of the office. Lay persons can also prepare standardized forms that are incidental to their business, especially when they are simply filling in the blanks on forms prepared by attorneys. Real estate agents, for example, are allowed in some states to draft sales contracts. Paralegals cannot, however, give clients guidance about what to put in the form; they can only use the information the client provides.

Paralegals are not allowed to set fees or accept cases. The two are inextricably interrelated. Because only a lawyer can establish a lawyer-client relationship, only a lawyer can enter into a fee agreement with a client.

Paralegals can perform legal tasks, to some extent at least, if they are under the adequate supervision of an attorney. Such legal practice is not unauthorized as long as the "lawyer maintains a direct relationship with his client, supervises the delegated work, and has complete professional responsibility for the work product," according to the Model Code. The problem is determining what constitutes "adequate supervision." To what degree must an attorney review a paralegal's work? Is the attorney required only to give general instructions? With no firm guidelines in place dictating what an attorney is required to do, individual attorneys must assess the amount of supervision necessary and usually base their degree of supervision on the paralegal's experience level and the complexity of the task assigned.

Other tasks paralegals can perform include contacting clients and individuals outside the office (as long as they identify their status as paralegals), relaying instructions, informing clients about the status of their case, and interacting with third parties on behalf of clients. They cannot, however, offer their opinions. In some states, paralegals can supervise the signing of wills, appear in court to answer calendar calls, and make routine motions in court.

Paralegals must always take great care in disclosing their non-attorney status so as to never mislead anyone to believe they are authorized to practice law. They must never misrepresent their status to other attorneys, government officials, the courts, or the general public. Paralegals must clearly reveal their non-attorney status on business cards and on correspondence.

NET NEWS

For another perspective on the issue of the unauthorized practice of law, go to *www.paralegals.org/reporter*, click on "Fall 1999," and then on the article "How Much is Too Much: Paralegals' Duties and the Unauthorized Practice of Law." Also click on "Spring 1996" and the article "UPL: A Different Perspective."

Figure 1-5
Unauthorized Practice of Law

> **What Constitutes Unauthorized Practice of Law**
>
> Appearing in court to present a case
>
> Appearing in court to argue a motion
>
> Cannot give legal advice (advice about how to achieve a legal result or to resolve a specific legal problem)
>
> Cannot set fees
>
> Cannot establish attorney-client relationship
>
> **What Work Can Be Performed by a Paralegal**
>
> Representing clients at certain types of administrative hearings
>
> Answering factual questions that do not fall within the realm of giving legal advice
>
> Preparing legal documents that are reviewed by an attorney
>
> Performing legal tasks under the adequate supervision of an attorney
>
> Contacting clients and third parties to relay instructions, inform about the status of a case, etc. as long as no legal opinions are offered

"Attorneys are Just Like Any Other Professional. Some of Them Are a Delight and Others Are, Well, More of a Challenge."

Having every intention of utilizing a placement agency to help secure another job, Martha experienced one of those delightful coincidences that brighten everyone's life on occasion. While bemoaning her trials and tribulations at the real estate office to a waitress at the coffee shop, Martha was overheard by another customer whose brother-in-law (as fate would have it) was **counsel emeritus** with a firm that was looking for a paralegal. The young woman was just about to give Martha his name and phone number when John, the brother-in-law, walked into the shop. After a round of introductions, Martha and John talked for an hour. John was immediately impressed by Martha's obvious intelligence, wit, pleasant demeanor, and candor. Trusting his instincts, he decided to invite her in for an interview.

Andrew's quiet clearing of his throat brought Martha out of her reverie. They quickly established a destination for lunch and immediately set about getting to know one another. "How do you like working for White and Treadwell so far?" Andrew deliberately made the question open-ended.

Martha thought for a moment and then carefully chose her words. "I've been really impressed by the quality of personnel, especially the attorneys I've gotten to know. Most of them have been wonderful to work for."

"I notice you said 'most' of the attorneys were wonderful. I take it you've found some to be not so 'wonderful.' "

"Attorneys are just like any other professional. Some of them are a delight and others are, well, more of a challenge," replied Martha diplomatically.

"Would Ernesto happen to be one of those 'challenges' you're referring to?" persisted Andrew.

"I've certainly found him to be one of the most intense people I've ever worked with. But that intensity can be a bit daunting at times."

"Especially when you're working for him and two other attorneys," added Andrew, remembering harried moments when he was helping Ernesto prepare for trial while carrying out research for another attorney and responding to discovery requests for yet another attorney. "As I recall, Ernesto seemed to think my world revolved around his every whim and that I had nothing to do except meet his every need as soon as he snapped his fingers."

"Do I sense a little hostility?" asked Martha, grinning.

"No, I got past the hostility. But he sure taught me to set some boundaries for myself. I finally had to sit down with him and tell him point blank how I felt when his voice got that edge in it and he pressured me to the point of bullying."

"Did you ever reach an understanding?" questioned Martha, curious to know if establishing a healthy working relationship with a driven workaholic were possible.

"Oh, yes. I found out he could be oblivious, but he wasn't callous. When he understood what I was feeling, he was very apologetic. After that, whenever he started to demand I do something for him, he caught himself, asked if I had other projects I was working on, and when I might be able to get to what he needed to have done. Not only have Ernesto and I found a way to work together amicably, but every other attorney in the firm knows that I will not allow myself to be abused."

"Thanks for the heads-up. Now that I know the secret to Ernesto, I think we'll get along a lot better."

"No secret," corrected Andrew, "just an awareness I cultivated by working with Suzanne. All the attorneys respected her and would have never even considered talking down to her. Suzanne was something else. She had a very clear sense of who she was and what she brought to the firm and no attorney, or anyone else for that matter, ever got away with treating her like she was a 'less than.' Or if they did, they never repeated it," smiled Andrew.

"What did she do?" asked Martha, seeing that she could benefit from a few of Suzanne's interpersonal skills.

"First of all, she had the good sense to avoid confronting people publicly, if at all possible. But she made sure they came into her office, where she was in charge, no matter what their status in the firm. She focused on how she felt rather than what they had done or said. She told me once that people become defensive when you evaluate their behavior and are more likely to actually hear you if you just tell them what you know."

"What if that didn't work and they still didn't hear her?" queried Martha.

"Then she asked them questions. She would say 'I believe you said _____ . Is that correct?' And if they agreed, she would ask 'Why did you say that?' She would continue with that line of questioning until it became apparent to the individual what the miscommunication was and how it might have affected her. She said this approach usually ended in a mutually agreeable resolution."

---

counsel emeritus   an attorney who has retired but who is still associated with a firm

Putting It Into Practice 1.10:

Marianne, Martha's fellow student, has also started working as a paralegal. One of the attorneys treats Marianne rudely, asks her to do things of a personal nature (such as pick up his laundry and purchase items for his personal use), provides her with little or no instruction, and then berates her publicly if she does anything wrong. What advice would you give Marianne?

"The Most Important Thing You Can Do for Yourself Is To Show Some Initiative."

By this time, Martha and Andrew had arrived at the restaurant and sat down. After they had ordered, Martha resumed the conversation.

"Did Suzanne give you any pointers about how to get ahead in the firm? I don't seem to be able to get anyone to give me what I consider 'real' paralegal work. I don't know if they don't trust me or if they don't think I'm capable of doing anything more than what I'm doing now," lamented Martha.

"I suspect it's none of the above," observed Andrew. "Most of the attorneys are so preoccupied with their cases, they don't take the time to train their paralegals. And you've probably discovered that most of the other paralegals in our firm are either so swamped they don't have time to help anyone else or they're rather protective of anyone encroaching on their domain."

"So how do I break into something new?" Martha was beginning to despair at the thought of what the future might hold.

"The most important thing you can do for yourself is show some initiative. Decide what you want to be able to do and ask your supervisor, Melinda, if she would let you do it. Show her you're willing to learn and to spend the extra hours needed to get this work done as well as accomplish your other assignments." Andrew became more enthused as he considered the possibilities. "Do you know how I got my job?"

"I thought you did some kind of internship and that they liked your work so much they hired you."

"Not exactly. I did do an internship, but when it was over they told me they didn't have any positions available. They did say they would like to hire me when something opened up. I thought about it and decided to create my own job. I knew the firm did some probate work just to accommodate some of its clients, but that no one had fully developed that aspect of the practice. I told them I would work for minimum wage for two months, and if, in that time, I couldn't build up the probate business, I would leave and they wouldn't be out anything. But if I was successful in justifying my salary, the **law office administrator** would have to agree to hire me for the salary I demanded. I was successful and I'm still here," proclaimed Andrew, obviously relishing his victory.

"You're such an inspiration," said Martha admiringly.

"I'm just tenacious and sometimes that's what it takes to be a successful paralegal," observed Andrew matter-of-factly.

law office administrator someone responsible for the hiring, recruitment, training, and supervision of paralegals and other non-attorney personnel. In some firms those who recruit, hire, train, and supervise paralegals are called *legal assistant managers* or *paralegal coordinators.*

QUALITIES OF SUCCESSFUL PARALEGALS

What are the attributes of a successful paralegal? He or she is each of the following.

- ◆ **P** repared
- ◆ **A** nalytical
- ◆ **R** esilient
- ◆ **A** ble to work with details
- ◆ **L** ogical
- ◆ **E** ffective communicator
- ◆ **G** ood professional judgment
- ◆ **A** ble to organize
- ◆ **L** iterate with computers

PREPARATION at all times is a must for successful paralegals. Their work must be completed within agreed-upon time frames no matter what their workload. Beyond that, they must anticipate what attorneys will need and be prepared to respond to these needs with little or no advance notice.

ANALYSIS is required when preparing and reviewing documents as well as reading and applying the law. The ability to think critically and to find creative answers is essential.

RESILIENCY allows paralegals to adapt to changing circumstances and to persevere no matter what transpires. The litigation process can be very grueling and unpredictable, and attorneys' moods can shift with the status of a case, so flexibility is a wonderful attribute.

ABILITY TO WORK WITH DETAILS is a key ingredient of paralegal success. Many paralegal tasks require astute attention to detail, and attorneys, who can sometimes be oblivious to the details of case management, rely on paralegals to attend to the minutiae they might overlook while attending to the planning of legal strategy.

LOGIC is the cornerstone of the law. Legal reasoning involves the application of legal principles to specific, factual situations and, therefore, requires the utilization of logic.

EFFECTIVE COMMUNICATION SKILLS in both writing and speaking are vital to competent paralegals. They must be able to express themselves clearly, concisely, logically, and persuasively. Such skills allow them to work well with clients and other members of the legal team as well.

GOOD PROFESSIONAL JUDGMENT includes using suitable language, dressing appropriately, taking direction, responding appropriately to requests and questions, working within time constraints, and knowing when to ask for help.

◆ **LOCAL LINKS** ◆

In what kinds of activities are paralegals allowed to engage in your state? Are they, for example, allowed to:

- answer calendar calls?
- represent clients before certain administrative agencies?
- supervise the execution of wills?
- conduct real estate closings?
- make routine motions?

Does your state have an ethical rule that specifically addresses the supervision of paralegals?

Figure 1-6
Qualities of a Successful Paralegal

QUALITIES OF SUCCESSFUL PARALEGALS

Prepared
Analytical
Resilient
Able to work with details
Literate with computers
Able to organize
Good judgment
Effective communicator
Logical

ABILITY TO ORGANIZE includes the ability to establish priorities, develop a work plan, delegate responsibility, and manage time. Efficiency allows successful paralegals to work for more than one attorney on more than one case simultaneously.

LITERACY IN COMPUTER TECHNOLOGY is a must in today's computer-based legal environment. The more proficient paralegals are in using a variety of software programs, the more invaluable they are to the attorneys for whom they work.

Putting It Into Practice 1.11:

Marianne has trouble focusing on tasks, tends to overlook the details, has trouble organizing her day (or her life), has never worked in any kind of office setting, requires being given detailed instructions before she can act, does not like to talk on the telephone, and is still using WordPerfect 5.1 on her computer. What do you think her chances of being a successful paralegal are? Do you have any suggestions you might offer her before she applies for a paralegal position?

BONUS POINTERS:

EMOTIONAL QUALITIES OF SUCCESSFUL PARALEGALS

(The following study is controversial in its findings about some members of the legal profession. We have included it not to disparage lawyers, but because it echoes the sentiments of many paralegals we have talked to over the years. Dealing with "difficult" attorneys is a reality for some paralegals; it need not be yours. As you read the following section, consider how you would respond to some of the situations and attorneys described.)

A field study by Jennifer L. Pierce, an associate professor of sociology and American studies at the University of Minnesota, showed the importance lawyers place on personality traits over work performance skills in hiring legal assistants. Pierce claims that personnel directors emphasize the importance of being "pleasant" and being able to work with "difficult" attorneys, and that attorneys list personal characteristics such as "pleasant" or "unflappable" before they mention task-related skills such as "well organized" or "detail oriented" when describing effective paralegals.

Two particular behaviors Pierce found to be important were deference and caretaking behaviors. Paralegals are expected to defer to attorneys in that attorneys are viewed as the authority and paralegals as the subordinate. This deference may manifest in the aversion of direct eye contact, but is more often seen in the suppression of feelings, particularly anger and irritation. By enduring being treated, in the words of one paralegal, like an "emotional punching bag," they implicitly affirm the attorney's status. To do this, paralegals must manage their own anger as well as their attorney's. The majority of legal assistants Pierce interviewed reported daily incidents of managing anger. Law firms apparently recognize this aspect of the job because they tend to seek paralegals who can "deal with difficult attorneys."

The caretaking aspect of desirable paralegal behavior involves "being pleasant," unflappably "cheerful," and generally optimistic. An unspoken expectation of paralegals, which reflects this caretaking behavior, is that they wear an ever-present smile. The paralegals that Pierce interviewed pointed out the grim consequences of failing to smile. Questions such as "Why aren't you smiling today?" or "What's the matter with you? You look like someone just died." confronted those who dared not smile. Paralegals were also expected to be reassuring, thereby alleviating the anxiety of the attorney. Reassurance might entail listening to the attorney's work-related anxieties or making repeated assurances that a deadline will be met.

Some of the paralegals Pierce interviewed felt compelled to perform this kind of emotional labor while others did not. Those who felt compelled believed that if they did not perform these functions, they would be viewed as "uncooperative," would not receive raises, would be given unrewarding assignments, or might be forced out of the law firm altogether. Pierce's research indicates that their fears were justified. Her findings also show that male paralegals do not seem to have to fulfill the same emotional requirements as women do. They seem to be able to bow out of the "playing Mom" aspect without any cost. On the other hand, the emotional tasks performed by the female paralegals received neither explicit recognition nor financial reward.

"Everyone on the Legal Team Has a Special Place."

As Andrew and Martha headed back to the office, Andrew asked Martha how she was getting along with Audrey, the **legal secretary** in Martha's department.

"She's been very helpful," acknowledged Martha. "Any time I have a question, I just have to ask and she's only too willing to help me out.

"That's good because Audrey and I got off to a rocky start. I was pretty brash when I started out and wanted to impress everyone with what I knew. Audrey, unfortunately, was not only unimpressed, she made a point of putting me in my place every chance she got. After awhile I realized that Audrey had been with the firm for years before I arrived and was doing a lot of paralegal-type work but was getting a legal secretary's salary. I'm sure she resented having to train someone who received a higher salary and who had a higher status in the firm. We eventually worked it out, but only after I learned to humble myself a little and ask her for some advice."

"That reminds me. I heard Audrey's sister, who is a paralegal with that firm down the block, filed a sexual harassment suit against one of the attorneys. No one in our firm has experienced any problems along that line, have they?"

"Not at all. Everyone knows the **senior partners** have zero tolerance for sexual innuendoes, sexist language, or sexual overtures while on the job. Suzanne was instrumental in seeing to that. Everyone knows the story about one of the **associates** who unadvisedly commented about Suzanne's "tush" one day. Much to his chagrin, Suzanne temporarily abandoned her rule prohibiting public confrontations and repeated his comment in front of everyone within hearing distance, asking him if she had heard him correctly. As he stuttered and stammered around for a suitable reply, a **law clerk** nearby grinned. A stern glance from Suzanne inspired the clerk to make a quick exit. The associate sought to silently disappear behind him, but Suzanne's commanding voice stopped him in his tracks. "Please remember, Mr. Jones, that you work in a law office, not a brothel, and that your mother would be relieved to know that the money she expended on your legal education enabled you to recognize the difference."

"I bet no one ever heard a remark like that from him again," piped up Martha, enjoying her visualization of the scene.

"Nor from anyone else in the firm. But most importantly, Suzanne taught all the paralegals she supervised to respect themselves. She herself was proud of being a paralegal. She knew she was well-organized and was particularly gifted at handling details. Although she was bright enough to have gone to law school, she had no need to prove that to anyone. She picked paralegalism, not as an alternative to being a lawyer, but as her chosen profession. She was dismayed by the number of paralegals who talked about becoming lawyers one day and who acted as if their paralegal career was only a stepping stone on their career path. Acknowledging that some, for personal or financial reasons, might have

---

legal secretary secretary whose primary task is the typing of legal documents; this person may also serve as a receptionist in a smaller firm and may perform some of the same tasks as a paralegal, such as keeping track of deadlines, scheduling meetings, preparing subpoenas, and so on

senior partners attorney in a law firm who receives shares of the firm's profits and who participates in the firm's management; a senior partner has seniority in the firm

associates an attorney with a firm who is being trained and evaluated to determine if he or she is partnership material and who, during that training period, receives a salary

law clerk law school student working in a law office

legitimately opted for paralegalism as an intervening step, she exhorted her charges to closely examine their motives for being a paralegal. 'Never be ashamed of being a paralegal or see yourself as being "beneath" an attorney. Everyone on the legal team has a special purpose. The attorneys can't do it by themselves, and although they are more visible than others on the team, they are no more important. The paralegal, the legal secretary, and all the other personnel in a law office contribute to the success of a law practice. So never allow an attorney or anyone else to treat you like a second-class citizen. You are a professional, and you are to be treated professionally just as you treat others professionally.' Makes you proud to be a paralegal, doesn't it?" beamed Andrew, enjoying his reminiscence.

"Sure does," agreed Martha. "Whatever happened to Suzanne anyway? Why did she leave the firm?"

"The firm really didn't have a career path for paralegals, so there was no opportunity for Suzanne to advance. Once she had gone as far as she could here, she began to feel stymied. I know they really tried to entice her to stay by offering her more and more money, but Suzanne wanted to grow and money alone didn't give her what she wanted," explained Andrew.

"I've heard that's generally a problem in the paralegal profession," commented Martha.

"Yes, and one that our firm is only beginning to address," responded Andrew. "But I want to mention something else to you before I forget. If you want to be given more responsibility, you have to let people know what you are doing. You can't be afraid to toot your own horn now and then. How else will anybody know you're around? Our firm is very large and it's easy to get lost in the shuffle. From the look on your face, this is obviously not something you're too comfortable with."

Martha reddened a little and admitted, "I am a little shy. But you're right. I've noticed that the paralegals in my department who seem to get the best assignments are very vocal about what they've accomplished. I guess I need to be a little more aggressive."

"Not aggressive, but more assertive. You don't need to get in anybody's face, but you do need to assert yourself. Competency isn't enough in a firm our size. People need to be aware of your existence and shown what you can do." Andrew assessed Martha's expression and concluded he had made his point.

As they arrived at the front door of the office, Martha expressed her appreciation to Andrew. "You've certainly given me a lot to think about. Thanks for being so honest with me. I hope we can do this again in the near future."

"My pleasure, Martha. How about if we plan for another lunch next month?" suggested Andrew.

"I look forward to it," responded Martha as they stepped out of the elevator and parted company. "See you around."

Putting It Into Practice 1.12:

Why do you want to be a paralegal? Do you ultimately plan to become a lawyer? If not, why would you rather be a paralegal than an attorney? If you do plan to go to law school, consider asking one or more of your instructors to assess your potential as a law school student and as a lawyer.

Putting It Into Practice 1.13:

Marianne does her work, but does not participate in any of the firm's "extra-curricular" activities, speaks as little as possible to her co-workers, and does what she is told to do and no more. How would you assess Marianne's chances of being given additional responsibilities and advancing in the firm?

LAW OFFICE ORGANIZATION

Private Practice

private practice law practice in which attorneys work for themselves or other attorneys

Attorneys in **private practice** work for themselves or other attorneys. These private practices are organized as sole proprietorships, partnerships, limited liability partnerships, or professional corporations.

Sole Proprietorship

sole proprietorship law practice owned by one attorney, who receives the profits

In a **sole proprietorship,** one lawyer owns the business and receives the profits. Although this lawyer typically works by himself or herself and employs paralegals and a legal secretary, he or she may hire other attorneys as salaried employees who do not share in the profits or participate in managing the firm.

Partnership

partnership law practice that employs associates and that is managed by partners

A **partnership** is a law firm comprised of partners and associates. The associates are salaried employees who are in training and being evaluated to determine if they are partnership material. In the past, associates were expected to leave the firm if they were not offered a partnership position after five or so years. Today, however, more and more partnerships allow associates to stay on as permanent salaried employees or be given additional time to prove themselves.

Partners receive shares of the firm's profits rather than salaries and participate in the management of the firm. In small partnerships, most decisions are made by all of the partners, but in larger firms, the managing partner is responsible for seeing that decisions made by committees of partners are properly implemented. In large firms, each partner is assigned to a committee in such areas as financing, office equipment, recruitment, and personnel. The percentage of profits received and the degree to which partners are allowed to participate in the management of the firm depend on how much business they generate, how many hours they bill, and how long they have been with the firm, among other factors. In a partnership, each partner is liable for the actions of all other partners.

Professional Corporation

professional corporation corporate form of a law practice that limits non-professional liability of attorneys without limiting their liability for legal malpractice

A **professional corporation** (designated as PC after the firm's name) is a corporate form that limits individual, non-professional liability of attorneys without limiting their liability for legal malpractice. Attorneys are paid salaries, but can receive dividends if they become shareholders of the corporation. Attorneys who are directors of the corporation are responsible for managing it.

Limited Liability Partnership

limited liability partnership partnership form of law practice that limits the liability of partners

A **limited liability partnership** (designated as LLP after the firm's name) functions as a partnership but without making the partners liable for each other's acts. Each partner is responsible for anyone she supervises and for her own malpractice. Limited liability partnerships are easier to form than corporations, but have the advantages of a corporation.

In addition to attorneys, paralegals, law clerks, and legal secretaries, large firms employ law office administrators or managers, librarians who maintain and update the

---

NET NEWS

To find out the advantages and disadvantages of working in large, medium-size and small firms, go to *www.paralegals.org/reporter,* click on "Winter 1999," and read the section entitled "Paralegal Roles and Responsibilities." Then click on "Summer 2000" and read the same section entitled "Paralegal Roles and Responsibilities." In that same edition, consult the articles "Paralegal's Perspective: From the Small to the Not-So-Small Firm" and "Working in a Small Firm Environment."

Figure 1-7
Private Law Practice

Law Office Personnel	Law Office Organization
Partners	Sole proprietorship
Associates	Partnership
Paralegals	Professional Corporation
Law clerks	Limited liability partnership
Law office administrators	
Legal secretaries	
Librarians	
Investigators	
Receptionists	
Document clerks	
Typists	
Filing clerks	
Bookkeepers	

firm's library, and legal investigators who gather documentary evidence, take photos of evidence, and locate and interview witnesses. Whereas in small firms legal secretaries handle all of the clerical work, in larger firms the clerical staff is more specialized and includes receptionists, typists, document clerks, filing clerks, and bookkeepers.

general counsel   top legal counsel in a corporate legal office

staff attorneys   attorney who reports to general counsel

Some businesses create internal legal departments rather than contract out for legal services. The top legal counsel in most companies is referred to as **general counsel** and those reporting to general counsel are referred to as **staff attorneys.** General counsel is responsible for advising corporate officials on legal issues and monitoring and responding to legislative and administrative proposals that could potentially affect the corporation. Governmental agencies may either hire private law firms on an as-needed basis or, if they have sufficient work, hire attorneys on a full-time basis. In-house law firms function much the same way as those in the private sector.

Legal clinics offer low-cost services by focusing on creating high volume, low overhead operations that rely extensively on the use of paralegals. Legal service offices, which are frequently confused with legal clinics, provide free legal services to the poor. They are affiliated with the federal government's Legal Services Corporation and rely on private donations in addition to public funds. Legal services also make extensive use of paralegals, who are often involved in representing clients before administrative agencies.

Putting It Into Practice 1.14:

Would you prefer working for a law firm, an in-house law firm, a legal clinic, or a legal service office? What do you consider the advantages and disadvantages of each?

BONUS POINTERS:

RETENTION

Retention is a problem in many large law firms. Their average turnover rate is over 20 percent, a substantially higher rate than that experienced by other businesses and organizations. Faced with these numbers, they have been forced to ask why so many associates leave. The major issues associates identify are imbalances between their work and non-work life, lack of meaningful work assignments, lack of partnership opportunities, relationships with co-workers, lack of support or recognition, and lack of challenging opportunities.

Because such high attrition is extremely costly, firms are discovering that, in addition to increasing compensation and creating more creative benefit programs, they must adopt flexible scheduling alternatives that include sabbaticals, job shares, and telecommuting, and develop work enhancements such as relaxed dress codes, retraining, and career development programs. Firms that want to reduce attrition are finding they benefit from establishing formal mentoring relationships, developing individualized training programs, using associates to conduct in-house training sessions to share information they obtain at outside seminars, training associates in client development and financial management, praising associates in public but criticizing them in private, addressing issues of stress, and doing their best to make associates feel like valued team members. These firms also are finding they must assist associates in their development. They can accomplish this by teaching partners to effectively communicate and monitor work assignments and to provide timely and specific feedback on the strengths and limitations of the work performed by associates.

"Because This Came on the Heels of Similar Shootings Across the Country, Some Were Speculating That the Shooters Were Part of Some Disenfranchised Fringe Group on Campus."

As Martha walked into the lunchroom to put her leftovers from lunch in the refrigerator, she heard a news bulletin on the radio. "We've just received word that Michael Johnson, the nationally acclaimed star quarterback of the Washington High School football team, has been shot." Martha stopped abruptly and groaned involuntarily, "Oh, my God."

Mike went to the same high school as two of her daughters and they, along with most of the female population at Washington High School, had a crush on him. Not only an athlete being courted by several major college teams, Mike was an honor student, Homecoming King, and President of the senior class. Easy-going and gregarious, Mike made friends easily and seemed to live a charmed life. Charmed until now, at least.

The announcer went on. Details were sketchy, but apparently he had been shot during the lunch break as he and his girlfriend were walking to his car. Several students had seen three young men with masks suddenly come around the corner of a building, shooting wildly into the air. Everyone dove for cover or fell instinctively to the ground. Mike had apparently lain on top of his girlfriend to protect her. One of the men had walked over to Mike and shot him deliberately in the back at close range before running away. Remarkably, no one else had been hurt, but Mike was in critical condition at a nearby hospital.

Reeling from the shock, Martha ran into her office to call her daughters. They were home and safe, but were understandably shaken by the shooting. They had been at the other end of the campus when the shooting occurred, but were aware that rumors were already spreading about the perpetrators and their motive. Because this shooting came on the heels of similar incidents in high schools throughout the country, some were speculating that the shooters were part of some disenfranchised, fringe group on campus.

"Why Mike?" asked Martha out loud as she stood in the doorway of the lunchroom, listening to an update on the radio.

"Do you know him?" asked Ernesto, who unbeknownst to Martha was standing behind her.

"Yes. He lives down the street from us. My girls and he used to play together as kids."

"Well, if he survives, he's got one hell of a lawsuit," declared Ernesto, oblivious to the look of horror on Martha's face.

"How can you think of lawsuits when a beautiful young soul like that is mortally wounded?" blurted Martha.

"Don't get hot," sputtered Ernesto, attempting to cover his embarrassment. "Of course, I feel bad for the kid and his family. I was just making an observation."

Martha stiffened as she excused herself and returned to her office.

Several weeks later, after Mike had regained consciousness, Ernesto knocked on Martha's door. The air between them was still somewhat tense, and Ernesto wanted to tread carefully but lacked the guile to cloak his purpose. He came right to the point.

"I've been thinking about that Johnson kid. Now that it looks like he's going to live, I've been wondering if he has any idea of the damages he could collect if he sued the school district and any other potential **tortfeasors.** Some of the news reports indicate that the kids that shot him might be part of some weird underground group. Apparently they're obsessed with watching that cult movie, *Teenage Stalkers.* If that's true, he might have a case against the production company that made that movie."

"Why are you telling me this?" asked Martha coldly.

"I figured that if your girls were such good friends with him, they might be able to make some subtle suggestions about filing suit, maybe they could remind him that their mother just happens to work for the biggest, and of course best, law firm in town."

"So basically you want me to use my kids to do what you can't do—solicit business for this firm?" Martha asked, the edge in her voice noticeable even to Ernesto.

"It's not **solicitation** unless an attorney or an agent of an attorney is involved. And your kids certainly aren't agents of this firm," retorted Ernesto.

"I don't care what you call it, I'm not going to involve my girls in anything that underhanded. Besides, I learned in my ethics classes that lawyers are supposed to avoid 'even the appearance of impropriety.' One of my ethics professors taught us that if we'd be ashamed to admit what we had done, we shouldn't do it. Well, I'd be embarrassed to tell anyone I'd used my kids to induce a severely injured and vulnerable teenager to do business with this firm."

ETHICAL ETIQUETTE

ETHICAL CODES

The Model Code of Professional Responsibility was published by the American Bar Association (ABA) in 1969 and serves as a model set of rules designed to govern the conduct of lawyers. The Model Code contains:

This Code was modified by the ABA in 1983, and was newly entitled the Model Rules of Professional Conduct. The new Model Rules are formatted differently than the Model Code and no longer distinguish between mandatory and aspirational rules, although they do contain interpretative commentary. Most states have patterned their ethical rules after the new Model Rules; some have retained the old Model Code. California has its own code based on neither the Model Code nor the Model Rules.

Several sanctions can be used against attorneys who engage in ethical misconduct. The mildest sanction is a reprimand, which is basically a "slap on the hand," warning the attorney against future misconduct. Reprimands can be communicated confidentially or publicly, but in either case become part of the attorney's record and are then considered if the attorney should commit a subsequent ethical violation. More serious than a reprimand is a suspension. An attorney who is suspended is not allowed to practice for a designated period of time. The most serious sanction, disbarment, is reserved for the most egregious violations. A disbarred attorney is no longer able to practice because his license is revoked. In some instances, disbarred attorneys who demonstrate their complete rehabilitation are allowed to be reinstated, but in most cases disbarment is permanent.

Because paralegals are not attorneys, they are not bound by the ethical rules promulgated by the states. They are, however, liable for negligent or intentional conduct that causes injury to clients. Furthermore, some states have adopted guidelines designed to assist attorneys in their use of paralegals, and the ABA has developed Model Guidelines for the Utilization of Legal Assistant Services that states are encouraged to look to when drafting their own guidelines. Both NALA and NFPA have created codes of ethics to guide the actions of their members.

NET NEWS

To determine which code of ethics your state has adopted, go to *www.legalethics.com*.

Figure 1-8
Sources of Ethical Codes

American Bar Association
Model Code of Professional Responsibility
Model Rules of Professional Conduct
Model Guidelines for the Utilization of Legal Assistant Services

National Association of Legal Assistants
Model Code of Ethics and Professional Responsibility
NALA Model Standards and Guidelines for Utilization of Legal Assistants

National Federation of Paralegal Associations
NFPA Model Code of Ethics and Professional Responsibility and Guidelines for Enforcement

tortfeasors   person who has committed a tort, which is a private wrong resulting in injury to one or more persons

solicitation   inducement by an attorney or an agent of an attorney to hire that attorney

ETHICAL ETIQUETTE

SOLICITATION AND ADVERTISING

Attorneys are prohibited from soliciting business from prospective clients unless the attorney has a family or prior professional relationship with that client. In the personal injury area, so-called "ambulance chasing" is condemned by the public as well as the legal profession because it involves preying on people who are vulnerable and unable to make clear rational decisions because of their injuries. Some states have instituted time periods after accidents during which lawyers are prohibited from contacting victims.

Although the ethical rules clearly prohibit paralegals and other agents of attorneys from engaging in solicitation on behalf of their attorney employers, such solicitation still occurs. Accident investigators can often be found at the scene of airline crashes, for example, soliciting business for attorneys. The problem is serious enough that some states have created disaster teams of lawyers who go out to the scenes of major crashes and warn victims about being solicited.

Although at one time lawyer advertising was banned and generally considered offensive by members of the bar, the U.S. Supreme Court in 1977 in *Bates v. State Bar of Arizona*, 433 U.S. 350 (1977), reversed tradition and allowed some forms of advertising. The Court did not find the same dangers in advertising that it found in solicitation. Attorneys are now allowed to advertise their services via radio, TV, newspaper, or other forms of public media as long as their ads are not false or misleading. (Model Rule 7.2) Attorneys cannot, however, make statements that contain material misrepresentations of fact or law, they cannot create an unjustified expectation about legal results, or compare their services to the services of other lawyers unless that comparison is factually substantiated. Many states prohibit testimonials because they are believed to be inherently misleading. Dramatizations are becoming more tolerated although they are usually disfavored by the organized bar.

Today, many attorneys pursue some form of advertising, although most simply pay for listings in the Yellow Pages. The ABA encourages dignity in advertising and offers annual awards for Dignity in Lawyer Advertising. It discourages "inappropriately dramatic music, unseemly slogans, hawkish spokespersons, premium offers, and slapstick routines or outlandish settings." (Aspirational Goals for Lawyer Advertising) Many attorneys feel that lawyer advertising is a major reason for the poor public image of lawyers, although some studies show that the public does not find ads as distasteful as lawyers do.

Putting It Into Practice 1.15:

Do you think Ernesto's suggestion to Martha that her daughters talk to Mike about suing constitutes solicitation? Why or why not?

"This Kind of Advertising Sullies the Image of the Legal Profession and Puts Us in the Same Category as Used Car Dealers and Cereal Manufacturers."

"You make it sound like I wanted you to put a gun to the kid's head. I just want to make him aware of his options so he can make an intelligent choice," argued Ernesto.

"If you're so sure of yourself, why don't we run your proposal by Mr. Morgan?" Martha knew she had put Ernesto in a bind.

"That old relic?" sneered Ernesto. "He hates advertising! If he had his way, we'd still be using word of mouth to let people know we're here!"

"And what's wrong with word of mouth? That's what got you here, isn't it?" snapped John.

"John, I didn't know you were here," muttered Ernesto. Although John was counsel emeritus, he retained an office at the firm and came in about once a week to read his mail and peruse the latest legal publications. He was enjoying his retirement, but still liked to feel a part of the practice and took pleasure in the fact that some of the partners dropped by on occasion to solicit his advice.

"Obviously. Now what is it you're trying to get Ms. Ferguson to do that you don't want me to know about?" Ernesto summarized their discussion and John smiled.

"Ernesto, if you really believe that White and Treadwell is the best firm for Mr. Johnson, why can't you simply allow him to find that out for himself? We have created a name for ourselves in this community based on the quality of legal work we have done for thousands of clients over the years. Our name speaks for itself. We do not need to enlist the services of two teenage girls to do our bidding for us. I find all these cloak-and-dagger shenanigans totally unnecessary." John's voice began to take on the tone he adopted when he was lecturing at the law school.

"Furthermore, I agree with Ms. Ferguson that what you propose crosses over the boundary of impropriety." John stopped to take a breath and Ernesto fired back his rebuttal, ignoring the solicitation issue momentarily.

"Your philosophy may have worked great when there were a couple hundred attorneys practicing in this city, but now there are thousands. The public has no way of assessing who is best able to represent them unless we help them out."

"And you think advertising offers an objective and reliable way of helping them do that? Can you stand there and honestly tell me that TV ads, with flying eagles and roaring lions, have any relevance to the quality of legal work done?" interrupted John.

"You're using the extreme case to make your point. Of course, I'm not talking about that kind of crass commercialization. But what about the monthly newsletters our firm puts out so that our clients know what we're doing and how changes in the law affect them? And the press releases we put in the bar journal? And the home page we've created on the Web? What's so offensive about letting people know we exist and telling them what we do?" demanded Ernesto.

"I admit that giving people information about our firm is good marketing, and I have come to accept that as an inevitable part of doing business today. But some lawyers don't stop at that. They engage in direct-mail advertising, TV and radio spots, billboards, flyers on cars, and ads on the back of grocery receipts and in the TV guide. This kind of advertising sullies the image of the legal profession and puts us in the same category as used car dealers and cereal manufacturers. In fact, some of those testimonials I've seen on TV lately make me seriously question whether I should have entered the legal profession," lamented John.

"You're getting a little theatrical, don't you think," chided Ernesto. He could understand John's point, but thought that John's passive approach to attracting clients was unrealistic. He fancied himself a potential **rainmaker** for the firm and took enormous pride in his impressive win-loss record, which he considered the ultimate measure of any attorney's value. John may battle for the Truth, he thought to himself, but I want to walk out of the courtroom a winner. "Anyway, advertising is not the point as far as this Johnson kid is concerned. I think we're making a big mistake by not going after his business, but I guess we'll just have to wait and see what happens. Right now I have to meet with a client—a client who came to this firm, by the way, after he heard me speak at a Kiwanis club meeting." Ernesto strode off, feeling triumphant at having volleyed the parting shot.

When Ernesto was out of earshot, John confided to Martha, "Ernesto has the potential of being a great litigator. He just has to conquer his ego. Now don't you feel any pressure about steering that young man in our direction. He needs to focus on healing, not suing."

Martha nodded gratefully and smiled as John walked away. She knew his renown as an elder statesman for the legal profession and his reputation as a formidable litigator, but now she saw the gentle heart that housed the keen mind.

BONUS POINTERS:

A CASE OF SOLICITATION

Keith S. Franz and Judson H. Lipowitz are two lawyers who were disciplined for trying to make clients of survivors and grieving relatives of people killed in a collision between Maryland Rail Commuter Service and Amtrak trains in Silver Springs, Maryland. On the night of the accident, the lawyers passed out their business cards to survivors watching late-night news accounts of the crash at a Washington hotel. They called the victims and visited their homes. Victims of the crash were confronted by lawyers (other than the two named above) in intensive care units and were phoned repeatedly for days afterward.

Franz and Lipowitz reported themselves to the Attorney Grievance Commission the day before a newspaper article appeared detailing their conduct. Before their confession, the pair had apparently recognized their wrongdoing and sent letters to all the clients they had obtained, telling them that they could no longer represent them. They promised to aid any attorney the relatives chose to hire and did not charge for any of the time they had spent or expenses they had incurred. The attorneys claimed that this was an isolated incident and that no harm had come to any of their clients.

---

rainmaker   attorney who attracts new clients to a firm

Mike fought his way through the fog in his head. He wanted to understand, to feel, to be part of his surroundings. The words coming at him touched his eardrums but seemed to ricochet off his brain and out into the vapory world that surrounded him. Some of the smiling faces seemed vaguely familiar, but most were unknown. Would they all stop moving for just one second and explain to him what was going on? What did they want from him? Where were they all going in such a hurry? Why couldn't he feel his body? Was he dead? The swirling in his head threatened to overcome him and he started to slip back into the darkness, but poking fingers and strident voices brought him back.

■ TIM'S TECHNO TIPS

Introduction to Hardware and Software

Hi! I'm Tim. I don't appear in the story line until Chapter Three but the authors have agreed to allow me to start giving you some tips about some of the technological issues germane to the practice of law. Let me begin by saying computer literacy is a must for today's paralegal. As a self-confessed computer geek myself, I'm delighted that computers have become the mainstay of most law offices, but I'm sure some of you are looking for a way to avoid developing your computer expertise. Sorry, but there's no way out of this one! The attorneys who began practicing before computers became a way of life look to paralegals to do all the things with computers they don't know how to do and don't want to learn. And the attorneys at the other end of the spectrum, who can't wait to get the latest hardware gadgets and software packages, expect their paralegals to be as well-versed as they are in everything technology has to offer the modern legal practitioner. So, the bottom line is, one way or the other, you're going to have to hone those computer skills.

Let's get you started by establishing the basic elements that comprise an automated office. In years past, an automated office consisted of an electric typewriter and a copier. Today the computer and its associated *hardware* (physical items) and *software* (electronic instructions) rule. The most popular desktop computer is called the *PC (personal computer)*. Other computers, generally more powerful and expensive, are referred to as *minicomputers* and *mainframe computers*.

The PC has several basic elements. The *CPU (central processing unit)* is the "brains" of the computer. The relative speed with which a computer processes data is considered important (especially if you're in a hurry to get some information or to complete a task) and it's described in terms of *megahertz* (500, 600, or higher megahertz). The sophistication of a computer and its relative state of the art is reflected in its name: a Pentium III, an AMD-2, Macintosh, etc. Be aware, however, that regardless of its level of sophistication, a computer's basic elements remain the same.

Another important feature of a computer is its *memory.* Memory is expressed in *RAM (random access memory);* this memory is volatile in that turning off the power to the computer causes the information stored in RAM to be lost. For this reason, a computer must be "*booted*" each time it's turned on. During the "booting" process, the RAM is loaded with all the information the computer needs to begin utilizing its programs.

Information is stored permanently in a computer's *hard drive.* Hard drives range from 1 or 2 *gigabytes* (a gigabit is 1,000,000,000,000 *bytes,* which is the means by which information is encoded in a computer) to a hundred gigabytes and more.

The time needed to access a hard drive is substantially more than to access RAM, which is why, generally speaking, the more RAM you have, the better your computer will run. Most computers still have a floppy drive that reads portable disks, which can contain up to almost 3 million bits. As new ways of communicating evolve (the Web, e-mail, local and wide area networks, etc.), however, the need for floppy disks is rapidly diminishing.

Today, we've moved from hard drives and floppies to compact and portable storage devices, such as *Zip drives,* which contain over 100 megabytes of data. Some portable hard drives can be connected to your computer through either the *printer port* (a parallel connection on the computer that attaches to the printer and other parallel devices), your *serial port* (a serial connection on the computer, usually two of them, that attaches to your mouse and other serial devices), the *USB* (the universal serial bus) or a *SCSI* card (SCSI cards allow the computer to communicate with numerous peripherals through one connection), that can store gigabits of information with access times similar to the main hard drive in your computer. Tape drives with massive storage capability (but much slower access and copy times) are also available.

Most computers come complete with a *modem* that can communicate over telephone lines with other computers. The standard modems now used are limited to transmitting data at a little more than 50,000 bits per second. With special modems and data lines (such as fiberoptic cable), communication speeds of over 1 megabit per second are possible. Modems can also be used to send and receive faxes and to handle voice mail. The information processed, or received, by your computer can be viewed on the *monitor,* a TV-like device that provides a color image on a screen size of up to 21 inches or more. Larger screens are desirable because they can be adjusted to provide larger images for better viewing. They are capable of producing two pages of data side by side. For "cut and paste" purposes, a large screen is not only an eye saver but a time saver.

The most common devices for inputting data are the *keyboard* and *mouse.* Data can also be input by your modem, through a microphone, from a scanner, or via infrared devices, as well as a multitude of new devices that are being designed and marketed on a regular basis. One of the primary sources of input to your computer is the *CD-ROM.* Almost all programs are put on CD-ROMs for inputting to your computer.

When you buy a computer, you will notice that the speed of the CPU is one of the main selling points the salesperson will stress. But keep in mind that the speed of the computer's "*bus*" is equally important. The bus is the multilane highway connecting the CPU to the various output and input devices. Today's systems have a bus speed of approximately 100 megahertz, less than one-fifth the speed of many CPUs. Because of the bottleneck that can be created by the bus, as well as the access and write speeds of associated devices, the maximum benefit of the CPU's speed cannot be realized and, therefore, is not nearly as beneficial as you might be led to believe. Another thing to bear in mind when purchasing a computer is the extent of its video memory. Lack of video memory may be hard to notice in word processing applications (except when viewing graphics), but picture and graphic-intensive users will need to maximize their available video memory.

So what should a typical paralegal's computer look like? It should have at least a 300 megahertz CPU with a minimum of 64 (preferably 128) megabits of memory, and have a standard or specialized keyboard and mouse. (Wireless keyboards and mice are readily available to reduce the clutter on your work station.) A quality 56K fax/voice modem should be included along with a standard floppy drive. Some type of backup medium should be attached. A Zip drive, an external hard drive, or a tape drive should be used to back up your data on a regular basis. Most paralegals also have a scanner to copy adverse party pleadings into appropriate files. *OCR* (optical character recognition) programs that convert a scanned image into text that can be manipulated are readily available. Basic word processing is a must. Most law offices still use WordPerfect, although Microsoft's Word is gaining market share. Being versed in both programs is a plus.

Many law offices use specialized programs for docketing and maintaining a calendar, conflict checks, time keeping and billing, e-mail security, database and litigation support, anti-virus programs, and other tasks. The primary program on which all these programs run is called the *operating system.* Windows is, by far, the primary operating system for the personal computer. In the past MS-DOS was the primary operating system and is still used on older, slower machines that do not have the disk space, RAM, or CPU speed to effectively run the Windows operating system. Other operating systems, each of which has very small percentage of PC operating system market, include UNIX (mainly for larger computers than the PC), the Macintosh operating system used by Macintosh compatible PCs, and OS/2, an IBM operating system that has not caught on. Presently, the most advanced version of Windows is Windows 2000. Users with more sophisticated or complex *LANs* and *WANs* (Local Area Network/Wide Area Network) are usually running on Windows NT or Novell Netware. A LAN is a local network of computers that are hardwired (usually) together in one office or a suite of offices in one building. A WAN often is connected by telephone lines, optic cable, or satellite, and links various computers in different cities or countries together. LANs and WANs are usually connected with a special card inside the computer. They may have dedicated wiring that prevents any non-connected computer from accessing the system.

TECHNO TRIP

And now, something to look forward to. In upcoming chapters, I'll be talking about some specialized programs and associated hardware. Until then, take time to get up close and personal with the computer of your choice. If you have a computer of your own, look at the instruction booklet and see if you can answer these questions. If not, go to a local computer store, pick out a computer, and find out the answers.

1. What is the CPU speed?
2. What is the Bus speed?
3. What is the amount of RAM?
4. How many gigabits does your hard drive have?
5. What kind of mouse and keyboard does it have?
6. What is the transmission speed of the modem?
7. Can it accommodate a Zip drive?
8. Does it have a CD-ROM?
9. What is its video memory?
10. Does it have a scanner and an OCR program?
11. What operating system does it use?

Now let's do a little Internet exercise. Find out what a computer you would want to have would cost.

1. What kind of search terms did you use?
2. Which search terms proved most effective?
3. Try using different search engines, such as Netscape, HotBot, Lycos, Google, and others. What differences do you find when you use these different search engines?
4. Did you shop at particular Web stores, such as Circuit City, Best Buy, Fry's Electronics, Damark, or Liquidprice.com?

To familiarize yourself with some of the most common terms used on the Internet and to describe aspects of the Internet, go to *www.paralegals.org/reporter* and click on "1999 Year-End." Go to the article "A Basic Glossary of Internet Buzz Words."

SUMMARY – PART B

Certification is not required by most employers, but it is viewed as a positive step toward the increasing professionalization of paralegals. The licensing of paralegals, on the other hand, has created considerable controversy. The American Bar Association and several states have considered the licensing issue, but have not adopted any licensing proposals to date. NALA has opposed attempts at licensing, while NFPA has drafted a Model Act for Paralegal Licensure.

Paralegals are employed by law firms, legal clinics, government agencies, in-house law offices, legal service clinics, and special interest groups. They can also do work on a freelance basis. Although most paralegals work in law firms and in-house legal departments, legal clinics and legal service clinics rely extensively on paralegals. Attorneys in private practice are organized as sole proprietorships, partnerships, limited liability partnerships, or professional corporations.

Paralegals are not governed by the same set of ethical rules as attorneys. They can, however, be liable for any negligent conduct that causes harm to clients. Both NALA and NFPA have created ethical codes for their members. One of the most important ethical violations paralegals must avoid is the unauthorized practice of law. Violation of this ethical prohibition can result in fines or even imprisonment. Although the definition of "practicing law" is not clear, paralegals cannot give legal advice, cannot appear in court or argue motions, cannot accept clients or set fees, and cannot prepare legal documents unless they do so under the supervision of an attorney. Furthermore, paralegals must avoid violating the ethical rules governing attorneys because they serve as agents of the attorneys for whom they work. One of those rules prohibits attorneys from soliciting clients and prevents them from advertising in any way that is false or misleading. As agents of attorneys, paralegals also are prohibited from engaging in any act of solicitation.

KEY TERMS

Associates	Law office administrator	Malpractice	Senior partners
Certification	Legal secretary	Partnership	Sole proprietorship
Counsel emeritus	Licensure	Private practice	Solicitation
General counsel	Limited liability	Professional corporation	Staff attorneys
Law clerk	partnership	Rainmaker	Tortfeasors

REVIEW QUESTIONS – PART B

1. What is the difference between certification and licensure?
2. Why do some groups question the wisdom of licensing paralegals? What is the status of the licensing issue today?
3. Name several actions that constitute the unauthorized practice of law. Under what circumstances can a paralegal engage in the practice of law?
4. What are some characteristics of successful paralegals?
5. How should a paralegal deal with an attorney who is unreasonable or disrespectful?
6. What can a paralegal do to be given more responsibilities on the job?
7. Compare the four forms of private practice.
8. What are the functions of general counsel and staff attorneys?
9. What is the difference between a legal service office and a legal clinic?
10. How does the Model Code of Professional Responsibility differ from the Model Rules of Professional Conduct?
11. Explain the difference between a canon, an ethical consideration, and a disciplinary rule.
12. Explain the ethical rule regarding solicitation.
13. What are some of the arguments for and against lawyer advertising? What is the status of the ethical rules regarding lawyer advertising?

PRACTICE EXAM – PART B

MULTIPLE CHOICE

1. The following arguments are made in reference to the licensing issue regarding paralegals:
   a. the legal needs of the poor are not being met
   b. consumers may not be able to assess when it is appropriate for a paralegal to represent them
   c. some cases are not economical for attorneys to handle
   d. all of the above

2. The unauthorized practice of law is prohibited
   a. in order to protect consumers from receiving bad legal advice
   b. because lay people are not governed by the same ethical code as lawyers
   c. to protect attorneys from competition by lay people
   d. all of these arguments have been used

3. Paralegals can never
   a. argue motions in court unless they are purely ministerial
   b. prepare legal documents
   c. give legal advice, even if it is procedural in nature
   d. engage in the practice of law

4. Advertising by lawyers
   a. creates a poor public image for lawyers
   b. assists consumers in selecting a lawyer
   c. has the potential of misleading the public
   d. all of the above arguments have been made

5. Solicitation
   a. differs from ambulance chasing
   b. is prohibited because it allows attorneys to prey on the vulnerable
   c. is not considered as dangerous as advertising
   d. is rarely a problem

FILL IN THE BLANK

6. _____ is a voluntary process undertaken by a paralegal organization to recognize individuals with certain qualifications, whereas _____ is carried out by government agencies.

7. An entry level certification exam created by NALA is the _____ exam, while an advanced exam created by NFPA is the _____ exam.

8. A _____ is responsible for the hiring, training, recruitment, and supervision of paralegals.

9. An _____ is an attorney who is being trained and evaluated by a firm. A _____ is a student who is working for a firm while attending law school.

10. Attorneys in _____ work for themselves or other attorneys; they can organize as _____ , in which they own the business and receive the profits, as a _____ , in

which partners receive shares of the profits and participate in the management of the practice, or as _____ , in which the attorneys are paid salaries or receive dividends, but in which their individual liability is limited.

11. A special form of a partnership, known as a _____ partnership, has the attributes of a partnership but protects the partners from being liable for each other's acts.

12. The top legal counsel in a company is called _____ counsel, whereas those who report to this attorney are called _____ attorneys.

13. Someone who causes personal injury to another is referred to as a _____ .

14. The ethical code for lawyers contains _____(statements of general principle), _____ (mandatory rules that attorneys must follow), and _____ (aspirational comments interpreting the rules).

TRUE OR FALSE

____ 15. The ABA has recommended that paralegals be licensed.

____ 16. NFPA opposes the licensing of paralegals, whereas NALA has drafted a model act for paralegal licensure.

____ 17. Some fear that licensure of paralegals could lead to confrontations with attorneys.

____ 18. Administrative issues, such as what kinds of degrees should be required and what agency should be responsible for administering paralegal licensure, complicate the licensing issue.

____*19. The wide-ranging licensing scheme proposed in New Jersey became the focus on impassioned national debate before being rejected by the New Jersey Supreme Court.

____20. Paralegals are prohibited from engaging in any activity that calls for the "exercise of professional judgment" unless they do so under the supervision of an attorney.

____21. Paralegals cannot represent clients, even at administrative hearings.

____22. Paralegals cannot advise anyone about how to resolve a legal problem, but they can respond to questions that are strictly procedural in nature.

____23. Paralegals cannot accept cases, but they can set fees.

____24. The ethical code clearly specifies what constitutes "adequate supervision" of a paralegal.

____25. Paralegals can never supervise the execution of wills, answer calendar calls, or make purely ministerial motions.

____26. Paralegals are allowed to inform clients of the status of their case.

____27. Paralegals need not clearly reveal their nonattorney status as long as they are working under the supervision of an attorney.

____28. In order to advance in a law firm, paralegals must learn to take the initiative and to be assertive.

____29. Successful paralegals are well-organized and logical, but they do not need to be detail-oriented.

____30. Computer literacy is no longer a high priority for paralegals.

____*31. Many attorneys expect paralegals to refrain from expressing anger or irritation and to smile without fail.

____*32. Some research indicates that those paralegals who fail to show deference to attorneys and who fail to exhibit certain care-taking behaviors are viewed as uncooperative.

____33. In a professional corporation, each attorney is liable for the acts of all other attorneys, but in a partnership, attorneys are not liable for the acts of other attorneys.

____34. A senior partner receives a larger percentage of the profits and participates to a greater degree in managing a practice than does a junior partner.

____35. General counsel advise corporate officials on legal matters and monitor pertinent legislative and administrative proposals.

____36. Legal clinics are associated with the federal government's Legal Services Corporation.

____*37. The turnover rate of associates is quite high in many large law firms.

____*38. To retain associates, many firms have discovered they must train partners to more effectively train associates and must provide associates with flexible scheduling alternatives and work enhancement programs.

____39. The Model Rules and the Model Code are synonymous.

____40. Paralegals are not bound by the ethical code of lawyers.

____41. Because paralegals work under the supervision of an attorney, they are not liable for their negligent conduct.

____42. Solicitation by lawyers is a rare occurrence.

____43. Attorneys are allowed to advertise as long as their advertisements are neither false nor misleading.

____44. Attorneys cannot include testimonials or dramatizations in their advertisements.

____45. Attorneys are not allowed to compare their services to the services of other attorneys.

____46. Few attorneys today advertise because they consider it offensive.

* Questions taken from Bonus Pointers

LEGAL LINGO

What's My Name?

1. I am working in a law firm while I go to law school.
2. I attract lots of clients to a firm.
3. I am a type of law firm dedicated to issues that are of great importance to the public.
4. I am what attorneys are sued for when they fail to conform to a reasonable standard of care.
5. I have caused injury to another.
6. I provide legal services to the public but am not under the supervision of an attorney.
7. I am a voluntary process undertaken by paralegals who want to be recognized for their special qualifications.
8. I hand deliver documents.

9. I work as an independent contractor for an attorney.
10. I am done by the government to validate the qualifications of individuals employed in a particular line of work.
11. I am an attorney who participates in the management of a law firm and who has seniority in the firm.
12. I am a statement of general principle in the ethical code of lawyers.
13. I am an attorney who is being trained and evaluated by a law firm.
14. I am known by many names: sole proprietorship, professional corporation, partnership, and limited liability partnership.
15. I am an aspirational comment that is used to interpret the disciplinary rules.
16. I am also known as "ambulance chasing."

LEGAL LOGISTICS

1. Why are independent paralegals more likely than other paralegals to cross over the line prohibiting the unauthorized practice of law?
2. Why do you think it has been difficult to define what a paralegal is and describe what a paralegal does?
3. Why is the licensing of paralegals such a controversial topic?
4. Develop a plan of action for finding a paralegal job.
5. Sometimes friction exists between experienced paralegals and new associates or between experienced legal secretaries and new paralegals. Why do you suspect this happens?
6. What potential challenges do you foresee in becoming a paralegal?
7. What advantages do you see in working for a large firm? For a sole proprietor? For a government agency?
8. Why is it important for paralegals to understand why they want to be a paralegal?
9. Begin developing your personal "Guide to Success as a Paralegal." What pointers will you include from this chapter?

A TRIP TO THE MOVIES

If you saw the movie *To Kill a Mockingbird,* you no doubt remember Gregory Peck, who played the role of Atticus Finch, the stellar attorney whose integrity was impeccable. Imagine that Atticus hires you as a freelance paralegal to assist him in his defense of Tom Robinson, the African-American man accused of raping a young white woman.

1. He asks you to find out whether he has grounds for arguing that the bail set for his client was excessive. Is a paralegal allowed to do this?
2. During the trial, Atticus is supposed to appear in another court on another case. Can he ask you to appear in the courtroom for the simple purpose of requesting a continuance?
3. While you are standing outside the courtroom during a recess, your client asks if you think the trial is going well. Atticus is in another part of the building. How should you respond?
4. The client then asks what the consequence will be if the judge admits some apparently incriminating evidence against him. How should you respond?
5. Can Atticus ask you to prepare a post-trial motion moving for a new trial?
6. Atticus has another client, Boo Radley, who is very shy about coming into town. He wants you to prepare a simple will. Can you do this without Atticus' assistance?
7. Atticus realizes that Boo may have a lawsuit against a pesticide company and knows that Boo is unaware that he has a right to such a claim. If Atticus goes to Boo's house and tells him about this lawsuit, has he committed solicitation?
8. Atticus's competition advertises that his rates are the best around and that he has the best win-loss record of anyone in the county. Does an ad of this nature violate the ethical code?
9. Scout, Atticus's daughter, introduces you to some folks in town as her father's assistant. Her introduction might lead some people to believe that you are an attorney. What should you do?

INTERNET INQUIRIES

1. Go to the Web page for your local or state bar association. (Use the name of this bar association as a search term.) If you cannot find a site this way, go to *www.findlaw.com*. Answer the following questions.
   a. What is the address for this site? (You might want to bookmark this site to facilitate future referencing.)
   b. Does it have links to local, state, and federal governmental agencies?
   c. Does it have information about how to locate attorneys in your area?
   d. Does it have links to law-related resources, such as legal search engines and directories?
   e. Does it have links to local, state, and federal courts?
   f. Does it have links to pertinent ethical opinions
   g. Does it provide information about upcoming legal seminars?
   h. Does it have links to other bar associations and legal organizations?
   i. Can you access the local and/or state court rules on this site?
   j. Can you find jury instructions using this site?
   k. List other information available from this site that you think could prove helpful to you in the future.
   l. What are the requirements for attorneys being licensed to practice law in your state?

2. Go to *www.legalethics.com* and answer the following questions.
   a. What version of the ABA's ethical rules has your state adopted? Hint: Under "Choose a Category" click on "States." Under your state's listings, look for a category relating to courts or court rules.
   b. What articles can you find dealing with client confidentiality and the use of email? Hint: Under "Choose a Category" click on "Ethics" and under "And Then a Topic" click on "Articles."
   c. Summarize an ethical opinion issued in your state relating to advertising or confidentiality.

2 Developing the Case

OBJECTIVES:

In this chapter you will learn:

- the rules regarding confidentiality
- what law is and what purpose it serves
- the sources of the law
- to distinguish between substantive and procedural law
- to distinguish between civil and criminal law
- how to organize and structure an initial interview
- what the attorney-client privilege is
- how to get information from a client

- how to interview a witness
- how to obtain records
- how to take photographs for litigation purposes
- how to collect physical evidence
- how to get expert witnesses
- how to evaluate a civil case
- how to organize files
- how to manage your time
- to recognize conflicts of interest

Mike overheard his parents talking about his mounting hospital bills and their concern that the continuing onslaught of medical expenses could bring them to the brink of bankruptcy. Their insurance coverage would soon lapse but there was no end in sight to Mike's rehabilitative needs. Despite his parents' insistence that he not worry about how they would pay for his treatment, Mike was concerned. He didn't want his hospitalization to jeopardize the business his family had worked so long and diligently to create.

When Martha's daughters came to visit him, he was preoccupied with how he was going to help his family. He was only half-listening to the girls chatter when he suddenly remembered that Martha worked for a law firm. He saw his chance to get some information. The girls had little to offer him, however. Their mother had so clearly explained to them the need for **confidentiality** in her work, they were reluctant to question her about what she did and so they had little idea about what happened in her office. The girls did give Mike their mother's number and he was on the phone as soon as they left his room.

ETHICAL ETIQUETTE

CONFIDENTIALITY

One of the fundamental cornerstones of law practice is the concept of confidentiality. It is premised on the assumption that an attorney must know everything about a client's case in order to fully serve that client. The assumption is that a client will not reveal information that is embarrassing or incriminating without an assurance that it will not be revealed outside of the attorney-client relationship. This protection continues even after the attorney-client relationship is terminated. Arguably, any information gleaned as a result of the attorney-client relationship is protected no matter how the information is obtained or the setting in which the attorney learns the information. The best advice, then, is to reveal nothing about a client.

Confidentiality can be broken if:

- the client consents
- a court orders it

confidentiality   the obligation to preserve the confidences and secrets of a client

- ◆ it is necessary to collect a fee
- ◆ it is necessary to protect oneself against an accusation of wrong-doing
- ◆ it is necessary to prevent the commission of certain future crimes

The question of which crimes allow a breach of confidentiality is controversial. Some argue that a client must threaten to commit a crime involving imminent bodily harm or death, whereas others believe that the threat of committing some kind of property crime warrants a breach of confidentiality.

Because paralegals are privy to confidential information from clients either through reviewing written materials or being included in client conferences, they, more than other law office personnel, are faced with the issue of confidentiality. An awareness of the need to protect the confidentiality of client communications should be paramount in the mind of the paralegal at all times. Because of the importance of this issue, many firms provide in-house training for paralegals in which they teach specific ways to preserve confidentiality. You can ensure client confidentiality by doing the following:

- ◆ Carry on conversations with clients in rooms that are private.
- ◆ Refrain from talking to people about a case unless they are essential to the representation of the client.
- ◆ Do not take calls from a client while another person is in the room.
- ◆ Do not leave a client's folder open on one's desk, in the car, on an airline seat, or in other locations.
- ◆ Do not allow others to see what is on your computer screen.
- ◆ Protect your database so others cannot access it.
- ◆ **Redact** confidential information in writing samples used for training purposes, or in job interviews.
- ◆ Avoid using fax machines to relay confidential information.
- ◆ Avoid discussing confidential information on a cellular or cordless phone or over a speaker phone or intercom.
- ◆ Use a shredding machine (with permission) to discard confidential materials.
- ◆ Restrict access to computers and network servers.
- ◆ Protect the security of e-mail communications.
- ◆ Clearly label all folders containing privileged information.
- ◆ Protect the security of materials you take from the office to work on at home or to an off-site meeting.
- ◆ MOST IMPORTANTLY, NEVER DISCUSS CLIENTS OR THEIR CASES WITH ANYONE OUTSIDE THE OFFICE.

redact   mark out

Putting It Into Practice 2.1:

Martha's fellow student, Marianne, who is a paralegal in another firm, often tells her friends stories about some of the firm's clients. She is careful to change the names of the parties so that others will not know their real identities. Is she breaching the confidentiality of the firm's clients?

Figure 2-1
Ways to Protect Client Confidentiality

WAYS TO PROTECT CLIENT CONFIDENTIALITY

Converse in rooms that are private.

Avoid talking about the case with those who are not essential to the case.

Do not take calls while someone is in room.

Do not leave the client's folder out in the open.

Obstruct view of your computer screen.

Protect access to database.

Redact confidential information.

Avoid transmitting confidential information by fax.

Avoid discussing confidential information on your cell phone, cordless phone, speaker phone, or intercom.

Use a shredding machine to discard confidential information.

Restrict access to computers.

Protect the security of your e-mails.

Clearly label folders containing privileged information.

Protect the security of materials you take out of the office.

NEVER DISCUSS CLIENTS OR THEIR CASES OUTSIDE OF YOUR OFFICE.

◆ LOCAL LINKS ◆

What is the rule of professional conduct in your state that establishes the confidentiality requirement? In your state, when can confidentiality be breached to prevent the commission of a future crime?

To read an article containing additional information about confidentiality, go to *www.paralegals.org/reporter*, click on "Online 1998," and then on "Loose Lips Sink Ships . . . and Paralegals."

For articles about the issue of confidentiality in reference to e-mail and cell phone communications, go to *http://resource.lawlinks.com* and click on "Attorney Client Relations" under "Ethics and Professional Responsibility." Then click on the articles "Confidentiality: A Lawyer's Duties with Regard to Internet E-Mail" and "Confidentiality, Cell Phones, and E-Mail."

"The Tort System is Based on the Premise that Those Who Create Risks Bear the Burden of Compensating Those Who are Injured as a Result of Those Risks."

Martha was surprised to hear Mike's voice. Only a few weeks ago, he had been teetering on the edge of unconsciousness. After making a few inquiries about his health, Martha was clear that Mike had a definite agenda and did not want to dwell on his physical condition.

"Mrs. Fletcher, I'm really worried about how this whole mess with me is going to affect my parents financially. They aren't the type of people who like to sue, but I don't think they should have to pay for what somebody else did to me." Mike's voice trailed off and Martha detected the strain this conversation was having on him. She jumped in to give him a rest as much as to enlighten him about the philosophy underlying **tort law.**

"Some people agree with your folks that we all have to bear the consequences of getting injured. But the tort system is based on the premise that those who create risks bear the burden of compensating those who are injured as a result of those risks. Businesses, for example, benefit from the sales of the products they create; by the same token, they're expected to compensate those who are injured as a result of defects in those products. Arguably they're better able to bear the burden of this **liability** than consumers because of the profits they've reaped. Also, they're better able than consumers to assess the risks created by their products."

"But the school isn't a business," protested Mike.

"No, but schools owe a special duty of care to their students. Schools serve as a kind of surrogate parent. Among other things, they have a duty to protect students from certain kinds of harm," explained Martha.

"So you're saying that Washington High had a duty to protect me from being shot?" questioned Mike.

"No, I'm not saying that, and I can't say anything like that because I can't give legal advice. You need to talk with an attorney to get the answer to that question."

"Is there anyone in your firm you'd recommend?"

"I really haven't been there long enough to make any recommendations, Mike, but I do know that one of the firm's founders, John Morgan, is considered one of the foremost experts in personal injury law. He's retired, but he does come in occasionally and might be willing to talk with you. Would you like me to try set up an appointment for you?"

"That would be great, Mrs. Fletcher. I'd sure appreciate it."

"I'll get back with you later today. Take care of yourself, Mike."

tort law also known as personal injury law, tort law involves the compensation of those who have been victims of private wrongs

liability responsibility for damages

LAW AND ITS PURPOSE

Tort law compensates those who have been injured and, to some degree, punishes those who have caused the injury. Contract law seeks to give those who have entered into a contract the benefit of their bargain. Criminal law punishes those who have committed offenses against the public. Each branch of law serves its own unique purpose, but the question remains: What is the essence of the law?

Legal theorists and philosophers have struggled with the definition of law for centuries, but an exact definition has eluded them. This lack of consensus can be seen in the following definitions.

◆ Law is a "prophecy of what the courts will do."—Oliver Wendell Holmes, a highly respected former U.S. Supreme Court justice

◆ "Law is the creation and interpretation of specialized rules in a politically organized society."—Richard Quinney, a well-known sociologist
◆ A law is "externally guaranteed by the probability that coercion (physical or psychological), to bring about conformity or avenge violation, will be applied by a staff of people holding themselves specially ready for that purpose."—Max Weber, a well-known sociologist and lawyer
◆ Law is a tool used by the ruling class to dominate the lower classes. —Karl Marx, a famous social and political philosopher

Setting aside for the moment this intellectual debate about what the law is, we will, for purposes of this text, define law as that which defines both prohibited and required conduct and sets forth the sanctions imposed for its violation. No matter how elusive the definition of law may be, its functions are easier to articulate. The law serves as a means of:

Social Control — law serves as a norm to control deviant behavior, acting as a formal control that goes beyond the informal mechanisms of gossip, ridicule, and ostracism. To achieve this purpose, the law must establish specific rules of conduct, sanctions that accompany violation of these rules, and officials who interpret and enforce the rules.

Dispute Settlement — law resolves disputes by setting forth legal rights and obligations and formal procedural rules by which these rights and obligations are carried out. As such, the law provides a means of resolving disputes that is an alternative to more informal mechanisms.

Figure 2-2
What Is Law?

WHAT IS LAW?
PURPOSE
Social control

Dispute settlement

Social change

DEFINITIONS
Prophecy of what courts will do

Creation and interpretation of specialized rules

Rules that can be enforced by coercion

Tool used to dominate lower class

THEORIES
Natural law

Positivism

Realism

Critical legal theory

Social Change — law initiates, supports, and guides social change. Although some believe that law should follow changes in society rather than create such changes, American history is full of examples of the law serving as an instrument of social change. The position of African Americans, for example, has improved largely as a direct result of changes in the law.

Philosophers continue the age-old debate about how the law should function in a just society. While an in-depth discussion of **jurisprudence** goes beyond the scope of this text, some consideration of the most common theories of law will help you better understand the functioning of the legal system and the reasoning of judges.

jurisprudence   study of the law and legal philosophy

[handwritten: most fair and civil of the law philosophies]

Natural Law Philosophy — is based on the belief that human law should be derived from divinely based principles of justice and equality. When human laws do not reflect these principles, they can be resisted, but when they conform with natural law they must be obeyed. Natural law is reflected in the Constitution (freedom of speech and religion) and the Declaration of Independence (inalienable rights of life, liberty, and the pursuit of happiness). Martin Luther King, Jr., Henry David Thoreau, and Gandhi all looked to natural law to justify their civil disobedience.

[handwritten: makes an error by assuming that the law as written has no flaws, and that previous cases were correctly judged]

Positivism — is based on the assumption that legal decisions should be based on legal rules formulated in earlier court decisions, and that judges should use logic in applying previous decisions to the facts of the case before them. Unlike the natural law theorists, positivists regard moral values as irrelevant in arriving at legal conclusions and believe judges must focus on the law as it is rather than what it ought to be.

One school of positivists that has been particularly influential in American jurisprudence is the utilitarian school. The basic premise of utilitarianism is that all human judgments are an attempt to achieve pleasure and avoid pain. Legislation should create the greatest good for the greatest number and the needs of the individual should be subordinated to the good of the community. Utilitarianists are, therefore, opposed to theories creating inalienable rights.

[handwritten: should be labeled "socialism" based on the definition]

Realism — is based on the premise that the law should create socially desirable consequences. Unlike the positivists, the realists believe judges should not be slaves to logic and past decisions, but should rather embrace the social realities of the time. Realists are pragmatic (practical) rather than idealistic (like the naturalists) and focus on results rather than universal principles. One of the most famous realists is Oliver Wendell Holmes, who believed that law could not be worked out from general axioms of conduct but must change based on time and place. Realists contend that the changeability of law is what allows it to adapt to changes in social and political conditions, and that, if it were straight-jacketed by rigid pre-existing rules, it would lose its social value.

[handwritten: just a fancy way of identifying corruption in our legal/government institutions]

Critical Legal Theory — is based on the premise that the law is designed to keep the powerful in power and the powerless without power. It is a relatively new theory of law that is assuming greater importance in American jurisprudence. Critical law theorists view social institutions as inherently unjust and unnatural and reject the notion that legal decision making can be either rational or value-neutral. They see law as an instrument of political propaganda that legitimizes the existing class structure and exploits the poor. To illustrate, they point to the child labor laws enacted in the 1800s. While these laws were said to protect children from unreasonable working conditions, critical legal theorists point out that the primary advocates of these laws were large businesses who were well aware that the prohibition of child labor would bankrupt many small businesses, which relied heavily on the use of child labor.

Putting It Into Practice 2.2:

What do you think the natural law theorists perceive as the source of the law? The positivists? The realists? The critical legal theorists?

SOURCES OF THE LAW

Thus far our discussion of law has been very abstract. Let us now take it to a more concrete level by looking at how the law is actually created by the executive, legislative, and judicial branches of government. In the United States, the ultimate law of the land is found in the Constitution. The Constitution controls all other laws. Similarly, each state has a constitution, which is the second highest law in that state (second only to the U.S. Constitution). The U.S. Constitution and each of the constitutions of the fifty states follow the "doctrine of separation of powers." Under that doctrine, the functions of government are divided among the legislative, judicial, and executive branches in order to prevent any one part of the government from becoming too powerful. Congress and the state legislatures make the laws; the executive branch, consisting of the President and the Cabinet departments, carries them out and has the power to veto laws passed by the legislature. Courts—the judicial branch—apply laws to individual cases and interpret them in case of dispute.

NET NEWS

To read the U.S. Constitution or any state constitution, go to *www.law.cornell.edu* and click on "Constitutions and Codes."

Figure 2-3
Sources of Law

Sources of Law	
LEGISLATIVE (Statutes; ordinances)	EXECUTIVE (Administrative rules)
JUDICIAL (Case decisions)	

Legislative Branch

statutes law created by a state or federal legislature

Legislatures at both the federal and state levels create **statutes** (sometimes called *laws* or *codes*), while city and county agencies create **ordinances.** Both statutes and ordinances are designed to define and regulate appropriate and inappropriate behaviors. They cannot, however, conflict with either the U.S. or relevant state constitutions, which are considered the supreme law of the land.

ordinances law created by city or county agencies

Congress (the legislative branch of the federal government) is comprised of two houses: the Senate and the House of Representatives. In most cases, either house can initiate a bill (a proposed law), but before a bill can become law, it must be passed by both houses. When both houses approve a bill (by a simple majority), it is sent to the President, who has the option of either signing the bill, vetoing it, or doing nothing. If the President signs the bill, it becomes a statute. If the President does nothing and the legislature is in session, the bill becomes law after 10 days. If the President does nothing and the legislature goes out of session before 10 days pass, the bill does not become law. (This is called a *pocket veto.*) If the President vetoes a bill, each house must override the veto by a two-thirds majority vote for the bill to become law.

Congress has the power to enact legislation only in those arenas in which it has been given power to do so by the U.S. Constitution. It has the power, for example, to impose taxes and to regulate interstate commerce—a very broad power as interpreted by the U.S. Supreme Court. Any powers not given to Congress are reserved for the states under the Tenth Amendment to the Constitution. Therefore, each state has the right to create its own laws in those areas not regulated by Congress.

Executive Branch

The President is the Chief Executive of the United States and is assisted in his administration by his advisors in the Cabinet. Although the President's influence on the development of the law through his veto power is significant, the most direct influence on the law is wielded through the administrative agencies, which are also part of the executive branch of government. These agencies, created by a state or federal government, are responsible for carrying out duties delegated to them by the legislative branch. This delegation is necessary because the legislature cannot possibly oversee the enforcement of the overwhelming number of statutes that exist. Administrative agencies also create rules to govern the process, and to some extent the substance, by which they carry out those duties. These rules spell out in some detail what individuals must do to be in compliance with legislative mandates. The Social Security Administration, for example, must allocate Social Security benefits according to the broad guidelines established by Congress and

---

NET NEWS

For information about Congress, including the names and e-mail addresses of its members, the committees, the House and Senate Rules, and related Web sites, go to *lcweb.loc.gov/global/legislative/Congress.html.* This site also has information about the legislative process in general. For information about the status of bills currently before Congress, the sponsors of bills, or to see a list of public laws or vetoed bills, go to *www.law.cornell.edu* and click on "Law by Source or Jurisdiction."

For a listing of and links to the Web sites for most federal administrative agencies, go to *lcweb.loc.gov/global/executive/fed.html.*

must also create procedures by which those allocations can be distributed as well as challenged. (An extensive discussion of administrative agencies and law is set forth in Chapter 8.)

Putting It Into Practice 2.3:
How do the executive and legislative branches work together?

Judicial Branch

case law   resolution of fact-specific disputes

Courts create law by virtue of their decisions (referred to as **case law**) and their rule-making powers (their authority to create procedural rules). Legal disputes are usually resolved at the **trial court** level (the first level of the court system), but when litigants are unhappy with this resolution, they may have the option of appealing to an **appellate court** (the court at the next level in the judicial hierarchy). Appellate courts are not empowered to take testimony, receive evidence, or conduct trials; they make their decisions by reviewing the trial record, hearing arguments, and researching the law.

trial court   first level of the court system in which trials are heard

appellate court   court that reviews decisions made by lower courts

Substantive vs. Procedural Law

substantive law   law setting forth the rights and duties of individuals

procedural law   law setting forth the rules that must be followed when working within the legal system

The case law created by the courts can be either substantive law or procedural law. **Substantive law** is the law defining individuals' rights and duties. Contract law, for example, is a type of substantive law that defines what parties must do to create a contract and what their rights are if the party with whom they contracted fails to honor his obligations under the contract. **Procedural law,** on the other hand, sets forth the rules that must be followed when working with the legal system. The primary source of procedural law in the federal courts, as well as in the courts of most states, is court rules. Judges, with the help of committees of attorneys and scholars, adopt their own rules for the conduct of cases in their courts. The U.S. Supreme Court created the Federal Rules of Civil Procedure, which set forth the procedure to be followed in all federal courts. Each lower federal court also has its own rules (referred to as *local rules*) for any situations not covered by the Federal Rules of Civil Procedure and that the local judges consider important enough to warrant a rule. Similarly, in most states, the highest court prescribes general rules of procedure that apply to all courts in the state. (In a few states, notably California, procedural rules are established by statute.) Lower courts then adopt local rules of their own.

Failure to comply with procedural law can result in a case being dismissed or other serious consequence. Plaintiffs who file a claim in a court that lacks proper authority to hear that claim, for example, will not be able to pursue their claim no matter how worthy it is. Although paralegals must learn a certain amount of substantive law, they must master the ins and outs of procedural law. Consequently, some of the most important classes paralegal students take are procedural in nature.

Putting It Into Practice 2.4:
Is the study of business law primarily a study of procedural or substantive law? What about the study of litigation?

Figure 2-4
Divisions of the Law

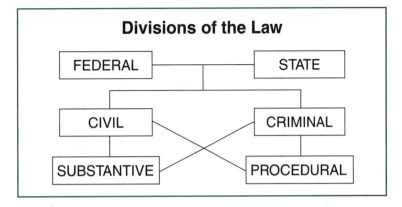

Civil vs. Criminal Law

Law can also be divided into civil law and criminal law. **Civil law** is the area of law that encompasses lawsuits brought by individuals (or business entities) who have suffered private wrongs for which they are seeking some form of compensation. Civil law includes tort law, property law, domestic relations law, contract law, and probate law. **Criminal law** is the area of law that deals with the wrongs done to an individual that result in harm to society as a whole. The purpose of criminal law is to punish those who commit crimes such as murder, robbery, theft, arson, and sexual assault.

Although the same act can be both a civil wrong and a criminal wrong (for example, a theft is both a civil wrong and a crime), several differences exist between civil and criminal law. The purpose of civil law is to compensate victims by providing them with some form of monetary damages, whereas the purpose of criminal law is to punish those who have committed a wrong. Punishment is accomplished by confining and/or fining the wrongdoer. The civil law acts on behalf of the individual wronged and that individual brings suit to recover damages. The criminal law acts on behalf of the state (or city), which is considered the offended party, and an agent of the state (known as the **prosecutor** (or attorney general, district attorney, public attorney, state's attorney, or city attorney) represents the state in the courtroom.

So if Dan steals a painting from Victor, Victor can file a civil suit, and if Dan is found liable (responsible), Victor can either recover the painting or monies in lieu of the painting. Additionally, Victor can contact the police and request that the state file a criminal action against Dan. If Dan is found guilty, he can be sentenced to a period of incarceration and required to pay a fine (which goes to the state) as well as **restitution** (payment as compensation to the victim) to Victor.

If Victor sues, he will have a lower burden of proof (preponderance of the evidence) than will the state in a criminal action (beyond a reasonable doubt). Under the **preponderance of the evidence** standard, the plaintiff must prove that it is more likely than not that the defendant committed the wrong. Under the **beyond a reasonable doubt** standard, the state must remove all reasonable doubts from the jurors' minds. Throughout the litigation process, the parties must adhere to the rules of civil procedure when they are pursuing a civil claim and the rules of criminal procedure when working within the criminal system. Practitioners of both civil and criminal law have to be familiar with the substantive and procedural components of the law with which they are working. Figure 2-5 summarizes the major differences between civil and criminal law.

Putting It Into Practice 2.5:

If a woman is sexually assaulted, has a civil or criminal wrong been inflicted on her?

---

civil law   law covering lawsuits brought by those who have suffered private wrongs for which they are seeking some form of compensation

criminal law   law covering wrongs done to an individual that result in harm to society as a whole

prosecutor   attorney representing the state in a criminal case

restitution   payment to victim of crime by defendant to compensate victim for losses suffered

preponderance of the evidence   standard of proof in civil cases requiring proof that it is more likely than not the defendant committed the wrong alleged by the plaintiff

beyond a reasonable doubt standard of proof in criminal cases requiring that all reasonable doubt is removed from the jurors' minds

Figure 2-5
Civil Law Compared to Criminal Law

CIVIL LAW COMPARED TO CRIMINAL LAW		
	CIVIL LAW	**CRIMINAL LAW**
Purpose	Compensation	Punishment
Remedies	Damages	Imprisonment; fines
Person wronged	Individual	Society
Burden of proof	Preponderance of the evidence	Beyond a reasonable doubt
Procedural rules	Rules of civil procedure	Rules of criminal procedure

guardian ad litem   a person appointed by the court to represent a minor or someone who is incompetent to sue on his own behalf

"We Need to Keep the Johnsons' World View in Mind if We End Up Litigating Because We Never Want to Override Them in Our Zealousness to Advocate on Their Behalf."

Martha was on the phone to John as soon as she hung up with Mike. She told him about her conversation with Mike and asked if he would be willing to meet with him.

"Martha, I'm not sure you understand the implications of retirement. I do love the law, but I also love being with my wife and family, working in the garden, and doing all those things a law practice made impossible. So as much as I'd like to help your young man, I really must decline and suggest you talk with a practicing attorney," explained John.

"Yes, sir, I do understand what I'm asking of you and I really don't expect you to take his case. I just thought that maybe you could talk with him and kind of steer him in the right direction. I've known Mike since he was a baby and I've seen him grow into such a wonderful person. I know how frightened and worried he is and I just want him to get some good advice. I've watched you with people and I know how good you are at giving them your undivided attention and making them feel at ease. I don't know if Mike has a case, but if he does, I know you'll give him a fair evaluation and you'll take the time to explain everything to him. If he doesn't, I know you'll be just as gracious and take just as much time with him as you would the firm's most important client. So I guess I'm asking that you do this as a favor to me. I'll pay you back whenever the opportunity arises." Having made her case, Martha waited for John's reply.

"You're a hard lady to refuse, Martha Fletcher. But one important question first. How old is Mike?"

"He just turned eighteen."

"Are you absolutely certain?" persisted John. "Otherwise he'll need to have his parents talk to me. As you know, in this state anyone under the age of eighteen is considered a minor and has to have a **guardian ad litem** appointed in order to sue."

"I'm certain," assured Martha. "Mike's birthday is the same day as one of my daughters and we usually invite him over to celebrate. This year he couldn't come because his friends had organized a big bash for his eighteenth birthday."

"Even so, I'd still feel better if his parents were involved. I feel very uncomfortable talking to someone so young without the knowledge of his parents," continued John.

"I know Mike's parents fairly well and I know why Mike is doing this on his own. They're good people—very conscientious, extremely hard-working, and fiercely independent. But they have a very strong ethic about taking responsibility for what comes their way and are adamant that people should not sue others except under the most extreme conditions. I have no doubt they would be opposed to Mike filing suit. In talking with Mike, I know that he carries some of these same feelings, but he is also concerned that his medical costs are going to ruin his family. He's desperate to find some way to bring them some relief."

"Good to know this," nodded John in acknowledgement. "It's important to understand what your client's motivations are from the get go. We need to keep the Johnsons' world view in mind if we end up litigating because we never want to override them in our zealousness to advocate on their behalf. That said, go ahead and give my home number to Mike and tell him to call if he still wants to talk with me. As Ernesto loves to remind me, I'm from the 'old school' and prefer that potential clients contact me. There's just something unseemly about me calling them. Also, Martha, since you know Mike so well, I'd like you to be there when I interview him. I'm sure he'll feel a lot more comfortable if you're there."

"I'd be honored, Mr. Morgan. I'll have Mike call you. And thank you so much. I owe you one."

SETTING UP AN INITIAL INTERVIEW

In some instances, paralegals may conduct initial interviews of potential clients although attorneys often prefer to reserve this task for themselves. You should be aware of what goes into creating a comfortable interview environment so that you can assist your attorney in setting the stage. And because, in some legal practices, paralegals do routinely interview clients before the attorney does, you should have some idea of how to structure an interview.

The opening moments of a conversation with a new client may very well establish the tenor of his relationship with your firm. In addition to obtaining essential biographical and background information and ascertaining potential claims the client may have, it is vital to establish such a rapport with the client that he feels free to speak openly and frankly. Eventually you may need to ask personal questions about such things as emotional damage, injuries sustained, sexual dysfunction, and scarring. People generally are not willing to make such sensitive disclosures unless they feel at ease with the interviewer. Additionally, you must glean sufficient information for your supervising attorney to decide whether the client has a cause of action, whether the claim is the type the firm would pursue, and, if not, to whom the client might be referred.

You can help create a relaxed environment by the way you arrange the furniture. Relegating the client to a low-backed reception chair while you look out from behind a formidable desk, seated in an imposing high-backed chair, does not promote trusting, uninhibited communication. You will appear more approachable if you position your chair alongside the client's or at right angles to each other at a small table. On the other hand, do not get so close that you make the client feel uncomfortable by invading his personal space.

To help break the ice, offer the client a cup of coffee, glass of water, or some tea or soda. Devoting a few minutes to small talk will give him an opportunity to acclimate to you and the surroundings, unless, of course, the client makes it clear he wants to get right to the point. Taking time to create a comfortable setting will certainly reap more benefits than immediately bombarding the client with questions.

Putting It Into Practice 2.6:

Some attorneys view client intake interviews purely as a means of finding out if the client has a viable claim. They spend little or no time getting acquainted with the client and, as quickly and efficiently as possible, get the pertinent information. Why might this approach to working with clients be counterproductive?

"Actually, Mike, Anything You Say to Me Is Confidential Because of the Attorney-client Privilege. But If You Allow Greta to Stay in the Room While We Talk, You Give Up That Privilege."

Because Mike was still in the hospital, John agreed to meet with him there. As he entered Mike's room, he took note of the dozens of flower arrangements, the get-well cards strung around the room, the pictures taped to the wall, and the other efforts of Mike's family and friends to make his room as homey as possible. John took in every detail and made a mental note of the photo of a beautiful young woman on the stand next to Mike's bed. After Martha introduced him to Mike, he deliberately avoided making any mention of his purpose in being there and allowed

Martha and Mike to reminisce about more pleasant times. He smiled encouragingly as they exchanged stories and then prodded them on with his questions. He knew that he was gathering information that could be useful if Mike were to choose the firm to represent him. He also knew that, by allowing this repartee between Mike and Martha, he was helping to build a rapport between himself and Mike. When their laughter subsided and they both fell silent, John knew it was time to begin his inquiry.

"Mike, I'm aware of the trauma you've suffered and Martha has told me you want to know if you might have a potential lawsuit. To answer that question, I'm going to need to ask you a few questions. First of all, what can you tell me about what happened the day you were shot?"

"Unfortunately, Mr. Morgan, I can't remember anything. The last thing I remember was walking across campus with Greta, my girlfriend. The next thing I knew I was here. That's it," said Mike, throwing up his hands in frustration.

"In that case, do you know the names of anyone who witnessed what happened?" suggested John.

"Not another detective," exploded Greta, pouncing into the room with the air of a mother tigress.

Without losing a beat, John wheeled around and extended his hand to Greta. "John Morgan, Greta, and no, I'm not another detective. I'm an attorney and I'm here at Mike's request."

"Oh. I had no idea," sputtered Greta, taken aback by John's pronouncement and perplexed by his knowledge of her name.

"How could you?" countered John reassuringly. "But perhaps I ought to wait outside to give you two some privacy. Mike and I can continue our conversation later."

"No, no, it's I who should leave," offered Greta, immediately picking up the subtle suggestion that the discussion John was having with Mike was not for her ears. "I apologize for butting in."

"If it's okay with you, Mr. Morgan, I'd just as soon she stay," interrupted Mike. "Maybe she can remember something that would be helpful."

"Actually, Mike, anything you say to me is confidential because of the **attorney-client privilege.** But if you allow Greta to stay in the room while we talk, you give up that privilege," explained John. "I strongly encourage you not to do that because the privilege may prove important to you at some later date. For that reason, I suggest that I talk with Greta and you separately."

"But," protested Mike, "I'm not even a client."

"The privilege extends to the initial conversation between a potential client and an attorney so long as they're discussing a legal issue," continued John patiently.

"If you think it's best, then I guess you and I should finish our discussion in private. But does that mean Martha can't stay either?" Mike inquired.

"No, the privilege extends to employees of attorneys, so anything you say in front of Martha is considered confidential as well," assured John.

"Not a problem, sweetie," cooed Greta. "I'll go down to the cafeteria for a few minutes and check back with you later. Nice to meet you, Mr. Morgan. Maybe we can talk later, Ms. Fletcher."

"I'll make a point of sticking around so we can," responded Martha.

attorney-client privilege
evidentiary rule that prohibits attorneys from testifying about communications made to them by their client and that prevents clients from having to testify about communications made to them by their attorney

ATTORNEY-CLIENT PRIVILEGE

The attorney-client privilege is a rule of evidence that encompasses some of the same concerns as the ethical rules regarding confidentiality. The attorney-client privilege prohibits an attorney from later testifying about any communications made by a client to the attorney unless the client consents. By the same token, the privilege prevents the client from being compelled to testify about any of those communications. Because the client is the holder of this privilege, only the client can waive it. The privilege survives even the death of the client.

While confidentiality covers any information relating to the representation of the client (according to the *Model Rules*) or any confidences or secrets no matter what their source (according to the *Model Code*), the privilege extends only to client statements made to an attorney or paralegal while receiving legal advice in confidence. The privilege does not apply to advice of a business or personal nature. It

Figure 2-6
Rules Regarding Attorney-Client Privilege

ATTORNEY-CLIENT PRIVILEGE

Prohibits attorney from testifying about client communications

Prevents client from being made to testify about communications made to attorney

Can be waived only by client

Survives death of client

Pertains to legal advice, not business or personal advice

Applies to initial consultations

Pertains to colleagues and employees of attorney

Must take steps to ensure privacy of communications

Privilege is lost if client's actions imply waiver of privilege or if document is inadvertently disclosed

---

NET NEWS

For more information about the attorney-client privilege, go to *www.paralegals.org/reporter*, click on "Online 1997," and then on "Attorney-Client and Attorney Work Product Privileges: Their Application to Paralegals." (The attorney work product privilege will be discussed in Chapter 6.)

---

does apply to initial consultations, even if the individual decides not to be represented by the attorney, and encompasses any exchange of information, even if the attorney does not charge a fee. The privilege covers communications with colleagues and employees of the attorney working on the case. This includes paralegals, investigators, experts, and outside agencies working with counsel.

In order to invoke the privilege, the attorney and client must take steps toward ensuring that their communications are in private and that they cannot be overheard by others. The privilege will be lost if a client implies by her actions that she is waiving the privilege. For example, if she allows a **third party** who is not working with the attorney to hear any communications, she loses the privilege. The privilege may also be lost if a protected document is inadvertently disclosed.

third party   an individual or entity not a party to the lawsuit

Putting It Into Practice 2.7:

Why should attorneys avoid discussing business with their clients over lunch?

GETTING THE INFORMATION

Having succeeded in relaxing the client, now determine why he has come to your office. Rather than asking for directed responses, begin by asking open-ended questions designed to encourage a free-flowing narrative that gives the client's side of the story. Doing this not only allows the client to tell his story without interruptions, but permits you to assess how he will present himself during testimony. When he is done, summarize what he has said to make sure you have heard everything accurately and to demonstrate that you have been listening carefully.

You can follow up later with more directed questions to fill in the gaps and clarify any points of confusion you might have with more closed questions.

(Closed questions are specific questions that elicit yes-no answers or short responses, such as "Did the man say anything before he hit you?" or "How much money did you owe the man who assaulted you?") You can use the five Ws of good journalism—who, what, where, when, and why— and "how" to structure your follow-up questions. Who are the key actors involved? What did they do? Where and when did they do it? Why did they do it? How did they do it? Making sure you can answer these key questions will minimize your chances of forgetting to ask relevant questions.

Be willing to probe beneath a client's opinions to find the underlying facts. What specific facts led him to formulate his conclusion and is that conclusion valid? Beginning interviewers are usually easily satisfied with the answers they receive and fail to dig deeper. For example, a client might say "The car hit me from behind while I was at the stoplight." The interviewer must get a more vivid picture of what happened. How fast does she think the vehicle was going? How does she know that? Did the client see the car in her rear-view mirror? When did she see it? Did she take any preventative measures before she was hit? Was she at a complete stop or had she started moving? Were there other vehicles around her? Were any of them hit as well? What time of the day was it? What were the weather conditions? Had she suddenly stopped? What did the other driver do immediately after hitting her? Follow up with questions of this sort to probe for details regarding the time and location of the incident, the identities and actions of the other participants, and the exact sequence of events. Further questioning is needed to verify the validity of the client's observations and beliefs and to test the certainty of her statements.

Putting It Into Practice 2.8:

One of the students Martha interviews says she saw a male with a mask point a gun at Mike and shoot at close range. Create examples of appropriate who, what, where, when, why, and how questions. Martha should ask.

Advance preparation for an interview is important. You can prepare by getting instructions from your supervisor, reviewing files of similar cases, and reading instructional materials about the interviewing process. Using notes and prepared questions to organize your thinking will be helpful if you know in general what you will be discussing with the client. You can use your notes to refresh your memory about key points you want to explore. Do not, however, become so dependent on your notes that you are unable to deviate in any way. Be flexible; adapt your questions to the client's statements.

Taking notes during the interview can be distracting to the person talking, but it also lets her know you are interested enough in what she is saying to record the highlights. In most legal interviews, note taking is essential to some degree because of the necessity of remembering so many facts. The best solution is to tell the client why you are taking notes and to assure him that you are listening even though you are writing. As frequently as possible, stop writing and make eye contact to demonstrate your interest and your connection to what is being said.

Listen to what the client is saying. Pay attention to the details. Note any omissions in his story. Be aware of his body language and the pace, volume, and pitch of his speech. These subtle clues may reveal more than verbal communication. Free yourself of any preconceived notions and be willing to explore avenues that you had not previously considered.

When you think you have gathered all the pertinent information, summarize again what you think the client has said to you. You may be surprised at how many discrepancies exist between what you think you heard and what he thinks he said.

An awareness of human nature comes in handy when conducting interviews. Some people will provide you with only the sketchiest of details. They will treat each piece of information you extract from them as if it were gold. Others will inundate you with details, digressing into so many subplots of their story you will begin to lose sight of their central theme. Some will re-experience the emotional trauma of the events and become so distraught that they will be unable to recount what happened to them.

Although you must distance yourself emotionally enough to be objective regarding the legal claims, you must remain sensitive to the emotional needs and psychological defenses of those you interview. A certain amount of detachment is necessary to do your job. You cannot become a client's counselor or therapist, but divorcing yourself from your own humanity is neither necessary nor desirable. You must develop your own means of cajoling information from the reclusive, channeling the storytellers, and reassuring the distressed.

Remember, too, that interviewing is a two-way street. Just as your are assessing the client, so he is assessing you. Be conscious of the messages you are sending. You must communicate a sense of receptivity, warmth, and competence if you want the client to trust you and cooperate with you fully.

Putting It Into Practice 2.9:

Marianne is asked to interview a prospective client who has sustained relatively minor injuries in a traffic accident. During the interview, Marianne says very little and never looks up because she is writing continuously. The only questions she asks are those she has prepared in advance. At the end of the interview, she thanks the client for coming in and promptly ushers her to the door, telling her that an attorney will get back with her. What suggestions might you make to Marianne?

Figure 2-7
The Initial Interview

INITIAL INTERVIEW

Put the client at ease

Reveal your paralegal status

Ask open-ended questions initially and follow up with more directed and closed questions

Summarize when appropriate

Probe beneath the surface to get the underlying facts

Prepare some questions in advance, but maintain flexibility

Take notes, but explain the purpose of note taking and stay focused on listening

Listen carefully to what is being said

Observe body language

Be objective, but remain sensitive to the emotional needs and psychological defenses of the client

Remember that the client is assessing the interviewer

NET NEWS

For one attorney's view of the importance of effective communication with clients and for some suggestions as to how to do that, go to *www.mindspring.com/~italco/com.html* and read the article "Effective Communication with Clients."

Figure 2-8

Information Needed from an Initial Interview

> ### QUESTIONS TO ASK
> Who are the adverse parties?
> What is the dispute about?
> What damages are involved?
> When did the dispute arise?
> Where can additional information be obtained?
> What additional administrative information is needed?

STRUCTURING AN INITIAL INTERVIEW

Checklists or questionnaires can be invaluable tools to ensure that important facts are not missed. Figure 2.9 shows a sample checklist. If you work in a firm whose practice is devoted mainly to a specialized type of case (such as automobile accidents), your employer will undoubtedly be using them already. If not, begin creating your own. As useful as checklists and questionnaires are, however, they are no substitute for good judgment. Before conducting an interview, take time to consider what you are trying to accomplish. Figure 2-8 identifies the primary information you want to get from an initial interview.

Determine Who the Adverse Parties Are

One of the first tasks in interviewing a new client is to find out who else may be involved in the dispute. For obvious ethical reasons, an attorney cannot represent a client if she already represents one of the adverse parties. (See the discussion regarding conflicts of interest later in this chapter.) Prospective clients know—or think they know—whom they want to sue. But often, after hearing the facts and evaluating the client's position, you will find that the best claim is against someone whom the client never thought of suing. Therefore, when you ask the prospective client who the adverse parties are, cast your net wide, and try to identify every person, every business entity, and every insurance company that may be involved in the dispute, however peripherally.

Determine What the Dispute Is About

One reason you need the facts of the dispute is so that you can give your supervising attorney enough information that she can decide whether to accept the case. Several factors will play a part in the decision. Does the case fit within the firm's area of practice? Does the firm have the necessary resources to devote to the case at this time? Is it in the client's best interests to pursue the case or are the chances of success too small to merit the required effort and expense?

Eventually, if your firm accepts the case, you will need all of the factual details (including names, dates, and places) before you can file suit. Your complete and accurate notes of your client's description of the facts will save you a great deal of effort, not to mention embarrassing phone calls to the client to obtain details that you were told but have forgotten.

Figure 2-9

Interview Checklist for Personal Injury Cases

INTERVIEW CHECKLIST FOR PERSONAL INJURY CASE

Date _____

Name _____ SS# _____

Address _____

Telephone (Work) _____ (Home) _____

Date of birth _____ Age _____ Driver's license # _____

Marital status _____ Children _____

- -

Date and time of accident _____

Place of accident _____

Description of accident _____
_____

Injuries _____
_____

Investigating officer _____

Witnesses _____

Doctors providing treatment _____

Ambulance _____ Hospital _____

Treatment provided _____
_____

Employer _____ Address _____

Lost time _____ Rate of pay _____

Other losses _____

Property damage _____

Pre-existing conditions _____

- -

Insured _____ Phone _____

Company _____ Agent _____

Adjustor _____ Phone _____

Claim number _____ Policy number _____

Med/pay limits _____ UM/UIM limits _____

Collision _____ Deductible _____

- -

Name of defendant _____

Address _____ Phone _____

Insurance company _____ Address _____

Adjustor _____ Phone _____

Claim number _____ Policy number _____

Policy limits _____

In any personal injury case, a complete insurance profile must be constructed. In an accident involving a motor vehicle, for example, you need to find out if the client has any automobile insurance for the vehicle and whether it provides medical payments and collision coverage. You need to inquire in some depth about the nature and extent of his injuries, how those injuries could interfere with his relationships, and whether any medical insurance is available. You should ascertain whether he was taken to the emergency room, who his treating physicians were, how many times he has seen them and for what reasons, whether his work has been affected and, if so, how it has been affected.

The client's medical history is also important. Who is his family physician? What physical examinations has he had, including those for obtaining employment, for permission to be involved in school activities, and to be involved in other activities?

An employment history is equally important. By whom is he employed and for how long? What kinds of promotions has he been given? Has he received any bonuses or does he perform a significant amount of overtime? How much work time has he lost because of his injuries? Has he or will he be denied promotions or other forms of advancement because of his injuries? This information can have a significant impact on the amount of compensation the client will be entitled to recover.

You need the client to describe the scene of the accident and the chain of events leading up to the accident in exquisite detail. Was his car functioning well before the accident? After the accident? What did the police officers do at the scene of the accident? You will also need to determine the nature and extent of the damages to the client's vehicle and whether any witnesses were at the scene.

The long-term effects of injuries on the client's daily life are also important. Can he prepare meals? Take out the trash? Participate in recreational activities that he enjoyed before being injured? Can he drive a car? Has he had to hire someone to do chores such as mow the lawn?

Determine What Damages Are Involved

Another important issue is whether the case makes financial sense, both to the client and the attorney. Is litigation the best approach, or would an alternative form of dispute resolution (discussed in Chapter 8) be more effective and efficient? For the client, the overriding question should be, "Does the value of the expected outcome, taking into account the chances of losing, exceed the expected cost of litigating?" From the law firm's standpoint, the issue is whether the case is one on which the firm can make money. Like it or not, a law firm is a business, and its continued existence depends on making a profit. Therefore, in deciding whether to take a case, one of the things an attorney ordinarily does is to assess the strength of the case and the amount of money likely to be won or lost. To do so, some preliminary fact-gathering is required.

To estimate the value of a claim, you need to be able to make an educated guess about both the plaintiff's chances of winning and the amount the plaintiff might win. For the attorney to estimate the amount the plaintiff might win, information must be gathered about the extent of the plaintiff's injuries and losses.

Begin by thinking about all the ways the plaintiff may have been damaged. For example, in a personal injury case, you need to know (1) how much the plaintiff's medical bills are; (2) how much income the plaintiff lost by missing work; (3) whether future medical treatment will be needed and how much it will cost; and (4) whether any of the plaintiff's injuries will be permanent, and, if so, what sort of value a jury might place on a permanent injury of that kind. Each case is different, and no checklist can anticipate every possible kind of damages; it is up to the lawyer (or paralegal) to apply her skill and judgment to be sure that no damages are overlooked.

At the initial interview stage, of course, you will not be able to obtain a complete breakdown of the plaintiff's damages. In fact, the plaintiff's damages may not all have happened yet—the plaintiff may still be undergoing medical treatment, for example. Therefore, your goals at this early stage are twofold: first, to get enough facts to allow the attorney to at least estimate the value of the claim; and second, to get as much information as you can to pull together the details later on (i.e., names and addresses of doctors, hospitals, employers, etc.). A good checklist is invaluable here.

judgments formal decision by a court with respect to the rights and claims of the parties before it

plaintiff party who is suing

defendant party who is being sued

Once the value of the claim is estimated, the decision about whether the case is worth pursuing still cannot be made. Not all **judgments** can be collected. From the **plaintiff's** standpoint, it is usually pointless to sue unless the **defendant** has either insurance or enough assets from which to collect a judgment. As a practical matter, judgments against ordinary individuals are essentially worthless unless there is insurance from which the judgment can be collected. Therefore, a final essential task in evaluating a claim is to get information about any insurance coverage that may apply, and about the extent of the defendant's assets.

Putting It Into Practice 2.10:

If the firm decides to take Mike's case, to what types of questions will Martha and John need answers?

Determine When the Dispute Arose

Time limits apply to the filing of lawsuits; these time limits arise from **statutes of limitations.** A statute of limitations is a statute that requires suit be filed on a particular type of claim within a specified length of time after the claim arises. For example, the statute of limitations for negligence claims may provide that all claims for negligence must be sued upon within two years after the claim arises. These time limits are extremely important. Failure to file a claim in a timely manner means the plaintiff will be forever barred from filing that claim (unless some exception exists).

When does a claim arise? It depends on the situation, and, as with most issues in litigation, there may be a dispute about what date the claim arose. Fortunately, in most cases, some date can be easily identified as the *earliest* possible date on which the claim could have arisen. Failure to file a lawsuit within the prescribed period of time after that date could result in a malpractice claim. Therefore, whenever you first talk to a prospective client about a possible suit, you must ascertain the relevant dates to be sure that the suit is filed before any applicable statute of limitations runs.

Try to obtain dates for every occurrence that a client tells you about. One of the important dates is the date the accident actually happened. Make sure you get the actual date rather than the date your client remembers. In other words, do not take your client's word for the date—check the documentation such as the police accident reports.

BONUS POINTERS:

STATUTE OF LIMITATIONS PROBLEMS

Statute of limitations law is riddled with exceptions. For example, the statutes of limitations "clock" is typically "tolled" (stopped) whenever the plaintiff is prevented from filing suit because of insanity, being incapacitated (e.g., in a coma), being imprisoned, or being under the age of majority. The clock is also "stopped" when the cause of action is concealed in some way so that the plaintiff does not find out about it until long after it has already accrued. Suppose, for example, the defendant embezzles funds from the plaintiff, and the plaintiff does not discover the embezzlement until an audit is conducted. In many states, the clock would not start running until the plaintiff had a reasonable chance to discover the facts supporting the cause of action.

Determine Where to Get More Information

One of the most important purposes of an initial interview is to obtain leads to all of the information that the client does not have. As you begin to notice gaps in your information, think about how you are going to fill them, and what information you can get from your client that will help you do so. As you conduct the interview, do not become so wrapped up in the tale you are being told that you fail to notice any time gaps or apparent inconsistencies. The appropriate time to discover problems with a case is when you first become involved, not after a great deal of time, money, and effort have been expended.

Inevitably, you will eventually need to obtain every document having any bearing on the case. Find out what documents are likely to exist and who has them. Obtain names, addresses, telephone numbers, and specific descriptions of any documents known to exist. You will need bills, statements, estimates, appraisals—whatever it takes to establish the amount of the plaintiff's losses. In personal injury cases, you will need copies of medical records; to get them, you need to know where and by whom the plaintiff has been treated as well as his date of birth and social security number. In accident cases, you will need investigation reports; to get them, you need the date, time, and location of the accident and the identities of the drivers. In business disputes, you need copies of any contracts involved in the suit, as well as copies of all of the written correspondence between the parties.

Make copies of any documents the client has brought with her and make arrangements to get copies of additional pertinent documents. Experience teaches that the best time to get a copy of a document is at the *first* opportunity. This may also be a good time to have the client sign authorization (release) forms, which will be needed to secure medical, employment, and other records pertinent to the case.

Sooner or later, a complete list of the names, addresses, and telephone numbers of every potential witness in the case must be prepared—that is, every person having any knowledge or information about any of the facts in dispute. This includes experts such as treating physicians and police investigating officers. Start the list now, fill in as much as the client knows, and start making plans to obtain the rest. Keep an ongoing witness list in the file, updating it whenever you obtain new information.

Putting It Into Practice 2.11:

Write a list of the witnesses John and Martha will need to interview if the firm accepts Mike's case.

Get Needed Administrative Information

Before concluding the interview, be sure you have obtained all of the administrative data you will need in processing the case. Use your checklist. Be sure you get the following information.

- ◆ residential address
- ◆ address where mail is to be sent
- ◆ address of employment
- ◆ marriages
- ◆ children
- ◆ date of birth
- ◆ Social Security numbers of those involved
- ◆ insurance carrier
- ◆ extent of insurance coverage and limits on policy (It is also a good idea to get a copy of the policy to put in the client's file.)

Inform the Client

At the end of the interview, summarize what you understood the client to have said and ask if you have misstated or omitted anything. Allow the client to ask any questions that he has not yet asked but be careful not to say anything that could be construed as giving legal advice. Find out what the client's goals and expectations are in reference to filing a suit and ascertain whether those goals and expectations are reasonable. If the client decides to retain your firm, he should be told what in general will happen in the future regarding his case. The client should be told if he needs to supply any documents, keep any records or receipts of expenses, maintain a journal, prepare a narrative describing the events of his case (written while these events are still fresh in his mind), or do anything else to facilitate the resolution of his case. The client should be told when a follow-up appointment needs to be made and when the attorney will get back to him.

Many attorneys like to send follow-up letters to clients expressing their pleasure at being retained, summarizing what was discussed and what was decided, delineating the terms of representation, and specifying what the attorney and client have agreed to do and by what date they have agreed to do it. Both the attorney and paralegal should review the notes they took during the interview, summarize and type them, and put them in the client's file. Some attorneys prefer that the paralegal prepare a more formal memorandum to the file that includes background information about the client, why the client is seeking legal advice, and a list of tasks that need to be completed along with copies of any records or documents that the client brought to the interview.

judgment proof without assets to pay off a judgment

"That Boy Is Hiding Something and We Need to Find out What it Is Because My Gut Tells Me That What He Knows Could Have a Significant Impact on this Case."

"Do you remember where we were before Greta arrived?" John asked Mike. He was well aware of his last question but wanted to evaluate Mike's short-term memory.

"Gosh, I kinda lost track of your questions after Greta came in, Mr. Morgan," apologized Mike.

"No problem, son. Let's see if I can remember." John paused for a moment as if deliberating. "Oh, yes. Can you give us the names of anyone else other than Greta who might have witnessed the shooting?" prompted John.

"Sure can. I've heard there were at least four kids other than Greta who saw what happened. The gunmen were all wearing masks, though, so I'm not sure how much help any of them will be."

"Martha, would you mind writing down the names of those students?" As Martha was getting her pen and pad, John saw his opportunity to probe Mike a little to see what he might know.

"Mike, I'm curious about a couple of things I read in the paper. Maybe you can help shed some light on them."

"I'll sure try, sir."

"I read that some people think the perpetrators might have been part of some fringe group on campus that is obsessed with emulating the characters in the movie *Teenage Stalkers.* Do you know anything about that?"

"Yes. I know there's this kinda freaky group on campus that spends half its time doing drugs and the other half watching sick movies. I've heard these guys had been looking to do something really rad that would prove to everybody how cool they are."

"You lost me on the 'rad' part, but I gather this group is looking to make a name for itself and that shooting someone of your caliber on campus would do the trick," suggested John.

Does this group have a name?"

"I don't think they have a name. I don't think they're that organized, but I could get you the names of some of the ones that everyone knows are involved," offered Mike.

"That would be a good start." Turning to Martha, John asked, "Are you ready to write down the names of those witnesses now?" As Martha asked Mike for the names and spellings of the witnesses, John pondered whether Mike could withstand many more questions. "Now, I know all these questions are beginning to wear you down, but I need to ask you one more very important question." John paused to allow Mike to feel the full import of the question. "I must ask that you be completely candid with me, Mike. Do you know of any reason why anyone would want to shoot you?" John let the question hang on its own without any further embellishment.

"No, sir, I do not," responded Mike, shifting his eyes downward and blanching almost imperceptibly. John watched as Mike shifted his body weight and distractedly scratched his chin.

John sat back and sighed. No one said anything while John sat quietly, apparently lost in thought. "Well, there's a lot of questions that need to be answered before I can tell you whether you have a potential lawsuit here. First, there is no doubt you have a right to sue the boys who shot you. But, of course, we don't know who they are. And even if we find out who they are, they're probably **judgment proof**—meaning they don't have any assets we can collect. Second, we could go after their parents, assuming they have any money or other assets, but once again we don't know who these people are and we don't know if they had any way of foreseeing that their sons would do anything this treacherous. Third, the school district is potentially liable but only if the school officials knew or reasonably could have known about the shooting. To find that out we need to talk with some of the school employees and I doubt that the district's attorney is going to let us do that unless we depose them, which we generally can't do unless we file suit. And finally, we have the company that produced *Teenage Stalkers.* Even if we could prove that this movie in any way motivated the shooting, current case law would make it extremely difficult to hold the company liable. **First Amendment** protections of speech make it very iffy that we could ever get in the courtroom door on this one. On the other hand, there've been several suits filed in other courts recently based on similar grounds, and I get the sense the law is about to change. So this might be a good time to file suit.

"The bottom line is, Mike, that we need to do a considerable amount of investigative work before we can realistically determine if you might have a **cause of action,** that is to say, a lawsuit. A lawsuit like this is very risky for a law firm because a great deal of time and money need to be expended up front with the chance of getting a zero recovery. On the other hand, there is the potential for a very handsome recovery in light of the suffering you have experienced, the expenses your parents have incurred, and the impact this experience has had and will continue to have on your life. I'm going to need to go before the partners in our firm and ask if they want to take on a case of this kind. That's assuming you would like us to represent you." John paused to give Mike a chance to respond.

"I would very much like your firm to represent me if you would. Mrs. Fletcher is like a mom to me and I know how highly she thinks of you and your firm."

"Very good, young man," said John, rising from his chair. "I'll get back with you as soon as I know something more definite. If we do decide to go forward with your case, someone from our firm will meet with you and your parents, assuming you want them involved, to discuss fees and other preliminaries."

"Won't you be handling my case?" asked Mike, ignoring John's reference to his parents.

"Well, this might just be the case to bring me out of my retirement. You never know," said John with a cryptic smile.

John and Martha said their good-byes and stepped out into the hall. "Martha, I'd like you to stick around and talk to Greta. Find out what she remembers about the incident. Tomorrow I'm going to call counsel for the school district and see if I can finagle some interviews with the school principal, the secretary, Mike's teachers, and anyone else that comes to mind. If I'm successful, I'd like you to conduct some of those interviews. I want to find out if anyone at the school had any inkling about a shooting. Meanwhile, I'd like you to get hold of the students whose names Mike just gave us. Find out what they saw, what they heard, and what the rumor mill is saying. Listen carefully to what they say but listen just as carefully to what they don't say. Pay particular attention to their body language. You'll get clues from that that you won't from their words."

"I'm not sure what you mean," interrupted Martha.

"Did you notice Mike's body language when I asked him if anyone had any motive to shoot him?"

"No, I guess I didn't," admitted Martha.

"His eyes darted momentarily before he looked downward, indicating he was uneasy about remembering something of an emotional nature. He paled slightly, which is what the body does when it goes into the 'fight-or-flight' response as a reaction to fear. And he appeared uneasy and scratched his face, both common physical reactions to lying. That boy is hiding something, Martha, and we need to find out what it is because my gut tells me that what he knows could have a significant impact on this case."

"I'm not sure I can get all this information out of an interview, Mr. Morgan. I've never heard of some of the things you're talking about," said Martha, beginning to wonder if she was in over her head.

"You don't have to," John assured her. "These are some things I learned from working with a **jury consultant.** Just trust your instincts. You know when someone is lying to you or when they're not telling you everything they know. I'm simply encouraging you to listen to your gut reactions and not just rely on what your logical mind tells you. Okay?"

"Okay."

First Amendment first amendment to the U.S. Constitution; this amendment protects the freedom of speech, press, and the exercise of religion

cause of action lawsuit

jury consultant expert in psychology or communications who assists attorneys in selecting jurors that fall within the ideal demographics for the case and sometimes helps assess jurors' reactions during the trial

EFFECTIVE LISTENING SKILLS

Listening effectively requires skill, concentration, and a lot of energy. It is not a passive experience. Indeed, the phrase "active listening" has been coined to denote the kind of listening required if you want to ferret out what others are really saying. It means going beyond words to the actual message the speaker is attempting to convey.

Active listening requires an attentiveness to non-verbal as well as verbal cues. What people are saying with their lips may differ from what they are saying with their bodies. You do not have to be an expert in communication to read this language well enough to sense when people are lying, when they are uncomfortable with what is being said, when they are agitated, and when they are hiding something. The more attention you give to non-verbal clues the better you will get at reading this language.

One caveat to the interpretation of non-verbal language: be aware of the effects of gender, race, and ethnic origin on this language. In some cultures, for example, direct eye contact is considered rude or even a challenge to authority, whereas in others the lack of direct eye contact is interpreted as hiding something or being deceptive. To some people, a light touch on the shoulder is perceived as reassuring, but to others it is seen as a sexual overture or a subtle act of aggression. In some cultures, shaking hands or making any kind of physical contact with someone of the opposite sex is forbidden, whereas in other cultures the failure to shake hands is considered an affront. Sensitivity to these cultural and experiential differences will reduce your chance of offending someone or inhibiting another's willingness to communicate with you.

Active listeners often paraphrase what they are hearing the speaker say to confirm they are hearing it correctly and to reassure the speaker they are not only listening but are receiving the real import of the speaker's words. Paraphrasing should not be done so frequently that it interrupts the speaker's train of thought, becomes annoying, or appears artificial. Paraphrasing is vital to accurate communication because the perceptions of listeners can easily distort the ideas being conveyed by the speaker. Good listeners do their best to recognize their perceptual filters so they are aware when they are likely to misunderstand or misinterpret what is being said. They take responsibility for their role in the communication process rather than blaming the speaker if there is a miscommunication.

Empathic listening goes beyond active listening in that it allows the listener to appreciate and sense the feelings of the speaker regardless of what is being said. This does not mean becoming enmeshed in the speaker's feelings and taking them on. However, it does mean going beyond the verbal content to the emotional underpinnings. Having this kind of sensitivity to the feelings of others allows the listener to convey a sense of acceptance to the speaker. Many of the actions and beliefs expressed in the context of an attorney-client relationship can be unsettling or even shocking to the attorney or paralegal, but it is important that the client never feels judged or belittled because of what she has revealed. Listening empathically does not imply that the listener condones or in any way agrees with the conduct or feelings of the speaker, but it does honor and accept the speaker's feelings and gives permission to unconditionally express them.

Most law practices are extremely busy and both attorneys and paralegals usually have a limited amount of time they can devote to each client. Some clients and witnesses either fail to appreciate this or get so wrapped up in their story that they go on and on with no regard to how much time they are using. In these situations, it is tempting for the listener to cut off the speaker and force him to "get to the point." At times this may be necessary, but the paralegal should be extremely careful not to lose some valuable insights or information because he is anxious to get to what he thinks is the important part of the client's story. Attorneys are notorious for interrupting others and doing what they can to get the essential information as efficiently as possible. This kind of efficiency can prevent the attorney from finding out information that later in the case may be prove to be helpful. Therefore, it is the paralegal to whom clients and witnesses frequently turn when they want someone to listen to them and it is the paralegal who often has the opportunity to ferret out information that the attorney overlooks. Patience, coupled with discernment about when to take charge, is an invaluable attribute of paralegals.

NET NEWS

To read a brief article by an attorney who adheres to a holistic view of lawyering and who interviews clients from that perspective, go to *www.consciouslaw.org/library/library.html* and click on "Interviewing the Whole Client."

Putting It Into Practice 2.12:

How can good listening skills be developed?

RECESS

SUMMARY – PART A

The attorney-client relationship is based on confidentiality. Any information obtained by the attorney from the client as a result of that relationship is protected.

Paralegals must be diligent in protecting that confidentiality in everything they do and say. An evidentiary rule that arises out of the concept of confidentiality is the attorney-client privilege. This privilege prevents attorneys from testifying about any communications between themselves and their clients and protects clients from having to testify about those communications. This privilege is considered waived if the client allows a third party who is not a colleague or employee of the attorney to hear any communications with the attorney.

The law cannot easily be defined, but its purpose is to resolve disputes, exert social control, and guide social change. Each school of jurisprudence perceives the purpose of law differently. The natural law theorists see the law as a derivation of divine law, positivists believe the law should be based on legal rules rather than moral values, realists believe the law must change in accord with the social realities of the time, and critical legal theorists view the law as a tool of the ruling class that is designed to exploit the poor.

The duties of government are divided among the legislative, executive, and judicial branches. Statutes and ordinances are created by the legislative branch, while administrative regulations are created by administrative agencies, who are responsible for carrying out the duties delegated to them by the legislative branch. The judicial branch creates case law, which includes both substantive and procedural law. The U.S. Supreme Court created the Federal Rules of Civil Procedure and the highest court in each state has written the rules for all the courts in that state. Failure to comply with these rules can result in serious consequences to the litigants. Civil law can be distinguished from criminal law in terms of purpose, burden of proof, remedies, and person considered wronged.

The first contact attorneys have with a client is during the initial interview. Because this first meeting generally sets the tone for the relationship, the interviewer should do everything possible to relax the client. Begin the interview by allowing the client to give a free-flowing narrative of his story and then follow up with more directed questions. Use the five Ws of good journalism to structure your follow-up questions. Take notes, but assure the client you are listening by asking questions and summarizing what he has said. Pay attention to body language as well as verbal language and be sensitive to the emotional needs and psychological defenses of those you are interviewing.

Checklists can be helpful in structuring the initial interview to ensure that you obtain all of the essential information. Begin by identifying all potential adverse parties to make sure that the attorney does not have a conflict of interest. Get as many as details as possible regarding the dispute to determine if this is the kind of case the firm will want to accept. With personal injury cases, for example, get information about the client's insurance coverage, the nature and extent of his injuries, how the injuries occurred, the type of medical treatment he received, and his medical and employment histories. To determine the potential value of the claim, find out all the ways the client has incurred damages and will continue to suffer damages and ascertain whether any judgments could be collected from the potential defendants. Next, determine whether all or part of the case is barred by the statute of limitations. Find out how to get additional documents and how to locate various witnesses who may be needed. Obtain any essential administrative information, summarize what has been discussed at the interview, and inform the client about what will probably happen with his case and what steps he will need to take. Send a follow-up letter and prepare a summary of your notes to put in the file.

KEY TERMS

Appellate court
Attorney-client privilege
Beyond a reasonable
   doubt
Case law
Cause of action
Civil law
Confidentiality

Criminal law
Defendant
First Amendment
Guardian ad litem
Judgments
Judgment proof
Jurisprudence
Jury consultant

Liability
Ordinances
Plaintiff
Preponderance of
   evidence
Procedural law
Prosecutor
Redact

Restitution
Statutes
Statute of limitations
Substantive law
Third party
Tort law
Trial court

REVIEW QUESTIONS – PART A

1. What information is considered confidential in the attorney-client relationship? Under what circumstances can confidentiality be broken?
2. What functions are served by the law?
3. Describe the basic premise of each of these schools of jurisprudence:
   a. natural law
   b. positivism
   c. realism
   d. critical legal theory
4. What is the function of the legislative branch of government? The executive branch? The judicial branch?
5. Describe the process used to pass a bill in Congress.
6. What is the difference between substantive law and procedural law? Give an example of each.
7. What are three differences between civil law and criminal law?

8. What steps should an interviewer take to relax a prospective client during an initial interview?
9. During an initial interview with a client, what should an interviewer do about each of the following?
   a. using prepared questions
   b. taking notes
   c. asking directed questions
   d. summarizing what the client has said
   e. a client who begins crying
10. What information should you obtain from the initial interview of a client?
11. In the event of a personal injury case, what information should you get about the accident and the client who was injured?
12. Why is it important to determine the value of a case up front?
13. Why is it important to obtain the dates of every occurrence related by the client?

PRACTICE EXAM – PART A

MULTIPLE CHOICE

1. Confidentiality in the attorney-client relationship
   a. terminates when the attorney-client relationship terminates
   b. does not exist if the information is obtained during an informal conversation outside the office
   c. can be broken to prevent the commission of certain crimes
   d. none of the above

2. Paralegals should
   a. refrain from talking about cases unless they change the names of the clients
   b. prevent others from seeing clients' folders or looking at information on their computer screen
   c. redact all non-confidential materials they use outside of the office
   d. feel free to carry on confidential conversations over cellular phones and via e-mail because they will be private

3. The law serves to
   a. formally control deviant behavior
   b. establish the rights and obligations of parties
   c. guide social change
   d. all of the above

4. The natural law theorists
   a. are like the realists in that they are idealists
   b. are like the positivists in that they are concerned about creating inalienable rights
   c. believe that human law must always be obeyed
   d. none of the above

5. According to the positivists
   a. judges should use logic in applying legal rules
   b. the law should embrace the social realities of the time
   c. moral values are extremely important in shaping the law
   d. none of the above

6. The law must change based on time and place and social conditions according to the
   a. natural law theorists
   b. positivists
   c. realists
   d. critical legal theorists

7. The child labor laws were actually designed to put small businesses out of business according to the
   a. natural law theorists
   b. positivists
   c. realists
   d. critical legal theorists

8. In order for a bill to become a statute
   a. it must be passed by either the Senate or the House
   b. it must be signed by the President
   c. the President can do nothing and the bill can still become law
   d. none of the above

9. Administrative agencies
   a. fall within the legislative branch of government
   b. create rules that spell out what they must do to be in compliance with legislative mandates
   c. delegate duties to the legislative branch
   d. carry out duties delegated to them by the judicial branch

10. Civil law differs from criminal law in terms of
    a. burden of proof
    b. purpose
    c. remedies
    d. all of the above

11. Under criminal law
    a. the attorney general must prove his case by a preponderance of the evidence
    b. the state's attorney must conform to the rules of criminal procedure
    c. the prosecutor acts on behalf of the victim
    d. the district attorney seeks punishment for the offender rather than restitution for the victim

12. During an initial interview of a client
    a. it is best to begin immediately asking questions about why the client has come to your office
    b. the interviewer should establish a position of authority
    c. the interviewer should devote a few minutes to small talk
    d. the interviewer should control the conversation as much as possible, giving the client little opportunity to speak

13. The attorney-client privilege
    a. is a subset of the concept of confidentiality
    b. can be waived only by the attorney
    c. begins once the client hires the attorney to represent her
    d. extends to personal and business advice as well as legal advice

14. During an initial interview with a potential client
    a. use the five Ws of good journalism
    b. begin by allowing the client to give a narrative of his story
    c. adapt your questions to the client's statements
    d. all of the above

15. Once a potential client has told you his story
    a. follow up with general questions
    b. summarize what you think you have heard
    c. tell him whether you think he has a case before pinning him down to the details
    d. none of the above
16. To accept a case
    a. it must be in the client's best interests
    b. the firm must have the resources to devote to the case
    c. it must fit within the firm's area of practice
    d. all of the above
17. At the initial interview
    a. it is not important to get enough information to estimate the value of a case
    b. the interviewer should get the date of every event the client mentions
    c. the interviewer must get a complete picture of the client's damages
    d. all of the above
18. At the end of the initial interview
    a. inform the client about what he needs to supply the firm
    b. refrain from discussing the client's goal and expectations until the firm decides whether to accept the case
    c. prepare a follow-up letter only if the firm and the client enter into a business relationship
    d. all of the above

FILL IN THE BLANK

19. The concept of _____ is based on the assumption that clients will not reveal information that is embarrassing or incriminating if they are not assured that information that will not be revealed outside the attorney-client relationship.
20. _____ theorists look at law as divinely created inalienable rights, while _____ deny the existence of inalienable rights and believe that the law is based on rules and the logic used in applying those rules. The _____, on the other hand, believe that the law should not be restricted to logic and past decisions but should be sensitive to the social realities of the time.
21. _____ theorists reject the idea that decision-making can be rational or value-neutral and see the legal as being inherently unjust.
22. The ultimate law of the land is found in the U.S. _____.
23. Under the doctrine of the _____, each function of government is divided among the legislative, executive, and judicial branches.
24. A _____ is a law created by a state or federal legislature, while an _____ is a law created by a city council or county board of supervisors.
25. Courts create _____ (a resolution of fact-specific disputes) that can be either _____ law (law that sets forth the rights and duties of parties) or _____ law (law that sets forth the rules that litigants must follow).
26. Cases are heard by the _____ courts and reviewed by the _____ courts.
27. _____ law deals with lawsuits brought by individuals who have suffered private wrongs for which they are seeking compensation, whereas _____ law deals with the wrongs done to an individual that result in harm to society as a whole.
28. In some cases, the _____ (who represents the state in a criminal case) seeks _____ in order to compensate the victim for losses she has suffered.
29. Civil cases require proof by a _____, whereas criminal cases require proof _____.
30. The _____ prevents attorneys from being able to testify about communications between themselves and their clients.
31. Even if a client has a viable _____ (lawsuit), a law firm will not accept his case if a _____ could not be collected because the defendant is _____.
32. A statute that requires a lawsuit to be filed on a particular type of claim within a specified time period is referred to as a _____.
33. _____ (personal injury) law establishes what the plaintiff must prove to show the defendant's _____ (responsibility) for the plaintiff's damages.
34. _____ are sometimes used by attorneys to help them select ideal jurors for their case.

TRUE OR FALSE

____ 35. Confidentiality pertains to any information obtained in the context of the attorney-client relationship no matter how that information is obtained.

____ 36. Paralegals should avoid saying anything about clients outside their office.

____ 37. Confidentiality cannot be broken even if the client consents or the court orders it.

____ 38. Paralegals should avoid taking calls from clients while another person is in the room.

____ 39. Folders containing privileged documents should be clearly labeled.

____ 40. Legal theorists and philosophers can agree on a definition of law, but cannot agree on its purpose.

____ 41. The law is designed to resolve disputes and serve as a kind of social control, but it is not intended to bring about social change.

____ 42. A study of jurisprudence helps one to better understand the legal system and the reasoning of judges.

____ 43. Natural law theory can be seen in the acts of civil disobedience of those who believe that human law should not be followed if it violates divinely based principles of justice.

____ 44. Utilitarianism, which is a school of positivism, advocates that the good of the community must be subordinated to the good of the individual.

____ 45. Both the positivists and the realists believe that judges should adhere to past decisions and should keep the law as unchanged as possible.

____ 46. Critical legal theorists perceive the law as a tool of social propaganda that exploits the poor.

____ 47. The separation of powers doctrine is designed to keep the legislative branch of government more powerful than the executive and judicial branches.

____ 48. A statute or ordinance cannot conflict with the U.S. Constitution or the constitution of the state in which it was enacted.

____ 49. If the President does nothing and the legislature is not in session, the bill becomes law after 10 days.

____ 50. The primary source of substantive law is court rules.

____ 51. Failure to comply with procedural law can result in a case being dismissed.

____ 52. The primary purpose of civil law is to compensate victims, while the primary purpose of criminal law is to punish offenders.

____ 53. The criminal law acts on behalf of the person wronged and seeks to recover damages for that person.

____ 54. The attorney representing a plaintiff in a civil suit has a higher burden of proof than the prosecutor in a criminal case.

____ 55. Being sensitive to the arrangement of furniture, offering the client something to drink, and engaging in small talk all contribute to relaxing the client during an initial interview.

____ 56. The attorney-client privilege prevents attorneys from being able to testify about communications between themselves and their clients, but does not prevent clients from being compelled to testify about any of those communications.

____ 57. The client is the holder of the attorney-client privilege, but the privilege does not survive the death of the client.

____ 58. The attorney-client privilege covers communications with paralegals, investigators, and experts working on a case.

____ 59. A client may lose the attorney-client privilege if her actions imply she has waived it.

____ 60. Inadvertent disclosure of a document can result in a loss of the attorney-client privilege.

____ 61. Begin an interview with the new client with directed, closed questions.

____ 62. Never takes notes when interviewing new clients because they will think you are not listening.

____ 63. A client's non-verbal cues can be as meaningful as the words he uses.

____ 64. An understanding of common psychological needs and defenses will help you to get information from clients initially.

____ 65. Use prepared questions and be careful not to deviate from them any more than necessary during an initial interview.

____ 66. An interviewer should determine who the adverse parties are when interviewing a potential client to determine if the attorney might have potential conflicts of interest.

____ 67. One of the reasons for finding out the facts of the dispute in some detail during the initial interview is to determine whether the attorney should accept the case.

____ 68. Going over the client's medical and employment histories is not necessary during the initial interview because that information is not needed until the firm decides whether to accept the case.

____ 69. To assess the value of a claim, you need to look only at the plaintiff's chance of winning.

____ 70. At the initial interview, the interviewer should get a complete breakdown of the plaintiff's damages.

____ 71. Assume everything a client is telling you at the initial interview is true.

____ 72. In deciding whether to accept a case, an attorney needs to consider only the value of the claim.

____ 73. Statutes of limitations problems can exist over when a claim arose.

____ *74. A plaintiff cannot bring suit if she is under the age of majority, in prison, or insane.

____ 75. You should assume that any dates a client gives you are accurate.

____ 76. At the initial interview, get the specific descriptions of documents, who has them, and how those people or entities can be located.

____ 77. You do not need to get the names of potential witnesses or copies of documents the client brings to the first meeting because the firm may not accept the case.

____ 78. At the end of the initial interview, summarize what the client has said and tell him what he will be expected to do should he decide to retain the firm.

____ *79. Active listening requires paying attention to non-verbal language and hearing the actual message the speaker is trying to convey.

____ *80. Non-verbal language is the same in every culture.

____ *81. Empathic listening implies that the listener agrees with and condones what the speaker is saying.

____ *82. Paralegals should always do their best to make sure the person they are interviewing gets to the point as quickly as possible.

*Questions taken from Bonus Pointers

PART B

INTERVIEWING A WITNESS

Many people are concerned about having to testify in court and will often "not recall" an event to ensure their testimony will not be required. Do everything possible to allay a witness's fears about talking with you. Meeting people at their home after work or for lunch can help make reluctant witnesses more comfortable and feel less "put out" than asking them to come to your office. You are more likely to earn witnesses' cooperation if you accurately assess and meet any needs they have. Some witnesses want to know they are helping your client, they want sympathy or attention, they want to be told how important they are, or they need assurance that what they are about to say will not get them in trouble.

Emphasize at the beginning of the interview that you are a paralegal and not an attorney. Explain why you want to do the interview and what the possible ramifications of talking with you could be, including the likelihood of the opposing attorney or paralegal wanting to conduct an interview as well. You must never discourage witnesses from talking with the other side. Doing this could not only get you fired, but in some jurisdictions could result in criminal charges being filed for attempting to influence a witness and could result in your attorney being disciplined.

If you know in advance that the witness will support your client's position, you may want to ask permission to tape record the interview. Providing a copy of such a tape to opposing counsel could conceivably speed up settlement. The presence of a tape recorder makes many people uncomfortable, however, and may be counterproductive. Therefore, if you opt to record the interview, make sure the witness feels comfortable before starting. Keep in mind that the opposing side may have a right to obtain a copy of the recording and that several evidentiary obstacles must be overcome before tape-recorded statements can be used in court.

Never tape record a conversation or statement without the witness's permission. If you are not a participant in a conversation, it is almost certainly illegal for you to record it. Even if you are recording your own telephone conversation with someone else, you may be committing a crime if the person you are recording does not know you are doing it. State laws vary on this issue. In most states it is not a crime to secretly record a face-to-face interview with a witness, but it may be unethical. Certainly the witness is unlikely to be pleased if he finds out. Always get your supervising attorney's approval before you get out your tape recorder.

As with the initial interview of a client, allow the person to give a free-flowing narrative of the events she observed. At some point, try to pinpoint the exact location of the witness at the time the events occurred to determine whether the observation was possible. It is not uncommon for witnesses to make materially false statements and be honestly unaware of their falsity.

impeached　discredited

If a witness is hostile, you will need to pin her down with as many specific facts and details as possible. Find out exactly where the witness was standing, what she was doing, who was at the scene, what they were wearing, who was doing what to whom, and so on. If nothing else, by restricting the witness to exacting factual details, she may be less easily **impeached** (discredited) at a later date should other witnesses or physical evidence conflict with her statements.

Remember that witnesses can often provide more than personal, firsthand information. They may lead you to legally admissible evidence. They might tell you, for example, that their friends also observed the incident but did not talk to the police officers so their names are not on the police report. They also might alert you to the fact that someone was taking photographs or videos of the scene. This information might allow you to obtain additional collaborative evidence to support your client's story or to impeach the recollections of a hostile witness.

Always be gracious. An interview is not a place for aggressive, hard-hitting questions. Witnesses do not have to talk to you. If you irritate them, they may terminate the interview. You cannot afford to burn bridges during the initial stages of an investigation. You may find out later that the witness you alienated is the one you most need.

Putting It Into Practice 2.13:

What does a paralegal want to accomplish when interviewing a witness?

BONUS POINTERS:

GETTING A WITNESS STATEMENT

Having interviewed a witness, you may decide that you want to take his statement. Several means can be used to do that. You may wish, with the permission of the witness, to tape record his statement. Alternatively, you may ask him to write out a statement, although it is rare that individuals do an adequate job. Frequently, investigators write out the person's statement and have the witness sign it. The obvious drawback to this procedure is that the witness can later deny having made the statement or can say he signed it even though he was never given an opportunity to read it. In such cases, the statement may be inadmissible and the investigator may be forced to take the stand to testify as to the witness's statement. Putting the statement in the witness's words makes it more difficult for him to later **recant** (deny having made the statement). In addition to having the witness sign the statement,

recant　deny having made a statement

have him initial each page, as well as sign a statement attesting to the truth and accuracy of the foregoing statement.

If a witness is unwilling to be recorded or to sign an affirmative statement, he may be willing to sign a written "negative" statement. Such a statement denies any knowledge on the part of the witness. Having this statement in writing may preclude the witness from coming back at a later date with new recollections.

Although expensive, another alternative is the use of a court reporter. This method virtually precludes the witness from denying that he made the statement, but if he does, a court reporter, who is a disinterested third-party rather than an investigator, will be called to testify.

Statements should be as specific as possible. Detailed, specific factual information rather than abstract generalizations are the goal. Be sure to get the witness's actual observations and not his opinions; opinions of lay witnesses are generally not admissible.

Witness statements can also be made from recorded telephone statements. When taking a statement over the telephone, identify yourself, the purpose of the phone call, the name of the person being interviewed, the date and time of the call, the telephone number of each party, and the fact that the conversation is being recorded and that the witness gave permission to record the statement. The witness should then be asked to give his full name, date of birth, address, driver's license number, and social security number. Having all of this information facilitates location of the witness two or three years later if the case ultimately goes to trial. This same identifying information should be obtained when recording a statement in person. During the conversation, be careful to avoid making extraneous comments or speaking while the witness is speaking. After the statement has been recorded, the tape should be labeled with the case name, witness name, and date of interview, and should be transcribed as soon as possible after the interview.

NET NEWS

To see articles written by private investigators about the process of interviewing and taking witness statements, go to *www.pimall.com/nais/n.indexc.html.* Articles are available for review and references are made to related books sold at this site.

Figure 2-10
Things to Keep in Mind When Interviewing Witnesses

Things to Keep in Mind When Interviewing Witnesses

Allay the witness's fears about being interviewed.

Assess and try to meet the needs of the witness.

Reveal your paralegal status.

Explain the purpose and ramifications of the interview.

Consider asking permission to tape record the interview.

Allow the witness to begin with free-flowing narrative and follow up with more directed questions.

Pinpoint details, especially if the witness is hostile.

Remember that the witness may lead to other admissible evidence.

Always be gracious.

"I Remember Now Getting a Strange Call about Two Days Before Mike Was Shot."

A few days later, Martha got a phone call from John. In his usual direct manner, he skipped the small talk and jumped to the reason for his call.

"Martha, I just heard from Ernie, our private investigator. I'd asked him to sniff around the police station and see if he could find out anything about the Johnson shooting. As luck would have it, a couple of his old buddies were setting out to arrest a couple of boys in connection with that shooting and they were only too happy to tell Ernie what they knew.

"It appears that a couple of the boys involved were bragging to some other kid about what they had done. He, in turn, was telling a friend about it when his mother overheard their conversation and confronted him. She dragged him down to the police station, and after a little subtle persuasion he finally gave up the names of the boys. It turns out both of them belong to this group that seems obsessed with the *Teenage Stalkers* movie. So it's looking like we might have the perpetrators and that we could conceivably have a cause of action against the company that made this movie."

"Great news, Mr. Morgan!" exclaimed Martha, relieved for Mike and excited about the prospects of working on a case of this caliber.

"Well, it's too soon to celebrate, but at least we have a start. Now, I've also been able to set up some interviews with some of the folks at the school."

"Wow, that's great," interjected Martha. "I thought you were pretty sure the district's attorney wouldn't allow that."

"I have to admit I'm pleasantly surprised. I called the attorney, who happens to be the daughter of an old buddy I went to law school with, and so we had a nice time catching up before I asked her about the interviews. She was understandably reluctant at first, but I told her that if we couldn't talk with anyone we would have to file suit so we could depose them. I also said that, if we interviewed their people and found out no one knew anything, we would obviously not file suit against the district. I guess she talked with the principal, who assured her they were just as shocked as everyone else by what happened to Mike and that he had no qualms about us talking with anyone on his staff. I've made up a list of people I'd like you to interview, beginning with Ms. Sinclair, secretary to the vice-principal, and Ms. Lee, secretary to the principal."

"I'd love to, Mr. Morgan. But to be honest, I've never conducted an interview before," admitted Martha.

"Then there's no time like the present to learn. Make yourself an outline of questions. With Ms. Sinclair, for example, you'll want some information about her background—her education and training, what other positions she may have held on campus, how long she's worked for the school, and what her responsibilities are. Then you'll want to ask what she knows about the Johnson shooting, if she saw or heard anything herself, and most importantly, whether she had heard any rumors or whether she or anyone else she knew had been aware that some kind of violence might occur on campus. Had there been any step-up in security? Had she and the other staff members been briefed or in any way warned about potential violence on campus? Was there a general climate of fear? Those are the kinds of questions you will want to follow up with after you've first asked her to tell you what she knows. Why don't you write out your questions and run them by me before you interview her?" suggested John.

"That would be great. When would you like me to get them to you?"

"I'll be in the office Friday. That should be soon enough. I've scheduled her interview on Monday afternoon at the school. I asked that you be able to use a small conference room in the administrative building so that you'll have privacy."

"Thanks for making the arrangements, Mr. Morgan. I'll have my questions ready on Friday. And thanks for giving me this opportunity."

"You're quite welcome. After all, I think it's about time we bring you out from behind that copy machine and put some of that hard-earned education into practice," teased John.

The days flew by. Before Martha knew it, she was standing at the entrance of the school administration building. She was grateful that she was carrying out her first interview in familiar surroundings. As she walked in the door, she immediately saw Ms. Lee, who had befriended her daughters, both of whom had worked part-time in the front office.

"Good afternoon, Ms. Fletcher. So nice to see you again," called out Ms. Lee.

"Thank you. It's nice to see you, too. How is the semester going?"

"Certainly more dramatic than most. This place has seen more camera crews in the last few months than it has in the whole time it's been in operation. And I think half the city police force has been here at one time or another," complained Ms. Lee.

"I'm sure it's been very traumatic for everyone," sympathized Martha. "Hopefully everything can return to normal now, whatever that is."

"Have you seen Mike lately?" asked Ms. Lee. "I hadn't heard anything recently about how he's recovering."

As Martha started to answer, Ms. Sinclair stuck her head out a door and asked if she was Ms. Fletcher. When Martha confirmed her identify, Ms. Sinclair motioned to Martha to follow her. Martha cursorily responded to Ms. Lee's question as she moved in the direction of Ms. Sinclair, who was briskly walking down the hall. When she reached the conference room, Ms. Sinclair silently waved Martha into the room and indicated where she should sit. Certainly not a "chatty Cathy" thought Martha, wondering how she was going to get this woman talking in anything other than monosyllables. Then she noticed the newspaper in Ms. Sinclair's hand and observed the unfinished crossword puzzle.

"Are you a crossword puzzle fan, too, Ms. Sinclair?"

"Why yes, I am," responded Ms. Sinclair enthusiastically.

"I had some real problems with 43 down this morning," Martha continued, hoping to engage Ms. Sinclair in something that was of mutual interest.

Ms. Sinclair glanced down to see if she had completed that one and grinned triumphantly. "Oh, I'm an avid gardener so I knew that one right away. Those dahlias are called 'dinner plate' dahlias because their flowers are so huge."

"Right! I remember having seen them once. They are magnificent flowers. Have you ever grown them?" Martha asked, hoping this conversation would relax Ms. Sinclair, whose stiffness went beyond formality.

"Yes, I do, as a matter of fact. Last year I had such a splendid crop that people stopped by my yard just to inquire about those flowers. This year I planted one hundred tubers," bragged Ms. Sinclair.

"Amazing! I'll bet you can hardly wait for the weather to warm so they'll start blooming," said Martha encouragingly. Martha continued the flower conversation for several minutes until she observed Ms. Sinclair sit back in her chair and breathe more deeply. Then she eased into the interview, explaining who she was and why she was there. After Ms. Sinclair indicated that the vice-principal had warned her about why she was being interviewed, Martha went on to get the background information John had suggested. She quickly discovered that Ms. Sinclair was not by nature a disclosing individual, and that open-ended questions reaped very little information. She changed her tack and began asking more directed questions.

"Do you remember anyone on the staff talking about the violence being experienced on high school campuses around the nation?" asked Martha.

"There was some talk, yes," responded Ms. Sinclair, making no offer to amplify her answer.

"Did anyone express concern that similar violence might erupt on your campus?" added Martha.

"I think some were concerned, but it wasn't a major topic of conversation." Ms. Sinclair was not deliberately secretive but she was clearly a woman of few words.

Martha thought for a moment and then asked, "Do you know if security was beefed up on campus in the time preceding the shooting?"

"No, not that I was aware of."

The interview went on in a similar fashion for about an hour, until Martha had exhausted every avenue of questioning she could come up with. Before wrapping up, she asked one more general question. "Ms. Sinclair, can you think of anything else that we haven't discussed that would help us understand why this senseless act occurred?"

Just then, the phone in the room rang, startling both women. After Ms. Sinclair answered it, she turned toward Martha and said, "You know, I just remembered getting a strange phone call about two days before Mike was shot. The person didn't give his name but he did tell me that a student was going to "get wasted" on campus in the next couple of days, and that if we knew what was good for us we would cancel classes."

Martha did her best to cloak her elation. "Did you tell anyone about the call?" asked Martha calmly.

"I told our vice-principal, Mr. Garcia, but he laughed it off as another prank call."

"Do you get many prank calls like that?" Martha gently but patiently pursued this line of inquiry.

"Well, not exactly like this one, but it's not uncommon for us to get one or two phone calls a month warning us that something is going to happen unless we cancel classes."

"Did this caller tell you anything specific? Did he give you a specific time or date or place?"

"He did say it would happen on Friday. I remember that."

"And did it happen on Friday?" asked Martha, a chill going down her back.

"Yes." Ms. Sinclair's expression never changed, but she did ask, "Is this going to get Mr. Garcia in trouble?"

Putting It Into Practice 2.14:

Why might Martha want to get a written statement from Ms. Sinclair?

BONUS POINTERS:

LOCATING WITNESSES

There are two kinds of non-party witnesses—people whom we are not suing, but who have information about the dispute. These are the "impartial" witness (someone who is not a part of the dispute and does not side with either party) and the "involved" witness (someone who can be expected to "take sides"). Whether we represent the plaintiff or the defendant, it is to our advantage to interview and take statements from as many of the impartial witnesses as we can find, as early as possible.

It can matter a great deal which side gets to these witnesses first. Ideally, the first side to talk to a witness will obtain (with the witness's permission) a tape-recorded or signed statement, locking the witness into one version of the facts for all time. A single answer to a single question can, at times, make or break a lawsuit.

How do we locate these witnesses? Oftentimes, clients know the whereabouts of the most important witnesses and records, such as police reports, that reveal the identities of others. But sometimes paralegals must consult other resources. Telephone books, neighbors, co-workers, friends, and relatives of potential witnesses can be good sources of information, especially when witnesses have simply moved, changed jobs, or changed their telephone number.

Other sources of information including the ones listed here, are frequently consulted.

- ◆ motor vehicle department
- ◆ voter registration lists
- ◆ post office
- ◆ utility companies
- ◆ Social Security office
- ◆ county assessor's office
- ◆ driver's license bureau

Private investigators and "skip tracing" companies can also be used to locate witnesses. Because of the cost of using these services, however, many firms have their paralegals do this kind of investigative work.

Putting It Into Practice 2.15:

Using one of the Internet addresses given in the Net News, try to locate someone you have lost track of and whose address you no longer know.

NET NEWS

The Internet can be useful in locating individuals. Some on-line sources include the following.

- ◆ Finding People on the Internet (*http://www.nova. edu/Inter-Links/phone.html*)
- ◆ People Search (*http//www.yahoo.com/search/people/*)
- ◆ Internet Address Finder (*http://www.iaf.net/*)
- ◆ The Big Book (*www.bigbook.com*)
- ◆ Switchboard, USA (*www.switchboard.com*)
- ◆ Telephone Directory and Reverse Directories (*www.anywho.com and www.whowhere.com*)
- ◆ Four11 (*www.four11.com*)

To get a paralegal's perspective of how best to locate witnesses, go to *www.paralegals.org/reporter*, click on "1996 Year-End," then on "Inside the Internet," and then on "Looking for Mister or Miss Netizen."

Figure 2-11
Investigative Process

Investigative Process

Locate and interview witnesses

Find and review records

Take photographs

Collect and preserve evidence

Find experts to evaluate case

Martha could hardly wait to get back to the office to tell John about her interview with Ms. Sinclair. The anonymous phone call provided evidence that the school officials had received a warning about the impending shooting and gave John further reason to pursue his investigation. He had already received permission from the partners to conduct a limited investigation, and now it appeared that he might be able to build a claim against the school district.

"I'm going to need to talk with Mr. Garcia now to substantiate what Ms. Sinclair told you. Were you able to get a written statement from her, Martha?"

"She has agreed to sign a written statement if I prepare it for her," responded Martha.

"Great. Get that over to her right away before she changes her mind or someone changes it for her. Now let's just hope that Mr. Garcia doesn't deny all knowledge of this call. Do you know if Ms. Sinclair mentioned the call to anyone else other than Mr. Garcia?"

"She indicated that she did mention it to one of the faculty members. I wrote her name down."

"Good, because I'd like you to talk with her as well and get a witness statement if you can. Let me see if I can get permission from the district's attorney for you to talk with her. If I can, I'd like you to set up an interview as soon as possible. Then there are several other things I need you to attend to as well. First, I need you to have Mike sign a medical authorization form. We need to get his existing medical records.

"Second, make yourself a note to get a copy of the police report when it's available. We won't be able to get it while Mike's case is still under investigation," continued John. "When it is available, I want to see it to find out what kinds of physical evidence the police have."

Martha looked up from writing notes to herself about what John wanted to have done. "You mean something like the bullets that were fired or the photographs of Mike's injuries or of shoeprints at the scene?" suggested Martha.

"Have you worked as a paralegal in the prosecutor's office or do you just read a lot of John Grisham novels?" teased John.

"Neither, actually," explained Martha. "But my father was a police officer."

"Oh, well, that explains it," laughed John. "So I guess I don't need to tell you what you'll find in a police report. Anyway, let me see it as soon as we receive it."

GETTING RECORDS

Before requesting records from any institution, contact its representative first to see what procedures you must follow. Find out, for example, if any fees are charged and if those fees must be paid before the records can be released. Many doctors charge nominal fees for their notes and several hundred dollars for their **narrative reports.**

narrative reports   reports prepared by medical doctors

Once you receive records, review them immediately to ensure that you can read any handwritten entries and that you understand any abbreviations or shorthand notations. Clarifying any ambiguities in advance may save time later, prevent misunderstandings, and open up new avenues of investigation. Treat each new document you receive as a potential "smoking gun" that is critical to winning the case. With this attitude, you will be less tempted to procrastinate in your reviewing of records.

Figure 2-12
Medical Authorization Release

Medical Authorization Release

To Whom it May Concern:

Please be advised that my attorney, John Morgan, Esq., WTHIE & TREADWELL, is hereby authorized to request, and to receive, all medical information which you may have in your possession concerning me.

You are hereby authorized to allow my attorney complete access to any and all of my medical records, including billing statements, diagnoses, medical test results, doctors' and nurses' notes and the like which are or may later be in your possession or in any way reflect anything concerning me. I hereby waive, in favor of my attorney, any and all confidential relationships.

I hereby authorize the use of a copy of this Release as though it were an original.

Michael Johnson
DOB: 11/05/82
SSN: 560-00-4321

Date: July 15, 2000

STATE OF ARIZONA   )
)   *ss.*
County of Maricopa   )

SUBSCRIBED AND SWORN TO *before me this 15th day of July, 2000, by Michael Johnson.*

Notary Public

My Commission Expires:

Medical Records

Medical records supply diagnostic information establishing the nature and extent of the illness or injuries, the treatment being used, and the prognosis for the patient's recovery (including any long-term effects and possible ongoing treatment). These records can be obtained from private physicians, who usually keep detailed records of their patients' visits, and from hospitals. Hospital records include admission forms, progress notes, physician's orders, lab and X-ray reports, operative reports (in the event of surgery), billing invoices, and discharge summaries. The technical terms in medical records can be hard to decipher without the assistance of a medical dictionary. An anatomy-physiology book is also handy as well as the *Physician's Desk Reference* (referred to as the *PDR*), which describes how various drugs are used, their side-effects, and the conditions under which they should not be used. In some firms, nurse paralegals (paralegals with a nursing background) or legal nurse consultants (nurses who do not have specific paralegal training) review and decipher medical records.

NET NEWS

To read more about the differences between nurse paralegals and legal nurse consultants and the qualifications for each, go to *www.law.net/nipal/nurseind.htm*. Both types of practice have become increasingly popular areas of employment for those with a nursing background.

Figure 2-13
Hints for Dealing with Records

Hints for Dealing With Records

Find out the procedures for obtaining records before requesting them.

Have the client authorization forms in advance.

Provide the custodian of records with appropriate fees and information.

Review records immediately after receiving them.

Clarify ambiguities in the records.

Use technical resources and consultants to interpret the records.

Because medical and employment records are confidential, you need the client to sign a written authorization (release), like that shown in Figure 2-12, before the doctor's office or employer will release any records. Most firms have standard release forms, but check the form before using it to make sure it provides everything you need. Explain to the client why these authorization forms are necessary and how they will be used. Having clients sign several authorization forms in advance prevents them from having to return to the office every time an authorization is needed. Because some institutions require authorizations to be notarized, you may save time by having them all notarized at the same time.

NET NEWS

To read more about the process of getting medical records, go to *www.paralegals.org/reporter*, click on "Winter 1998," and then on "Medical Records Acquisition in Litigation."

Police Records and Other Official Records

To obtain accident reports, you must submit a written request to the law enforcement agency and enclose any required fees. Many agencies require forms to be filled out and some require that a need be established before the records will be provided because the records may not be available to the public. A similar process must often be followed to secure birth and death certificates (usually from the department of health services), motor vehicle registration records, and driver's license information (although the information available from these other records is often restricted).

Putting It Into Practice 2.16:

Look on the Internet to see if your local police department has a Web page. Use the name of the department as your search term. If so, is information available on this site regarding how to order accident reports online?

County Recorder's Office and Court Clerk's Office

Become familiar with the location, procedures, and personnel in the county recorder's and court clerk's offices. Paralegals are often asked to obtain records and file documents with these offices. The county recorder's office, for example, may have information about mortgages, bankruptcies, trusts, and judgments. The court clerk's office has court case files, which, unless they have been sealed by the courts, are public

The home page of NACO, the National Association of Counties at *http://www.naco.org*, is a valuable resource that has direct links to all counties that are members and to the Web pages of all of its members that maintain them. On the Web page for your county, you will most likely find a link to the county recorder's office. Alternatively, you can enter the search term "[your county] recorder's office" to find the Web page for your county recorder. By the same token, you can probably find the home page for your local court clerk's office by using its name as a search term.

A well-known public records search company is "KnowX" at *www.knowx.com*. This company has multiple databases that can be used to find assets, people, and businesses at the same time. It is very comprehensive in its coverage, easy to use, and provides detailed pricing information.

records. You can determine anyone's litigation history by accessing records found in the court clerk's office. To expedite your investigations, find out if the records in these offices are online and whether this service is free or subscription-based.

Putting It Into Practice 2.17:

Does your county trial court have a Web page? Use the name of this court as your search term. If so, can you access an individual's court records online? Can you find out online the status of a case currently in litigation?

Other Public Records

Other documents that are usually a matter of public record include those listed here.

- ◆ property deeds
- ◆ tax liens
- ◆ marriage licenses
- ◆ business certificates
- ◆ partnership filings
- ◆ annual reports of corporations
- ◆ professional licenses
- ◆ telephone records
- ◆ highway department records

State and local records are usually easily accessible; individuals can walk in and request copies of documents. (Call first, however, because some agencies do not allow the public to inspect records on certain days.) At the federal level, however, requests for information often require going through the **Freedom of Information Act** (FOIA). This Act requires federal agencies to make certain records related to such issues as consumer product safety, environmental hazards, public health, labor relations, and government spending available to the public. Individuals can also request that they be provided any records that the government has regarding them. The FOIA does not apply to Congress, the federal courts, the White House staff, state and local agencies, schools, and private organizations and businesses. Federal agencies can refuse to release certain types of exempted information: trade secrets, defense and foreign policy secrets, personnel and medical files, confidential financial information, internal agency rules and government memos, and investigative reports prepared for law enforcement purposes.

Freedom of Information Act
federal act requiring federal agencies to make certain records available to the public

BONUS POINTERS: **HOW TO MAKE A FREEDOM OF INFORMATION ACT REQUEST**

If you are not sure which agency has the records you want, go to the library and check the United States Government Organization Manual or call the local office of your representative in Congress. In writing your request, you should do the following.

- ◆ Reasonably describe the records you want with sufficient specificity that an employee of the agency familiar with records can locate the records in a reasonable amount of time and without an unreasonable amount of effort.
- ◆ Restrict your request to the records you really want rather than asking for "all the files relating to."
- ◆ Address your request to a specific agency.
- ◆ Provide identifying information such as social security number, date of birth, and address, if requesting personal records.
- ◆ Specify the purpose for which the records are requested and your status in requesting these records. (This is done so that the appropriate fees can be assessed.)
- ◆ Mark your envelope "Attention: Freedom of Information Act."

The agency has a right to charge fees for the costs of searching for the documents, reviewing documents to determine if they should be included in the agency's response to your request, and duplicating documents. Those making requests for commercial use can be charged all three fees, while those making requests for non-commercial use will be charged only the duplicating and searching fees. If a request is made on behalf of an educational or non-commercial scientific institution or as a representative of the media, only the duplicating fees will be charged. Ask the agency from which you are making an FOIA request for the current agency fee schedule, which will explain the cost of different types of searches and the cost per page for photocopying.

Figure 2-14 shows a sample FOIA request letter.

Figure 2-14
FOIA Request

Agency Head (or Freedom of Information Officer)
Name of Agency
Address of Agency
City, State, Zip Code

Re: Freedom of Information Act Request

Dear _____ :
This is a request under the Freedom of Information Act, 5 U.S.C. Sec. 552.

I request that a copy of the following documents be provided to me:
_____ .

In order to help determine my status to assess fees, you should know that I am affiliated with an educational institution, and that this request is made for a scholarly purpose and not for a commercial use.

I am aware I am entitled to make this request under the Freedom of Information Act, and if your agency response is not satisfactory, I am prepared to make an administrative appeal. Please indicate to me the name of the official to whom such an appeal should be addressed. I am aware that if my request is denied, I am entitled to know the grounds for this denial.

I am aware that while the law allows your agency to withhold specified categories of exempted information, you are required by law to release any segregable portions that are left after the exempted material has been deleted from the documents that I am seeking.

I am willing to pay fees for this request up to a maximum of $ _____ . If you estimate that the fees will exceed this limit, please inform me first.

Sincerely,

Name
Address
City, State, Zip Code

NET NEWS

For more information about preparing FOIA requests, go to *www.paralegals.org/reporter*, click on "Online 1998," and then on "FOIA and Public Disclosure Requests: Don't Become Road Kill on the Information Super Highway." Another site that will guide you through the process of preparing FOIA requests is at *www.aclu.org/library/foia.html*.

Additional Sources of Information

Other sources of information include those listed here.

◆ public libraries (consult with the reference librarian)
◆ specialized libraries, such as medical libraries
◆ trade associations, such as the American National Standards Institute and the American National Safety Council
◆ technical references, such as the *Lawyer's Desk Reference: Technical Sources for Conducting a Personal Injury Action*
◆ computer databases

Putting It Into Practice 2.18:

Go to the Internet and find out if your local library is online. If it is, what kinds of resources are available online? If your library is not online, go to the Web page for the Phoenix Public Library (*http://pac.lib.ci.phoenix.az.us/enhanced/index.html*), click on "Databases and Websites." What resources are available online for this library?

"Third, Martha, I'd like you to go over to the campus sometime in the afternoon next week when most of the kids have left and look around at the scene of the shooting. You've interviewed some of the students who were at the scene, so you have a sense of what happened. I'd like you to review what they said in their interviews and see if what they say happened could actually have happened."

"Do you think they're lying?" inquired Martha.

"No. I just don't want any surprises later. I don't want to find out after taking this case that they couldn't possibly have seen what they said they did because a tree or something else was obstructing their view. I'm not suggesting that they're lying, but experience has taught me that people's perceptions can be skewed, especially when they've experienced something as traumatic as these kids did. They may be filling in the blanks in their memories now, and they've had enough time to compare stories that they may be inadvertently adopting some of the details they heard from others rather than what they observed themselves."

"I understand," concurred Martha. "My dad mentioned some of the problems with eyewitness identification."

"Good. Then you're aware of how easy it is for people to make misidentifications. My main concern with a civil case, however, is that the story our witnesses give is plausible and that they're not going to be blown out of the water at trial. So what I'd like you to do is to take some photos of the scene from as many perspectives as you can think of. Pinpoint as closely as you can where each of the students was when the shooting occurred and take photos from each of those perspectives. Keep in mind that if we decide to take Mike's case, I'll have Ernie take the photos we would introduce at trial. The photos you're taking are for my eyes only, so don't be concerned if they don't turn out perfect," assured John.

"I assume the firm has a camera I can use?" questioned Martha.

"Yes, we have a 35mm. Nothing fancy, but it takes good enough pictures for what we need," confirmed John.

NET NEWS

For information about photography of crime scenes (which applies to photography of civil matters), go to *http://police2.ucr.edu/csi.html* and click on "Crime Scene Photography." One of the best articles at this site is entitled "Crime Scene Photography." Although this article is clearly an outline used to teach a class, it is sufficiently detailed to give you some good general information about photographing evidence.

PHOTOGRAPHING THE SCENE

Photographs can be worth "a thousand words." Therefore, careful attention must be paid to the photographic process. Keep in mind that these photos are for evidentiary, not aesthetic, purposes. Although photos are often taken by professional photographers because of their expertise and to avoid having to call a paralegal to testify at trial, paralegals should still be aware of what constitutes good photography for litigation purposes.

◆ Black-and-white film is often better than color film because it produces sharper details.
◆ Fill the frame as much as possible, avoiding any distracting background.
◆ Make sure photos accurately reflect the scene they are depicting; try to take photos at the same time of day that the incident occurred.
◆ Record camera speed, lighting and weather conditions, and camera placement for every photo.
◆ Never alter any evidence while photographing it.
◆ Photograph from every conceivable angle.
◆ Take a series of photos when necessary. (E.g., to show the changes in bruises or to recreate the sequence of events leading up to an accident.)
◆ Have aerial photos taken to orient jurors to the conditions existing at a particular location.
◆ Take close-up photos of damaged vehicles and other forms of evidence.
◆ Create videos to demonstrate procedures or processes that entail movement.

Putting It Into Practice 2.19:

What photos other than the ones John mentioned might the firm want to get if it takes Mike's case?

GETTING PHYSICAL EVIDENCE

Physical evidence, such as skid marks, bullets, consumer products, and vehicles are sometimes needed to prove the facts at issue at trial. When physical evidence is in the possession of a law enforcement or investigative agency, it must be obtained by means of a **subpoena,** a written court order compelling a third party to produce evidence. But if it is in possession of the client, it must be clearly labeled or put in a sealed container that must be labeled. The label should identify the person who collected it, when and where it was found, and what it is. This labeling is required in order to properly **authenticate** the evidence so that it is admissible at trial. In other words, the court must be assured that the evidence is in substantially the same condition as when it was found. This process of authenticating physical evidence is

subpoena   written court order compelling a person to appear before the court or to produce evidence

authenticate   verify evidence is in substantially the same condition as when it was found

---

For information about the collection and preservation of physical evidence, go to *http://police2.ucr.edu/csi.html*, click on "Evidence Collection," and then on "Evidence Collection Guidelines." Although this information is designed for law enforcement officers, it is equally relevant to the collection of evidence in civil cases.

---

chain of custody proof of the location and condition of physical evidence from the time it is created until it appears in the courtroom

called preserving the **chain of custody.** Generally, an investigator collects and preserves evidence for trial so that the investigator rather than a paralegal can be called as a witness to testify to the chain of custody.

Evidence is usually destroyed or changed if it is not preserved soon after the incident occurs. Consequently, efforts should be made to find and collect evidence as soon as you learn of its existence. Personal injury and product liability cases, in particular, can be won or lost based on the availability of physical evidence.

Putting It Into Practice 2.20:

What kinds of physical evidence might be available in Mike's case? Where would this evidence be located and how could it be obtained?

"Fourth, Martha, I need some help in locating a Ph.D. in psychology to educate me about the effects of violence in the media on teenagers. I've read a lot in the popular media, but I have no idea if what I'm reading is in the least bit supported by any kind of data. If we go to trial, we're undoubtedly going to need to present expert testimony in this regard, so whoever we get should have some experience on the witness stand," explained John.

"Any ideas about where to begin looking for such an expert?" asked Martha, whose only frame of reference was the educational community.

"Let's ask Ernesto when we meet tomorrow if he's aware of any cases that have been litigated recently that are factually similar to ours. If he does, the best place to begin would be to contact the attorneys involved in that case and find out who they used and who they might recommend," offered John.

"Do you think they would actually take the time to talk to me?" Martha knew how busy most of the attorneys she knew were, and she seriously doubted very many attorneys would take the time to respond to such a request.

"Remember that 'imitation is the sincerest form of flattery.' Never underestimate the size of a lawyer's ego," John joked. "Most of them love to talk about themselves, especially about the cases they've successfully litigated. Trust me, your call will be the highlight of their day."

OBTAINING AN EXPERT WITNESS

expert witnesses witness who, because of experience or training, has acquired special knowledge in a particular field; expert witnesses are allowed to present their opinions at trial whereas lay witnesses are not

Expert witnesses are becoming more and more essential to the trial process. Attorneys have found that if their opponent puts an expert witness on the stand, they are virtually compelled to counter with their own expert. In a personal injury case, for example, experts are often required to establish damages and to prove who or what was the cause of the plaintiff's injuries. Experts are also used to review a case file and serve as consultants to help the attorneys prepare for trial.

Paralegals are often asked to locate potential expert witnesses. One way to do this is to consult with other attorneys who have litigated in the field in which you need an expert and ask them to recommend someone who is not only knowledgeable but effective as a witness. You may become aware of such an attorney by reading a court decision or an article about a particular case. But how do you get the telephone number of this attorney in order to contact her?

For more information about how to find an appropriate expert, go to *www.paralegals.org/reporter*, click on "Winter 1995," and then on "Find the Right Expert."

"One final thing," added John as Martha was leaving. "I'm going to want to meet with you and Ernesto to evaluate Mike's case. Before we get together, I'd like you to review a brief synopsis of tort law I've prepared. Reading this will help get in the right mind set for this evaluation process. As you're reading through it, keep in mind the potential defendants we have in his case. Ask yourself whether we have the evidence we'll need to prove negligence or any intentional torts against each of these defendants."

"I'll read it tonight, Mr. Morgan," Martha assured him.

If the article or decision gives the name of the city and state in which the attorney practices, you can look in *Martindale Hubbell* (*www.martindale.com*), a publication that provides a compilation of the names of attorneys, their areas of practice, and personal data, including phone number, fax number, address, e-mail and Web site. West's Legal Directory (*www.lawoffice.com*) is another source of this information, as is the American Bar Association (*www.abanet.org*). Alternatively, if you know the trial court in which the litigation occurred, you can use that court's indexing system to pull the court file, which will have names, addresses, and telephone numbers of the attorneys involved. The Court Clerk's office has both a plaintiff and defendant's index and the plaintiff's or defendant's name can be found in this index.

The American Trial Lawyers Association (ATLA), whose Web site is at *www.atla.org*, has a directory of expert witnesses, as do many local bar associations. You can also consult the law library, which often has a directory for various specialties.

Putting It Into Practice 2.21:

Look on the Internet under "expert witness." Once there, look for an organization known as Technical Advisory Service for Attorneys (TASA). Go to its home page and look at the areas in which TASA provides experts. Check your home state for experts in psychology. What are the names of two experts you would recommend to your supervising attorney in a case like Mike's?

ELEMENTS OF A PERSONAL INJURY CLAIM

In order to realistically evaluate a personal injury claim, you must be familiar with the elements of negligence, intentional torts, and strict liability.

Negligence

negligence conduct that creates an unreasonable risk of harm to another

In a personal injury claim for **negligence,** the plaintiff must be able to prove the following.

◆ duty—that the defendant owed a duty of care to the plaintiff
◆ breach of duty—that the defendant breached, that is, failed to fulfill, that duty of care
◆ causation—that the defendant's breach of duty caused the plaintiff's injuries
◆ damages—that the plaintiff suffered damages for which she is entitled compensation

DUTY

The notion of duty arises out of the legal obligations that result from our relationships with others. Parents, for example, owe a duty of care to their children; airline companies and their employees owe a duty of care to their passengers. The nature of this duty varies depending on the nature of the relationship. Landowners owe a different duty of care to trespassers than they do to those whom they invite onto their premises. In some cases, the tortfeasor may owe a duty of care to those with whom he has no direct contact, such as third parties that he could reasonably anticipate being injured by his conduct. A tavern owner, for example, could owe a duty of care to those injured by an intoxicated patron whom the tavern owner recognizes as being so intoxicated as to constitute a danger to those about him.

BREACH OF DUTY

As a practical matter, the key issue that arises in most negligence cases is not whether the defendant owed a duty of care to the plaintiff, but whether she breached that duty. A key question that must be answered when dealing with breach of duty is whether the defendant conducted herself as a reasonable person would have under similar circumstances.

objective standard standard in which the defendant's actions are compared to those of a hypothetical reasonable person

In making this determination, the courts use what is referred to as an **objective standard.** Under this standard the defendant's actions are compared to those of a hypothetical "reasonable person." In contrast, under a **subjective standard** one asks whether the tortfeasor herself believes she acted reasonably.

subjective standard standard in which the question is whether the tortfeasor herself believes she acted reasonably

Suppose, for example, a woman believes that she is about to be burglarized and, fearing for her safety, shoots a would-be burglar. Using an objective standard, one would ask whether the woman acted as a reasonable person would have in that same situation. Using a subjective standard, one would question whether the woman herself believed that she had acted in a reasonable fashion.

The difference in outcome resulting from using two different standards is most evident if the woman in question were unusually fearful of being attacked. Suppose the woman, having been burglarized several times in the past, became hysterical when she saw a man's outline in her window and shot him through the window before he made any actual attempt to enter her home. Under an objective standard, her actions probably would not qualify as reasonable. A reasonable person in those circumstances most likely would have waited to ascertain whether the individual outside the window actually posed a threat. From a reasonable person's standpoint, it would have been just as likely that the person was a solicitor or a friend as a burglar. Under a subjective standard, however, the only question would be whether the woman herself, in fact, believed that her life was in danger.

Even under an objective standard, however, the physical characteristics of the tortfeasor are taken into consideration. A defendant who is blind, for example, is held to the standard of care expected of persons similarly impaired and not to the standard of care of a sighted person. The circumstances in which the defendant acts are also taken into consideration. The rescuer who responds in an emergency situation is not held to the same standard of care as one who acts under less demanding conditions.

Those blessed with a higher degree of knowledge, skill, or experience are held to a higher standard of care than the ordinary reasonable person. Because police officers, for example, have received training and presumably have experience in the handling of firearms, they are held to a higher standard of care when they discharge their weapons than the average person. Police officers are held to a "reasonable police officer" standard rather than a reasonable person standard. Therefore, a civilian might be justified under the reasonable person standard in taking another's life whereas a police officer under equivalent circumstances might not be. Specialists in a particular field are held to an even higher standard. A police officer trained as a hostage negotiator, for instance, is held to a higher standard of care in a hostage situation than the average police officer.

In some cases, statutes will determine the reasonable standard of care. Statutes that set forth safety standards, for example, in essence define minimal standards of reasonable conduct. Violation of those statutes will be treated as **negligence per se** (negligence in itself). A traffic ordinance mandating a speed of fifteen miles per hour in school crossing zones sets forth the standard of conduct expected of a reasonable driver in a school crossing zone. A driver who injures someone in the crossing zone as a result of violating the ordinance is negligent *per se*. In other words, the driver's negligence is presumed.

In some cases, the plaintiff is unable to prove the defendant's negligence because she is unable to gain access to information regarding the defendant's conduct. In such cases, the plaintiff can rely on the doctrine of ***res ipsa loquitur,*** which means "the thing speaks for itself." To utilize this doctrine, the plaintiff must show that: (1) the event that injured the plaintiff was one that does not ordinarily happen except through negligence; (2) the instrument that caused the plaintiff's injury was under the exclusive control of the defendant; and (3) the plaintiff's injuries were not due to her own actions. In some courts, the plaintiff must further show that the explanation underlying the events that occurred is more readily accessible to the defendant than to the plaintiff.

A plaintiff injured in a modern-day airplane crash could use this doctrine to allow the jury to infer that negligence was more than likely the cause of the crash. Notice how the elements mentioned earlier are applicable to such a case: (1) airplane crashes do not normally occur except through negligence; (2) planes are under the exclusive control of the defendant airline company; (3) the plaintiff in such instances does not ordinarily contribute to the cause of the crash; and (4) the defendant airline company is generally more capable of assessing the cause of the accident than the plaintiff.

CAUSATION

The third element the plaintiff must prove is causation. Causation is divided into two categories: **actual cause** and **proximate cause.** Actual cause, or causation in fact, is a factual question that asks whether the defendant's conduct was the actual, factual cause of the plaintiff's injuries. Actual causation is not generally a legal problem unless there are multiple causes of the plaintiff's injuries. Suppose, for example, three different assailants throw rocks at the plaintiff. Only one of the rocks hits its mark, causing the plaintiff to sustain a serious eye injury. The question would be which of the three assailants actually caused the plaintiff's injury. In such cases, courts generally find that each of the events was a cause of the injury, thereby forcing the defendants to apportion the damages.

Proximate cause, referred to by some writers as "legal cause," revolves around the issue of **foreseeability.** The concept arises from the notion that even the most negligent defendant should not be responsible for consequences that are too remotely connected to his conduct. Suppose the plaintiff is knifed by the defendant and is hospitalized for his injuries. If the plaintiff refuses medical treatment, contracts gangrene, and dies from wounds that, under the ordinary course of treatment, would have been minimal, should the defendant be held responsible for his death? In other words, was the defendant in this case the proximate cause of the plaintiff's

negligence per se presumed negligence; arises from the violation of a statute

res ipsa loquitur doctrine the plaintiff can turn to in proving negligence when it is difficult to obtain information about the defendant's conduct

actual cause factual cause of the plaintiff's injuries

proximate cause legal cause of the plaintiff's injuries

foreseeability reasonable predictability

death or was the plaintiff's death due to some intervening factor, namely, the plaintiff's decision to reject medical care?

Another example of a situation in which proximate cause is an issue in one in which the plaintiff dies as a result of an injury that, if sustained by an ordinary person, would have resulted in only minor injuries. In these "eggshell skull" cases, so-called because the plaintiff has a skull of eggshell thinness, the rule often expressed by the courts is that the defendant must "take his plaintiff as he finds him." In other words, the defendant is responsible for the full extent of the plaintiff's injuries even if the average person in the same circumstances would have sustained far less serious injuries.

The issue of foreseeability also arises in what is sometimes referred to as the "unforeseeable plaintiff" problem. The question in this case is whether the defendant's conduct posed any foreseeable risk of harm to the plaintiff. Suppose the defendant's conduct is unquestionably negligent in reference to a third party, but the plaintiff, rather than the third party, is injured as a result of the defendant's conduct. Should the defendant be held liable for the plaintiff's injury even if she did not act negligently in reference to the plaintiff?

The question was posed in one of the most famous American tort cases, *Palsgraf v. Long Island Railroad,* 162 N.E. 99 (N.Y. 1928). One of the defendant's employees, attempting to assist a man running to board the defendant's train, accidentally dislodged a package from the passenger's arm. Unbeknownst to anyone, the package contained fireworks, which exploded when they fell. As a result of the shock of the explosion, some scales at the other end of the train platform fell and hit the plaintiff. Arguably, the defendant's employee was negligent in pushing the passenger in the effort to assist him. The real question, however, was whether the defendant's negligence toward the passenger should give rise to liability to the plaintiff, who was injured by a series of fluke events. In a decision written by Judge Cardozo, the court held that the defendant was not liable because the plaintiff was not a foreseeable plaintiff, in that it was not reasonably foreseeable that she would be injured by the defendant's misconduct. According to the Cardozo rule, which is generally followed today, "[a] wrong is defined in terms of the natural and probable, at least when unintentional." Judge Andrews, in his dissent, argued that the defendant owed a duty of care to everyone in society to protect them from unnecessary danger. Everyone, he said, has a duty to refrain from any acts that unreasonably threaten the safety of others.

Putting It Into Practice 2.22:

Zina is eating a hamburger at a local fast food restaurant when she bites into something that has a strange taste and texture. When she spits it out onto her plate, she realizes to her horror that she has bitten into part of a cockroach. Zina becomes hysterical and has to be taken to the emergency room to be sedated. Subsequently, Zina becomes phobic about eating at any restaurant.

(a) Did the restaurant breach its duty to Zina? How can Zina prove that breach if the restaurant owner insists his people did nothing wrong? (b) Suppose the restaurant argues that Zina's reaction was abnormal and that it should not be held responsible for her ongoing psychological trauma and continued need for therapy. Will the restaurant prevail? (c) Suppose that Zina finds evidence that a health inspection conducted the week before her incident reveals that the restaurant was cited for failure to comply with certain city ordinances relating to pest and rodent control for eating establishments. Why might this be helpful to her case?

Figure 2-15
Tort Causes of Action

TORT CAUSES OF ACTION

NEGLIGENCE
DUTY

BREACH OF DUTY
Objective standard
Higher standard for specialists
Negligence per se
Res ipsa loquitur

CAUSATION
Actual cause
Proximate cause

DAMAGES

INTENTIONAL TORTS
Assault
Battery
False imprisonment
Intentional infliction of emotional distress
Trespass to land
Trespass to chattels
Conversion

STRICT LIABILITY
Defective products
Wild animals or domestic animals with vicious propensities
Abnormally dangerous activities

Intentional Torts

intentional tort   tort in which the tortfeasor intends or has a desire to bring about a particular consequence

Intentional torts are those torts in which the tortfeasor intends or has a desire to bring about a particular consequence. The tortfeasor need not necessarily desire to harm the person, but he must be aware that certain consequences are substantially certain to result from his conduct. If a defendant knows with substantial certainty that a result will occur, he will be liable for the consequences. An individual who throws a firecracker into the middle of a dense crowd, for example, may not actually want to hit anyone, but if he knows with substantial certainty that someone will get hit, he has acted intentionally.

The primary intentional torts follow.

Assault—intentionally causing apprehension of harmful or offensive contact

Example: A strikes at B but misses, because B ducks behind C.

Battery—intentional infliction of harmful or offensive contact

Example: A hits B.

False imprisonment—intentional confining of another

Example: A store detective unlawfully and unreasonably detains B, who is suspected of shoplifting.

Infliction of mental distress—intentional infliction of severe emotional or mental distress as a result of extreme and outrageous conduct

Example: A tells B that her husband has been critically injured in an accident when in fact he has not and A knows he has not.

Trespass to land—intentionally entering or wrongfully remaining on another's land

Example: A walks on B's land without B's permission.

Trespass to chattels—intentional interference with another's use or possession of chattel (personal property)

Example: A takes B's car for a "joy ride" without B's permission but returns it the following day.

Conversion—intentional interference with another's use or possession of chattel to the extent fairness requires that the defendant pay the full value of the chattel

Example: A takes B's car without B's permission and keeps it for a year.

Putting It Into Practice 2.23:

Suppose that the cook knew Zina and, wanting to get back at her for something, deliberately put a cockroach in the hamburger he served to her. What intentional torts has he committed?

Strict Liability

strict liability imposition of liability without showing of intent or negligence

Strict liability is applicable when a defendant is neither negligent nor intended any wrongdoing. It is a particularly useful theory in situations involving abnormally dangerous activities. Injuries involving defective products and dangerous animals are two other areas in which strict liability is imposed. Animal owners who are or should be aware of the vicious propensities of their domesticated pets are strictly liable for damages caused by those pets. People who keep wild animals are strictly liable for all damage caused by such animals if the damage results from a "dangerous propensity" typical of that particular species. Some courts have moved to a negligence standard, however, when dealing with those who display wild animals to the public (as in a zoo, for example). In cases involving strict liability, defendants who engage in particularly dangerous kinds of activities must pay for any damage that results even if they carry out those activities in the most careful manner possible. Liability is imposed even though a defendant is not at fault. This lack of fault is what distinguishes strict liability from negligence.

In determining whether an activity is "abnormally dangerous," the courts generally consider the following.

- ◆ high degree of risk
- ◆ likelihood of serious harm is great

- risk cannot be eliminated by due care
- activity is not a matter of common usage
- activity is inappropriate to the place it is carried on
- the value of the activity to the community is outweighed by its dangerousness

Any one factor alone is generally not sufficient to warrant strict liability; however, all of the factors need not be present to find strict liability. The essential question is whether the risk created is so unusual (either because of its magnitude or because of the circumstances surrounding it) to justify strict liability even though the activity was carried out with all reasonable care. Examples of such activity are the transportation of nuclear materials, the storage of flammable liquids in an urban area, or the disposal of hazardous waste.

The rationale underlying strict liability in the area of product liability is that it is easier for the defendant to bear the risk of loss than for the plaintiff. Advocates of strict liability reason that merchants and manufacturers have the ability to internalize the costs of accidental losses and can distribute such losses among the consumers who purchase their products. Another reason given for imposing strict liability is that product safety is better promoted by a strict liability theory than by traditional negligence theory. Once courts render decisions imposing strict liability on defendants even though they were not negligent, defendants arguably have a strong incentive to prevent the occurrence of future harms. Preventing future harm is a primary goal for those who advocate strict liability.

Putting It Into Practice 2.24:

Suppose that the cockroach was in a bottle of soda Zina opened while eating at the restaurant rather than in her hamburger. The soda manufacturer presents evidence that it has done everything humanly possible to prevent animals and insects from getting into their bottles. If Zina is unable to prove negligence, can she still recover from the manufacturer for her damages? Explain.

EVALUATING THE CASE

After the initial interview with the prospective client and the preliminary investigation, the attorneys and paralegals usually meet to discuss the case. The primary purpose of this meeting is to determine whether to take the case. Typically the attorneys focus on identifying the legal issues and determining whether the damages are sufficient to justify litigation. If an attorney believes that the cost of litigation will exceed what could realistically be collected from the defendant, she is likely to advise against suing.

Under certain circumstances, attorneys will represent clients even though they will not receive any money. If, for example, an attorney believes that a client is pursuing a cause that needs to come before the courts and knows that it will cost more to litigate than can possibly be recovered, the attorney may very well accept the case on principle rather than for economic gain. Attorneys are expected to accept a limited number of ***pro bono publico*** cases, that is, cases that are undertaken for no compensation. Although some states require attorneys to do a prescribed amount of pro bono work each year, most merely encourage rather than require pro bono work. Paralegals are also encouraged to lend their services to the community by means of doing pro bono work, although they are not required to do so.

A case will not be accepted unless the attorneys are reasonably certain they can prove each **element** (those factors that need to be proved) of the cause of action,

pro bono publico an attorney's representation of a client for no fee; means literally "for the good"

element specific factors that must be proved in order to win a lawsuit

Figure 2-16
Evaluating a Case

Evaluating a Case

Is there evidence to support each element of the cause of action?

Do the potential damages justify litigation?

Does the defendant have viable defenses?

How credible are the client and the witnesses that will be called to testify?

Is additional information needed?

How can that information be obtained?

---

that some kind of legal relief is available, and that the defendant will not be able to raise a defense that totally absolves him of liability.

At this initial meeting, paralegals are often asked to share their impressions of the client and any witnesses they have interviewed, the types of information they believe need to be gathered, and the sources of that information. At the conclusion of this meeting, the attorneys hope to identify any problems with the case and formulate an investigative strategy for resolving those problems. If the problems appear insurmountable, the attorneys may decide to reject the case altogether.

"Recently Someone Managed to Convince a Court That the Entertainment Industry Should Not Enjoy Unlimited Protection, and That If the Film Actually Encouraged Viewers to Commit Violent Acts, the Makers of That Film Could Be Held Liable."

John called a meeting with Martha and Ernesto to brainstorm the Johnson case. He knew that discussing the case with others would assist him in evaluating the feasibility of litigating the matter, in determining whom to sue, and in deciding what additional information needed to be gathered before a final decision could be made. He respected Ernesto's knowledge of constitutional issues and knew that, having recently represented the plaintiff against a media defendant in a defamation case, he was abreast of First Amendment trends in the entertainment industry.

"Ernesto, have you had a chance to review Martha's and my notes regarding the interviews we have conducted so far?" inquired John.

"Yes, and I think you might have a shot against the producer of *Teenage Stalkers*," responded Ernesto, anticipating John's next question. "Up until recently, no one who sued the maker of one of these trash films could make a case. The courts consistently found that the film makers were protected by the First Amendment. But recently someone managed to convince a court that the entertainment industry should not enjoy unlimited protection, and that if the film actually encouraged viewers to commit violent acts, the makers of that film could be held liable. Of course, proving this would be incredibly difficult, but if you had the right facts and the right court, you might be able to make a claim stick." Privately, Ernesto hoped that this case had just those facts because he knew this was exactly the kind of case he could really sink his teeth into. He aspired to making a name for himself at a young age and he knew this case had the potential to do just that.

John was well aware of Ernesto's aspirations and wanted to make sure his career plans did not interfere with his evaluation of the case. "Are you aware of the current status of the case to which you're referring? And do you know if there have been any similar cases in which the plaintiff has got the matter before the court?"

"No to both questions. I don't even remember the name of the case and I haven't read anything about it for the last few months. It's the only case I'm aware of where the plaintiff has made it to trial without getting dismissed."

"So it sounds to me like our first step is to get hold of that case so we can review the arguments made by both sides and find out where it is in the litigation process. Once we do that, we're going to need to re-interview some of our witnesses and see if we're going to be able to meet the **standard of proof** required by the courts," said John, thinking out loud.

"You're right," agreed Ernesto. "And remember that a case like this has the potential of setting precedent, so you want to make sure you have the kind of facts that will help a judge decide in your favor. It appears you have a sympathetic plaintiff, and from what I hear you have a movie that's off the chart in terms of gratuitous violence. So you might have the right combination. Some courts are beginning to lean in the direction of curtailing First Amendment freedoms where violence is involved. They might be looking for a case that allows them to do that in good conscience."

"I'd rather rely on the soundness of my legal argument than the appeal of my client. At this point, I think we need to focus on whether we have any chance of making a plausible argument that the movie company breached its duty of care to Mike. For that matter, we need to find out exactly how the courts have defined that duty. Do you have time to get the case you're talking about?"

"Not really, John. I'm going to trial next week. But maybe the following week," offered Ernesto.

"No, I want to get on with this case and I'm going to be out of town next week myself. Martha, could you go over to the law library next week and see if you can track down this case? I'll have some other things I'll need you to look up as well."

Martha gulped. She had not done any legal research since her classes at the college and she wasn't sure she was up to this assignment. Then she remembered her conversation with Andrew and immediately concluded that she must take advantage of this opportunity if she was ever going to advance in the firm. "I'd be glad to, Mr. Morgan. Perhaps you could give me some more direction after our meeting," suggested Martha.

"You bet. Also, Martha, what did you gather about this *Teenage Stalkers* movie from interviewing some of the students? Did they give you the impression that this movie actually encouraged viewers to commit copycat crimes?"

"No, none of them said any like that. But they certainly indicated it was incredibly violent. Apparently the boys in this cult group watched it repeatedly and often quoted from it. Some of them even bragged that they had done some of the things depicted in the movie."

"Like what?" John asked, looking for more details.

"I know some of them had apparently committed some minor burglaries and had defaced some buildings, leaving suggestive symbols and warning messages. We probably need to watch this movie, as much as I dread doing so," added Martha.

"No doubt that will be a necessity," agreed John. "But for now, let's move on. Let's consider where we're at with the school district," continued John. "A school clearly has a duty to protect its students from harm that is *foreseeable*. And while the shooting of one of their students is generally not foreseeable, it becomes foreseeable when they are forewarned. I'm a little nervous about this being an anonymous phone call, however. They can argue they receive phone threats all the time and they can't possibly take the time to investigate every single crank call they get."

"True, but this caller gave them a specific day of the week and said that one of the students would be shot. I would argue they were obligated to at least call the police, step up security, and conduct some kind of minimal investigation. They didn't do any of these things as far as I can tell," argued Ernesto.

"We can certainly get a better feel for how the courts have viewed the duty of the schools by doing some preliminary research. With the increasing violence in the schools I would expect to find some cases where the courts have discussed this issue. Martha, add that to your list of things to research next week. And while you're at it, check the statutes to see what kinds of **immunities** the schools have in this state."

"Got it, Mr. Morgan," assured Martha.

"Now let's consider the issue of causation for the district." John systematically evaluated each of the elements. "The district will argue that the boys, not the district, were the cause of Mike's injuries and that they should not be held liable for the criminal acts of a third party. I would argue, however, that the district's failure to intervene was just as much a cause of Mike's injuries as the shooting itself."

"And I think you would prevail on this one," concurred Ernesto. "The biggest problem with the district, as you pointed out, is whether they had sufficient notice to alert them to the possibility that their students were in danger. We need to get more facts on this one."

---

standard of proof   amount of evidence required by law to prevail in a lawsuit

immunities   exemption from being sued

"Okay. Now let's look at the boys and their parents. As a legal matter, the boys are no doubt responsible for Mike's injuries, but we're going to have to look to the parents for damages. We're eventually going to need to depose the parents to find out what they knew. I can't imagine they'll talk with us if they know we're lawyers."

"I don't suppose you'd consider sending Martha in to talk with them under some pretense," suggested Ernesto.

"And not tell them she's a paralegal and that she works for us? I think you know the answer to that one, Ernesto. I don't go in for that kind of chicanery and you know it, young man," retorted John.

"Well, technically we're not representing anyone at this point," argued Ernesto.

"I'm not interested in the technicalities. I'm interested in what is ethical. I'm not about to participate in duping these people into giving us information and that's that," John declared with finality.

"All right, I get it," huffed Ernesto. "But you better find out if these people have any money before you get too excited about suing them. I suggest you have Martha go to the county recorder's office and find out what properties they might own. Along that same line, I would have her contact Dun & Bradstreet or some other credit reporting service as well as the SEC's filings to see what you can find out about the financial status of the movie company. We don't even know if it's solvent, and there's no sense going to all the trouble of making a case against this company if it's just going to fold if we get a judgment."

"Good point. Martha, why don't you do that before you go to the library to conduct your research. Ernesto's right: the best case against an **insolvent** defendant is no case at all. Martha, can you think of anything else we have overlooked?"

"Something you said at the hospital about Mike has been bothering me. You said you thought he might be hiding something. I've replayed that conversation over and over in my head and I think you're right. But does that mean that he might not have a case? I mean, even if he did something wrong, did that give those kids a right to shoot him in cold blood?"

"No, of course not. The problem is that if those kids shot him because of some feud or if they were motivated by something other than the movie, that would negate any claim we might have against the movie company. We have to be able to show that the movie prompted them to shoot Mike; in other words, that it was the cause of them doing what they did. But you raise an important point, Martha. We all need to be alert when we talk to witnesses about any possible motives anyone might have had for shooting Mike. If we get wind of anything, and I mean anything that could remotely connect to this shooting, we need to follow up on it immediately," warned John.

"Why don't we reconvene after Martha's had a chance to do some research on the finances of the defendants and on the relevant law? Ernesto will be done with his trial after next week and I'll be back in town then, so let's get together a week from tomorrow. Will that give you enough time to do everything I've asked, Martha?" John was aware that Martha had other responsibilities and, unlike many of the other attorneys in the firm, was careful not to overwhelm the paralegals with more than they could handle. Martha wasn't sure she could get everything done in a week if she worked on it full time and she knew she had a number of other jobs she needed to complete for two other attorneys.

"Actually Mr. Morgan, one week is not enough time. I have a number of other deadlines I have to meet for next week. As much as I'd love to devote all of my time to this investigation, I can't. Two weeks would be a more realistic time," Martha said firmly but respectfully.

"Then two weeks it is. I appreciate your honesty, Martha, and your reminding me that you do have cases other than the Johnson matter," grinned John. As Martha was going out the door, John reminded her to begin organizing the case file. Even though the firm had not decided whether to accept Mike's case, some place was needed to store his medical records and the interview notes John and Martha had prepared.

"Oh, and please write a letter to Mike telling him what we discussed in our meeting today, what our plan of action is, and when we anticipate getting back to him. I like to keep clients apprised of what's going on with their case. Even if Mike never becomes a client, I believe it's important to set a good tone for any possible future relationships. When you're finished, bring it back for my signature."

insolvent　lacking money or assets

ORGANIZING THE FILE

File organization is extremely important. Attorneys and paralegals must be able to retrieve documents easily and rapidly. Therefore, organizing a case file is not postponed until the case is accepted by the firm. A preliminary file should be opened as soon as you have met with and collected materials from the client. The file should contain all the notes you and your attorney took while interviewing the client as

To see a demonstration of computer software that can be used to organize all information pertaining to a case, go to *www.trialworks.com* and click on "TrialWorks Overview."

well as the names and telephone numbers of potential witnesses. The file should also contain all the client's documents that you have received at this point and an inventory listing all those documents. Do not alter these original documents in any way because they may need to be introduced at trial or may end up being returned to the client if the case is not accepted. The easiest way to organize these documents is usually chronologically.

Then prepare a list to put at the front of the file. This list should enumerate each task that needs to be accomplished, its projected date of completion, and its actual date of completion. Using this list can help you budget your time and can also help keep you on task so that you do not get distracted by all the demands on your time. Checking off each task as you complete it provides a feeling of accomplishment and reduces the sense of frustration you are likely to feel when there are interruptions to your anticipated work plan. The tasks that you do not complete can be rolled over to the next day, thereby eliminating the risk of forgetting prior assignments when new ones are given. By recording both projected and actual dates of completion, you can begin to assess your efficiency and how realistically you budget time.

Putting It Into Practice 2.25:

What should Martha put in the preliminary file for Mike? What should be on Martha's to-do list at this point?

MANAGING YOUR TIME

Time management is a crucial skill for paralegals. Unfortunately, most firms assume that the paralegals they hire intuitively know how to organize their time and offer little or no instruction on how to be both efficient and effective. In many law practices, paralegals work for more than one attorney, and in almost every area of practice they are expected to work on more than one case at a time. Consequently, most paralegals are juggling work for a number of attorneys (with a variety of working styles) while having to keep track of multiple cases in varying stages of completion (sometimes referred to as the "multiple boss dilemma"). The challenge is how to do this while meeting all deadlines, attending to all details, and doing it without forgetting anything or alienating anyone.

To accomplish this, you need to develop some basic skills.

Prioritize Tasks — Not every task is equally important. The well-organized paralegal knows how to assign the relative importance of assignments quickly. This classification is based not only on the critical nature of the task involved (for example, tasks relating to trial preparation assume more importance—especially a few days before the trial—than tasks relating to the initial investigation of a case) and the time period in which the task must be completed, but also the individual who assigned it. An assignment by a senior partner who has made it clear that he needs it done immediately obviously takes priority over an assignment by an associate who has given you no immediate deadline.

Estimate Completion Times — Estimate the amount of time you think you will need to complete each task and then double the estimated time for tasks you have never carried out before. Doing this allows you to predict more accurately how much time you will actually need to complete all of your tasks. Doubling the amount of time for unfamiliar tasks takes into account the learning curve required when learning how to do something new.

Be Flexible — Give yourself enough flexibility in your timetable to account for all those unanticipated events. Life is inherently unpredictable. Undoubtedly, when you are the busiest is when you will be interrupted the most. Some interruptions and a certain amount of "down" time is to be expected. By factoring that into your allotted time, you can more realistically assess your completion time.

Beware of Procrastination — Some jobs are less pleasant than others. Once you have prioritized your tasks, finish those with equal priority first and get them behind you so you can focus on the tasks you find more enjoyable. Many books and motivational speeches have been written about how to beat the procrastination habit, but the bottom line is that most people procrastinate because they are afraid of failing. By avoiding what they fear doing, they can hide behind the excuse that they have not had time. Procrastination simply delays the inevitable. Doing the most dreaded tasks first not only saves time but conserves the energy expended on worry.

Schedule at Least Part of Your Day so that You Will Be Uninterrupted by Phone Calls — To do this, you will probably need to come in early, stay late, or go to the law library unless your office will allow you to hold your calls for one or two hours a day. You will be amazed at what you can accomplish if you are able to give your undivided attention to what you are doing.

Avoid situations and people that you know will distract you. Invariably you will work with people who love to spend as much time as possible doing anything but what they are paid to do. These are usually the same people who love to gossip and to keep the office in a stir. Although they may be amusing and entertaining, socialize with these "time vampires" after work. If you want to establish your reputation as a professional, you cannot afford to invest your time unproductively.

Learn to Say "NO" — Most first year law students are warned that the law is a jealous mistress. But they do not realize the full import of that admonition until they become an associate. In a relatively short time, they discover that their personal and family lives have been consumed by the practice of law. Soon they are not only devoting their evenings and weekends to fulfilling their billing obligations (many law firms still require their associates to bill an incredible number of hours), but they are spending most of their free time thinking about legal questions.

NET NEWS

For additional information on time management, go to *www.mindtools.com/page5.html.* Click on those lessons about time management you think would be most beneficial to you.

Figure 2-17
Time Management

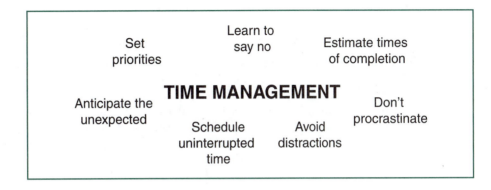

These same slaves to the law then look for assistants who will likewise enslave themselves. To avoid becoming ensnared in this unhealthy lifestyle, you must clearly set your parameters when you begin your employment. Decide how much time you want to spend with your family and attending to your personal needs and desires, and then commit to zealously protecting that time. Doing this may anger the more deeply devoted workaholics, but even they will respect your commitment to preserving a balanced life.

Putting It Into Practice 2.26:

In light of these benchmarks of good time management, assess your own time management skills. What could you start doing now, while you are still in school, to improve those skills?

BONUS POINTERS:

COMMUNICATIONS WITH CLIENTS

The primary culprit behind many malpractice claims is a breakdown in communication between client and attorney. Poor client relations is probably the single most important factor contributing to these claims. In fact, the most common complaint registered against attorneys, according to most state bar organizations, is lack of communication. The failure of lawyers to communicate with their clients has resulted in so many disciplinary and civil complaints that the American Bar Association's *Model Rules of Professional Conduct* now include Rule 1.4, which requires clients to be kept "reasonably informed about the status" of their case.

One simple way attorneys can keep clients informed is to send them copies of everything that is done in their case. In this way, clients are immediately aware of the shifts and turns their case is taking and they have an ongoing sense of the status of their case. They are then less resistant to observations and suggestions made by counsel and they feel more involved in their cause of action. Without such efforts at communication, clients have a tendency to feel they have lost ownership of their case and begin to feel as if the attorney/firm is working against them instead of on their behalf.

Therefore, the simple act of keeping clients apprised as to the current status of their case and making them aware of the strengths and weaknesses of their case can minimize exposure to malpractice claims. Additionally, regular communication helps create realistic expectations on the part of the client and reassures the client that his case is important to the firm.

▰▰▰ *Putting It Into Practice 2.27:*

The attorney for whom Marianne works rarely returns phone calls from his clients until they have called two or three times. He believes it is unnecessary to inform clients about what he is doing until they receive a bill, and he thinks it is frivolous to send them copies of any of the documents he has prepared or received. What are his chances of receiving a complaint from clients? Why?

conflict of interest conflict between the interests of one party and the interests of another party

"One final thing I need you to attend to is a conflicts check," added John. "We have a computer program available to check for any possible **conflicts of interest** that may exist for anyone in the firm, including the paralegals. When anyone is hired, we require her to provide information about any matters she has worked on for previous employers, any significant business or financial interests that could potentially create a conflict of interest, and any family or personal relationships that could result in a conflict of interest. Andrew usually runs these conflict checks for us. You will need to give him the names of the potential defendants, the names of Mike's parents, and the names of any businesses with which they have been associated."

ETHICAL ETIQUETTE

CONFLICTS OF INTEREST

Attorneys are not allowed to represent parties whose interests are adverse to one another or to former clients. They cannot zealously represent one client when doing when so would compromise the interests of another client. Martha's firm, for example, could not advocate on behalf of Mike if it were already representing the school district. Doing so could put the firm in a position of breaching its duties of loyalty and confidentiality to both clients. If the firm had confidential information from the school district that was favorable to Mike, it would be obligated to use that information to benefit Mike, but doing so would breach its duty of confidentiality to the school district and not doing so would breach its duty of loyalty to Mike.

Attorneys' duties of confidentiality and loyalty to their clients are also compromised when they have interests that are adverse to their clients. If they have personal or business interests contrary to their client's interest, they cannot give their client their undivided loyalty. Suppose John's wife represented one of the defendants in Mike's case. Could she be wholly loyal to her client during settlement negotiations if she knew that she would personally benefit if her client offered Mike a substantial settlement proposal (because her husband would receive some part of that settlement as part of his fee for representing Mike)? By the same token, would she be able to diligently preserve her duty of confidentiality to her client if breaching that duty would benefit Mike and consequently benefit her if her husband was able to secure a larger settlement for Mike as a result of the disclosure? The ethical rules protect attorneys and their clients from becoming involved in such conflicts of interest by prohibiting representation under those conditions.

A conflict of interest sometimes does not exist initially but can arise during the course of developing the case. One common area in which the potential for conflict exists occurs when spouses seek a divorce and, for economic reasons usually, opt to be represented by a single attorney. Although some courts allow spouses to be represented by one attorney, a potential conflict exists if the parties find themselves at odds with one another. While spouses may initially desire an amiable divorce, their interests oftentimes run counter to one another and the attorney is faced with advising one spouse to the detriment of the other. Co-parties in litigation can also end up becoming adversaries even though they are initially aligned together against an opposing party. A driver and passenger who sue the driver who hit them may become adverse parties if it becomes in the best interest of the passenger to sue the driver of the vehicle in which she was riding. Representing co-defendants in a criminal case is particularly problematic because their interests are very likely to become adverse to one another even if they are in alignment initially.

Conflicts of interest are particularly troublesome in this day of increasing mobility of both attorneys and clients, the growing size of many firms, and the mergers of firms. The most problematic conflict today involves the representation of a client whose interest may be adverse to a former client. This so-called "successive representation" is prohibited only if the past and present matters are substantially related. The premise is that the attorney may be in a position to breach confidentiality to the former client out of a need to convey confidential information necessary to the representation of the current client and that the duty of loyalty would be violated. To illustrate, suppose White & Treadwell had previously represented Washington School District in a suit involving a student injured while playing football. Information obtained from this representation could conceivably be useful in Mike's case, but detrimental to the school district if it were revealed. The question the courts have had to grapple with is whether a "substantial relationship" exists between the current and former clients' representations.

Clients can consent to simultaneous representation of adverse interests if there is a potential conflict of interest, but not if there is an actual conflict. Such consent must be given voluntarily and only after full disclosure by the attorney. The client must be given sufficient information to be able to fully appreciate the significance of what he is waiving. Some states require this consent to be in writing. Courts will not honor consent if the two clients' interests are so adverse as to make it impossible for the attorney to adequately represent both of them.

If one attorney in a firm is disqualified from representing a client, the whole firm is disqualified. This creates problems when attorneys switch firms, thereby causing the new firm with whom they are now associated to be disqualified from representing the clients of their former firm. Whether this rule applies to paralegals as well is debatable. Conflicts of interest of this sort are so problematic in this day of increasing mobility that the courts in some instances allow firms to construct a so-called "ethical wall" or "screen" around a lawyer or paralegal who has a conflict of interest with a client, thereby allowing the firm to represent that client. This "wall" prevents the lawyer or paralegal from having any connection with the legal matter involving that client. With this "wall," the attorney or paralegal cannot disclose any information gained from representing the client of their former employer and must not do any work on any matter relating to work done for the former employer.

Most law firms maintain a conflict data base of some kind. In larger firms, the conflict data base will be computerized, often under the control of a single employee who is responsible for maintaining it, and to whom lists of names are submitted for checking. If it appears that a new client's case may involve someone whom the firm has represented in the past, the firm's attorneys have to decide whether to accept the representation.

To run a thorough conflicts check, you need to get the names of the following individuals.

◆ the client (including names before marriage)
◆ the client's children and spouse
◆ key employees, officers, and directors of corporate clients
◆ major shareholders for corporate clients
◆ members of associations to which the client belongs

NET NEWS

To read more about ethical walls, go to *www.paralegals.org/reporter*, click on "Winter 1998," and then on "Ethical Quandaries."

Figure 2-18
Rules Pertaining to Confidentiality

> ## RULES PERTAINING TO CONFIDENTIALITY
> Attorneys cannot represent clients whose interests are adverse to another client or a former client.
> Attorneys cannot represent clients whose interests are adverse to their own.
> Attorneys cannot represent clients whose interests may be adverse to a former client if the past and present matters are substantially related.
> Clients can consent to simultaneous representation if they do so voluntarily and after full disclosure.
> Firms should run "conflict checks" before accepting a case.
> If one attorney from a firm is disqualified from representing a client, the whole firm is disqualified.
> In some cases, a firm may be allowed to create an "ethical wall" around an attorney or paralegal who has a conflict of interest with a client so that the firm can still represent that client.

Putting It Into Practice 2.28:

Suppose Ernesto's wife is on the school board for the Washington High School district. Does this create a conflict of interest for the firm?

"Something Tells Me She's Going to Be a Key to Unlocking the Mystery Surrounding Mike's Attack."

Martha went to the hospital to visit with Mike and to give him the letter she had written to him summarizing what the firm had done with regard to his case. When she returned, she stopped by John's office to see if he was in. He welcomed her warmly, but immediately queried her about the look of concern on her face.

"Mr. Morgan, I'm really worried about Mike," began Martha. "I've never seen him this depressed. I'm not sure exactly what the doctors told him, but he seems convinced that he's never going to be able to walk again. Apparently they're planning to move him next week to the county rehab center. Unfortunately, that means he won't get the kind of quality care he's receiving now. Considering the gravity of the injuries to his spinal cord, I'm afraid this could mean the difference between Mike's walking again and not walking," lamented Martha.

"That tells me the insurance has run out," interjected John. "We need to get with his parents immediately. I have a pretty good rapport with St. Joseph's Rehab Center just outside of town, and I think I can get them to accept a **lien** on his lawsuit if he decides to sue. Of course, the parents are going to have to agree to pay for Mike's expenses if we don't file suit or if we aren't able to collect anything. But at least this would give him a shot at getting the best medical care possible."

"That would be wonderful if you could pull it off." Martha allowed herself to hope for the best. "I know Mike doesn't think he'll ever be able to walk again let alone play football, but if there is even a one percent chance he could have a professional football career, I would hate to think of that being denied him simply because he didn't get adequate follow-up care."

"Something else is bothering you, isn't it, Martha?" observed John.

"Actually, yes. When I visited with Mike today, a young girl named Carmela was there at the same time. She seemed really sweet and obviously adores Mike—but then, as I told you before, most of the female student body adores Mike—but I was puzzled by how Mike acted. He seemed very anxious to get her out of the room and away from me."

"How could you tell?" prompted John.

"For one thing, she had made some sopapillas [a Mexican pastry] for him. He took the basket they were in, and without even looking inside, thanked her and put them on the table next to his bed. He said he would get to them later and then looked at her as if he were expecting her to leave. She didn't pick up the hint, but when I said I would find another chair so we could both sit down, he told her that he really needed to talk with me privately. After she left, I asked him point blank why he had been so rude and he just stammered something about 'needing his space'."

"I take it his response didn't satisfy you," observed John.

Martha shook her head.

"Well, you know maybe he's not as mature as you think he is and he was just embarrassed by having this girl hanging around him."

"No way," responded Martha adamantly. "One thing I know about Mike is his compassion for others. On more than one occasion, I've seen him reach out to kids that others ridiculed or ignored. It's not his nature to be so ungracious."

"Well, then, what do you think is going on?" John knew that Martha did not bring this up just for the sake of idle chat.

"I think he didn't want me to talk with Carmela. And the only reason I can think of is that he's afraid she'll tell me something that he doesn't want us to know," blurted out Martha.

"I suspect you may be right. But what could she possibly know? From what you're telling me, she's unlikely to have any connection with the group that shot him," mused John. "Nevertheless, we need to pay attention to this and follow up. I'd like you to arrange to talk with Carmela as soon as possible. Something tells me she's going to be a key to unlocking the mystery surrounding Mike's attack."

Docket Control And Case Management Software

After reading this chapter, you can understand why maintaining a complete and accurate calendar is a necessity in any law office. Originally, lawyers relied on a piece of paper labeled "calendar," on which they made their entries sequentially. As the complexity of the legal profession grew, monthly and annual bound volumes became available to maintain an attorney's appointments, court dates, due dates for responses, and the like. In a small firm of only one or two attorneys, a paper calendar was workable, but in larger firms the paper calendar loomed as an ominous reminder of the potential malpractice claim lurking behind one erroneous entry or one typographical error.

Most of today's law firms, both small and large, have computerized their calendar and use specialized programs for calendaring their docket (court related activities and appointments). Some have turned to Personal Information Managers (PIMs) and Personal Data Assistants (PDAs), fairly complex calendars and associated databases (names, telephone numbers, addresses, e-mail addresses, etc.). These general, low-power programs can be adapted for use in a law office and can be maintained in an electronic device smaller than a pack of cigarettes.

A far superior approach to calendaring can be found in the many programs for case management that have been developed for the legal profession. One, **VirtuaLaw,** is available for free. An extensive listing of available case management software for the legal profession, and links to the manufacturer's Web sites, can be found at *http://tech.findlaw.com/general_software/case_management.html.* That site also has a link to the "freeware" site where VirtuaLaw can be downloaded for free. You can also go directly to *http://dunsinane.net/bryan/index.htm* to review the VirtuaLaw programs.

What are the attributes of a good case management program? It should ensure that information has to be inputted only once. When changes to telephone numbers, addresses, and other data are made, these modifications should be recognized in any future references to that data, regardless of which portion of the program is utilized. Inputing of data should be easy to perform and the data's function should be obvious. It is also necessary that

ticklers and reminders can be made to appear on the responsible person's calendar and will remain there until intentionally deleted. Most case management programs also provide for document templates that allow the user to prepare various documents and form letters by merging the database with the template. As the complexity of case management programs grows, more and more functions are available. Timekeeping and billing can be integrated. Local rules of court regarding various time calculations, such as local holidays and response times, can be made part of the docketing system. In network applications, the system administrator, or other authorized user, can search the program database to determine when all attorneys are available for a firm meeting. Conflict checks can be made by searching the database and comparing all prior clients and witnesses to see if any conflict exists.

Today's case management programs sometimes include features generally considered to be litigation support functions (such as VirtuaLaw). Graphics files can be attached to a client's file. Optical character recognition (OCR) can be included to allow conversion of written information contained in a graphics file to a text file. A text file can be searched for relevant terms or phrases. All documents and pleadings generated in a case can be accessed from these hybrid case management/litigation support/timekeeping-billing programs.

As the complexity of the case management program increases, the need for freedom of choice also increases. Many programs are licensed on the basis of how many program users are on a single system or network. Many of the "bells and whistles" important to a large firm are a waste of resources for a smaller firm. Because of the varying needs of each firm (depending on the number of attorneys, type of practice, billing practices, etc.), the "one-size-fits-all" program is difficult, if not impossible, to come by. As you will see if you visit the site referenced above, case management programs come in specialized forms, depending not only on the size of the firm but also its practice area. Case management programs directed to specialized areas such as personal injury, collections, corporate law, and bankruptcy are readily available.

TECHNO TRIP

Take your browser to *http://tech.findlaw.com/general_software/case_management.html.* Compare the offerings of *abacuslaw.com* with *www.amicus.ca* and VirtuaLaw (*http://dunsinane.net/bryan/index.htm*). Which of the three case management programs best

suits your expectations? If you take the downloadable tours, briefly take notes about the features that each has. Should price be a factor in selecting your case management program if a single-user version is less than $300?

SUMMARY – PART B

The first step in interviewing witnesses is to attempt to secure their cooperation. If you know in advance that a witness will support your client's position, you may want to tape record the interview or you may want to get a statement from the witness later. Pin down hostile witnesses with as many details as possible so they can more easily be impeached if necessary. Use witnesses to get additional leads.

Obtaining records is a task usually given to paralegals. Before requesting records from an institution, find out what kinds of fees are charged and when those fees must be paid. Review records immediately after obtaining them to make sure you can read them. Medical records usually require the aid of a medical dictionary, *PDR,* or nurse paralegal to be deciphered. Have clients sign authorization forms to obtain confidential records such as medical and employment records. Become familiar with the process for obtaining police reports as well as records from the court clerk, county recorder, secretary of state, corporation commission, and other agencies that contain public records. Also familiarize yourself with how to secure records from federal agencies by means of a Freedom of Information Act request.

Investigators rather than paralegals usually gather physical evidence, but either can be asked to take photographs. Photos are taken for evidentiary purposes and should be taken with that in mind. Black-and-white film is usually used to take photos from every conceivable angle and with the intent of representing what is being photographed as realistically as possible. All physical evidence and every photo must be carefully marked so that they can be readily identified at trial. The marking of physical evidence is necessary to preserve the chain of custody.

Expert witnesses are becoming increasingly important at trial and are often used to review files and to help attorneys prepare for trial. Paralegals often are asked to help locate experts and can sometimes do this by consulting with attorneys who have litigated in the area in which an expert is needed. ATLA, local bar associations, and the law library are also potential sources of expert witnesses.

Shortly after the initial interview with a client, attorneys and paralegals meet to evaluate the case and decide whether to accept it. The attorneys must be confident they can prove each element of the case, that some kind of legal relief is available, and that the defendant will not be able to raise defenses that absolve him of liability.

A plaintiff in a negligence cause of action must prove that the defendant owed a duty of care to the plaintiff, that the defendant breached that duty, and that the breach caused the plaintiff to be injured, for which she is entitled to compensation. The plaintiff can look to the doctrine of *res ipsa loquitur* and the concept of negligence per se to help prove breach of duty. An objective standard is used in determining whether a defendant acted reasonably. Defendants are liable for any reasonably foreseeable injuries they cause to a plaintiff although they may also be liable for injuries to unforeseeable plaintiffs and to plaintiffs that are unusually sensitive. Plaintiffs can also sue for damages resulting from intentional torts, which include assault, battery, false imprisonment, intentional infliction of emotional distress, trespass to land, and trespass to chattels. Even defendants who did not intend to commit a wrongdoing or who were not negligent can be held strictly liable for damages to the plaintiff. Strict liability is raised in cases involving dangerous animals, defective products, or abnormally dangerous activities.

Even before a case has been accepted, a preliminary file should be set up. The interview notes prepared by the attorneys and paralegals should be included in this file as well as the names and telephone numbers of potential witnesses, all the documents the client has brought in, and an inventory of those documents. A to-do list should be put at the front of the file to help focus the paralegal on the tasks that need to be done. Measures that paralegals can take to better manage their time include prioritizing their tasks, estimating the amount of time they will need to complete their tasks and then adding time for unanticipated events and doubling the time for new tasks; avoiding procrastination and people/events that cause distractions; scheduling time during which they will be uninterrupted by phone calls; and learning to say "no."

Attorneys are forbidden from representing parties whose interests are adverse to other clients they are representing. Doing so can actually or potentially compromise the attorney's duties of loyalty and confidentiality. For the same reasons an attorney cannot represent a client if she has personal or business interests that are adverse to the client's nor can she represent a client whose interests may be adverse to a former client. Because successive representation can be so stifling it is prohibited only if the present and former matters are substantially related. Under some circumstances clients can consent to simultaneous representation of adverse interests. Before accepting clients, attorneys should conduct thorough conflicts checks.

KEY TERMS

Actual cause
Admissible
Authenticate
Cause of action
Chain of custody
Conflict of interest
Element

Expert witnesses
Foreseeable
Freedom of Information
   Act
Immunity
Impeached
Insolvent

Intentional Tort
Lien
Narrative reports
Negligence *per se*
Objective standard
Pro bono
Recant

Res ipsa loquitur
Standard of proof
Strict liability
Subjective standard
Subpoena

REVIEW QUESTIONS – PART B

1. How should you initiate an interview with a witness?
   a. What might you consider doing if the witness supports your client's position?
   b. How should you handle hostile witnesses?
2. What steps should you take to get medical records for a client? In addition to medical records, what kinds of other records are paralegals often asked to obtain?
3. What should be kept in mind when taking photographs that could be used in court?
4. What must be done to preserve the chain of custody?
5. What can a paralegal do to find an expert witness in a particular field?
6. What kinds of questions must be answered before a firm will be willing to pursue a cause of action for a client?
7. What must a plaintiff prove in a negligence cause of action?
   a. What is the doctrine of *res ipsa loquitur*?
   b. What is negligence *per se*?

   c. What is the difference between actual cause and proximate cause?
   d. What is the "eggshell skull" rule?
8. Describe the basic intentional torts available to a plaintiff.
9. Under what circumstances can a plaintiff allege strict liability? What is an "abnormally dangerous" activity?
10. What kinds of things should be included in a preliminary file for a case that has not yet been accepted?
11. What can a paralegal do to better manage her time?
12. Under what conditions should an attorney not represent a client due to a conflict of interest?
   a. For what reasons are attorneys forbidden from representing clients with whom there exists a conflict of interest?
   b. Under any circumstances can an attorney represent a client even if a conflict of interest does exist?

PRACTICE EXAM – PART B

MULTIPLE CHOICE

1. When interviewing witnesses
   a. insist that they come to the office
   b. tell them up front that you are a paralegal
   c. discourage them from talking with the other side
   d. always tape record witnesses who you know will support your client's position

2. With witnesses
   a. it is important that you initially take everything they say as factually true
   b. you need to ask focused questions rather than allowing them to tell you what they observed
   c. you need to pin down those who are hostile with as many factual details as possible
   d. ask aggressive, hard-hitting questions

3. Before obtaining records
   a. find out whether any fees will be charged
   b. find out if the fees must be paid before the records will be released
   c. find out if any forms must be filled out
   d. all of the above

4. Medical records
   a. are usually easy to decipher
   b. do not need to be reviewed until the case is set for trial
   c. cannot be obtained unless the client signs a medical authorization form
   d. are not confidential

5. Photographs for evidentiary purposes
   a. should be marked to show the camera speed and lighting conditions
   b. should be in color
   c. should be taken from only a few angles to minimize the total number of shots taken
   d. be aesthetically pleasing

6. Physical evidence
   a. need not be collected as soon as possible
   b. should be placed in a sealed, marked container to preserve the chain of custody
   c. need not be labeled when it is collected
   d. is usually collected by paralegals

7. Expert witnesses
   a. are rarely used today
   b. can be located through *Martindale Hubbell*
   c. are used as consultants as well as witnesses
   d. all of the above

8. An attorney whose name appears in a court decision
   a. can be located through *Martindale Hubbell* even if the state in which he practices is unknown
   b. can be located through the trial court in which the case occurred
   c. cannot be located
   d. none of the above

9. Before a firm will accept a client's case, it must know that
   a. the damages justify the cost of litigation
   b. at least some of the elements of the cause of action can be proved
   c. that the defendant has no possible defense
   d. all of the above

10. A preliminary file
    a. should not be opened until a case has been accepted
    b. should contain all the documents received from the client
    c. need not include the names of potential witnesses until the interviewing process has been initiated
    d. all of the above

11. Time management includes
    a. learning to say "no"
    b. scheduling time that is not interrupted by phone calls
    c. prioritization
    d. all of the above

12. A plaintiff who alleges negligence must prove
    a. negligence *per se*
    b. *res ipsa loquitur*
    c. breach of duty
    d. all of the above

13. To prove breach of duty
    a. a plaintiff must show that the defendant breached a subjective standard of care
    b. a plaintiff may have to resort to the doctrine of *res ipsa loquitur* if evidence of the defendant's conduct is unavailable
    c. a plaintiff must show that the defendant was negligent *per se*
    d. a plaintiff must show that the defendant actually caused the plaintiff's injury

14. A plaintiff who is injured by the negligence of her surgeon can use the doctrine of *res ipsa loquitur* to prove the surgeon's negligence
    a. if she can show that what happened does not ordinarily happen except through negligence
    b. even if whatever caused her injuries was not under the defendant's exclusive control
    c. even if she contributed to her own injuries
    d. all of the above

15. If three men shoot in the direction of the plaintiff but only one of their bullets strikes the plaintiff
    a. the question is one of actual causation
    b. the question is one of proximate causation
    c. the plaintiff cannot recover unless she can prove which of the defendants' bullets struck her
    d. the plaintiff has a problem of foreseeability

16. Proximate cause
    a. revolves around the issue of foreseeability
    b. is implicated in the "eggshell skull" rule
    c. sometimes involves unforeseeable plaintiffs
    d. all of the above

17. In *Palsgraf*
    a. the defendant was held liable even though the plaintiff's injuries were not reasonably forseeable
    b. the majority reasoned that a wrong should be defined in terms of the "natural and probable"
    c. the majority reasoned that defendants owe a duty to everyone in society and not just those to whom injury is foreseeable
    d. none of the above

18. A person commits an intentional tort if
    a. he does something knowing with substantial certainty that harm will occur to the plaintiff
    b. he hits at someone but misses that person and hits someone else
    c. takes someone's property
    d. all of the above
19. Strict liability is imposed
    a. on an animal owner whose pet injures another even if the animal owner could not reasonably have known of the pet's dangerous propensities
    b. only if fault can be proved
    c. when someone is injured by a defective product
    d. all of the above
20. An activity is considered "abnormally dangerous"
    a. if, among other factors, the value of the activity to the community is outweighed by its dangerousness
    b. even if the risk of harm is minimal and can be eliminated by due care
    c. even if the activity carries a minimal risk and can be carried out safely if it is done with reasonable care
    d. all of the above
21. The rationale for strict liability is
    a. that it is easier for manufacturers to bear the risk of loss from a defective product than it is for consumers
    b. that merchants can internalize the costs of accidental losses
    c. that it promotes product safety
    d. all of the above

FILL IN THE BLANK

22. Obtaining a witness statement using the witness's own words allows the attorney to _____ (discredit) the witness at trial if he tries to _____ (deny what he said).
23. One way to _____ evidence is to label it to make sure it is in the same condition when it is introduced in court as when it was found; doing this preserves the _____ of physical evidence.
24. Physical evidence that is in the custody of a law enforcement or investigative agency can be obtained using a _____.
25. An _____ witness is often needed by the plaintiff at trial because the opinion of a such a witness can be used to help prove the plaintiff's case.
26. To accept a case, attorneys must believe that sufficient _____ evidence (evidence that the court will allow to be introduced) exists to meet the _____ of proof for each _____ of the cause of action.
27. In a personal injury case, the plaintiff must be able to prove that the defendant breached its duty to prevent _____ harm from occurring to the plaintiff.
28. A defendant that is protected by some kind of statutory _____ cannot be sued, and a defendant that is _____ is not worth suing because he has no recoverable assets.
29. Under the _____ Act, a private citizen can secure records pertaining to himself that are in the possession of a federal agency.
30. Attorneys are encouraged to perform a certain amount of _____ work so that those who cannot afford representation can still be represented.
31. A _____ prevents an attorney from representing a client if he has personal or business interests that are adverse to those of the client.
32. In a personal injury claim for _____, a plaintiff must prove that the defendant's breach of duty caused her injury. The plaintiff must prove this breach using an _____ standard (comparing the defendant's actions to those of a hypothetically reasonable person).
33. When a statute defines minimal standards of reasonable conduct, violation of that statute will be treated as _____ (negligence in itself).
34. If a plaintiff is unable to prove the defendant's negligence because she is unable to gain access to information regarding the defendant's conduct, she may be able to rely on the doctrine of _____.
35. A plaintiff must prove that the defendant was the _____ (factual) cause of her injuries. She must also prove _____ cause, which revolves around the question of _____ (reasonable predictability) because even the most negligent defendant should not be responsible for consequences that are too remotely connected to his conduct.
36. Under the _____ rule, a defendant takes his plaintiff as he finds him.

37. If A hits B, A has committed the tort of _____, but if A strikes at B but misses because B ducks, A commits the tort of _____. If A locks B in a room and will not let her go, A commits the tort of _____. If A walks on B's land without B's permission, A commits the tort of _____, but if A takes B's car without B's permission, A commits the tort of _____, and if A does not return the car for a year, A commits the tort of _____. If A tells B that she ran over B's prized and cherished dog and she did not, A commits the tort of _____.

38. A defendant whose pet fox bites his neighbor is probably _____ for the neighbor's injuries.

39. Dynamiting is considered an _____ activity for which a defendant is liable if anyone is injured, even if he uses the utmost care.

TRUE OR FALSE

____ 40. In order to get the cooperation of a witness, you may have to meet her needs and allay her fears.

____ 41. Never discourage witnesses from talking with opposing counsel.

____ 42. Tape recording witnesses' interviews can be counter-productive even if what they say will support your client.

____ 43. Hostile witnesses can be more easily impeached if you let them ramble during their interview.

____ 44. Witnesses commonly make false statements that they honestly believe.

____ 45. In addition to providing personal, first-hand information, witnesses can provide you leads to other evidence that supports your client.

____ *46. The best way to record a witness's statement is to have an investigator write out the statement and have the witness sign it.

____ *47. Witness statements should be generalized and should include the witness's opinions.

____ *48. It is often important to be the first side to get to talk with a witness.

____ *49. The driver's license bureau, the county assessor's office, the motor vehicle department, and the Social Security office are potential sources of information about witnesses.

____ 50. Doctors usually do not charge fees for their reports and notes.

____ 51. Treat every document as if it were a "smoking gun."

____ 52. Medical records are easier to understand with the help of the *PDR* and a medical dictionary.

____ 53. Some institutions require authorization forms to be notarized.

____ 54. Some police agencies require that a need be shown before records will be released.

____ 55. Paralegals rarely have to get records from the county recorder's and court clerk's offices.

____ 56. The Freedom of Information Act requires state agencies to make agency records available to the public.

____ 57. No exemptions to the FOIA exist.

____ *58. FOIA requests should be specific enough that an employee of the agency can find the records in a reasonable period of time without an unreasonable amount of effort.

____ *59. All records provided through the Freedom of Information Act are free of charge.

____ 60. Photos of evidence should fill the frame as much as possible and should accurately reflect the scene being depicted.

____ 61. Aerial photos have no value at trial.

____ 62. Labels on physical evidence need only indicate where the evidence was found.

____ 63. Evidence cannot be admitted at trial unless the chain of custody has been broken.

____ 64. Physical evidence can be lost or destroyed if it is not collected soon after an incident occurs.

____ 65. When one side uses an expert witness at trial, the opposing side is almost compelled to put an expert on the stand.

____ 66. Paralegals have little to do with locating expert witnesses.

____ 67. Both ATLA and local bar associations have directories of expert witnesses.

____ 68. Paralegals are not asked to participate in meetings with attorneys where potential causes of action are evaluated.

____ 69. Attorneys will generally not accept a case if the damages do not justify the cost of litigation.

____ 70. A preliminary file should be opened as soon as someone has met with and collected materials from the client.

____ 71. The easiest way to organize the documents in a file is by subject matter.

____ 72. To-do lists help paralegals budget their time and keep them on task.

____ 73. Most paralegals work for only one attorney and are able to focus on only one case at a time.

____ 74. Tasks should be prioritized based only on the critical nature of the task, regardless of who assigned the task.

____ 75. When estimating the amount of time needed to complete a number of tasks, add time for unanticipated events and double the estimated time for performing new tasks.

____ 76. Most people procrastinate because they are lazy.

____ 77. To avoid being consumed by the practice of law requires carving out and protecting the time needed to meet personal needs and the needs of family and friends.

____*78. The most common complaint registered against attorneys is lack of communication.

____*79. One way that attorneys can improve communications with their clients is to send them copies of everything that is done in their case.

____ 80. Attorneys cannot represent clients whose interests are adverse to their own personal or business interests, but they can represent clients whose interests are adverse to the interests of former clients.

____ 81. Attorneys can represent clients if no conflict of interest exists initially even if one could potentially develop.

____ 82. Representing co-defendants in criminal cases is a good strategy.

____ 83. The biggest problem with conflicts of interest exists in the area of successive representation.

____ 84. Clients can always consent to simultaneous representation.

____ 85. To run a thorough conflicts check, you need only the client's name, including any previous names.

____ 86. The nature of the duty we owe to others arises out of the nature of our relationship.

____ 87. In no case does anyone owe a duty of care to someone with whom he has not had direct contact.

____ 88. The key issue in most tort cases is whether the defendant owed a duty of care to the plaintiff.

____ 89. The reasonableness of a defendant's conduct is generally determined using a subjective standard.

____ 90. The physical characteristics of a defendant are taken into consideration when determining whether the defendant breached his duty of care.

____ 91. A rescuer who responds in an emergency situation is held to the same standard of care as one who acts under less demanding conditions.

____ 92. A civilian might be justified in taking another's life whereas a police officer under equivalent circumstances might not be.

____ 93. Specialists are held to a higher standard of care than non-specialists.

____ 94. In some cases, statutes will determine the reasonable standard of care.

____ 95. In some courts, the plaintiff must further show that the explanation underlying the events that occurred is more readily accessible to the defendant than to the plaintiff if the plaintiff relies on the doctrine of *res ipsa loquitur.*

____ 96. A negligent defendant is responsible for any consequences connected to his conduct even if that connection is remote.

____ 97. A defendant is responsible for the full extent of the plaintiff's injuries even if the average person in the same circumstances would have sustained far less serious injuries.

____ 98. With an intentional tort, the tortfeasor must have an intent to harm the plaintiff.

____ 99. Keepers of wild animals are generally held to a negligence standard.

____100. In cases involving strict liability, defendants who engage in particularly dangerous kinds of activities must pay for any damage that results even if they carry out those activities in the most careful manner possible.

____101. The transportation of nuclear materials is considered an abnormally dangerous activity.

____102. Preventing future harm is a primary goal for those who advocate strict liability.

LEGAL LINGO

Word Scramble

Unscramble the letters to form words using the clues provided.

1. MTEENLE — What must be proved in a lawsuit
2. TENJMGUD — Decision by a court
3. HEPMICA — Discredit a witness
4. YINTUMMI — Exemption from being sued
5. EJUSPERCIRNUD — Study of the law and legal philosophy
6. BILYATILI — Responsibility for damages
7. NIHCA FO SUCDYOT — What must be preserved to admit physical evidence into court
8. NOYDEFICTENLAIT — Attorney's obligation to keep client's secrets
9. ECTRAPMELAI — Professional misconduct
10. CATDER — Mark out
11. OBOPRON — Representation without charge
12. MDALETI — Guardian _____
13. ECUSA FO NITOCA — Lawsuit
14. PENBOUSA — Court compelling person to appear or to produce evidence
15. FESEREBOLAE — Reasonably anticipated
16. NEIL — Security interest
17. MATOINSILIT — Statute requiring a lawsuit to be filed within a certain time period
18. TREPEX — Witness that can offer opinions
19. SIBELSIMDA — Evidence that the court will allow to be introduced
20. OTTR — Private wrong
21. XIMROPTEA — Legal cause
22. SER PAIS QUIRUOLT — Thing speaks for itself

LEGAL LOGISTICS

1. How do you plan to respond to questions from your family and friends about your daily activities as a paralegal in light of what you now know about confidentiality?

2. Suppose that you have a client who is arrested for harboring an illegal immigrant who has been unable to gain political asylum but who fears for his life if he is made to return to his country. Your client has clearly and knowingly violated the law, but did so because she believes the law is wrong. What would a natural law theorist say about the law and your client's reaction to that law? A positivist? A realist? A critical legal theorist?

3. You work for a personal injury law clinic. You have been asked to interview a prospective client who slipped and fell on something on the floor in a supermarket. List the areas of questioning you will need to pursue, keeping in mind the elements of negligence as you do this. Prepare a brief summary of what you learn for your attorney.

4. You have been asked to interview one of the students who witnessed Mike being shot. You have been warned that the student is terrified of telling anyone what he saw for fear of retribution.

   a. What will you do to allay his fears?
   b. Where will you conduct the interview?
   c. Make a list of potential questions you will want to ask.

5. You are asked to obtain records from an administrative agency. Before sending for these records, you call the agency. What questions do you ask?

6. A woman comes into your office wanting a divorce. She has recently been released from the hospital, recovering from injuries her husband inflicted when he went into a rage because she had not prepared dinner to his liking. What kinds of photos should you take immediately? What kinds of physical evidence might the police have collected?

7. One attorney asks you to write a letter to a client, locate some financial records and medical records for another client, and conduct some preliminary legal research on another matter that he is considering for possible litigation. Another attorney wants you to review some medical records, locate an expert witness, and interview several lay witnesses for an upcoming trial as well as draft a settlement proposal on another case. How will go you about deciding what order to do each of these tasks?

To see some of the actual people involved in this case and to participate in an experiment conducted by a Harvard law evidence class in relationship to this case, go to *lawschool.mtcibs.com*, click on "Web Lectures," then on "Civil Procedure" and go to the series of lectures connected to "A Civil Action." Another site that will provide you with additional information about this case is *cyber.law.harvard.edu/acivilaction*.

A TRIP TO THE MOVIES

The movie *A Civil Action,* starring John Travolta, documents the true story of a small personal injury firm that took on Beatrice and W. R. Grace, two major companies that were polluting the waters going into a nearby town, resulting in serious illness and death to several children. Although they ultimately won a settlement, the Woburn case bankrupted the firm and almost destroyed the careers of its attorneys.

Assume you work as a paralegal in the firm that is now considering whether to take on the Woburn case. Respond to the following questions.

1. You have been asked to assist in interviewing a single parent whose child has died from leukemia that the parent believes was caused by the contaminated drinking water. The attorney, who has no children, believes that your presence will be helpful because you have two children, and has asked you to arrange the interview.
   a. Explain what you will do to set up the interview and where you will try to conduct it.
   b. What will you plan to do at the beginning of the interview?
   c. How will you respond if the woman you are interviewing begins crying inconsolably?
   d. How will you respond if the woman is obsessed with telling you about her child and keeps diverting the conversation back to stories about her child when you try to ask about events leading up to the child's illness?
   e. During the interview, the woman admits that she is so distraught about her child's death that she has fantasized about sabotaging the operations of Beatrice. When she tells you about what she has thought about doing, you realize that someone could get killed or seriously hurt if she follows through. Does the attorney-client privilege prevent you from notifying Beatrice and/or the police?
   f. Why is it important to find out when the child first became ill and when the mother first suspected that the cause of the child's illness may have been the water?
2. You conduct a conflicts check in reference to the Woburn matter and discover that one of the partners owns 500 shares of stock in Beatrice and that another partner represented the president of Grace in a custody battle ten years ago. Do either of these situations create a conflict of interest that precludes your firm from representing the plaintiffs?
3. A paralegal comes in from the opposing firm to pick up some documents. What can you do to minimize the chance of breaching the confidentiality of any of your firm's clients?
4. The laws make it extremely difficult for plaintiffs in environmental hazard cases to prove that the chemical they claim caused their injuries was in fact the actual of their injuries. Some argue that the standard of proof of causation is too high in these cases and that plaintiffs should not be required to exclude all other possible causes of their injuries (for example, smoking, diet, etc.). What comments do you anticipate would be made by representatives of each of the following schools of jurisprudence about such laws?
   a. natural law
   b. positivism
   c. realism
   d. critical legal theory
5. You are asked to find witnesses who observed the companies dumping toxic wastes into the river.
   a. How will you locate these witnesses?
   b. Under what circumstances will you want to record any statements and how will you record them?
   c. What strategy will you use if any of these witnesses are hostile?
6. What kinds of experts will be needed in this case? Where will you look for these experts?
7. You are asked to open a file on the Woburn matter. What will you include in the file at this point?
8. What things do you think the attorneys will consider when deciding whether to go forward with this case?
   a. Which elements of negligence do you think will be challenging to prove? Why?
   b. Has the company committed any intentional torts?
   c. Is there any basis for a strict liability claim?

INTERNET INQUIRIES

1. Suppose your firm has a client who was injured in a horseback riding incident and that you need to find an expert in equine behavior. Find the names of at least two experts in this area. In this process, use not only the sites suggested in the chapter, but go to the Web page for your state bar association and find out if this site gives links to expert witness directories. Try to obtain individuals who are local or who reside in states near your own.

2. Find out if the county recorder's office in your jurisdiction is on the Internet. If it is, input your name, your parent's name, or the name of someone you know who owns property, and find out what information is available. Then go to the county assessor or county treasurer and bring up your or this person's tax records. Find out how much information is available regarding the value of any properties you or this person own.

3. Using the search terms "telephone numbers" or "telephone records," find at least two companies that locate phone numbers, including unlisted and unpublished numbers. Answer the following questions for each company.
   a. What is the cost of doing a national search for a listed number?
   b. What is the cost of doing a national search for an unlisted or unpublished number?
   c. What other numbers can the company locate (e.g., pager numbers, cell phone numbers, etc.)?
   d. What is the turnaround time for these searches?
   e. Does the company guarantee the accuracy of these searches?

4. Using the search term "skip tracing," go to the Web sites and answer the following questions. (Because skip tracing companies abound, let us suggest two sites to compare: www.skiptracing.com and www.1800ussearch.com. Do not equate our suggestion to look at Web sites as a recommendation for using these particular companies, and do not restrict your analysis to these two companies alone.)
   a. What kinds of searches does this company perform?
   b. What ranges of costs are involved in doing a skip trace?
   c. Does the company indicate what kind of accuracy you can expect? If yes, how accurate are its searches?
   d. What is the turnaround time for a typical search?
   e. How long has the company been in business?

5. Using the search term "[your state] vital records," answer the following questions. If your state participates in the VitalChek program (*www.vitalchek.com*), you can answer these questions by going to the VitalChek site.
   a. What is the cost of obtaining a birth certificate?
   b. To whom will birth certificates be given?
   c. What information must be provided to get a birth certificate?
   d. What is the cost of obtaining a death certificate?
   e. To whom will death certificates be given?
   f. What information must be provided to get a death certificate?
   g. In your state, can you order birth/death certificates by mail? In person? By fax? By telephone? Online?

6. Using the search term "[your state] driving records," see if you can find the Web page for the agency in your state that houses driving records.
   a. What is the name of the agency in your state that has driving records?
   b. What information must be provided to get a driving record?
   c. For what period of time are the records given?
   d. What is the cost of obtaining these records?
   e. Prepare a letter to the appropriate agency in your jurisdiction requesting your driving record for the applicable number of years. Make sure you include the necessary fee.
   What information is included in your driving record? What time frame does this record cover? How accurate is the information in this record?

3

Researching the Case

OBJECTIVES:

In this chapter you will learn:

- how the courts are organized
- where cases are reported
- to read and brief a case
- to read citations
- to distinguish between primary and secondary authority

- how legal encyclopedias, treatises, digests, American Law Reports, restatements, and legal periodicals can be used to do legal research
- how to update legal materials
- the limitations placed on appellate courts
- to analyze and compare case law
- to find and interpret statutes
- to write a legal memorandum

Martha Remembered One of Ms. Barnes's Admonitions to Begin with What You Do Know.

Martha snapped to attention as she drove into the parking lot of the law school. On the drive over she had been pondering her dilemma about whether to say anything to Mike about Carmela and had been only partially aware of where she was driving. But when she saw the maze that greeted her, she shifted her full attention to the task at hand. Having outmaneuvered another vehicle jockeying for a parking spot, she began looking for access into the law school, whose modern architecture masked any signs of a front entrance. After walking almost all the way around the building, she finally negotiated her way toward the law library. "Not a sign of things to come, I hope," she thought to herself, reflecting on the challenges she had faced just in getting from her office to the law library.

She positioned herself close to the front desk because she figured she would probably need a lot of help from the librarians. She reviewed all of her assignments and found herself sinking into a state of overwhelm. She froze in fear, unable to think about anything except John's expectation that she produce all this information for him by next week. Her mind raced. She could not decide where to begin.

Martha sat motionless for several minutes, trapped in a veritable iceberg of panic until she thought of her research instructor, Ms. Barnes, and her incessant reminders about the calming effects of deep breathing. "When in doubt, BREATHE!" Martha smiled in spite of herself and took a few deep breaths. As she felt her jaw muscles beginning to loosen a little, she remembered another of Ms. Barnes's admonitions to always start with what you do know.

"So what do I know?" thought Martha. "Well, for this first assignment I know that I need a court opinion. So I know that I start with case law, and I know that this opinion has been written so it probably reached the appellate level. I know that it's a civil case and that it was heard in the Louisiana courts, but I don't know whether it was heard in the state or federal courts."

ORGANIZATION OF THE COURTS

Federal Courts

district court *trial court of general jurisdiction at the federal level*

Federal courts are those courts belonging to and deriving their power from the federal government. In the federal system, three main "levels" of courts exist. (Figure 3-1 illustrates the three-tiered hierarchy of the federal courts.) The trial court in the federal system is the United States **district court**. Each federal district has a

Figure 3-1
Organization of Federal Courts

ORGANIZATION OF FEDERAL COURTS

United States Supreme Court

↓

Courts of Appeal (Circuit Courts)

↓

District Courts

general jurisdiction   power of a court to hear all types of civil and criminal cases

magistrates   judge who assists the district court judge by performing certain limited functions

bankruptcy judges   federal court judge who hears bankruptcy cases

appeals   a formal request in which a party asks a higher court to review the decision of a lower court and change it in some way

circuit court   second level of courts in the federal system; also formally known as the U.S. Court of Appeals

U.S. District Court; each state has at least one district and some of the more populous states have two to four. District courts are courts of **general jurisdiction** in that they can hear cases that are not specifically assigned to specialty courts and that are within the power of the federal courts to hear. U.S. District court judges preside over lawsuits filed in federal court. Ordinarily, lawsuits in U.S. district courts are heard by a single judge; in special situations, a panel of three judges may preside. District court judges are assisted by magistrates and bankruptcy judges. **Magistrates** hear motions and minor criminal cases and conduct pretrial hearings for civil cases. **Bankruptcy judges**, as the name implies, handle bankruptcy cases.

The second level of courts is responsible for **appeals.** An appeal is a formal request in which a party asks a higher court to review the decision of a lower court and change it in some way. In the federal system, this second level of courts is called the *U.S. Court of Appeals* or **circuit court,** as it is popularly called. The U.S. Court of Appeals is divided into thirteen circuits, eleven of which are divided geographically to encompass all 50 states. (Figure 3-2 shows the geographic lay-out of these courts.) Each of these geographical circuits is numbered from one to 11 and is responsible for the appeals from all the U.S. District Courts within its region. (The regions are called *circuits* because, in times past, appellate court judges had to travel from district to district to hear appeals. This was called "riding the circuit.)" Today, judges usually stay in one place and make litigants come to them.) In addition to the eleven geographical circuits, the District of Columbia has a circuit court of appeals because of all the government activities there that generate so much litigation. A thirteenth circuit, called the Federal Circuit, handles appeals in specialized cases from across the country. If you are dissatisfied with the judgment of a U.S. District Court, your appeal will ordinarily be sent to the court of appeals for the circuit in which your state is included. Lawyers often refer to a U.S. court of appeal simply as a "circuit." For example, the U.S Court of Appeals for the Second Circuit, which hears appeals from districts in New York and several northeastern states, is referred to in popular lawyer jargon as "the Second Circuit."

The highest court in the federal system is, of course, the U.S. Supreme Court. The main function of the U.S Supreme Court is to offer a final level of appeal. A party that loses an appeal in the U.S. Court of Appeals can ask the U.S. Supreme

NET NEWS

For more information about the structure and history of the circuit courts, go to *www.courts.net/fed/index.html*. Click on "Circuit Courts" and then on "9th Circuit" and then "History and Structure" under "Points of Interest." This site also provides information about each circuit and district court and the United States Supreme Court. Another site that has information about the circuit courts is *www.uscourts.gov*. At that site, click on "Frequently Asked Questions" and "Links."

Figure 3-2
Map of the 13 Federal Circuits

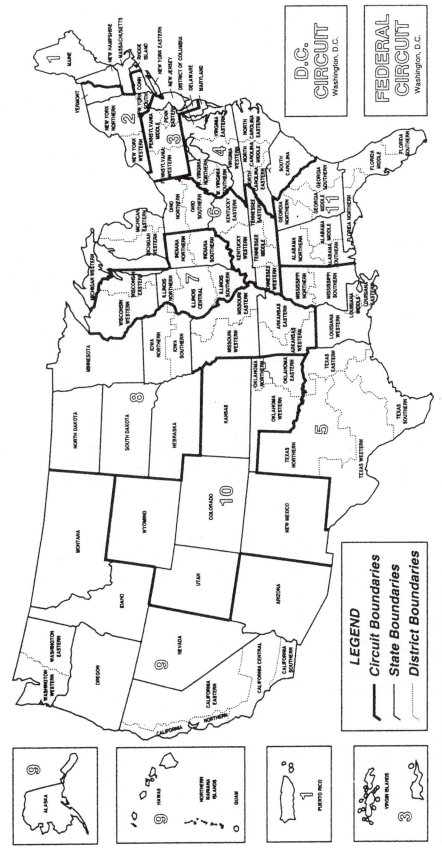

ADMINISTRATIVE OFFICE OF THE UNITED STATES SUPREME COURTS

APRIL 1988

NET NEWS

To take a virtual tour of the U.S. Supreme Court, go to the Northwestern University site at *http://oyez.nwu.tour*. You will need to download "Quick Time" to take the tour.

discretionary   within the discretion of the court

writ of *certiorari*   written request asking an appellate court to review a lower court's decision

◆ **LOCAL LINKS** ◆

What titles are used in reference to the judges in your state?

Court to review the case. In most situations, review by the U.S. Supreme Court is **discretionary**, in that it is up to the Court whether to hear the appeal. In contrast, the circuit courts, because they represent the first level of appeal, must hear all properly filed appeals. (The Court of Appeals can, however, impose penalties on litigants who waste its time with "frivolous" appeals that are clearly without merit.) Most of those cases are chosen by the U.S. Supreme Court after the losing party on appeal has requested a **writ of *certiorari***, a written request asking that an appellate court review a lower court's decision. *Certiorari* is a Latin term meaning "to be informed of."

The Supreme Court will review the case only if four of the nine justices vote to hear it. If the Court decides that a case is "*cert* worthy," it will direct the lower court to send its records and files to the Supreme Court for review. If it denies "*cert*," the decision of the lower court will stand. In practice, the U.S. Supreme Court chooses its cases carefully; of the more than six thousand petitions for certiorari filed, less than four hundred are accepted. Full written opinions are rendered in only about two hundred cases, while the rest are disposed of without oral argument or formal written opinions.

Judges who sit on the U.S. Supreme Court or a state court of last resort are referred to as *justices* in most states. At present, nine justices (eight associate justices and one chief justice) sit on the U.S. Supreme Court. The chief justice is responsible for the administration of the Court and the leadership of the federal judicial system. Under Article III of the U. S. Constitution, no mandatory retirement exists for U.S. Supreme Court justices; thus, some of these justices have served incredibly long periods. (Justice John Marshall, often regarded as one of the Court's finest justices, was on the bench for 34 years.) The average time of service, however, is 15 years.

Putting It Into Practice 3.1:

If your goal is to get a case before the U.S. Supreme Court, what must you do to get there?

BONUS POINTERS:

appellant   person who files an appeal; sometimes known as the *petitioner*

brief   written argument explaining why a party believes the trial court's decision was or was not in error

appellee   person responding to an appeal; sometimes known as the *respondent*

COURT TRADITIONS

The justices continue to recognize several long-standing traditions, including the "conference handshake." Before meeting in conference to review a case, the justices formally shake hands with each other. They also sit on the bench in accordance with their seniority. The chief justice sits in the middle, the most senior justice sits to his right, the next most senior justice to his left, and so on until the newest member, who sits on the far right. Pictures of the Supreme Court reflect this arrangement.

Appeals in the U.S. Court of Appeals are heard and decided by panels of three judges. The party who began the appeal—the **appellant**—furnishes the court with a written argument called a **brief** that details the reasons why the appellant thinks the trial court was in error. The other party—the **appellee**—prepares a brief in response.

Figure 3-3
*Picture of the U.S. Supreme
Court Justices* (Collection,
The Supreme Court
Historical Society)

oral arguments period during which attorneys have an opportunity to explain their arguments and answer any questions the appellate court judges assigned to their case have

en banc all of the appellate judges sitting together to hear a case

affirmed when an appellate court leaves a trial court's decision unchanged

reversed when an appellate court changes a trial court's decision

remand when an appellate court sends a case back to the trial court to either change its judgment or redo a trial

constitutional courts courts whose existence is derived from Article III of the U.S. Constitution; also known as *Article III* courts

legislative courts specialized federal courts created by Congress

---

◆ LOCAL LINKS ◆

Draw a chart showing the organization of the courts in your state. Your chart should be similar to that shown in Figure 3-4. Where is each court located?

The court of appeals may schedule **oral arguments,** at which attorneys for each party are given a short time (usually less than an hour) to explain their arguments and answer any questions the judges may have. Or, the court may decide the appeal on the briefs submitted, without hearing arguments. Occasionally, and usually at the request of a party who has lost an appeal before a panel and requested a hearing before the full membership of the court, all the judges will sit together and decide a case *en banc.*

The Court of Appeals may choose to affirm, reverse, or modify the trial court's decision. If the trial court's decision is **affirmed,** it is left unchanged. If it is **reversed,** the Court of Appeals will **remand** the case back to the trial court to correct its error either by changing its judgment or redoing the trial.

The authority for the three-tiered federal system arises out of Article III of the U.S. Constitution, which provides that "[t]he judicial Power of the United States, shall be vested in one supreme court and in such inferior Courts as the Congress may from time to time ordain and establish." In the Judiciary Act of 1789, Congress established thirteen district courts and three circuit courts. Through further legislative action over the years, the court system has grown to the ninety-four district courts and thirteen circuit courts in existence today. Judges who serve on these so-called **constitutional courts** (or Article III courts) serve for life. They are appointed by the U.S. President and their appointments must be approved by the U.S. Senate. Their service is terminated only by resignation or impeachment for improper behavior.

Congress has also created more specialized **legislative courts,** such as the U.S. Tax Court (which hears appeals from Internal Revenue Service rulings), the U.S. Military Court of Appeals (which hears final appeals for court-martial convictions), and the U.S. Claims Court (which hears cases involving claims against the U.S. government). Judges appointed to these courts, bankruptcy judges, and magistrates serve for set terms and do not enjoy the independence of the judges who serve on the constitutional courts.

Putting It Into Practice 3.2:

What do you think is the purpose in making it so difficult to remove a judge who serves on a constitutional court? What do you think are the advantages and disadvantages of having lifetime judicial appointments?

State Courts

In many states, the courts are organized along the same three-tiered system used in the federal system: a trial court of general jurisdiction, an appeals court, and a supreme court. (Figure 3-4 shows the organization of a common state court system.) In many states, the trial court is called the Superior Court. Several exceptions exist, including New York, where the general civil trial court is called the Supreme Court, and Louisiana, whose court system is derived from French law and is based on a different

---

NET NEWS

To read the biography of each U.S. Supreme Court justice, go to *http://oyez.northwestern.edu* and click on "Justices."

To hear audiotapes of oral arguments made before the U.S. Supreme Court in selected cases, go to the Northwestern University site *http://oyez.nwu.edu* and click on "Cases." Search by Title and ask to return only those cases with "real audio."

"Isn't This the Case Involving the Plaintiffs Who Sued the Producers of the Movie Natural-Born Killers?"

Martha was oblivious to the watchful gaze of one of the student assistants. Unlike many of the students who worked in the law library, Tim took a real interest in helping those in distress. He enjoyed seeing others experience the thrill of discovery when they found that case or statute or article that clearly addressed the issue they were researching. An avid observer of human nature, Tim quickly recognized the signs of someone drowning in fear. Like a lifeguard to the rescue, Tim zeroed in on Martha. Not wanting to be too obvious, he casually stood nearby. When Martha glanced up, she looked into the most penetrating but gentle blue eyes she had ever seen.

"Anything I could help you find?" asked Tim quietly. A quick assessment of the expression on her face and Tim knew that this was an intervention that would require some time. Probably a paralegal being thrown into the waters to sink or swim, he thought, knowing that Martha was not a law school student, all of whom he recognized at this point in the semester.

"Uh, I'm not sure. Maybe," stuttered Martha, doing her best to keep her composure. The look of compassion on Tim's face, however, brought out the truth in Martha and she blurted out, "Actually, I can use all the help I can get. So if you have some time and you could help me get started, I'd be eternally grateful." The tension in Martha's face did not go unnoticed by Tim, and he immediately regaled her with a story about his first day in the law library. Soon Martha was laughing delightedly at the images conjured up by Tim's recounting of his embarrassing tale.

When Tim was certain that Martha was feeling better about herself and the task that lay before her, he asked, "So where would you like to start?"

"I guess the easiest place to begin is with this case that I know was tried in the Louisiana courts," responded Martha.

"Do you have any idea if this is a recent case or an older one?" followed up Tim.

"Recent. I think it's probably not more than six months old."

"Good. That's helpful. And do you know if it's a state or federal case?" continued Tim.

"No, but I do know that one party's name is Byers," offered Martha hopefully.

"Great. The case should be in the hard-bound volumes of the reporters by now. You know, this case would be really easy to find using **Westlaw** or **LEXIS/NEXIS**. Any particular reason you came to the library to find it?"

"Yes. Our firm hasn't accepted this case yet, so we don't have a billing code we can charge our research to."

"Makes sense. Did you try the Internet by any chance?" pursued Tim.

"No, I never thought about that," admitted Martha. "And you know, it's likely this case would have been on the 'Net because it caused quite a stir, especially with the legal community and the media."

"This isn't the case involving the plaintiffs who sued the producers of the movie *Natural-Born Killers,* is it?" Martha's comment about the media triggered a memory in Tim about a case in which he thought the plaintiff might have been Byers.

"Yes, in fact, it is," confirmed Martha.

"Well, then, this may be your lucky day. One of our professors who teaches a class on law and the media has been actively following *Byers*. She gave her students a research project involving this case and had us keep several copies on reserve so all of the students wouldn't be trying to use the same **reporter** simultaneously. Let me get you a copy so you can make sure this is the same case." A quick scan of the **headnotes** convinced Martha that this was indeed the case she was seeking.

Westlaw; LEXIS/NEXIS two of the most commonly used online databases for legal research

reporter   set of books containing reported cases

headnotes   short, numbered paragraphs at the beginning of an opinion that summarize points of law discussed by the court

Figure 3-4
Organization of Arizona State Courts

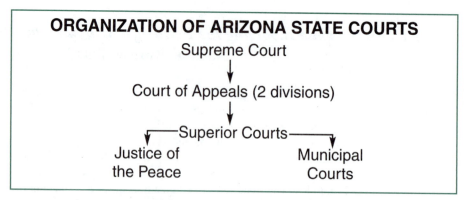

philosophy entirely. Superior courts are state courts in the sense that they are created by state law, but they are usually funded and administered by county governments.

Appeals from the decisions of state courts are taken to the intermediate appellate state courts (although some states have no intermediate level of appellate court). In Arizona, this court is called the Court of Appeals; in New York, the intermediate appellate court is called the Appellate Division. Some states have more than one intermediate appellate court. The appellate procedure is like that described for the U.S. Court of Appeals. State courts of appeals are located in the state's capital city, but may have branches in a few other cities in the state.

Each state has a court of last resort (often called a supreme court) whose function is to hear appeals regarding issues it considers important. The name varies, however; in New York the highest court is called the Court of Appeals. Courts of last resort are often located in the capital city.

Most states have many trial courts (one for each county), but only one court of appeals (which may have several divisions or departments), and one court of last resort. Many states also have courts of **limited jurisdiction** (courts that are allowed to hear only a narrow range of cases) in such areas as domestic relations, probate, and traffic.

States develop their own system for selecting and retaining judges. Many use some version of the so-called Missouri Plan, which requires that a panel of lawyers and lay persons select a number of candidates from which the governor makes an appointment. In many states, the newly appointed judge must within a year or two of being appointed go before the electorate, who decides whether to retain this judge. Such retention elections are then held on a periodic basis thereafter until the judge resigns or is not retained. In other states, judges are appointed by the legislature or governor; in still others, they are elected.

limited jurisdiction   power of the courts to hear only a narrow range of cases

---

◆ **LOCAL LINKS** ◆

How are your state court judges selected and retained?

WHERE CASES ARE REPORTED

official reporter   set of books containing cases that are authorized by the court

unofficial reporter   set of books containing cases that are published by private companies

Cases are published in sets of books called reports or reporters. **Official reporters** are authorized by the court and are usually published by governmental authorities; **unofficial reporters** are published by private companies, such as West Publishing Company or the former Lawyers' Co-operative Company. Most legal researchers prefer using the unofficial reporters because they contain research aids (which will be discussed later) that official reporters generally do not.

NET NEWS

===

For links to all state courts, go to *www.courts.net*. If you do not know how the courts are organized in your state, you can find out by going to your state court Web site or to the site for the Center for Information Law and Policy at *www.cilp.org*.

Figure 3-5
Map of Regional Reporters

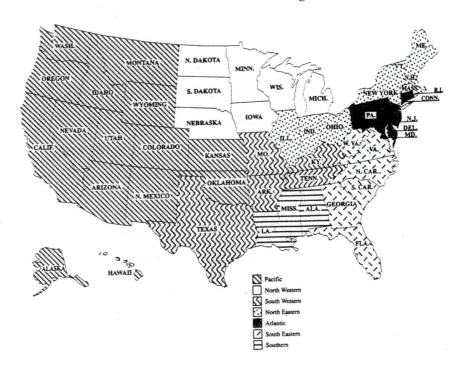

State Courts

State court cases can be found in seven regional reporters.

Pacific Reporter (P.)
Atlantic Reporter (A.)
North Eastern Reporter (N.E.)
North Western Reporter (N.W.)
Southern Reporter (So.)
South Eastern Reporter (S.E.)
South Western Reporter (S.W.)

These are all unofficial reporters, published by West, that cover designated geographic areas (see Figure 3-5 showing a map of these regions). Each of these regional reporters has a first and second (and, in some cases, third and fourth) series. After a designated number of volumes is published, West begins a new series.

About two-thirds of the states also publish an official state reporter; for some states, West publishes a separate unofficial reporter. In essence, most state court opinions can be found in two places: in the regional West reporter system and in the state court reporter, if one exists.

Selected cases are also published in *American Law Reports,* published by the former Lawyers' Co-operative Publishing Company. Unlike the reporters, this specialized research tool contains only a limited number of cases. These cases are, however, extensively **annotated** (referenced to other cases and legal sources). Such annotations are invaluable to the researcher because they identify related sources.

When cases are first written they are published as **slip opinions,** which are simply reproductions without any headnotes or other editorial features. Slip opinions for the U.S. Supreme Court usually appear in libraries within five to 10 days of the date the decision is rendered and online within 24 hours. Within a few weeks after an opinion is issued, publishers of official (and some unofficial reporters) prepare **advance sheets,** which are pamphlets of groups of cases. The advance sheets are placed next to the hard-bound reporters until the newest reporter is published, usually within a few months, at which point the advance sheets are destroyed.

◆ **LOCAL LINKS** ◆

What reporters are used to publish your state's cases?

---

annotated   contains references to cases and other legal sources

slip opinions   form in which a case is originally published

advance sheets   pamphlet forms in which cases are first put together before they are bound

Federal Courts

U.S. Supreme Court decisions are published in the following reporters.

U.S. Reports (official reporter) (U.S.)
Supreme Court Reporter (S. Ct.) (unofficial reporter)
United States Reports (L. Ed.) *Lawyers' Edition* (unofficial reporter)
United States Law Week (U.S.L.W.)

U.S. Court of Appeals opinions are published in these reporters.

Federal Reporter (F.; F.2d; F.3d) (published by West)
A.L.R. Fed. (A.L.R. Fed.) (published by former Lawyers' Co-operative selected cases only)

U.S. district court opinions are published in these reporters.

Federal Supplement (F. Supp.) (published by West)
A.L.R. Fed. (A.L.R. Fed.) (published by former Lawyers' Co-operative selected cases only)

Availability of Cases

Not all appeals are published. The highest courts in the states generally publish all of their opinions, but the intermediate courts usually select only certain opinions to be published. In some states, important trial court decisions are also published, but this is the exception rather than the rule. At the federal level, not only are all decisions rendered by the district and circuit courts published, but all decisions rendered by the U.S. Supreme Court are published. All court decisions are considered public records and can be obtained from the court clerk's office even if they are not published.

Figure 3-6
Coverage of Regional Reporters

Atlantic Reporter (A. and A.2d)
    Connecticut, Delaware, District of Columbia, Maine, Maryland,
    New Hampshire, New Jersey, Pennsylvania, Rhode Island, Vermont
North Eastern Reporter (N.E. and N.E.2d)
    Illinois, Indiana, Massachusetts, New York, Ohio
North Western Reporter (N.W. and N.W.2d)
    Iowa, Michigan, Minnesota, Nebraska, North Dakota, South Dakota,
    Wisconsin
Pacific Reporter (P. and P.2d and P.3d)
    Alaska, Arizona, Colorado, Hawaii, Idaho, Kansas, Montana, Nevada,
    New Mexico, Oklahoma, Oregon, Utah, Washington, Wyoming
South Eastern Reporter (S.E. and S.E.2d)
    Georgia, North Carolina, South Carolina, Virginia, West Virginia
South Western Reporter (S.W. and S.W.2d)
    Arkansas, Kentucky, Missouri, Tennessee, Texas
Southern Reporter (So. and So.2d)
    Alabama, Florida, Louisiana, Mississippi

NET NEWS

To read both federal and state court opinions online, go to *www.law.cornell.edu* and click on "Court Opinions." Be aware that only relatively recent cases are available online, that not all courts have opinions available online, and that these cases have not been edited and so are not necessarily accurate. Court opinions can also be accessed by going to *www.courts.net*. U.S. Supreme Court and federal court decisions can be accessed by going to *www.findlaw.com*. Select the court you are interested in ("Laws: Cases and Codes") before doing a search.

Putting It Into Practice 3.3:

In what reporters will Martha find *Byers?*

Electronic Research

Cases are also available online. Westlaw and LEXIS/NEXIS are two of the most commonly used commercial legal databases today, while LOIS (Law Office Information Systems) is a relative newcomer to the world of computerized legal research. Although neither has eliminated the need for hard-copy research, they are becoming increasingly accessible to legal researchers. Competent paralegals should have a working knowledge of either Westlaw or LEXIS. Many recent cases are also available on court Web sites and law school library Web sites. Although these sources are more limited in scope than what can be found using either Westlaw or LEXIS/NEXIS, they are free to access.

The greatest advantage of online research is its ability to offer up-to-date information without the inconvenience of going to a law library. Online databases provide the most current information available. The primary disadvantage of online research is its cost. Online research (except for the free searches that can be conducted on the Internet) is very expensive: a half-hour search can easily add up to $100 or more. (For more information about online research, see the Techno Tip at the end of this chapter.)

Putting It Into Practice 3.4:

Where should Martha look for a case if she knows it has been issued by the U.S. Supreme Court within the last few weeks?

READING CASES

Format of Court Opinions

caption beginning of a court opinion where the parties and their relationship are identified

Court opinions begin with a **caption** that identifies the parties and their relationship to one another. (See Figure 3-7 to see the elements of a court opinion illustrated using the first page of *Byers.*) Directly above the caption is the case **citation,** which provides information that identifies where the case can be found in the reporter. (See below for more information about citations.) Directly beneath the caption is the **docket number,** which is the number assigned to the case by the court clerk for administrative purposes. Beneath the docket number is the identity of the court that rendered the decision and the date it was rendered. Also included are the names of the attorneys who represented each side as well as the judges who heard the case and wrote the opinion.

citation (also known as a *cite*) part of a court opinion that provides information identifying where the case can be located

docket number number assigned by the court clerk to a case

BONUS POINTERS:

READING CAPTIONS

To facilitate your reading of captions, familiarize yourself with these commonly used phrases.

Et al.—and others

    May Chang, et al., Plaintiffs,

       v.

    Linda Miller, et al., Defendants.

In re—in the matter of

    In re Jack Dreyer, Petitioner

Ex rel.—in report to (applies to cases instigated by private parties and then brought by a government agency, such as the state)

    Ex rel. Maria Sanchez

Et ux.—and wife

    Finlayson, et ux., Plaintiffs

       v.

    Ramirez, et ux., Defendants

712 So.2d 681
(Cite as: 97-0831 (La.App. 1 Cir. 5/15/98), 712 So.2d 681)   CITATION

Patsy Ann BYERS, et al.
v.
Sarah EDMONDSON, et al.   CAPTION

No. 97 CA 0831.   DOCKET NUMBER

Court of Appeal of Louisiana,   COURT RENDERING
First Circuit.   DECISION

May 15, 1998.   DATE DECISION WAS RENDERED

A shooting victim brought an action for negligence and intentional tort against, among others, the producers of a movie and videotape that the shooter had allegedly viewed shortly before beginning the crime spree that included the shooting. The Twenty-First Judicial District Court, Parish of Tangipahoa, No. 9502213, Robert H. Morrison, III, J., dismissed the claim. The victim appealed. The Court of Appeal, Carter, J., held that: (1) the victim stated a cause of action for intentional tort against the producers of the movie, and (2) the allegations of the petition brought the case into the exception to the First Amendment for incitement to imminent lawless activity.   SYLLABUS

Reversed and remanded.

Fitzsimmons, J., assigned additional reasons.

HEADNOTE   **[1] PLEADING k228.17**   WEST KEY NUMBER
302k228.17
Evidence is generally not admissible on an exception raising the objection of no cause of action unless the pleadings are expanded through the admission of the evidence by the trial court without objection from the other party.

[2] PLEADING k228.20
302k228.20
For the purposes of determining the issues raised by the exception of no cause of action, the well-pleaded facts in the petition must be accepted as true, and the court must determine if the law affords the plaintiff a remedy under those facts.

[3] PLEADING k228.11
302k228.11
When a petition states a cause of action as to any ground or portion of the demand, an exception raising the objection of no cause of action must be overruled.

Figure 3-7
First Page of Byers

One of the research aids offered by West reporters are **headnotes,** which are short numbered paragraphs that precede the opinion. These headnotes identify the point of law being discussed using the **West numbering system.** Headnotes, which are written by West editors, summarize specific principles of law discussed by the court. In the West key numbering system, legal issues are organized alphabetically by topic and numerically by subtopic. Each key contains a topic name (key name) and section number (key number). Headnote 7 (indicated by the "7" in brackets) in *Byers* relates to negligence, and keynote k210 relates specifically to what constitutes a duty.

You can use headnotes to read cases more efficiently. If you are interested only in certain issues, you may read only the section of the opinion dealing with those issues by looking for the applicable headnotes. In *Byers,* for example, if you were interested in reading only about the constitutional issues in the case, you would focus on the parts of the opinion dealing with headnotes 13-21. Beware, however, of relying too heavily on headnotes. Reading headnotes is no substitute for reading the actual case. Analyzing a case requires that you read the court's actual words, not an editor's interpretation of those words.

In both official and unofficial reporters, you will also usually find a **syllabus,** which is a brief synopsis of the court's opinion. In official reporters, the syllabus is prepared by a designee of the court, but in unofficial reporters, it is written by an editor. Never rely on a syllabus or a headnote in preparing a memorandum because they do not necessarily accurately or completely reflect what the court actually said.

Use the briefing format described below to structure your reading of cases, making sure that you pull out the procedural history of the case, the essential facts, the issues and holdings, and the rationale used by the court. Read the entire opinion, including any concurring and dissenting opinions. **Concurring opinions** are written by judges who agree with the opinion of the majority, but who reach that conclusion using different or additional reasoning. Sometimes judges believe that the majority has not adequately explained or illustrated its reasoning and wish to offer additional examples, supporting case law, and arguments. Concurring opinions can be helpful because they offer additional support for a legal conclusion and sometimes are easier to read than the majority opinion. **Dissenting opinions** (written by those judges who disagree with the outcome of the case) are also helpful because the losing argument today may become the prevailing argument in the future when, as the make-up of the court changes, the dissenting judge in the minority today becomes part of the majority down the road. Dissenting opinions can also assist you in formulating a response to an opponent who cites the majority's argument. If the case law the opposing party is citing is not **binding** on the court (in that the court is not obligated to follow it), you can certainly use the dissenting opinion to mount your rebuttal. Sometimes the issue is stated more clearly by the judges writing the concurring or dissenting opinions.

West numbering system
numbering system used by West by which legal issues are organized alphabetically by topic and numerically by subtopic

syllabus   brief synopsis of an opinion

concurring opinions
opinion written by a judge who has reached the same conclusion as the majority but for different or additional reasons

dissenting opinions   opinion written by a judge who disagrees with the majority's conclusion

binding   law that the court is obligated to follow

Putting It Into Practice 3.5:

Look over *Weirum v. RKO* (an edited case found in Appendix B) and find the following: caption, docket number, and headnote dealing with negligence.

Figure 3-8
Anatomy of a Citation

ANATOMY OF A CITATION				
Pastorini v. Hobbs CASE NAME	101 VOLUME	U.S. REPORTER	437 PAGE	1992 DECISION DATE

CITATIONS

Case citations (commonly referred to as *cites*) provide the information necessary to find a case or any other legal resource. They identify the name, volume, and page of the reporter in which the case is located. The date the case was decided is also included. Examine the following citation.

Pastorini v. Hobbs,   101   U.S.   437   (1992).

The citation begins with the case name, Pastorini v. Hobbs. The first number that follows the case name refers to the volume number of the reporter. (In this case, the volume number is 101.) The reporter is identified by the abbreviation (in this case, U.S., which refers to the *United States Reports*). The number following the reporter is the page number in the reporter (page 437). The date in parentheses indicates the year the opinion was rendered.

Conveniently, all citations for cases follow the same basic format: volume number, name of reporter, page number, and date. In opinions written by courts other than the United States Supreme Court, the level of the court is given in parentheses. In the following example, "5th Cir." refers to the Fifth Circuit Court, which rendered the opinion.

Flynn v. Brown, 106 F.2d 987 (5th Cir. 1972).

The "F.2d indicates that the opinion appears in the *Federal Reporter, Second Series.* Note that "2d" rather than "2nd" is used to designate a second series. You might understandably assume that the number following the name of the reporter refers to the edition; however, the number actually refers to the series. Therefore, *Pacific Reporter* (2d) refers to the second series of *Pacific Reporters* and not to a second (or revised) edition. If the case had been tried in the district before being heard in the Fifth Circuit, its citation might appear as follows.

Flynn v. Brown, 96 F. Supp. 456 (S.D.N.J. 1971).

The "S.D.N.J." indicates that the case was tried in the southern district court of New Jersey. District court opinions are published in the *Federal Supplement,* as indicated by "F. Supp." in the citation.

State court cases follow the same general format. The volume number precedes the abbreviation for the reporter, and the page number follows that abbreviation. The information in parentheses, in addition to the date, designates the court that rendered the opinion. The following example illustrates this.

Singh v. Thomas, 167 Ariz. 22 (Ct. App. 1989).

The "Ct.App." in parentheses identifies the Court of Appeals as the court that delivered the opinion. Such identification is necessary because opinions for both the Arizona Court of Appeals and the Arizona Supreme Court are published in the *Arizona Reports.* If the Arizona Supreme Court had issued the opinion, only the date would appear in the parentheses.

Singh v. Thomas, 167 Ariz. 22 (1983).

Parallel cites include both the official and unofficial reporters.

parallel cites cite containing reference to both the official and unofficial reporters

Wallace v. Ladmo, 156 Ariz. 99, 201 P.2d 234 (Ct. App. 1993).
Official   Unofficial

The "P.2d" refers to the *Pacific Reporter,* which is the regional (unofficial) reporter that publishes Arizona cases. The "2d" indicates that this case is found in the second series of the *Pacific Reporter.*

To find out everything you could possibly want to know about citations, look to *The Bluebook: A Uniform System of Citation,* also called the *Bluebook* because it always comes with a blue cover. Designed to maintain a consistent system for citing references, the *Bluebook* is considered the "Bible" to those lawyers who wish to conform their writing to standard citing practices. This reference will enlighten you about the proper format for citing every type of legal and nonlegal reference you could possibly allude to in your research, and it is followed in federal and many state courts. It will also provide you with proper abbreviations, guide you in the use of underlining, advise you as to the order in which you cite references, and so on.

Cite checking—checking the accuracy of legal citations—is a task often relegated to paralegals. (This term is used by some lawyers to mean the process of checking to see that the correct authority is cited or that the authority is still valid.) Your familiarity with the rules of the *Bluebook* at the early stages of your education will assist you in conforming to these rules when you begin your active practice. Note that the *Bluebook* citations for the reporters are shown in parentheses in Figure 3-6 and in the list of federal reporters shown on page 120.)

LOCAL LINKS
What are the names and abbreviations for the state reporters in your state? Which court opinions are published in which reporters?

cite checking checking the accuracy of legal citations

Putting It Into Practice 3.6:

Where would you find the following cases?

101 F.2d 595

99 S.E.2d 104

95 Colo. 54, 105 P.2d 67

BONUS POINTERS:

WHY READING CASES IS SO CHALLENGING

If you recognize that reading cases is a challenging prospect, you are less likely to become discouraged when you discover that understanding case law is a very time-consuming and potentially frustrating experience. What makes reading cases so challenging?

First, many of the legal concepts you will be confronted with will be complex. After all, the "easy" cases rarely go up on appeal. Some of the issues that courts must grapple with are very abstract, and others require juggling of existing case law that is inconsistent or highly convoluted.

Second, some judges do not write clearly and simply. Their writing may be obtuse and pretentious. Judges are not required to demonstrate their competency to express themselves clearly and concisely before assuming their judicial duties. Consequently, readers may be

NET NEWS

For more information about the basis of legal citations, go to *www.law.cornell.edu/citation.*

forced to wend their way through a language maze that further complicates an already complex thought process.

Third, judges assume that their readers understand basic legal principles and concepts. They do not explain legal processes and terminology that they presume are common knowledge to the lawyers who constitute the bulk of their readership.

To make reading case law less frustrating, be patient with yourself. Give yourself time, and realize that you will have to read hundreds of cases before you become reasonably proficient.

Have a dictionary in hand every time you sit down to read a case, and assume that you are going to have to consult it frequently. Two of the best known legal dictionaries are *Black's Law Dictionary* and *Ballentine's Law Dictionary*. In addition to definitions, both dictionaries contain a pronunciation guide to Latin legal terms, and *Black's* has a table of common legal abbreviations, an organizational chart of the United States government, a text of the U.S. Constitution, and a chart showing the composition of the United States Supreme Court from 1789 until today. Avoid the temptation of guessing what a word means or a process entails. The time you invest when you start reading cases will save you time eventually. As your knowledge base grows, you will have to rely on the dictionary and other references less and less.

Remember that your ability to read and understand cases is a reflection of your experience, not your intelligence. Give yourself the time and opportunity to build your skill level and never compare your proficiency with that of those who have been reading case law for years. Briefing cases will help you better understand them. By virtue of preparing a case brief, you will immediately recognize your weaknesses in understanding a case and will know where you have to focus your efforts in order to remedy your misunderstanding.

Having found *Byers* and read it, Martha was now prepared to **brief** the case, which John had instructed her to do with the integral cases she found. She had heard his lectures to the new associates about the importance of briefing, and she knew he would not tolerate any shortcuts. She began by writing down the citation for *Byers*.

brief (v.) to prepare a written summary of a case

case brief a written summary of a case

BRIEFING

The key to reading cases is learning to transform legal abstractions into workable principles. One of the best ways to accomplish this is to brief cases. A **case brief** dissects and summarizes a case. It is a condensed version (usually one or two pages) of case law and contains only the most pertinent information. Reading a case brief allows you to quickly determine what the facts of the case are, what issues were before the court, and what the court decided and why. A brief allows you to refresh your memory about a case without having to reread it. Likewise, an attorney can read a brief that you have prepared to understand the legal principles involved and to decide whether the actual case is significant enough to warrant reading it.

You will not find universal agreement among law professors and practitioners as to the optimal makeup of a case brief. But here is a suggested format.

- ◆ citation
- ◆ procedural history
- ◆ facts
- ◆ issues
- ◆ holdings
- ◆ rationale

Figure 3-9
Elements of a Brief

ELEMENTS OF A BRIEF

CITATION
PROCEDURAL HISTORY
FACTS
ISSUES
HOLDINGS
RATIONALE

◆ **LOCAL LINKS** ◆
Find out what your instructor's preferred format for briefing is.

Modify this format to meet the demands of your instructor or employer. In some respects, briefing cases is similar to taking notes. Your style of note-taking should reflect your unique listening and analytical preferences. So, too, should your case briefs reflect your own needs and preferences (unless you are preparing them for someone else).

Briefs are more helpful if they are written in your own words rather than simply copying from the opinion. Remember that the purpose of briefing is to summarize the primary elements of the case; this is not accomplished by compiling a list of extensive quotations. Also, resist the temptation to brief while you are reading the case. Read the case until you feel like you really understand it and then brief it. If you are reading a series of cases dealing with the same topic, you may find it more useful to read all of the cases before you begin briefing.

BONUS POINTERS:

BRIEFS COME IN TWO FORMS

Briefs come in two forms in the legal world. Case briefs are truly brief and are intended to condense the essentials of a case into one or two pages. Legal briefs, on the other hand, are anything but brief, typically consisting of twenty pages or more. They are aimed at convincing a judge to adopt a particular legal position.

Case briefs are used to help the reader understand and compare case law. Legal briefs are written by attorneys and are the culmination of considerable research. They are used to persuade a third person to adopt a particular position. Most university and state law libraries have such briefs available for review.

Citation

At the top of the page, copy the citation of the case you are briefing. Having this citation readily available will allow you to quickly locate the case if you need to read it again.

Putting It Into Practice 3.7:

Write out the citation for *Weirum v. RKO*.

Procedural History

The procedural history consists of the nature and result of all proceedings that occurred previously in regard to the case you are briefing as well as the nature of the current proceeding. For example, the procedural history may show that a case that is now before the U.S. Supreme Court originated in a superior court in Arizona, that it was appealed to the Arizona Court of Appeals and the Arizona Supreme

Cir. 5/15/98), 712 So.2d 681)
Patsy Ann BYERS, et al.

v.

Sarah EDMONDSON, et al.
No. 97 CA 0831.
Court of Appeal of Louisiana,
First Circuit.
May 15, 1998.

A shooting victim brought an action for negligence and intentional tort against, among others, the producers of a movie and videotape that the shooter had allegedly viewed shortly before beginning the crime spree that included the shooting. The Twenty-First Judicial District Court, Parish of Tangipahoa, No. 9502213, Robert H. Morrison, III, J., dismissed the claim. The victim appealed. The Court of Appeal, Carter, J., held that: (1) the victim stated a cause of action for intentional tort against the producers of the movie, and (2) the allegations of the petition brought the case into the exception to the First Amendment for incitement to imminent lawless activity.

Reversed and remanded.
CARTER, Judge. . . .

FACTS

This suit arises from the shooting of plaintiff, Patsy Byers (Byers) by Sarah Edmondson (Edmondson) and Benjamin Darrus (Darrus). According to the **allegations** of Byers's [FN2] **petition,** Edmondson and Darrus acted together when Edmondson shot and seriously wounded Byers during an armed robbery of a Time Saver convenience store in Ponchatoula, Louisiana. Darrus accompanied Edmondson upon the shooting spree, encouraged her to engage in the shooting spree and assisted Edmondson by driving her to and from the armed robbery and shooting. Neither Edmondson nor Darrus attempted to obtain medical assistance for Byers after shooting her. The shooting, which took place on March 8, 1995, rendered Byers a paraplegic.

> FN2. This petition was filed on behalf of Patsy Byers, her husband, and their three children. While this appeal was pending, Patsy Byers died. Her estate has been substituted as a plaintiff in her petition. For purposes of this appeal, we will refer to all of the plaintiffs collectively as Byers.

On July 26, 1995, Byers filed suit against Edmondson and Darrus for the damages sustained by Byers and her family as a result of the armed robbery and shooting. In early March 1996, Byers filed a first **supplemental and amending petition** for damages, adding Edmondson's parents and several insurance companies as defendants. In this petition, Byers alleged that the gun used in the shooting was obtained from a cabin owned by Edmondson's parents.

On the same date, Byers filed a second supplemental and amending petition for damages, through which she named Warner Home Video, Inc., Warner Brothers, Inc., Time Warner Entertainment Company, L.P., Time Warner,

allegations   statements in pleading (documents filed with court in which parties explain what the dispute is about) in which a party sets forth its version of what caused the dispute

petition   formal written request to a court asking that something be done

supplemental and amending petition   formal request to court modifying the original petition

Inc., Regency Enterprises [Regency was later dismissed], Alcor Films, J.D. Productions, and Oliver Stone as additional defendants. Byers restated the same prior allegations with respect to the occurrence of the shooting and the obtaining of the weapon used in the shooting. The new allegations asserted that Edmondson and Darrus "went upon a crime spree culminating in the shooting and permanent injury to Patsy Ann Byers as a result of seeing and becoming inspired by the movie *Natural-Born Killers* produced, directed, and distributed by the Hollywood defendants." The amended petition further alleged that "[a]ll of the Hollywood defendants are liable, more particularly, but not exclusively for, distributing a film which they knew or should have known would cause and inspire people such as . . . Edmondson and . . . Darrus, to commit crimes such as the shooting of Patsy Ann Byers, and for producing and distributing a film which glorified the type of violence [Edmondson and Darrus] committed against Patsy Ann Byers by treating individuals who commit such violence as celebrities and heroes, as well as for such other negligence as will be learned during discovery and shown at trial of this matter."

On September 25, 1996, defendant Time Warner Entertainment Company, L.P. (TWEC), . . . a **peremptory exception** raising the objection of no **cause of action.** Additionally, TWEC, Alcor Film & TV GMBH & Co. Produktions KG, Jane and Don Productions Inc., and Oliver Stone (the Warner defendants) [footnote omitted] filed their own peremptory exception raising the objection of no cause of action on September 25, 1996. In the exception, the Warner defendants asserted that they owed no duty to plaintiffs to ensure that none of the viewers of the movie would decide to imitate actions depicted in the fictional film. The Hollywood defendants also denied that they owed a duty to prevent harm inflicted by others absent a "**special relationship**" obligating the defendant to protect the plaintiff from such harm. They further asserted that imposition of such a duty would violate the First Amendment to the United States Constitution and Article 1, Section 7 of the Louisiana Constitution. A hearing on the exception was set for December 16, 1996.

A week before the hearing, on December 9, 1996, Byers filed a third supplemental and amending petition for damages through which she added and supplemented the allegations with respect to the actions and liability of the Warner defendants. Paragraph 1 of plaintiffs' third supplemental and amending petition for damages provides:

> Plaintiffs desire to supplement and amend paragraph V. (E). of their Petition to read as follows:

> V. (E).

> All of the Hollywood defendants are liable, more particularly, but not exclusively:

> (A) for producing and distributing a film (and marketing same on videotape) which they knew, intended, were substantially certain, or should have known would cause or incite persons such as defendants, Sarah Edmondson, and Benjamin Darrus (via subliminal suggestion or glorification of violent acts) to begin, shortly after repeatedly viewing

peremptory exception pleading that questions the sufficiency of law in a petition

cause of action facts giving rise to a legal right to sue

special relationship legal relationship between individuals that requires one individual to take steps toward protecting the other. For example, a parent has a duty to protect her child from certain types of harm.

same, crime sprees such as that which led to the shooting of Patsy Ann Byers;

(B) for negligently and/or recklessly failing to take steps to minimize violent content of the video or to minimize glorification of senselessly violent acts and those who perpetrate such conduct;

(C) by **intentionally, recklessly, or negligently** including in the video subliminal images which either directly advocated violent activity or which would cause viewers to repeatedly view the video and thereby become more susceptible to its advocacy of violent activity; [FN7]

FN7. At oral argument, counsel for Byers acknowledged that he had to abandon the subliminal message allegations in the petition because an examination of the *Natural-Born Killers* video by Byers's expert failed to reveal the presence of the type of subliminal messages alleged in the petition. Thus, for purposes of this appeal, we will ignore the subliminal message allegations contained in the petition.

(D) for negligently and/or recklessly failing to warn viewers of the potential deleterious effects upon teenage viewers caused by repeated viewing of the film/video and of the presence of subliminal messages therein; and

(E) as well as for other such intentional, reckless, or negligent acts will [sic] be learned during discovery and shown at trial of this matter.

intentionally, recklessly, or negligently types of intent. An individual acts intentionally if she intends a particular result. She acts recklessly if she acts with wanton indifference to the consequences of her actions, ignoring a substantial and unjustifiable risk that harm will occur. She acts negligently if she fails to use the care that a reasonable person in those circumstances would use. Intentional conduct is more egregious than reckless conduct, which is more egregious than negligence.

memorandum document setting forth legal arguments and explaining issues of law

Two days later, Byers filed a **memorandum** opposing the Warner defendants' exceptions raising the objection of no cause of action. In this opposition, Byers asserted that Edmondson and Darrus (1) repeatedly viewed the movie on videotape, sometimes under the influence of mind-altering drugs; (2) desired to emulate the protagonists of the video by obtaining a gun and ammunition; and (3) began their own reenactment of the "Mickey and Mallory" story from the film, resulting in the murder of a Mississippi cotton gin owner and brutal attempted murder of Patsy Byers.

reply memorandum memorandum filed in response to an opposing party's memorandum

On the morning of the hearing, the Warner defendants filed a **reply memorandum,** noting that a similar claim filed in Georgia against the Warner defendants as a result of a Georgia murder by a couple who was allegedly imitating the actions of the characters "Mickey and Mallory" from *Natural-Born Killers,* had recently been dismissed for the failure to state a cause of action. Subsequently, on December 23, 1996, defendant Time Warner, Inc., filed . . . a peremptory exception raising the objection of no cause of action in response to Byers's third supplemental and amending petition.

Byers appealed the judgment of the trial court, assigning as error the trial court's finding that Byers's cause of action was proscribed by Louisiana law and United States and Louisiana constitutional guarantees of free speech.

taking the matter under advisement judge's decision to make a decision regarding the matter before him or her at a later date

After **taking the matter under advisement,** the trial court granted [Time Warner's] objection of no cause of action, finding that the "law simply does not recognize a cause of action such as that presented in [Byers's] petition." . . . A **judgment** was signed on January 23, 1997, . . . dismissing Byers's suit as to those claims against the Warner defendants. [footnote omitted] Byers

judgment formal decision by a court

filed a **motion for new trial,** which was denied by the trial court. [footnote omitted] Byers appealed the judgment of the trial court, assigning as error the trial court's finding that Byers's cause of action was proscribed by Louisiana law and United States and Louisiana constitutional guarantees of free speech.

PEREMPTORY EXCEPTION RAISING OBJECTION OF NO CAUSE OF ACTION

The objection of no cause of action is properly raised by the peremptory exception. The exception of no cause of action questions "whether the law extends a remedy to anyone under the factual allegations of the petition." The purpose of an exception pleading the objection of no cause of action is to determine the sufficiency in law of the petition. . . .

Generally, no evidence may be introduced to support or controvert the exception. . . However, . . . the jurisprudence recognizes an exception to this rule, which allows the court to consider evidence which is admitted without objection to enlarge the pleadings. . . . Otherwise, the exception is triable on the face of the pleadings, and, for the purposes of determining the issues raised by the exception, the well-pleaded facts in the petition must be accepted as true. . . The court must determine if the law affords plaintiff a remedy under those facts. . .

When a petition states a cause of action as to any ground or portion of the demand, an exception raising the objection of no cause of action must be overruled. Any doubts are resolved in favor of the sufficiency of the petition. . .

In resolving the issue of whether Byers has a cause of action against the Warner defendants for the shooting, we must determine if the Warner defendants owed a duty to Byers to prevent her from being shot by two people who viewed *Natural-Born Killers* and went on a crime spree shortly thereafter. If we find that such a duty exists under Louisiana law, we must further decide whether the imposition of such a duty violates the guarantee of free speech contained in the First Amendment to the United States Constitution and in Article 1, Section 7 of the Louisiana Constitution.

DUTY

In the petition and supplemental and amending petitions, Byers alleges that the Warner defendants are liable to Byers under Louisiana tort law in that they were negligent and committed an intentional tort. However, before we can find that a cause of action has been set forth based on a negligence or intentional tort theory of recovery under the facts of this case, we must first determine whether a duty was owed by the Warner defendants to Byers. A duty represents a legally enforceable obligation to conform to a particular standard of conduct. . . Louisiana courts have traditionally applied a duty-risk analysis to determine whether a plaintiff has stated a cause of action in tort against a particular defendant. . . This approach is most helpful in cases where the only issue is whether the defendant stands in any relationship to the plaintiff as to create any legally recognized obligation of conduct for the plaintiff's benefit. . . The existence of duty is a question of law for the court

matter of law   disputed legal question, which is usually left for a judge to resolve

to decide from the facts surrounding the occurrence in question. . . When no duty exists, a court will dismiss a petition as a **matter of law** for failure to state a cause of action. . .

The factual allegations which must be accepted as true are that Edmondson and Darrus viewed *Natural-Born Killers* and began a crime spree shortly thereafter; Byers was shot while Edmondson and Darrus were on this crime spree; the Warner defendants produced, directed, and marketed *Natural-Born Killers* for the movie theatres and for video; the Warner defendants did not warn viewers of the film or video of the potential deleterious effects that repeated viewing of the film could have on teenage viewers; the Warner defendants were negligent through the production of a film which they knew, should have known, or intended would incite people such as Edmondson and Darrus to commit violent acts such as the one committed against Byers; the film glorified the type of violence committed by Edmondson and Darrus against Byers through its treatment of individuals in the film who committed such acts as celebrities and heroes; and the Warner defendants failed to take steps to minimize the violent content of the film or the glorification of senselessly violent acts in the film. Thus, Byers essentially contends that the Warner defendants owed her a duty to not produce this film in the form in which it was released and/or to protect her from viewers who would imitate the violent acts or crimes committed by the film's two main characters and cause her harm.

We recognize that in Louisiana, a defendant does not owe a duty to protect a person from the criminal acts of third parties absent a special relationship which obligates the defendant to protect the plaintiff from such harm. . . We further note that in the present case, Byers has not, nor can she allege the existence of such a special relationship.

However, we agree with Byers that based on the allegations of the petition which we must accept as true for purposes of . . . [this] cause of action, the Warner defendants are liable as a result of their misfeasance in that they produced and released a film containing violent imagery which was intended to cause its viewers to imitate the violent imagery. If the intentional action allegations contained in the petition can be proven at trial, the imposition of a duty would be warranted based on the same rationale used by the California court in Weirum v. RKO General, Inc., 15 Cal.3d 40, 123 Cal.Rptr. 468, 539 P.2d 36 (1975) to impose a similar duty.

In Weirum, a radio station was liable for injuries caused by the negligent acts of its listeners responding to a broadcast by one of the radio's disc jockeys. The specific broadcast was made in conjunction with a contest sponsored by the station wherein listeners were encouraged and directed to be the first to locate a traveling disc jockey. The station would periodically announce the most recent location of the traveling disc jockey. The reward was money and prizes. While two listeners were rushing to find the traveling disc jockey, in response to the most recent broadcast by the station regarding the traveling disc jockey's whereabouts, they forced a third vehicle off the road. The driver of this third vehicle died as a result of the accident. The deceased driver's family filed a civil suit against the radio station. The California court, in imposing liability upon the radio station, found that a duty was owed to prevent the type of harm befallen by the deceased because the risk of harm to the deceased was imminently foreseeable. The court focused on the fact that the radio station directly urged motorist/listeners to immediately speed to a destination if they wanted to receive a prize. . .

If in fact, plaintiffs can prove their allegation that the Warner defendants, through the creation and release of *Natural-Born Killers*, intended to urge viewers to imitate the criminal conduct of Mickey and Mallory, the main characters in the film, then the risk of harm to a person such as Byers would be imminently **foreseeable,** justifying the imposition of a duty upon the Warner defendants to refrain from creating such a film. The breach of this duty would render the Warner defendants liable for the damages inflicted on innocent third parties such as Patsy Byers by viewers of the film imitating the violent imagery depicted in the film.

While we note that courts across the nation have generally refused to hold filmmakers, producers, directors, and/or promoters liable for injuries allegedly sustained from others imitating actions or scenes depicted in a film, television broadcast, or magazine, or described in a song, many of these dismissals came after the filing of a **motion for summary judgment,** or even after a trial on the merits and thus, after the parties had the opportunity to conduct **discovery** pertinent to the alleged facts. See Way v. Boy Scouts of America, 856 S.W.2d 230 (Tex.App. 5th Dist.1993) (motion for summary judgment granted dismissing plaintiff's claims against the publisher of a firearm advertisement in a magazine which advertisement allegedly caused a fatal firearm injury to plaintiff's son); Yakubowicz v. Paramount Pictures Corporation, 404 Mass. 624, 536 N.E.2d 1067 (1989) (motion for summary judgment granted dismissing plaintiff's claim that the producer of a gang violence film was liable for the murder of plaintiff's son who had viewed the film); Bill v. Superior Court of the City and County of San Francisco, 137 Cal.App.3d 1002, 187 Cal.Rptr. 625 (1st Dist.1982) (motion for summary judgment granted dismissing plaintiff's claim that the producer of a gang violence film was liable for the shooting of plaintiff's daughter by a third party shortly after both saw the film); DeFilippo v. National Broadcasting Co., Inc., 446 A.2d 1036 (R.I.1982) (motion for summary judgment granted dismissing plaintiff's claim that the broadcast of a hanging stunt on a television program caused the death of plaintiff's son who tried to imitate the stunt); Walt Disney Productions, Inc. v. Shannon, 247 Ga. 402, 276 S.E.2d 580 (1981) (motion for summary judgment granted dismissing plaintiff's claim that the broadcast of a television program caused plaintiff's son to be injured when the son imitated an experiment performed on the television program); and Olivia N. v. National Broadcasting Co., Inc., 126 Cal.App.3d 488, 178 Cal.Rptr. 888 (1st Dist.1981) (**judgment of non-suit** granted at trial when plaintiff admitted that the film at issue in the suit did not incite the unlawful behavior which injured the plaintiff). It was a rare situation where the dismissal was granted based solely on the allegations contained in the petition. See Zamora v. Columbia Broadcasting System, 480 F.Supp. 199 (S.D.Fla.1979); see also McCollum v. CBS, Inc., 202 Cal.App.3d 989, 249 Cal.Rptr. 187 (2nd Dist.1988). We do not find these two latter cases to be persuasive to our decision in the present case.

foreseeable   something that a person of ordinary caution would expect to occur

motion for summary judgment   request for judgment in favor of the moving party on the grounds that no genuine issue of fact is in dispute

discovery   process by which parties can obtain information pertinent to their dispute

judgment of non-suit termination of an action based on lack of evidence

In Zamora v. Columbia Broadcasting System, 480 F.Supp. 199, the pleadings did not contain any allegations of intentional conduct by the film producers. In this case, the petition contains allegations that the Warner defendants intended to cause the viewers of *Natural-Born Killers* to imitate the conduct of Mickey and Mallory and go on crime sprees involving the type of crime committed upon Patsy Byers. In McCollum v. CBS, Inc., 202 Cal.App.3d 989, 249 Cal.Rptr. 187, the lyrics of a song were at issue and the court had the opportunity to examine all of the lyrics before deciding to dismiss the suit. Presently, the entire film is not before the court for examination as it was not introduced as evidence at the hearing . . . raising the objection of no cause of action. Accordingly, based on the allegations contained in Byers's petition, we find that Byers has stated a cause of action for an intentional tort against the Warner defendants under Louisiana tort law.

Because we find that under the allegations of the petition, accepted as true, the Warner defendants may owe a duty to Byers and thus, the petition states a cause of action under Louisiana law, we must address the Warner defendants' claim that the imposition of a duty would be in contravention of the guarantee of free speech contained in the First Amendment to the United States Constitution and Article 1, Section 7 of the Louisiana Constitution. Byers contends that the conduct of the Warner defendants in creating *Natural-Born Killers* is not protected speech because it falls into two of the exceptions to the First Amendment guarantee of free speech: the obscenity exception and the incitement to imminent lawless activity exception.

First Amendment rights are accorded a preferred place in our democratic society. First Amendment protection extends to a communication, to its source, and to its recipients. Above all else, the First Amendment means that government has no power to restrict expression because of its message, its ideas, its subject matter, or its content. . . The fact that a case does not involve government restriction of speech does not prevent the barring of an action by the first amendment. The chilling effect of permitting the imposition of civil liability based on negligence is obvious—the fear of damage awards may be markedly more inhibiting than the fear of prosecution under a criminal statute. . . Motion pictures are a significant medium for the communication of ideas and are protected by the First Amendment, just like other forms of expression. . .

However, the freedom of speech guaranteed by the First Amendment is not absolute. There are certain limited classes of speech which may be prevented or punished by the state consistent with the principles of the First Amendment: (1) obscene speech; (2) libel, slander, misrepresentation, obscenity, perjury, false advertising, solicitation of crime, complicity by encouragement, conspiracy, and the like; (3) speech or writing used as an integral part of conduct in violation of a valid criminal statute; and (4) speech which is directed to inciting or producing imminent lawless action, and which is likely to incite or produce such action. . .

Byers argues that *Natural-Born Killers* falls within the incitement to imminent lawless activity exception to the First Amendment. The constitutional guarantee of free speech does not permit a state to forbid or proscribe advocacy of the use of force or of law violation except where such advocacy is directed to inciting or producing imminent lawless action and is likely to incite or produce such action. . . Thus, to justify a claim that speech should be restrained or punished because it is (or was) an incitement to lawless action, the court must be satisfied that the speech (1) was directed or intended toward the goal of producing imminent lawless conduct and (2) was likely to produce such imminent conduct. Speech directed to action at some indefinite time in the future will not satisfy this test. Moreover, speech does not lose its First Amendment protection merely because it has "a tendency to lead to violence." . . .

In Byers's third supplemental and amending petition, it is alleged that the Warner defendants intended to incite viewers of the film to begin, shortly after viewing the film, crime sprees such as the one that led to the shooting of Patsy Byers. We must accept this allegation as true for purposes of the peremptory exception raising the objection of no cause of action. Once accepted as true, the film *Natural- Born Killers* would fall into the unprotected category of speech directed to inciting or producing imminent lawless action and which is likely to incite or produce such action.

We note that in Rice v. Paladin Enterprises, Incorporated, 128 F.3d 233 (4th Cir.1997), the United States Fourth Circuit Court of Appeal held that the publisher of a book which contained step-by-step instructions on how to be a hit man could be civilly liable for the deaths of victims killed by a third person who followed the instructions in the book to murder the victims. The issue before the court was whether the book was protected under the First Amendment. The court found that the particular book was not protected speech. The United States Supreme Court **denied writs**. . . .

denied writs   court refused to review the lower court's decision

In Rice, it was stipulated by Paladin that it not only knew that the book's instructions might be used by murderers, but, it actually intended to provide assistance to murderers and would-be murderers.

The U.S. Fourth Circuit further stated:

> In other words, the First Amendment might well circumscribe the power of the state to create and enforce a cause of action that would permit the imposition of civil liability, such as aiding and abetting civil liability, for speech that would constitute pure abstract advocacy, at least if that speech were not "directed to inciting or producing imminent lawless action, and . . . likely to incite or produce such action." . . . The instances in which such advocacy might give rise to civil liability under state statute would seem rare, but they are not inconceivable. . .

* * * * * *

After carefully and repeatedly reading *Hit Man* in its entirety, we are of the view that the book so overtly promotes murder in concrete, nonabstract terms that we regard as disturbingly disingenuous both Paladin's cavalier suggestion that the book is essentially a comic book whose

amici friend of the court; a non-party who provides information to the court

"fantastical" promotion of murder no one could take seriously, and **amici**'s reckless characterization of the book as "almost avuncular," see Br. of Amici at 8-9. The unique text of *Hit Man* alone, boldly proselytizing and glamorizing the crime of murder and the "profession" of murder as it dispassionately instructs on its commission, is more than sufficient to create a triable issue of fact as to Paladin's intent in publishing and selling the manual.

* * * * * *

Paladin, joined by a spate of media amici, including many of the major networks, newspapers, and publishers, contends that any decision recognizing even a potential cause of action against Paladin will have far-reaching chilling effects on the rights of free speech and press. See Br. of Amici at 3, 22 ("Allowing this lawsuit to survive will disturb decades of First Amendment jurisprudence and jeopardize free speech from the periphery to the core. . . . No expression—music, video, books, even newspaper articles—would be safe from civil liability."). That the national media organizations would feel obliged to vigorously defend Paladin's assertion of a constitutional right to intentionally and knowingly assist murderers with technical information which Paladin admits it intended and knew would be used immediately in the commission of murder and other crimes against society is, to say the least, breathtaking. But be that as it may, it should be apparent from the foregoing that the indisputably important First Amendment values that Paladin and amici argue would be imperiled by a decision recognizing potential liability under the peculiar facts of this case will not even arguably be adversely affected by allowing plaintiffs' action against Paladin to proceed. In fact, neither the extensive briefing by the parties and the numerous amici in this case, nor the exhaustive research which the court itself has undertaken, has revealed even a single case that we regard as factually analogous to this case.

Paladin and amici insist that recognizing the existence of a cause of action against Paladin predicated on aiding and abetting will subject broadcasters and publishers to liability whenever someone imitates or "copies" conduct that is either described or depicted in their broadcasts, publications, or movies. This is simply not true. In the "copycat" context, it will presumably never be the case that the broadcaster or publisher actually intends, through its description or depiction, to assist another or others in the commission of violent crime; rather, the information for the dissemination of which liability is sought to be imposed will actually have been misused vis-a-vis the use intended, not, as here, used precisely as intended. It would be difficult to overstate the significance of this difference insofar as the potential liability to which the media might be exposed by our decision herein is concerned.

And, perhaps most importantly, there will almost never be evidence proffered from which a jury even could reasonably conclude that the producer or publisher possessed the actual intent to assist criminal

stipulated mutually agree to avoid the need to present arguments

activity. In only the rarest case, as here where the publisher has **stipulated** in almost taunting defiance that it intended to assist murderers and other criminals, will there be evidence extraneous to the speech itself which would support a finding of the requisite intent; surely few will, as Paladin has, "stand up and proclaim to the world that because they are publishers they have a unique constitutional right to aid and abet murder." Appellant's Reply Br. at 20. Moreover, in contrast to the case before us, in virtually every "copycat" case, there will be lacking in the speech itself any basis for a permissible inference that the "speaker" intended to assist and facilitate the criminal conduct described or depicted. Of course, with few, if any, exceptions, the speech which gives rise to the copycat crime will not directly and affirmatively promote the criminal conduct, even if, in some circumstances, it incidentally glamorizes and thereby indirectly promotes such conduct. . .

As previously indicated, plaintiffs have alleged the very intent on the part of the Warner defendants referred to by the Rice court. Because this case is before us on a peremptory exception pleading the objection of no cause of action, we must accept this allegation as true. However, in holding that plaintiffs' allegations of intent state a cause of action, we do not address the issue of whether the Warner defendants may later invoke the protection of the First Amendment guarantee of free speech to bar Byers' claim after discovery has taken place. It is only by accepting the allegations in Byers' petition as true that we conclude that the film falls into the incitement to imminent lawless activity exception to the First Amendment. We agree with Rice v. Paladin Enterprises, Incorporated, 128 F.3d 233, that the mere foreseeability or knowledge that the publication might be misused for a criminal purpose is not sufficient for liability. Proof of intent necessary for liability in cases such as the instant one will be remote and even rare, but at this stage of the proceeding we find that Byers' cause of action is not barred by the First Amendment. Since we have determined that the allegations of plaintiffs' petition bring the case at this stage into the incitement to imminent lawless activity exception, we need not address Byers' claim that the film constitutes obscene speech.

CONCLUSION

remanded send back to the lower court

For these reasons, the judgment of the trial court is reversed and the matter is **remanded** to the trial court for further proceedings consistent with the views expressed herein. Costs of this appeal are assessed to the Warner defendants.

REVERSED AND REMANDED.

(1998).

Court, and that it was ultimately granted *cert* in the U.S. Supreme Court. This history includes the following:

- ◆ names and relationships between the parties
- ◆ why the parties appealed
- ◆ claims and defenses that have been raised
- ◆ names of courts involved
- ◆ results of each court proceeding

disposition practical effect of a court's decision

Pay particular attention to the disposition of the case at each level. The **disposition** is the practical effect of the court's decision. For example, an appellate court may dispose of a case by remanding it back to the lower court, or a trial court may dispose of a case by entering an award for damages for the plaintiff.

Knowing the procedural history is important because the status of a case is affected by several factors.

LEVEL OF THE REVIEWING COURT

precedential extent to which a court is controlled by an earlier court's decision

An opinion written by a state's highest court holds more weight than one written by a lower court, just as an opinion by the U.S. Supreme Court has more **precedential** value than one written by a lower federal court.

RESOURCES COURT DEVOTES TO CASE

per curiam **opinion** court opinion with no identified author

memorandum decision decision that identifies the court's decision or order but offers no explanation

An opinion that is rendered *en banc* usually involves issues that are more critical than those heard by a panel of judges. On the other hand, a ***per curiam* opinion** (which has no designated author) or a **memorandum decision** (which identifies a court's decision or order but offers no reason for the opinion) involves little or no discussion. Although such decisions have precedential value, they lack the persuasiveness of more fully developed opinions.

CLOSENESS OF VOTE

Opinions that are supported by a clear majority of the judges tend to carry more weight than those in which the vote is close. An opinion supported by seven out of nine justices is more likely to stand over time than an opinion in which the vote is five to four. With the latter opinion, the majority could shift if one justice were to be replaced or change votes.

plurality opinions opinion in which no majority exists

Plurality opinions carry less weight than decisions commanding a clear majority. In plurality opinions, no majority exists because the judges come to the same conclusion but for different reasons; seven of the nine justices may reach the same conclusion, but four may decide on the basis of reason A while three decide on the basis of reason B. The plurality opinion is the one authored by the four justices who subscribe to reason A.

REACTION OF HIGHER COURT

overturned to change the decision of a lower appellate court

Opinions that are implicitly endorsed by higher courts have greater precedential value than those that are accepted for review. If a petition for *certiorari* is denied by the U.S. Supreme Court or by the highest court in the state, the lower court's decision stands, because the higher court has refused to review it. If *cert* is accepted, on the other hand, the lower court's decision may be **overturned** (changed), resulting in the lower court's opinion being vacated. (Note that reversal occurs when a reviewing court changes the decision of a lower trial court, and overturning occurs when a reviewing court changes the decision of a lower appellate court or one of its own earlier decisions.) Obviously, greater reliance can be placed on a decision in which appellate remedies have been exhausted than on one in which review is still possible.

Figure 3-10
Status of a Case

STATUS OF A CASE

Level of Reviewing Court
Resources Court Devotes to Case
Closeness of Vote
Plurality Opinion
Reaction of Higher Court

Having read the opinion carefully once, Martha was aware that understanding some of the unique procedural aspects of *Byers* was critical to understanding what the court had done. She knew that it was important that Time Warner, one of the defendants in this case, had filed a "peremptory exception" because the court alluded to this procedural point throughout the opinion. Not knowing what a "peremptory exception" was, she relied on the court's explanation that the purpose of such a pleading is to "determine the sufficiency in law of the petition."

Then she summarized the procedural history.

The plaintiff filed a suit, followed by two supplemental and amended petitions for damages in which she added defendants. One of the defendants, TWEC, filed several motions, one of which was a peremptory exception objecting that no cause of action existed. In response, the plaintiff filed another supplemental and amended petition for damages in which she added allegations and filed a response memorandum objecting to TWEC's exceptions, to which TWEC filed a reply memorandum. The district court granted the peremptory exception raising the objection of no cause of action and dismissed plaintiff's suit against most of the defendants. Plaintiff appealed the judgment of the district court.

Putting It Into Practice 3.8:

Write out the procedural history for *Weirum v. RKO*.

Facts

Facts are an integral part of case law. In fact, case law is basically legal principles woven around facts. Without facts to flesh them out, legal principles are hollow recitations. A brief should contain all the essential facts (those facts whose absence or modification would alter the outcome of a case) as well as any background or historical facts that enhance an understanding of the nature of the dispute. Essential facts in an abortion case might be that the female seeking the abortion is a juvenile and that she was the victim of a sexual assault.

Martha Knew That the Facts In Byers Were Important.

Martha knew that the facts in *Byers* were important because the court stated that its decision was based on the plaintiff's allegations and premised its conclusion on the plaintiff's ability to prove those allegations at trial. The court had summarized the facts of the case and the procedural facts at the beginning of the opinion, making it easy for Martha to pull out the essential facts of what had led up to the plaintiff's injury.

Defendants Edmonson and Darrus shot and severely wounded the plaintiff while robbing a convenience store. Having repeatedly watched the depiction of a violent killing spree in the movie *Natural-Born Killers,* the defendants decided to emulate the protagonists in the movie by attempting to murder the plaintiff. The movie was produced by Time Warner Entertainment Company (TWEC).

███████ *Putting It Into Practice 3.9:*

Write out the facts for *Weirum v. RKO.*

Issue and Holding

issue the question of law the court is answering in its opinion

The essential facts must be included in the statement of the issue. The **issue** is the question of law the court is answering in its opinion. In most cases, more than one issue is at stake. Understanding the issue is critical to the understanding of a case. Oftentimes, when people read a court opinion and find the court's conclusion or reasoning process invalid, it is because they have misinterpreted the legal issue.

Writing a statement of the issue is often challenging for novices to the law. Students frequently err by writing issues that are far too broad and that lack the essential facts. An example of an issue that has been stated too broadly follows.

Did the defendant commit a burglary?

Notice that without some factual information detailing the circumstances under which the defendant was accused of committing a burglary, this statement alone is virtually meaningless. Issue statements are written with more detail for three reasons: (1) spelling out the issue in concrete terms forces you to analyze the issue to ensure that you really understand it; (2) the case should be distinguishable from other case law; and (3) you should be able to ascertain the issue without having to reread the facts section. In light of these factors, a more appropriate issue statement might be the following.

Can a defendant who legally enters a building but who remains unlawfully in order to steal documents be convicted of burglary?

holding answer to the question raised in the issue

Notice that this phrasing allows the issue to be answered with a "yes" or "no." The answer to the question of law identified in the issue statement is the **holding.** Having a simple holding not only relieves you of some writing, it makes it easier to remember case law. Therefore, while your issue statements may be rather complex, your holdings will generally be very simple. Of course, issues cannot always be answered "yes" or "no," and an accurate answer may require a brief explanation. If, for example, the issue before the court is what standard of care is required of a driver, the holding must reflect an explanation of that standard and cannot be answered "yes" or "no."

dicta plural of *dictum* (coming from the Latin phrase *obiter dictum*) gratuitous remarks by the court in a court opinion regarding issues that were not raised by any of the parties

It is possible to confuse ***dicta*** with the holding of a court. *Dicta* refers to remarks by the court that are unnecessary to the court's decision and, most importantly, pertain to issues not raised by any of the parties. *Dicta* are not binding on the court and other parties and cannot be cited to another court as the law. In fact, presenting *dicta* to a court as legal precedent is unethical because to do so could mislead the court.

Finding the Issue Was Straightforward Because the Court Had Neatly Summarized the Two Questions Before It.

Finding the issue was straightforward in this case because the court had neatly summarized the two questions before it. (See paragraph immediately preceding headnotes 7–10.) Martha generalized the court's characterization of the issue by taking it beyond the parties in this case and then put it in the form of a question. She phrased the issues so that they could be simply answered "yes" or "no."

Issue 1: Does a movie company owe a duty to third parties who are injured by those who view one of its movies that depicts a violent crime spree and who injure others in the process of emulating that crime spree?

Holding 1: Yes

Issue 2: Is the constitutional protection of freedom of speech violated by the imposition of such a duty?

Holding 2: No

███ *Putting It Into Practice 3.10:*

Write out the issues and holdings for *Weirum v. RKO.*

Rationale

rationale reasoning used by the court

Lawyers and litigants are rarely satisfied with simply knowing a court's holding. They want to know the reasons supporting the court's conclusion because that reasoning serves as a guide to how future cases will be decided. For this reason, the **rationale** (reasoning) offered by courts must be mastered by those who practice law. Understanding case law is based on an understanding of rationale, not a mere knowledge of holdings. Students of the law sometimes focus their energies on committing holdings to memory, but then skim briefly over the rationale. They ulti-

black letter law law that is standard and not subject to change

mately discover that knowledge of **black letter law** (law that is standard and not subject to change, such as the elements of a tort) is important, but that complete comprehension of a court's reasoning is even more important if black letter law is to be applied to a client's particular facts.

public policy questions of fairness and justice that courts use to guide their decisions

In their reasoning process, most courts do one or more of the following.

◆ define an ambiguous term or concept
◆ choose between conflicting provisions of the law

case of first impression case pertaining to an issue that the court hearing the case has not considered before

◆ apply legal principles to a fact situation that differs to some degree from the fact patterns in other appellate decisions
◆ decide how **public policy** would best be served

The Court Explained Why the Defendants, Who Generally Owe No Duty to Persons Harmed by the Criminal Acts of Third Persons, Did Have a Duty Under the Facts Alleged In the Plaintiff's Petition.

Martha had to read the court's discussion about duty more carefully to pull out the essential aspects of its reasoning. She zoomed in on the paragraph corresponding to headnote 11 in which the court explained why the defendants, who generally owe no duty to persons harmed by the criminal acts of third persons, did have a duty under the facts alleged in the plaintiff's petition. Knowing that this was probably a **case of first impression** for the First Circuit and aware that the court was one of the first courts to find the existence of a duty, she was careful to explain how the court had distinguished its facts from the facts in other opinions in which no duty had been found.

As she went on to summarize the court's reasoning regarding the issue of free speech, she carefully read the court's explanation about speech that is unprotected by the First Amendment because it is intended to incite imminent lawless action. As someone unfamiliar with the basic tenets of constitutional law, she appreciated the court's nutshell version of the law in that area.

Then she wrote:

(1) Generally, defendants owe no duty to protect persons from criminal acts of third parties unless some kind of special relationship exists that requires the defendant to protect the plaintiff. When, however, those who produce and release a film containing violent imagery with the intent of causing the viewers to imitate that violence, they have a duty to those who are injured as a result of that acting out. This duty is contingent on the plaintiff's ability to prove that the defendants intended viewers to imitate the conduct of the actors and go on a crime spree.

(2) A film that is intended to incite viewers to go on a crime spree like that depicted in *Natural-Born Killers* falls within the incitement to imminent lawless activity exception to the First Amendment. Proof of intent is necessary to fall under this exception; merely knowing that someone might misuse the film for criminal purposes is not sufficient.

Synthesis

When briefing two or more cases, you must synthesize the rules of law that can be derived from those cases. To ascertain these rules, you must compare the issues and rationale considered in each case. Do the issues involve similar or dissimilar fact patterns? What kind of reasoning process did each court use and how do those reasoning processes compare? A synthesis goes beyond merely restating each court's holdings. It compares the outcomes of the cases and attempts to harmonize these outcomes into a set of logically consistent rules of law.

Synthesis prods you to see the interrelationships among cases. After reading several cases dealing with the same issue, you may be hard pressed to see the similarities and dissimilarities. Through synthesis, you begin to see a consistent pattern and formulate a general principle applicable in similar scenarios. Or, to the contrary, you may see a divergence in rationale and then may be able to identify some criteria for distinguishing cases. In synthesis, you begin to understand why courts with similar fact patterns arrive at dissimilar results. You also see connections between cases that are ostensibly unrelated factually.

In *Byers,* the court synthesizes case law from other courts, refusing to find producers liable for injuries sustained from others imitating acts depicted in films. The court explains that the connection between these cases is that they were dismissed after the parties had been able to discover the facts. After listing numerous cases, the court points out that the last two cases are not persuasive because they contain no allegations of intentional conduct. The court uses this litany of cases to demonstrate why it came to a different conclusion: the facts before it were different from the facts before the other courts. The *Byers* court had to accept the allegations in the plaintiff's petition that the defendants had engaged in intentional conduct. Based on those unique facts, the court found the movie producers had a duty, but the court made it clear that if the plaintiff were unable to prove those facts, the producers would have no duty.

Case synthesis is the crux of legal analysis. Without it, legal research is reduced to stockpiling cases. If you cannot synthesize what you have gathered, you will never go beyond merely having an impressive collection of cases. Ferreting out relevant case law is an important skill, but if you cannot synthesize these cases on the basis of their similarities and dissimilarities, your value to an attorney is limited. Therefore, synthesis is a skill you need to cultivate.

NET NEWS

For more insights about the importance and process of briefing, go to *www.vcsun.org/~djordan/legalwrite.htm* and click on "Briefing Cases."

Figure 3-11
Diagram of Synthesis

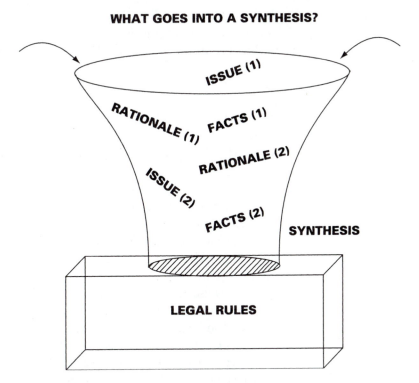

WHAT GOES INTO A SYNTHESIS?

ISSUE (1)

RATIONALE (1) FACTS (1)

RATIONALE (2)

ISSUE (2)

FACTS (2)

SYNTHESIS

LEGAL RULES

BONUS POINTERS:

IMPORTANCE OF BRIEFING

While doing legal research, you will find briefing cases to be absolutely essential to gaining an understanding of case law. Simply reading cases fosters passive participation. In other words, you can read a case over and over without gaining any real understanding of the court's reasoning. But if you put pen to paper and translate what you have read into your own words, you become actively engaged. The active engagement dramatically enhances your ability to critically reflect on the case. Writing forces the brain to engage in a creative process. In this process, you begin to see connections and interrelationships, to ask critical questions, and to postulate possible extensions of legal principles. Without engaging in such a critical thinking process, you might never get past a superficial understanding of a case. You might also find that you are confused or do not really understand what the court is saying.

To better understand the difference between active and passive learning, reflect for a moment on the difference between your preparation for a multiple-choice exam and your preparation for an essay exam. Is it not true that your understanding of a subject need be only fairly superficial for you to pass a typical multiple-choice test? Do you not have to be much better prepared and possess a much higher level of understanding to pass an essay exam on the same material? By the same token, reading a case several times may allow you to pass a superficial multiple-choice test on it, but writing a case brief better prepares you for an in-depth essay exam.

RECESS

SUMMARY – PART A

Legal disputes are resolved at the trial court level. When litigants are unhappy with that resolution, they can appeal to the appellate courts. At the federal level, trials are held in the district courts; decisions made in those courts are reviewed in the U.S. circuit courts of appeal (circuit courts). Each state has at least one district court; some states have two or three. District court judges are assisted by magistrates and bankruptcy judges. Thirteen circuit courts have been created (eleven geographical regions plus a circuit for the District of Columbia and a Federal Circuit Court that handles specialized cases). Review by the U.S. Supreme Court, the highest court in the federal system, is discretionary and is initiated when a party files a writ of certiorari. If four of the nine justices deem the case to be *cert* worthy they will direct the lower court to send its records and files to the Supreme Court for review. Very few cases are accepted for review. The district courts, circuit courts, and U.S. Supreme Court are all constitutional courts, but Congress has also created legislative courts, such as the U.S. Tax Court and U.S. Claims Court.

Appellate courts do not hear testimony or receive evidence, so they must render their decisions based on the court record prepared at trial. The appeal process begins when the appellant files a brief and the appellee responds. The court may or may not allow oral arguments. Most appeals are heard by a panel of judges, but on occasion may be heard by the court *en banc*. The appellate may either affirm, reverse, or modify the lower court's decision and has the option of remanding the case back to the trial court to remedy the error.

Most state court systems follow the same three-tiered hierarchy used in the federal system, with the trial court usually being designated as superior court, the appellate court being the court of appeals, and the highest court being the supreme court. Many states also have additional courts of limited jurisdiction. The appellate process is similar to the one used in the federal system. Judges are either elected, appointed, or selected and retained in accordance with some form of the Missouri Plan.

Cases can be found in both official and unofficial reporters. The latter have headnotes, which facilitate the research process. Cases are also available online via Westlaw and LEXIS/NEXIS. Cases can be located through the information provided in case citations. Case briefs assist one in understanding case law and usually consist of a citation, procedural history, facts, holding, and rationale. Knowing the procedural history of a case is important because the status of a case is affected by the level of the reviewing court, the resources the court devotes to the case, the closeness of the vote, and the reaction of the higher court to the case. Briefs should contain all essential facts, which must be included in the issue statement. The rationale is important to master because understanding case law is based on understanding the rationale of the courts.

KEY TERMS

Advance sheets
Affirmed
Allegations
Amici
Annotated
Appeals
Appellant
Appellee
Bankruptcy judges
Binding
Black letter law
Brief (n. and v.)
Caption
Case brief
Case of first impression
Cause of action
Circuit court
Citation
Cite checking
Concurring opinions

Constitutional courts
Denied Writ
Dicta
Discovery
Discretionary
Disposition
Dissenting opinions
District court
Docket number
En banc
Foreseeable
General jurisdiction
Headnotes
Holding
International, reckless, or
   negligent
Issue
Judgment
Judgment of non-suit
Legislative courts

LEXIS/NEXIS
Limited jurisdiction
Magistrates
Matter of law
Memorandum
Memorandum decision
Motion for a new trial
Motion for summary
   judgment
Official reporter
Oral arguments
Overturned
Parallel cites
Per curiam opinion
Peremptory exception
Petition
Plurality opinions
Precedential
Public policy
Rationale

Remand
Remanded
Reply memorandum
Reporter
Reversed
Slip opinions
Special relationship
Stipulated
Supplemental and
   amending petition
Syllabus
Taking the matter under
   advisement
Unofficial reporter
West numbering system
Westlaw
Writ of *certiorari*

REVIEW QUESTIONS – PART A

1. Describe the structure of the federal court system.
2. Describe how cases are accepted for review by the U.S. Supreme Court and what happens once they are accepted for review.
3. What is the difference between constitutional courts and legislative courts?
4. How does your state court system compare with the federal system? How are judges selected in your state?
5. What is the difference between official and unofficial reporters? Give an example of each.
6. Identify the following components of a court opinion.
   a. caption
   b. citation
   c. docket number
   d. syllabus
   e. headnotes
7. Where would you find the following cases?
   a. 297 A.2d 596
   b. 105 U.S. 235
   c. 150 F. Supp. 58
   d. 89 F.2d 678
8. What is the purpose of a case brief? What are its elements?
9. Why is it important to be aware of the procedural history of a case?
10. What are some things to keep in mind when writing an issue statement in a case brief?
11. What kinds of approaches do courts usually take in creating their rationale?

PRACTICE EXAM – PART A

MULTIPLE CHOICE

1. District courts
   a. are the trial courts at the federal level
   b. are found in some states but not others
   c. house magistrates who preside over most trials
   d. are courts of limited jurisdiction
2. The U.S. Court of Appeals
   a. has 13 geographical circuits
   b. is the highest appellate court in the federal system
   c. has a separate circuit for the District of Columbia
   d. none of the above
3. The U.S. Supreme Court
   a. has ten judges
   b. accepts most cases for review
   c. must deem a case *cert* worthy before it can be reviewed
   d. issues a full written opinion for every case it reviews
4. Appeals
   a. may result in the appellate court remanding the case back to the trial court
   b. begin when the appellee files a brief
   c. are usually heard by the court sitting *en banc*
   d. always include an opportunity for the attorneys to make oral arguments
5. Examples of legislative courts are
   a. district and circuit courts
   b. U.S. Tax Court and U.S. Claims Court
   c. U.S. Supreme Court and state supreme courts
   d. none of the above
6. Judges who serve on constitutional courts
   a. are appointed for life
   b. cannot be terminated unless they resign or are impeached
   c. must be approved by the Senate
   d. all of the above
7. In the state court system
   a. in New York the trial court is called the supreme court
   b. the superior court in most states is a court of limited jurisdiction
   c. appeals are made to the circuit courts
   d. all of the above
8. Under the Missouri Plan
   a. judges are elected
   b. judges are appointed by the governor and then retained by election
   c. judges are appointed for life
   d. none of the above
9. Unofficial reporters
   a. are easier to use because they contain headnotes
   b. are always annotated
   c. are published by government agencies
   d. all of the above
10. Online databases
    a. are relatively inexpensive to access
    b. offer some of the most current information
    c. are available but not widely used by most legal researchers
    d. all of the above

11. Headnotes
    a. are written by the court
    b. summarize particular factual issues
    c. allow you to read cases more efficiently
    d. can be relied on to accurately reflect what the court has said in its opinion

*12. Reading cases can be challenging because
    a. the courts assume the reader has an understanding of basic legal principles
    b. case law generally deals with complex issues
    c. some cases are poorly written
    d. all of the above

13. If the citation for a case is 156 P.2d 127 (N.M. 1996)
    a. the case can be found on page 156 of the *Pacific Reporter*
    b. the case was heard in the New Mexico Court of Appeals
    c. the case can be found in the *Pacific Reporter, Second Series* in volume 156
    d. none of the above

14. Case briefs
    a. should be written in your own words
    b. summarize the facts, issues, and holdings of a case
    c. should be prepared as you read a case
    d. should be prepared in accordance with the standard format used by all law professors

15. The status of a case is affected by
    a. the reaction of the higher court to that case
    b. the level of the court reviewing it
    c. the closeness of the vote
    d. all of the above

16. A well-written issue statement in a case brief
    a. should contain all the essential facts
    b. should be written as broadly as possible
    c. must be able to be answered either "yes" or "no"
    d. all of the above

17. In its reasoning process, a court will usually
    a. consider public policy
    b. define an ambiguous term or concept
    c. consider conflicting provisions in the law
    d. all of the above

FILL IN THE BLANK

18. At the federal level, the _____ courts are the trial courts and the _____ courts are the courts of first appeal.

19. District court judges are assisted by _____ judges and _____ .

20. Parties who want the U.S. Supreme Court to review their case must file a _____ .

21. The appeal process begins when the _____ (person initiating an appeal) files a _____ (written argument) to which the _____ (party responding to an appeal) must respond. The parties may then be given an opportunity to present _____ at which they present their arguments and answer the court's questions.

22. An appellate court has the option of _____ (letting it stand) a lower court's decision or _____ (changing it) it; if it does the latter, the appellate court will probably _____ the case back to the trial court so it can remedy its error.

23. If all the appellate court judges hear a case, they are said to sit _____ .

24. A state superior court is a court of _____ jurisdiction, but a probate court is a court of _____ jurisdiction.

25. _____ reporters are published by the government and are not as easy to use as _____ , which are published by private companies. The latter contains _____ , which are numbered, short paragraphs that summarize the principles of law discussed by the court.

26. A reporter that contains references to other cases and legal sources is said to be _____ .

27. Court opinions contain a _____ , which identifies the parties and their relationship, a _____ , which provides information identifying where the case can be located, a _____ , which is a number assigned by the court clerk to a case, and a _____ , which is a brief synopsis of the opinion.

28. _____ facilitate the research process by summarizing specific points of law discussed by the court and the _____ also facilitates research by organizing legal issues alphabetically by topic and numerically by subtopic.

29. _____ opinions are written by judges who agree with the opinion of the majority but reach that conclusion using different or additional reasoning.

30. A _____ provides information about how to locate a case in both official and unofficial reporters.

31. A court opinion just issued by a court will first be published as a _____ and later in the form of _____ , which are filed at the end of the bound volumes.

32. A case of _____ is one that involves an issue that has never been heard by that court before.

33. The best way to learn to transform legal abstractions in a case into workable principles you can work with is to _____ the case.

34. The _____ of a case brief contains the names of the courts involved, the results of each court proceeding, and the names of the parties who appealed and why.

35. One possible way for an appellate court to _____ of a case is to remand it back to the trial court.

36. A _____ decision is an opinion with no identified author, whereas a _____ decision is one that identifies the court's decision or order but offers no explanation.

37. If seven justices reach the same conclusion, but four decide on the basis of reason A while three decide on the basis of reason B, the opinion written by the four justices is referred to as a _____ opinion.

38. An appellate court that changes the decision of a lower appellate court is said to _____ the lower court.

39. It is possible to confuse the _____ of an opinion, which is the court's answer to the issue, with _____ , which are gratuitous remarks by the court regarding issues that were not raised by any of the parties.

40. The rationale of most courts goes beyond a consideration of _____ (the law that is standard and not subject to change) to a consideration of such things as _____ , which encompasses questions of fairness and justice.

TRUE OR FALSE

____ 41. Each state has at least one federal district court.

____ 42. District court judges are assisted by magistrates and bankruptcy judges.

____ 43. The U.S. Courts of Appeals consists of a total of eleven circuit courts.

____ 44. The Federal Circuit handles appeals in specialized cases from across the country.

____ 45. The circuit courts hear appeals from the district courts.

____ 46. Review by the U.S. Circuit Courts of Appeal is discretionary, but review by the U.S. Supreme Court is obligatory.

____ 47. If the U.S. Supreme Court denies *cert*, the decision of the lower court will stand.

____ 48. The chief justice is responsible for administering the Court, including the nine associate justices.

____ 49. Most justices on the U.S. Supreme Court serve terms of four or five years.

____ *50. One of the traditions maintained by the Supreme Court justices is the conference handshake.

____ 51. All the judges on the appellate court hear each and every appeal.

____ 52. Parties to an appeal are always allowed oral arguments if they request them.

____ 53. The authority for the legislative courts arises out of Article III of the U.S. Constitution.

____ 54. Judges who serve on the constitutional courts are appointed for life and cannot be terminated unless they resign or are impeached for improper behavior.

____ 55. Bankruptcy judges and magistrates serve for set terms and are less independent than the judges who serve on the constitutional courts.

____ 56. The organization of most state court systems is radically different than that used by the federal system.

____ 57. Judges in the state courts are appointed by either the governor or the legislature.

____ 58. Most state court cases can be found in two places.

____ 59. The number behind the name of the reporter refers to the edition of the reporter.

____ 60. All appeals are published.

____ 61. Westlaw and LEXIS have basically eliminated the need for hard-cover research.

____ 62. U.S. Supreme Court decisions can be found in three different reporters.

____ 63. Reading headnotes allows you to forego reading the case.

____ 64. Headnotes allow you to read only those legal issues in a case in which you are interested.

____ 65. Sometimes judges write concurring opinions because they believe that the majority has not adequately explained or illustrated its reasoning.

____ 66. Reading dissenting opinions is generally a waste of a researcher's time.

____ 67. Parallel cites include both the official and unofficial reporters.

____ 68. Two of the most commonly used law dictionaries are *Black's* and *Ballentine's*.

____ 69. Case briefs should contain extensive quotations to make sure you correctly state the law.

____ 70. Legal briefs are designed to convince a judge to adopt a particular legal position, whereas a case brief is designed to help the reader understand and compare case law.

____ 71. *Per curiam* opinions and memorandum opinions have more precedential value than those reviewed by the court sitting en banc.

____ 72. A plurality opinion has less precedential value than an opinion carrying a clear majority.

____ 73. Greater reliance can be placed on a decision in which appellate remedies have been exhausted than on one in which review is still possible.

____ 74. Case law is basically legal principles woven around facts.

____ 75. An issue statement should contain those facts whose absence or modification could change the outcome of the case.

____ 76. *Dicta* are binding on a court and can be cited as authority to support a legal position.

____ 77. An understanding of black letter law is sufficient for most paralegals.

____ 78. Simply reading cases fosters passive participation, but briefing cases encourages active engagement.

*Questions taken from Bonus Pointers

PART B

"I Need to Find a Case In Arizona Dealing with the Duty of Public Schools to Protect Their Students from Harm."

"What's next?" asked Tim, noticing that Martha was beginning to stir after a couple of hours of intense concentration.

"Do you provide this much service to everyone?" Immediately, Martha wished she could withdraw her question. Tim's obvious embarrassment showed on his face and she felt bad that she had been so flippant. "I'm sorry. I really do appreciate all your help and I'll take as much as you can offer."

"Okay, then," said Tim, hoping that Martha didn't realize how much he was enjoying helping her. "Do you need to find another case?"

"Actually, yes. Only this time I don't know the name of the case. I need to find a case in Arizona dealing with the duty of public schools to protect their students from harm. I think I'll begin by checking out the state and regional **digests.**"

"Good idea. But before doing that, you might want to take a few moments and review the law regarding duty in general. Your best bet is to consult a **secondary source,** like a legal encyclopedia, or a **treatise,** such as **Prosser on Torts.** Now, would you excuse me? Someone's waiting for me at the front counter."

---

digests set of books arranging cases by subject matter; used to locate cases

secondary source finding tool for the law

treatise volume devoted to one area of law, which is usually examined in depth

Prosser on Torts shorthand title for the popular treatise *Prosser and Keeton on the Law of Torts*

Figure 3-12
Primary vs. Secondary Authority

PRIMARY VS. SECONDARY AUTHORITY	
PRIMARY AUTHORITY	**SECONDARY AUTHORITY**
Case Law	Dictionaries
Constitutions	Encyclopedias
Statutes	Periodicals
Ordinances	Restatements
Administrative Regulations	Treatises

◆ **LOCAL LINKS** ◆
Your instructor might very well approach the research of the duty issue very differently. Take notes regarding your instructor's suggestions.

primary authority law generated by a government body, such as a court legislature, or administrative agency

binding authority authority that a court is required to follow

persuasive authority authority that a court has the option of following or ignoring

PRIMARY AND SECONDARY AUTHORITIES

Primary authority is the law generated by a government body, such as a court, legislature, or administrative agency. Case law, statutes, and administrative regulations are all primary authority. The tools used to find primary authority and to understand it are called *secondary authority*. Encyclopedias and treatises are both examples of secondary authority because both are used to direct you to cases, statutes, and administrative regulations.

Primary authority can be either binding (mandatory) or persuasive. Courts are required to follow **binding authority,** but have the option of following or not following authority that is merely **persuasive.** If, for example, a decision is rendered by the Alaska Supreme Court, the lower courts in that state are obligated to adhere to the decision. In other words, the decision would be considered binding primary authority for the lower courts in Alaska. It would be considered persuasive primary authority, however, for the Oregon courts because the Alaska courts have no authority over the Oregon courts.

ENCYCLOPEDIAS

A good place to start when you have no knowledge of an issue in the law is with encyclopedias. Legal encyclopedias, like any encyclopedia, divide the realm of law into broad topic areas and cover each topic in alphabetical order and with broad, sweeping brushstrokes. Reading an encyclopedia's coverage of a topic will introduce you to basic legal terminology and the most important general rules in that area of law. Because encyclopedias reference their topics, they are a wonderful source of citations that can lead you to primary authority. They are not, however, to be used as a substitute for reading primary authority.

The two most popular legal encyclopedias are *American Jurisprudence (Am.Jur.)* and *Corpus Juris Secundum* (*C.J.S.*).

C.J.S. is published by West and features the West key numbering system. (See Figure 3-13 for sample page from *Am.Jur.* and Figure 3-14 for sample page from *C.J.S.*) Any key number you find in *C.J.S.* can be used to find cases in the West digest system. *Am.Jur.,* as a publication of the former Lawyers' Co-op, refers to other Lawyers' Co-op resources. One primary difference in the two encyclopedias is that *C.J.S.* aims at providing all cases that support a given statement of the law, whereas *Am.Jur.* intends to provide only a representative cross-section of cases. Many states have state-specific legal encyclopedias (e.g., California has *California Jurisprudence*).

▰ *Putting It Into Practice 3.13:*

Using the Index to *Am.Jur.,* locate "Products Liability." Find a section dealing with tobacco products. Read the summaries (including any pocket parts) until you find a reference to *Cipollone v. Liggett.* Do the same with *C.J.S.* What differences do you notice between the two encyclopedias?

negligence necessary to establish the liability of any private party,[44] failing which there will be no liability.[45] Thus, the general rule that there can be no tort liability in the absence of a duty owed to the injured person applies,[46] as does the generally applicable standard of ordinary or reasonable care by which compliance with or breach of that duty is appraised,[47] and it must be established that the plaintiff suffered personal injury or property damage proximately caused by the government's breach of its duty.[48] Some jurisdictions, however, qualify the traditional test for a duty owed the plaintiff where a governmental defendant is involved, and condition liability on the breach of a special duty owed the plaintiff, apart from the duty owed by the government to the general public.[49]

b. DUTY [§§ 138–144]

(i) IN GENERAL [§§ 138, 139]

§ 138. Generally

In the absence of sovereign or governmental immunity from suit or liability in tort, the threshold issue in a negligence action against a state or local governmental entity is whether the defendant owes a duty of care to the plaintiff.[50] The general rule that there can be no tort liability in the absence of a duty owed to the injured person applies to negligence actions against state and local governmental entities as it would in an action against any private party,[51] since the government is not an insurer or injuries not caused by its

State (3d Dept) 25 App Div 2d 912, 270 NYS2d 140; Melendez v Philadelphia, 320 Pa Super 59, 466 A2d 1060; Rice v Granite School Dist., 23 Utah 2d 22, 456 P2d 159; Warden v Grafton, 99 W Va 249, 128 SE 375, 42 ALR 259.

As to the elements and principles governing negligence actions, generally, see 57A Am Jur 2d, NEGLIGENCE.

44. Ryan v State, 134 Ariz 308, 656 P2d 597, 38 ALR4th 1188, later proceeding (App) 150 Ariz 549, 724 P2d 1218; Ankers v District School Bd. (Fla App D2) 406 So 2d 72; Ferentchak v Frankfort, 105 Ill 2d 474, 86 Ill Dec 443, 475 NE2d 822; Bockelman v State, Dept. of Transp. (Iowa) 366 NW2d 550; Irwin v Ware, 392 Mass 745, 467 NE2d 1292, 48 ALR4th 287; St. John Bank & Trust Co. v. St. John (Mo App) 679 SW2d 399; Schear v Board of County Comrs., 101 NM 671, 687 P2d 728; Applegate v Duncanside Park (Portage Co) 28 Ohio App 3d 88, 28 Ohio BR 130, 502 NE2d 249, motion overr.

45. Lane v Brookhaven (2d Dept) 23 App Div 2d 689, 257 NYS2d 721; Shaver v Rotterdam (3d Dept) 22 App Div 2d 834, 253 NYS2d 893.

45. § 138.

47. § 145.

48. § 147.

49. § 140.

50. Stark v. City of Los Angeles (2d Dist) 168 Cal App 3d 276, 214 Cal Rptr 216.

51. Kotzebue v McLean (Alaska) 702 P2d 1309; Adams v State (Alaska) 555 P2d 235 (superseded by statute on other grounds as stated in Wilson v Anchorage (Alaska) 669 P2d 569); Ryan v State, 134 Ariz 308, 656 P2d 597, 38 ALR4th 1188, later proceeding (App) 150 Ariz 549, 724 P2d 1218; Chavez v Tolleson Elementary School Dist. (App) 122 Ariz 472, 595 P2d 1017, I ALR4th 1089; Hoyem v Manhattan Beach City School Dist., 22 Cal 3d 508, 150 Cal Rptr 1, 585 P2d 851; Leake v Cain (Colo) 720 P2d 152; Commercial Carrier Corp. v Indian River County (Fla) 371 So 2d 1010, on remand (Fla App D3) 372 So 2d 1022, later app (Fla App D3) 398 So 2d 488 and on remand (Fla App D3) 372 So 2d 1182; Ankers v District School Bd. (Fla App D2) 406 So 2d 72; Cootey v Sun Invest., Inc. (Hawaii) 718 P2d 1086; Norman v Turkey Run Community School Corp., 274 Ind 310, 411 NE2d 614; Anderson v East, 117 Ind 126, 19 NE 726; Wilson v Nepstad (Iowa) 282 NW2d 664; Trout v Koss Constr. Co., 240 Kan 86, 727 P2d 450; Dunne v Orleans Parish School Bd. (La) 463 So 2d 1267; Smith v Howard (La App 1st Cir) 489 So 2d 1037; Schear v Board of County Comrs., 101 NM 671, 687 P2d 728; Taylor v state (3d Dept) 25 App Div 2d 912,

Figure 3-13
Sample Page from American Jurisprudence

§ 464 SCHOOLS AND SCHOOL DISTRICTS 78A C.J.S.

ineffective,[70] but they are not exempted from liability for conduct which is considered operational[71] or otherwise not discretionary.[72]

The fact that an employee is not immune from suit for failing to provide proper supervision carries no implication that the employee's activities were such as to render the school authority liable.[73]

§ 465. —— Scope and Extent of Duty and Liability

A school authority's duty to supervise its students exists to the extent that the authority has physical custody and control over the student, or to the extent that the authority and its employees have the power to control the behavior of the student.

Library References

Schools 89.11-89.11(2).

A school authority's duty to supervise its students exists to the extent that the authority has physical custody of and control over the student,[74] or to the extent that the authority and its employees have the power to control the behavior of a student.[75]

In the absence of a special, dangerous condition or circumstance,[76] a school authority is under no duty to supervise all movements of all pupils at all times,[77] and the fact that each student is not personally supervised every moment of each school day does not constitute fault on the part of a school authority.[78] A school authority's duty to supervise includes taking precautions against crimes or torts inflicted by third parties,[79] as well as taking reasonable steps to protect students from assaults by other students.[80]

The supervisorial duty of a school authority may extend to periods before the beginning of classes,[81] and has been stated to commence upon entry of a student to the school bus[82] or upon arrival at school.[83] Once a student is beyond the school authority's lawful control, the authority generally owes no legal duty to supervise the activities of the student,[84] and it is, generally, the case that school authorities are not legally responsible for accidents that students may suffer once they have been released from school.[85] Supervisorial responsibility may, however, under some circumstances, extend to times after the end of classes.[86] A school must provide supervision for students who are participating in an after hours activity sanctioned by the school,[87] and, even when students are not in custody or compulsory attendance, liability may attach

---

70. Or.—Mosley v. Portland School Dist. No. 1J, 813 P.2d 71, 108 Or.App. 7, affirmed in part, reversed in part on other grounds 843 P.2d 415, 315 Or. 85.

71. Fla.—Comuntzis v. Pinellas County School Bd., App. 2 Dist., 508 So.2d 750.

Deployment of supervisory personnel in accord with school board manual

School was not entitled to sovereign immunity in action by student assaulted by classmate, who alleged that school principal negligently failed to carry out operational duty of deploying supervisory personnel at school in accord with school board manual.

Fla.—Bonica By and Through Avant v. Dade County School Bd., App. 3 Dist., 549 So.2d 220.

72. Routine decisions

Decisions on how to supervise students and to stop attack of students before weapon was used were routine decisions made by school employees in course of day-to-day activities and thus district and school employees were not immune from negligence claims based on failure to supervise students.

Or.—Mosley v. Portland School Dist. No. 1J, 813 P.2d 71, 108 Or.App. 7, affirmed in part, reversed in part on other grounds 843 P.2d 415, 315 Or. 85.

73. Ind.—Borne by Borne v. Northwest Allen County School Corp., App. 3 Dist., 532 N.E.2d 1196, transfer denied 558 N.E.2d 828.

74. N.Y.—Palella by Palella v. Ulmer, 518 N.Y.S.2d 91, 136 Misc.2d 34.

75. Fla.—Rupp v. Bryant, 417 So.2d 658.

76. La.—Narcisse v. Continental Ins. Co., App. 3 Cir., 419 So.2d 13. Wyo.—Connett v. Fremont County School Dist. No. 6, Fremont County, 581 P.2d 1097.

77. La.—Narcisse v. Continental Ins. Co., App. 3 Cir., 419 So.2d 13, Wyo.—Commett v. Fremont County School Dist. No. 6, 581 P.2d 1097.

78. La.—Nicolosi v. Livingston Parish School Bd., App. 1 Cir., 441 So.2d 1261, writ denied 444 So.2d 1243.

79. Or.—Fazzolari By and Through Fazzolari v. Portland School Dist. No. 1J, 734 P.2d 1326, 303 Or. 1.

80. Fla.—T.J. v. State, App. 2 Dist., 538 So.2d 1320.

81. School breakfast period

La.—Laneheart v. Orleans Parish School Bd., App. 4 Cir., 524 So.2d 138.

82. N.Y.—Hurlburt by Hurlburt v. Noxon, 565 N.Y.S.2d 683, 149 Misc.2d 374

83. Cal.—Perna by Perna v. Conejo Valley Unified School Dist., 2 Dist., 192 Cal.Rptr. 10, 143 C.A.3d 292.

84. N.Y.—Palella by Palella v. Ulmer, 518 N.Y.S.2d 91, 136 Misc.2d 34.

85. Cal.-Perna by Perna v. Conejo Valley Unified School Dist., 2 Dist., 192 Cal.Rptr. 10, 143 C.A.3d 292.

86. Fla.—Broward County School Bd. v. Ruiz, App. 4 Dist., 493 So.2d 474.

While awaiting bus

La.—Laneheart v. Orleans Parish School Bd., App. 4 Cir., 524 So.2d 138.

While awaiting pickup by parents

La.—Sutton v. Duplessis, App. 4 Cir., 584 So.2d 362.

87. La.—Laneheart v. Orleans Parish School Bd., App. 4 Cir., 524 So.2d 138.

Club meeting

Because the school authorities assumed control over the club where the student was injured as well as the meetings of the club, the school,

---

Figure 3-14
Sample Page from Corpus Juris Secundum

TREATISES

Treatises are secondary sources of the law that analyze and criticize the law. They
are scholarly works that provide a very detailed analysis of specific points of law
and examine it in some depth. Usually written in multiple volumes, they are helpful to researchers not only because they explain the law, but because they provide
numerous references to cases and statutes. **Hornbooks** are a special type of treatise
written specifically for law students. They are usually one volume and contain
questions designed to guide students through their study of the law. Both hornbooks and treatises cover general rules of law, exceptions to those rules, and the
evolution of the law. (See Figure 3-15 for a sample page from *Prosser and Keeton
on the Law of Torts.*)

Consult treatises at the beginning of your research to better understand the
basic concepts and issues in the area of law you are researching. To find a treatise,
look in the catalog under the topic you are interested in or go directly to the
shelves housing the area of law in which you are interested. Because some treatises are more helpful than others, you will find it to your advantage to ask the
reference librarian which treatises are recommended for a particular area of law.
Consult state-specific treatises whenever they are available and issues of state law
are involved.

Putting It Into Practice 3.14:

Find out if your library has a copy of *Prosser and Keeton on the Law of Torts.* Look
in the table of contents and index under "Products Liability" for a discussion on
liability of the tobacco industry for injuries caused by smoking.

DIGESTS

Digests are finding tools that are used to locate cases. They arrange cases by subject
matter and provide brief summaries of cases (called *headnotes*) relating to a specific
topic. Each case can then be found using the case citation at the end of the summary. (See sample from *Pacific Digest* in Figure 3-16.)

The most comprehensive digest system is published by West and is called the
American Digest System. This system brings together all of the cases reported in the
National Reporter System (all of the reporters identified earlier, such as the *Supreme
Court Reporter,* the *Federal Reporter,* the *Pacific Reporter,* and so on). The *General
Digests* contain headnotes for all of the cases published by West in its National
Reporter System. The *General Digest,* which is printed annually, has been organized
in ten-year groups called "Decennials" (meaning ten-year period).

United States Supreme Court decisions can be located using the *U.S. Supreme
Court Digest* and all federal cases can be located using West's *Federal Practice Digest.*
West has also prepared four regional digests: *Atlantic, North Western, Pacific,* and
South Eastern digests. Cases from those regions in which no regional digest exists
(north eastern, southern, and south western) can be found using the *General Digest*
and the state digests. West also publishes digests for each state and the District of
Columbia. (Figure 3-17 lists the primary digests published by West and shows the
dates of coverage, where applicable.)

All these problems deal with policy issues—the last four even more than the first. The attempt to deal with all of them in terms of causation is at the bottom of much of the existing confusion.

**WESTLAW
REFERENCES**

Generalizations About Proximate Cause
headnote("proximate cause" /s jur*** /5 instruct)
topic(torts negligence) /p "legal cause"
foresee! /3 injur*** /s jur***

Relation to Duty
topic(negligence torts) /p proximate legal /2 cause
  /p duty

Confusion With Standard of Conduct
automobile car /p unattended /p negligen! foresee!

Confusion With Defenses to Negligence Action
proximate /2 cause /p comparative /2 negligence

Proposed Formulae
formula* /s proximate /2 cause % formula /2
  instruction

The Nearest Cause
"nearest cause" & topic(negligence torts)

The Last Human Wrongdoer
topic(negligence torts) & final last +3 wrongdoer
  tortfeasor

Cause and Condition
restatement −s torts ÷4 431 433 435

The Substantial-Factor Test
substantial /s factor /s "proximate cause"
topi(torts negligence) /p "substantial factor"

Justly Attachable Cause
"justly attachable" /s cause

Systems of Rules
topic(torts negligence) /p rule* /s determin! /s
  cause* causation

Problems Involved
headnote("proximate cause" /p foresee! /p risk)
topic(negligence torts) /p owe* /p duty /p protect!
topic(negligence torts) /p standard +2 conduct

§ 43. Unforeseeable Consequences

Negligence, it must be repeated, is conduct which falls below the standard established by law for the protection of others against unreasonable risk. It necessarily involves a foreseeable risk, a threatened danger of injury, and conduct unreasonable in proportion to the danger. If one could not reasonably foresee any injury as the result of one's act, or if one's conduct was reasonable in the light of what one could anticipate, there would be no negligence, and no liability.[1] But what if one does unreasonably fail to guard against harm which one should foresee, and consequences which one could in no way have anticipated in fact follow? Suppose, for example, that a defect in a railway platform offers at most the foreseeable possibility of a sprained ankle; but as a result of it a passenger dies of inflammation of the heart?[2] Or one's negligent driving threatens another with something like a broken leg, but instead causes the other to be shot?[3]

There is perhaps no other one issue in the law of torts over which so much controversy has raged, and concerning which there has been so great a deluge of legal writing.[4] At the risk of becoming wearisome, it must be repeated that the question is primarily not

§ 43

1. Stephens v. Mutual Lumber Co., 1918, 103 Wash. 1, 173 P. 1031; Mendelson v. Davis, 8th Cir., 1922, 281 F. 18; Nunan v. Bennett, 1919, 184 Ky. 591, 212 S.W. 570; Sears v. Texas & New Orleans Railroad Co., Tex. Civ.App.1932, 247 S.W. 602; Gaupin v. Murphy, 1928, 295 Pa. 214, 145 A. 123.

2. Keegan v. Minneapolis & St. Louis Railroad Co., 1899, 76 Minn. 90, 78 N.W. 965 (liable).

3. Lynch v. Fisher, La.App.1947, 34 So.2d 513 (liable). Cf. Walmsley v. Rural Telephone Association, 1917, 102 Kan. 139, 169 P. 197 (liable); Gouna v. O'Neill, Tex.Civ.App.1941, 149 S.W.2d 138 (not liable).

4. See the articles cited supra, § 41, n.1. Also Dias, The Duty Problem in Negligence, 1955, 13 Camb.L.J. 198; Dias, The Breach Problem and the Duty of Care, 1956, 30 Tulane L.Rev. 377; Fleming, The Passing of Polemis, 1961, 39 Can.Bar Rev. 489; Goodhart, The Imaginary Necktie and the Rule in Re Polemis, 1952, 68 L.Q.Rev. 514; Goodhart, Liability and Compensation, 1960, 76 L.Q.Rev. 567; Green, Foreseeability in Negligence Law, 1961, 61 Col.L.Rev. 1401; Payne, The "Direct" Consequences of a Negligent Act, 1952, 5 Curr. Leg.Prob. 189; Payne, Foreseeability and Remoteness of Damage in Negligence, 1962, 25 Mod.L.Rev. 1; Williams, The Risk Principle, 1961, 77 L.Q.Rev. 179; Wilson and Slade, A Re-examination of Remoteness, 1952, 15 Mod.L.Rev. 458; Wright, Re Polemis, 1951, 14 Mod. L.Rev. 393.

Figure 3-15
Sample Page from Prosser and Keeton on the Law of Torts.

◆89.6 SCHOOLS

For later cases see same Topic and Key Number in Pocket Part

threw rock and school district was not liable for student's eye injury.
Fagan v. Summers, 498 P.2d 1227.

◆89.7. Injuries to persons other than pupils.

Library references
C.J.S. Schools and School Districts § 321.

Artz.App. 1980. Spectator who slipped and fell on ramp while leaving school property after watching little league game could not recover for injuries where she was aware that ramp had been slippery in the past and still continued to use ramp and ramp was not unreasonably dangerous.
Jackson v. Cartwright School Dist., 607 P.2d 975, 125 Ariz. 98.

Okl.App. 1983. Suit by invitee who attended chili supper on school property and was injured when she tripped on metal grate on school property, against school district was not barred by statutory exemption from limited liability imposed by Political Subdivision Tort Claims Act which provides that political subdivision or an employee of a political subdivision who enters upon any property on or under express or implied authority of law shall not be liable if a loss results from such entry. 51 O.S.1981, §§ 151 et seq., 155.
Smith v. Broken Arrow Public Schools, Independent School Dist. No. 3, 665 P.2d 858.

Or.App. 1987. Allegation by plaintiff who was injured when attacked by three students at basketball game that basketball game was sponsored by school districts and that students from both schools were invited to attend basketball game was sufficient to establish relationship giving rise to duty on part of school districts to take precautions to protect plaintiff from reasonably foreseeable acts of third parties.
Cook v. School Dist. UH3J, 731 P.2d 443, 83 Or.App. 292.

Or.App. 1975. Assuming that State Board of Higher Education had duty to select "safe place" in which to hold "Indian Powwow," act of selecting a site was obviously exercise of "discretionary function" within purview of statute providing that every public body is immune from liability for any claim based upon performance of discretionary function or duty, and thus liability to plaintiff for injury suffered as result of encounter with horse found somewhere upon fairgrounds adjacent to fairgrounds area building leased by Board for powwow did not attach. ORS 30.265.
Baker v. State Bd. of Higher Educ., 531 P.2d 716, 20 Or.App. 277, appeal after remand 558 P.2d 1247, 28 Or.App. 53, appeal after remand 586 P.2d 114, 37 Or.App. 87.

Wash. 1965. School district must observe that degree of care, precaution, and vigilance which circumstances demand in order to provide for safety of its invitees.
Perry v. Seattle School Dist., No. 1, 405 P.2d 589, 66 Wash.2d 800.

Whether spectator injured when football player was knocked out of bounds and into spectator had been completely ignorant of the game did not control issue whether school district supervising the game had been negligent.
Perry v. Seattle School Dist. No. 1, 405 P.2d 589, 66 Wash.2d 800.

Spectator attending football game sponsored by school district which charged no admission had duty to protect herself not only against dangers of which she had actual knowledge but such dangers incident to game as would be apparent to reasonable person in exercise of due care.
Perry v. Seattle School Dist. No. 1, 405 P.2d 589, 66 Wash.2d 800.

◆89.8 Motor vehicles in general.

Library references
C.J.S. Schools and School Districts § 322.

Colo. 1986. School district did not, by placing crossing guards at intersection during afternoon, assume duty to provide crossing guards in the morning when kindergartners walked home.
Jefferson County School Dist. R–1 v. Gilbert by Gilbert, 725 P.2d 774.

◆89.9. —— Contributory negligence.

For other cases see earlier editions of this digest, the Decennial Digests, and WESTLAW.

◆89.10. Nuisance.

Library references
C.J.S. Schools and School Districts § 321.

Kan. 1973. Action of school board in allegedly permitting students to gather, for short time before classes started, on school grounds without access to school building and without prescribing supervision though some racial tension existed did not constitute nuisance within exception to governmental immunity rule.
Sly v. Board of Educ. of Kansas City, 516 P.2d 895, 213 Kan. 415.

◆89.11. Supervision of other pupils.

Library references
C.J.S. Schools and School Districts § 321.

Ariz.App. 1979. School district and classroom teacher owe duty of ordinary care toward student during time student is under their charge and that duty is breached when

Figure 3-16
Sample Page from Pacific Digest

Figure 3-17
American Digest System

American Digest System	
Century Digest	1658–1896
First Decennial	1897–1906
Second Decennial	1907–1916
Third Decennial	1926–1926
Fourth Decennial	1926–1936
Fifth Decennial	1936–1946
Sixth Decennial	1946–1956
Seventh Decennial	1956–1966
Eighth Decennial	1966–1976
Ninth Decennial (Parts I and II)	1976–1986
Tenth Decennial (Parts I and II)	1986–1996
General Digest, 9th Series	1997–date
Federal Courts	
U.S. Supreme Court Digest	
Federal Practice Digest	1754–1938
Modern Federal Practice Digest	1939–1961
West's Federal Practice Digest 2d	1961–1975
West's Federal Practice Digest 3d	1975–1983
West's Federal Practice Digest 4th	1983–date
State Courts	
West Regional Digests	Atlantic
North Western	Pacific
South Eastern	

"Another Way to Get Into Digests Is to Generate a List of Possible Terms. I Like to Use the Six Journalism Questions: Who, What, Where, When, Why, and How."

"Okay, I'm back. Did you find anything helpful in the encyclopedias or treatises?" asked Tim.

"I only got as far as the encyclopedias, but I did find something interesting in *C.J.S.* Let me find it," said Martha, searching through her notes. "Right here. 'A school authority's duty to supervise includes taking precautions against crimes or torts inflicted by third parties, as well as taking reasonable steps to protect students from assaults by other students.' "

"And does this statement go directly to what you are researching?" checked Tim.

"Absolutely," confirmed Martha.

"Okay. Does *C.J.S.* cite any cases to support this statement?"

"Yes, but neither of them is in Arizona."

"But remember you can use these cases to get into the Arizona and Pacific digests. If you look up these cases and find the key numbers that discuss the points of law you're interested in, you can go to the digests and look under those same key numbers."

Heeding Tim's advice, Martha found one of the referenced cases and skimmed through the headnotes until she found one discussing a school's duty to protect students from crimes committed by other students. The number assigned to this headnote was "Schools k89.11(1)." (See Figure 3-18 showing headnotes.) Martha then went to the *Arizona Digest* and looked under "Schools" until she found the key number 89.11(1). (See Figure 3-19 showing page from digest.) Under that key number was a summary for *Chavez v. Tolleson Elementary School District,* a case involving a lawsuit against a school district filed by the father of a 10-year-old girl who left school without permission and who was subsequently abducted and slain.

"So how did it go?" asked Tim, when he dropped by to check on Martha's progress.

"Well, I found a pretty good case. It's not exactly on point, but I wasn't sure I'd find any relevant cases." Martha's shoulders relaxed a little as she allowed herself to contemplate the possibility of success.

"Good for you. But let me remind you that it's not always that easy," Tim pointed out. "Another way you can get into digests is to generate a list of possible terms. I like to use the six journalism questions: who, what, where, when, why, and how. Who are the parties? What is the issue? Where did the issue arise? When did it arise? Why are the parties suing? How did the issue arise?"

As Tim clicked off these questions, Martha quickly applied them to Mike's case. "Who is involved: students, school, school board. What is the issue: negligence, duty. When did the issue arise: during school. Where did the issue arise: school grounds. Why are the parties suing: damages, compensation. How did the issue arise: shooting, violence, assault, battery." After this brief silent analysis, Martha continued her thoughts out loud. "And then I would take the words I generated and select the ones I thought the West editors would most likely use."

"Absolutely," Tim concurred. "And remember, if you get stuck you can always check the legal thesaurus to help you come up with additional terms."

538 So.2d 1320
52 Ed. Law Rep. 851, 14 Fla. L. Weekly 497
(Cite as: 538 So.2d 1320)
< KeyCite Citations >
District Court of Appeal of Florida,
Second District.

T.J., a child Appellant,
v.
STATE of Florida, Appellee.

No. 88-1971.

Feb. 15, 1989.

Student was adjudicated delinquent in the Circuit Court, Sarasota County, Emanual LoGalbo, Jr., Acting J., for possession of cocaine. Student appealed. The District Court of Appeal, Altenbernd, J., held that assistant principal's examination of plastic bag containing cocaine in zippered side pocket of student's purse exceeded scope of search for knife.

Reversed.

West Headnotes

[1] Schools k169.5
345k169.5

Assistant principal's examination of plastic bag containing cocaine in zippered side pocket of student's purse exceeded scope of search for knife; principal took everything out of purse and did not locate weapon, did not see any bulges in side pocket, and only felt plastic bag when she placed her hand inside it. U.S.C.A. Const.Amend. 4.

[2] Schools k89.11(1)
345k89.11(1)
(Formerly 345k89.11)

School boards have potential civil liability if school officials fail to take reasonable steps to protect students from assaults by other students.
*1320 James Marion Moorman, Public Defender, and Julius J. Aulisio, Asst. Public Defender, Bartow, for appellant.

Robert A. Butterworth, Atty. Gen., Tallahassee, and David R. Gemmer, Asst. Atty. Gen., Tampa, for appellee.

ALTENBERND, Judge.

T.J., a juvenile, appeals her adjudication of delinquency. Following an adverse ruling on a dispositive motion to suppress, she reserved the right to appeal and pleaded nolo contendere to felony possession of cocaine. The cocaine had been unexpectedly discovered in her purse by a school official conducting an extensive search for a knife. Recognizing the seriousness of the drug problem which confronts our public schools, we reluctantly reverse the trial court and direct that the evidence of cocaine be suppressed.

The essential facts establish that the appellant was a fifteen‑year‑old student attending eighth grade at a middle school. She had a school history of minor disciplinary problems, but no prior history of problems relating either to drugs or weapons.

[1] On the day preceding her search, T.J. had been involved as a spectator at a fight between two other female students which occurred at a school bus stop. During the fight, one student pulled a knife and threatened the other. The fight at the bus stop ended without a stabbing. The victimized student, however, was told that the knife would be brought to school in the morning and that the fight would continue.

The following morning, the victimized student reported her fears to a school disciplinary supervisor. She believed that either the girl who had fought with her or T.J. would have the knife. [FN1] The school disciplinary supervisor reported the student's problem to an assistant principal.

> FN1. Apparently, this belief was based upon a friendship between T.J. and the girl with the knife. The record, however, does not clearly explain why the victimized student believed the knife would be in T.J.'s purse.

The assistant principal decided to search both girls. The search of the girl who had had the knife the prior evening did not produce a weapon. When T.J. was searched, the assistant principal opened her purse. The assistant principal did not see a knife or any other weapon. She took everything out of the

Figure 3-18
Example of Headnotes

§ 54–416, subd. 11 (A.R.S. §§ 15–432, 15–438 et seq.).

Sawaya v. Tucson High School Dist. No. 1 of Pima County, 281 P.2d 105, 78 Ariz. 389.

Ariz.App. 1980. Spectator who slipped and fell on ramp while leaving school property after watching little league game could not recover for injuries where she was aware that ramp had been slippery in the past and still continued to use ramp and ramp was not unreasonably dangerous.

Jackson v. Cartwright School Dist., 607 P.2d 975, 125 Ariz. 98.

◆**89.8. Motor vehicles in general.**

Library references

C.J.S. Schools and School Districts § 322.

Ariz. 1990. School district which applied for and established specially marked crosswalk where none previously existed owed common law duty of care, for negligence purposes, to high school student who was struck by motor vehicle and injured as she was crossing in crosswalk, despite district's contention that crosswalk was established only for students of adjacent elementary school.

Alhambra School Dist. v. Superior Court In and For County of Maricopa, 796 P.2d 470, 165 Ariz. 38.

Where school district followed statutory procedure to establish marked crosswalk, district assumed statutory duty of care, for negligence purposes, to persons using crosswalk, not just to students of abutting school. A.R.S. § 28–797.

Alhambra School Dist. v. Superior Court In and For County of Maricopa, 796 P.2d 470, 165 Ariz. 38.

Ariz.App. 1989. Neither agreement between city and school district requiring school district to operate crossing in conformance with Arizona school crossing manual nor statute dealing with marking of crosswalks abutting school grounds where children "shall be required" to cross imposed duty on district to protect high school student, who was struck by vehicle while using crosswalk at which portable crossing signs had not been placed and crossing guard had not arrived, but was using crosswalk away from school in order to get ride to school in another district when accident occurred; student was not "required" to use crosswalk to go to school. A.R.S. §§ 28–641, 28–792, subd. A, 28–797, 28–797 subds. A, C-E, G.

Alhambra School Dist. v. Superior Court In and For County of Maricopa, 780 P.2d 401, 161 Ariz. 568, review granted, opinion vacated 796 P.2d 470, 165 Ariz. 38.

Statute dealing with school district's marking of crosswalks in front of school building or abutting school grounds where children

"shall be required" to cross streets creates duty only to children who are required to use crosswalk to attend school. A.R.S. §§ 28–797, 28–797, subd. A.

Alhambra School Dist. v. Superior Court In and For County of Maricopa, 780 P.2d 401, 161 Ariz. 568, review granted, opinion vacated 796 P.2d 470, 165 Ariz. 38.

Statute dealing with school crosswalks does not, by use of word "persons," place duty upon school district with respect to all persons using crosswalk between specified hours; rather, term "persons" was intended to mean "children." A.R.S. §§ 28–792, 28–792, subd. A, 28–797, subds. C-E, G.

Alhambra School Dist. v. Superior Court In and For County of Maricopa, 780 P.2d 401, 161 Ariz. 568, review granted, opinion vacated 796 P.2d 470, 165 Ariz. 38.

◆**89.9–89.10.** *For other cases see tge Decennial Digests and WESTLAW.*

Library references

C.J.S. Schools and School Districts.

◆**89.11. Supervision of other pupils.**

Library references

C.J.S. Schools and School Districts § 321.

Ariz.App. 1979. School district and classroom teacher owe duty of ordinary care toward student during time student is under their charge and that duty is breached when conduct creates unreasonable risk of harm to student. A.R.S. § 15–142 [A][14].

Chavez v. Tolleson Elementary School Dist., 595 P.2d 1017, 122 Ariz. 472, 1 A.L.R. 4th 1089.

School personnel could not reasonably have foreseen that ten-year-old student would leave elementary school grounds without permission and thereafter be abducted and slain; thus district and school personnel were not liable for death of child.

Chavez v. Tolleson Elementary School Dist., 595 P.2d 1017, 122 Ariz. 472, 1 A.L.R. 4th 1089.

Law Rev. 1968. Torts—school districts—liability for negligent supervision of extracurricular activities.

9 Ariz.Law Rev. 530.

◆**89.12-89.19.** *For other cases see the Decennial Digests and WESTLAW.*

Library References

C.J.S. Schools and School Districts.

For legislative history of cited statutes see Arizona Revised Statutes Annotated

Figure 3-19
Sample Page from Arizona Digest

USING DIGESTS

Digests are organized according to topics, which are arranged alphabetically, and subtopics, each of which is assigned a key number, depicted by a picture of a key, followed by a number. Key numbers are the foundation for the West key numbering system, which is an indexing system for points of law identified by West's case reporters. Each key number corresponds to a specific area of law. Remember that Martha looked under "Schools" in the digest and then under the key number 89.11(1), where she found *Chavez.*

But how do you know where to look in the digest? If you know the general topic to look under, such as "Negligence," you can consult the topic outline at the beginning of the volume containing the cases on negligence. Scan the outline, looking for key numbers that might be relevant to what you are researching.

Alternatively, you could consult the *Descriptive Word Index,* an index created for each West digest. This index is an alphabetical listing of certain words and phrases. Each of these words and phrases indicates a topic name identifying where this word or phrase is listed in the digest and a key number that refers to the key number used in the digest. If, for example, you looked in the *Descriptive Word Index* under "Negligence," you could then find the subtopic "Duty to protect against act of third parties" (see Figure 3-20 for a sample page from the *Descriptive Word Index*), which the *Index* indicates is found under Negligence k2 in the digest.

Putting It Into Practice 3.15:

Look under "Products Liability" in the *Federal Practice Digest Index* and find a reference to "Tobacco Products." Scan the headnotes until you find a reference to *Cipollone v. Liggett.*

"Don't Forget to Check the Pocket Parts."

"Don't forget to check the pocket parts," reminded Tim, as he breezed past Martha.

"Right." Tim's reminder brought back memories of Ms. Barnes's incessant admonitions to "Update, update." When she looked under "Schools k89.11(1)" in the pocket parts, Martha found a summary of *Hill v. Safford Unified School District,* which dealt with a shooting of a high school student by another student.

"Wow, this is right on point," thought Martha to herself, surprised to find a case so apparently similar to Mike's.

UPDATING CASES

Pocket parts are pamphlets inserted in the slots at the end of bound books. These pamphlets contain the most current cases and also refer to other legal sources. To find cases in the pocket parts, look under the topic of interest (topics are arranged alphabetically) and then look under the appropriate key number. Pocket parts are published once a year, but they are supplemented halfway through the year with paperback supplements.

The advance sheets contain mini-digests of the cases in those pamphlets. You can find cases in the mini-digest the same way you find them in the pocket parts. Look for the topic (arranged alphabetically) and then the key number.

SCHOOLS

60 P.D. (367 P.2d)—356

References are to Digest Topics and Key Numbers

SCHOOLS AND SCHOOL DISTRICTS—Cont'd
TORTS of districts—Cont'd
Falls, auditorium floor—
Neglig 136(15)
Schools 122
Governmental functions in general.   Schools 89.1
Governmental immunity doctrine, decision overruling, retroactivity.   Schools 89
Initiation in school club.   Schools 89.11
Injuries to persons other than pupils.   Schools 89.7
Motor vehicles, see this index Automobiles
Negligence in general.   Schools 89.2
Nuisance.   Schools 89.10
Physical education.   Schools 89.4
Play, supervising other pupils at play.   Schools 89.12
Proprietary functions in general.   Schools 89.1
Recess, supervision of other pupils during recess.
Schools 89.12
Rock thrown by fellow student, dismissal of claim against teacher disposing of actions against officials.
Schools 122
School grounds, condition of.   Schools 89.6
Statute precluding judgment against school board with no liability insurance to cover, declaratory judgment action.
Schools 114
Storeroom of manual training class, stacking of plywood.
Schools 121
➤ Supervision of other pupils.   Schools 89.11, 89.12
Transportation of pupils, see this index Pupils
Vocational training and equipment.   Schools 89.19
TOWNS. see this index Towns
TRANSFER of pupils—
Failure of district to offer vocational subject desired.
Schools 154
Request by student.   Schools 154
TRANSFER of pupils by court order. Prohib 30
TRANSFER of warrants, orders and certificates of indebtedness.
Schools 95(3)
TRANSPORTATION of child by parents—
Reimbursement child attending school out of district.
Schools 159 1/2
TRANSPORTATION of pupils—
School buses. see, generally, this index School Buses
TRESPASS. student, appearance as member of public six days after warning to leave. Mun Corp 631(1)
TRIAL.   Schools 122
TRUANTS. see this index Truants
TRUSTEES.   Schools 51-63
Permitting or requiring attendance if pupils in particular schools or districts.   Schools 38, 154
TUITION see this index Tuition
ULTRA VIRES torts, defenses.   Schools 89.11
UNEMPLOYMENT compensation, see this index Unemployment Compensation
UNIFICATION, constitutional requirement, uniform school system.
Schools 22
UNION districts.   Schools 33
UNITED States service academies, see this index Service Academies
UNIVERSITIES. see this index Colleges and Universities
UNMARRIED teachers becoming pregnant, dismissal.
Schools 141(4, 5)
UNORGANIZED territory.   Schools 29
USE of—
Property.   Schools 65
VACANCIES in boards.   Schools 48(3), 53(4)
VACATIONS.   Schools 162
VAGRANCY—
Loitering on school property, constitutionality of statute   Vag 1
VALIDITY—
Bonds.   Schools 97(7)
Contracts.   Schools 80
Rules and regulations governing pupils.   Schools 172
Tax levy and assessment.   Schools 103(1)

SCHOOLS AND SCHOOL DISTRICTS—Cont'd
VALIDITY—Cont'd
Warrants, orders and certificates of indebtedness.
Schools 95(2)
VENUE of action by or against.   Schools 114
VILLAGES—
Independent districts, creation or organization of.
Schools 25
System of schools, application to villages.   Schools 12
VOCATIONAL training and equipment, liability for torts.
Schools 89.19
WARRANTS.   Schools 95
WEALTH, financing system reflecting disparity among districts, permissibility.   Schools 91
WEALTH of district, discrimination in educational opportunity.
Const Law 242.2(2)
WEAPONS—
Discharge injuring student, instructor's negligence.
Schools 5
WORKING cash fund.   Schools 92(1)
WORKMEN'S compensation proceedings, see this index Worker's Compensation
WORKSHOP, failure to attend because of aversion to the use of Federal funds in public schools, refusal of transfer as insubordination justifying dismissal.
Schools 141(1, 4)
ZONING regulations—
Construction and operation.   Zoning 288
Particular uses.   Zoning 76
Permits and certificates.   Zoning 388
Variances or exceptions.   Zoning 508

SCIENCE
ADMINISTRATIVE agencies, etc., judicial review of scientific evidence.   Admin Law 792
COMPETENCY of scientific works as—
Documentary evidence—
Crim Law 439
Evid 363
EMPLOYMENT taxes, see this index Employment Taxes
ESTATE tax, deduction of devises for scientific purposes.
Int Rev 1009-1009.4
JUDICIAL notice of scientific facts and principles.
Evid 9
OPINION and expert evidence, see this index—
Expert Testimony
Opinion Evidence
PATENTABILITY of scientific phenomena or principles.
Pat 16.3
REFERENCE by expert witness to scientific or other authorities.
Crim Law 487

SCIENTER
See, also, this index Notice
ADMISSIBILITY of evidence, similar offenses to prove.
Crim Law 370
ALLEGATION in indictment or information.
Ind & Inf 89
FALSITY of representations.   Fraud 13(2)
OBSCENITY, moving pictures, inherent requirement of proving scienter under ordinance.   Mun Corp 594(1)
POLICE officer's duties, interference.   Mun Corp 594(1)
PREFERENTIAL transferee of corporation.
Corp 547(4)
WILD animals, notice of character imputed to owner.
Anim 74(5)
WILLFUL acts, presumption, LSD-laced mushrooms delivered to detective.   Drugs & N 107

SCIENTIFIC ASSOCIATIONS OR CORPORATIONS
EMPLOYMENT taxes, see this index Employment Taxes
EXCESS profits and war profits taxes, liability.
Int Rev 971

Figure 3-20
Sample Page from Descriptive Word Index

SHEPARDIZING

To **Shepardize** a case is to check on the history and treatment of that case—to find out about the decisions made by different courts in relationship to the case and to see how it was treated by other courts in subsequent decisions. Did another court review the decision and affirm it or, more importantly, reverse it? Or did other courts consider the decision and follow the same reasoning or did they criticize it? One of the most important reasons to Shepardize cases is to ensure they are still good law. Attorneys have an obligation to know if a higher court has reversed or overruled a lower court's decision. Suggesting that a trial court follow the lead of a case that is no longer considered valid law is unethical. Another good reason to Shepardize is that doing so can lead to other cases as well as relevant statutes, law review articles, and *American Law Reports.*

Shepardizing a case requires the use of the *Shepard's* citator system, which is found in printed form and electronically. *Shepard's* can be accessed online at its Web site (http://www.shepards.com) or with LEXIS. The online *Shepard's* is more current than the print *Shepard's* and it automatically provides a complete list of all citations. The online version, however, does not give the treatment of a case, such as whether it was reversed or followed. It does have a "Signal" feature that alerts you to cases that are no longer good law and warns you to use some authorities with caution.

Westlaw now provides a comparable feature, called KeyCite, which allows the researcher to retrieve all citing references, including case law and secondary authorities. A series of colored flags is used to alert the reader to cases that are no longer good law or that contain some kind of negative history. LEXIS also has an updating system, which it calls Auto-Cite. Using KeyCite and Auto-Cite along with *Shepard's* increases the accuracy of your research and also introduces you to secondary sources you would not necessarily find by using *Shepard's* alone.

Shepard's Tells You Whether the Case In Question Has Been Questioned By Other Authorities, Discussed In a Dissenting Opinion, Harmonized with Other Cases, or Explained By Another Court.

Martha began her second day feeling considerably more optimistic than she had the day before. She decided to begin by shepardizing the cases she had found. She started with *Chavez v. Tolleson Elementary School District.* She located *Shepard's Arizona Citations* (the name of the citator) and found the volume number of *Chavez,* number 122, in bold print at the top corner of the page. Then she found the page number for *Chavez,* page 472, in bold in the middle of the page. (See Figure 3-21 to see this page out of *Shepard's.*) Several cases that cited *Chavez* were listed below. She remembered that the citations in parentheses were parallel citations for *Chavez* and that the citations below the parallel cites referred to the history of *Chavez* or showed how other cases had treated *Chavez.* She could tell from the ascending volume number that the cases were arranged in chronological order.

She could not remember what the letter "d" meant that preceded one of the citations, so she looked at the beginning of the volume to find an explanation. She found a table of abbreviations entitled "Abbreviations for History of Case" and another table entitled "Abbreviations Relating to Treatment of a Cited Case." (See Figures 3-22 and 3-23 showing these tables.) The "d," she discovered, meant that the cited case was significantly different from *Chavez,* indicating that the court in the cited case had distinguished *Chavez.* Martha then noted that all of the "f"s further down the page indicated that *Chavez* had been followed by a number of other courts in the Ninth and Tenth Circuits (the citations following "Cir. 9" refer to Ninth Circuit cases and the citations following "Cir. 10" refer to Tenth Circuit cases). She quickly scanned the list of abbreviations and noticed that *Shepard's* also told about whether the case in question had been questioned by other authorities, discussed in a dissenting opinion, harmonized with other cases, or explained by another court.

"How are you doing today?" Tim's cheerful inquiry startled Martha, but she was grateful for the interruption.

"Great timing. I don't remember what the small elevated numbers that appear immediately after the name of the reporter are."

"Good question. Those numbers refer to the headnotes in your case, which I see is *Chavez*," observed Tim, leaning over Martha's shoulder to get a better look at the page in *Shepard's*. For example, the case in volume 600, page 769, of the Pacific Reporter (2d) discusses the point of law raised in headnote 14 of *Chavez*. So if you want to research only those issues discussed in headnote 14, you would look only at those cases referencing headnote 14."

"That's good to know. Now, another thing. I notice that most of the cited cases don't have any letter in front of them. Does that mean those cases aren't worth looking up?"

"Not at all," answered Tim. "The absence of a letter simply means that the *Shepard's* editors made no judgment about the impact this case had on your case. The cited case does, however, mention your case and may still be helpful. One thing to look out for is repeated criticism or questioning of your case. When that happens, consider finding a case that has been more widely accepted." Tim took a minute to skim over the cites to see if there was anything of particular interest and he zoomed in on the A.L.R. annotation. "Good news! Your case has been the subject of an annotation," Tim announced.

"And you know that because . . ." prompted Martha.

"See that funny looking "A" with a "4" next to it?"

"Oh, yes. I was just getting ready to look that up."

"That refers to an annotation, fourth series, of the *American Law Reports*. Get hold of that annotation right away because it may do a lot of your research for you. At the very least, it will give you a feel for how other courts have handled your issue."

"I'm on it," said Martha, giving a mock salute.

Putting It Into Practice 3.16:

To Shepardize *Cipollone v. Liggett,* look in *Shepard's United States Citations* under Volume 505 (in the upper right-hand corner) and then find page 504 (bold print). Answer the following questions.

    a. Was *Cipollone* heard in the district court more than once?
    b. Have any courts in the First Circuit followed *Cipollone?*
    c. Have any courts in the Fourth Circuit distinguished it?
    d. Has the Supreme Court ever justified this decision?

AMERICAN LAW REPORTS (A.L.R.)

The *American Law Reports* (A.L.R.) contain annotations in connection with particular cases that prompted consideration of key legal issues. Up until 1969, the A.L.R. contained both federal and state law, but since that time the A.L.R. Fed., which contains federal cases, is published separately from the other A.L.R.s, which are now in their fifth series.

A.L.R.	1919-1948 (state and federal)
A.L.R.2d	1948-1965 (state and federal)
A.L.R.3d	1965-1969 (state and federal)
	1969-1980 (state cases)
A.L.R.4th	1980-1992 (state only)
A.L.R.5th	1992-date (state only)
A.L.R.Fed.	1969-date (federal only)

Vol. 595	Pacific reporter, 2d Series, (Arizona Cases)

r 595P2d662
597P2d²995
q 600P2d²1098

—183—

Eaton v Unified
School District
No.1 of Pima
County
1979

(122Az391)
a 595P2d169
636P2d¹92
660P2d¹1207
e 680P2d¹149

—186—

Highlands
Insurance
Co. v Fischer
1979

(122Az394)
f 603P2d¹113
f 603P2d⁴113
f 603P2d⁵114
791P2d¹1089
Cir. 10
723F2d³1501

—189—

Finfrock v
Finfrock
1979

(122Az397)

—191—

Aspell v
American
Contract
Bridge League
of Memphis,
Tennessee
1979

(122Az399)
685P2d⁶1306
688P2d¹624
j 716P2d1031
732P2d³1110
737P2d³1096
d 757P2d⁶109
770P2d368
786P2d1067
804P2d135
20$A_.^2$ 344s
20$A_.^3$ 988s

—196—

Arizona v
Salazar
1979

(122Az404)
j 631P2d526
635P2d³847
o 635P2d³849
643P2d¹1024
653P2d³12
f 692P2d³320
692P2d¹994
692P2d³995
15A⁴721n

—200—

Thorneycroft v
Emery Air
Freight Corp.
1979

(122Az408)
666P2d¹81
88A⁴553n

—203—

Anderson
v Mobile
Discount Corp.
1979

(122Az411)
628P2D⁴596
628P2D⁷597
632P2D¹1004
636P2d¹1230
Cir. 8
d 703F2d³288
15COA347 § 14
73$A_.^2$ 403s
30$A_.^3$ 9s
85$A_.^4$ 297n

—206—

Continental
Bank v Wa-
Ho Truck
Brokage
1979

(122Az414)
f 605P2d¹1283
650P2d⁷1284
d 650P2d⁷1284
e 671P2d⁶430
e 671P2d⁷430
685P2d⁸153
707P2d⁵963
712P2d⁹969
712P2d⁶974
796P2d²890
796P2d¹891
808P2d²1232

836P2d⁵979
842P2d¹1376
Cir. 5
782F2d⁸1349
Cir. 10
788FS⁹1191
11COA143 § 15
23$A_.^3$ 932s
67$A_.^3$ 144s
23$A_.^4$ 868n

—214—

Estate of
Hansen
1979

(122Az422)

—657—

Fullen v
Industrial
Commission
1979

(122Az425)
627P2d⁶697
636P2d⁸1267
678P2d⁸501
699P2d⁸395
761P2d1039
786P2d⁸1073
f 787P2d¹1110
f 787P2d²1110

—662—

In re the
Marriage of
Furimsky
1979

(122Az430)
s 595P2d177
597P2d¹995
j 600P2d1099
604P2d²649
606P2d¹835
634P2d²405
q 634P2d²406
q 657P2d²906
659P2d¹1346
663P2d¹593
q 663P2d594

—665—

Arizona v
Newman
1979

(122Az433)
609P2d⁴55
639P2d⁴1029
647P2d⁴181
653P2d⁴712
676P2d1112
708P2d¹85

708P2d108
735P2d⁶770

—670—

Arizona v Gin
1979

(122Az438)

—671—

Underdown
v Reche
1979

(122Az439)
688P2d¹1074
e 792P2d²777
799P2d²814

—674—

In the Matter
of 1969
Ford Truck
1979

(122Az442)
639P2d¹371
d 687P2d¹947
688P2d¹1091

—990—

Arizona v Gray
1979

(122Az445)
cc 662F2d569
618P2d⁹591
643P2d¹¹1029
648P2d⁸122
665P2d⁵66
696P2d⁸708
696P2d⁹709
760P2d1068
780P2d⁹1069
f 795P2d¹¹1304
795P2d¹²1304
816P2d¹¹239
450US¹467
67LR¹441
101SC¹1203
Cir. 9
625F2d¹221
640F2d¹237
99$A_.^3$ 140n

—995—

Michael v Cole
1979

(122Az450)
s 595P2d1006
637P2d⁹729
663P2d⁷1023
667P2d⁴1315
683P2d¹295

685P2d⁷1306
728P2d683
f 732P2d²198
751P2d⁴972
Cir. 7
803F2d⁹308
Cir. 9
710F2d⁷559
4$A_.^2$ 761s
87$A_.^4$ 167n

—998—

Arizona
v Porter
1979

(122Az453)
s 595P2d1003
s 609P2d1055
617P2d⁸787
631P2d⁴1107
649P2d275
690P2d⁵61
715P2d⁵765
742P2d⁴1358
742P2d⁵1359
762P2d⁵1324
784P2d⁵300
800P2d¹1280
69$A_.^2$ 361s
69$A_.^2$ 384s

—1003—

Arizona
v Porter
1978

(122Az458)
v 595P2d998
s 609P2d1055

—1006—

Michael v Cole
1978

(122Az461)
m 595P2d995

—1010—

Dennis
Development
Co. Inc. v
Department
of Revenue
1979

(122Az465)
d 641P2d1320
f 644P2d⁴907
f 669P2d¹1020
674P2d¹882
685P2d³1334
726P2d¹245
d 822P2d⁴503

—1014—

Barrasso v First
National Bank
of Arizona
1979

(122Az469)
623P2d¹15
627P2d⁶1091
645P2d⁶1266
669P2d⁵992
697P2d¹679

—1017—

Chavez v
Tolleson
Elementary
School District
1979

(122Az472)
(1A⁴1089)
600P2d¹⁴769
d 611P2d¹³550
613P2d¹⁵954
617P2d¹⁵773
625P2d¹⁵934
630P2d¹⁴560
673P2d954
728P2d295
d 763P2d¹⁴989
775P2d1125
782P2d¹³742
825P2d⁵22
d 825P2d¹⁴25
831P2d⁷383
Cir. 4
778FS¹⁴291
Cir. 9
f 587FS⁷1528
f 587FS⁸1528
587FS¹⁴1528
Cir. 10
f 671FS¹³1327
f 671FS¹⁴1327
18COA555§ 8
32$A_.^2$ 1163s
38$A_.^3$ 830s
34$A_.^4$ 264n

—1023—

Arizona v
Contreras
1979

(122Az478)

—1026—

Arizona v
DeWoody
1979

(122Az481)
650P2d¹458

Figure 3-21
Sample Page from Shepard's

Figure 3-22
Abbreviations for History of Case and Treatment of Case

ABBREVIATIONS—ANALYSIS

History of Case

a	(affirmed)	Same case affirmed on appeal.
cc	(connected case)	Different case from case cited but arising out of same subject matter or intimately connected therewith.
D	(dismissed)	Appeal from same case dismissed.
m	(modified)	Same case modified on appeal.
r	(reversed)	Same case reversed on appeal.
s	(same case)	Same case as case cited.
S	(superseded)	Substitution for former opinion.
v	(vacated)	Same case vacated.
US	cert den	Certiorari denied by U.S. Supreme Court.
US	cert dis	Certiorari dismissed by U.S. Supreme Court
US	reh den	Rehearing denied by U.S. Supreme Court.
US	reh dis	Rehearing dismissed by U.S. Supreme Court.

Treatment of Case

c	(criticised)	Soundness of decision or reasoning in cited case criticised for reasons given.
d	(distinguished)	Case at bar different either in law or fact from case cited for reasons given
e	(explained)	Statement of import of decision in cited case. Not merely a restatement of the facts.
f	(followed)	Cited as controlling.
h	(harmonized)	Apparent inconsitency explained and shown not to exist.
j	(dissenting opinion)	Citation in dissenting opinion.
L	limited)	Refusal to extend decision of cited case beyond precise issues involved.
o	(overruled)	Ruling in cited case expressly overruled.
p	(parallel)	Citing case substantially alike or on all fours with cited case in its law or facts.
q	(questioned)	Soundness of decision or reasoning in cited case question.

ABBREVIATIONS—COURTS

Cir. DC—U.S. Court of Appeals, District of Columbia Circuit
Cir. (number)—U.S. Court of Appeals Circuit (number)
Cir. Fed.—U.S. Court of Appeals, Federal Circuit
CCPA—Court of Customs and Patent Appeals
CIT—United States Court of International Trade
ClCt—Claims Court (U.S.)
CtCl—Court of Claims (U.S.)
CuCt—Customs Court
ECA—Temporary Emergency Court of Appeals
ML—Judicial Panel on Multidistrict Litigation
RRR—Special Court Regional Rail Reorganization Act of 1973

Each A.L.R. is organized according to the following format.

1. Annotation outline—shows how the annotation is organized
2. Total Client Service Library reference—shows other resources related to the topic in the annotation
3. Scope—describes issues discussed in the annotation
4. Related matters—directs the reader to other annotations and other legal sources related to the annotation
5. Index—alphabetical index of the topics discussed in the annotation
6. Table of Jurisdictions Represented—table showing which sections discuss cases from which states
7. Summary—overview of the entire annotation
8. Case—includes a brief synopsis of the case and headnotes
9. Annotation—analyzes case and the issues it presents

Figures 3-23 and 3-24 show an annotation for *Chavez*.

Annotations can be found using the alphabetical *Index to Annotations* (used like any index) or the *A.L.R. Digest* (used like any other digest). The *Index* is often easier to use because no index is found in the digest volumes. Pocket parts are used to update the A.L.R.3d, 4th, 5th, and Fed. annotations.

Putting It Into Practice 3.17:

Look in the *A.L.R. Digest* (to the 3rd, 4th, 5th, and Federal A.L.R.) under "Landlord and Tenant." Find "Acts of third persons generally" and then find "Landlord's obligation to protect against criminal activities of third persons." Find an annotation for *Kline*—43 ALR3d 331 and answer the following questions.

a. Does the annotation address liability for the rape of tenants?
b. Which section discusses the duty to protect against robbery?
c. What New York case is discussed in that section?

By the time Tim next checked on Martha's progress, she was in the middle of reading one of the cases she had found.

"There's a cite in this case to the "Rest." and I can't for the life of me remember what that is referring to," lamented Martha.

"To one of the Restatements," responded Tim.

"That's right. I remember now," sighed Martha, feeling foolish.

"Could I help you find the Restatement you need?" asked Tim encouragingly.

"Sure. That would save me wandering down the aisles for awhile." Martha's head was beginning to swim after poring through digests and reporters for a couple of hours.

"Looks like you could use a break," observed Tim. "Why not take a breather, walk around, get something to drink, and come back in a few minutes. You'll think more clearly and get more accomplished in the long run."

"Good idea, coach," teased Martha. "But I'd like to take a rain check on that Restatement offer."

"You got it," promised Tim, admiring Martha's quiet sense of humor.

RESTATEMENTS

The Restatements, one of the most prestigious forms of secondary authority, are prepared by the American Law Institute. Since 1923, a group of judges, preeminent lawyers, and law professors have met with the intent of clarifying the ambiguities in case law and "restating" it in a clear and orderly manner. Today, the Institute not only presents the law created by the courts in a rule-like manner, but it also

Figure 3-23
Subject of Annotations for Chavez

SUBJECT OF ANNOTATION

Liability of university, college, or other school for failure to
protect student from crime

Antonio M. CHAVEZ, personal representative and father of Deceased,
Regina Chavez, Appellant and Cross-Appellee,

v

TOLLESON ELEMENTARY SCHOOL DISTRICT and Ida Moriarity,
Appellees and Cross-Appellants

Court of Appeals of Arizona, Division 1, Department B
March 22, 1979
122 Ariz 472, 595 P2d 1017, 1 ALR4th 1089
Rehearing denied April 27, 1979
Review denied May 22, 1979

SUMMARY OF DECISION

The Superior Court of Maricopa County, Arizona, Sandra D. O'Connor,
J., entered judgment N.O.V. in a wrongful death action brought against a
school district and certain school personnel by the father of a ten year old elementary school pupil, who left the school grounds without permission and
was abducted and slain.

The Court of Appeals of Arizona, Division 1, Department B, Froeb, J.,
affirmed. The court held that a school district and a classroom teacher owe a
duty of ordinary care toward a student during the time the student is under
their charge and that that standard is not one which requires specific proof in
order to be correctly applied by a jury. Hence the plaintiff was not required
to produce evidence relating to specific standards of care. The court held that
there were no facts in the record indicating that school personnel should have
been aware of the potential of criminal conduct in the area of the school and
held that, as a matter of law, the defendants could not reasonably have foreseen that the pupil would leave the school grounds without permission and
thereafter be abducted and slain. The court also held that although it was error for the trial court to grant judgment N.O.V. on the ground that the plaintiff failed to introduce proof relating to the standard of care, the trial court's

---

does its best to predict what courts will do in the future. Although courts are not
obligated to follow the Restatements, they often cite them.

The Restatements are organized in chapters and divided into sections, each of
which deals with a principle of law, which is restated in boldface in clear, unambiguous terms. Each restatement is followed by a "comments" section, which analyzes the principles of law, and "illustrations," which give examples that demonstrate
the practical application of the principle. The Reporter's Note that follows the illustrations references cases citing the Restatement principle. (Figure 3-25 shows a page
from the Restatement (Second) of Torts.) Restatements have been prepared for a

Figure 3-24
Total Client Service Library

ANNOTATION

**LIABILITY OF UNIVERSITY, COLLEGE, OR OTHER SCHOOL
FOR FAILURE TO PROTECT STUDENT FROM CRIME**

by

Joel E. Smith, J.D.

TOTAL CLIENT-SERVICE LIBRARY® REFERENCES

15A Am Jur 2d, Colleges and Universities § 39; 57 Am Jur 2d, Municipal
School and State Tort Liability §§ 74, 75; 68 Am Jur 2d, Schools
§§ 319–322

Annotations: See the related matters listed in the annotation, infra.

5 Am Jur Pl & Pr Forms (Rev). Colleges and Universities, Forms 41–44;
18 Am Jur Pl & Pr Forms (Rev). Municipal, School, and State Tort
Liability, Forms 1–3, 171–213

13 Am Jur Legal Forms 2d, Municipal, School, and State Tort Liability
§§ 181:11–181:15, §§ 181:31–181:36

4 Am Jur Proof of Facts 2d 87, Teachers's Failure to Supervise Students:
9 Am Jur Proof of Facts 2d 729, School's Failure to Maintain Children's
Play Area Properly

US L Ed Digest, Colleges and Universities § 1; Schools §§ 1–2

ALR Digest, Colleges and Universities § 6; Schools §§ 16–17

L Ed Index to Annos, Colleges and Universities; Criminal Law; Privileges
and Immunities; Schools

ALR Quick Index, Colleges and Universities; Criminal Law; Governmental Immunity or Privilege; Schools Torts; Victim

Federal Quick Index, Colleges and Universities; Criminal Law; Privileges
and Immunities; Schools and School Districts; Torts; Victim of Crimes

variety of legal topics: Torts, Contracts, Property, Trusts, and many others. Some are
in their second or third edition (e.g., Restatement (Second) of Torts).

Putting It Into Practice 3.18:

Assuming the Restatement (Second) of Contracts has been adopted in your state,
how old must someone be in your state to enter into a binding contract? To
answer this question, look in the Table of Contents of the Restatement (Second)
of Contracts under "Parties to Contract" and find the subsection "Infants."

NET NEWS

To learn more about the American Law Institute and the *Restatements of the Law,* go to the ALI Web site at *www.ali.org.*

Figure 3-25

*Sample Page from Restatement
(Second) of Torts*

§ 319

Illustrations:

1. A operates a private hospital for contagious diseases. Through the negligence of the medical staff. B, who is suffering from scarlet fever, is permitted to leave the hospital with the assurance that he is entirely recovered, although his disease is still in an infectious state. Through the negligence of a guard employed by A, C, a delirious smallpox patient, is permitted to escape. B and C communicate the scarlet fever and smallpox to D and E respectively. A is subject to liability to D and E.

2. A operates a private sanitarium for the insane. Through the negligence of the guards employed by A, B, a homicidal maniac, is permitted to escape. B attacks and causes harm to C. A is subject to liability to C.

§ 320. Duty of Person Having Custody of Another to Control Conduct of Third Persons

One who is required by law to take or who voluntarily takes the custody of another under circumstances such as to deprive the other of his normal power of self-protection or to subject him to association with persons likely to harm him, is under a duty to exercise reasonable care so to control the conduct of third persons as to prevent them from intentionally harming the other or so conducting themselves as to create an unreasonable risk of harm to him, if the actor

    (a) knows or has reason to know that he has the ability to control the conduct of the third persons, and

    (b) knows or should know of the necessity and opportunity for exercising such control.

See Reporter's Notes.

Comment:

    a. The rule stated in this Section is applicable to a sheriff or peace office, a jailer or warden of a penal institution, officials in charge of a state asylum or hospital for the criminally insane, or to teachers or other persons in charge of public school. It is also applicable to persons conducting a private hospital or asylum, a private school, and to lessees of convict labor.

    b. Helplessness of other. The circumstances under which the custody of another is taken and maintained may be such

---

See Appendix for Reporter's Notes, Court Citations, and Cross References

[2 Restatement of Torts 2d]

As Martha was copying a section from the Restatement of Torts, she sensed someone standing behind her and looked around to see Tim grinning sheepishly.

"I didn't want to disturb you," he began to apologize. "You seemed so intent on what you were doing."

"No problem. You can't disturb me any more than I already am," smiled Martha.

"It just occurred to me that you might want to check out the legal periodicals. The issue you're dealing with is the kind of topic legal scholars like to sink their teeth into. If I were you, I'd look especially for some law review articles because they not only give you some creative approaches to your problem but they are an awesome source of references. Why reinvent the wheel? If they've done all the research, why not take advantage of it?

"I like how you think, Mr.—? You know, I've been monopolizing your time the last two days and I just realized I don't even know your name." Martha was not being completely truthful. She had been looking for an excuse to ask Tim his name all afternoon.

"McFay. Tim McFay."

LEGAL PERIODICALS

Legal periodicals are secondary sources that encompass such publications as law reviews published by law schools, publications by bar associations and paralegal associations, and legal newspapers. Law reviews are published by law schools and contain extensive scholarly articles written by judges, law professors, or attorneys and edited by selected law students. They also have book reviews and shorter articles written by law students.

Bar associations (organizations to which attorneys are usually required to belong in order to practice law in a particular state) publish journals that offer features focusing on the practical aspects of practicing law. While law reviews are scholarly in their approach, bar association (and paralegal association) publications are very pragmatic. One of the better known publications for paralegals is *Legal Assistant Today,* which provides practical information and suggestions to paralegals.

Local and national law newspapers are published weekly or daily and offer articles on a wide variety of legal topics of interest to practicing attorneys and paralegals. One of the better known national newspapers is the *National Law Journal,* which is published weekly. In addition to having features discussing current topics of concern to the legal community, this newspaper highlights recent federal and state court decisions and provides professional announcements and advertisements for career opportunities.

Several indexes can be used to locate legal periodical articles, including *Index to Legal Periodicals and Books* and *Current Law Index.* Articles can be accessed by looking under the topic name or author. You can also look for articles discussing a particular case or statute.

■■ *Putting It Into Practice 3.19:*

Ask your instructor what legal periodicals he or she subscribes to or recommends. Find out what legal periodicals your library carries and examine them.

NET NEWS

For links to major law reviews and journals online, go to *www.ilrg.com/journals.html.*

"Sometimes I Think We Forget That Judicial Decisions Are Not Necessarily a Reflection of a Judge's Personal Philosophy."

"How are you enjoying the law review articles?" asked Tim, eyeing the journals stacked up next to Martha.

"I wish some of these professors were judges. They have some great ideas about how the law should be."

"But keep in mind that they're not subject to the same kinds of restrictions that appellate court judges are," Tim reminded her.

"I'm not sure what you mean."

"For one thing, judges are bound by the facts before them. The facts may not permit them to go in the direction they would like to. And for another, they have to adhere to the case law that has preceded them. Depending on their judicial philosophy, they may be very restricted in what they believe they are able to do. Sometimes I think we forget that judicial decisions are not necessarily a reflection of a judge's personal philosophy."

Judicial philosophy was a far cry from the pragmatic concerns that occupied Martha's world at the firm, but she was impressed with Tim's knowledge and his obvious love for the law. She was deeply entrenched in the practicalities that defined the law for her, but she found she enjoyed visiting the ethereal realm of abstractions and ideals in which judges and legal scholars played.

LIMITATIONS ON APPELLATE COURTS

Questions of Fact vs. Questions of Law

issues of law issue relating to the application or interpretation of the law

Appellate courts do not hear testimony or receive evidence because they decide only **issues of law.** Issues of law involve the interpretation and application of the law, such as whether the law applied in the case at hand was constitutional or whether the actions taken by the trial court were proper. An appellate court may review lower court decisions on **issues of fact,** but only to the extent necessary to determine whether the trial court "clearly abused its discretion." Issues of fact involve factual questions as to who did what to whom, when and where they did it, why they did it, and so on. If a trial court, for example, finds that the defendant was present at the crime scene, the appellate court cannot disturb this finding as long as the evidence in the record supports it. The question of presence at the crime scene involves a factual question rather than a legal one. But if the question before the trial court is whether testimony regarding the defendant's presence at the crime scene is admissible, this question is a legal one. The rationale behind this rule is that the trial court, by virtue of being present during presentation of evidence, is in a better position to evaluate testimony and other evidence than the appellate court, which reviews only the record prepared at trial.

issues of fact issue relating to a factual question in the dispute between parties

Appellate courts have more discretion in reviewing questions of law than they do in reviewing issues of fact. They examine the legal principles and reasoning used by the lower court. Appellate courts are obligated to correct any legal errors committed by the lower court. They cannot, however, resolve legal questions that are not properly presented to them. If a party fails to make a timely objection, thereby preserving it in the court record, the appellate court is denied any opportunity to correct that error.

By the same token, if a party fails to adhere to a multitude of rules governing appellate practice, the appellate court may deny legal review of any errors committed. Appellate practice is highly structured and bound by rules. Procedural obstacles exist at every turn. Unwary litigants may be unwittingly deprived of access to an appellate court if they fail to comply with any one requirement dictated by the rules of appellate practice.

Stare Decisis

Under the principle of **stare decisis** (which literally means "let the decision stand"), courts are obligated to adhere to their previous decisions as well as the decisions of those courts that review their opinions. A state court of appeals, for example, must render decisions that are consistent with its previous decisions and the decisions rendered by the court of last resort in that state. *Stare decisis* is an integral feature of the American legal system and is revered because of the desire to retain stability and predictability in the law.

Stare decisis can be somewhat confining if fairness dictates a different outcome. Not all people who commit crimes, for example, deserve the same treatment. Someone who steals bread to feed his children arguably should be treated differently than someone who steals out of greed. A legal system that mandated strict conformance to precedent in such cases could be stifling. Courts escape this rigidity by **distinguishing** (differentiating) cases that are factually different. If the facts vary significantly, a court is justified in altering its conclusion and possibly even its analysis. A court that finds a legal right to an abortion for an adult, for example, may come to a very different conclusion for a juvenile seeking an abortion, even if all the other facts are identical. Similarly, the law in reference to abortion is dependent on the stage of the abortion, the funding source of the abortion, and the immediacy of the abortion (whether a waiting period is required), among other things. In short, the law is usually contingent on a number of factors.

Adherence to Statutes and Constitutions

Appellate courts are also constrained by the legislature to some extent. They cannot ignore a statute they find distasteful unless they believe it to be unconstitutional. If the legislative intent is clear, the courts must adhere to the statute. Because legislative intent is often unclear, however, appellate courts frequently find leeway in their interpretation of a statute's purpose.

Appellate courts are bound to follow the U.S. and state constitutions, but the extent to which they are bound depends on their judicial philosophy. Judges whom some commentators categorize as **conservative** believe that they are limited to a strict interpretation of statutes and constitutions. So-called **liberal** judges perceive their role as going beyond such literal interpretation and view themselves as protectors of minority groups and the politically disadvantaged.

A relatively conservative U.S. Supreme Court wrote *Plessy v. Ferguson*, which allowed the maintenance of segregation in this country. This opinion did not mean that the judges themselves philosophically agreed with the principles of segregation, but rather that they felt obliged to defer to the legislature. In later years, their more liberal counterparts in *Brown v. Board of Education* found segregated schools to be in violation of the Constitution. The difference between these two panels of judges lay not necessarily in their personal philosophies but in their judicial philosophies. The *Brown* Court perceived its role as a protector of the politically powerless, a protector that intervened when the legislative branch failed to represent all of its constituents. The *Plessy* Court, on the other hand, perceived itself as confined by the will of the legislature.

All of these rules shape appellate court practice and prevent appellate judges from behaving capriciously and frivolously. While personal philosophy no doubt colors the opinions of appellate judges to some degree, the rules of appellate decision-making preclude the appellate process from becoming a forum for personal agendas.

Putting It Into Practice 3.20:

Very few cases are overturned on appeal. Why do you think this is so?

Figure 3-26
Constraints on Appellate Courts

CONSTRAINTS ON APPELLATE COURTS
Confinement to Questions of Law
Stare Decisis
Adherence to Statutes
Adherence to Constitutions

"Finding a Case on All Fours Rarely Happens."

"Have you exhausted all of the digests now"? asked Tim.

"Well, I've certainly exhausted myself, but I'm not sure I've exhausted all of the digests," quipped Martha.

Tim grinned, grasping for a quick comeback. "Will you be back tomorrow?" was all that came out.

"No doubt. And probably the next day too, at the rate I'm going."

"I thought you were pleased at the cases you'd found."

"I was until I read the cases more carefully. In the case most similar to ours factually, the court found no liability. That's not good for the home team. I need to find a case more like ours where the court did find liability." Images of a ceaseless quest for the perfect case filled Martha's imagination. "But whether I find the perfect case or not, I have to get back to my boss with what I find by the first of next week."

"Finding a case on all fours rarely happens. . ." began Tim.

"On all fours?" frowned Martha. "Sounds like some kind of animal."

"I mean a case that's right on point," explained Tim, hoping he wasn't coming off as being pretentious.

"Okay. But what do you mean—that rarely happens?" Martha had expected just such a case to appear and she was feeling very unsettled by Tim's suggestion that that might not happen.

Tim could see by the alarm on Martha' face that he was fueling her anxiety. "All I'm saying is that we rarely find cases that have the same facts or even close to the same facts as the facts in our client's case. The best we can usually hope for is to find a case where the facts are reasonably similar enough that we can analogize our case to the reported case." Tim wasn't sure his explanation was helping. "Say, the librarians have prepared a little booklet for beginning researchers. Why don't you take it home with you and I can answer any questions you might have tomorrow."

"All right," agreed Martha, not too certain that she wanted to think about research any more that night, but comforted by the fact that Tim would be around to help her.

LEGAL ANALYSIS

Legal analysis, the thinking process of lawyers, can be reduced to four essential elements, as expressed in the acronym IRAC.

I = Issue
R = Rule
A = Application
C = Conclusion

Figure 3-27
Legal Analysis

LEGAL ANALYSIS
I = ISSUE
R = RULES
A = APPLICATION OF RULES
C = CONCLUSION

Issue

As with a brief, the issue statement sets forth the problem being resolved. No one can sensibly respond to any question until that question is understood. Although this statement may seem self-evident, stating the issue is often a stumbling block for those learning legal analysis and a point of contention for those engaging in the litigation process. Do not treat the process of constructing an issue statement lightly.

Rule

The rules of law that govern legal analysis are much like the rules in any game. These rules establish the parameters within which you must operate. For purposes of legal analysis, these rules include case law, statutes, ordinances, administrative regulations, court procedural rules, and constitutional provisions.

In most legal writing, a large percentage of the analysis is devoted to establishing the rules. Before you can even consider the problems presented in your situation, you must logically and systematically set forth the principles that will guide your reasoning process.

Application

Once you have identified the rules, you must apply them to the facts in your situation. Many times, conflicting or ambiguous rules are involved, and you have to determine which is most applicable. You may, for example, have a group of related cases, none of whose holdings directly resolve the question in your case. After explaining each case and discussing the similarities and dissimilarities between cases, you have to explain which holding is most analogous to your case and, therefore, dictates a certain outcome.

If the application of rules can lead to conflicting outcomes, how neutral should you be when constructing your arguments? The answer depends on your purpose. If you are preparing your writing for an attorney for informational purposes or for a professor for instructional purposes, you should apply the rules in every imaginable way. Because you are not trying to persuade your reader to reach a certain outcome, you should consider every reasonably conceivable argument. This way the reader can anticipate likely arguments of opponents and mull over likely rebuttals. If, on the other hand, your audience is a court and your intent is to persuade, you should present your arguments in a manner that best reflects your client's position.

Conclusion

Having pondered all sides of an issue, you must finally render a conclusion. Some find themselves paralyzed by indecision when asked to do this and will complain that they cannot reach a conclusion because they do not know all the facts. Unfortunately, the practice of law often requires practitioners to draw conclusions without knowing the whole picture. Until both sides in a lawsuit have completed the fact-finding process (part of something called *discovery*, which will be discussed in the next chapter), each side has a one-sided perception of the problem because most of its information has come from the client. Some factual questions may never be resolved because the parties continue to disagree about what happened. In truth, conclusions can be drawn even from incomplete data. Simply admit that the conclusion is a tentative one. If the unknown facts turn out one way, your conclusion will be X, but if they turn out another way, your conclusion will be Y. In this way, the reader knows that you have considered all the contingencies. The bottom line, however, is that you must reach a conclusion—no excuses.

When writing your conclusion, make sure you explain the reasoning behind it. Certainly your supervising attorney will expect such an explanation. To omit your reasoning leaves the reader hanging, wondering why that particular conclusion was drawn. This is called **conclusory writing.** Your conclusion must not appear to be the result of a coin toss. To give the reader confidence in your decision, you must provide a rationale.

conclusory writing   coming to a conclusion without offering any explanation for how the conclusion was drawn

---

ANALYSIS of *In re Charlotte* (found in Appendix B)

ISSUE
    Is a girdle a burglary tool?

RULE
    A burglary tool is a tool, instrument, or other article adapted, designed, or commonly used for committing or facilitating offenses involving larceny by physical taking.

APPLICATION
    A girdle is neither a tool, instrument, nor article adapted, designed, or commonly used for purposes of committing larceny. It is simply an article of clothing.
    Some would argue, however, that a girdle may indeed be adapted for purposes of larceny. Because of its design, it is especially helpful in committing shoplifting because it provides the perfect place for hiding clothing and relatively small items.

CONCLUSION
    The legislative intent of Sec. 140.35 of the Penal Law was to include tools used to take items but to exclude tools used to hide them. Even though burglary tools could logically include girdles, the legislature apparently did not intend to do so. Therefore, for purposes of our penal code, a girdle is not considered a burglary tool.

◆ **LOCAL LINKS** ◆
Your instructor may have additional or differing suggestions about how to analyze case law. Record those suggestions.

Putting It Into Practice 3.21:

Find the issue before the court in *Hill.* Identify one of the rules used by the *Hill* Court. How does the court apply that rule? What conclusion does the court come to in its application?

COMPARING CASE LAW

The first step in analyzing relevant case law is to examine the facts. Decide which facts are essential. Then compare these facts to the facts in your client's case. To help objectify this comparison, make three columns on a sheet of paper. Label the first column "Similar Facts," the second "Dissimilar Facts," and the third "Unknown Facts." Doing this will help you visualize the extent of the differences that exist. Having done this, you must then evaluate the relative importance of the similarities, dissimilarities, and unknowns. If, for example, the factual similarities involve relatively unimportant facts, while the dissimilarities or unknowns pertain to critical facts, then you may be hard pressed to convince a court to apply the case. If the essential facts are, for the most part, similar and the dissimilarities and unknowns are relatively trivial, then a court will be likely to apply the case to your facts.

Comparison between Mike's Case and *Hill*

SIMILARITIES
Shooting
Student assaulted by another student
Assailants members of a gang
Assault occurred after school

DISSIMILARITIES
School received warning of threat to kill vs. no warning
On campus vs. off campus
During school hours vs. during after hours
Fatal shooting vs. non-fatal shooting
Previous altercation vs. no previous altercation

UNKNOWNS (in Mike's case)
Prior discipline of assailant by school officials
Where assailants got guns
Whether assailants were known to have "dangerous propensities"
Reason behind shooting

Putting It Into Practice 3.22:

What do you think are the best reasons to cite to a court as to why it should distinguish *Hill* from Mike's case? Which dissimilarities would you emphasize? Which unknown facts are most important to determine in that they could best serve to convince a court to distinguish *Hill*?

Martha could not concentrate on the task before her—selecting a dress to wear. Her mind kept flitting back and forth from what she had read about legal analysis in the booklet Tim had given her to snippets of her conversations the day before with Tim. What was it about that man that intrigued her? she wondered. Images of his smiling face kept floating in and out of her awareness. She pushed them away as she forced herself to focus on what to wear. Not generally a woman of indecision and certainly not one to be overly concerned about her appearance, she was becoming increasingly irritated with her inability to make a choice. "Come on, Martha, this is not a major life decision," she chided herself; yet somehow she could not shake the feeling that today was a red letter day.

"Bright-eyed and bushy-tailed, I see." Tim greeted Martha with genuine enthusiasm.

"Indeed, I am, and looking forward to finding exactly what I need," beamed Martha.

"That's the spirit," commended Tim.

"And with that, I bid you farewell as I venture into the land of statutory authority." Martha waved her arms dramatically to punctuate her proclamation.

"Fare thee well, fair maiden." Tim bowed with mock fanfare. "Oh, and by the way, the Arizona statutes are in the other direction."

STATUTES

codified law   laws that have been arranged according to subject matter; also referred to as *codes*

slip laws   laws that have recently been enacted and have been published in sheet form

Statutes come in three forms as they evolve from recently passed bills to **codified law.** Immediately after they mature from bills to laws, statutes can be found in the form of **slip laws,** which are simply sheets of paper on which the newly created laws are printed. At the federal level, slip laws are identified by public law numbers, such as Pub. L. No. 105-90. The number 105 refers to the fact that this law was enacted by the 105th Congress and the 90 means that it was the 90th bill passed by that Congress.

session laws chronologically ordered volumes of laws

At the end of a congressional session, all of the slip laws are compiled into one or more chronologically ordered volumes called **session laws,** which are published in the *Statutes at Large.* An example of a citation for a session law is 115 Stat. 800. This means that this session law can be found in volume 115 of the *Statutes at Large* on page 800. Because it can take up to a year for a news *tatutes at Large* to be available, other publications, such as *United States Law Week,* and online sources, provide more up-to-date publications of new statutes. (*U.S. Law Week* is printed weekly.)

The laws in a *Statutes at Large* volume are in chronological order, but when they are codified, they are grouped by subject and arranged according to their title. Federal statutes, for example, are arranged according to 50 subject categories, and bound in three different publications. The official government publication of the federal statutes is the *United States Code* (U.S.C.). The U.S.C. is organized by title, each of which covers a specific subject. For example, Title 18 contains all the statutes relating to crime and criminal procedure. (See Figure 3-28, which shows a section from Title 18 in the U.S.C.A.) So a law designated as 18 U.S.C. Sec. 111 refers to title 18 of the U.S.C., section 101.

Two unofficial versions of the federal statutes are found in the *United States Code Annotated* (U.S.C.A.) and the *United States Code Service* (U.S.C.S.). Both of the unofficial codes are annotated in that they contain references to cases that interpret and apply the code. For this reason, most researchers prefer to use the U.S.C.A. (which, as a West publication, ties into other West publications) and U.S.C.S. (which, as a publication of the former Lawyers' Co-op, ties into *Am. Jur.* and the A.L.R.) rather than the official version of the U.S.C. Another reason to use the unofficial versions is that they are updated regularly using pocket parts and supplements, whereas the U.S.C. is published every six years. The U.S.C. can also be accessed online at *http://law.house.gov/usc.html.*

Federal statutes can be located via an index using any significant terms in the statute or under the title number, if you know it. Alternatively, if you know the popular name of a section of the code, you can use the Popular Name Table, which is found in the last index volume. For example, if you look under "Tort Claims Act" in the Popular Name Table, you will discover that this Act could be found in Title 28. (See Figure 3-29 showing a page from the Popular Name Table.) In addition to using the pocket parts and supplements to update your statutory research, you can

Figure 3-28
Sample Section from U.S.C.

> **Sec. 111. Assaulting, resisting, or impeding certain officers or employees**
> - (a)   In General.—Whoever—
>   - (1) forcibly assaults, resists, opposes, impedes, intimidates, or interferes with any person designated in section 1114 of this title while engaged in or on account of the performance of official duties; or
>   - (2) forcibly assaults or intimidates any person who formerly served as a person designated in section 1114 on account of the performance of official duties during such person's term of service, shall, where the acts in violation of this section constitute only simple assault, be fined under this title or imprisoned not more than one year, or both, and in all other cases, be fined under this title or imprisoned not more than three years, or both.
> - (b)   Enhanced Penalty.—Whoever, in the commission of any acts described in subsection (a), uses a deadly or dangerous weapon (including a weapon intended to cause death or danger but that fails to do so by reason of a defective component) or inflicts bodily injury, shall be fined under this title or imprisoned not more than ten years, or both.

Ton   **FEDERAL AND STATE ACTS CITED BY POPULAR NAME**

Wis Laws 1989, 341.25 et seq.

Tonapah Chapter
Nev. Statutes 1903, Ch. 89, p. 163

Tonawanda City Court Act
N.Y. Laws 1942, ch. 906

Tongass Timber Reform Act
U.S. Code 1988 Title 16, §§472a, 539d, 539e
Nov. 28, 1990, P.L. 101-626, 104 Stat. 4426

Tongass Timber Sale Act
U.S., Aug. 8, 1947, c. 516, 61 Stat. 920

Tonkin Gulf Resolution
U.S., Aug. 10, 1964, P.L. 88-408, 78 Stat. 384

Tonnage Duties Act
U.S. Code 1988 Title 46, Appendix §121 et seq.
July 20, 1789, c. 3, 1 Stat. 27
July 31, 1789, c. 5, 1 Stat. 29
Sept. 16, 1789, c. 15, 1 Stat. 69
Mar. 2, 1799, c. 22, 1 Stat. 627, §§63, 64
June 19, 1878, c. 318, 20 Stat. 171
Aug. 5, 1909, c. 6, 36 Stat. 11, §36

Tonnage Measurement Simplification Act
U.S. Code 1988 Title 46, §§12102, 14102, 14104,
    14501, 14502, 14504, 14511, 14521, 14522
Dec. 24, 1980, P.L. 96-594, 94 Stat. 3461

Tonnage of Vessels Act
U.S. Code 1988 Title 46, §§14502, 14512
May 6, 1864, c. 83, 13 Stat. 69, §3

Tostine Company Act
Mich. Comp. Laws 1948, 494.1 et seq.

Tool Act (Burglary Tools)
N.C. Gen. Stat. 1943, §14-55

Tool and Die Lien Act
Ill. Rev. Stat. 1991, Ch. 82, §350 et seq.

Tool Equipment Act (Railroad Cars)
Mich. Comp. Laws 1979, 469.141 et seq.

Topographic Mapping Act
Cal. Public Resourse Code §8831 et seq.

Torrens Act (Instruments Creating Liens)
Ill. Rev. Stat. 1991, Ch. 30, §103 et seq.

Torrens Act (Land Title Registration)
Cal. Statutes 1915, p. 1932.
Colo. Rev. Stat., 38-36-101 et seq.
Ga. Official Code Anno. 44-2-40 et seq.
Haw. Rev. Stat. 1985, §501-1 et seq.
Ill. Rev. Stat. 1991, Ch. 30, §44h et seq.
Mas. Gen. Laws 1990, 185:1 et seq.
Min. Stat. 1990, 508.01 et seq.
N.C. Gen. Stat. 1943, §43-1 et seq.
Neb. Laws 1915, Ch. 225
N.Y. Real Property Law (Consol. Laws Ch. 50) §370
    et seq.
Ohio Rev. Code 1953, 5309.01 et seq.
Ore. Rev. Stat. 1953, 94.005 et seq.
Ten. Public Acts 1917, Ch. 63
Utah Laws 1917, Ch. 28
Va. Code 1950, §55-112
Wash. Rev. Code 1976, 65.12.005 et seq.

Torrens Act (Mechanics' Lien-Notice of Claim)
Ill. Rev. Stat. 1991, Ch. 82, §24

Torrens Act (Registered Titles)
Ill. Rev. Stat. 1991, Ch. 30, §4th et seq.

Torrens Repeal Law
Ill. Rev. Stat. 1991, Ch. 30, §1201 et seq.

Torres-Felando Long Term Care Reform Act
Cal. Statutes 1982, Ch. 1453

Tort Actions General Survival Act
D. C. Code 1981, § 12-101

Tort Claims Act
U.S. Code 1988 Title 28 §§1291, 1346, 1402, 1504,
    2110, 2401, 2402, 2411, 2412, 2671 to 2680
Aug. 2, 1946, c. 753, 60 Stat. 812, Title 4
Alk. Stat. 1962, §09.05.250 et seq.
Cal. Government Code §900 et seq.
Del. Code of 1974, Title 10, §4001 et seq.
Ida. Code 1947, 6-901 et seq.
Ind. Code 1988, 34-4-16.5.1 et seq.
Iowa Code 1991, 25A.1 et seq.
Kan. Stat. Anno. 75-6101 et seq.
Md. Code 1974, CJ. §5-401 et seq.
Me. Rev. Stat. Anns. 1964, Title 14, §8101 et seq.
Mont. Code Anno., 1991, 2-9-301 et seq.
N.J. Stat. Anno. 59:1-1 et seq.
N.M. Stat. Anno. 1978, 41-4-1 et seq.
N.Y. Laws 1939, Ch 860, §8 et seq.
Okla. Stat. 1991, Title 51, §151 et seq.
Ore. Rev. Stat. 1991, 30.260 et seq.
S.C. Code of Laws 1976, §15-78-10 et seq.

Figure 3-29
Sample Page from Popular Name Table

also refer to *Shepard's,* which will tell you whether a statute has been interpreted as being unconstitutional or is in any way invalid.

Putting It Into Practice 3.23:

Look at Figure 3-29, showing the Popular Name Table, and find out where you could locate North Carolina's "Tool Act."

Research of state statutes is conducted in much the same way. Like federal statutes, they appear first as slip laws, then as session laws, and are ultimately codified as state codes. Most states have annotated codes that are organized by subject matter and have prepared a general index that can be used to locate specific statutes. Statutes are kept current using pocket parts and supplements. In Martha's search, she found a statute 12-820.01, in the Arizona Revised Statutes, an annotated version of the Arizona statutes, setting forth the immunities for public entities (see Figure 3-30).

Putting It Into Practice 3.24:

Does any part of A.R.S. 12-820.01 indicate that schools are absolutely immune in regard to their supervision of students? How does this statute define a "public entity"? Look under "No Immunity" in the annotations that follow the statute. Do you notice any cases involving a school district?

The greatest challenge to statutory research is generally not in finding statutes but in interpreting them. Statutory analysis often boils down to decoding vague or ambiguous words or phrases. To do this, you must determine the purpose of the statute, that is, the *legislative intent* behind it. Was the legislature attempting to remedy some social ill? Was it trying to close a loophole? Were the legislators addressing a particular problem, or were they trying to write a statute general enough to apply to a wide variety of circumstances? Were they attempting to thwart some future acts that they anticipated might be a problem? Was this legislation part of a package designed to remedy a common problem?

To get an insight into legislative intent, consider the following factors.

Definitions Section of Statute

Some statutes are preceded by a section defining certain terms used in the statute, especially any terms that have a technical meaning that differs from ordinary usage. To illustrate, consider a case in which a suspect shoots a woman who is three months pregnant, resulting in the death of her fetus. If the state wants to charge the suspect with murder and the murder statutes in that state refer to the killing of a "human being," the question that must be answered is whether a

---

NET NEWS

To read the *United States Code* or any state statutory code, go to *www.law.cornell.edu* and click on "Constitutions and Codes."

Analysis
"Political Subdivision."
"Public Entity."

"Political Subdivision."

Cities are political subdivisions within the meaning of paragraph 6. City of Tucson v. Fleischman ex rel. County of Pima, 152 Ariz. 269, 731 P.2d 634 (Ct. App. 1986).

"Public Entity."

The claims statutes apply to cities even though they are not specifically included in paragraph 6 of this section. City of Tucson v. Fleischman ex rel. County of Pima, 152 Ariz. 269, 731 P.2d 634 (Ct. App. 1986).

Case References.

12-820.01. Absolute immunity.

A. A public entity shall not be liable for acts and omissions of its employees constituting:
1. The exercise of a judicial or legislative function; or
2. The exercise of an administrative function involving the determination of fundamental governmental policy.
B. The determination of a fundamental governmental policy involves the exercise of discretion and shall include, but is not limited to:
1. A determination of whether to seek or whether to provide the resources necessary for:
(a) The purchase of equipment,
(b) The construction or maintenance of facilities,
(c) The hiring of personnel, or
(d) The provision of governmental services.
2. A determination of whether and how to spend existing resources, including those allocated for equipment, facilities and personnel.
3. The licensing and regulation of any profession or occupation.

1984

CASE NOTES

Analysis
Constitutionality.
In General.
Purpose.
Applicability.
- Article.
- Nondecisions.
- Section.

Figure 3-30
Sample Page from Arizona Revised Statutes

fetus is a human being. The place to begin answering this question is by looking at the definitions section of the statute defining murder.

Plain Meaning

If no definitions are available (which is frequently the case), you should consider the plain meaning (everyday meaning) of the word in question. The rules of statutory construction require adherence to the language used by the legislature, and other sources cannot be consulted unless the language is ambiguous or some inconsistency exists within the statute. Because the meaning of "human being" is ambiguous, its plain meaning is not apparent and, if it is not clearly defined in the statute, other sources will need to be consulted.

Context of Other Statutes

If the plain meaning is subject to equally reasonable but different interpretations, then plain meaning does not solve the dilemma. In those cases, the statutory context must be considered. How is the term used in other sections of the statute or other statutes addressing the same issue? The problem with applying the definition of another statute that defines "human being" is that the purpose of the two statutes might differ. A civil statute dealing with the wrongful death of a human being, for example, may very well have a different purpose than a criminal statute dealing with the killing of a human being.

Public Policy

The historical context of the statute may be enlightening. The events and conditions that shaped the passage of the statute may reveal the legislature's motivation. These public policy considerations may be found in other statutes, in case law, or in the legislative history (discussed below). If, in our case involving the defining of the term *human being*, the legislature had drafted a statute intended to make it easier for the state to prosecute those whose actions resulted in the death of a fetus, we might infer that the term *human being* was intended to encompass a fetus.

Case Law

Interpretations by other courts, administrative agencies, or legal scholars may also shed light on the legislature's intent. If other courts within your state have interpreted the terms at issue, their conclusions will guide you. If courts in other states have interpreted the terms, their conclusions may be persuasive, but not binding. How other courts defined *human being* could be helpful in our case, but only to the extent the context in which these courts had defined the term was similar to ours.

Legislative History

legislative history history behind a statute, including the events that took place before the statute's passage and during its consideration that reflect on its purpose

If none of these approaches yields the legislature's intent, the **legislative history** of the statute should be examined. This history includes the events that took place before the statute's passage and during its consideration (statements made by legislators during debates or committee reports discussing its passage) that reflect on the bill's purpose. In our quest to define *human being*, we would certainly want to find any documentation of legislative debates or committee reports in which the term had been the subject of discussion.

A statute's legislative history does not, however, necessarily impart the legislative intent behind the statute. Determining the collective intent of any group of

Figure 3-31
Determining Legislative Intent

> **DETERMINING LEGISLATIVE INTENT**
> Definitions Section of Statute
> Plain Meaning
> Context of Other Statutes
> Public Policy
> Case Law
> Legislative History

people is difficult, but determining such intent in the context of political agendas is almost impossible. Legislators vote to pass bills for a variety of reasons, and their actual motivation is often known only by them. Furthermore, legislators are ill-equipped to predict the future, and frequently situations arise that they never contemplated when they passed the bill. Such novel situations demand creative interpretations of applicable laws.

To illustrate statutory interpretation, consider one court's analysis of a statute regarding a school district's duty to those who used its crosswalks (*Alhambra School District v. Superior Court*, 796 P.2d 470 (Ariz. 1990). The plaintiff in this case was a high-school student who was injured while using the crosswalk next to a grade school. The school argued that it owed a duty of care solely to the students of the grade school. It reasoned that, because the signs alluded to in the statute had to read "Stop when children in crosswalk" and another subsection required vehicles to stop for any person in the crosswalk when the signs were in place, the term *person,* as used in the statute, really referred to children who were required to use the crosswalk. The court reasoned otherwise.

> "The [district's] construction of the statute strains the language beyond the bursting point. The common meaning of *person* clearly is not students of Cordova Elementary School. The legislature has not expressed its intention that person should be read to mean students of Cordova Elementary School, or even children. Surely we are not to infer that because the sign says children, drivers are free to run down any adult who may be using the crosswalk. The legislature's intention is clear in this case. If it had intended to limit the protection only to students of Cordova, it could easily have done so. Therefore we must give effect to the statute's unambiguous meaning. By following the statutory procedure to establish a marked crosswalk, the District assumed a duty of care to persons using the crosswalk, not just students of the abutting school."

BONUS POINTERS:

canons of construction
rules that guide courts in interpreting statutes

CANONS OF CONSTRUCTION

Although the pursuit of legislative history is a worthy and sometimes fruitful quest, you may have to enlist the **canons of construction** in the process of interpreting a statute. These canons are rules that guide courts in interpreting statutes and include the following.

- ◆ Words and phrases should be construed in the context of the statute of which they are a part.
- ◆ Statutes should be construed in light of the harm the legislature intended to address.
- ◆ Statutes on the same subject should be construed together.
- ◆ Statutes should be construed in such a way as to preserve their constitutionality.
- ◆ Statutes in conflict with case law should be construed narrowly.

It was noon by the time Martha had finished reading all of the cases and statutes she had identified. She was organizing her notes and gathering up her briefcase and purse when Tim appeared. It was the first time she had seen him since she had run into him earlier in the morning, and she was beginning to think he was avoiding her.

"I've been so swamped today I couldn't get by to see how you were doing until now," explained Tim, as if sensing her question.

"No need to apologize, Mr. McFay. I know you have a lot more things to do than just watch over me."

"Tim. Please call me Tim. And let me say that 'watching over you' has been one of my more enjoyable tasks." Martha blushed appreciatively. "Actually, I came over to see if I could take you out to lunch."

"How kind of you, Tim. But I was planning on taking a really quick lunch and beginning work on the memo I need to write for my boss. I don't think I would be very good company." Martha's mind was racing. She had not gone out with anyone since her divorce. She had known this man for only 48 hours. She quickly checked off all the reasons she should say no.

"Not to be pushy, but maybe I could help you with the memo. I've had quite a bit of experience with memo writing and would be glad to give you some pointers."

Martha felt her resolve weakening. A little voice in her head cried out to say yes. "Well, that's an offer I can't refuse, Tim. Where do you have in mind?" Martha took a deep breath and hoped for the best.

WRITING A MEMORANDUM

memorandum document setting forth legal arguments and explaining issues of law

office memorandum informative memo prepared for internal use within a law office; also called an *internal memorandum*

advocacy memoranda persuasive memo prepared for the court; also called a *points and authority memorandum*

Before drafting a **memorandum,** you must be clear on your purpose. A memorandum written by a paralegal, law clerk, or associate for an attorney in the office is called an **office memorandum** or *internal memorandum.* Because the purpose of such a memo is largely to inform, both sides of every issue must be presented. When writing to the trial court or appellate court, the purpose is to persuade, and such memos are referred to as **advocacy memoranda** or *points and authority* memoranda.

While it is important to recognize that a balanced analysis must be given, you must not totally abandon your advocacy position. Too often novices to the law forfeit the game before it is even begun. After researching a question and deciding that the law clearly favors the opposition, they give up all hope of mounting any kind of defense and suggest surrender as the only realistic option. If any viable arguments exist, they must be explored and creative applications of legal principles should be pondered. Realistic assessment of the weaknesses of a case is good, but premature capitulation of a position (and therefore of a client) is unprofessional.

Format

Several organizational formats exist for legal memoranda. A few variations are presented here for your consideration, but remember that your choice of formats will be dictated by the preferences of the attorney for whom you are preparing the memo.

Format A	Format B	Format C
Heading	Heading	Heading
Overview	Issue	Issue
Facts	Answer	Conclusion
Issue; Answer	Facts	Facts
Analysis	Analysis	Analysis
Conclusion	Conclusion	
Recommendations		

Figure 3-32
Memo Format

MEMO FORMAT

Heading

Overview

Facts

Issues and Holdings

Analysis

Conclusions

Recommendations

◆ **LOCAL LINKS** ◆
What format does your
instructor prefer?

The advantage of format A is that readers are given an overview of the case and the pertinent facts before being presented with all of the details. Readers are thus better able to recognize the relevance of the facts and connect them with the pertinent legal issues. This format also leaves the readers with recommendations to consider in terms of further research, investigation that may need to be conducted, or procedural options that might be pursued.

Formats B and C have their own advantages, but because format A encompasses all of the elements of formats B and C, we will use it as the basis for the following discussion.

Heading

The heading of a memo contains basic identifying information: your name, the name of the person to whom the memo is being addressed, the date the memo was submitted, the case name, the office file number, and the court docket number. A "re" statement in the right-hand corner of the memo identifies the basic subject matter being discussed. This statement allows anyone looking through a case file to quickly identify the subject matter of the memo and facilitates the filing of the memo if it is stored in the law office library. Therefore, the information in this statement must be detailed enough to distinguish this memo from others.

Overview

The overview provides a brief summary of the memo. Before diving into the forest of facts and legal principles, the reader is afforded an aerial view of the contents. This synopsis allows the reader to know what issues are presented and how they are resolved. Readers can then decide whether they need to read the entire memo or can skim through it with an eye as to what the outcome is. While you may argue that giving away the conclusion at the beginning takes away some of its impact, remember that you are writing a memo and not a suspense novel. You do not want to shock or amaze your readers. You want to convey ideas as efficiently, systematically, and painlessly as possible.

In the overview, you should include the issues discussed in your analysis, your resolution of each issue, and, ever so briefly, the reasoning used to arrive at your conclusion. The overview should be restricted to one or two paragraphs. If you write much more, you defeat the purpose of providing a brief summary.

Facts

Although the attorney is no doubt familiar with the pertinent facts, you must nevertheless commit them to paper. Doing so will not only refresh the attorney's memory, but will help you clarify which facts are important to the case. Additionally, memos are filed in the office and may be read later by others who lack any familiarity with the case. Providing a detailed discussion of the facts puts the legal issue into a meaningful context for future readers.

Any fact you discuss in your analysis must be included in the statement of facts. To help you honor this fundamental rule of memo writing, review your analysis after you have completed it to ensure that every fact you have discussed in the analysis is recorded in the statement of facts.

Issue

The issue should be stated as completely as possible. It should contain the legal question at stake, but it should be clothed in the factual context that makes the issue unique to the case at hand.

Issues should be written in such a way that they can be universalized. In other words, the way the issue is written should indicate that the legal principles are applicable to persons other than the parties in the case. An issue such as "Did Mr. Smith breach the contract when he failed to begin construction on the date specified in the contract?" focuses on what Mr. Smith did rather than the general legal principles at issue. A better statement of the issue would be "Is the failure to begin construction on the date specified in a contract a breach of that contract?"

Because the reader has already been apprised as to the resolution of the issues in the overview, a very brief answer to the question raised in the issue is appropriate. A simple "yes" or "no" may be sufficient. If the issue was not clearly resolved but involves some contingencies, those contingencies should be identified in the answer. Brevity should be the watchword. Remember that the reader can go to the analysis and conclusion sections for more detail.

Analysis

IRAC is the linchpin for analysis. Begin every discussion of an issue with a disclosure of all the relevant case law, statutes, constitutions, and other "rules." After clearly articulating the rules, offer an argument as to how the rules might be applied and explain which rules are most persuasive. Present any reasonable counterarguments, followed by a conclusion explaining which argument you find most persuasive and why.

Remember that the soundness of your reasoning is the criterion by which your arguments will be evaluated by the attorney. Therefore, you must do more than suggest arguments. You must explain in as much detail as possible how each argument emanates from the legal rules and how you arrived at your conclusion. In essence, you must construct a mental footpath for your readers to prevent them from getting lost along the way. Your goal is to see that your readers arrive at the same destination (conclusion) you do. To ensure this, eliminate any gaps in your mental walkway. Your readers should not have to leap from point A to point B, but should be able to trace the logical path you laid and arrive with as little effort as possible at the end point you intended.

Conclusion

Although it may seem repetitious, summarize your resolution of each issue in your conclusion (what you decided and how you decided it). Why restate what you have already said in your analysis? The conclusion section may be the only section the reader actually reads. In the frantic pace of law practice, attorneys frequently "cut to the chase." Initially, they may be interested only in how you resolved the legal issues and may thoroughly digest the "hows" of your reasoning later. You can fulfill this need for instant information by succinctly paraphrasing the discussion in your analysis. Highlight the conclusion you reached for each subissue and explain briefly,

NET NEWS

For some hints about good legal writing, go to *www.sims.berkeley.edul,pam/papers/goodwriting.html.* To review some of the more important rules of grammar, go to *http://webster.commnet.edulgrammar/index.htm.*

if necessary, what facts and/or reasoning dictated the outcome of your decision. The identification of the facts that affected your decision-making process may be particularly important, since those facts may change as your case progresses. Knowing which facts dictate the outcome of a case is essential to any attorney in the negotiation and litigation phases of a case.

In your concluding paragraph, come to an overall conclusion. Explain how you arrived at that conclusion, particularly if your subconclusions suggest conflicting final conclusions. An explanation of your reasoning process is essential if the reader is to evaluate the soundness of your conclusion.

Make sure that your subconclusions are consistent with your ultimate conclusion. Before writing your conclusion, review the arguments in your analysis and summarize them, first in your mind, and then on paper. Then, and only then, commit your ultimate conclusion to paper.

Recommendations

In the last section of the memo, recommend how you think the case should be handled. You might, for example, recommend that the case be settled or that a claim be filed. This is the appropriate place to indicate where further investigation is needed and what specific factual questions need to be addressed. In your analysis, you undoubtedly had to draw tentative conclusions in the absence of sufficient data. Before writing the recommendation section, review your analysis and take note of every unknown factor. Use this section as a platform for drawing attention to all unknown variables that need clarification.

"Essentially, You Need to Show What Facts In Your Case Support a Finding of Foreseeability, What Facts Do Not Support a Finding of Foreseeability, and What Facts You Need to Gather If You Are Going to Be Able to Make a Case For Foreseeability."

Tim cleared the dishes aside so Martha had some room to write. Martha appeared to be fixated on the clean piece of paper in front of her. Finally, she broke the silence. "I have no idea where to start with this memo. I have read so many cases and looked at so many articles, I just don't know how to put it all together."

"All right, let's begin with something you know," stated Tim calmly. "What were you assigned to do? Think about that and you'll probably be able to write out your issues."

Martha thought for a moment and then began writing. As she did, she was careful to prevent Tim from seeing what she was writing, not out of modesty, but because she did not want to commit any breach of confidentiality.

Issue 1: Did the school district breach its duty of care to Mike by not doing anything to prevent him from being shot?

Issue 2: Is the school district protected from liability for Mike's shooting by any kind of statutory immunity?

"Okay. The second issue is very straightforward," observed Martha. "The statute clearly addresses the issue and I really don't have to do any kind of analysis. But the first issue is not clear at all. I have several cases and they all seem to say something different."

"So are all of those cases in Arizona?" began Tim.

"No."

"Then set those aside until you have worked with the Arizona cases. As you know, anything outside of Arizona is persuasive but not binding on the Arizona courts."

"And I should probably focus on the Arizona Supreme Court cases before I consider the Court of Appeals cases," suggested Martha.

"Not necessarily. I would look at the cases that are most analogous to the facts of your case first. Then you can consider precedential value, age of the case, and so on."

"Of course." Tim's advice seemed logical enough. Martha wondered why she hadn't thought of it first. "And when you look at it that way, I have only one Arizona case where the facts are close to the facts of our case."

"Great. Then you can start by outlining the legal rules the court laid down in that case. If I remember correctly, your issue has something to do with the duty of schools to protect their students from harm caused by other students." In response to Martha's affirmative nod, Tim continued. "Can you summarize in a sentence or two what the court says about that duty?"

Martha scanned through the opinion until she found the section on duty. Skimming through the paragraphs, she found a sentence that seemed to encapsulate the court's characterization of the duty. "The essence of those duties is to exercise reasonable care in light of foreseeable and unreasonable risks," she read.

"Excellent. Underline that so you can include it in the memo. Now does the court go on to explain what a 'foreseeable and unreasonable risk' is?" questioned Tim.

"In a sense it does. The court summarizes the plaintiff's argument here: 'the school "knew or should have realized that Scott Fast might avail himself of the opportunity to commit a tort or crime towards Clint Hill," and "[it] failed to provide any security or disciplinary measures to protect [him]." ' "

"So the plaintiff is arguing that what happened to Hill was reasonably foreseeable," suggested Tim.

"In a nutshell, yes," confirmed Martha.

"And the court agrees?" continued Tim.

"No. Let me see if I can find it in the opinion. Yes, here it is." Martha read through her copy of the opinion. "Appellant repeatedly asserts that Hill's death was 'foreseeable' and 'predictable.' We find nothing in the record, however, to support that claim.' Then the court goes on to cite all the evidence that is lacking to support the plaintiff's contention of foreseeability."

"Good. You'll want to include this discussion in the analysis section of your memo where you summarize the legal rules applied by the courts. Does the court give any specific, factual examples of what is and is not foreseeable?" asked Tim.

"As a matter of fact, yes. In the next section, the court gives examples of a number of cases where courts in other states had found sufficient evidence to support foreseeability and those cases where they had not found sufficient evidence."

"That information will be extremely helpful to your attorneys because it will give them an idea about what the courts are looking for in these cases to impose liability. So you're going to want to really focus on the facts in each of these cases."

"Does that mean I should go back and read all of these cases now?" asked Martha, hoping that the answer would be no.

"Not unless any of them are Arizona cases and their fact patterns are more analogous to your case than the facts in this case," Tim explained. "Now, does the court explain or give examples of what does constitute sufficient evidence to support a claim of foreseeability?"

Martha skimmed through the opinion to refresh her memory. "Yes, the court does cite another case (*Jesik*) where a student repeatedly requested help and kept warning school officials that someone was trying to kill him. The court in that case found that the school 'had specific and repeated notice of both the actor and the exact type of harm that did in fact occur.' (611 P.2d at 551.) I have a copy of that case somewhere as well," remembered Martha.

"So now your job boils down to showing where your case stands in relationship to these two cases, and any other cases you have where the facts are similar to your case. Essentially, you need to show what facts in your case support a finding of foreseeability, what facts do not support a finding of foreseeability, and what facts you need to gather if you are going to be able to make a case for foreseeability."

"So, in essence, I have to show whether the fact differences between our case and *Hill* are substantial enough that we could convince a court to distinguish *Hill* and find that what happened to our client was reasonably foreseeable," summarized Martha.

"Well put. And by the same token, you need to show how the facts of your case are analogous to the facts in *Jesik* and other cases where the courts have found liability. Of course, don't forget to make counterarguments, considering the arguments your opponents will make. You want your analysis to be well-balanced." Tim glanced down at his watch and immediately jumped to his feet. "I had no idea how late it was, Martha. I've got to get to back to the library. I'm sorry to do this to you but I have to run."

And with that he was gone. As Martha reorganized her papers, she felt conflicting emotions. Part of her was relieved that she had not had to decide whether to go out with Tim and the other part was disappointed that he had never asked. She felt very alone as she found her way back to her car. And then she remembered: he did know the name of the firm where she worked.

Putting It Into Practice 3.25:

Suppose Martha was asked to address the issue of liability of the producers of *Teenage Stalkers* in Mike's case. How would you suggest she organize her analysis?

■ TIM'S TECHNO TIPS

Computer Assisted Legal Research

Doing legal research does not necessarily entail going to the library, taking a large table, and covering it with legal research materials piled several books high. Computer-based legal research allows most research to be performed at your office or home over a phone line. Using the computer's modem to connect with various research databases is faster, and in some cases, less expensive than a trip to the closest law library.

Legal research can be performed on the World Wide Web by connecting with any of the numerous sources of legal materials available. For subscribers to legal databases produced on CD-ROM, the modem is not required (except to update cases and materials published since the date the CD-ROM was published); only a CD-ROM drive is necessary. West Publishing, LEXIS, LOIS, and others produce searchable legal materials on CD-ROM and also have materials available for research on their own Web sites or through a direct telephone connection to their own computer.

The primary advantage of CD-ROM research is that no telephone connection is required. The downside is the relative lack of storage space (about 650 million bits). While most state cases and statutes (or the United States Supreme Court cases and United States Code) can be stored on one CD-ROM, national or sectional searches are not yet possible. More storage capability is necessary to have all the federal circuit court decisions available, let alone the federal district court decisions. Some advancement has been made through the use of "jukeboxes" that allow several CD-ROMs to be loaded onto one mechanism. The computer can then switch to different drives as the search goes from state to state or circuit to circuit. No such system has yet begun to approach having the materials available that the major legal databases provide.

The major legal publishers have extensive databases. Westlaw and LEXIS/NEXIS, for example, have both reported United States cases in their databases along with almost all law review articles, bar publications, major treatises, legal periodicals, and foreign legal sources. The biggest drawback is the cost of accessing the data and the speed limitations inherent in using a modem. Bigger users such as large law firms and corporate law departments are often wired into a non-traditional telephone line hookup that allows data transfer rates of hundreds of thousands of bits per second compared to the maximum transfer rate with the standard modem of some fifty thousand plus bits per second.

All commercial legal databases are searchable. Although they differ in some respects, they all allow word and **Boolean** expressions to be used. To illustrate the process involved in a word search, let us use the phrase "bad faith insurance." Using those words would, depending on the search engine, find all sentences, paragraphs, or other word groupings that contained the three selected words. If you were searching for all cases, for example, that contained the three selected words in the sequence listed, the search engine might require that the words be entered with quotation marks: "bad faith insurance." Most search engines are not case sensitive, so capitalization is not considered. A more sophisticated search allows you to search for any case in which the words appear within a certain number of words, such as five, from each other. Or such a search may be structured so as to require that the words appear in a specific order. For example, if "faith" appears before "bad," the case will not appear as a "hit."

In addition to commercial sites that charge a fee to do research on their database, several organizations have developed Web sites that allow various degrees of sophistication of legal research. Cornell Law School hosts a site at *www.law.cornell.edu* that has a very good database of its own as well as links to other sources. United States Supreme Court decisions can be found on *www.law.cornell.edu/supct* or *www.findlaw.com,* and information about federal courts in general can be found on *www.uscourts.gov.* Most state bar associations, and the American Bar Association, have Web sites that can provide information, much of it searchable, and links to other Web sites of interest. Your state courts, trial and appellate, may also have their own Web sites with recent cases, court rules, and the like. Many trial courts now have their docket online so that case histories of trials can be followed, attorney's court dockets confirmed, and a person's or company's litigation history determined. In like manner, many states now provide for online Uniform Commercial Code (UCC) searches, access to recorded information, tax data, corporate/LLC/Partnership records, as well as other public information maintained by the various state agencies. The same is also true for the federal government.

TECHNO TRIP

Go to the LOIS (Law Office Information Systems) Web site at *www.pita.com.* Sign up for the free 10-day trial subscription and check out its capabilities. You should also use its Law Links function to see what materials in your state it can take you to. Now go to the Westlaw site at *www.westlaw.com.* Sign up for their free 14-day subscription and compare Westlaw with LOIS. Go to the LEXIS/NEXIS site at *www.lexis.com.* Try to find a free trial subscription. Compare LEXIS/NEXIS's offerings to Westlaw and LOIS. Note: At the time of this writing, LOIS offers a student subscription to its database for a semester or a year (varies) for $5.00. The passwords must be obtained through your instructor.

SUMMARY – PART B

The secondary authorities used to locate primary authority are encyclopedias, treatises, digests, reporters, Restatements, and legal periodicals. The two primary legal encyclopedias are *American Jurisprudence* and *Corpus Juris Secundum,* both of which are helpful in gaining a general understanding of the law in a particular area. A detailed analysis of specific points of law can be found in treatises, which are scholarly works prepared on a number of legal topics. Both encyclopedias should be consulted at the beginning stages of legal research to gain a better understanding of the area of law being researched.

Digests are the finding tools used to locate case law. The *American Digest System,* which is the most comprehensive digest system, is organized into Decennials. Federal cases can be found in West's *Federal Practice Digest,* United States Supreme Court cases can be found in the *U.S. Supreme Court Digest,* and state cases can be found in one of the four regional digests published by West. Specific topics in a digest can be found by looking at the topic outline at the beginning of each volume or by consulting the Descriptive Word Index. All topics are arranged in alphabetical order using the West key numbering system. Digests are updated by pocket parts and mini-digests. An essential aspect of the updating process is Shepardizing, which also alerts you to the existence of related cases and other legal resources and indicates how other courts have treated the case in question. Another source of case law is the *American Law Reports,* which is now in its fifth series. The A.L.R. presents selected cases, analyzes each, indicates how other courts have dealt with the same issue, and references additional cases and legal resources. One of the most prestigious forms of secondary authority is the Restatements, which restate the law in a clear, unambiguous, rule-like format. Restatements have been prepared for a number of different areas of law and each contains comments and illustrations that explain and illustrate the principles articulated in each restatement. Legal periodicals are another secondary source; they include such publications as law reviews/journals, publications by bar associations and paralegal associations, and legal newspapers.

Federal slip laws can be found in *U.S. Law Week* and session laws in the *Statutes at Large.* When these laws are codified, they can be found in the United States Code (official version) or the two unofficial versions, *United States Code Annotated* and United States Code Service. The unofficial versions not only contain annotations that analyze and interpret the code, but they are updated more regularly than the official code. Statutes can be located in an index using any significant terms in the statute, the title number, or the statute's popular name. Research of state statutes is conducted in much the same way as research of federal statutes. Interpreting ambiguous terms in a statute is done by determining what the legislative intent behind that statute is. To ascertain this intent, you should consider the definitions section of a statute, the plain meaning of the words in question, public policy, the context of other statutes, case law, and the legislative history of the statute.

Appellate courts are under several constraints. They are allowed to review issues of law, but cannot review issues of fact unless the trial court "clearly abused its discretion." They cannot review an issue unless a party has made a timely objection on the record. Appellate courts are obligated under the doctrine of *stare decisis* to adhere to their previous decisions as well as the decisions of those courts that review their opinions. To overcome the potential rigidity of this doctrine, courts are allowed to distinguish those cases that are factually different. Appellate courts are also obligated to honor the U.S. and state constitutions and statutes unless they are unconstitutional. Judges adhering to a conservative judicial philosophy feel more constrained in their interpretation of statutes and constitutions than do those adhering to a more liberal judicial philosophy. The latter are more inclined to protect minorities and the politically disadvantaged.

The essence of legal analysis can be condensed into the acronym IRAC: Issue, Rule, Application, and Conclusion. The issue must be clearly and accurately stated, but the bulk of the analysis is devoted to laying out the rules, which includes case law, statutes, and administrative regulations. After applying the rules, you must come to a conclusion and explain how you reached the conclusion. When comparing the facts of your case to case law, make a list of the factual similarities, dissimilarities, and unknowns, and then evaluate the relative importance of these differences and similarities.

Memoranda can be either an internal or advocacy memoranda. The former requires a more balanced analysis than the latter, but both necessitate an allegiance to one's role as an advocate. Several organizational formats for memoranda exist and each one has its own advantages, but the choice of format should be dictated by preferences of the attorney asking to have the memo prepared. If an overview is provided, it should be a brief summary of the memo, allowing the reader to know what issues are presented and how they are resolved. All facts that are discussed in the analysis must be included in the statement of facts. The statement of the issue should be complete but written in such a way that it can be universalized. The analysis should open with a disclosure of all the relevant rules followed by an application of those rules, a presentation of reasonable counterarguments, and conclude with an explanation of which argument you find most persuasive and why. The resolution of each issue should be summarized in your conclusion, followed by an overall conclusion, explaining how you arrived at that conclusion.

The last section of the memorandum should contain recommendations about how the case should be handled and where further investigation is necessary.

KEY TERMS

Advocacy memoranda
Binding authority
Canons of construction
Codified law
Conclusory writing
Conservative
Digests

Distinguishing
Hornbook
Issues of fact
Issues of law
Legislative history
Liberal
Memorandum

Office memorandum
Persuasive
Primary authority
Prosser on Torts
Secondary source
Session laws
Shepardize

Slip laws
Stare decisis
Treatise

REVIEW QUESTIONS – PART B

1. What is the difference between primary and secondary authority? Give an example of each.
2. What is the difference between persuasive and binding authority?
3. Give an example of each of the following and describe how they can be used in conducting legal research.
   a. legal encyclopedia
   b. treatise
   c. digest
   d. Restatement
   e. legal periodical
4. What is the difference between a hornbook and a treatise?
5. What can be found in the following tools?
   a. Fourth Decennial
   b. *Federal Practice Digest*
   c. *General Digest*
   d. *Atlantic Digest*
6. How would you find information in a digest about the duty of landlords to protect their tenants?
7. How can you go about updating the cases you find in the bound section of a digest?
8. What can you learn from Shepardizing a case?
9. What information can be found in the A.L.R. that is not found in an official reporter containing the same case?
10. Why were the Restatements created?
11. How do law review articles differ from legal newspapers?
12. Explain the difference between an issue of fact and an issue of law. Why is that difference important to the appellate courts?
13. What is the doctrine of *stare decisis?* What is its purpose? How can courts get around this principle and why would they want to?
14. Describe the difference between a conservative and liberal judicial philosophy.
15. Explain IRAC and how it is used to construct a legal analysis.
16. What is the best way to compare your case to existing case law?
17. What is the difference between an internal (or office) memorandum and an advocacy (or points and authority) memorandum?
18. What should be covered in each of the following parts of a memo?
   a. heading
   b. overview
   c. facts
   d. issue and answer
   e. analysis
   f. recommendations
19. What are the differences among a slip law, a session law, and codified law?
20. What are the advantages of using the U.S.C.A. and U.S.C.S. over the U.S.C.?
21. What factors should you consider in interpreting an ambiguous term in a statute?

PRACTICE EXAM – PART B

MULTIPLE CHOICE

1. To find detailed information about a specific legal topic, it would be best to consult
   a. *Am. Jur.*
   b. *C.J.S.*
   c. a treatise on the subject
   d. *General Digests*
2. To find a recent district court case, it would be best to consult
   a. a regional digest
   b. West's *Federal Practice Digests*
   c. the Restatement
   d. First Decennial
3. References to other West resources can be found using
   a. *C.J.S.*
   b. *Am. Jur.*
   c. Restatements
   d. *American Law Reports*
4. In a West digest
   a. the key numbers correspond to specific topics of law
   b. topics can be found by looking through the topic outline at the beginning of each volume
   c. topics are organized alphabetically by topic
   d. all of the above
5. Shepardizing a case allows you to
   a. find out if the case is still good case law
   b. learn about the history of a case
   c. find out if other courts have criticized or questioned the case
   d. all of the above

6. An A.L.R. annotation
   a. is similar in format to the format used by West in its reporter system
   b. contains a synopsis of a case but no headnotes
   c. has a list of related legal resources
   d. does not indicate how other courts have dealt with the same issue
7. A Restatement
   a. has been prepared for every area of the law
   b. contains principles of law but no explanation of those principles
   c. is designed to clarify the law in unambiguous terms
   d. is rarely followed by the courts
8. Legal periodicals include
   a. law reviews but not bar journals
   b. law journals and legal newspapers
   c. the *National Law Journal* but not *Legal Assistant Today*
   d. none of the above
9. Appellate courts are constrained
   a. in that they are allowed to review only questions of fact
   b. by statutes, even if they are unconstitutional
   c. by the doctrine of *stare decisis*
   d. all of the above
10. Legal analysis
    a. requires that a conclusion be drawn even in the absence of all the facts
    b. requires a neutral application of the rules even if the memo is being written to the court
    c. requires conclusory writing
    d. all of the above

11. When comparing your case to existing case law
    a. consider what the essential facts are
    b. objectify the difference by listing all the factual similarities, dissimilarities, and unknowns
    c. evaluate the importance of each similarity and dissimilarity
    d. all of the above
12. An office memo should
    a. always contain an overview
    b. contain arguments and counterarguments
    c. contain a statement of the issue but not a statement of the facts
    d. have a conclusion that comes at the end of the memo
13. When researching federal statutes
    a. use the U.S.C.A. because it is updated more frequently than the U.S.C.
    b. use the U.S.C. because it contains annotations
    c. use the U.S.C.S. to get the most recently enacted slip laws
    d. none of the above
14. An ambiguous term may be clarified by considering
    a. the definitions section of the statute
    b. the legislative history of the statute
    c. public policy
    d. all of the above

FILL IN THE BLANK

15. Case law, statutes, and administrative regulations are examples of _____ authority, which can be located using _____ authority, such as a digest.
16. Courts are obligated to follow _____ authority, but do not have to follow _____ authority.
17. Law students use _____ to learn the legal principles in a given area of the law.
18. The most comprehensive digest system is called the _____ System; it has been organized in ten-year periods called _____ .
19. _____ are the pamphlets inserted in the slots at the end of digests; they are used to update the digests.

20. By _____ a case, you can find out about the history of the case, how other courts have treated it, and whether any other legal sources refer to it; to do this you must a Shepard's _____ , which is in both printed and electronic form.
21. Appellate courts are allowed to review issues of _____ , but cannot review issues of _____ unless the trial court clearly abused its discretion.
22. Under the doctrine of _____ , courts are obligated to follow case precedent unless they can _____ the case because it is factually different.
23. Judges who adhere to a _____ judicial philosophy strictly interpret statutes and

constitutions, whereas judges who adhere to a _____ judicial philosophy go beyond a literal interpretation of statutes and constitutions so that they can protect minorities and the politically disadvantaged.

24. Legal analysis consists of setting forth the I_____ , R_____ , A_____ and C_____ .

25. _____ writing (drawing a conclusion with no explanation) should be avoided even if the writer lacks all of the facts.

26. A more balanced analysis is required in an _____ memorandum, written for an attorney within the office, than in an _____ memorandum, prepared to persuade the court to adopt a particular position.

27. When bills are first enacted into laws, they can be found in the form of sheets of paper called _____ ; at the end of a legislative session the _____ laws are compiled in the *Statutes at Large.*

28. The two unofficial versions of the codified federal law are _____ and _____ .

29. When interpreting a vague or ambiguous term in a statute, one should consider the _____ of the statute, that is, what the legislature had in mind when creating the statute.

30. The _____ of a statute, which includes the events that took place before the statute's passage and during its consideration, can be considered when interpreting terminology in that statute.

*31. The _____ are rules that guide courts in interpreting statutes.

TRUE OR FALSE

_____ 32. A legal encyclopedia can be used to learn legal terminology and the general rules of law.

_____ 33. *C.J.S.* can be used to locate other Lawyers' Co-op resources and *Am. Jur.* can be used to locate other West resources.

_____ 34. *Am. Jur.* provides a broader coverage of case law than *C.J.S.*, which provides only a representative cross-section of cases.

_____ 35. Treatises are helpful to researchers not only because they explain the law, but because they provide numerous references to cases and statutes.

_____ 36. Treatises should be consulted in the latter stages of legal research, after you have a basic understanding of the legal principles involved.

_____ 37. Treatises can be located using the catalog or by consulting a librarian.

_____ 38. West publishes seven regional digests.

_____ 39. The *General Digests* contain all of the cases published by West in its National Reporter System.

_____ 40. West does not publish digests for the states.

_____ 41. Key numbers are the foundation for the West key numbering system.

_____ 42. The only way to find topics in any West digest is by using the Descriptive Word Index.

_____ 43. Pocket parts are published about once a month.

_____ 44. Advance sheets can be updated using the mini-digests they contain.

_____ 45. Attorneys have an ethical obligation to Shepardize cases to ensure they are still good law.

_____ 46. Shepardizing cases can lead to relevant statutes, law review articles, and *American Law Reports.*

_____ 47. The A.L.R. contains annotations for state cases only.

_____ 48. The members of the American Law Institute, which publishes the Restatements, avoid predicting what courts will do in the future.

_____ 49. The Restatements contain illustrations and comments sections that explain and illustrate the principles articulated in each restatement of the law.

_____ 50. Law journals are published by bar associations.

_____ 51. Law review articles are scholarly in their approach, while bar association publications tend to be very pragmatic.

_____ 52. An appellate court can review testimony that the defendant was observed talking with the informant, but cannot review the admissibility of that testimony.

_____53. Appellate practice is highly structured and bound by rules.

_____54. *Stare decisis* is honored because it retains stability and predictability in the law.

_____55. Under the doctrine of *stare decisis,* courts cannot deviate from case precedent even if the facts are substantially different.

_____56. If the legislative intent is unclear, an appellate court has some leeway in its interpretation of the statute's purpose.

_____57. Conservative courts, more so than liberal courts, view themselves as protectors of minorities and the politically disadvantaged.

_____58. The rules of appellate decision making preclude the appellate process from becoming a forum for personal agendas.

_____59. For purposes of legal analysis, the rules include case law, statutes, ordinances, administrative regulations, court procedural rules, and constitutional provisions.

_____60. When analyzing a legal issue, you should apply the rules in as neutral a fashion as possible if you are writing the memo for informational purposes.

_____61. Sometimes a conclusion cannot be drawn because the writer lacks sufficient data.

_____62. If the essential facts in your case are, for the most part, similar to existing case law, and the dissimilarities and unknowns are relatively trivial, a court will probably be willing to apply that case to your facts.

_____63. A paralegal preparing an internal memorandum should avoid taking an advocacy position.

_____64. The choice of format for a memorandum usually depends on the preference of the attorney for whom the memo is being prepared.

_____65. The "re" statement in a memo should be detailed enough to distinguish this memo from others.

_____66. The overview in a memo should be at least one page in length and should contain a fairly detailed summary of the primary issues presented in the memo.

_____67. Any fact discussed in the analysis must be included in the statement of facts.

_____68. The issue statement in a memo should be written to apply only to the parties involved.

_____69. The answer to the question raised in the issue statement should be as brief as possible.

_____70. It is not necessary in a memo to explain in any detail how you arrived at your conclusion.

_____71. The presentation of counterarguments is inappropriate in an office memorandum.

_____72. In the conclusion section of your memo, you need not mention how you resolved each issue in your analysis because to do so would be repetitious.

_____73. The conclusion in a memo should contain an explanation of how you arrived at that conclusion and should be consistent with the subconclusions in the analysis section.

_____74. The recommendation section in a memo should suggest where further investigation is needed and how the case should be handled.

_____75. Slip laws are identified by public law numbers, indicating the year they were enacted and the order in which they were enacted.

_____76. *Statutes at Large* provides a more updated version of federal laws than *United States Weekly.*

_____77. The U.S.C. contains an annotated version of the federal code.

_____78. Federal statutes can be located using any significant terms in the statute, the title number, or the popular name of the statute.

_____79. Research of state statutes is carried out in much the same way that research of federal statutes is.

_____80. The plain meaning of a statute must be honored unless the language is ambiguous or some inconsistency exists within the statute.

_____81. How a term is used in other sections of a statute or other statutes addressing the same issue cannot be considered when interpreting an ambiguous or vague term in a statute.

_____82. How courts in other states have interpreted a particular term in a statute cannot be considered when interpreting that term.

_____83. A statute's legislative history gives a clear insight into the legislative intent behind the statute.

*Questions taken from Bonus Pointers.

LEGAL LINGO

ACROSS

2. When an appellate court sends a case back to a lower court
4. Summaries of points of law discussed by the court
8. Law setting forth the rules litigants must follow
10. To change a lower trial court's decision
13. Law setting forth the rights and duties of parties
14. Practical effect of a court's decision
16. Containing references to cases and other legal resources
18. An opinion that has no author is a per _____
20. Case summary
21. Citation that indicates both the official and unofficial reporters
24. Type of opinion in which no majority exists
25. Type of writ requesting review by an appellate court
28. Original form of a newly enacted law
29. Differentiate a case based on a difference in facts
30. Abbreviation of a prestigious secondary authority prepared by the American Law Institute
31. Precedence of case law is set forth in principle of _____ *decisis*
32. Type of treatise used by law school students

DOWN

1. To organize law according to subject matter
3. Written analysis that can be either internal or advocacy
5. To change the decision of a lower appellate court
6. Abbreviation for an annotated reporter system
7. Type of law dealing with compensation of those who have suffered private wrongs
9. Abbreviation for an unofficial reporter of the federal code
11. Gratuitous remarks by a court
12. Abbreviation for legal encyclopedia published by West
15. Law created by city council or a county board of supervisors
17. Federal court at which trials are heard
18. Part of a court opinion identifying the parties and their relationship
19. To check on the status of a case using a citator
20. Sets standard for citations
22. Person responding to an appeal brought by the opposing party
23. Payment by defendant to victim of crime
26. Finding tool used to locate cases
27. Law that a court must follow

LEGAL LOGISTICS

1. Why is it important to understand how the court system is organized and how it functions before reading case law?

2. Find *Rice v. Paladin Enterprises, Inc.*, 128 F.3d 233 (4th Cir. 1997).

   a. Read the caption. Who are the parties? Who are all the amici curiae? (Look this phrase up in a law dictionary if you are not familiar with it.) Why do you think the press is so interested in this case?

   b. Read the synopsis. What are the essential facts? What had the district court decided? Did the 4th Circuit agree with the district court?

   c. When was the case argued? When was it decided?

   d. Who wrote the opinion?

   e. Look at headnote 11. Why does this court conclude that the First Amendment is not violated by holding the defendants liable?

   f. Why do you think the court includes excerpts from *Hit Man* at the beginning of the opinion?

   g. Did Paladin intend to provide assistance to murderers and would-be murderers in his book?

3. Read *Yakubowicz v. Paramount Pictures Corp.*, 536 N.E.2d 1067 (Mass. 1989) (found in Appendix B).

   a. What events led to the plaintiff's filing suit? Who is the plaintiff? Who are the defendants?

   b. Use IRAC to analyze the breach of duty issue.

      (1) State the issue in your own words, making sure to include the essential facts in this case.

      (2) What rules of law does the court cite?

      (3) What conclusion does the court reach and how does it reach that conclusion?

   c. Prepare a written brief of this case.

4. If you are researching an unfamiliar area of law, where will you look before you actually start looking for primary authority?

5. Why might you want to consult the Restatement even though it is a secondary authority?

6. Why would law review articles be particularly helpful when researching the liability of those engaged in e-commerce?

7. Why would you want to look for A.L.R. annotations even though you had already found cases using your regional digest?

8. Do you think it is more challenging to find cases or read them? Why? What can you do to help clarify your understanding of any particular series of cases?

9. Compare *Rice v. Paladin* and *Yakubowicz v. Paramount Pictures*. Explain why these two courts came to different conclusions.

   a. What essential facts differed in these two cases?

   b. What rule of law can you derive from these two cases?

   c. Write a memo to John, Martha's supervising attorney. Assume that *Rice, Yakubowicz,* and *Byers* are the only applicable cases you have found. John has asked you to determine if the producer of *Teenage Stalkers* has a duty to those injured by viewers emulating the violence they saw depicted in the movie and if it has breached that duty by creating and releasing a movie that glorifies teenage violence.

10. Read the following summary of facts taken from *Brum v. Dartmouth,* 704 N.E.2d 1147 (Mass. 1999).

    Jason Robinson, son of the plaintiff Elaine Brum, was stabbed to death at Dartmouth High School in April, 1993, by three armed individuals, at least one of whom was not a student at the school. Earlier that morning, the three assailants had been involved in a violent interaction at the school with two of Robinson's classmates and possibly with Robinson as well, but had left the school immediately afterward. After the altercation, the school principal detained Robinson's two classmates, but not Robinson, and one of the classmates informed the principal that the three individuals who had fled planned to return to the school and retaliate against him and his friends, including Robinson. Later that morning, the assailants, visibly armed, did return to the school and proceeded to a second floor classroom, unimpeded by school officials, where one of them stabbed Robinson to death.

    Robinson's mother sued the town of Dartmouth and several town and school officials under the Massachusetts Tort Claims Act, alleging that the defendants' negligent failure to maintain adequate security measures at the school and specific failure to protect her son in the presence of a known threat resulted in his death.

    Defendants argue that the plaintiffs' claims against them are barred by the statutory public duty rule of G.L. c. 258, § 10(j), which exempts from the Tort Claims Act "any claim based on an act or failure to act to prevent or diminish the harmful consequences of a condition or situation, including the violent or tortious conduct of a third person, which is not originally caused by the public employer or any other person acting on behalf of the public employer."

The plaintiff responds that § 10(j) does not confer immunity on the defendants because the defendants "originally caused" the dangerous "condition or situation" that resulted in the killings by the "violent . . . conduct of a third person."

The court says, "But it is also true that those killings came about because the defendants 'failed to prevent' them. We are thus forced to construe the first sentence of § 10(j) to give meaning both to what appears to be its announced principal purpose, which is to confer immunity on public employees for harm that comes about as a result of their 'failure . . . to prevent' the 'violent or tortious conduct of a third person,' and to do so in the presence of the clause which removes that immunity where the 'harmful consequences' were 'originally caused by the public employer.' "

a. Where would you look to find the statute in question?

b. What is the ambiguity in the statute?

c. What will the court have to do to resolve this ambiguity?

d. How might it go about doing that?

11. Read the following excerpt from a concurring opinion by Judge Ireland.

In the present case, the school principal was told that the assailants had threatened to return to the school and retaliate against the students who were involved in a prior altercation. Apparently, the school took no action in response to that warning. Several school officials then witnessed three armed individuals enter the school, but again they took no action. Those armed individuals then stabbed Robinson to death in front of his classmates as he sat in a classroom. At the time that he was stabbed, the school's security "standards and procedures"—if one could refer to them as such—consisted of a "no-trespassing" sign and a sign asking visitors to report to the school office. See ante at. On such facts, parents should be able to submit to a jury the claim that the school breached a duty owed to them.

While G.L. c. 71, § 37H, G.L. c. 258, § 10(j). . . may compel the outcome we reach today, I believe that parents should be entitled to believe that the school officials to whom they entrust their children will not be deliberately indifferent and simply stand by and do nothing when made aware of an imminent threat to the safety of their children. I believe, too, that school officials should not be allowed to figuratively shrug and say "the problem did not originate with us, so we are not responsible." While not absolute guarantors of safety, school officials should, at the least, be expected to take reasonable measures to protect children when they have advance notice of danger.

This entire matter is within the control of the Legislature, which, I hope, will act to impose an obligation on school districts, and to ensure that the restrictions in the Massachusetts Tort Claims Act do not apply to these cases.

If the court could have construed this statute to allow the plaintiffs to maintain their claim and did not do so, how would you characterize the philosophy of this court? Do you agree with the public policy argument made by the concurring judge?

A TRIP TO THE MOVIES

The movie *The Insider* is based on a true story. One of the producers for CBS (Lowell Bergman) lines up an interview for Mike Wallace with Dr. Jeffrey Wigand, a former vice-president and head of research at a major tobacco company, Brown and Williamson. Enormous pressures are brought to bear on both Wigand and CBS to keep the interview from being aired because of the damning information Wigand reveals about what this company knew about nicotine addiction and how the company deliberately enhanced the addictive qualities of the cigarettes it produced.

Imagine that you are an assistant to one of the corporate counsel at CBS and answer the following questions.

1. You are asked to find out about a tort called *tortious interference.*

a. What are the possible legal references you could consult?

b. Look up *tortious interference* in one of these resources. What is its definition?

c. Could CBS be liable for this tort in light of the fact that it is asking Wigand to sit for an interview during which he is asked to violate a broadly-worded confidentiality agreement he had signed with Brown and Williamson?

d. Where would you look to find out how the Kentucky state courts have applied the concept of tortious interference?

2. Suppose CBS is sued for tortious interference and is found liable. What will it have to do if it does not want to pay the damages?

3. Suppose you want to find out more about how the courts have dealt with claims against the tobacco industry. You know about *Cipollone v. Liggett,* 505 U.S. 504 (1992).
   a. Who wrote the opinion?
   b. When was the case argued? When was it decided?
   c. Who argued the case for the petitioner? (Ask your instructor who this man is.) Were there any *amici curiae?* Did the attorney general from your state submit an *amicus* brief? Why are so many people interested in this case?
   d. Did any of the justices write any concurring or dissenting opinions?
   e. Read the syllabus. Would any part of the claim made by the plaintiff be supported by Wigand's testimony?
   f. How could you use Shepard's to find a copy of *Cipollone* in one of the unofficial reporters? Why might you find it helpful to read the unofficial version?
   g. How would you go about getting a copy of the Federal Cigarette Labeling and Advertising Act referenced in this opinion?
   h. The district court ruled that the plaintiff's claims were "preempted" by the federal statutes. What does this mean? How does preemption illustrate the interplay between the legislative and judicial branches of government and the doctrine of "separation of powers"?
   i. In what sense is statutory interpretation the cornerstone of *Cipollone?*
   j. Do the justices agree on how the statutes should be interpreted?

INTERNET INQUIRIES

1. Go to the Internet and get information about the federal district and circuit courts in your jurisdiction.
   a. Can you obtain information about ongoing cases at this site? If so, is there a fee for accessing this information?
   b. Are the local rules for this court posted here?
   c. Is there a link to the clerk's office for this court?
   d. Can you pull up court opinions at this site? If so, how far back in time are these cases available online?
   e. Can you pull up recommended jury instructions at this site?
2. Go to the Internet and get information about your state trial courts.
   a. Can you get information about ongoing cases at this site?
   b. What kinds of basic information can you get about the court at this site?
   c. If you were called for jury duty, could you go to this site to get information?
   d. Is there a link to the clerk's office for this court?
   e. What law-related links are provided?
3. Go to *www.law.cornell.edu* and find a 1998 First Circuit case involving a lawsuit against a cigarette manufacturer in reference to nicotine-yield ratings. Prepare a brief of this case.
4. Go to *www.law.cornell.edu* and find a 1991 U.S. Supreme Court opinion involving a suit by the Primate Protection League. Prepare a brief of this case.

4

Initiating a Case

"The Bottom Line Is, I Came Away from This Assignment a Little Bit Concerned about Whether We Have Much of a Case Against the School."

Martha sat impatiently, waiting for John to get off the phone so they could begin their meeting with Ernesto. She knew John had read her memo and she felt a sense of dread coupled with anticipation as she waited for his appraisal of her first stab at legal analysis. Her fears were soon allayed.

"Excellent job on your first memo, Martha," began John as soon as he hung up. "Your writing was clear and concise and I found it very easy to follow your reasoning. Having read it, I have a good idea of where we need to go if we're going to find the school liable in this case—which leads to the subject of our meeting today, folks. We need to decide if we're going to go forward with Mike's case. And, if we are, we need to decide whom we're going to sue."

"Let me second John," chimed in Ernesto. "I've seen first-year law students who didn't write that well."

"Thank you both for your kind words. I appreciate your encouragement. But I have to tell you that I did get some help writing it." Martha was extremely gratified to hear their praise but did not want to mislead them into thinking she had done it all on her own.

"Oh, yes. I remember your telling me how helpful the young man in the library was." Turning to Ernesto, John continued. "Martha had a personal escort who guided her through the library and who even took her to lunch. I don't remember the law librarians being that helpful when I went to law school. Do you, Ernesto?" asked John, winking conspiratorily.

Before Ernesto could respond, Martha jumped in, doing her best to deflect this unwanted attention. "I guess I was just very fortunate. But the bottom line is, I came away from this assignment a little bit concerned about whether we have much of a case against the school."

"Well, it's certainly not going to be a slam-dunk," agreed John, taking the hint that Martha clearly wanted to keep her personal relationships private. "But one thing I can tell you for sure is that we're not going to get any more information from anyone at the school unless we file suit. I got a call from counsel for the school district yesterday, and she made it very clear that we are not to talk with any more of the school's employees."

ETHICAL ETIQUETTE

IMPROPER COMMUNICATIONS WITH OPPONENTS

Attorneys are not permitted to communicate directly with the opposing attorney's client. A lawyer for a party must channel all communications about the case through the other party's attorney. An exception is allowed if opposing counsel gives consent. However, once litigation is anticipated, no competent litigator would ever willingly allow a client to communicate with the opposing attorney outside her presence.

For litigators, the main significance of the prohibition against direct contact with the opposing party is that it limits the kinds of investigation that can be done when litigating against an organization, such as a corporation. An attorney must not interview anyone having managerial responsibility in an organization or anyone who is directly involved in the events giving rise to the lawsuit. In effect, as a practical matter, the rule prohibits attorneys from speaking to anyone in the corporation who would be likely to have any information of interest to them. State law varies somewhat as to how far down the corporate hierarchy the prohibition extends.

"Just Like the Publisher for the Hit Man, This Group Seems to Take Pleasure in Admitting Its Role in Advocating Violence."

"Her reaction is a good sign for us. She obviously thinks there's an issue of liability or she wouldn't have been so quick to cut off communications," opined Ernesto.

"I think you're right," concurred John, "and I'm inclined to believe we have enough information at this point to be in good faith if we decide to file a claim against the school district. Based on Martha's research, I believe we can safely argue that the school had a duty to protect Mike from the violent acts of other students if those acts were foreseeable, that it breached that duty by failing to follow up on the anonymous phone call, and that it is not immune from suit for its negligence. And since we're obviously going to have to file suit before we can find out what else those at the school might have known about Mike's shooting, I think we should file immediately if Mike decides he wants us to go forward. We have nothing to lose by filing quickly, and we might be able to get information before the people at the school have a chance to totally close their ranks."

"I'm with you on this one, John." Ernesto had a quick mind matched only by the speed of his tongue, and he was eager to get beyond what he perceived as a foregone conclusion for the school. "Now, let me tell you what I found out about the company that produced *Teenage Stalkers.* Its name, CODA, stands for Citizens of a Decentralized America. I did a little background check on this group and found out that their mission is to free Americans from the 'tyranny' of the federal government and return to the loose confederation of states that existed before our independence from Britain. They want power to be restored into the hands of the individual states and they're willing to use whatever means is necessary to make this happen. Now here's the really interesting part." Ernesto's eyes gleamed with the thrill of his discovery. "In their mission statement—which is one of the scariest things I've ever read—they explicitly target certain groups they believe are particularly receptive to their message." Ernesto could hardly contain his enthusiasm.

"Teenagers," muttered John, almost inaudibly. "Of course," he thought out loud. "Who is any more alienated than teenagers? I bet they focus on the ones who are the most marginalized—the ones angry at the world in general, rejected by their peers—the outcasts. Am I right?"

"Yeah, the 'freaks,'" confirmed Ernesto, disappointed that John had stolen his thunder. "And, just like the publisher for *Hit Man,* this group seems to take pleasure in admitting its role in advocating violence."

"Does their mission statement actually advocate the use of violence to overthrow the American government?" asked John, quickly honing in on the element of intent.

"Yes. Isn't it incredible?" asked Ernesto. "Their acknowledged purpose is to educate their viewers about the tyranny of the American government and to inspire and encourage them to engage in acts and activities that 'will result in the demise and destruction of the federal government as it currently exists.'" Ernesto read from a portion of the mission statement.

"How frightening," remarked Martha incredulously.

"You bet. But how perfect for us. We're actually going to be able to prove that they intended to provoke imminent acts of violence by their viewers," exclaimed Ernesto triumphantly.

"Even if we can prove this—" began John cautiously, still stunned by Ernesto's reading of the mission statement.

"Not if—*when* we prove it," insisted Ernesto.

"All right, all right. But even if we're able to prove breach of duty, we're still going to have show causation and we don't have any proof at this point that Mike's attackers were provoked by what they saw in the movie to attack Mike." John did not want to lose sight of the legal hurdles they had to jump.

"Maybe not, but we do know that they watched the movie repeatedly, that they're members of the group targeted by the makers of the movie, and that they bragged about emulating some of things they'd seen in the movie. I think we can make a reasonable inference that the movie incited them to shoot Mike. And the only way we're going to be able to prove that is by doing some **discovery**," reasoned Erneto.

"So it seems we have grounds to sue the boys, their parents, the school, and CODA," summarized John. "Which reminds me, I was going to check on the statute pertaining to **vicarious liability** for parents. Seems to me that there's a $10,000 limit in Arizona for parental liability for the malicious acts of children." John pulled up the appropriate statute using a CD-ROM that contained all of the Arizona statutes. (LEXIS-NEXIS publishes annotated state statutes on a separate CD-ROM.) "Unfortunately, I'm right," he announced after checking the statute. "But even if we can't get much from them, I think we should still include them as defendants. They may have information about the school or the movie or something else that could prove helpful to us. They're more likely to help us as defendants than as non-parties."

"You know my theory on that one, John. I like to sue everyone I can and then let the defendants duke it out. As long as no one can claim I've filed a frivolous suit, I say the more the merrier," laughed Ernesto.

ETHICAL ETIQUETTE

FRIVOLOUS LAWSUITS—RULE 11

Although lawyers should consider all possible claims when preparing a complaint, they are forbidden from bringing "frivolous" or unmeritorious claims. Such claims can arise if an attorney fails to confirm information supplied by a client and prepares a complaint based on erroneous information. An attorney that assists a party in bringing a lawsuit simply to generate fees or to maliciously harm, harass, or intimidate his opponent violates several ethical rules. Attorneys are also prohibited from preparing claims that are unwarranted under existing law unless they can make a good faith argument that the law should be changed.

In addition to being censured for committing ethical violations, attorneys who bring frivolous suits in a federal court can be sanctioned under Rule 11 of the **Federal Rules of Civil Procedure** (FRCP). Rule 11 requires that complaints be "well grounded in fact" and "warranted by existing law or a good faith argument for the extension, modification, or reversal of existing law" and that they not be filed for any "improper purpose, such as to harass or to cause unnecessary delay or needless increase in the cost of litigation."

Violation of this rule may result in being ordered to pay the attorney's fees and expenses of the opponent or in having the complaint **dismissed with prejudice**. In some cases, attorneys or their clients or both have also been required to pay fines. Rule 11 applies to all documents filed with the court. Carefully conducting thorough, factual investigations and checking out all details in preparation for drafting a complaint can protect attorneys from Rule 11 sanctions. Most states have a rule similar to FRCP 11.

discovery   process by which parties can obtain almost any information pertinent to their dispute, under compulsion of a court order, if necessary

vicarious liability   liability for the torts of another. Employers, for example, are vicariously liable for the torts of their employees.

Federal Rules of Civil Procedure   procedural rules created by the U.S. Supreme Court that dictate the procedures followed in all federal courts

dismissed with prejudice judicial dismissal of case that precludes the case from being brought again

Putting It Into Practice 4.1:

The attorney for whom Marianne (Martha's fellow student) works likes to file suit as soon as he has completed the initial client interview. He does this without conducting any investigation to validate his client's claims. Why might this be a risky practice?

"So It's Not Outside the Realm of Reason to Assume That This Kid Has or Will Be Coming Into Some Money of His Own."

"I think it's safe to assume," concluded John, "you think we have a good faith claim against CODA. The next question is whether the company is solvent. What did you find out when you checked out CODA, Martha?"

"Even though the company appears undercapitalized, it is solvent at this point. I'm afraid that if we sue and get a judgment, however, the company would file for bankruptcy and we'd get nothing," reasoned Martha.

"But the interesting thing is," pointed out Ernesto, "they're in a bit of a philosophical conundrum if they do that. In their mission statement they blast the court system and pledge to bring about its downfall. If they stay true to their beliefs, they're not going to be able to turn to that system to protect them."

"I don't think we should count on that happening," countered John. "But I'm willing to pursue a claim against the company if it's solvent for the present."

"And remember, John, the case against these guys is more than just a PI (personal injury) claim. This is an opportunity to create some case precedent and, who knows, maybe even get to the Supreme Court." Ernesto had already envisioned himself holding the justices spellbound with his compelling arguments.

"For you, maybe, but for Mike it's about collecting a judgment and nothing more. So let's stay focused on what our client needs and not what we might aspire to." John's terse reminder was accompanied by a stern look of reproval. Having made his point, John continued. "I would say the school district is going to be our most viable defendant unless one of the boys turns out to be a closet millionaire."

"Actually, that may not be so far-fetched," piped up Martha. "The thought occurred to me the other day that the Hendershott boy might be one of THE Hendershotts—the family that owns about half the ranch land in northern Arizona. I thought I recognized his parents' names as people whose names I'd seen in some of the society columns in the paper. I went to the library and checked the archives for the newspaper and confirmed that he really does belong to this family." She watched Ernesto's eyes widen at her conclusion.

"So it's not outside the realm of reason to assume that this kid has or will be coming into some money of his own," reasoned Ernesto.

"Certainly something we need to follow up on," said John matter-of-factly. "Excellent work, Martha. Talk about taking the initiative! Wouldn't it be nice to be able to collect a judgment against the actual tortfeasor instead of having to go against the **deep pocket**? Well, at any rate, all of these defendants are **jointly liable**, so we can let the jury sort out degrees of culpability. For now, it's enough to know we can actually recover something if we get a judgment. So let me meet with Mike, tell him what we've discovered, and find out how he wants to proceed."

Putting It Into Practice 4.2:

Is the firm violating Rule 11 of the *Federal Rules of Civil Procedure* by filing a claim against CODA when the law regarding liability is not clearly established in reference to the media? Explain.

deep pocket defendant who may or may not be the primary tortfeasor but who pays all or most of a judgment because of his financial status

jointly liable liability of each defendant for the entire loss suffered by the plaintiff

GOING AFTER THE DEEP POCKET

A practical problem that attorneys face when initiating a lawsuit is whom they should sue. When more than one defendant is involved, it is not unusual for the attorney to find, after a little research, that the defendant who is the least culpable has more substantial financial resources and is better able to pay a judgment than the defendant who is the most culpable. If the defendant who is most responsible for the plaintiff's injuries is judgment proof, the attorney may resort to going after the "deep pocket" if she intends to recover any damages for the plaintiff.

One doctrine that allows plaintiffs to recover from the deep pocket is the doctrine of **joint and several liability. Joint tortfeasors** (two or more people who act together to produce a single tort) are "jointly and severally liable" in that they are totally liable for the entire loss suffered by the plaintiff if that loss cannot be apportioned among the defendants. Under the rule of joint and several liability, each defendant can be held responsible for paying for the entire harm or any designated portion of the harm. It is up to the plaintiff to decide whether to recover from one or all of the joint tortfeasors. The defendants can later try to recover from one another the inequitable portion of the monies they had paid to the plaintiff. Consequently, one defendant can be held responsible for payment of all damages even though his contribution to the plaintiff's injuries was relatively minor. For example, if a plaintiff suffered damages in the amount of $10,000 and five defendants acted together to cause the injuries, the plaintiff could recover $2,000 from each defendant, $10,000 from one defendant, or $1,000 from four defendants and $6,000 from one defendant, and so on.

Another doctrine that allows recovery from the deep pocket is the doctrine of vicarious liability. Under this doctrine an individual is held liable for the torts of another because of the special relationship he holds to the tortfeasor. The most common special relationship is the one between employer and employee. This doctrine allows the plaintiff to recover from the employer (deep pocket) rather than the employee. The rationale used to justify this doctrine is that employers should consider the expense of reimbursing those injured by their employees as part of the cost of doing business. For the doctrine to apply, the employee must be acting "within the scope and furtherance of his employment." An employee is considered to be doing that as long as he is intending to further his employer's business purpose. An employer is liable even if she explicitly forbids an employee to engage in certain acts and the employee does so anyway as long as the acts are done within the scope and furtherance of employment. An employer is not, however, vicariously liable when an employee goes on a "frolic" or "detour" of his own, unless his deviation from his business purpose is reasonably foreseeable.

To illustrate vicarious liability, consider an employee of a pizza parlor who, having completed his deliveries, drives twenty miles out of his way for a little rendevous with his girlfriend. His twenty-mile side trip would very probably be considered a "frolic" or "detour" and, if so, the employer would not be vicariously liable for any acts of negligence the employee might commit along the way. However, if the employee became involved in an accident while enroute back to the pizza parlor, the employer would again become vicariously liable because once the employee got back on track, he would be acting within the scope of his employment.

As you might expect, the idea of tapping nominally responsible defendants to pay a plaintiff's damages is controversial. Critics argue that minimally negligent defendants should not be required to shoulder the burden for harm caused by others. They further maintain that, even if business (which is often the deep pocket) can pass on its tort-related costs to the public through higher prices, these higher prices hurt the business. Using business to provide "insurance" only encourages plaintiffs to find wealthy business defendants to sue, resulting in a tort system that is no longer grounded in moral obligation and that serves up defendants as scapegoats. Without such doctrines as joint and several liability, however, the injured

joint and several liability rule by which each defendant, can be held responsible for paying for the entire harm to the plaintiff or some designated portion of the harm as long as the harm cannot be apportioned among the defendants

joint tortfeasors two or more tortfeasors who act together to produce a single tort

◆ **LOCAL LINKS** ◆
Does your state have some form of the doctrine of joint and several liability?

plaintiff ends up bearing the loss, being either uncompensated or undercompensated. Pared to its essentials, the question is one of social policy: where society wants to assign the burden when a liable party cannot pay damages. Because of the concern about "deep pockets," joint and several liability has been abolished in some states. Other states have placed statutory limits on the doctrine by requiring that the liability of a tortfeasor whose contribution to the plaintiff's damages is below a certain percentage be limited to the tortfeasor's equitable share of the damages.

Putting It Into Practice 4.3:

(a) Could Mike decide to recover from the school district only and ignore the other defendants even though the other defendants were primarily responsible for his injuries? Assume that he is filing suit in your state. (b) Why will Mike want to sue the school district as well as any faculty who might have been negligent?

COLLECTABILITY OF JUDGMENTS

One of the most important considerations in deciding whether a lawsuit is worth filing in the first place is the question of whether the person to be sued has assets from which a judgment could be collected. Lawyers regularly turn down great cases that would be fantastic moneymakers—except that the person to be sued has no insurance and no reachable assets. The loser can, of course, simply pay the judgment, or the parties can agree to settle the case for some lesser amount. But if the loser refuses to cooperate, the winner must somehow find the loser's property and have it seized and sold to pay the judgment, which may be difficult or even impossible.

Like it or not, the importance of collectability is a central fact of litigation. As a practical matter, however, there is often no good way to know whether a judgment can be collected until after it is obtained. In most states, the defendant is not required to allow the plaintiff to invade his financial privacy before judgment.

This does not mean, however, that plaintiffs are always flying blind on the question of whether a judgment can be collected. For one thing, a plaintiff can use the discovery process to find out if the defendant has insurance coverage. If the defendant has enough insurance to cover the judgment the plaintiff is seeking, the collectability problem evaporates. Also, if the defendant is a large corporation and not visibly teetering on the edge of bankruptcy, it is usually safe to assume that a judgment can be collected.

In many situations, it will be obvious that a judgment can not be collected. The prime example is the automobile collision where the driver at fault has no insurance. As a practical matter, collecting any significant amount of money from an ordinary working person who has no insurance is difficult if not impossible. How can this be? In the American system, winners of lawsuits are not allowed to strip the losers down to their underwear and leave them to sleep in the street. The law allows a **judgment debtor** (the loser in a lawsuit) to keep enough money and property to be able to survive. Each state has exemption statutes that list a number of items that any judgment debtor is entitled to keep. These lists have been added to and adjusted upward from time to time, to the point that today, in some states, the "survival" level can be luxurious indeed. A typical middle-class judgment debtor will be able to keep his house, at least one car, some clothes, books, furniture, tools, jewelry—most of the common badges of middle-class existence. As for wages, federal law allows the judgment debtor to keep either three-fourths of his take-home pay or the equivalent of thirty hours at minimum wage, whichever is greater. This leaves, at most, one-fourth of the judgment debtor's take-home pay that can be seized, and even that

judgment debtor defendant who loses a lawsuit

meager source of payment will likely dry up quickly if targeted. The judgment debtor will change jobs, move to another state, or simply file for bankruptcy.

Putting It Into Practice 4.4:

Why might a firm refuse to represent someone even though that person has a winnable claim against a defendant and the damages are substantial?

"I Want You to Remember That This Is Your Lawsuit. We Are Here to Guide You, Not to Tell You What You Have to Do."

After explaining to Mike and his parents what legal claims Mike had and what would have to be done in order to get a judgment, John asked if they had any questions or comments. Mike's parents immediately made it clear that they did not want Mike to sue the parents of the boys.

"Mr. Morgan, we have a son who is twelve years older than Mike and that boy has been in trouble all his life. We understand the heartbreak of having a child who destroys his life and brings pain to everyone who loves him. We have searched our souls for a reason—What did we do wrong?—and we still do not understand. How could Mike and his brother have come from the same flesh and blood, been raised in the same house, and turn out so different? We could never hold other parents responsible for the sins of their children. We would no more want to judge another parent than we would want others to judge us for what our son has done." Terell Johnson was normally a man of few words; the torrent of speech that burst forth from him was a reflection of the mental anguish he had been harboring for years.

John could read the torment on Terell's face and rushed to assure him that Mike did not have to sue anyone he did not want to. "In Mike's case, relatively little would be served by suing the parents because of the statutory cap on damages I told you about. Plus, in all likelihood the parents had no idea what their sons were planning. Proving their negligence would be difficult and not financially worth the effort."

After Mike confirmed that he did not want to sue the parents, John continued. "I want you to remember, Mike, that this is your lawsuit. The firm and I are here to represent you, to advise you. The ultimate decision with regard to every choice that has to be made is yours. We will tell you what the implications are of every turn you take and will keep you apprised of the risks involved, but we will never try to persuade you to do something you don't want to do. We are here to guide you, not to tell you what you have to do."

"I understand, Mr. Morgan, but I don't know much of anything about the legal system, except what I've seen on TV and in the movies. So I'm not sure I'm going to be much help to you," conceded Mike.

"That's why part of my job is to educate you so you know enough to be able to make those tough decisions. It's also why I will be keeping you informed every step of the way about what we are doing and what we have discovered." When neither of Mike's parents or Mike appeared to have anything to say, John moved on to another matter. "Unless any of you has any further questions about the case, I'm going to show you what is called a **contingency fee agreement.** This is the kind of fee agreement we normally use in personal injury cases, such as yours. Under this agreement, we will not receive any compensation unless we are able to secure a settlement for you or win a judgment. You will, however, be required to pay many costs, such as court costs and expert witness fees. All of this is outlined in the agreement. Let me walk you through it."

---

contingency fee agreement
agreement in which an attorney provides services for no charge (except for payment of costs) in exchange for receiving a percentage of the client's recovery

FEE ARRANGEMENTS

Attorneys use a variety of billing methods to charge for their services. The most common are contingency fees, hourly rates, and fixed fees.

Personal injury, medical malpractice, and collections cases are often handled on a contingency fee basis, in which the attorney agrees to provide services for a fee based on a percentage of the client's recovery. If there is no recovery, the attorney receives nothing. Typically the percentage of the fee depends on whether the case is settled or litigated. A common contingency fee arrangement provides for payment of 33 percent if the case settles before it goes to trial, 40 percent if it goes to trial, and 50 percent if the case is appealed.

The contingency fee arrangement has been the subject of frequent criticism. Some maintain that it creates a conflict of interest between the attorney and the client in reference to settlement offers. They argue that an attorney may agree to settle a case prematurely in order to collect a fee with as little investment of time and energy as possible even though it is not in the best interest of the client to settle. Critics of contingency fee agreements also point out that, in some cases, attorneys receive much more than would be considered a reasonable fee for the efforts they expended. On the other hand, such a fee arrangement allows those who would ordinarily be financially incapable of pursuing their claims to do so. Also, attorneys do not win all their cases and so those cases in which they receive nothing may balance those for which they may be overcompensated.

Attorneys doing defense work or work for a corporation usually charge by the hour. The fee varies with who is performing the work (a partner, an associate, or a paralegal) and with the type of work being done. Because of this fee structure, clients benefit when as much work as is within the competency of paralegals to perform is assigned to paralegals, whose hourly billing rate is substantially lower than attorneys'.

For certain types of services—drawing up a will, handling an uncontested divorce, or filing a simple bankruptcy—some attorneys charge a fixed fee (flat or set fee). Firms that delegate some or most of this work to paralegals find themselves at a competitive advantage over those who assign the same tasks to attorneys, who cost the firm considerably more.

The fee agreement is one of the key terms of the attorney-client agreement. This is a written agreement entered into between the attorney and the client once the attorney has agreed to accept the case. This agreement articulates the work that the attorney has agreed to do (and what he will not do). It should specify how the fee amount is determined and when it must be paid. In a personal injury case, for example, the agreement should indicate whether the attorney's percentage is computed before or after the costs of litigation (any out-of-pocket expenses incurred by the attorney) are deducted and whether the fee is due when the judgment is actually collected. The agreement should also indicate the types of costs that can be anticipated (such as filing fees and other court costs, the costs of expert witnesses, court reporter fees, the cost of photocopying, mailing, and making long distance phone calls) and should clarify whether the client is obligated to pay these costs even if no recovery is obtained. Any attorney's liens (claims by an attorney on any recovery obtained by the client) should be disclosed in this agreement.

In some cases, attorneys demand a **retainer,** which is an advance from which the attorney pays fees and covers expenses. Attorneys have an obligation to put retainers in a trust fund for that client. They cannot withdraw any monies from that trust fund unless they incur expenses or perform services for which they earn a fee.

Additional forms of fee agreements can be found at many of the "legal" Web sites referred to throughout this book. Additional examples can also be found at *www.lectric.com/forma.htm.*

◆ LOCAL LINKS ◆

In your state, what percentages are customarily used in contingency fee agreements? Are there customary fees?
In your state, what specific provisions must attorney fee contracts contain?

---

retainer advance received by an attorney from which she must pay expenses and from which she can collect her fees

---

NET NEWS

To get more information about fee arrangements, including the national averages for fixed fees and the hourly rates for attorneys and paralegals, go to *www.lawyers.com/lawyers-com/content/hiring/hiring.html.* Click on "How, and How Much, Do Lawyers Charge?" For some pointers about negotiating fees with lawyers, go to *www.lectlaw.com,* click on "Rotunda," and then "Laypeople's Law Lounge." Under "Dealing with the Lawyer System," click on "General Information on Attorney Fees."

Figure 4-1
Retainer Agreements

RETAINER AGREEMENT

Agreement dated this ___ day of October, 2000, by and between Michael Johnson and White & Treadwell, PLLC, Attorneys at Law.

1. I do hereby employ White & Treadwell to represent me and my interests in any and all matters and/or causes of action that I may have arising out of an incident in which I was involved on May, 5, 2000.

2. I hereby agree that the attorney's fees are to be based upon a contingency fee basis of thirty-three and one-third percent (33 1/3%) of the gross recovery received. It is my understanding that there will be no attorney's fees if no sums are recovered. I hereby further agree to be responsible for all out-of-pocket expenses arising out of any action taken in this matter and that no settlement shall be made without my consent.

_____
Michael Johnson
White & Treadwell, PLLC

By_____
John Morgan

Figure 4-2
Types of Fee Agreements

FEE AGREEMENTS

Contingency Fee—agreement to provide legal services in exchange for fee based on percentage of client's recovery

Hourly Rate—charge for services by the hour

Fixed (Flat or Set) Fee—fee that is based on the type of work being done rather than what is recovered or how much time is spent doing the work

---

◆ **LOCAL LINKS** ◆

What are typical billing rates for the attorneys and paralegals in your area?

Putting It Into Practice 4.5:

Why do you think fee disputes are one of the more commonly litigated disputes between clients and attorneys? What issues do you anticipate would arise?

NET NEWS

For more information about the ethical standards in regard to fee setting and collection, go to *www.lectlaw.com*, click on "Rotunda," "Legal Professional's Lounge," and then on "Lawyers." Go to the article entitled "Overview of the Ethical Aspects of Attorney Fees."

ETHICAL ETIQUETTE

FEES AND FEE ARRANGEMENTS

One of the most common causes of attorney disciplinary actions is the mishandling of client funds. Because paralegals are often asked to carry out an attorney's instructions relating to client funds and because in smaller firms they will often be responsible for the bookkeeping and record keeping functions, they must know the ethical rules by which attorneys are bound.

Two major rules guide attorneys in relation to client funds. First, they should never commingle (mix) their funds with a client's funds. They should have a separate bank account that contains only client funds. A client may warrant a separate account if the attorney handles enough money for them. All funds must remain in the trust account until the attorney has performed the work necessary to earn the fee. If a dispute arises between the client and attorney about the appropriateness of a fee, the amount in contention must remain in the trust account until the dispute is resolved.

Second, an attorney must never draw funds from a trust account for personal use. The fact that the attorney intends to (or in fact does) return the funds at a later date is not a defense. An attorney's financial problems or mismanagement issues are also not acceptable excuses. Attorneys have a duty to maintain accurate and complete records of a client's funds.

All states (except Indiana) have mandatory or voluntary IOLTA (Interest on Lawyers' Trust Accounts) programs. The interest on these IOLTA accounts are used to fund such things as legal services for the poor or the bar's disciplinary program. These programs usually pertain only to those accounts that would not earn interest for the client because they are too small or are being held for too short of a period of time. The funds generated by these programs are substantial, however, and each state has developed its own rules about how the monies are to be expended.

Paralegals should not discuss fees with new clients. Although paralegals often serve as a liaison between attorneys and clients and may answer questions about fees and costs, they cannot enter into contractual agreements with clients on behalf of attorneys and they cannot establish fees.

Putting It Into Practice 4.6:

Around the holidays, Marianne's attorney is short of cash and has Marianne withdraw some money from his trust account. He promises her that he will pay it back right after the holidays. Before she can say anything, he tells her that he is leaving for the morning and that a new client has just phoned and is stopping by to sign an attorney-client agreement. The attorney tells Marianne to prepare a standard agreement for a personal injury case and to answer any questions the client might have about their fee arrangement. What should Marianne do?

◆ **LOCAL LINKS** ◆

How does your state use IOLTA funds?

Mike's mother, Marian, had said nothing up to this point. But after John's explanation of the fee agreement, she sat forward in her chair. "Mr. Morgan, my husband and I run a catering business. One of our clients has threatened to sue us because we weren't able to cater for his company when Mike was in the hospital. We didn't know if he was going to live or die and we couldn't bear to leave his side." Marian's voice caught as she remembered how close Mike had come to dying. "We called this company and told them they would have to get somebody else to cater for them, and they told us they couldn't get anybody at that late date. It turns out they did get somebody, but it cost them a lot more money. Now they want us to pay them the difference in costs. We don't have the kind of money they're talking about, Mr. Morgan, and we don't think it is right that they should ask for it. But if they sue us, I'm not sure we can afford to pay an attorney. Do you lawyers have some way to handle cases like ours?"

"Unfortunately, Mrs. Johnson, the contingency fee arrangement doesn't work in a case like yours because you are being sued. You won't recover anything; if you win, you won't have to pay your client, but you still have to pay your attorney. The judge can, under certain circumstances, decide to make your opponent pay your attorney's fees, but you can't count on that happening. No. In your case, we would need to charge you by the hour."

"What do you charge by the hour?" inquired Marian.

"That depends on who is doing the work. A senior partner charges $250 per hour, our junior associates begin charging at $150 per hour, and we charge $80-100 per hour for work done by our paralegals."

"I had no idea attorneys were that expensive," gasped Marian. "We'd have all we could do to pay for a paralegal."

"What we could do," suggested John, "is arrange for you to make monthly payments so that you wouldn't have to pay us all at once and we could make sure that as much work as possible was done by paralegals. Do you mind my asking how much they say you owe them?"

"I think they said $20,000, didn't they, Terell?" asked Marian. Terell nodded his agreement.

"In Arizona, any disputes with damages less than that set by local rule—$50,000 in our county—must go to **arbitration.** With arbitration, a neutral third party hears your case. It's a much more relaxed process than a trial and a lot less expensive." Seeing the worried look on the Johnsons' faces, John hastened to add, "Of course, in cases like this, we can write a letter on your behalf and get the opposing party to settle right away. If you get any phone calls from their attorney, you can feel free to have the attorney call me. I'll bet we could get it straightened out without anybody having to file suit."

"You would do that for us?" asked Marian, looking greatly relieved.

"Well, it's outside of my bailiwick, but I know how to be pretty persuasive when I want to. I'd be glad to make a few phone calls on your behalf. If for any reason we can't get it resolved, we'll work out some kind of payment plan that you can afford." John knew that the partners would be less than delighted with this proposition, but he believed that firms should provide their clients the best service possible. He also knew the firm was in a position to make a handsome fee on Mike's case that would offset any losses it incurred in taking on the contractual dispute.

arbitration hearing held before a neutral third party who renders a decision and issues an award

TIMEKEEPING

The importance of paralegals maintaining accurate timekeeping records cannot be over-emphasized. The practice of law is both a profession and a business. As such, the generation of profits is essential to the success of any law practice (other than government law offices, such as the county attorney's office or federal district attorney's office). A law office's profits arise out of the hours billed by each attorney and paralegal on staff. These billable hours are the staple of any law practice.

Therefore, it is absolutely essential that all attorneys and paralegals maintain accurate records of the hours they have expended in working on each case to which they have been assigned.

Firms use a variety of procedures for recording time spent , and many have employed computerized timekeeping procedures. (See "Tim's Techno Tips" at the end of this chapter for a discussion of computerized procedures.) Regardless of the details, however, every procedure requires paralegals to maintain records of the clients for whom they have done work, the type of work they did (e.g., phone call, document review, preparation of letter, travel, or research), the date they performed the work, and the time they spent doing it. Not all work is considered billable. The time Martha spent familiarizing herself with the law in Mike's case, for example, would probably not have been billable if the firm had been billing Mike on an hourly fee basis. For this reason, inexperienced paralegals spend more time accomplishing the same goal as more experienced paralegals, but amass fewer billable hours.

To maintain an on-going tally of the time spent on each project and/or task, paralegals and attorneys use some kind of timesheet on which to record the time expended. These time sheets are then typed onto time tickets or into some kind of computer database. Remembering to note the time spent on each task (e.g., reviewing a file, talking on the phone, preparing a document) requires incredible discipline. To assist them in integrating this recording process into their routine, some paralegals place a small digital clock in a visible place on their desk; others use a

◆ **LOCAL LINKS** ◆
What kinds of billing practices are common in the area where you live? Does your instructor have any helpful hints regarding timekeeping?

NET NEWS

For more information about paralegal billing practices, go to *www.paralegals.org/reporter,* click on "Winter 1999," and then on "Billing Paralegal Time."

dictating machine to record time only. Well-organized paralegals recommend making a list of each task entailed in any project and then recording the time each task was begun as well as completed.

Being intimately familiar with the billing practice of a firm is extremely important. Some firms have minimum billing practices. Every phone call, for example, may be billed as 0.1 hour (6 minutes) or 0.2 hour (12 minutes) even if the client does not answer and even if the conversation actually takes less time. Every letter may be billed at a minimum of 0.5 hour even if it is a form letter that can be completed in a few minutes. Other firms are less rigid in their billing practices, but do require paralegals to log every hour expended and then review these records to determine which hours will actually be billed.

By routinely assessing your billing rate, you can evaluate your efficiency. If, in an eight-hour day, you are typically billing only four hours, you need to reassess how you are using your time. To keep accurate records, you should fill out your time sheet immediately after you complete a task. Otherwise you may be forgetting the time you expended and you may, at the end of the day, be unable to account for the time you expended.

Beyond the economic necessity of maintaining accurate records, the court in some instances may need to be able to determine the amount of time spent on a case. The awarding of attorney's fees, for example, requires that the court be able to review the amount of time spent in preparing a case to determine if that amount of time falls within the realm of standard practice. This caveat also applies to paralegals because paralegal fees are sometimes recoverable as part of attorney's fee awards. Any time attorney's fees becomes an issue, a law firm must be able to bolster its claims of reasonableness by producing records of the time expended by each staff member. Failure to keep accurate and consistent records may result in a loss of fees to the firm. Furthermore, inability to justify fees to a client can result in a client who not only resents the amount of monies being paid, but harbors such hostility toward the firm that any future relations become impossible.

Putting It Into Practice 4.7:

For one week, maintain an ongoing time sheet, keeping track of the time you spend on each thing you do. Estimate these times in terms of 0.1 hour (six minutes). How frequently do you remember to record your time? Review your timesheet at the end of the week. What are you able to observe about how you use your time?

BONUS POINTERS:

ACCESSIBILITY OF LEGAL SERVICES

The poor and even many of the middle class cannot afford legal representation. As of 1992, 45 million persons had incomes that were low enough to qualify for legal services. Another 15 million people were near-poor and could not reasonably afford counsel. This means that, in 1992, there was one lawyer for every 9000 financially eligible poor persons, and one lawyer per 14,200 poor or near-poor persons. Several surveys have demonstrated that close to half of poor persons at any given time face at least one legal problem and often more than one. [67 Fordham L. Rev. 2475 (1999) "Acting 'A Very Moral Type of God'; Triage Among Poor Clients"; Paul Tremblay]

Those who cannot afford an attorney can seek assistance through publicly or privately funded legal services, such as Community Legal Services. Applicants must be able to prove their indigency and must have a case that falls within the parameters set by these agencies. The areas of law focused on by these agencies are landlord-tenant, consumer, family, housing, and welfare.

Many people who cannot afford even a modestly priced attorney either do not meet the indigency requirements of Legal Services or their case does not fall within the relatively narrow guidelines. These people can also seek representation through programs sponsored by the local bar association, a legal clinic, or through a pre-paid legal plan.

A legal clinic is a high-efficiency law firm that can afford to charge lower fees because of the high volume of cases it accepts. These firms can handle a large volume of cases because they tend to use standardized forms and procedures and delegate a great deal of their work to paralegals. They generate their caseloads through extensive advertising and tend to focus on fairly routine cases, such as divorces, wills, traffic offenses, and simple bankruptcies.

Pre-paid legal plans work like most medical plans. Under such plans, people can either select from a group of lawyers or are allowed to pick any lawyer they prefer. In the latter plan, there are usually limits as to what will be covered. Some of the largest plans are union-based. The money deducted from each paycheck is put into a fund that finances the establishment of union employee law firms or independent firms that service plan members nationwide. Other plans mass market through credit unions, hospitals, universities, or other large employers. Most plans require the lawyer to charge a discounted hourly rate for plan members—typically $70-100 per hour.

Unrepresented litigants can also obtain information from various sheets, booklets, and court forms that are available in many courthouses, or they can obtain information from Web sites. In Maricopa County Superior Court in Arizona, a "self-service" center has been created to assist unrepresented litigants in filling out forms, learning about court procedures, and alerting them to appropriate referral resources. Some courts organize information tables staffed by non-lawyers, court clinics staffed by law students, and "lawyers-for-the-day" programs staffed by volunteer lawyers. In addition, some states, such as California, have statutorily recognized "legal document assistants"—non-lawyers who can fill out routine paperwork for litigants representing themselves.

◆ **LOCAL LINKS** ◆
What agencies in your area are available to represent clients for free or a reduced fee?

Putting It Into Practice 4.8:
Do you think the Johnsons would qualify to be defended by Community Legal Services?

"Your Standard Response to Anyone Who Wants to Talk with You about This Case or Who Wants Information Is That You are Represented by an Attorney and They Will have to Talk with Me."

"Now, I have a few more things to tell you about your case. I want you to know up front what you can expect so you're not surprised later on." John went on to explain the basic process for civil litigation, describing what would probably happen at each stage of the process and what role Mike would play at each stage. He gave an estimate of how long he thought it would probably take before Mike's case went to trial, if, in fact, a trial was necessary.

"Now, Mike, I want to re-emphasize that you should not discuss this matter with anyone. If members of the press should try to interview you, you just tell them they should talk with me. If any attorney should try to talk with you, call me immediately. Your standard response to anyone who wants to talk with you about this case or who wants information is that you are represented by an attorney and he or she will have to talk with me. Are you clear on that?" asked John emphatically.

"Crystal clear, sir," responded Mike.

"Good. Also, you need to send all your medical bills to Martha as soon as you receive them. We need to keep a current tally of any and all expenses you incur as a result of your injuries. As I indicated to you earlier, I'll be communicating with you regularly, sending you copies of documents we send out and those we receive from the other parties so that you know what's going on at all times. So, I guess that wraps it up for now."

As John stood up and ushered the Johnsons to the door, he continued to explain what his next steps would be. "I'll prepare a complaint, which will initiate the lawsuit, and send it out probably the first of next week. We'll start the discovery process immediately in this case because there are several unknowns we want to clear up as soon as we can. I'll send you a copy of the complaint and will let you know as soon as we receive answers from the defendants." As soon as he and the Johnsons had said their good-byes, John sat down to formulate a litigation plan.

PLANNING LITIGATION

Before rushing headlong into litigation, seasoned attorneys develop a litigation plan. In doing so, they consider several factors.

◆ the client's objectives and cost constraints
◆ the theory of the case
◆ writing a **demand letter**
◆ any pre-filing requirements
◆ the litigation timetable

demand letter letter sent by the plaintiff's attorney to the defendant's attorney or insurance company demanding a specific sum of money in return for a release of plaintiff's claims

Client Objectives

Attorneys begin by reviewing what the client has indicated she wants to accomplish, what her priorities are, and under what financial constraints she is operating. The attorney must then construct litigation objectives that are aligned with the client's objectives. If an attorney believes that trial will be necessary, for example, he will conduct a more thorough discovery in preparation for trial than if he believes that settlement is likely early on.

Theory of Case

Attorneys follow up with a review of their client's position—their theory of the case—and consider the contested and uncontested facts. They will hone in on missing facts and begin contemplating how to fill in those facts. They will look at the jury appeal of their case: how believable are their witnesses, their client? How does their client's story compare with the opponents' stories? They begin the process of constructing their case.

Demand Letter

Because of the high cost of lawsuits, a plaintiff may be better served by settling the case before suit is filed. If appropriate, the plaintiff's attorney may send a demand letter to the defendant or the defendant's insurance carrier. This letter begins with an explanation of what the dispute is about, followed by an analysis of the liability issue. It emphasizes the facts in the plaintiff's favor and explains how these facts enhance the plaintiff's chances of winning. The plaintiff's damages are spelled out in as much detail as possible. Copies of whatever documents the plaintiff will be relying on to prove damages—bills, receipts, physician's reports, repair estimates,

NET NEWS

To see a sample demand letter, go to *www.alllaw.com/forms/pleadings* and click on "Demand Letter."

employer's verification of time lost from work—are enclosed. The demand letter concludes by demanding a specific sum of money in return for a release of plaintiff's claims. A time limit is set, specifying a deadline after which the offer to settle will terminate.

Submitting a pre-suit settlement demand in a given case is a strategic choice. Some plaintiff's lawyers, even in garden-variety accident cases, always file suit first, believing that this shows determination and that their demands will be taken more seriously. Some opponents—usually large corporations or insurance companies—deliberately cultivate a reputation for being tough litigants and for fighting every claim to the bitter end. Settlement overtures with such opponents are usually futile.

Pre-filing Requirements

Injured parties are not always free to fire off a lawsuit as their first offensive move. Some legal actions, usually involving situations coming under the regulation of a government agency, require the aggrieved party to first "exhaust administrative remedies" before filing suit. In other words, the party must conform to the prescribed review procedures set forth by the agency before resorting to a court of law. Injured employees covered by worker's compensation laws, for example, are usually prohibited from suing their employer; they must instead apply for compensation from the worker's compensation fund. Resort to the courts is possible only after the applicable state agency has made its decision. Claims involving illegal discrimination often must first be brought to the Equal Employment Opportunity Commission or a state administrative agency having jurisdiction; the agency must investigate and give permission before the aggrieved party can sue.

Suits against government agencies and departments are particularly demanding of careful pre-suit planning. Historically, the government was immune from suit altogether. Although this absolute **sovereign immunity** no longer applies, vestiges remain in the form of statutes that require anyone intending to sue a government agency to give notice of his claim before filing suit. Notices of claims must be in the correct form and delivered to the correct government official within the allowed time period, which is typically short. Often, even a seemingly trivial defect in the notice will cause the suit to be dismissed, perhaps forever.

Certain types of contracts provide that any dispute under the contract must be arbitrated rather than taken to court. Usually, such contracts specify time limits for commencing arbitration. Many contracts have "notice and claims" provisions that require notice of intent to sue; usually such notice must be given in a shorter time period than the applicable statute of limitations.

Some people, such as minors, are considered incompetent to sue in their own name. Before suit can be filed, they must be appointed a guardian or conservator or some other form of legal representative.

Litigation Timetable

Once the plaintiff's attorney has decided whom to sue, which court to sue in, what claims to assert, and what relief to demand, she must plan her discovery in a way that fulfills the client's objectives within the client's cost constraints. Without such

sovereign immunity
governmental immunity from suit

motions formal request by a party for a judge to enter an order or make a ruling of some kind

planning, discovery can easily become outrageously expensive and unfocused. In addition to determining which facts need to be found and which ones need to be confirmed, the attorney must decide which discovery methods will be most effective (discovery will be discussed in Chapter 5) and in what order they should be used. As part of this process, the attorney should consider what **motions** she will probably need to file and which motions are likely to be filed by her opponent. Then she needs to gear the discovery process toward finding the facts necessary to prevail when filing or responding to these motions.

Once these steps in the litigation process have been identified, the attorney must create a realistic timetable in which to carry out these steps. This timetable should indicate the probable times needed to complete each of the anticipated steps leading up to trial. While such a timetable needs to be flexible enough to accommodate the inevitable changes that will occur along the way, it should also be complete enough that the attorneys and paralegals involved in the case have a good idea of the time frame during which they will need to complete particular tasks. Creating a timetable at the onset of litigation greatly facilitates personal time management. Software programs are available to produce timetables electronically.

Putting It Into Practice 4.9:

Do you think John should prepare a demand letter to any of the defendants before he files suit? Are there any pre-filing requirements of which he should be aware?

Figure 4-3
Factors to Consider in Planning Litigation

FACTORS TO CONSIDER IN PLANNING LITIGATION
Client's Objectives and Cost Constraints
Theory of Case
Demand Letter
Pre-Filing Requirements
Litigation Timetable

NET NEWS

To read about some things a client should consider before filing suit, go to *www.lectlaw.com,* click on "Rotunda," "Legal Professional's Lounge," "Litigation," and then on "Assorted Rules." Read the article entitled "Considerations Before Filing a Civil Lawsuit."

After completing the litigation plan, John briefly considered which court he should file suit in. Although in some cases this was a complex issue fraught with a number of strategic and procedural considerations, in the Johnson matter the choice was very straightforward. Because he had no grounds for filing in federal court, he was relegated to suing in the Arizona state court, known as the Superior Court.

JURISDICTION

forum   court in which a lawsuit is filed

A decision that must be made at the onset of litigation is which **forum** (the court in which the lawsuit is filed) is best for the plaintiff. Two considerations are most important in making this choice. First, a court must be chosen that has legal authority to hear the case, which is to say, the court must have **jurisdiction.** Second, out of all the possible courts in which suit could be filed, the one in which the plaintiff is most likely to win is obviously the best choice for the plaintiff. All courts are not created equal, nor do all courts apply the same laws.

jurisdiction   authority of a court to hear a case

Generally, a plaintiff must file in the appropriate court in the county in which the parties reside if the following are true.

◆ All parties to the lawsuit are now, and were at the time of the events in dispute, residents of the forum county.
◆ The dispute is over some set of circumstances that occurred entirely within the forum county.
◆ The case is a suit for money damages.
◆ The case does not involve any government agencies as plaintiff or defendant.
◆ The amount of money in question is above the local county court threshold (i.e., not so small as to force the case into small claims court).
◆ None of the claims on which the suit will be based arises from federal law or from the law of some other state or country.

Putting It Into Practice 4.10:

Which of these factors exists in the Johnson case?

However, a plaintiff has many local courts from which to choose. At a minimum, in a suit for damages, the plaintiff could choose her local county or superior court, the defendant's local county or superior court, the local county or superior court where any significant part of the events in dispute happened, or the federal district court for the district in which the plaintiff or defendant resides or in which any significant part of the events in dispute happened (assuming a basis for federal jurisdiction exists).

Subject Matter Jurisdiction

subject matter and personal jurisdiction   power of a court to hear cases of a given type

In deciding which of these courts would be most appropriate the plaintiff must consider which have both **subject matter** and **personal jurisdiction.** Subject matter jurisdiction is the power to hear and decide cases of a given type. This kind of jurisdiction is extremely important because defects in the court's subject matter jurisdiction cannot be waived and can be raised at any time, even when the case is on appeal. If the court finds that it lacks subject matter jurisdiction, it must dismiss the case. This means that a case could be fully litigated, the plaintiff could obtain a judgment, and the case could be thrown out on appeal if the appellate court determined that the trial court lacked subject matter jurisdiction. Fortunately, this sort of thing does not happen often, but the possibility is enough to make litigators very wary about subject matter jurisdiction.

general subject matter jurisdiction   power of a court to hear all types of cases

State trial courts have the power to hear all types of cases and so are considered courts of **general subject matter jurisdiction.** Some exceptions to the "generality" of state court subject matter jurisdiction do exist. For example, divorce cases must

◆ **LOCAL LINKS** ◆

What kinds of subject matter jurisdiction restrictions exist in your state?

limited subject matter jurisdiction power of a court to hear only a few specific categories of cases

federal question jurisdiction authority of federal courts to hear all civil case arising out of the Constitution, laws, or treaties of the United States

diversity of citizenship jurisdiction authority of federal courts to hear civil cases between citizens of different states

domicile state in which a person is physically present or in which a corporation is incorporated or has as its principal place of business

jurisdictional amount amount in controversy in a diversity case; at this point that amount must be $75,000 or more

personal jurisdiction authority of a court to render a decision that will be binding on a party

be filed in some states in specialty divorce or family courts; probate cases must be filed in probate court in some localities, and small claims cases (i.e., cases in which the amount in dispute is below a certain threshold amount of money, typically on the order of a few thousand dollars), may have to be filed in a court designated to handle small claims.

Federal courts, on the other hand, are courts of **limited subject matter jurisdiction.** Their jurisdiction extends only to a few specific categories of cases for which Congress has passed laws allowing suit. Federal district courts have subject matter jurisdiction over "all civil actions arising under the Constitution, laws, or treaties of the United States." 28 U.S.C. § 1331. This is called **federal question jurisdiction.** In practice, this means that if a cause of action is based on a federal statute, the plaintiff can sue in federal court. Merely because a case is based on a federal statute does not mean it must be filed in federal court, however, and many such cases are filed in state court.

The other main category of federal subject matter jurisdiction is **diversity of citizenship jurisdiction.** The idea here is that the federal courts should provide an impartial forum for suits between residents of different states. Presumably, state courts might tend to favor their own residents over "foreigners." Therefore, the federal district courts have original jurisdiction over all civil actions between "citizens of different states." "Citizenship" as used here means **domicile.** Usually, a person's domicile is the state in which the person lives and intends to remain. A corporation is considered to be a citizen of any state in which it is incorporated and also of the state in which its" principal place of business" is located. In cases involving a number of plaintiffs and defendants, "complete diversity" is required. In other words, no defendant can be a resident of the same state as any plaintiff.

The other requirement for diversity jurisdiction is that the "matter in controversy" must exceed "the sum or value of $75,000." This is referred to as the **jurisdictional amount.** This amount is determined by how much the plaintiff asks for in the complaint, not by how much is actually won. This jurisdictional amount is set by statute and is subject to change.

Putting It Into Practice 4.11:

Why does the federal court not have jurisdiction in the Johnson case?

Personal Jurisdiction

Personal jurisdiction (in personam jurisdiction) is the power to render a decision that will be binding on the parties. The issue that personal jurisdiction addresses is: "Is it fair under these circumstances to force the defendant to litigate in this forum?" The answer depends on whether the defendant in question has sufficient "contacts" with the forum state to make it fair to force him to litigate there. The easy way to

---

NET NEWS

For more information about subject matter jurisdiction, go to *www.west.net/,smith/smjuris.htm.*

Figure 4-4
Jurisdiction

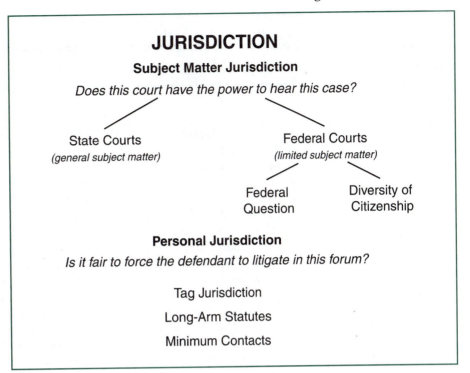

JURISDICTION

Subject Matter Jurisdiction

Does this court have the power to hear this case?

State Courts
(general subject matter)

Federal Courts
(limited subject matter)

Federal
Question

Diversity of
Citizenship

Personal Jurisdiction

Is it fair to force the defendant to litigate in this forum?

Tag Jurisdiction

Long-Arm Statutes

Minimum Contacts

serve process   physically hand
a defendant a complaint and
summons

long-arm statutes   statute that
authorizes suits against non-
residents in certain situations

get personal jurisdiction is to get the consent of the party being sued or to sue in
the state in which the defendant resides (or the corporation is present). To get personal jurisdiction of a defendant who refuses to consent to suit in the plaintiff's
choice of states and does not reside there, the plaintiff must either **serve process** on
the defendant within the boundaries of the forum state or take advantage of the so-
called **long-arm statutes.** (Serving process consists of having a copy of the summons and complaint delivered to the defendant.)

Because courts have jurisdiction of anyone located within the boundaries of the
state, whether or not the person is a resident of the state, the plaintiff can get personal jurisdiction over a defendant if she can manage to catch the defendant in the
state in which she wants to sue. She must then get a process server to serve process
on the defendant before he leaves the state. As a practical matter, this so-called "tag"
jurisdiction is not a particularly impressive way to acquire personal jurisdiction.

A more efficient way is to look to the *long-arm statute* each state has that authorizes suits against non-residents in certain situations specified by the statute. These
statutes must meet the U.S. Supreme Court requirement that defendants have
"minimum contacts" with the forum state before they can be dragged into court
against their will. To illustrate the fundamental fairness of this requirement, consider the following. Suppose Sam Snowbird from Duluth, Minnesota is driving
through Albuquerque, New Mexico, when he is involved in a collision with Larry
Local, a New Mexico resident. It seems perfectly reasonable to allow Larry to sue
Sam in New Mexico—after all, it was Sam's choice to drive there. On the other
hand, it would be fundamentally unfair to allow Sam to sue Larry in Duluth—
Larry has not done anything to subject himself to the authority of Minnesota. Minimum contacts requires that the defendant (1) caused an act or event to occur
within the forum state; and (2) the cause of action which the plaintiff is suing on
arises from that act or event.

NET NEWS

For more information about personal jurisdiction, go to *www.west.net/.smith/jurisdiction.htm.*

BONUS POINTERS:

PERSONAL JURISDICTION CASES

To get a feel for the concept of minimum contacts, consider the following brief summaries of two leading federal cases and one state case.

World-Wide Volkswagen Corp. v. Woodson, 444 U.S. 286, 100 S. Ct. 559 (1980). involved a suit in an Oklahoma court by New York plaintiffs against a New York car distributor and a dealership that sold plaintiffs a car that burned up in Oklahoma injuring the plaintiffs. Neither of the defendants conducted any business in Oklahoma and did not regularly sell to Oklahoma buyers. HELD: Defendants had insufficient contacts with Oklahoma to allow assertion of jurisdiction; foreseeability of injury alone is an insufficient basis for asserting personal jurisdiction.

Burger King Corp. v. Rudzewicz, 471 U.S. 462, 105 S. Ct. 2174 (1985). Florida corporation sued Michigan residents in Federal Court in Florida (based on diversity) for breach of a franchise agreement. Defendants alleged breach occurred in Michigan, not Florida, and that Florida court did not have jurisdiction over them. Florida's long-arm statute provided that it had jurisdiction over any breach of contract to be performed in Florida. (The franchisees' payments were made to plaintiff in Florida.) HELD: Defendants had sufficient contacts with Florida to allow assertion of jurisdiction.

Hoskins v. California, 168 Ariz. 250, 812 P.2d 1068 (1990), *review denied,* 168 Ariz. 177, 812 P.2d 1034 (1991). California parolee killed an Arizona resident in Arizona. Plaintiff alleged that the State of California failed to control the killer in California. Plaintiff also alleged that the State of California was doing business in Arizona for purposes of general jurisdiction. HELD: Defendant State of California had insufficient contacts with Arizona to allow assertion of jurisdiction.

At the federal level, there are no long-arm statutes; therefore, to sue people who are not residents of the forum state, plaintiffs must refer to the long-arm statute of the state in which the district court sits. The long-arm jurisdiction of the federal courts is determined by state law, not federal law.

Putting It Into Practice 4.12:

Does Arizona have personal jurisdiction over CODA?

VENUE

Jurisdiction allows us to answer the question, "Would a court in this state have the power to render a binding decision in this case?" Jurisdiction does not, however, answer an important related question: "Is this court a *reasonable and convenient* place in which to litigate this case?"

venue limitation on place of suit based on convenience

Venue is a further limitation on the place of suit, based on convenience. Even if a given court would have personal and subject matter jurisdiction over a suit, the plaintiff cannot proceed there if venue is not proper. In theory, the venue rules are designed to channel lawsuits into the courts that can hear them most efficiently, preferably without making the parties and witnesses travel great distances. In practice, venue rules are made by legislatures, and tend at times to be arbitrary and illogical.

NET NEWS

For additional information about venue, go to *www.west.net/,smith/jurisdiction.htm.*

Under the venue rules of most states, plaintiffs are free to choose a county in which any defendant resides. Depending on the state and the circumstances of the case, other permissible choices may include the plaintiff's county of residence, or the county in which the events in dispute occurred. In federal court, the plaintiff may sue in any district in which any of the defendants reside or in which most of the events giving rise to the dispute occurred. Generally speaking, if a plaintiff can get "long-arm" jurisdiction over the defendants, venue will be proper.

In routine cases, venue issues rarely arise. Quite commonly, the parties, the attorneys, and the dispute are all tied to one county, and that is where the suit is filed. In the rare case in which there is some compelling reason to file in a county in which venue is not obvious, it will be necessary to read the venue statute for the forum state to decide whether the case can proceed there.

Putting It Into Practice 4.13:
Will CODA likely prevail if it requests a change in venue?

DECIDING WHICH COURT IS THE BEST

The plaintiff wants to file in the place that gives her the best possible shot at winning. The choice of forum will have a huge impact on what procedure will be followed, what rules of substantive law will be applied, and how the case will be decided. It is entirely possible—even likely—that a given lawsuit could succeed in State A and fail in State B, due simply to differences in the laws of the two states.

Procedural Law

Every court applies its own procedural law. In the federal courts, the source of procedural law is the *Federal Rules of Civil Procedure.* Thus, procedural law is theoretically uniform in all federal district courts, whether the court is sitting in Alaska or Washington, D.C. As a practical matter, procedure under the federal rules is sufficiently uniform that most attorneys who have experience litigating in federal court in one district feel perfectly comfortable litigating in another district.

In state courts, procedure is determined by state law. In most states, the highest court issues rules of procedure, which are often patterned after the *Federal Rules of Civil Procedure.* In a few states, such as California, which has its procedural rules contained in the *California Code of Civil Procedure,* the legislature prescribes court procedure by statute. In all states, the interpretation of procedural rules is up to the appellate courts of the state. The details of state court procedure are extremely variable from state to state. Few competent attorneys would even dream of handling suits in the state courts of some other state without having a license to practice there and a thorough familiarity with the court system. Preferably, cases should be referred to a litigator in the state in which the suit will proceed.

◆ **LOCAL LINKS** ◆

Who created the procedural rules in your state?

Substantive Law

A given cause of action may be based on federal substantive law or state substantive law—it is up to the plaintiff to decide which substantive laws to sue under. With federal causes of action, deciding what substantive law will apply is relatively easy. Almost always, the cause of action will be based on some federal statute. Assuming personal jurisdiction can be obtained, the suit can be filed in any U.S. District Court in any state, or in the state courts of any state, and the substantive law applied will always be the same.

Every state has its own legislators, each free to "legislate" accordingly, and appellate judges, each with their own opinions about what the law should be. Although generally every state applies its own substantive law, in some cases, a case must be decided under the substantive laws of some other state.

In diversity cases, federal courts apply federal *procedural* law (the Federal Rules as interpreted by the federal courts), but the *substantive* law is the law of the state in which the court sits. That seems easy enough, until you realize that the line between "procedure" and "substance" is not always clear. Is, for example, a "statutes of limitations" problem a procedural one or a substantive one? (Substantive, according to the U.S. Supreme Court.)

Other Factors to Weigh in Choosing a Forum

A number of other important factors must be considered in deciding which forum offers the best chances of winning.

Crowded dockets are a modern fact of life. In some forums, as many as five years are needed to get a case to trial; in others, parties may get in front of a jury in as little as a year after filing the complaint. Long delays usually favor the defendants, because defendants ordinarily prefer to delay the possibility of having to pay the plaintiff anything for as long as possible.

The judge to whom a lawsuit is assigned may greatly influence the outcome. Judges are people, who possess the usual array of biases and prejudices. Intellectual abilities vary, as do judges' level of interest in particular areas of the law. Most urban courts have a number of judges, and cases are assigned at random, so usually the plaintiff does not get to select a particular judge. However, it seems that the **bench** (meaning all the judges taken together) of a particular court often develops its own "personality," enough so that the plaintiff has a discernibly higher probability of being assigned a "good" judge (defined as one more likely to decide important issues in the plaintiff's favor) if the plaintiff files in (say) U.S. District Court than if she files in her state court (or vice versa).

bench all of the judges taken together

Another important variable is the way in which judges are assigned. In some courts, once a judge is assigned, the parties are stuck with the assignment. In others, there is a procedure by which a party can **strike** or **notice** (disqualify) a judge and get a different one. (Attorneys are circumspect about availing themselves of this option because they may appear before this judge in the future and many judges view being struck with some degree of displeasure.) Some courts take the type of case into account in assigning cases to judges, so that judges can develop specialty expertise; in other courts, case assignments are totally random.

strike; notice disqualify a judge

Still another factor to consider is the effect of a forum choice on the demographics of the eventual jury pool, as graphically demonstrated by such notorious cases as those involving Rodney King and O.J. Simpson. Trial lawyers usually have very definite ideas about the kinds of jurors they would prefer in a particular case. Choosing a forum in which the desired kinds of people are prevalent in the local population is one easy way to gain an advantage in jury selection.

Figure 4-5
Factors to Consider in Choosing a Court

> # FACTORS TO CONSIDER IN CHOOSING A COURT
>
> Substantive law
> Procedural Law
> Crowded court dockets
> Judges' predispositions
> Jury demographics
> Home state of attorney

> ◆ **LOCAL LINKS** ◆
>
> Are parties allowed to strike (notice) judges in your jurisdiction?

All other things being equal, attorneys usually prefer to litigate in their home state. The procedure and the court systems are familiar and the judges and the local substantive law are known quantities. Filing in another state, whether in federal or state court, will usually require bringing in a local lawyer in the forum state to share the responsibility, and necessitates travel back and forth to the forum state, all of which add to the costs.

Putting It Into Practice 4.14:

If John could file Mike's lawsuit in federal court, what factors might make him choose federal court rather than state court?

"Office Politics Are a Reality of Law Practice and Any Other Organization."

Martha knocked on John's door to see if he was in. She took a deep breath and slowly exhaled in response to his "It's open."

"Would you have a moment sometime today to spare me?" Martha inquired.

"Now is actually a good time," responded John graciously. "What did you want to talk about?"

"I'm really uncomfortable talking about this, so I guess the best way is for me to just spit it out." John could read the discomfort in Martha's posture and immediately did his best to put her at ease.

"Why don't we sit over here," he said, motioning toward the overstuffed chairs he had arranged to give the feel and appearance of being in someone's living room. "Take your time, Martha. The nice thing about being retired—or at least semi-retired—is that I have more time to be with the people I care about."

Martha smiled at the subtle compliment and then braced herself to disclose what was bothering her. "I've recently become aware of some of the gossip in the office. Apparently some of the paralegals think it's unfair that I'm working on the Johnson case and the word is out that I did something, uh," Martha paused a moment looking for the right word, " 'unprofessional' to get this assignment."

"I believe they call it 'kissing up' in today's vernacular," commented John, hoping to ease the tension. Martha smiled briefly, but immediately pressed on, determined to make her point.

"I've been doing a lot of soul-searching since I first heard these rumors and I admit that I did look at Mike's case as an opportunity to get ahead. I thought that whatever I might learn from this case would help me to advance in the firm, but I never intended to step over anyone else. In fact, I assumed from the beginning that I would be given some kind of secondary role and that another paralegal would be brought in to do most of the work."

When Martha took a breath, John jumped in. "Martha, Martha, stop right there. You don't have to justify yourself to me. I'm fully aware of your level of experience and I made a judgment call when I decided to use you rather than a more experienced paralegal in Mike's case. But so that you're clear, let me tell you exactly why I chose you. I saw firsthand how close you and Mike are and I knew that he would be much more comfortable having you involved in his case than a paralegal he didn't know. Based on that, I decided to give you a chance to do some things

I knew you hadn't done before. And here's the key thing for you to remember. Everything you did, you gave 100 percent or more of your efforts and, just as importantly, you proved yourself competent every step of the way. If I had seen at any point that you were in over your head, I would have pulled in another paralegal at once. My point is this. You got this assignment initially because of your relationship with Mike and because I saw no harm in your doing some preliminary work. Now that we have decided to actually pursue his case, you have the assignment because you *earned* it," said John.

"Oh," replied Martha humbly, not quite knowing how to respond. "But what about the paralegals who are miffed? I have to work with them in the future and I don't want to destroy any working relationship I might have with them."

"Look, Martha. Office politics are a reality of law practice, and any other organization, I'm sure. I'll be willing to bet you that the ones who are the most bitter about your getting this case either lack the ability or personality to advance in a law firm. I venture to say you will lose very little if you lose their friendship. The others respect competence and initiative in their co-workers and will wholeheartedly support you once they know the facts. Now, the best way I know to take care of office gossip is to nip it in the bud."

"And how do you suggest I do that?" asked Martha.

"In this situation, it's probably best if I do it. At our next staff meeting, I'll tell them I've been hearing something through the rumor mill that I want to address. Then I'll tell them the same thing I just told you about why I picked you—in more detail, obviously—and ask if they have any questions. In my experience, bringing these kinds of issues into the light has a way of resolving them before they fester into big misunderstandings and resentments," explained John.

"Thank you so much, Mr. Morgan. I've never worked in such a large office before and I guess I'm naïve about these kinds of things. I'll do everything I can to make sure your trust in me is well-deserved," assured Martha.

"I've no doubt you will. Now go on about your business and don't worry about the naysayers."

NET NEWS

To read more about office politics, go the following Web sites: *www.fastcompany.com/online/14/politics.html;* *www.mapnp.org/library/intrpsnl/off_pltc.htm;* or *www.smartbiz.com/sbs/arts/bly59.htm*

BONUS POINTERS: **OFFICE POLITICS**

Office politics are a reality of every organization; it is certainly not isolated to the practice of law. We bring it up here simply to sensitize you to the issue. The "games people play" in offices can transform the most ideal of professions into a miserable work environment. If you should be confronted with co-workers or supervisors who make your life problematic, just remember that any number of books have been written and seminars organized around the challenges of working with "difficult" people.

RECESS

SUMMARY – PART A

Attorneys are prohibited from filing frivolous or unmeritorious lawsuits. Doing so is not only a violation of the ethical rules but a violation of Rule 11 of the *Rules of Civil Procedure.* A major consideration in deciding whether to file a lawsuit is the question of whether the defendant has assets from which a judgment could be collected. Collectability is generally not an issue if the defendant has adequate insurance coverage, but it is problematic in the absence of such coverage because of the difficulty involved in seizing a judgment debtor's assets. The doctrines of joint and several liability and vicarious liability allow plaintiffs to go after the "deep pocket" when the most culpable defendant is judgment proof.

The most common fee arrangements used by attorneys are contingency fee agreements, fixed billing rates, and hourly rates. Although some criticize contingency fee arrangements as overly compensating attorneys and as creating conflicts of interest between attorneys and clients, they remain popular because they allow plaintiffs to pursue litigation who would otherwise be unable to afford to do so. Attorney-client agreements, which should be in writing, should set forth the details of the fee agreement and should specify what the attorney has agreed to do as well. Attorneys who demand retainers must deposit those funds in a trust fund and are prohibited from withdrawing any funds until they have earned them. One of the most common complaints against attorneys is fee mishandling. Attorneys should never commingle clients' fees with their own monies or use money from a client's trust account for personal use under any circumstances. Paralegals should not set up fee arrangements with new clients, although they can answer some questions regarding fees and costs.

In developing a litigation plan, attorneys consider their client's objectives and cost constraints, the theory of the case, whether a demand letter should be written, whether any pre-filing requirements must be met, and what a realistic litigation timetable is. Part of the plan may include the preparation of a demand letter, which sets forth the basis for the plaintiff's claim and specifies the nature and extent of the plaintiff's damages. Attention must be paid to pre-filing requirements, such as statutory notice requirements, assigning a guardian or conservator, and arbitration provisions in contracts. A litigation timetable should be prepared, which sets forth the estimated time periods needed to carry out the anticipated steps in the discovery process as well as prepare and respond to the expected motions.

In choosing a forum court, a plaintiff must consider both subject matter and personal jurisdiction. As courts of general subject matter jurisdiction, state courts can hear most cases but as courts of limited subject matter jurisdiction, federal courts are limited to cases involving federal questions or where there is diversity of citizenship. Even if a court has subject matter jurisdiction over a case, it may not have personal jurisdiction over the defendants. Personal jurisdiction requires proper service of the defendants, which can be done using "tag jurisdiction" or the "long-arm" statutes of the forum state, which require that the defendant has "minimum contacts" with the forum state. Having decided which courts have jurisdiction, the plaintiff must also consider which courts would be an appropriate venue. Other considerations for the plaintiff to contemplate are the substantive and procedural laws the court will apply, the caseload of the court, the nature of the jury pool and the bench as a whole, and the cost and convenience of litigating in that court.

KEY TERMS

Arbitration
Bench
Contingency fee
  agreement
Deep pocket
Demand letter
Discovery
Dismissed with prejudice
Diversity of citizenship
  jurisdiction

Domicile
Federal question
  jurisdiction
Federal Rules of Civil
  Procedure
Forum
General subject matter
  jurisdiction
Joint tortfeasors
Joint and several liability

Jointly liable
Judgment debtor
Jurisdictional amount
Limited subject matter
  jurisdiction
Long-arm statutes
Motions
Notice
Personal jurisdiction
Retainer

Serve process
Sovereign immunity
Strike
Subject matter and
  personal jurisdiction
Venue
Vicarious liability

REVIEW QUESTIONS – PART A

1. What are the possible consequences of an attorney filing a frivolous lawsuit?
2. Why is collectability such an important aspect of litigation? How can plaintiffs avoid wasting time and energy suing a defendant against whom a judgment cannot reasonably be collected?
   a. How do the doctrines of joint and several liability and vicarious liability assist plaintiffs?
   b. Why has the doctrine of joint liability been abolished in some states?
3. What types of fee agreements are used by attorneys and in what types of cases are they used?
4. What should be included in an attorney-client agreement?
5. What are two things an attorney should avoid doing in reference to the trust accounts he establishes for his clients?
6. What goes into a litigation plan?
   a. What is included in a demand letter?
   b. What kinds of pre-filing requirements may need to be complied with prior to filing a lawsuit?
7. Under what conditions should a plaintiff file in state court? Under what conditions can a plaintiff consider filing in federal court?
8. In what ways can a court obtain personal jurisdiction over a defendant?
9. What factors other than jurisdiction must a plaintiff consider when choosing a forum court?

PRACTICE EXAM – PART A

MULTIPLE CHOICE

1. A claim is considered frivolous if
   a. it is not well-grounded in fact
   b. it is filed with the intent of causing unnecessary delay
   c. it is filed with the intent of increasing the cost of litigation
   d. all of the above
2. An attorney who brings a frivolous lawsuit
   a. can be sanctioned only under the ethical rules
   b. can be required to pay the attorney's fees of the opposing party
   c. can have the complaint dismissed but will suffer no personal consequences
   d. none of the above
3. A lawsuit is "good" only if
   a. liability can be proved
   b. damages can be shown
   c. a judgment can be collected
   d. all of the above
4. Plaintiffs can reasonably assume that a judgment can be collected if
   a. the defendant has adequate insurance
   b. the defendant has a job, a house, and at least one vehicle
   c. the defendant is a corporation
   d. none of the above
5. The doctrine of joint and several liability
   a. is in effect in every state
   b. allows plaintiffs to go after the deep pocket
   c. requires injured plaintiffs to bear their loss
   d. is a popular doctrine

6. Vicarious liability is
   a. justified because employers should consider the cost of reimbursing those injured by their employees as part of the cost of doing business
   b. applicable when an employee is on a "frolic" or "detour"
   c. not applicable when an employee injures a plaintiff while doing something she was strictly forbidden to do
   d. all of the above
7. Some view going after the deep pocket
   a. as being unfair to business
   b. as an unfair means of requiring minimally negligent neligent defendants to shoulder the burden of harm caused by others
   c. as a means of preventing plaintiffs from having to bear the burden of their loss
   d. all of the above
8. Contingency fee agreements
   a. are not commonly used except in corporate work
   b. sometimes prevent plaintiffs from pursuing their claims
   c. are criticized because they can result in an attorney being overcompensated
   d. restrict attorneys from receiving more compensation if they go to trial than if they settle a case

9. An attorney-client agreement
   a. does not need to be in writing
   b. should specify how the fee will be determined and when it should be paid
   c. need not get into such details as the types of costs that can be anticipated
   d. none of the above

10. In reference to clients' monies
    a. attorneys are allowed to mix their clients' funds with their own personal funds
    b. attorneys may be required to put those monies in an IOLTA account
    c. attorneys are allowed to borrow from their trust accounts as long as they pay the money back immediately
    d. none of the above

11. A litigation plan includes
    a. a litigation timetable
    b. a client's objectives
    c. a theory of the case
    d. all of the above

12. Factors that affect a plaintiff's choice of forum are
    a. jury demographics
    b. jurisdiction but not venue
    c. substantive law but not procedural law applied
    d. all of the above

13. A plaintiff should file in a local court if
    a. the case is a suit for something other than money damages
    b. some of the parties are residents in the forum county
    c. the circumstances of the dispute occurred in the forum county
    d. some of the claims are based on federal law

14. A plaintiff may decide to sue in federal court
    a. because federal court is a court of general subject matter jurisdiction
    b. if all of the plaintiffs and defendants reside in different states
    c. if the amount in controversy is less than $75,000
    d. none of the above

15. Personal jurisdiction of a defendant can be obtained by
    a. getting consent of the defendant
    b. tag jurisdiction
    c. long-arm statutes
    d. all of the above

FILL IN THE BLANK

16. Through the process of _____ , parties can obtain almost any information pertinent to their dispute.

17. If a case is dismissed with _____ , it cannot be brought again.

18. Employers are _____ liable for the torts of their employees.

19. One of the problems that arises with _____ tortfeasors (two or more tortfeasors who act together to produce a single tort) is the doctrine of _____ , which allows a defendant to be liable for the entire loss suffered by the plaintiff. This doctrine allows plaintiffs to go after the _____ , who is not the primary tortfeasor but who, because of his financial status, ends up paying all or most of the judgment.

20. _____ fee arrangements are commonly used in personal injury cases whereas _____ billing is used for most defense and corporate work. Attorneys preparing simple wills or doing straightforward bankruptcies usually charge a _____ rate.

21. Attorneys are allowed to ask for an advance called a _____ from which they can pay expenses and collect their fees.

22. An alternative to litigation is _____ , in which a neutral third party renders a decision and issues an award.

23. If a plaintiff's attorney decides that his client is better served by settling a claim prior to filing suit, he may write a _____ letter, which sets forth the basis of the plaintiff's claim and the full extent of the plaintiff's damages.

24. A party that wants a judge to enter an order or make a ruling should file a _____ .

25. Choosing a _____ court (the court in which the lawsuit will be filed) is based in part on which courts have _____ , i.e., the authority to hear a case, and also on what the appropriate _____ is, based on the convenience of the parties.

26. Some courts may have _____ jurisdiction in that they can hear that type of case, but lack _____ jurisdiction because they cannot render a decision that will be binding on a party.

27. Federal courts have _____ subject matter jurisdiction, whereas state courts have _____ subject matter jurisdiction.

28. A federal court has jurisdiction over cases involving a _____ or where there is _____; in the latter case, the _____ must be $75,000 or more.

29. The _____ of a person is any state in which he is physically present.

30. In order to _____ (physically hand a defendant a copy of the complaint and summons) on a defendant, a plaintiff can rely on _____ jurisdiction (getting the defendant before he leaves the state) or _____ statutes, which permit service of non-residents so long as they have _____ with the forum state.

31. Each _____ (meaning all of the judges taken together) takes on its own "personality."

32. In many states, a party can _____ a judge it finds objectionable.

TRUE OR FALSE

____ 33. An attorney who files a lawsuit without confirming information supplied by the client is likely to be in violation of Rule 11 of the *Rules of Civil Procedure* if the claim is later found to be unmeritorious.

____ 34. Attorneys are absolutely prohibited from bringing claims that are unwarranted under existing law.

____ *35. An employer is vicariously liable for any torts committed by an employee in the scope and furtherance of his employment unless the employee is engaged in a frolic or detour.

____ *36. Joint and several liability has been abolished in some states and modified in others because of a concern that the doctrine is used to go after "deep pocket" defendants.

____ 37. The doctrine of joint and several liability is applicable only when the loss suffered by the plaintiff cannot be apportioned among the defendants.

____ 38. A defendant who is jointly and severally liable cannot be held responsible for paying all of the plaintiff's damages if he is minimally negligent.

____ 39. An employer is vicariously liable for the acts of an employee committed during the scope and course of his employment unless the employee is engaged in a frolic or detour.

____ 40. The essential question raised by the doctrine of joint and several liability is where society wants to assign the burden when a liable party cannot pay damages.

____ 41. Winning a final judgment automatically results in a plaintiff's getting paid.

____ 42. Collectability is a central fact of litigation.

____ 43. State exemption statutes allow a judgment debtor to keep enough money and property to be able to survive.

____ 44. A plaintiff is assured of being able to collect a judgment debtor's wages even if the debtor has no other viable assets.

____ 45. A common contingency fee arrangement provides for payment of 10 percent if the case settles before it goes to trial, 20 percent if it goes to trial, and 30 percent if the case is appealed.

____ 46. Some criticize contingency fee agreements because they create a potential conflict of interest between the attorney and the client in reference to settlement offers.

____ 47. Clients who are being charged an hourly rate save money when as much of their work as possible is delegated to paralegals.

____ 48. Most firms charge an hourly rate for doing an uncontested divorce or preparing a simple will.

____ 49. An attorney-client agreement should disclose any liens an attorney might have on a client's judgment and should indicate what costs a client can anticipate paying and when those costs should be paid.

____ 50. Attorneys have an obligation to put retainers in a trust fund for a client, but they can withdraw money from that trust fund immediately if they need it for any reason.

____ 51. In serving as liaisons between attorneys and their clients, paralegals are allowed to establish fees with new clients.

____ 52. One of the most common causes of attorney disciplinary actions is the mishandling of client funds.

____ 53. It is unethical for paralegals to be responsible for the bookkeeping and record keeping functions of a firm.

_____54. Attorneys are allowed to remove monies from a trust account as long as they know they will be earning the fees in the near future.

_____55. If a dispute arises between the client and attorney about the appropriateness of a fee, the amount in contention must remain in the trust account until the dispute is resolved.

_____56. An attorney can draw funds from a trust account for personal use as long as he returns the funds at a later date.

_____57. Attorneys are required to maintain accurate and complete records of clients' funds.

_____58. Only a few states have IOLTA programs, which are used to fund social activities for attorneys.

_____*59. Anyone who cannot afford to hire legal representation can always receive representation from an attorney at community legal services.

_____*60. Legal clinics can charge lower fees because they handle large volumes of relatively routine cases.

_____61. Sometimes plaintiffs are better served by settling rather than filing suit.

_____62. Demand letters should always be sent as a matter of course.

_____63. Some government agencies have strict time limits that must be complied with or suit can never be filed.

_____64. Contractual "notice and claims" often have shorter time periods than the applicable statute of limitations.

_____65. In most states, minors can file in their own name.

_____66. A litigation timetable cannot include time frames for discovery because the discovery process cannot be planned in advance.

_____67. All courts are created equal and apply the same laws, so which forum is chosen has little effect on the outcome of a case.

_____68. Once a plaintiff selects a forum, the defendant has no grounds for changing that forum.

_____69. A plaintiff can choose to sue in any county in which any significant part of the events in dispute occurred.

_____70. Defects in subject matter jurisdiction cannot be waived , but they cannot be raised once a case has been decided.

_____71. Any cause of action involving a federal statute can be raised in federal court because it involves a federal question.

_____72. A corporation is considered to be domiciled in any state in which it is incorporated or in which its principal place of business is located.

_____73. Complete diversity is not required in diversity cases; in other words, some plaintiffs and defendants can reside in the same states.

_____74. Personal jurisdiction addresses the question of whether it is fair to force a defendant to litigate in a particular state.

_____75. Long-arm statutes require that defendants have certain minimum contacts with the forum state before they can be dragged into court against their will.

_____*76. New York plaintiffs buy a car in New York and are injured in Oklahoma when their car burns up there. The Oklahoma court has personal jurisdiction over the New York dealership and distributorship even though neither conducted any business in Oklahoma and did not regularly sell to Oklahoma buyers.

_____77. At the federal level, there are no long-arm statutes.

_____78. If a court has jurisdiction over a case, it necessarily is the proper venue.

_____79. Venue rules are designed to channel lawsuits into the courts where they can be heard most efficiently.

_____80. Because all states pattern their procedural rules after the _Federal Rules of Civil Procedure_, procedural law in the state courts is essentially the same as it is in federal courts.

_____81. In diversity cases, the federal courts apply the procedural law of the state in which the court sits and federal substantive law.

_____82. Long delays before a case can be heard favor defendants.

_____83. Because each bench has its own "personality," a plaintiff may experience a different outcome in a district court than in a state court.

_____84. In some courts, you can "strike" a judge and get a different one.

_____85. Jury demographics can have an impact on the outcome of a case.

_____86. All things being equal, most attorneys prefer litigating in their home state.

*Questions taken from Bonus Pointers

PART B

Martha was standing at the elevator thinking about why Tim had not called her when John approached. "Heard any more from your friend at the law library?" asked John innocently.

"My God, he reads minds," thought Martha, struggling not to look shocked. "No. Actually, I haven't had any reason to go there," responded Martha, doing her best to conceal her disappointment in Tim's apparent lack of interest in furthering their relationship. "Maybe he just needs a little encouragement," began John, immediately changing the subject after casting a furtive glance in Martha's direction. "Well, I'm just getting ready to work on the body of the complaint for Mike," John continued, somewhat lamely. "I think it's safe to say that his life will never be the same after this complaint is served."

DRAFTING A COMPLAINT

Overview of a Complaint

complaint a formal, written statement in which the plaintiff describes, in summary fashion, what the dispute is about and what plaintiff wants the court to do

allegations numbered paragraphs in which the plaintiff spells out her version of what happened to cause the dispute

counts section of a complaint establishing the elements of a particular cause of action

prayer for relief a concluding section of the complaint stating specifically what the plaintiff wants the court to do

A civil lawsuit begins when the plaintiff files a **complaint** with an appropriate court. A complaint is a formal, written statement in which the plaintiff describes, in summary fashion, what the dispute is about, and what the plaintiff wants the court to do. The plaintiff spells out her version of what happened to cause the dispute in statements called **allegations,** which are organized in numbered paragraphs so they can easily be referred to by both parties in subsequent court papers. Customarily, the complaint is also divided into separate sections, or **counts,** for each separate cause of action being asserted. The complaint ends with a **prayer for relief,** a concluding section stating specifically what the plaintiff wants the court to do (typically, award a money judgment for damages). The complaint is signed by the plaintiff's attorney. In some federal and state courts, complaints can be filed electronically; procedures are evolving in this area of "cyber-practice," but most courts are not yet this technologically advanced.

A complaint, no matter how artfully drafted, will not be accepted by the court clerk if it does not conform to the requirements in the court's local rules. Caption, paper size, type size, line spacing, margins, backing sheets if required,—all must be correct. The clerk may reject a complaint that fails to meet any mechanical requirements, no matter how trivial the violation may seem (see Bonus Pointers: Mechanical Requirements).

BONUS POINTERS:

MECHANICAL REQUIREMENTS

The court file is the official record of the case kept by the clerk of the court. The clerk keeps a separate file for each case, and every important event in the lawsuit must be recorded in the file. The importance of this file cannot be overstated. The court file is the single permanent and complete record of everything that has happened in the case, the record that all participants rely on. From the judge's standpoint, the court file *is* the case—the judge will usually refuse to consider any papers that are not part of this file.

When a court paper is presented for filing, the clerk of the court examines it to ensure that the paper complies with the formal requirements of the local rules. If a party has not

NET NEWS

To read about the status of electronic filings and to find out which courts accept electronic filings, go to *www.nscs.dni.us/NCSC/TIS/TIS99/ELECTR99/Elecfil1.htm.*

followed the rules, the clerk will likely refuse the paper. The clerk does not care about the content of a court paper; however, court clerks often exhibit near-zero tolerance for deviations from correct form. Urban court clerks often handle millions of pages of paper each year, and seemingly minor mistakes may be enough to bring the clerk's automated processing to a standstill, or, worse, cause court papers to disappear forever into the wrong file.

Most courts specify a number of mechanical details that parties must follow in preparing a court paper. Some of the common considerations follow.

1. *Size, weight, and type of paper* The rules of most courts place limits on the types of paper that are acceptable. The clerk's job of segregating papers into the correct files, and of microfilming or electronically imaging papers for archiving, can be carried out more efficiently if the items being processed are uniform.

2. *Whether line-numbered paper should be used* Traditionally, court papers were prepared on "pleading paper," which has line numbers pre-printed along the left margin. Many courts no longer require it, although many law firms continue to use it. Word processing programs number lines automatically.

3. *Margins* Again, uniformity is the goal. Court clerks tend to be particularly fussy about the top margin on the first page, which many courts require to be several inches wide to provide room for the clerk's stamps.

4. *Font, type size, line spacing, and length limits* Many courts specify a minimum type size, and most require court papers to be double-spaced. This is done mainly to ensure readability, especially after copies have been made. Some courts specify the font (the design of the individual letters) to be used. Even if the rules are silent, stick with a widely used font such as Courier. This is not a good place to show off your computer's font-making versatility.

Courts commonly place limits on the overall length of court papers—for example, limiting motions to no more than fifteen pages. Resist the temptation to get more words into the same number of pages by using a different or smaller type or by "fudging" the margins.

5. *Backings* Some courts require court papers to be prepared with a colored backing, which serves as a visible separator between papers in the file.

6. *Other details not covered by the rules* Many other formal details, although not specifically covered by the rules, are the subject of such long-standing custom that failure to observe them will instantly be noticed. These include such minutiae as the wording of the name of the court; whether to use parentheses or colons to make the vertical line down the middle of the caption; whether various parts are indented or kept on the left margin; and how many spaces to indent paragraphs.

◆ **LOCAL LINKS** ◆

Where are the local rules that set forth the mechanical requirements in your courts?

Putting It Into Practice 4.15:

After Marianne has prepared a complaint, her supervising attorney tells her to make sure she has conformed with the local rules. She has no idea what her supervisor is talking about and thinks she is just being picky. Explain to Marianne what she needs to be looking for in the local rules and why her attorney supervisor is not simply being picky.

NET NEWS

Law firms keep a file of forms to serve as models for the drafting of documents that are frequently used. More and more, these forms files are being computerized. To see the types of legal forms available on the Internet, go to *www.lectlaw.com/form.html* and *www.legaldocs.com.*

Figure 4-6
Caption of a Complaint

WHITE & TREADWELL
John Morgan, Esq., SBN 00123
Ernesto Esparanza, Esq. SBN 012345
2020 North Central Avenue, Suite 3200
Phoenix, Arizona 85005
(602) 555-1234

Attorneys for plaintiff Michael Johnson

IN THE SUPERIOR COURT OF MARICOPA COUNTY
PHOENIX, ARIZONA

Michael Johnson, a single man,   )
)
)
                      Plaintiff,   )   NO. _____
)
)   Complaint
                         vs.   )   (Tort - non-motor
)   Vehicle)
Daniel Hendershott, Max Evans and   )
Alan House, all single men; CODA,   )
Inc., a foreign corporation, and   )
Washington High School District.   )
)
                      Defendants.   )
_____)

Caption

caption title page of a complaint

The complaint opens with the **caption,** which serves as a kind of "title page." The caption lists the names of all the parties, including spouses, (in subsequent court papers, only the first plaintiff and first defendant will be listed); the name, address, and telephone number of the attorney filing the complaint; the name of the court in which the complaint is being filed; and the title of the paper (in this case, "Complaint"). The space for the case number is left blank; the clerk of the court will assign a number when the complaint is filed. Some local rules require that the type of case, whether it is subject to arbitration, or whether a jury trial is demanded, be included in the caption.

Sometimes the name of a party is unknown. If a party is married, for example, the plaintiff may not know the name of the spouse. Some courts (although by no means all courts) allow the plaintiff to designate parties using fictitious names. If the defendant's name is Arnold McCullom, the plaintiff would refer to the parties as Arnold McCullom and Jane Doe McCullom, husband and wife. A similar tactic can be used with designations for business organizations whose names are unknown: "XYZ Corporation" or "ABC Partnership."

Putting It Into Practice 4.16:

Suppose you have a client, Molly Running Deer, who is injured when another motorist, Stuart Thames, runs a red light. Assume that Molly is single and that Stuart is married but that you do not know his wife's name. You are preparing a complaint for Molly in your local county or superior court. Following the rules in your jurisdiction, prepare the caption of this complaint.

Figure 4-7
Body of a Complaint

Body of the Complaint

Plaintiff, by and through counsel undersigned, for his complaint against the defendants, alleges as follows:

Jurisdictional Allegation

1. Plaintiff Michael Johnson (hereinafter Michael) is an adult single man residing in Maricopa County, Arizona.
2. Defendants Daniel Hendershott (hereinafter Daniel), Max Evans (hereinafter Max) and Alan House (hereinafter Alan) are adult single men residing in Maricopa County, Arizona.
3. Defendant CODA, Inc. (hereinafter CODA) is a foreign corporation with its principal place of business in the state of Colorado. CODA is an acronym for Citizens Of a Decentralized America.
4. Washington High School District (hereinafter WHSD) is a political subdivision in Maricopa County, Arizona.
5. That defendants caused an act to occur in Maricopa County, Arizona out of which plaintiff's cause of action arises.
6. Plaintiff's monetary claims against defendants exceed the jurisdictional prerequisites of this court.
7. This case is not subject to mandatory arbitration as plaintiff's monetary claims exceed $50,000.
8. Notice of claim, as required by law, has been given to defendant WHSD.

Body

preamble introductory paragraph or phrase of a complaint

Following the caption is the **preamble** (also called a *jurisdictional statement*), which is an introductory paragraph or phrase, such as "Plaintiff alleges." Federal court rules require that this jurisdictional statement tell the court specifically the grounds for its jurisdiction. The body of the complaint begins with a statement of the grounds upon which the court's jurisdiction is based and an identification of the parties and their residences. In the remainder of the body of the complaint, the plaintiff must state her claim, showing why she is entitled to relief. To do this, the plaintiff must give a short summary of the facts of her case and state the particular facts necessary to establish each element of each cause of action. This is best done by first telling what happened in a section called "General Allegations"; then, in separate counts, establishing the elements for each cause of action.

Allegations

In the "General Allegations" section, the plaintiff simply tells her story in the most convincing way she can. This section is usually a page or two in length and represents a golden opportunity for the plaintiff to begin persuading the judge of the rightness of her cause. This narrative should, at a minimum, include the dates on which the main events happened, the places where the events happened, the main "bad acts" of the defendant, a description of how the plaintiff suffered losses, and how those losses were caused by the defendant's conduct. The narrative should be in chronological order and should include enough factual detail to make the sequence of events easy to follow.

At the time an attorney drafts a complaint, she usually does not have all of the facts. A standard shorthand phrase that is used to identify a fact as one that is likely to have evidentiary support after a reasonable opportunity for discovery is "upon information and belief." For example, "Upon information and belief, John Doe was intoxicated."

Figure 4-8
Allegations of a Complaint

General Allegations:

11. Daniel, Max, and Alan attacked Michael, without provocation or warning to Michael, on property controlled by WHSD on May 5, 2000.
    …
15. Michael has incurred and continues to incur, substantial damages for medical and other health care related expenses.
16. Michael has sustained substantial financial damages due to the loss of educational, vocational, and professional opportunities directly caused by the injuries Michael sustained in the attack of May 5, 2000.
    …
19. Michael is entitled to punitive damages against Daniel, Max, and Alan.
    …
21. CODA produced and distributed the movie "*Teenage Stalkers*."
22. CODA knew, or should have known, and with reasonable and responsible diligence would have known, that individuals, such as defendants Daniel, Max, and Alan could react violently against individuals such as the plaintiff, after prolonged viewing of "*Teenage Stalkers*."
23. …
25. WHSD had notice that violent acts were about to occur on its campus on the day of Michael's injuries.
26. WHSD failed to take reasonable precautions, to protect Michael from a known risk of harm.
27. WHSD breached its duty to Michael.
28. ….

███████   *Putting It Into Practice 4.17:*

Write the general allegations in your complaint for Molly Running Deer. Assume that the accident occurred on January 18, 2000, at 9:00 P.M., and that Molly was flown by helicopter to a local hospital where she required surgery to repair a subdural hematoma she sustained as a result of the accident. She also had severe lacerations and bruises on her head and upper torso. She continues to experience mood swings and memory loss that the doctors attribute to her head injuries. One witness to the accident said that Stuart's car never slowed as he entered the intersection and estimated his rate of speed at 40-50 mph. A police report indicates that Stuart's blood alcohol level was 0.15 percent an hour after the accident (indicating he was under the influence of alcohol at the time of the accident). Fill in any other details you believe are necessary and use locations and institutions specific to your locale.

Counts

Having told her story, the task that remains in the counts of the complaint is to allege every element of each cause of action. The plaintiff's purpose now shifts from that of persuasively telling her story to that of forestalling a motion to dismiss for failure to state a claim (discussed on p. 262). Now the plaintiff should recite the elements of the causes of action in the exact language of the cases or statutes from which they are derived. One count should be used for each separate theory of liability or cause of action. Each count should begin with a centered heading, with the counts numbered in sequence. After the heading, the elements of the pertinent theory of liability should be alleged in a very summary fashion in a few short paragraphs.

Figure 4-9
Counts of a Complaint

Count One—Battery

39. Michael realleges all of the allegations contained in the complaint.
40. [Add more specific factual allegations if appropriate]
    ...
46. Michael has stated a cause of action in battery against Defendants Daniel, Max, and Alan.
    ...

Count Six—Negligence

67. Michael realleges all of the allegations contained in the complaint.
68. WHSD owed a duty to Michael to take reasonable precautions to protect Michael from known risks.
69. WHSD breached its duty to Michael when it failed to take reasonable precautions regarding a known risk.
70. Michael was injured as a direct result of WHSD's breach of duty.

Figure 4-10
Prayer for Relief

Prayer for Relief

Wherefore Michael demands judgment against the defendants as follows:

On Count One against Daniel, Max, and Alan, jointly and severally;
1. For general damages in an amount to be shown by the evidence;
2. For special damages in an amount to be shown by the evidence;
3. For punitive damages in an amount to be shown by the evidence;
4. For such other and further relief as the Court deems just and equitable.

On Count Six against WHSD;
1. For general damages in an amount to be shown by the evidence;

Putting It Into Practice 4.18:

Prepare one count of negligence for your complaint for Molly Running Deer. (Before doing this, you might want to review the elements of negligence as discussed on pages 92 and 93 of Chapter 2.)

---

compensatory damages
damages designed to compensate the victim for her losses and restore her to the position she was in before she sustained her injuries

punitive damages damages designed to punish defendants who have acted with ill-will or in conscious disregard for the welfare of others

nominal damages damages awarded when no actual damages are proved but a tort is shown to have been committed

The final section of the body of the complaint is the prayer for relief. It is here that the plaintiff says what she is asking the court to do. The prayer for relief is worded in standard language, usually copied from a form complaint in some other suit. The following "stock" prayer for relief, with the appropriate dollar amount inserted, should be at least adequate in any American court. Remember that this dollar amount helps determine which court has proper jurisdiction.

Wherefore, plaintiff requests that the Court enter judgment in favor of Plaintiff and against Defendants and each of them as follows:

1. For general and special damages in the amount of $100,000.00.
2. For Plaintiff's reasonable costs and attorney's fees incurred herein.
3. For such other and further relief as the Court deems just and equitable.

The issue of damages is a factual one decided by a jury (in jury trials). In tort, cases, damages are divided into three basic categories: **compensatory damages, punitive damages,** and **nominal damages.** Compensatory damages are designed to compensate the victim for her losses and restore her to the position she was in

Figure 4-11
Damages in Tort Cases

DAMAGES IN TORT CASES

COMPENSATORY DAMAGES
(compensate plaintiff for losses)

GENERAL DAMAGES
(losses expected to occur)

SPECIAL DAMAGES
(losses unique to plaintiff)

PUNITIVE DAMAGES
(punish defendant)

NOMINAL DAMAGES
(no actual damages proved)

general damages   losses that would naturally be expected to occur in every case based on the same theory of liability

special damages   particular losses that a client has suffered

before she sustained her injuries. Compensatory damages are further divided into **general damages** and **special damages.** General damages are those losses that would naturally be expected to occur in every case based on the same theory of liability. Pain and suffering is a type of general damages that would be expected if a plaintiff were seriously injured. Special damages are the particular losses that a client has suffered, such as medical expenses, lost wages, or future impairment of earnings. Punitive damages are intended to deter the defendant and others from future misconduct. Not designed to make the plaintiff whole, punitive damages are intended to punish defendants who have acted with ill will or in conscious disregard for the welfare of others. Such awards are reserved for defendants who act in a particularly egregious manner. If a claim is included for punitive damages and if the judge agrees that punitive damages are warranted—a big "if"—the plaintiff is entitled to take discovery aimed at finding out how much money the defendant has. Nominal damages are awarded when no actual damages are proved but a tort is shown to have been committed.

The request for general and special damages is fairly standard and usually appears in the complaint. In some courts, the rules require plaintiffs to ask for a specific amount of damages. In others, plaintiffs are permitted (or required) to substitute a request for "general and special damages in an amount which Plaintiff will prove." The latter is preferable because deciding exactly how much to ask for at the time of filing a complaint is difficult in that the plaintiff does not yet have all the facts. If the plaintiff's complaint specifies a low amount and the plaintiff later finds that the evidence would support a higher demand, she may have to ask the court for permission to amend the complaint, and she may not get it. If she errs on the high side, she can be sure that her "unreasonable" demand will come flying back at her in front of the jury as her opponent tries to paint her as a greedy opportunist.

BONUS POINTERS:

PROVING DAMAGES

Paralegals are often called on to provide the evidence necessary to prove or disprove claims for damages. Some of the practical implications of proving past and future medical expenses, loss of earning capacity, and pain and suffering are summarized here.

Past Medical Expenses

The plaintiff has the burden of proving the amount of medical expenses and that the expenses were necessary and reasonable. The best way to prove past expenses is through the use of bills that reflect the charges made. It is important to keep a running account of all bills. These bills should be tabulated on a monthly basis and may be submitted to the insurance company and to defense counsel on an ongoing basis. In most jurisdictions, proof of medical bills plus proof of payment raises the presumption that the bill was necessary and reasonable. In some states, however, testimony from a doctor, druggist, or other expert is required.

The reasonableness and necessity of treatment become problematic when dealing with **preexisting conditions** (conditions existing prior to the plaintiff's injuries). If the plaintiff was not suffering from the preexisting condition at the time of the injury, the expenses will probably be recoverable. If, however, the plaintiff was under treatment for that condition at the time of the injury, she will have difficulty proving which expenses were necessitated by the aggravation caused by the defendant's negligence and which expenses stemmed from the preexisting condition. The plaintiff may therefore be unable to recover any of the medical expenses.

preexisting conditions
condition that existed prior to the plaintiff's being injured by the defendant

Future Medical Expenses

Future medical expenses are much less subject to quantification. No doctor can state with absolute certainty how long future treatment will be needed or what exact amount of future medical expenses will be incurred. Courts are aware of this ambiguity and do not require the same degree of mathematical proof that they do for past expenses. In some jurisdictions, future medical expenses are left for the jury to determine based on the amount of past medical expenses, the nature of the plaintiff's injuries, and the condition of the plaintiff at the time of trial. Other jurisdictions require medical testimony regarding a dollar amount and do not allow a jury to award more than the amount supported by testimony.

Loss of Earning Capacity

To prove loss of earning capacity, a plaintiff must first prove that the injuries creating her disability impaired her ability to work and earn money. To prove the latter, the paralegal must obtain copies of the plaintiff's wage stubs, W-4 forms, and/or IRS records. The defense will want to show that the plaintiff's work record was sporadic, that the earnings for the years at issue were unusually high, or that for some reason the plaintiff would not have been able to earn comparable wages in the years ahead for reasons other than the disability sustained.

Other types of evidence that can be used to show a plaintiff's earning potential are evidence of education and on-the-job training, as well as evidence of fringe benefits, such as bonuses, insurance programs, tips, and pensions. Prospective earnings from reasonably anticipated promotions or advancements may also be submitted, as well as evidence that the plaintiff was studying or was taking steps to advance into better paying work.

Pain and Suffering

Damages for pain and suffering are, by their very nature, not amenable to quantification. Therefore, all a plaintiff can do is prove that the physical pain and mental anguish were in fact experienced. The most direct evidence of pain and suffering is testimony by the plaintiff as to objective symptoms, such as the actual injuries received, and subjective symptoms, such as headaches. Mental anguish may take the form of fear, worry, depression, or humiliation.

Detailed descriptions must be elicited from the plaintiff, complete with specific incidents that illustrate the nature and depth of the pain and anguish and the limitations such suffering imposed on her lifestyle. In major personal injury lawsuits, plaintiffs' attorneys frequently use "day-in-the-life-of" videotapes to illustrate graphically to the jury the full extent of the plaintiff's injuries. Such videos chronicle in a simple but poignant way the everyday suffering of the plaintiff and those who care for her.

Doctors, as well as others who are familiar with the plaintiff, can testify regarding their observations of her pain and suffering. In working with these potential witnesses, it is important to strive for detailed information that can be used to create a vivid picture for

Figure 4-12
Conclusion of a Complaint

Dated this 22nd day of January, 2001

WHITE & TREADWELL

By John Morgan
Attorney for plaintiff Michael
Johnson

the jury. Generalizations and vague statements are not helpful and will not create the kind of jury empathy plaintiff's counsel desires. The defense, on the other hand, will want to rebut the plaintiff's claim of physical and mental anguish by presenting evidence that the plaintiff is pain-free and relatively happy or, alternatively, that the plaintiff's suffering was caused by factors other than the injuries induced by the defendant.

In most states, the winner of a lawsuit is entitled to judgment for her court costs. The request for costs should be included in every complaint. The costs that can be awarded are limited to certain categories of expenses. In federal court, the allowed categories include such things as filing fees, court reporter fees, witness fees, and process server fees, but do not include attorney's fees. The winner of a lawsuit may or may not be entitled to judgment for attorney's fees; it depends on the type of case (awards of attorney's fees are common in breach of contract actions, uncommon in tort cases) and on the substantive law on which the claims are based. Because plaintiffs cannot be penalized for asking, they should include a request for attorney's fees unless they clearly have no basis for doing so.

Putting It Into Practice 4.19:

Prepare a prayer for relief for Molly Running Deer's complaint. Assume that her medical bills are already $50,000 and that the doctors estimate that she will probably require another $20,000 in ongoing therapy and medical treatment. Her present and future lost wages are estimated at $10,000.

Conclusion

The complaint concludes with the standard date and signature lines used in all court papers. The format for the attorney's signature is somewhat variable, but typically consists of the name of the law firm, if the attorney is a member of one; below that, a horizontal line on which the attorney signs; and on succeeding lines, the attorney's name and, in some states, address and/or bar number, and finally the words "Attorney(s) for (whomever it is that the attorney represents—plaintiff, defendant, defendant John Doe, etc.)" Be aware that the wording of an attorney's signature line may carry subtle implications about whether the attorney is or is not a partner in the firm, a matter about which some attorneys have little sense of

◆ LOCAL LINKS ◆
Complaints may differ in some respects in your jurisdiction. Find out from your instructor what those differences are and make note of them here.

humor. Therefore, obtain a sample of the way your employer wants his signature line to read and follow it verbatim.

In times past, clients in many jurisdictions were required to furnish a sworn affidavit attesting to the truth of the allegations of the complaint. This is called "verifying" the complaint, and is accomplished by following the signature line for the attorney with a verification. The verification is pure boilerplate, and typically looks like this.

VERIFICATION

Plaintiff [put in name], being first duly sworn, upon his [her] oath deposes and says: That he [she] is the plaintiff in the above-entitled action; that he [she] has read the foregoing complaint and the allegations thereof are true of plaintiff's own knowledge, except such allegations as are made upon information and belief, and these plaintiff believes to be true.

_____
Plaintiff

SUBSCRIBED AND SWORN to this ___ day of _____, 20___, before me, the undersigned Notary Public.

_____
Notary Public

---

summons court order requiring the defendant to appear before the court and defend the suit

conformed stamp copies of the complaint with the case number assigned by the court clerk when the complaint is filed

The verification is signed by the plaintiff and notarized; it is the notarization that makes the verification "sworn." The federal rules have, for the most part, abolished verification. State court verification requirements vary from one state to another.

Once John had finalized the complaint, he asked Martha to see that it was filed with the clerk of the court. Martha began by making six copies of the complaint, one for each of the defendants plus one for the office files. She also prepared a **summons** for each defendant and a copy for her file. Along with the complaint, she included a check for the required filing fee, a completed information sheet for the clerk (giving summary information about the case, the parties, and the lawyers), and an instruction sheet for the process server, indicating how, where, and upon whom she wanted the summons and complaint served. The clerk of the court retained the original complaint for the court's file and **conformed** the other copies by stamping them with the case number (assigned at the time of filing) and with the clerk's stamp or seal. As was her custom, Martha immediately recorded the time it had taken her to file the complaints.

Martha sighed with relief when she finally got everything off her desk pertaining to Mike's complaint. Except for confirming that everyone was properly served, her part was complete for now and the ball was in the defendants' court. Her heartbeat quickened, however, when she saw the note on her desk, dated two weeks earlier, indicating that Tim had phoned and asked her to call him back.

NET NEWS

The mechanics of putting together a complaint using a word processor can be challenging. To get some hints about how to do that and to see a sample complaint, go to *www.lamission.cc.ca.us/law/compsteps.htm*.

Figure 4-13
Complete Complaint

WHITE & TREADWELL
John Morgan, Esq., SBN 00123
Ernesto Esparanza, Esq. SBN 012345
2020 North Central Avenue, Suite 3200
Phoenix, Arizona 85005
(602) 555-1234

Attorneys for plaintiff Michael Johnson

IN THE SUPERIOR COURT OF MARICOPA COUNTY
PHOENIX, ARIZONA

Michael Johnson, a single man,))) Plaintiff,)) vs.)) Daniel Hendershott, Max Evans, and) Alan House, all single men; CODA,) Inc., a foreign corporation, and) Washington High School District.)) Defendants.) _____)	NO. _____ Complaint (Tort - non-motor Vehicle)

Jurisdictional Allegations

1. Plaintiff Michael Johnson (hereinafter Michael) is an adult single man residing in Maricopa County, Arizona.
2. Defendants Daniel Hendershott (hereinafter Daniel), Max Evans (hereinafter Max), and Alan House (hereinafter Alan) are adult single men residing in Maricopa County, Arizona.
3. Defendant CODA, Inc. (hereinafter CODA) is a foreign corporation with its principal place of business in the state of Colorado. CODA is an acronym for Citizens Of a Decentralized America.
4. Washington High School District (hereinafter WHSD) is a political subdivision in Maricopa County, Arizona.
5. That defendants caused an act to occur in Maricopa County, Arizona out of which plaintiff's cause of action arises.
6. Plaintiff's monetary claims against defendants exceed the jurisdictional prerequisites of this court.
7. This case is not subject to mandatory arbitration as plaintiff's monetary claims exceed $50,000.
8. Notice of claim, as required by law, has been given to defendant WHSD.
  ... .

General Allegations:

11. Daniel, Max, and Alan attacked Michael, without provocation or warning to Michael, on property controlled by WHSD on May 5, 2000.
  ... .
15. Michael has incurred and continues to incur substantial damages for medical and other health care related expenses.
16. Michael has sustained substantial financial damages due to the loss of educational, vocational, and professional opportunities directly caused by the injuries Michael sustained in the attack of May 5, 2000.
  ... .

Figure 4-13
Complete Complaint
(continued)

19. Michael is entitled to punitive damages against Daniel, Max, and Alan.

   ... .

21. CODA produced and distributed the movie *Teenage Stalkers*.
22. CODA knew, or should have known, and with reasonable and responsible diligence would have known, that individuals such as defendants Daniel, Max, and Alan could react violently against individuals such as the plaintiff after prolonged viewing of *Teenage Stalkers*.
23.

   ... .

25. WHSD had notice that violent acts were about to occur on its campus on the day of Michael's injuries.
26. WHSD failed to take reasonable precautions to protect Michael from a known risk of harm.
27. WHSD breached its duty to Michael.
28. ... .

... .

Count One—Battery

39. Michael realleges all of the allegations contained in the complaint.
40. [Add more specific factual allegations if appropriate]

   ... .

46. Michael has stated a cause of action in battery against Defendants Daniel, Max, and Alan.

   ... .

Count Six—Negligence

67. Michael realleges all of the allegations contained in the complaint.
68. WHSD owed a duty to Michael to take reasonable precautions to protect Michael from known risks.
69. WHSD breached its duty to Michael when it failed to take reasonable precautions regarding a known risk.
70. Michael was injured as a direct result of WHSD's breach of duty.

   ... .

Wherefore Michael demands judgment against the defendants as follows:
On Count One against Daniel, Max, and Alan, jointly and severally;
   1. For general damages in an amount to be shown by the evidence;
   2. For special damages in an amount to be shown by the evidence;
   3. For punitive damages in an amount to be shown by the evidence;
   4. For such other and further relief as the Court deems just and equitable.

   ... .

On Count Six against WHSD;
   1. For general damages in an amount to be shown by the evidence;
   2. For special damages in an amount to be shown by the evidence;
   3. For such other and further relief as the Court deems just and equitable.

   ... .

DATED this 22nd day of January, 2001

WHITE & TREADWELL

_____

by John Morgan
Attorneys for Plaintiff

Figure 4-14
Affidavit of Service

IN THE SUPERIOR COURT OF THE STATE OF ARIZONA
IN AND FOR THE COUNTY OF MARICOPA

Michael Johnson, a single man,)
)
) NO. _____
Plaintiff,)
) Affidavit of Service
vs.) of Process by a
) Private Process Server
Daniel Hendershott, Max Evans, and) (Defendant Max Evans)
Alan House, all single men; CODA,)
Inc., a foreign corporation, and)
Washington High School District.)
)
Defendants.)
_____)

STATE OF ARIZONA)
) ss.
County of Maricopa)

I, the Affiant, being sworn, state: That I am qualified to serve process in this cause; that I received the following judicial documents on the following date from the following attorney:

Documents: Summons, Complaint and Certificate of Compulsory Arbitration
Date Received: January 22, 2001
Received from: John Morgan

That I personally served true copy(ies) of the documents on those named hereafter at the time, place, and in the manner indicated and/or pursuant to Arizona Rules of Civil Procedure, Rule 4.1 copy(ies) was/were left at the party(ies) usual place of abode with a person of suitable age and discretion who resides therein at party(ies) usual place of abode.

If the named party(ies) was/were a corporation, that the person served below is an officer, managing agent, or statutory agent of said corporation(s).

Upon: Max Evans, a single man by leaving one copy with him, in person, while at 2341 North Thunderbird Avenue, Phoenix, Arizona, on January 29, 2001 at the hour of 5:50 p.m. on said day. Affiant also attempted service on January 22, 24, and 26, 2000.

_____
Jack Harrison, Affiant

Subscribed and sworn to before me the undersigned Notary Public, this 29th day of January, 2001, by Jack Harrison.

My commission expires:_____
Notary Public

SERVING PROCESS

Purpose of Service

A defendant's obligation to respond to the suit does not begin until the plaintiff has properly served the complaint on that defendant. Until then, the defendant is unlikely even to be aware that suit has been filed. The summons and complaint cannot be served using ordinary mail, although, in some cases, it can be served by certified mail, return receipt requested. Formality is insisted upon because when a summons and complaint are served, the courts want to be sure of getting the undivided attention of the person being served—they do not want a lawsuit being mistaken for junk mail! It would be fundamentally unfair to allow a lawsuit to proceed and judgment to be taken against someone who had not even been made aware that there was a suit. Because defendants have a right to defend themselves, the U.S. Supreme Court has ruled that a person being sued is entitled to be notified of that fact by the best means possible under the circumstances. Therefore, proper service of the complaint is a jurisdictional requirement without which the court has no power to enter a binding judgment.

Procedures for Serving Process

The summons and complaint must be served on the defendant himself, rather than on the attorney representing the defendant because the defendant is the person being sued and he must receive proper notice in order to defend himself. A summons and complaint can be served in a number of different ways. The most common way is **personal service.** Personal service means having someone locate each defendant and physically hand the papers to that person. The person who serves the summons and complaint may be a sheriff or other government official, or, in many courts, the job is done by a private process server. After serving a copy of the summons and complaint on each defendant, the sheriff or process server signs and files an **affidavit of service** (in some areas it is known as a *return of service* or *proof of service*) with the court, which serves as proof that delivery was actually made. See figure 4-14 for a sample *affidavit of service.* The specific form and content of the paper may vary, but the purpose is to establish that the court record was delivered.

Bowing to practicality, nearly all courts allow **abode service** (also known as *substituted service*). Abode service is accomplished by leaving a copy of the summons and complaint at the defendant's "usual place of abode with some person of suitable age and discretion then residing therein" (Federal Rule 4(e)(2)). In other words, the process server can hand the papers to whoever answers the door at the defendant's house, providing that person is "of suitable age and discretion" and "residing therein." Some courts require a follow-up mailing.

Serving process on a corporation requires delivery to an agent of the corporation. One of the usual requirements that a corporation must meet when filing incorporation papers is to appoint an agent to receive service of process. Most states also require out-of-state corporations to appoint an agent to receive service before doing business in that state. The name and address of a corporation's appointed agent can easily be determined by calling the state agency that regulates corporations (Corporations Commission or Department of Corporations are two of the common names.) Therefore, serving process on a corporation is usually as simple as making one phone call to get the name and address of the agent, and instructing the process server to deliver the papers there.

Sometimes the defendant already knows that the plaintiff is filing suit, and is willing to waive formal service of process. Usually, this is perfectly permissible as long as both parties agree, but the plaintiff must carefully follow the rules of the particular court in filing the appropriate documents to establish the waiver.

To arrange for out-of-state personal service, plaintiffs can look to process server firms, many of which have offices in other states or correspondent arrangements with process servers in other states. A "full-service" process server firm can usually arrange for personal service in any state. In modern litigation practice, this is by far the preferred method.

The summons and complaint can be served by mail in either federal or state court as long as the plaintiff follows the procedures prescribed in the state in which service is to be made. To serve a summons and complaint by mail, the plaintiff must first mail the papers to the defendant using the class of mail prescribed by the state

personal service locating a defendant and personally handing papers to that person

affidavit of service filed with the court, this serves as proof that delivery of a summons and complaint was actually made

abode service to leave a copy of the summons and complaint at the defendant's usual place of residence with a person of suitable age and discretion who resides therein

NET NEWS

For additional information about service of process, go to *www.west.net/~ smith/jurisdiction.htm.*

◆ **LOCAL LINKS** ◆

Find out from your instructor how the procedures and terminology for serving process may differ in your jurisdiction from what has been described.

court rules—usually registered or certified, with a return receipt. After receiving the return receipt, the plaintiff must prepare and file an affidavit reciting the circumstances making mail service appropriate. The affidavit serves as a return of service—that is, it provides a record in the court's file showing that service was made. Notice that the defendant can easily defeat service simply by refusing to sign.

Putting It Into Practice 4.20:

What should Martha do before she calls the process server in Mike's case? Assume that the students whom Mike is suing have been expelled from school.

Martha Posted a Note on Her Calendar for a Week from Then to Remind Herself to Verify That Service had Been Validly Made.

The firm had an established account with a process server firm, so all Martha had to do was fill out the instructions for service on a printed form. Because she believed all of the local defendants could easily be located, she provided the process server with only the name and address of each defendant (or the defendant's agent). Had she thought they might be difficult to find, she would have also given the process server work addresses, social security numbers, and/or physical descriptions.

After providing the process server with sufficient instructions to allow him to serve all of the defendants, Martha posted a note on her calendar for a week from then to remind herself to verify that service had been validly made. She did this so she would be aware of any problem situations that might arise and could take steps to rectify them. When she received the affidavits of service, she verified with the court that the original affidavits had been filed.

Before she turned to the work that lay before her in other cases for which she was responsible, Martha took a few minutes to update Mike's file and make some entries to the central index in his file. Martha prided herself on having all of her files in order and up-to-date so that anyone accessing a file could find what she needed easily.

CREATING AND ORGANIZING FILES

A uniform filing system is essential in any law office to maximize efficiency, simplify storage, speed up the retrieval process, and minimize confusion. One important aspect of any legal filing system is some type of central index, which allows anyone to either find or file case materials in a particular case. The central index lists every file and describes its contents. Central indexes usually include several categories.

- ◆ pleadings
- ◆ correspondence
- ◆ notes and file memoranda (memos written by attorneys and paralegals to the file)
- ◆ legal research
- ◆ discovery
- ◆ client documents
- ◆ opponent's documents

Each time a new file is opened up, it must be included in the central index because this index is the key to knowing where each and every document is located.

Additionally, a paralegal should organize her own working file for each case she is working on. This file could contain the following items.

- personal notes (from interviews and research)
- central index
- other indexes (such as pleading and discovery indexes)
- witness directory (providing the information necessary to locate any witness in the case)
- deposition schedules
- chronology of events
- case calendar
- case memorandum (an ongoing synopsis of the facts and legal contentions as they develop)
- record of all case costs

Paralegals should take this file with them to every meeting and out-of-office assignment. Because this is the single most utilitarian file to a paralegal, it should be copied on a backup diskette.

How files are organized depends on the complexity of the case and the system adopted by the firm. Although no details about the specifics of organizing can (or should) be offered in an introductory text, it is important to remember that every document should be filed immediately after it is received. No matter what system is used, it should allow anyone to find any single document easily and quickly. Furthermore, it should be flexible enough to allow the organization to be modified as more documents are amassed during the course of litigation.

Putting It Into Practice 4.21:

docket put on the office calendars

What documents should Martha have placed in Mike's file at this point?

Martha Knew How Critical It was to Meet Deadlines, that Point Having Been Reinforced Vividly when One of Her Friends Was Fired for Miscalculating a Discovery Deadline.

Martha made a mental note to calculate and **docket** (or *calendar*) the deadlines for each of the defendant's answers as soon as she received their return of service. She anticipated, however, that the attorneys for all of the defendants would probably be asking for extensions. Martha had a reputation for being extremely conscientious about noting and checking deadlines: some of the other paralegals even teased her about being paranoid. But she knew how critical it was to meet those deadlines, that point having been reinforced vividly when one of her friends was fired for miscalculating a discovery deadline, which resulted in her firm having a malpractice claim filed against it.

When Martha had a moment to herself, she decided after some hesitation to return Tim's call. "He probably thinks I blew him off," thought Martha to herself. "The only decent thing to do is to at least let him know why I didn't call back," she rationalized, assuring herself that she had no intention of beginning any kind of relationship with this man. "Is Mr. McFay in?" she asked in her most business-like manner.

"Hello. This is Tim."

At the sound of his voice, all of Martha's resolve melted away and she immediately realized how much she wanted to see Tim again.

COMPUTING DEADLINES

Importance of Meeting Deadlines

Most law firms follow a strict policy whereby all incoming mail and deliveries must go first to some employee who is responsible for checking each paper for potential deadlines, computing the dates if necessary, and making appropriate notations on the office calendar. This process is referred to as docketing or calendaring. The docket is the office calendar, and may be kept in a regular (paper) calendar book or, increasingly, on some kind of computer system. Typically, a central docket is kept containing all deadlines for all attorneys in the office; each attorney and paralegal may also keep her own calendar, or, in a computerized system, may simply access her portion of the central docket.

After a plaintiff serves a complaint, the defendant has a fixed number of days to file and serve an answer. The defense attorney must do several things: (1) consult the rules of procedure and determine the deadline date (the last day on which the answer can be filed and still be considered on time); (2) record the deadline in the office calendaring system so that appropriate reminders will be generated; (3) prepare the answer before the deadline; and (4) file the answer and serve it on the opposing party in the correct manner. A mistake anywhere along the way may result in a **default judgment** being entered against the defendant.

default judgment judgment entered against the defendant if the defendant fails to appear and respond to the plaintiff's complaint within the time period allowed by the rules and the plaintiff takes steps to obtain a judgment by default

BONUS POINTERS:

DEALING WITH DEADLINES

Each step in the litigation chain of events must be carried out correctly. A complaint that is not served exactly in accordance with the rules may be treated as if it were not served at all—even if the opposing party clearly received it. If the judge is about to rule on a motion, and a party's response has not been filed, it does not matter whether the party is "only" a day late or a month late—the result will likely be the same. When dealing with the paper-processing requirements of the rules, "approximately correct" and "nearly on time" are not good enough.

Office procedures in a litigation law office are specifically designed to facilitate this process of time-sensitive moves and countermoves. The smooth operation of all this paper-processing is absolutely critical to a successful litigation practice. Any law office, large or small, that fails to approach all tasks carefully and systematically will, sooner or later, have some important paper "fall through a crack," and find itself on the receiving end of a malpractice suit.

Good management of deadlines in a law firm begins with proper mail handling practices. Most of the deadlines paralegals deal with arise either from the need to respond to papers sent by opponents or from court orders requiring the completion of some task by a particular date. Even relatively small law firms may receive several mailbags full of documents each day. Clearly, if each paper in this daily river of documents were to be routed directly to the person it is addressed to, at least some of them would be overlooked. The attorney to whom a paper is addressed may be out of town, and the document may sit unread on her desk for a week; a secretary may accidentally put an incoming motion in the case file instead of giving it to the attorney to respond to. The potential for oversights is enormous.

In a properly run system, no one—not even the senior partner of the firm—is allowed to touch an item of mail before the docketing clerk has processed it. The docketing clerk stamps each incoming paper with a "received" stamp that automatically imprints the date. This is important in case a dispute arises later about when the paper was actually received. The docketing clerk also makes a notation on the paper, again using a rubber stamp, indicating any deadlines that are being docketed. After a paper has been docketed, the docketing clerk determines which attorney is responsible for the case to which the paper pertains, and routes the paper to that attorney (or perhaps to her secretary) for the actual preparation of the required response. To demonstrate the importance of calendaring, many insurance carriers require law offices to use at least two calendaring systems before the carrier will provide insurance coverage to the law firm.

One of the reasons information about calculating deadlines is important for paralegals is that they are sometimes assigned to do docketing. Another is that, even with the most carefully planned docketing system, mistakes occasionally occur. Therefore, in a first-rate firm, everyone—partners, associates, paralegals, even the lowliest clerical employee—is responsible for deadlines. Every paralegal should cultivate the following habit: Every time she sees or comes in contact with a new court paper in a case, she should give it a quick "deadline check." If it has already been stamped with a response date, the paralegal should double check the deadline by re-computing it; if not, she should consider whether a response requirement may have been overlooked. In the long run, this is a habit that will pay rich dividends in terms of malpractice claims avoided.

Putting It Into Practice 4.22:

How might the failure to meet a court deadline result in a malpractice claim against an attorney and the firing of a paralegal?

All response deadlines, deadlines for filing papers with the court, and other court-related deadlines *must* get into the central calendar—even ones that have been entered in attorneys' and paralegals' personal calendars. One of the things that a proper central calendaring system does is to generate daily reports for each attorney and paralegal in the office, showing the upcoming deadlines for all matters for which they are responsible, including projects assigned to subordinates. This provides a fail-safe mechanism in case an attorney or paralegal becomes ill or incapacitated, or simply "drops the ball." The next person up the ladder of authority will automatically be made aware of any pending deadlines. A good docketing system also keeps track of the opponent's deadlines. This way the firm is prepared to take appropriate action if an opponent's filings are not received when they are due.

It is also imperative that all paralegals, regardless of their area of practice, keep a personal calendar, but it is especially important for litigation paralegals. Too many time-critical events in the practice of law are possible to allow reliance on memory alone, and some of these events will be of a type (i.e., appointments with witnesses, progress checks for assigned tasks, etc.) not appropriate for the central office calendar. It goes without saying that all deadlines for projects should be entered in personal calendars, even though they are already entered in the office calendar.

Martha received the first return of service from the school district. She sat down to compute the deadline for its answer. Under the Arizona Rules of Civil Procedure a defendant has 20 days in which to file an answer. Knowing that the district was served by the process server on December 3, 2000, she could easily compute the date its answer was due. She began counting the day after the date of service (because the first day of service does not count) and found the twentieth day to be December 23 (because the last day is included in the count). Because that day fell on a weekend (Saturday) and the Monday that followed was Christmas, she knew that the answer would not actually be due until December 26. (The rules prohibit a deadline from falling on a weekend or holiday.)

Computing Deadlines

To compute the deadline, a starting point from which to count the required number of days is needed. The starting point is the date on which the opposing party served the paper to which a response is required. That date depends on the mode of service.

◆ For papers personally served by a process, the date of service is the date that the process server actually delivered the paper. Therefore, to compute the due date for an answer to a a complaint, the exact date on which the client was served must be known.

◆ For a paper that was hand-delivered, the date of service is the date on which the paper was actually delivered.

◆ For a paper that was served by mailing, the date of service is the date on which the paper was given to and accepted by the post office. Be sure not to drop mail into boxes that have already had their last pick-up for the day.

Their Brief Conversation Confirmed Martha's Suspicion that Carmela Was Avoiding Her, and She Decided to Begin Asking Some Questions about Carmela's and Mike's Relationship.

In the process of computing the deadlines, Martha noticed a reminder on her calendar to speak with Carmela. A glance at the clock told her Carmela would probably be home from school and Martha decided to call her while she was thinking about it. Carmela was polite but obviously hesitant to speak with Martha, and it took some cajoling to get her to agree to a meeting time. Martha could not shake the feeling that she and Mike were hiding something.

For that reason, Martha was not surprised when Carmela did not show up at the agreed upon time. When Martha called and asked Carmela for an explanation, she was apologetic but distant and hesitated to make another appointment immediately. They agreed to wait until her finals were over and the Christmas season past. Their brief conversation confirmed Martha's suspicion that Carmela was avoiding her and she decided to begin asking some questions about Carmela's and Mike's relationship. Something told her that they were more than casual friends. If so, why was Mike so uneasy when Carmela was around?

Meanwhile, the answers from the defendants began coming in. As Martha had anticipated, all of them had requested extensions of time to file an answer and John had **stipulated** (agreed) to all of them. John examined each of the answers carefully, trying to read between the lines to infer each defendant's strategy.

stipulated   agree to

Putting It Into Practice 4.23:

Assume that defendant Hendershott receives personal service of the complaint on December 12, 2000. When will his answer be due?

ANSWERING THE COMPLAINT

Objectives of the Answer

Just as the complaint defines the issues that the plaintiff intends to present to the court, the answer defines the issues from the defendant's standpoint. An answer is, first and foremost, a point-by-point response to the allegations of the complaint. As with complaint drafting, however, the defendant has some homework to do before he can start writing. Before being able to admit or deny the facts alleged in the plaintiff's complaint, the defendant must investigate each of those facts. Even seemingly trivial and insignificant facts need to be checked out because these facts may later turn out to be the facts that decimate the defendant's case.

More than this, however, the defendant must be able to correctly allege all of the required elements of each affirmative defense to be raised, and to identify any missing elements in the plaintiff's causes of action. The legal and factual research required to prepare an answer is not, therefore, very different from that required to draft a complaint.

Figure 4-15
Answer to Complaint

Barbara Tsosie, Esq. SBN 08766
SIMON & PORTER
1000 North Central Avenue, Suite 2800
Phoenix, Arizona 85004
602-255-7070
Attorneys for defendant Washington High School District.

IN THE SUPERIOR COURT OF MARICOPA COUNTY
PHOENIX, ARIZONA

Michael Johnson, a single man, 　　　　　　　　Plaintiff, 　　　　vs. Daniel Hendershott, Max Evans, and Alan House, all single men; CODA, Inc., a foreign corporation, and Washington High School District. 　　　　　　　　Defendants.	NO. _____ Separate Answer of Defendant Washington High School District

Defendant Washington High School District, by and through counsel under-signed, in answer to Plaintiff's complaint, admits, denies and alleges as follows:
1. Admits the allegations contained in paragraphs 1, 2, 4, 6, 7, 8, & 68 of the complaint.
2. Denies the allegations contained in paragraphs 5, 25, 26, 27, 68, 69 and 70 of the complaint.
3. Alleges that this defendant is without sufficient information so as to be able to form a belief as the allegations contained in paragraphs 3, 11, 15, 16, 19, 21, 22 and 46 of the complaint and therefore denies same.
4. Denies each and every allegation not specifically admitted herein.

Affirmative Defenses

As affirmative defenses this answering defendant alleges assumption of risk and contributive or comparative negligence.

This answering defendant further alleges that Plaintiff's complaint fails to state a cause of action upon which relief can be granted.

WHEREFORE, having fully responded to Plaintiff's complaint Defendant Washington High School District requests that this court dismiss Plaintiff's com-plaint and award defendant its costs incurred herein.

　　　　　　　　　　　　　SIMON & PORTER

　　　　　　　　　　　　　_____

　　　　　　　　　　　　　by Barbara Tsosie, Esq.
　　　　　　　　　　　　　Attorneys for defendant Washington
　　　　　　　　　　　　　High School District.

Copy of the foregoing mailed
this 23rd day of March, 2001 to:

Dana Ferraror, Esq.　　　　　　　　William Yakamura, Esq.
500 Main Street　　　　　　　　　　59 Plain Street
Scottsdale, Arizona　　　　　　　　 Durango, Colorado 95660
Attorney for defendant Hendershott　Attorney for defendant CODA, Inc.

John Morgan, Esq.
WHITE & TREADWELL
Ernesto Esparanza, Esq.
2020 North Central Avenue, Suite 3200
Phoenix, Arizona 85005

Attorneys for Plaintiff

_____

Martha Fletcher

Basically, the defendant's objectives in writing an answer are to (1) make sure he has a reasonable basis for believing the truth of whatever he asserts in the answer; (2) avoid a default; (3) concisely convey to the judge the defendant's side of the dispute and enable the judge to easily discern which issues the plaintiff and defendant disagree on; and (4) avoid losing any potential defenses by accidentally leaving them out.

Steps to Drafting an Answer

The defense attorney's first job—and the first job of a paralegal given responsibility for screening prospective clients—is to nail down the answer deadline, which can be done by calling the court and confirming the date the complaint was served on the defendant. Often, complaints are brought in by a prospective client only a day or two before the answer is due. The easiest way to solve this deadline problem is simply to ask the plaintiff's attorney to stipulate that the answer will be due on an agreed upon date. In many jurisdictions, extensions of time to file answers are requested and given routinely. The attorneys involved must, of course, satisfy any formalities required by local rules in documenting the extension. In any event, a short letter should be sent to the plaintiff's attorney confirming the extension.

The defense attorney needs to fully grasp the facts of the case before answering the complaint. To do that the attorney needs to obtain as much information as possible from the client. The paralegal can assist by obtaining the following.

1. a complete narrative of what happened
2. names, addresses, and phone numbers of everyone involved
3. names, addresses, and phone numbers of any possible witnesses
4. a list of all documents that may bear on the case

Putting It Into Practice 4.24:

What do you think the attorney who represents CODA will do upon receiving Mike's complaint?

Third-party Claims

Next, the defense attorney must decide whether any claims should be made against others who are not parties to the lawsuit. To do this, the attorney must file a

Figure 4-16
Counterclaims, Cross-claims, and Third-party Claims

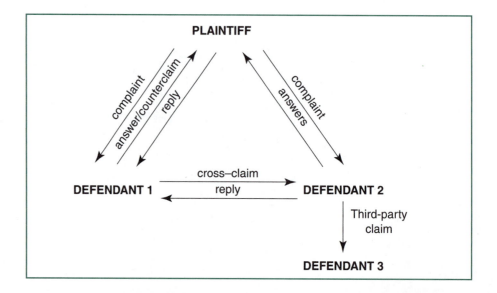

third-party claim claim against someone who is not already a plaintiff or defendant in the suit

third-party claim, which is a claim made against someone who is not already named as a plaintiff or defendant in the suit. A simple example will illustrate the need for third-party claims. Suppose your cousin Al is trying to buy a car, but, Al's credit history being what it is, the dealer will not write the loan without a cosigner. You agree to cosign, the loan is made, and off goes Al with the car. Later (as inevitably seems to happen to cosigners) Al falls upon bad times and is unable to make the payments. The lender sues you for the money. Your reaction, quite correctly, is: "Wait a minute—if I have to pay this, Al has to pay *me*." But because Al is not named as a defendant in the lawsuit, you must bring him into the lawsuit yourself, via a third-party claim.

third-party plaintiff party bringing a third-party claim

third-party defendant party defending against a third-party claim

You then become the **third-party plaintiff** and Al becomes a **third-party defendant.** The third-party claim must, of course, be served on the third-party defendant in the same way that a complaint would be served, and the third-party defendant must file an answer to it. Typically, the third-party claim is tacked on at the end of the answer.

indispensable party party without whose presence in a lawsuit a just result cannot be achieved

Sometimes a claim needs to be made against someone who is not named in the complaint, but that person cannot be brought into the suit. Suppose cousin Al is living somewhere in Brazil, address unknown, and you have no way to serve process on him. The judge must decide whether Al is an **indispensable party,** that is, whether he is someone without whose presence a just result cannot be achieved. If the judge deems Al an indispensable party, he will dismiss the suit; if not, the suit goes on without the benefit of Al's presence.

Putting It Into Practice 4.25:

Are there any third-party claims CODA or the school district might want to bring?

Affirmative Defenses

Essentially a defendant can defeat a cause of action asserted in a complaint in three ways.

affirmative defense defense relying on factual issues not raised in the complaint

1. The plaintiff's complaint leaves out a required element.
2. The plaintiff is unable to prove the facts supporting a required element.
3. The defendant establishes an **affirmative defense.** An affirmative defense is an excuse or justification that protects the defendant from liability to the plaintiff and that relies on factual issues not raised in the complaint. Instead of contesting the plaintiff's facts, it adds some new ones. A defendant who has been sued for battery, for example, can assert the affirmative defense of self-defense. A defendant who persuades a jury that he acted in self-defense wins even if the plaintiff proves that he committed battery. For purposes of drafting an answer, affirmative defenses work much the same way that causes of action do in the complaint. Affirmative defenses have elements, and the defendant must allege the facts supporting each element in the answer. A few common affirmative defenses are contributory and comparative negligence, assumption of risk, fraud, discharge in bankruptcy, duress, and statute of limitations.

Defenses to Tort Claims

If a plaintiff alleges that a defendant was negligent, a defendant can allege the following in return.

contributory negligence
doctrine that bars a plaintiff who contributed to her own injuries from recovering any damages

Contributory Negligence In a state that has adopted a **contributory negligence** system, a plaintiff that was in the least bit negligent (i.e., contributed to her own injuries) is totally barred from any recovery. The plaintiff is barred even though the defendant was negligent and, in most cases, was more negligent than the plaintiff. The rationale for this rule is that negligent plaintiffs should be punished for failing to protect their own safety.

Several exceptions have been created to contributory negligence because of the harshness of its consequences for the plaintiff. One of those exceptions is the "last clear chance doctrine." Under this doctrine, if the defendant has an opportunity that is unavailable to the plaintiff to prevent the harm that occurs (the last clear chance) and does not take advantage of it, the defendant remains liable despite the plaintiff's contributory negligence.

comparative negligence
doctrine that reduces the amount of damages a plaintiff who contributed to her own injuries can recover

Comparative Negligence In those states that have adopted the **comparative negligence system,** a plaintiff's recovery is reduced in direct proportion to his own degree of negligence. If a plaintiff suffers damages of $10,000, for example, and is shown to be 20 percent negligent, his recovery would be reduced 20 percent to $8,000. Under some systems, a plaintiff can recover no matter how extensive his negligence, but in others he cannot recover if he is more than 50 percent responsible for his own injuries.

assumption of risk doctrine that bars a plaintiff from recovery or reduces her recovery if the defendant can show that the plaintiff voluntarily consented to take a chance that harm would occur

Assumption of Risk Under the doctrine of **assumption of risk,** a plaintiff is either barred from recovery or her recovery is reduced if the defendant can show that the plaintiff voluntarily consented to take a chance that harm would occur. The difference between contributory negligence and assumption of risk is not always clear. Some courts, however, perceive contributory negligence as being "reckless" and assuming the risk as being "adventurous." A plaintiff who deliberately walks down defective steps when others, only slightly more inconvenient, are available may voluntarily assume the risk but would not necessarily be considered contributorily negligent.

Assumption of risk can be raised as a defense to strict liability but generally contributory negligence cannot. Considerable controversy exists as to whether comparative negligence is a viable defense to strict liability.

The following are defenses to intentional torts.

Consent A defendant it not liable for an intentional tort if the plaintiff consents to the defendant's intentional interference. Consent is not a defense if the plaintiff is incapable of or incompetent to give consent.

> Example: A doctor removes a patient's appendix. As long as the patient has given informed consent to the operation, no battery has been committed.

Self-defense A defendant is entitled to use reasonable force to protect himself or another against imminent harm if he reasonably believes it is necessary to do so.

> Example: A attacks B with a knife. B is entitled to use deadly force to defend herself if she reasonably believes she is in danger of death or serious bodily harm.

Defense of Property A defendant is entitled to use reasonable (but not deadly) force to protect his property against imminent harm if he reasonably believes it is necessary to do so and he verbally demands that the intruder stop first (if circumstances permit).

> Example: A is in the process of stealing B's car. B can yell at A to stop and if A refuses, B can use non-deadly force to stop A.

◆ **LOCAL LINKS** ◆

Does your state have a contributory negligence or comparative negligence system?

Necessity A defendant may harm the property interest of another when necessary to prevent a disaster to the community or to protect his own interests because no less damaging way to prevent the harm exists. Reimbursement of the plaintiff may be required.

Example: A can trespass on B's land to avoid a criminal attack.

Other defenses include the following.

immunity absolute defense derived from a defendant's status (e.g., government official) or relationship to the plaintiff (e.g., spouse of the plaintiff)

Immunity This is a complete defense to any tort. Four basic kinds of **immunity** are available.

(1) *Governmental Immunity* Many governmental agencies are immune from suit, although both Congress and state legislatures have passed laws limiting the extent of this immunity. State tort claims acts exist in many states that place limits on the damages that plaintiffs can collect against a state agency. Public officials, such as judges and legislators, also receive complete immunity as long as the act complained of is within the scope of their duties. The rationale for this type of immunity is that public officials must be given free rein to carry out the difficult tasks of their offices, unfettered by fear of being sued.

(2) *Interspousal Immunity* In some states, individuals are immune from suit by their spouses although most states have rejected interspousal immunity. The rationale for this doctrine was that allowing suit would result in a flood of litigation, create family discord, and encourage fraud.

(3) *Parent-Child Immunity* Some states prohibit suits by children against their parents and vice versa for the same reasons underlying spousal immunity.

(4) *Charitable Immunity* Charitable organizations, including educational and religious organizations, used to receive immunity so that their very existence was protected. Most states have abolished charitable immunity altogether while others have abolished it in reference to charitable hospitals only.

Statutes of Limitation Statutes of limitations limit the time in which an action can be brought. Any action not commenced within that time period is barred. The purpose of such statutes is to protect individuals from having to defend stale lawsuits. They also allow people to have some measure of stability and predictability in their lives by limiting the time frame in which they can anticipate being sued.

Statutes of limitations begin to run at the time of injury. Because some injuries may not be apparent for several years after they occur (injuries caused by medical malpractice, for example, may not be obvious for years after treatment), some courts have decided that the statute does not begin to run until the injury is, *or should have been,* discovered.

◆ **LOCAL LINKS** ◆

What is the status of interspousal immunity in your state?
What is the status of parent-child immunity in your state?
What is the status of charitable immunity in your state?

Putting It Into Practice 4.26:

(a) What potential defenses might Stuart raise in response to Molly Running Deer's complaint? Would these defenses necessarily preclude Molly from recovering anything? (b) Could Stuart raise immunity as a defense if the reason he ran the red light was that he was a judge in a hurry to get back to the courtroom? (c) Would necessity be a viable defense for Stuart if he ran the red light because he was rushing to get his little girl to the hospital? (d) Suppose Molly did not suffer any significant injuries in the accident and decided not to sue immediately, but that two years later she began suffering from migraines, which her doctors believe could possibly stem from the head injuries she sustained in the accident with Stuart. What problem does this pose for Molly if the statute of limitations for negligence in her state is one year? How might she get around this problem?

Figure 4-17
Defenses

DEFENSES

NEGLIGENCE

Contributory negligence

Comparative negligence

Assumption of risk

INTENTIONAL TORTS

Consent

Self-defense

Defense of property

Necessity

Immunity
Governmental
Interspousal
Parent-child
Charitable

Statute of limitations

STRICT LIABILITY

Assumption of risk

Writing the Answer

The caption can be copied from the plaintiff's complaint, except that the title is now "Answer." Immediately below the caption begins the body of the answer. First comes the preamble. A common phraseology is: "Defendant(s), for his (her, its, their) answer to plaintiff's complaint, admits, denies, and alleges as follows:" (If the defense attorney represents fewer than all defendants, then he would write: "Defendants Smith and Jones, for their answer to plaintiff's complaint, admit, deny, and allege as follows:".)

Like complaints, answers are organized in numbered paragraphs. Note that the numbers of the paragraphs in the answer have nothing to do with the numbers of the paragraphs of the complaint. The paragraphs of the answer are numbered sequentially; the answer will refer to each of the paragraphs of the complaint by number, but its own paragraphs are numbered in their own sequence.

At this point, the defendant has an opportunity to respond to what the plaintiff alleged in the complaint. The defendant can choose to respond in several ways.

1. He may deny the whole paragraph.
2. He may admit the whole paragraph.
3. He may admit part and deny part.
4. He may state that he is "without knowledge or information sufficient to form a belief as to the truth" of the paragraph.
5. After admitting or denying, he may allege something new in order to get an important point across.

To illustrate how answers are done, consider the following examples.

Example 1: *A simple admission* Suppose paragraph 1 of Mike's complaint alleges:

1. Plaintiff Michael Johnson is a resident of Maricopa County, Arizona.

Suppose we represent defendant CODA. We would need to find out whether Michael Johnson was, in fact, a resident of Maricopa County, Arizona. If our research showed he was, we would answer:

   1. Answering paragraph 1, admits the allegations thereof.

Example 2: *A denial for lack of information* Suppose paragraph 2 of Mike's complaint alleges:

   2. Defendants Max Evans and Daniel Hendershott are residents of Maricopa County, Arizona. Defendants Max Evans and Daniel Hendershott caused an act or event to occur in the state of Arizona out of which plaintiff's claims arose.

As representatives of CODA, we have no idea who these defendants are or where they live or whether they did anything in Arizona out of which the plaintiff's claim arose, so we would certainly not admit that. On the other hand, we really have no factual basis to deny these things either. This is a perfect opportunity to deny on account of lack of knowledge.

   2. Answering paragraph 2, defendant CODA is without knowledge or information sufficient to form a belief as to the truth of the allegations of said paragraph, and therefore denies them.

Example 3: *Admit in part, deny in part*

The third paragraph of Mike's complaint alleges:

   3. Defendant CODA is a corporation organized and existing under the laws of the state of Delaware, and doing business in the state of Arizona out of which plaintiff's claim arose.

As representatives of CODA, we may agree that we are a Delaware corporation and that we do business in Arizona, but we certainly are not going to admit that the plaintiff's claim arose from anything we did. Therefore, we would respond:

   2. Answering paragraph 3, defendant CODA admits that it is a corporation organized and existing under the laws of the state of Delaware, admits that it does business in the state of Arizona, and denies that plaintiff's claim arose from the business done by it.

Under the federal rules, any allegations in a complaint that are not denied in the answer are deemed admitted. Because Arizona follows the federal rules in this regard, CODA should, to protect itself against the possibility of failing to deny something in Mike's complaint, include a boilerplate denial:

  10. Defendant CODA denies each and every allegation of plaintiff's complaint not expressly admitted herein.

The question of which allegations to deny and which ones to admit is a strategical one. Some litigators, preferring an aggressive style, deny everything, forcing the plaintiff to prove everything. They argue that if the plaintiff has to spend energy

Figure 4-18
*Defendant's Options in
Answering Allegations*

> # DEFENDANT'S OPTIONS IN ANSWERING ALLEGATIONS
>
> Deny in whole
> Admit in whole
> Admit in part and deny in part
> State that he is "without knowledge of information sufficient to
> form a belief as to the truth" of the assertion
> Allege something new

and money proving the obvious, she will have that much less energy and money to spend proving facts that might actually hurt the defendant. Others prefer to concede the facts that the plaintiff will clearly be able to prove and save their ammunition for the truly contested issues. They point out that excessive contentiousness over trivia has a way of annoying judges and juries.

■ *Putting It Into Practice 4.27:*

Suppose paragraph 2 of Molly Running Deer's complaint says: "Defendant Stuart Thames is a resident of Pima County, Arizona. Defendant Thames caused an act or event to occur in the state of Arizona." How do you think Stuart's attorney will answer this allegation?

Having taken care of the elements of the causes of action alleged by the plaintiff, the defense attorney must now allege any affirmative defenses.

Example: Here is a paragraph alleging self-defense as it might appear in a response to an allegation of battery.

11. In using physical force against plaintiff, defendant acted for the purpose of defending himself against plaintiff, who was at the time brandishing and repeatedly firing a pistol with the evident intention of injuring or killing him. The acts of plaintiff in doing so were not privileged. Defendant did not intend to cause death or serious bodily harm to plaintiff, and used force which was reasonable in the circumstances and was not likely to cause death or serious bodily harm.

Next comes the prayer for relief. Here is typical verbiage.

WHEREFORE, having fully defended, defendant CODA prays that plaintiff's complaint be dismissed, that plaintiff take nothing thereby, for defendant's costs and attorney's fees incurred herein, and for such other and further relief as to the Court seems just in the premises.

Now the defendant must consider what claims he may have against the plaintiff or other defendants. If he has any claims he could bring against the plaintiff in a separate suit, he can assert them now. If the plaintiff's cause of action against the defendant and the defendant's cause of action against the plaintiff arise from the same factual setting, they are said to be **transactional** and they will be lost if

transactional   causes of action
that arise out of the same factual
setting

counterclaim claim that a defendant brings against the plaintiff

compulsory counterclaim claim that must be brought because it will be lost if it is not raised

cross-claim claim that a defendant brings against another defendant in the same lawsuit

reply answer to a counterclaim

they are not raised in the existing lawsuit. A claim that the defendant brings against the plaintiff is referred to as a **counterclaim** and one that must be brought because it will be lost if it is not raised is called a **compulsory counterclaim.** A claim that a defendant brings against another defendant in the same lawsuit is referred to as a **cross-claim.** (In some states, such as California, cross-claims, counterclaims, and third-party claims are all brought via a cross-complaint.) In most courts, counterclaims and cross-claims are tacked on at the end of the answer rather than put into a separate filing, and they are written in the same fashion as complaints.

If the defendant asserts a counterclaim, the plaintiff is required to file a **reply,** which is a kind of "mini-answer" directed at the counterclaim. This reply is written in exactly the same way that an answer is written.

Putting It Into Practice 4.28:

Under what conditions could Stuart Thames bring a counterclaim against Molly Running Deer? Suppose Stuart claims he ran the red light because his brakes did not work. How could he bring into the lawsuit the mechanic who had checked his brakes a week earlier?

◆ **LOCAL LINKS** ◆

How are counterclaims, cross-claims, and third-party claims brought in your state?

The date and signature lines are the same as they were for the complaint (and for any other court paper). Answers are signed by the attorney for the defendant rather than by the defendant himself unless some specific statute or rules require otherwise. The defendant should, however, read the answer to make sure there are no inaccuracies.

Additionally, a **certificate of service** (also known as *proof of service*) must be included at the end of the answer. Answers must be delivered in the right way to the right people. (In a few jurisdictions, service by fax is permissible.) The proof that an answer was served correctly is the certificate of service, which consists of a statement that appears at the end, following the attorney signature, reflecting the fact that the answer was mailed (or hand-delivered), recording the date of mailing, and listing the names and addresses of each recipient. The form shown below is one of the common styles, but many localities have a different preferred style. The mailing certificate must be separately signed, in theory, by someone with personal knowledge of the fact that the paper was actually placed in the mail to the people listed. In practice, mailing certificates are routinely signed by the attorney or by a secretary, either of whom is likely relying on a runner or clerk to do the actual mailing. Some states have standard proof of services forms litigants can use.

certificate of service statement at the end of a court paper reflecting that the paper was mailed (or hand-delivered), recording the date of mailing, and listing the names and addresses of each recipient

◆ **LOCAL LINKS** ◆

Is the certificate of service different in your jurisdiction? If so, how?

CERTIFICATE OF SERVICE

The undersigned certifies that the foregoing was served in accordance with the requirements of Rule 5, ARCP, by mailing / hand-delivering a copy thereof this ____ day of _____, 2001 to:

John Morgan, Esq.
WHITE & TREADWELL
2000 North Central Avenue, Suite 2900
Phoenix, Arizona 85004
Attorney for plaintiff

_____
[signature goes here]

NET NEWS

To see a sample answer, go to *www.alllaw.com/forms/pleadings* and click on "Answer (Response to Preliminary Allegations)." To read an article about the consideration that goes into answering a complaint, go to *www.paralegals.org/Reporter,* click on "Spring 1999," and read the article entitled "Considerations in Answering in Civil Lawsuits."

For more information about what default judgments are and the procedures for securing them, go to *www.hrothgar.co.uk/YAWS/rules/part-12.htm.*

Usually, a runner files an original answer with the clerk of the court or an answer is filed by mail. Many courts charge a filing fee for filing an answer, and the firm's check in the required amount accompanies the filing. Answers are served in the same way as other court papers subsequent to the complaint: they can either be mailed or hand-delivered. In practice, an answer is usually served either by mailing it to the office of the party's attorney, or by sending a runner who will hand the paper to the receptionist in the attorney's office. If an attorney has appeared for a party, service is always on the attorney (unless otherwise provided for by applicable rule or statute), and not on the party. (In fact, the ethical rules prohibit sending any communication to an opposing party known to be represented by an attorney—all communications must be with the attorney.) Papers to be served on parties who are not represented by attorneys must be mailed or delivered to the party himself.

John was relieved to receive an answer from each of the defendants. He was particularly concerned about CODA. In light of its precarious financial situation, he fully anticipated that the company would fail to answer the complaint and then file for bankruptcy if he secured a default judgment against it.

ALTERNATIVES TO FILING AN ANSWER

Filing an answer is not, however, the only option. Alternative options are explained here.

Do Nothing, Default

As a result, the plaintiff will almost certainly obtain a judgment by default for the full amount she is suing for. This outcome is not necessarily bad if the defendant has no assets from which a judgment could be collected. Because the judgment debtor is allowed to keep any exempt property, possibly the only "bad effects" of having a judgment are that his credit rating is ruined, and that if the defendant later finds himself with more money, he could be forced to pay.

On the other hand, if a defendant decides to defend the suit, he will have to hire a lawyer, which will probably cost a great deal of money—at least thousands of dollars, perhaps tens of thousands. Faced with doing nothing and keeping his assets, or hiring a lawyer and having to take out a second mortgage on his house to pay an attorney, a defendant may decide that default is the lesser of two evils.

discharge in bankruptcy
court order by the bankruptcy court wiping out a judgment debtor's debts

File for Bankruptcy

If the defendant qualifies to file for bankruptcy, he can not only keep all exempt property, he can get a **discharge in bankruptcy,** which is a court order by the bank-

For more information about bankruptcy, go to *www.law.cornell.edu* and click on "Law About," "Commercial Transactions," and then on "Bankruptcy."

ruptcy court wiping out all of his debts. In addition, when a defendant first files the bankruptcy proceeding, all lawsuits against him are immediately and automatically stayed. (An **automatic stay** is an order by the bankruptcy court ordering plaintiffs to refrain from proceeding further with their suit.) Filing for bankruptcy is not free. The cost of a typical consumer bankruptcy is approximately $1,000, including attorney's fees and court filing fees. This amount, however, is a good deal less than expenses incurred in defending a lawsuit.

automatic stay   an order by the bankruptcy court ordering plaintiffs to refrain from proceeding any further with their suits

The bottom line is that, unless the person being sued is either wealthier than the average middle-class American wage earner or is covered by insurance, there may be little to be gained and much to be lost by filing an answer and defending.

Seek a Different Forum

If the plaintiff's attorney is doing a good job, the court in which the suit is filed is the one best for the plaintiff and worst for the defendant. But the defendant is not necessarily stuck with the plaintiff's choice. If the plaintiff has filed in state court, and the case qualifies for federal jurisdiction, the defendant may be able to **remove** (transfer) the case to the U.S. District Court sitting in the same state. If the plaintiff has filed in U.S. District Court in State X, it may be possible to get the case removed to the U.S. District Court for State Y, if the case can be more conveniently litigated there. Removal applies only to certain types of cases and can be expensive to pursue.

remove   transfer to another court

Move to Dismiss for Lack of Jurisdiction, Improper Service, Etc.

If the defendant files an answer to the complaint, he is, by definition, addressing the merits of the plaintiff's case. But before the court can adjudicate the merits of the case, the plaintiff must cross a number of procedural hurdles. The court must have jurisdiction of the subject matter and of the defendant's person; venue must be proper; process must have been correctly served; any indispensable parties must be included; and any other procedural prerequisites must have been satisfied.

If there are procedural defects of this kind, the federal rules authorize a defendant to file a motion to dismiss instead of an answer. A defendant who files a motion to dismiss under these circumstances does not have to file an answer until 10 days after the court rules on the motion to dismiss. If the defendant is successful, he will not have to file an answer at all.

Negotiate a Settlement

In most lawsuits, one of the first things that the defendant's attorney does after receiving the complaint is to contact the plaintiff's attorney and explore whether there is some way to make the suit go away. A settlement may simply involve the defendant's paying the plaintiff some money to drop the case, or it may require a much more complicated deal between the plaintiff and defendant. Either way, the parties avoid the risk, expense, and aggravation of litigating on the merits.

Move to Dismiss for Failure to State a Claim

Suppose plaintiff sues defendant for doing something that is not actionable, that is, something that the law simply does not regard as illegal. A motion to dismiss for failure to state a claim upon which relief can be granted says, in effect, "Even if everything happened exactly the way it says in the plaintiff's complaint, the plaintiff is still not entitled to judgment. The allegations of the plaintiff's complaint, even if every one of them is true, do not describe something that the law regards as actionable." If the defendant does decide to move to dismiss for failure to state a claim, and the court rules in the plaintiff's favor, then, as with other motions to dismiss, the defendant has until 10 days after the court's ruling to file an answer.

A defendant's objectives in a lawsuit are (usually) several: (1) to avoid having to pay money to plaintiff, if possible; (2) if it is necessary to pay, to delay payment as long as possible (although an attorney cannot ethically make moves in a lawsuit whose only purpose are to cause delay); and (3) to keep the costs of the suit (legal fees, discovery costs, etc.) to a minimum.

Which of the options discussed above best achieves those goals depends on the circumstances.

Putting It Into Practice 4.29:

Suppose Stuart Thames is uninsured and has few non-exempt assets. What would you advise him to do in response to Molly Running Deer's complaint? What would you advise him to do if he were a successful plastic surgeon with a lucrative practice and Molly's damages exceeded the coverage provided by his automobile insurance?

Figure 4-19
Defendant's Alternatives to Filing an Answer

DEFENDANT'S ALTERNATIVES TO FILING AN ANSWER

Default
File for bankruptcy
Seek a different forum
Move to dismiss for lack of jurisdiction
Move to dismiss for failure to state a claim
Negotiate a settlement

DEFENDANT'S OBJECTIVES

Avoid having to pay plaintiff
Delay payment as long as possible
Keep costs of suit to a minimum

What Possible Reason Could Jorge Have had for Wanting to Shoot Mike?

As Martha walked to her car, she mulled over an earlier conversation with John.

"Appears that the Hendershott kid is going to sing like a bird. His attorney practically begged me to make a deal. But what really caught my attention, Martha, is this Jorge Boroquez he brought in as a third-party—says this kid was the real instigator of the attack on Mike. Isn't *Boroquez* Carmela's last name?" inquired John.

Martha could feel the chill going down her spine again just recounting this question. Was Jorge related to Carmela, she wondered, and if so, what possible reason could Jorge have had for wanting to shoot Mike? The sick feeling in her stomach warned her that she might not want to know the answers to these questions.

She put aside these disturbing thoughts as she tightened her seat belt and started the engine. After all, tonight was her first date with Tim. The new year was still in its infancy and Martha sensed she was opening a new chapter in her life.

■ TIM'S TECHNO TIPS

Timekeeping and Billing Software

Before computers and dictation machines, timekeeping was a manual process. Oftentimes, time records were kept on "tear-off" sheets like those now used for telephone messages. Each billable activity had to be separately entered with identifying information regarding the client, the matter being billed, and the activity completed. Either the timekeeper's secretary or a billing clerk would "round up" the billing slips, sort them appropriately and, at the time of billing, enter the data onto the billing invoice. The pre-billing report (invoice) would then be reviewed, adjustments made, and a final invoice prepared. Unless billing memos were prepared on a daily or weekly basis, neither the firm nor the timekeeper knew exactly how much and at what rate time had been billed. Managing cash flow was basically a monthly function.

We've come a long way! With the advent of computers and specialized billing and timekeeping programs, billing management has changed drastically and definitely for the better. Programs like Timeslips (*www.timeslips.com*) provide the ability to manage timekeeping on an almost real-time basis. The system administrator can review the output of any member of the firm on a daily, weekly, monthly, or project basis and compare that information with prior billing cycles. Each client, and each activity for that client, can be reviewed and adjusted and compared with the budget for the activity. In many instances, the database for the billing and timekeeping program is, or can be, integrated with the case management database so that one data entry is all

that is needed to start a new client file. Address, telephone, fax, and e-mail changes are done only once but appear in every facet of a firm's database, including its billing program.

Amicus Attorney and VirtuaLaw (the freeware case-management program) integrate the billing function (although in not as sophisticated a manner as a full-blown version of Timeslips) with case management. When a legal service item is completed, a billing button is activated to enter the billing information for the activity. Most programs allow for entry and compilation of time whether or not it is billed (pro bono activities, project time, etc.). When the actual invoice is prepared (automatically using a template created to the firms specifications), unbilled time can be shown or left off the invoice. The client can be billed separately for each different activity, or a "super bill" can be created grouping each activity with subtotals, if desired.

Billing programs greatly improve firm efficiency and promote better tracking of timekeeper production. For firms that use a budgeting process with their clients, the programs allow management to determine if a project is on, under, or over the budget and to track the source(s). Financial analysis of "what ifs" is easy and instantaneous. The effects of changing the billing structure of partners, associates, and paralegals can be determined. Project-based budgets have become far more feasible due to the controls that can be exercised and the ease with which a firm's work product can be analyzed.

TECHNO TRIP

Go to *http://dunsinane.net/bryan/index.htm* and download the billing module for VirtuaLaw, if you have not already done so. You will need to download VirtuaLaw to use the billing module. After experimenting, go to *www.abacuslaw.com* and see what type of billing module comes with it. Next go to *www.amicus.ca* and view its billing module. Finally, go to *www.timeslips.com* and download its demo version. Compare its features with those of VirtuaLaw. Which billing/timekeeping program would you prefer, aside from the reason that one of them is free?

SUMMARY – PART B

A complaint initiates a lawsuit. It consists of a caption, preamble, allegations, counts, and a prayer for relief. To prevent it from being rejected by the clerk of the court, it must conform to the requirements set forth in the local rules regarding paper size, font, margins, line spacing, line numbering, and a number of other details.

The defendant is not obligated to respond to a lawsuit until he has been properly served. The plaintiff can accomplish this through personal service, abode service, or mail service. Corporations can be served through agents they have identified as having the authority to be served. Once service is completed, the process server or sheriff must file an affidavit or return of service. Service can be waived if both parties agree, but the plaintiff must be careful to comply with the local rules regarding waiver. Service can also be accomplished using certified mail or registered mail with a return receipt.

A copy of the complaint must be put in the client's file along with all other documents sent out and received in the case. Once a case has been accepted by a firm, a central index should be prepared for that case and every new file should be added to that index. Additionally, a paralegal should organize her own working file, which she can take with her to every meeting regarding that case. Any filing system that is used should be easily accessible to everyone and should be flexible enough that it can be modified if necessary.

A central docketing system is essential in any law office to keep track of all deadlines. Once a defendant is served with a complaint, he must answer within the prescribed period of time or risk having a default judgment entered. In addition to the central calendaring system, every litigation paralegal should maintain a personal calendar. When computing deadlines for answers, the starting point must first be determined. That date depends on the mode of service. The rules for computing deadlines must be carefully followed (e.g., the first day of the count begins the day after service, a deadline cannot end on a weekend or holiday, etc.).

The defendant defines the issues in his answer. In drafting the answer, the defense attorney wants to avoid a default, convince the judge of his client's side of the dispute, make sure there is a reasonable basis for whatever he asserts, and avoid losing any potential defenses. Before answering the complaint, the defense attorney should compute the deadline by which the answer must be filed and should ask opposing counsel to stipulate to an extension if necessary. Then he should investigate the facts alleged in the plaintiff's complaint and decide whether any third-party claims should be filed. A defendant can defeat a plaintiff's cause of action by asserting that the plaintiff has omitted a required element or lacks the facts needed to prove a required element or the defendant can raise an affirmative defense. The defenses a defendant can raise include contributory and comparative negligence, assumption of risk, immunity, consent, self-defense or defense of property, necessity, and bar by reason of the statute of limitations. In answering the complaint, the defendant can either admit or deny allegations in whole or in part, or can say he is "without knowledge or information sufficient to form a belief as to the truth" of a particular allegation. The defendant can then bring any counterclaims or crossclaims he thinks are appropriate. In addition to the caption, preamble, date, and signature lines (similar to those in the complaint), the answer must have a certificate of service. Answers can be served by mailing or hand-delivery to the attorney representing the plaintiff or to the plaintiff herself if she is unrepresented.

In lieu of filing an answer, a defendant can choose to do nothing, file for bankruptcy, move to dismiss for lack of jurisdiction or failure to state a claim, seek a new forum, or negotiate a settlement. Which option is most advantageous depends on the defendant's financial status, whether he has insurance coverage, the strength of his case, the amount of damages in question, and whether any legal issues exist that might be resolved in the defendant's favor.

KEY TERMS

Abode service	Complaint	General damages	Reply
Affidavit of service	Compulsory counterclaim	Immunity	Special damages
Affirmative defense	Conformed	Indispensable party	Stipulated
Allegations	Contributory negligence	Nominal damages	Summons
Assumption of risk	Counterclaim	Personal service	Third-party claim
Automatic stay	Counts	Prayer for relief	Third-party defendant
Caption	Cross-claim	Preamble	Third-party plaintiff
Certificate of service	Default judgment	Preexisting conditions	Transactional
Comparative negligence	Discharge in bankruptcy	Punitive damages	
Compensatory damages	Docket	Remove	

REVIEW QUESTIONS – PART B

1. What are the primary parts of a complaint and what purpose does each serve?
2. What kinds of details can cause a court clerk to reject a complaint?
3. Why are the courts so adamant that defendants be properly served?
4. Describe each of the ways that an individual and a corporation can be properly served.
5. What general considerations should kept in mind in reference to creating and organizing files?
6. What steps should be taken in a law office to ensure that all deadlines are complied with?
7. In computing a deadline for an answer, what rules must a paralegal keep in mind?
8. What are the elements of an answer?
9. Describe these basic defenses.
   a. Contributory negligence
   b. Comparative negligence
   c. Assumption of risk
   d. Consent
   e. Self-defense or defense of property
   f. Immunity
   g. Necessity
   h. Statute of limitations
10. Differentiate between a third-party claim, a counterclaim, and a cross-claim.
11. What options does a defendant have in response to a complaint other than filing an answer? Under what circumstances is each of those options most viable?

PRACTICE EXAM – PART B

MULTIPLE CHOICE

1. A court clerk may reject a complaint if
   a. the body of the complaint is done poorly
   b. the margins are not wide enough or the font size is wrong
   c. the plaintiff has inadvertently omitted one of the parties
   d. none of the above

2. A caption includes
   a. the name and address of the attorney preparing the complaint
   b. the name of the court in which the complaint is being filed
   c. the names of the parties and their spouses
   d. all of the above

3. In preparing a complaint, a plaintiff must
   a. establish the elements of each cause of action
   b. set forth the specific amount of damages she is requesting
   c. have evidentiary support for every fact she asserts
   d. verify the complaint

4. In a complaint, the plaintiff should
   a. convince the judge of the rightness of his position as he prepares each count
   b. establish the elements of each cause of action in the "General Allegations" section
   c. include a request for costs
   d. all of the above

5. In federal court, costs include
   a. filing fees and court reporter fees
   b. attorney's fees
   c. witness fees but not process server fees
   d. none of the above

6. Formal service is required
   a. but it is not a jurisdictional requirement
   b. because the U.S. Supreme Court has said that defendants are entitled to the best notification possible
   c. and it cannot be waived
   d. although a court can issue a binding decision without it

7. A complaint
   a. cannot be served by mail
   b. unlike other court papers, must be served on the defendant personally
   c. can be served on someone residing at the defendant's home as long as that person is of suitable age and discretion
   d. served on a corporation must be served on one of the corporations officers or managers

8. A central index
   a. includes such categories as pleadings and correspondence
   b. need not be used except in complex cases
   c. does not need to be updated to include newly created files
   d. none of the above

9. File organization
   a. is standard from firm to firm and case to case
   b. should allow those familiar with the case to easily access documents but should be inaccessible to others
   c. requires that documents be filed immediately after they are received
   d. all of the above

10. When a defendant's attorney receives a complaint
    a. he must immediately compute the deadline date
    b. he can assume that the opposing attorney will stipulate to an extension
    c. he should record the deadline on his personal calendar but need not record on the central calendar
    d. all of the above

11. In computing the due date for an answer to a complaint, the paralegal must know
    a. the date the process server received the complaint
    b. that a deadline cannot end on a weekend or holiday
    c. that she begins counting on the day that service is made
    d. all of the above

12. An answer
    a. does not define the issues for the defendant because the plaintiff does that in the complaint
    b. can be created before the defense attorney knows any of the facts about the case
    c. is a point-by-point response to the allegations in the plaintiff's complaint
    d. all of the above

13. In drafting an answer, the defense attorney
    a. must be concerned that she has a reasonable basis for believing the truth of whatever she asserts
    b. avoid losing any potential defenses
    c. must try to convince the judge of the rightness of her client's position
    d. all of the above

14. A defendant can respond to a plaintiff's complaint by
    a. asserting that the plaintiff left out a required element, but cannot allege that the plaintiff lacks the facts to prove that element
    b. asserting that the plaintiff lacks the required elements of a cause of action and the facts to support those elements
    c. asserting an affirmative defense but not necessarily alleging the elements of that defense
    d. none of the above

15. In answering a complaint, a defendant can
    a. admit or deny a whole paragraph, but not part of it
    b. admit or deny allegations, but cannot claim to be without sufficient information to form a belief regarding the truth of an allegation
    c. allege something new
    d. none of the above

16. In response to a complaint, a defendant
    a. can file a motion to dismiss for failure to state a claim upon which relief can be granted
    b. must do something—ignoring it is not an option
    c. cannot file a motion to dismiss until after filing an answer
    d. cannot file for bankruptcy until after a judgment is entered
17. A defendant's objectives in defending a lawsuit are
    a. to avoid having to pay the plaintiff money
    b. to delay any payments to the plaintiff for as long as possible
    c. to minimize the costs of the lawsuit
    d. all of the above
18. In response to an intentional tort claim, a defendant can raise the defense of
    a. contributory negligence
    b. comparative negligence
    c. consent
    d. all of the above
19. The defense of immunity includes
    a. governmental immunity
    b. spousal immunity
    c. charitable immunity
    d. all of the above

20. Under a contributory negligence system
    a. a plaintiff can recover if she is only slightly negligent
    b. plaintiffs are punished for failing to protect their own safety
    c. plaintiffs cannot recover even under the "last clear chance" doctrine
    d. nothing mitigates the harshness to the plaintiff
21. Governmental immunity
    a. is justified by the need to allow government officials to have free rein in carrying out the difficult tasks of their office
    b. applies only to federal governmental agencies
    c. does not apply to government officials such as judges and legislators
    d. all of the above
22. Statutes of limitations
    a. begin to run when an injury is discovered
    b. bar any action that does not conform to certain statutory mechanical requirements
    c. protect individuals from having to defend stale lawsuits
    d. none of the above

FILL IN THE BLANK

23. A civil lawsuit begins when the plaintiff files a _____ , which is a formal, written statement in which the plaintiff describes what the dispute is about and what she wants the court to do.
24. A complaint ends with a _____ , which is a concluding section stating specifically what the plaintiff wants the court to do.
25. A complaint begins with a title page called the _____ and an introductory paragraph or phrase called the _____ .
26. The plaintiff tells her version of what happened in numbered paragraphs called _____ , and then establishes the elements of each cause of action in sections referred to as _____ .
27. Plaintiffs must request both _____ damages, such as pain and suffering, and _____ damages, such as medical expenses incurred in undergoing surgery.
28. Both general and special damages are a sub-category of _____ damages (damages that restore the plaintiff to the position she was in before she was injured). A plaintiff can

also request _____ damages if she thinks the defendant's conduct was egregious enough to warrant punishment. If no actual damages occurred even though the defendant committed a tort, the plaintiff can still ask for _____ damages. She can recover no damages, however, if she suffers from a _____ condition (one that existed prior to her being injured by the defendant).
29. The court clerk _____ each copy of the complaint by stamping it with the case number she has assigned at the time of filing.
30. The most common way to serve papers is through _____ service (physically hand papers to someone), although most courts allow _____ service (leaving papers at someone's home with someone of suitable age and discretion residing there).
31. After serving a complaint, the process server signs and files a(n) _____ .
32. The _____ (office calendar) may be kept either in a regular paper calendar book or on a computer system of some kind.

33. Failure of a defendant to file an answer in a timely manner may result in a _____ being entered against him.

34. A plaintiff's attorney will often _____ (agree) to an extension of time by which the defense attorney must file an answer.

35. In answering the complaint, the defense attorney has the option of filing a _____ against parties who are not named in the plaintiff's suit, a _____ against the plaintiff, or a _____ against another defendant in the lawsuit.

36. A lawsuit cannot proceed without the inclusion of an _____ party, without whom a just result cannot be achieved.

37. In addition to admitting and denying the allegations in a plaintiff's complaint, a defendant has the option of raising an _____ , which is a defense relying on factual issues not raised in the complaint.

38. In a state that has adopted _____ , a plaintiff who in any way contributed to her own injuries cannot recover anything. In a state that has adopted _____ , that plaintiff's recovery would be reduced, but she would not be completely barred from recovery.

39. Under the doctrine of _____ , a plaintiff who voluntarily takes a chance that harm will occur cannot recover or, at the least, her recovery will be reduced.

40. _____ is a complete defense to any tort. It includes _____ , which protects government agencies from suit, _____ , which protects spouses from suit, _____ , which protects parents from being sued by their children, and _____ , which protects charitable organizations from suit.

41. A _____ limits the time during which suit can be brought.

42. Two causes of action that arise out of the same factual setting are called _____ claims.

43. A _____ is a statement at the end of a court paper reflecting that the paper was mailed, recording the date of mailing, and listing the names and addresses of each recipient.

44. In some cases, a defendant who is unhappy with the plaintiff's choice of forum can seek to have the case _____ (transferred) to another forum.

45. When a defendant first files for bankruptcy, he is entitled to an _____ , which is an order by the bankruptcy court ordering plaintiffs to refrain from proceeding any further with their suits, and can get a _____ , which is a court order wiping out all of his debts.

TRUE OR FALSE

____ 46. A complaint is signed by the plaintiff but need not be signed by the plaintiff's attorney.

____ 47. A clerk of the court may reject a complaint that has improper line spacing or lacks the required backing papers.

____ *48. A court file is the single permanent and complete record of everything that has happened in a case.

____ *49. Some local rules limit certain court papers to a specified number of pages.

____ 50. The preamble identifies the parties, the attorney filing the complaint, and the title of the paper.

____ 51. The space for the case number is left blank on the complaint.

____ 52. The identities, addresses, and relationships of all the parties must be identified somewhere in the complaint, but the jurisdictional grounds for the case need not be specified.

____ 53. The plaintiff can use the general allegations section as an opportunity to convince the judge of the rightness of her cause.

____ 54. If a plaintiff wants to indicate that a fact is likely to have evidentiary support after she has a reasonable opportunity for discovery, she may use the phrase "upon information and belief."

____ 55. Some courts allow the plaintiff to designate parties whose names are unknown at the time the complaint is drafted using fictitious names.

____ 56. One count can be used to establish all the plaintiff's causes of action.

____ 57. A count should recite the elements of the cause of action using the exact language of the cases or statutes from which they are derived.

____ 58. If possible, a plaintiff should ask for "general and special damages in an amount which plaintiff will prove."

_____ 59. The issue of damages is decided by a jury because it is a factual issue.

_____ 60. Damages for pain and suffering are a type of special damages.

_____ *61. Compensatory damages are designed to restore a plaintiff to the position she was in before being injured by the defendant, and punitive damages are designed to punish the defendant.

_____ *62. Plaintiffs have an obligation to prove future medical expenses with the same degree of certainty with which they are required to prove past medical expenses.

_____ *63. In most jurisdictions, proof of medical bills plus proof of payment raises the presumption that the bill was necessary and reasonable.

_____ *64. To prove loss of earning capacity, the only evidence that needs to be considered are wage stubs, W-4 forms, and IRS records.

_____ *65. Details from the plaintiff's life coupled with specific incidents are needed to prove pain and suffering.

_____ 66. A party who wins a lawsuit must still pay his own costs.

_____ 67. The winner of a lawsuit is always entitled to a judgment for attorney's fees.

_____ 68. The format for the attorney's signature line is standard in all firms.

_____ 69. Verification is required in federal courts and most state courts.

_____ 70. In many courts, the plaintiff must include a check for the filing fee and an information sheet when she files the complaint.

_____ 71. A lawsuit does not begin until the defendant is properly served.

_____ 72. Ordinary mail can be used to serve a summons and complaint.

_____ 73. The summons and complaint must be served on the defendant's attorney, not the defendant himself.

_____ 74. The purpose of a return of service is to establish the fact of delivery in the court record.

_____ 75. Serving process on a corporation is usually as simple as making one phone call to get the name and address of the agent and instructing the process server to deliver the papers there.

_____ 76. Service of process can be waived, and there is no requirement necessary to verify the waiver.

_____ 77. After receiving the return receipt from a complaint served by registered mail, the plaintiff must prepare and file an affidavit

reciting the circumstances making mail service appropriate.

_____ 78. A defendant cannot legally refuse to accept a complaint served by certified mail.

_____ 79. A "full-service" process server firm can usually arrange for personal service in any state.

_____ 80. Paralegals should create working files they can take with them to meetings and to out-of-the-office assignments.

_____ 81. File organization should be flexible enough to allow modification as documents are gathered.

_____ 82. In most law offices, mail goes directly to the attorneys before it is checked by the docketing clerk or paralegal.

_____ 83. In a firm that has a central calendaring system, the attorneys and paralegals do not have to maintain a personal calendar for docketing purposes.

_____ *84. Deadlines must be strictly complied with because being "nearly on time" is not good enough in the practice of law.

_____ *85. It is important that the docketing clerk stamp each piece of incoming mail with a "received" stamp that automatically imprints the date.

_____ 86. Fortunately for paralegals, compliance with deadlines is the responsibility of attorneys.

_____ 87. Deadlines that are entered on the master calendar in a law office need not be entered on personal calendars of attorneys and paralegals.

_____ 88. Paralegals need not maintain personal calendars as long as they have a good memory.

_____ 89. A good docketing system keeps track of an opponent's deadlines.

_____ 90. To compute the due date for an answer to a complaint, the paralegal must know the date the client was served with the complaint.

_____ 91. For a paper served by mail, the date of service is the date on which the paper was put in the mail.

_____ 92. Because deadlines sometimes fall on weekends or holidays, attorneys may find it necessary to ask the opposing attorney to stipulate to an extension.

_____ 93. Very little legal and factual research is needed to prepare an answer.

_____ 94. Often the easiest way for a defense attorney to deal with a deadline problem regarding an answer is to ask the plaintiff's attorney to stipulate to an extension of time.

____ 95. Defense attorneys do not need to check out all the facts in a plaintiff's complaint until after they have filed an answer.

____ 96. A third-party complaint is very different in form than a plaintiff's complaint.

____ 97. If an indispensable party is not included in a lawsuit, the judge will dismiss the suit.

____ 98. The caption of an answer in a lawsuit is identical to that of the complaint.

____ 99. Answers are numbered like complaints, but the numbers of the paragraphs of an answer have nothing to do with the numbers of the paragraphs of the complaint.

____100. Litigators agree that the defendant should deny everything, forcing the plaintiff to prove everything.

____101. The "last clear chance" doctrine gives an opportunity to negligent plaintiffs to recover their damages.

____102. Under all comparative negligence systems, plaintiffs can recover no matter how negligent they are.

____103. The difference between assumption of risk and contributory negligence is not always clear.

____104. If a plaintiff voluntarily assumes a risk, she can never recover.

____105. Consent is not a defense if the plaintiff is incapable or incompetent to give consent.

____106. A defendant is entitled to use reasonable force to protect himself against future harm if he reasonably believes it is necessary to do so.

____107. A defendant is never entitled to use force to protect his property.

____108. A defendant may never harm the property interest of another even if it is necessary to prevent a disaster to the community.

____109. The rationale behind interspousal immunity is the prevention of a flood of litigation, family discord, and fraud.

____110. All states prohibit children from suing their parents.

____111. Some state tort claims acts limit the damages plaintiffs can recover against state agencies.

____112. Any action not commenced within the time limit set by the appropriate statute of limitations is barred.

____113. Transactional claims will be lost if they are not alleged in the defendant's answer.

____114. Counterclaims and cross-claims are filed separately from the answer.

____115. If a defendant asserts a counterclaim, the plaintiff is expected to file a reply.

____116. Answers must be served in the same way that complaints are.

____117. An answer must be served on the defendant himself rather than his attorney.

____118. Although the defense attorney usually signs the answer, the defendant should read it to make sure there are no inaccuracies.

____119. If a defendant is uninsured and has few non-exempt assets, default may be a better strategy than defending the lawsuit.

____120. The defendant must accept the plaintiff's choice of forum.

____121. If a defendant believes the forum court lacks subject matter or personal jurisdiction, the defendant should file a motion to dismiss rather than an answer.

____122. A defendant who believes that the plaintiff's claim is not actionable should file a motion to dismiss for failure to state a claim.

____123. A defendant who files a motion to dismiss must still file an answer.

____124. If the defendant has a weak case and the amount of money at stake is large compared to the legal costs, the defendant may want to do what he ethically can to delay the outcome of the case.

*Questions taken from Bonus Pointers

LEGAL LINGO

Fill in the missing letters.

1. __ __ __ __ N __   Section of a complaint establishing the elements of a cause of action
2. __ __ V __ __ S __ __ __ __   Type of federal court jurisdiction
3. __ __ M __ __ __ L __   Where person is physically present
4. __ P __ __ __ __ L   Type of damages
5. __ __ L __ __ A __ __ __ __ __   Numbered paragraphs in a complaint
6. __ I __ __ __ V __ __ __   Process by which parties obtain information about a case
7. __ __ P __ __ O __   Title page of a complaint
8. V __ __ __ R __ __ __ __   Liability for the torts of another

9. _ _ _ S _ _ _ L   Type of jurisdiction
10. _ _ N _ _ R _   What a court clerk does to a copy of a complaint
11. _ _ _ K _ _ _   Office calendar
12. _ B _ _ _ _ _   Type of service
13. _ _ F _ _ L _   Result of failure to file an answer
14. _ _ R _ _   Court that hears a case
15. _ _ _ P _ _ _ _ _   Agree to something
16. _ _ _ R _—_ A _ _ _ _   Claim against someone who is not a party to the lawsuit
17. _ F _ _ _ M _ _ _ _ _   Type of defense relying on factual issues not raised in the complaint
18. _ _ V _ _ _ L   Joint and _____ liability
19. C _ _ _ _ _ _—_ _ A _ _   Claim against another defendant
20. _ _ _ U _ _ _ R _ _ _ _ _ _   Claim against the plaintiff
21. _ _ _ N _ _ N _ _ N _ _ _   Type of fee agreement
22. _ _ _ _ U _   Location based on the convenience of the parties
23. _ _ _ T _ _ _ _ Y   Intentional infliction of harmful or offensive contact
24. R _ _ _ _ _ _ _   Transfer to another court
25. _ T _ _   Order from bankruptcy court to refrain from proceeding with lawsuit
26. _ _ T _ _ _ _ _ R   Advance paid to an attorney
27. _ _ _ _ G—_ R M   Type of statute that permits service on non-resident defendants
28. R _ _ _ R _   Process server must sign and file a _____ of service

LEGAL LOGISTICS

1. Your attorney asks you to prepare to draft a complaint for a client who wants to sue a supermarket after falling in the store. What should you do before you begin actually preparing the complaint?
   a. Suppose your firm's client fell in a courthouse rather than a supermarket. What kinds of things would you need to check on before filing suit?
   b. What kind of fee arrangement do you anticipate your attorney will make in a slip-and-fall case?
   c. Would it be appropriate to send a demand letter in this case? What would you have to know before such a letter could be written?
   d. Assume you are suing the supermarket. What information will you need before you can prepare the caption?
   e. If the supermarket is incorporated in your state, the client resides in your town/city, and the damages appear to be around $10,000, in what court will you want to sue?
   f. Will this case be subject to arbitration under the laws or your jurisdiction?
   g. If the supermarket is a corporation, how will you go about serving the complaint and summons on it?
   h. Prepare the general allegations for the complaint.
   i. Will you have more than one count?
   j. Prepare the prayer for relief for the complaint.
   k. For what reasons might the court clerk reject this complaint?
   l. How do you anticipate the corporation will respond to your complaint? What kinds of defenses will it raise?

2. Suppose you represent a woman who has suffered a history of physical, mental, and emotional abuse from her husband in a divorce. What type of fee arrangement do you anticipate your attorney will make if the divorce involves child custody and spousal maintenance issues that are fairly complicated?
   a. Under what circumstances could your attorney use some of the monies from the retainer he collects from this client?
   b. What options might this woman have if your attorney decides not to accept her case because she cannot afford to pay his retainer?
   c. How will you go about serving process on the husband if he now resides in another state?
   d. Suppose the husband is personally served the complaint on June 14, 2000. When is his answer due? What should his attorney do if he does not think he can get the answer completed by that date?

3. Molly Running Deer, who was injured by Stuart Thames, comes into your office to seek representation. She wants your firm to sue Stuart for her damages. What will your firm probably do before deciding whether to take her case? Why might the firm reject her case even if Molly has an excellent case?

a. What procedural tactic might the firm employ in drafting the complaint that might allow them to get a better picture of Stuart's financial status?

b. Suppose Stuart was delivering pizza at the time he was involved in the accident. Whom might the firm want to sue and why? Would it be possible for Molly to collect an entire judgment from a tortfeasor other than Stuart even if he is the one who is actually responsible for her injuries?

c. Suppose Stuart is a businessman who was just passing through the state when he was involved in the accident with Molly. What would you have to know to determine if Molly could sue in federal court? Why might Molly want to sue in federal court rather than in state court?

d. What affirmative defense(s) do you anticipate Stuart raising in his answer? Why will his attorney want to check on the date the accident occurred?

e. What advice would you give Stuart about how he should respond to Molly Running Deer's complaint? What would you have to know before you could give this advice?

f. Suppose paragraph 3 of Molly's complaint says:

Plaintiff was sitting in the intersection of 60th Street and Thomas waiting to make a left-hand turn. When the light turned red, Plaintiff began to proceed cautiously through the intersection when she saw Defendant's car speeding toward her. Although Plaintiff swerved to avoid colliding with Defendant's car, Defendant slammed into her vehicle in the middle of the intersection, spinning her vehicle around.

Stuart says that the light was green when he entered the intersection, but the police report indicates four separate witnesses viewed the accident and each says the light was red. How would you answer this allegation?

A TRIP TO THE MOVIES

In the movie *Philadelphia,* Tom Hanks plays the role of Andrew Beckett, a successful attorney in a large firm in Philadelphia who is terminated when the firm discovers he has contracted AIDS. Beckett pursues a wrongful termination suit against the firm, but in the process has to deal with prejudices against gays and against those afflicted with the AIDS virus.

1. Joe Miller (Denzel Washington) is the attorney who ultimately accepts Beckett's case after initially refusing to do so. Do you think Miller was ethically or morally bound to accept Beckett's case?

a. What ethical obligations do attorneys have with regard to cases involving unpopular causes or situations?

2. What courts would have jurisdiction over Beckett's case? What factors would have been important to Miller in selecting a forum court?
(Note: Remember that Beckett alleged a violation of the Federal Vocational Rehabilitation Act.)

3. What kind of fee arrangement do you think Miller established with Beckett?

4. What do you think the weakest link in Beckett's case was?

a. What would you have done to remedy this weak link in his case?

b. What do you think was the strength of his case?

c. Would you have presented a demand letter in this case?

5. Had Wyant and Wheeler been a law clinic rather than a well-established law firm, why might Miller have wanted to allege punitive damages?

6. What individuals and entities do you think Miller should have included as defendants?

a. Why would it be important for Miller to know the nature of the law firm's organization?

b. What impact might the doctrine of joint and several liability have on this case?

7. What would you say was the "theme" of Miller's case against the law firm? How did he develop this theme throughout the trial?

8. What kinds of damages do you think Beckett should have claimed?

9. What facts make it unlikely that Miller could be accused of filing a frivolous lawsuit?
10. At the stage in Beckett's case in which answers have been filed, what would you anticipate finding in Beckett's file?
11. What strategy do you think Wyant and Wheeler used in answering Beckett's complaint?
12. Assume that Beckett had clear evidence that he was fired because he had AIDS. What strategy do you think the firm should have taken when it received his complaint?

INTERNET INQUIRIES

1. Go to *www.law.cornell.edu* and find the answers to the following questions about jurisdiction.
   a. What is meant by the "res" of jurisdiction?
   b. What provisions in the U.S. Code pertain to federal jurisdiction and venue?
   c. Find a recent U.S. Supreme Court decision regarding jurisdiction and write down its citation.
2. Find and download samples of pleadings forms (complaints and answers) that are used in your jurisdiction. You might find these by going to the Web page for your local or state bar associations or the Web page for your local courts.
3. Go to *www.lectlaw.com* and answer the following questions.
   a. What are examples of billing abuses that have been committed by some attorneys?
   b. What types of questions should a client consider asking an attorney he is considering hiring?
   c. Where might a client look to find an attorney who will work free of charge or for a reduced fee?

5

Discovery and Motion Practice

OBJECTIVES:

In this chapter you will learn:

- what discovery is
- how and why the discovery process has been reformed
- what mandatory disclosure is and why some attorneys object to it
- the purpose of depositions
- how to compare depositions with written discovery
- how to arrange, prepare for, notice, and assist at depositions
- how expert witnesses are used
- what an I.M.E. is
- the purpose of document discovery and how it is conducted

- the purpose of written discovery and how it is conducted
- how to prepare interrogatories and requests for admissions and when they are used
- what a disclosure statement is and what is included in it
- the consequences of inadequate disclosure
- how motions are presented and decided
- a suggested format for a motion
- suggested ways to summarize depositions
- grounds for objecting to discovery requests
- the consequences of non-compliance with discovery requests

"Whatever We Find Out in the Discovery Process Is Either Going to Make or Break Mike's Case."

"Carmela, does your brother dislike Mike for some reason?" Martha asked pointedly, having confirmed that Jorge knew Mike.

"Why do you ask me that?" asked Carmela, obviously uncomfortable with the question.

"Look, Carmela, one of the defendants in Mike's lawsuit has named Jorge as a party. The only reason he would do that is if he thought Jorge had something to do with Mike's attack. Now it's only a matter of time before someone tells us the truth about whatever you and Mike are hiding. I'd really rather hear it from you than from someone else," pleaded Martha.

"Please, Mrs. Ferguson, talk to Mike. Please don't make me tell you. Mike is my friend," protested Carmela, bursting into tears.

"All right, I'll talk to Mike. But then I need to get the straight scoop from you."

"The 'straight scoop'?"

"The whole story," explained Martha, forgetting in her exasperation that Carmela's knowledge of American idioms was still somewhat limited. She had come to the United States only two years ago and had not yet mastered all of the intricacies of the English language. "I want you to know that we've not yet begun the discovery process in Mike's case. That's a process in which both sides exchange information in a case. Whatever we find out in that process is either going to make or break Mike's case. If you're truly Mike's friend, you'll help us make sure we know what's going on without having to learn it from the other side," warned Martha.

evidence factual information about a dispute presented to a judge or jury

common law court-made law originating in England with the Norman Conquest. Prior to the Conquest, England had no centralized court system and disputes were resolved based on local custom. When William, Duke of Normandy, was crowned King of England, he appointed judges who "rode the circuit," settling disputes in the name of the king. Although at first the judges decided each case as if it were the first of its kind, over time they realized they could be more efficient if they shared their decisions with each other. The resulting law became known as the common law.

request for production of documents discovery tool used to get documents from opposing parties

interrogatories written questions submitted to opposing parties

request for admissions discovery tool used to elicit admissions from opposing parties

depositions taking and recording of oral testimony

independent medical examination (I.M.E.) discovery tool that allows a party to have an opposing party examined by a physician of choice

OVERVIEW OF DISCOVERY

Ultimately, trials are decided on the basis of evidence. **Evidence** is the factual information about the dispute that is presented to the judge or jury. How is all this evidence acquired? Each side possesses some of the evidence that is critical to the other side's case. But few suits could go forward without some means of prying evidence away from opposing parties. At **common law**—lawyer shorthand for court-made law originating in England—litigants pretty much went to trial with whatever evidence they had and took their chances. Nowadays, however, parties can obtain almost any information pertinent to their dispute by means of a number of mechanisms, under compulsion of a court order, if necessary. These mechanisms are collectively called discovery, and their use is governed by the rules of procedure.

How much information can a party to a lawsuit be forced to disclose? In general, the limits are broad indeed: under the federal rules, any information that is "reasonably calculated to lead to admissible evidence" is fair game. Litigants can expect to be forced to turn over plenty of information that might ordinarily be considered private.

Discovery in American courts has traditionally been "request-centered": parties wanting some piece of information must request it. The procedural tools most frequently used for doing so are described below.

- ◆ **Requests for Production of Documents** are used to obtain documents that are in the possession of an opposing party. A subpoena duces tecum is used to obtain documents from non-parties.
- ◆ **Interrogatories** are written questions that are submitted to an opposing party, who must then provide written answers. **Requests for Admissions** are used to extract admissions from opposing parties.
- ◆ **Depositions** provide a means of taking and recording testimony from potential witnesses.
- ◆ **Independent Medical Examinations (I.M.E.)** allow a party to have a physician of its choice examine an opposing party (commonly used by defendants in personal injury cases to verify the extent of the plaintiff's injuries).

Putting It Into Practice 5.1:

Why might parties find it difficult getting the evidence they need in a request-centered discovery system?

DISCOVERY REFORM AND MANDATORY DISCLOSURE

The last decade has seen the emergence of a reform movement advocating "disclosure-centered" discovery, in which parties are required to disclose information voluntarily without waiting for a request. Traditional discovery tools are still available,

---

NET NEWS

To read more about the common law, go to *www.britannica.com*, enter "common law" as a search term, and then click on "common law" when it appears.

"My Gut Tells Me That Whatever Game Mike Is Playing Is a Dangerous One—One That Could Blow Up in His Face, and Ours, if He's Not Careful."

Before their meeting, Martha snagged John and warned him that they needed to talk with Mike as soon as possible.

"Thanks for the heads-up. Why don't we begin today by hearing what you found out from Carmela? Something tells me this may have a bearing on how we coordinate our discovery efforts," suggested John.

As soon as Martha and Ernesto were settled, John began. "Discovery in this case is going to be a mammoth undertaking. I'd like to set up a plan today so we can get started at once. Martha, would you please prepare a summary of our discussion today and make a chart showing our estimated dates for sending out discovery requests and setting up depositions?" requested John.

"Absolutely," assured Martha. "When would you like that done?"

"By Friday, please," responded John. "Now before we discuss our deposition timetable, I'd like Martha to tell us about her interview with Carmela."

Martha succinctly summarized her interaction with Carmela, emphasizing Carmela's behavior and reminding John and Ernesto about Mike's discomfort when Carmela was in the room with him at the hospital.

"We've definitely got to talk with Mike immediately. We can't have our client sabotaging his own case." John's suspicions were once again aroused by what Martha had observed.

"Wait just a minute," protested Ernesto, holding up his hands to demonstrate his point. "Don't forget that we have a **disclosure statement** due in a few weeks. Whatever Mike tells us we may have to disclose at that time. If Mike really does have some kind of bombshell he's going to drop on us, I think we'd be far better off delaying talking with him until after we've submitted our disclosure statement. That way we'll have some time before we have to **supplement** our disclosure statement. Even if we end up having to include his revelations in our supplementation, at least we'd have bought ourselves some time to deal with the situation. I really don't like coming out of the gate looking vulnerable." Ernesto firmly believed that winning lawsuits was largely a matter of strategy and fancied himself far more adept at such gamesmanship than John.

"Very good point," began John, "but I think we have to also keep in mind that all of the defendants are going to want to depose Mike immediately. We can't afford to have them finding out something during his deposition that we don't already know, and, based on the fact that Hendershott has included a third-party whom we know nothing about, I think that's a very strong possibility." Turning to Martha, he asked, "Do you think Mike is hiding something significant? Or am I overreacting?"

"My gut tells me that whatever game Mike is playing is a dangerous one—one that could blow up in his face, and ours, if he's not careful," confirmed Martha.

"I may come to rue this decision, but I want to interview Mike again before we depose anyone or send out any discovery requests," announced John calmly, knowing that his decision irritated Ernesto but trusting his own instincts more than Ernesto's.

"All right, I can live with that," conceded Ernesto. "But I think you're making a serious mistake." At that moment, John's phone rang.

"It's your secretary," said John, handing the phone to Ernesto.

While they were waiting for Ernesto, John reminisced about the changes in the discovery process. "There's no doubt that the process needed to be changed and I'm proud that Arizona was in the forefront of discovery reform. Frankly, small firms and sole practitioners oftentimes took a real beating from the larger firms, who had the capacity to inundate them with reams of meaningless and unnecessary discovery requests in the hope they would fold out of sheer exhaustion. Discovery became more about survival than a quest for the truth. I think that mandatory disclosure has put a real damper on the use of this kind of strategy. But at the same time, it's created some thorny ethical dilemmas for attorneys and has made it very tempting for the unscrupulous members of the profession to cheat."

---

disclosure statement a document each party is required to prepare and serve on opposing parties shortly after a lawsuit commences. This document must contain certain categories of information about that party's case.

supplement to amend a disclosure statement to include additional information a party finds out after filing the original disclosure statement

Figure 5-1
Tools of Discovery

TOOLS OF DISCOVERY

Depositions
Independent Medical Examinations
Interrogatories
Requests for Admissions
Requests for Production of Documents

---

but their use is greatly restricted so as to reduce costs. To understand what the reformers are trying to accomplish, consider the historical background discussed in the Bonus Pointers "Historical Context of Discovery Reform."

BONUS POINTERS:

HISTORICAL CONTEXT OF DISCOVERY REFORM

When the *Federal Rules of Civil Procedure* were adopted in 1938, the discovery rules they embodied were seen as a radical change from prior practice. Before the federal rules, a party needing information or evidence from an opposing party could generally get it only by filing a motion and obtaining a court order. This state of affairs was wasteful, inefficient, and tedious for judges.

With the adoption of the federal rules, the pendulum swung hard in the opposite direction. Now litigants could, in effect, write their own tickets. Instead of needing a motion and a court order to make an opponent produce a document or answer a question, all that was needed was a written request, signed by the requesting attorney, that was enforceable as though it were a court order.

The federal rules contemplated "open discovery." Litigants could ask for—and opponents were required to turn over—not only evidence but anything "reasonably calculated to lead to admissible evidence." Open discovery, however, brought its own set of problems.

In the first place, it could easily be used as a tactical weapon. Litigators became adept at creating discovery requests whose real purpose was not to obtain useful information, but rather to force an opponent to expend huge quantities of money and legal talent compiling the data requested. Another problem was that lawyers were almost forced to carry open discovery to its limits. If the rules allowed fishing through every single record that an opponent had ever committed to paper in the last decade, many attorneys felt it was malpractice to stop short of doing so.

By the 1970s and 1980s, in the view of many judges, the discovery tail was wagging the dog. The cost of discovery in a typical lawsuit was out of proportion to its contribution to the justness of the outcome. What could be done, short of requiring judges to micromanage the discovery in each lawsuit?

A few progressive courts experimented with tentative—and usually minor—changes. A typical change consisted of limiting the number of interrogatories allowed. Where before, any party could send out long sets of written questions to be answered by an opposing party, with no limits on how many sets or how many questions in each set, henceforth each party was limited to, say, 25 questions for the entire lawsuit. Such measures did little to contain the rising cost of litigation, but did serve to improve the skill of litigators in writing single questions that would take enormous work to answer. (Here is an example, only slightly exaggerated: "State the substance of each and every communication had by any employee of defendant General Motors Corp. with any other person during the last ten years, the subject matter of which involved any customer complaint regarding the quality or safety of any General Motors vehicle.") In the 1990s, judicial dissatisfaction with perceived abuses came to a full boil, and, in jurisdiction after jurisdiction, the decision was made to shift to a different system of discovery, based on mandatory disclosure.

For a more in-depth discussion regarding the problems of discovery abuse, go to *www.uchastings.edu/plri/fal95tex/discov.html.*

Under the traditional request-centered system, an attorney who wanted information had to ask for it—and describe it in clear enough terms that an opponent could not get away with hiding some crucial bit of evidence by claiming that the request was ambiguous. That process was inherently inefficient: because the requesting party had no knowledge of what information was there to be discovered, she had to ask to see everything. In some ways, traditional discovery was like the game "Battleship," in which each player tries to guess where the other player's ships are.

The basis of mandatory disclosure is full and open disclosure. Instead of putting the requesting party to the impossible task of firing off requests in the dark, mandatory disclosure requires each party to disclose—without being asked—every bit of information in her possession that is relevant to any issue being litigated. This approach eliminates a great deal of the game-playing of traditional discovery and much of the paperwork as well. Traditional discovery tools are still needed to flesh out the information voluntarily provided, but their use is now greatly curtailed.

Putting It Into Practice 5.2:

How is mandatory disclosure more efficient and economical than the traditional system?

Local Variations

Discovery procedures are not uniform throughout the federal system. When the U.S. Supreme Court adopted the 1993 amendments, it made them optional, allowing the district courts to decide for themselves whether to follow all of the changes, some of them, or none of them. Today, almost no two U.S. District Courts follow exactly the same discovery rules. Some adhere to the old system; others completely embrace the new; and a great many operate with some mixture of the two. State courts have not, on the whole, rushed to a wholesale adoption of the federal, disclosure-based system of discovery, and many states continue to experiment with their own solutions to the problems of discovery abuse.

Nevertheless, much about discovery is relatively uniform, regardless of place. The raw materials on which the discovery process operates—mainly paper records and testimony of live witnesses—are the same everywhere. Discovery revolves around analyzing the information obtained (a fertile source of work for paralegals); disclosure rules change only the way in which information is gathered, not what is done with it thereafter. The goals and motivations of the litigants are largely unchanged, regardless of the system used.

◆ **LOCAL LINKS** ◆

How is discovery handled in your jurisdiction? Is it a "request-centered" system or a "disclosure-centered" system?

To read about both sides of the issue of discovery reform, go to *www.uchastings.edu/plri/fal95tex/discov.html.*

ETHICAL ETIQUETTE

ETHICAL CONCERNS SURROUNDING MANDATORY DISCLOSURE

Some argue that mandatory disclosure drives a wedge between an attorney's loyalty to her client and loyalty to the court. Attorneys are ethically bound to zealously represent their clients, but they are also ethically bound as officers of the court to serve the interests of fairness and justice. Critics maintain that mandatory disclosure may place attorneys in situations where they are unable to fulfill either obligation. The defense attorney, in particular, appears to be put in the position of having to advocate against her client's interests.

Others respond that mandatory disclosure should not be rejected because it requires honest behavior from parties. An obligation to disclose serves the public interest of efficiently and accurately resolving civil disputes.

Criticisms of Mandatory Disclosure

Not every litigator is a fan of disclosure-based discovery. Some make the following criticisms.

Litigants are naturally tempted to hide evidence they think will hurt their case. By severely restricting the use of the traditional discovery tools, the new rules make it harder to detect such cheating, and the punishment for parties who are caught "hiding the ball" is neither certain enough nor severe enough to have much deterrent effect. In short, mandatory disclosure rules—or, more accurately, the limitations on traditional discovery that accompany them—make the outcome of litigation overly dependent on the ethics and honesty of one's opponents.

Mandatory disclosure rules also have put lawyers in the uncomfortable position of having to, in effect, build an opponent's case for him. Disclosure rules may require a diligent lawyer to reveal evidence that will lead to new claims or defenses that a lazy opponent would otherwise never have generated. This seems unfair to the diligent lawyer's client, who is paying for work that undercuts his or her own case.

Finally, disclosure rules undermine the attorney-client privilege. If a client discusses some damaging bit of evidence with his or her lawyer, the lawyer has no choice but to reveal it to the opposing party under the disclosure rules. A client who understands the system will be motivated not to tell his or her lawyer about "bad" evidence.

Putting It Into Practice 5.3:

Which do you think is the more equitable system: mandatory disclosure or the traditional system? Why?

BONUS POINTERS:

REPORT CARD ON MANDATORY DISCLOSURE

A preliminary evaluation of the mandatory disclosure rules adopted by some of the federal courts indicates that the new rules have had little impact on federal civil litigation. So concludes a report issued by the American Bar Association's Subcommittee on Mandatory Prediscovery Disclosure Rules. The subcommittee conducted its survey by randomly mailing questionnaires to approximately one-half of the Section of Litigation's 60,000 members and sending a separate mailing to every judge and magistrate judge in each federal court district. Of those responding, approximately 75 percent said that the mandatory disclosure rules should not be continued. Furthermore, the survey provided no evidence that the new discovery rules have decreased discovery costs, delays, or conflict between opposing attorneys. But it also showed that the effects have not been as negative as the critics predicted. The sub-

pretrial conference (known as a *scheduling conference* in many jurisdictions) conference at which the judge discusses the case with the attorneys and issues a scheduling order, specifying, at least in a general way, what motions will be filed, what discovery will be taken, and setting firm deadlines for the completion of each task

committee acknowledged that no definite conclusions could be drawn from this cursory study, conducted only one year after the implementation of the new rules.

Studies conducted by the Rand Corporation and the Federal Judicial Center have drawn similar conclusions. Both concluded that mandatory disclosure has done no harm, but that it has had little impact on discovery abuse. They also confirmed what other researchers have suggested: discovery abuse usually occurs in complex, high-stakes lawsuits and not in small and medium-sized cases, where mandatory disclosure has had little effect. (Kathleen Blaner et al., *Federal Discovery: Crown Jewel or Curse?*, 24 LITTIG. 8 (1998)).

NET NEWS

To read more about the RAND evaluation of mandatory disclosure in the federal courts, go to *www.rand.org/publications/MR/MR941*.

When Ernesto got off the phone, John picked up the thread of their meeting.

"Setting aside for the moment the issue with Mike, I think we should go ahead and set up a tentative deposition schedule." John liked to orchestrate the discovery process as best he could although he was fully aware that only so much could be planned.

"Let's be real, John. You know we're never going to get this many attorneys to agree to our proposed schedule. I say we go straight to the court, don't pass "Go," don't collect $200, and set up a **pretrial conference.** That way we can present our plan to the judge, get his approval, and avoid spinning our wheels with these other attorneys."

"Certainly more efficient," agreed John, "but not very honoring of our colleagues, who may actually have previous commitments that make it impossible for them to attend depositions at the times we've scheduled. Perhaps you consider professional courtesy a secondary concern, but I like to handle things as much as I can without getting the judges involved. I'd prefer to send out a proposed deposition schedule to all of the attorneys, let them give their input, and not go to the judge unless we reach an impasse."

"You're our fearless leader, so never let it be said I stood in your way." Ernesto wondered, somewhat bitterly, why they called themselves a "team" when it seemed more like a monarchy to him.

OVERVIEW OF DEPOSITIONS

deponent witness being deposed

The mainstay of witness discovery is the deposition. A deposition is a proceeding in which the attorneys asks questions and the witness, referred to as the **deponent,** answers them.

Usually, a deposition is conducted at the office of one of the attorneys. The witness is placed under oath, usually by a court reporter who is authorized to administer oaths. The judge is not present. The attorneys' questions and the deponent's answers are recorded, either electronically or in shorthand by a court reporter. Later, the court reporter uses the recording or shorthand notes to produce a written **transcript** of the testimony—that is, a typed or printed booklet in which the questions and answers are reproduced, word for word. The attorney who scheduled the deposition questions the witness first; then the opposing attorney may take a turn, if desired.

transcript typed or printed booklet in which the questions and answers are reproduced, word for word

Advantages of Depositions Over Written Discovery

Why take a deposition? Depositions can be used for a number of important purposes that cannot be achieved with written discovery.

1. Interrogatories, document requests, requests for admissions, and disclosure statements are certainly useful, but they fall short in one

important respect: they do not allow attorneys to evaluate how witnesses will perform while actually testifying. Interrogatories help determine the general shape of a witness's testimony, but the impact that the witness has on the jury depends greatly on the witness's demeanor, manner of speech, body language, and a host of other intangible factors that can never be assessed without actually seeing the witness in action.

2. Depositions can be used to take discovery from non-party witnesses, whereas interrogatories can usually be directed only to parties.

3. If a witness gives an evasive answer in a deposition, the attorney can immediately follow up with more questions.

4. The attorney can follow the thread of the witness's story wherever it may lead by asking additional questions.

5. The deposition transcript is a particularly effective tool for cross-examination at trial because it reflects the witness's own words. If the witness gives an answer at trial that contradicts the answer given to the same question in the deposition, the attorney can read the witness's earlier answer from the deposition transcript and show the jury that the witness is not being truthful.

6. Depositions can be used as a substitute for trial testimony in situations where the witness cannot testify in person. For example, a witness may be dying and not expected to be available when the trial takes place, or may be at some distant location. The witness's deposition can be read (or, in an increasing number of courts, a video recording of the deposition can be shown) at trial as a substitute for live testimony.

Putting It Into Practice 5.4:

Why will John probably want to depose Ms. Sinclair, the vice-principal's secretary? Why might he want to depose one of the students who witnessed the shooting but who is planning to move out of state when he graduates in a few months? What will John be assessing when he deposes the Hendershott boy accused of shooting Mike?

Figure 5-2
Depositions

DEPOSITIONS
Goals of Depositions

Obtain information
Pin down witness's story
Create a usable transcript
Develop idea of how to handle witness at trial
Lay groundwork for cross-examination at trial

Advantages of Depositions

Assess how witness will come across at trial
Discover information from non-parties
Can follow up on evasive answers
Can follow up thread of witness's story
Can use deposition testimony during cross-examination at trial
Can use deposition testimony as substitute for trial testimony

Goals of a Deposition

The goals to be achieved through deposition discovery are several.

◆ To obtain information. One of the main purposes of a deposition is to find out what facts the witness can provide, and to get leads to other sources of information.

◆ To pin down the witness's story. An attorney's questions need to cover the subject matter thoroughly, excluding all possible alternate versions of the facts, so that the witness has no room to tell a different story at trial.

◆ To create a useable transcript. This means avoiding procedural errors that would render the deposition or the transcript invalid. It also means making sure that the deposition covers the right questions and answers, asked in the right way.

◆ To develop a clear idea of how to handle the witness at trial. What is the witness's personality like? Are there particular kinds of questions with which he has trouble? Is he easily led? Prone to blurt out poorly thought-out answers? Easily provoked to anger?

◆ To lay the groundwork for cross-examination at trial. A deposition is a perfect place to get a witness to commit to essential facts that will prevent him from deviating from the story the attorney wants told at trial.

One thing to keep in mind is that ammunition that could better be saved for trial should not be used at a deposition. No judge or jury is present at a deposition. So although it may feel good to "score points" at a deposition and demonstrate that a witness is lying, doing so merely gives that person plenty of time to think up a better story before trial.

A deposition is not, of course, the only tool available for accomplishing these goals. The cost of taking a deposition can be prohibitive, especially in small cases. In fact, many litigators depose a witness only if the witness is adverse or uncooperative, or if the witness might not be able to attend the trial.

Putting It Into Practice 5.5:

Considering the goals of depositions, do you think attorneys should write out all of their questions in advance?

"Although we may not be able to depose everyone in the order we'd like, we still need to decide whom we want to depose. I think we can safely assume we need to depose all the parties and their employees. Who else?" began John.

"Do we need to depose the kids who witnessed the shooting?" asked Martha.

"Normally, I would say yes, but in this case, I'm not sure they have much to tell us. The perpetrators were all wearing masks so they can't identify them and most of them were down on the ground and covering their heads when Mike was shot," responded John.

"I'd say we'd be better off waiting to depose them until after we've deposed the three boys involved in the shooting, especially the Hendershott kid," agreed Ernesto. "Him I think we should depose as soon as possible. Get him while he still wants to talk."

"Agreed. We also need to depose the school secretary that Martha talked to as soon as we can, even though we have a witness statement from her. I'd like to see if we can get any more information from her. And we need to find out right away what the vice-principal's position is going to be," John cautioned.

"We need to think about whether we want to depose all of the medical personnel who have treated Mike and the officers involved in the investigation of his case," suggested Ernesto.

"Well, to begin with, we'll need to get permission of the court to depose them because most of the them aren't going to be called as expert witnesses," said John, thinking out loud.

"May I ask why we'd need court permission?" interjected Martha hesitantly.

"Certainly. The rules in Arizona don't limit the number of depositions you can take, but they allow depositions only of certain people, such as parties and expert witnesses. All other depos have to be approved by the court. Of course, in this case, I'm sure we'd have no trouble getting the judge to go along with deposing these folks. I'm just not sure we need to spend our money deposing them. We've interviewed all of them, and what they know certainly supports our position, so I don't think we'd be in for any surprises. And we know that the other parties are going to be chomping at the bit to depose them."

"I think you're right, John. Why don't we hold off with them unless it looks like we're going to need to preserve their testimony for trial," concurred Ernesto. "One group of people we haven't mentioned are the **custodians of the records** for the school and CODA. I think we should depose them early on."

custodian of the records
someone in an organization who knows about its filing system and records. The custodian is often deposed so that the attorney can find out how the entity keeps its records. Also, many records today are kept electronically rather than on paper, so trying to guess what records a company has is foolhardy.

◆ **LOCAL LINKS** ◆

Ask your instructor if there are any limits in your jurisdiction as to the number of depositions you can take or whom you can depose.

ARRANGING DEPOSITIONS

Before depositions can be arranged, the attorneys must determine which witnesses need to be deposed and when and where the depositions will take place. This seemingly easy task is more complicated than it appears. Some participants prefer not to be deposed and will do everything possible to resist and delay. The order in which depositions are taken and the timing of depositions in relation to other discovery can give one side an advantage over the other. Typically, each side likes to depose the other side's witnesses first to find out exactly what its opponent's witnesses will say and get their stories pinned down on the record before having its own witnesses testify.

The current federal rules place some limits on the freedom of attorneys to schedule depositions and give judges a more active role in the management of deposition discovery. For example, each side may schedule up to 10 witnesses without court permission. (All the plaintiffs are considered one side and all the defendants the other.) To depose additional witnesses, a party has to file a motion and get the court's permission. Depositions cannot be taken after the cutoff date specified in the scheduling order, unless the judge gives permission. But absent an order by the judge to depose witnesses in a particular sequence, depositions can be taken in any order. Some state court rules impose much stricter limitations on the parties' freedom to take depositions, and call for correspondingly greater involvement by the judge in deposition scheduling.

If the number of depositions that can be taken is limited, attorneys often begin by preparing a list of every potential witness that could testify. Then they select the best names from the list, focusing on what facts need to be proved, ranking each potential witness in order of importance. The most difficult aspect of this process is assigning priorities and deciding which witnesses are the most important to depose. Certain categories of witnesses will almost always be deposed unless the amount of money at stake in the lawsuit is too small to justify the expense. These include the opposing parties, any expert witnesses designated to testify for the opposing party, eyewitnesses, individuals directly involved in a disputed transaction, and any other witnesses considered key to the case.

Depositions are usually conducted in the law office of the attorney requesting the deposition to create an atmosphere of formality and control. Under these conditions, witnesses are more likely to take the proceeding seriously and opposing counsel finds it more difficult to distract the attorney conducting the deposition.

For information about arranging out-of-town depositions, go to *www.paralegals.org/reporter*, click on "Winter 1995," and go to "Setting the Out-of-Town Deposition."

There are a few exceptions, however. If an attorney is deposing his opponent's star medical expert, for example—for whose time he will be billed at rates sometimes in excess of $1000 per hour—the attorney would rather not pay for the witness to sit around in traffic. And attorneys may have no choice but to travel to depose out-of-town witnesses; under the federal rules, attorneys cannot force a witness to travel more than 100 miles to attend a deposition.

The opposing party is often deposed as early as possible. This allows the attorney to find out exactly what the opponent is claiming and make her go on the record with as much factual detail as possible. Document-gathering depositions and custodian of records' depositions are also taken early in the case to build a full set of documents as early as possible for use as a basis for other factual development. Expert witness depositions are usually left for later in the discovery cycle because expert witnesses typically offer opinions based on the facts they are given, and those facts often emerge, in part, from depositions of other witnesses. In the end, timing and sequence of depositions is a matter of judgment, usually involving choices between imperfect alternatives.

Putting It Into Practice 5.6:

In the case involving Molly Running Deer and Stuart Thames, whom would you want to depose if you represented Mr. Thames and in what order would you probably depose them?

"We're going to need to depose the experts any of the parties intend to call. But, of course, we don't need to think about that until we get their disclosure statements," indicated John.

"Do we need to get court permission to depose them?" inquired Martha, trying to get all of the rules straight in her mind.

"No. In Arizona, the rules automatically permit the deposition of all experts," answered John.

EXPERT WITNESSES

Most of the witnesses who testify in a trial are "lay" witnesses—people who describe an event they themselves observed and who are not allowed to testify regarding their opinions. Another category of witnesses—expert witnesses—is becoming more important as society becomes increasingly dominated by complex technologies. Expert witnesses are employed to give opinions on specialized subjects that ordinary jurors might not be able to grasp on their own. Expert witnesses are those people who have training and experience in some specialized field involved in the suit, often some branch of medicine. The following kinds of experts are commonly used.

criminalists forensic scientist who analyzes evidence and testifies regarding the results of that analysis

forensic used in court

◆ **criminalists** (forensic scientists, usually chemists) who analyze physical evidence and testify regarding the results of their analysis
◆ **forensic** experts (psychiatrists, medical doctors, engineers, dentists, and anthropologists) who have expertise in a specific field and who offer that expertise in the courtroom

To read more about obtaining and using expert witnesses, go to *www.lectlaw.com* and click on "The Library's Rotunda," "Legal Professional's Lounge," and "Lawyers." Look for the article entitled "Who, What, Where, Why and How of Best Using Experts."

- ◆ vocational consultants, who testify about the vocational prospects of those who have been injured
- ◆ economic and financial consultants, who testify regarding the economic ramifications of injury

Usually, each party locates, hires, and pays his own expert witnesses. Although expert witnesses are theoretically impartial in their opinions, lawyers naturally try to find experts whose "impartial" opinions will most help their cases. Thus there is often a certain element of advocacy in expert testimony.

Predictably, each party will want to find out, well before trial, who the opposing party's experts are, what their opinions are, and how those opinions were formed. Because expert testimony represents a substantial investment of work and money by the party who hires the expert, the discovery of experts has special limitations.

Putting It Into Practice 5.7:

What experts do you anticipate the school district will use in Mike's case?

Once they had reached agreements with the other attorneys about scheduling dates for the upcoming depositions, John asked Martha to prepare **deposition notices.** Martha was relieved to have finally been given an assignment that she was accustomed to doing.

deposition notices
notification of a pending
deposition

NOTICING DEPOSITIONS

Under the federal rules, a party who wants to take a deposition must give reasonable notice in writing to every other party in the case. The purpose of this notice is to let the other litigants know about the deposition so that they can attend, participate, and make objections. Notices of deposition are usually one-page printed or word processor forms, containing blanks in which the paralegal fills in the name and address of the witness and the date, time, and place of the deposition. A copy of the notice of deposition must be served on the attorney for each other party, which is usually done by mailing or hand-delivering a copy to each attorney's office. (See Figure 5.3 for a sample notice of deposition.)

The federal rules also require attorneys to state in the notice how the testimony will be recorded. Most often, depositions are recorded stenographically by a court reporter using a shorthand machine. The machine operates in a manner similar to a typewriter, but it "types" in a special shorthand code onto a paper strip and/or computer disk. Its keys are designed for fast input, so that an experienced court reporter can take down testimony faster than a witness can talk. The court reporter later uses a computerized transcription device to "read" the shorthand code and produce a printed booklet containing a word-for-word transcript of everything said at the deposition. It is up to the party noticing the deposition to arrange for a court

Figure 5-3
Notice of Deposition

WHITE & TREADWELL
John Morgan, Esq., SBN 00123
Ernesto Esparanza, Esq. SBN 012345
2020 North Central Avenue, Suite 3200
Phoenix, Arizona 85005
(602) 555-1234
Attorneys for plaintiff Michael Johnson

IN THE SUPERIOR COURT OF MARICOPA COUNTY
PHOENIX, ARIZONA

Michael Johnson, a single man,	)
	)
	) NO. CV99-01456 PHX JL
Plaintiff,	)
	) NOTICE OF DEPOSITION
vs.	)
	)
Daniel Hendershott, a single man, et. al.	)
	)
	)
Defendants.	)

Notice is hereby given pursuant to Rule 30, Arizona Rules of Civil Procedure, that the deposition upon oral examination of the person whose name and address appear below will be taken at date, time and place indicated.

Name Of Deponent: Jordan Washington, a football coach for Washington High School, concerning the following matters:
Communications with or from Michael Johnson, from April—May, 2000; performance of Michael Johnson.on football team.

Address Of Deponent: 6366 N. 76th St.
Scottsdale, AZ

Date And Time: 9:00 a.m., February 14, 2001

Location: Law Offices of White & Treadwell
2020 North Central Avenue, Suite 3200
Phoenix, Arizona 85005

A subpoena duces tecum is being served on the person to be examined. A copy of the designation of the materials to be produced as set forth in the subpoena is attached hereto.

DATED this 21st day of January, 2001.

WHITE & TREADWELL

_____
John Morgan
Attorneys for plaintiff Michael Johnson

CERTIFICATE OF SERVICE
The undersigned certifies that the foregoing was served in accordance with the requirements of Rule 5, ARCP, by mailing / hand-delivering a copy thereof this 21st day of January, 2001 to:

Barbara Tsosie, Esq.
SIMON & PORTER
1000 North Central Avenue, Suite 2800
Phoenix, Arizona 85004

Figure 5-3
Notice of Deposition (continued)

Dana Ferraror, Esq.
500 Main Street
Scottsdale, Arizona
Attorney for defendant Hendershott

William Yakamura, Esq.
59 Plain Street
Durango, Colorado 95660
Attorney for defendant CODA, Inc.

_____ [signature goes here]

reporter to be present. If a law firm has an ongoing relationship with a firm of court reporters, this is done by sending a copy of the notice of deposition to the court reporter firm.

Court reporter fees comprise a significant part of the cost of deposition discovery. The party noticing the deposition pays for the court reporter's services, and for the original transcript to be filed with the court (no charge in federal court). Court reporters typically bill at a fixed rate per page of transcript. At this writing, customary West Coast metropolitan area court reporter fees are upwards of $5.00 per double-spaced typed page. A typical two- or three-hour deposition can easily run well in excess of 100 pages.

◆ **LOCAL LINKS** ◆
What are typical court reporter fees in your jurisdiction?

Putting It Into Practice 5.8:

What should Martha anticipate doing after John develops a deposition schedule?

BONUS POINTERS:

DEPOSITIONS IN THE ELECTRONIC AGE

You may be wondering why the practice of taking down deposition testimony in shorthand continues in an age of tape recorders, video cameras, and even computers with voice-recognition capabilities. In fact, the current federal rules allow attorneys to choose between "sound, sound-and-visual, or stenographic" recording. Why not get out a video camera, save hundreds of dollars, and, as a bonus, finish up with a recording that reflects not just the words spoken but also gestures, tone of voice, and body language?

Court reporters are unlikely to be rendered extinct by video cameras for several reasons. One is that a deposition must be taken in the presence of someone authorized to administer an oath and court reporters are so authorized. Beyond that, however, stenographic recordings have certain advantages over video. Experienced court reporters are able to distinguish and correctly transcribe words under conditions that would render an electronic recording unintelligible, such as when the witness is mumbling or facing away from the microphone, or when two people speak at the same time. And video recordings record everything, warts and all. If the attorney doing the questioning seems to be struggling, pausing frequently, or saying "umm" a lot, the resulting video may be rather unflattering.

As a practical matter, even when using sound or video recording to take a deposition, most attorneys hire a court reporter to operate the recording equipment. Most court reporting firms now offer video recording as an option. Better to pay a court reporter and be sure of a usable record than to save a few dollars and risk losing some crucial bit of testimony because someone forgot to turn over the tape! Also, even if the deposition is recorded electronically, a written transcript will still be needed to work from and to use in the courtroom, and the court reporter hired to make the recording can also make a transcript.

To read about the advantages of videotaping depositions, go to *www.bizjournals.com/atlanta/stories/1998/06/22/focus19.html.*

"Another thing, while I'm thinking about it, Martha. I think we need to warn Mike about probable upcoming I.M.E.s. Could you please explain the process to him and why it's important that he cooperate? Then let him know as soon as we get notice of a requested I.M.E." John knew that he would be very preoccupied with all the details of discovery in the near future and wanted to make sure that Mike did not get lost in the whirlwind of activity.

INDEPENDENT MEDICAL EXAMINATION (I.M.E.)

independent medical examination (I.M.E.) examination of a party by doctors selected by the opposing party

notice of independent medical examination court paper directing the person to be examined to appear at a specified doctor's office at a designated date and time

Lawsuits often involve physical injuries, and the amount of money to be won or lost depends on how severe and how permanent the injuries are. Proof usually requires testimony by doctors. For example, Mike's doctors will be asked to testify about Mike's injuries—how he was treated, how much the treatment cost, whether any future treatment will be needed—and to give an opinion about whether any impairment is permanent.

Naturally, the other parties' lawyers will not take Mike's doctors' word for these things. They will want doctors of their own choosing to examine Mike and give their opinion. The federal rules allow them to do this by filing and serving a **notice of independent medical examination** (I.M.E.). An I.M.E. can be conducted on a party whose medical condition is a legitimate issue in the suit. This notice, which is usually a single page court paper, simply instructs the person to be examined to appear at the specified doctor's office at the date and time stated. See Figure 5-4 for a sample notice of independent medical examination.

John Also Knew That Being Painstakingly Thorough Is What Had Helped Him Win Cases In the Past and Would Likely Help Them Prevail in a Case Such as This One, in Which So Many Details Needed to Be Nailed Down.

"Ernesto, you and I need to prepare a list of all the documents we anticipate requesting," suggested John.

"Okay, but we could just wait until we receive their disclosure statements. Then we could build on the list of documents they provide," countered Ernesto.

"I'd rather put some thought into it before that. If we rely on their list, we'll start thinking along their lines rather than thinking this case through independently. It's nice that the mandatory disclosure rules require parties to be so forthcoming, but I think the traditional approach required lawyers to think through their cases more fully without relying on the assistance of their opponents. Why don't you give it some thought in reference to CODA at least and I'll do the same for the school and the district." John realized that Ernesto's ego was taking a bruising in having to pander to what he knew Ernesto thought were out-dated strategies. But John also knew that being painstakingly thorough is what had helped him win cases in the past and would likely help them prevail in a case such as this one, in which so many details needed to be nailed down.

"I'll give it my best shot," conceded Ernesto, having finally concluded that they were going to approach this case John's way.

"Great. Then when we've both arrived at our lists and identified documents that the other parties haven't disclosed, I'd like you to prepare the requests for production. I probably don't need to remind you of this, Martha, but be sure to docket when those responses are due so none of them gets by us without our noticing. When we receive any documents, I'd like all of us to review them so we're all familiar with every document." A firm believer that cases could be won or lost on a sentence or two in a document, John relied on his paralegals to review all documents received, but familiarized himself with them as well.

Figure 5-4
Notice of I.M.E.

SIMON & PORTER
Barbara Tsosie, Esq.
1000 North Central Avenue, Suite 2800
Phoenix, Arizona 85004
(602) 555-6789
Attorneys for defendant Washington High School District

IN THE SUPERIOR COURT
MARICOPA COUNTY, ARIZONA

Michael Johnson, a single man,	)	
	)	
	)	NO. CV99-01456 PHX JL
Plaintiff,	)	
	)	NOTICE OF INDEPENDENT
vs.	)	MEDICAL EXAMINATION
	)	OF PLAINTIFF
DANIEL HENDERSHOTT, ALAN	)	
HOUSE, and MAX EVANS; CODA,	)	
INC., a Delaware corporation;	)	
WASHINGTON HIGH SCHOOL	)	
DISTRICT	)	
	)	
Defendants.	)	

Notice is hereby given pursuant to Rule 35, Arizona Rules of Civil Procedure, that independent medical examination of the plaintiff, Michael Johnson, will be taken at date, time and place indicated.

Name Of Person to be Examined   Plaintiff Michael Johnson

Examiner   Dr. Harold Smith

Date And Time: 10:00 a.m., March 24, 2001

Location: Southwest Medical Group
2022 North 3rd Street, Suite 29
Phoenix, Arizona 85004

DATED this 21st day of January, 2001.

SIMON & PORTER

_____
Barbara Tsosie
Attorneys for defendant
Washington High School District.

CERTIFICATE OF SERVICE

The undersigned certifies that the foregoing was served in accordance with the requirements of Rule 5, ARCP, by mailing / hand-delivering a copy thereof this 21st day of June, 2001 to:

John Morgan, Esq.   Dana Ferraro, Esq.
WHITE & TREADWELL   500 Main Street
2020 North Central Avenue, Suite 3200   Scottsdale, Arizona
Phoenix, Arizona 85005   Attorney for defendant Hendershott
Attorneys for plaintiff Michael Johnson

William Yakamura, Esq.
59 Plain Street
Durango, Colorado 95660
Attorney for defendant CODA, Inc.

_____
    [signature goes here]

GOALS OF DOCUMENT DISCOVERY

The goal of document discovery is to assemble a complete set containing every single piece of paper that could conceivably bear on the case, whether the information is helpful or harmful. "Good" documents are needed as evidence and "bad" documents are necessary so they can be countered when they are produced by the other side. But the goal goes far beyond merely gathering documents to use as evidence. In fact, many of the documents will never see the light of day in a courtroom. Some of them will not be admissible at trial because the concept of "relevance" for discovery purposes is far broader than "relevance" under the applicable evidentiary rules. The main purpose of gathering documents is to provide a body of data that can be used to track down other evidence. Every document was written by someone—someone who is a potential witness, if he knows something about the facts at issue. Documents often refer to other documents. Even if the document at hand is not helpful, the one it refers to may be.

Often, another goal of document discovery is to establish that given documents do not exist. If a particular category of documents is properly requested from a defendant, and none are produced, then for practical purposes, the requesting party has proved that the defendant does not have any documents of the type requested. Framing document requests clearly and concisely is important so that opposing parties do not have room to "wiggle out" by later claiming that the request was ambiguous.

In reality, however, opponents are not about to willingly turn over documents that are likely to cement their undoing. Resistance is a given. Additionally, in this age of record proliferation, being confronted with rooms full of potentially relevant documents and computer disks full of data is not unusual in complex cases. Analyzing every page may not be cost-effective. Finally, the time allowed by the court for completing discovery is limited. Discovery consists of chasing the facts from lead to lead, and the process must end somewhere. Although the goal is to find all the information that exists, attorneys usually settle for finding enough to prove their case.

Putting It Into Practice 5.9:

Marianne, Martha's fellow student, is reviewing documents in a contract dispute. She quickly scans each document, but discards it if she does not immediately recognize it as providing the information she is seeking. What might she be missing by this cursory review?

DOCUMENT DISCOVERY IN A NUTSHELL

Document discovery begins with a very broad request for production of documents on each opponent. (In courts requiring disclosure statements, this step is unnecessary; each party simply waits for its opponent's initial disclosure package.) Each document and category of documents that could conceivably be useful is requested. Eventually, a written response is received, stating which items are being provided and which are being objected to, accompanied by a stack of papers. In disclosure-based discovery courts, this stack of papers accompanies the opposing party's initial disclosure statement.

Invariably, the pile of papers contains some, but not all, of the documents to which the party is entitled. All of the disclosed papers must be read and analyzed. The information gained from this analysis along with information from other sources, such as deposition testimony, answers to interrogatories, and informal interviews of witnesses, will doubtless point to other documents or categories of documents previously unheard of. As a result, new requests and subpoenas must be sent out asking for additions to the list.

NET NEWS

To learn about the mechanics of organizing documents in the litigation process, go to *www.paralegals.org*, click on "Spring 1988," and then on "Establishing a Document Trail."

Meanwhile, steps must be taken to pursue any documents missing from the responses (or disclosure packages) that were received. First, a letter is sent to opposing counsel politely asking for the missing items; if they are not promptly forthcoming, a motion asking the court to order the party to produce them is filed. Unfortunately, chasing after documents is a routine part of document discovery.

As the documents flow in, they must be organized using a suitable filing and indexing system. In small cases, this can be done by hand; in big-document cases, a computerized litigation support data base is almost certainly necessary. No matter what system is used, anyone accessing the file must be able to ascertain where each document came from, how it was obtained, where the original is, and who might be called as a witness to testify that it is authentic. In all but the smallest cases, some way of indexing documents by subject must be devised so that important papers can be located quickly.

After receiving the second or third set of documents and subpoenaed records from other sources, the attorney and paralegal should be well on their way to assembling a complete set of documents. After analyzing them, they will indubitably discover still more gaps and need to continue sending out requests for production, issuing subpoenas, and filing motions, until either they get everything they need or the discovery cutoff date arrives—a date set by the court (or procedural rules) after which no further discovery is permitted.

Each move in this basic plan should be made as early as reasonably possible. A party who is resisting disclosure will often try to stall until the cutoff arrives; therefore, a party must react immediately when an opposing party tries to get away with an incomplete response. Moreover, documents often reveal new evidence and time is needed to locate and follow up on those new facts.

> ◆ **LOCAL LINKS** ◆
> What kind of document discovery process does your instructor recommend?

Putting It Into Practice 5.10:

Why should litigation paralegals be detail-oriented?

Figure 5-5
Document Discovery

DOCUMENT DISCOVERY

Goals

Obtain every document bearing on the case
Find other evidence
Establish that documents do not exist
Establish facts that prove case

Process

Begin with broad request for every conceivable document
Read and analyze documents
File and index documents received
Send out new requests asking for additional documents
Obtain documents not received as result of initial request

THE TOOLS OF DOCUMENT DISCOVERY

In general, to obtain documents from someone who is a party to the lawsuit, a "Request for Production of Documents" is used. This request is prepared in the form of a court paper, with the usual caption and formal parts. The body of the request lists the documents being requested. In addition to producing the requested documents, a party who receives a request for production must also file and serve a written response. Figure 5-6 shows an example of a request for production of documents.

To obtain documents from someone who is not a party to the lawsuit, a subpoena is used. A subpoena is the modern descendant of what was, at common law, a formal court order commanding a witness to appear and testify. Under traditional subpoena practice (and even today in some state courts), there were two types of subpoenas: *subpoenas ad testificandum,* ordering a witness to appear at a specified time and place to give testimony; and *subpoenas duces tecum* (Latin for "bring with you"), ordering a witness to appear and also bring specified documents or items to be examined.

Modern courts have streamlined subpoena procedures considerably over the years in an effort to eliminate unnecessary burden on the clerk's office. Originally, subpoenas had to be signed by judges; all modern courts long ago abandoned that time-wasting practice in favor of authorizing the clerk of the court to issue subpoenas. In many courts, the clerks eventually began issuing stacks of subpoenas to attorneys in blank—already stamped, sealed, and ready for the attorney to fill in the name of the witness and other information, and thus eliminating the burden on the clerk's office of having to issue subpoenas one at a time. Finally, in 1991, the federal courts authorized attorneys to sign subpoenas, thereby taking the clerk's office completely out of the loop. Under the federal rules, a subpoena signed by an attorney has the force and effect of a court order.

◆ **LOCAL LINKS** ◆

Who has the authority in your jurisdiction to issue subpoenas?

Putting It Into Practice 5.11:

What will Martha need to do to get records from a security company hired by the school?

"One last thing, Ernesto. When the time is right, I'd like you to prepare whatever interrogatories and requests for admission you deem appropriate for CODA and I'll do the same for the school district. Martha, I'd like you to assist both of us. The more heads, the better," indicated John.

"And I suppose you want us to get going on those right away as well. No sense relying on our opponents for ideas." Ernesto's sarcasm was not lost on John, but he ignored it.

"I'll let you be the judge of when to start on them. Keeping in mind that we are limited to 25 interrogatories to each party without a stipulation or court order, we need to be somewhat judicious in how we select to use them. We'll no doubt have a better idea of the gaps we need to fill in after we've seen the defendants' disclosure statements and wrapped up some of our depos. On the other hand, there's probably some information we know we're going to need. For example, I think we should try to get some admissions from CODA about their philosophy if we possibly can. At any rate, Ernesto, I trust you've had enough litigation experience to organize this."

Inwardly, Ernesto shook his head. John was a paradox to him. One moment he was directing his every move and the next he was bowing to his expertise. "I don't think I'll ever understand the old man," Ernesto thought to himself.

Figure 5-6
Request for Production of Documents

WHITE & TREADWELL
John Morgan, Esq., SBN 00123
Ernesto Esparanza, Esq. SBN 012345
2020 North Central Avenue, Suite 3200
Phoenix, Arizona 85005
(602) 555-1234
Attorneys for plaintiff Michael Johnson

IN THE SUPERIOR COURT OF MARICOPA COUNTY
PHOENIX, ARIZONA

Michael Johnson, a single man, Plaintiff, vs. Daniel Hendershott, Max Evans, and Alan House, all single men; CODA, Inc.,a foreign corporation; Washington High School District. Defendants.	NO. _____ Plaintiff's Request for Production of Documents to Washington High School District

Pursuant to ARCP Rule 34 Plaintiff requests that Defendant Washington High School District produce the documents and things listed herein for inspection and copying at 10:00 a.m. on June 12, 2001 at the law offices of White & Treadwell, 2020 North Central Avenue, Suite 3200, Phoenix, Arizona 85005.

INSTRUCTIONS AND DEFINITIONS

1. "Document" means and includes writings, letters, memoranda, contracts, agreements, conveyances, drawings, graphs, charts, photographs, computer printouts, electronic mail messages, phone records, computer disks and/or disk files, audio, video, or data tape recordings, and any other data compilations from which information can be obtained.
2. You are required to produce all documents of the kinds described herein that are in your possession or control, including without limitation all documents that are now or at any time during the pendency of this lawsuit in your own possession or that of your attorneys, partners, officers, employees, agents, or other representatives or which you have the power or ability to obtain from others
3. In the event that you claim that any document requested herein is not subject to production by reason of any privilege, you are required to state the basis for your claim of privilege in your written response hereto, which statement shall include a description stating, for each and every document as to which you claim privilege, the general nature or type of document, the name of the author of the document, the date of the document, the specific privilege claimed, and the legal and factual basis for the claim of privilege as to that document.
4. "Incident" shall refer to the activity of May 5, 2000 out of which Plaintiff's complaint arises.

DOCUMENTS TO BE PRODUCED

1. Any and all correspondence, memoranda, notes, telephone records, calendar entries, and the like, in any way relating to the incident of May 5, 2000 involving Plaintiff.
......
......
6. Copies of any and all procedures, policies, notes, memoranda, correspondence, and the like providing instructions, recommendations, cautionary advise or similar information regarding Defendant's processing , or how it should process, any telephonic or other communicated threat of violence on or near its facilities.

DATED this 2nd day of May, 2001.

WHITE & TREADWELL

_____
by John Morgan
Attorneys for Plaintiff

OVERVIEW OF WRITTEN DISCOVERY

Strategically, written discovery serves a fundamentally different purpose than do depositions. Answers to interrogatories and responses to requests for admissions are not very well suited for ferreting out the proof needed to establish the elements of a case. Here are a few of the disadvantages of written discovery.

proponent party preparing interrogatories

- ◆ Answers to interrogatories and responses to requests for admissions are invariably written by that party's lawyer, not by the opposing party herself (although, theoretically, they come from the opposing party). Therefore, they are usually carefully drafted to give away as little as possible.
- ◆ The answering party has at least 30 days to think about the questions and hone the answers. The responses are thoroughly edited.
- ◆ Attorneys have no immediate opportunity to follow up evasive or ambiguous answers with additional questions, as they do in a deposition.
- ◆ Interrogatories may reveal information about the strengths and weaknesses of the case of the **proponent** (party preparing the interrogatories).
- ◆ To answer interrogatories and requests for admissions, the opposing attorney has to research issues and think about the claims and defenses involved in the case. In effect, one's opponent is prodded into action when it might be preferable to let him drift along in a state of complacency.

Although written discovery is very unlikely to pry loose any "smoking guns," it does serve several important uses. These uses fall into four general categories.

- ◆ Getting background facts. Names, addresses, locations of documents, and similar information can be obtained.
- ◆ Placing limits on an opponent's case. Open-ended questions can be used asking an opponent to disclose all evidence that he has on a given issue. Here, opposing counsel's natural tendency to disclose as little as possible works in the proponent's favor: within reasonable limits, evidence not disclosed in response to a proper interrogatory will not be allowed at trial.

◆ **LOCAL LINKS** ◆

How do attorneys in your area generally use interrogatories? What limits, if any, on the use of interrogatories are imposed in your jurisdiction?

- ◆ Pinning down known facts. Knowing a fact and being able to prove it are two different things. Interrogatories and requests for admission provide a simple and inexpensive way of establishing non-controversial details by getting an opponent to admit them.
- ◆ Getting information about the opponent's theories and actions.

Figure 5-7
Advantages and Disadvantages of Written Discovery

ADVANTAGES AND DISADVANTAGES OF WRITTEN DISCOVERY

Advantages of Written Discovery
Get background facts
Place limits on opponent's case
Pin down known facts
Get information about opponent's theories and actions

DISADVANTAGES OF WRITTEN DISCOVERY

Answers are written by lawyer rather than the party
Answering party has time to think about answers
Cannot follow up on ambiguous or evasive answers
Interrogatories may reveal information about proponent's case
May prod opponent into action

▓▓▓   *Putting It Into Practice 5.12:*

Why might John prefer to use interrogatories and requests for admission before using a deposition to get CODA to admit its philosophy regarding the advocacy of violence?

REQUESTS FOR ADMISSION

Why would parties ever want to help out an opposing party by admitting facts? Why not refuse to admit anything and force opponents to prove each and every detail of their case? Because a party that refuses to admit facts that are not really in dispute may find itself paying for its lack of cooperation. Under the federal rules, if a party refuses its opponent's request for admission of a fact, and the judge later determines that the party did not have reasonable grounds for its refusal, the judge is required to make the party pay the cost incurred by the opponent in proving the fact, including attorneys' fees.

As a practical matter, judges are apt to become annoyed with litigants who make trials take longer by forcing others to put on formal proof of facts that are not really in doubt. Judges who are annoyed have plenty of subtle ways of getting even with the offending party. Excessive obstructiveness in admitting facts may also provoke an opponent into being equally obstructive in responding to requests for admissions, making the case more expensive and time-consuming to prove for everyone.

> ◆ **LOCAL LINKS** ◆
> What are the consequences in your jurisdiction for refusing to admit facts that are not in dispute?

▓▓▓   *Putting It Into Practice 5.13:*

What will be the possible consequences for Stuart Thames if he refuses to admit that he ran the red light if, in fact, he knows that he did?

PREPARING INTERROGATORIES AND REQUESTS FOR ADMISSIONS

propound submit

An interrogatory is simply a written question that we **propound** (submit) to an opponent. Interrogatories are submitted in sets containing a series of unnumbered questions. The following interrogatory gives you an idea of what an interrogatory looks like.

Interrogatory No. 3
State the name, address, and telephone number of each and every person who witnessed the automobile collision described in plaintiff's complaint.

A request for admission looks nearly the same as an interrogatory, except that instead of being worded as a question, it begins with the words "Admit that . . ." followed by a statement expressing the fact to be admitted.

Request for Admission No. 7
Admit that the Real Estate Purchase Agreement dated March 15, 1999, a copy of which is attached as Exhibit 1 to plaintiff's complaint, bears the genuine signature of defendant John Smith as seller.

Given that interrogatories and requests for admission are so similar in form and purpose, why not combine both in the same document and title it "Interrogatories and Requests for Admission"? In fact, many attorneys favor this practice. But beware that some state rules prohibit combining them. Sending one's opponent both a request for admission and an interrogatory covering the same topic can be useful. For example, an admission that Document X is a true and accurate copy and bears a genuine signature might be requested. An interrogatory could then be added that would be answered if the request were denied, asking for the facts on which the denial was based.

Request for Admission No. 5
Admit that the document attached to plaintiff's complaint as Exhibit 1 is a true and correct copy of a contract entered into between plaintiff and defendant on or about March 15, 2000 and that said contract bears the genuine signatures of plaintiff and defendant.

Interrogatory No. 5
In the event that you deny the foregoing request for admission, state each and every fact tending to show that the document attached to plaintiff's complaint as Exhibit 1 is not a true and correct copy of a contract entered into between plaintiff and defendant on or about March 15, 2000 or that said contract does not bear the genuine signatures of plaintiff and defendant.

Both interrogatories and requests for admission can be submitted only to a party, and in both cases a written response is expected. Under the federal rules, the responding party has 30 days to respond unless a shorter or longer response time is ordered by the court or agreed to by the parties.

Sets of interrogatories and sets of requests for admission are nearly identical in form and appearance. Both take the form of a court paper, with the usual caption, date, and signature lines, and certificate of mailing. Following the caption is a preamble, then perhaps a list of instructions and definitions. The numbered questions or requests for admission comprise the body of the document. A copy of the set of interrogatories or requests for admission is served on the party who is to respond to them.

One of the judicial responses to using interrogatories as weapons for running up opponents' costs was to limit the number of interrogatories allowed. The federal rules allow interrogatories "not exceeding 25 in number including all discrete subparts." A number of state courts have adopted similar rules. In jurisdictions that impose numerical limits on the number of interrogatories that can be propounded, judges retain the power to authorize parties to exceed the limits in appropriate situations.

◆ **LOCAL LINKS** ◆
Ask your instructor if any limits have been imposed on the propounding of interrogatories.

Putting It Into Practice 5.14:

Write one request for admission and one interrogatory pertaining to some aspect of CODA's philosophy.

NET NEWS

To learn more about the use and drafting of interrogatories, go to *www.sound.net/~dadman/legal/interogs.htm*. This site also has sample interrogatories.

USING INTERROGATORIES AND REQUESTS FOR ADMISSION

Under the federal rules, and in many state courts, discovery is permitted only after the suit has gotten underway. Under the federal rules, the discovery process begins with a meeting between the opposing attorneys to plan out the discovery that needs to be accomplished, schedule it, and set deadlines. At the scheduling conference after this meeting, the judge reduces the discovery plan to an order. Neither side may engage in discovery at all until they have met and conferred, unless all parties agree to allow earlier discovery or permission is obtained from the judge. Once discovery has begun, anyone can use any discovery procedure at any time unless the scheduling order says otherwise. Therefore, the sequence and timing of discovery becomes largely a matter of strategy and depends considerably on the rules in force in the forum court.

In courts that have adopted mandatory disclosure rules, interrogatories are used mainly for pinning down important factual issues and hardly at all for "fishing" for evidence. Both interrogatories and requests for admission are most likely to be used late in the discovery process, after the mandatory disclosures have been made and the factual issues of the case are well defined. In more traditional courts, where there is no mandatory disclosure and no limits on written discovery, interrogatories may be used much earlier to try to obtain all of the background information that would flow in automatically as a result of the disclosure rules in a jurisdiction that has adopted them.

> ◆ **LOCAL LINKS** ◆
>
> When does your instructor recommend that interrogatories and requests for admission be used?

RECESS

SUMMARY – PART A

Through discovery, parties can obtain almost any information they want about their opponent's case. Under the federal rules, any information that is "reasonably calculated to lead to admissible evidence" is discoverable. Discovery in the American courts has traditionally been request-centered, but is now becoming more disclosure-centered. The primary tools that were used under request-centered discovery were depositions, interrogatories, requests for production of documents and things, requests for admission, subpoenas *duces tecum,* and independent medical examinations. While these same tools are used under the new disclosure-centered approach to discovery, their use is restricted so as to reduce the costs of discovery. Mandatory disclosure evolved because of the abuses that existed under open discovery. Discovery procedures are not uniform throughout the federal court system, and many states have developed their own solutions to the problems with discovery.

Depositions are the cornerstone of witness discovery. They can be used to evaluate how a witness will testify at trial, to substitute for trial testimony, if necessary, and to cross-examine a witness at trial. Unlike interrogatories and other discovery tools, attorneys can ask follow-up questions of deponents. Attorneys use depositions in order to obtain information, to pin a witness down to a position, to create a transcript that can be used at trial, to lay the groundwork for cross-examination at trial, and to decide how to handle the witness at trial.

Deciding whom to depose and the order in which to take depositions can be strategically important. Under the current federal rules and the rules of many state courts, parties are limited in the number of depositions they can conduct and when they can conduct them. Opposing parties, expert witnesses designated to testify for the opposing party, eyewitnesses, individuals directly involved in a disputed transaction, and any other key witnesses will almost always be deposed. Depositions are typically conducted in the law office of the attorney requesting the deposition, unless the deponent is from out of state or is an expert witness. Opposing parties, custodians of the records, and those connected with documents are usually interviewed early in the discovery process, whereas expert witnesses are usually reserved for later in the discovery cycle. Because expert testimony has become increasingly important with today's complex technology, parties want to find out who the opposing parties' experts are, what their opinions are, and how those opinions were formed. Under the federal rules, parties who want to depose someone must give reasonable notice in writing to every other party. This notice must indicate how the deposition will be recorded; most depositions are recorded stenographically. The person noticing the deposition must pay for the court reporter's services.

Under the federal rules, a party is entitled to conduct an independent medical examination of a party whose medical condition is a legitimate issue in the dispute. To do this, the party must serve a notice of an I.M.E.

One goal of document discovery is to get hold of all relevant documents in a case, whether they are "good" or "bad," because those documents may lead to other evidence. Another goal is to establish that a given document does not exist. As a practical matter, however, parties usually do their best to resist requests for documents because sometimes it is not cost-effective to analyze every document, and discovery must be completed in a limited time frame that may not permit an exhaustive review of all possible documents. Document discovery begins with a broad request for production of documents on each opponent, except in those courts requiring a disclosure statement. After the documents are analyzed, new requests are usually made for additional documents and efforts are made to retrieve those documents missing from the responses or disclosure packages. An indexing and filing system should be developed that allows anyone to locate documents easily and determine the source of each document, how it was obtained, where the original is, and who might be called as a witness to testify that it is authentic. Discovery of documents must be carefully planned because most courts set discovery cut-off dates. Because of this limited time frame, parties need to react immediately when an opposing party resists a discovery request.

To obtain documents from a party to a lawsuit, a request for production of documents is used, and to obtain documents from someone who is not a party, a subpoena *duces tecum* is used. Subpoenas no longer have to be signed by judges but can, in fact, be signed by court clerks or, in federal court and some state courts, by attorneys.

Requests for admissions and interrogatories are not particularly suited for finding the proof necessary to establish the elements of a case because the responses are usually drafted by the attorney rather than the party, they are carefully edited, and ambiguous answers cannot be immediately clarified. Furthermore, they reveal the strengths and weaknesses of the proponent and prod the party answering the questions into action. On the other hand, written discovery can be useful in getting background information, in pinning down the facts, and placing limits on a party's case. Interrogatories are sets of a series of numbered questions; requests for admission are similar except that they begin with the phrase "Admit that." If a party refuses to admit facts that are not really in dispute, the judge must, under the federal rules, make the party pay the cost incurred by the opponent in proving the fact, including attorneys' fees. Many attorneys combine interrogatories and requests for admission in the same document. Both can be submitted only to a party and, under the federal rules, must be responded to within 30 days. The federal courts and many state courts have imposed limits on the number of interrogatories that can be propounded, although judges retain the power to allow more in appropriate situations.

Under the federal rules, parties cannot engage in discovery until they have met and conferred and the judge has reduced their agreement to an order. Once discovery has begun, however, parties can use any discovery procedure at any time that does not conflict with the scheduling order. In courts that have adopted mandatory disclosure, interrogatories are used mainly for pinning down important factual issues and used late in the discovery process. In courts where there is no mandatory disclosure, interrogatories are used earlier to try to obtain background information.

KEY TERMS

Common law
Criminalists
Custodian of the records
Deponent
Depositions
Deposition notices

Disclosure statement
Evidence
Forensic
Independent medical
    examination (I.M.E.)
Interrogatories

Notice of independent
    medical examination
Pretrial conference
Proponent
Propound
Request for admissions

Request for production of
    documents
Supplement
Transcript

REVIEW QUESTIONS – PART A

1. What is the common law and how did it evolve?
2. What is the purpose of discovery? What are the primary tools that are used in discovery?
3. What is the difference between request-centered discovery and disclosure-centered discovery?
4. What criticisms have been levied against mandatory disclosure?
5. What advantages do depositions have over other forms of discovery?
6. What does an attorney usually hope to achieve at a deposition?
7. What kinds of things need to be taken into consideration when scheduling depositions?
8. What must an attorney do to arrange a deposition? Why is he required to notify the other parties?
9. What are the goals of document discovery?
10. Describe the general process for locating and storing documents.
11. What is the difference between a request for production of document and a subpoena *duces tecum*?
12. What are the advantages and disadvantages of written discovery?
13. At what point and for what purpose would an attorney use interrogatories?

PRACTICE EXAM – PART A

MULTIPLE CHOICE

1. Discovery
   a. is a means of prying evidence from the opposing side
   b. was very broad under the common law
   c. is becoming more request-centered
   d. all of the above
2. The common law
   a. originated in France
   b. arose in England before there was a centralized court system
   c. evolved from decisions shared by judges who rode the circuit after the Norman Conquest
   d. none of the above
3. The best way for a party to obtain detailed information from a witness is through
   a. interrogatories
   b. a deposition
   c. a subpoena *duces tecum*
   d. an independent medical examination

4. The best way for a party to obtain documents from a non-party is through
   a. interrogatories
   b. request for production of documents
   c. a subpoena *duces tecum*
   d. a deposition

*5. When the federal rules were initially adopted
   a. open discovery was the goal
   b. litigants could request anything that was reasonably calculated to lead to admissible evidence
   c. litigants no longer had to resort to court orders to obtain evidence
   d. all of the above

*6. Mandatory disclosure evolved because
   a. some lawyers used open discovery as a weapon rather than as a tool
   b. the discovery process had become unduly expensive
   c. the discovery process had become an excuse to go on "fishing expeditions"
   d. all of the above

7. Some people argue that mandatory disclosure rules
   a. make the outcome of litigation overly dependent on lawyer's ethics and honesty
   b. force lawyers to build an opponent's case for him or her
   c. undermine the attorney-client privilege
   d. all of the above

8. Depositions
   a. allow attorneys to evaluate how a witness will testify in the courtroom
   b. can be used only with parties
   c. result in transcripts that can be used by the attorney privately but cannot be introduced at trial
   d. cannot be used as a substitute for trial testimony

9. The purpose of a deposition is
   a. to obtain information and nothing more
   b. to find out how to handle a witness at trial
   c. to discredit the witness
   d. to learn about the witness but to avoid pinning down the witness to a particular position

10. In the federal courts
   a. each side can schedule only 10 depositions without getting court permission
   b. judges have very little involvement in relationship to the scheduling of depositions
   c. judges decide what order depositions will be taken
   d. parties can take depositions at any time before trial

11. If a limited number of depositions are permitted, attorneys will almost always depose
   a. opposing parties but not expert witnesses
   b. expert witnesses, but not eyewitnesses
   c. opposing parties, expert witnesses, and eyewitnesses
   d. opposing parties, but no one else because only parties can be deposed

12. A notice of deposition
   a. is not required under the federal rules
   b. must be served on the party rather than the attorney for the party
   c. provides parties an opportunity to attend and/or object to a deposition
   d. is in the form of a motion

13. Court reporters
   a. are paid by the party being deposed
   b. usually charge at a fixed rate per page
   c. are not used if the deposition is recorded by video
   d. usually charge about $1 per page

14. The goal of document discovery is to
   a. find all relevant documents whether they are "good" or "bad"
   b. find those documents that will lead to other evidence
   c. establish that a certain document does not exist
   d. all of the above

15. A good filing and indexing system allows one to
   a. determine where the original of any document is
   b. determine the source of any document
   c. identify who can be called to testify about a document's authenticity
   d. all of the above

16. Subpoenas
   a. can be issued by attorneys in federal court
   b. must be signed by a judge
   c. must be signed by a clerk of the court
   d. none of the above

17. Interrogatories and requests for admission are useful
   a. in getting information without disclosing the strengths and weaknesses of one's own case
   b. in pinning down the facts
   c. because they are usually written by the parties rather than the attorneys
   d. because they allow the attorney to follow up on evasive or ambiguous answers

18. Requests for admission and interrogatories
   a. must be responded to within 30 days under the federal rules
   b. can be submitted only to parties
   c. take the form of court papers
   d. all of the above

19. Discovery
    a. can be conducted at any time and in any order under the federal rules
    b. cannot, under the federal rules, be conducted until the judge has signed a scheduling order
    c. is always permitted as soon as the complaint is filed
    d. none of the above

20. Interrogatories are used
    a. to fish out evidence in those jurisdictions where disclosure is mandatory
    b. early in the discovery process in those jurisdictions mandating disclosure
    c. to obtain background information in those jurisdictions where disclosure is not mandatory
    d. late in the discovery process in those jurisdictions where disclosure is not mandatory

*Questions taken from Bonus Pointers

FILL IN THE BLANK

21. Through the process of discovery, parties can obtain _____ (factual information relating to their case) that can be presented at trial.

22. Under the_____ (judge-made law), parties went to trial knowing little or nothing about their opponent's case.

23. A_____ can be used to obtain documents that an opposing party has possession of, whereas a _____ can be used to obtain documents from people who are not parties to a lawsuit.

24. _____ are used to obtain admissions from a party, _____ are written questions used to obtain information from parties, and _____ are a means of taking and recording testimony from witnesses.

25. If a defendant wants to verify the extent of the plaintiff's injuries, he should request an _____.

26. In some states, parties are required to prepare _____, which contain certain specific categories of information about that party's case.

27. At a _____ conference, a judge discusses the case with the attorneys and issues a scheduling order.

28. The court reporter at a deposition prepares a _____ (record) of the testimony of the _____ (person being deposed) testimony.

29. A lawyer often deposes the _____ to find out everything about how an organization keeps its records.

30. _____ witnesses are allowed to give opinion testimony, whereas _____ witnesses are not allowed to testify as to their opinions.

31. A party that wants to assess the medical condition of a party whose condition is a legitimate issue in a dispute can do so by filing and serving a _____.

32. Interrogatories are questions that are _____ (submitted) to opponents.

TRUE OR FALSE

____ 33. The discovery process provides parties with some means of prying evidence from the other side.

____ 34. Under the federal rules, any information that is "reasonably calculated to lead to admissible evidence" is subject to discovery.

____ 35. Discovery in the American courts has traditionally been disclosure-centered.

____ 36. The common law is judge-made law that originated with the Norman Conquest of England.

____ 37. Parties are not required to supplement disclosure statements once they have prepared them.

____ 38. Request-centered discovery places more reliance on interrogatories, depositions, and other discovery tools than does disclosure-centered discovery.

____*39. Under the federal rules that were first adopted, a party needing information from an opposing party generally had to file a motion and obtain a court order.

____ *40. Open discovery encouraged unlimited "fishing expeditions" and could be used as a tactical weapon rather than as a tool for gaining information.

____ 41. Open discovery was inherently inefficient because parties had to guess what information their opponents had.

____ 42. Under the new federal rules, judges have little involvement in the discovery process.

____ 43. Discovery procedures are uniform throughout the federal court system.

____ 44. State courts have, for the most part, wholeheartedly adopted the federal disclosure-based system.

____ 45. Much of discovery work consists of analyzing information obtained—work that is often done by paralegals.

____ 46. Written discovery can generally be used only against parties, but depositions can be used to get information from non-parties.

____ 47. An attorney is forbidden from asking follow-up questions of a deponent.

____ 48. A deposition is a good place to prove that a witness is lying.

____ 49. A transcript of a deposition can be used to cross-examine a witness at trial.

____ 50. Deciding whom to depose and the order in which to conduct depositions is a relatively straightforward task.

____ 51. Typically, each side would like to depose the other side's witnesses first.

____ 52. In the federal courts, parties have a right to an unlimited number of depositions.

____ 53. Depositions can be taken only of parties.

____ 54. Attorneys usually like to conduct depositions in their own office to make it easier to maintain control over the deposition and to ensure that the deponent takes the deposition seriously.

____ 55. Attorneys can require deponents who are out of state to attend depositions that are hundreds of miles away.

____ 56. Expert witnesses are usually deposed as early as possible in the case, while opposing parties are usually left for later in the discovery cycle.

____ 57. Expert witnesses can offer their impartial opinions but are not allowed to express any kind of advocacy.

____ 58. Some limitations have been imposed by the courts on the discovery of experts.

____ 59. The federal rules require attorneys to notify the other attorneys how the testimony at a deposition will be recorded.

____ 60. Court reporters' fees are usually a minimal part of discovery costs.

____ *61. In the near future, court reporters probably will be replaced by video cameras because of the superior accuracy of those cameras.

____ 62. The goal of document discovery is to get hold of only those documents that are helpful to one's case.

____ 63. Document requests should be framed in such a way that opposing parties can later claim that the request was ambiguous.

____ 64. In complex cases, it is not unusual to be confronted with rooms full of documents.

____ 65. Although the goal of document discovery is finding every existing document, the reality is settling for enough to prove one's case.

____ 66. In all cases, document discovery begins with a broad request for a production of documents from each opponent.

____ 67. In courts that do not require disclosure statements, parties submit a written response, stating which items are being provided and which are being objected to.

____ 68. Chasing after documents is often a routine part of document discovery.

____ 69. Attorneys need not send out requests for documents until the latter stages of a case.

____ 70. Unlimited time frames are usually allowed for discovery in most courts.

____ 71. Parties should react immediately when an opposing party tries to get away with an incomplete response to a request for documents.

____ 72. To obtain documents from someone who is not a party to a lawsuit, a request for production of documents is used.

____ 73. A party who receives a request for production must file and serve a written response to the request.

____ 74. A subpoena *duces tecum* and a subpoena *ad testificandum* are the same thing.

____ 75. Subpoenas have to be signed by judges.

____ 76. Requests for admission and interrogatories are particularly well suited for finding the proof necessary to establish the elements of a case.

____ 77. Answers to interrogatories are usually carefully edited to reveal as little information as possible.

____78. Interrogatories may reveal as much about the strengths and weaknesses of the proponent's case as their answers may reveal about the case of the party responding to the interrogatories.

____79. Interrogatories are less useful than depositions in getting background information.

____80. Evidence not disclosed in response to a proper interrogatory will not be admitted at trial.

____81. Written discovery is an inexpensive way of establishing non-controversial details by getting opponents to admit them.

____82. There are no consequences for a party if it refuses to admit facts that it knows not to be in dispute.

____83. Requests for admission and interrogatories must be submitted in separate documents.

____84. Interrogatories and requests for admission can be submitted to both parties and non-parties.

____85. Some jurisdictions have imposed limits on the number of interrogatories that can be propounded.

____86. Under the federal rules, discovery cannot begin until the opposing attorneys have met and planned out the discovery that needs to be accomplished and the judge has reduced their agreement to a scheduling order.

____87. The sequence and timing of discovery is largely a matter of strategy and depends considerably on the rules of the court in which the litigation is taking place.

* Questions taken from Bonus Pointers

PART B

"You Mean You're Going to Tell Everyone About Me and Carmela?"

"Mike, the bottom line is, we know there's something you're keeping from us. Carmela won't talk to me. In fact, she practically begged me not to ask her any questions. Said I should talk with you. What is it you're hiding?" Martha insisted. She and John were meeting with Mike in John's office and had to this point been unsuccessful in extricating Mike's secret. Martha's rising frustration was reflected in the tone of her voice. But she could see, much to her relief, that John's admonition about needing to know all the facts to adequately represent him had hit home.

Mike sat quietly with his head bowed; after awhile, he took a deep breath. With his exhalation, his shoulders dropped and all his defenses seemed to evaporate. His voice barely audible, he told them his story.

Carmela had begun popping up unexpectedly in his life ever since an incident at the school in which Mike had intervened, bringing an end to the taunting Carmela had been subjected to after dropping her tray of food in the cafeteria. His reprimand had immediately silenced the jeers of the ninth-grade boys, who were quick to pounce on anyone lower in the school hierarchy than they. Mike had helped Carmela pick up the spillage and had gone on his way, oblivious to the hero's status he had instantly acquired in her mind. After that day, her eyes shyly followed him wherever he went on campus and she spent days patiently plotting how to make their paths cross again.

With the singularity of purpose found in a woman who believes she has discovered the man of her dreams, she finally found a way to ingratiate herself into his life. She volunteered at the hospital where she knew Mike worked part-time, asking to be assigned to the children's ward, where she knew he spent most of his time. For two days a week, she was now in his presence and was at last rewarded with an opportunity to begin forging a relationship. For his part, Mike found Carmela easy to talk with and relished the chance to dominate the conversation. He found it difficult to express himself this freely with anyone, including Greta, his girlfriend, who usually dictated what they did, where they went, and generally how they functioned as a couple. He was flattered by Carmela's unabashed adoration and bemused by her unveiled attempts to please him.

At Carmela's invitation, he went to her house one evening for dinner. Coming from a closely knit family, he appreciated the warm love and acceptance he saw between members of Carmela's family. He would have gladly spent more time with them had it not been for Jorge's obvious disdain. Jorge had been watching Carmela with Mike and could read the signs of her growing infatuation with him. Hardened by what he had seen in his war-torn country and by his spurning at the hands of young Americans who rejected anyone they did not understand, he was inordinately protective of his sister. Certain that Mike would take advantage of her naivete, Jorge confronted Mike directly, warning him through clenched teeth to stay away from his sister and their family.

"Touch my sister and you're a dead man," he had warned. Mike could read the anger smoldering in his eyes and he reluctantly stayed away.

But the more he pulled away from Carmela and threw himself into his relationship with Greta, the more he found his thoughts turning toward Carmela. Drawn to her simple candor and her quiet beauty, he could not force himself to dismiss her. Over time, they began to know each other with an easy intimacy they shared with no one else, an intimacy that found no physical expression until one afternoon when they stopped by Mike's house to pick something up. At this point, Mike's narrative became pointedly nebulous and he would say only that an accidental brush of the skin ignited an unspoken passion that had grown between them.

"We were together only once, but we have been cursed for our sins." Mike's strong religious convictions provided him an easy explanation for Carmela's resulting pregnancy. "I didn't know where to turn, what to do, and Carmela was terrified to tell her family." Mike scanned Martha's eyes for a sign of understanding.

When Mike said nothing further, Martha asked gently, "Did Jorge find out that Carmela was pregnant?"

"Yes," said Mike woodenly. "Carmela and I had made an appointment with Planned Parenthood. Neither one of us wanted an abortion, but we wanted to talk with someone who could give us some options. Jorge was downtown the afternoon we went to see the counselor and saw us walking through the doors together."

"And apparently drew his own conclusions," added John.

Appearing not to hear John's comment, Mike continued. "We needn't have bothered to go there. The next day Carmela miscarried."

"I'm so sorry, Mike." Martha put her hand on Mike's arm but he seemed not to notice. She and John allowed Mike to sit quietly for a few minutes before they asked any further questions. John was the first to break the silence.

"How long after all this happened were you shot, Mike?"

"Around two months."

"Did Jorge ever threaten you after he saw you and Carmela together that day?"

"No. I saw him a few times on campus, but he avoided looking at me."

"I have to ask you this, Mike," prefaced John. "Do you think Jorge was responsible for your getting shot?"

"I've thought about that a lot. I've even thought that maybe I deserved to get shot after what I put Carmela through."

"But do you know for a fact that Jorge was involved?" persisted John.

"No. In fact, I can't see any connection between Jorge and the guys who actually attacked me. He's always been a real loner on campus. He'd be the last person I'd expect to join any gang and I've never seen him hanging around any of those guys."

"All right, then. At this point, we're not going to have to disclose what you've told us to the other defendants."

"You mean you're going to tell everyone about me and Carmela?" burst out Mike, a look of sheer horror on his face.

"I don't think your relationship with her is necessarily relevant, but we will have to disclose Jorge's participation in the crime if we discover that he was, in fact, the motivating force behind your shooting. If that happens, the other attorneys are bound to question you about your relationship with Jorge. In fact, Mike, we can be reasonably certain that the Hendershott boy knows something about Jorge by virtue of the fact that he included him as a third-party. The bottom line is that your relationship with Carmela is likely to come out whether we disclose it or not. I think you need to be prepared for this. If I were you, I would give serious thought to telling your parents, your girlfriend, and anyone else you would rather find out from you before they hear about this from some other source. This is bound to be a high profile case and you're somewhat of a celebrity on campus." John paused for a moment, reflecting on whether he wanted to make his next statement. "It is possible that the newspapers might get hold of this."

"Oh, my God," moaned Mike, running his fingers frantically through his hair. "It would destroy Carmela."

"We'll certainly do our best to protect yours and Carmela's privacy in this matter, Mike. But lawsuits do have a way of unearthing those things we'd sometimes rather keep hidden. I just think you need to be prepared for the worst."

After Mike had left their office, John turned to Martha and said, "Well, at least the secret is out. Now we have to decide how we're going to deal with it. I guess we'd better send out our disclosure statement before we talk with Hendershott. Something tells me Jorge is at the bottom of all this, and we're going to need some time to piece things together before we have to make our disclosures to the other parties."

DISCLOSURE STATEMENTS

Disclosure statements must be filed with the court and so must take the form of court papers (although state rules vary). Under the federal rules, the body of the disclosure statement must address four areas of subject matter.

The first category of required disclosure is the name, address, and telephone number of each individual likely to have discoverable information. All persons likely to have information about disputed facts must be identified, whether or not they might actually be called to testify. Because this disclosure is required early in the case, at a time when a party's investigation is usually not very far along, complying with this requirement may not be easy.

The following are among those individuals always listed.

- all individual parties to the suit
- employees of a corporation believed to have been involved in the events out of which the lawsuit arose
- all individuals from whom statements have been taken
- all individuals listed as witnesses in any police investigative report or similar document
- all individuals having custody of documents that may be relevant to the suit
- all individuals expected to be called as witnesses
- all individuals who are associated with the client and who may possess discoverable information

The subjects of the information expected from each person must also be specified, briefly and to the point. Describing the information expected or disclosing what each person's testimony might be is unnecessary.

◆ LOCAL LINKS ◆
Does your jurisdiction require the submission of disclosure statements?

Putting It Into Practice 5.15:

What witnesses other than the parties and employees of the parties do you think Mike will have to disclose at this time?

Figure 5-8
Information Required in Disclosure Statements

INFORMATION REQUIRED IN DISCLOSURE STATEMENTS

Names, Addresses, and Telephone Numbers of Individuals Having Discoverable Information

Parties to suit
Employees of corporation involved in events resulting in suit
Those from whom statements have been taken
Those listed as witnesses in investigative reports
Those having custody of documents relevant to suit
Those expected to be called as experts
Those associated with client who may have discoverable information

All Documents Relevant to Disputed Facts in Pleadings

Documents that are part of dispute
Communications about subject matter of suit
Business records relating to factual matters at issue

Computation of Damages and All Documents Used to Make Those Computations

Concrete provable expenses
Expenses that are difficult to quantify
Expenses requiring estimation or computation

Insurance Coverage

INADEQUATE DISCLOSURE: THE CONSEQUENCES

Disclosure statements, like discovery responses, provide information—potential ammunition—to an opponent. Obviously, a party would rather not give away any more of it than necessary. Suppose a party files a disclosure statement that is incomplete, either because information was deliberately withheld or because the party was less than diligent in gathering the facts to be disclosed.

Is there a downside to this kind of behavior? Yes. In the first place, some judges are apt to react to blatant and deliberate infractions of the disclosure rules by making an ethics complaint against the offending attorney, resulting in bar disciplinary proceedings and possible censure, suspension, or disbarment. Such severe measures are uncommon, however, and imposed only in extreme cases.

What about more subtle omissions? The federal rules give the judge a veritable arsenal of weapons with which to punish a party who, "without substantial justification," fails to disclose required information.

◆ The judge may prohibit the offending party from using the witness or document that was not disclosed. This threat alone is usually not much of a deterrent: if the witness's testimony is adverse enough to tempt the attorney to withhold disclosure, calling her as a witness at trial is likely the last thing that the party would want to do.

◆ The judge may order the offending party to pay the opposing party's expenses, including attorney's fees, caused by the failure to disclose.

◆ The judge may order particular facts as being deemed established.

◆ The judge may inform the jury of the nondisclosure.

◆ The judge may prohibit the offending party from introducing particular evidence. This allows the judge to "level the playing field" by taking away some of the evidence that would have favored the non-disclosing party.

◆ Finally, the judge may strike claims or defenses from the pleadings, dismiss claims, or render judgment by default against the offending party. If the nondisclosure is sufficiently compelling, the judge has the power to end the lawsuit then and there and enter judgment in favor of the other party.

Figure 5-9
Sanctions for Non-Disclosure

SANCTIONS FOR NON-DISCLOSURE

Prohibit offending party from using witness or document that was not disclosed

Order offending party to pay opposing party's expenses

Order facts as being deemed established

Inform jury of nondisclosure

Prohibit offending party from introducing evidence that would have favored it

Strike claims or defenses from pleadings, dismiss claims or enter default judgment

The second category of disclosure requires that each party provide a copy of, or a description of, all the documents in its possession, custody, or control that are relevant to disputed facts alleged in the pleadings. Some lawsuits are document-intensive; some are not. In a simple automobile accident case, aside from perhaps a police report, no documents may be relevant to the issue of liability. At the other extreme, in some kinds of commercial litigation, such as antitrust lawsuits and securities fraud cases, the relevant documents may literally fill many rooms.

Usually, the documents that need to be disclosed fall into one of three main categories.

1. Documents that, in and of themselves, form part of the dispute. For example, if the lawsuit involves a claim of breach of a written contract, the contract is a document that would be disclosed. So would any other documents relating to it: prior drafts, notes, correspondence, etc.
2. Documents comprising communications about the subject matter of the suit. These may include letters, memos, telephone messages, and electronic mail messages, which are fast becoming an important source of evidence in lawsuits.
3. Business records relating to factual matters at issue in the suit.

Putting It Into Practice 5.16:

What documents do you think John will need to disclose in Mike's case?

The next subject of required disclosure is the computation of damages and the documents and other evidentiary materials upon which such computations are based. The items comprising a party's damage claims usually fall into one of three categories.

The first category relates items involving concrete, provable expenses that are easy to establish, such as a doctor's bill for treatment of injuries. For such items, a description and amount, separately or by categories, is all that is needed along with attached copies of the bills.

The second category involves items such as damages for pain and suffering that are difficult or impossible to quantify. At trial, treating physicians or physician experts will be called to describe how the injury in question affects the plaintiff. Medical records may be introduced to show the nature of the plaintiff's injuries. The plaintiff's attorney does not want to risk having any of this evidence excluded because of nondisclosure, so the disclosure statement should list the main factors comprising such claims and all supporting documents.

The third category involves items that are based on provable quantities, but nevertheless require estimates or computations, such as a claim for future income lost due to an injury. The amount of the claim is not mere guesswork—it can be computed if the salary the plaintiff would have received and the period of time before she can return to work are known. Some of the quantities needed to make the calculations need to be estimated, but an expert witness can do that. For these items, the damages disclosure must include all of the data on which the computation will be based and must show how the computation will be made.

Putting It Into Practice 5.17:

Marianne is sloppy about keeping all of a client's medical bills in one place. She does not keep an ongoing tally of each client's medical bills as they come in. Why is this a problem?

The final category of information to be disclosed is any insurance policy covering the defendant for the liabilities claimed in the suit. Because judges want to encourage settlement, insurance coverage is discoverable even though evidence of insurance coverage is inadmissible at trial. The availability of insurance is usually an important factor in settlement decisions. Like it or not, the settlement value of a claim often depends greatly on whether a judgment, if won, could be collected. If a defendant has no insurance coverage and no other assets from which a judgment could be collected, the plaintiff will be much more likely to accept a low cash payment rather than spend several years and tens of thousands of dollars obtaining an uncollectable judgment.

BONUS POINTERS:

MORE COMPREHENSIVE DISCLOSURE SCHEMES

The federal rules do not carry the disclosure philosophy to its logical limit. The disclosure of potential witnesses, documents, damage calculations, insurance, and expert witnesses is enough to provide litigants with a good start to their factual development, but the intent of the federal rules is that interrogatories, depositions, and other traditional discovery tools will still be needed to fill in the gaps. The federal rules provide the litigants with the sources of information—potential witnesses and documents—but each party must extract the desired information from those sources using other discovery methods.

Some judges and scholars favor much more comprehensive disclosure schemes. In some state courts, the rules require more detailed disclosure encompassing not only the sources of information, but the information itself. In Arizona, for example, state court rules require additional disclosure: (1) the factual basis of each claim or defense (not just the subject matter—the rule requires a party to state in detail the facts underlying each claim or defense), and (2) the legal theory underlying each claim or defense, including citation of authorities where necessary.

Ernesto Could See Their Case Against CODA Slipping Away.

Ernesto's face sobered after he heard the news of Mike's disclosure about Jorge. He could see their case against CODA slipping away. If it turned out that the boys assaulted Mike at Jorge's urging rather than being incited by the movie, they would not be able to prove causation against CODA.

"Guess we better see if we can interview Jorge and that Hendershott boy right away. It looks like CODA's motion to dismiss may be the least of our worries right now," Ernesto offered, trying not to show his discouragement.

"We don't know what those boys are going to say until we talk with them, so let's stay focused on the immediate issue before us. Now, I hear we've been assigned Judge Salt." John's ability to cast aside any matters that might distract him from his present task was one of the reasons he was such a formidable litigator. "I went to law school with Ben and I've been before him any number of times. He'll give us a fair hearing and, if anything, he tends to favor expansion of tort liability. He likes to shoot from the hip, however, so you're going to need to make a strong case during **oral arguments.** Unlike most judges, he probably won't take the case **under advisement:** he'll tell you immediately what his decision is or at least let you know the direction he's leaning."

"Good to know. Oral arguments are tomorrow. I'll let you know what happens. Thanks, John."

---

oral arguments verbal presentations made by attorneys to a judge

under advisement judge's declaration that he will issue a decision later, after having time to consider a matter; sometimes referred to as under submission

ETHICAL ETIQUETTE

EX PARTE COMMUNICATIONS

Attorneys and paralegals are bound by the ethical rules to not engage in **ex parte communications,** i.e., communications about a pending case with a judge outside of the presence of opposing counsel. The rationale for this prohibition is that allowing such communications would give the party communicating with the judge an unfair advantage. At the very least, it gives the appearance of favoritism and improper influence on the judge. Therefore, in the name of fairness, attorneys cannot contact a judge about a case unless opposing counsel is present except in rare circumstances specified under the law.

---

ex parte communications communications with a judge outside the presence of opposing counsel

motions formal request for a judge to do something

MOTION PRACTICE

Motions comprise a significant part of the workload of attorneys and paralegals. **Motions** are simply formal requests for the judge to do something—usually, to enter an order or to make a ruling of some kind. Because litigation is a contest between adversaries, it is crucial that judges hear from both sides before making important rulings. As a practical matter in modern court systems, this is accomplished by requiring essentially all communication with the judge to be by motion.

HOW MOTIONS ARE PRESENTED

movant party filing a motion

memorandum of points and authorities written legal argument that accompanies a motion

respondent party responding to a motion

response court paper explaining why a judge should not rule as requested in the motion to which the response is responding

reply court paper rebutting the arguments made in the response

motion papers motions, responses, replies, and the accompanying memoranda

Except during trial, motions are submitted in writing. Written motions are court papers, beginning with a caption, stating briefly what the moving party (the **movant**) is asking the judge to do and which rule of civil procedure authorizes the request. All motions except the very simplest are accompanied by a written legal argument, called a **memorandum of points and authorities,** which is usually several pages long and lays out in detail all of the reasons why the judge should do as the movant is asking.

The motion and the supporting memorandum must be filed with the clerk of the court and copies must be served on all other parties. The opposing party (the **respondent**) is then given some period of time in which to file and serve a written **response.** This is a court paper, similar to a motion, that is also supported by a memorandum of points and authorities, this time giving all of the respondent's reasons why the judge should *not* do what the motion is asking.

How does the responding party know when the response is due? The answer depends on the court. Some courts set a briefing schedule and notify the attorneys. In others, the rules of procedure or local rules establish a set number of days for response. Many judges simply dispose of unopposed motions summarily—that is, they grant the motion unless there is some obvious reason not to.

After the opposing party responds, the moving party is allowed to file a written **reply,** which has the same format as the motion and response. The reply, however, rebuts arguments made in the response. Notice the three-stage sequence: party A makes a motion, party B responds, and party A replies to the response. This pattern of argument occurs over and over in litigation: motions, jury summations, and appellate briefs. Motions, responses, replies, and the accompanying memoranda are referred to generically as **motion papers.**

Putting It Into Practice 5.18:

Why do attorneys who write clearly and concisely have an advantage as litigators?

Figure 5-10
Motion Practice

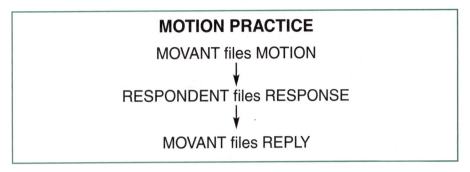

Judge Salt insisted on holding oral arguments, on the rare occasions he allowed them, in the open courtroom. Well-known for "going by the book", he maintained tight control over courtroom activities and tolerated little deviance from the strict protocol he thought appropriate. Not standing on ceremony, he immediately turned to Mr. Yakamura, CODA's attorney, and said, "You've got an uphill battle, sir, if you're going to convince me to dismiss the claims against your client. I found Mr. Esparanza's arguments to be very persuasive, and I'm inclined to agree with him unless you can show me good cause to decide otherwise. The ball's in your court, Mr. Yakamura. Please proceed."

HOW MOTIONS ARE DECIDED

hearing proceeding in which the judge listens to oral arguments and asks the attorneys questions

After all the motion papers have been filed and served, the most important motions will be decided after a **hearing** before the judge. A hearing is a proceeding at the courthouse in which the judge listens to oral arguments from each of the opposing attorneys, and has an opportunity to ask them questions. Depending on the court and the judge, hearings can be very formal affairs, held in the courtroom with a bailiff and court reporter present and the attorneys standing at a lectern to deliver argument. Or, they can be quite informal, held in the judge's **chambers** (the judge's private office), with the judge and the attorneys seated comfortably around the judge's desk, usually with a court reporter present.

chambers judge's private office

In theory, oral argument follows a three-stage sequence with the moving attorney speaking first, the responding attorney second, and the moving attorney then giving a brief reply. In practice, most judges feel free to interrupt with questions at any time, and some do not enforce the idea of the attorneys taking turns. In some courts, arguments can deteriorate into a kind of verbal free-for-all.

Not all motions are scheduled for hearings. Given their increasingly impossible caseloads, many judges prefer not to spend time listening to attorneys give speeches repeating the same arguments they made (or should have made) in their written memoranda. In many courts, hearings are scheduled only if specifically requested, and even then the judge may be free to cancel the hearing and issue a decision based on the written memoranda alone. Consequently, points and authorities supporting a motion must always be written as if they will be the only argument the judge will entertain. Never assume holes in an argument can be patched up at the hearing.

minute entry formal communication of a judge's order to the parties; also known as a *minute order*

Sometimes judges announce their decision at the conclusion of the hearing. More commonly, however, they take the motion under advisement. This gives them time to reflect on the arguments and re-read the memoranda. It also avoids the potentially awkward task of giving the loser the bad news face-to-face. The judge's order (a written decision either denying or granting the motion) is formally communicated to the parties via a **minute entry** (or *minute order*). The term is another of those throwbacks to the courts of yore, where the clerk meticulously recorded everything that happened in court in a "minute" book.

Putting It Into Practice 5.19:

At Marianne's law firm, one of the new associates has little time to prepare a response adequately and writes it without reviewing or editing it, consoling herself that she will have the opportunity to redeem herself at oral arguments. What is the flaw in her reasoning?

EXAMPLE OF A MOTION: MOTION TO DISMISS

motion to dismiss   motion requesting that a judge keep a claim or defense from going forward because it is lacking in merit

Some motions pertain to procedural details or to discovery disputes; others, such as **motions to dismiss,** call for the judge to decide whether a party's claim or defense is good enough to go forward, or so lacking in merit that it should be declared dead on the spot. As you can imagine, judges dislike wasting weeks of trial time on a case that could never be won in the first place, and these procedures give them the power to weed out such cases early on.

A motion to dismiss asks the judge to find that there is something wrong with a claim as it appears in the plaintiff's complaint. The judge does not consider any evidence or worry about whether the claim can be proved. In fact, the judge must assume that every allegation in the plaintiff's complaint is true and can be proven. The claim will be dismissed only if the judge decides that the plaintiff must lose even if she proves everything alleged in the complaint.

If a claim is defective because the law simply does not allow that kind of claim, the motion to dismiss is for failure to state a claim. Other reasons for moving to dismiss are lack of jurisdiction (a common ground), improper venue, insufficiency of process, insufficiency of service of process, and failure to join a party.

Putting It Into Practice 5.20:

Suppose Stuart Thames believes that Molly Running Deer has no evidence to show that he caused the accident. Assume there are no witnesses and that the police report does not indicate who caused the accident. Would it be appropriate for him to file a motion to dismiss?

NET NEWS

To see an example of a motion to dismiss, go to *www.alllaw.com/forms/pleadings*. To see examples of other types of motions, go to *www.plf.net/links.htm*.

Ernesto was thankful he had taken the extra time to rewrite his motion as many times as he had. It was the final revision that captured the essence of his argument and articulated it in a way that made it difficult to rebut. Judge Salt had obviously done his homework—he could tell from the pointed questions he was asking Mr. Yakamura. As he listened to the judge hammering away at the increasingly flustered Mr. Yakamura, Ernesto began to feel more confident that the judge would rule against CODA.

It is convenient to think of a motion as having three parts: (1) the motion proper, (2) the memorandum of points and authority, and (3) the attachments, consisting of any supporting papers that must be submitted with the motion. The purpose of the motion is to tell the judge what is being requested and the purpose of the memorandum is to tell the judge why she should grant the request.

The body of the motion (the motion, not the memorandum) consists of two paragraphs stating who is making the motion, what the motion is asking for, what rule the motion arises under, and what other documents support the motion.

> Defendant respectfully moves pursuant to Rule 12(b)(6), *Federal Rules of Civil Procedure,* for an order of the Court dismissing Count II of plaintiff's complaint.
>
> This motion is based upon the accompanying memorandum of points and authorities.

A suggested basic memorandum format is comprised of four main parts, described here.

Summary of Argument

If the judge sees only one thing in a memorandum, it will most likely be whatever is on the first page below the caption. This is the "prime real estate" in a memorandum. The "Summary of Argument" lays out the main points of the argument in a few short, easy-to-grasp sentences. Ideally, the judge should be able to skim this section in less than a minute and come away with a reasonable understanding of the argument being made.

Factual Background

Never assume that the judge is familiar with the facts of the case. Judges are often responsible for hundreds of cases and cannot possibly remember even the broad outlines of each one, let alone the details. If the judge needs to know any particular facts to understand a motion, those facts must be included in this section. Factual statements must be supported by evidence; this can be done by quoting from deposition transcripts and/or by attaching affidavits and other supporting documents.

Argument

This section is the main part of the memorandum and is usually the largest. Its organization depends on the issues being addressed and how they can be most convincingly presented. Often the argument begins with a short section stating the conclusion and summarizing the main points supporting the conclusion in a few sentences. Then each of the main points is explained in detail in a series of subsections.

Conclusion

The memorandum ends with a short conclusion in which the main proposition is restated and the main points supporting it are again briefly summarized. Why so much repetition? Because the reality is that a judge will not necessarily read the entire memorandum. Repetition improves the odds that the judge will read at least the main points.

Putting It Into Practice 5.21:

Describe the basic organization of CODA's motion to dismiss.

Figure 5-11
Motion Format

MOTION FORMAT

Body of Motion

Memorandum of Points and Authorities
Summary of Argument
Factual Background
Argument
Conclusion

Attachments

"Why Did the Police Arrest Jorge if All He Did was 'Inspire' Them?"

"We've tried repeatedly to talk with Jorge and he absolutely refuses to speak to any of us. Martha has talked with Carmela, however. She told Martha that Jorge is convinced the police are out to persecute him and his family and he's resolved not to say anything," explained John.

"I don't follow." Ernesto's confusion was written on his face.

"It's a long story, but the short version is this. Apparently Jorge's father was a political prisoner in their country, which is why the family was granted political asylum here. Jorge was about 16 when they came to the U.S. and seems to have been deeply scarred by what he experienced in his country. At any rate, he has a great fear of the police, having seen his family members all tortured repeatedly by the police for their refusal to cooperate. He firmly believes he's a political prisoner even though he's been told by everyone, including his **public defender**—with whom he apparently refuses to communicate—that he's being held for Mike's attempted murder."

"So it doesn't look like we're going to get much out of him," said Ernesto, shaking his head. "How about the Hendershott boy? Could you get an interview with him?"

"Oh, yes. Dana Ferraro was falling all over herself to arrange that. Turns out she wants to enter into a **Gallagher agreement.**"

"Really," said Ernesto, somewhat shocked. "Little early for that, isn't it?"

"Maybe. But Dana's a pretty savvy litigator, so if she wants to settle I say we consider her proposal seriously. First of all, it's true that Hendershott did plead guilty in exchange for a reduced sentence and that he gave the police enough information to make a really good case against the other two boys. I gather they'll probably be pleading guilty shortly."

"Great! That makes our job a little easier," commented Ernesto.

"Exactly. Now, I was able to interview Hendershott yesterday. Sorry I had to do it without you, but the opportunity arose suddenly and you were in depositions all week. Anyway, the kid seemed to be pretty straight with me. Told me about their little group and their fantasies about doing something to make a statement about the so-called 'tyranny' of the American government."

---

public defender attorney paid by the government to represent criminal defendants who qualify for representation because of their financial status

Gallagher agreement agreement in which the defendant agrees to guarantee the plaintiff a certain amount of money if the plaintiff loses or recovers less than a designated amount and the plaintiff agrees to refund part of the defendant's payment if the verdict against the defendant is greater than a stated amount

"What did he say about *Teenage Stalkers?*" Ernesto was eager to find out if they still had a case against CODA, whose motion to dismiss had been denied by Judge Salt in accordance with John's prediction.

"Said they watched it at least once a week, that they liked to act out some of the best parts, and that they'd been looking for a way to do something as 'awesome' as the heroes in the movie."

"So the movie did incite them to attack Mike," suggested Ernesto encouragingly.

"That's where it's not clear. Apparently their paths crossed with Jorge's one afternoon after school. They were hanging out behind the convenience market next to the school, talking about what heroic acts they planned to carry out when Jorge, who had stopped by to smoke a cigarette, overheard them. Unfortunately, Hendershott was, in his own words, 'pretty wasted' during the ensuing conversation and so he's not really sure who said what. But I gather that, at the very least, Jorge planted the idea of going after Mike in their minds. They decided, with Jorge's encouragement, that Mike was the personification of everything evil in the educational system today: the glorification of athletes, the elitism perpetuated by grades and other competitive practices, and so on. I had to sift through a lot of rhetoric, but that seemed to be the gist of their reasoning."

"Did Jorge help them plan their attack?"

"No."

"Did he participate in any way?"

"Not that I'm aware of."

"Well, then, it doesn't make any sense. Why did the police arrest Jorge if all he did was 'inspire' them?"

"I can't answer that for certain. But I'm guessing that when Hendershott decided to open up to the police, he needed some kind of scapegoat and Jorge fit the bill. He said to me in passing that this whole thing was really Jorge's idea. But when I pressed him a little on that point, he admitted that Jorge hadn't actually been involved in carrying out the assault. He was also very vague about what exactly Jorge had said that encouraged his group to go after Mike. I think we need to depose him to see if we can pin him down more precisely because we're unlikely to get much assistance from Jorge."

"So what kind of deal does Dana want to make and why?"

"We already know that the Hendershott family is well endowed and I suspect that Daniel himself has some assets because Dana seems to see him as the proverbial deep pocket. Since his guilt is a given, she's doing her best to minimize his liability."

"What's she offering?"

"To pay $500,000 if no judgment is entered against either CODA or the school," explained John. "This will be reduced 50 cents on the dollar for whatever we receive from either the school or CODA . Hendershott will guarantee a minimum payment of $150,000, to be paid once we have signed an agreement, with the balance to be paid after trial or after a judgment is entered against the school or CODA."

"Don't you think it's a bit premature for us to be considering settling with Hendershott?" asked Ernesto reflectively. "For all we know, he could have millions of dollars at his disposal. We might be throwing away a bundle in the future just to have a little security now."

"We're certainly taking a risk by settling," agreed John, "but we have to consider Mike's needs. What's most important to him right now is to pay his medical bills and prevent his parents from having to go through a bankruptcy, which, frankly, is looking more and more like a possibility. Of course, it's ultimately up to Mike whether he wants to accept this offer, but I'm inclined to think he's probably going to take it."

BONUS POINTERS: ### GALLAGHER OR MARY CARTER AGREEMENTS

Plaintiffs and defendants sometimes enter into agreements known as "Mary Carter" or "Gallagher" agreements. Under these agreements, the defendant (or some of the defendants) agrees to guarantee the plaintiff a certain amount of money if the plaintiff loses or recovers less than a stated amount. The plaintiff agrees to refund part of the defendant's payment in the event of a verdict against the defendant in excess of a stated amount. Funds may actually change hands prior to trial or may be transferred on paper alone. Numerous variations on this theme exist, but the important feature is that the contracting defendant, although still a party in the case and usually a participant at the trial, benefits by the size of the judgments against the other defendants.

Plaintiffs benefit from such arrangements because they pressure settling defendants, who have a substantial interest in a sizeable plaintiff's recovery, to cooperate with the plaintiff in discovery and at trial. Besides obtaining security by being guaranteed payment, the plaintiff is able to present a more streamlined, simplified case merely by reducing the number of defendants.

Likewise, settling defendants benefit by eliminating the risk of paying more than the amount agreed on. The cost of litigation is reduced because the need for an aggressive defense is no longer warranted. Most importantly, the settling defendant has in effect purchased part of the plaintiff's claim, giving him a chance to recover all or part of what he has paid or agreed to pay. If the parties to a Mary Carter or Gallagher agreement succeed in their attack on the remaining defendants, the settling defendants may end up paying nothing—even if the jury finds substantial fault on their part.

The vast majority of courts tolerate these agreements even though the secrecy of their terms is subject to great controversy. These agreements may promote settlement, but they can also be abusive to nonsettling defendants, who may be faced with a lower chance of resolving the dispute as well as an increased exposure for damages. Although most courts now require the disclosure of such agreements—at least to the court and the nonsettling parties—these agreements continue to affect trials covertly. They skew the litigation process by hiding from the jury the full extent of the allegiance between the plaintiff and the settling defendant. They may also pressure attorneys into questionable ethical situations and can encourage settling defendants to share with the plaintiff information obtained from other defendants during joint defense efforts.

◆ **LOCAL LINKS** ◆

Are Mary Carter or Gallagher agreements permitted in your jurisdiction?

Putting It Into Practice 5.22:

How would Mike benefit from entering into a Gallagher agreement with Hendershott? How would Hendershott benefit? How could it be unfair to the school district and CODA?

As John and Ernesto took depositions, the case against CODA began to look stronger, but the case against the school district weakened. Ms. Sinclair wavered about when she had received an anonymous call warning about an impending attack and Mr. Garcia was adamant that she had never told him about such a call. Without clear evidence that the school was aware of the potential threat to its students' security, Mike would not be able to establish liability. John rolled the facts over in his mind and kept coming back to Mike's revelation about Jorge. Suddenly, it dawned on him. What if Mike had told someone at the school about Jorge's threat? By disclosing this to the right person, he could have conceivably put the school on notice that Mike's life was in danger. He called Mike immediately.

As soon as Mike answered the phone, John knew that something was very wrong.

"What's the matter, son? You sound as if you just lost your best friend."

"You're half right, Mr. Morgan. I told Greta about Carmela," admitted Mike.

"I take it she wasn't as understanding as you'd hoped."

"That's putting it mildly, sir. She threatened to ruin me and Carmela—said she'd tell everyone about me getting Carmela pregnant. I don't know what she's going to do. Right now, she won't even acknowledge me."

"I'm very sorry to hear this, Mike, but I still think in the long run you'll be glad you came clean with Greta."

"Actually, I'm already relieved. I think I've known for a long time that Greta and I weren't right for each other and I guess I just didn't want to tell her. But I'm really afraid for Carmela. She'd be devastated if word ever got out about her pregnancy."

"Let's just hope and pray that Greta takes the high road."

"Thanks. But I'm sure you had another reason for calling."

"Actually, I do. I've been going over the facts of your case and just realized I never asked you something. Did you ever tell anyone at the school—a teacher, a counselor, any employee—about Jorge's threat against you?"

"Yes," said Mike, after a long pause. "Is that a problem?"

"No, actually that's a good thing. With whom did you talk?"

"My coach," confided Mike. "After I found out about Carmela's being pregnant, I lost it. I needed someone to talk to and I knew I couldn't tell my parents—they'd have just freaked. So I went to Coach and told him what had happened and about Jorge threatening me."

"Did he think you should take this threat seriously?" asked John without revealing how important Mike's answer was.

"Yes. He said I should watch my back."

"Did he indicate you might want to notify security or that he would do that?"

"No. But I'd made him promise to never tell anyone what I'd told him." Mike thought for a moment. "This doesn't mean you're going to get Coach involved, does it?"

"I'm afraid so. We're going to need to depose him. If he knew you were being threatened and he took that threat seriously, he had a legal obligation to notify someone—an administrator, a security officer, someone. The fact that he didn't gives us grounds to argue that the school, as his employer, was negligent."

"But I really don't want to get Coach Washington in trouble," protested Mike.

"I know you don't, Mike. But you also don't want your parents to have to pay all your medical bills. In order for us to prevail against the school, we're going to have to show someone was at fault. And right now, that's beginning to look like the coach."

As soon as John got off the phone, he called Martha into his office. "I'd like you to arrange a deposition for Coach Jordan Washington as soon as possible."

PREPARING FOR A DEPOSITION

A paralegal can assist an attorney in preparing for a deposition by assembling the information she will need at that deposition. This can be done by preparing an outline setting forth suggested topics and questions, accompanied by copies of all pertinent discovery documents. The final product the paralegal produces should ideally be so complete that the attorney will find no need to go through the files looking for additional facts. The attorney can use the outline and documents as a starting point from which to plan the questioning.

One of the most important sources of deposition subject matter is the set of documents gathered in discovery. Any documents in which the witness's name appears—especially those authored by the witness—should be set aside, copied, and considered as possible material to ask about in the deposition. Any documents describing events that the witness observed or transactions in which the witness participated should be set aside, as should any documents needing authentication by this witness.

In a smaller case where the quantity of documents is manageable, the paralegal may go through the documents by hand, looking for potential deposition documents. In a complex case where the discovery documents may comprise many thousands of pages, reviewing every document for every deposition is impractical. In those cases a computerized document retrieval database should be set up and all of the document information entered into it as the documents come in. Then the database can be queried for a list of all the documents in which the witness's name appears or other relevant factors. (See Tim's Techno Tips at the end of this chapter.)

ASSISTING AT A DEPOSITION

Although paralegals do not question deponents, they do commonly attend and assist at depositions. Some of the functions commonly assigned to paralegals follow.

◆ Keeping track of documents and exhibits. When an exhibit is marked, copies are provided for each opposing attorney. Particularly in depositions involving large numbers of documents, having a paralegal present to locate exhibits and distribute the copies is helpful.

◆ Helping keep track of what topics have been covered and what loose ends remain. Questioning often jumps unpredictably from topic to topic as the attorney follows new threads raised by the witness's answers. The paralegal can help by keeping notes of the extent to which each topic has been fully explored and sharing this information with the attorney during breaks.

◆ Observing the witness and making notes of the witness's demeanor and reactions to questions. A good deal of the attorney's attention is occupied with the mechanics of phrasing questions. The paralegal is in a position to pay closer attention to the witness's body language and behavior.

◆ Helping detect evasive or unresponsive answers. As absorbed in the questioning as the attorney often is, she will sometimes fail to notice when the witness does not fully answer the question asked.

Putting It Into Practice 5.23:

What might Martha do to assist John at Mr. Washington's deposition?

WHAT TO EXPECT AT A DEPOSITION

Customarily, the court reporter sits at the head of the conference table, so as to have the best vantage point from which to hear all participants. The witness sits at one side of the table adjacent to the court reporter. The attorney conducting the questioning sits at the opposite side of the table, facing the witness, and the assisting paralegal sits next to the attorney. Usually, the opposing attorney sits next to the witness.

After introductions and, perhaps, a few moments of polite exchange of pleasantries, the court reporter swears in the witness. Then the questioning begins. The attorney begins by asking the witness to state her name for the record as well as her current address and telephone number (to make it easier to contact the witness.) After these identification questions, many attorneys ask whether the witness has ever been deposed before, and then describe the ground rules for the proceeding. Here is a typical introductory speech by an attorney taking a deposition.

Atty: Have you ever been deposed before?

Witness: No.

Atty: Let me begin by explaining a few ground rules. I will be asking you a number of questions, which you are required to answer. The court reporter, whom you see seated here on your right, will take down my questions and your answers, and everything else that is said here today, word for word, and prepare a printed transcript. The testimony you give here today will appear verbatim in the transcript, and can be used or quoted at the trial or in other proceedings in this lawsuit. Do you understand all that?

Witness: Yes.

Atty: Your testimony here is under oath, the same as if you were testifying in court in front of the judge. Do you understand that?

Witness: Yes.

Atty: Please take care to answer questions audibly, because the court reporter cannot interpret nods and shakes of the head, okay?

For more information about what to expect at a deposition (discussed in the context of divorce cases), go to *www.dadsdivorce.com/guide/custody/33.html.*

Witness:	Okay.
Atty:	Mr./Ms. _____ [the opposing attorney] may object to one of my questions from time to time. If that happens, the court reporter will record the objection so that the judge can consider it later, but you will go ahead and answer the question unless instructed by your attorney not to answer. Do you understand that?
Witness:	Yes.
Atty:	If you do not understand any of my questions, it is important that you tell me so that I can rephrase the question until you do understand it. Will you do that?
Witness:	Yes.

With the preliminaries attended to, the questioning gets underway in earnest. Typically, the first phase of questioning is aimed at getting the witness to tell her story in her own words. The attorney asks, "What happened next?" until the witness has related the whole story. Useful testimony is more likely to be elicited by letting the witness narrate as much as possible rather than trying to force testimony into preconceived factual theories using narrow questions. Unlike cross-examination in court, attorneys do ask questions to which they do not know the answer. Better to find out what a witness can say that can hurt a case at a deposition than to have the bombshell dropped in the courtroom.

After the witness has related her story, the attorney can fill in gaps and pin down details. While narrating, witnesses are often imprecise about times and locations; it is important to go back and ask the witness when and where each event took place and who else, if anyone, was present. The witness may have referred to documents or may have been asked to make a rough drawing or map as an aid in clarifying where people or objects were during events the witness is describing. If so, these must be marked as exhibits and the witness must identify them on the record.

Putting It Into Practice 5.24:

Describe basically what you think would transpire at the deposition of a witness who observed the accident involving Molly Running Deer and Stuart Thames. Assume the deposition is conducted by Molly Running Deer's attorney.

BONUS POINTERS:

THE OPPOSING ATTORNEY'S ROLE

The attorney for the opposing party will do her best to weaken any damaging testimony in several ways. First, she may make objections. Because no judge is present, the court reporter normally notes the objection on the record. The witness then answers the question despite the objection (otherwise the deposition would have to be taken again if the judge overruled the objection). Attorneys sometimes make so-called "speaking objections" when a witness is getting into trouble—objections that, in effect, tell the witness how to answer. Although the federal rules prohibit this, attorneys, when faced with a choice between the possibility of a scolding from the judge for a suggestive objection and the

---

NET NEWS

To read a deposition taken of Dr. Jeffrey Wigand (the former vice-president and head of research for Brown & Williamson, whose testimony was the focus of the movie *The Insider* and was crucial in subsequent litigation against the tobacco companies), go to *www.gate.net/~jcannon/deposit.html*. To read depositions taken in the Department of Justice case against Microsoft, go to *www.zdnet.com/zdnn/special/msdojdepos/msgates0827.html*.

certainty that a witness is about to torpedo the case with a bad answer, sometimes opt to bend the rules.

Opposing attorneys may also confer with the witness if the witness is the attorney's client. A witness is free to confer with her attorney during a deposition. A recess may be taken, or the witness and attorney may engage in a whispered conference during questioning. This is, in fact, the proper tactic to use when one's client is obviously having trouble with a question. However, the attorney conducting the questioning can, and usually should, note the conference on the record. ("Let the record show that the witness is conferring with his attorney before answering the question.")

Finally, the opposing attorney may instruct the witness not to answer a question. This tactic is proper only if the witness is the attorney's client, and only if the question calls for privileged information, violates a court-ordered limitation on discovery, or is so unreasonable that the attorney is prepared to stop the deposition and track down the judge for an order then and there. Instructing a witness not to answer is not a recommended move except under the most compelling of circumstances.

"Now, Looking Back, Do You Regret Not Having Done Something, Told Somebody Something, That Might Have Prevented Mike from Being Attacked?"

Martha began to feel sorry for the coach as John bore down on him. She knew that John had to pin him down if he was going to preserve Mike's case against the school, but she could see the coach beginning to squirm in his chair and wished there was some other way this could be accomplished. Mike had often talked to her about his coach and how much he trusted and admired him. She understood why Mike could not bring himself to be present to watch his coach being subjected to the rigors of intense questioning.

MORGAN: Did you believe that Jorge's threat was a serious one?

WASHINGTON: Yes.

MORGAN: Did you tell anyone about this threat?

WASHINGTON: No.

MORGAN: Why not?

WASHINGTON: Because Mike had asked me to keep what he had told me confidential. He practically begged me never to reveal what he had said to anyone.

MORGAN: Did you think Mike's life might have been in danger from Jorge?

WASHINGTON: I didn't think he'd actually kill him, no.

MORGAN: But did you think he might seriously injure him?

WASHINGTON: Not likely.

MORGAN: But possible?

WASHINGTON: Yes, possible.

MORGAN: Was it also possible that in the process of injuring Mike, Jorge might have gone too far and killed him?

TSOSIE: Objection. Calls for speculation.

MORGAN: This is a deposition, not a trial. He can speculate. Go ahead, Mr. Washington, and answer the question.

WASHINGTON: I suppose it was possible. But then, just about anything's possible, isn't it?

MORGAN: Let me remind you, Mr. Washington, we're not talking about hypotheticals here. One of your best athletes and someone you've told us here today is very dear to you was, in fact, seriously injured and almost died. Now, we don't have to speculate about that, do we, sir?

WASHINGTON: No.

MORGAN: Now, looking back, do you regret not having done something, told somebody something, that might have prevented Mike from being attacked?

TSOSIE: Objection. We all know hindsight is perfect. The question is whether Mr. Washington acted reasonably at the time.

MORGAN: Do you have an objection, Ms. Tsosie, or are you trying to testify for your client? You may answer (looking at the witness).

WASHINGTON: Knowing what I know today, I do wish I had done something.

MORGAN: Would it have been possible for you to have contacted security, for example, and told them that one of your athletes had been threatened and that you thought he was in danger of being attacked?

WASHINGTON: Yes.

MORGAN: And could you have done this without revealing the details of what Mike had told you?

WASHINGTON: Yes.

MORGAN: And could you have also told someone in the administration the same thing?

WASHINGTON: Yes.

MORGAN: And do you wish you had done this?

WASHINGTON: Yes.

The coach's last answer was barely audible, but he answered before Ms. Tsosie could object. John's strategy in asking a series of questions to which he was fairly certain he would get a "Yes," then interjecting the question to which he really wanted to get a "Yes" down on the record had proved successful. John had guessed correctly that the coach probably felt deeply guilty about not having intervened in some way, and had used that guilt to get the answer he needed to keep Mike's case against the school alive.

John was a masterful but compassionate litigator. His questioning at both trial and depositions was usually brief and to the point. Having created the transcript he was looking for, he ended the deposition. Martha knew that the next responsibility fell to her: summarizing the deposition.

SUMMARIZING A DEPOSITION

In a lawsuit of average complexity, the transcripts of the depositions taken by both sides may amount to several thousand pages. Litigators and their paralegals, who are usually dealing with a number of such lawsuits simultaneously, cannot be expected to locate important deposition testimony on command by memory alone. Searching through reams of transcripts whenever some particular bit of testimony is needed is highly impractical. Therefore, a systematic way of cataloging and indexing deposition transcripts is necessary.

Traditionally, paralegals often had to go through a transcript question by question and prepare an outline or index. In the last decade or so, as court reporters have embraced computerized note-taking and transcription, several innovations have been introduced that make organizing deposition testimony easier. One such innovation is the computer-generated index. A modern, computer-generated transcript comes with a word index that lists every single word in the deposition (except words like *a* and *the*), and gives page and line numbers of every place where each word appears in the transcript.

Transcripts can also be maintained on disk. Most court reporters can provide, for an extra charge, a diskette with a word processing file containing the entire transcript. This allows one to do word searching and other processing using word processing software. This also saves typing when quoting long passages in another document.

A third innovation is the "min-u-script" transcript. In addition to the usual transcript, a transcript can be ordered in which the questions and answers appear in single-spaced fine print, with several columns per letter-sized page. This way, testimony that occupies ten or more pages in the standard transcript can be seen at a glance on a single page.

But all of this wonderful technology has not eliminated the need for paralegals to laboriously wade through transcripts making outlines. Computerized indexing is no substitute for trained legal judgment. The computer can locate words, but it cannot decide which ones are important, nor can it assess meaning and relevance. Someone who is properly trained and familiar with the facts and issues of the case must read the transcripts, analyze the testimony, identify the questions and answers that may prove useful or need follow-up, and preserve the analysis in such a way as to allow the attorney to find needed testimony quickly.

digest summarize

A common solution is to have a paralegal summarize or **digest** each deposition. In a typical deposition, even though the questioning may jump around from topic to topic, "chunks," or short sequences of questions and answers, can be identified that together add up to one main point. When summarizing a deposition, the main point of each "chunk" must be expressed in a few, well-chosen words. If possible, the witness's words should be used rather than paraphrasing, if that can be done without sacrificing brevity.

No one format is correct. As with case briefs, this tool is prepared for individual use and must be tailored to meet the individual's needs. Commonly, a deposition outline has a narrow column on the left for the page and line number of each entry, with the summary of the main point of each "chunk" to the right.

The trick to identifying the main point of each segment is to focus not on the words, but on the relationship of the testimony to the issues in the case. Extraneous details and facts that are not in doubt are ignored. The main point that needs to be captured in each segment is the tendency of the testimony to prove or disprove some disputed issue.

Here are a few examples of formats that can be used to summarize depositions. The first—a narrative summary—is merely a summation of the testimony. It is used to summarize the testimony of minor witnesses or as an adjunct to other more complete summations.

Deposition of Officer Jones (First Officer at Scene)
3/24/01

Circumstances of Call: Jones arrived at school in response to 911 call from secretary.

Observations at Scene: Immediately saw that several students were highly agitated, milling around in confusion. Pl. was face down, apparently unconscious, with what appeared to be bullet wounds in his back.

Actions Taken: Called for backup officers; secured scene after trying to control bleeding from Pl.'s back.

Testimony can also be summarized by subject matter. This method requires more time to complete and is especially helpful when the deposition is lengthy and complex. The beauty of this approach is that it can greatly assist an attorney attempting to impeach a witness at trial because the attorney can zoom into a specific subject very efficiently.

Deposition of Emergency Room Physician Carrigan
4/1/01

ASSESSMENT OF CONDITION AT ADMISSION:	PAGE	LINES
Initial exam: Pl. was unconscious; pupils pinpoint; breathing shallow; profuse bleeding around L-2	4	1–19
Tests ordered: Ordered X-rays of spine; called in neurological consult	9	10–22

If establishing the sequence of events is what is most important to the attorney, a chronological summation is probably the best way to organize the deposition summary. The format can be basically the same as the previous summation, but arranged according to chronology rather than subject matter.

A whole-page summary can be used to summarize in a few sentences the testimony on each page of the deposition. This kind of summary is easier to prepare and generally easier to read than summaries prepared according to page and line numbers.

Deposition of Examining Physician Carrigan
4/1/01

PAGE	TESTIMONY
2	Witness: Cathryn Carrigan resides at 2020 E. Central, Tempe. Explanation of depo procedure.
3	Educational Background: B.S. Chemistry - 1973 from ASU; M.D. - 1980 from U of A; residency at Good Samaritan Hosp. in Phoenix
4	Initial exam of Pl. showed him to be unresponsive to any stimuli; pinpoint pupils; shallow breath; profuse bleeding from L-2

Alternatively, this summary can be further defined using line numbers as well.

PAGE	LINES	TESTIMONY
4	1–10	Initial exam of Pl. showed Pl. was unresponsive to stimuli
	11–16	Pupils were pinpoint; breathing shallow
	17–21	Profuse bleeding from L-2; also signs of bullet wound around T-12

◆ **LOCAL LINKS** ◆
What format does your instructor recommend for summarizing depositions?

███ *Putting It Into Practice 5.25:*

Summarize Coach Washington's testimony as you would do if you were preparing a deposition summary. Use the format recommended by your instructor.

GROUNDS FOR OBJECTING TO DISCOVERY REQUESTS

Work Product

Under what is referred to as the "work product doctrine," an attorney's work product can be obtained only if the requesting party has a "substantial need" for the information and has no other practical way to get it. An attorney's work product includes any documents prepared in anticipation of litigation or for trial.

Work product issues most commonly arise in connection with statements taken by an attorney or paralegal from a non-party witness and reports obtained from expert witnesses. For example, reports prepared by an expert witness hired by an attorney are probably protected from discovery, but those same reports prepared by an expert hired by the client are probably not considered a work product and are therefore discoverable.

Martha's mind wandered briefly from the task of drafting responses to interrogatories to her discussion the previous evening with Tim about the impact of discovery reform on the litigation process. How nice, she thought to herself, to have someone with whom she could share professional as well as personal interests. Her mind immediately shifted gears, however, when she saw John walking by her office.

"John," she called out. "Could you help me with one of interrogatories we received from CODA? I'm not sure how to respond."

" 'Identify each and every expert from whom you have obtained information or statements in connection with this matter, and, separately for each such person, state the substance of the information so obtained, whether or not you intend to use them as witnesses,' "Martha read out loud.

"**Work product.** Object and decline to answer on the grounds it's calling for an attorney work product," he announced matter-of-factly, scarcely missing a beat.

work product   documents prepared by an attorney in anticipation of litigation or for trial; such documents are protected from being discovered by opposing counsel

Questions Calling for Privileged Communications

A witness who validly asserts a privilege cannot be forced to testify. Common privileges are described here.

◆ Physician-patient privilege. Communications between a doctor and patient involving medical treatment are usually privileged and cannot be inquired into.
◆ Husband-wife privilege. Spouses cannot be compelled to testify about private communications between each other.
◆ Attorney-client privilege. An attorney is not permitted to answer questions about what a client has said to the attorney in confidence while seeking legal advice.
◆ Priest-penitent privilege. Under the laws of most states, a statement made privately to a member of the clergy in the course of confession or counseling is privileged.
◆ Privilege against self-incrimination. The Fifth Amendment of the U.S. Constitution gives each person the right to refuse to answer a question if the answer would tend to incriminate him.
◆ Other privileges. Some states also grant privileged status to communications with accountants, journalists, social workers, and others.

Putting It Into Practice 5.26:

Will Hendershott be able to claim the privilege against self-incrimination?

Questions Exceeding the Scope of Discovery

Any discovery question that is not reasonably calculated to lead to admissible evidence is objectionable and need not be answered unless rephrased. Questions that are objectionable are ambiguous, misleading, or burdensome.

AMBIGUOUS QUESTIONS

A question capable of more than one meaning is objectionable. The question must be clear enough that the answering party knows what is being asked.

MISLEADING QUESTIONS

Misleading questions are another example of questions that are improper because of their form. The subject matter of the question may be perfectly appropriate, but the answer is likely to be misinterpreted. A classic misleading question is "When did you stop beating your wife?"

BURDENSOME QUESTIONS

Any competent litigator can dictate in an hour a set of interrogatories that will take a team of paralegals months of full-time work to answer. Traditionally, an otherwise proper interrogatory had to be answered, regardless of how much work was required to do so. Today, however, courts are less tolerant of discovery requests designed primarily to make the responding party spend time and money. Although considerable variability exists from one jurisdiction to another and even from one judge to another, many judges today will refuse to require answers to discovery requests deemed unreasonably burdensome.

Putting It Into Practice 5.27:

Why is it important for paralegals to learn the grounds for objecting to discovery requests?

contempt of court willful disobedience of a court order; an act that embarrasses the court or obstructs it in administering justice; contempt of court can result in a fine or incarceration

---

"I'm Fairly Certain That Jorge's Participation Was Pretty Minimal in This Whole Affair, but We Need Him to Admit That."

After months of depositions and supplementation of disclosure statements, John, Ernesto, and Martha were starting to get a fairly complete picture about the events leading up to Mike's attack. But one question still haunted them: how important had Jorge been in launching Mike's assault? Jorge was still incommunicado and the Hendershott boy could not seem to decide what had provoked their attack. He vacillated between portraying himself as a rebel bent on destroying the American way and painting himself as an innocent victim of Jorge's manipulations. The other two teenagers were of little help. One of them had been so high during their encounter with Jorge, he did not even remember Jorge's being present. The other was so obviously terrified by Jorge that he refused even to acknowledge that he knew him.

"We need to file a motion to compel against Jorge," argued Ernesto.

"What makes you think he's going to respond to that any more than he's responded to any other overtures to get him to talk?" asked John petulantly.

"Because if he refuses to cooperate, we can ask the judge to find him in **contempt of court**."

"That should really scare him considering he's already been in jail for two months."

"But he might change his mind if he finds out that the judge can keep him there until he talks," insisted Ernesto.

"Ernesto, get real," snapped John. "We're not going to get anywhere by threatening this boy. He's not afraid of us. The more we try to force him to speak, the more resistant he's going to get."

"So what's your solution?" asked Ernesto stiffly.

"We have to find a way to convince him to tell the police what happened," said John.

"And how are we going to do that? He won't even talk with us."

" 'We' are not. We're going to have Carmela talk with him. Jorge may not care about getting out of jail, but I'd be willing to wager his sister wants him out of there. Maybe she can get him to open up to his public defender. I'm fairly certain that Jorge's participation was pretty minimal in this whole affair, but we need him to admit that. If we can get him to talk to his public defender, maybe he'll be willing to talk to us as well."

"Sounds pretty iffy to me, but I suppose it's worth a try. When do you plan to talk with her?"

"Actually, I was planning on asking Martha. She seems to have a good rapport with Carmela. Maybe between the two of them they can figure out how to get Jorge to see his situation differently."

Figure 5-12
Grounds for Objecting to Discovery Requests

> # GROUNDS FOR OBJECTING TO DISCOVERY REQUESTS
>
> Work Product
> Privileged Communications
> Questions Exceeding Scope of Discovery
> Misleading Questions
> Ambiguous Questions
> Burdensome Questions

NET NEWS

To read more about the work-product and attorney-client privileges as they relate to discovery requests, go to *www.lectlaw.com* and click on "The Library's Rotunda," "Legal Professional's Lounge," and then on "Lawyers." Examine the article entitled "Discovery Protection: Work-Product, Attorney-Client and Common-Interest Privileges."

NON-COMPLIANCE WITH DISCOVERY REQUESTS

Sometimes a party simply refuses to provide requested information or to participate voluntarily in the discovery process. In this case, what can be done? First, the party seeking the information can simply decide to look for it elsewhere. Waging a motion battle to force a proper response can be time-consuming, expensive, and distracting from the primary task of preparing for trial. Some information is simply not worth the effort required to get it. In a typical real-life lawsuit, inadequate responses to discovery requests are common and litigants cannot afford to do battle over all of them. Furthermore, actually winning the motion does not guarantee the information will be given. On the other hand, having an opponent on the record with an answer that is later shown to be false or at least misleading can be good jury ammunition.

In some situations, however, the information is vital and can be obtained only from the opponent. Then, there is no choice but to try to get the opposing party to comply with the rules, either by persuasion or by force. The federal rules (and those of many state courts) require parties to try to resolve discovery disputes on their own before asking the judge to intervene. To comply, the attorney may be required to phone opposing counsel or to send a demand letter followed by a phone call.

If the recalcitrant party still refuses to cooperate, the next option is to file a **motion to compel,** which is a motion requesting the judge to order an opposing party to respond to a discovery request. For example, if a party fails to answer some of the interrogatories in a set, the proponent can file a motion to compel asking the judge to order the party to provide answers by a certain date. Go to Figure 5-13 to see an example of a motion to compel.

As a last resort, a party can file a **motion for sanctions,** asking the judge to impose a sanction—in effect, a punishment—on a party who is willfully disobeying the rules. With a motion to compel, the worst that can happen to the disobedient party is that the judge may order him to make a proper response and possibly pay

motion to compel motion requesting a judge to order a party to respond to a discovery request

motion for sanctions motion asking the judge to punish a party

Figure 5-13
Motion to Compel

WHITE & TREADWELL
John Morgan, Esq., SBN 00123
Ernesto Esparanza, Esq. SBN 012345
2020 North Central Avenue, Suite 3200
Phoenix, Arizona 85005
(602) 555-1234

Attorneys for plaintiff Michael Johnson

IN THE SUPERIOR COURT OF MARICOPA COUNTY
PHOENIX, ARIZONA

Michael Johnson, a single man,	)	
	)	
	)	NO. _____
Plaintiff,	)	
	)	Plaintiff's Motion to
vs.	)	Compel Prodution
	)	of Documents from
Daniel Hendershott, Max Evans, and	)	Washington High School
Alan House, all single men; CODA,	)	District
Inc.,a foreign corporation;	)	
Washington High School District.	)	
	)	
Defendants.	)	
	)	

Pursuant to ARCP Rule 37, Uniform Rule IV (g) and Local Rule 3.2 (h), and the following Memorandum of Points and Authorities, Plaintiff requests that this court compel Defendant Washington High School District to produce the documents and things requested pursuant to Plaintiff's Request for Production of Documents served on May 2, 2001. Defendant has refused to produce the requested documents based on an alleged claim of attorney-client privilege and work product.

The documents requested by Plaintiff and which Defendant has refused to produce are:

6.   Copies of any and all procedures, policies, notes, memoranda, correspondence, and the like providing instructions, recommendations, cautionary advise or similar information regarding Defendant's processing , or how it should process, any telephonic or other communicated threat of violence on or near its facilities.

The undersigned hereby certifies that after personal consultation with Defendant's attorney and good faith efforts to do so, the parties are unable to satisfactorily resolve this discovery dispute

DATED this 22nd day of July, 2001.

WHITE & TREADWELL

_____
John Morgan
Attorneys for plaintiff Michael Johnson

. . . .

. . . .

some attorney's fees. With a motion for sanctions, the disobedient party could conceivably lose the entire lawsuit and be thrown in jail for contempt of court. (Judges rarely impose such severe sanctions; usually, the threat is enough to induce obedience.) A motion for sanctions is allowed if a party has completely failed to respond to a discovery request or a motion to compel has been filed, the judge has issued an order compelling the party to provide the requested discovery, and the party has not obeyed the order.

Some of the punishment options a judge can resort to, singly or in combination, are presented here.

◆ assess attorney's fees
◆ make factual rulings (with the intent to deter parties from hiding adverse facts via the threat that, if the deception is caught, the facts will be made even more adverse)
◆ disallow designated evidence
◆ prohibit any evidence on particular claims or defenses
◆ strike claims or defenses
◆ render judgment (a relatively severe punishment, imposed only in unusually compelling situations)
◆ hold the offending party or attorney in contempt of court

Putting It Into Practice 5.28:

John has requested that the school provide its telephone logs for a period of one month preceding Mike's shooting. The school does not respond in a timely manner. What should John do? Is a motion for sanctions appropriate?

Figure 5-14
Consequences of Failure to Comply with Discovery Request

CONSEQUENCES OF FAILURE TO COMPLY WITH DISCOVERY REQUEST

Options when Opposing Party fails to Comply with Discovery Request

Get information elsewhere
Contact opposing counsel by phone or letter
File motion to compel
File motion for sanctions

Court Sanctions for Non-Compliance with Discovery Request

Assess attorney's fees
Make factual rulings
Disallow designated evidence
Prohibit evidence on designated claims or defenses
Strike claims or defenses
Render judgment
Hold in contempt of court

Martha was glad to be able to help out in Mike's case, but she had just about had her fill of men with secrets. The relationship between her and Tim was continuing to deepen and she knew they had the potential to forge a lasting partnership, but she was troubled by Tim's obvious discomfort with discussing his past, or at least certain parts of it. Whenever she nudged him to tell more about himself, he balked and found ways to change the subject. She was certain he was hiding something, and whatever it was frightened her. If there were such a thing as a "soul mate," she believed Tim to be hers, but she feared that the secret between them could destroy everything they had built together over the last several months.

■ TIM'S TECHNO TIPS

Litigation Support Software

Litigation support software has been around for some time. One of the oldest, and most popular, is Summation. Summation was first introduced by two San Francisco attorneys in the late 1980s. It now has numerous features that allow for complete database management, OCR (optical character recognition—a program that reads graphic files and deciphers what the images represent) of scanned documents, electronic folders for deposition transcripts, automatic numbering of scanned documents, and other tasks. (Documents are scanned by taking a picture of the document and translating the picture into a digital code.) A visit to Summation's Web site at *www.summation.com* will provide you with testimonials, a virtual demonstration, and a free CD. (You must buy the product if you want to use it in a case.)

While Summation appears to be primarily useful in cases involving lots of documents and numerous depositions, that is not the case. It is also invaluable to the attorney who has a caseload of countless standard "fender benders." Summation can maintain these cases on a large hard drive, or if necessary, copy them to a CD-ROM so that a solo practitioner's entire caseload can be carried with him and viewed from a notebook computer. In order to do so, all pleadings, correspondence, and documents, would have to be inputted into the program, scanned as graphic images and, if desired, OCR'd so that the words they contained could be searched. Depositions would be loaded from a floppy—court reporters can now produce the transcript in ASCII text or your favorite word processor format.

One of the principal advantages of Summation is the ability to post and keep track of electronic notes on the deposition transcript or scanned documents. These notes can be coded so that if the document is being presented at trial, only the base document would be shown on other monitors or computers. Information can also be redacted from a scanned file. This feature is useful when some parts of a document are inadmissible and cannot be shown to the jury, or contain privileged information that should not be given to the adverse party. The redacted information appears on the screen as a black area so that it is relatively easy to recognize as being redacted.

Other companies have their own version of litigation support programs. Entering the search term "litigation support software" in your Internet browser will give you a very long list of "hits." Two of the other companies that produce litigation support software are Lawpro, Inc. (*www.lawproinc.com*) and Legal Resources Group, a division of Questsoft, Inc. (*www.legalrg.com*). Lawpro, Inc. claims its program will do it all: case management, billing, litigation support, etc. Legal Resources Group has a smaller vision, but claims its program (The Ultimate Bucket) is far easier to use than its competitors. Numerous other companies have offerings in this area. Some concentrate on document control, others on database management. VirtualLaw has some attributes of many of the non-freeware programs, but lacks many of the bells and whistles.

TECHNO TRIP

It's time to find out for yourself which litigation support program feels right for you. Go to Summation's Web site and take the virtual demo. If interested, order the free demonstration CD. Next, head over to Lawpro's Web site and take their virtual demo. Lastly, go to Legal Resource Group's Web site and download their demo package. Take the time to check the price of each offering. Compare the three for "feel" and intuitiveness. Which program would you feel most comfortable with at this stage in your education? Finally, how do they compare with VirtualLaw? Are they worth the asking price?

SUMMARY – PART B

Under the federal rules, a disclosure statement must provide four areas of information: (1) the name, address, and telephone number of every person likely to have discoverable information; (2) a copy of, or a description of, all the documents in the possession, custody, or control of a party that are relevant to disputed facts alleged in the pleadings; (3) a computation of damages and the documents and other evidentiary materials upon which such computations are based; and (4) any insurance policy covering the defendant for the liabilities in the suit. Judges in the federal courts have the power to punish parties who file incomplete disclosure statements. They can prohibit the party from introducing the evidence at trial that would have favored that party, declare the facts in question as being established, order the party to pay the opposing party's fee, inform the jury of the nondisclosure, or declare the issue relating to the non-disclosed material adjudicated.

Almost all communications with judges are by motion. Motions are formal court papers stating what the party wants the judge to do and which rule of civil procedure authorizes the type of motion being made. Motions are accompanied by a memorandum of points and authorities. After the movant files a motion with the court and serves it on the attorneys representing the other parties, the respondents have an opportunity to file responses, which the movant can then rebut in a reply. After the motion papers have been filed, the judge may grant oral arguments, although such arguments are optional and parties should not count on them to first make their arguments. Typically, judges take motions under advisement and communicate their decision to the parties by means of a minute entry. Motions can revolve around procedural details or discovery disputes or can, as in the case of motions to dismiss, decide whether a case has enough merit to proceed forward. Motions to dismiss are granted only if the judge determines that the plaintiff must lose even if he or she is able to prove everything alleged in the complaint. The motion itself states who is making the motion, what the motion is asking for, what procedural rules govern the motion, and what documents support the motion. The accompanying memorandum consists of a summary of the argument, the factual background, the argument, and the conclusion.

Paralegals can assist attorneys in preparing for depositions by collecting the documents and other information the attorney will need. One way that paralegals can assist attorneys in preparing their questioning is by assembling an outline of potential topics. At the deposition itself, paralegals can help by keeping track of all documents and exhibits, by keeping notes about what topics have been covered and which ones remain to be covered, by observing the witness's demeanor, and by helping detect when a witness gives evasive or unresponsive answers. Typically, an attorney begins a deposition by establishing the ground rules and then allows the witness to tell her story, after which the attorney will ask questions that try to fill in the gaps. Documents, drawings, maps, or any evidence referred to must be marked as exhibits and identified by the witness on the record. After depositions, paralegals are often assigned to prepare an outline or index that summarizes the testimony. Although computerized indexing has made this process easier, a computer is no substitute for a paralegal's legal judgment. No one format for summarizing depositions is correct, but whatever form is used must allow an attorney to find relevant testimony quickly and easily.

Discovery requests can be objected to on the grounds that they constitute an attorney's work product, that they call for privileged communications, that they exceed the scope of discovery, or that they are ambiguous, misleading, or burdensome.

If a party refuses to respond to a discovery request, the party requesting the information has several options. He can look for the information elsewhere; this is the wisest choice when the information is not worth the time and expense that may be necessary to obtain it. Before looking to the court for assistance, the party should try to resolve the dispute by writing a demand letter and talking with the attorney representing the non-responding party. If that fails to produce results, the party may then choose to file a motion to compel and, if that fails, a motion for sanctions. If the court grants a motion for sanctions, it has several punishment options, including the assessment of attorney's fees, making adverse factual rulings, disallowing certain evidence or defenses or claims, and even holding the party or attorney in contempt of court.

KEY TERMS

Chambers
Contempt of court
Digest
Ex parte communications
Gallagher agreement
Hearing

Memorandum of points
    and authorities
Minute entry
Motions
Motion for sanctions
Motion papers

Motion to compel
Motion to dismiss
Movant
Oral arguments
Public defender
Reply

Respondent
Response
Under advisement
Work product

REVIEW QUESTIONS – PART B

1. According to the federal rules, what information must be provided in a disclosure statement?
2. What are the possible consequences of incomplete disclosure in the federal system?
3. Describe the procedures followed in motion practice.
4. What does a motion and supporting memorandum consist of?
5. How can a paralegal assist an attorney before, during, and after a deposition?
6. Describe a typical deposition.
7. On what grounds can a party object to a discovery request?
8. What options does a party have if the opposing party refuses to provide requested information?

PRACTICE EXAM – PART B

MULTIPLE CHOICE

1. Disclosure statements
   a. need not be filed with the court
   b. are not court papers
   c. unlike motions, are not required to have captions and other formal parts
   d. none of the above
2. A disclosure statement (under the federal rules) should identify
   a. anyone who may be called as a witness
   b. anyone having custody of a relevant document
   c. anyone from whom a statement has been taken
   d. all of the above
3. Documents that must be disclosed in a federal case are
   a. those in the possession of a party's attorney, but not in the possession of a party's insurance company
   b. business records, but not communications about the lawsuit
   c. those that are part of the dispute
   d. none of the above
4. Some damages are
   a. concrete, provable expenses that are easy to prove
   b. items such as pain and suffering, which are difficult to quantify
   c. items such as loss of future income, which are provable but require estimates
   d. all of the above
5. A party that fails to prepare a complete disclosure statement can be punished by the judge
   a. by being prohibited from using the non-disclosed evidence at trial
   b. but the attorney cannot be ethically censured
   c. by having the non-disclosed facts deemed proved but the jury cannot be informed of the party's non-disclosure
   d. but the judge cannot enter a default judgment against the offending party

6. A motion to dismiss can be based on
   a. lack of jurisdiction
   b. failure to state a claim
   c. improper venue
   d. all of the above
7. The summary of the argument section of a memorandum
   a. should lay out the main points of the argument
   b. is unlikely to be read by the judge
   c. should stimulate the judge's curiosity but should not reveal what is discussed in the argument
   d. none of the above
8. The argument section of a memorandum
   a. should open with an immediate discussion of the main points of the argument
   b. must follow a set organizational pattern
   c. usually has a series of subsections explaining each of the main points of the argument in detail
   d. none of the above
*9. A Mary Carter or Gallagher agreement
   a. encourages settlement
   b. protects defendants but not plaintiffs
   c. benefits all of the defendants, whether they enter into the agreement or not
   d. promotes a sense of openness and fairness in the trial process
10. When preparing for a deposition, a paralegal should
    a. set aside all documents describing events the witness observed
    b. set aside all documents the witness needs to authenticate
    c. in large, complex cases use a computerized document retrieval database to locate documents bearing the witness's name
    d. all of the above
11. At a deposition, a paralegal
    a. should keep track of what topics have been covered but should not be distracted by the witness's demeanor
    b. should keep track of documents and exhibits
    c. need not pay attention to evasive and unresponsive answers because that is the attorney's job
    d. all of the above
12. At a deposition
    a. the attorney usually begins by asking the witness some identification questions and explaining the ground rules
    b. the attorney asking the questions swears in the witness

   c. the attorney is careful not to ask questions to which she does not know the answer
   d. the attorney tries to avoid allowing the witness to tell his story
13. The opposing attorney at a deposition
    a. is not allowed to confer with a witness
    b. is not allowed to make objections
    c. may instruct a witness not to answer a question
    d. none of the above
14. Today's computers
    a. have eliminated the need for paralegals to summarize depositions
    b. create indexes that accompany a transcript
    c. cannot only locate words in a transcript, but can assess the legal meaning and relevance of those words
    d. all of the above
15. When summarizing a deposition, it is important to
    a. keep in mind that there is only one ideal format
    b. focus on the relationship between the testimony and the issues in the case
    c. identify the main point of each segment of testimony by focusing on the words used by the deponent
    d. all of the above
16. Information that is privileged includes
    a. communications between a patient and a physician
    b. communications between spouses
    c. communications that tend to incriminate the person giving the information
    d. all of the above
17. A party is not required to respond to a discovery request that
    a. is burdensome
    b. has misleading or ambiguous questions
    c. calls for questions that exceed the scope of discovery
    d. all of the above
18. A court that grants a motion for sanctions
    a. has the option of holding the offending attorney in contempt of court
    b. can prevent the party from using the evidence that was not provided, but cannot actually render a judgment in favor of the requesting party
    c. cannot make factual rulings that are adverse to the offending party
    d. can assess attorney's fees but cannot strike any claims or defenses

FILL IN THE BLANK

19. After _____ (verbal presentations made by attorneys to a judge), a judge will usually take the case _____ and will not issue a decision until later.
20. Motions are accompanied by a written legal argument called a _____.
21. After the _____ (the party filing a motion) files a motion, the _____ (the party opposing the motion) will be allowed to file a _____, and in rebuttal the party filing the motion will be allowed to file a _____. All of these papers are referred to generically as _____.
22. If a judge decides to allow a _____ in which he will listen to the attorneys' arguments, he may opt for an informal affair in his private _____.
23. Judges communicate their decisions and orders to parties by means of a _____.
24. The purpose of a _____ is to tell the judge what the movant is asking for; the purpose of a _____ is to tell the judge why she should grant the movant's request.
25. A _____ is an attorney who represents criminal defendants who cannot afford counsel.
*26. Plaintiffs and defendants who want to minimize the risks of going to trial may enter into a _____, which the defendant guarantees the plaintiff a minimal recovery and the plaintiff agrees to refund the defendant if the verdict is greater than a certain amount.
27. An attorney's _____ includes any documents prepared for trial or in anticipation of litigation and is protected from discovery.
28. A party that wants the judge to order a party to comply with a discovery request should file a _____; if the party still refuses to respond, the party making the request may want to file a _____, which asks the judge to punish the offending party.

TRUE OR FALSE

____ 29. Only those individuals likely to testify need to be identified in a disclosure statement.
____ 30. Under the federal rules, the name, address, and telephone numbers of persons likely to have discoverable information must be provided, but no information need be given about the subjects of the information they have.
____ 31. Insurance coverage is discoverable even though evidence of insurance coverage is inadmissible at trial because judges want to encourage parties to settle.
____ 32. A federal judge has the power to "level the playing field" by taking away evidence that would have favored the party that failed to disclose it.
____ *33. The federal rules require more detailed disclosure in disclosure statements than any of the states do.
____ 34. Essentially all communications with a judge are by motion.
____ 35. The ethical rules are permissive about allowing attorneys to talk without judges without opposing counsel being present.
____ 36. A motion consists of a paragraph requesting the judge to do something and giving the procedural rule supporting the request and is accompanied by a memorandum of points and authorities.
____ 37. Motions must be filed with the court and must be served on the attorneys for all of the parties.
____ 38. The rules of procedure always establish the number of days in which a response must be filed.
____ 39. A response and a reply are the same thing.
____ 40. Motions are always heard in the judge's chambers.
____ 41. Oral arguments are always formal affairs in which the attorneys take turns speaking and are not allowed to interrupt each other.
____ 42. Judges must allow parties to give oral arguments if they request them.
____ 43. Judges commonly take motions under advisement and convey their decision to the parties via a minute entry.
____ 44. Judges like to take motions under advisement so they have time to reflect on the arguments made to them and so they can avoid having to give the loser the bad news face to face.

____ 45. Minute entries are sent to the parties but are not put in the court's file.

____ 46. A motion to dismiss can be granted if the judge determines that there is not enough evidence to support the plaintiff's claim.

____ 47. When preparing a memorandum, the attorney can assume that the judge is familiar with the facts of the case.

____ 48. Any factual statements made in a memorandum must be supported by evidence.

____ 49. Repetition should be avoided in a memorandum because it insults the judge reading it.

____ *50. A defendant that enters into a Gallagher agreement is no longer a party in the case and does not participate at trial.

____ *51. A plaintiff who enters into a Mary Carter agreement can present a more streamlined case at trial.

____ *52. Mary Carter agreements allow defendants to eliminate the risk of having to pay more than the amount agreed upon with the plaintiff.

____ *53. Settling defendants who have entered into a Gallagher agreement with the plaintiff may end up paying nothing even if the jury finds them to be substantially at fault.

____ *54. Mary Carter and Gallagher agreements can skew the litigation process and pressure attorneys into unethical situations.

____ 55. A paralegal can assist an attorney in preparing for a deposition by generating an outline of possible topics and questions and assembling all documents that may be relevant.

____ 56. No matter what the size of the case, a paralegal preparing for a deposition should go through all the documents by hand looking for pertinent documents.

____ 57. Useful testimony is more likely elicited by asking focused questions than by allowing a witness to narrate his story.

____ 58. Once an attorney understands the gist of what a witness observed, he should use interrogatories to fill in the gaps and pin down the details.

____ 59. Any documents that a witness referred to in the deposition and any drawings or maps he might have made should be marked as exhibits and identified by the witness of the record.

____ *60. Attorneys are encouraged to make speaking objections.

____ 61. A typical transcript of a deposition taken by both sides usually runs about one hundred pages.

____ 62. Today, paralegals usually have to go through transcripts question by question to prepare a deposition outline.

____ 63. Most court reporters can provide a transcript on disk that allows one to search for words and phrases.

____ 64. A "min-u-script" allows a paralegal to see ten or more pages of standard transcript on one page.

____ 65. When summarizing a deposition, a paralegal should use the same words used by the witness if that can be done without sacrificing brevity.

____ 66. The main point that a paralegal needs to capture in a deposition summary is how the testimony proves or disproves a disputed fact.

____ 67. An attorney's work product cannot be obtained by an opposing party unless that party has a substantial need for it and has no other practical way to get it.

____ 68. Sometimes waging a motion battle does not warrant the time and money necessary to be successful, but winning the motion does guarantee the information will be given.

____ 69. Under the federal rules, parties do not have to try to resolve discovery disputes before filing a motion to compel.

____ 70. A motion for sanctions is called for when a motion to compel has been granted and disobeyed by the offending party.

* Questions taken from Bonus Pointers

LEGAL LINGO

What's My Name?

1. I am a witness at a deposition.
2. Each party must serve me on the opposing party shortly after a lawsuit begins and then must update me periodically.
3. I am a meeting at which the judge discusses the case with the attorneys and issues a scheduling order.

4. I am used to obtain documents from an opposing party.
5. I am a process by which a defendant can verify the extent of the plaintiff's injuries.
6. I am a witness who is allowed to give opinion testimony.
7. I am something a judge usually does after hearing the attorneys make arguments regarding a motion.
8. I am lawyer short-hand for judge-made law.
9. I am the party making a motion.
10. I am someone who knows about the filing system and records in an organization.
11. I am the party who is sending out interrogatories to be answered.
12. I am prepared by a court reporter.
13. I accompany a motion and explain why the judge should do as the moving party is requesting.
14. I am written questions used to obtain information from parties.
15. I am the documents prepared by an attorney in anticipation or preparation for litigation and I cannot be the subject of discovery.
16. I am a chemist who analyzes physical evidence.
17. I am filed by the respondent.
18. I am a judge's private office.
19. I am an agreement parties enter to minimize the risks of going to trial.
20. I am the formal document by which a judge conveys his or her decisions to the parties.
21. I am used to punish a party that refuses to comply with a reasonable discovery request.

LEGAL LOGISTICS

1. Summarize what you think the primary abuses in the discovery process have been to date.
   a. How would you resolve those abuses?
   b. What is your assessment of mandatory disclosure?
   c. How well do you think mandatory disclosure has dealt with the problems in the discovery process?
2. Suppose you represent Molly Running Deer in her case against Stuart Thames. What things will you have to include in a disclosure statement if you are suing in federal court?
   a. What experts might you want to call in this case?
   b. Whom would you depose?
   c. How might you use interrogatories and requests for admission before deposing Stuart?
   d. If you interviewed a witness to the accident whose perception is that Stuart clearly and blatantly ran the red light, why might you want to depose this witness?
   e. Why might you want to depose Stuart early in the case?
   f. What should Molly's attorney do if Stuart did not show up for his deposition and his attorney refused to return her phone calls?
   g. Suppose Stuart claims that he tried to use his brakes but that they suddenly failed; he files a cross-claim against the manufacturer. What kinds of documents should he request and how should he get them?
3. Suppose you are a paralegal in a law office in your jurisdiction representing a woman filing for divorce. Outline the discovery process as you would plan it.
4. Suppose your firm is representing a store that has recently been sued by a customer who fell while in the store. How will you go about determining the extent of the plaintiff's injuries?
   a. Prepare an outline of the subjects you would want to see covered in a deposition of the plaintiff.
   b. What will you have to include in a disclosure statement?
5. Do you think Gallagher and Mary Carter agreements enhance the judicial process or inhibit it? Explain your reasoning.

A TRIP TO THE MOVIES

The movie *Erin Brockovich* is based on a true story about a young woman who enters the legal field as a file clerk, with no experience and no legal training, and who ends up involving her firm in a suit against a multi-billion-dollar company, Pacific Gas & Electric. The resulting judgment—$333 million—was the largest judgment ever awarded in a civil action in the United States up to that time. Brockovich's tenacity and compassion for the plaintiffs and their families cause the suit to escalate from a minor real estate case to a massive toxic tort case that rocked the legal and corporate worlds.

1. Why did Brockovich have to do such extensive research before a toxic tort case could be filed against PG&E?

a. Why would it not have been appropriate to file suit and then send a request for production of documents in this case?

b. Why did PG&E pay for the medical treatment for the people next to the plant?

2. Would the implementation of mandatory disclosure have assisted the plaintiffs in making their case?

3. What ethical and moral dilemmas faced the attorneys who represented PG&E?

4. What people would you have wanted to depose if you represented the plaintiffs? How might PG&E have used depositions of the plaintiffs to their advantage?

5. How could PG&E have used the traditional discovery process to demoralize and bankrupt the plaintiff's firm?

6. Why would the plaintiffs rely on depositions more than interrogatories to get information from the parties in this case?

7. Based on the statements made by the attorney originally representing PG&E, what stance do you think the company was prepared to take in reference to the element of causation? What do you predict would have been the results of any I.M.E.s they had conducted on the plaintiffs?

8. How might the plaintiffs have used a disclosure statement to their advantage?

a. What would be the possible consequences to PG&E if it failed to disclose the water testing documents in its possession?

b. What options would the plaintiffs have if PG&E refused to disclose the water testing documents?

9. On what basis do you think PG&E filed its motion to dismiss? (Look up *demurrer* and see how it compares to a motion to dismiss.)

10. How might Brockovich have assisted Ed Masry if he had deposed one of the engineers at the PG&E plant?

11. If the plaintiffs had gone to trial, why would deposition summaries have been crucial to Masry and the other attorneys?

12. If Brockovich had needed to notify the clerk at the Water Office that he was going to be deposed and that he should bring relevant records to the deposition, what would she have had to do?

13. Why was this case such a difficult one for a sole practitioner to undertake? Why was Masry forced to involve a bigger law firm?

14. Why was it in the plaintiffs' best interests to have their case arbitrated rather than taken to trial?

INTERNET INQUIRIES

1. Go to the Internet, enter the search term "deposition," and look for transcripts of depositions. Find a deposition that is of interest to you and prepare a brief summary of the substantive testimony—testimony that is directly related to the legal issues at stake, and not simply background information.

2. Suppose your attorney asks you to work with a client who is very nervous about her upcoming deposition in her divorce case. Go to the Internet and write down the addresses of at least three Web sites that you think would be helpful to her.

3. You have been asked by your attorney to prepare a motion to strike. Go to the Internet and find out what procedural rules govern motions to strike in your state. (Try www.courts.net to link to the Web

page for the highest court in your state, which may have the procedural rules for your state online.) Then find samples of motions upon which you might pattern yours.

a. What are the pertinent procedural rules?

b. List the Web addresses of the sites you find that have samples of motions.

4. Find out if your local trial court has a Web page. (Try www.pac-info.com and *www.lexisone.com*.)

a. If it does, can you get information about the status of cases pending before this court?

b. Using a name given to you by your instructor or the name of someone you know to be currently involved in a case with this court, go to this Web site and make a list of all the information you can find out about this case.

6

Pre-Trial, Trial, and Post-Trial

OBJECTIVES:

In this chapter you will learn:

- the basis for a motion for summary judgment and what is included in such a motion
- how to set a trial date
- what a pretrial statement is and what it includes
- the ethical implications of responding to inquiries from the press
- what a motion *in limine* is
- what goes into preparing jury instructions
- the considerations underlying the preparation and submission of trial exhibits
- what goes into a trial notebook
- the jury selection process
- the purpose of opening statements and closing arguments
- the rules and practices that govern the presentation of evidence and the examination of witnesses

- the burdens of proof that dictate each party's actions and the consequences of not meeting those burdens
- how a judge decides what instructions to give a jury
- what types of verdicts can be requested
- how a verdict is translated into a judgment
- the options available to the loser at a trial
- why such issues as the form of judgment and the assessment of costs provoke contention between the parties
- the process that must be followed in order to collect a judgment
- options available to a judgment debtor who chooses to resist collection of a judgment
- the steps in the appellate process and the rules that govern that process

"I Just Found Out That the Man I Thought I Might End Up Marrying Has Been Deceiving Me All These Months."

"How could you have kept this a secret?" Martha lashed out. "This changes everything. I can never trust you again!"

"You don't know how many times I've tried to tell you but I was afraid you'd react this way."

"Did it ever occur to you that I might not have reacted this way if you'd been truthful with me up front?"

"I was afraid you'd never give me a chance if you knew who I was." Tim looked down to avoid seeing what he knew was revulsion in Martha's eyes.

"I have to go. I have to get back to work," said Martha mechanically.

"But we have to talk this out, Martha," pleaded Tim.

She turned to him coldly. "No, I don't *have* to do anything. Please do not call me or try to make contact with me. Goodbye, Tim." Martha turned rigidly and walked away, her resolute cadence masking the anguish ripping at her heart.

Ernesto read the look of devastation on Martha's face as soon as she walked into his office, but wanted to avoid prying. "So how are you doing on that list of exhibits for the response to CODA's *motion for summary judgment?*" asked Ernesto, pretending not to notice Martha's reddened eyes.

"They're all right here. I'll have the affidavits you requested today before I leave," responded Martha in her most professional voice.

"Great," replied Ernesto uncomfortably. He wasn't accustomed to seeing what he perceived as the perennially unflappable Martha so obviously distraught. "The more I work on this response, the more certain I am that we can convince the judge that there are genuine issues of fact at stake in our case against CODA." Ernesto was talking to fill the silence rather than to inform Martha, who he knew was intimately familiar with the status of his response. When Martha continued to stand impassively before him, offering no comment and making no movement toward leaving his office, Ernesto could no longer bear the tension. "Did something happen while you were at lunch? You look kind of upset," he added almost apologetically.

"Oh, nothing much. I just found out that the man I thought I might end up marrying has been deceiving me all these months."

"Another woman?"

"No, another life."

"What do you mean?"

"Tim is a convicted felon. He spent two years in the Arizona State Penitentiary on drug charges. Turns out my Prince Charming is a fraud," announced Martha flatly.

MOTIONS FOR SUMMARY JUDGMENT

motion for summary judgment   motion asking the judge to dismiss a case on the grounds that no genuine issues of material fact are raised in the complaint

The question raised by a **motion for summary judgment** is whether the evidence supporting any element of a cause of action in a complaint is so weak as to not raise a genuine issue of material fact. The purpose of a motion for summary judgment is to weed out claims or defenses that are so weakly supported by the evidence that submitting them to the jury would be a waste of time. If the facts on which a claim depends are so clear that no one can dispute what happened, the judge can decide the claim immediately.

To understand how motions for summary judgment work, consider a claim for battery. The elements of battery are (1) an act by defendant; (2) intent; (3) harmful or offensive contact; and (4) damages. Suppose the defendant proves that he did not touch or in any way contact the plaintiff. If the plaintiff has no evidence to support the element of "harmful and offensive contact," the defendant is entitled to a summary judgment. Notice that the defendant can, by moving for summary judgment, force the plaintiff to "put up or shut up"—either show evidence supporting the claims or see them dismissed. A motion for summary judgment may seek to dispose of all claims—in effect, ending the entire lawsuit—or may be aimed at only certain claims.

A basic principle of summary judgment procedure is that the judge does not decide factual disputes. In fact, one good way to defeat a motion for summary judgment is to convince the judge that the evidence is genuinely conflicting. Then the judge must let the jury sort out the evidence and decide what the facts are.

Because the trial has not yet begun, on what evidence can a judge base his decision? When a defendant files a motion for summary judgment, the plaintiff must put forward whatever evidence she has to support the claim being attacked. The plaintiff can do this by submitting the following.

declarations   another term for *affidavit*, which is used to show what a witness's testimony would be

affiant   person signing an affidavit

◆ Affidavits. In summary judgment practice, affidavits (also known as **declarations**) are routinely used as a kind of substitute for live testimony to show what a witness's testimony would be. Under the federal rules, affidavits must be based on personal knowledge and must show that the **affiant** (the person signing the affidavit) is competent to testify about the matters in the affidavit.

◆ Document exhibits attached to the affidavits. Just as in court, these documents must be admissible in evidence and submitted in a form complying with the procedural rules.

◆ Copies of discovery responses and/or excerpts from deposition transcripts. As a practical matter, the judge will usually consider only what the parties submit. Judges do not have time to browse through all of the pleadings and discovery in the case file. (Note that discovery responses are not filed in many courts.)

Putting It Into Practice 6.1:

What do you think CODA probably argued in its motion for summary judgment?

trial setting   minute entry specifying a date, time, and place for trial

---

"I Think It's Time We Put Our Case to the Test."

"Great job on keeping our claims against CODA alive," John congratulated Ernesto after hearing that Judge Salt had denied CODA's motion for summary judgment.

"Thanks," replied Ernesto appreciatively. "I'm sure glad we had that affidavit from Jorge clarifying his role. For awhile I thought the judge was beginning to buy CODA's argument that Mike's shooting was all part of some vendetta orchestrated by Jorge, and that seeing *Teenage Stalkers* was only a fortuitous happenstance that had no impact on the boys' decision to assault Mike. By the way, I never heard how Martha carried that off—getting Jorge to talk."

"Actually, I think Mike and Carmela are responsible for that happening. They went to see Jorge—together— after they both went to meet with her parents and confess everything that had happened, including Carmela's pregnancy. Apparently they convinced her parents and Jorge that they're serious about each other and that they intend to marry when they're both old enough."

"Marry?" interjected Ernesto incredulously. "Since when did they get that serious? Correct me if I'm wrong, but didn't Mike have another girl in tow when he came into our office the first time I met him?"

"That would be Greta. They broke up when Mike told her about Carmela. Over the last few months, he and Carmela seemed to have gotten much closer. I know she's been fiercely loyal to him throughout this whole thing. Anyway," continued John, getting back to Ernesto's original question, "Jorge apparently was impressed with Mike's willingness to face the music as far as his and Carmela's parents were concerned. Meanwhile, Carmela kept hammering at Jorge until he finally realized that he was in deep trouble if he didn't start talking about what had happened. Finally, he capitulated and agreed to speak to his public defender, who was able to get the criminal charges against him dismissed."

"I see. Thanks for the update on our continuing saga. Mike's love life alone could fill several volumes," quipped Ernesto before turning his attention to the current status of the case. "So what are we left with now in terms of defendants? Just CODA, the school district, and Hendershott?"

"Right. Hendershott dismissed his complaint against Jorge, and the other two boys—House and Evans— defaulted," confirmed John.

"I think we're ready to request a **trial setting,** don't you?" asked Ernesto.

"I do. I think it's time we put our case to the real test."

NET NEWS

To read samples of complex motions for summary judgment, go to *www.findlaw.com* and enter "LawCrawler" in the "FindLaw Guide." Use "Motion for summary judgment" as a search term.

SETTING A TRIAL DATE

motion to set and certificate of readiness   form that provides the court with the information necessary to schedule a block of time for a trial

◆ **LOCAL LINKS** ◆
How are trial dates set in your jurisdiction?

A trial cannot begin until a trial setting, which consists of a minute entry specifying a date, time, and place for trial, is obtained. The court issues a trial setting in response to some triggering event, such as the filing of a **motion to set and certificate of readiness.** This is typically a one- or two-page printed form that informs the court how many trial days are needed, whether a jury trial is demanded, and any other information the calendar clerk needs to schedule the necessary block of time. Other courts set cases for trial automatically when the filed pleadings or discovery reach a certain stage, or do so early in the case as part of a scheduling order.

Ideally, the trial setting would be firm and unchangeable; few, if any, courts operate that way, however. In practice, courts—like airlines—nearly always overbook their reservations, and may schedule as many as a half dozen cases for trial at the same time before the same judge. Otherwise, judges would be sitting around with nothing to do every time a case settled "on the courthouse steps," as so frequently occurs.

Moreover, there are plenty of ways in which a trial setting can be vacated or postponed, even at the last moment. Attorneys, parties, witnesses, or even the judge can become sick or sustain an injury. Attorneys can be ordered to trial at the same time in other cases having a higher priority. Judges can be transferred to a different division, or retire, or take vacations. Surprise evidence or witnesses can come to light at the last minute, requiring additional preparation time. The trial that the judge is already hearing can drag on unexpectedly for a few extra days, wiping out an allotted time slot. A defendant can file for bankruptcy, bringing all proceedings in any lawsuits involving that defendant to a screeching halt. Judges can and do grant continuances and vacate trial dates for all of these reasons and many others. Thus, cases rarely make it to trial on their first setting.

Putting It Into Practice 6.2:

John and Ernesto estimate that Mike's trial will last about one week. For what reasons should they not be surprised if their trial date has to be reset?

As Mike's case got closer to trial, the media exposure became more intense. "I know the press is really getting antsy about this case," empathized John, "but please stand firm in refusing to give them any information, Martha. Just keep referring them to me. At our **pretrial conference** next week, I'm going to ask Judge Salt to issue a **gag order** against Don Yakamura, CODA's attorney. I know he probably won't do that, but maybe he'll put his foot down about Don's trying this case in the papers. Speaking of the pretrial conference, how are you coming with the list of witnesses and documents for our **pretrial statement?**" asked John.

---

pretrial conference
conference between the attorneys and the judge at which the judge specifies what the attorneys can and cannot present at trial

gag order   court order prohibiting attorneys from discussing a case with the media

pretrial statement
court paper setting forth the parameters of what the attorneys can and cannot present at trial

PRE-TRIAL STATEMENTS/ORDERS

Modern court rules prescribe a series of procedural steps that must be completed before a trial can begin. These procedures are designed to ensure that the attorneys have fully prepared their cases and honed the issues. More and more, trials are carefully planned and choreographed events, with every step carefully thought out in advance. Most judges have little patience with unprepared attorneys who fumble around trying to "wing it."

pretrial order similar to a pretrial statement except signed by the judge rather than the attorneys

The main weapon used to enforce the requisite level of preparedness is (depending on the court) the **pretrial order** or joint pretrial statement. Regardless of whether the rules of the particular court call for a pretrial order (signed by the judge) or a joint pretrial statement (signed by the attorneys), the procedure and content are essentially the same. The finished pretrial order or pretrial statement is a filed court paper that sets out the parameters of what the attorneys can and cannot present at trial. The rules require the opposing attorneys—the ones who will actually conduct the trial—to meet, confer in good faith, and prepare this document together. (In practice, each side usually prepares proposed drafts of their contributions, which they then mark up and pass back and forth by fax until something resembling a finished product emerges.)

The pretrial statement or pretrial order delineates the boundaries of what is allowed at trial by specifying an agreed list of witnesses and documents that can be used at trial. This pretrial listing of documents saves a good deal of trial time because the parties must articulate any anticipated objections to a particular exhibit. If a document is listed and no objections are specified, that document can be admitted at trial without further debate.

The pretrial order or statement also includes lists of issues of fact and issues of law to be decided at trial. These lists of issues supersede the pleadings at trial: the court may refuse to allow evidence that is outside the scope of the issues listed in the pretrial order. Naturally, the parties do not always agree on what the issues are, or how they should be worded, or whether a given document is admissible as an exhibit. The pretrial order has separate sections in which each party can stake out his position on any disputed issues. The goal is for the attorneys to cooperate in defining the issues in such a way that the trial focuses on questions in serious dispute.

> ◆ **LOCAL LINKS** ◆
>
> Do the rules in your jurisdiction require a pretrial order or a pretrial statement?

Putting It Into Practice 6.3:

How do pretrial statements and orders streamline the trial process?

ETHICAL ETIQUETTE

RESPONDING TO INQUIRIES FROM THE PRESS

Dealing with the press involves an ongoing and delicate balance between the right to freedom of speech versus the right to a fair trial. This issue is particularly problematic in jury trials where the need to protect the litigants' right to express themselves clashes with the administration of the courts and the right of litigants (especially criminal defendants) to a just hearing. These tensions are most apparent when the press wants to place a camera in the courtroom, when a judge issues a gag order, or when attorneys attempt to try their cases in the press. Although the constitutionality of the provisions of the *Model Rules* relating to the press have been questioned, there is general agreement that lawyers are admonished from making statements outside the courtroom that they know have a "substantial likelihood of materially prejudicing an adjudicative proceeding." The *Rules* also encourage lawyers to take reasonable steps to prevent employees from making statements that violate this rule.

Putting It Into Practice 6.4:

Why are courts reluctant to issue gag orders?

NET NEWS

To read a pretrial statement prepared in *Microsoft v. DOJ*, go to *http://techlawjournal.com/courts/dojvmsft2/81006ms.htm.*

"The Most Important Thing to Remember Is That You're Here to Tell the Jurors Your Story."

Martha was almost grateful for the extra hours she had to put in the last week before Mike's trial was scheduled to begin. It took her mind off Tim and allowed her to channel her restless energies into something constructive. She had worked every evening that week and was prepared to work the weekend, preparing exhibits, working on the **trial notebook**, and making final arrangement with all of the witnesses.

This evening she had agreed to stay late to assist in preparing Mike to testify. John and Ernesto were planning to conduct a mock trial so that Mike could get the feel for the types of questions he would be asked. But before they conducted their examination of Mike, John gave him some general pointers.

"The most important thing to remember, Mike, is that you're there to tell the jurors your story. So you need to look at them when you testify. Even though you'll be tempted to look at the attorneys because they're asking you the questions, remember that you're going to lose the jury if you don't look at them." Martha was on a roll, her mind clicking off a list of caveats. "And another thing. Listen to the questions carefully and answer only what you're being asked. Don't volunteer anything and don't be afraid to say you don't know. No witness has ever gotten in trouble for saying 'I don't know,' but many a witness has dug himself a hole by pretending to know something he didn't."

"Will the attorneys try to get me to lose my temper like they do on TV?" Mike was conjuring up images of dramatic courtroom scenes he had seen.

"Some of them use that as a tactic. But if they try to do that and fail, they end up looking like the 'bad guys' to the jury. Look, there're all kinds of techniques lawyers can use to confuse and rattle witnesses. No matter what happens, just remember to look at the jury and listen carefully to what you're being asked."

trial notebook indexed compilation of the most important documents and resources that an attorney needs to access during trial

COUNTDOWN TO TRIAL

After the pretrial order has been hammered out, signed by the attorneys for both sides, and filed with the court, the attorneys spend the last few days before trial (often including evenings and weekends) pulling all the pieces together. This is a hectic time for trial lawyers and the paralegals, secretaries, and associates who work under their direction. Working hours lengthen as the simplest tasks develop unforeseen complications, and at times it seems as though a platoon of lawyers working twenty-four hours a day could not get the job done in time. Not every lawyer—or paralegal—is cut out for this kind of intense work.

During this time, in addition to preparing the witnesses, rehearsing the arguments, and attending to all the paperwork, the opposing lawyers are usually negotiating intensively in an effort to reach a settlement. The reason is simple: trying a civil suit costs a great deal of money—often thousands of dollars per day for attorney's fees alone. The money is better spent on a settlement that makes the case go away forever than on a trial that might be lost.

Important direct testimony—that is, the testimony of one's own, friendly witnesses—may be scripted word for word, or nearly so, and rehearsed with the witnesses. Far better to be skewered by some surprise answer in the privacy of one's own office than in open court in front of the jury. Cross-examination of opposing witnesses is outlined, question by question. Opening statements and closing arguments are written out or outlined, rehearsed in the presence of others, and adjusted as needed. Not all lawyers take such great pains in every case—the expense is not always justified—but every well-tried case is, to a great degree, scripted and rehearsed in advance.

NET NEWS

To get an idea about what goes into preparing witnesses for trial, go to www.jri-inc.com/psycholo.htm.

"Martha, I can't find a copy of the **motion** *in limine* we're filing regarding Carmela's pregnancy. Do you have one?" asked Ernesto, abruptly sticking his head inside Martha's office.

"Yes, but it will take me a minute to put my hands on it. I'll bring it in to you as soon as I find it." Martha could hear the edge in Ernesto's voice. She noticed that despite all their efforts to plan everything as much as possible in advance, several last-minute preparations were inevitable.

"Good. I can't seem to find anything," sighed Ernesto.

motion *in limine*   motion asking a judge to rule in advance on an admissibility of evidence

Figure 6-1
Motion in Limine

WHITE & TREADWELL
John Morgan, Esq., SBN 00123
Ernesto Esparanza, Esq. SBN 012345
2020 North Central Avenue, Suite 3200
Phoenix, Arizona 85005
(602) 555-1234
Attorneys for plaintiff Michael Johnson

IN THE SUPERIOR COURT OF MARICOPA COUNTY
PHOENIX, ARIZONA

Michael Johnson, a single man,)	
)	NO. _____
Plaintiff,)	
)	Plaintiff's Motion
vs.)	in *Limine* re Carmela
)	Boroquez
Daniel Hendershott, Max Evans, and)	
Alan House, all single men; CODA,)	
Inc.,a foreign corporation;)	Assigned to the
Washington High School District.)	Honorable
)	Benjamin Salt
Defendants.)	

Plaintiff respectfully requests that this court grant this Motion *in Limine* to preclude any Defendant from inquiring of any witness, or mentioning in opening or closing argument, any reference to the pregnancy of Carmela Boroquez. Any such inquiry or revelation would not be material to this trial and would result in unfair prejudice to plaintiff. Plaintiff's position is more fully set forth in the attached Memorandum of Points and Authorities.

Respectfully submitted 22nd day of December, 2001.

WHITE & TREADWELL

_____
by John Morgan
Attorneys for Plaintiff

Figure 6-2
Pre-Trial Tasks

PRE-TRIAL TASKS

Prepare witnesses to testify
Outline cross-examination
Prepare opening statement and closing arguments
Negotiate settlement
Prepare motions *in limine*
Prepare jury instructions
Prepare exhibits
Assemble trial notebook

Motions in Limine

Television shows depicting trial scenes often show lawyers jumping to their feet making an impassioned objection to some bit of evidence. Objections may be high drama, but once a prejudicial question has been asked, the cat is out of the bag and an objection does not prevent the damage that is done. Questions about whether the defendant has insurance, for example, are improper (with a few exceptions), but once a plaintiff's lawyer asks the defendant if he has liability insurance, every juror is likely to assume that any verdict is going to come from an insurance company, no matter how much the judge instructs the jury to disregard the question.

Lawyers preparing for trial can usually anticipate many of the "improper" questions that their opponent will likely try to ask. They can seize the initiative, outside the hearing of the jury, and, in effect, make the objection before the question is asked by filing a motion *in limine*. This motion asks the judge to rule in advance on the admissibility of evidence. If the judge rules in the movant's favor, the opposing party will be prohibited from mentioning or referring to the objectionable evidence. An attorney who deliberately defies the judge's order *in limine* is inviting a mistrial, jeopardizing his license to practice law, and risks being jailed for contempt of court.

 Putting It Into Practice 6.5:

Why do you think Ernesto wants to file a motion *in limine* in reference to Carmela's pregnancy?

John leaned back in his chair and took a break from his least favorite task: preparing jury instructions. "Nothing like a trial to get your juices flowing," he mused to himself. Despite the anxiety, frustration, and sleep deprivation, he savored the final days before trial, enjoying the camaraderie as everyone pitched in to pull everything together. A rap at the door roused him from his brief reverie. "I just got off the phone with Judge Salt's secretary and found out how he likes to have exhibits marked," announced Martha.

NET NEWS

To see a sample motion *in limine,* go to *www.quojure.com/archives/excludetest.htm.*

Jury Instructions

In the American court system, the jury is in charge of deciding questions of fact (what happened), but it is the judge's job to decide questions of law (what legal rules to apply to the dispute). Because the jurors must render the verdict, the judge must communicate to the jurors the legal principles he wants them to apply. To do this, the judge reads formal instructions on the law, referred to as **jury instructions,** to the jury just before it retires to deliberate. This process is sometimes called **charging the jury.** (Some courts are experimenting with instructing the jury on undisputed, relevant issues of law at the start of trial, hoping that the jury will be better able to assess the evidence as it is presented.) The jury instructions specify, in concise terms, the elements of each cause of action submitted to the jury.

Most trial lawyers believe that jury instructions have little influence on the jury's decision, but the exact wording of jury instructions is very important on appeal. If the court of appeals decides that an instruction does not correctly explain the elements of the cause of action to which it pertains, the case will likely be sent back for a new trial. Trial judges, who are perfectly aware of the importance that courts of appeals place on jury instructions, react by putting the burden on the attorneys to get them right. Both sides are required to submit any instructions they want the judge to give the jury. A party may not complain to the court of appeals about an instruction not being given if it was never requested.

Many judges require the submission of jury instructions just prior to the start of trial. This gives the judge and the opposing attorneys a chance to digest the proposals and to do any last minute legal research required to get the wording exactly right. After each side has presented its case, but (usually) before closing arguments, the judge will hear arguments and decide exactly what instructions will be read to the jury.

Many jurisdictions have books of recommended jury instructions, referred to as **uniform** or **patterned instructions,** published by the court, the state bar association, or some other authoritative body, covering the most common causes of action: motor vehicle negligence, breach of contract to pay a debt, and the like. These instructions have been used in prior trials and their validity has been well established. They can be modified as necessary to fit a particular case.

jury instructions formal instructions to the jury on points of law they will be asked to apply

charging the jury process of giving jury instructions

> ◆ **LOCAL LINKS** ◆
> What does your instructor recommend as good sources of jury instructions?

uniform or **patterned instructions** recommended jury instructions that have been used successfully in previous trials

Putting It Into Practice 6.6:

Why must John and Ernesto be conscientious about preparing jury instructions?

NET NEWS

To see jury instructions used in specific state courts, go to *http://resource.lawlinks.com/content/Legal_Research/Jury_Instructions/state_court.htm* and click on the state court in which you are interested. To see sample jury instructions from the 9th Circuit, go to *www.think.org/jury/index.html*. To read about how jury instructions and the whole jury system might be improved, go to *www.uchastings.edu/plri/spr96tex/juryinst.html*.

Figure 6-3
Jury Instruction Request

WHITE & TREADWELL
John Morgan, Esq., SBN 00123
Ernesto Esparanza, Esq. SBN 012345
2020 North Central Avenue, Suite 3200
Phoenix, Arizona 85005
(602) 555-1234
Attorneys for plaintiff Michael Johnson

IN THE SUPERIOR COURT OF MARICOPA COUNTY
PHOENIX, ARIZONA

Michael Johnson, a single man,	)	
	)	
	)	
	)	NO. _____
Plaintiff,	)	
	)	Plaintiff's Jury
vs.	)	Instruction Request
	)	Boroquez
Daniel Hendershott, Max Evans, and	)	
Alan House, all single men; CODA,	)	
Inc.,a foreign corporation;	)	Assigned to the
Washington High School District.	)	Honorable
	)	Benjamin Salt
	)	
Defendants.	)	
	)	

Pursuant to Rule 51, Arizona Rules of Civil Procedure, the above-indicated party requests that the Court give the *RAJI (Civil) 2nd* Instructions indicated by a mark on this Request, and any additional Instructions that are submitted with this Request.

Standard   Negligence

1. Duty of Jurors........... ....1[.]
2. Evidence................. ....[ ]
3. Rulings of the Court...... ....3 [.]
4. Arguments of Counsel...... ....[ ]
5. Stipulations.............. ....3[.]
6. Credibility of Witnesses.. ....[ ]
7. Expert Witness............ ....4[.]
8. Felony Conviction........ ....[ ]
9. Burden of Proof (More Probably True) 5.[ ]
10. Burden of Proof (Clear ....6.
and Convincing)........... ....7[ ]
11. Closing Instruction....... ....8[.]
   . . . .
   . . . . .9.
Distress . . . .
   . . . . .10.

Violation of Statute
Negligence Per Se) . . . .[ ]
Driving Under the
Influence of Alcohol . . . .[ ]
Presumptions of In
toxication . . . .[ ]
Assume Laws Obeyed-
Duty to Observe . . . .[ ]
Negligence of a Child-Duty of Adult . .[ ]
Sudden Emergency . . . .[ ]
Res Ipsa . . . .[ ]
Negligent Infliction
of Emotional Distress (Indirect) . . . . .[ ]
Negligent Infliction of Emotional
(Direct) . . . .[ ]
Wilful or Wanton Conduct . . . .[ ]

Fault . . . . .Personal Injury Damage

1. Claims; Definitions....... ....[1]..
2. Causation................ ....2 [.]
3. Plaintiff's Burden of Proof . . . . .3.[ ]
4. Statement of Liability . . . . .4.[ ]
   Issues .5[.]
5. Claims; Definitions....... ....[ ]
6. Causation................ ....[ ]
7. Burden of Proof (All Parties) . . . .[ ]
8. Statement of Liability Issues . . . .[ ]
9. Plaintiff's Fault (Contributory
   Negligence) . . . .[ ]
10. Plaintiff's Fault (Assumption of Risk) . .[ ]
11. Determining Relative
   Degrees of Fault . . . .[ ]

Measure of Damages . . . .[ ]
Pre-Existing Condition . . . .[ ]
Damages for Wrongful Death . . . . . .[ ]
Punitive Damages . . . .[ ]
Mortality Tables
and Life Expectancy . . . .[ ]

Respectfully submitted 22nd day of December, 2001.

WHITE & TREADWELL
_____
by John Morgan
Attorneys for Plaintiff

Figure 6-4
Sample Jury Instructions

> A sample of the jury instruction covered by the RAJIs (Recommended Arizona Jury Instructions):
>
> Standard No. 1 - I will now tell you the rules you must follow to decide this case. I will instruct you on the law. It is your duty to follow the law whether you agree with it or not.
>
> It is also your duty to determine the facts. You must determine the facts only from the evidence produced in court. You should not speculate or guess about any fact. You must not be influenced by sympathy or prejudice. You must not be concerned with any opinion you may feel I have about the facts. You are the sole judges of the facts.
>
> You must take account of all my instructions on the law. You are not to pick out one instruction, or part of one, and disregard the others. However, after you have determined the facts, you may find that some instructions do not apply. You must then consider the instructions that do apply, together with the facts as you have determined them.
>
> Decide the case by applying the law in these instructions to the facts.
>
> Fault No. 1 - Plaintiff claims that defendant was at fault. Fault is negligence that was a cause of plaintiff's injury.
>
> Negligence is the failure to use reasonable care. Negligence may consist of action or inaction. Negligence is the failure to act as a reasonably careful person would act under the circumstances.

Exhibits

By the time the trial date arrives, the attorneys should know precisely what documents each side may use as exhibits during the trial. Many courts mandate an exchange of exhibits well in advance of the trial date. Even in courts that do not require this exchange, any competent litigator automatically sends out a set of interrogatories and a request for production of documents requiring the opposing party to identify and supply copies of all trial exhibits.

Two important considerations govern the preparation of exhibits for use at trial. The first is admissibility: the law of evidence imposes various requirements, depending on the type of document and its source. At a minimum, for example, all documents used as exhibits must be authenticated—that is, a witness must testify that the document is what it appears to be and not a forgery. To save time, judges prefer that attorneys stipulate to the admissibility of all documents except those few for which they have a serious basis to challenge. The pretrial order commonly includes such stipulations. By the time the trial starts, each attorney (or the paralegal in charge of the exhibits) should have checked off each individual document and made sure that whatever is required to have it admitted—be it a stipulation or a witness's testimony—is in place and ready to be presented.

The second consideration is the physical handling of the documents themselves. In times past (and even now in rural courts or in small cases), introduction of an exhibit at trial required a time-consuming ritual in which the document was first handed to the clerk for marking with an exhibit number, then passed around for the opposing lawyer and perhaps the judge to examine, and only then shown to the witness to be identified. In busy metropolitan court systems, where the exhibits in many civil cases may number in the hundreds, judges usually require the attorneys to bring in their exhibits before the trial starts so that the clerk can mark them and list them in advance. Either way, all the physical documents that will actually be used at trial must be readied and organized so that each can be located quickly when needed in the hectic atmosphere that may prevail in the courtroom during trial.

◆ **LOCAL LINKS** ◆
What procedures do the courts in your jurisdiction follow in reference to the marking of exhibits?

Figure 6-5
Presentation of Exhibits

PRESENTATION OF EXHIBITS

Exhibits Must Be Admissible
Have they been authenticated?
Do they comport with all evidentiary rules?

Exhibits Must Be Properly Marked
What process is to be followed?
When are they to be marked?

---

demonstrative evidence
visual aids used to help the jury understand the facts

In this electronic era, charts, diagrams, pictures, and blowups have also become part of the courtroom scene. These visual aids—called **demonstrative evidence**—are not really evidence in the same way as the documents that are used to help prove the facts of the case. They are employed to make the facts easier for the jury to understand. Well designed visual aids can be quite compelling, but they take time to create, and the specialty graphic arts services required are not usually available within the law office. The trial attorney must plan in advance what demonstrative evidence will be needed, and the person responsible for making it happen—often a paralegal—must see that all the pieces come together in time for the start of trial.

Putting It Into Practice 6.7:

What kinds of exhibits would you introduce at Mike's trial? What kinds of demonstrative evidence?

As Martha put the finishing touches on the trial notebook, she experienced a sense of pride in all the work this notebook represented. Turning off the lights in her office, she felt comforted in knowing that everything within the realm of her responsibility was complete. Her stomach tightened, however, when she thought about the next day. Tomorrow Mike's trial would begin.

Trial Notebook

A trial attorney needs access—sometimes instantaneous access—to a huge variety of papers. One of the most important ways in which paralegals can be useful in trial is by anticipating what papers may be needed at any point and having them ready to hand.

As a way of locating the most important papers quickly, most trial lawyers use a trial notebook. Traditionally, this consists of a loose-leaf binder with tabbed sep-

---

NET NEWS

To see an example of computer-generated demonstrative evidence, go to *www.cyberbar.net/street.html*.

---

arators and an index. As computer technology becomes more and more widespread, laptop computers, which can hold many more documents and also facilitate searching, are becoming a more common substitute.

What goes into the trial notebook is determined partly by personal preference and partly by the document requirements of the particular case. Some of the items that trial lawyers usually include are described here.

◆ An index or outline of the notebook's contents so that specific documents can be located quickly.

◆ An outline and schedule of the trial indicating which witnesses are expected to testify each day, in what order, and at what times.

◆ The pleadings.

◆ The readily accessible pretrial statement or order that determines which issues are "fair game" during the trial.

◆ Minute entries in chronological order; which can be used to establish exactly what the judge's ruling was on a particular point, should the need arise.

◆ ***Voir dire*** questions and jury selection notes. To the extent that the court allows attorney-conducted *voir dire,* an outline or draft of the questions to be covered is helpful.

◆ Jury instructions and supporting notes. Both parties' proposed jury instructions, together with argument notes and supporting authorities, are needed when the judge hears arguments to decide which instructions to give. Once the judge has settled on the instructions, this section is replaced with the set of instructions that will actually be given. These are especially essential during closing arguments so that the attorneys can quote from the instructions.

◆ Notes, memoranda, and copies of important case law pertaining to legal issues expected to arise during trial.

◆ Outline or draft of opening statement. Most trial lawyers would consider it poor technique to read from notes when delivering an opening statement or closing argument. Nevertheless, good opening statements are prepared in advance, and reviewing an outline or notes can help an attorney fix the main points firmly in her mind before beginning.

◆ Outline of direct examination of favorable witnesses.

◆ Outline of cross examination of opposing party's witnesses.

◆ Copies of principal exhibits. In most lawsuits, a few documents bear directly on the claims and defenses and will be referred to frequently.

◆ Outline or draft of closing argument.

voir dire   questioning of prospective jurors

Putting It Into Practice 6.8:

What could you do as a paralegal in Mike's case to help prepare a trial notebook?

NET NEWS

To see an example of an electronic trial notebook, go to *www.paralegals.org/Reporter,* click on "Online 2000," and read the article entitled "Trial Preparation." An article relating to the issue of technology in the courtroom is "Second Opinion: Going High Tech in the Courtroom When You Are Low Tech at Home." (Another site that has a sample computerized trial notebook is *www.cyberbar.net/expaper/ctnote.html.*)

CONTENTS OF A TRIAL NOTEBOOK

Index
Trial schedule
Pleadings
Pretrial statement/order
Minute entries
Voir dire questions
Jury instructions
Notes
Memoranda
Case law
Opening statements
Closing arguments
Direct examination outlines
Cross-examination outlines
Exhibits

This was Martha's first jury trial and she was nervous with anticipation. As she checked the VCR for the final time to make sure that it was ready to play the tape she had set in place, she wondered what was going on in the judge's chambers. She knew that John and Ernesto had prepared for every possibility they could conceive of, but John had warned her that trials were inherently unpredictable and to be prepared for anything. She was reviewing a mental checklist to make sure she had not forgotten anything when she saw John striding toward her, Ernesto not far behind. From the expression on their faces, she knew that they were ready for battle.

TRYING THE CASE

On the morning of the first day of trial, the judge begins by holding a conference with the attorneys, probably in chambers. In part, this is to tie up any remaining loose ends: check that all pending motions have been decided, discuss the scheduling and order of presentation of witnesses, go over the pretrial order, perhaps work on jury instructions. Here, too, the judge has an opportunity to express any individual preferences about the way the trial is to be conducted. Increasingly, judges also take advantage of the chance to twist the parties' arms and encourage them to settle.

The formal commencement of trial occurs in the courtroom. A court reporter is present and, using a shorthand machine, will take down every word spoken until the trial is over. The judge or the clerk calls the case by number, and the judge asks first whether the plaintiff is ready, then whether the defendant is ready.

Jury Selection

The first task in a jury trial is to select a jury. The procedure for accomplishing this varies considerably from one court to another. The details often depend in large part

In That Moment, Martha Realized What Courage a Litigator Has to Have to Make Decisions That Could Alter the Outcome of a Case.

John motioned to Martha to stay when the judge announced a break in the *voir dire* process. "What's your gut feeling about juror #5?" John inquired.

"The guy that owns the car dealership?" Martha clarified. In response to John's affirmative nod, Martha's mouth puckered up slightly while she thought. "From what I've read about jury selection, he's not the kind of guy you'd want in a case like ours, but something tells me to keep him. I can't really tell you why."

"Exactly," echoed John. "He seems to have a strong personality—the kind that's likely to lead a jury. I just can't shake this feeling that if we get him on our side he'll be a powerful ally. Of course, we also run the risk that he won't be sympathetic to our facts and that he'll sway the rest of the jurors against us." John thought for a moment and then declared, "I'm going to take a chance with him. I'll use my last **peremptory challenge** to strike juror #10. Thanks for your input, Martha."

In that moment, Martha realized what courage a litigator has to have to make decisions that could alter the outcome of a case. Having made his choice, she knew that John would move on now without looking back to second guess himself.

peremptory challenge
removal of a potential juror for no cause

◆ **LOCAL LINKS** ◆

How many jurors are used to hear a civil case in your jurisdiction?

---

on the preferences of the individual judge, so consulting the judge's staff may be necessary. First, a predetermined number of prospective jurors are sent to the courtroom; the number depends on the local customs and the type of case. These are ordinary citizens who have been drawn at random from voter registration lists, driver's license records, or some other public source, and sent jury summonses ordering them to appear for jury duty. Each prospective juror has filled out a questionnaire; the resulting information, typically including such things as education, occupation, and previous involvement with the court system, is given to the attorneys.

The purported goal of jury selection is to start with a sizeable panel of prospective jurors who comprise a broad cross-section of typical citizens, weed out those that the judge or the attorneys think may not be able to act fairly and impartially, and end up with the required number of jurors to decide the case. (How many? Traditionally, twelve; but nowadays, to cut costs and save time, more likely six or eight plus an alternate or two.) The real goal of the attorneys is somewhat different: a trial attorney wants a jury composed, not of the fairest jurors, but of the ones most likely to find in her client's favor.

The first step in the weeding-out process is to ask the prospective jurors questions about their backgrounds and about any feelings or beliefs they have that may interfere with their ability to follow the judge's instructions. This questioning is called *voir dire* (which literally means "to speak the truth"). *Voir dire* customs vary considerably from one court to another. In some courts, the attorneys must submit all *voir dire* questions beforehand and the judge addresses the questions to the jurors; in others, attorneys are given great freedom to ask jurors pointed questions about their personal habits and prejudices. Attorneys who are allowed to conduct their own *voir dire* often craft questions that are really thinly disguised arguments designed to get a jump start on selling the jury on the merits of their cases: "If the evidence shows that the school district, by failing to maintain adequate security, set in motion the chain of events that led to Michael Johnson's being injured, is there any reason why you could not vote to grant him a substantial sum of money to fairly compensate him for those injuries?"

Prospective jurors may be excused for any of a number of reasons. These may involve personal problems, such as family duties or illness, making it unreasonably

NET NEWS

To read about how jury consultants can assist attorneys in the jury selection process, go to *www.psychologylaw.com* and click on "Recent Presentations." Examine the article entitled "Social Psychology of the Courtroom."

To read in more depth about the jury selection process, go to the following sites: *www.212.net/crime/jury.htm; http://expertpages.com/news/voir_dire_getting_jurors_to_talk.htm; www.jri-inc.com/tipson.htm; www.jri-inc.com/voirdire.htm.*

difficult for a juror to attend. (Usually, a fairly compelling story is required; judges become quite unreceptive to the usual excuses for not serving after hearing them all a few hundred times.) Prospective jurors who are relatives or close friends of any of the parties or attorneys or who are already familiar with the facts of the case are also likely to be excused.

challenge for cause removal of a potential juror because the judge believes that the juror is likely to base a decision on personal beliefs or prejudices rather than on the evidence and the judge's instructions

Attorneys are allowed to use a **challenge for cause** to excuse a juror. This occurs when a prospective juror says something or reveals something about his background that persuades the judge that the juror may be prone to base a decision on personal beliefs or prejudices rather than on the evidence and the judge's instructions. In the Johnson case, for example, a prospective juror who has strong religious beliefs against any depictions of violence in a film could not fairly decide the claims at issue between CODA and Michael Johnson and would be excused for cause.

After *voir dire* is completed, each side is allowed a specified number of peremptory challenges; that is, to strike some small number of prospective jurors from the panel. Naturally, each attorney will use the allotted strikes to remove the jurors she thinks are least likely to vote in the desired way. No "cause" is needed when an attorney uses a peremptory challenge to strike a juror. The decision of which jurors to strike is based entirely on the attorney's best guess as to what sorts of people will least improve the chances of winning. This guess may be based on almost anything, from astrology to psychology to personal experience. Peremptory challenges may not be used, however, to exclude racial groups from jury panels.

The end result of all this maneuvering is a panel of the required number of jurors, all of whom have managed to avoid being excused or stricken. They are sworn in as jurors and seated in the jury box. Jury selection usually consumes a substantial part of the first day. It can take much longer in highly publicized cases, where it is hard to find jurors who have not already heard all about the case from the news media. With jury selection completed, the judge will take a recess, perhaps until the next day.

Putting It Into Practice 6.9:

Will John be able to remove a juror who is a friend of the Hendershott family? A movie producer who believes that the right to freedom of speech is an absolute right with no exceptions? A member of a radical student group on a college campus?

BONUS POINTERS:

TRIALS TO THE COURT

Not all trials are jury trials. A plaintiff may fail to demand a jury trial in time, both parties may agree that a jury is not necessary, or the case may be the kind for which no right to a jury exists (e.g., divorce).

In a non-jury trial, the judge takes over the functions of the jury and decides both the factual and legal issues. So that the parties know which rules of law the judge applied (in

findings of fact and conclusions of law court paper listing each of the factual and legal findings on which a judge's decision is based

order to appeal the judge's decision), the procedural rules require that the judge make **findings of fact and conclusions of law.** That is, the judge must sign a court paper listing each of the factual and legal findings on which his or her decision is based. In practice, before announcing a decision, the judge orders both parties to submit proposed findings and then adopts the findings of the winning party.

Judges often relax the formal rules of evidence in non-jury cases. Because judges have the training and presumably the impartiality to resist being swayed by improper evidence, they often become irritated when attorneys insist on constantly jumping to their feet with objections. For similar reasons, judges commonly encourage attorneys to skip closing arguments and ask for a written argument instead. As with oral arguments, judges usually take matters under advisement and inform the parties of the verdict via a minute entry later—often weeks later.

John stood up slowly and deliberately, carefully buttoning the top button of his suit. When he was certain he had the jury's attention, he began to speak. "It was a day like any other day. The sun shone, birds prepared their nests in anticipation of spring, and people everywhere were going about the business of daily living. But it was a day that would dramatically alter the life of Michael Johnson. For him, it was not just another day."

Opening Statements

Next on the agenda are the opening statements. Each attorney makes what amounts to a speech, giving the jury his client's version of the facts. The plaintiff's attorney goes first; the defendant's attorney can reply immediately, or wait until he calls his witnesses.

Opening statements are not the time to present arguments. The attorney may describe the evidence he intends to present; he is free to read to the jury from the complaint or answer; and he may tell the jurors what will be asked of them at the end of the case. The attorney may not, however, launch into impassioned oratory about how dangerous the world is for students today—that sort of speechmaking must be saved for closing argument. Most attorneys use opening statements simply to tell their client's story in the most sympathetic and persuasive way possible.

Putting It Into Practice 6.10:

Most attorneys create a "theme" during opening statements that they follow throughout the case. What do you think the theme of Mike's case should be?

Martha found it fascinating to listen to each attorney's opening statements. She marveled at the ability of the attorneys to take what were presumably the same facts and create such different perspectives. Having heard that most jurors made up their minds about a case during opening statements, she wondered what the jurors were thinking at this point. She had little time to pursue this question, however. The time for examining witnesses had begun and it was incumbent on her to make sure that their first witness, Daniel Hendershott, was ready to take the stand.

NET NEWS

For some insights about writing persuasive opening statements, go to *http://members.aol.com/jtf1952/openings.htm.* To read articles about opening statements, go to *http://resource.lawlinks.com,* and click on "Courtroom Trial Procedure," and then on "Closing/Opening Statements."

Presentation of Evidence

Now comes the main event: the presentation of each side's case. This is done in turns, in the familiar, three-step pattern: plaintiff's case first, defendant's case second, and finally the plaintiff is given a chance to rebut the defendant's case. A trial consists of questioning witnesses, one after the other. Documents and other exhibits can, of course, be used, but they are often presented via the testimony of witnesses: the witness identifies, describes, and reads from the document.

To understand the parties' objectives in a trial, imagine that each of the plaintiff's theories of liability is a chain. To win the lawsuit, the plaintiff must construct at least one complete chain sufficiently strong to lift the load (the plaintiff's burden of proof). Each chain has one link for each element of that cause of action.

Thus, a cause of action for negligence has four links in the chain: one labeled "duty," one labeled "breach of duty," one labeled "causation," and another labeled "damages." The plaintiff's goal is to have a chain made of those four links at the end of the trial. The plaintiff creates each link by putting on some evidence supporting each element. The defendant tries to sever, or at least weaken, the plaintiff's chain. If the defendant can put on enough evidence to cut even one of the links, and the plaintiff is unable to repair the damage, the chain is broken and the plaintiff loses.

If, at the end of the trial, the judge believes that the plaintiff's chain has all of its links and the defendant has failed to refute any of those links, she can grant a **directed verdict** for the plaintiff. If the judge believes that one or more of the links has clearly been cut, she can grant a directed verdict for the defendant.

If the judge believes that it is uncertain whether all of the links in the plaintiff's chain have held up under the defendant's attacks (i.e., if reasonable jurors could disagree about whether the evidence supports each of the elements of the cause of action), the judge must submit the case to the jury for decision.

directed verdict   verdict directed by a judge for the defendant because of the plaintiff's failure to prove one or more elements of her cause of action, or a verdict for the plaintiff because the plaintiff has clearly proven all the elements of her case and the defendant has failed to prove a defense

Figure 6-7
Chain of Evidence

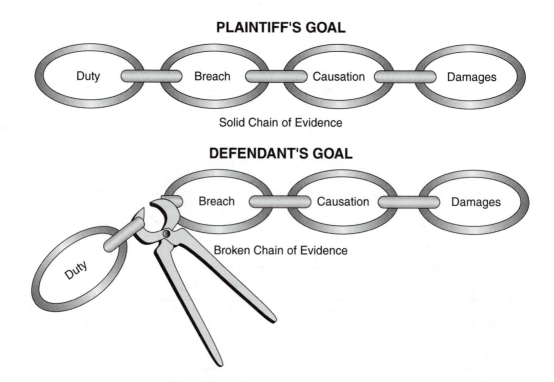

PLAINTIFF'S GOAL

Duty — Breach — Causation — Damages

Solid Chain of Evidence

DEFENDANT'S GOAL

Breach — Causation — Damages

Duty

Broken Chain of Evidence

In theory, the jury will test each of the links in the chain and find for the plaintiff only if the evidence supporting each link is more than fifty-fifty in the plaintiff's favor. In practice, however, jury deliberations are seldom so analytical. Once the case is submitted to the jury, fairness and common sense dictate.

Putting It Into Practice 6.11:

What do you think is the weakest link in Mike's case against the school district? Against CODA?

Only the Second Day of Trial and Already One of Those "Little Surprises" John Warned Me About.

John was careful to avoid asking Daniel any **leading questions** when he **examined** him. If only the jury knew, he thought to himself, how much wrangling had preceded the judge's decision that John would not be allowed to treat Hendershott as a **hostile witness** even though he was a defendant. (The judge reasoned that, because of the Gallagher agreement the two parties had entered into, Hendershott would be more cooperative than defendants typically are.) The beauty of pretrial orders, John thought, is that the jury is spared all the legal posturing and can focus on the testimony.

Having completed his **direct examination** of Hendershott, John sat down and allowed the other attorneys to cross-examine him. Hendershott was, as John expected, taking pains to portray himself as a reluctant participant in Mike's attack. CODA's attorney, Don Yakamura, who was obviously getting irritated with Hendershott's efforts to deflect responsibility from himself, committed a strategically fatal error: he asked a question to which he did not know the answer.

"So if you were so concerned about what was going to happen to the plaintiff, why didn't you do something about it?" asked Mr. Yakamura defiantly.

"I did," retorted Hendershott belligerently.

The jury was unaware that all of the attorneys looked up in unison upon hearing this response. Mr. Yakamura himself was mortified that he had let himself ask this question, but knew that having opened the doorway, he would have to go through it.

"What did you do?" Mr. Yakamura stood with his back to the jury, hoping they did not hear the panic in his voice.

"I called the school," admitted Hendershott. He himself had not wanted to disclose this, but had been so incensed at Yakamura's demeaning questions that he had momentarily forgotten his fear of the other boys' reaction.

John caught a quick glimpse of Dana Fletcher's face and knew that her client's disclosure was as much of a shock to her as it was to everyone else. After Yakamura had returned to his seat with as much dignity as he could muster, John began **re-direct examination** of Hendershott. Although he was nervous about continuing in Yakamura's misguided steps, he reasoned that Hendershott's revelation gave him potential ammunition against the school and felt he had no real choice but to pursue this line of questioning.

"When did you call the school, Daniel?" asked John as nonchalantly as he could.

"Two days before Mike was attacked."

"That would have been on Wednesday of that week?"

"Yes, sir."

---

leading questions question that tells the witness what the attorney expects the witness to answer

examined question

hostile witness uncooperative witness

direct examination examination by an attorney that calls the witness to testify

re-direct examination examination to repair any damage done during cross-examination

"What did you say?"

"I said that something really bad was coming down on Friday of that week and that they should shut down the school."

"Did you indicate what that something was?"

"I said someone—maybe even some student—was going to get shot."

"Did you indicate a specific time when it would occur?"

"No, I don't think so."

"Did you say anything that would indicate they should take what you said seriously?"

Hendershott thought for a moment and then said, "Before I hung up, I said 'Freedom to the People!' "

"And why would that have meant anything to the people at the school?" asked John, holding his breath as he waited for Hendershott's response.

"Because me and the guys had spray-painted those exact words all over campus several weeks before."

Only the second day of trial and already one of those "little surprises" John warned me about, thought Martha. She was shocked, but pleased, at this sudden turn of events.

The Plaintiff's Case

After the opening statements, the judge instructs the plaintiff's attorney to call the first witness. The witness comes forward, is asked to take the familiar oath to "tell the truth, the whole truth, and nothing but the truth," and takes a seat on the witness stand to the side of the judge's bench. The plaintiff's attorney examines the witness first. An attorney's examination of a witness that he called to the stand is called direct examination; the opposing attorney's examination of the witness is called **cross-examination.** If the plaintiff's attorney feels a need to shore up any of the damage inflicted by his opponent's cross-examination, he may conduct re-direct examination. On rare occasions, the judge may allow the questioning to go back and forth several times in a series of re-direct and recross examinations.

In some courts, the **scope** (extent of subject matter covered during examination) of cross-examination is limited to the scope of direct examination. In direct examination, an attorney is free to ask about any aspect of the case, but in cross-examination the attorney may not ask questions on subjects not covered during direct examination. The rationale is that if the scope of cross-examination were unlimited, nothing would prevent the defendant from putting on his entire case by cross-examining the plaintiff's witnesses, resulting in both parties putting on their cases simultaneously.

Although not all courts limit the scope of cross-examination, almost all limit re-direct examination to the subjects raised during cross-examination. This forces the attorney who calls the witness to ask all the questions she has for that witness all at once rather than piecemeal.

In general, a party may not cross-examine her own witnesses. (Witnesses "belong" to the party who calls them.) An exception is made (in most states) if the witness's answers demonstrate hostility. Then the judge declares the individual to be a hostile witness and allows the witness to be treated as if belonging to the opposing party. The practical effect of this ruling is that the attorney can ask a hostile witness leading questions. Also, if the plaintiff calls the defendant as a witness, the plaintiff can treat him as an adverse witness.

In direct examination, leading questions are forbidden. A leading question is a question that tells the witness what answer the attorney wants to hear. "Didn't you spend last Saturday night at home watching television with your wife?" is a leading question. The same question, rephrased so as not to be leading, would be "What

cross-examination examination by opposing counsel

scope extent of subject matter covered during examination

◆ **LOCAL LINKS** ◆
Do the courts in your jurisdiction limit the scope of cross-examination?

Figure 6-8
Scope of Examination

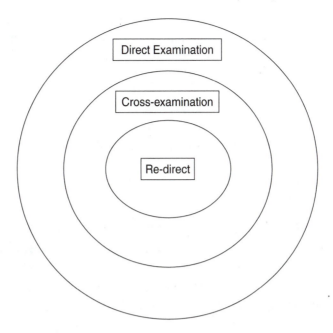

did you do last Saturday night?" In the leading version, the attorney is telling the story, not the witness.

In cross-examination, leading questions are not only allowed, they are often essential. The purpose of direct examination is for the witness to tell his story in his own words. The purpose of cross-examination is to test the witness's credibility and truthfulness—in other words, to poke as many holes in that testimony as possible. This is best done by asking questions that must be answered with a "yes" or "no," and making sure that if the witness picks the wrong answer, the attorney has plenty of ammunition to discredit him. Although skillful, well-planned cross-examination can be spectacular and fun to watch, skillful, well-planned direct examination wins cases.

The plaintiff's attorney decides which witnesses to call and the order in which to call them. Cooperative witnesses will show up voluntarily; the plaintiff's attorney (or paralegal) is responsible for staying in contact with them as the trial progresses and making sure that each witness arrives in time to testify. The plaintiff can also subpoena uncooperative or hostile witnesses (although subpoenas allow even cooperative witnesses to be released from work with no repercussions). The plaintiff can even call the defendant as a witness. One common tactic is to call the defendant as the first witness, thereby depriving the defendant of the chance to listen to all of the plaintiff's witnesses and adjust his story accordingly.

Before the questioning begins, either side may ask the judge to put witnesses **under the rule** (also called *sequestering of witnesses*). The judge will then order all witnesses who are not parties to the suit to remain outside the courtroom and to refrain from talking with anyone about the case, except while actually testifying. The purpose of this measure is to preclude witnesses from changing their testimony in response to what other witnesses say. The parties themselves are entitled to remain in the courtroom during the entire trial; parties cannot be put under the rule. Also, many judges allow each party to select one person, who may also be a witness, to remain in the courtroom to assist the attorney.

The plaintiff must, at a minimum, establish a ***prima facie*** case for each theory of liability. A *prima facie* case means that at least some credible evidence has been presented in support of each element of the cause of action. In terms of the "links

under the rule　court order that witnesses leave the courtroom and not discuss the case with anyone; also called *sequestering of witnesses*

prima facie　presentation of credible evidence to support each element of a cause of action

in a chain" metaphor, putting on a *prima facie* case means putting on at least some evidence establishing each of the links. Although the links need not necessarily be very strong, no link can be missing entirely.

Putting It Into Practice 6.12:

Why do you think John and Ernesto opted to put on Hendershott as their first witness? Why would they have liked to have had him classified as a hostile witness?

John Saw the Look of Awareness Flash Across Her Face and He Knew She Was Not Feigning Surprise When She Answered.

After Hendershott was dismissed, John called Ms. Sinclair. Ms. Tsosie requested a brief recess, but John managed to convince the judge that Ms. Sinclair's testimony would be brief and that the completion of her testimony would be around lunch time. In actuality, John wanted Ms. Sinclair to testify before Ms. Tsosie had a chance to prepare her for his questions. He ignored Ms. Tsosie's glare in his direction. John's initial questions were exactly as Ms. Sinclair anticipated and she answered them as she had been rehearsed, emphasizing that she could not remember when the anonymous phone call had been made.

"So you would be surprised to learn that Daniel Hendershott just testified that he called the school two days before Mike's shooting?" asked John matter-of-factly.

Ms. Sinclair sat in stunned silence, answering only after John repeated the question. Before she could recover her composure, John asked his next questions.

"Did his use of the phrase 'Freedom to the People' have any particular significance to you?" John had positioned himself directly in front of Ms. Sinclair, being careful not to block the jury's view of her. He was close enough to see into her eyes when he asked the question. He saw the look of awareness flash across her face and he knew she was not feigning surprise when she answered.

"You know, I forgot all about that. But the caller did use those words."

"And what did those words mean to you?"

"They were the same phrase some kids had painted all over campus."

"Do you remember when they were painted?"

"No."

"But it was before you received the phone call warning you that someone was going to get shot?"

"Yes."

"Do you know which kids painted that phrase?"

"I don't know exactly, but I think they were part of that kooky group that wanted to start a revolution."

"The group that Hendershott and the other boys who shot Mike belonged to."

"I believe so," responded Ms. Sinclair slowly, only now beginning to put everything together.

"And did you tell Mr. Garcia about this phone call?"

"Yes."

"And what did he say?"

"**Objection. Hearsay,**" interjected Ms. Tsosie forcefully.

---

objection formal challenge made by an attorney when opposing counsel is trying to introduce evidence

hearsay secondhand information used to prove the truth of the matter asserted

Rules of Evidence

The rules of evidence dictate what kinds of evidence can and cannot be introduced at trial and what attorneys must do to get that evidence introduced. Before a document or physical evidence can be introduced, for example, a **foundation** must be laid, in essence setting forth the background information necessary to establish that the document or physical evidence is authentic. If the proper foundation is not laid, opposing counsel will probably object. If the judge **sustains** (upholds) the objection, the evidence cannot be admitted, but if the judge **overrules** (denies) the objection, the evidence can be admitted. John, for example, cannot introduce the bullets retrieved from the scene of Mike's shooting unless he presents testimony showing that the police who found the bullets marked them in an easily distinguishable way and then maintained a complete record of who came into possession of the bullets thereafter (i.e., preserved the chain of custody).

Evidence cannot be presented unless it is **relevant.** Evidence is relevant if it logically leads an individual to the conclusion that a fact is either more or less probable. Hendershott's political beliefs are relevant in Mike's case because they help the jury understand his motivation in shooting Mike. They would not be relevant if he were the plaintiff in an automobile accident in which his political beliefs played no part. Evidence that is relevant is still not admissible if it is prejudicial, that is, if it would unduly inflame the passions of the jury. Gory photographs of murders are sometimes excluded even though they are relevant because they could interfere with the jury's ability to render an impartial verdict.

One type of evidence that is inadmissible is hearsay. Hearsay is secondhand information. Essentially a witness (in the courtroom) is testifying about what another person (outside of the courtroom) said and this testimony is used to prove the truth of the matter being asserted. Suppose the question is whether Dr. Smith went into the bar before he went into surgery. Lucy, who is on the witness stand, testifies that Wanda told her that she saw Dr. Smith go into the bar. Lucy's testimony is hearsay. She did not actually see Dr. Smith go into the bar and is relying on secondhand information she heard from Wanda. Wanda cannot be examined to determine her credibility and her competence, which is why hearsay is prohibited.

An out-of-court statement is not hearsay if it is used to impeach a witness. If a witness tells a police officer at the scene of an accident that the defendant ran the red light and then says on the stand that the defendant did not run the red light, the witness's out-of-court statement can be used to show his lack of reliability. The statement is not hearsay because it is not being used to prove whether the defendant, in fact, ran the red light. Instead, it is being offered to show that the person said something different previously. Admissions by parties are also not considered hearsay according to the *Federal Rules of Evidence.* Therefore, parties' statements can be introduced against them in court, even if those statements are harmful to them.

Numerous exceptions to the prohibition against hearsay (known as the **hearsay rule**) exist. These exceptions are based on the rationale that the circumstances under which the statements are made gives them a certain degree of trustworthiness. Some of the more commonly used exceptions are noted here.

Dying declarations are statements made while a declarant (the person making the statement) believes he is dying and under circumstances giving rise to his dying. This exception is allowed because important evidence might otherwise be lost and

foundation background information necessary to prove that a document or physical evidence is authentic

sustains uphold an objection

overrules deny an objection

relevant evidence that logically leads to the conclusion that a fact is either more or less probable

hearsay rule rule that hearsay is inadmissible

NET NEWS

To read the *Federal Rules of Evidence*, go to *www.law.cornell.edu/rules/fre/overview.html*. To learn more about the rules of evidence (in an easy-to-read summary format prepared by a California-based attorney), go to *www.dicarlolaw.com/ RulesofEvidenceSummary.htm*.

because it is assumed that people dying generally will not lie. The exception applies only if the declarant is unavailable to testify.

"Excited utterances" are spur-of-the-moment comments that are admissible because the nature of their spontaneity suggests a degree of trustworthiness. A witness can testify, for example, to hearing a bystander scream out right before an accident, "Oh my God, she's going to run over that child!"

"Declarations against interest" are those statements that could expose the declarant to civil or criminal liability or that are in opposition to the declarant's financial interests. The declarant must be unavailable to testify for this exception to apply. A witness might testify, for example, that he heard Jorge threaten to kill Mike. His testimony would be admissible, even though it was hearsay, if Jorge refused to testify.

Certain business records and public records are admissible even though they are hearsay. Mike's medical records would be admissible under this exception.

Statements made for the purposes of diagnosing and treating a medical condition are admissible. Under this exception, Mike's doctor could testify that, when he was examining Mike, Mike told him he had a terrible pain in his lower back.

Putting It Into Practice 6.13:

Determine which of the following testimony would be considered hearsay in the case involving the injury of Molly Running Deer.

(a) The police officer interviews Tyrone at the scene of the accident, who says that he saw Stuart run the red light. The officer testifies to this on the witness stand.

(b) Tyrone testifies that he was the first one to reach Stuart after the accident and that Stuart, who was seriously injured, appeared to think he was dying. Tyrone testifies that Stuart said over and over, "Forgive me for running the red light."

(c) Myra testifies that she was talking with her friend, Susanna, at the intersection when Susanna suddenly cried out, "Watch out! That blue car's going to run the red light!" Myra testifies to Susanna's statement.

(d) Jason, the paramedic who treated Stuart, testifies that in the ambulance Stuart kept asking whether he had hurt anyone.

(e) The police officer who investigated the accident testifies that when he talked with Stuart in his hospital room, Stuart told him that he had planned to take his car in to have the brakes checked. In his deposition, Stuart claims that he had had his brakes checked the day before the accident. Molly's attorney wants to use the officer's testimony to impeach Stuart.

Max's Reaction to the Tape was All Ernesto Needed to Make His Point.

"Objection overruled," stated Judge Salt firmly, without explanation.

"What did Mr. Garcia say when you told him about the phone call?" repeated John.

"He said not to worry about it. That those kids were just a bunch of crackpots and that I should forget about it."

"And did you?" asked John.

"Did I what?"

"Forget about it?"

"Yes, I guess I did—quite literally," conceded Ms. Sinclair.

Wanting to leave the jury on this note, John requested that he be allowed to call his next witness after the lunch break. He wanted Ms. Tsosie to have an opportunity to talk with Mr. Garcia before he took the stand. The rest of the case went smoothly and without additional surprise until Ms. Tsosie cross-examined one of Mike's attackers, Max Evans. For reasons that were still unclear to John, one of her questions provoked Max into a political diatribe that sent Judge Salt furiously pounding his gavel. But Max was not to be interrupted until he had had his say.

Shortly thereafter, John and Ernesto decided to **rest**. Both felt more confident about their case against the school district in light of Hendershott's admission, but were still uneasy about their case against CODA. When CODA moved for a directed verdict, the judge called the attorneys into his chambers so that he could hear their arguments outside the earshot of the jurors. Ernesto whispered something in John's ear and stayed in the courtroom as the other attorneys filed obediently behind the judge.

"Martha, where's our copy of *Teenage Stalkers?*" asked Ernesto urgently. When Martha found it for him, he began to frantically fast forward through the tape, stopping now and then to listen to the dialogue. When he finally found the part he was looking for, he stopped and told Martha to listen.

She looked at Ernesto and shook her head. "I can't believe it. Those are the *exact* words Max Evans used."

Ernesto nodded his concurrence. "And I'd be willing to bet the kid doesn't even know he's quoting the movie word for word. I'd better get in there right away."

Ernesto let himself in just as Judge Salt was announcing his reasons for directing a verdict in favor of CODA. "Therefore, I have come to the conclusion that the plaintiff has failed to meet his burden of proof in establishing that the movie *Teenage Stalkers* incited the assailants to carry out their attack on the plaintiff."

"Your honor, if I might have just one word," said Ernesto as he worked his way past the other attorneys. "I think I have something here you're going to want to hear."

"Very well, Mr. Esparanza. But make it quick."

"Your honor, I have a section of tape from *Teenage Stalkers* that I would like you to hear. When I was listening to Max Evans go on his tirade, I knew what he was saying sounded very familiar. Then it suddenly occurred to me that I'd heard those same words in the movie. I have fast-forwarded to that exact dialogue in the movie and I'd like you to hear it."

The VCR was wheeled into the judge's cramped quarters and all the attorneys hovered around it as Ernesto pushed the "Play" button.

"Why, it sounds almost as if the boy memorized those lines," said Judge Salt in amazement. "It does sound like what he said on the witness stand. So what do you propose, Mr. Esperanza?"

"I'd like to recall Max Evans to the stand and have the court reporter read back the relevant testimony. Then I'd like to play the tape for the jury and ask Max if he deliberately tried to memorize that dialogue. I'm certain, your honor, that Max has no idea that he's spouting dialogue from the movie. I think this goes to show that even though the boys aren't sure why they attacked Mike, they were motivated by the movie in a way that even they are unaware of."

This last statement drew strong argument from Mr. Yakamura, who objected strenuously to the concept of holding his client responsible for the unconscious motivations of its customers. The judge, however, relented and Ernesto called Max back to the stand.

Max's reaction to the tape was all Ernesto needed to make his point. His subdued silence after hearing the excerpt told more than his quiet admission that he did not realize he had been quoting the dialogue.

"Great save!" whispered John to Ernesto. "All those hours you listened to that horrendous movie finally paid off."

rest action taken when a party
is finished putting on witnesses

Figure 6-9
Trial Process

TRIAL PROCESS

Opening Statements

Plaintiff's Case
Direct examination
Cross-examination
Re-direct examination

Motions

Defendant's Case
Direct examination
Cross-examination
Re-direct examination

Plaintiff's Rebuttal

Motions

Closing Arguments

Charging the Jury

"Half-Time"

When the plaintiff has called and examined all of her witnesses, the plaintiff's attorney announces to the judge that "Plaintiff rests." When a party rests, it means that the party is finished putting on evidence for his side of the case.

For the plaintiff's attorney, resting is a somewhat anxious event because it means that the plaintiff has now taken her best shot, and the plaintiff's claims must stand or fall on what has been presented. Once the plaintiff rests, the defendant is entitled to have the judge decide whether the plaintiff has made out a *prima facie* case for each cause of action. If the defendant thinks that the plaintiff has failed to put on evidence in support of some element of one of her causes of action, the defendant may move for a directed verdict as to that cause of action. If the judge agrees with the defendant, that cause of action will be dismissed. Therefore, before resting, a wise plaintiff's attorney reflects carefully to be sure that each of plaintiff's chains has all of its links.

If there are motions to be heard, the jury leaves the room and returns when the defendant is ready to begin calling witnesses. If not, the defendant's case may begin immediately, or the judge may allow a recess to give the defendant's attorney a short time to prepare. Some plaintiffs' attorneys prefer to rest near the end of the trial day, making it likely that the defendant will not be able to begin until the following day. Then the jury will have the whole night for the plaintiff's case to sink in, with no interference from the defendant's evidence. Most lawyers like to time their presentations so that the last thing on the jurors' minds at the end of the day is some strong and favorable bit of evidence.

Putting It Into Practice 6.14:

Why is a directed verdict in favor of the defendant such a devastating decision for the plaintiff?

Yakamura hammered away at what he obviously perceived to be the weakest link in Mike's case against CODA: the role of the movie in the boys' decision to attack Mike. Not content with having shown that none of the defendants knew exactly what had motivated him to go after Mike, he zeroed in on Mike, turning to a theory Mike had never even considered.

"Isn't it true, Mike, that for all you know the defendants could have attacked you for racial reasons rather than because they had been watching *Teenage Stalkers?*"

"You mean because I'm African American?" asked Mike, his shock at the question apparent in his voice.

"That's exactly what I mean," shot back Yakamura.

"I suppose so," agreed Mike after a momentary pause.

When Ernesto had the opportunity to question Mike, he followed up on Mike's answer. "Do you think it's likely that you were attacked for racial reasons, Mike?"

"Not really."

"Why not?"

"I grew up with Max and Daniel, and they may be a lot of things but racists they're not. In all the years I've known them, I've never heard either of them use a racial slur." "So why would two boys you've known since childhood suddenly attack you and try to kill you?" asked Yakamura in rebuttal.

"I really don't know why. I can't speak for them, sir. All I can tell you is that they've really changed. And when they began spouting all this anti-American propaganda, I didn't want to have anything to do with them. I couldn't begin to tell you why they did what they did." A subtle crack in Mike's voice betrayed the hurt and anger he was trying to conceal as he sought to maintain his composure.

Judge Salt declared a brief recess after Mike's cross-examination was complete. Martha was walking to the restroom when she was accosted by one of the jurors, who obviously wanted to engage her in conversation.

"I'm sorry, ma'am, but I'm not allowed to talk with anyone on the jury. I don't mean to be rude, but our talking could get me in real trouble. Please excuse me." And with that, Martha walked away.

ETHICAL ETIQUETTE

CONTACT WITH JURORS

Attorneys are expressly prohibited from having *ex parte* communications with jurors before and during trial. As agents of attorneys, paralegals must be extremely conscientious about violating this rule. In addition to the attorney's being censured, a mistrial could possibly be granted regardless of whether there was any intent to influence a juror. Even an apparently innocent social encounter during a break can conceivably lead to a mistrial.

Many attorneys like to talk with jurors after a trial to assist in evaluating their performance by finding out what influenced the jurors' deliberations. However, in some states, attorneys are not allowed to communicate with jurors after the trial. The *ABA Model Rules* and *Model Code* permit post-trial communications as long as they are allowed by law and are not intended to embarrass or harass a juror or to influence a juror's actions during future jury service.

Defendant's Case

After the plaintiff rests, the defendant takes a turn at calling witnesses. Naturally, the plaintiff may cross-examine each witness.

The defendant may use either (or both) of two main strategies. The first is a direct attack on some part of the plaintiff's evidence. The defendant's task is, in some ways, easier than the plaintiff's. The plaintiff must offer evidence establishing every single element of a cause of action. The defendant can succeed in defeating the plaintiff's case by knocking out just one of those elements. Defendants commonly choose the tactic of mounting a strong attack on the weakest link in the plaintiff's chain and letting the rest of the plaintiff's case go basically unchallenged.

Moreover, the defendant need not actually disprove one element of the plaintiff's cause of action—the burden of proof is on the plaintiff. The defendant can win merely by casting enough doubt on the evidence supporting one element of the plaintiff's case.

preponderance of the evidence evidence showing that it is more probable than not that a given fact occurred

For most causes of action, the plaintiff must establish each element by a **preponderance of the evidence.** The preponderance-of-evidence test works like a balance scale. In Mike's case, for example, suppose Hendershott had not admitted attacking Mike and that Mike had to prove the element of intent for the battery cause of action. Place all the evidence tending to show that the boys intended to harm Mike on one side of the scale and all the evidence tending to show that the boys did not intend to attack Mike on the other side. If the scale tips, even slightly, in the direction of the evidence showing intent, Mike has sustained his burden of proof in reference to the element of intent. To put it another way, the preponderance-of-evidence test requires Mike to present enough evidence to persuade the jury that it was more probable than not (i.e., greater than a 50-50) chance that the boys intended to harm him.

An alternative strategy is for the defendant to raise an affirmative defense. An affirmative defense is some circumstance that allows the defendant to win even after the plaintiff has established each element of her cause of action. Often, affirmative defenses involve some legitimate excuse or justification for doing whatever the defendant did. If the defendant raises an affirmative defense, the defendant has the burden of establishing the defense by a preponderance of the evidence. Suppose, for example that Mike proves Hendershott intended to shoot him but Hendershott argues that he did so in self-defense. Under the substantive law pertaining to battery, self-defense is an affirmative defense. Hendershott would have the burden of proving, by a preponderance of the evidence, each element of self-defense.

clear and convincing evidence burden of proof that requires more proof than a preponderance of the evidence and less proof than beyond a reasonable doubt

Sometimes a higher burden of proof than preponderance of the evidence applies, even in a civil suit. In some states, for example, proof of civil fraud carries a burden of **clear and convincing evidence,** which is greater than a preponderance but less than the criminal standard of beyond a reasonable doubt. The burden for proving the right to punitive damages may also be by clear and convincing evidence.

Putting It Into Practice 6.15:

What will the school district have to do to win in Mike's case?

Because Mr. Garcia clung fast to his claim that he did not remember Ms. Sinclair telling him about an anonymous phone call, Ernesto recalled Ms. Sinclair to the stand. A few questions quickly reaffirmed her conviction that she had relayed this information. At that point, Ernesto knew it was matter of whom the jury believed.

The district's defense had centered around minimizing the future impact of Mike's injuries. Believing as John did in the importance of keeping a case as simple as possible for a jury to follow, Ernesto opted to recall only one other witness: an economist. This expert systematically explained why the conclusions drawn by the district's economist were erroneous. Believing that the issue of damages was probably going to be the most difficult issue for the jury to grapple with, at least as far as the district was concerned, Ernesto wanted this witness: words to be the last testimony the jury heard before retiring to render their decision.

Figure 6-10
Burdens of Proof

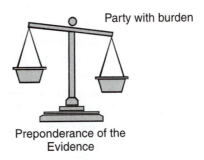

Party with burden

Preponderance of the
Evidence

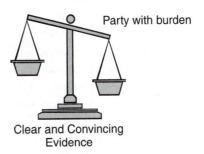

Party with burden

Clear and Convincing
Evidence

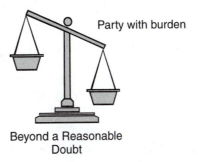

Party with burden

Beyond a Reasonable
Doubt

Rebuttal

rebuttal   opportunity for the
plaintiff to present arguments that
contradict arguments made by the
defendant

When the defendant is through calling witnesses, the defendant rests, and the plaintiff gets one last turn. This phase is called **rebuttal.** During rebuttal, the plaintiff may call witnesses and the defendant may cross-examine them.

The scope of the evidence that the plaintiff is allowed to present during rebuttal is quite limited: it must directly rebut some item of evidence offered during the defendant's part of the case. Allowing the plaintiff to bring up new matters at this late stage would not be fair because the defendant's part of the trial is over, and the defendant will have no chance to give his side of the story. Naturally, plaintiffs' attorneys are sometimes tempted to save some juicy bit of evidence and sneak it in during rebuttal so that the defendant will have no chance to offer evidence to disprove it. This practice is referred to as "sandbagging." Most judges vigorously enforce the restrictions on the scope of rebuttal, however, so trying to get important evidence in during rebuttal is risky.

More Motions

After rebuttal is over, the trial enters another "housekeeping" phase, again outside earshot of the jury. Both parties may now move for a directed verdict. In principle, the judge is always free to bypass the jury and render an immediate verdict, for either party, if he has been persuaded that the facts are so clear that no reasonable juror could reach a different conclusion. As a practical matter, directed verdicts at the close of the evidence do not gain very much in terms of efficient use of the court system—at most, some jury deliberating time will be saved. On the other hand, if an appellate court disagrees with the judge, the entire trial will have been wasted and the case will have to be tried again. Therefore, most judges are reluctant to grant a directed verdict and do so only in circumstances where the correct outcome is clear.

At this time, the judge must make a final decision about what instructions to give the jury, if that has not already been done. The attorneys need to know the exact wording of the jury instructions to prepare their closing arguments. Otherwise, they run the risk of arguing some point only to have the judge instruct the jury to the contrary a few minutes later. In all but the simplest cases, settling jury instructions usually requires argument—and plenty of it—as the attorneys debate the case law pertaining to the applicable theories of liability. Plaintiffs' attorneys want jury instructions that do not require proof of elements for which their evidence is weak. Defendants' goal is the opposite: the more elements the plaintiff has to prove, the better. The wording of instructions is also a battleground. The party with the best case—which may be either plaintiff or defendant—will prefer instructions that are clearly worded and easy to apply; the opposing party, on the other hand, will be perfectly happy for the judge to give instructions that are confusing and difficult to comprehend.

closing arguments final arguments made by attorneys after the close of their presentation of evidence

Putting It Into Practice 6.16:

Is Judge Salt likely to entertain a request for a directed verdict from CODA at this point in the trial? Why or why not?

"There Is Only One Innocent Person in This Courtroom—Only One Person Who Has Paid the Price of What Everyone Else Has Only Given Lip Service to."

In his **closing arguments,** John reiterated the theme he had begun in his opening statements. He talked of the "war" that CODA and others of its kind were engaging in against mainstream America and of the "soldiers" that it had commandeered from the ranks of the disenchanted and disenfranchised. He described Mike as an unwitting "casualty" of this war—a casualty that could have been avoided had school officials responded to the warning they had been given.

In his rebuttal, John alluded to CODA's argument that a verdict against CODA would endanger free speech. He reiterated that the right to free speech was not absolute and that speech that invites others to violence is not protected. He went on to restate the evidence showing how the movie incited the three defendants into attacking Mike, emphasizing the insidious nature of the movie's message as it was revealed in Max Evans's chilling demonstration of how unconsciously he carried that message.

"Do not be misled by Mr. Yakamura'a beguiling pleas to protect freedom of speech and by Ms. Tsosie's protestations that the school is but an innocent bystander. There is only one innocent person in this courtroom—only one person who has paid the price of what everyone else has only given lip service to. And he is going to continue to pay that price for the rest of his life.

"CODA had a choice, and it chose to enlist the services of Max Evans, Alan House, and Daniel Hendershott in its war against the American system. Max Evans, Alan House, and Daniel Hendershott had a choice, and they chose to vent their rage and frustration through physical violence. Washington High School had a choice, and it chose to ignore the warning signs. Mike Johnson is the only one who did not have a choice to be the target of these misguided forces. But you, ladies and gentlemen of the jury, have an opportunity to provide Mike with some choices as he picks up the pieces of his life and goes on from here. I trust *you* will choose wisely."

Closing Arguments

In closing arguments, the attorneys pull all of the pieces of their case together into a (hopefully) coherent and persuasive unit. Up to this point, most of the trial is devoted to listening to witnesses, one after the other. This results in a "piecemeal" presentation. Imagine what a movie would be like if actors appeared only once and spoke all of their lines for the whole movie at that time. The plot would be pretty hard to follow. You would probably need someone to explain afterward what was supposed to have happened. That is exactly what closing arguments do. Some trial lawyers like to draw an analogy between a trial and a puzzle. In the evidentiary phase, all of the pieces are laid out without showing how they all go together. In the closing arguments, all the pieces are assembled into a single picture. Because closing arguments serve as a blueprint for the rest of the case, many trial lawyers believe that trial preparation should begin with closing arguments.

Closing arguments differ from opening statements. In opening statements, lawyers are limited to saying what the evidence will be. Closing arguments are much less restricted and attorneys may argue what they think the evidence means. In addition to talking about the testimony presented during the trial, attorneys are free to draw inferences, to talk about common sense, to bring up facts and ideas that everyone knows from experience, to argue about what is good or bad for society, and—especially—to talk about what is the fair and just outcome. In an opening statement, if an attorney begins to argue—to stray much beyond the cold facts to be presented—the opposing attorney will object and the judge will remind the offender to stick to the evidence. In a closing argument, objections are considered poor form and will be tolerated only if the arguer is clearly misrepresenting the evidence on an important point. The assumption is that the jury knows that this is argument, not evidence, and that if one attorney's reasoning is flawed, the other is free to point out the flaws when it is his turn to speak.

Closing arguments follow the familiar three-step sequence: plaintiff first, then defendant, then plaintiff again. The plaintiff has the right to the first and last word to the jury because she has the burden of proof.

Paralegals assist in closing arguments by preparing charts, pictures, and "blowups"—poster-sized enlargements of juicy excerpts from document exhibits—that are often indispensable as a way of explaining complicated evidence. If, for example, an attorney reads a few sentences out of a contract to the jury, few jurors will follow and none will likely remember any of it an hour later. If the attorney instead puts a huge blowup of the few sentences on an easel in front of the jury while arguing (and, with luck, manages to leave the blowup where the jury can still see it while the opposing attorney is arguing), the point is much more likely to be understood and remembered. Paralegals are often responsible for designing these visuals and having them made up.

◆ *Putting It Into Practice 6.17:*

In your opinion, are closing arguments important? Defend your position. Do you think closing arguments are likely to change a juror's mind? What would you have argued in your closing arguments if you had represented Mike?

When John sat down, Judge Salt turned to the jury and began the painstaking process of charging the jury. After several hours, he dismissed the jury for the evening, with instructions to return in the morning to begin their deliberations.

After the jury left the room, John and Ernesto were chatting with Mike when Ms. Tsosie approached them. The serious expression on her face belied her mission of reconciliation. Mike was stunned to hear her offer: $350,000 if they settled before the jury returned the next day. He was utterly unprepared for this turn of events and was shocked at John and Ernesto's casual and noncommitted response: they would discuss it and get back to her.

Charging the Jury and Submitting the Case to the Jury

After both sides have finished their closing arguments, the judge instructs the jury. (In some states, jury instructions are read before the closing arguments.) First, the judge reads a series of instructions that are given in every civil suit—instructions about how to deliberate, how to select a foreperson, how to reach a verdict, and other housekeeping matters. Second, the judge reads the instructions on the rules of substantive law that the jury is to use in deciding the case. By now, these are thoroughly researched and honed to perfection.

In the federal courts, and in a few state courts, the judge is also allowed to comment on the evidence. In practice, most federal judges use this privilege sparingly. Refraining from commenting on the evidence is safe. The judge is not required to do it, even in federal court, so keeping quiet cannot cause a reversal on appeal. On the other hand, the wrong kinds of comments can be reversible error. If the court of appeals perceives the judge's comments as misstating the evidence or as overly argumentative in favor of one side, the court of appeals may send the case back for another trial.

The judge concludes the instructions by submitting the case to the jury for deliberation. The jurors are given verdict forms on which to record their decision and sent off to the jury room.

◆ LOCAL LINKS ◆

Are the judges in your jurisdiction allowed to comment on the evidence? When are jury instructions read in your jurisdiction?

Figure 6-11
Form of Verdict

We, the Jury, duly empaneled and sworn in the above entitled action, upon our oaths, do find in favor of plaintiff Michael Johnson and find the full damages to be $_____ .

We find the relative degrees of fault to be: (If a party listed below is not at fault, put a zero (0) on the percentage line for that party.

Defendant Max Evans   _____%

Defendant Daniel Hendershott   _____%

Defendant Alan House   _____%

Defendant CODA   _____%

Defendant Washington District High School   _____%

                                        Total: 100%

(1) _____   (5) _____

(2) _____   (6) _____

(3) _____   (7) _____

(4) _____   (8) _____
                                                    FOREMAN

We, the Jury, duly empaneled and sworn in the above entitled action, upon our oaths, do find in favor of defendants.

(1) _____   (5) _____

(2) _____   (6) _____

(3) _____   (7) _____

(4) _____   (8) _____
                                                    FOREMAN

RECESS

SUMMARY – PART A

A motion for summary judgment raises the question of whether genuine issues of material fact are raised in the complaint or defense. To defeat a motion for summary judgment, a party should submit evidence that an actual conflict of evidence exists. The party can do this by submitting affidavits, documents, or discovery responses that demonstrate this conflict.

Trial settings are not firm because judges usually schedule more cases for trial than they can possibly handle, anticipating that most of them will settle before going to trial and that other contingencies will arise that will result in delays. Judges set trial dates after some triggering event, such as filing a motion to set and certificate of readiness. To help ensure that attorneys will be prepared to go to trial, courts prepare a pretrial order or require the attorneys who will actually be going to trial to prepare a joint pretrial statement, which sets forth the boundaries of what can and cannot be presented at trial. The pretrial order or statement contains a list of the witnesses and documents that will be presented at trial as well as a list of the issues of fact and law that must be decided at trial. The rules generally require attorneys to exchange names of witnesses and copies of documents months before trial. Listing the documents saves trial time because any documents to which an attorney does not object in the pretrial statement will be admitted at trial. Judges encourage attorneys to compromise on issues as much as possible so that the trial can focus on the most serious issues in dispute.

Immediately before trial, witnesses are carefully prepared and cross-examination questions as well as opening and closing arguments are outlined. Motions *in limine* must be submitted to the judge, thus establishing the boundaries within which the attorneys must ask their questions. Jury instructions are prepared prior to trial. The exact wording of these instructions is important because of the potential importance this wording may play on appeal. Trial exhibits must be marked by the clerk before or during trial so that they can be located quickly. The authenticity of exhibits must be established although most pretrial orders contain stipulations of authenticity except for those the attorneys plan to challenge. Demonstrative evidence must be planned for well in advance of trial because the assistance of a graphics service is frequently required.

On the first day of trial, many judges meet with the attorneys in their chambers to—among other things—try once more to convince the attorneys to settle. If the trial moves forward, jurors are selected through the process of *voir dire*. Some courts control the *voir dire* process while others allow the attorneys to ask the questions. Jurors may be excused for personal reasons or "for cause." The attorneys also have the option of striking jurors by using a specified number of peremptory challenges.

The trial opens as both sides give opening statements during which they tell their client's story. The plaintiff then presents evidence, followed by the defendant, and concluding with the plaintiff, who is given an opportunity to rebut the defendant's case. This evidence is presented and rebutted through direct examination, during which leading questions are prohibited, and cross-examination, during which leading questions are essential. Attorneys cannot cross-examine their own witnesses unless those witnesses are hostile. Either side can ask that witnesses be placed "under the rule." Some courts limit the scope of cross-examination to areas that were covered on direct examination; all courts limit redirect examination to the scope of cross-examination. After the plaintiff rests, the defendant can move for a directed verdict on one or more claims if the defendant believes the plaintiff has failed to establish a *prima facie* case for those claims. The judge will allow a claim to go before the jury if reasonable jurors could differ as to whether the evidence supported the plaintiff's claim. Judges are reluctant to enter directed verdicts unless the outcome of the case is very clear.

The defendant then has the choice of attacking the plaintiff's case or raising an affirmative defense. Because the plaintiff has the burden of proving each element of her case by a preponderance of the evidence, the defendant need go after only the weakest link in the plaintiff's case to prevail. The defendant, however, has the burden of proving an affirmative defense. The plaintiff has the opportunity of rebuttal once the defendant has rested, but is restricted to rebutting evidence that was brought in by the defendant. Introducing new evidence at this point is called "sandbagging" and is vigorously opposed by judges. Motions are generally made both when the plaintiff rests and when the defendant rests.

At the end of the case, jury instructions are once again debated and both parties are careful to get their objections to these instructions on the record so they are preserved on appeal. Attorneys pull all the pieces of their case together in the closing arguments, where they are allowed to explain the evidence, to draw inferences, and to talk about commonly accepted ideas and general principles, such as fairness and justice. Objections are seldom made during closing arguments. Because closing arguments serve as a blueprint for the case, many trial attorneys believe that trial preparation should begin with the outlining of closing arguments.

Before the jury retires to deliberate, the judge reads them two sets of jury instructions. The first is a set of general instructions that is used in every civil case and the second is a set of specific instructions addressing the substantive law to be applied in the case at hand. In federal courts and some state courts, judges are permitted to comment on the evidence, but few do because of the possibility of committing reversible error.

KEY TERMS

Affiant
Challenge for cause
Charging the jury
Clear and convincing evidence
Closing arguments
Cross-examination
Declarations
Demonstrative evidence
Direct examination
Directed verdict
Examined
Findings of fact and conclusions of law
Foundation
Gag order
Hearsay
Hearsay rule
Hostile witness
Jury instructions
Leading questions
Motion for summary judgment
Motion *in limine*
Motion to set and certificate of readiness

Objection
Overrules
Peremptory challenge
Polled
Preponderance of the evidence
Pretrial conference
Pretrial order
Pretrial statement
Prima facie
Rebuttal
Re-direct examination
Relevant
Rest
Scope
Sustains
Trial notebook
Trial setting
Under the rule
Uniform instructions/patterned instructions
Voir dire

REVIEW QUESTIONS – PART A

1. What is the purpose of filing a motion for summary judgment? What should a party do to defeat such a motion?

2. How is a trial setting obtained? For what reasons will a trial date often have to be reset?

3. What do modern courts do to ensure that trials are well-orchestrated events?

4. What tensions are created when attorneys talk to the press about their case?

5. Why might an attorney file a motion *in limine?*

6. Why are jury instructions important?

7. What two things must be considered when preparing exhibits for trial?

8. What is the purpose of a trial notebook? What kinds of items should be included in it?

9. What is the purpose of *voir dire?* How are peremptory challenges and challenges for cause used in this process?

10. Compare opening statements with closing arguments.

11. Explain the differences in purpose behind direct examination, cross-examination, and re-direct examination. During which of these can leading questions be asked?

12. Give an example of hearsay. What exceptions to the hearsay rule exist?

13. What is the significance of a directed verdict in favor of the defendant?

14. In what respect is the defendant's job easier than the plaintiff's? What two strategies can a defendant rely on in order to win?

15. Explain the preponderance-of-evidence test.

16. What kinds of information are included in jury instructions?

PRACTICE EXAM – PART A

MULTIPLE CHOICE

1. A motion for summary judgment
   a. should be raised before the complaint is filed
   b. can be used to weed out claims and defenses for which no genuine issue of material fact exists
   c. is inappropriate when the facts are so clear that the judge has no doubt about what will happen at trial
   d. none of the above

2. To defeat a motion for summary judgment, a party should
   a. submit affidavits of witnesses
   b. submit documents
   c. submit discovery responses and deposition excerpts
   d. all of the above

3. Trial dates are rarely firm because
   a. courts usually overbook trials
   b. cases settle on the courthouse steps
   c. judges grant continuances because witnesses or attorneys are injured or become ill
   d. all of the above

4. Modern judges
   a. encourage parties to be prepared in advance of trial by having the attorneys prepare pretrial orders
   b. encourage parties to be prepared by signing joint pretrial statements
   c. do their best to ensure that trials are carefully orchestrated events
   d. encourage attorneys to "wing it" at trial

5. Pretrial statements and orders include
   a. lists of witnesses and documents to be presented at trial
   b. lists of issues but not of facts to be decided at trial
   c. lists of documents to be introduced but no lists of issues and facts because those are contained in the pleadings
   d. none of the above

6. An attorney who deliberately defies a judge's order *in limine*
   a. risks a mistrial
   b. can lose his license to practice law
   c. can be found in contempt of court
   d. all of the above

7. Jury instructions are important because
   a. they often determine the outcome of a jury's decision
   b. they may serve as the basis for appeal
   c. they represent each party's interpretation of the law
   d. all of the above

8. Before an exhibit can be introduced at trial
   a. it can be proven authentic by witness testimony
   b. the opposing attorney must stipulate to its authenticity
   c. the clerk must mark it before trial begins
   d. all of the above

9. A trial notebook may include
   a. outlines of direct and cross-examination
   b. minute entries in chronological order
   c. a proposed trial schedule
   d. all of the above

10. The jury selection process
    a. always involves prospective jurors drawn from voter registration lists
    b. always involves selection of jurors from twenty-four prospective jurors
    c. depends on the individual preferences of the judge
    d. does not require jurors to reveal anything about themselves

11. *Voir dire*
    a. is conducted by the judge
    b. is conducted by the attorneys
    c. is done in accordance with the procedures dictated by the judge conducting the trial
    d. does not allow attorneys to ask questions about jurors' personal habits and prejudices

12. Jurors can be excused
    a. for personal reasons
    b. because they are biased
    c. for no cause
    d. all of the above

13. During opening statements, an attorney should
    a. present arguments
    b. present his client's story in the best light possible
    c. make impassioned philosophical speeches
    d. all of the above

14. Cross-examination
    a. is limited in scope by some courts to subjects that were covered on direct examination
    b. usually contains many leading questions
    c. is allowed when the plaintiff calls the defendant as a witness
    d. all of the above

15. Being put under the rule
    a. prevents witnesses from changing their testimony in response to what they hear other witnesses say
    b. applies to parties as well as other witnesses
    c. means the parties cannot have someone present to assist counsel
    d. none of the above

16. Hearsay includes
    a. out-of-court statements used to impeach a witness
    b. admissions by a party
    c. out-of-court statements used to prove the truth of the matter asserted
    d. dying declarations

17. An exception to the hearsay rule is
    a. an excited utterance
    b. a statement made for purposes of medical diagnosis
    c. certain business and public records
    d. all of the above

18. The plaintiff
    a. has an easier job than the defendant
    b. loses if she is unable to prove one element of her case
    c. wins if the defendant is unable to prove an affirmative defense
    d. wins as long as the defendant fails to disprove any elements of the plaintiff's case

19. After all of the evidence has been heard
    a. the judge will make a final decision regarding jury instructions
    b. the judge is more likely than ever to grant a directed verdict
    c. "housekeeping" matters are heard in the presence of the jury
    d. jury instructions are discussed by the attorneys but rarely hotly debated

20. During closing arguments
    a. attorneys should not argue
    b. objections are encouraged
    c. the plaintiff gets to give the first and last argument
    d. attorneys may not argue what they think the evidence means

FILL IN THE BLANK

21. A _____ is a motion asking a judge to dismiss a case on the grounds that no genuine issues of material fact are raised in the complaint.

22. Under the federal rules, affidavits must show that the _____ (the person signing the affidavit) is competent to testify about the matters in the affidavit.

23. A trial cannot begin until a _____ , which consists of a minute entry specifying a date, time, and place for trial, is obtained. This can be done by filing a _____ , which is a printed form that tells the court how many trial days are needed and whether a jury is needed.

24. At a _____ , the judge specifies what the attorneys can and cannot present at trial after reviewing the _____ prepared by both attorneys setting forth what they believe they should and should not be able to present at trial.

25. Dealing with the press involves a balancing between freedom of _____ and the right to a _____ . This is most apparent when a court issues a _____ prohibiting attorneys from talking to the press about a case.

26. An attorney who is concerned that opposing counsel may try to ask potentially prejudicial questions at trial should file a _____ , asking the judge to rule in advance of trial on the admissibility of evidence.

27. _____ (formal instructions to the jury on points of law they will be asked to apply) are carefully researched and argued by the attorneys and are read by the judge in the process of _____ the jury. _____ instructions are those that have been used in prior trials and whose validity has been well established.

28. Before a document can be introduced at trial, it must be proven _____—that it is what it purports to be.

29. Blowups, charts, diagrams, and other types of _____ help explain the facts to the jury.

30. Paralegals are often asked to prepare a _____ , which is an indexed compilation of the most important documents and resources that an attorney needs to access during trial.

31. The process of asking prospective jurors about their backgrounds and about any feelings or beliefs they have that may interfere with their ability to follow the judge's instructions is called _____ .

32. An attorney can use a _____ to remove a juror who is prone to base a decision on personal beliefs or prejudices rather than on the evidence and the judge's instructions. An attorney can use a _____ to remove a juror for no cause.

33. If, after the plaintiff rests, the judge concludes that the plaintiff has clearly failed to prove one of the elements of her cause of action, he can grant a _____ for the defendant.

34. An attorney can ask _____ questions (questions that suggest the answer the attorney wants to hear) when conducting _____

of a witness, but cannot ask such questions when conducting _____ examination, unless the witness is a _____ (uncooperative) witness.

35. The _____ (extent of subject matter that can be covered) is more limited on _____ examination (conducted in response to cross-examination) than direct examination.

36. A witness who has been put _____ cannot remain in the courtroom and is prohibited from discussing the case with anyone.

37. Before a document can be introduced, the attorney must lay the proper _____ to establish the authenticity of the document.

38. If an attorney tries to introduce testimony that is arguably _____ (secondhand information), opposing counsel must make an _____ (a formal challenge). If the judge _____ the objection, the attorney can present the testimony, but if the judge _____ the objection, the attorney will not be allowed to present the testimony.

39. Attorneys are not allowed to present evidence unless it is _____ , that is, it logically leads to a conclusion that a fact is either more or less probable.

40. When a plaintiff _____ (finishes putting on witnesses), she faces the possibility of a _____ if the judge determines that she has failed to prove one or more elements of her cause of action.

41. In a civil lawsuit, the plaintiff must prove each element of her cause of action by a _____ (more than 50 percent of the evidence). Some causes of action require proof of _____ , which is an even higher standard of proof required in some civil cases.

42. A defendant can win by proving an _____ defense, (a legitimate excuse for doing what he did).

43. When the defendant rests, the plaintiff gets one last turn during _____ to call more witnesses.

44. Deliberately introducing evidence during rebuttal that the defendant did not raise during his part of the case is called _____ .

45. Attorneys pull all the pieces of their case together in their _____ .

TRUE OR FALSE

____ 46. A defendant can, by moving for summary judgment, force a plaintiff to "put up or shut up."

____ 47. A judge is not allowed to grant a partial motion for summary judgment.

____ 48. A judge often has to resolve factual disputes when reviewing a motion for summary judgment.

____ 49. In summary judgment practice, affidavits are routinely used as a kind of substitute for live testimony.

____ 50. In some courts, cases rarely make it to trial on their first setting.

____ 51. Joint pretrial statements are usually prepared by paralegals.

____ 52. Pretrial orders are signed by the attorneys and presented to the judge.

____ 53. If an attorney fails to object to a document that is listed in the pretrial statement, the judge will admit that document at trial without debate.

____ 54. A pretrial order contains sections in which the parties can stake out their positions on disputed issues.

____ 55. Lawyers should not make comments outside the courtroom that they know are likely to materially prejudice a courtroom proceeding.

____ 56. Once attorneys begin the actual trial preparation process, settlement is rarely an option.

____ 57. Important direct testimony is rehearsed with witnesses and cross-examination is outlined question for question in well-tried cases.

____ 58. Some courts instruct the jury on undisputed, relevant issues of law at the beginning of trial.

____ 59. Many trial lawyers believe that jury instructions have little impact on jurors' decisions.

____ 60. A party may complain to the court of appeals about a jury instruction even if the party never requested that instruction.

____ 61. Jury instructions are usually decided by the judge before the trial even begins.

____ 62. Attorneys must always draft jury instructions from scratch.

____ 63. Judges prefer that attorneys stipulate to the admissibility of all documents except those that they have a serious basis to challenge.

____ 64. All physical documents that will be used at trial should be organized before trial so that each can be located quickly during the trial.

____ 65. Planning for demonstrative evidence is usually one of the last things attorneys and paralegals undertake in preparing for trial.

____ 66. A trial notebook usually includes copies of the pretrial order, jury instructions, *voir dire* questions, and an outline of closing argument.

____ 67. When judges meet with the attorneys on the first day of trial, they discourage attorneys from settling at that point.

____ 68. Jury panels always consist of twelve jurors.

____ 69. Attorneys' intent in *voir dire* is to find the fairest jurors possible.

____ 70. Attorneys who are allowed to conduct their own *voir dire* often use questions that are really designed to sell the jury on the merits of their cases.

____ 71. Attorneys can use peremptory challenges to remove jurors whom they believe will not vote in the desired way, but they cannot use them to remove racial minorities from a jury panel.

____*72. Judges take over the functions of the jury in non-jury trials and decide both the factual and legal issues.

____*73. Judges are required to make findings of fact and conclusions of law in non-jury trials so that the parties know which rules of law the judge applied if they decide to appeal the judge's decision.

____*74. Judges do not relax the formal rules of evidence in non-jury cases.

____ 75. If a judge believes that the links in the plaintiff's chain may or may not have held up under the defendant's attacks, he will grant a directed verdict for the defendant.

____ 76. Attorneys are not allowed to continue their examination of a witness after they have completed redirect examination.

____ 77. The scope of cross-examination is unlimited.

____ 78. An attorney may not cross-examine his own witness unless the witness is hostile.

____ 79. "Was the car blue?" is an example of a leading question.

____ 80. The purpose of cross-examination is to test a witness's credibility and truthfulness.

____ 81. Cases are generally won as a result of skillful cross-examination.

____ 82. The judge decides the order in which witnesses will be called.

____ 83. A common tactic for plaintiffs is to call the defendant as their first witness.

____ 84. To avoid a directed verdict, the plaintiff must establish a *prima facie* case for each theory of liability.

____ 85. Relevant evidence is not admissible if it is unduly prejudicial.

____ 86. Bob's testimony that James told him that Myrna did not go to school on the day in question is hearsay.

____ 87. Bob's testimony that James told him that Myrna (a party in the case) bragged about not going to school the day in question is not hearsay.

____ 88. Bob's testimony that James told him that he saw Myrna at the movies is hearsay if Bob's statement is used to show that Myrna was lying when she testified that she was in school.

____ 89. If the defendant thinks that the plaintiff has failed to put on evidence in support of some element of one of her causes of action, the defendant may move for a directed verdict as to that cause of action.

____ 90. Plaintiffs like to time their presentations so they finish at the end of a trial day.

____ 91. Defendants need to challenge every aspect of the plaintiff's case; they cannot afford to attack only the weakest link in the plaintiff's chain.

____ 92. A defendant can win by casting enough doubt on the evidence supporting one element of the plaintiff's case.

____ 93. The preponderance-of-evidence test requires a party to present enough evidence to persuade a jury that it was more probable than not that the alleged facts occurred.

____ 94. Defendants need not meet the requirements of the preponderance-of-evidence test in proving an affirmative defense.

____ 95. An affirmative defense allows a defendant to win even after the plaintiff proves each element of her cause of action.

____ 96. Most judges are very liberal about allowing plaintiffs to delve on rebuttal into areas that were never raised by the defendant.

____ 97. Judges are generally reluctant to enter directed verdicts after all of the evidence has been introduced.

____ 98. The party with the worst case generally prefers jury instructions that are clearly worded and easy to apply.

____ 99. In closing arguments, all the pieces of the puzzle that the attorneys collected during the evidentiary phase are put together into a single picture.

____ 100. Many attorneys begin their trial preparation with the writing of closing arguments.

____ 101. During closing arguments, attorneys cannot draw inferences, talk about common sense, or describe fair and just outcomes.

____ 102. Paralegals have nothing to do with the preparation of closing arguments.

____ 103. Judges are encouraged to comment on the evidence before submitting a case to the jury.

____ 104. Judges instruct the jury on the substantive law as well as on general issues regarding how to deliberate, how to select a foreperson, and how to reach a verdict.

*Taken from Bonus Pointers

PART B

These Are Not the Kinds of Decisions They Prepare You for in Law School

John sat pensively in his office chair, reflecting on his recommendation that Mike not accept the school's offer. These are not the kinds of decisions they prepare you for in law school, he thought. He would have been pleased to know that his and Martha's hunch about Mr. Hom, the businessman on the jury, had proved to be accurate.

Mr. Hom fell effortlessly into his role of foreperson, unobtrusively guiding the other jurors through the process of assessing liability. An avid aficionado of the arts, he would have, under ordinary circumstances, fiercely argued on behalf of protecting CODA's First Amendment rights. But he was also an expert on advertising and knew first-hand the power of brainwashing. Max Evans's unconscious regurgitation of the movie dialogue deeply disturbed him. Also appreciating the power of advertising from the vantage point of a successful entrepreneur, he could not bring himself to argue against the other jurors' unequivocal rejection of CODA's arguments regarding the First Amendment.

Once the jurors decided that the boys should be liable for 60 percent of Mike's damages, the district 30 percent liable, and CODA 10 percent liable, they focused on assessing Mike's total damages. They relied heavily on the testimony of Mike's economist and concluded that Mike's damages ranged somewhere between $5 and

$9 million. At this point, Mr. Hom stepped forward and talked about the realities of collecting judgments. As a veteran of two major lawsuits, he surmised that Mike was unlikely to collect anything from the boys and that he might not collect anything from CODA either if it was successful in appealing the jury's verdict. For these reasons, he suggested that they opt for a figure in the higher part of their range. He reminded them, too, that after Mike's attorneys had taken their share of the judgment and had their costs reimbursed, Mike would be left with substantially less money. With these factors in mind, the jury reached its final verdict.

Deliberation and Verdict

The jury's first task is to elect a foreperson; then the jurors discuss the case and try to arrive at a decision. In general, jury members must decide how to accomplish this. Few restrictions exist so, as a practical matter, jurors are free to decide the case in any way they wish, taking as little or as much (within reason) time as they wish, based on whatever reasons seem sufficient to them. In theory, there are a few cardinal sins. Using a coin toss or other game of chance to decide the case is one which, if proven, can lead to a finding of jury misconduct and a mistrial. In practice, losing a case because two jurors think one lawyer has a better tailor still means the case is lost.

Lawyers often find it instructive to talk to the jurors after a case is over as a means of learning which tactics were persuasive and which ones fell flat. Attending such "post-mortems" (also called "exit interviews") allows paralegals to quickly learn that many factors besides the law and the evidence influence jurors. The wise lawyer learns to identify and use these other factors rather than rail against them. Among other things, experience teaches that many verdicts come down to nothing more complicated than that the jury believed that some important: witness was lying to them. Lawyer demeanor is also important: a professional appearance, good grooming, and a likable, pleasant, and confident attitude are usually helpful.

general verdict   finding for plaintiff or defendant

In the vast majority of cases, only a **general verdict** is called for; that is, the jury is asked merely to find for the plaintiff or defendant, and if the verdict is for the plaintiff, to decide the amount of money to be awarded. In cases involving multiple parties, separate verdicts are needed for each one. In Mike's case, for example, the jury must render a verdict for each defendant.

special verdict   written findings on particular issues of fact

In some courts, judges can require the jury to be more specific about what they are deciding. A **special verdict,** for example, consists of written findings on particular issues of fact. In a battery case, for example, the jury could be asked to render separate verdicts on whether the defendant made physical contact with the plaintiff; whether the defendant acted intentionally; whether the plaintiff suffered damages; and whether the damages were caused by the defendant's conduct. The judge would then decide whether the specific facts found in the special verdict were enough to support liability and render judgment accordingly.

general verdict with interrogatories   finding for plaintiff or defendant and answering of questions about specific facts

Another procedure is to submit the case to the jury for a **general verdict with written interrogatories,** asking the jury about specific facts upon which the verdict depends. Here, the judge might ask the jury to reach a general verdict, in the usual way, on whether the defendant is liable to the plaintiff for battery, and, in addition, to answer the question, "Did the defendant intend to make physical contact with the plaintiff?" If the answers to any of the factual questions are inconsistent with the verdict, the judge can send the jury back to try again, or order a new trial.

NET NEWS

To learn more about the jury deliberation process, go to *www.jri-inc.com/jury.htm.*

Most judges try to avoid using these procedures, seeing them as a way for the parties to plant the seeds of reversible error and set up an appeal. The judge's power to use special verdicts or interrogatories with the jury is discretionary: that is, the judge is not required to use them, but may do so if she wishes. Therefore, the court of appeals is highly unlikely to send the case back for a new trial just because the judge used a general verdict. If the judge uses special verdicts or jury interrogatories, however, and the jury comes back with the wrong answers—inconsistent findings, for example—the judge may have no choice but to order a new trial.

hung jury jury unable to reach a verdict

If the jurors cannot agree on a verdict and a unanimous verdict is required, one determined holdout juror can cause a **hung jury**—a jury unable to reach a verdict. Judges dislike wasting time retrying cases, so a deadlocked jury will likely be sent back several times with increasingly adamant exhortations to come to some agreement. In many cases, jurors can negotiate with each other and reach some compromise. If the judge becomes convinced that breaking the deadlock is hopeless, the only solution is to order a new trial with a new jury.

In courts where a majority verdict is permitted, a hung jury is still possible because the majority required is almost always more than a simple majority. Nevertheless, majority verdicts make hung juries much less likely, which is one of the reasons why some states use them.

◆ **LOCAL LINKS** ◆

Is a unanimous verdict required in your jurisdiction?

polled asking each juror whether he agreed with the verdict

When the jurors reach a decision, they send word to the judge. Because no one can predict how long it will take the jury to reach a decision, the judge and the attorneys usually go back to their offices. The judge's secretary notifies the attorneys that the jury has returned, everyone returns to the courtroom, and the judge has the verdict read. Any party then has the right to have the jury **polled** (except in some states where post-trial contact with jurors is prohibited). Polling the jury consists of the judge asking each juror, in open court, whether he agreed to the verdict. Polling provides a safeguard against coercion, giving any jurors who feel they were pressured into a decision an opportunity to say so.

motion for judgment notwithstanding the verdict request that the judge disregard the jury's verdict and enter a verdict in favor of the party who lost at trial

Putting It Into Practice 6.18:

Why would a judge probably prefer having a trial requiring a general verdict and a majority vote?

Eight million dollars! Martha could scarcely wrap her mind around the verdict. The foreman's pronouncement was still ringing in her ears when Mike grabbed her and hugged so hard she thought he might break her ribs. Carmela was beside him almost immediately, crying and laughing simultaneously, and Martha breathlessly guided Mike into her waiting arms. How wonderful, she thought, that they have each other to share in this victory. And for just a moment, she realized how alone she had felt since her break-up with Tim. But this was a time to revel in their victory, and she allowed herself to be swept away by the giddy elation that, at this moment, transcended everything in her personal life.

But the celebration was short-lived. A few days after the trial, the judge granted CODA's **motion for judgment notwithstanding the verdict.** Although Mike was shocked that his newly acquired fortune could so quickly be taken from him, John and Ernesto were not surprised. Both knew that the judge had been waffling when CODA moved for a directed verdict at the close of its case.

NET NEWS

To find out about jury verdicts across the country, including the amounts of damages awarded, go to *www.morelaw.com.*

Getting from Verdict to Judgment

The path to this point in the case is long and arduous, having taken a year or probably more and tens of thousands of dollars in attorney time and costs to prepare. But the end is not yet in sight. All that has been obtained is a verdict. What is needed is a final judgment: a court order declaring that one party owes the opposing party money. Several potential hurdles must be overcome before a judgment can be secured, and even then the opposing party can appeal. Because judgments are not self-executing, the prevailing party must still figure out how to collect the money once obtaining the judgment.

The loser at trial has several possible procedural moves from which to choose. The first is a **motion for a new trial.** A motion for new trial must be based on some error committed during the trial, usually a procedural error that affects the fairness of the proceedings (e.g., juror misconduct). In effect, it is a way of short-circuiting the appeal process when some mistake has been made that the judge knows will lead the court of appeals to order a new trial. Time and money should not be wasted on an appeal whose outcome is a foregone conclusion. It is better and cheaper for the trial judge to bite the bullet, acknowledge the error, and retry the case. As you might expect, motions for a new trial are hard to win. No judge wants to try the same case twice, so if the alleged error is reasonably debatable, the motion will be denied and the losing party can then appeal.

A motion for judgment notwithstanding the verdict (often called **judgment n.o.v.**—the initials stand for the Latin phrase *non obstante verdictum*) is a request for the judge to disregard the jury's decision completely and enter judgment in favor of the party who lost the trial. The judge does this if she is persuaded that the jury reached a verdict that no reasonable person could have arrived at from the evidence by following the judge's jury instructions.

The typical sequence of events is this: One party moves for a directed verdict after both sides have finished their evidence. The judge may be inclined to grant the directed verdict, but if she does so, and the court of appeals disagrees, the whole case will have to be retried. Having already invested days or weeks in a jury trial, letting the jury render a verdict is more sensible. If the jury makes the same decision the judge would have, the judge lets the jury verdict stand. If the jury reaches the "wrong" decision, the judge grants a motion for judgment n.o.v. Then, if the court of appeals decides that the judge should not have taken the decision away from the jury, it can simply reinstate the jury verdict, and a second trial is avoided. It is safer for the judge to deny the motion for directed verdict and grant the motion for judgment n.o.v. after the verdict than it is to grant the motion for directed verdict, send the jurors home, and risk reversal on appeal.

Still another option available to a losing defendant is to ask for a *remittitur.* Suppose the jury finds in favor of the plaintiff and awards an unexpectedly large sum of money for damages. If the defendant persuades the judge that the award is unreasonable and excessive, the judge has the power to let the verdict stand and reduce the amount of the award. The plaintiff can appeal, of course. By the same token, a plaintiff can ask for an *additur* when a jury awards inappropriately low damages in light of uncontroverted evidence.

motion for a new trial
motion requesting that the judge grant a new trial based on alleged judicial error

remittitur   request that a jury award be reduced by the judge on the grounds that it is unreasonable and excessive

additur   increase by a court in the amount of damages awarded by the jury

Putting It Into Practice 6.19:

If the judge granted CODA's motion for judgment n.o.v. on the basis of the element of causation, what had the judge concluded?

Figure 6-12
Parties' Options After Verdict

PARTIES' OPTIONS AFTER VERDICT

Motion for a New Trial
Motion for Judgment N.O.V.
Remittitur
Additur
Appeal

GETTING FROM VERDICT TO JUDGMENT

entry of judgment   day that the judgment is formally entered

The event that formally ends the trial phase of the litigation is the **entry of judgment.** Knowing exactly when a judgment is entered is important, because various deadlines—especially the deadline for filing an appeal—are counted from the entry of judgment. In federal court, judgment is entered when it is signed by the court and recorded in the clerk's docket. In state courts, procedures vary, and the winning party may have to **lodge** a proposed **form of judgment** (the exact wording of the decision) with the court (i.e., prepare and deliver the actual judgment that the party wants the judge to sign).

lodge   prepare and deliver a judgment

form of judgment   exact wording of a judgment

Skirmishes can occur over the contents of the judgment. With a garden-variety judgment on a general verdict involving only an award of money damages, argument about the wording of the judgment is unnecessary and the judge will sign it immediately. In more complicated cases (such as the disposition of property in a divorce case), the exact wording can become quite important and the court may need to hear argument about the form of judgment.

taxable court costs   expenses related to a lawsuit

Another potential battleground is the assessment of costs. The winning party is entitled to have judgment against the loser for **taxable court costs.** Taxable costs do not include all expenses related to the suit. (Federal and state statutes list the categories of expenses that can be assessed against the losing party.) Typically, the most expensive category of taxable costs are the court reporter fees for depositions, filing fees, and process service fees. Two of the greatest expenses of litigating are generally not taxable: attorney's fees and expert witness fees, both of which can add up to tens of thousands of dollars even in relatively ordinary cases.

Does the loser also have to pay the winner's attorney's fees? This is an important question, because the attorney's fees may add up to more than the amount of damages being sued for. In the American system, the general rule is that each party must pay his own attorney, although many exceptions exist. Because most contracts written by lawyers include an agreement that, in case of a dispute, the loser pays the attorney's fees, attorneys' fees are often awarded in breach of contract lawsuits. Many recent statutes create new causes of action (for such things as consumer fraud, securities fraud, and the like) that provide for an award of attorneys' fees to the winner. And in many courts, the judge has the power to award attorneys' fees if the judge believes that a party deliberately abused the system—filing a frivolous lawsuit merely to harass the opposing party, for example. Some advocates of reform believe that the laws should be changed to require the loser to pay the winner's attorneys' fees in all cases (as is the case in Great Britain). Such proposals are particularly popular with defense lawyers because they anticipate that fewer plaintiffs will sue if losing means getting assessed tens of thousands of dollars for the defendant's attorneys' fees.

◆ LOCAL LINKS ◆

In your jurisdiction, what does the winning party have to do to enter a judgment?

statement of costs   document prepared by the winner of a lawsuit itemizing the costs incurred in the suit

One way a court determines the amount of costs to assess is for the winner to file a **statement of costs,** after which the loser can file written objections to any

Figure 6-13
Notice of Appeal

William Yakamura, Esq.
59 Plain Street
Durango, Colorado 95660
(303 555-12134
Admitted Pro Hoc Vice

Attorney for defendant CODA, Inc.

IN THE SUPERIOR COURT OF MARICOPA COUNTY
PHOENIX, ARIZONA

Michael Johnson, a single man,	)	
	)	
	)	NO. _____
Plaintiff,	)	
	)	Notice of Appeal
vs.	)	
	)	
Daniel Hendershott, Max Evans, and	)	
Alan House, all single men; CODA,	)	
Inc., a foreign corporation;	)	Assigned to the
Washington High School District.	)	Honorable
	)	Benjamin Salt
Defendants.	)	
	)	

Defendant CODA, by and through counsel undersigned, does hereby give notice of its appeal from the judgment entered against it in favor of the Plaintiff in the above entitled matter on the 25th day of October, 2001.

Dated this 22nd day of November, 2001.

_____
William Yakamura, Esq.
Attorney for Defendant CODA

items deemed improper. Attorneys' fees are a different matter: proceedings to determine the fees to be awarded can become quite complex and drawn out, possibly requiring evidentiary hearings as the parties argue over the reasonableness of various charges.

Putting It Into Practice 6.20:

Why might it be important for John and Ernesto to know exactly when the judgment is entered in Mike's case? What aspect of this judgment might be disputed by the parties? Will Mike have to pay CODA's attorneys' fees in light of the judge's granting of CODA's motion for judgment n.o.v.?

"It's Entirely Possible That, After All Is Said and Done, We'll Still Have to Chase after the Company, Looking for Collectable Assets."

Mike thought that all the tough decisions were behind him as far as his case was concerned. But now that the reality of the verdict was really beginning to sink in, he found himself at another crossroads.

"So basically you want to know if I want to pursue an appeal against CODA?" clarified Mike.

"Yes," affirmed John. "And I want to remind you about our retainer agreement. If we are successful in our appeal, the firm's percentage of whatever is recovered will increase from 33 percent to 40 percent. Although you will not pay our fees, normally you'd be expected to pay the costs of the appeal. But because your case has the potential of going to the U.S. Supreme Court and because the partners in our firm would like to see that happen, the firm is willing to bankroll the appeal."

"Doesn't sound like I have much to lose. If you win, I win, and if you lose, at least I'm not out any more money. And after the final appeal, it's all over, right?" asked Mike hopefully.

"Well, not exactly," admitted John. "As we told you earlier, CODA's financial status is somewhat shaky. So it's entirely possible that, after all is said and done, we'll still have to chase after the company, looking for collectable assets."

"More hearings? More fighting?" groaned Mike.

"I'm afraid so," conceded John.

COLLECTING A JUDGMENT

judgment creditor party to whom money was awarded

Entry of judgment marks the end of the trial phase of the lawsuit, but it is by no means the end of the road for the parties to the dispute. The parties' strategies and options depend on who won and on whether a significant amount of money has been awarded. Now each of the parties has a potential weapon in hand: the judgment debtor (the party ordered to pay the money) can appeal, and the **judgment creditor** (the party to whom the money was awarded) can try to collect the money awarded in the judgment. Although, procedurally, appeal and collection are separate processes, as a matter of strategy, they are related. Appealing can be one way for the loser at trial to delay collection of the judgment, but the threat of collection while the appeal is pending can put a serious damper on the loser's enthusiasm for the appeal.

stay court order prohibiting the judgment creditor from collecting on the judgment

As a general rule, a judgment is effective and enforceable as soon as it is entered, and the judgment creditor can begin collection proceedings immediately. But if a judgment debtor wants to prevent a judgment creditor from collecting the judgment while the case is on appeal, it must obtain a **stay.** A stay is a court order, either by the trial court or the court of appeals, prohibiting the judgment creditor from trying to collect on the judgment while the stay is in effect. One common way to obtain a stay is by posting a **supersedeas bond.** Another is to file for bankruptcy, which results in an automatic stay of all proceedings against the judgment debtor.

supersedeas bond promise by the judgment debtor to pay when the appeal is over, accompanied by some form of security

A supersedeas bond allows the judgment debtor to keep the money while the appeal is in process if it guarantees that the money will be available when the appeal is over. The bond is a promise to pay, accompanied by some form of security. The security can be cash deposited with the court—in effect the court will hold the money during the appeal—or, more commonly, it will be an insurance contract from an approved insurance company. If the bond is secured by an insurance contract, the court can order the insurance company to pay the judgment creditor if she wins on appeal. Naturally, the insurance company will make sure that, if it has to pay, it has some way of getting the money back from the judgment debtor. Before an insurance company issues a supersedeas bond, it insists on getting some security—perhaps a mortgage on the judgment debtor's property or a written guarantee from a large corporation that is clearly able to pay the amount in question. If the judgment debtor has few assets, probably no insurance company will issue a bond, and the judgment debtor will be forced to try to dodge the judgment creditor's collection efforts while the appeal is going on.

Putting It Into Practice 6.21:

Suppose Molly Running Deer obtains a judgment against Stuart Thames. What can Stuart do to prevent Molly from collecting this judgment or to make it more difficult for her to do so?

Debtor's Examination

execution seizing of property to pay for a judgment

In order to seize the judgment debtor's property and apply it to pay the judgment—a process referred to as **execution**—the judgment creditor must find out what assets the judgment debtor has. Asset discovery begins with a judgment debtor's examination, often called a **debtor's exam** or *post-judgment discovery.* A debtor's exam is, in effect, like a deposition of the judgment debtor, in which the judgment creditor's attorney asks questions about the judgment debtor's assets. Some debtor's exams are held at the court, under the supervision of a court officer who is not a judge but is appointed to handle routine matters in the judge's place. The supervising officer does not actually attend the examination—there are too many—he merely swears in the judgment debtor and stands by in case a ruling or order of some kind is needed. The judgment creditor's attorney and the judgment debtor are sent into any available conference room to do the questioning. If, as not uncommonly happens, the judgment debtor is evasive or uncooperative, she can be easily hauled back before the supervising court officer, who will likely administer a dose of reality. The court will force the judgment debtor to answer any reasonable questions about her property under threat of jail if she refuses to answer. Debtor's exams can also be held at the judgment creditor's attorney's office, in a manner similar to a deposition, although a court reporter is often not present.

debtor's exam questioning of judgment debtor to determine what assets he or she has; also called a *post-judgment discovery*

The objective of a debtor's exam is to find property or money belonging to the judgment debtor. The modern reality is that most kinds of property have some kind of paperwork associated with them: real estate has deeds, cars have title certificates, bank accounts have statements. Therefore, it is customary to summon the judgment debtor to the debtor's exam via a subpoena *duces tecum,* which includes a long and detailed list of documents for the judgment debtor to bring. The examination consists of going through these records one by one, noting the information necessary to find and seize the property in question. Of equal importance, the attorney questions the judgment debtor about the categories of property for which no documents have been produced. Questions will be asked about the judgment debtor's income and expenses, and where any excess money has gone.

◆ **LOCAL LINKS** ◆

How are debtor's exams set up in your jurisdiction?

Putting It Into Practice 6.22:

What will Molly Running Deer's attorney do at the debtor's exam of Stuart Thames?

BONUS POINTERS:

LOCATING ASSETS OF JUDGMENT DEBTORS

Once you have obtained a final judgment against a defendant, the process of collecting on the judgment begins. Many states have enacted the Uniform Enforcement of Foreign Judgments Act, or some amended version, that allows for the registration of any judgment not entered by that state's courts to be registered—and enforced—as if the judgment were rendered by that state's court.

Usually before, but certainly after, registration of the judgment, the county recorder's records should be checked to see if any real property is held in the county by the judgment debtor. The county assessor's records should also be checked for records of certain personal property (such as mobile homes) and to give an idea of the value of the property.

The state's corporation commission should always be reviewed for corporate debtors to make sure they are still lawfully doing business. In many states, some "bare bones" financial records are part of the corporation's annual report. Usually the names of officers and directors, and their addresses, are also available.

Some databases can be searched to find out if an individual defendant is a shareholder in or officer or director of a corporation or a partner of a partnership. Many states that mandate disclosure, however, require that only 10 percent or 20 percent or greater equity owners be listed. If your state registers partnerships at the corporation commission, you can get information on either entity at the commission. Some states make it the responsibility of the secretary of state to maintain entity information.

When searching for the assets of debtor, be sure to search the debtor's and his spouse's name separately. Some search engines search for the exact search term submitted. If the phrase "John Doe and Jane Doe" is used, many search engines will not list any "Jane Doe" hits that do not have a "John Doe" preceding it. All possible combinations should be used if you are not positive how the search engine functions: "John Doe and Jane Doe," "Jane Doe and John Doe," "John and Jane Doe," "Jane and John Doe," "John Doe," "Jane Doe," "Doe, John," "Doe, Jane."

Execution

judgment lien security interest giving the lienholder the right to sell the property to pay off a judgment

Once assets are found, several procedures can be used to translate these assets into money. To execute (seize and sell property to pay a judgment) on real estate, the first step is usually to obtain a **judgment lien.** A lien is a security interest, similar to a mortgage, giving the lienholder the right to have the property sold to pay off a debt. A lien that comes from recording a judgment is called a *judgment lien.*

Once a judgment lien exists, the judgment debtor can have the property sold and the proceeds applied to pay the judgment. In some states, the judgment creditor must foreclose the judgment lien in the same way that a lender forecloses a delinquent mortgage. In general, this is done by filing a suit for foreclosure in court, and obtaining a court order to have the sheriff (or some other court officer) sell the property at auction. This may be problematic because the judgment debtor may not be the only one with rights to the property. Lenders, co-owners, lessees, spouses, and partners may also have an interest in the property and they must be notified and given a chance to salvage what is theirs. If the property is the judgment debtor's house, the situation is even more complicated because the exemption laws may apply to all or part of the judgment debtor's equity.

writ of execution court order directing the sheriff to seize property and sell it at public auction

levy seize

Tangible personal property includes things such as furniture, cars, tools, jewelry—anything that can be physically held or touched. To execute on tangible personal property, a **writ of execution** must be obtained from the clerk of the court. A writ of execution is a court order directing the sheriff (or other law enforcement official) to **levy** upon (seize) specific property and sell it at public auction. The judgment creditor's lawyer (or the court clerk) prepares the writ of execution: a court paper, typically a one- or two-page printed form with an attached list of property to be levied upon. The clerk of the court issues it more or less on request, without the judge's having to be involved. Each state has statutes setting forth the procedure to be followed by the sheriff in seizing and selling the property.

As a practical matter, writs of execution on tangible personal property are rarely of much use for several reasons. First, by the time a judgment is entered and a writ issued, the judgment debtor has had plenty of warning, and any tangible property of any value is likely to be long gone or well hidden. Second, when the deputy sheriff goes out to levy on the property, he cannot enter private property and conduct a search without permission. If the owner of the premises refuses to let the deputy sheriff in, telling him that the property sought is not there, the sheriff will simply return the writ *nulla bona*—nothing found. And finally, most of the common kinds of used personal property are unlikely to sell for much money at an auction. Execution on tangible personal property works best when there is some object that is large and difficult to hide—machinery, say—and the judgment creditor knows exactly where it is and can lead the deputy sheriff to it.

The best and easiest assets to execute on are money and other financial assets, except cash, which is too easy to hide. A judgment creditor's best targets are accounts in banks, stockbrokerages, and other financial institutions, because they generate a constant flow of statements and records, all of which can be subpoenaed from the institution if necessary, making the money relatively easy to trace. If the judgment debtor transfers money from a known account trying to make it disappear from the radar screen, the judge can simply order him to transfer it back, under threat of jail.

Garnishment is the process used to execute on a bank account. Garnishment is a procedure that can be used when someone who owes money to the judgment debtor is required to pay the money to the judgment creditor rather than the judgment debtor. When a bank account is garnished, for example, the court orders the bank to take the money that it owes to the judgment debtor and pay it to the judgment creditor. Although the process is more complicated than this discussion will show, in principle, any time a judgment creditor finds a debt owed to the judgment debtor, she can, via a **writ of garnishment,** step in and collect it on behalf of the judgment creditor. A writ of garnishment is a court order directed to the person who owes the judgment debtor money. It is issued by the clerk under procedures that vary from state to state.

The same procedure is used to seize the judgment debtor's wages. Wages are, again, in essence a debt owed by the employer to the employee. Remember, however, federal law imposes limits to what can be seized: no more than one-fourth of the employee's take-home pay.

garnishment process by which someone who owes money to the judgment debtor is made to pay it to the judgment creditor

writ of garnishment court order directing person who owes money to the judgment debtor to pay it to the judgment creditor

Putting It Into Practice 6.23:

What are Molly Running Deer's options in executing on her judgment against Stuart Thames? Which of those options would you recommend?

Figure 6-14
Collecting a Judgment

COLLECTING A JUDGMENT

Judgment Creditor's Options
Real Property - Judgment Lien
Personal Property - Writ of Execution
Financial Assets – Writ of Garnishment

Judgment Debtor's Options
Incorporate
Convert Vulnerable Assets into Exempt Assets
File for Bankruptcy
Move

NET NEWS

For some helpful hints about collecting judgments, go to *www.nolo.com/encyclopedia/articles/cm/CM45.html.*

BONUS POINTERS: **ROLE OF THE PARALEGAL IN COLLECTION PRACTICE**

Some lawyers make a specialty of collecting debts. They represent doctors, dentists, hospitals, collection agencies—anyone with a large volume of delinquent bills to collect. In a debt collection practice, obtaining judgments is usually easy and routine because most delinquent debtors do not contest the suit. Here, judgment collection becomes a large part of the practice. Debt collection practices are high volume operations because of the relatively small amounts usually involved in each case. To keep the volume of cases flowing efficiently, paperwork is usually computerized and highly dependent on the use of forms.

Much of this work is perfectly suited to paralegals. The dollar amounts involved are too small to justify extensive attorney time, yet more legal judgment is needed than a clerk is capable of bringing to bear. The paralegal in such practice will be given tremendous responsibility, and the attorneys may never even review most of the files.

The Judgment Debtor's Options

Obviously, the judgment debtor who is willing to resist collection aggressively and who is not afraid to bend the rules can make it extremely tedious and difficult to convert a judgment into actual money. Litigation is an adversarial process and defendants will not necessarily throw in the towel and pay up merely because the plaintiff won a judgment.

One of the best ways for defendants to protect themselves against lawsuits is to incorporate. A primary reason to incorporate a business is the fact that any lawsuit arising from the business goes against the corporation, not the shareholders. In fact, limited liability is one of the primary advantages enjoyed in the corporate form of business organizations. Say you have a million dollars in the bank, and you decide to go into the roller blade rental business. Every time one of your customers falls down, you risk losing your million in a lawsuit. But if you form a corporation, of which you are the sole stockholder, and you fund the corporation with a reasonable amount of capital—say, $25,000—your customers are stuck with suing the corporation, and the most you can lose is (in theory) $25,000.

Naturally, plaintiffs' lawyers are always chipping away at the corporate shield (often referred to as "piercing the veil"), and every once in a while they manage to break through and get judgments against the shareholders—no defense is perfect. In the professions, for example—law and medicine—the corporate shield does not always work because ethical rules make the individual lawyer or doctor liable for malpractice even if her practice is incorporated.

If a judgment debtor is a natural person—a live human being as opposed to a corporation or other entity—the first line of defense is to take advantage of the exemption statutes. A judgment debtor can legally take vulnerable assets that could be seized and convert them into exempt assets, even after the judgment has been entered. A judgment debtor who has $50,000 in the bank may be able to render it unreachable simply by using it to pay down the mortgage on his house. Cash is subject to execution, but the equity in a debtor's personal residence is exempt in most states (at least to a set amount, such as $100,000).

Merely rearranging assets to take advantage of the exemption statutes does not, of course, extinguish the judgment. The instant that the judgment debtor acquires any non-exempt property, the judgment creditor can swoop down and levy on it. And if the judgment creditor wants to "play hardball," nothing prevents him from garnishing each of the judgment debtor's paychecks, even if the amount to be collected that way is limited.

◆ **LOCAL LINKS** ◆
To what extent is the equity in your personal residence exempt from execution in your jurisdiction?

NET NEWS

To read about some of the details of Chapter 7 and Chapter 13 bankruptcy, go to *www.nolo.com/encyclopeida/dc_ency.html* and click on "Chapter 7 Bankruptcy" and "Chapter 13 Bankruptcy."

Can the judgment debtor do anything to escape this aggravation? Certainly. She may file for bankruptcy. The bankruptcy court will allow the debtor to keep all exempt property and grant a discharge in bankruptcy which will extinguish the judgment.

Another tactic is for the judgment debtor simply to move to another state with his or her assets—again, perfectly legal. In theory, the judgment creditor can pursue the assets in the new state, but doing so takes time and money, and will likely require hiring a lawyer in the new state—and if the judgment creditor gets close, the judgment debtor can always move again. And if moving to another state is not enough to seriously dampen the judgment creditor's enthusiasm, moving to another country almost certainly will be. In theory, collecting judgments in other countries is possible; in practice, except for a few friendly countries like Canada, doing so is difficult and expensive to the point of futility unless a huge amount of money is at stake.

When the judgment is against a business entity instead of an individual, exemption laws do not apply. Now the bankruptcy laws take on great importance. Chapter 11 of the Bankruptcy Act allows corporations and other business entities to file for reorganization under bankruptcy laws. The bankruptcy court has the power to approve a plan for dealing with creditors that will allow the business to remain viable. Usually, the plan will involve paying off debts over a long period of time and at a substantial discount. Reorganization does not usually result in the judgment debtor making a clean getaway—some amount will have to be paid sooner or later—but once a Chapter 11 filing has occurred, the judgment creditor is unlikely to see his money any time soon.

Perhaps, by now, you are beginning to understand why most lawyers avoid suing individuals unless they have insurance. As a practical matter, individuals (and small businesses) who are sufficiently determined can make judgment collection so difficult as to be not worth the expense.

Putting It Into Practice 6.24:

What can Stuart Thames do to discourage Molly Running Deer from executing on her judgment?

BONUS POINTERS:

BANKRUPTCY

Bankruptcy is one way individuals and businesses can deal with the problem of over-indebtedness. It provides relief to debtors and protects creditors by permitting the debtor's assets to be gathered and distributed equitably to creditors. Bankruptcy falls within the exclusive control of the federal courts and falls within Title 11 of the U.S. Code. Chapters 7, 11, and 13 are the chapters that cover individual and commercial bankruptcies.

Chapter 7, which is called the "Liquidation" chapter, involves the process of collecting a debtor's assets and distributing them to creditors. To apply for bankruptcy, an individual must not have declared bankruptcy within the previous six years. A trustee is appointed by the court to determine which creditors' claims are valid and to then distribute the debtor's non-exempt assets in accordance with the priorities established by law. Some debts, such as alimony and child support, are not dischargeable and some property is exempt from being included in the assets. When the process is complete, the bankrupt is no longer responsible for those debts that have been discharged.

Chapter 11—the "Reorganization" chapter—is geared toward saving businesses that are financially distressed. Under this approach, the debtor must propose a reorganization plan, which must be approved by certain creditors and stockholders and ultimately by the court. Approval allows the debtor to make a fresh start, subject to any requirements imposed by the court.

Chapter 13 ("Adjustment of Debts of an Individual with Regular Income") allows a debtor to defer payment of debts so that they can eventually be paid. (Some are paid in full.) This chapter applies to individuals and sole proprietorships who have a source of income that will allow them to pay their debts in the future. The debtor must devise a plan that can either be accepted or rejected by creditors and that must be approved by the court.

Paralegals who work in bankruptcy law are often allowed great latitude in the tasks they perform. Because bankruptcy is very form driven, paralegals can do just about everything except sign paper and offer clients legal advice. Most paralegals work for law firms that represent creditors, debtors, or trustees, but a few work for bankruptcy judges. Their duties include the following.

- ◆ help clients fill out questionnaires regarding their assets and debts
- ◆ help clients assemble documents
- ◆ check UCC filings and real property records
- ◆ prepare inventories of debts and assets
- ◆ request documentation from creditors regarding claims
- ◆ draft bankruptcy petitions and status reports
- ◆ serve as liaison with trustee in bankruptcy
- ◆ attend bankruptcy proceedings

"Is There No End to This Nightmare?"

"I have one more thing for you to consider, Mike, and this is going to take a little more reflection on your part. Ms. Tsosie called me today and informed me that the school district is planning to appeal the verdict against it." Mike's groan stopped John from proceeding.

"Is there no end to this nightmare?" asked Mike bitterly. "I thought it was all over, but I'm beginning to think it's going to haunt me for the rest of my life."

"This is probably no consolation, but appeals are commonly a threat made by the losers in a lawsuit as a means of settling the case," explained John.

"But why should we settle, Mr. Morgan, when we've won? I mean, aren't we entitled to get what the jury awarded us?"

"Because if the district appeals, it can keep you from getting your money for a long time. Plus it will cost you money to fight the appeal and you have no guarantees that you'll win. The district is banking that you'd rather have some money in your hands now than more money down the road."

"So what are they offering?" Mike did not like what he was hearing, but he was starting to see how it fit into his increasingly jaded perception of litigation as a very elaborate and highly structured game of chance.

"Of the $2.4 million verdict against them, they are willing to pay $1.5 million and promise to forgo an appeal."

"Is that a reasonable offer?" asked Mike, not having a clue about how to play the cards that had been dealt him.

"I think it's low. I would suggest countering at $2.2 million, although I think an even $2 million would probably be reasonable."

Mike, who was feeling more like a pawn than a victor, gave John permission to make the counteroffer. He wasn't sure whether the depression he felt descending on him was the result of his pain medication or the feeling of impotence he had when he reflected on the events of his life over the last year. He had lost his chance at a professional sports career; his short-term memory loss had jeopardized his hope of getting into medical school; he was in constant pain; and he might never regain full mobility. How was any amount of money ever going to make up for what he had lost? And now the people most responsible for his suffering were doing everything they could to take what he had begun to see as rightfully his.

At that moment, he heard a knock at his door. He looked up and saw Carmela smiling at him. In her smile, he forgot his pain and anger and disappointment and remembered only how lucky he was to be alive.

APPEALS

An appeal is a procedure for challenging the trial court's decision. The court of appeals has the power to reverse the trial court's decision—that is, to set it aside—or to affirm, and let the trial court's judgment stand as it is. If the court of appeals reverses, the case will ordinarily be remanded (sent back) to the trial court for a new trial. However, if the court of appeals can determine from the record what the trial court's decision should have been, the case may not need to be retried. The court of appeals will simply instruct the trial court to enter a different decision.

Grounds for Reversal

reversible error   error by a trial judge that justifies reversal or modification of the trial court's decision

harmless error   error by a trial judge that does not affect the outcome of a case

Appeals are about error. Before the court of appeals will reverse or modify a trial court judgment, the court must be persuaded that **reversible error** was committed in the trial court. Most error is not reversible error. Probably no case makes it all the way to judgment without a few errors along the way, but if the errors are trivial, or if they did not affect the ultimate outcome of the case, they will be branded **harmless error** and the judgment will be affirmed in spite of them. Reversible error comes in many flavors. A few common ones are allowing evidence that should have been excluded, refusing to allow evidence that should have been admitted, misstating the law in a jury instruction, or refusing to give a jury instruction that should have been given. More often than not, error is considered harmless and the trial court's verdict stands.

One kind of error that courts of appeals generally never address is error committed by the jury in deciding the facts. Because the jury has the opportunity to hear and observe the witnesses in person while the court of appeals has only the cold, sterile record, the court of appeals will not substitute its judgment for that of the jury. The court of appeals reviews the process of a trial, not the outcome. The court will reverse if the process was not conducted according to the rules, but will not reverse merely because the members of the court of appeals would have reached a different verdict than the jury did.

Normally, appeals involve only one or a few specific claimed errors. The court of appeals does not comb through the whole record looking for mistakes. It is up to the appellant (party filing the appeal) to do that and to specify exactly what errors the appellant is asking the court of appeals to consider. (All parties other than the appellant are called *appellees.*)

Notice that the appellant may be either the plaintiff or the defendant. Usually, the appellant is the party that lost the case, but the winner may also appeal. For example, the plaintiff may win a substantially smaller amount of money than expected, and decide it is worth going through the delay and expense of an appeal in order to get another shot with a different jury. (Of course, for this tactic to suc-

cross-appeal an appeal by the appellee

ceed, the plaintiff will have to find some reversible error on which to base the appeal.) Parties can also **cross-appeal;** in fact, when the loser appeals, it is quite common for the winner to cross-appeal. Otherwise, the court of appeals will hear about and possibly reverse those of the trial judge's rulings that the appellant did not like, but will never hear about whatever erroneous rulings went against the appellee.

Putting It Into Practice 6.25:

What will the school district have to prove to prevail on appeal?

Interlocutory Appeals

interlocutory appeals appeal taken before a case is over and judgment is entered

An appeal can be taken only after a final judgment is entered. Why should a party have to waste time and money litigating to a final judgment, only to have the case sent back for a new trial? The reason for prohibiting **interlocutory appeals**— appeals taken before the case is over and judgment entered—is simple expediency. Appellate courts are afraid that cases would be appealed piecemeal, with one attorney or the other running off to the court of appeals every time the trial judge made a decision on some minor motion.

◆ **LOCAL LINKS** ◆
Under what conditions are interlocutory appeals allowed in your state?

Interlocutory review is allowed in a few limited situations. Attorneys can file a so-called "extraordinary writ" requesting review by the appellate court. These petitions are designed to give courts of appeal an excuse for reaching down and fixing particularly egregious errors by the trial court; they are often tried and seldom successful. In federal courts and in some state courts, the trial judge has the power to **certify** a ruling for immediate appeal. Trial judges do this only if the ruling is important and the judge is in some doubt about its correctness.

certify decision by a trial judge that a ruling can be appealed before the case is over

Putting It Into Practice 6.26:

Mr. Yakamura believes that, as a matter of law, Judge Salt should have granted his motion for a directed verdict. What are his options?

Appellate Process

The appeal process begins with the appellant filing a *notice of appeal* with the clerk of the trial court. The notice of appeal is a court paper, typically one page, which simply says that the party filing it is appealing. After the notice of appeal is filed, several things must happen more or less simultaneously; the exact procedure for doing them varies from court to court. The trial court must transmit the record to the court of appeals. The entire record can be huge: it includes the transcript of the trial, the trial exhibits, the entire court file containing the pleadings and other court papers, and, potentially, papers pertaining to discovery that, under modern practice, may not have been filed with the court. Therefore, the parties must designate the parts of the record they intend to use in the appeal so as to avoid having to prepare and transmit unnecessary items. Arrangements must be made for the court reporter to transcribe the shorthand notes and prepare a typed or printed transcript of the testimony. Preparing and transmitting the record typically takes several weeks to several months.

Once the record has been transmitted, the parties have a short time to submit written arguments called *briefs.* The content of a brief is similar to that in a legal

Figure 6-15
Judgment on Jury Verdict

WHITE & TREADWELL
John Morgan, Esq., SBN 00123
Ernesto Esparanza, Esq. SBN 012345
2020 North Central Avenue, Suite 3200
Phoenix, Arizona 85005
(602) 555-1234
Attorneys for plaintiff Michael Johnson

IN THE SUPERIOR COURT OF MARICOPA COUNTY
PHOENIX, ARIZONA

Michael Johnson, a single man,)
 	
)
 	
)
Plaintiff,   )
)
vs.   )
)
Daniel Hendershott, Max Evans, and   )
Alan House, all single men; CODA,   )
Inc.,a foreign corporation;   )
Washington High School District.   )
)
Defendants.   )
_____)
	NO. _____
	
	Judgement on Jury
	Verdict
	
	Assigned to the
	Honorable
	Benjamin Salt

The above-entitled and numbered Cause having come on regularly for trial before a jury on August 5, 2001, and the Plaintiff, Michael Johnson, being present in person and represented by his attorneys, John Morgan, Esq. and Ernesto Esparanza, Esq. of White & Treadwell, the Defendants Alan House and Max Evans having been regularly defaulted and not appearing, Defendant Daniel Hendershott being present in person and represented by Dana Ferraror, Esq., Defendant Washington High School being present by its duly authorized representatives and represented by Barbara Tsosie, Esq. Simon & Porter, and Defendant CODA being present by its duly authorized representatives and represented by William Yakamura, Esq., *pro hoc vice,* and all sides having announced ready; and the Plaintiff having introduced evidence in support of his Complaint; and the Defendants having introduced evidence in opposition thereto; and the matter having been submitted to the jury for determination on August 12, 2001; and the jury having returned a verdict for Plaintiff.

NOW, THEREFORE, IT IS HEREBY ORDERED, ADJUDGED AND DECREED:

1.   That Judgment be entered in favor of the Plaintiff Michael Johnson against Defendants Alan House, Max Evans and Daniel Hendershott, jointly and severally, in the sum of Four Million Eight Hundred Thousand Dollars ($4,800,000.00)

2.   That Judgment be entered in favor of the Plaintiff Michael Johnson against Defendant Washington High School District in the sum of Two Million Four Hundred Thousand Dollars ($2,400,000.00).

3.   That Plaintiff is awarded taxable costs expended in the amount of Twelve Thousand Six Hundred Eighteen and 45/100 Dollars ($12,618.45).

DONE IN OPEN COURT this 25th day of October, 2001.

_____
The Honorable Benjamin Salt
Judge of the Superior Court

To see sample briefs, go to *www.quojure.com*, click on "Archives," and then page down to "Briefs in Appellate Proceedings."

memorandum in support of a motion in the trial court. That is, it consists of an argument, citing authorities (statutes and reported appellate cases), giving reasons why the court of appeals should or should not reverse the case. Briefs are, however, much more formal documents than trial court motions. Appellate court rules may require briefs to be bound like a booklet, to include a table of contents, table of cases cited, and to conform to very particular rules of style and layout. Briefs must also comply with page-limit requirements that, if ignored, are grounds on which the court clerk can refuse to accept the brief.

Briefs are filed with the clerk of the court of appeals in the familiar three-stage sequence: appellant's opening brief, giving reasons why the court of appeals should reverse the trial court's decision; appellee's responding brief, arguing the contrary; and finally, appellant's reply brief, typically much shorter than the other two, in which appellant answers any new arguments raised in appellee's responding brief. Appellate court rules provide for time deadlines for filing these briefs that are typically about a month apart. In practice, the opposing lawyers often agree among themselves to extend the deadlines. Preparing a quality brief is a major undertaking, and a few extra weeks spent on the brief make little difference in the context of an appeal that will likely drag on for at least another year.

Tedious and slow though it may be to take a case from complaint to verdict, trial courts move at supersonic speed compared to the glacial pace of most appellate courts. After all the briefs have been filed, the appeal is said to be "at issue"; the next step is to wait for the court of appeals to take up the case for decision. This may take anywhere from six months to several years, depending on the court and its backlog.

panel group of appellate court judges assigned to a case

At some point, the appeal will be assigned to the **panel** of judges that will decide it. A panel typically consists of at least three appellate court judges. Often the judges making up the panel will meet with each other periodically and divide up their pending cases so that each appeal will be assigned to one judge for a preliminary work-up. Each appellate judge has one or more law clerks (clerking for an appellate judge is a much sought-after apprenticeship for new lawyers) who will be assigned the work of reading the briefs, researching the legal issues, and making recommendations to the judge.

Appellate cases can be decided with or without oral argument. In some cases, the parties may decide to waive argument (or not request it) and submit the case for decision on the written briefs alone. Why? Typically, because it gets the case decided faster. In other cases, the court of appeals may not wish to hear argument or, in some states, oral arguments are simply not an option.

When argument is allowed, the attorneys present a formal argument. Unlike arguments on trial court motions, appellate arguments are formal affairs, never done in chambers. Each side is under strict time limits: the court will sometimes cut lawyers off in mid-sentence if they try to keep talking after the time runs out. As a rule, appellate judges tend to be well prepared for argument and will have read and understood the briefs. Therefore, the attorneys are not allowed to simply repeat what is in the briefs. Most of the argument time is spent answering pointed questions from the judges, not only about the case being decided, but also about any cases cited as authorities in the briefs. Skillful appellate lawyers learn to work their best arguments into their answers to the judges' questions.

At some time after hearing arguments, the panel of judges holds a conference, makes a tentative decision, and assigns one of their number to write an opinion. This written opinion will not only decide the case, it will also describe the pertinent facts, indicate what questions the court is deciding, and explain the decision and the reasons underlying it. Other members of the panel may, if they wish, write concurring or dissenting opinions. Copies of the completed opinions are sent to the attorneys. Several months typically elapse between oral argument and announcement of the decision. At the same time, or within some short time prescribed by the rules, the court of appeals issues a **mandate.** A mandate is an order telling the trial court what to do next. The appellate court's decision may require a new trial, require the trial court to change the judgment in some way or follow other specific instructions, or simply sustain the trial court's judgment.

The party who loses the appeal can ask the state's highest appellate court (in many cases called the supreme court) to review the court of appeals' decision. The procedure for asking for this additional review varies, but it is almost always discretionary. The state's highest court can, and usually does, refuse to consider the matter, in which case the court of appeals' mandate will stand and little if any additional time will be lost. If review is accepted, the decision process will begin again, and additional months or years will pass before the highest court issues its own written opinion and mandate.

mandate order by the court of appeals telling the trial court what to do next

Putting It Into Practice 6.27:
Why do you think attorneys discourage their clients from appealing?

Figure 6-16
Appeal Process

APPEAL PROCESS

Notice of Appeal is Filed
Trial Court Transmits Record
Appellant Files Opening Brief
Appellee Files Responding Brief
Appellant Files Reply Brief
Appeal is Assigned to Panel
Panel Reviews Briefs
Panel May Allow Oral Arguments
Panel Meets in Conference
Judges Prepare Opinions
Mandate is Issued
Losing Party May Appeal to Next Level of Appellate Court

NET NEWS

For more details about the appellate court process, go to *www.ce9.uscourts.gov/web/sdocuments.nsf/History?OpenView*. Click on "Operation of 9th Circuit Courts" and then on "Appellate Court Participants." To see the *Federal Rules of Appellate Procedure*, go to *www.law.cornell.edu/topics/archive/appellate_procedure.html*.

Martha had just finished reorganizing the trial notebook and all the files that had suffered the ramifications of being plundered during the trial. As she put each document in place, she mused about how much work had gone into Mike's trial and how far she had come professionally since she had first been assigned to his case. Having been given so many opportunities to learn new skills and to prove her abilities, she was confident that many doors would now be opened to her. Pity, she thought, that my personal life is not faring as well.

With a sigh, she closed Mike's files and bundled them up to take them into the file room. Her arms full, she struggled momentarily to open the door. "Thanks," she said gratefully to the kind person on the other side of the door who must have heard her fighting with the door handle.

"You're welcome."

Martha almost dropped everything when she recognized Tim's voice. She didn't know whether she was more shocked to see Tim standing in front of her or John affectionately slapping him on the back.

■ TIM'S TECHNO TIPS

Courtroom of the Future

The so-called "courtroom of the future" exists now. Many jurisdictions are upgrading their courtrooms to utilize new technology. Voice-activated recording systems, computer monitors, documents pre-packaged on CD-ROM, and real-time court reporting that shows the testimony as it is being given are being implemented. Large-document cases will, in some jurisdictions, be required to utilize these courtrooms of the future to cut down on trial time and jury fatigue. In these types of cases, the actual documents will be exchanged as graphic files on CD-ROM. Formats for the files will be set by court order to insure compatibility with the court's equipment.

In Maricopa County, Arizona, the Superior Court (the trial court) is converting eight of its old court rooms into new, high-tech courtrooms. Each of these courtrooms will have 12 flat-screen monitors (10 to 12 inches) which will be used to display documents and other evidence. Jurors' chairs will be similar to those used on the airlines to allow note-taking and facilitate juror participation (which is allowed in Arizona). The chairs will also be equipped with ear phone jacks to assist the hearing impaired.

Videoconferencing ability will allow witnesses to testify from external locations, including jail. This will greatly facilitate the appearance of experts, especially medical experts, who are often from out-of-town or out-of-state. The podium will have its own computer and monitor, camera, VCR (or perhaps DVD) and other niceties to assist in the electronic presentation of evidence. At least six voice-activated video cameras, with audio, will be used. One will be in the judge's chambers for recording arguments on motions, jury instructions, and the like. The court reporter will be "plugged-in" to the computer system so that the transcript of the proceeding will be available in real time on counsel's computers and, if necessary, can be shown to the jury on their monitors.

This $3 million investment will probably reduce trial time by 25 percent. Such a reduction would greatly enhance jurors' ability to follow the presentation of evidence without burnout or boredom.

To read about the "e-courtrooms" of the future, which are being constructed now in Arizona, go to the April, 2001 edition of the *Arizona Attorney* (published by the Arizona State Bar). These computer-integrated courtrooms are designed to reduce trial time, enhance the accuracy of communication, and elevate the quality of trial presentations.

TECHNO TRIP

Use your browser to search the phrase "courtroom of the future" or similar term. Ignore the articles and listings more than a few years old. What other courts are going "digital"? Go to the University of Arizona Web site at *www.law.arizona.edu*. Click on Courtroom and Law Office of the Future and then go to the First Annual Institute on Technology in the Courtroom. (Yes, it happened in 1995, but it is still applicable.) Read the remarks of the speakers and their forecasts for the future of technology in the courtroom. Were their "visions" accurate? How about their timing?

SUMMARY – PART B

Jurors are allowed to render their decision on almost any basis except a coin toss or other game of chance. Juries usually give a general verdict, although judges have it within their discretion to order a special verdict or a general verdict with written interrogatories. If a jury becomes deadlocked, resulting in a hung jury, a judge must order a new trial. Hung juries are less likely to result when a majority verdict is allowed. Once a verdict is entered, attorneys have the option of polling jurors. Attorneys are advised to poll jurors after trial to learn what entered into their decision-making process.

The loser has the option of filing a motion for a new trial, thereby circumventing the appeal process, or a motion for a judgment notwithstanding the verdict, which allows the judge to disregard a jury decision the judge believes is unreasonable. The defendant can also ask for a *remittitur.*

The trial phase formally ends with an entry of judgment. In federal courts, judgment is entered when it is recorded in the clerk's docket, but in some state courts the winning party must lodge a proposed form of judgment with the court. The form of judgment, the assessment of taxable costs, and the determination of attorneys' fees are potential sources of further disagreement. Taxable costs, for which the loser is liable, include court reporter, filing, and service fees. Courts sometimes determine the assessable costs by reviewing a statement of costs prepared by the winner. An ongoing philosophical as well as personal debate is whether the loser should have to pay the winner's attorneys' fees. Generally each party is required to pay its own fees, although exceptions exist in cases involving contractual disputes, where state statutes provide otherwise, or where the judge believes that the losing party deliberately abused the legal system.

The entry of judgment marks the end of the trial phase of a lawsuit, but not necessarily the end of the dispute. If the judgment is in favor of the defendant for costs but not for attorney's fees, the plaintiff has the option of giving up or appealing. The situation is more complicated if the judgment involves a significant amount of money. In that case, the judgment creditor may try to collect the monies awarded in the judgment and the judgment debtor may appeal. A judgment creditor can begin collection proceedings immediately after the judgment is entered unless a motion for a new trial has been filed or a stay has been obtained. A stay can be obtained by posting a supersedeas bond or occurs automatically when the judgment debtor files bankruptcy. In federal court, a ten-day waiting period is required before collection proceedings can begin.

Collectability of a judgment is a key fact of litigation. Prior to filing suit, the plaintiff should take steps to ensure that a judgment can be collected. A judgment can probably be collected against a defendant corporation that appears solvent or a defendant that has sufficient insurance coverage. If a plaintiff can prove that punitive damages are justified, she is warranted in doing discovery that will reveal the defendant's assets. Judgment debtors' property and wages are protected to some extent by exemption statutes, but the judgment can be executed through the seizure of any non-exempt property.

A judgment debtor's examination is used to determine the assets of a judgment debtor. These exams may be conducted at the court under the indirect supervision of a court officer or at the office of the attorney representing the judgment creditor. These exams are similar to a deposition; a court reporter may or may not be used. Judgment debtors are often summoned using a subpoena *duces tecum* so that they bring the documents containing the information necessary to locate and seize the debtor's assets. Tenacity is required when dealing with corporations of any size because they will do all they can to stonewall the process.

A judgment lien must be obtained before executing on real estate. This lien arises automatically in some states when the judgment is entered and must be recorded with the county recorder in other states. The judgment creditor can then file a suit for foreclosure, have the property sold, and apply the proceeds to the judgment. This process becomes more complicated if others also have rights to the property or if the property in question is the judgment debtor's home. Judgment creditors are strongly urged to record a judgment in the county recorder's office of every county in which the judgment debtor may own real estate.

To execute on tangible personal property, a writ of execution must be obtained from the court clerk. As a practical matter, these writs are of little value. By the time they are issued, judgment debtors have often hidden or disposed of the property. Additionally, the judgment debtor can refuse to allow the sheriff to enter his property when the sheriff arrives to levy on the property, and most such property is unlikely to sell for much at an auction.

The best assets to execute on are money and other financial assets that can be easily traced, such as bank accounts. To execute on a bank account, a writ of garnishment must be filed. The same procedure is used to seize a judgment debtor's wages; the procedures for garnishment vary from state to state.

To execute any judgment, a copy of the final judgment must be presented. If the judgment comes from a court in the same state, a certified copy from the court clerk that issued it will suffice. If the judgment comes from a state other than the one in which the judgment creditor is seeking to execute property, the procedures can be more complicated. In some states, it is necessary to sue on the judgment by filing another lawsuit.

Judgment debtors can escape paying judgments by converting their vulnerable assets into exempt assets (which can be done even after a judgment is entered), by filing for bankruptcy, or moving to another state or foreign country. Doing the latter does not prevent the judgment creditor from pursuing the judgment, but makes it more difficult and expensive to do so. Debtors can avoid personal liability by incorporating, although the corporate shield does not protect lawyers and doctors from being liable for malpractice. Exemption laws do not apply to businesses, and creditors can reach judgment debtors who have declared Chapter 11 bankruptcy, but they are delayed in satisfying their judgment. Judgment debtors who are involved in fraudulent conveyances can frustrate judgment creditors (even though such transfers are illegal) by requiring them to get a judgment against the individual to whom the property was given.

Collection of judgments is rarely a problem in personal injury practice because the target of litigation is almost always an insurance company. Collection problems often do arise in commercial litigation, however, because the targets are often able to afford to take considerable effort in escaping payment. Attorneys with debt collection practices often rely extensively on legal assistants because of the high volume and routine nature of their cases.

Appellate courts will reverse or modify a trial court's judgment if they believe reversible error has been committed. Reversal usually requires a new trial, although an appeals court may simply instruct the trial court to enter a different decision if the record reveals what the decision should have been. Appellate courts review the process followed by the trial court and not the outcome; therefore, they will not substitute their judgment for that of the jury. Appellants must specify the errors they believe were committed at the trial level; the appellate court will not comb the record looking for errors. Appellees also have an opportunity to file cross-appeals. Appeals cannot be taken before a final judgment is entered. Interlocutory appeals are prohibited out of a desire to prevent appeals from being made on a piecemeal basis. In the federal courts, a trial judge can "certify" a ruling for immediate appeal if the ruling is very important and the judge has some doubt regarding the correctness of his ruling.

To initiate an appeal, the appellant must file a notice of appeal with the clerk of the trial court. The trial court must then transmit the trial record to the appellate court. The parties can indicate the parts of the record they intend to use in the appeal so that not all of the record has to be transmitted. The court reporter prepares a transcript of the testimony. Once the record is transmitted, both parties submit written briefs, which must conform to strict stylistic rules and fall within designated page limits. The appellant's opening brief is followed by the appellee's responding brief, which is followed by the appellant's reply brief. Several months or even years may transpire after the appeal is at issue until the appellate court hears the appeal.

Appeals are typically heard by panels of three judges. Each of the judges has one or more law clerks who read the briefs, research the issues, and make recommendations to the judge. Oral arguments, which may be waived by the parties, are formal arguments made within strict time limits during which the attorneys must respond to pointed questions posed by the appellate judges. After oral arguments, the judges meet in conference, make a decision, and assign one of the panel to write an opinion. Other judges may prepare concurring or dissenting opinions. Copies of the opinion are sent to the attorneys and a mandate is issued to the trial court. The party who loses the appeal can try to appeal to the supreme court, although supreme courts usually deny such requests. If the supreme court denies review, the mandate of the court of appeals stands.

KEY TERMS

Additur	Harmless error	Motion for judgment notwithstanding the verdict	Reversible error
Certify	Hung jury		Special verdict
Cross-appeal	Interlocutory appeal		Statement of costs
Debtor's examination	Judgment creditor	Motion for a new trial	Stay
Entry of judgment	Judgment lien	Notice of appeal	Supersedeas bond
Execution	Levy	Panel	Taxable court costs
Form of judgment	Lien	Polled	Writ of execution
Garnishment	Lodge	Post-judgment discovery	Writ of garnishment
General verdict	Mandate	*Remittitur*	
General verdict with interrogatories			

REVIEW QUESTIONS – PART B

1. Explain the difference between a general verdict, a general verdict with interrogatories, and a special verdict.
2. Describe the options available to the party who loses at trial.
3. Why is the entry of judgment such an important date? What aspects of a judgment do parties typically dispute?
4. What can a judgment debtor do to delay or prevent a judgment creditor's execution on a judgment?
5. What is the purpose of a debtor's exam? How is it carried out?
6. Describe the process used to execute on each of the following
   a. real estate
   b. tangible personal property
   c. bank accounts
7. What options are available to judgment debtors to protect themselves against the actions of judgment creditors?
8. On what grounds are appeals filed? When can they be filed? Under what circumstances will some courts allow an immediate appeal of a ruling?
9. Describe the appellate process.

PRACTICE EXAM – PART B

MULTIPLE CHOICE

1. If a judge wants a jury to answer specific questions about facts upon which its final verdict depends, the judge should request a
   a. general verdict
   b. general verdict with interrogatories
   c. special verdict
   d. none of the above

2. A party that believes that the judge made a significant error during the trial should file
   a. a motion for a new trial
   b. a motion for judgment n.o.v.
   c. a *remittitur*
   d. all of the above

3. Taxable court costs include
   a. attorneys' fees
   b. expert witness fees
   c. court reporter fees
   d. all of the above

4. In the American system, attorneys' fees
   a. are always paid by the loser
   b. are always paid by each party
   c. are often paid by the loser in breach of contract cases
   d. cannot be awarded by the judge even if one of the parties deliberately abused the system

5. To prevent a judgment creditor from collecting a judgment, a judgment debtor can
   a. file for bankruptcy
   b. obtain a stay
   c. file a supersedeas bond
   d. all of the above

6. A debtor's examination
   a. is always held in the office of the judgment creditor's attorney
   b. is often held at the court under the supervision of a court officer
   c. is presided over by a judge
   d. is supervised by an officer of the court who actually attends the examination

7. At a debtor's exam, the judgment creditor's attorney questions the judgment debtor about
   a. records containing information about the property in question
   b. property for which no documents are produced
   c. his income and expenses
   d. all of the above

8. Once a judgment lien is obtained
   a. the judgment creditor can immediately sell the property
   b. the judgment creditor can sell the property even if others have an interest in the property
   c. the judgment creditor may need to foreclose the lien
   d. all of the above

9. A writ of execution
   a. authorizes the sale of tangible personal property at a public auction
   b. is a court paper listing the items of property to be levied upon
   c. is issued by a court clerk
   d. all of the above

10. Writs of execution on tangible personal property
    a. are valuable to judgment creditors because the sheriff can enter private property to levy on the property
    b. are not valuable because the judgment debtor has plenty of time to hide the property
    c. are valuable to judgment creditors because such property often sells for a lot at public auction
    d. are not valuable because they are so hard to obtain

11. Bank accounts are one of the easiest assets to execute on because
    a. they generate a constant flow of records
    b. they are easy to trace
    c. they can be subpoenaed
    d. all of the above

12. A lawyer who has been sued for malpractice can protect his assets by
    a. filing for bankruptcy
    b. incorporating
    c. converting his business assets into exempt assets
    d. moving to another state

13. An example of harmless error is
    a. giving an improper jury instruction
    b. allowing evidence that should have been excluded
    c. refusing to allow evidence that should have been admitted
    d. none of the above if it affected the outcome of the case

14. Courts of appeal
    a. review the trial process, not the outcome
    b. comb through transcripts looking for error
    c. often substitute their judgment for that of the jury
    d. all of the above

15. Interlocutory appeals are
    a. never allowed
    b. allowed only to correct the most egregious errors by the trial court

c. are prohibited when a judge has "certified" a ruling

d. none of the above

16. Before a notice of appeal is filed
   a. the transcript must be transmitted from the trial court to the court of appeals
   b. the parties must designate which parts of the transcript they want transcribed
   c. a judgment must be entered
   d. all of the above

17. Briefs
   a. must be filed with the clerk of the trial court
   b. must conform to certain rules of style and layout
   c. are not restricted to any particular page limits
   d. are relatively informal

18. At appellate oral arguments
   a. attorneys must conform to strict limits
   b. attorneys usually repeat the arguments they made in their briefs
   c. the appellate judges are not allowed to ask the attorneys questions
   d. none of the above

19. Appellate court decisions
   a. are usually written by all of the judges
   b. give the outcome of the case but do not describe the pertinent facts
   c. explain the court's decisions and the reasons underlying it
   d. do not indicate what questions the court is deciding

FILL IN THE BLANK

20. In most cases, a jury is asked to render a _____ verdict, deciding either for the plaintiff or defendant and how much money is to be awarded. In some cases, jurors are asked to render a _____ verdict, consisting of written findings on particular factual issues.

21. One determined juror can lead to a _____ if a unanimous verdict is required.

22. Any party can _____ the jury to determine whether each juror agreed with the verdict.

23. A _____ is based on a party's belief that the judge committed an error during the trial and that that error is likely to result in a new trial.

24. A judge grants a _____ if he believes that the jury reached a verdict that no reasonable person could have arrived at from the evidence.

25. If the jury awards the plaintiff an unexpectedly high amount of damages, the defendant can request a _____ ; if the jury awards inappropriately low damages, the plaintiff can request an _____ .

26. The event that formally ends the trial phase of litigation is the _____ .

27. In some state courts, the winning party must _____ (prepare and deliver) a proposed _____ (exact wording of the judgment) with the court.

28. The winning party is entitled to have judgment against the loser for _____ (some of the expenses related to the lawsuit).

29. A court can determine the amount of costs to assess by having the winner file a _____ .

30. Appealing is one way for a judgment debtor to delay collection of a judgment by a _____ . To do this, the judgment debtor must obtain a _____ , which is a court order prohibiting the judgment to be collected. This order can be obtained by filing a _____ (a promise to pay accompanied by some form of security).

31. The _____ (seizing of a judgment debtor's property and applying it to pay the judgment) of a judgment begins with a _____ (deposition-like process in which the judgment creditor's attorney asks questions about the judgment debtor's assets).

32. Because the purpose of a debtor's exam is to find property or money belonging to the judgment debtor, the judgment creditor typically summons the judgment debtor to the debtor's exam via a _____ , which includes a long and detailed list of documents for the judgment debtor to bring.

33. The first step in executing on real estate is obtaining a _____ (a security interest enabling the lienholder to sell the property to pay off a judgment).

34. To execute on tangible personal property, one must obtain a _____ , which is a court order directing the sheriff to _____ upon (seize) specific property and sell it at public auction.

35. _____ is the process used to execute on a bank account. This is done by filing a _____ , which is a court order issued by the court clerk and directed to the person who owes the judgment debtor money.

36. One of the best ways for businesses to protect themselves against lawsuits is to _____ because then any lawsuit arising from the business goes against the corporation, not the shareholders.

37. A judgment debtor can legally take assets that could be seized and convert them into _____ assets that cannot be seized.

38. An appellate court will not reverse a lower court's decision unless it determines that a _____ error was committed; most errors are, however, deemed _____ in that they would not affect the outcome of the case.

39. If one party files an appeal, the appellee commonly files a _____ (counter appeal).

40. _____ appeals—appeals taken before the case is over and judgment entered—are generally prohibited.

41. If a federal court judge is uncertain of a ruling, he has the power to _____ that ruling for immediate appeal.

42. The appeal process begins with the appellant filing a _____ with the clerk of the trial court.

43. Appellate _____ are similar in content to legal memoranda in that they provide arguments and supporting authority.

44. Once all the briefs are filed, an appeal is said to be _____ .

45. Appeals are often heard by a _____ of judges, consisting typically of three appellate judges.

46. _____ are often assigned to read briefs, research the legal issues, and make recommendations to the judge.

47. Appellate court judges can, if they wish, write _____ opinions, agreeing with the result but disagreeing with all or part of the reasoning in the majority opinion, of _____ opinions, disagreeing with the result reached by the majority.

48. After a court of appeals renders its decision, it will issue a _____ to the trial court, ordering what to do next.

TRUE OR FALSE

____ 49. Jurors can legally decide cases in any way they wish, including tossing a coin.

____ 50. Attorneys and paralegals are not allowed to talk with jurors after a case is over.

____ 51. Judges avoid using special verdicts and general verdicts with interrogatories because they set the stage for appeal.

____ 52. Hung juries are less likely in states where a majority verdict is allowed.

____ 53. Polling of jurors is not allowed in most states.

____ 54. Because judgments are self-executing, litigation is essentially over when a judgment is obtained.

____ 55. Motions for a new trial are relatively easy to win.

____ 56. It is safer for a judge to deny a motion for directed verdict and grant a motion for judgment n.o.v. than to grant the motion for a directed verdict and risk reversal on appeal.

____ 57. The deadline for filing an appeal is determined by counting the day that the judgment is entered.

____ 58. In federal court, a judgment is entered once it is lodged by the winning party.

____ 59. In some cases, parties cannot agree about the form of judgment and must involve the court.

____ 60. Taxable court costs include all the expenses related to a lawsuit.

____ 61. In some cases, attorneys' fees end up being more than the total amount being litigated.

____ 62. A reform measure popular with the defense bar is that the losers in lawsuits should always be required to pay the winners' attorneys' fees.

____ 63. Proceedings to determine attorneys' fees can become quite complex, sometimes requiring evidentiary hearings.

____ 64. A judgment is not effective as soon as it is entered, so a judgment creditor cannot begin collection proceedings immediately.

____ 65. Filing for bankruptcy results in an automatic stay of all proceedings against a judgment debtor.

_____ 66. By filing a supersedeas bond, a judgment debtor does not have to pay a judgment until after the appeal process is completed.

_____ 67. Insurance companies usually post supersedeas bonds even when judgment debtors have few assets.

_____ 68. A judgment creditor has no real recourse if a judgment debtor is evasive or uncooperative at a debtor's exam.

_____ 69. In some states, a judgment creditor must foreclose the judgment lien before being able to sell the property and use the proceeds to pay the judgment.

_____ 70. To foreclose on a judgment lien, the judgment creditor files a suit for foreclosure and obtains a court order to have the sheriff sell the property at auction.

_____ 71. Garnishment is a procedure used when someone who owes money to the judgment creditor is required to pay the money to the judgment debtor rather than the judgment creditor.

_____ 72. A writ of garnishment must be issued by a judge.

_____ 73. A judgment debtor's wages cannot be garnished by the judgment creditor.

_____ 74. The corporate shield protects even lawyers and doctors against judgment creditors who have sued for malpractice.

_____ 75. A judgment debtor can legally convert assets into exempt assets after a judgment has been entered.

_____ 76. Using the exemption statutes to protect assets in essence extinguishes the judgment.

_____ 77. Filing for bankruptcy allows the judgment debtor to keep all exempt property and receive a discharge in bankruptcy, which extinguishes the judgment.

_____ 78. A judgment debtor can inhibit a judgment creditor from collecting a judgment by moving to another state or country.

_____ 79. Exemption laws do not apply to businesses.

_____ 80. Chapter 11 bankruptcies allow the bankruptcy court to approve a "reorganization plan" for dealing with creditors that allow the business to remain viable.

_____ 81. Chapter 11 bankruptcies allow judgment creditors to get paid fairly quickly.

_____ *82. A debt collection practice is often highly computerized and highly dependent on the use of forms.

_____ *83. Paralegals who work in high-volume debt collection practices are often given extensive responsibility and have little attorney supervision.

_____ 84. If the court of appeals reverses a lower court's decision, the case must be sent back to the trial court for a new trial.

_____ 85. Courts of appeal frequently substitute their judgment for that of the jury because they believe they better understand the law.

_____ 86. The winner at the trial court level has no reason to file an appeal.

_____ 87. Interlocutory appeals are generally prohibited to prevent piecemeal appeals.

_____ 88. Preparing and transcribing a record for the appellate court can take several months.

_____ 89. The parties have no voice in deciding which parts of the court record will be transcribed for the appellate court's review.

_____ 90. Appellate briefs are less formal than trial court motions.

_____ 91. An appellant's responding brief responds to the arguments made in the appellee's reply brief.

_____ 92. Opposing attorneys frequently agree to extend the deadlines for submitting appellate briefs.

_____ 93. The appellate process is a much more expeditious process than the trial process.

_____ 94. Oral argument is required in all appellate cases.

_____ 95. Appellate oral arguments are formal affairs, never conducted in a judge's chambers.

_____ 96. Skillful appellate lawyers work their best arguments into their responses to the judges' questions.

_____ 97. An appellate court's mandate may simply sustain the trial court's judgment or may order a new trial.

_____ 98. The party that loses an appeal at the appellate court level is entitled to an appeal by the supreme court.

*Questions taken from Bonus Pointers

LEGAL LINGO

Fill in the missing letters.

1. __ X __ __ U __ __ O __
2. __ __ T __ __ L __ __ U __ O __ __
3. __ __ F __ A __ __
4. __ O __ __
5. __ __ I __ __ I __ __
6. __ __ __ Y
7. __ __ R __ S __ __ __ __ T
8. __ __ R __
9. __ __ E __ A __
10. __ __ R __ __ E __ __
11. __ N __ __ M __ N __
12. __ __ A __
13. __ E __ N __ __ R __ __ __ V __
14. __ __ M __ __ T __ __ __ R
15. __ __ E __ __ __ A __
16. __ __ N __ __ T __
17. __ __ D __
18. __ U __ __ R __ __ D __ __ __
19. __ __ T __ __ __ T __ __
20. __ __ T __ __ __ G

1. Seizing of property to pay off a judgment
2. Appeal before final judgment
3. Person making a signed sworn statement
4. What an attorney can do to a jury after a trial is over
5. Questioning of prospective jurors
6. Seize
7. Process used to seize wages
8. Exact wording of a judgment
9. Type of verdict requiring written findings
10. Error that does not affect case outcome
11. Motion to prevent questions from being asked at trial
12. Order stopping collection of judgment
13. Type of evidence that helps jurors understand the facts
14. Reduction in award
15. Order setting parameters at trial
16. Order to trial court
17. Prepare and deliver
18. Type of bond
19. Requirement for document to be admitted
20. Trial date

LEGAL LOGISTICS

1. Consider Molly Running Deer's suit against Stuart Thames for injuring her when he allegedly ran a red light.

   a. On what grounds might she file a motion for summary judgment?

   b. What would this motion force Stuart to do?

   c. Suppose Stuart's attorney has been threatening to bring in several high-powered accident reconstructionists to prove that Stuart could not have possibly run the red light. How will preparing the pretrial statement assist Molly's attorney in evaluating these threats?

   d. It is two weeks before trial. You are a paralegal in the office of Molly's attorney. What are you doing to prepare for trial?

   e. Your attorney wants you to draft jury instructions for this case. Where will you look for assistance in doing this?

   f. What kinds of jurors would you be looking for if you represented Stuart?

   g. What kinds of *voir dire* questions would you want to ask?

   h. Suppose Molly intends to present evidence that Stuart had been drinking prior to the accident and that one of the prospective jurors belongs to M.A.D.D. (Mothers Against Drunk Driving).

   What might Stuart's attorney do to remove this juror?

   i. Suppose Molly calls Stuart as her first witness. What kinds of questions will her attorney be allowed to ask? What might be the advantage of calling Stuart first?

   j. Will Molly be allowed to present testimony by the police officer that a driver stopped at the scene and told him that Stuart had almost smashed into him at the previous intersection?

   k. What if the officer testifies that Stuart told him at the scene that he probably should not have had that last drink?

   l. Molly wants to introduce copies of her medical records. What will she have to prove before she can get them admitted as evidence?

   m. Suppose Stuart introduces expert testimony that Molly's injuries were relatively minor and that she will suffer no ongoing effects of those injuries. What can Molly do in response if she has already rested?

   n. What will Stuart's attorney try to convey during closing arguments?

   o. With what impression will Molly's attorney want to leave the jury?

p. What can both attorneys do during closing arguments they could not do during opening statements?

q. Suppose the judge awards Molly $250,000, with $100,000 coming from Stuart's insurance coverage and the remainder from Stuart himself. What steps should Molly take if she is not sure what assets Stuart has? What would probably be the easiest way for her to execute on her judgment? What options does Stuart have to prevent her from collecting her award?

2. Assume you are representing a client who was injured when she slipped and fell in a supermarket.

a. What can your firm do to prevent opposing counsel from asking your client at trial about a previous fall she had a few years ago?

b. Suppose the supermarket has filed a motion for summary judgment in regard to liability.

c. Your client has just found out she has won tickets for a Caribbean cruise. Unfortunately, the dates for the cruise conflict with the trial setting for her case. She wants to know how likely it is that she will actually go to trial on the date set. What will you tell her?

d. Your attorney has asked you to prepare the client for trial. What can you tell her to help her be a better witness?

e. What started out as a simple slip-and-fall has become increasingly complicated. Your attorney wants you to prepare a trial notebook, in part to help her keep the testimony of all the different witnesses straight. What kinds of things will you include in this trial notebook and how will you organize it?

f. What will your attorney want to do in opening statements?

g. What must your attorney prove if she is going to avoid a directed verdict against her?

h. During cross-examination of a witness, your attorney asks, "Isn't it true that the stock clerk, Don Tuttle, told you that the store had five previous accidents related to spills on the floor?"

i. Why might the attorneys expend a great deal of time debating how the jury should be instructed in reference to the element of "breach of duty"?

j. Would it be to your client's advantage to ask the jury to render a general verdict or a special verdict?

k. Why might you and your attorney want to talk with the jurors after they complete their deliberations?

l. The supermarket decides to appeal the jury's verdict. At what point can it begin the appeal process? What steps will it need to take if it does not want to pay your client her award until after the appeal is over? What will the supermarket's attorneys need to do to get their case before the court of appeals?

3. Your firm is representing a woman who has filed for divorce. She does not have a right to a jury trial.

a. In what ways will the preparation for and presentation at her trial be different from a jury trial?

b. Suppose your client wants to introduce photographs a private investigator took of her husband having sex with another woman. Assume that child support is the only issue being contested. On what grounds might opposing counsel object to the introduction of these photographs?

c. Can opposing counsel bring up the issue of your client's education while cross-examining her if your attorney did not raise the issue during direct examination?

d. Your client is unhappy with one of the judge's rulings and wants to appeal it. What arguments could you offer to help her understand why it may not be in her best interest to do this?

A TRIP TO THE MOVIES

In the movie *The Rainmaker,* Rudy Baylor, a recent law school graduate, takes on Great Benefit Insurance Company, whose policy is to categorically deny all claims. Be aware that this movie's jaded view of the bar confronts the viewer with example after example of unethical conduct and presses the question of whether the practice of law is still a noble profession.

1. Was Great Benefit's motion to dismiss a legitimate motion? Should it have moved for summary judgment?

2. Why was the case on the "fast track"?

3. What was unusual about the deposition of Donny Ray?

4. If this case had been in federal court, could the plaintiff have introduced Jackie LaManchak as a witness at the last minute?

5. Why did the judge sustain the defendant's objection that Rudy's initial questions to Ms. Black were leading?
   a. Why was Mr. Drummond allowed to ask leading questions?
   b. Why did Rudy have a hard time introducing the employee's manual? How did he finally get it admitted?
   c. Why did the judge admit the letter from the Blacks' treating physician?
   d. In real life, how would these issues of admissibility been dealt with before the trial?

6. Why didn't Rudy accept Great Benefits' initial offer?
   a. Do you think he should have settled the case at that point?
   b. Suppose Great Benefit offered $100,000 the first day of trial. Would it have been wise for Rudy to settle?

7. Why did the judge dismiss Mr. Porter as a juror?
   a. Why did the defense not challenge Mr. Porter for cause?
   b. Could the defense have used a peremptory challenge to strike Mr. Porter?

8. How might Rudy have benefited from having a trial notebook?

9. What kinds of demonstrative evidence did Rudy use?

10. What was the gist of the defendant's closing arguments? Of the plaintiff's closing arguments? Do you think Rudy's closing was effective?

11. What kind of verdict did the judge require the jury to give?
    a. What did you infer from the jury's verdict?
    b. Why might it have been wise for Great Benefit to poll the jury?
    c. Were you convinced that Rudy had met his burden of proof in showing that Great Benefits had acted in bad faith toward the Blacks? Do you think the punitive damage award was justified?

12. What aspects of the trial did you find unrealistic?

13. What procedural options did Great Benefit have (that it did not pursue in the movie) after the jury rendered its verdict?

14. How did Great Benefit avoid paying the judgment?
    a. Why do you think the CEO was trying to leave town?
    b. What other alternatives did Great Benefit have to avoid collection?
    c. What could Rudy have done before trial that might have averted this outcome?
    d. If Great Benefit had been solvent, how might Rudy have gone about collecting the judgment?
    e. In light of the ultimate outcome, do you think Rudy was successful?

15. Based only on what you saw in the movie, what grounds might Great Benefit have had for appeal?
    a. What would it have had to do to stay execution of the judgment while pursuing an appeal?
    b. How could it have used the threat of appeal to its advantage?

16. What ethical violations did you see depicted in the movie?

INTERNET INQUIRIES

1. Go to www.law.umkc.edu/faculty/projects/ftrials/ftrials.htm, which has information about numerous famous American trials. Select one of the trials in which you have an interest and answer the following questions.
   a. Describe the historical background of this trial.
   b. What were the issues at stake in this trial?
   c. What is the historical significance of this trial?

2. Go to the Internet to find jury instructions that could be used in a negligence case being tried in your jurisdiction. One of the possible Web sites that may have this information is your local or state bar association Web site. Links to state bar associations can be found at Hieros Games (www.hg.org/northam-bar.html.) Write down the addresses of the sites you find.

3. Your supervising attorney has asked you to help prepare a witness to testify for her first time. Consult the Internet for the addresses of at least three Web sites that would give her some pointers about what to do and what not to do.

4. Go to the Internet and find some sites discussing Chapter 11 bankruptcy. Write a paragraph explaining the major characteristics of Chapter 11 bankruptcy.

5. Go to www.dicarlolaw.com/RulesofEvidenceSummary.htm to answer the following questions.
   a. What are the four types of evidence?
   b. When is evidence
      a. material
      b. competent
      c. prejudicial
   c. What is real evidence? How is it authenticated?

d. What is the best evidence rule?

e. When is a witness competent to testify? In what four ways can you help refresh a witness's memory?

f. How do bias, interest, prejudice, and other factors that create doubt about a witness's credibility affect the value of his testimony?

g. In general, who can and cannot give opinion testimony?

h. In what ways can a witness be impeached?

6. Find out if your county recorder's office has a Web page. If it does, use a name provided by your instructor or the name of someone you know to be a judgment debtor and write down the information you are able to find from this Web site about this judgment debtor.

7. Does your local trial court have a Web page? If it does, use the same name you used in the previous question. Write down all the information you can find about this judgment debtor.

8. Find the Web page for Dun & Bradstreet. List the information you could find about an individual's or business's assets at this site.

9. Why do you think it would be wise to obtain a Dun & Bradstreet report on a party against whom you plan to collect a judgment?

7

Criminal Law and Procedure

OBJECTIVES:

In this chapter you will learn:

- the basic rules of search and seizure law
- what is involved in obtaining a warrant
- when an officer can conduct a warrantless search
- when an officer can stop and frisk a suspect
- what *Miranda* warnings are and when they must be given
- what occurs when at a suspect's booking, initial appearance, and arraignment
- the difference between a preliminary hearing and a grand jury hearing
- what plea bargaining is and why some criticize this practice
- how attorneys deal with clients who threaten to perjure themselves or to commit future crimes
- the tasks a paralegal practicing in the criminal law area performs

- when a defendant has a right to counsel
- what the basic elements of any crime are
- how offenses are classified
- what basic defenses are available and under what circumstances they can be raised
- what the exclusionary rule is, when it can be raised, and the exceptions to this rule
- what types of sentencing schemes are possible and what considerations go into sentencing an offender
- the basic assumptions underlying the four theories of punishment
- what alternatives to incarceration are available
- the standards for being admitted to the Bar

"Why Don't You Start By Telling Martha What Led Up to Your Arrest?"

"He wants to talk to you about going to *law school*?" Martha repeated John's last statement to make sure she had heard correctly. He's got some gall, she thought smugly. Apparently Tim hasn't got around to telling him about being an ex-con.

"And, yes, I know about Tim's past, if that's what you're wondering," continued John, anticipating Martha's unspoken objection. "He's got an uphill battle ahead of him, but I think he's got a shot at becoming a lawyer. Of course, he's going to need all the friends he can get. It's not easy dealing with all the prejudice out there directed at ex-felons." John looked steadily at Martha as he talked, hoping to make some dent in the armor she had put up since Tim had appeared.

"So what are you suggesting?" asked Martha rigidly.

"That maybe it's time for you to bury the hatchet and sit down and listen to what Tim has to say. You might learn something," said John pointedly.

Martha felt the sting of John's subtle remonstration and was confused. John acted as if she, rather than Tim, was the villain. While she foundered for an appropriate response, John made a suggestion: "Tell you what. Why don't we all go out to dinner and talk about this over a nice meal?"

Both Tim and Martha began sputtering excuses, but John prevailed and within a few minutes they had made the necessary arrangements to go to John's favorite restaurant. Before she had time to sort through her conflicting emotions, Martha found herself sitting across from Tim, with John serving as the convivial moderator.

"Tim, why don't you start by telling Martha what led up to your arrest?" suggested John after they had ordered their food.

"Well, I'm not sure where to start," began Tim uncomfortably. He thought for a moment and then began. "I started working for my uncle in his real estate business while I was still in college. I was really lucky to get the right properties at the right time and made some really big sales. In hindsight, I can see that I wasn't ready for instant success—I got hooked on being a wheeler dealer and all that went with it. The whole thing was very seductive. Before I knew it, I had a beautiful home, a gorgeous wife, and all the 'toys' that go with the good life," recalled Tim. "My life was frenetic. I became a kind of thrill-seeker, bouncing from one high to the next. One of the highs I discovered was cocaine. From the first time I was introduced to it, I loved it—how it made me feel, how everything seemed so clear, and how much energy I seemed to have. My nights revolved around getting high and I spent my days anticipating the nights.

"It all started to unravel when my sales began to go down a little, which probably wouldn't have been a problem if I hadn't been living on the edge. But no matter how many creditors I had breathing down my neck, I made sure I scored some coke. I'm sure you could probably write the rest of the script: I got into a drug dealer for several thousand dollars, he put the squeeze on me, I couldn't pay, he offered me a deal—make a couple deliveries and he'd cut me some slack." Tim shook his head and chuckled. "My first delivery turned out to be my last."

"You got caught your first time? How unfortunate—or maybe fortunate, depending on how you look at it," observed John.

"Very fortunate," agreed Tim. "I've always felt that if I do have a guardian angel, he was working overtime that night."

"Don't you think he should have intervened a little sooner?" Martha's sarcasm was not lost on Tim.

"I wasn't ready. Sometimes you need a wake-up call and, unfortunately, it took going to prison for me to finally see how much I'd messed up my life," explained Tim.

"So how did you get arrested?" asked Martha, deliberately sidestepping Tim's comment.

"It turned out to be a real comedy of errors. Unbeknownst to me, an informant had told the narcs [undercover narcotics officers] about the delivery I was making. They were tailing me so they could arrest me when the deal went down. They weren't expecting a beat cop in the neighborhood to get suspicious and start questioning me. Anyway, I was supposed to meet the buyer in front of a bar at 8:00 p.m. I got there a few minutes early and waited out front. I was incredibly nervous and was pacing back and forth, oblivious to the cop watching me. When it got to be about 8:15 and the buyer still hadn't showed, I got nervous and decided to leave. When I turned to walk away, I heard this voice yell out, 'Stop, I want to talk to you!' I had no idea whose voice I was hearing—I hadn't seen the cop—but I knew I didn't want to find out. I panicked and ran. The cop took off after me and threw me down to the ground when he caught up with me. It wasn't until I stood up that I realized I'd run from a cop. He immediately **arrested** me, searched me, and found the cocaine I'd brought to deliver.

NET NEWS

For links to over 12,000 criminal justice related sites, go to *www.talkjustice.com/cybrary.asp.*

---

arrested interfering with a suspect's freedom to the extent that the suspect is no longer free to go

OVERVIEW OF FOURTH AMENDMENT SEARCH AND SEIZURE LAW

The Fourth Amendment of the U.S. Constitution protects us from "unreasonable searches and seizures." Specifically, it provides that "The right of the people to be secure in their persons, houses, papers, and effects, against unreasonable searches and seizures, shall not be violated, and no Warrants shall issue, but upon probable cause, supported by Oath or affirmation, and particularly describing the place to be searched, and the persons to things to be seized."

The Fourth Amendment is implicated only if a "search" or "seizure" has occurred. The U.S. Supreme Court has determined that a search or seizure occurs only when an individual's "expectation of privacy" is violated. To illustrate, consider the police search of a trash bag. A person who has a trash bag inside her home has a reasonable expectation of privacy. Therefore, if officers look through that bag, they have conducted a search. But if that same person carries the trash bag out to the garbage can in back of her home, she loses any expectation of privacy. The courts have decided that when people remove their trash from inside their home it becomes abandoned property; therefore, the police are not conducting a search when they rummage through it.

For more information about "expectation of privacy," go to *www.nolo.com/encyclopedia/crim_ency.html,* click on "Search and Seizure," and go to the article entitled "Understanding Search and Seizure Law."

Examples of contexts in which individuals have no expectation of privacy include the following.

curtilage land around a dwelling

- ◆ Anything done in a public setting that an officer overhears or sees.
- ◆ Open fields. The land around a dwelling, called the **curtilage** (e.g., the flower bed adjacent to a house) is protected by the Fourth Amendment, but the area beyond the curtilage (open fields) is not protected. Therefore, if an officer sees marijuana growing in an open field, he can enter that field and take photographs without legally violating the owner's right to privacy.
- ◆ Anything in "plain view." Anyone who leaves contraband (illegal materials) in plain view of an officer loses any expectation of privacy with regard to that contraband. The officer can lawfully seize an object he recognizes as contraband as long as he has a lawful right to be present. An officer who is called to the scene of a domestic dispute, for example, and who sees a baggie of marijuana on the coffee table can seize the marijuana because it is in "plain view" and the officer has a lawful right to be present.
- ◆ An inmate in a jail or prison cell. Because inmates lose many of their rights upon incarceration, their "house" is not afforded the same constitutional protection as the house of someone who lives outside of prison. Therefore, guards have no Fourth Amendment limitations on their search of an inmate's cell and their seizure of its contents.

Putting It Into Practice 7.1:

In which of the following contexts does the defendant have a reasonable expectation of privacy?

(a) a 100-acre field next to a farmhouse

(b) a garage attached to the defendant's house

(c) Tim in the holding tank of the jail

(d) an officer walking by the street in front of the defendant's home, glances in the window to see the defendant striking his wife

(e) the defendant and her husband sitting in a restaurant counting their proceeds from a recent robbery, unaware that a police officer is sitting in the booth next to them

(f) an officer called to the defendant's home begins looking through the defendant's trash can while he is there

ARREST AND SEARCH WARRANTS

search warrant court document authorizing the police to search and seize certain items

When an individual has a lawful expectation of privacy, the Fourth Amendment protects that person from unreasonable searches and seizures. The highest expectation of privacy is in the home. For that reason, the police cannot (with some exceptions) search inside the home without first obtaining a **search warrant** (a court doc-

probable cause belief based on facts that go beyond reasonable suspicion that a crime has been committed or is about to be committed

ument authorizing the police to search and seize certain items). The courts encourage officers to secure a warrant whenever possible because the process of obtaining a warrant involves review by a neutral third party (a judge or magistrate) to determine if the search or seizure is justified. The search warrant requires the officer to describe with particularity the places to be searched and the things to be seized. This means that the descriptions must be precise enough that an officer not connected with the case could figure out where to search and what to seize. An officer must also sign an affidavit, attesting to the basis upon which he believes **probable cause** supports the finding of incriminating evidence. The judge's signature indicates her review of the officer's affidavit and her concurrence with the officer's assessment of probable cause.

Probable cause defies precise definition and officers must learn through experience when their suspicions rise to the level of probable cause. Generally speaking, however, it must be based on specific facts that would lead a reasonable person to believe that a crime has been or is about to be committed. For probable cause to conduct a search, it must be more likely than not that the objects being searched for are connected with criminal activity and that those objects will be found in the place being searched. For probable cause to arrest someone, it must be more likely than not that a crime was committed and that the person being arrested committed it.

arrest warrant court document authorizing the police to arrest a suspect

While search warrants are used to get judicial approval to conduct a search, **arrest warrants** (court documents giving the police permission to arrest a suspect) are used to get judicial approval to arrest someone. The police can use their own knowledge of a suspect or information supplied by victims and witnesses to establish probable cause to obtain an arrest warrant. Arrest warrants are rarely required. If officers are present when they have probable cause to believe that a crime has been or is about to be committed, they can arrest the suspect immediately: having to stop and get a warrant would unduly interfere with the ability of the police to do their job.

hot pursuit police pursuit of a suspect into a private home

exigent circumstance emergency

Arresting someone at home, however, requires the use of an arrest warrant. Homes are considered sacrosanct and the police are not allowed to enter without a warrant unless they are in "**hot pursuit**" or some other **exigent** (emergency) **circumstance** exists. The "hot pursuit" exception takes into consideration the practical circumstances that sometimes make securing an arrest warrant impracticable. Officers chasing a suspect need not stop their pursuit and get an arrest warrant just because the suspect runs into his home.

Many states impose statutory requirements for making arrests as well. For example, many states prohibit officers from making warrantless misdemeanor arrests unless the person commits the crime in their presence.

Putting It Into Practice 7.2:

How might an informant assist an officer in securing a search warrant?

WARRANTLESS SEARCHES

Search warrants are generally required unless some grounds for a warrantless search exist. Under the following circumstances, the courts have permitted searches to be conducted without a search warrant.

CONSENT SEARCH—A person may consent to a search as long as that consent is voluntary. (The police cannot use deception or coercion to induce consent.) Officers cannot exceed the scope of the search consented to by the suspect.

CONSENT BY THIRD PARTY—People who share control of a place with the suspect may consent to a search if they have the capacity and authority to do so. A roommate, for example, can consent to a search of rooms shared with the suspect, but may not be able to consent to a search of a room to which the suspect has denied her access.

SEARCH INCIDENT TO A LAWFUL ARREST—Officers can search the area within the suspect's immediate control to ensure that the suspect is unable to destroy any evidence or obtain any weapons. If the arrest takes place in a person's home, the police can do a "protective sweep" of the premises if they reasonably believe that another person who might be dangerous to the officers might be in the areas to be swept. For searches to be lawful under this rule, the arrest must be lawful. Therefore, if the arrest turns out not to have been based on probable cause, any items seized pursuant to the search incident to arrest may have to be **suppressed** (not able to be used as evidence against the defendant).

suppressed prevent from being presented as evidence

VEHICLE SEARCH INCIDENT TO A LAWFUL ARREST—When the police lawfully arrest an occupant of a vehicle, they may search the vehicle's entire passenger compartment and the contents of any containers found in those compartments. More specifically, they can search open or closed glove compartments as well as luggage, bags, and boxes found in the vehicle. Searches of trunks are not allowed under this rule.

VEHICLES SUSPECTED OF CARRYING CONTRABAND—Because of the inherent mobility of automobiles, the courts have created an exception to the warrant requirement if officers have probable cause to believe that a car is being used to transport contraband. Under this exception, officers can search the entire vehicle as well as closed containers within it.

PLAIN VIEW—An officer is allowed to seize any evidence that is readily visible to the officer as long as he has a lawful reason for being present. The incriminating nature of the items seized must be immediately apparent to the officer. The officer cannot move the item to be seized to get a better view of it. He must immediately have probable cause to seize it.

The so-called "plain-view doctrine" also applies to other senses (hearing, touch, and smell) and may apply even if the police use a mechanical device, such as a flashlight, to get a better view of the defendant or his property. Plain view even extends to aerial searches as long as the police are flying in navigable, public air space.

ADMINISTRATIVE INSPECTIONS—Certain businesses are subject to inspections by administrative agencies as part of their licensing requirements. For most health, safety, and fire inspections, search warrants are not required. Border and customs officials can search baggage and vehicles at the border without a warrant (and without probable cause) if they believe the suspect is involved in smuggling or immigration violations. Also, government employers can search the office of a government employee without a warrant as long as the search is work-related.

NET NEWS

To read more about search warrants and when they are needed, go to *www.nolo.com/encyclopedia/crim_ency.html*, click on "Search and Seizure," and read the article entitled "Search Warrants: What They Are and When They're Necessary."

DESTRUCTION OF EVIDENCE—Officers who reasonably believe that the suspect is about to destroy evidence or that the evidence will be destroyed if the time is taken to get a search warrant can forgo getting a warrant.

INVENTORY SEARCH—Officers can inventory a vehicle they have impounded and in the process of that inventory, search the entire vehicle. Inventory searches are justified by the need to protect (1) the suspect's property from being stolen or damaged; (2) the police from later claims of theft by the suspect; and (3) others from being hurt by the contents in the suspect's vehicle (e.g., a bomb).

Putting It Into Practice 7.3:

In which of the following circumstances would an officer be required to secure a search warrant?

(a) An officer stops a suspect for driving erratically and smells the odor of marijuana in the car.

(b) An officer wants to get fingernail scrapings from a man suspected of killing his wife.

(c) An officer arrests a suspect for driving under the influence, and before taking him into custody searches the inside of the defendant's vehicle, including his glove compartment.

(d) The suspect's friend is visiting overnight when the police arrive and ask if they can search the suspect's house. The friend makes it clear he is only a guest.

(e) Officers trespass on the suspect's front lawn, and while there look inside the suspect's window and see him snorting cocaine.

(f) Federal agents inspect a weapons dealer.

Figure 7-1
Warrantless Searches that are Permitted

WARRANTLESS SEARCHES THAT ARE PERMITTED

Consent search
Consent by third party
Search incident to lawful arrest
Vehicle search incident to lawful arrest
Vehicle suspected of carrying contraband
Plain view
Administrative search
Destruction of evidence
Inventory search

"So if you hadn't run, you'd never have been arrested," clarified Martha.

"Actually, if the officer had reasonably suspected I was about to commit a crime and that I was armed, he could have stopped and frisked me." Taking the lead from Martha's puzzled expression, Tim went on to explain, "A **frisk** is a cursory search of the outer clothing only and is justified by an officer's need to protect himself and others from a suspect who may be armed."

"But you weren't armed, were you?" insisted Martha.

"No."

"Then he couldn't have seized the cocaine if he hadn't found any weapons on you," reasoned Martha.

"That would have been true traditionally. But under most recent case law, the U.S. Supreme Court has allowed an extension to the 'plain view' rule, which some people call the 'plain touch' rule. Basically, this rule allows officers who are conducting a lawful frisk to seize anything they immediately identify as contraband. So if the officer had frisked me for a weapon and had instead felt a baggie containing something he immediately recognized as some kind of drug, he could have seized it."

frisk   pat-down search of a suspect's clothing if the officer has reasonable suspicion to believe the suspect has committed or is about to commit a crime

---

508 U.S. 366, 113 S.Ct. 2130

Supreme Court of the United States
MINNESOTA, Petitioner,
v.
Timothy **DICKERSON.**
No. 91-2019.
Argued March 3, 1993.
Decided June 7, 1993.

Justice WHITE delivered the opinion of the Court.

In this case, we consider whether the Fourth Amendment permits the seizure of contraband detected through a police officer's sense of touch during a protective patdown search.

I

On the evening of November 9, 1989, two Minneapolis police officers were patrolling an area on the city's north side in a marked squad car. At about 8:15 p.m., one of the officers observed respondent leaving a 12-unit apartment building on Morgan Avenue North. The officer, having previously responded to complaints of drug sales in the building's hallways and having executed several search warrants on the premises, considered the building to be a notorious "crack house." According to testimony credited by the trial court, respondent began walking toward the police but, upon spotting the squad car and making eye contact with one of the officers, abruptly halted and began walking in the opposite direction. His suspicion aroused, this offi-

cer watched as respondent turned and entered an alley on the other side of the apartment building. Based upon respondent's seemingly evasive actions and the fact that he had just left a building known for cocaine traffic, the officers decided to stop respondent and investigate further.

The officers pulled their squad car into the alley and ordered respondent to stop and submit to a patdown search. The search revealed no weapons, but the officer conducting the search did take an interest in a small lump in respondent's nylon jacket. The officer later testified:

"[A]s I pat-searched the front of his body, I felt a lump, a small lump, in the front pocket. I examined it with my fingers and it slid and it felt to be a lump of crack cocaine in cellophane.". . .

The officer then reached into respondent's pocket and retrieved a small plastic bag containing one fifth of one gram of crack cocaine. Respondent was arrested and charged in Hennepin County District Court with possession of a controlled substance.

Before trial, respondent moved to suppress the cocaine. The trial court first concluded that the officers were justified under *Terry v. Ohio,* 392 U.S. 1, 88 S.Ct. 1868, 20 L.Ed.2d 889 (1968), in stopping respondent to investigate whether he might be engaged in criminal activity. The court further found that the officers were justified in frisking respondent to ensure that he was not carrying a weapon. Finally, analogizing to the "plain-view" doctrine, under which officers may make a warrantless seizure of contraband found in plain view during a lawful search for other items, the trial court ruled that the officers' seizure of the cocaine did not violate the Fourth Amendment:

"To this Court there is no distinction as to which sensory perception the officer uses to conclude that the material is contraband. An experienced officer may rely upon his sense of smell in DWI stops or in recognizing the smell of burning marijuana in an automobile. The sound of a shotgun being racked would clearly support certain reactions by an officer. The sense of touch, grounded in experience and training, is as reliable as perceptions drawn from other senses. 'Plain feel,' therefore, is no different than plain view and will equally support the seizure here.". . .

His suppression motion having failed, respondent proceeded to trial and was found guilty.

On appeal, the Minnesota Court of Appeals reversed. The court agreed with the trial court that the investigative stop and protective patdown search of respondent were lawful under *Terry* because the officers had a reasonable belief based on specific and articulable facts that respondent was engaged in criminal behavior and that he might be armed and dangerous. The court concluded, however, that the officers had overstepped the bounds allowed by *Terry* in seizing the cocaine. In doing so, the Court of Appeals "decline [d] to adopt the plain feel exception" to the warrant requirement.

The Minnesota Supreme Court affirmed. Like the Court of Appeals, the State Supreme Court held that both the stop and the frisk of respondent were valid under *Terry,* but found the seizure of the cocaine to be unconstitutional. The court expressly refused "to extend the plain view doctrine to the sense of touch" on the grounds that "the sense of touch is inherently less immediate and less reliable than the sense of sight" and that "the sense of touch is far more intrusive into the personal privacy that is at the core of the [F]ourth [A]mendment.". . . The court thus appeared to adopt a categorical rule barring the seizure of any contraband detected by an officer through the sense of touch during a patdown search for weapons. The court further noted that "[e]ven if we recognized a 'plain feel' exception, the search in this case would not qualify" because "[t]he pat search of the defendant went far beyond what is permissible under *Terry*.". . . As the State Supreme Court read the record, the officer conducting the search ascertained that the lump in respondent's jacket was contraband only after probing and investigating what he certainly knew was not a weapon.

We granted certiorari, . . ., to resolve a conflict among the state and federal courts over whether contraband detected through the sense of touch during a patdown search may be admitted into evidence. [FN1] We now affirm. [footnote omitted]

FN1. Most state and federal courts have recognized a so-called "plain-feel" or "plain-touch" corollary to the plain-view doctrine. . . . *Some state courts, however, like the Minnesota court in this case, have rejected such a corollary.* . . .

Terry further held that "[w]hen an officer is justified in believing that the individual whose suspicious behavior he is investigating at close range is armed and presently dangerous to the officer or to others," the officer may conduct a patdown search "to determine whether the person is in fact carrying a weapon.". . . "The purpose of this limited search is not to discover evidence of crime, but to allow the officer to pursue his investigation without fear of violence. . . .". . . Rather, a protective search—permitted without a warrant and on the basis of reasonable suspicion less than probable cause—must be strictly "limited to that which is necessary for the discovery of weapons which might be used to harm the officer or others nearby.". . . If the protective search goes beyond what is necessary to determine if the suspect is armed, it is no longer valid under *Terry* and its fruits will be suppressed . . .

These principles were settled 25 years ago when, on the same day, the Court announced its decisions in *Terry* and *Sibron.* The question presented today is whether police officers may seize nonthreatening contraband detected during a protective patdown search of the sort permitted by *Terry*. We think the answer is clearly that they may, so long as the officers' search stays within the bounds marked by *Terry*.

B

We have already held that police officers, at least under certain circumstances, may seize contraband detected during the lawful execution of a *Terry* search. In *Michigan v. Long, supra,* for example, police approached a man who had driven his car into a ditch and who appeared to be under the influence of some intoxicant. As the man moved to reenter the car from the roadside, police spotted a knife on the floorboard. The officers stopped the man, subjected him to a pat-down search, and then inspected the interior of the vehicle for other weapons. During the search of the passenger compartment, the police discovered an open pouch containing marijuana and seized it. This Court upheld the validity of the search and seizure under *Terry*. The Court held first that, in the context of a roadside encounter, where police have reasonable suspicion based on specific and articulable facts to believe that a driver may be armed and dangerous, they may conduct a protective search for weapons not only of the driver's person but also of the passenger compartment of the automobile. . . Of course, the protective search of the vehicle, being justified solely by the danger that weapons stored there could be used against the officers or bystanders, must be "limited to those areas in which a weapon may be placed or hidden.". . . The Court then held: "If, while conducting a legitimate *Terry* search of the interior of the automobile, the officer should, as here, discover contraband other than weapons, he clearly cannot be required to ignore the contraband, and the Fourth Amendment does not require its suppression in such circumstances.". . .

The Court in *Long* justified this latter holding by reference to our cases under the "plain-view" doctrine. . . Under that doctrine, if police are lawfully in a position from which they view an object, if its incriminating character is immediately apparent, and if the officers have a lawful right of access to the object, they may seize it without a warrant. If, however, the police lack probable cause to believe that an object in plain view is contraband without conducting some further search of the object—*i.e.,* if "its incriminating character [is not] 'immediately apparent,'" . . .—the plain-view doctrine cannot justify its seizure. . .

We think that this doctrine has an obvious application by analogy to cases in which an officer discovers contraband through the sense of touch during an otherwise lawful search. The rationale of the plain-view doctrine is that if contraband is left in open view and is observed by a police officer from a lawful vantage point, there has been no invasion of a legitimate expectation of privacy and thus no "search" within the meaning of the Fourth Amendment—or at least no search independent of the initial intrusion that gave the officers their vantage point. . . . The warrantless seizure of contraband that presents itself in this manner is deemed justified by the realization that resort to a neutral magistrate under such circumstances would often be impracticable and would do little to promote the objectives of the Fourth Amendment. . . . The same can be said of tactile discoveries of contraband. If a police officer lawfully pats down a suspect's outer clothing and feels an object whose contour or mass makes its identity immediately apparent, there has been no invasion of the suspect's privacy beyond that already authorized by the officer's search for weapons; if the object is contraband, its warrantless seizure would be justified by the same practical considerations that inhere in the plain-view context. [footnote omitted]

The Minnesota Supreme Court rejected an analogy to the plain-view doctrine on two grounds: first, its belief that "the sense of touch is inherently less immediate and less reliable than the sense of sight," and second, that "the sense of touch is far more intrusive into the personal privacy that is at the core of the [F]ourth [A]mendment.". . . We have a somewhat different view. First, *Terry* itself demonstrates that the sense of touch is capable of revealing the nature of an object with sufficient reliability to support a seizure. The very premise of *Terry*, after all, is that officers will be able to detect the presence of weapons through the sense of touch and *Terry* upheld precisely such a seizure. Even if it were true that the sense of touch is generally less reliable than the sense of sight, that only suggests that officers will less often be able to justify seizures of unseen contraband. Regardless of whether the officer detects the contraband by sight or by touch, however, the Fourth Amendment's requirement that the officer have probable cause to believe that the item is contraband before seizing it ensures against excessively speculative seizures. [footnote omitted] The court's second concern—that touch is more intrusive into privacy than is sight—is inapposite in light of the fact that the intrusion the court fears has already been authorized by the lawful search for weapons. The seizure of an item whose identity is already known occasions no further invasion of privacy. . . . Accordingly, the suspect's privacy interests are not advanced by a categorical rule barring the seizure of contraband plainly detected through the sense of touch.

III

It remains to apply these principles to the facts of this case. Respondent has not challenged the finding made by the trial court and affirmed by both the Court of Appeals and the State Supreme Court that the police were justified under *Terry* in stopping him and frisking him for weapons. Thus, the dispositive question before this Court is whether the officer who conducted the search was acting within the lawful bounds marked by *Terry* at the time he gained probable cause to believe that the lump in respondent's jacket was contraband. The State District Court did not make precise findings on this point, instead finding simply that the officer, after feeling "a small, hard object wrapped in plastic" in respondent's pocket, "formed the opinion that the object . . . was crack . . . cocaine.". . . The District Court also noted that the officer made "no claim that he suspected this object to be a weapon," *id.,* at C-5, a finding affirmed on appeal, . . . (the officer "never thought the lump was a weapon"). The Minnesota Supreme Court, after "a close examination of the record," held that the officer's own testimony "belies any notion that he 'immediately'" recognized the lump as crack cocaine. . . . Rather, the court concluded, the officer determined that the lump was contraband only after "squeezing, sliding and otherwise manipulating the contents of the defendant's pocket"—a pocket which the officer already knew contained no weapon. . . .

Under the State Supreme Court's interpretation of the record before it, it is clear that the court was correct in holding that the police officer in this case overstepped the bounds of the "strictly circumscribed" search for weapons allowed under *Terry* . . . Where, as here, "an officer who is executing a valid search for one item seizes a different item," this Court rightly "has been sensitive to the danger . . . that officers will enlarge a specific authorization, furnished by a warrant or an exigency, into the equivalent of a general warrant to rummage and seize at will.". . . Here, the officer's continued exploration of respondent's pocket after having concluded that it contained no weapon was unrelated to "[t]he sole justification of the search [under *Terry:*] . . . the protection of the police officer and others nearby.". . . It therefore amounted to the sort of evidentiary search that *Terry* expressly refused to authorize, . . ., and that we have condemned in subsequent cases. . . .

Once again, the analogy to the plain-view doctrine is apt. In *Arizona v. Hicks,* 480 U.S. 321, 107 S.Ct. 1149, 94 L.Ed.2d 347 (1987), this Court held invalid the seizure of stolen stereo equipment found by police while executing a valid search for other evidence. Although the police were lawfully on the premises, they obtained probable cause to believe that the stereo equipment was contraband only after moving the equipment to permit officers to read its serial numbers. The subsequent seizure of the equipment could not be justified by the plain-view doctrine, this Court explained, because the incriminating character of the stereo equipment was not immediately apparent; rather, probable cause to believe that the equipment was stolen arose only as a result of a further search—the moving of the equipment—that was not authorized by a search warrant or by any exception to the warrant requirement. The facts of this case are very similar. Although the officer was lawfully in a position to feel the lump in respondent's pocket, because *Terry* entitled him to place his hands upon respondent's jacket, the court below determined that the incriminating character of the object was not immediately apparent to him. Rather, the officer determined that the item was contraband only after conducting a further search, one not authorized by *Terry* or by any other exception to the warrant requirement. Because this further search of respondent's pocket was constitutionally invalid, the seizure of the cocaine that followed is likewise unconstitutional. . . .

IV

For these reasons, the judgment of the Minnesota Supreme Court is
Affirmed.

Putting It Into Practice 7.4:

(a) Describe the search conducted by the officer in this case. (b) What is the issue before the Court? (c) What is the purpose of a *Terry* patdown search? (d) At what point is a *Terry* search no longer valid? (e) What is the "plain view" doctrine? (f) What is the rationale of a "plain view" search? (g) How does that rationale apply to searches involving "tactile discoveries"? (h) How did the U.S. Supreme Court respond to the Minnesota Supreme Court's contentions that "the sense of touch is inherently less immediate and less reliable than the sense of sight" and that the "sense of touch is far more intrusive into the personal privacy"? (i) Why did the Court in *Arizona v. Hicks* conclude that the seizure of the stereo equipment was not justified? (j) Why did the Court refuse the admit evidence of the cocaine?

STOP AND FRISK

reasonable suspicion   a belief based on specific, articulable facts that a person has committed or is about to commit a crime

stop   temporarily detain a suspect

When police officers have **reasonable suspicion** (a belief based on specific, articulable facts) that a person has committed or is about to commit a crime, they have a right to **stop** (temporarily detain) that person and conduct a frisk (a patting down of the outer clothing). In essence the officer must observe some kind of unusual conduct that leads him to believe that criminal activity is afoot. On that basis he can briefly detain the suspect. If nothing in this initial encounter dispels his fears for his or other's safety, he can conduct a limited search of the suspect's outer clothing.

The concept of stop and frisk originated in *Terry v. Ohio,* 392 U.S. 1 (1968), a seminal case that articulated the basis for reasonable suspicion. In that case, the officer observed several suspects, whom he believed to be "casing" a store. When the officer approached the suspects and asked them to identify themselves, they mumbled something incoherently. Based on the suspects' evasive and suspicious behavior, the Court held that the officer was constitutionally protected when he patted down one of the suspect's outer clothing and removed a gun he felt in his pocket. The court announced that reasonable suspicion had to be based on "specific and articulable facts which, taken together with rational inferences from those facts, reasonably warrant that intrusion." Frisks are limited to searches of outer clothing and cannot be extended to inner clothing or pockets. They are searches for weapons only and cannot extend to searches for contraband or incriminating evidence. If, in the process of frisking the suspect for weapons, the officer feels something he immediately recognizes as contraband, he can seize it under the so-called "plain touch" rule (see *Minnesota v. Dickerson* on page 411).

Not every encounter with a police officer constitutes a "seizure." "Stops" are covered under the Fourth Amendment and must, therefore, be reasonable, whereas other encounters that fall short of a "stop" are not protected by the Fourth Amendment. A person is considered "seized" for purpose of the Fourth Amendment when a reasonable person would believe he was no longer free to leave. Circumstances that would lead a reasonable person to this conclusion include an officer's display of a weapon, an officer's threatening tone of voice or language, some kind of physical touching by the officer, or the threatening presence of several officers. Interestingly, the U.S. Supreme Court has concluded that a suspect being chased by the police is not "seized" until he submits to the chase. Therefore, an officer's actions are not governed by the Fourth Amendment until the suspect is actually restrained or stops voluntarily.

For an overview of search and seizure law, go to *www.fsu.edu/,crimdo/fagan.html.*

At some point, a "stop" can turn into an arrest. The significance of this difference is that reasonable suspicion is all that is required for a "stop," but reasonable suspicion must blossom into probable cause before an officer can carry out an arrest. If the officer cannot establish probable cause in a timely manner, he must release the suspect. The U.S. Supreme Court has cautioned officers that they can detain a suspect no longer than is reasonably necessary to verify or dispel their suspicions. Although some police departments suggest officers detain suspects for no more than 20 minutes if possible, the Court in *U.S. v. Sharpe,* 470 U.S. 675 (1985), observed that the police are involved in a "swiftly developing situation" and that the courts "should not indulge in unrealistic second-guessing." The Court refused to limit officers to 20-minute detentions.

Putting It Into Practice 7.5:

Narcotics agents identify themselves to someone they suspect of smuggling drugs. At the airport where they have been watching him, they ask for and examine the suspect's ticket and his driver's license, and retain his ticket and driver's license while they ask him to accompany them to a room 40 feet away. They give him no indication that he can leave. Is he seized for purposes of the Fourth Amendment? How long can they detain him before they must arrest him?

"The whole nightmare had just begun. But it really came home to me when the officer *Mirandized* me. All of a sudden, those words, which had previously just been empty phrases I'd heard from actors, became very personal. And when the officer said, 'and anything you say can be used against you in a court of law,' I came out of the daze I'd been in and felt a cold terror creep over my body."

INTERROGATION

The questioning of suspects implicates the Fifth and Sixth Amendments. The Fifth Amendment prevents officers from forcing suspects to provide testimonial evidence that could be used to incriminate them. The rationale for this prohibition is that the state must prove its own case against a defendant without trying to coerce the defendant into providing evidence that could be used to convict him. The Sixth Amendment provides for representation by an attorney.

custodial interrogation
being questioned while in police custody, i.e., being significantly deprived of one's freedom

In *Miranda v. Arizona,* the U.S. Supreme Court concluded that both rights applied to those in **custodial interrogation.** (Custodial interrogation begins when a suspect's freedom has been deprived in a significant way and questioning has begun.) The Court reasoned that having the right to an attorney and to be protected against self-incrimination were meaningless if the suspect did not know about these rights until after he or she had already confessed. The ritualized *Miranda* **warnings** notify suspects that (1) they have the right to remain silent; (2) that anything said can be used against the suspect in a court of law; (3) that they have the right to an attorney; and (4) that if the suspect cannot afford an attorney, one will be appointed prior to any questioning.

***Miranda* warnings**   warnings an officer must give a suspect who is in custodial interrogation

Mirandized   to give *Miranda* warnings

Once a suspect invokes her right to counsel, she cannot be questioned unless she waives that right. Nor can the police try to resume questioning at a later time.

Instead, they must give the suspect an opportunity to consult with an attorney. Any statements obtained in violation of *Miranda* are inadmissible as part of the prosecution's case, although such statements can be used to impeach the defendant.

A suspect can choose to waive her right to an attorney. Any waivers must be voluntary, that is, they cannot be the result of mental impairment, intoxication, language barriers, or anything else that would impair the suspect's ability to knowingly and intelligently waive her rights. To help ensure proper waivers, many police departments now require suspects to sign a card indicating they understand their rights as they have been explained and that they want to talk with the officer. Additionally, many departments tape record or videotape suspects receiving and waiving their rights.

Because *Miranda* warnings apply only to "custodial interrogations," the question of when a suspect is "in custody" and when a suspect is being "interrogated" are subjects of more than academic interest. Generally, a suspect is considered "in custody" when a reasonable person in the suspect's position would believe he was not free to leave (i.e., he was in custody). Interrogations that occur at a station house are, more likely than not, custodial, and certainly once people are placed under arrest they are in custody of the police. But the lack of a formal arrest does not necessarily indicate that the suspect is not in custody. If, for example, during the course of voluntary questioning, the police indicate to the suspect that they consider him a prime suspect, his questioning is likely to be considered custodial. Questioning that occurs at a suspect's home before being placed under arrest or at the scene of a traffic stop for a minor traffic violation are most likely not custodial.

Interrogation goes beyond mere questioning and instead requires asking questions that the police "should know are reasonably likely to elicit an incriminating response from the suspect." (*Rhode Island v. Innis,* 446 U.S. 291 (1980).) In *Innis,* the police arrested a suspect for a murder committed in the vicinity of a school for handicapped children. They believed the suspect used a sawed-off shotgun to commit the crime and had not yet found the gun when they arrested him. In front of the suspect, one of the officers commented to another officer, "God forbid one of the children might find a weapon with shells and they might hurt themselves." The suspect then told the officers where the gun could be found. The Supreme Court concluded that no interrogation had occurred because the officers should not necessarily have known that their conversation was "reasonably likely to elicit an incriminating response." Routine questions asked for identification purposes only, such as a defendant's name, address, height, and weight, are not considered interrogation and do not require *Miranda* warnings.

Miranda has been experiencing a gradual erosion as a result of U.S. Supreme Court interpretations over the years. *Miranda* warnings are not required, for example, when police questioning is motivated by a "concern for public safety." In *New York v. Quarles,* 467 U.S. 649 (1984), officers apprehended a rape suspect when he ran to the back of a grocery store. After handcuffing him, the officers asked the suspect, without *Mirandizing* him, if he had a gun and where it was. The Court held that *Miranda* warnings were unnecessary because the police needed to ask the question to protect the public safety.

In a more startling case, *Moran v. Burbine,* 475 U.S. 412 (1986), the Court upheld a suspect's waiver of his *Miranda* rights even though the police declined to tell the suspect his family had retained counsel for him. Furthermore, the police actually deceived the lawyer by falsely telling her they did not intend to interrogate the suspect. Shortly after the conversation with the lawyer on the phone, the police read the suspect his *Miranda* rights and obtained a signed waiver of those rights. The Court reasoned that "events occurring outside of the presence of the suspect and entirely unknown to him surely can have no bearing on the capacity to comprehend and knowingly relinquish a constitutional right." Although knowing that a lawyer had been retained "would have been useful" to the defendant and

NET NEWS

To read the arguments about *Miranda* made by the attorneys who argued the Fourth Circuit case when it was reviewed by the U.S. Supreme Court, go to *www.pbs.org/newshour/bb/law/jan-june00/miranda_1-6.html.*

For additional discussion regarding *Miranda* and its impact on law enforcement, go to *www.law.about.com/newsissues/law/cs/mirandarights/*

perhaps even "affected his decision to confess," the police are not required to "supply a suspect with a flow of information to help him celebrate his self interest in deciding whether to speak or stand by his rights." The Court considered the motives of the police to be irrelevant to the defendant's decision to waive his *Miranda* rights.

At the time of this writing, *Miranda* has survived its latest challenge, this time by the Fourth Circuit, which reverted to an old federal statute that based the admissibility of confessions solely on whether they were voluntary. In reviewing the Fourth Circuit's decision to admit a confession even though the officer failed to properly *Mirandize* the defendant, the U.S. Supreme Court, confirmed the sanctity of *Miranda,* negating the Fourth Circuit's contention that *Miranda* was not a constitutional holding. In a 7-2 decision, the Court declared the federal statute unconstitutional and reaffirmed that despite the erosion of *Miranda,* it remains a viable constitutional precedent.

Putting It Into Practice 7.6:

Two police officers see Joe carrying a jacket that matches the description of a jacket worn by a murder victim the day before. They stop Joe and ask him where he got the jacket. His answers are evasive and they decide to take him to the station house for further questioning.

(a) Do they need to *Mirandize* him before they question him further?

(b) On the ride to the station house, one of the officers comments to the other officer, "Too bad about that Millhouse woman. Shame they can't find her body and give her a decent Christian burial." Joe then tells them where they could find her body. What issue is raised by his incriminating statements?

(c) Suppose Joe is *Mirandized* but is not told that his attorney will be coming in a few hours to see him. Joe decides to confess before his attorney arrives. Will the officers' failure to inform him about his attorney render his confession inadmissible?

booked the administrative process involved in bringing a suspect into the jail or police facility

initial appearance first appearance of a suspect before a judge at which the suspect is formally charged, counsel is appointed, and bail is set

"Few things are as humiliating as being **booked** into jail. No matter how nice the jail personnel try to be, the process itself is dehumanizing—from having your mug shots taken to being fingerprinted to being strip-searched."

"I never did understand the need to strip-search all arrestees," commented Martha.

"Well, I understand it, even though I certainly didn't appreciate having to go through it," replied Tim. "After all, drugs and other contraband are frequently smuggled into the jails and some people bring it in on their person. Just because I was there for less than 24 hours before I went to my **initial appearance** didn't preclude me from being subject to the same regulations as every other inmate."

Figure 7-2
Procedures Preceding Trial

PROCEDURES PRECEDING TRIAL

Booking
Administrative Process

Initial Appearance
Announcing of Charges
Appointing of Counsel
Setting of Bail

Preliminary Hearing or Grand Jury
Determining if Probable Cause Exists to Bind Defendant Over for Trial

Arraignment
Informing Defendant of Charges in Indictment or Information
Entering of Plea
Imposing of Sentence or Setting Time for Sentencing

NET NEWS

To see live video transmissions of real events in the Maricopa County, Arizona jail (courtesy of Sheriff Joe Arpaio), go to *www.crime.com/info/jailcam.html.*

BOOKING AND INITIAL APPEARANCE

◆ **LOCAL LINKS** ◆
How soon must an arrestee be brought to an initial appearance in your state?

bail   the security given by the defendant to the court to guarantee his or her presence at trial in exchange for immediate release from custody

posting a bond   process of paying money and promising to appear later in court in exchange for immediate release from custody

bond   a document signed by the defendant and a bail bondsman requiring the bondsman to pay the court if the defendant fails to appear in court

After being arrested, a suspect is booked. Booking involves taking the defendant's personal information, fingerprinting and photographing him, conducting any tests (such as testing for blood alcohol or drugs), and allowing the defendant to use the telephone. If the defendant is to be detained, he is also searched and his possessions are inventoried. At this point, some defendants are cited and released with instructions that they must appear in court at a later date.

Those who are detained must be taken promptly before a judge or magistrate for their initial appearance. At this hearing, the judge will formally announce the charges against the defendant, appoint a public defender or court-appointed counsel if the defendant is entitled to legal representation (based on the defendant's economic status), and set **bail.**

Bail is the security given by the defendant to the court to guarantee his presence at trial in exchange for immediate release from custody. Bail may be denied if the judge believes that the defendant is likely to flee or that he poses a risk to the community. Bail cannot be excessive, but can be based on such factors as the seriousness of the offense, the weight of evidence against the defendant, the defendant's ties to the community, and the defendant's financial abilities and character. The judge must consider the defendant's individual circumstances in fixing bail.

A defendant has the option of **posting a bond. A bond** is a document signed by the defendant and a bail bondsman requiring the bondsman to pay the court if the defendant fails to appear in court. In exchange for making this promise, the bail bondsman charges a substantial fee (usually ten percent of the bail set by the court). Bail bondsmen typically secure their risk with collateral (such as mortgages, stocks, bonds, and other valuables) and are noted for going to great lengths to recover from clients who "skip" or "jump" bail (fail to appear in court).

For many people, any amount of bail is excessive because they have no assets with which to secure a bail bond. The federal courts and some state courts allow

NET NEWS

For more specific information about the types of bonds that can be posted and what is involved in posting a bond, go to *www.bailbondservices.com* and *www.gottrouble.com/legal/criminal/bail* resource/ .

such people to be **released on their own recognizance** (OR), essentially by promising in writing that they will appear in court. Failure to reappear or to meet any conditions of the release can result in a rearrest or a requirement that the accused pay a sum of money to the court.

◆ **LOCAL LINKS** ◆
Do your state courts allow defendants to be released on their own recognizance?

Putting It Into Practice 7.7:

Why is it to a defendant's advantage to have counsel present at his initial appearance?

"If You've Never Been in a Jail, You Have No Idea What I'm Talking About. Believe Me—It's an Experience You Don't Want to Have."

"I'd never been in a jail before that night and I tell you I was never so happy to get out of someplace as I was to get out of there. I was in a holding tank with a bunch of drunks, some guy who was obviously mentally ill, and another guy I was sure would kill me if he had the chance."

"You couldn't have been in that much danger," objected Martha. "There were guards all around, weren't there?"

"Actually, I went for hours without seeing a guard. The jail downtown is seriously understaffed. And even if they're around, you find out pretty quickly that if some guy wants to hurt you, he can. Makeshift weapons are pretty common and easy to make. But, frankly, getting hurt wasn't my primary concern. I just wanted to get away from the stench and the incessant noise. If you've never been in a jail, you have no idea what I'm talking about. Believe me— it's an experience you don't want to have."

"I always wanted to take a shower as soon as I got out of there and my ears would ring for hours afterward," concurred John. "I was a public defender when I first graduated from law school and I spent a considerable amount of time in the jails meeting with clients," he explained to Martha.

"Oh," was all Martha could find to say. "Well, at least you didn't have to stay there long, did you?" she added lamely to Tim.

"No. My Dad found an attorney who helped me post bond, and I was released early the next morning. Fortunately, I was out on bail until I was sentenced. But it wasn't long before I received a subpoena from the prosecutor's office, summoning me to appear before the **grand jury.** I wasn't aware of it at the time but the state was really going after my dealer and so the prosecutor subpoenaed me to testify against him. Right before the hearing, the prosecutor really pressured me to **plea bargain**—promising me a great deal if I just agreed to identify my dealer."

"So you got a reduced sentence," concluded Martha summarily.

"Actually, no. I didn't agree to testify—although the prosecutor still called me before the grand jury."

"Could I infer from your refusal to testify that your dealer threatened you?" surmised Martha.

"Yes, and my wife as well. But how did you—?" Tim was puzzled by Martha's awareness about the realities of the drug world.

"My dad was a cop. Remember? He used to regale me with stories about pushers, pimps, fences, and the other 'denizens of the dark,'" explained Martha, enjoying her opportunity to prove that she was not as naïve about the criminal element as Tim and John had supposed.

---

released on their own recognizance   a defendant's promise in writing to reappear in court at a later date

grand jury   jury that listens to evidence presented by the prosecutor to decide if probable cause exists to bind the defendant over for trial

plea bargain   agreement by the defendant to plead guilty in exchange for the prosecutor's dropping or reducing some charges or recommending a lesser sentence to the judge

PRELIMINARY HEARING AND GRAND JURY INDICTMENT

preliminary hearing hearing at which the judge determines if the state has shown probable cause to bind the defendant over for trial

In many states, a **preliminary hearing** or a grand jury proceeding is used to review the prosecutor's case in felony cases to determine if probable cause exists to warrant binding the defendant over for trial. At a preliminary hearing, the prosecutor calls witnesses and presents evidence supporting the charges against the defendant. The defendant has no obligation to present a case because he is presumed innocent, but he may opt to cross-examine the state's witnesses. If the judge concludes that the state has presented sufficient evidence to proceed, the prosecutor is allowed to file an **information**: a charging document issued by the prosecution accusing the defendant of having committed a crime. In cases involving misdemeanors, the prosecutor can file an information after the initial appearance. If an attorney concludes that his client has nothing to gain from having a preliminary hearing, he may opt to waive this hearing.

information charging document issued by a prosecutor accusing the defendant of having committed a crime

---

◆ **LOCAL LINKS** ◆

Are grand juries used in your state?
In what capacity?

Alternatively, the prosecutor may take a felony case before a grand jury: a group of people whose job is to determine if probable cause exists to believe that the defendant committed a crime. The federal government and about half of the states use a grand jury. Some states do not use grand juries and, in others, prosecutors have the option of going to the grand jury. Grand jury proceedings are conducted in secret. The prosecutor is in charge of calling witnesses and presenting evidence; the defendant is not allowed to attend. Any one called as a witness before the grand jury is not allowed to bring his attorney into the hearing. If the grand jury votes to bind the defendant over for trial, the defendant is said to be **indicted.**

indicted grand jury's written accusation that a defendant has committed a crime

Grand juries can also be used as investigative tools by the prosecutor's office. A grand jury has the power to subpoena witnesses and investigate people who have not yet been arrested. If the grand jury decides that someone should be brought to trial, an arrest warrant will be issued and the defendant will go directly from an initial appearance to **arraignment.**

arraignment hearing at which the judge informs the defendant of the charges being brought and the defendant enters a plea

---

■ *Putting It Into Practice 7.8:*

Why might it be to a defendant's advantage to have a grand jury proceeding rather than a preliminary hearing?

Figure 7-3
Grand Jury Compared to Preliminary Hearing

GRAND JURY COMPARED TO PRELIMINARY HEARING

Grand Jury	Preliminary Hearing
Determines probable cause	Determines probable cause
Prosecutor presents case but defense is not present	Prosecutor presents case and defense can rebut
Hearing is secret	Hearing is open to public
Grand jury determines if probable cause exists	Judge determines if probable cause exists
Indictment is issued by grand jury	Information is issued by prosecutor

---

For more in-depth information about federal and state grand juries and to see an indictment issued in the Oklahoma bombing case, go to *www.udayton.edu/~grandjur/*.

To read more about the comparison between the grand jury and preliminary hearing processes, go to *http://consumerlawpage.com/article/grand.shtml*.

For more information about arraignments, go to *www.gottrouble.com/notfound.html*. Click on "Sitemap," "Criminal Law," "Criminal Court System," and then "Arraignment."

ARRAIGNMENT

At an arraignment, the court informs the defendant of the charges in the information or indictment and then asks the defendant to enter a plea. If the defendant pleads guilty, the judge must question the defendant to ensure that he understands the nature of the charges, the possible punishment prescribed by law, and the nature of the constitutional rights he is waiving (the right to a trial and to confront witnesses). Once the judge determines that the guilty plea is voluntary, the judge may either impose a sentence immediately or set a time for sentencing. If the defendant pleads not guilty, a tentative date is set for trial.

nolo contendere plea of no contest to criminal charges

A defendant can also plead ***nolo contendere***—no contest. With this plea, the defendant agrees that the prosecution has sufficient evidence to prove its case beyond a reasonable doubt but neither admits nor denies the charges. The defendant is treated as if he pleaded guilty, but his plea is not considered an admission of guilt and cannot be used against him at a later civil trial.

PLEA BARGAINING

Frequently, the defense attorney and the prosecutor have engaged in plea bargaining prior to the arraignment. In essence, the defendant agrees to plead guilty to the charges alleged or, more frequently, to some lesser offense in exchange for the prosecution's agreement to a lesser punishment. (Note that plea agreements cannot be created without being reviewed and approved by a judge.) Plea bargaining is a way of life for most lawyers engaged in criminal practice, but it is highly criticized. Somewhere between 75 and 90 percent of all criminal cases are resolved by a plea bargain.[1] Probably because of this fact, more than 80 percent of all people charged with crimes plead guilty or are convicted after trial.[2]

Although plea bargaining facilitates the efficient administration of the criminal justice system, it does not ensure justice. Not only does it allow those who are guilty of a crime to serve shorter sentences than they might have had they been found guilty by a jury, but innocent defendants can be pressured into pleading guilty for fear of not being able to prove their innocence. Although some states claim to have abolished plea bargaining, the sheer volume of cases the courts and criminal justice agencies must deal with necessitates some kind of bargaining process to expedite the resolution of cases.

◆ **LOCAL LINKS** ◆

Is plea bargaining permitted in your jurisdiction?

Putting It Into Practice 7.9:

Can you imagine a circumstance in which a defendant charged with a serious crime, such as child molestation, might accept a plea bargain from the state rather than go to trial?

For more information about plea bargaining, go to *www.nolo.com/encyclopedia/crim_ency.html*, click on "Understanding Plea Bargaining: How Most Criminal Cases are Settled," and go to the articles entitled "Plea Bargains: Why and When They're Made," "Defendants' Incentives for Accepting Plea Bargains," and "Prosecutors' and Judges' Incentives for Accepting Plea Bargains."

"Let Me Assure You, Criminal Defense Attorneys Aren't the Only Attorneys Who Sometimes Walk Ethical Tightropes."

"I can't begin to tell you how grateful I was to have Celandra, my attorney, to advise me. In fact, after it was all over I decided that when I got out of prison I wanted to become a defense attorney. I wanted to be there for others the way she was for me," confided Tim.

"But how much could an attorney really do for you?" protested Martha. "It sounds like they had you dead to rights."

"Well, for openers, she warned me the first night she talked to me that the police would probably get a warrant to search my house."

"So in essence she advised you to destroy evidence. That's exactly why I could never understand how any self-respecting lawyer could do criminal defense work. Pretty soon they're no better than their clients!" Remembering John's history as a public defender, Martha backtracked. "I'm sorry, Mr. Morgan, but I really don't know how you could have done that kind of work."

"Obviously. First of all, Celandra told Tim what the law was; I'm sure she didn't tell him to destroy evidence. What did you expect her to do? Let the police find cocaine, add it to the charges against Tim, and potentially allow Tim's home to be forfeited to the state?" John's patience with Martha's ongoing judgments was exhausted by her last remarks.

"The state can actually seize your home?"

"Yes, and your car, your bank accounts, and any personal property connected to any illegal transactions," added John. "And let me assure you, criminal defense attorneys aren't the only attorneys who sometimes walk ethical tightropes. Civil attorneys often have to advise clients about the legal consequences of their actions knowing full well that they'll probably choose to do something that violates the law."

"But they can't allow a client to lie on the stand?"

"Not intentionally. If they know in advance that a client is planning to perjure himself, they can ask the judge's permission to withdraw from the case or they can refuse to ask the client questions, just allowing him to narrate the story. Of course, both of these actions telegraph to the judge and the jury that the client is lying."

"So what? Isn't that what the client deserves?" Martha was indignant that anyone should think an attorney should protect a client from being revealed as a perjurer.

"Ideally, yes. Zealous representation is not supposed to include allowing your client to lie. The realities of practice, however, sometimes make that a difficult standard to uphold." Seeing that Martha did not understand his last comment, John went on. "Let's not get sidetracked. We're here to hear Tim's story. It's just that you've been shielded from seeing the extremely difficult choices attorneys sometimes have to make and you've apparently arrived at the conclusion that only criminal defense attorneys are put in positions that potentially compromise their integrity. That's categorically untrue."

When Tim saw John sit back, he returned to Martha's earlier comment. "Let me respond to your earlier remark about how any 'self-respecting' attorney could do defense work. Keep in mind that the state has an obligation to prove its case against the defendant and that it must follow the law in doing so. One of the defense attorney's primary tasks is to ensure that the state does its job fairly and honestly."

"Oh, please. I heard those kinds of rationalizations in school. The problem is that guilty people get off on some of those technicalities that defense attorneys are so worried about."

"That's true. Some guilty people do get off. But those 'technicalities' you refer to are the constitutional rights that protect you just as much as they protect those who commit crimes."

"I'm not planning on committing any crimes, so I'm not really worried about how many rights I have," replied Martha tersely.

"But, having been in that situation, I can tell you that if you or someone you love is ever accused of committing a crime, you'll be very grateful to know that the police and the prosecutors are required to follow certain procedures," pointed out Tim. "I know I was. And on a more philosophical note—you know, the integrity of our whole criminal justice system depends on all of its players following the rules. If the law enforcers don't obey the law, why should anyone else?"

Before Martha could think of a retort, their server appeared. "Who had the pasta?"

To understand law enforcement's perspective of the benefits of the forfeiture laws, go to *www.usdoj.gov/marshals/seizure.html*. To get a defense attorney's perspective of the criminal forfeiture laws, go to *www.afnlaw.com* and click on "How to Defend a Criminal Forfeiture."

ETHICAL ETIQUETTE

CANDOR IN ADVOCACY

Attorneys have an obligation to be honest in their dealings with the court. They cannot:

- ◆ make false statements of law or fact
- ◆ offer false evidence
- ◆ alter, conceal, or destroy evidence
- ◆ allow a client to perpetrate a fraud on the court
- ◆ counsel a client to commit a crime or
- ◆ assist a client in committing a crime

If they discover later that false evidence was presented to the court, they are required to rectify the fraud.

The issue of perjury is a difficult and controversial problem with which lawyers wrestle. If an attorney knows in advance that a client intends to perjure himself, the attorney should not call the client to the stand, but if the client insists on testifying, the courts do not provide uniform guidance to attorneys. The *Model Rules* recommend that the attorney advise the client to retract the false testimony, or ask the court's permission to withdraw from the case, or, if neither of those suggestions works, to disclose the false testimony to the court. This situation is particularly difficult when dealing with criminal defendants, who have a constitutional right to testify and to be represented by competent counsel. Courts frequently refuse to allow attorneys to withdraw in the middle of a trial. If a criminal defendant insists on perjuring himself, the courts are split on whether the attorney should disclose the perjury if the judge refuses to allow withdrawal.

Another potentially troublesome area, particularly for criminal defense attorneys, is the prevention of future crimes. Although a client's revelations are normally confidential and an attorney cannot reveal information the client discloses regarding past criminal conduct, an attorney can disclose revelations regarding future criminal acts if he believes the crime "is likely to result in imminent death or substantial bodily harm." (Model Rule 1.6 (b) (1).) This provision of the Model Rules is very controversial and many states have modified this rule. Some states requires attorneys to reveal information likely to result in death or substantial bodily harm while others permit revelations regarding future crimes, whether those crimes are serious or not. Still others allow attorneys to disclose information that could lead to the commission of a crime or fraud or any act that could substantially injure the property of financial interest of another.

◆ **LOCAL LINKS** ◆

What are the rules in your state regarding an attorney's right/obligation to disclose that a client has threatened to commit future crimes?

Putting It Into Practice 7.10:

Why might a criminal defense attorney struggle with whether to tell the judge that his client intends to take the stand and perjure himself?

"The Frightening Truth Is That They—and the Prosecutors as Well—Depend on Plea Bargaining to Get Through Their Caseload."

"Is it true that you're better off with a private attorney than a public defender?" Martha asked, breaking the silence.

"I've met several public defenders and I know some **assigned counsel** and all of the ones I've met are very competent," responded Tim, eager to find a more neutral topic of conversation. "The problem, particularly with public defenders, is their impossible caseload. I don't think they can possibly do justice to all of their clients."

"Which is why most of them have very little time to spend with individual clients," added John. "The frightening truth is that they—and the **prosecutors** as well—depend on plea bargaining to get through their caseload. When I was with the public defender's office, we used to threaten periodically to refuse all plea bargains."

"What good would that have done?" asked Martha.

"It would have brought the whole criminal justice system to its knees in a month. The system relies on plea bargaining to get cases resolved as quickly and with as few resources being expended as possible."

"Sounds like bargain basement justice to me," observed Martha.

"Sometimes that's what you get, despite everyone's best intentions," agreed John.

"But aren't you entitled to competent representation?" inquired Martha. "I think I remember learning something about 'effective assistance of counsel' in one of my classes."

"To some extent, that's true." explained John. "But defendants face a difficult burden in proving their counsel was ineffective. An attorney can do a pretty rotten job and still be considered effective for purposes of the Sixth Amendment."

NET NEWS

To read an interesting article about the role and future of criminal defense attorneys, go to *dpa.state.ky.us/advocate/jan99/ asicus.html.*

SIXTH AMENDMENT RIGHT TO COUNSEL

Both state and federal court defendants have a right to appointed counsel if they are **indigent** (lacking adequate financial resources to afford counsel) and if they can be sent to jail. Therefore, defendants have a right to be provided an attorney if they are charged with a **felony** (crime for which the authorized punishment is a prison sentence of a year or more) or with a **misdemeanor** (crime for which the authorized sentence is less than a year in jail) for which the defendant is to be sentenced to any amount of jail time. A defendant can appear *pro se* (without representation) but must do so "knowingly and intelligently." A defendant who insists on appearing *pro se* cannot later claim ineffective assistance of counsel on appeal.

In addition to having a right to counsel at the trial itself, indigent defendants have a right to counsel at any stage of the criminal proceedings considered a "critical stage." A stage is considered critical if the defendant will be required to make a decision that

---

assigned counsel private attorney paid by the state on a contractual basis to represent indigent defendants

prosecutors attorney who presents the state's case against criminal defendants; also known as *district attorneys* and *state's attorneys* at the state level and *U.S. attorneys* at the federal level

indigent lacking adequate financial resources to afford legal representation

felony crime for which the authorized punishment is a prison sentence of a year or more

misdemeanor crime for which the authorized sentence is less than a year in jail

pro se without legal representation

can formally be used against him at a later time. Therefore, the initial appearance, preliminary hearing, and arraignment are all considered critical stages at which counsel must be provided. Counsel must usually be provided at a post-trial sentencing as well.

lineup where a witness picks the suspect out of a group of people

Defendants also have a right to have an attorney present at a pre-trial **lineup**, where a witness picks the suspect out of a group of people. This right applies only when the police have formally charged the suspect by indicting him or having a preliminary hearing. The right to counsel does not apply if the witness picks out pictures of the suspect in a photo identification session with the police. Similarly, defendants do not have a right to counsel if the police conduct some kind of scientific procedures, such as drawing blood, taking fingerprints, extracting samples (handwriting, voice, hair), or getting evidence from the defendant's clothing.

The right to counsel means more than having a warm body occupying counsel's chair in the courtroom. Defendants have a right to effective assistance of counsel. The Supreme Court, however, has made it difficult for defendants alleging ineffective assistance of counsel to meet their burden of proof. They must prove both that their attorney's performance was "deficient" (in that the attorney was not reasonably competent) and that this deficiency was prejudicial to the defense (in that there is a "reasonable probability that, but for counsel's errors, the result of the proceeding would have been different.") (*Strickland v. Washington,* 466 U.S. 668 (1984).) Under this standard, most attorneys will be considered competent and, indeed, the Court admonished appellate courts to apply a "strong presumption" that any attorney's performance being reviewed falls within the wide range of acceptable conduct.

Putting It Into Practice 7.11:

Why do you think the courts have provided indigent defendants with the right to counsel? Why do you think the U.S. Supreme Court has made it difficult for defendants to claim ineffective assistance of counsel?

NET NEWS

For more information about what criminal defense attorneys do and how they can be obtained, go to *www.nolo.com/encyclopedia/crim_ency.html.* Click on "Criminal Defense Lawyers and Public Defenders" and go to the articles entitled "What a Good Criminal Defense Lawyer Does," "Developing a Defense Strategy," and "Obtaining a Criminal Defense Lawyer."

"Sounds to me like some of those attorneys need a really good paralegal to get them on the straight and narrow," teased Martha.

"Absolutely," jumped in Tim, missing Martha's attempt to lighten the tone of their conversation in his earnestness to find some common ground on which they could agree. "Matthew—Celandra's paralegal—was the first paralegal I'd ever come in contact with. And let me tell you, that man was like a whirling dervish—everywhere at once. He did everything—from finding witnesses to working with private investigators to making arrangements for bail. Celandra told me many times she didn't know what she'd do without him."

"He sounds pretty impressive," remarked Martha.

"He was. But he had years of experience. In fact, he was one of the first paralegals to work in the criminal area around here."

"From what one of my friends, who works at the county attorney's office, told me, I gather the criminal area is really beginning to open up for paralegals. In fact, I heard the public defender's office just hired two new paralegals last month," reported Martha.

"I certainly got the impression from talking to Matthew that it was a good field to go into if you like variety in your work. He assured me he never got bored."

PARALEGALS IN THE PRACTICE OF CRIMINAL LAW

The tasks that paralegals perform in both criminal defense and criminal prosecution are similar in nature to those performed in civil practice. Both undertake tasks that include the following.

- ◆ conducting initial interviews with clients
- ◆ gathering factual information
- ◆ conducting legal research
- ◆ managing and reviewing documents
- ◆ interviewing and obtaining statements from witnesses
- ◆ locating experts and other witnesses
- ◆ assisting in discovery, pretrial, and trial procedures
- ◆ preparing clients for trial
- ◆ maintaining office calendar
- ◆ drafting post-trial motions

Other tasks that those in the practice of criminal defense law perform include these.

- ◆ reviewing arrest and search warrants
- ◆ reviewing police reports
- ◆ arranging bail
- ◆ assisting clients in obtaining information related to bail
- ◆ determining eligibility for free representation (if working for the public defender)
- ◆ serving as a liaison with criminal justice agencies and judicial offices

Some specific tasks that are unique to criminal prosecution practice are

- ◆ referring victims to appropriate agencies
- ◆ screening out cases that are appropriate for diversion programs
- ◆ and preparing statistical caseload reports

NET NEWS

To read about what it is like to practice in various criminal justice agencies, go to the following articles at *www.paralegals.org/Reporter*.

"Life As an Oregon DOJ Paralegal" (Summer 1999)

"At the City Attorney's Office" (Summer 1999)

"Paralegal Roles and Responsibilities" (Summer 1999)
(working with the Attorney General and DOJ)

"Paralegal Roles and Responsibilities" (Year-End 1999)
(working with public defender and FBI)

RECESS

SUMMARY – PART A

The Fourth Amendment protects people from unreasonable searches and seizures and is not implicated if no search or seizure has occurred. A search or seizure occurs only if it violates the individual's expectation of privacy. An officer has a right to seize contraband that is in plain view, in an open field, in a public place, or in a jail/prison cell. Officers are encouraged to obtain search warrants, although they can bypass getting a warrant under certain circumstances. To secure a warrant, an officer must sign an affidavit, which establishes probable cause that incriminating evidence will be found and that describes with particularity where the search will be conducted and what is to be seized. Arrest warrants are not necessary unless an officer plans to arrest the suspect in his home, which he can do without a warrant if he is in hot pursuit or some other exigency exists. Officers can conduct a search without getting a warrant if (1) they get the consent of the defendant or of a third party who has the capacity and authority to give consent; (2) they are searching incident to a lawful arrest; (3) they have probable cause to believe a vehicle contains contraband; (4) they are conducting an administrative or inventory search; (5) they observe something in plain view; or (6) they believe the evidence will be destroyed. Officers can stop and frisk someone if they have reasonable suspicion to believe that the suspect committed or is about to commit a crime. Frisks are limited to searches of outer clothing and must be confined to a search for weapons. A suspect is not considered "seized" unless a reasonable person in this situation would have concluded he was not free to leave. If an officer cannot establish probable cause after a brief detention of a suspect, he must release that individual. A suspect cannot be detained longer than is reasonably necessary to verify or dispel the officer's suspicions.

The Fifth Amendment protects suspects from being forced to incriminate themselves and the Sixth Amendment provides the right to legal representation. Suspects are advised of both rights when they are given *Miranda* warnings. *Miranda* warnings do not have to be given until a suspect is the subject of a "custodial interrogation." A suspect is considered to be in custody when he is significantly deprived of his freedom to leave. Interrogation occurs when the police ask questions they "should know are reasonably likely to elicit an incriminating response from the suspect." Once a suspect has invoked her right to counsel, she must be given an opportunity to consult with counsel and further questioning is not allowed. Any waiver of *Miranda* rights must be shown to be voluntary. Any statement made by a defendant in violation of his *Miranda* rights cannot be used by the prosecution except to impeach the defendant. The protection of *Miranda* has gradually eroded, allowing officers today, for example, to ask questions of a suspect for purposes of public safety without first *Mirandizing* him.

After a suspect is arrested, he is booked. Shortly thereafter, he is taken to an initial appearance, where the judge announces the charges against him, sets bail, and appoints a public defender or assigned counsel. A judge can deny a defendant bail if the judge believes the defendant is likely to flee or that he poses a risk to the community. Bail cannot be excessive, but can be based on the seriousness of the offense, the weight of evidence against the defendant, the defendant's financial abilities, and his character. A grand jury proceeding or a preliminary hearing is used to determine if probable cause exists to bind a defendant over for trial. While grand jury proceedings are held in secret and the defendant is not allowed to attend, preliminary hearings are open hearings at which defense counsel can opt to cross-examine witnesses. If the grand jury finds probable cause exists, it issues an indictment against the defendant, and if the judge determines that probable cause exists at the preliminary hearing, the prosecutor issues an information. At an arraignment, the court informs the defendant of the charges against him and asks the defendant to enter a plea. If the defendant pleads guilty, the judge must ensure that the defendant entered the plea voluntarily and with full knowledge of the consequences of that plea. Many cases are resolved by means of plea bargaining, which facilitates the resolution of criminal cases but does not necessarily ensure that justice is done.

Attorneys have an ethical obligation to be honest. They cannot, for example, present false evidence, make false statements of law or fact, destroy evidence, or allow a client to perpetrate a fraud on the court. Ethical conflicts arise for criminal defense attorneys when a client makes it clear that he intends to perjure himself on the witness stand. Another controversial ethical question is whether attorneys can reveal a client's intent to commit future crimes.

Indigent defendants have a right to be appointed counsel if they are charged with a felony or a misdemeanor that entails jail time as a sentence. This right to counsel extends to any critical stage of the process. No right to counsel exists when a defendant is subjected to scientific procedures or the extraction of samples. Any defendant has the option of appearing *pro se*. A defendant who alleges the ineffective assistance of counsel must prove that her attorney's performance was deficient and that this deficiency was prejudicial to her defense. Appellate courts presume that the conduct of attorneys they are reviewing fell within the range of competence.

KEY TERMS

Arraignment	Exigent circumstance	Lineup	Prosecutors
Arrested	Felony	*Miranda* warnings	*Pro se*
Arrest warrant	Frisk	*Mirandized*	Reasonable suspicion
Assigned counsel	Grand jury	Misdemeanor	Released on their own
Bail	Hot pursuit	*Nolo contendere*	recognizance
Bond	Indicted	Plea bargain	Search warrant
Booked	Indigent	Posting a bond	Stop
Custodial interrogation	Information	Preliminary hearing	Suppressed
Curtilage	Initial appearance	Probable cause	

REVIEW QUESTIONS – PART A

1. What does the Fourth Amendment provide?
2. Under what circumstances does an individual have no expectation of privacy?
3. What must an officer do to obtain a search warrant?
4. What must an officer show to establish probable cause to obtain a search warrant? An arrest warrant?
5. Under what conditions can an officer conduct a warrantless search?
6. Under what conditions can an officer stop and frisk a suspect? At what point does a stop occur?
7. Why are *Miranda* warnings given? What are those warnings? At what point must an officer give them?
8. When is a suspect considered to be in "custody"? At what point does an interrogation occur?
9. In what respects has the protection of *Miranda* gradually eroded over the years?
10. What occurs at each of the following?
    a. booking
    b. initial appearance
    c. preliminary hearing
    d. grand jury hearing
    e. arraignment
11. How does plea bargaining affect the criminal justice system?
12. What ethical problems arise for an attorney when a criminal defendant indicates he intends to perjure himself on the stand or that he intends to commit a criminal act?
13. When is an indigent defendant entitled to representation? When is he not entitled to representation?
14. What must a defendant prove if he alleges ineffective assistance of counsel?

PRACTICE EXAM – PART A

MULTIPLE CHOICE

1. The Fourth Amendment
   a. prohibits unreasonable searches and seizures
   b. requires the use of warrants whenever a search is conducted
   c. requires that warrants be supported by reasonable suspicion
   d. allows for the issuance of a warrant based on an officer's unsworn statements

2. The Fourth Amendment
   a. is involved even when the courts determine that no search or seizure occurred
   b. is implicated only if the suspect has an expectation of privacy
   c. protects people equally no matter where they are located
   d. none of the above

3. An individual has an expectation of privacy
   a. in an open field
   b. in his curtilage
   c. in his jail cell
   d. when he is in a public place

4. The plain-view doctrine
   a. applies only to the sense of sight
   b. does not apply to aerial searches
   c. applies even if the officer uses a flashlight to augment his sense of sight
   d. has been rejected by the U.S. Supreme Court

5. A search warrant
   a. can be obtained if an officer is able to show that it is more likely than not that evidence connected to the crime will be found
   b. can be obtained if the officer describes in general what she plans to search for
   c. can be obtained without judicial review
   d. is not something the courts encourage officers to obtain

6. Probable cause
   a. is easily defined
   b. exists if it is more probable than not that a crime was committed
   c. can be based on generalized suspicion
   d. is less than reasonable suspicion

7. Arrest warrants
   a. are frequently required by the courts
   b. must be based on information personally observed by an officer
   c. can be obtained when an officer is present and has probable cause to believe a crime has been or is about to be committed
   d. is not required when an officer is arresting someone in his home

8. A search warrant is needed to search
   a. something in plain view
   b. a curtilage
   c. an open field
   d. incident to a lawful arrest

9. In order for an officer to seize something in plain view
   a. the incriminating nature of the object must at some point be apparent to the officer
   b. the officer can rely only on her sense of sight
   c. the officer must be present lawfully
   d. none of the above

10. Inventory searches are permitted without getting a warrant
    a. to protect the contents of the suspect's vehicles from theft and damage
    b. to protect the police from later claims of theft by the suspect
    c. to protect others from being hurt by the contents in the suspect's vehicle
    d. all of the above

11. A warrant is not necessary if a search is made
    a. for purposes of a health, safety, or fire inspection
    b. by officials at the border who believe the suspect is involved in smuggling or immigration violations
    c. by a government employee and the search is work-related
    d. all of the above

12. A stop and frisk
    a. is permitted only if an officer has probable cause to believe that the suspect committed a crime
    b. can be used to search for evidence of a crime
    c. allows an officer to search a suspect for weapons
    d. can be conducted of both inner and outer clothing

13. A person is probably considered "seized" if
    a. an officer displays a weapon
    b. an officer physically touches the suspect
    c. an officer uses a threatening tone of voice
    d. all of the above

14. A suspect cannot be detained
    a. indefinitely
    b. longer than is reasonably necessary to confirm or dispel the officer's suspicions
    c. for as long as it takes the officer to establish probable cause
    d. none of the above

15. *Miranda* warnings
    a. apply only to custodial interrogations
    b. implicate the Fifth Amendment only
    c. notify defendants of the right to bail
    d. all of the above

16. *Miranda* warnings include
    a. the right to remain silent
    b. the right to have counsel appointed
    c. the fact that anything you say can be used against you in the courtroom
    d. all of the above

17. A waiver of *Miranda* rights is voluntary
    a. even if it is the result of intoxication
    b. as long as it is done intelligently and knowingly
    c. despite resulting from a language barrier
    d. cannot be recorded or videotaped

18. A custodial interrogation
    a. occurs when a reasonable person would not feel free to leave
    b. is more likely to occur in someone's home than at the station house
    c. takes place even when a suspect is stopped and questioned regarding a minor traffic violation
    d. does not take place until a suspect is formally arrested

19. Interrogation
    a. is basically synonymous with questioning
    b. includes asking identification questions
    c. occurs when the police ask questions they know are reasonably likely to lead to incriminating responses
    d. all of the above

20. *Miranda* warnings
    a. are more essential to police work today than they were 20 years ago
    b. are not required when public safety is threatened
    c. cannot be legally waived if the police fail to tell a suspect that an attorney has been retained and wants to speak with him before he is questioned
    d. all of the above

21. When a suspect is booked, he is
    a. photographed
    b. fingerprinted
    c. tested for blood alcohol and/or drugs (if appropriate)
    d. all of the above

22. Bail can be based on
    a. the defendant's financial status
    b. the weight of evidence against the defendant
    c. the defendant's character
    d. all of the above

23. At a grand jury proceeding
    a. the prosecution is seeking an information
    b. the defendant and his attorney are present
    c. the prosecutor is in charge of calling witnesses
    d. the defense attorney has an opportunity to cross-examine the witnesses

24. A grand jury has the power to
    a. subpoena witnesses
    b. investigate people who have not yet been arrested
    c. issue an arrest warrant if it decides probable cause exists
    d. all of the above

25. If a defendant enters a guilty plea, the arraignment judge must ensure that he
    a. understands the nature of the charges
    b. understands the possible punishment
    c. understands the nature of the rights he is waiving
    d. all of the above

26. If a defendant enters a plea of *nolo contendere*
    a. he agrees that the prosecution has sufficient evidence to prove its case but neither admits nor denies the charges
    b. he is treated as if he entered a plea of not guilty
    c. his plea is considered an admission of guilt
    d. his plea can be used against him in a later civil trial

27. Plea bargaining
    a. ensures that justice is done
    b. is highly criticized
    c. resolves only about 10 percent of all criminal cases
    d. has been abolished in about half the states

28. Attorneys
    a. cannot say anything if their client perpetrates a fraud on the court
    b. must withdraw immediately if they discover that their client intends to perjure himself or herself
    c. cannot make false statements of law or fact
    d. must advise the court if their client indicates he or she may commit a crime sometime in the future

29. The *Model Rules* suggest that an attorney who knows a client intends to perjure himself or herself on the stand
    a. counsel with the client to change his or her mind
    b. ask the court's permission to withdraw
    c. disclose the false testimony to the court
    d. do each of the above in the order given

30. In all states
    a. attorneys must reveal information likely to result in death or substantial bodily harm
    b. attorneys can reveal future crimes, whether those crimes are serious or not
    c. attorneys can disclose information that could lead to the commission of a crime that could substantially injure the property or financial interests of another
    d. none of the above

31. An indigent defendant
    a. must be appointed counsel if he is charged with a felony
    b. must be appointed counsel if he is charged with a felony or a misdemeanor
    c. is not allowed to represent himself *pro se*
    d. need not be appointed counsel if he is a state court defendant

32. Critical stages in the criminal justice process during which counsel must be provided indigent defendants include
    a. preliminary hearing
    b. arraignment
    c. post-trial sentencing
    d. all of the above

33. A defendant is entitled to representation
    a. during a photo identification
    b. during a pretrial lineup if he has been formally charged
    c. when the police draw blood
    d. when the police take a handwriting sample

34. A criminal defendant who alleges ineffective assistance of counsel
    a. must prove that his attorney was less competent than the average attorney
    b. must prove that his attorney was not reasonably competent
    c. must prove that his attorney's deficient performance could possibly have prejudiced his defense
    d. must prove that his attorney's deficient performance undoubtedly resulted in his conviction

FILL IN THE BLANK

35. A suspect is under _____ when a reasonable person believes that he is no longer free to leave.

36. Individuals have a high _____ _____ in their homes and in their _____ (the area surrounding their dwelling place), which is why the police cannot search those places without a warrant or under some exception to the warrant requirement.

37. An officer has a right to enter a field next to a suspect's barn because individuals have no expectation of privacy in an _____.

38. An officer who is called to someone's home because that person is said to be disturbing the peace has a right to seize drugs he sees in _____.

39. Generally speaking, officers must obtain a _____ (a court document authorizing the police to search and seize certain items) before searching a home.

40. When an officer has _____ to believe that a crime has been committed and that the person he wants to arrest has committed it, he has grounds to obtain an _____ _____ (a court document authorizing arrest).

41. An officer can arrest a suspect in his home without getting a warrant if the officer is in _____ of the suspect or if some other _____ (emergency) circumstance exists.

42. If an arrest turns out to unlawful, any evidence gathered from a search incident to that arrest will have to be _____.

43. When officers have _____ _____ (a belief based on specific, articulable facts) that a person has committed or is about to commit a crime, they have a right to _____ (temporarily detain) that person and conduct a _____ (pat down of the outer clothing).

44. A person is considered _____ for purposes of the Fourth Amendment when a reasonable person would conclude he was no longer free to go.

45. A suspect need not be given _____ (warnings about his right to remain silent, to have counsel, etc.) until he is the subject of a _____, which begins when a suspect's freedom has been deprived in a significant way and questioning has begun.

46. At a defendant's _____ _____ (when he is first taken before the judge), the judge sets _____, which is the security given by the defendant to the court to guarantee his presence at trial in exchange for immediate release from custody. A judge can require the defendant to _____ (pay money and promise to appear later in court) or can _____ _____ (requiring only that the defendant promise to return to court).

47. A defendant's case is reviewed to determine if probable cause exists to bind the defendant over for trial at either a _____ (in which a jury listens to evidence presented by the prosecutor) or a _____ (in which a judge listens to evidence presented by the prosecutor). If the jury finds the existence of probable cause, it will issue an _____ (a written accusation that the defendant committed a crime), and if the judge concludes probable cause

exists, the prosecutor will issue an _____, accusing the defendant of having committed a crime.

48. At a defendant's _____, the judge informs the defendant of the charges being brought and the defendant enters a plea.

49. Most criminal cases do not go to trial but are instead resolved by a _____, an agreement by the defendant to plead guilty in exchange for the prosecutor dropping or reducing some charges or recommending a lesser sentence to the judge.

50. An _____ defendant (one lacking the financial resources necessary to retain counsel) must be appointed either a public defender or _____ (a private attorney paid by the state on a contractual basis) if he is charged with a _____ (crime for which the sentence is one year or more in a prison) or a _____ (a crime for which the sentence is less than a year in jail) if the possibility of a jail sentence exists.

51. Any criminal defendant has the option of appearing _____ (without legal representation).

52. Counsel must be provided to indigent defendants at any _____ in the process.

53. Indigent defendants have a right to counsel at a pretrial _____ (where a witness picks the suspect out of a group of people) if they have been formally charged.

TRUE OR FALSE

_____ 54. The highest expectation of privacy exists in one's automobile.

_____ 55. A suspect has an expectation of privacy in his trash even when he puts that trash in the garbage can outside his home.

_____ 56. An officer can seize an object that he recognizes as contraband as long as he has a lawful right to be present.

_____ 57. The courts encourage officers to get arrest warrants more than they encourage them to get search warrants.

_____ 58. Many states prohibit officers from making warrantless misdemeanor arrests unless the person commits the crime in their presence.

_____ 59. An officer can lawfully search if the defendant consents to that search, even if her consent is not voluntary.

_____ 60. A third party can never consent to the search of a suspect's premises.

_____ 61. Officers are allowed to search the area in the immediate control of a suspect after arresting that suspect.

_____ 62. If a suspect is arrested in his home, the police can do a "protective sweep" of the premises if they reasonably believe that another person who might be dangerous to the officers is in the home.

____ 63. If an officer arrests an occupant of a vehicle, he can search the passenger compartment but not the glove compartment, luggage, or boxes in the vehicle.

____ 64. If an officer has probable cause to believe that a vehicle contains contraband, she can search the vehicle and any closed containers in the vehicle.

____ 65. If an officer reasonably believes that a suspect is about to destroy evidence, she can forgo getting a warrant.

____ 66. If nothing in an officer's initial encounter dispels his fears for personal safety as well as the safety of others, he can conduct a limited search of the suspect's outer clothing.

____ 67. Any encounter between a suspect and a police officer constitutes a "stop."

____ 68. A suspect is considered seized when he is being chased by the police.

____ 69. An officer must release a suspect he has temporarily detained if he cannot establish probable cause.

____ 70. The rationale for the Fifth Amendment is that the state must prove its own case against a defendant without trying to coerce the defendant into providing evidence that could be used to convict him.

____ 71. Even though a suspect has invoked her right to counsel, she can still be questioned.

____ 72. Many police departments videotape or record suspects waiving their *Miranda* rights.

____ 73. Any statement obtained in violation of a defendant's *Miranda* rights cannot be used by the prosecution except to impeach the defendant.

____ 74. An officer must *Mirandize* a suspect before asking for such information as the suspect's name, address, height, and weight.

____ 75. An officer cannot ask a suspect that he arrests in a public place where he left his gun without first *Mirandizing* the suspect.

____ 76. If the police deceive a suspect or his attorney, the suspect's waiver of *Miranda* rights will undoubtedly be considered invalid.

____ 77. If a suspect is to be detained after being booked, the police have the right to search him and inventory his possessions.

____ 78. A judge cannot deny a defendant bail even if she believes the defendant is likely to flee or that he poses a risk to the community.

____ 79. In exchange for posting a bond, a bailbondsman charges a minor fee, usually about one percent of the bail set by the judge.

____ 80. Bailbondsmen typically go to great lengths to recover from clients who jump bail.

____ 81. Defendants who lack sufficient assets to post a bond must stay in jail until trial because the courts refuse to allow defendants to be released on their own recognizance.

____ 82. The federal government and about half of the states no longer use grand juries.

____ 83. Grand jury proceedings are open proceedings.

____ 84. Many defendants waive their right to a grand jury and opt for the expediency of a preliminary hearing.

____ 85. Anyone called as a witness before a grand jury can be represented by counsel at the proceeding.

____ 86. Grand juries can be used as investigative tools.

____ 87. The only two possible pleas a defendant can enter are "guilty" or "not guilty."

____ 88. Plea bargaining works to the benefit of guilty defendants, but has no effect on innocent defendants.

____ 89. Plea bargaining expedites the resolution of criminal cases, but does not necessarily ensure that justice is done.

____ 90. Attorneys cannot counsel a client to commit a crime or assist a client in committing a crime.

____ 91. Attorneys cannot present false evidence, but if they discover at a later time that false evidence was presented to the court, they are not required to rectify the fraud.

____ 92. If a criminal defendant insists on perjuring himself, the courts are uniform in requiring attorneys to disclose the perjury if the judge refuses to allow them to withdraw.

____ 93. Under the *Model Rules*, an attorney must disclose a client's intent to commit future crimes if she believes the criminal act "is likely to result in imminent death or substantial bodily harm."

____ 94. A defendant who appears *pro se* must do so knowingly and intelligently and cannot later claim ineffective assistance of counsel.

____ 95. Indigent defendants always have a right to counsel at a pretrial lineup.

____ 96. Defendants have a right to counsel when the police take a hair sample or fingerprints.

____ 97. Appellate courts should presume that an attorney's performance that is being reviewed fell within the wide range of acceptable conduct.

PART B

"Assault Charges?" Repeated Martha Incredulously, Rolling Her Eyes. "Gee, Tim, This Just Keeps Getting Better and Better."

"I've met several folks in the law library doing their own legal research and I always try to dissuade them from going the *pro se* route," commented Tim. "I know that I'd have been in much worse shape if I hadn't had Celandra and Matthew working for me." Seeing the question mark on Martha's face, he added, "For one thing, they got the assault charges against me dismissed."

"*Assault charges?*" repeated Martha incredulously, rolling her eyes. "Gee, Tim, this just keeps getting better and better. Being a convicted drug pusher is bad enough, but now you're telling me you assaulted someone."

"I believe he said those charges were dismissed," corrected John. "Why don't we give Tim a chance to tell us what happened?"

"Please do," said Martha stiffly.

"If you remember, I ran away when I heard someone say 'Stop, I want to talk to you.' I didn't know I was running away from a cop. When he tackled me, I fought to get away and landed a few good kicks before he handcuffed me and turned me over. That was the first time I realized I'd hit a cop."

◆ **LOCAL LINKS** ◆

How are felonies and misdemeanors defined in your state?
What term is used to describe offenses that carry penalties of fines but no incarceration?

◆ **LOCAL LINKS** ◆

Has your state adopted all or parts of the *Model Penal Code?*

Model Penal Code   a set of uniform criminal laws proposed by the American Law Institute, parts of which have been adopted by most state's legislatures

corpus delicti   body of a crime

mens rea   intent

actus reus   act

causation   link between the intent and the act

ELEMENTS OF A CRIME

Crimes can be divided into three categories: felonies, misdemeanors, and *petty offenses*. In most states, felonies are crimes carrying a prison sentence of one or more years; misdemeanors are those crimes resulting in a fine or a jail sentence of less than a year; petty offenses are violations of state law resulting in a fine but no incarceration. Some felonies are classified as *capital crimes* because they carry a death sentence (capital punishment).

Every state has the right to create its own criminal code, which has resulted in considerable diversity among the states. What constitutes a crime in one state is not necessarily a crime in another state; by the same token, the punishment for similar crimes can vary significantly from state to state. Motivated by this lack of uniformity, the American Law Institute—a group of law professors, judges, and practicing lawyers—gathered in 1956 with the intent of simplifying and standardizing American criminal law. They developed the *Model Penal Code,* a proposed set of uniform criminal laws, parts of which have been adopted by most state legislatures.

No matter whether a crime has been defined in accordance with the **Model Penal Code** or derived from the common law, or some combination thereof, the ***corpus delicti*** (body) of every crime consists of three elements: (1) ***mens rea*** —intent; (2) ***actus reus***—act; and (3) **causation**—direct link between the *mens rea* and the *actus reus*.

Mens Rea

The *Model Penal Code* assigns one of four mental states to every crime.

◆ A criminal act may be purposeful—that is, intending to cause a specific harm.
◆ A second mental state is knowing. An individual who perpetrates a crime may do it knowingly knowing, that is, being aware that a specific harm could occur as a direct result of his or her act.

For more information about what crimes are and how they are defined, go to *www.nolo.com/encyclopedia/crim_ency.html*, click on "Criminal Law: An Overview," and go to the articles entitled "What Is a Crime?" and "How to Interpret Criminal Statutes."

◆ A third mental state is recklessness. A perpetrator is reckless if he is aware of and consciously disregards a substantial and unjustifiable risk that harm will occur (conscious risk creation).

◆ A fourth and final mental state is criminal negligence, the failure to perceive a substantial and unjustifiable risk that harm will occur (unconscious risk creation). With both recklessness and criminal negligence, the risk must be of such a nature and degree that failure to perceive it is a gross deviation from the standard of care a reasonable person would observe in that situation.

The differences in mental states are most clearly demonstrated using homicide. If David aims a gun at Victoria and shoots her, intending to kill her, he kills her purposefully. If David walks into a crowded bar and begins firing his gun and strikes Victoria, he kills her knowingly. Even though he did not intend to kill Victoria, he knew that firing a weapon into a crowded room could result in someone's getting shot; thus, he acted knowingly. If David is celebrating the Fourth of July in his backyard by firing gunshots into the air and one of the bullets strikes his next-door neighbor, Victoria, he kills her recklessly. Firing a gun into the air in an area where people may be present constitutes a conscious disregard of a substantial risk of harm and is, therefore, reckless. If David is cleaning his gun while talking with Victoria and the gun (which, unbeknownst to David, is loaded) accidentally discharges, David is criminally negligent. Although David may not have perceived a risk of the gun discharging, a reasonable person would have checked the gun before cleaning it. Failure to do so constitutes criminal negligence. Note that criminal negligence goes beyond tort negligence in that it is a *gross* deviation from the reasonable standard of care.

infer draw a conclusion based on given facts

As you might suspect, defendants rarely explicitly state their mental state. Therefore, jurors must **infer** from witnesses' observations and the defendant's statements and actions what the defendant's mental state was. Suppose a defendant claims, for example, that he killed his wife's lover out of a sudden rage of passion upon catching the two of them in bed together. If witnesses testify that the defendant knew of his wife's affair, that he talked of getting even with her someday, and that when he purchased a gun he told the gun dealer that he would now be able to "even the score with someone," the jury could reasonably conclude that the defendant killed purposely and not simply recklessly.

The distinction between mental states is not always clear. In homicide cases, for example, jurors may find it difficult to distinguish recklessness from knowing or from criminal negligence. In those circumstances, they are likely to be swayed more by the atrocity of the murder than they are by fine legal distinctions.

For more information about criminal mental states, go to *www.nolo.com/encyclopedia/crim* ency.html, click on "Criminal Law: An Overview," and go to the article entitled "How a Defendant's Mental State Affects His or Her Responsibility."

Figure 7-4
Corpus Delicti

CORPUS DELICTI

Mens Rea
Purposely
Knowingly
Recklessly
Criminal Negligence

Actus Reus
Affirmative action
Omission
Possession
Incomplete act

Causation

![Putting It Into Practice 7.12:]

Putting It Into Practice 7.12:

What is the highest mental state that could exist under the *Model Penal Code* in each of the following cases?

(a) Gordon beats his wife to teach her a lesson. He does not want to kill her, but he is aware she could die.

(b) Gordon aims a gun at his wife while he knows she is sitting on the toilet and fires a shot through the door, killing her instantly.

(c) Gordon and his wife are playing around with a gun they both think is unloaded. The gun discharges and Gordon's wife dies.

(d) Gordon is playing around with his gun while he and his wife are camping. He shoots at a noise he hears in the bushes, not realizing it is his wife. She dies from the bullet wound.

Actus Reus

The *actus reus* can be an affirmative action taken by the defendant, such as hitting another person. This act must, however, be voluntary. Hitting someone as a result of having an epileptic seizure, for example, is not a voluntary act. (Although some courts have held those suffering from epilepsy criminally responsible for the harm caused in a motor vehicle accident resulting from their seizure, reasoning that seizures can be prevented with proper medication.)

Possession itself constitutes the *actus reus* of cases involving illegal possession of drugs, weapons, or pornographic materials. In some instances, failure to do something required by law (an omission) can constitute the *actus reus*. A mother, for example, can be charged with child abuse for failing to take reasonable steps to intervene when her husband beats her child. The law requires her to do what is reasonably necessary to protect her child.

People can be charged with a crime even if they are prevented for some reason from completing it. Inchoate (incomplete) crimes include **attempt, solicitation,** and **conspiracy**. A defendant commits an attempt if he takes some steps that go beyond mere preparation toward committing a crime; those preliminary steps are

attempt taking steps that go beyond mere preparation toward committing a crime

solicitation asking another person to commit a crime

conspiracy agreement between two or more people to commit a crime

considered the *actus reus*. If David attempts to shoot Victoria, but is unable to do because he is unaware that the gun is unloaded, he can be charged with attempted murder.

Solicitation occurs when a defendant asks another person to commit a crime in exchange for some kind of reward; the *actus reus* is the communication made by the solicitor. If David asks Duncan to shoot Victoria and Duncan pretends to agree and then tells the police about David's request, David can be charged with solicitation of murder.

Conspiracy involves an agreement between two or more people to commit some kind of criminal act; a conspiracy is complete once one of the parties commits some kind of "overt" act (the *actus reus*). If David and Duncan plotted to kill Victoria, but their plans were foiled because the police discovered the plot, they could be charged with conspiracy if one of them committed an "overt" act, such as purchasing a gun. Prosecutors are usually fond of the crime of conspiracy because it is relatively easy to prove, it often carries the same penalties as the crime being conspired to commit, and it can be used in factual circumstances that would make proof of a completed crime difficult.

Causation

As with tort cases, criminal law requires proof of causation. If the connection between the defendant's intent and the ultimate consequence is too remote, the defendant will not be held responsible. If, for example, David chases after Victoria with a knife and she runs outside into a storm where she is struck by lightning, the courts will not hold David responsible for Victoria's death. Her death would be considered an "act of God" and that act would supersede David's act of chasing Victoria as the cause of her death. If, however, Victoria were to have run out into traffic and be injured by an oncoming car and then die as a result of negligent medical care, David could be charged with her murder. To reach this conclusion, a court would have to conclude that dying as a result of negligent medical care is a "natural and probable consequence" (in other words, a foreseeable consequence) of having been chased by someone with a knife.

"Isn't hitting an officer an aggravated assault?" asked Martha.

"Oh, yeah," confirmed Tim. "I was in big trouble. Hitting someone is an assault and that's a misdemeanor. But hitting a police officer is an aggravated assault, which is a felony. In Arizona, it's a class six felony."

GRADATION OF OFFENSES

Crimes are commonly divided into the following categories.

Crimes Against People

1. Homicide

   ◆ Murder—intentionally or knowingly causing the death of a human being
   ◆ Manslaughter—recklessly causing the death of a human being
   ◆ Negligent homicide—negligently causing the death of a human being

2. Assault—intentionally, knowingly, or recklessly causing physical injury to another person

3. Kidnapping—knowingly restraining another person with the intent of committing specified felonies
4. Robbery—theft of personal property using force or threatening to use force
5. Sexual assault—intentionally or knowingly engaging in sexual intercourse with any person without the consent of that person

Crimes Against Property

1. Arson—knowingly and unlawfully damaging a property or structure by knowingly causing a fire or explosion
2. Burglary—entering a structure with the intent of committing a theft or any felony
3. Forgery—making, completing, or altering a written instrument with the intent to defraud
4. Theft—knowingly controlling the property of another with the intent of depriving him or her of such property
5. Trespass—knowingly entering or remaining unlawfully on the property of another

Crimes Against the Government

1. Bribery—conferring or agreeing to confer any benefit upon a public servant or party officer with the intent to influence that person's vote, opinion, judgment, or exercise of discretion in that person's official capacity
2. Interfering with judicial proceedings—knowingly disobeying or resisting the lawful order or mandate of the court
3. Perjury—making a false sworn statement in reference to a material issue

Crimes Against the Public Order

1. Carrying a concealed weapon—knowingly carrying a deadly weapon without a permit
2. Disorderly conduct—engaging in fighting or seriously disruptive behavior with the intent of disturbing the peace or quiet of a person, family, or neighborhood
3. Possession of drugs—possession of drugs whose use is outlawed or that can be possessed only when prescribed by a licensed physician
4. Prostitution—engaging in, agreeing to, or offering to engage in sexual conduct with another person under a fee arrangement

Each of these crimes is graded according to the seriousness of the harm created. Under the *Model Penal Code*, for example, felonies are divided into three categories, with first degree felonies being the most serious and third degree felonies being the least serious. In Arizona, where Tim was arrested, felonies are divided into six degrees (ranging from the most serious—class 1 felony, to the least serious—class 6 felony) and misdemeanors into three degrees (ranging from the most serious—class 1 misdemeanor, to the least serious—class 3 misdemeanor). Tim was charged with an aggravated assault (because he assaulted a police officer), which is a class 6 felony. The class of felony, along with other factors, determines the sentence the judge can impose. (See discussion on sentencing later in this chapter.)

◆ **LOCAL LINKS** ◆

How are felonies and misdemeanors graded in your state?

Figure 7-5
Criminal Defenses

CRIMINAL DEFENSES

Self-Defense
Defense of Property
Defense of Third Party
Duress
Necessity
Infancy
Intoxication
Insanity
Entrapment

"But Wasn't It Your Word Against the Officer's?"

"So how did your attorney get the assault charges dropped?" inquired Martha.

"By arguing that I acted in self-defense. I truly thought someone was attacking me when the officer pulled me down to the ground. I did everything I could to get away."

"But you were wrong. You were actually attacking a police officer. How could you claim self-defense?" questioned Martha.

"Because in my mind I thought I had to defend myself. The courts refer to that as a **subjective** belief. Celandra argued that a reasonable person in my circumstances would have believed he was under attack—an **objective** belief. Celandra apparently proved to the prosecutor's satisfaction that I was subjectively and objectively justified in using physical force to defend myself."

"But wasn't it your word against the officer's?" Martha persisted.

"When we deposed the officer, I could see that he really was convinced that I'd seen him and that he'd identified himself as an officer before I began to run. But when Celandra pressed him, he couldn't remember exactly what he'd said. It obviously hadn't occurred to him that, with the lights across the street from the bar shining directly into my eyes, it would have been difficult for me to see anyone standing between me and those lights."

"And, I take it, that's where he was standing."

"Yes. One night Matthew took me back to the scene to help him understand exactly what had happened. When I stood next to the bar and he stood where the officer said he'd been, I couldn't see Matthew at all because I was looking right into the glare of the lights. Based on this argument and the officer's shaky testimony about what he'd said, the prosecutor opted to drop the assault charges."

"Which is precisely why it's so important to go back and check out the scene," remarked John enthusiastically. "This is what I try to get new attorneys to understand, but some of them just don't seem to get it until they have an experience like you did."

---

subjective   standard that considers the actual belief of the defendant

objective   standard that considers what a reasonable person in the same situation as the defendant would have believed

DEFENSES

Defendants have several defenses they can raise. Some of them completely exonerate defendants, thereby relieving them of all responsibility, while others negate certain aspects of their crime, reducing their culpability (responsibility) but not totally absolving them.

Use of Force

An individual is allowed to use physical force to defend himself if he reasonably believes such force is imminently necessary for self-protection. He can use only a reasonable amount of force (no more than is necessary to repel the attack), and must

◆ **LOCAL LINKS** ◆

Does your state require an individual to retreat before using deadly force?

stop using force as soon as the aggressor indicates an intent to withdraw. Self-defense cannot be raised by those who initiate an attack.

Deadly physical force (force that could cause death or serious physical injury) can be used only when reasonably necessary to protect oneself against a threat of deadly physical force. The use of excessive force invalidates the defense. Someone who is being attacked by an aggressor using fists is most likely unjustified in using a gun to defend himself. Many jurisdictions require defendants to retreat before using deadly force. Retreat is not required, however, of a defendant in his home (the so-called "castle exception") or if retreat would further endanger him.

Force can be used to protect property although in most states deadly force cannot be used. The rationale for denying the use of deadly force is that property can be replaced (most property is insured), and even if the thief were convicted, he would not receive the death penalty. Therefore, the person whose property is being stolen or damaged is not justified in imposing the death penalty. Spring guns and other mechanical devices generally cannot be used to defend property in the home-owner's absence because they are considered deadly force.

◆ **LOCAL LINKS** ◆

How much force can be used in your state to defend property?

In some states, force can be used to defend a third person under attack as long as that person is justified in using self-defense. If, for example, a defendant were to come across a person being subdued by an undercover police officer and mistakenly believe that the person was under attack, he would not be justified in using physical force to defend that person. In other states, a defendant is justified in defending a third person as long as he reasonably believes the use of force is necessary. In those states, the defendant would be justified in using force to defend the person being subdued by the undercover officer.

◆ **LOCAL LINKS** ◆

Under what circumstances can an individual defend a third person in your state?

Duress and Necessity

Because a criminal act must be voluntary, a person forced to commit a crime can claim duress as a defense. If a defendant can prove that he committed a crime only because he was threatened with the use of physical force, he will not be held responsible for those criminal acts. If, for example, a defendant steals something because someone is holding a gun to his head, he will not be held responsible for the theft because he was under duress. Duress is not a defense if the threat is to destroy the defendant's property or reputation. It is also not a defense to certain crimes, such as murder, and it is not a defense to threats of future harm. The threat must be to cause imminent—not future—physical harm.

Necessity requires the defendant to prove that he took an action to avoid a greater harm than the harm he caused. If a defendant is in a boat and a big storm comes up, he is justified in tying the boat to someone's dock to prevent it from being destroyed and himself from drowning. The defendant may have to pay for any damages incurred by the dock, but he will not be criminally responsible for the trespass committed. Some defendants have raised necessity as a defense when they stole food to feed their family, but the law generally does not allow such a defense. The rationale is that social service agencies are available to feed the poor and that allowing people to raise economic necessity as a defense would result in abuse of that defense.

Infancy

conclusive presumption a presumption that could not be rebutted

Under the common law, a **conclusive presumption** (a presumption that can not be rebutted) existed that children under the age of seven were incapable of forming criminal intent. During the writing of this text, a six-year-old boy obtained a gun and killed one of his classmates. No matter what the prosecution might be able to prove about this boy, he cannot be held responsible for his act because he is conclusively incapable of forming the *mens rea* required of homicide. There is a **rebuttable presumption** (a presumption that can be overcome with the presentation of evidence) that children between the ages of seven and fourteen are not capable of forming a criminal intent.

Intoxication

For certain crimes, being under the influence of alcohol or drugs can sometimes be used as a defense. The reasoning behind this defense is that the defendant is unable to form the requisite intent because of his intoxicated state. If the defendant formed the intent before becoming intoxicated, he cannot use this defense. Nor can this defense be used in cases having a mental state of recklessness (such as drunk driving). It can be used in crimes having a mental state of purposefulness (such as first degree murder), not to absolve the defendant, but to reduce his culpability. In a murder case, for example, an intoxicated defendant could have first degree murder charges reduced to manslaughter if he could prove that he was too drunk to have purposefully killed the victim. Involuntary intoxication is a complete defense as long as the defendant formed the intent to commit the crime after unintentionally becoming intoxicated. Such cases occur when someone "doctors" another person's drink or gives a person something to ingest that is laced with a drug.

Insanity

Insanity is a defense because an individual who is incapable of forming a mental intent (no *mens rea*) or has no control over his actions (no *actus reus*) cannot be held responsible for his actions. Legal insanity has little or no relationship to medical insanity. Someone who is institutionalized in a facility that treats the mentally ill may be considered sane for legal purposes. Although all states allow insanity as a defense, considerable disagreement exists about the standard that should be employed for assessing insanity. Three standards are in use today: the M'Naughten test, the irresistible impulse test, and the substantial capacity test.

The M'Naughten test is the oldest and most commonly used of the three tests, and is sometimes referred to as the "right-wrong" test. It originated in England in a case in which the defendant, M'Naughten, was tried for killing the secretary to the prime minister of England, having confused the secretary with the prime minister. M'Naughten was not held responsible for the murder because he suffered from a mental disease or defect that prevented from him from knowing what he did and that what he did was wrong. Under this test, a defendant is considered insane if he does not know the difference between right and wrong or if he does not comprehend what he is doing.

The irresistible impulse test is more liberal in defining insanity than the M'Naughten test. Under the M'Naughten test, a person who commits criminal acts knowing them to be wrong but who cannot control himself is considered sane; under the irresistible impulse test, that same person would be considered insane. Under this test, a person who knows an act to be wrong but who commits it because of an irresistible impulse to do so is thought to be insane. This impulse cannot simply be one that the defendant failed to resist, but one that he lacked the ability to control.

The most liberal test is the one proposed by the American Law Institute: the substantial capacity test. Under this test, an individual who lacks the ability to "appreciate" the wrongfulness of his conduct or lacks the ability to "conform" his

Figure 7-6
Insanity Tests

INSANITY TESTS

M'Naughten
Does the defendant know what he is doing and, if so, does he know that what he is doing is wrong?

Irresistible Impulse
Even if the defendant knows that what he is doing is wrong, does he have an irresistible impulse to do it anyway?

Substantial Capacity
Does the defendant appreciate the wrongfulness of his conduct or does he lack the ability to conform his conduct to what he knows to be right?

◆ **LOCAL LINKS** ◆
What test is used to determine legal insanity in your state?

conduct to what he knows to be right is insane. The lack of ability to control one's conduct is less restrictive than that defined by the irresistible impulse test. Many people who would not be considered insane under either the M'Naughten or irresistible impulse tests would qualify under the substantial capacity test.

In addition to being able to claim insanity at the time the criminal act was committed, defendants can also claim insanity at any stage of their trial. If they are unable to cooperate in their own defense and to understand the nature of the charges against them, they cannot be tried. Although the issue of insanity is frequently and fiercely debated, insanity is rarely successful as a defense. In fact, is it raised successfully in less than one percent of all criminal cases.

Traditionally, a successful plea of insanity was equivalent to a "not guilty" verdict. The defendant was committed to a mental institution, and when treatment was completed, he was released—even if the treatment time was less than the time that would have been served for a prison sentence. Some states now use a "guilty but mentally ill" verdict. Under this verdict, defendants are put in a hospital for treatment, and if they have time remaining on their sentence when they are released from the hospital, they serve that time in prison.

Entrapment

entrapment law enforcement inducing someone to commit a crime

Entrapment occurs when law enforcement induces a defendant to commit a crime. In some states, entrapment applies only to those defendants who are innocent (who are not predisposed toward committing the crime), and in other states, the predisposition of the defendant is irrelevant. In the latter states, the rationale is that the

---

NET NEWS

To read a transcript of a debate about abolishing the insanity defense, go to *www.debatesdebates.com/programs/transcript110.hmtl.*

For more information about common defenses, go to *www.nolo.com/encyclopedia/crim_ency.html*, click on "Criminal Law: An Overview," and go to the article entitled "Common Defenses to Criminal Charges."

444   ◆   Chapter 7

◆ **LOCAL LINKS** ◆

In your state, can defendants who are predisposed toward committing a crime claim entrapment?

government should not, as a matter of public policy, use its resources to entice its citizens into committing crimes. In essence, entrapment is designed to punish law enforcement for its use of inappropriate enforcement techniques.

Entrapment arises most frequently in sting operations, in drug and vice enforcement (e.g., in arrests for illegal drug transactions and prostitution where an undercover officer is used), and with other consensual crimes where victims and witnesses are hard to find. The question of entrapment may arise if an officer (posing as someone buying narcotics) asks to buy heroin from someone who does not first approach him. In some states, the police will arrange for a series of "buys" from the same defendant to prove the defendant's predisposition toward committing the crime and negate the defendant's argument that he was entrapped.

Entrapment applies only to inducement by the government. If a private individual induces someone else to commit a crime and then contacts the police, entrapment has not occurred. The entrapment defense focuses on the wrongdoing of the government, not the actions of private citizens.

Putting It Into Practice 7.13:

Consider the following situations.

(a) Ed owns a shop that has been burglarized repeatedly. He tries all kinds of security alarms and a watchdog, but to no avail. In his frustration, he rigs together a mechanical device with a gun that goes off if somebody triggers the device. Some kids break into the shop one night and the gun goes off, striking one of them in the leg, causing him to have his leg amputated. Is Ed criminally responsible for the boy's injuries?

(b) Mildred is home alone one evening when she hears a noise. She calls out and asks who is there. No one answers, but the person continues to struggle with the lock. Mildred runs to get a gun and fires it when the door opens. To her horror, she discovers that she has shot her son, who was intoxicated and could not find his key. Should she be tried for his death?

(c) Brian comes home one evening in a drunken rage and kills his wife. Can he raise his intoxication as a defense?

(d) Suppose Brian has been treated for schizophrenia and that, when he killed his wife, he had not been taking his medication for several days. What will he have to show in a state that uses the M'Naughten test if he argues that he was insane?

(e) Billie, who is five, kills his three-year-old brother while they are playing cowboys and Indians with their father's gun. Billy has been warned repeatedly not to touch any guns in the house. Can the state prosecute Billy?

(f) Duane steals some money from the bank where he works because his next-door neighbor, Bruce, threatens to expose Duane's extramarital affair to his wife if he does not steal the money. Can he raise any legitimate defense?

 (1) Supposer Bruce is a security guard at the bank and that, instead of threatening Duane, he encourages him to commit the heist and then calls the police after Duane is successful. Can Duane claim entrapment?

 (2) Would your answer change if Bruce were doing this at the request of a police officer?

"The Court Created the Exclusionary Rule as Its Remedy Because It Knew Officers Would Be Deterred from Engaging in Unlawful Conduct If They Knew They Would Be Prevented from Introducing Any Evidence They Obtained."

"Well, at least you had a legitimate defense. You didn't just use some technicality to get yourself off," commented Martha.

"Some technicality like the **exclusionary rule**?" asked Tim, an edge in his voice.

"Isn't that the rule that allows criminals to get off just because the police made some minor mistake?" responded Martha uneasily, sensing she was about to get another lecture.

"Some little mistake like violating your constitutional rights?" asked John testily. "Did you know that historically the Supreme Court urged the states to find some way to prevent the police from blatantly obtaining evidence illegally? The Court discovered that threats of disciplinary measures being taken and of potential civil lawsuits did not dissuade the police because such consequences rarely occurred. In exasperation, the Court created the exclusionary rule as its remedy because it knew officers would be deterred from engaging in unlawful conduct if they knew they would be prevented from introducing any evidence they obtained."

"All right, Mr. Morgan, I get the point. Did you use the exclusionary rule or some other, uh—" Martha searched for the right word.

"Constitutional defense?" said Tim, filling in the blank. "Yes. As a matter of fact, Celandra was able to get some of the evidence against me suppressed by raising a constitutional defense."

"You aren't going to tell me you committed another crime, are you?" moaned Martha.

"No, but I was carrying some cocaine in the trunk of my vehicle. I had agreed with my dealer to transport it to another buyer the following day but, for obvious reasons, I never made it that far. The officer found it when he searched my vehicle."

"Why did he search your vehicle? Did he see you drive in?" asked Martha.

"No. After I'd asserted my right to keep silent, he asked me whether I'd driven or come on foot. Like an idiot, I told him that I'd driven and even told him where I'd parked the car. The officer decided to impound the car, which gave him the right to inventory it. Celandra argued that the officer's questions constituted an interrogation that violated my assertion of my *Miranda* rights. The court agreed and suppressed evidence of the cocaine found in the car."

---

exclusionary rule prohibition against the prosecution introducing evidence that was obtained in violation of the defendant's constitutional rights

standing a right to make an argument before the Court because one's own constitutional rights have been violated

EXCLUSIONARY RULE

The exclusionary rule prevents the prosecution from introducing evidence that was obtained in violation of the defendant's constitutional rights. If an officer stops a motorist without having reasonable grounds for doing so, any contraband that the officer discovers in the vehicle cannot be introduced at trial because it was discovered as a direct result of the illegal stop. This rule was developed by the Supreme Court as a means of deterring unconstitutional conduct by police officers. The Court reasoned that officers would have little motivation for using illegal means to obtain evidence if they knew they would be unable to present such evidence at trial. A decidedly more liberal Court (known as the "Warren Court" because Chief Justice Earl Warren presided over the Court at that time) than the current Rehnquist Court reasoned that the preservation of judicial integrity dictated that the court not be implicated in unconstitutional invasions of the American people.

The exclusionary rule can be asserted only by those with **standing** (a right to make an argument before the court because one's own constitutional rights have been violated). If a man puts drugs he has in his possession into his girlfriend's purse because

---

NET NEWS

To see an example of a motion to suppress arguing that, under the Exclusionary Rule, evidence should not be admitted because the officer lacked probable cause to seize it, go to *www.quojure.com/archives/seizure.htm*.

case-in-chief the part of the prosecutor's case providing direct proof of the defendant's guilt

he fears that he is going to be searched, and the police illegally search his girlfriend's purse, the man has no standing to argue that his constitutional rights were violated. The violation of the girlfriend's constitutional rights gives her standing, but not him.

Although illegally obtained evidence cannot be introduced by the prosecutor during his **case-in-chief** (the part of the case providing direct proof of the defendant's guilt), it can be introduced to impeach the defendant's testimony made during direct and cross-examination. Illegally obtained evidence can also be used at grand jury hearings.

While the Warren Court represented the heyday for the development of constitutional protections of criminal defendants, the Burger and Rehnquist Courts (both named after their Chief Justice) have been slowly chipping away at the exclusionary rule, creating exception after exception to its applicability. The arguments for and against the exclusionary rule boil down essentially to this: On one side it is argued that the Fourth Amendment was meant to be obeyed, and that if it is obeyed, improperly obtained evidence cannot be used. On the other side, as Justice Cardozo, a famous Supreme Court justice so eloquently articulated, the price to society is too high if the "criminal is to go free because the constable has blundered." *People v. Defore,* 242 N.Y. 13, 21, 150 N.E. 585, 587 (1926).

In 1984, in two landmark cases, *U.S. v. Leon,* 468 U.S. 987, and *Massachusetts v. Sheppard,* 468 U.S. 981, the Burger Court created the "good-faith exception" to the exclusionary rule. In *Leon,* the police relied on a warrant that appeared valid on its face but that was later determined by the appellate courts to be lacking in probable cause. In *Sheppard,* the officers used an improper warrant form (a narcotics form rather than a murder form for the murder they were investigating), but the affidavit correctly described the items for which they were searching. The Court concluded that evidence could be used in the prosecutor's case-in-chief if it was obtained by officers who reasonably relied on a facially valid search warrant that later turned out to be unsupported by probable cause. The exception applies only to cases involving search and arrest warrants and has not yet been considered by the Court in reference to warrantless searches.

The arguments made in these two cases capture the essence of the debate about the pros and cons of protecting the constitutional rights of the accused and of the current concern of policymakers that the price of this protection is too high. In reaching its conclusion, the majority of the Court conducted a "cost-benefit" analysis to determine if the exclusionary rule served any valid purpose. On the "cost" side of the equation was the risk "that some guilty defendants may go free or receive reduced sentences." In contrast, the Court considered the "benefit" side to be minimal in cases, such as these, where the police acted in "objectively reasonable reliance" on a magistrate's issuance of a warrant.

The dissent's cost-benefit analysis relied on different factors. The dissent argued that prosecutors rarely drop cases because of search and seizure problems. The benefit, on the other hand, was not to deter individual officers, but to encourage compliance by police officers across the country. The argument made, in essence, was that the exclusionary rule encouraged police departments to educate their officers and develop procedures that fulfilled the Constitution; the good faith exception would, as one dissenting justice said, "put a premium on police ignorance of the law."

NET NEWS

For a more in-depth discussion of the Exclusionary Rule, go to
http://supreme.lp.findlaw.com/constitution/amendment04/06.html.

Putting It Into Practice 7.14:

Suppose an officer forgets to *Mirandize* Toby before he confesses to his and his friend David's involvement in a crime. Will the prosecution be allowed to introduce evidence of Toby's confession against him? Against David? Can the prosecution argue that the officer acted in good faith and that he simply forgot to give timely *Miranda* warnings?

BONUS POINTERS:

VICTIM RIGHTS

Every American is affected in some way by crime. Eighty-three percent of Americans will be victims of violent crime sometime during their lifetime (Congressional Record, 1990).[3] Out of a desire to meet the needs of crime victims, former President Reagan established a Task Force on Victims of Crime in 1982. In its final report, the Task Force proposed greater victim access to and participation in criminal proceedings. An explosion of federal and state activity has transpired since the issuance of that report, centering on establishing and interpreting crime victims' rights to notice of and presence at critical stages of criminal justice proceedings.

The federal government moved to preserve victims' rights by passing such acts as the Federal Victim and Witness Protection Act of 1982 and the Victims of Crime Act of 1984. The Federal Victim and Witness Protection Act provided model legislation for the states to improve and safeguard victims' roles in the criminal justice process without encroaching upon the constitutional rights of defendants by, among other things, criminalizing threats or retaliation against victims. The Victims of Crime Act of 1984 was designed to induce the states to create victim compensation programs and to aid in the maintenance of local programs assisting victims. It established the Crime Victims' Fund, which compensates victims and supports victim service programs.

Several states have enacted victims' bills of rights and more than half the states have ratified "victim rights" constitutional amendments. Most of these bills of rights focus on strengthening the victim's role in courtroom attendance, the plea-bargaining process, and the sentencing process. Other common provisions in victims' bill of rights include requiring that a victim be notified of crucial developments of the case; preventing defendants from profiting from the sales of their stories about their crime; and permitting victims to consult with the prosecutor about key prosecutorial decisions. Only a few states extend these rights to victims of virtually all crimes. Most limit victim participatory rights to victims of felonies, or crimes involving physical or sexual violence or injury, or specifically enumerated offenses. For crime victims to exercise their participatory rights, they must first be made aware that such rights exist. The federal system and most states require that victims be given notice of their participatory rights by the investigating law enforcement agency, the prosecutor, or victim services personnel.

While victims have clearly gained from these legislative reforms, many fear that current law amounts to paper promises and that victims' feelings of helplessness are exacerbated by the impotency of some laws. Many states treat victims' rights as privileges that can be granted or denied at the state's whim. Inadequate laws create the false expectation that a victim is entitled to participate in the legal process. Victims then feel angry and powerless when the exercise of their rights is denied.

probation   release of an offender from custody in exchange for the offender agreeing to meet certain conditions

---

"So after all was said and done, did you go to trial?" asked Martha.

"Celandra and the prosecutor entered into a plea agreement, but unfortunately the judge refused to accept it and ended up sentencing me to two years in prison."

"I take it you were shocked by this?" pursued Martha.

"Let's just say I went to the sentencing hearing expecting to walk out of the courtroom a free man. I thought I was going to be on **probation.** I didn't expect to be handcuffed and carted away to prison that day. I'll never forget the look on my family's faces as the sheriff escorted me out of the courtroom. That day rocked my world in ways you can never know," reflected Tim soberly.

◆ **LOCAL LINKS** ◆
Are victims allowed to participate in sentencing hearings in your state?

SENTENCING

Except in capital cases, the judge is usually responsible for imposing a defendant's sentence after the jury has entered a guilty verdict. At the sentencing hearing, the judge hears evidence presented by the prosecution and defense in reference to the nature of the appropriate punishment. The prosecution typically presents evidence of "aggravation," showing why the defendant deserves the punishment recommended by the state, and defense counsel presents evidence of "mitigation," showing why the defendant deserves minimal punishment. The judge also reviews a **presentence report,** prepared by the probation department. This report summarizes the defendant's criminal record, work history, family background, and any other factors relevant to sentencing. In some states, judges also listen to victim impact statements, in which victims describe the impact the defendant's actions had on their lives.

presentence report report summarizing the defendant's criminal record, work history, family background, and other factors relevant to sentencing

Indeterminate vs. Determinate Sentencing

Historically, many states utilized an **indeterminate sentencing** system in which offenders' sentences were a range of years (e.g., 5-20 years). Neither the defendant nor the judge knew how many years he would serve. The actual sentence was in the hands of the correctional institution where the defendant served. Prison officials recommended when a prisoner be released based on his conduct in prison. This system was intended to foster good behavior in inmates and to facilitate their rehabilitation. In practice, those who could best manipulate the system were rewarded. Critics contended that prison officials were given unfettered control over inmates' lives.

indeterminate sentencing sentence that is given as a range of years; the actual length of time served is determined by the correctional institution

Consequently, most states adopted some form of **determinate sentencing,** in which offenders were given a set sentence. To promote good behavior in the prison, many states adopted a "good time" credit system whereby inmates could reduce their sentence in accord with the number of credits they earned by abiding by prison rules. The purpose of this system was to give prisoners incentive to cooperate with prison officials and to involve themselves in programs offered by the institution. Because of concerns that prisoners were not serving the full length of the sentence imposed ("truth in sentencing" laws), several states have abandoned good-time credit programs.

determinate sentencing a set sentence determined by the court

Putting It Into Practice 7.15:

Why might an inmate prefer receiving a determinate sentence? Are there any reasons he might prefer an indeterminate sentence?

Presumptive Sentencing

In some states, such as Arizona, where Tim was sentenced, **presumptive sentencing** is used. Such sentencing takes discretion away from the judges, who some policy makers believed were abusing their discretion. As a result, critics believed that unjustified disparity in sentencing existed because of differences in judicial philosophies about punishment. To ensure that defendants who committed similar crimes in similar circumstances received the same sentences, some legislators introduced presumptive sentencing.

presumptive sentencing set sentence that can be increased if the judge finds aggravating circumstances or decreased if the judge finds mitigating circumstances

Figure 7-7
Sample Presumptive Sentence

SAMPLE PRESUMPTIVE SENTENCE		
Mitigating Circumstances 8 yrs	Presumptive Sentence 10 yrs	Aggravating Circumstances 15 yrs

◆ **LOCAL LINKS** ◆

What kind of sentencing scheme is used in your state?

Under this scheme, judges must impose a presumptive sentence unless they can cite aggravating circumstances (e.g., the heinousness of the crime or the fact that the offender had an accomplice) to increase the presumptive sentence or mitigating circumstances (e.g., the age or mental capacity of the defendant) to reduce the presumptive sentence. Discretion in sentencing, however, is inevitable. Interestingly, in the presumptive sentencing system described above, the discretion has shifted from the judiciary to the prosecution. It is the prosecution that chooses which crimes will be charged (and which ones will be dropped) and which aggravating circumstances to allege, as well as other factors that go beyond the scope of this text but that do affect the sentencing outcome.

Putting It Into Practice 7.16:

If a presumptive sentence for robbery is 20 years, why might an offender receive a sentence of 25 years?

Federal Sentencing Guidelines

The Federal Sentencing Guidelines, which were enacted in 1987, rigidly limit a sentencing judge's discretion. They were brought on, in part, by the lack of truth in sentencing once characteristic of the federal courts. At one time, a defendant convicted of assault could have received a multiyear sentence and yet have been released after a few months due to parole, early release, or good time credits. To correct this skewing of sentences, Congress enacted a sentencing guideline system in which the sentence announced in court is the actual time served (minus fifty-four days of annual "good time" after the first year).

Congress also wanted to address the disparity in federal sentencing. Prior to the guidelines, two defendants could be charged with the same crime and get two different sentences: one might get ten years and the other probation. Although critics contend disparity in sentencing still exists, proponents argue that the guidelines have created greater uniformity.

The Guidelines focus on the offender's conduct, not his character. The judge assigns points in reference to two factors: the defendant's prior offenses and the offense level of the crime. Each crime is given a base offense level, based on the offender's "relevant conduct," which the judge can adjust according to the circumstances of the crime, such as the defendant's role in the offense, the amount of drugs in question, whether justice was obstructed, and the degree to which the defendant has accepted responsibility for his conduct.

These two factors—the defendant's criminal history and the offense level of the crime—create a guideline sentencing range. Offenses are grouped into

NET NEWS

To read the federal sentencing guidelines and explanations of their application, go to *www.ussc.gov/guidelin.htm*. For information about the United States Sentencing Commission, federal sentencing statistics, reports to Congress, and other aspects of federal sentencing, go to *www.ussc.gov/sitemap.htm*. To read an interview with the chairperson of the United States Sentencing Commission and a report called "U.S. Sentencing Guidelines Impact on Federal Drug Offenders," go to *www.lectlaw.com/tcri.html* and click on the appropriate articles.

forty-three base offense levels and six criminal history levels. Once the seriousness of the offense and the extent of the offender's criminal history have been determined, the sentencing judge finds a range of months for which the offender must be imprisoned. The ranges are very narrow. For example, an offense level of fourteen, combined with a criminal history category of II, creates a sentencing range of eighteen to twenty-four months. To award a greater or lesser sentence, the judge must find aggravating or mitigating circumstances that she believes were not adequately addressed by the U.S. Sentencing Commission in drafting the sentencing guidelines.

As with presumptive sentencing, the federal guidelines shift sentencing discretion from the judge to the prosecutor. The prosecutor initiates the criminal charges, which determine the base offense level by which the defendant's sentence is calculated. The government—not the defendant—can ask the court to decrease the sentence when the government has determined that the defendant has substantially assisted them in prosecuting another crime. The prosecutor has total discretion in deciding whether to file this motion.

Critics point out that the guidelines are extremely complex and that they force judges to sentence crimes rather than criminals. The individuals that are treated most harshly by the guidelines are the minor criminals, whereas the more serious criminals sometimes outmaneuver the system. The guidelines have led to an increase in the prison population because more drug offenses have been made into federal crimes.

BONUS POINTERS:

THE MYTH OF LENIENCY

Is the United States, as some argue, really too lenient toward offenders?[4] Consider the following statistics.

◆ The United States has the highest per capita incarceration rate of any Western nation.

◆ As of 1994, the United States incarcerated more people than any other country except Russia.

◆ The propensity to incarcerate and the length of time served for homicide in the United States is not radically different from that in other institutionally similar countries. But in the case of property crimes and drug offenses, the United States clearly incarcerates more often and for longer periods than other similar nations.

◆ The United States is the only Western industrialized nation that has not abandoned the death penalty.

Is this difference in incarceration due to a higher crime rate?[5]

◆ Victimization statistics suggest that our property is actually more secure against crime in comparison to other industrialized countries.

If you are interested in getting more statistical information about prisons and prisoners, go to *http://crime.miningco.com/ newsissues/crime/*. Click on "Prison/Punishment," and then on "Statistics: Prisoners, Prisons, and Punishment." A number of articles will come up for you to access.

◆ The United States is less secure against personal violence. Our homicide rates are much higher and the rates for other crimes of violence—rape, robbery, aggravated assault, and assault—are also higher, but less strikingly so.

Has the United States become more lenient in recent years?[6]

◆ From 1972 to 1994, the numbers of inmates sentenced to state and federal institutions increased fivefold.
◆ From 1978 to 1994, the jail population tripled.
◆ As of 1994, more than one percent of the American population was either on probation or parole.
◆ In 1996, more than 5.5 million people were either incarcerated, on probation, or on parole—84 percent more than in 1985.[7]

PHILOSOPHY OF PUNISHMENT

Four theories are generally called upon in justifying punishment.

1. retribution
2. deterrence
3. rehabilitation
4. incapacitation

Retribution

retribution punishment based on revenge and on the notion that the offender owes a debt to society

Retribution is best known for its Biblical support: "an eye for an eye, and a tooth for a tooth." The premise for retribution is that the offender has committed a wrong against society—a wrong over which he has conscious control—for which society deserves to be "paid back." Vengeance is the primary motive. Retribution is the justification often cited by those who advocate the death penalty. What is not frequently understood about retribution is that it was originally designed to impose limits on punishment. No more pain was to be imposed on the offender than he caused his victim. In other words, no more than an eye could be extracted from the offender who blinded another; the offender could not be killed or further mutilated.

The question retributionists are faced with is this: How much pain must offenders endure before they have "paid back" their debt to society? How many years must an offender serve in prison, for example, before he has paid back society for sexually assaulting a woman? Because such questions are not easily answered, retributionists focus on ensuring that punishment is justly proportionate. If the crime of theft carries a sentence of 10 years, then justice demands that the crime of manslaughter carry a sentence that is proportionately more punitive. Retribution is the primary rationale for the "get-tough-on-crime" agenda of many politicians.

Deterrence

deterrence punishment based on the belief that people will not commit crimes if the pain of punishment exceeds the pleasure they derive from committing the crime

The other justification for punishment that is popular today is **deterrence.** It is based on the premise that offenders rationally decide to commit crimes because they are seeking pleasure (e.g., money, sexual gratification, power, etc.). Punishment is seen as effective because the pain of punishment is worse than the pleasure derived from committing the crime. The argument is that rational people seek to minimize their pain and maximize their pleasure. Policy makers continue to increase sentences because they believe that, at some point, the prospect of punishment (pain) will exceed any possible pleasure people derive from committing the crime and thereby discourage them from breaking the law.

general deterrence preventing the general population from committing crimes

Deterrence comes in two forms: general and specific. **General deterrence** is aimed at preventing the general population from committing crimes. When a judge imposes a sentence on a particular offender with the intent of sending a message to the whole community, general deterrence is his motivation. **Specific deterrence** is aimed at the specific offender. When a judge imposes a sentence with the intent of scaring a particular offender into changing his ways, specific deterrence is the motivation.

specific deterrence preventing a specific offender from committing future crimes

Although an in-depth critique of these theories is beyond the scope of this text, one fact that advocates of both retribution and deterrence have to reckon with is that the vast majority of crimes are committed by those under the influence of alcohol or, in fewer cases, drugs. This fact undermines the contention that offenders have control over their actions and that they enter into crimes rationally. By the same token, crimes of passion (e.g., a barroom brawl that results in a killing or a husband killing his wife when he finds her in bed with another man) are, by definition, irrational crimes.

While space prohibits thoughtful consideration of the numerous studies that have been conducted to determine the efficacy of imprisonment as a deterrent, one hypothesis is that certainty and swiftness of punishment are better predictors of deterrence than severity of punishment. In other words, efforts by the criminal justice system to impose swift sentences and to enhance the chances that offenders will actually get apprehended more effectively curb crime than simply increasing sentences. As one inmate said, "The law don't make no difference to me because I ain't gonna get caught. I mean, if I really thought I was gonna get caught, I wouldn't commit a crime in the first place, would I?"[8]

So how likely is an offender to be caught and punished? In 1992, of the 10.3 million violent crimes committed, only 165,000 led to convictions, and of these, only 100,000 led to prison sentences. Fewer than one convicted criminal was sent to prison for every hundred violent crimes. The more serious the crime, the higher the clearance rate, however. Thirteen percent of burglaries were cleared by arrest, whereas fifty-one percent of reported rapes and sixty-five percent of homicides were cleared.

As to swiftness of punishment, how quickly are offenders punished? The average time between arrest and conviction for murder is 267 days, while the average time between arrest and conviction for an individual charged with burglary, theft, drug trafficking, or a driving-related offense is 40 days.[9] For a number of reasons, the more serious the crime, the longer the delay between arrest and conviction.

Rehabilitation

rehabilitation punishment designed to heal the offender; based on the assumption that people's actions are influenced by factors outside of themselves

Rehabilitation is aimed at changing the behavior of offenders and is based on the premise that circumstances outside of the offender's control (e.g., heredity, environment, social forces, mental illness, etc.) cause him to commit crimes. Based on a medical model of treatment, the focus is on keeping the offender institutionalized until he is changed. Although this model of punishment was popular in the 1960s, it is rarely relied on today and, in all fairness, was never fully implemented even in its heyday.

Treatment and punishment are, in essence, diametrically opposed, making it unrealistic to expect institutions whose primary function is exacting punishment to direct their resources and intent into treatment. Critics point out that assuming offenders have little or no control over their actions is demeaning and can result in inhumane and interminable punishment if the offender refuses or cannot meet the expectations of the person conducting the treatment.

Incapacitation

incapacitation   punishment that incapacitates the offender and prevents him from committing future crimes

Incapacitation is the most pragmatic of the four theories. The reasoning is simply this: Offenders who are taken off the streets or who are otherwise "incapacitated" cannot commit crimes. Incarceration is the most common choice of incapacitation, but chemical castration of rapists and the death penalty are other examples of incapacitation. This approach makes no attempt to change the offender or to prevent future misconduct. The focus is on the present and keeping the offender away from others. This approach focuses on the immediate problem of controlling the offender rather than on what will happen when the offender is eventually released. It is extremely effective in the short term, even if terribly costly. (See Bonus Pointers: The Cost of Imprisonment.) That is a price, however, many are willing to pay for immediate security. The following argument is representative of that reasoning.

Stiffen the backbone of the system, make it more certain that criminals pay for their crimes, and pay hard: surely crime will dwindle as a consequence. Deterrence—that is the key. Moreover, a burglar in jail can hardly break into your house. This effect is called "incapacitation." It, too, seems like plain common sense. If the crooks are all behind bars they cannot rape and loot and pillage. The death penalty, of course, is the ultimate incapacitator.

Never mind soft-headed worry about causes of crimes; forget poverty, unemployment, racism, and slums; forget personality and culture. Use the steel rod of criminal justice to stamp out crime, or to reduce it to an acceptable level. Get rid of sentimentality; take the rusty sword down from the wall; let deterrence and incapacitation do their job.[10]

Evidence exists that prison is an effective tool for reducing crime not primarily because it works as a deterrent, but for reasons of incapacitation. In recent study, Steven Levitt (1996) concludes that "incarcerating one additional prisoner reduces the number of crimes by approximately fifteen per year," and that "the marginal social costs of incarceration are at or below the accompanying social benefits of crime reduction."[11] The author notes that, while incarceration rates more than tripled in the last two decades, victimization rates for violent crimes remained unchanged and fell for property crimes. From this data, the author concluded that our harsh incarceration practices have been effective. He bases his conclusions on self-reporting by offenders of the average number of crimes they commit while not in prison, and that

---

NET NEWS

To read a discussion about the death penalty in the context of the theories of punishment, go to *www.utm.edu/research/iep/c/capitalp.htm.*

Figure 7-8
Philosophies of Punishment

PHILOSOPHIES OF PUNISHMENT

Retribution

Offender has committed a wrong for which society deserves to be paid back
Assumes offender has control over actions

Deterrence

Punishment is effective when pain of punishment exceeds pleasure
of committing crime
Assumes offenders are rational and seek to maximize pleasure
and minimize pain

Rehabilitation

Punishment is aimed at changing behavior of offenders
Assumes forces outside of offenders' control cause them to commit crimes

Incapacitation

Offender is incapacitated to prevent commission of crimes

those subject to imprisonment have a constant disposition to offend such that, if left at large, they predictably will offend and at a predictable rate.

Putting It Into Practice 7.17:

How might someone arguing on behalf of the death penalty use retribution, deterrence, and incapacitation to bolster her argument?

BONUS POINTERS:

COST OF IMPRISONMENT

The average annual cost in 1996 of incarcerating a prisoner ranged from $9351 in Alabama to $38,424 in Alaska. Some of the variation in costs probably reflects different bookkeeping methods across states. Compared to incarceration, probation and parole are cheap. State data show that probation tends to cost close to $1000 per year and parole tends to cost somewhere between $1000 and $2000 a year, with significant variation from state to state. On the average, incarceration is more than fifteen times more costly per person than probation or parole.

The cost of running prisons represents an increasing share of the growing sum that society is spending to protect itself from crime. In 1996, state governments expended more than $27 billion on corrections, three times the $9 billion spent on corrections in 1985.[12]

ALTERNATIVES TO INCARCERATION

Because of the high cost of imprisonment, the tremendous overcrowding in most of our prisons today, and because some crimes simply do not warrant incarceration, alternatives to incarceration are frequently employed. One of the primary alternatives is probation, in which the defendant is released from custody after agreeing to meet certain conditions. These conditions can include not going to certain places

probation officer individual responsible for supervising offenders to ensure they fulfill the conditions of their probation

or parts of town or seeing certain people, submitting to alcohol or drug testing, reporting to the **probation officer** on a daily basis, getting psychological treatment, or attending classes. The probation officer is responsible for supervising the probationer to ensure that he adheres to these conditions. Violation of these conditions can lead to a revocation of probation and result in the probationer being sentenced to jail or prison. As of 1996, more than 3.1 million people were on probation. This resulted in probation officers having caseloads of 150 or more probationers, making effective supervision extremely difficult.

work furlough program that allows offenders to work during the day and serve time on the weekends or evenings only

Other alternatives include **work furlough** (allowing the offender to work during the week and serve time on the weekends or in the evenings only), **restitution** to the victim to compensate her for the harm caused, and monitoring the offender using an electronic device attached to the wrist or ankle that allows the offender's location to be determined.

restitution payment by an offender to his victim to compensate the victim for the harm caused

A final alternative is **intensive supervisory probation** (ISP), which includes any probation program that involves closer monitoring and more stringent conditions for the offender than ordinary probation. An ISP probation officer monitors about 25 to 30—a caseload about one-sixth the average for a probation officer. In practice, such programs are often combined with house arrest, drug treatment or testing, and electronic monitoring.

intensive supervisory probation any probation program that involves close monitoring and more stringent conditions than ordinary probation

Putting It Into Practice 7.18:

Suppose an offender is the sole provider for a family. What alternatives might the judge consider to avoid sending the offender to prison and thereby creating economic hardship for the family?

BONUS POINTERS:

RESTORATIVE JUSTICE

Restorative justice traces its roots to the system of justice employed by indigenous peoples around the world, including many American Indian tribes. In these systems, emphasis is on restoring the offender, the victim, and the community back to wholeness: repairing the damage caused to all three by the actions of the offender. Frequently, the offender and victim are invited to sit together to talk as a first step toward getting the offender to take responsibility for his actions. Often times, community members sit in some form of "sentencing circle," which includes the judge, the prosecuting and defense attorneys, the social worker or probation officer, the victim and offender and members of their families, and neighbors and concerned members of the community. The circle arrives at a sentence, which must be ratified by the judge, and commits to take whatever steps are necessary to support both the victim and the offender. If the offender violates any of the agreed-upon conditions, he will be returned to court, where he will be sentenced to jail or prison. The focus of these circles is on accountability rather than vengeance—making the offender accountable and returning both the victim and the offender to their rightful places in the community. Restorative justice programs are currently finding their way into small towns and big cities all around the country.

NET NEWS

For more information about restorative justice, go to *www.restorativejustice.org*.

"I Found Out What It Was Like to Live in an Alien Land Filled with Alien People, Governed by Alien Rules."

"I had no idea when I walked out of that courtroom how much my life was going to change." Tim grimaced at the memories. "At that moment, I lost whatever control I thought I had over my life. I found out what it was like to live in an alien land filled with alien people, governed by alien rules. From that day until I was released, I had no control over when I slept, when I ate, when I took a shower, or whom I associated with. I learned to be on constant alert. To this day, I can't stand being in a crowd—a crowd in prison means something's going down and someone's going to get hurt. I learned how to protect myself, how to play the game, how to get what I needed. But the one thing I never got used to was the constant noise. It's never really quiet in prison, even at night." Tim's voice trailed off as he relived the sights and sounds of prison life.

"But at least you had your family, didn't you?" asked Martha hopefully, looking for something positive to talk about.

"My parents stuck by me," agreed Tim. "It was hard on them, but they tried to make it out to see me every other weekend."

"And your wife?" inquired Martha.

"She didn't see herself as the wife of a con," replied Tim wryly. "She left me shortly after I was sentenced."

"Sorry." Martha could see the sadness on Tim's face despite his protestations that her leaving had not been unexpected.

After a long silence, she continued. "Would you say that prison changed you?"

"In ways you'll never know," replied Tim gravely. "If you mean, was I rehabilitated—yes, I grew up very fast and my priorities changed dramatically. I began to see myself and the world I'd created for myself very differently."

"So, as bad as prison life was, it must have done something good for you," persisted Martha.

"The changes I made came from inside me," replied Tim firmly, emphasizing that he credited himself—not the institution—with the changes he had made. "No one ever encouraged me to enroll in classes—I made that choice. No one said, 'Tim, you have a drug problem; you need some help.' I was the one who decided to get counseling and to begin looking at what I'd done with my life. Don't get me wrong. I met some guards and other staff that were supportive of what I was trying to do but I never, ever had anyone take the initiative and begin working with me."

"But look at you now," Martha encouraged. "You've got a good job, you're taking classes—"

"And it's been a struggle every step of the way," interrupted Tim, unaware of the bitterness in his voice. "If it hadn't been for the support of my parents, I don't think I'd have made it." He took a sip of water and then remembered. "Of course, I'll always be grateful to the dean of the law school, who took a chance and gave me a job in the law library. I began writing to him about six months before I was released and I guess he decided I was really serious when I showed up at his doorstep the day after I was released."

"And now you're talking about law school," added Martha, forgetting for a moment her earlier scoffing at this possibility.

"Right. I'm *talking* about it and that's all that may ever come of it. Do you have any idea how hard it is for an ex-felon to get admitted to the bar in this state?"

IMPRISONMENT

While prison is theoretically a place offenders go *as* punishment rather than *for* punishment, in reality imprisonment in American institutions is the embodiment of physical, social, economic, and psychological losses that go beyond the deprivation of liberty.

"The prisoner is confronted by a hostile or indifferent prison environment in which denial of personal problems and manipulation of others are primary ingredients of interpersonal life. The result is that the prison's survivors become tougher, more pugnacious, and less able to feel for themselves or others, while the nonsurvivors become weaker, more susceptible, and less able to control their lives."[13]

Severe restriction of freedom of movement is the most obvious impingement on the prisoner's freedom; for some, freedom of movement becomes almost non-existent. In some of the most modern prisons, the maximum-security units are windowless cells built of stainless steel and concrete block in which the inmates are in almost total lockdown. Some are so automated that the inmates have almost no human interaction. (Prisoners are served food, for example, by motorized conveyors that circumvent the need for human contact.) Their every movement is monitored by guards sitting at closed-circuit televisions, thereby depriving them of any privacy.

This loss of liberty includes separation from friends and family. Most prisons are located in remote areas that are not accessible by public transportation. For those who do have the means to travel to the prison, the journey is a time-consuming one that makes regular visitations onerous. This lack of contact puts a severe strain on family bonds, resulting in the dissolution of marriages and loss of contact with children. The lack of heterosexual contact adds to the existing tensions within a prison.

Double-bunking, which has become the norm in many overcrowded institutions today, also adds to inmate stress. A typical cell is 6 × 9 with two bunks and a toilet—a room originally designed for habitation by one person is now occupied by two people. Such overcrowding leads to increased security problems, increased spread of disease, absence of any privacy, deterioration of sanitary conditions, and decreased availability of programs and services.

Loss of autonomy is an intangible but significant deprivation. Prisoners are told when to eat, sleep, shower, get out of their cells, and perform all other activities. Making such decisions is part of being an adult, and its loss results in a process called "institutionalization," in which the individual becomes subordinate to and dependent on the institution. All inmates experience institutionalization to some degree and, therefore, find reintegration into society difficult when they are released.

BONUS POINTERS: ## VICTIMIZATION IN PRISON

Most inmates face some form of psychological, economic, social, and physical victimization in prison. Psychological victimization ranges from the verbal manipulations used to gain advantages over other inmates to spreading rumors designed to damage the reputation of an offender or to cause him emotional distress. Economic victimization begins with the exorbitantly high prices inmates pay for illicit goods and services and continues when they lose them to the predatory activities of other inmates. Social victimization occurs when inmates become targets because they are members of a particular religion, race, ethnic group, or ideology. Frequently inmates are attacked because they belong to a rival gang. Physical victimization is what inmates fear most. Although sexual assaults are relatively rare, many inmates are propositioned, threatened, or fondled. Nevertheless, physical attacks are per capita much greater in prison than on the outside. The high level of violence is due in part to the substantial number of offenders who are prone to violence but also due to the lack of adequate supervision and the high level of tension that exists when individuals with varying conflicts are housed in close proximity.

Most inmates are seriously disadvantaged when they enter prison. Most come from broken families, have a poor education, enjoy few job skills, have a history of alcohol or drug abuse, and suffer from strained interpersonal relationships. They generally leave prison with these same disadvantages plus the stigma of a felony conviction. These factors make finding employment difficult and render some jobs totally unobtainable. Failure to notify a potential employer of one's felon status can be grounds for return to the institution. Finding a place to live can be equally problematic. Most prisoners have only a few hundred dollars when they are released from custody and may be unable to supply satisfactory references to landlords.

NET NEWS

To read more about prisons and the impact of imprisonment, go to *www.criminology.fsu.edu/cjlinks*, click on "Corrections," and go to any of the sites that might be of interest to you. This site has a staggering number of links to criminal justice Web sites that cover the gamut of criminal justice topics.

parole suspension of prison sentence to assist prisoners in reintegrating back into community

Psychological adaptation to the outside world is exacerbated by the institutionalization process. Going from the highly controlled, routinized, slow-paced world of the prison to the frenetic, complex world on the outside is problematic for all inmates. They must transition from an environment in which they have almost no autonomy to one in which they must make a myriad of decisions in one day—from what to buy at the grocery story to maneuvering busy streets in their vehicle. Tasks that most people take for granted are obstacles to their survival on the streets. This reintegration process is aggravated by the abolition of **parole** in some states and the lack of sufficient halfway houses, both of which are designed to facilitate inmates' return to society.

recidivate return to prison

Many would argue that all of these implications of imprisonment may be true, but that we should remember the plight of the victims of these offenders. Justice, they say, demands that those who create pain for others must expect to suffer the consequences of what they have created. While those sentiments are certainly understandable, the stark reality is that most prisoners return to the streets, where, if they have not changed, they will be free to prey on yet more victims. In truth, the majority of inmates **recidivate** (return to prison). A study conducted by the Department of Justice following the release of 108,580 inmates from prison to parole in 11 states in 1983 revealed that 63 percent returned to prison within three years on either felony or serious misdemeanor charges.[14] Many of those who do not return to prison end up working menial jobs, becoming dependent on the state, or joining the ranks of the homeless.

commuted reduction of a sentence by the governor or President

Putting It Into Practice 7.19:

In what respects might an offender be a greater detriment to society after having been in prison than before being sentenced?

ETHICAL ETIQUETTE

ADMISSION TO THE BAR

Attorneys must pass a bar exam, which includes both multiple-choice and essay question components, before they can be admitted to their state bar. Additionally, they are subjected to an investigation whose purpose is to determine if they are morally fit to assume the role of an attorney. What constitutes "moral fitness" is often debated, and the standards for its measurements have changed with the times. In the past, attorneys have been prohibited from practicing law because they were cohabiting with someone of the opposite sex (a crime in many states) or because they engaged in sexual practices the committee on fitness found objectionable.

In Arizona, the question of moral fitness is currently being pressed by James Hamm, who was convicted of murder and who served more than 18 years in prison before his sentence was **commuted** by the governor. While in prison, Hamm obtained an advanced degree, served as a jailhouse lawyer for many of the inmates, and organized Middle Ground, which advocates on behalf of inmates and their families. When he was released, Hamm was accepted into Arizona State University law school, where he continued his work with Middle Ground while he studied. He ultimately graduated, passed the bar exam, and is now asking to be admitted to the practice of law in Arizona. The bar is divided about whether someone who has committed murder should ever be allowed to practice law, no matter how exemplary a life he has lived in the interim.

Putting It Into Practice 7.20:

Do you think James Hamm should be admitted to the practice of law? Is there anything else you would need to know before answering this question?

"No Matter What I do, No Matter How Many Amends I Make, I Know I'm Probably Always Going to Get That Look."

Tim took Martha aside while they were standing outside the restaurant, waiting for the valet. "Martha, the hardest part about everything I've been through is the look I get when I tell people I'm an ex-con. I saw that look on your face the day I told you. No matter what I do, no matter how many amends I make, I know I'm probably always going to get that look. It's the reason I didn't tell you right away. I was hoping that if you got to know me well enough, it wouldn't matter. But I guess I was wrong. I'm sorry I didn't tell you earlier. I know now I should have been honest with you up front. It would have been much easier on you if you'd never let me into your life."

"Tim, your car's here," announced John.

"Thank you for listening to my story, Martha," concluded Tim quietly, turning on his heel and walking away, head bowed and shoulders drooping.

■ TIM'S TECHNO TIPS

Criminal Case Management

Just like the civil practitioner, the criminal defense attorney and prosecutor need to docket court appearances, schedule appointments, draft form letters, keep track of witnesses, discover and analyze evidence, and prepare for trial. What sets the criminal bar (defense and prosecution) apart from their counterparts on the civil side is the differences in the criminal rules of procedure, the constitutional issues that occur in criminal trial, and the difference in the burden of proof. Speedy trial rules, which do not exist in the civil realm, for example, require that a case be heard within certain time limits or the charges are dismissed, usually without prejudice so that the state can file the charges again. Because of the restraints and interplay of criminal practice, it makes sense that the case management software we have already looked at might not be sufficient for the criminal attorney.

Criminal case management software has developed along two lines: those for defense attorneys and those for prosecutors. Many of the prosecution versions are designed to produce the types of reports expected of city, county, state, and federal prosecutors. The defense side is often more concerned with keeping track of witnesses—a notoriously difficult task in criminal cases—as well as the client. The client may be in jail, out on bond, or on probation or parole for prior offenses. The defense attorney must also keep track of required appearances in the case at issue and must log in each client's required visits to probation or parole officers, drug or alcohol screenings, various counseling sessions that might be a requirement of probation or parole, and so on.

TECHNO TRIP

Begin this trip with a search of the phrase "criminal case management software." You will find literally thousands of hits, many of which will not appear to be related to the subject matter of your search. Look at three software packages and compare them to each other and, after selecting a "winner," compare it to the civil case management programs we reviewed earlier.

Go to *www.microfirm.com* and review the company's Prosecutor II (or latest version) program. A download demo is available. Next go to *www.key-point.com* and check out the Case-in-Point criminal case management program by running its demo package. Finally, go to *www.legaledge.com* and demo the defense and prosecution packages offered by that company.

Which of the programs do like best? How do they compare with the civil case management programs you have reviewed? Do you believe that a specialized software package is required for criminal case management, or do you believe that the better civil packages could be easily modified for use in criminal cases?

SUMMARY – PART B

Crimes are classified as felonies, misdemeanors, and petty offenses; a few felonies are considered capital crimes. Many states have adopted parts of the *Model Penal Code*, prepared by the American Law Institute, in an effort to standardize and simplify criminal law. Every crime is composed of three elements: *mens rea, actus reus,* and causation. Under the *Model Penal Code*, every crime is assigned the *mens rea* of purposely, knowingly, recklessly, or criminal negligence. The distinction between mental states is not always clear; a defendant's mental state must often be inferred from witness observations and statements and actions by the defendant. The *actus reus* can be an affirmative action or an omission, but any act must be voluntary. Possession alone can constitute the *actus reus.* Three inchoate crimes are attempt, solicitation, and conspiracy. To hold a defendant responsible for his actions, a court must conclude that the consequences were the "natural and probable consequences" of those actions. Crimes are graded according to the seriousness of the harm committed. Under the *Model Penal Code*, there are three classes of felonies and three classes of misdemeanors. The class of felony, along with other factors, determines the sentence the judge can impose.

An individual can use a reasonable amount of physical force to defend himself if he reasonably believes such force is imminently necessary for self-protection. Deadly physical force can be used only when reasonably necessary to protect oneself against a threat of deadly physical force. Many states require individuals to retreat before using deadly force except in their home or where retreat would create more danger for them. Deadly force cannot be used to protect property. In some states, force can be used to defend a third person under attack, but only if the person being defended is justified in using self-defense. In other states, the defendant must reasonably believe the use of force is necessary. Duress is a defense if the defendant can prove that he committed a crime only because he was threatened with the use of physical force. Threat to property or reputation is not sufficient, nor is a threat of future harm. Necessity requires the defendant to prove that he took an action to avoid a greater harm. Economic necessity is not allowed as a defense. Children under the age of seven are conclusively presumed incapable of forming criminal intent; a similar rebuttable presumption exists for children between the ages of seven and fourteen. In some circumstances and for certain crimes, intoxication can be used as a defense to reduce the crime for which the defendant is held responsible. All states allow insanity as a defense because neither the defendant's intent nor his act is voluntary. Three tests are used to determine whether someone is legally sane: the M'Naughten test, the irresistible impulse test, and the substantial capacity test. Traditionally, an insanity verdict was equivalent to a "not guilty" verdict, but some states today use a "guilty but mentally ill" verdict. Entrapment occurs when law enforcement induces a defendant to commit a crime and is designed to punish law enforcement. The predisposition of the defendant is relevant in some states and not in others.

The Supreme Court adopted the exclusionary rule as means of deterring unconstitutional conduct by police officers and because the judicial integrity of the Court required that it not be a party to constitutional invasions of its citizens. Only those with standing can assert the exclusionary rule. Under the good-faith exception to this rule, evidence can be used in the prosecutor's case-in-chief if it was obtained by officers who reasonably relied on a facially valid search warrant that later turned out to be unsupported by probable cause.

At the sentencing hearing, the judge hears evidence of aggravation and mitigation and reviews the presentence report. Because indeterminate sentencing gave correctional institutions unfettered control over when inmates would be released, most states adopted some form of determinate sentencing. To encourage the good behavior of inmates, many institutions developed "good-time credit" programs that allowed inmates to reduce their sentence. Because some critics believed that judges were abusing their discretion in sentencing, some states have developed some form of presumption sentencing, in which judges can deviate from a presumptive sentence only if they cite aggravating or mitigating circumstances. Under the federal sentencing guidelines, the judge must determine the appropriate sentence based on an intricate point system unless she can cite aggravating or mitigating circumstances not considered by the U.S. Sentencing Commission.

Punishment is based on several theories: retribution, deterrence, rehabilitation, and incapacitation. Under the retribution and deterrence theories, offenders are assumed to be in control of their actions, whereas rehabilitationists believe that people commit crimes because of factors outside of their control. With both general and special deterrence, the assumption is that people make a rational choice to commit crimes to further their pleasure and will not be deterred unless the potential punishment exceeds the pleasure they derive from committing the crime. Incapacitation is costly and short-sighted; rehabilitation can be inhumane and demeaning. Alternatives to incarceration that are used to avoid the high cost of imprisonment are probation, restitution, work furlough, and monitoring of offenders using electronic devices.

Prisoners experience more than deprivation of movement, which can be severely restricted in some institutions. They are also faced with loss of contact with family and friends, loss of autonomy, and overcrowding. Psychological, physical, social, and economic victimization are common consequences of being imprisoned. Most inmates find it difficult to reintegrate back into the community when they are released and many recidivate.

KEY TERMS

Actus reus
Attempt
Capital crime
Case-in-chief
Causation
Commuted
Conclusive presumption
Conspiracy
Corpus delicti
Determinate sentencing

Deterrence
Entrapment
Exclusionary rule
General deterrence
Incapacitation
Indeterminate sentencing
Infer
Intensive supervisory
   probation

Mens rea
Model Penal Code
Objective
Parole
Presentence report
Presumptive sentencing
Probation
Probation officer
Rebuttable presumption
Recidivate

Rehabilitation
Restitution
Retribution
Solicitation
Specific deterrence
Standing
Subjective
Work furlough

REVIEW QUESTIONS – PART B

1. How are crimes classified?
2. What is the *Model Penal Code* and why was it developed?
3. What are the three elements of any crime?
4. Describe the four mental states used in the *Model Penal Code*.
5. In addition to affirmative acts, what constitutes the *actus reus*?

6. What are three inchoate crimes and what is the *actus reus* of each?
7. What must the state prove to show causation?
8. How are crimes graded under the *Model Penal Code*?
9. Under what circumstances can one use force to defend oneself? To defend one's property? To defend another?

10. Under what circumstances is deadly physical force not justified?
11. When can the following defenses be raised?
    a. infancy
    b. intoxication
    c. insanity
    d. duress
    e. necessity
    f. entrapment
12. Describe the differences in the three tests used to evaluate legal insanity.
13. What is the Exclusionary Rule and why was it adopted? How is it being eroded today?
14. What does a judge consider in deciding what sentence to impose on an offender?
15. What is the difference between determinate and indeterminate sentencing?
16. What is presumptive sentencing and why was it developed?
17. How are sentences determined under the federal sentencing guidelines?
18. Explain each of the following theories of punishment.
    a. retribution
    b. deterrence
    c. rehabilitation
    d. incapacitation
19. What alternatives to incarceration are available?
20. What losses do prisoners typically experience while they are imprisoned and how do these losses affect their reintegration back into the community?

PRACTICE EXAM – PART B

MULTIPLE CHOICE

1. The American Law Institute
   a. created a set of uniform laws the states could use as a model
   b. wrote the *Model Penal Code*, which has been adopted in every state
   c. is composed of legal scholars only
   d. all of the above
2. An *actus reus*
   a. cannot be an omission
   b. can be an affirmative act even if it is not voluntary
   c. can be the act of possession by itself
   d. is not required in every case
3. An example of an inchoate crime is
   a. assault
   b. conspiracy
   c. causation
   d. homicide
4. A crime against property is
   a. bribery
   b. forgery
   c. disorderly conduct
   d. perjury
5. Self-defense cannot be used
   a. by those who initiate an attack
   b. by those who use deadly force
   c. by those who repel an attack
   d. all of the above
6. Deadly physical force
   a. can never be used to defend oneself in one's home
   b. can be used only after an attempt to retreat
   c. can be used to protect property
   d. can be used to protect oneself in one's home if the use of such force is reasonably necessary
7. Duress is a defense
   a. when a threat is made to a defendant's property or reputation
   b. when a threat of future harm is made to the defendant
   c. when a threat of imminent violence is directed toward the defendant
   d. all of the above
8. Economic necessity
   a. is not generally allowed as a defense
   b. is not a defense because the poor can seek social service agencies when they are in need
   c. is discouraged as a defense to prevent its abuse
   d. all of the above
9. Intoxication
   a. can be used as a defense in all types of crimes
   b. can be raised as a defense if the defendant was unable to form the required intent because of his or her intoxicated state
   c. completely absolves the defendant of responsibility
   d. all of the above
10. Entrapment
    a. is designed to punish law enforcement
    b. applies only when the defendant is predisposed toward committing the crime for which he has been charged
    c. is completely unrelated to the predisposition of the defendant
    d. applies to private citizens as well as government officials

11. The exclusionary rule
    a. is a rule required by the Constitution according to the current Court
    b. was designed to deter police misconduct
    c. is considered an effective deterrent by today's Court
    d. none of the above
12. In conducting its cost-benefit analysis in reference to the exclusionary rule, the majority in *Leon* and *Sheppard* argued that
    a. prosecutors rarely drop cases because of search and seizure issues
    b. the exclusionary rule encourages the police to comply with constitutional procedures
    c. the exclusionary rule exacts a substantial social cost because of the criminal defendants who go free or receive reduced sentences
    d. none of the above
13. At the sentencing hearing
    a. only the prosecution is allowed to present evidence
    b. the judge considers evidence of aggravations and mitigation
    c. the jury decides what sentence should be imposed
    d. none of the above
14. A presentence report reviews an offender's
    a. prior convictions
    b. work history
    c. family history
    d. all of the above
15. With indeterminate sentences
    a. the length of the sentence was unaffected by an inmate's behavior
    b. inmates knew exactly when they would be released
    c. length of sentence was largely in the hands of the correctional institution
    d. inmates were protected from the politics of the prison in which they were housed
16. Presumptive sentencing
    a. may shift discretion from the judiciary to the prosecution
    b. requires the judge to consider aggravating circumstances, such as the defendant's age
    c. gives judges additional discretion
    d. minimizes the prosecution's role in sentencing
17. Under the federal sentencing guidelines
    a. a judge must assign points to the defendant's criminal history

    b. a judge must assign points to the offense level for the crime
    c. each crime is assigned a base offense level
    d. all of the above
18. Retribution is based
    a. on the concept of forgiveness
    b. on the concept that no more pain can be imposed on the offender than the offender imposed on his or her victim
    c. on the belief that the pain imposed in the form of punishment must exceed the pleasure the offender derived from committing the crime
    d. on the assumption that offenders are not responsible for their conduct
19. The premise of deterrence is that
    a. people make a rational decision to commit crimes
    b. people seek to maximize their pleasure and minimize their pain
    c. if sentences are long enough, people will decide not to commit crimes because the pleasure they may derive from committing the crime is outweighed by the pain of imprisonment
    d. all of the above
20. Rehabilitation
    a. is based on the medical model
    b. assumes that offenders have little or no control over their actions
    c. can be inhumane and demeaning
    d. all of the above
21. Incapacitation focuses on
    a. changing the offender
    b. preventing future misconduct
    c. keeping offenders from committing crimes
    d. the future rather than the present
22. The terms of probation can include
    a. being tested for drugs or alcohol
    b. attending classes
    c. daily reporting to the probation officer
    d. all of the above
23. Overcrowding in prisons leads to
    a. increased security problems
    b. increased spread of contagious diseases
    c. exacerbation of the lack of privacy
    d. all of the above
24. Which of the following is uncommon in prison?
    a. sexual assault
    b. verbal manipulation
    c. economic victimization
    d. targeting of members of religious, ethnic, or racial groups

25. Most inmates
    a. come from stable families
    b. have a poor education
    c. develop job skills in prison that make employment relatively easy to find
    d. have good interpersonal skills

26. When leaving the prison, most inmates
    a. have a job lined up for them
    b. have a fairly easy time of finding a place to live
    c. find psychological adaptation to the fast-paced, impersonal life on the streets to be difficult
    d. none of the above

FILL IN THE BLANK

27. Someone who commits a _____ for violating a state law may be fined but cannot be incarcerated.

28. A _____ is any crime that carries the death penalty.

29. The three elements of any crime are the _____ (intent), the _____ (the act), and _____ (which connects the act to the intent).

30. Someone who commits a crime intending to cause a specific act does so _____, whereas someone who commits a crime being aware that a specific harm could occur does so _____. If a defendant is aware of and consciously disregards a substantial and unjustifiable risk that a harm will occur, he commits the crime _____, but if he fails to perceive a substantial and unjustifiable risk that a harm will occur, he or she commits the crime with _____.

31. Typically, jurors must _____ (draw a conclusion based on specific facts) a defendant's mental state from the defendant's actions and statements and witness observations.

32. A defendant who inadvertently kills someone while cleaning a gun because he is unaware that the gun is loaded has a mental state of _____, whereas a defendant who kills someone when he fires shots into a crowded room just to see what people will do has a mental state of _____.

33. A defendant who takes some steps that go beyond mere preparation toward committing a crime but does not complete the crime, commits the *actus reus* of an _____. A defendant who asks another to commit a crime for him or her commits the *actus reus* of _____ when he or she makes the communication. A defendant who commits an overt act after agreeing with other individuals to commit a crime, commits the *actus reus* of _____. All of these crimes are examples of _____ crimes.

34. Arson is a crime against _____, sexual assault is a crime against _____, and perjury is a crime against _____.

35. Under the _____ test, a defendant is legally insane if he does not know the difference between right and wrong. Under the _____ test, a defendant is legally insane even if he does know right from wrong, but has a compelling urge that he cannot control to commit the act he knows is wrong. Under the _____ test, a defendant is legally insane if he cannot "appreciate" the wrongfulness of his conduct and cannot "conform" his actions to what he knows is right.

36. _____ occurs when law enforcement induces a defendant to commit a crime.

37. Only those with _____(a right to make an argument before the Court because one's own constitutional rights have been violated) can claim their constitutional rights were violated.

38. Because of the exclusionary rule, illegally obtained evidence cannot be introduced during the prosecutor's _____ (the part of the case providing direct proof of the defendant's guilt).

39. Under the _____, a prosecutor can introduce evidence in his case-in-chief that was obtained by officers who reasonably relied on a facially valid search warrant that later turns out to unsupported by probable cause.

40. Inmates who have been assigned an _____ sentence do not know how long they will serve because their sentence is a range of years. Inmates who are given a _____ sentence are given a set sentence that may be changed only on the basis of _____, which are given for good behavior.

41. Some states have adopted some form of _____ sentencing as a means of preventing disparity in sentencing.

42. Those who advocate _____ maintain that an offender deserves to be punished

for the wrongs he has committed in order to "pay back" society. Those who advocate _____ emphasize the need to make the pain of imprisonment greater than the pleasure of committing the crime. Those who believe in _____ are not concerned about why people commit crime or how they are changed; they simply want to prevent offenders from being able to commit crimes. Those who believe that offenders can be treated are advocates of _____.

43. If a judge imposes a sentence with the intent of discouraging the offender from committing another crime, she is relying on the theory of _____. But if the judge imposes a sentence with the intent of discouraging others from committing similar crimes, she is relying on the theory of _____.

44. In lieu of incarcerating an offender, a judge has the option of sentencing him to _____, which is a release from custody in exchange for an agreement to meet certain conditions. The offender is then supervised by a _____, whose job is to ensure that these conditions are met.

45. Some offenders are sentenced to make _____ (repay the victim for harm caused) or to a _____, in which they work during the day and serve time in the evenings or on the weekends.

46. The loss of autonomy in prison leads to _____, in which the inmate becomes subordinate to and dependent on the prison.

47. The majority of inmates _____ (return to prison).

TRUE OR FALSE

____ 48. The punishment for crimes varies considerably from state to state.

____ 49. The intent of the American Law Institute was to standardize and simplify criminal law.

____ 50. The difference between criminal negligence and recklessness is that, with the former, the defendant perceives a risk and ignores it, whereas, with the latter, the defendant fails to even perceive the risk.

____ 51. With both recklessness and criminal negligence, the failure to perceive a risk must be a gross deviation from the standard of care a reasonable person would observe in that situation.

____ 52. Jurors are usually able to easily distinguish one mental state from one another, as those mental states have been defined by the *Model Penal Code.*

____ 53. A defendant who takes steps that go beyond mere preparation toward committing a crime commits the crime of attempt.

____ 54. A defendant who asks another person to kill someone can be charged with solicitation if the solicited person carries out the killing.

____ 55. Attempt requires proof of an "overt act."

____ 56. Even if the connection between a defendant's intent and the ultimate consequence is very remote, the defendant will still be held responsible for his actions under the criminal law.

____ 57. To hold a defendant responsible for his actions, a court must conclude that the consequences were the natural and probable consequences of the defendant's actions.

____ 58. Under the *Model Penal Code,* there are five classes of felonies and six classes of misdemeanors.

____ 59. The class of felony is one of the factors a judge can consider in imposing a sentence.

____ 60. All defenses completely exonerate defendants.

____ 61. Someone claiming self-defense can use no more force than is necessary to repel the attack.

____ 62. Someone acting in self-defense has a right to continue using force even after the aggressor has withdrawn.

____ 63. Many jurisdictions require defendants to retreat before using deadly force, even in their own homes.

____ 64. Spring guns can be used to defend property.

____ 65. Because of insurance and because the death penalty is not a penalty for theft, deadly force cannot generally be used to defend property.

____ 66. A defendant is always justified in defending a third person as long as he reasonably believes the use of force is necessary.

____ 67. With the necessity defense, the defendant must prove that he took an action to avoid a greater harm.

____ 68. A rebuttable presumption exists that children under the age of seven are incapable of forming criminal intent.

____ 69. Intoxication cannot be raised as a defense to recklessness.

____ 70. Intoxication can be used to reduce a defendant's charge of first degree murder to manslaughter.

____ 71. People who are insane are not criminally responsible for their actions because they are incapable of forming criminal intent and their actions are not voluntary.

____ 72. Legal insanity and medical insanity are closely connected.

____ 73. Many people who would be considered legally insane under the M'Naughten test would not be considered insane under the substantial capacity test.

____ 74. Insanity is often claimed as a defense and is usually successful.

____ 75. A defendant's sanity is not an issue during trial and the proceedings preceding trial.

____ 76. Traditionally, an insanity verdict was the equivalent of a "guilty" verdict.

____ 77. In states that use a "guilty but mentally ill" verdict, a defendant may still serve some time in prison.

____ 78. The enforcement of drug laws and vice laws is more likely to lead to claims of entrapment than other areas of law enforcement.

____ 79. A defendant who hands contraband over to his friend for safekeeping can still assert the exclusionary rule if the police search his friend in violation of the Fourth Amendment.

____ 80. Illegally obtained evidence cannot be used by the prosecutor either as part of her case-in-chief or to impeach the defendant.

____ 81. Illegally obtained evidence can be used in a grand jury proceeding.

____ 82. The good-faith exception is an expansion of the exclusionary rule.

____ 83. The good-faith exception applies only to the Fourth Amendment.

____ 84. Juries never impose sentences on offenders.

____ 85. Judges are not allowed to review victim impact statements.

____ 86. When "good-time credit" programs are dropped, prisoners have little incentive to cooperate with prison officials.

____ 87. Presumptive sentencing is one means of controlling judicial discretion in sentencing.

____ 88. Presumptive sentences help ensure that defendants who committed similar crimes in similar circumstances receive the same sentences.

____ 89. In presumptive sentencing schemes, the judge must impose a presumed sentence unless the defense can prove the existence of mitigating circumstances.

____ 90. Under the federal sentencing guidelines, judges are given considerable discretion.

____ 91. The federal sentencing guidelines shift discretion from judges to the prosecution.

____ 92. Under the federal sentencing guidelines, judges must focus on the offense rather than the offender who committed the offense.

____ *93. The U.S. has the highest per capita incarceration rate of any industrialized Western nation.

____ *94. In more recent years, the U.S. has become increasingly lenient in its sentencing.

____ *95. The average cost of housing a prisoner is around $2000 per year.

____ *96. Putting an offender on probation is considerably cheaper than institutionalizing him in prison.

____ *97. The community has little involvement in restorative justice approaches to punishment.

____ *98. The focus of a sentencing circle is holding the offender accountable and returning both the victim and the offender to their rightful places in the community.

____ 99. Rehabilitation is the most popular rationale for punishment today.

____ 100. Retributionists struggle with the question of how much an offender must suffer before he has paid back his debt to society.

____ 101. According to the theory of retribution, criminals have no control over their actions.

____ 102. Deterrence is based on the argument that rational people seek to minimize their pain and maximize their pleasure.

____ 103. One of the criticisms of the deterrence theory is that many people commit crimes while under the influence of alcohol or drugs.

____ 104. Harshness of punishment is a more effective deterrent than the certainty and swiftness of punishment.

____ 105. Rehabilitation is based on the premise that circumstances outside of the offender's control cause him to commit crimes.

____ 106. Rehabilitation is easily implemented in correctional institutions.

____ 107. Incapacitation is costly but very effective in the short term.

___108. A probationer who violates the terms of her probation can be sentenced to jail or prison.

___109. Programs in which probationers' movements were monitored using electronic devices were determined to be constitutionally invalid.

___110. In some modern maximum-security prisons, inmates are locked down almost all the time and have virtually no human contact.

___111. Most prisons do everything possible to promote prisoners' contacts with family and friends.

___112. Double-bunking is prohibited in most prisons today.

___113. Some inmates experience institutionalization; others do not.

___*114. Physical attacks are rare in prison because of the high level of security.

___115. Most inmates leave prison with the same disadvantages with which they entered.

___116. Because most states put a great deal of time and effort into reintegrating inmates back into society, most do not return to prison.

*Questions taken from Bonus Pointers

LEGAL LINGO

Across

4. Revenge as a motive for punishment
8. Treatment as a motive for punishment
10. An officer can ask the court to issue this if she has probable cause to believe that a crime has been committed
11. Crime for which the penalty can be death
13. To induce someone to commit a crime (as a police officer)
15. To prevent a suspect from leaving (for purposes of the Fourth Amendment)
19. Punishment as a means of preventing an offender from committing any crimes
22. Act
25. Emergency
28. Panel of jurors convened to review cases to determine if probable cause exists to bind defendants over for trial
30. Without legal representation
31. Prevention of future crimes based on the theory that people seek pleasure and avoid pain
32. Temporarily detain a suspect for questioning
33. To return to prison
34. An officer can do this (interfere with the suspect's freedom to go) when he has probable cause to believe the suspect has committed a crime
35. Payment to victim as compensation for harm caused

Down

1. Document a prosecutor files if the judge finds probable cause to bind the defendant over for trial
2. Corpus _____ (body of the crime)
3. Hearing at which a judge determines if there is probable cause to bind a defendant over for trial
5. Lacking sufficient resources to hire counsel
6. Cursory search of a suspect's outer clothing
7. Link between intent and act
9. Draw a conclusion based on given facts
12. Hearing at which a defendant enters a plea
14. To find that probable cause exists to bind the defendant over for trial
16. Rule that prevents state from introducing illegally obtained evidence
17. What a defendant posts in exchange for immediate release from custody
18. Security given by the defendant to the court in exchange for immediate release from custody
20. Land around a dwelling
21. An officer can seize contraband in _____ as long as he has a lawful right to be present and immediately recognizes the objects as being contraband
23. Right to argue to the court that one's own constitutional rights have been violated
24. To prevent evidence from being admitted at trial
26. Intent
27. Set sentence
29. Police following a suspect into a private home when they are chasing him

LEGAL LOGISTICS

1. An officer follows you for several miles before pulling you over. He claims you have been driving erratically and, after asking you a few questions about where you are going and where you have been, asks you to step out of the vehicle and perform a roadside sobriety test. After you fail the test, he tells you that he is arresting you for driving under the influence and that he wants to take you to the station where he can get a blood alcohol sample from you.
   a. Must he get an arrest warrant before he can arrest you? What must he prove to the court to justify your arrest?
   b. What grounds could the officer use to justify the search of your vehicle and the contents of any closed containers in it?
   c. The officer sees a marijuana cigarette lying on the seat beside you. Does he have any grounds for seizing the cigarette or must he get a search warrant?
   d. The officer does not *Mirandize* you immediately after putting you under arrest. Can he lawfully ask you your name, age, and address?
      1. Can he lawfully ask you how many drinks you had before you drove?
      2. If you assert your right to counsel, can he lawfully continue asking you questions about what you were doing before you were stopped?
   e. Do you have a right to counsel while the officer is testing your breath for its blood alcohol content? Do you have a right to counsel at your preliminary hearing?
   f. What options do you have if you cannot afford the bail the judge sets?

2. Your office has a client, Jim, who is accused of sexually assaulting a young woman, Marjorie, while they were on a date.
   a. Jim has already been to his initial appearance. Explain to him what procedures follow the initial appearance.
   b. Under the laws of your state, what is the *mens rea* of sexual assault? What is the *actus reus*? What is the potential punishment?
   c. Jim has been charged with burglary and kidnapping as well. Explain why these charges are possible. Check the burglary and kidnapping statutes in your state to see if the state could allege burglary and kidnapping in cases of sexual assault.
   d. Ther state agrees to drop the burglary, kidnapping, and sexual assault charges in exchange for a guilty plea to simple assault and promises to recommend probation because this is Jim's first criminal offense. Jim insists he did nothing wrong and that Marjorie willingly agreed to have sex with him. Marjorie disagrees vehemently and threatens to destroy Jim and any possible hopes he might have of a career in medicine. Explain to Jim why he might want to consider a plea bargain.
   e. Assume Jim did not accept the plea bargain and that he was sentenced under a presumptive sentencing system. Explain how his sentence will be determined by the judge.
      1. If Jim were convicted of being involved in a prostitution ring, how would his sentence be calculated under the federal sentencing guidelines?
      2. How would his sentence compare if he were given an indeterminate sentence?
3. Your clients, the Myers, are accused of arson. They tell you that the firefighters who fought the blaze that destroyed their home searched the premises after the fire was out. If the courts consider the immediate search of a place destroyed by fire to be an exigent circumstance, do you think the courts will require firefighters to get a search warrant?
   a. Police investigators search an area around the Myers' home that the court considers outside the Myers' curtilage. Do the police need to obtain a search warrant?
   b. If the police want to get a search warrant to look for possible incendiary devices in the house, what will they have to do?
   c. The officers get a search warrant that the trial court later determines to be invalid. On what basis might the state get the incendiary devices the police found admitted into evidence?
   d. Several of the firefighters notice some people hanging around watching them fight the fire. They tell the police who arrive at the scene and the police start asking some of the people questions. One of them, Peter, refuses to answer their questions. He starts to walk away and two policemen step in front of him. Has he been stopped for purposes of the Fourth Amendment? Do the officers have grounds for stopping him?
   e. Peter pushes the policemen away and tries to walk past them. One of the officers grabs him and frisks him. In the process, he finds a baggie of heroin on him. Can the officer lawfully arrest him for possession of heroin?
   f. The police arrest Mr. Myer and tell him that his attorney will not get there for several hours when they know, in fact, that his attorney is waiting to see him. In a moment of remorse, Mr. Myer decides to confess. The police videotape his waiver of his *Miranda* rights. Your office argues that his waiver is invalid because the police deceived him. Are you likely to prevail?
   g. Create a scenario in which the following defenses would be appropriate for the Myers to raise.
      1. duress
      2. insanity
      3. intoxication
      4. infancy
4. Kenneth has been charged with the theft of a Snickers candy bar worth $1 from a grocery store. Kenneth has a history of ten prior convictions, including theft (of a bag of Oreo cookies), criminal mischief, assault, and possession of a controlled substance. Under the laws of Texas, Kenneth is now considered a "habitual offender" and can be charged with a felony. The state prosecutes under this statute, and his resulting sentence is 16 years. One observer says that it will cost over $200,000 to incarcerate Kenneth if he serves his entire sentence, but the chief prosecutor responds that "it's an appropriate use of taxpayers' dollars if it keeps a habitual criminal off the streets." Under each of the four theories of punishment, make arguments on behalf of the state that justify

Kenneth's punishment. Then form counterarguments on behalf of Kenneth that negate the justness of his punishment. (This was the actual sentence imposed on Kenneth Payne by a Texas jury in 2000 under the circumstances described in this hypothetical.)

a. If you were the judge in this case, what kind of punishment would you have imposed?

b. Why might prison be an inappropriate place to punish Kenneth?

A TRIP TO THE MOVIES

The movie *A Time to Kill* depicts a murder trial in Mississippi in a time of simmering racial unrest and a re-emergence of the Ku Klux Klan. Carl Lee Haley, an African-American father whose ten-year-old daughter has just been brutally raped, kills her assailants in the halls of the courthouse as they are walking to their arraignment. It is his murder trial and the ensuing search for justice that engulf the life of his attorney, Jake Brigands, his family, and assistants.

1. Could Sheriff Walls have arrested Carl Lee in the courthouse if he had apprehended him, or did he need to get an arrest warrant?

   a. Suppose Sheriff Walls had chased Carl Lee until he ran into his home. Would the Sheriff have had to secure an arrest warrant at that point?

   b. If the sheriff had arrested Carl Lee in his home, are there any grounds by which he could have seized a shotgun he saw on a table in an adjoining room without getting a search warrant?

   c. If the sheriff had to resort to getting a search warrant to find the weapon Carl Lee used in the shooting, what would he have had to show to get the warrant?

   d. Suppose a magistrate issued a search warrant that a judge later determined was invalid. Would any evidence derived from that warrant necessarily be inadmissible?

2. Should Sheriff Walls have *Mirandized* Cobb and Willard (the men who raped Tanya) before he asked them where they had been that day?

   a. Suppose Sheriff Walls gave Cobb and Willard their *Miranda* rights but gave them incorrectly, neglecting to mention their right to counsel. Will Cobb's confession be admissible if he confesses after being read these incomplete *Miranda* rights?

   b. Could his confession be used in any way even if the courts determined it was obtained improperly?

   c. Suppose that Sheriff Walls properly *Mirandized* Cobb and Willard and that Willard invoked his right to counsel. Could the sheriff continue to ask Willard questions while waiting for his attorney to arrive?

3. Why do you think the judge denied bail to Carl Lee Haley?

4. Do you think Jake Brigands had an ethical obligation to warn Sheriff Walls that Carl Haley might try to kill Cobb and Willard?

5. Why was getting a change of venue so important to the defense?

6. For what type of juror was the defense looking?

   a. Could the state use its peremptory challenges to exclude African Americans on the jury?

7. Under the test for insanity used in this case, what did Jake have to prove?

   a. Why was it so difficult for him to prove insanity under this test?

   b. Under what test might he have had an easier time of proving insanity?

   c. Jake confronts the expert witness, Dr. Wilbert Rodeheaver, with the fact that he was treating a patient he had declared legally sane. Explain why this was not necessarily a valid reason to impeach Dr. Rodeheaver.

8. Do you think Carl Lee should have accepted the state's plea offer?

9. Under which of the four theories of punishment do you think the death penalty could be justified in Carl Lee's case?

10. If Carl Lee had been found guilty, how would his sentence have been determined in federal court?

    a. If a federal judge had been sympathetic to Carl Lee's reasons for committing his crimes, what could he have done?

11. Do you think justice was served in this case?

INTERNET INQUIRIES

1. Locate the Web pages for the following criminal justice agencies in your area. Record these. If you plan on practicing in the criminal law arena, consider bookmarking these sites.
   a. Local and state police agencies
   b. County and city prosecutor's offices
   c. County and federal public defender's offices
   d. State and federal attorney general's offices
   e. Local probation department
2. Use the Internet to find out about criminal justice diversion programs.
   a. What is the purpose of a diversion program?
   b. Give three examples of diversion programs.
   c. Find the Web page for a diversion program in your area.
      (1) What does this program provide?
      (2) What are the eligibility requirements for getting into this program?
      (3) How might a client benefit from going through this program?
3. Your firm is representing a client who has been charged with aggravated assault. You have been assigned the task of gathering information relating to bail.
   a. What are his options in your jurisdiction in terms of posting a bond?
   b. What information will you need to gather in relationship to setting bail?
4. Go to the Internet and find a local or state police departments that has a Web page.
   Does this page indicate how to obtain an accident report? If it does, answer the following questions.
   a. What information must be provided?
   b. How much does a report cost?
5. Use the Internet to find the article entitled "Navigating the Maze of Criminal Records Retrieval" by Lynn Peterson, president of a public records research firm in California. After reading this article, summarize how you would approach doing a nationwide criminal records search.
6. Find out if you can access criminal records online through your local court. If you can, give the Web site of that court and summarize the process you must follow to get those records.
7. Go to *www.criminology.fsu.edl/cjlinks* and follow the links that are of interest to you. Write down the addresses of three sites that you think would be of value to you in the future and summarize the types of information available at each.

END NOTES

[1] J. Reiman, The Rich Get Richer and the Poor Get Prison (4th ed. 1995).

[2] C. Fried, *Reflections on Crime and Punishment,* 30 SUFFOLK U. L. REV. 681 (1997).

[3] 136 CONG. REC. S6374-75 (daily ed. May 16, 1990).

[4] All statistics cited in relation to this question are extracted from C. Fried, *Reflections on Crime and Punishment,* 30 SUFFOLK U. L. REV. 681 (1997).

[5] *Id.*

[6] All statistics cited in relation to this question are extracted from V. KAPPELER ET AL., MYTHOLOGY OF CRIME AND CRIMINAL JUSTICE, 292–295 (2d ed. 1996).

[7] *Developments in the Law: Changes in Prison and Crime Demographics,* 111 HARV. L. REV. 1875 (1998).

[8] J. Smolowe, *Going Soft on Crime,* TIME, NOV. 14, 1994, at 63.

[9] C. Fried, *Reflections on Crime and Punishment,* 30 SUFFOLK U. L. REV. 681 (1997).

[10] L. FRIEDMAN, CRIME AND PUNISHMENT IN AMERICAN HISTORY 456 (1993).

[11] Stephen D. Levitt, *The Effect of Prison Population Size on Crime Rates: Evidence from Prison Overcrowding Litigation,* 111, Q. J. OF ECON. 319, 319 (1996).

[12] *Developments in the Law: Changes in Prison and Crime Demographics,* 111 HARV. L. REV. 1875 (1998).

[13] R. JOHNSON & H. TOCH, THE PAINS OF IMPRISONMENT 19 (1982).

[14] J. IRWIN & J. AUSTIN, IT'S ABOUT TIME: AMERICA'S IMPRISONMENT BINGE (1994).

8

Alternative Dispute Resolution (ADR), Tribal Court Advocacy and Administrative Law

OBJECTIVES:

In this chapter you will learn:

- what ADR options are available
- what arbitration is, what types are available, and how an arbitration is typically conducted
- what mediation is, what types are available, and how a mediation is typically conducted
- what med-arb, summary jury trials, and mini-trials are and when they are appropriate to use
- what ethical rules govern mediators
- the advantages and disadvantages of ADR
- what a tribal court advocate is
- how tribal courts differ from Anglo-American courts
- what an administrative agency is

- what the role of an ALJ is
- how an administrative hearing differs from a trial
- what a centralized panel is and its impact on ALJs
- what the rule-making power of an administrative agency is and what rules govern the use of that power
- the constraints that limit the actions of an administrative agency
- the basics of researching administrative law
- the kinds of investigative actions an administrative agency can take
- when paralegals can practice before administrative agencies

---

"There's Always ADR, If You Two Need Some Help Getting This Resolved."

"What happened to you?" asked John as he spotted Martha coming around the corner. "You look like you've just seen a ghost."

"No, just my ex-husband. He called and asked if I would meet him for lunch today." Martha was still reeling from George's unexpected announcement at lunch.

"So how is George doing these days?"

"He's off to pursue a new career." George had clerked for John while he was attending law school. John had admired George's sharp intellect, but had wondered at the time whether the day-to-day practice of law would satisfy his restless mind. He had not been surprised when he found out after hiring Martha that George (whose former marriage to Martha had been a surprise to John) had gone on to earn a doctorate in computer sciences after practicing law for a few years. "I thought he just got into the computer field."

"Oh, you know George. He changes careers faster than some people change underwear. Only this time he thinks I should relieve him of his financial responsibilities for the girls while he goes to medical school."

"Can you do that on your salary?" John was aware of Martha's struggle to get her financial affairs in order after divorcing George.

"Not and stay in the house we're living in now and certainly not without changing our lifestyle pretty dramatically," replied Martha despondently.

"Do you think you can work this out?"

"I sure hope so. I don't have the energy to take it through the courts."

"Well, there's always **ADR** if you two need some help getting this resolved," offered John.

Figure 8-1
Forms of ADR

FORMS OF ADR

ARBITRATION
Neutral holds hearing, renders decision, and issues award

MEDIATION
Neutral facilitates parties in finding resolution to problem

MED-ARB
Mediation followed by arbitration if problem remains unresolved

SUMMARY JURY TRIAL
Parties present evidence to jury in abbreviated fashion

MINI-TRIAL
Parties present evidence to neutral who issues advisory opinion

PRIVATE JUDGING
Private judge has a formal trial and issues binding decision

NEUTRAL EXPERT FACT-FINDING
Neutral with expertise in matter at issue hears evidence and makes recommendations

OMBUDSMAN
Person working for organization in which problem arose hears dispute and recommends resolution

WHAT IS ADR?

alternative dispute resolution (ADR); approaches to dispute resolution that save individuals the time, expense, and psychological trauma of going to trial

Alternative dispute resolution (ADR) encompasses all those approaches to dispute resolution that allow individuals their "day in court," but saves them some of the time, expense, and psychological trauma of going to trial. The primary forms of ADR in use in the United States today are presented here.

ARBITRATION—

hearing held before a neutral third party, also referred to as a "neutral" who renders a decision and issues an award.

MEDIATION—

problem-solving process involving a neutral third party who facilitates the parties in reaching a resolution but who has no authority to render a decision.

MED-ARB—

a mediation conducted by a neutral third party followed by an arbitration using the same neutral third party if the mediation fails to resolve the conflict.

SUMMARY JURY TRIAL—

an abbreviated trial in which the parties present evidence in summary fashion to a jury, thereby allowing the attorneys to have their case evaluated.

MINI-TRIAL—

settlement process in which the parties present their case to a neutral third party who issues an advisory opinion that the parties use to negotiate a settlement.

Although other variations of ADR exist, these are the most commonly used forms in the United States at this time and will serve to illustrate the nature and scope of ADR.

The Beauty of Voluntary Arbitration Is That You Can Get the Input of a Detached Third Party, But You Can Still Reserve the Option of Going through the Courts If You're Dissatisfied with the Outcome.

Martha and George met several times but could not reach any consensus regarding child support. After their last encounter, Martha decided to ask John about arbitration because he was a member of the American Arbitration Association.

"I've heard arbitration can be a lot less expensive than litigation. But what happens if I'm unhappy with the arbitrator's decision? Am I stuck with it?" inquired Martha.

"With voluntary arbitration, you and George can set your own rules," clarified John. "So you two can decide if you want the arbitrator's decision to be **binding**. This is the beauty of arbitration, at least if it's voluntary: you can get the input of a detached third party, but you can still reserve the option of going through the courts if you're dissatisfied with the outcome."

binding final; non-appealable

arbitration allows parties to enjoy all the benefits of a trial without the inordinate expenditure of time and money.

arbitrator the neutral third party who hears the evidence and renders a decision in an arbitration

mandatory arbitration arbitration that parties must try before being granted a conventional trial

voluntary arbitration arbitration that parties use by choice as a means of attempting to resolve their dispute

binding arbitration arbitration in which the arbitrator's decision is final and non-appealable

non-binding arbitration arbitration in which the arbitrator's decision can be appealed

ARBITRATION

One of the first forms of ADR to be used, arbitration was embraced originally by the business community as a means of resolving labor disputes. **Arbitration** allows parties to enjoy all the benefits of a trial without the inordinate expenditure of time and money. Attorneys still play the role of advocate and a neutral third party still serves as an arbitrator. Arbitration's primary advantage lies in its reduction—or in some cases, elimination—of the discovery process. Control of the discovery process lies with the **arbitrator** (the neutral third party who hears the evidence and renders a decision). Many arbitration statutes allow discovery only as a "permissible" process.

Arbitration has been used longer than any other form of ADR in this country and continues to be one of the most popular. Arbitration can be ordered by the court, sometimes one party can demand it, or the parties can enter into it voluntarily. Many states have adopted statutes that compel parties to arbitrate disputes (at least if the disputed amount falls below a statutory limit) before going to trial.

Forms of Arbitration

Arbitration can take a number of different forms. In some cases, arbitration is **mandatory,** which means that the parties must try arbitration before being granted a conventional trial; in other cases, it is **voluntary,** which means it is used by the parties by choice as a means of attempting to resolve their dispute. The mandate to arbitrate can come from a statute, a contractual agreement, a court rule, or a custom. Note that the parties cannot usually be forced to settle their dispute under mandatory arbitration but can be required to at least try.

Arbitration can also be either **binding** or **non-binding.** Binding arbitration is final and generally non-appealable. The courts rarely overturn binding arbitration awards. Binding arbitration is usually found in the private sector and is entered into

---
NET NEWS

To get a sense of the history of the arbitration movement, go to *www.lectlaw.com/ref.html*, click on "Alternative Dispute Resolution," and then on "Events in the History of the AAA and ADR."

private arbitration
arbitration based on a contractual agreement

court-annexed arbitration
arbitration that takes place within the court system and that is governed by local rules

trial *de novo*   may be requested if either party is dissastified with the arbitrators award.

◆ **LOCAL LINKS** ◆
In your jurisdiction, is arbitration required for certain types of cases? If so, under what circumstances?

by agreement or custom. Non-binding arbitration is generally mandated by the courts and is appealable.

Furthermore, arbitration can be **private,** which is based on a contractual agreement, or **court-annexed,** which takes place within the court system and is governed by local rules. Private arbitration typically arises from a contract clause that specifies that the parties must arbitrate any disputes. Real estate agreements and labor union contracts often contain such clauses. Stockbrokers, lawyers, healthcare organizations, and automobile manufacturers commonly use arbitration clauses in their contracts. The parties choose an arbitrator or go through a private provider, such as the American Arbitration Association, and must pay for the arbitrator's services.

With court-annexed arbitration, the parties are notified after filing their pleadings that they must present their claim to an arbitrator. Often the statutes allow the courts to refer matters to arbitration by their own motion or by motion of a party requesting it. Parties can, however, object to arbitration by showing cause why it should not be attempted. The parties generally do not choose the arbitrators nor the rules of arbitration to be followed. The award, however, is non-binding and the parties generally do not have to pay for the arbitrator's services. If the parties are satisfied with the arbitrator's award, a judgment is entered, but if either party is dissatisfied, a **trial *de novo*** is scheduled. Disincentives to request a trial *de novo* exist in the form of fees required to make the request and potential liability for costs and attorney's fees if the requesting party fails to improve his position at trial.

Arbitration can be any combination of the above. You can, for example, have binding, voluntary, private arbitration; similarly, you can have non-binding, mandatory, court-annexed arbitration. A dispute involving a contract that contains an arbitration clause, such as a collective bargaining agreement with a union, will go to private, binding arbitration. The procedure for this arbitration will be governed by the contract. A matter involving a complaint filed in the courts that falls under a statute requiring arbitration (e.g., a federal statute requiring all civil claims involving a disputed amount less than $100,000 in monetary damages to be arbitrated) is considered non-binding, court-annexed arbitration.

Putting It Into Practice 8.1:

Suppose Mike Johnson's parents decide that the bill submitted by the neurologist who treated Mike is unreasonable because they believe that some of the charges were for services never rendered and that some of the tests the neurologist ordered were unnecessary. Under what circumstances could the Johnsons' claim be subject to mandatory arbitration? If the Johnsons are required by statute to arbitrate their claim, will the arbitrator's award be binding?

BONUS POINTERS:

AMERICAN ARBITRATION ASSOCIATION (AAA)

The American Arbitration Association (AAA) is a private, non-profit organization that provides rules for parties to follow in private arbitrations. It also maintains a list of qualified arbitrators with knowledge in specific areas. Although the AAA does nothing to render or enforce arbitration awards, it will assist in the logistics of arbitration hearings by, among other things, providing meeting places. The AAA's primary office is in New York, but it has regional offices around the country.

In some cases, contracts will specify the use of AAA rules. In other cases, the parties agree to modify the AAA rules to meet their own needs or they use rules developed by some other organization. Another commonly used private organization that has established arbitration rules and procedures is the Center for Public Resources (CPR).

For additional information about the AAA, go to *www.adr.org*. At this site, you will find publications pertaining to ADR, get information about the rules and procedures governing arbitration, see a roster of neutrals, and view the Federal Arbitration Act and the Administrative ADR Act of 1996.

For more information about the arbitration process, go to *www.lectlaw.com/ref.html*, click on "Alternative Dispute Resolution," and review the articles entitled "Article About Arbitration by AAA V.P.," "Beginner's Guide to Alternative Dispute Resolution," and "AAA Guide to Arbitration for Business Folks."

Arbitration Process

Preparation for arbitration can be much less demanding than for trial. Motion practice in arbitration, for example, may be very limited. While access to discovery tools is not a right under many statutes, arbitrators do have the authority to permit discovery to the extent they deem it reasonable. Because of the informality of the procedures, parties are not as well informed about their opponent's position as they are in litigation. Some complain that this amounts to "playing blind man's bluff" at the hearing.

The arbitrator initiates the hearing by swearing in the parties and witnesses who will testify. The parties then give opening arguments and present both documentary and testimonial evidence. The attorneys are allowed to question witnesses and the arbitrator may ask questions if necessary. Rebuttal questions are also allowed. While the rules of evidence are not followed, they may be used as guidelines. At the end of questioning, the parties may either present closing arguments or prepare post-hearing briefs. Some arbitrators may not allow both or may require submissions of a brief when the hearing is over.

Arbitration hearings, unlike trials, are not open to the public. Everything discussed in the context of the hearing is confidential and matters disclosed often are not discoverable in future proceedings.

Arbitrators usually take the matter under advisement after the hearing. By statute, agreement, or organizational rule, they are limited in the amount of time they can consider the matter. Arbitrators are not required to commit their reasons for their decisions in writing, although sometimes they do so voluntarily. An award that is binding on the parties can be set aside only if the arbitrator engaged in misconduct, refused to hear material testimony or admit material evidence, failed to decide the issues submitted for arbitration, or exceeded the limits of her authority. Courts reviewing arbitration decisions may not retry the issues of the case, but are instead limited to deciding whether the award was valid.

Putting It Into Practice 8.2:

Why might the Johnsons prefer to arbitrate their claim rather than go to trial? Why might some attorneys be uncomfortable with the arbitration process?

Role of the Paralegal

The paralegal's role in arbitration is similar to that in litigation: preparing the file, preparing witnesses, conducting research, and so forth. If the efforts to arbitrate in a court-annexed arbitration fail, the case will go to trial eventually. Therefore, the paralegal must enter into preparations for arbitration with the anticipation that a trial is a possible outcome.

Some concerns unique to arbitration may confront the paralegal, including the question of jurisdiction: Is arbitration appropriate under the governing statute or

---

NET NEWS

For assistance in finding neutrals to arbitrate disputes in the corporate world, go to *www.cpradr.org*.

---

contract clause? The paralegal must also ensure that the parties are following the most current rules governing the arbitration. Paralegals are often responsible for drafting demands for arbitration and the responses to such demands.

Assisting in the selection of arbitrators is another task that falls to paralegals. When appropriate they conduct background checks on potential arbitrators as well as conduct conflict checks to make sure no conflict of interest exists between any member of the firm and potential arbitrators.

During the hearing, paralegals must be even more familiar with documents than they are in litigation because of the impromptu nature of arbitration hearings. Being able to "think on your feet" is a particularly important attribute of paralegals in the arbitration field.

Litigation paralegals are not the only paralegals potentially connected to the arbitration process. Paralegals working in the corporate and real estate areas must research jurisdictional arbitration requirements to ensure that the arbitration clauses in their contracts comply with these requirements. This can be particularly tricky in the international arena, where arbitration laws vary greatly. Careful drafting of arbitration clauses prevents jurisdictional disputes at a later date.

Paralegals with expertise in a particular field may want to look into becoming an arbitrator. The AAA accepts nonlawyers who are experts in their field and some organizations use nonlawyers as arbitrators. To get experience as an arbitrator, consider consulting the Better Business Bureau, which uses arbitrators on a volunteer basis to preside over consumer disputes.

Over the Long Haul, People Who Use Mediation Are Less Likely to End Up in Court Fighting over the Outcome Than Those Who Allow the Decision to Be Made By a Third Party, Such as a Judge or Arbitrator.

"Before you make your decision, remember that our domestic relations court requires parties to go through mediation before they're allowed to go before a judge. You might prefer mediation to arbitration if you want to have more of a say in the outcome of your case," offered John.

"I've never experienced mediation, but I've heard a lot of good things about it from people who've used it," agreed Martha.

"I've been involved in only two mediations, but I was very impressed with the process. It doesn't work for everyone, but if you're dealing with reasonable people who are willing to take some responsibility for working things out themselves, it can be very effective. From what I've read, over the long haul, people who use mediation are less likely to end up in court fighting over the outcome than those who allow the decision to be made by a third party, such as a judge or arbitrator."

"If we choose mediation, we won't be represented by attorneys, correct?"

"In our court-mandated mediation process, attorneys are not allowed to be involved. But if you choose mediation rather than going through the courts, you can choose to be represented by counsel. I would say that if George decided to be represented, you should be represented as well. To be frank, however, many advocates of mediation maintain that attorneys are not generally well-suited for mediation because they're trained to advocate rather than compromise."

"The only thing I worry about with mediation is that George will have an advantage because he used to be a lawyer."

"Normally, I'd agree. But I know you well enough to know that you'll educate yourself thoroughly before you enter into mediation. And while George may be a bit eccentric, I don't see him doing anything manipulative or mean-spirited. I suspect the two of you could, with a little guidance, create a mutually agreeable solution."

To answer Martha's question about getting a lawyer, go to *www.nolo.com/encyclopedia/cm_ency.html* and click on "If You Choose Mediation, Will You Still Need a Lawyer?" For more insights about mediation in the context of divorce, go to *www.nolo.com/encyclopedia/div_ency.html* and click on "Divorce Mediation Myths" and "Divorce Mediation FAQ."

For more information about mediation in general, go to *www.nolo.com/encyclopedia/cm_ency.html* and click on "Why Consider Mediation," "What Kinds of Cases Can Be Mediated?" and "Some Types of Cases Should Not Be Mediated."

MEDIATION

mediation uses a neutral third party to facilitate communication between disputing parties.

mediator a neutral third party who facilitates communication between disputing parties.

Mediation uses a neutral third party to facilitate communication between disputing parties, assisting them in defining key issues, identifying possible options and alternatives, and enabling them to reach a mutually agreeable compromise. Unlike an arbitrator, a **mediator** cannot force a decision on the parties; therefore, a mediator must rely on effective communication skills to encourage parties to express their feelings and to listen to their opponent's position. For mediation to be effective, the parties often must undergo a perceptual shift. Winning at any cost is such a predominant theme in American culture that parties have to be brought to understand that mediation is designed to create a "win-win" situation that meets everyone's needs.

Mediation is usually voluntary although participation is sometimes mandated by contract or by the court. Settlement, however, can never be mandated. When settlement is reached, studies show that mediated agreements are more likely to be complied with than decisions imposed by arbitrators or judges. This success may be because the parties essentially control the decision-making process.

Types of Mediation

Several models of mediation exist. Under some models, such as the community model, the mediator takes a very nondirective role, helping the parties brainstorm and keeping the lines of communication open. The mediator does little or nothing to suggest resolution. Her primary role is to encourage the parties to express their feelings and explore possible solutions. Although some preliminary research indicates that agreements reached under this approach appear to be longer lasting than those obtained under the direction of a more controlling mediator, this approach can be very time consuming and thus impractical when time constraints exist.

The approach more likely to be used when attorneys are involved is the model typically used in the business community. Here the mediator participates more actively, suggesting resolutions and urging the parties to accept these resolutions. Under this approach, the expertise of the mediator can be helpful in assisting the parties understand their conflict, evaluate their position, and forge some kind of agreement. This approach seems to result in higher rates of settlement than the non-directive approach described above, but not necessarily in settlements that are as permanent.

transformative mediation less directive form of mediation in which parties are encouraged to speak freely until finished; no expectation of settlement exists

One of the newest approaches to mediation is called **transformative mediation;** it is used extensively by the U.S. Postal Service. This approach is even less directive than the community model. No expectation exists that any settlement will necessarily be reached. The primary purpose of this type of mediation is to allow the parties to speak until they have nothing else to say. If at the end of the mediation, the parties have not reached any consensus but have experienced some kind of "transformation" in that they understand the conflict and feel they can live with a lack of resolution, the mediation is considered successful. Very few guidelines limit the parties' conduct and emotional flare-ups are expected and permitted. The rationale is that, by fully ventilating pent-up feelings and thoughts, the parties can eventually get to what is at the core of their dispute. This kind of mediation seems to work well in employment disputes and in domestic relations cases.

Attorneys may or may not attend mediation sessions. If, however, one side is represented by counsel, the opposing side most certainly should be represented; nothing is served in mediation by having one of the parties feel besieged. Advocates of mediation often recommend that an attorney serving as litigation counsel should not also serve as mediation counsel because the roles are so different. Litigators in particular often find it difficult to switch to a mediator role because they are so geared for combat in the courtroom.

◆ **LOCAL LINKS** ◆

In what ways is mediation used in your jurisdiction?

Putting It Into Practice 8.3:

How might mediation where attorneys are involved differ from mediation where attorneys are not involved?

Mediation Process

Although the mediation process will vary depending on the type of model used, certain general procedures are followed. The mediator sets the date for the mediation and informs the parties of the rules that will be followed during the mediation. Some mediators will meet with the parties separately before the mediation begins so they had better understand the dispute. Some mediators also allow the parties to submit position papers outlining their position and the reasons they have assumed this stance. Other mediators believe that any foreknowledge about the dispute will create preconceived notions that make it more difficult for the mediator to be neutral. They contend that preparing position papers allows the parties to become more deeply entrenched and committed to their positions, thereby inhibiting resolution of their dispute.

Figure 8-2
Comparison Between Arbitration and Mediation

COMPARISON BETWEEN ARBITRATION AND MEDIATION

Arbitration Process
Limited discovery and motion practice
Swearing in of witnesses
Opening arguments
Evidence presentation
Closing arguments or post-hearing briefs
Decision is rendered

Mediation Process
Possible meeting with mediator and position papers
Setting of ground rules
Fact gathering; possible venting of feelings
Caucusing with parties separately
Guiding parties toward agreement
Clarification of tentative agreement
Writing of agreement
Possible review by court

At the beginning of the formal mediation, the mediator explains her role, the confidential nature of the proceedings, any ground rules (e.g., no name-calling), the benefits of mediation, and the procedural steps that will be followed (if any). She begins to establish a rapport with the parties, identifies any potential conflicts of interest, encourages the parties to mediate in good faith, solicits their active participation, and asks if they have questions.

During the fact-gathering stage that follows this introduction, the party who brought the dispute to the mediator is usually asked to tell his story first and then the opposing party is given an opportunity to respond. The mediator is not obliged to follow this order, however, and if multiple issues are involved, the parties may prioritize the issues before beginning the mediation. Depending on the level of participation of the mediator, she may assist the parties in practicing good communication skills, may reword judgmental language used by anyone, and may ensure that the parties have equal opportunity to speak. This first phase of mediation can be highly charged if the parties ventilate their feelings and opinions.

After this "venting," the mediator may choose to caucus with the parties separately. This is done if the mediator believes the session is getting out of control or if he needs to clarify an issue outside the hearing of the other party. Caucuses cannot be done without the consent of the other party and nothing discussed during a caucus can be disclosed to the other party without consent of each party.

During the fact-gathering, the mediator will begin to define the issues, helping the parties to focus on the issues rather than their positions. At appropriate times the mediator will reinforce points of agreement as well as conduct "reality checks" whenever necessary. The mediator steers the parties away from past events and focuses them on what they want to see happen in the future. The mediator is responsible for creating an environment in which the parties feel free to brainstorm possible options and to offer solutions without fear of censure. If no suggestions are forthcoming, the mediator may, depending on the style of mediation, offer some suggestions or ask questions that may lead to creative problem solving. In the event of an impasse, the mediator uses all of her skills to circumvent the obstruction so that the discussion can continue. As solutions are proposed, the mediator must guide the parties in assessing the practicality and reasonableness of their proposals. Doing this often requires focusing the disputants on the consequences of their decisions in terms of potential future litigation, economic and emotional costs, stress on relationships, and other practical concerns.

Once a tentative agreement is reached, the mediator clarifies the terms of the agreement and makes sure all parties understand the terms of this agreement. One way this can be accomplished is by having the parties restate the agreement in their own words. The essence of the agreement is then prepared in writing, although the parties may want to have the agreement reviewed by an attorney before signing a formal agreement. In a court-ordered mediation, the parties may be required to appear before a judge to finalize their agreement. Whatever the formal requirements for closure, advocates of mediation recommend some kind of personal closure as well, symbolized, perhaps, by a handshake or a sharing of coffee.

NET NEWS

For more information about the mediation process, go to *www.nolo.com/encyclopedia/cm_ency.html* and click on "The Six Stages of Mediation." At that same site, you can get an idea about the cost of mediation by clicking on "How Much Will Mediation Cost?" To read about an actual mediation, go to *www.lectlaw.com/ref.html*, click on "Alternative Dispute Resolution," and look for the article entitled "Story of an Actual Construction Mediation."

Putting It Into Practice 8.4:

Why do you think some courts require parties in domestic relations cases to try to mediate their disputes?

Role of the Paralegal

Paralegals who want to remain in litigation can still play a role in mediation. The same tasks that must be completed to prepare for litigation are also needed to prepare for mediation. With those matters that do not begin with litigation, investigative research is still necessary to ascertain information about assets, background of the parties, basic information relating to the issues, and so on to ensure that any negotiations are conducted in good faith and that any settlement reached is as fair as possible. If a matter starts down the litigation path but is referred by the court to mediation, the paralegal may assist in drafting such documents as a Motion for Referral to Mediation. If mediation becomes a reality, the paralegal may help prepare a position paper to educate the mediator about the case; if settlement is reached, the paralegal may prepare a settlement agreement and any related documents.

Non-litigation paralegals are often responsible for drafting agreement-to-mediate clauses in real estate contracts and other commercial transactions. As with arbitration clauses, preparation of such clauses requires research of the ADR laws in the relevant jurisdiction.

BONUS POINTERS: **SKILLS OF EFFECTIVE MEDIATORS**

Mediators are not required, or even necessarily encouraged, to be attorneys. Mediators must be nonjudgmental in both attitude and behavior. They must avoid even the appearance of evaluation if they are to preserve their role of neutrality. Accordingly, they must know how to use non-value-laden verbal language and to exhibit neutral body language.

Mediators must model active and empathic listening. They must be able to discern what is actually being said, which is sometimes different from the words being used. Similarly, they must be able to reframe what a party has said in a nonjudgmental way that reduces the "charge" (sting) on the communication so that the receiving party can respond rather than react. It is this capacity to keep the lines of communication clean that enables mediators to keep parties on track rather than going down emotional "rabbit holes" that jeopardize the possibility of settlement.

In addition to excellent listening skills, mediators must be flexible enough to adapt to the particular needs of the participants. Some individuals respond better to gentle, restrained intervention while others need more forceful guidance. The interpersonal skills required to be an effective mediator are quite sophisticated. Mediators must know, for example, how and when to steer people through impasses, how to help them save face, and how to stimulate creative problem solving without suggesting the resolution.

In general, successful mediators have patience, a sense of humor, a strong sense of caring, and a desire to help others solve challenging problems. They are able to stay calm in the presence of strong emotions. They express themselves clearly and hear others with minimal distortion. Above all, they genuinely like people and are tolerant of human eccentricities.

Putting It Into Practice 8.5:

What types of people are best suited to be mediators? Do you think you would be an effective mediator?

NET NEWS

If you are interested in getting more information about mediation as a career, go to *www.mediate.com* or *www.acctmorg* (the Web page for the American College of Civil Trial Mediators). Both of these sites provide means of locating mediators.

To see examples of and discussion about ethical standards set by various organizations for mediators, go to *www.mediate.com.*

E T H I C A L   E T I Q U E T T E

ETHICAL RULES FOR MEDIATORS

The American Bar Association (ABA), the American Arbitration Association (AAA), and the Society of Professionals in Dispute Resolution (SPIDR) have developed a set of standards to be used as guidelines in the practice of mediation. These standards are designed to be a first step in the process of assisting practitioners. The developers of this code recognize that these standards may have to be altered due to statutes or contractual agreements. They are designed, however, to guide mediators, to inform parties, and to enhance public confidence in the mediation process.

The following are the standards outlined in the Standard of Conduct for Mediators. The discussion and comments following each standard are not included.

1. Self-Determination: A mediator shall recognize that mediation is based on the principle of self-determination by the parties.
2. Impartiality: The mediator shall conduct the mediation in an impartial manner.
3. Conflicts of Interest: A mediator shall disclose all actual and potential conflicts of interest reasonably known to the mediator. After disclosure, the mediator shall decline to mediate unless all parties choose to retain the mediator. The need to protect against conflict of interest also governs conduct that occurs during and after the mediation.
4. Competence: A mediator shall mediate only when the mediator has the necessary qualifications to satisfy the reasonable expectations of the parties.
5. Confidentiality: A mediator shall maintain the reasonable expectations of the parties with regard to confidentiality.
6. Quality of the Process: A mediator shall conduct the mediation fairly, diligently, and in a manner consistent with the principle of self-determination of the parties.
7. Advertising and Solicitation: A mediator shall be truthful in advertising and solicitation for mediation.
8. Fees: A mediator shall fully disclose and explain the basis of compensation, fees, and charges to the parties.
9. Obligations to the Mediation Process: Mediators have a duty to improve the practice of mediation.

Putting It Into Practice 8.6:

Would ethical standard #1 in the Standard of Conduct for Mediators be applicable to a code of ethics for arbitrators?

"Another possibility for you to consider is med-arb. If you and George were unable to reach an agreement through mediation, the neutral party who facilitated the mediation would then be required to render a decision," explained John.

"But if that happened, wouldn't we end up presenting our case twice?" asked Martha.

"No. The same party is used for both the mediation and the arbitration, so you need to present your evidence only once. The obvious problem with this approach is that the neutral is no longer truly neutral after hearing what each party has disclosed during the mediation."

"Maybe This Would Be an Opportunity for You to Reconnect with Tim and to Get Some Valuable Information at the Same Time."

"Are you aware that Tim has just finished being trained as a mediator?" asked John cautiously, not knowing the current status of Martha's relationship with Tim.

"No. I haven't talked with Tim since we all met for dinner," admitted Martha. "But I have been thinking about calling him." Martha had taken their dinner conversation as a challenge to educate herself and had been reading articles and books about the criminal justice process as well as talking to people she knew who worked in the system. Although she was not prepared to fully relinquish all of her beliefs about the value of a punitive system, she was ready to acknowledge that the criminal justice system and its processes were in need of renovation. She had also come to a point where she was willing to open the door, if only a crack, toward re-establishing some kind of relationship with Tim.

"Maybe this would be an opportunity for you to reconnect with Tim and to get some valuable information at the same time," suggested John.

"And you'd really like that, wouldn't you?" teased Martha. "You try to be subtle, Mr. Morgan, but sometimes I can feel your hands on my back pushing me along."

"Well, maybe sometimes you need a little pushing," replied John with mock gruffness.

Tim was almost beside himself when he heard Martha's voice. He had given up hope that she would ever call and had steeled himself against making any further overtures at reconciliation. They agreed to meet the following day. Neither of them mentioned anything about their past, choosing instead to focus on Martha's dilemma.

"Are there any other options I should be aware of other than arbitration or mediation?" asked Martha after summarizing her discussion with John and explaining why the child support issue had suddenly arisen.

"Not really. There are a couple of other forms of ADR that are becoming increasingly popular: summary jury trials and mini-trials. But both of these approaches are designed for more complex cases and would not be appropriate in your case," advised Tim.

MED-ARB

med-arb combination of mediation and arbitration

A hybrid form of ADR created by combining mediation and arbitration is **med-arb**. In this approach, mediation is attempted first; if the parties fail to agree to a settlement, the same neutral that facilitated the mediation conducts an arbitration. The obvious problem that arises in this case is that the so-called "neutral" is no longer neutral, having heard information that could influence the arbitration. On the other hand, the med-arb approach is efficient and cost-effective in that the parties present their evidence only once.

Some critics of med-arb point out that parties are less likely to be fully disclosing to a mediator who may then have information that could be used against their interests in the arbitration. If, for example, a party during mediation admits that it would be willing to accept a settlement of $10,000, the mediator-turned-arbitrator would then know that it could award $10,000 rather than the $20,000 being demanded by that party. If, on the other hand, the party failed to disclose its bottom line during the mediation for fear of how this information would be used in the event of an arbitration, the mediation process would be compromised and settlement would be less likely. By the same token, an arbitrator who wanted to obtain referrals for future mediations/arbitrations would be reluctant to grant an award based on disclosures made during a mediation for fear of the disclosing party's reaction. Therefore, the integrity of both the mediation and the arbitration can be compromised when the two are combined.

The best use of med-arb seems to be with parties who like the cost savings and efficiency of this approach, who trust the integrity of the mediator/arbitrator being used, and who stand in relatively equal bargaining relationship with each other, thereby minimizing the chances of one party manipulating the process to its advantage. Parties who feel they run the risk of being out-maneuvered in this process are probably better advised to go through mediation and then a separate arbitration using a different neutral.

ROLE OF THE PARALEGAL

Paralegals have the potential of serving the same functions as they would in a traditional mediation or arbitration. Additionally, they may be asked to research the potential uses of med-arb when drafting ADR provisions in contracts.

> ### *Putting It Into Practice 8.7:*
>
> Do you think med-arb is a viable form of dispute resolution in the Johnsons' case?

SUMMARY JURY TRIAL

summury jury trial   only ADR approach that uses an actual jury

The only ADR approach that uses an actual jury is the **summary jury trial**. In this approach, the attorneys present an abbreviated version of the evidence; sometimes no "live" testimony is allowed. The jury is selected from an actual jury pool using a modified *voir dire* process (generally only two strikes are allowed). After hearing the summarized evidence (each side being given a short time, usually an hour or two), the jurors are allowed to deliberate and asked to deliver a consensual verdict, if possible. If consensus proves impossible, each juror is asked to submit separate and anonymous findings. Although the jury's verdict is non-binding (which the jurors may or may not be told), the attorneys are encouraged to engage in a roundtable discussion with the jurors to gain some insights into how the jurors reached their conclusions.

To participate in this form of ADR, the litigants must have completed discovery and essentially be ready to go to trial. Summary jury trials seem to work best when only one or two key issues are involved, the financial stakes are high, each party wants to go trial and is convinced that it will win, and a normal trial would be probably take at least one week to complete. After seeing the outcome of a summary jury trial, the litigants are sometimes more willing to settle or to settle for a more reasonable amount. Parties that stubbornly refuse to believe they could lose at trial become less recalcitrant when a verdict is rendered against them or they receive an award that is substantially less than what they anticipated.

A major criticism of summary jury trials is that, because they present the evidence in such an abbreviated manner, jurors are left with an incomplete picture and, therefore, their conclusion is inconsistent with the verdict that would have been rendered had they been presented with all the evidence. Similarly, some point out that the jury is being asked to evaluate evidence based on the attorneys' presentation of that evidence, whereas they might decide differently if they were exposed to all of the actual witnesses. Although summary trials reduce the expense of litigation, the costs can actually increase if the parties refuse to accept the jury's verdict and insist on going to trial.

> ### *Putting It Into Practice 8.8:*
>
> Suppose the Johnsons decided to sue the neurologist for malpractice, claiming that the neurologist's care for Mike fell below the standard of care in the medical community. Would a summary trial be a viable tool for resolving this claim?

◆ **LOCAL LINKS** ◆

Is med-arb used in your jurisdiction?

◆ **LOCAL LINKS** ◆

Are summary jury trials used in your jurisdiction?

mini-trial a voluntary proceeding where attorneys prepare as if they were going to trial but then present their cases in an abreviated fashion

MINI-TRIAL

A process that shares some similarities with the summary jury trial is the **mini-trial**. As with the summary jury trial, the attorneys prepare as if they were going to trial but then present their cases in an abbreviated fashion. Unlike the summary jury trial, their case is put before party representatives who have the authority to settle. Also unlike the summary jury trial, the mini-trial is a voluntary proceeding (not mandated by a judge) and the referee is usually an expert in the matter at hand rather than a judge. Because of this arrangement, parties have the freedom, as they do in mediation, to create their own solutions.

No exact format for mini-trials exists because the parties are encouraged to create their own format. However, certain steps are taken in every mini-trial. The parties agree in advance to the procedural rules, including the limits on discovery that will be followed. Live testimony can be presented, but often is not and the trial process is abbreviated, usually lasting less than one week. A neutral third party serves as referee, but representatives of the party decide how the case will be resolved. If the parties fail to settle, the neutral may advise the parties of the strengths and weaknesses of their case.

As with summary jury trials, mini-trials help the parties focus on the key issues of their case and help reduce the posturing that parties typically engage in. Hence, this process reduces the time and cost spent litigating relatively minor issues. Advocates of mini-trials point out that this form of ADR is favored by business executives because it allows them rather than their attorneys to be in control of the dispute. Therefore, mini-trials are most successful when the parties have an ongoing business relationship that they would like to continue. Mini-trials are not recommended when high emotional stakes are involved or an individual is suing a company. The process works best when equally sophisticated business representatives sit on opposite sides of the issue. They also satisfy some parties' need to have their "day in court." Attorneys find them particularly useful for clients who overestimate the strength or value of their case. Clients who are adamantly opposed to negotiations sometimes soften to the notion of settlement after hearing both sides of the case presented.

ROLE OF THE PARALEGAL

The role of the paralegal in both mini-trials and summary jury trials is similar. The work done during the pre-filing, filing, and discovery phases of such cases is the same as what would be done in preparing a case for litigation. If the parties decide to have a mini-trial, however, the paralegal may participate in drafting the Mini-Trial Agreement, which will set forth the agreed upon procedures to be followed.

In preparation for the summary presentation of evidence, the paralegal will review all documents and depositions with an eye toward refining and condensing them. Good summarization skills are essential to carry out this crucial task because all of the evidence must be crystallized into a form that captures the essence of the case. As part of this process, the paralegal may be asked to retrieve selected excerpts from various documents and depositions. Therefore, an intimate knowledge of all relevant documents is critical if this task is to be manageable. As in litigation preparation, the paralegal will be asked to prepare evidentiary displays that can be used during the presentation of evidence. If the case is settled, the paralegal may be allowed to assist in drafting the settlement agreement as well as in organizing any confidential materials that are either to be destroyed or stored. But throughout this process, the paralegal must have in mind that the case may not settle and be prepared to get ready to go to trial.

◆ **LOCAL LINKS** ◆
Are mini-trials used in your jurisdiction?

▬▬ *Putting It Into Practice 8.9:*

How might the Johnsons benefit from having a mini-trial to resolve their malpractice claim?

Tim thought for a moment and then suggested, "I suppose you could consider private judging if you wanted to expedite the hearing. But from what I know about George, I think the two of you would probably be best served by going to mediation." Although Tim knew that the remaining forms of ADR were not appropriate in Martha's case, he went on to explain Martha's other options, appreciating her need to have all the information before making a decision.

OTHER OPTIONS

private judging the parties involved agree to have a neutral, usually, a retired judge, hear and decide their case

Other options that exist as alternatives to litigation are private judging, neutral expert fact-finding, and the ombudsman. With **private judging**, the parties agree to have a neutral, who is usually a retired judge, hear and decide their case. This option gives the parties the power to select their own judge (including one who has expertise in the matter at hand), to schedule an expedited hearing, and to establish their own rules governing the procedure. This process can occur outside the realm of the court's jurisdiction by private agreement between the parties or can occur when a judge or the parties request a private judge. In the latter case, the so-called "rent-a-judge" statutes require that the private judge follow the procedural requirements of a formal trial and apply the law of that jurisdiction. The private judge must then submit his findings of fact to the presiding judge (the judge with whom the case had been filed). The private judge's decision is binding but can be appealed.

neutral expert fact-finding presentation of evidence to a neutral who has expertise in the question at issue

Neutral expert fact-finding can be voluntary (private and outside the court's intervention) or involuntary (court-ordered); in both cases it is non-binding. A neutral with expertise in the question at issue is used to make recommendations. This approach is used to resolve complex disagreements in the securities, patent, medical malpractice, and anti-trust areas of the law. Such proceedings tend to be very informal and of an investigatory nature. They focus on obtaining impartial feedback from someone whose expertise in the area of question is respected by both parties. This process is sometimes followed by an arbitration, mediation, or litigation.

ombudsman individual hired by an organization to hear disputes and complaints and recommend solutions

A final form of ADR that is used involves the use of an **ombudsman,** who is accustomed to hearing disputes or complaints and recommending how they might be resolved. Hospitals, corporations, and educational organizations use ombudsmen to resolve employee as well as customer complaints. These people work for the organization but report to the chief executive of the agency and remain outside of the internal chains of command. Ombudsmen typically engage in a wide range of activities including mediation, arbitration, fact-finding, counseling, problem-solving, and exchanging information.

◆ **LOCAL LINKS** ◆

Are private judging, neutral expert fact-finding, and ombudsmen used in your jurisdiction?

▬▬ *Putting It Into Practice 8.10:*

Which of the options described above might assist the Johnsons in resolving their malpractice claim?

"Mediation Tends to Work Better When the Parties Are in a Position of Relatively Equal Bargaining Power."

When Tim could see that Martha was leaning toward mediating the child support issue with George, he suggested she consider a few things. "You might want to consider having an attorney as a mediator, specifically an attorney who has or has had a domestic relations practice in the recent past. This way, she would be familiar with the child support guidelines the courts are following and would know how your situation would most likely be resolved if you went before a judge in our county. On the other hand, some people would argue that a non-lawyer could just as effectively, or in some people's minds, even more effectively, mediate your case because such a mediator would not be influenced by a knowledge of the law."

"That's a good point and something I hadn't even considered. I'll have to think about that," said Martha appreciatively. "Along those same lines, I'm still a little apprehensive about the fact that George has a better knowledge of substantive law than I do. And while I don't think he had much experience in the area of domestic relations, I'm afraid he might have an advantage when it comes to arguing his position."

"You have a valid concern," agreed Tim. "Mediation tends to work better when the parties are in a position of relatively equal bargaining power. I would suggest you get some legal advice before you enter into any kind of mediation so you're well aware of what your legal rights are. You'd probably be upset if you found out after the mediation that you'd agreed to forfeit something to which you're legally entitled. On the other hand, no one has a more sincere interest in the welfare of your children than you and George and no one knows what your finances can bear better than you two. So in many respects, despite what guidelines the law may offer, you two are in a better position to negotiate a fair agreement than anyone."

BRIGHT AND DARK SIDE OF ADR

ADR is still in its infancy. As such, little research has been done to date to test its efficacy either as it is used privately or in the court system. However, both proponents and skeptics agree that ADR can potentially save time and money. In light of the alleged litigation explosion, ADR represents a means of resolving disputes more expeditiously and without the inordinate costs of litigation. Businesses in particular, especially those who engage in international commerce, have found ADR to be a viable form of dispute resolution. Furthermore, by relieving some of the congestion in the courts, ADR opens the door for cases that truly demand litigation.

On the other hand, one of the criticisms levied against ADR is that it actually adds time and creates more expense to resolve disputes. This criticism is particularly applicable to court-annexed arbitration that mandates that cases below a certain dollar amount must go to arbitration. The parties must prepare for a hearing, take time off work to attend the hearing, wait for the arbitrator's award, and then notify the court they are dissatisfied with the award before they are entitled to a trial *de novo*. Mediation can also require more time to complete than would litigation, particularly where the issue involves several people in a community and has a strong emotional context.

In rebuttal, however, efficiency is not necessarily the best measure of success in cases of this nature. Giving people the time to vent their frustrations and express their feelings may save time in the long run because the solution that is eventually crafted may resolve the problem permanently. A more expeditious resolution, on the other hand, may result in the parties coming back to court at a later date because of their unwillingness or inability to conform to a court's dictate. Furthermore, evidence exists that supports the premise that compliance with the resultant decision is greater with those who are given an opportunity to participate in the decision-making than those to whom the outcome is simply dictated.

NET NEWS

Not surprisingly, ADR can be done online. To read an assessment of the fusion of ADR and the Internet and to get sites for on-line ADR services, go to *www.paralegals.org/Reporter* and click on "Online 2000." Look for the article entitled "Electronic ADR."

Another benefit of ADR is that the availability of all the varieties of ADR allows parties to enjoy more flexibility than found in traditional litigation. They can choose from a simplified hearing process or can assert control over the decision-making process through mediation. They can enjoy the privacy and non-binding nature of some forms of ADR, which allow them to air their grievances simply and efficiently, and still fall back on the traditional forms of litigation if they decide to. All the preparation they put in toward preparing their case for ADR can be applied to litigation. Even when ADR fails, it can still simplify the litigation process and allow attorneys to prepare cases more efficiently and less expensively. (This efficiency is further enhanced by the use of paralegals.) It also helps parties avoid the uncertainty of litigation and provides them remedies that are more flexible than typically available in the judicial process.

Some are concerned, however, that ADR may force those who cannot afford to litigate to lose some of the rights to which they are entitled in litigation. They point out that inexpensive and expeditious adjudication is not necessarily synonymous with fair and just adjudication. Because parties do not always possess equal power and resources, the concern is that informal processes lacking procedural protection will result in ill-informed decisions. These critics point to family law as one area where ADR may bring about a "second-class" justice. They argue that the rights that women have gained over the last decade may be lost if domestic relations disputes are pushed into ADR. Although studies show that mediation program participants are often pleased with the process and the results, divorce mediation raises concerns about power imbalances between the mediating parties. Where there is a history of domestic violence, for example, the party being abused may feel incapable of negotiating on her own behalf. Critics of ADR believe that disadvantaged individuals benefit most from formal legal processes, that the more intimate ADR processes may actually prejudice weaker individuals, and that even after agreement is reached, judicial oversight may be necessary to protect the weaker parties.

Despite the possibility of not protecting less powerful individuals, ADR often preserves relationships that might otherwise be severed after enduring the travails of litigation. With mediation in particular, parties are able to communicate directly with another. After venting their feelings, they can then focus on a rational cost/benefit analysis of the difference between litigating and settling.

To the contrary, however, some point out that some disputes cannot be resolved by mutual agreement and good faith because these disputes reflect sharply contrasting views about fundamental public values that cannot be eliminated by simply encouraging disputants to understand each other. These critics maintain that a potential danger of ADR is that disputants who seek only reconciliation may ignore public values reflected in rules of law established by the legislature. Some controversies, they argue further, should be brought to the public's attention. Difficult issues of constitutional or public law and matters that affect large groups, such as pollution and corporate fraud, should be adjudicated to ensure the proper application of public values. Environmental disputes, which they cite as illustrative of this problem, are often settled by mediation. The danger, they maintain, is

◆ **LOCAL LINKS** ◆

How well has ADR been accepted in your jurisdiction?

that environmental standards will be created by private groups without the democratic checks of governmental institutions.

Ultimately, one of the greatest strengths of ADR is that it helps people focus on their real needs and interests and overcome perceptual differences. Neutrals who facilitate the ADR process assist parties in realistically evaluating their case by pointing out its weaknesses. As a result, proposals suggested by these third parties can avoid the knee-jerk negative reactions that might be precipitated by proposals suggested by the other party.

◼ *Putting It Into Practice 8.11:*

What is your overall assessment of ADR as an alternative to litigation? Would you advise Martha to mediate her dispute with George?

BONUS POINTERS:

QUALITY CONTROL

ADR works only if the neutrals are well trained. The question is what kind of training should be required. Some believe that neutrals must have substantive expertise in the field in which the dispute arose, as do most arbitrators, who are experts in their field and certainly more knowledgeable about the issue at hand than the average juror. Others argue that a lack of substantive knowledge is an asset because the neutral will be less likely to prejudge the situation (in arbitration) or offer options (in mediation). They point out that those who opt for ADR can select another neutral if they believe the one they have been assigned is unqualified, whereas litigators have little or no choice about the judge they are given.

A corollary to the training issue is the question of whether ADR should be regulated and, if so, by whom it should be regulated. Bar associations often see themselves as best equipped to moderate ADR, but non-lawyer facilitators often see it differently. Their concern is that the legal profession will make ADR the province of those with legal training and will strip ADR of its unique characteristics by making facilitators become mini-lawyers.

Figure 8-3
Pros and Cons of ADR

PROS AND CONS OF ADR	
Pros	**Cons**
Saves time	Can take more time than litigation alone
Saves money	In some cases costs more money than litigation alone
Relieves court congestion	Some parties have to take extra steps
Increases compliance with decision rendered	Not always efficient
Gives parties more flexibility	Don't get their day in court
Allows parties to avoid uncertainty of litigation	Denies litigation to those who need it
Assists in preparing for litigation	Increases cost of eventual litigation
Gives alternative form of dispute resolution	Provides "second "class" justice to poor
Helps preserve relationships	Fails to protect weaker parties
Allows venting of feelings and opinions	Some disputes cannot be resolved just through understanding
Helps people realistically assess their case	Denies procedural protections to some

To get the perspective of three paralegals working in the field of ADR, go to *www.paralegals.org/Reporter* and click on "Fall 1997." Go to the section entitled "Paralegal Roles and Responsibilities."

"I'd be glad to help you get prepared if you decide to go ahead with the mediation," Tim offered. "No strings attached," he added quickly when he saw Martha's head whirl around.

"Really?" Martha asked, somewhat stunned. "After all the terrible things I've said to you? And the way I've treated you?"

"I should never have kept you in the dark about my past. It was wrong and I'm really, really sorry," continued Tim contritely.

"Please, don't apologize," interrupted Martha. "I feel bad enough already. Can't we just start over? I'd like to get to know you—the whole you—if you'll give me a another chance. Do you think we could be friends?"

RECESS

SUMMARY – PART A

The primary forms of ADR used in this country are arbitration, mediation, med-arb, summary jury trials, and mini-trials. Arbitration was one of the first forms of ADR to be used. It allows attorneys to present their case to a neutral third party, but saves the time and money required to go to trial. Arbitration can be mandatory or voluntary, binding or non-binding, and private or court-annexed. Private arbitration typically arises out of a contract clause requiring the parties to arbitrate disputes, whereas court-annexed arbitration is usually dictated by statute. With private arbitration the award is usually binding and the parties must pay for the arbitrator's services. With court-annexed arbitration, the award is usually non-binding and the parties can request a trial *de novo*; the parties do not have to pay for the arbitrator's services. Appeals are often discouraged, however, by requiring fees or by holding parties liable for costs if they do not improve their position at trial. Disputes involving contracts containing arbitration clauses will go to private, binding arbitration, whereas matters filed in the courts governed by statutes requiring arbitration will go to non-binding, court-annexed arbitration.

The procedures for private arbitration are set forth in the contract requiring arbitration. Many contracts specify the use of AAA rules. Under these rules, arbitrators are selected from a list of names provided by the AAA. The parties strike those names that are unacceptable, allowing the AAA to select an arbitrator from the remaining names. Parties can also choose arbitrators from private sources.

Arbitrations are generally informal procedures, where the rules of evidence are used only as guidelines. Because of the informality of the process and the lack of extensive discovery, some believe that going into an arbitration is like playing "blind man's bluff." Hearings follow the same outline as trials, beginning with opening statements and the presentation of evidence, and ending with closing arguments and/or the presentation of post-hearing briefs. They differ from trials in that they are closed to the public.

Arbitrators usually take the matter under advisement but must render a decision within a specified time period. Binding awards cannot be set aside except for specific misconduct on the part of the arbitrator. Courts reviewing these decisions can decide only whether the award was valid and cannot retry the issues.

Mediation allows parties to find their own way to resolution. The neutral facilitates communication, assists in defining the issues, identifies possible solutions, and generally aids the parties in working toward compromise. The level of directiveness of the neutral depends on the type of mediation being used. The community and transformative models of mediation are very non-directive, whereas the business model most often used when attorneys are involved encourages the mediator to be more participatory. Some studies indicate that the latter approach results in a higher rate of settlement, but that settlements arising out of the less directive approaches are longer lasting.

Mediation is usually voluntary, but can be mandated by contract or by the court. Although attorneys need not be present, if one side is represented by counsel, it is usually best that the opposing side is also represented. When attorneys participate in the mediation process, they must manifest different skills than are required in litigation. Above all, they must keep in mind that their primary function is to facilitate compromise, not to win.

The mediation process varies. Some mediators like to meet with the parties before the mediation and ask them to prepare position papers. Other mediators believe that any prior knowledge about the dispute makes it more difficult for the mediator to be neutral. Most mediators open the process by establishing the rules, explaining their role and the process, identifying any conflicts of interest, and encouraging the full participation of the parties. During the fact-gathering stage, the parties tell their stories and vent their feelings. The mediator may then choose to caucus with the parties separately. Nothing said during a caucus can be disclosed to the opposing party without consent of each party. The mediator then helps the parties focus on the issues rather than their positions and on what they want rather than what has happened in the past. As the parties offer solutions, the mediator encourages them to assess the practicality and reasonableness of their proposals, and if no solutions are proposed, may suggest some herself. If an agreement is reached, she clarifies the terms of the agreement, making sure that everyone understands what the agreement is. Once the agreement is formalized, the mediator brings closure to the process.

A hybrid of arbitration and mediation, med-arb, begins with a mediation, which, if unsuccessful, culminates in an arbitration. The same neutral serves as both arbitrator and mediator. One primary criticism of this approach is the tainted neutrality of the facilitator, which can potentially compromise the integrity of both the arbitration and mediation. Efficiency and cost-effectiveness are the primary benefits of this process. Med-arb works best when the parties have relatively equal bargaining power and trust the neutral.

Summary jury trials and mini-trials are both means of presenting evidence in an abbreviated fashion and of obtaining feedback from neutral third parties. With summary jury trials, the evidence is presented to a jury with whom the attorneys can engage in a roundtable discussion after the jury has rendered its verdict, or if no consensus is reached, after individual jurors have submitted their verdicts. With mini-trials, the evidence is presented to a neutral who is usually an expert in the question at hand. Summary jury trials work best when only a few key issues are at stake, when a regular trial would last a week or more, and when the financial stakes are high and each party is convinced it would win at trial. They do not work unless the parties are substantially prepared to go to trial and they may result in a skewed outcome because the jurors do not get to hear all of the evidence and what evidence they do hear is presented by the attorneys rather than the actual witnesses. Mini-trials also assist the parties to focus on the key issues and to avoid the costs of conventional litigation.

Business executives often like this form of ADR because it gives them rather than their attorneys control of the dispute. Mini-trials work best when the parties have an ongoing relationship they want to preserve and when no highly emotional issues are at stake. They give parties their "day in court" and often encourage those who are adamantly opposed to negotiations to see the value of settlement.

Other less popular ADR options include private judging, neutral expert fact-finding, and the use of an ombudsman. Private judging allows parties to select their own judge, to schedule an expedited hearing, and to establish their own rules to govern the procedure. Neutral fact-finding is often used when complex issues are involved and is frequently followed by arbitration, mediation, or litigation. Ombudsmen are used by hospitals, corporations, and educational organizations to resolve employee and consumer complaints.

Ideally, ADR can save parties time and money and relieve the courts of some of their congestion. Parties who use ADR often comply better with the final decision than those who litigate. Parties also have more flexibility when they choose ADR rather than litigation and can avoid some of the uncertainties of litigation. Furthermore, ADR assists parties in realistically assessing their case and preserving relationships. On the other hand, ADR can take more time and cost more money than litigation. Parties sometimes experience "second hand justice" when they turn to ADR and weaker parties may not receive the protection they need. Some disputes simply require more than mutual understanding because they involve public values that need to be aired in the courtroom.

KEY TERMS

Alternative dispute resolution (ADR)	Court-annexed arbitration	Neutral	Private judging
	Mandatory arbitration	Neutral expert fact-finding	Summary jury trial
Arbitration	Med-Arb		Transformative mediation
Arbitrator	Mediation	Non-binding arbitration	Trial *de novo*
Binding	Mediator	Ombudsman	Voluntary arbitration
Binding arbitration	Mini-trial	Private arbitration	

REVIEW QUESTIONS – PART A

1. Describe the following forms of arbitration.
   a. private
   b. court-annexed
   c. mandatory
   d. voluntary
   e. binding
   f. non-binding
2. Describe the basic arbitration process.
3. How does mediation differ from arbitration?
4. What are the various types of mediation?
5. Describe the various stages of a typical mediation.
6. What are the qualities of an attorney advocating well for a client during a mediation?
7. What are the qualities of a good mediator?
8. Describe each of the following.
   a. med-arb
   b. summary jury trial

   c. mini-trial
   d. private judging
   e. neutral expert fact-finding
   f. ombudsman
9. Explain the advantages and disadvantages of the following.
   a. med-arb
   b. summary jury trial
   c. mini-trial
10. Under what circumstances would you use each of the following?
    a. private judging
    b. neutral expert fact-finding
    c. ombudsman
11. Discuss at least four reasons that ADR should be utilized as a means of conflict resolution. Give a counterargument to each of these reasons.

PRACTICE EXAM – PART A

MULTIPLE CHOICE

1. Alternative dispute resolution includes
   a. arbitration
   b. mediation
   c. private judging
   d. all of the above

2. Binding arbitration
   a. results in awards that are appealable
   b. is not allowed in the context of private arbitration
   c. results in awards that are rarely overturned by the courts
   d. none of the above

3. With court-annexed arbitration
   a. the parties are referred to arbitration after filing their pleadings
   b. parties cannot object to arbitration
   c. the award is binding
   d. all of the above

4. A binding arbitration award can be set aside if
   a. the arbitrator engaged in misconduct
   b. the arbitrator exceeded the limits of her authority
   c. refused to hear material evidence
   d. all of the above

5. At arbitration hearings
   a. no rebuttal questions are allowed
   b. the discovery rules vary from jurisdiction to jurisdiction
   c. no closing arguments are allowed
   d. the rules of confidentiality do not apply

6. A mediator
   a. facilitates communication between the disputants
   b. renders a decision and issues an award
   c. must do everything possible to steer the parties toward compromise
   d. tries to get the parties to accept her proposed solution

7. Mediation
   a. requires a directive approach by the mediator
   b. exists in a variety of forms
   c. is usually mandated by the courts
   d. agreements are less likely to be complied with than decisions rendered by arbitrators

8. All mediators
   a. require parties to submit position papers
   b. meet with the parties prior to the mediation
   c. help the parties identify the key issues
   d. allow parties to vent without restriction

9. During the mediation
   a. the party bringing the dispute to the mediator is always allowed to speak first
   b. the parties are allowed to express their feelings
   c. the parties can caucus with one another
   d. an impasse automatically terminates the mediation

10. Once a tentative agreement is reached
    a. the mediation is over
    b. the parties must find some way to create closure
    c. the parties' attorneys negotiate a settlement
    d. the mediator makes sure that each party understands the terms of the agreement

11. Good mediators
    a. are tolerant
    b. are interested in helping others solve their problems
    c. know how to help people save face
    d. all of the above

12. Med-arb
    a. works best when the parties have unequal bargaining power
    b. is cost effective but not efficient
    c. can be problematic because the same neutral is used for the arbitration and mediation
    d. uses a different arbitrator and mediator

13. Summary jury trials
    a. work best when the financial stakes are low
    b. allow attorneys to gain insights from how the jury reached its verdict
    c. allow parties to go before a mock jury without having to actually prepare for trial
    d. are open to the public

14. Mini-trials
    a. allow parties to have their "day in court"
    b. are particularly useful for parties who are adamantly opposed to settlement
    c. are favored by business executives
    d. all of the above

15. Hospitals, educational organizations, and corporations often resolve customer and employee disputes using
    a. ombudsmen
    b. neutral expert fact-finding
    c. summary jury trials
    d. private judging

16. The strength of ADR is
    a. that it always reduces the cost of resolving disputes
    b. that it always protects weaker parties
    c. that is always takes less time than litigation
    d. relieves court congestion

17. ADR
    a. is most appropriate when there is a need to establish precedent
    b. is inappropriate when there is need to bind non-parties
    c. can effectively be used to resolve every controversy
    d. is particularly effective when fault needs to be assigned or rights need to be established

FILL IN THE BLANK

18. _____ involves a third-party neutral who facilitates the resolution of the conflict but who lacks authority to render a decision.

19. _____ involves a third-party neutral who hears the presentation of evidence by the attorneys and who issues an award, whereas _____ involves a third-party neutral who hears presentation of evidence by the attorneys and who issues an advisory opinion that the attorneys can use to negotiate a settlement.

20. _____ uses the same neutral third-party to mediate and, if necessary, arbitrate.

21. A _____ requires the use of a jury, but the jury's decision is not binding on the parties.

22. _____ _____ arbitration awards cannot be appealed (unless the arbitrator engaged in misconduct), whereas _____ arbitration awards can be set aside and result in a trial _____ .

23. Under _____ arbitration, the parties must try arbitration before they can go to trial.

24. A _____ arbitration takes place within the court system and is governed by local rules, whereas a _____ arbitration is based on contractual agreement and is governed by rules agreed upon by the parties.

25. In the _____ model of mediation the mediator encourages the parties to communicate but does little to suggest resolution. In the _____ model of mediation, the mediator takes an even less directive approach and does not necessarily expect the parties to reach settlement.

26. A hybrid form of ADR involving both arbitration and mediation is called _____ .

27. The only form of ADR that actually uses a jury is called a _____ .

28. _____ help parties focus on key issues by having the parties present an abbreviated form of the evidence to representatives of the parties who have the authority to settle.

29. With _____ , the parties hire a neutral (usually a retired judge) who hears their case and renders a decision, whereas with _____ , a neutral with expertise in the matter at hand is used to listen to the evidence and make recommendations.

30. _____ are used by hospitals, corporations, and educational organizations to resolve employee and customer disputes.

TRUE OR FALSE

____ 31. Arbitration can never be mandated by a court.

____ 32. Private arbitration usually arises out of a contract clause requiring parties to arbitrate any disputes.

____ 33. An award arising out of non-binding arbitration cannot be appealed.

____ 34. Under mandatory arbitration, parties can be forced to settle their dispute.

____ 35. Parties engaged in a court-annexed arbitration can request a trial *de novo* if they are dissatisfied with the arbitrator's award.

____ 36. A contract containing an arbitration clause will go to private, binding arbitration and the contract will dictate the procedures to be followed in the arbitration.

____ 37. A matter filed in the courts that by statute must be arbitrated is considered non-binding, court-annexed arbitration.

____ 38. Parties involved in binding arbitration do not have to pay for the services of the arbitrator, but parties involved in non-binding arbitration do have to pay for the services of the arbitrator.

_____ 39. Some courts have held parties who appeal arbitration awards liable for costs if they fail to improve their position at trial.

_____ 40. Parties have an absolute right to discovery if they agree to arbitration.

_____ 41. Some attorneys believe that going into an arbitration hearing is like playing "blind man's bluff."

_____ 42. The rules of evidence are usually followed in arbitration hearings.

_____ 43. Attorneys who are involved in an arbitration are required to file post-hearing briefs as well as to give closing arguments.

_____ 44. Arbitration hearings are open to the public.

_____ 45. Arbitrators are limited in the amount of time they can take a matter under advisement.

_____ 46. Courts reviewing arbitration awards are allowed to basically retry the issues.

_____ 47. Unlike arbitrators, mediators do not impose decisions on the parties.

_____ 48. Mediation itself is usually voluntary, but settlement is mandatory.

_____ 49. The community and transformative models of mediation require a directive approach from the mediator.

_____ 50. The business model of mediation results in higher rates of settlement than less directive approaches, but those agreements are not as long-lasting.

_____ 51. The transformative model considers mediation successful if the parties understand the conflict and decide they can live with it even if they do not reach a consensus.

_____ 52. Attorneys are not allowed to attend mediation sessions.

_____ 53. Litigators sometimes find it difficult to advocate in mediations because the roles are so different.

_____ 54. All mediators require parties to submit position papers before the mediation.

_____ 55. The fact-gathering stage of mediation is usually very quiet because the parties are simply listening to each other.

_____ 56. The mediator has a right to reveal anything disclosed to her during a caucus with the opposing party.

_____ 57. The mediator tries to steer the parties away from past events and focus them on what they want to achieve.

_____ 58. A mediator may never suggest solutions.

_____ 59. Mediators help parties assess the practicality and reasonableness of their proposals and assist them in doing "reality checks."

_____ 60. Mediators should model passive and reactive listening.

_____ 61. Mediators should develop a technique for mediation and use that same technique with every mediation they conduct.

_____ 62. Paralegals generally make poor mediators because they do not have a law degree.

_____ 63. Once a tentative agreement is reached, the mediator's job is over.

_____ 64. Med-arb can create problems for both the parties and the neutral because the neutrality of the latter can be called into question.

_____ 65. Med-arb works best when the parties are looking for a cost-effective and efficient method of resolving their dispute and believe they have comparable bargaining power.

_____ 66. Parties in med-arb are usually more willing to disclose confidential information than they are in a simple mediation.

_____ 67. With summary jury trials, the attorneys often present an abbreviated form of the evidence themselves rather than using "live" testimony.

_____ 68. Mini-trials and summary jury trials work best when the litigants are still involved in the discovery process and not yet prepared to go to trial.

_____ 69. Summary jury trials are the most appropriate form of ADR when the financial stakes are low and several key issues are involved.

_____ 70. Summary jury trials reduce the cost of trial even if the parties refuse to accept the jury's verdict and go to trial.

_____ 71. The conclusion of a summary jury trial can be inconsistent with the verdict that would have been rendered if the jury had been able to hear all of the evidence.

_____ 72. The neutral in a mini-trial is usually a retired judge.

_____ 73. Parties are encouraged to create their own format for a mini-trial.

_____ 74. Business executives favor mini-trials because they, not their attorneys, decide how the case will be resolved.

_____ 75. Mini-trials are most appropriate when high emotional stakes are involved and when an individual is suing a company.

_____ 76. With private judging, parties can select their own judge, schedule their own hearing time, and establish their own procedural rules.

____ 77. The neutral expert fact-finding process is used most frequently in complex cases because experts in the field in question are used to make recommendations to the parties.

____ 78. Ombudsmen are successful in resolving disputes for organizations because they are employed outside of those organizations.

____ 79. In some cases, ADR can actually add time and create more expense to resolve disputes.

____ 80. Allowing people to participate in the decision-making process may actually increase the likelihood of their complying with the resultant decision.

____ 81. When ADR fails, it further complicates the litigation process.

____ 82. In some cases, ADR may bring about a "second-class" justice.

____ 83. ADR helps preserve relationships that might otherwise be severed in the litigation process.

____ 84. A potential danger of ADR is that parties may be content with seeking resolution at the expense of sacrificing public values that should be brought to the public's attention.

____ 85. Neutrals are required to have substantive expertise in the field in which they are serving as a neutral.

____ 86. ADR is currently regulated by local bar associations.

____ 87. ADR is inappropriate when a judicial precedent is needed or when non-parties need to be bound by a decision.

____ 88. Some believe that courts should not be allowed to annex ADR.

____ 89. Some believe that cases where rights need to be established or fault assigned should be channeled into ADR, whereas those cases where settlement is the goal should be channeled into litigation.

*Questions taken from Bonus Pointers

PART B

"I Feel Comfortable with the Indian Ways and Thought That Being a Tribal Court Advocate Might Be a Way for Me to Go."

"I have a favor to ask you, Martha," Tim said hesitantly, after they had cleared the air about their past and had agreed to the parameters of their newly-forged friendship.

"Sure. What can I do for you?" Martha was happy for an opportunity to show Tim that she truly wanted to preserve their friendship.

"I'm thinking about applying for a new real estate license so I can get back into selling again," began Tim.

"Really? I thought you were going to put all your energy into getting admitted to law school."

"Actually, I received notice a few weeks ago that I've been accepted for the fall semester."

"How wonderful! Congratulations! I'm so happy for you!" exclaimed Martha, hiding her misgivings about not being in his life to celebrate his acceptance when he received it. "So why go back to what got you into trouble to begin with?"

"It wasn't selling real estate that got me into using coke. Besides, I'm a very different person now. Have no fear, Martha, I'm not going to get sucked back into that lifestyle," affirmed Tim when he saw the look of consternation on Martha's face. "I'm going to need money to support myself during law school and this is the best way I can think of to make money and have flexible hours. Plus, I've got to be realistic. There's a very good chance that, because of my felony conviction, I may never get admitted to the bar even if I do really well in law school. I've got to be prepared to have alternative means of bringing in income. So I'm exploring a number of income-generating possibilities."

"Including being a **tribal court advocate,** I see." Martha had just noticed the pamphlets on Tim's coffee table advertising a course in tribal court advocacy at one of the local community colleges. "You never mentioned that you had an interest in tribal law."

"To be honest, I'd stopped thinking about that as a possible career when you and I were dating because I knew you wouldn't have wanted to uproot the girls from their school and I didn't want to have a commuting relationship. But I did spend the first ten years of my life on the Navajo reservation—my father was a teacher there—and I have very fond memories of the 'res.' I feel comfortable with the Indian ways and thought that being a tribal court advocate might be a way for me to go."

---

tribal court advocate   a non-attorney who is allowed to represent individuals before the tribal court

TRIBAL COURT ADVOCACY

Courts of Indian Offenses courts organized by the Bureau of Indian Affairs to keep order on Indian reservations and educate the tribes in Anglo-American norms

Tribal courts exist in two forms: the **Courts of Indian Offenses,** organized by the Bureau of Indian Affairs (BIA), and specific tribal courts, created and controlled by tribal governments pursuant to their inherent sovereignty. The Courts of Indian Offenses were originally established by the federal government to keep order on Indian reservations while educating tribal people in Anglo-American norms. They are often called CFR courts after the extensive Code of Federal Regulations (a codification of the rules and regulations issued by federal administrative agencies) that govern them. In contrast, some traditional tribal courts operated before and after the formation of the United States.

The two types of courts differ significantly. The origin of the court—federal or tribal—determines its power over particular individuals and actions. Both types of courts, however, can use tribal law. Today, most tribes have taken over the Courts of Indian Offenses. At the same time, the tribal courts' jurisdiction has broadened from primarily criminal to civil suits of increasing complexity. The law in modern tribal courts varies from jurisdiction to jurisdiction. These differences reflect the creativity of tribal courts as they balance tribal traditions and needs against the traditions and requirements of Anglo-American law.

Undoubtedly, no other ethnically identifiable population has so complex a relationship with the national government and its legislature. The status of American Indian nations as dependent sovereigns creates continuous disputes before the federal courts as tribal activities intersect with state or federal concerns. These disputes range from the most personal matters of family relations (such as child custody), to gaming, environmental regulation, regulation of the producers of crafts and arts, and broad jurisdictional issues.

judicial notice agreement by a judge to take note of certain readily verifiable facts without requiring the parties to provide evidence

For tribal courts, indigenous customs and usages that have survived the five-hundred-year struggle with Euro-American cultures are an important foundation of tribal law. Custom does not necessarily mean unwritten, inconsistent rules of law. Customary principles may be established when the court takes **judicial notice** of custom, uses it for the decision, and then publishes the opinion.

Essentially, the indigenous perspective can be traced to the close relationship tribal communities enjoy with nature. Balance and harmony in one's relationships with other members of the community, all life forms, and the physical universe are core tribal values. These values then underpin the goal of reconciliation in the resolution of disputes. While Anglo-American models of dispute resolution focus on determining the guilt of the offender and on imposing a punishment, indigenous models focus on restitution and making amends to all of the affected parties. When parties consent to or seek resolution through the Navajo Peacemaker Court, for example, the dispute is converted from a criminal matter into a civil case. Even if the matter remains a criminal action, under Navajo law the court can order punishment for the offender and compensation for the victim. The criminal code retains the Navajo custom that requires the offender to compensate the victim and the victim's clan.

NET NEWS

To read definitions of terms important to Indian law, such as "jurisdiction" and "Indian country," go to *www.indianz.com*. This site also has links to the Bureau of Indian Affairs (BIA) and Indian law court decisions. Other sites with information about tribal law are *www.nativesense.com* and *www.ndnlaw.com*.

Figure 8-4
Core Values of Tribal Law

Harmony with community

Balance   Compensation

CORE VALUES OF TRIBAL LAW

Restitution   Harmony with all life

Figure 8-4
Core Values of Tribal Law

◆ **LOCAL LINKS** ◆
Are there any tribal courts operating in your jurisdiction?
If so, is tribal court advocacy in those courts open to non-Indians?

Another aspect of Indian law that accommodates custom is in tort law. The standard for a defendant's conduct, for example, is "carelessness" rather than negligence. This standard allows the trier of fact to decide whether the defendant's conduct appeared careless under the circumstances without requiring a rigid determination of such elements as duty and standard of care. Some tribally authorized courts also preclude the use of such Anglo-American concepts as contributory and comparative negligence. Disallowing these defenses permits a broader view of what occurred and who was injured. These approaches to tort law are consistent with the expanded viewpoint of life held by many native peoples: that humans are in relationship with the earth and all living forms, not just other human beings.

Tribal court advocates are non-lawyers who, through experience and training, are allowed to represent individuals in tribal courts. Certification programs are available for those who have functioned in traditional dispute resolution as elders, peacemakers, advocates, and community representatives. This advocacy role is open to paralegals who receive the appropriate training and, in some states, is a career possibility for non-Indians as well as Indians.

Putting It Into Practice 8.12:

What similarities do the tribal courts and the restorative justice model (Bonus Pointers in Chapter 7) share?

"So If You Can Establish That You've Been Clean for the Last Five Years, That You've Held Responsible Jobs, and Been Involved in Your Family and Community Activities, I Think You Stand a Good Chance of Getting Reinstated."

"I have to admit, I'm a little apprehensive about seeing you get back into real estate just because I hate to see you get around the same people and in the same environment you were in when you got into drugs. But I also trust you and I know you wouldn't do this if you weren't sure you could handle it." Martha could see that Tim really wanted to get back into real estate, and she wanted to demonstrate her willingness to support him as he sought to put his past behind him.

"Thanks, Martha. That means a lot to me," replied Tim, quietly reaching for Martha's hand and giving it a gentle squeeze of appreciation. Sensing that Martha was responsive to his subtle overtures, Tim ventured to take his efforts at reconciliation one step further. "Would you be open to the possibility of dating again?" he asked shyly.

"Why don't we just stay friends for the time being," Martha suggested tactfully, not wanting to hurt Tim's feelings, but wanting to make it clear that she was not yet ready to commit to anything beyond a platonic relationship. The long silence was awkward for both of them.

Finally, Tim cleared his throat and continued. "In order to get my license back I have to take a test prepared by the Real Estate Commission. Because of my felony conviction, however, they're probably going to make me prove that I'm worthy of having a real estate license before they let me take the test."

"So you're going to have to call a series of character witnesses to attest to the 'new and improved' you," filled in Martha.

"You took the words out of my mouth," chuckled Tim, somewhat surprised by Martha's familiarity with the process.

"Remember, I used to work in a real estate office," explained Martha. "One of our clients lost his license and had to have a hearing to get it back. I remember having to contact all those witnesses to make sure they were available to testify."

"Was he successful?" asked Tim, trying to assess the likelihood of his getting a new license.

"No, but his situation was very different from yours," added Martha reassuringly. "He'd been convicted of embezzlement and the hearing officer wasn't convinced that he'd proven himself trustworthy. But I don't think a conviction on drug charges necessarily impugns your honesty. So if you can establish that you've been clean for the last five years, that you've held responsible jobs, and been involved in your family and community activities, I think you stand a good chance of getting reinstated."

Figure 8-5
Functions of Administrative Agencies

FUNCTIONS OF ADMINISTRATIVE AGENCIES

Legislative
Writing rules and regulations

Executive
Seeing that rules and regulations are carried out

Judicial
Interpreting regulations and statutes

ADMINISTRATIVE AGENCIES

administrative law the law concerning the powers and procedures of administrative agencies

administrative agencies agency that creates and enforces rules on behalf of the legislative and executive branches of government

administrative decisions decision that resolves a dispute between an individual and an agency regarding the application or interpretation of a rule or regulation

Administrative law is law concerning the powers and procedures of **administrative agencies.** Administrative agencies create and enforce rules on behalf of the legislative and executive branches of government. For example, Congress has created laws establishing that each person is to be taxed, but it is the Internal Revenue Service (IRS)—an administrative agency—that is responsible for establishing the rates of taxation and for enforcing this taxation. An administrative agency can be known as a commission, board, authority, bureau, office, department, corporation, administration, division, or agency.

Agencies have three basic functions. The first is quasi-legislative. Agencies write the rules and regulations that make up administrative law. The volumes of administrative law created by the multitude of administrative agencies far exceed the volumes created by both the legislatures and courts combined.

The second function is executive. Agencies ensure that the administrative regulations created by the agency and the statutes created by the legislature are carried out.

The third function is quasi-adjudicative. Agencies interpret the regulations and statutes governing the agency. Administrative agencies resolve disputes by means of hearings at which **administrative decisions** are rendered. An administrative decision resolves a dispute between an individual and an agency regarding the application or interpretation of a rule or regulation.

Examples of Administrative Agencies

FEDERAL LEVEL

Central Intelligence Agency (CIA)
Consumer Product Safety Commission (CPSC)
Department of Defense (DOD)
Department of Transportation (DOT)
Environmental Protection Agency (EPA)
Equal Employment Opportunity Commission (EEOC)
Federal Communications Commission (FCC)
Interstate Commerce Commission (ICC)
Internal Revenue Service (IRS)
National Labor Relations Board (NLRB)
Nuclear Regulatory Commission (NRC)
Occupational Safety and Health Administration (OSHA)
Securities and Exchange Commission (SEC)
Social Security Administration (SSA)

STATE LEVEL

Corporation Commission
Department of Education
Fire Department
Health Services
Motor Vehicle Department
Real Estate Commission
State Revenue Service
Workers' Compensation Department

◆ **LOCAL LINKS** ◆
What are the names of some of the state administrative agencies in your jurisdiction?

Putting It Into Practice 8.13:

Give examples of the quasi-legislative, quasi-adjudicative, and executive functions of the IRS.

"I'm not sure what types of felonies constitute grounds for revocation of a real estate license. Do you know?" asked Tim.

Martha thought for a moment before responding. "No, but you may be in luck. I'm pretty sure I read in the paper recently that the Real Estate Board is getting ready to reconsider grounds for real estate licensure and revocation."

"Great! That means they'll be having hearings that are open to the public."

"And they might very well be interested in your comments, considering your background," encouraged Martha.

RULE-MAKING POWER

enabling statute statute that creates an administrative agency by broadly defining its powers

An administrative agency is created when Congress or a state legislature passes legislation that broadly defines the powers of that agency. As a result of that **enabling statute,** that agency then has the authority to create rules and regulations. In essence, the legislature delegates its powers to the administrative agency. This delegation is lawful as long as it is not overly broad and includes guidelines for

Figure 8-6
Sample Rules Taken from the Illinois Income Tax Act

SAMPLE RULES TAKEN FROM THE ILLINOIS INCOME TAX ACT

A tax return may not be able to be filed because of various errors or omissions contained on the return. An error or omission that is termed a "mathematical error" will result in a correction notice (i.e., Notice of Additional Tax Due) being issued to the taxpayer. The term "mathematical error" is defined in IITA s 1501(a)(12) as follows:

The term "mathematical error" includes the following types of errors, omissions, or defects in a return filed by a taxpayer which prevents acceptance of the return as filed for processing:

(A) arithmetic errors or incorrect computations on the return or supporting schedules;

(B) entries on the wrong lines;

(C) omission of required supporting forms or schedules or the omission of the information in whole or in part called for thereon; and

(D) an attempt to claim, exclude, deduct, or improperly report, in a manner directly contrary to the provisions of the Act and regulations thereunder any item of income, exemption, deduction, or credit.

---

the agency's actions. Such delegation is permitted because of the necessity of having experts to oversee the necessarily complex rules that structure government regulation.

Consider the IRS, an agency familiar to everyone and with which some have probably had disturbingly "close encounters." Congress has neither the time nor the expertise necessary to create all of the intricate rules that govern taxation. Nor is Congress in a position to ensure that individuals and business entities pay their fair share of taxes or to respond to inquiries about how to compute what is owed. Toward this end, Congress delegated its power to collect taxes by creating the IRS. As anyone who has filed a tax return can attest, the IRS has used these delegated powers to create a multitude of complex rules and regulations. (See the sample rules in Figure 8-6 from the Illinois Income Tax Act.)

Administrative agencies must conform to various requirements mandated by the constitution and by statute when creating these rules. They must, for example, provide adequate notice that proposed rules are being considered by the agency so that interested parties can attend public hearings at which the proposed rules will be discussed. If the proposed rules are adopted, they must be published in the *Federal Register,* a publication of the rules and regulations issued by federal administrative agencies. These rules then have the same power as any statute created by the legislature.

Most federal administrative agencies' procedural rules and rule-making practices remained a mystery until the 1946 passage of the **Administrative Procedure Act** (APA). The APA requires agencies to (1) keep the public currently informed of their organization, procedures, and rules; (2) provide for public participation in the rule-making process; and (3) prescribe uniform standards for the conduct of formal rule-making.

LIMITATIONS ON ADMINISTRATIVE AGENCIES

Although administrative agencies wield tremendous power in their domain, they always serve at the pleasure of the legislature that created them. If they make decisions that alienate their "creator," they may experience loss of revenues, a reduction of their powers, or, in the worst case, extinction. The conflict that arose between the National Endowment for the Arts (NEA) and Congress in 1989 regarding the fund-

Administrative Procedure Act act that sets forth the guidelines by which federal administrative agencies must operate

---

NET NEWS

The federal Administrative Procedure Act (APA) can be found at *www.law.cornell.edu/uscode/5/ch5.html.*

ing of photography exhibits demonstrates the sometimes uneasy balance of power between Congress and administrative agencies.

Congress created the NEA in 1965 to provide financial support to the arts. Congress intended to prevent the federal government from interfering with the grant-making process and NEA grant recipients. The enabling statute was purposely drafted to ensure that federal funds would be disbursed to artists based on the expert judgment of the NEA and free from governmental interference. Rather than specifying the exact criteria for a grant, Congress allowed the NEA to distribute its grant awards, reasoning that a small group of experts can more efficiently perform the grant-making function than can all the members of Congress.

The Institute of Contemporary Art in Philadelphia (ICA) and the Southeastern Center for Contemporary Art in Winston-Salem (SECCA) received federal grants from the NEA to fund art exhibits. ICA exhibited a retrospective of photographic works by the late Robert Mapplethorpe, including portraits, floral arrangements, and works depicting homosexual and heterosexual erotic acts. SECCA exhibited a photograph that showed a crucifix submerged in the artist's urine. The controversial subject matter of those photographs, and the fact that the NEA had partially funded each exhibit, caused Congress to reconsider whether the NEA's grant-making standards were proper.

After many congressional debates on proposed legislation to amend the NEA's grant-making process, Congress enacted two significant changes. One required the NEA to notify the Committee on Appropriations of the House and the Senate of any direct grant it intended to make to ICA or SECCA. The second restricted the NEA from granting funds to works of art considered obscene. Both provisions were suspect from a constitutional perspective.

One year later, Congress passed a new bill reauthorizing the NEA to fulfill its mandate as federal financier of the arts, but without any restrictions regarding either obscenity or advance notice. In the same bill, however, Congress incorporated a requirement that grant applicants give a detailed explanation of their work to the NEA when seeking federal funds.

centralized panel
organization of ALJs so that they are detached from any particular agency

Putting It Into Practice 8.14:

In what respect is the democratic process a part of administrative rule-making?

"Now We Have a Centralized Panel in Which a Whole Staff of ALJs Is Housed in a Central Facility and Agencies Can Ask to Be Provided an ALJ to Adjudicate a Particular Case."

"Did you get to attend your client's hearing?" pursued Tim.

"Yes, I did, as a matter of fact. And it was very different in some respects from the trial I observed in Mike's case."

"In what ways?" asked Tim, eager to get a sense of what he could expect when he attended his hearing.

"Well, in the first place, the atmosphere is much more informal and relaxed. More like an arbitration than a trial. And the hearing officer, or I guess now they're usually called ALJs, takes a much more active role in questioning the witnesses than a judge does. No one seemed to get too hung up on the rules of evidence either. They let a lot of things into the record that certainly would have been considered inadmissible at a trial."

"I've heard people allege that some ALJs are biased. I gather that comes from the fact that the ALJ who hears your case works for the same agency for whom he's supposed to make an unbiased decision. Have you ever heard that?"

"Frequently. The attorneys who interacted with the Real Estate Board often groused about that. But I've heard that things have changed in the last few years. Now we have a **centralized panel** in which a whole staff of ALJs is housed in a central facility and agencies can ask to be provided an ALJ to adjudicate a particular case. This way the ALJ is not associated with any one agency and is much better able to retain independence."

NET NEWS

ALJs have formed a national organization called the Association of Administrative Law Judges. Their Web page can be found at *www.aalj.org.*

ADMINISTRATIVE LAW JUDGES

administrative law judges
judge who resolves disputes between individuals and agencies regarding the application or interpretation of rules and regulations; also known as *hearing examiners* and *hearing officers*

Administrative law does not attract much attention. In fact, **administrative law judges** (ALJs) also known as **hearing officers** and **hearing examiners**) are sometimes referred to as the "invisible judiciary." And yet, these judges are responsible for a staggering number of decisions that affect everyone in every aspect of their lives.

Decisions made by administrative law judges include the following.

◆ establishment of rates for gas, electrical, communication and transportation services
◆ licensing of radio and television broadcasting
◆ compliance with federal standards relating to interstate trade, labor relations, advertising, consumer products, and food and drugs
◆ regulation of health and safety in transportation and industry
◆ adjudication of claims relating to Social Security benefits, workers' compensation, and international trade

hearing officers term also used in reference to administrative law judges

hearing examiners term also used in reference to administrative law judges

Putting It Into Practice 8.15:

It has been said that the lower in the administrative hierarchy an individual is, the more discretion he has. For example, the police officer on the street has more opportunity to use discretion than does the police chief in the same agency. In what ways might ALJs have more discretion than trial court judges who review the decisions of those ALJs?

ADMINISTRATIVE ADJUDICATORY HEARINGS

Resolution of disputes through the administrative process is designed to reduce some of the load on the court system. The procedures followed in these hearings vary from state to state and in agencies within a single state. Federal and state administrative procedure acts provide guidelines that must be used in all administrative proceedings, but agencies rely on their rule-making powers to create procedures unique to their particular agency.

settlement conference
conference involving the judge and the attorneys representing all of the parties at which an attempt is made to resolve the dispute between the litigants

Pleadings are not as important in administrative adjudication as they are in court litigation, but they do serve to notify all parties that a hearing is going to be held. Discovery is generally very limited, although subpoenas can be issued if necessary (by the ALJ) and depositions can be taken (as ordered by the ALJ). Agencies typically provide a list of exhibits that are to be presented and a list of witnesses who will appear. As in litigation, parties are encouraged to settle and the ALJ is likely to hold a **settlement conference.**

adjudicatory hearing
hearing before an administrative agency to resolve a dispute between an individual and an agency

The ALJ (or hearing officer) presides over the **adjudicatory hearing** and has the power to administer oaths. Because of the relative informality of such hearings, ALJs have more latitude than judges in organizing hearings and establishing the environment in which they are held. A court reporter or hearing assistant is responsible for recording the proceedings, although tape recorders are used more frequently than shorthand machines to do the recording. The agency may or may not be represented by counsel. The claimant has a right to be represented by counsel but the government is not obligated to provide such representation. Paralegals are allowed to represent clients in some agencies and legal aid organizations may under certain circumstances provide counsel to those who fall within their income guidelines. Individuals commonly represent themselves at such hearings.

Hearings begin when the ALJ reads the case name and number into the record, identifies who is present, and explains the purpose of the hearing. Opening statements are rarely given. The ALJ allows the parties to review all documents that are to be offered into evidence and to make any objections they deem relevant; the ALJ then decides which documents will be admitted into the record. Witness testimony is similar to that in a courtroom trial although the ALJ may take a more active role in examining witnesses than a trial judge does. The rules of evidence are very relaxed and evidence that would be considered inadmissible in a trial setting will often be admitted in an administrative hearing. Closing arguments, if allowed at all, are usually submitted in written form to the ALJ.

The ALJ normally takes time to review the evidence presented before issuing a written decision. In the decision, the ALJ usually identifies the key issues, cites any relevant statutes or regulations, and summarizes witness testimony. The ALJ then evaluates the evidence (indicating how much weight was given to the testimony and documents presented), states his findings of fact, and sets forth his decision, explaining the legal ramifications of the decision.

Putting It Into Practice 8.16:

Why do you think the courts are more likely to allow paralegals to represent clients in administrative hearings than at trial?

exhausted his administrative remedies conform to the prescribed review procedures set forth by the agency before resorting to a court of law

Rulings of administrative agencies are subject to judicial review but only after the individual seeking relief has **exhausted his administrative remedies.** This means that the individual must conform to the prescribed review procedures set forth by the agency before resorting to court review. Generally speaking, courts are reluctant to overturn administrative rulings unless they were made "arbitrarily" or "capriciously" or conflict in some way with the law. Typically the party is allowed only to submit written documents and must state specific grounds for appeal, such as gross abuse of discretion or misapplication of the law. State and federal statutes dictate the grounds and procedures for judicial review of agency decisions.

Ferguson v. Arizona Department of Economic Security is representative of judicial review of an administrative agency's decision. The question before this court is whether a decision by the Department of Economic Security was "arbitrary and capricious."

Cite as: 122 Ariz. 290, 594 P.2d 544

Court of Appeals of Arizona, Division 2.
Hugh **FERGUSON,** Plaintiff-Appellant,

v.

ARIZONA DEPARTMENT OF ECONOMIC SECURITY, John L. Huerta, Director, Arizona
Department of Economic Security, and the Tanner Companies (United Metro),
Defendants-Appellees.
No. 2 CA-CIV 3060.
March 30, 1979.

HOWARD, Judge.

The issue here is whether an appeal tribunal of the Department of Economic Security was arbitrary and capricious when it found that appellant voluntarily quit his job without good cause.

The tribunal's findings of fact show that on April 28, 1977 appellant told his supervisor that he was looking for other employment. On May 5, 1977, his employer told him that a replacement had been found and his employment would be terminated on May 11. Instead of working until the termination date, on May 6 appellant submitted his resignation. He did not continue working until the discharge date because to do so would have been "demeaning" and "untenable." In his testimony before the tribunal appellant stated that it would have been embarrassing for him to continue working after he had been fired.

The appellate tribunal found that appellant left work in violation of Regulation No. R6-3-50135, Arizona Compilation of Rules and Regulations, and was therefore ineligible for benefits from May 1, 1977 until he becomes reemployed and earns $425. The trial court affirmed.

The purpose of the Employment Security Act, A.R.S. Secs. 23-601- 799, is to allow compensation for a limited period to those who are capable of working and available for work and are involuntarily unemployed through no fault of their own. . . .

A.R.S. Sec. 23-775 deals with an employee's disqualification from benefits. It states:

"An individual shall be disqualified for benefits:
1. For the week in which he has left work voluntarily without good cause in connection with his employment, if so found by the department, and in addition to the waiting week, for the duration of his unemployment and until he has earned wages in an amount equivalent to five times his weekly benefit amount otherwise payable."

Regulation No. R6-3-50135, cited by the appeals tribunal as the basis for its decision, states:

"D. Leaving prior to effective date of discharge (V L 135.25)
1. Generally a worker would leave without good cause in connection with his work if he quits before the effective

date of discharge even though he has been told that the duration of his employment is limited.
2. He would leave with good cause connected with the work if:
a. He can show that he would suffer substantial detriment by remaining at work until the date of discharge, or
b. He quits to accept a definite offer of work with another employer."

Appellant contends that the above regulation conflicts with the purpose and intent of the Employment Security Act because it disqualifies him from receiving benefits for the entire statutory period when he would have been entitled to benefits if he had merely remained on the job instead of resigning. We do not agree.

A.R.S. Sec. 23-775(1) makes it clear that if an employee leaves work voluntarily and does so without good cause in connection with his employment, he is disqualified from benefits.

Rules of an administrative body are valid if reasonably related to the purposes of the enabling legislation. . . Furthermore a rule or regulation of an administrative agency should not be inconsistent with or contrary to the provisions of a statute, particularly the statute it seeks to effectuate. . . Since A.R.S. Sec. 23-775 requires, in the case of an employee leaving work voluntarily, that such leaving be with good cause in order to entitle the employee to benefits, we do not believe that the rule is unreasonable or inconsistent with the purposes of the Employment Security Act. While it may have been arguably wiser to have a rule which merely would disqualify appellant in a situation such as this from receiving unemployment compensation for the period of time between his resignation and when he would have been discharged, it is clear that A.R.S. Sec. 23-775(1) does not prohibit the department from adopting such a rule. Under the statute there are only two choices. Departure of the employee was either with or without good cause. We cannot fault the department for its decision that there is no good cause for an employee leaving prior to the effective date of discharge unless he can show that he would suffer substantial detriment by remaining at work until the date of discharge or if he quits to accept a definite offer of work with another employer.

Affirmed.

▰▰▰▰ ***Putting It Into Practice 8.17:***

(a) What are the essential facts in this case? (b) What is the purpose of the Employment Security Act and what does Sec. 23-775(1) provide? (c) What does the appellant contend? (d) Why does the court uphold Regulation R6-3-50135? (e) Under what two conditions might an employee have good cause for leaving prior to the effective date of his discharge?

CENTRALIZED PANEL

The administrative judicial system has been heavily criticized because of the potential bias of an ALJ, who is attached to an agency and who presides over litigation between a private party and that agency. Despite all alleged guarantees of independence, the fact that the ALJ is housed in the same building as the agency staff and that he is assigned to the case by the agency whose actions he is reviewing, taints the image of impartiality.

> ◆ **LOCAL LINKS** ◆
> Does your state use a centralized panel?

Because of the appearance of judicial bias and other concerns, many states have adopted the concept of a centralized panel, in which the ALJ is detached from any particular agency. In this system, a staff of ALJs is employed and assigned, upon request of an administrative agency, to preside over an agency proceeding that is within the jurisdiction of the central office. The centralized panel separates ALJs from all internal agency processes. ALJs hear cases involving a variety of agencies rather than being attached to a single agency. As a result, ALJs are truly independent. Having a centralized panel also results in significant cost reductions, greater caseload and workload efficiency, greater public confidence, and more hearing officer professionalism.

▰▰▰▰ ***Putting It Into Practice 8.18:***

Why do you think so many states have turned to a centralized plan in their use of ALJs?

EXAMPLE OF ADMINISTRATIVE PROCESS

To get a better idea of what parties must do to get a hearing before an ALJ, let us walk through the process dictated by the Individuals with Disabilities Education Act (IDEA) as implemented by the state of Nevada. This act mandates that all students who are learning challenged be provided a "free appropriate public education." A free appropriate public education is defined under the statute as "special education and related services, provided at public expense, that meet the standards of the state educational agency." These services must conform with the individualized education program (IEP) of the student with the disability. Students who are learning challenged must be mainstreamed. In other words, they must be educated to the maximum extent possible with students who are not learning challenged; they are not to be sent to segregated classrooms or schools unless the nature or severity of their learning challenge is such that education in regular classes cannot be achieved satisfactorily.

Before parents can file an action in state or federal court under IDEA, they must exhaust their administrative remedies. Nevada provides a two-tiered administrative review process: a due process hearing and an administrative appeal. To pursue a claim under IDEA parents must do the following.

First, they must set up an IEP meeting with the school at which the student's unique needs and supplemental aids and services necessary for him to benefit from education are outlined.

If no resolution occurs at the IEP meeting, the parents must then file for an administrative due process hearing. In a letter addressed to the superintendent of the school district, the parents must identify the child, her address, and the school she is attending; describe the facts relating to the problem; and propose a solution to the problem. This hearing request is then forwarded to the State Superintendent of Public Instruction, who appoints a hearing officer.

The hearing officer arranges a pre-hearing conference to discuss the issues presented, identify witnesses, and set deadlines for hearing briefs and disclosing documents. At the hearing, the parents have a right to be represented by counsel, to present evidence, to cross-examine witnesses, to obtain a record of the hearing, to obtain written findings of fact and decisions, to have their child present, and to open the hearing to the public. Parents can opt to participate in mediation while the administrative due process hearing is pending.

If the parents are dissatisfied with the administrative due process hearing decision, they can appeal the decision to the State Superintendent of Public Instruction. The Superintendent must appoint a state review officer who will examine the record of the hearing, ensure that due process was followed at the hearing, and obtain additional evidence if necessary. The reviewing officer must render a written decision.

If the parents are dissatisfied with the review officer's decision, they can file a civil action in either state or federal court.

Putting It Into Practice 8.19:

Do you suspect that many parents file actions in state or federal court under IDEA?

"I can see I have a lot to learn before I go before an ALJ. Guess I better get busy doing some research in my spare time," remarked Tim wryly.

"I haven't done any research in administrative law," admitted Martha. "But I've heard that you really need to be familiar with the resources in that area if you're going to do a decent job."

"It's easier if you have a penchant for detail and are willing to wade through tons of verbiage to get what you need," agreed Tim. "One young associate I knew was assigned the grueling task of reviewing the *Federal Register* on a weekly basis to help his office keep abreast of all changes to the *CFR* that pertained to them."

"That would be right up there with reading the phone book," grimaced Martha.

"He actually found it interesting, surprisingly enough." Tim thought for a moment before adding, "But maybe that was because he had an engineering background and enjoyed reading technical data."

NET NEWS

Several good Web sites provide links to numerous administrative law resources. These include Hieros Gamos (*www.hg.org/adm.html*) and Catalaw (*www.catalaw.com/topics/Administrative.shtml.*)

RESEARCH OF ADMINISTRATIVE LAW

Any research in the area of administrative law requires familiarity with how the *Code of Federal Regulations* (*CFR*) and the *Federal Register* can be used in tandem to find the relevant agency ruling or regulation, to update the rule, or to determine whether the rule remains effective. The Federal Register Act (passed in 1935) required the publication of every regulation and amendment issued by a federal administrative agency in the *Federal Register.* The *Federal Register* provides a chronological publication of agency rules and regulations, thereby assuring uniformity and predictability in the implementation and application of administrative rules and regulations. Because the sheer number of rules and regulations continued to confuse those practicing administrative law, Congress amended the Federal Register Act in 1937 to provide for the publication of the *CFR.*

Code of Federal Regulations

The *CFR* is a compilation of the rules published in the *Federal Register* by the executive departments and agencies of the federal government. The *CFR* is divided into 50 titles that represent broad areas subject to federal regulation. For example, Title 42 concerns public health. (Note that these 50 titles do not necessarily match the 50 titles of the *United States Code.*) Each title is broken down into chapters, chapters are divided into parts and subparts, and subparts are subdivided into sections. The *CFR* is published annually, in quarterly installments. The *CFR* also publishes a monthly cumulative list of changes in regulations since they were published in the latest annual *CFR* (called the *List of Sections Affected* (*LSA*). This list informs the researcher if a regulation has been changed, revoked, renumbered, or added to since it was printed in the *Federal Register.*

To locate regulations in the *CFR,* one can consult a separate volume, *The CFR Index and Finding Aids,* which includes subject entries and the names of administrative agencies. It also has a parallel table of statutory authorities and rules listing all sections of the *U.S. Code* and the *U.S. Statutes at Large* that are cited as rulemaking authority for the *CFR.* Regulations can also be found using the *Index to the Code of Federal Regulations,* loose-leaf services, Westlaw, or LEXIS.

Figure 8-7
Sample Page from CFR

[Title 25, Volume 1]
[Revised as of April 1, 2000]

From the U.S. Government Printing Office via GPO Access

[<STRONG>CITE</STRONG>:
<STRONG>25CFR1</STRONG>.<STRONG>2</STRONG>]

[Page 9]

Title 25—Indians

Chapter I—Bureau of Indian Affairs, Department of the Interior

Part 1—Applicability of Rules of the Bureau of Indian Affairs—Table of Contents

Sec. 1.<STRONG>2</STRONG> Applicability of regulations and reserved authority of the Secretary of the Interior.

The regulations in chapter I of title 25 of the Code of Federal Regulations are of general application. Notwithstanding any limitations contained in the regulations of this chapter, the Secretary retains the power to waive or make exceptions to his regulations as found in chapter I of title 25 CFR in all cases where permitted by law and the Secretary finds that such waiver or exception is in the best interest of the Indians.

[25 FR 3124, Apr. 12, 1960]

Federal Register

The *Federal Register,* which serves primarily to update the *CFR,* is published daily except Saturday, Sunday, and official federal holidays. All agencies are required to publish their final rules in the *Federal Register* 30 days before the rules are to take effect. Several kinds of finding aids are published in the *Federal Register.* The most important of these is the list of *CFR Parts Affected.* This list is cumulated monthly and is a numerical guide to each title of the *CFR* affected by documents published in that day's issue of the *Federal Register.* The list also provides the citation to the *CFR* and the page number in that day's *Federal Register* where the action may be found.

Figure 8-8
Sample Page from Federal Register

[Federal Register: February 1, 2001 (Volume 66, Number 22)]
[Rules and Regulations]
[Page 8519]
From the Federal Register Online via GPO Access [wais.access.gpo.gov]
[DOCID:fr01fe01-4]

DEPARTMENT OF EDUCATION

34 CFR Part 606

Developing Hispanic-Serving Institutions Program; Delay of

Effective Date

AGENCY: Department of Education.

ACTION: Final regulations; delay of effective date.

SUMMARY: In accordance with the memorandum of January 20, 2001, from the Assistant to the President and Chief of Staff, entitled "Regulatory Review Plan," this regulation temporarily delays the effective date of the regulations entitled Developing Hispanic-Serving Institutions Program published in the Federal Register on January 8, 2001 (66 FR 1262).

EFFECTIVE DATE: The effective date of the regulations amending 34 CFR Part 606 published at 66 FR 1262, January 8, 2001, is delayed 60 days until April 8, 2001.

FOR FURTHER INFORMATION CONTACT: Kenneth C. Depew, Acting Assistant General Counsel for Regulations, Office of the General Counsel, U.S. Department of Education, 400 Maryland Avenue, SW., room 6E227, FB-6, Washington, DC 20202-2241. Telephone: (202) 401-8300.
   If you use a telecommunications device for the deaf (TDD), you may call the Federal Information Relay Service (FIRS) at 1-800-877-8339.

Dated: January 24, 2001.

Rod Paige,
Secretary of Education.
[FR Doc. 01-2779 Filed 1-31-01; 8:45 am]
BILLING CODE 4000-01-P

NET NEWS

The *CFR* is available online at *www.access.gpo.gov/nara/cfr/cfr-table-search.* The *Federal Register* is available online at *www.access.gpo.gov/nara/#frl.*

The *United States Government Manual* is available online at *www.access.gpo.gov/nara/nara001.html.*

Information About Administrative Agencies

The *United States Government Manual* is the official handbook of the federal government, published by the Office of the Federal Register. The *Manual* provides comprehensive information on administrative agencies. A typical agency description includes a list of principal officials, a summary statement of the agency's purpose and role, a brief history, and a description of the agency's programs and activities.

The *Federal Regulatory Directory* is another source for basic information concerning administrative agencies. In a concise, easy-to-use format, this directory presents the information needed to deal with the multitude of federal regulatory agencies. It contains extensive profiles of 13 of the largest, most important agencies, including the Consumer Product Safety Commission, the EPA, the ICC, and the SEC, and briefer profiles of most other federal administrative agencies. An appendix summarizes how to use the *Federal Register* and the *CFR*.

Final decisions of federal agencies are usually appealable to federal court. These federal court decisions can be found in the *Federal Reporter, Federal Supplement, United States Reports,* or in the commercial loose-leaf services. Administrative decisions that are not appealed are more difficult to find because most agencies do not publish their decisions in any kind of systematic way and some do not publish them at all. Still other agencies, such as the Federal Trade Commission, do publish their decisions. To find out if an agency officially publishes its decisions and the name of that publication, consult the *Uniform System of Citations* (*Bluebook*); look in the section entitled "U.S. Tables."

Publication of Administrative Decisions

In most states, numerous agencies publish their own decisions, which are generally appealable to state courts of record. While some administrative agency decisions are neither published nor readily accessible, other administrative agencies periodically publish their decisions and frequently make them available on computer research systems. While many similarities between state and federal administrative agencies exist, one must always refer to applicable state law and agency rules and regulations to ascertain how to proceed in reference to state administrative law issues.

NET NEWS

Administrative rules and decisions from federal agencies are available online. Some representative Web sites follow.

- ◆ Bureau of Census—*www.cb.gov*
- ◆ Department of Justice—*www.usdoj.gov*
- ◆ Environmental Protection Agency—*www.epa.gov*
- ◆ Federal Election Commission—*www.fec.gov*
- ◆ Federal Housing Authority—*www.fha.gov*
- ◆ Internal Revenue Service—*www.irs.ustreas.gov*
- ◆ Occupational Safety and Health Administration—*www.osha.gov*
- ◆ Securities and Exchange Commission—*www.sec.gov*
- ◆ Social Security Administration—*www.ssa.gov*

Links to federal administrative agencies can be found at *lcweb.loc.gov/global/executive/fed.html*. To obtain more information in reference to finding both federal and state government Web sites, go to *www.paralegals.org/Reporter*, click on "Summer 1999," and then on "Inside the Internet."

▰▰ *Putting It Into Practice 8.20:*

Indicate where would you find (a) a rule issued by the Social Security Administration two days ago; (b) a list of changes made in the last two months to regulations issued by the Department of Transportation; (c) information about the Securities Exchange Commission; (d) section 10 of Title 18 dealing with federal regulations.

Are Administrative Agencies Governed by the Same Restrictions Under the Fourth Amendment as the Police When They Conduct an Investigation?

"What little research I've done in administrative law has whet my appetite to learn more. It seems like a fascinating area of practice and I know so little about it. But the little exposure I've had has convinced me that administrative agencies have created their own little "fiefdoms," and if you're going to be an effective player, you have to learn the rules that govern these fiefdoms," observed Tim.

"I suspect that's true for every area of law," agreed Martha. "But one thing I'm curious about—the question that was raised by one of our clients yesterday. Do these agencies have to get a warrant before they can conduct an on-the-spot inspection? I mean, are they governed by the same restrictions under the Fourth Amendment as the police when they conduct an investigation?"

"You'd have to research it to be sure, but it seems to me that since they're considered part of the executive branch of government, they would be governed by the same rules," reasoned Tim.

"I'll ask Ernesto on Monday and let you know if you're right."

"Are you doing a lot of work for Ernesto now?"

"Quite a bit."

"Has he gotten any easier to work for?" asked Tim, knowing the challenges Martha had had with Ernesto in the past.

"Actually, yes. We seem to have gotten along much better since we worked together on Mike's trial. I suppose we developed a respect for one another. And I think he benefited from John's taking him under his wing," grinned Martha, thinking back to John's subtle and sometimes not-so-subtle coaching.

INVESTIGATIVE ACTIONS

Agencies are also responsible for seeing that their administrative responsibilities are executed. As such, agencies must sometimes investigate and prosecute those who violate their rules. Because administrative agencies are part of the executive branch of government, they are required to comply with the search and seizure requirements of the Fourth Amendment. They must, for example, obtain a warrant before conducting a search (some exceptions do exist) although the requirements for obtaining administrative warrants are less stringent than for obtaining criminal search warrants.

A warrant is not required if the owner consents to a search. In most cases, consent is given so inspectors representing administrative agencies do not usually apply for a warrant until they have been refused entry. In emergency situations, no warrant is required because of the need to take immediate action. If firefighters perform an investigation while they are fighting a blaze, they are not required to stop and get a warrant. But once the blaze is extinguished, they must obtain a warrant to pursue their investigation. The warrant requirement may also not apply to businesses subject to special licensing provisions, especially when frequent, unannounced inspections are the primary way used to enforce licensing requirements. A weapons dealer, for example, can be searched by a federal agent without a warrant because this is a business subject to intense federal licensing regulations that require frequent, unannounced inspections.

"Quite a few of my classmates were hired by DES (Department of Economic Security) to do work in child support enforcement, so I know there's a lot of work available in administrative agencies," Martha said as she inched her way toward the door. She could feel their conversation winding down, but was reluctant to bring it to a close.

"The folks working at DES are given a lot of responsibility and independence, aren't they?" Tim, too, was doing his best to prolong their time together.

"That's what I hear," confirmed Martha, as she turned to open the door. "Well, I guess I better be going. Thanks for all of the info about mediation. Let me know if and when you need me to testify on your behalf."

"Hopefully we'll talk before that but, yes, I'll call you as soon as I know what's happening."

Putting It Into Practice 8.21:

Do you think OSHA (Occupational Safety and Health Administration) would need to get a warrant before inspecting a laboratory to ensure that it was meeting OSHA's standards?

ROLE OF THE PARALEGAL

Describing the role of the paralegal in the realm of administrative law is not easy because administrative law encompasses so many aspects of law practice. A paralegal who works for a law firm or a corporate department has very different responsibilities than a paralegal working for an administrative agency. A paralegal working for a law firm may be responsible for analyzing administrative regulations and helping determine their applicability to a client's activities. A paralegal in a corporate department for a regulated industry, such as banking, utilities, healthcare, and insurance, may be responsible for helping attorneys review applicable administrative regulations and evaluate corporate compliance with those regulations. A paralegal working for an administrative agency may be responsible for drafting proposed rules, gathering facts to determine whether an individual or entity has complied with agency rules, or analyzing surveys to assess whether a new rule is appropriate.

In any of these settings, a paralegal may be called upon to assist in resolving disputes between an agency and a private party. Those who work with the elderly or the homeless will need to work with a number of administrative agencies in order to secure needed benefits for their clients. In limited circumstances, paralegals are allowed to actually represent clients before certain administrative agencies.

The specific tasks a paralegal in this area performs vary tremendously. Some do an extensive amount of research and report on their findings while others never do any kind of legal research. Some have daily contact with members of the public; others virtually never meet the public. Some appear at administrative hearings; others do not. To get a more concrete idea about what paralegals in representative areas of administrative law do, consider reviewing the articles identified in the following "Net News," taken from the *Paralegal Reporter.*

Although administrative law practice for paralegals cannot be concisely described, we can assure you that employment in this area has grown for several years and promises to continue growing. As government regulations become more numerous and more complex, those affected will find it increasingly necessary to seek legal help in interpreting and complying with these regulations, just as the government will experience an increasing need for more assistance in meeting its paperwork demands.

NET NEWS

For a sampling of articles related to different aspects of administrative law practice, go to *www.paralegals.org/Reporter* and consider the following articles.

Environmental Law (Fall 1999)—"Paralegal Roles and Responsibilities"; also two articles by paralegals about their experiences in environmental law practice

Immigration Law (Spring 2000)—"Paralegal Roles and Responsibilities," "Immigration Law and Practice," "Basic Principles of U.S. Immigration"

Banking (Fall 1998)—"Are You a Paralegal or a Banker?" (describes a variety of roles for paralegals in the banking industry)

Advocacy (Winter 1995)—"Paralegal Advocates for Low Income Elderly"

ETHICAL ETIQUETTE

PARALEGAL REPRESENTATION OF CLIENTS IN ADMINISTRATIVE AGENCIES

The trend is clearly toward increased non-attorney representation before administrative agencies. Consequently, the role of paralegals in the practice of administrative law is continuing to expand. At the federal level, the following agencies allow non-attorneys to practice before them: Small Business Administration, National Labor Relations Board, Bureau of Indian Affairs, and Social Security Administration. State agencies are not at all consistent about allowing non-lawyer practice, so it is important to check out the rules of each agency to avoid allegations of the unauthorized practice of law. In those states that allow the practice of non-attorneys, paralegals may or may not be allowed to practice. In those states that do allow attorneys to delegate authority to a paralegal, the attorneys remain responsible for supervising the paralegal.

Any paralegal who is allowed to practice before an administrative agency must know the law and procedures used by the agency; be able to apply the law to the facts of her case; and competently advocate for her client in an adversarial setting.

◆ **LOCAL LINKS** ◆

What agencies in your state permit paralegal representation of clients?

BONUS POINTERS:

Putting It Into Practice 8.22:

Why are paralegal students well advised to take an administrative law class if it is offered at their institution?

WORKERS' COMPENSATION

One type of administrative law that is open to paralegals is workers' compensation—a concept conceived in Germany in the late 1800s to circumvent certain problems of the tort system and to protect workers who are injured on the job whether or not by fault of their own negligence. It also relieves employers from tort responsibility for on-the-job injuries to their employees. Workers' compensation systems were intended to provide fast and efficient relief to injured workers without regard to fault. In theory, an injured worker gave up her right to sue her employer in return for the implied promise that her reasonable medical expenses would be taken care of, and that she would be compensated for the wages she lost as a result of the injury. What has actually evolved is a system that rivals the entire tort system in cost and that has become so complicated that many states recognize workers' compensation as a legal specialty. The system is driven by statutory rules that legislators tinker with on a regular basis.

What appears to be a straightforward goal—the compensation of injured workers without regard to fault—has not been easily implemented. To process disputed or questioned claims outside of the court system, an entire administrative hierarchy had to be created. Judges and juries were replaced with administrative law judges. The rules of civil procedure were replaced and/or supplemented by administrative rules and regulations. The delays in processing claims, disputes regarding compensable and noncompensable injuries, and the adversarial nature of the process have made the workers' compensation system less than ideal.

An extensive amount of paperwork is required in processing workers' compensation claims. Paralegals can perform almost all of the functions necessary to handle these claims. The caseload in this area of law is tremendous (as many as several hundred files may be worked on each week) and entails a great deal of client contact. Paralegals are responsible for reviewing claimants' files, calendaring and assembling medical reports, outlining issues, communicating with adjustors, drafting claims for compensation, and helping to prepare for hearings. In many states, paralegals are permitted to represent clients at hearings before the state workers' compensation board.

Martha turned into the parking garage for White & Treadwell at the same time that John did. She waited for him to get out of his car, and they walked to the elevator together. After exchanging a few pleasantries, John inquired, "So have you decided what you're going to do to resolve things between you and George?"

"Yes. I've decided mediation is probably the best way for us to go. Tim's going to give me the names of some mediators he recommends and then we'll go from there."

"How's Tim doing these days?" asked John innocently.

"Just fine," replied Martha without volunteering any additional information. They waited in silence for a several seconds. When John saw Martha was not going to disclose any more, he asked the question that was really on his mind. "So how did it go with the two of you?"

"Oh, we decided to name our first child after you," replied Martha nonchalantly, wanting to see John's expression but afraid she would start laughing.

"Smart aleck," muttered John.

"All right, not that it's anybody's business. We had a good time together. We're going to make a stab at being friends—nothing more."

"He's a nice guy," stated John matter-of-factly.

"I know that. I just haven't been able to get past the fact that he lied to me."

"He didn't exactly lie—he just didn't tell you everything. And I know I have no business getting involved in your personal life, so I'll keep my mouth shut."

"Thank you," responded Martha with mock primness.

As they got out of the elevator and walked in opposite directions, John couldn't resist adding, "But someday you may be sorry."

"I know," whispered Martha to herself.

■ **TIM'S TECHNO TIP**

Spreadsheets

Spreadsheets—they're not for your bed! Next to word processing, a paralegal is most likely to use a program known as a *spreadsheet*. The three most popular spreadsheets are Microsoft Excel, Lotus 1-2-3, and Quattro Pro. Microsoft Excel is part of Microsoft Office and can also be purchased as a stand-alone product. Quattro Pro is by Corel and can also be purchased as a stand-alone product; it comes with WordPerfect Office 2000. Lotus 1-2-3 is the oldest spreadsheet program and is compatible with Word and WordPerfect.

Spreadsheets are used in the legal environment for a variety of tasks. Budgets are prepared, damages are listed, future damages are calculated, real estate and stock holdings are tracked, real estate closing statements are prepared, taxes are calculated, and tax planning is performed. The main value of the spreadsheet is that it keeps track of changes in value automatically. If, for example, a real estate closing statement is being prepared and the taxes and interest prorated to the day of closing, inputting the new values will cause the program to automatically calculate the correct amounts that the buyer would have to pay and the funds the seller would receive. In a like manner, a personal injury practice keeps track of the client's medical expenses on a spreadsheet. As new bills are received and input into the spreadsheet the total of all expenses is automatically calculated.

Family law practitioners use spreadsheets to set up asset division schedules for their clients. As assets are disposed of or transferred to one party or the other, the spreadsheet gives an up-to-date total so that the relative equity of the division can be constantly monitored. Child support payments and arrearages, together with accrued late charges and interest, if any, can also be quickly calculated.

Estate practitioners use spreadsheets to keep track of assets and their values. Estates with heavy stock portfolios are especially well suited for spreadsheet analysis. The sophisticated practitioner can tie the spreadsheet into a stock quotation program to have up-to-the-minute data on the estate.

Most spreadsheet programs also include various statistical functions that can calculate averages, medians, standard deviations, percentages, and the like. Transferring the data to a graph or pie chart requires only a few mouse clicks.

TECHNO TRIP

Visit Excel at *www.microsoft.com/office/excel,* Lotus 1-2-3 at *www.lotus.com* and Quattro Pro at *www.corel.com.* Compare the three spreadsheets for functionality and ease of use. Next, compare the price of each program, first as a stand-alone product, and then with the office suite with which it can be packaged. Do any of these spreadsheets appear to be vastly superior or easier to use than the others? How do they compare in terms of price?

SUMMARY – PART B

The two types of tribal courts—the Court of Indian Offenses and specific trial courts created by the tribal government—have different powers. Tribal laws vary, reflecting trial judges' efforts to balance tribal tradition and needs against the traditions and standards of Anglo-American law. The tribal courts have an extremely complex relationship with the federal government. Tribal law is highly influenced by custom and focuses on the importance of restitution and restoration of relationships. Tribal court advocacy is a possible career for paralegals who receive the appropriate training.

Administrative agencies create and enforce rules on behalf of the legislative and executive branches of government. They have executive, quasi-legislative, and quasi-judicial functions. Administrative law judges (ALJs), also known as hearing officers or hearing examiners, are sometimes referred to as the "invisible judiciary" and are responsible for making a staggering number of decisions that affect everyone in every aspect of their lives. Federal and state administrative procedure acts provide guidelines that must be used in all administrative adjudicatory hearings, but agencies create procedures unique to them. Discovery is generally limited and the hearing is usually more relaxed and informal than a trial. Agencies may or may not be represented by counsel; claimants may be represented, but do not have a right to be provided with counsel. Non-lawyers have a right to represent clients in some administrative agencies. Opening statements and closing arguments are rarely given, but the parties are given an opportunity to review and object to the admission of any documents that are to offered into evidence before the ALJ decides while documents will be admitted. In a written decision, the ALJ evaluates the evidence, states findings of fact, and explains the legal ramifications of the decision. An ALJ's decision is subject to judicial review, but only after the claimant exhausts his administrative remedies. Courts are reluctant to overturn administrative rulings unless they were made "arbitrarily" or "capriciously" or conflict in some way with the law. Because of the appearance of judicial bias and other concerns, many states have adopted the concept of a centralized panel of ALJs. As a result, ALJs are more independent, they are more efficient, the public has greater confidence in their decisions, and the hearing process is less expensive.

The enabling statute that creates an administrative agency must not be overly broad and must contain guidelines for the agency's actions. Legislative delegation of power is essential because of the need for experts to oversee the complex rules that structure government regulation. When creating new rules, agencies must provide adequate notice so that interested parties can attend public hearings at which the proposed new rules are discussed. The APA requires that the public be kept informed about an agency's operations, that the public be allowed to participate in the rule-making process, and that uniform standards be maintained for the rule-making process. Administrative agencies serve at the whim of their creators and can be eliminated or have their powers reduced if they conflict with those who created them.

Research in administrative law requires familiarity with the *CFR* and the *Federal Register*. The *Federal Register* is a chronological publication of agency rules and regulations. The *CFR* is a compilation of the rules published in the *Federal Register;* it is published annually with quarterly installments, whereas the *Federal Register* is published daily. The *CFR Index and Finding Aids* can be used to locate rules in the *CFR*. The *United States Government Manual* and the *Federal Regulatory Directory* can be used to gather information about administrative agencies. Final decisions of federal agencies that are appealed can be found in the reporters, but those decisions that are not appealed may not be published anywhere. Some state agencies publish their own decisions.

Because agencies are responsible for seeing that their administrative responsibilities are executed, they must sometimes investigate and prosecute those who violate their rules. As members of the executive branch of government, they are required to comply with the provisions of the Fourth Amendment, although the requirements for obtaining a warrant are less stringent than for obtaining a warrant in a criminal case. Warrants are not required if the individual being inspected gives consent, if an emergency exists, or if the business being inspected is subject to special licensing requirements.

Practice in the area of administrative law is increasingly opening up to paralegals, both within agencies and as representatives of clients before agencies. Because of unauthorized practice of law concerns, paralegals should check the regulations of an agency before agreeing to represent someone. Any paralegal that does represent a client must be fully knowledgeable of the law in that area, must be able to apply the law to the facts of the case, and must be competent to represent someone in an adversarial setting.

KEY TERMS

Adjudicatory hearing	Administrative Procedure Act	Exhausted his administrative remedies	Settlement conference
Administrative agencies			Tribal court advocate
Administrative decisions	Centralized panel	Hearing examiners	
Administrative law	Courts of Indian Offenses	Hearing officers	
Administrative law judges	Enabling statute	Judicial notice	

REVIEW QUESTIONS – PART B

1. Describe the basic structure of the tribal courts. How does tribal law compare with Anglo-American law?
2. What are administrative agencies and what basic functions do they serve?
3. What kinds of decisions are ALJs responsible for making?
4. Compare an administrative hearing with a trial.
5. Under what condition can an individual appeal an ALJ's decision? What must the individual prove to get the decision overturned?
6. What is a centralized panel? Why was it developed? What is gained by having this kind of organization?

7. Why are administrative agencies created? How are they created?
8. What guidelines must an agency comply with when involved in the formal rule-making process?
9. What can be found in each of the following?
   a. *Code of Federal Regulations*
   b. *Federal Register*
   c. *U.S. Government Manual*
   d. *Federal Regulatory Directory*
10. Does an agent of an administrative agency necessarily have to obtain a warrant to conduct an inspection? Explain.

PRACTICE EXAM – PART B

MULTIPLE CHOICE

1. The Courts of Indian Offenses
   a. are also known as the CFR courts
   b. cannot use tribal law
   c. operated before the creation of the United States
   d. all of the above

2. Tribal court law
   a. is the same from jurisdiction to jurisdiction
   b. jurisdiction has become increasingly narrow
   c. reflects tribal traditions as well as the requirements of Anglo-American law
   d. all of the above

3. Under tribal law
   a. a defendant's conduct in a tort case is measured by carelessness rather than negligence
   b. the defenses of contributory and comparative negligence may not be allowed
   c. a criminal defendant may be required to compensate the clan of the victim
   d. all of the above

4. Administrative agencies have the task of
   a. writing rules and regulations
   b. enforcing rules and regulations
   c. interpreting rules and regulations
   d. all of the above

5. At an administrative adjudicatory hearing
   a. the parties are usually allowed extensive discovery
   b. subpoenas can be issued and depositions taken
   c. pleadings serve the same purpose as they do in litigation
   d. all of the above

6. An ALJ typically
   a. records testimony made by witnesses
   b. follows the rules of evidence very carefully
   c. is given a lot of latitude in organizing hearings
   d. none of the above

7. At an administrative adjudicatory hearing
   a. parties have an opportunity to review all documents and make objections before the ALJ decides which ones will be admitted
   b. opening statements are usually given
   c. oral closing arguments are usually allowed
   d. the ALJ rarely questions witnesses

8. An ALJ's written decision usually contains
   a. an explanation of the ramifications of the decision but no findings of fact
   b. an indication of how much weight was given to testimony and documents presented
   c. an identification of key issues but no summary of witness testimony
   d. none of the above

9. A centralized panel of ALJs
   a. improves an ALJ's image of impartiality
   b. allows the ALJ to be housed in the same agency whose actions he is reviewing
   c. costs more money than the traditional administrative judicial system
   d. results in ALJs being less efficient

10. An enabling statute
    a. creates a centralized panel
    b. enables ALJs to have more power
    c. establishes guidelines for an agency's actions
    d. is an illegal delegation of power

11. The APA requires that
    a. the public be kept informed about an agency's procedures and rules
    b. the public be allowed to participate in the rule-making process
    c. uniform standards be created to govern the rule-making process
    d. all the above

12. The *Federal Register*
    a. is published annually
    b. is a chronological publication of administrative rules and regulations
    c. can be indexed using the *CFR Index and Finding Aids*
    d. contains a *List of Sections Affected (LSA)*

13. The *CFR*
    a. is divided into titles representing broad subject areas subject to federal regulation
    b. is published in quarterly installments
    c. has a section that informs the researcher whether a regulation has been added, revoked, or modified
    d. all of the above

14. Before conducting a search, an inspector of an administrative agency
    a. need not get a warrant if consent is given
    b. is not governed by the Fourth Amendment
    c. must always get a warrant and the requirements for securing that warrant are the same as the requirements for securing a criminal warrant
    d. none of the above

15. Paralegals
    a. are never allowed to represent a client before an administrative agency
    b. can practice before an administrative agency as long as state laws allow non-attorneys to practice
    c. can be delegated authority to practice before an administrative agency in some states
    d. none of the above

FILL IN THE BLANK

16. The tribal courts organized by the Bureau of Indian Affairs are called _____ .

17. The Environmental Protection Agency is an example of an _____ , which creates and enforces _____—the law (rules and regulations) created by agencies such as the EPA.

18. _____ resolve disputes between administrative agencies and individuals by means of rendering an _____ .

19. An individual _____ by following the review procedures set forth by the agency before resorting to a court of law.

20. In a _____ , the ALJs are detached from any particular agency.

21. Legislation that creates an administrative agency by broadly defining its powers is called an _____ .

22. The _____ dictates the procedures an agency must follow in creating formal rules.

23. To obtain up-to-date information regarding agency rulings, proposed regulations, and adjudicatory proceedings requires proficiency in using the _____ and the _____ .

24. Information about administrative agencies can be found in either the _____ or the _____ .

25. Administrative agencies are considered part of the _____ branch of government and so must obtain a _____ before conducting an inspection (although some exceptions exist).

TRUE OR FALSE

____ 26. Some tribal courts are created and controlled by tribal governments pursuant to their inherent sovereignty.

____ 27. The CFR Courts were established by the government to keep order on Indian reservations while educating tribal people in Anglo-American norms.

____ 28. Knowing whether the sovereign of a tribal court is the federal government or the tribe is irrelevant because both have the same jurisdiction over people and actions.

____ 29. The tribal courts have a very complex relationship with the federal government.

____ 30. Indigenous customs have been virtually abandoned by the tribal courts.

____ 31. Anglo-American courts focus on determining the guilt of the offender and on imposing a punishment whereas tribal courts focus on restitution and making amends to all of the affected parties.

____ 32. Only lawyers are allowed to practice before the tribal courts.

____ 33. The volume of administrative law pales in comparison to that created by both the courts and legislatures combined.

____ 34. Hearing officers and examiners are part of what is known as the "invisible judiciary."

____ 35. ALJs are responsible for making decisions that affect the licensing of radio and television broadcasting, the establishing of health and safety standards in industry, and the setting of rates for gas and electrical services.

____ 36. Although the administrative hearing process varies from state to state, every agency within a state must follow the exact same procedures.

____ 37. Administrative agencies are usually represented by attorneys at administrative hearings and claimants are provided with counsel if they cannot afford them.

____ 38. ALJ rulings are subject to judicial review, but only after the individual seeking relief has exhausted his or her administrative remedies.

____ 39. Courts are generally eager to overturn the decisions of ALJs.

____ 40. State and federal statutes dictate the grounds and procedures for judicial review.

____ 41. The traditional administrative judicial system in which the ALJ was housed in the agency whose actions he was reviewing was criticized because of the potential bias of the ALJ.

____ 42. The centralized panel separates ALJs from all internal agency processes and allows them to hear cases involving a variety of agencies.

____ 43. A legislature cannot delegate its powers to an administrative agency.

____ 44. An enabling statute must not be overly broad.

____ 45. Enabling statutes allow experts to be used to oversee the complex rules that guide government regulation.

____ 46. Rules created by an administrative agency do not carry the same power as statutes created by a legislature.

____ 47. The public need not be informed of an agency's intent to create new rules.

____ 48. An uneasy balance of power exists between Congress and some administrative agencies.

____ 49. Once the legislature has created an administrative agency, it cannot reduce its power or eliminate it.

____ 50. Every regulation and amendment issued by a federal administrative agency must be published in the *Federal Register*.

____ 51. The *Federal Register* has a monthly cumulative list of changes in regulations since they were published in the latest annual *Federal Register*.

____ 52. The *CFR* serves to update the *Federal Register*.

____ 53. The *Federal Register* includes a list of "CFR Parts Affected."

____ 54. To find information about an agency's purpose, history, and programs, one could consult the *United States Government Manual*.

____ 55. Final decisions of administrative agencies cannot be found in the reporters because they are not published.

____ 56. Research of state administrative law issues requires reference to applicable state law and agency rules and regulations.

____ 57. Because consent is given in most cases, inspectors representing administrative agencies do not usually have to apply for a warrant.

____ 58. The requirements for an administrative warrant are the same as those for a criminal warrant.

____ 59. The warrant requirement may not apply to businesses subject to special licensing provisions.

____ 60. The trend is toward restricting the practice of non-attorneys before administrative agencies.

____ 61. Non-attorneys are allowed to represent clients before the Social Security Administration and the Bureau of Indian Affairs.

____*62. Workers' compensation systems provide fast and efficient relief to injured workers without regard to fault.

____*63. The workers' compensation system has resulted in the creation of an administrative hierarchy and the replacement of the rules of civil procedure.

____*64. Paralegals who work in the area of workers' compensation usually have very high caseloads involving an extensive amount of paperwork.

____*65. Paralegals are never allowed to represent clients at hearings before the state workers' compensation board.

*Questions taken from Bonus Pointers.

LEGAL LINGO

Fill in the missing letters.

1. _ _ B _ _ S _ A _   Used to resolve consumer complaints
2. _ E _ _ R _   Hybrid form of ADR
3. _ _ _ _   Judge in administrative setting
4. _ _ _ _   Act that provides guidelines for rule making
5. _ _ A _ _ F _ _ _ _ A _ _ _ _ _   Very non-directive form of mediation
6. _ _ N _ _ N _   Arbitration decision that is non-appealable
7. _ X _ _ I _ _ _ _   Hearing officer
8. _ _ A _ _ _ _ N _   Statute that creates an agency
9. _ _ D _ _ T _ _   Person who facilitates dispute resolution but who cannot render a decision
10. _ _ N _ -_ _ I _ _   Abbreviated trial presented to neutral third party who issues an advisory opinion
11. _ _ M _ _ _ Y _ _ _ Y   Abbreviated trial presented to jury
12. _ X _ _ U _ _   What one has to do before appealing an agency's decision
13. _ _ N _ _ _ _ L _ Z _ _   Type of plan to house administrative law judges
14. _ R _ _ T _ _ T _ _   Neutral third party who renders decision and issues award
15. _ N _ _ X _ _   Court arbitration, which occurs within the court system
16. _ _ V _ _ _ T _   Tribal court _____
17. _ F _ E _ _ _ _ _   Court of Indian _____
18. _ _ J _ _ I _ A _ _ R _   Hearing before an agency to resolve a dispute

LEGAL LOGISTICS

1. Your office has a client, Jorge, who has a contractual dispute with Eager Electronics, Inc. Jorge would like to resolve this dispute as expeditiously and as cheaply as possible. What could you recommend to him?
   a. Suppose this is a multimillion dollar dispute and both Jorge and Eager believe they will undoubtedly win if they go to trial. What types of ADR might you recommend Jorge consider?
   b. Your attorney is obsessed with knowing everything about a case before going to trial, and he likes to be in control of the litigation process every step of the way. He is a ruthless litigator and avoids compromise at all costs. How do you think he will fare if Jorge decides he wants to mediate his case?
   c. Suppose Jorge's claim is for $10,000 and that the courts in your state require arbitration of all claims under $50,000. Will the arbitrator's decision be binding?
      1. What can Jorge do if he believes the arbitrator's award is unreasonable?
      2. What is the consequence if a clause in Jorge's contract requires private, binding arbitration?
      3. How will your preparation for arbitration differ from your preparation if you were going to trial?
      4. Describe to Jorge what will probably happen at the arbitration hearing.
2. You do volunteer work in a shelter for abused women. One of the women wants to get a divorce. She knows that you work for a law firm and asks you about the process for getting a divorce. In your state, couples must try to mediate a divorce before they will be allowed to go to trial. Explain the mediation process to her. Assume the mediation model used in your community is the one used most frequently by the business community.
   a. Would you recommend the transformative model to her if she tells you that her husband is very manipulative?

b. Why might mediation not be the best path for this woman if her husband has controlled the finances all of their married life and is better educated and more sophisticated regarding business transactions?
3. One of your friends reads an article in the paper about the sentence a Native American received after he was convicted of theft. Your friend complains that the offender would have received a prison sentence if he had been sentenced in state court and complains that it is unfair that Native Americans are treated differently than other ethnic groups. Explain to him why Native Americans have been treated differently for historical reasons.
   a. Explain why his sentence may have been appropriate for this individual and his community than a sentence imposed under Anglo-American law.
   b. How might the goal of sentencing under tribal law have differed from the goal of sentencing under state law?
4. A client who is supposed to attend a hearing regarding her workers' compensation claim asks you to explain what an adjudicatory hearing is like.
   a. Tell her what will be contained in the ALJ's written decision.
   b. If she is unhappy with the decision, what must she do if she wants to appeal the decision to the state court?
   c. She has heard that ALJs are biased because they are working for the agency whose actions they are reviewing. Explain how the centralized plan has addressed that concern.
   d. Your attorney has asked you to find out whether you can represent this client at an upcoming hearing. Explain how you will find the answer to this question.
   e. An inspector for the agency drops by your client's home unannounced and wants to look inside. Does he need an administrative warrant to do this?

A TRIP TO THE MOVIES

1. Suppose that Tom Robinson, in *To Kill a Mockingbird*, was a Native American rather than an African-American and that he was accused of raping a white girl on the reservation where he lived.

a. In what ways would his trial have differed from the trial depicted in the movie?
b. If Tom were convicted, what would the tribal court do that an Anglo-American court would never consider?

2. In *Kramer v. Kramer*, the parents of Billy, a seven-year-old- boy, become embroiled in a bitter custody battle when the mother returns to reclaim the son she left behind when she left the marriage to "find her voice."

   a. In what ways might this family have been better served by mediation than it was by litigation?

   b. Do you think the parents were good candidates for mediation?

   c. Some argue that women can be put in an unfair bargaining position if they go to mediation. Do you see that as a problem in Joanna's case?

   d. Do you think arbitration or med-arb would have been a better option than mediation for the Kramers? If not a better option, would it have been a viable option?

3. In *Erin Brockovich*, a mass tort action arose out of what appeared to be a simple real estate case. For the benefit of the plaintiffs the case was arbitrated rather than sent to trial.

   a. How did the plaintiffs benefit from having their case arbitrated?

   b. What was the implication of the fact that the arbitration was binding?

   c. What had to happen before the case could be arbitrated?

      1. How many plaintiffs were involved?

      2. What did Brockovich do in order to collect the requisite number of consents?

   d. What kind of investigative work did she do to prepare for the arbitration?

   e. With what kind of local administrative agency did Erin have to deal? Suppose this agency had refused to give her the paperwork she requested. What would she have to do to get these papers?

   f. Suppose that the arbitrator had found in favor of Pacific Gas & Electric. What federal administrative agency might have gotten involved? Where would Brockovich have had to look to find the regulations governing Pacific Gas & Electric that were promulgated by this administrative agency?

4. What administrative agency did Jan Schlictmann turn to in *A Civil Action?* Why did he do this? What did this agency accomplish? Go to *www.epa.gov/region01/remed/sfsites/wellsgh.html* to find out the status of the clean-up of the toxic sites. Briefly summarize what you discover.

INTERNET INQUIRIES

1. What kinds of ADR are available in your state? Record the Web addresses of these agencies and describe the services they provide.

2. Choose two federal administrative agencies and go to their Web pages. Describe the information and services available on this Web page.

3. Choose two state administrative agencies in your state and go to their Web pages. Describe the information and services available at these sites.

4. Your supervising attorney has asked you to find a list of possible arbitrators that could be used to arbitrate a complex tort case. Use the Internet to find sources of arbitrators. Summarize what you find; include Web addresses of relevant sites.

5. What factors are involved in determining whether a tribal court has jurisdiction over an individual? Use the Internet to answer this question. Summarize what you discover and give the Web addresses for the sites that provide this information.

6. Find an attorney who does divorce mediation in your area. Several online resources are available for locating attorneys including

West Lawyer Directory (*www.lawoffice.com*); Legal Industry Directory (*www.lawinfo.com*); USA Law Attorney Directory (*www.usalaw.com/firmsrch.cfm*).

You can also go to *www.findlaw.com* as well as contact the bar association in your area by going to its Web page. You might also go to the Web pages for organizations providing mediation services. Describe the process you follow in finding the names of at least two attorney-mediators in your area; include the Web addresses you use and the names of the attorneys you locate.

7. You have been asked to find information for a client about the process she must go through to secure her Social Security benefits now that her husband had died. She wants to know how to find this information on the Internet. Summarize the steps you follow in getting this information on the Web. Give the names of publications and other resources you find that might be of help to her.

8. Using the Internet, find out what federal regulations govern food stamp eligibility for non-citizens. How did you find this answer?

(a) With what does 21 CFR 170 deal? How did you find this answer?

(b) Can you get the List of *CFR Sections Affected* online? If so, how?

(c) Can you read a federal regulation online on the same day that it is published? If so, how?

9

Business Law

OBJECTIVES:

In this chapter you will learn:

- the requirements of contract formation
- the basics of contract interpretation
- how a contract can be discharged
- the possible defenses to a contract
- the possible legal and equitable remedies
- the different types of warranties that are possible and how they can be disclaimed
- the advantages and disadvantages of forming sole proprietorships, partnerships, corporations, LLCs, and LLPs

- how to form partnerships, corporations, and LLCs
- how corporations are financed
- the basics of a secured transaction
- the duties of principals and agents
- how to distinguish between employees and independent contractors
- how corporate paralegals differ from paralegals who work in law firms

"So When is the Wedding?"

Martha was mulling over John's comment to her about Tim and almost walked by the Johnsons without seeing them. "Mr. and Mrs. Johnson, what are you two doing here?" she blurted out in her surprise.

"We've got a few legal questions about our business and your boss, Mr. Morgan, made us an appointment with a Ms. Yuen. But we got here a few minutes early and hoped we might run into you," explained Mrs. Johnson as she stood up to embrace Martha.

"Well, I'm so glad you did. Why don't you come into my office and wait there? That way we can catch up a little. It's been so long since I've seen either of you. How's Mike doing? It's been awhile since I've seen him, too." Martha led the way to her office.

"He's just great! In fact," said Mrs. Johnson, pausing to beam at her husband before she continued, "we've got quite a surprise for you."

"Really. And what might that be?"

"Mike and Carmela are getting married!" exclaimed Mrs. Johnson, as she squeezed her husband's arm affectionately.

"Wow!" was Martha's immediate response. All she could think of was how young they were. But the look of joy on the Johnsons' faces prompted her to put her concerns aside and she hugged them both in celebration. "I'm so happy for you and for Mike! Carmela is such a sweet girl and I know she just adores Mike."

"We couldn't have picked a better daughter-in-law, Martha, and we like her family, too. We think Mike has made a very good choice and we're happy to welcome her into our family," announced Mr. Johnson with a kind of formality that Martha found endearing.

"So when is the wedding?" she inquired, trying not to reveal her uneasiness about their age.

"Oh, definitely not until Carmela has graduated," Mrs. Johnson assured her. Sensing the unexpressed equivocation behind Martha's question, she added, "By then Mike will be 20 and Carmela 18. I know they're young, but they've both been through a lot. With what she experienced in her country and in coming to this country, Carmela is more mature now than most American girls are at 21. And Mike—well, he's a very different person than he was before the shooting. He's grown up a lot."

"Almost dying will do that to you," agreed Martha.

525

"We have faith in both of them and in their good judgment," stated Mr. Johnson confidently.

"What a wonderful thing to be able to say," said Martha admiringly. For several more minutes they exchanged neighborhood news. When there was a lapse in their conversation, Martha finally asked, "So what is it that brings you here?"

"After almost losing the business when Mike was hurt, we decided it was time to create a contract for our customers to sign," explained Mr. Johnson succinctly.

"You mean you've been doing business based on oral agreements all these years?" Martha was incredulous.

"Yes." confirmed Mr. Johnson, "And until this last year we never had any problems. But in light of our most recent experiences, we've decided to take steps to better protect ourselves and our business."

"Say, we thought we might be working with you on this," suggested Mrs. Johnson. "Is that possible?"

"No way," laughed Martha. "All I remember of contract law is endless, archaic rules: mailbox rules, mirror image rules, and what not. No, the only contracts I've seen since I've been out of school have been real estate contracts. So I've never worked with the UCC or dealt with anything but standardized contracts where all you have to do is fill in the blanks."

"Does that mean we'll be dealing with this 'UCC'?" asked Mr. Johnson, pronouncing the abbreviation deliberately and slowly.

"You won't, but your attorney will," explained Martha. "UCC stands for Uniform Commercial Code. It's nothing more than a set of laws designed to make contract law more uniform from state to state and to make it simpler than the endless set of rules found under the common law."

UNIFORM COMMERCIAL CODE

Contract formation is governed by the common law and by the Uniform Commercial Code (UCC): a model set of statutes created by preeminent legal scholars. The goal of the UCC has been to standardize the law regarding commercial transactions—a goal that has been highly successful in that the UCC has been adopted with only minor variations in all states except Louisiana, which has adopted only four of its articles. Another goal of the UCC, articulated in Section 1-1-2(2), has been to "simplify, clarify, and modernize the law governing commercial transactions" and to promote the expansion of commerce.

In this chapter, we will focus our attention on Article 2 of the UCC. Article 2 deals with sales of goods only, which means that it does not apply to sales of services, real estate transactions, and employment contracts. The distinction between a sale of goods and a sale of services is not always clear. Does a blood transfusion, for example, involve the sale of a product (blood) or is it part of a package of services provided by a hospital and therefore not a sale but a service? This issue has arisen in the so-called "bad blood" cases where a patient contracted a disease after receiving contaminated blood. In cases involving a combination of sales and services, the court determines which aspect is predominant and applies the UCC only if the transaction is primarily a sale of goods.

Certain provisions in the UCC apply only to merchants. Therefore, knowing whether parties are considered merchants may be important for purposes of analysis under the UCC. Merchants, for example, are not only required to be fair and honest in their dealings with others but are also expected to be aware of the normal business practices in their trade. The UCC (sec. 2-104(1)) defines a merchant as someone who deals in the goods that are the subject of the contract or that "holds himself out as having knowledge or skill peculiar to the practices or goods involved" in the contract.

When analyzing a contract situation, begin by asking whether the contract involves a sale of goods or services and then consider whether the parties are mer-

NET NEWS

To read in detail about the UCC and its provisions, go to *www.fullertonlaw.com/chapt12.htm*. The UCC itself is available at *www.law.cornell.edu/uniform/ucc.html*. At this site, you can also see each section of the UCC as it has been enacted by each state as well as proposed revisions to the UCC.

chants. If the contract in question is governed by the UCC, remember also that contracts must be reviewed in light of the over-arching goal of the UCC, which is to "permit the continued expansion of commercial practices" (UCC Sec. 1-102(2)). In this chapter, we will look at contracts from both the common law and statutory (UCC) perspective.

Putting It Into Practice 9.1:

Deedee has agreed to breed one of her best Arabian show mares to Chamberlain's stallion. Deedee is a well-known horse trainer who also breeds and sells Arabian horses. Chamberlain owns several businesses that have nothing to do with horses, but has a breeding and showing operation that employs several people on a full-time basis. Both are considered experts on the subject of Arabian horse bloodlines. (a) Would Chamberlain and Deedee be considered merchants under sections 1 and 2 of the UCC? (b) Construct an argument that their contract is governed by the UCC and a counterargument that it is not. In your arguments, consider the fact that many Arabian breeders currently use artificial insemination rather than naturally breeding their horses.

Boilerplate standardized language in a contract, often in fine print and difficult to understand

"Boilerplate. It's One of the Reasons It's a Good Idea To Have Any Contract You Sign Reviewed By a Lawyer."

"I think you're wise to have written agreements with your clients. If nothing else, it will help you avoid those 'he said, she said' situations," affirmed Martha. "Parties are always better off if they know from the very beginning what they're expected to do, what they can expect to receive, and what the consequences are if either is not able to perform."

"We learned the hard way what happens when you sign a contract that hasn't been reviewed by an attorney. We did that and almost lost our business when we weren't able to follow through on a big party we were supposed to cater. The week of the party was the week Mike got shot. We didn't have time or the presence of mind to get the final preparations together and we didn't have the kind of personnel that knew how to handle that kind of affair. Anyway, we were supposed to cater a seven-course formal meal and the company ended up having to get a cowboy-beans-and-barbecued-chicken dinner as a last-minute substitute."

"And they weren't very pleased," interrupted Mrs. Johnson.

"To say the least," continued Mr. Johnson. "This deal involved one of their biggest clients. They had planned an elaborate awards ceremony, their guests were all dressed to the T, and they ended up eating barbecued chicken. I guess it was quite a fiasco." Martha did her best to keep from smiling at the images Mr. Johnson's description was conjuring up in her mind. "Anyway, if Mr. Morgan hadn't negotiated a deal for us, we'd have ended up losing a lot of money. And part of it was that we hadn't read all the fine print in the contract so we didn't know what we were agreeing to."

"**Boilerplate,**" commented Martha. "It's one of the reasons it's a good idea to have any contract you sign reviewed by a lawyer."

"Well, we certainly learned our lesson," concurred Mr. Johnson.

ELEMENTS OF A CONTRACT

What is a contract? The Restatement (Second) of Contracts looks at contracts from a traditional approach, defining one as an exchange of enforceable promises. In the Restatement's words, a contract is a "promise or set of promises for the breach of which the law gives a remedy, or the performance of which the law in some way recognizes as a duty." The UCC, on the other hand, omits the promissory language, casting a contract as an enforceable agreement: "the total legal obligation which results from the parties' agreement as affected by this Act and any other applicable rules of law" (UCC Sec. 1-201(1)).

consideration exchange of something of value

A binding contract can be written or oral, but to be valid, it must contain three elements: (1) offer, (2) acceptance, and (3) **consideration**. We will examine each element separately.

Offer

offeror person who makes an offer

offeree person who receives an offer

The person making the offer is called an **offeror** and the person receiving the offer is called an **offeree.** For an offer to be valid, the offeror must intend to enter into a bargain. A statement that is merely an invitation to negotiate or to deal is not an offer. If Sam says to Brian, "Are you interested in buying my car?", no offer has been made; Sam and Brian are engaged in negotiations. But if Sam says to Brian, "I will sell you my car for $2,000," Sam has made an offer. In deciding whether an offer has been made, the courts look not only at the words of the parties but at the circumstances surrounding their statements.

Another requirement of a valid offer is that it must contain definite terms. An offer is generally considered definite if it includes the subject matter of the proposed bargain, the price, and the quantity involved. Because advertisements generally lack this kind of definiteness and because they are directed to the general public rather than to an individual, they are usually viewed as invitations to deal rather than as offers. The legal significance of finding a statement to be an offer is that it creates a power of acceptance in the offeree. In other words, an offeree has the power to accept the offer and create a contract that is binding on the offeror.

requirements contract contract in which a buyer agrees to buy all of a product that he needs from a particular seller

Under the UCC, a contract may be formed even if it lacks definiteness because of a lack of terms. If, for example, a term for price is missing, the UCC makes it a "reasonable price" (UCC Sec. 2-305(1)), and if the time and place of payment is missing, payment becomes due at the time and place where the buyer is to receive the goods (UCC Sec. 2-310(a)). If too many terms are missing, no contract is created. Generally, quantity must be included in the terms of the agreement, but even that can be missing if a **requirements contract** or **output contract** is being formed. A requirements contract occurs when a buyer agrees to buy all of a product that he needs from a particular seller. With an output contract, the seller agrees to sell all of his output to a particular buyer. In these cases, even though a specific quantity is not identified, an objective standard is available by which a court can enforce the contract.

output contract contract in which the seller agrees to sell all of his output to a particular buyer

Putting It Into Practice 9.2:

Deedee offers to buy every filly that Chamberlain's stallion, TeraZon, produces in the upcoming foaling season and that Chamberlain owns. She adds that she is willing to pay at least $50,000 for each filly, but no more than $1,000,000 total. Is this a valid offer?

An offeree's power of acceptance ends under the following conditions.

◆ when the offer expires
◆ when the offer is rejected
◆ when the offeree makes a counteroffer
◆ when the offeror revokes the offer
◆ by operation of law

Most commonly, offers expire because they have a limited time period for which they are open, which is stated in the offer. If no time for acceptance is established by the offer, it terminates after a reasonable time as determined by the circumstances in which the offer is made (e.g., business custom, rapidity of price fluctuation, or whether the offer was made face-to-face or by some other form of communication).

An offeree causes an offer to terminate by rejecting the offer or making a counteroffer. If, for example, Susie offers to sell her condo to Bernadette for $100,000 and Bernadette refuses, the offer terminates. By the same token, if Bernadette says she will buy it for $80,000, Bernadette's counteroffer causes Susie's offer to terminate. If Bernadette changes her mind later and says she will buy the condo for $100,000, she cannot create a contract because Susie's offer is no longer open.

An offeror can revoke (retract) an offer as long as that revocation is communicated to the offeree before the offeree accepts. In the majority of states, a revocation is effective when it is received by the offeree; in a minority of states, it is effective when it is sent out. (Notice the correct terminology: an offeror *revokes* an offer whereas an offeree *rejects* an offer.)

Bilateral contract offer that is to be accepted by a promise

unilateral contract offer that is to be accepted by performance

An offer that is to be accepted by a promise creates a **Bilateral contract** and the foregoing rules for revocation apply, but an offer that is to be accepted by performance creates a **unilateral contract**. If, for example, I say to you, "I will give you $5 if you will promise to wash my car," and you respond "Sure, I'll do it for $5," we have formed a Bilateral contract that is binding on both of us. If, however, I say, "I promise to pay you $5 if you wash my car," we have not formed a contract until you actually wash my car because a unilateral contract is created by performance, not a promise to perform. The problem with revocation with unilateral contracts is this. Suppose I decide I don't want you washing my car. Can I still revoke my offer once you have started hosing down the car? Under the traditional view, a unilateral contract was not formed until performance was complete so I could revoke my offer any time before you finished washing the car. Because of the obvious unfairness to the offeree, under the modern view the offeror cannot revoke once performance has begun. So in our case, once you begin hosing my car down, I cannot revoke my offer.

Finally, an offer can be terminated by operation of law, which means essentially that circumstances make it impossible for the offeree to accept the offer. If one of the parties dies or if the subject matter of the agreement is destroyed, the offer is deemed to have expired.

option contract promise by an offeror to keep an offer open for a specified time period

merchant firm offer merchant's creation of an offer that is irrevocable for a reasonable time period

An offeree can avert the previous causes of revocation by giving the offeror some form of consideration, usually money, in exchange for a promise by the offeror to keep the offer open for a specified time period. Doing this results in a separate contract between the buyer and seller called an **option contract.** Under the UCC, a merchant can create an offer that is irrevocable for a reasonable time period, called a **merchant firm offer,** even without consideration.

▬ *Putting It Into Practice 9.3:*

(a) Deedee asks Chamberlain if he will agree to sell her every filly that his mares produce this year that come out of his stallion, TeraZon. Is Deedee seeking to form a unilateral or Bilateral contract? (b) Chamberlain says he'll have to think about it and does not get back to her until after the foaling season is over. Under the common law, can he still accept her offer? (c) What could Chamberlain do if he wanted to make sure that Deedee would give him 90 days to make up his mind? (d) Suppose Deedee decides she would rather buy fillies from a different bloodline. She calls Chamberlain to tell him this, but he does not get her phone call. Two weeks later, he calls her to accept her offer. Can he still accept her offer? (e) Suppose Deedee said she would buy one of Chamberlain's yearlings for $10,000 and he said he would sell the yearling for $15,000. A few days later, Chamberlain says he will sell the horse for $10,000 but Deedee says she has changed her mind. Can Chamberlain claim they have an enforceable contract?

Acceptance

Once an offer clearly has been made, the question of acceptance, which involves two key questions, arises. First, what kind of acceptance is required? As mentioned previously, a Bilateral contract calls for acceptance by a promise whereas a unilateral contract requires acceptance by performance. Under the common law "mailbox rule," if an offer is accepted by a communicated promise using the mail, the acceptance is effective as soon as it is sent. Even if the acceptance is lost in the mail and never reaches the offeror, it still goes into effect as soon as it is dispatched. This rule is designed to facilitate the creation of contracts when the parties are at a distance from one another. When a unilateral contract is involved, the offeror is more likely to be unaware that the offeree has begun or perhaps even completed performance. In those cases, an offeror's obligation under the contract will be discharged if the offeree does not notify the offeror within a reasonable time that she has completed performance.

The second question regarding acceptance is: What is the result when the purported acceptance differs from the offer? Under the common law "mirror image" rule, an acceptance had to be a mirror image of the offer; if not, it was considered a counteroffer and the offer expired. The UCC has changed this rule for the sale of goods and established that an agreement "operates as an acceptance even though it states terms additional to or different from those offered or agreed upon, unless acceptance is expressly made conditional on assent to the additional or different terms" (UCC Sec. 2-207(1)). This provision anticipates the "battle of the forms" problem that occurs when parties use pre-printed contract forms in which they sim-

Figure 9-1
How Offers Terminate

HOW OFFERS TERMINATE
Offer expires
Offeree rejects offer
Offeree makes a counteroffer
Offeror revokes offer
By operation of law

ply add specific terms for price and quantity. These forms typically contain Boiler-plate language that result in the offer and acceptance having details that do not match. Under the UCC, between merchants these new terms become part of the contract unless these terms "materially alter" the contract, the offeror objects to them, or the original offer limited acceptance to its terms (UCC Sec. 2-207).

▌ *Putting It Into Practice 9.4:*

While Deedee is walking around Chamberlain's grounds, she comes across his farrier (a horse shoer), Antonio, working on one of Chamberlain's horses. She tells him that if he can get over to her barn and shoe one of her horses before tomorrow, she will pay him $60, which is $10 more than his standard fee. (a) What kind of contract is she seeking to form? (b) Antonio shows up around 10:00 that night, but Deedee has already had the horse shod by another shoer. Must Deedee still pay him? (c) Suppose that Antonio does show up that day to shoe Deedee's mare. Unaware that he has done this, Deedee contacts another shoer the next day, who shoes the horse again. Does Antonio have a right to collect his $60 from Deedee? (d) Deedee's friend, Darlene, who is a novice in the horse business, has signed a breeding contract with Chamberlain. After signing it, she reads it and discovers that she must pay a boarding fee of $10/day while the mare is being bred. She had agreed to pay Chamberlain a total of $10,000 to breed the mare and had never agreed to pay any additional fees. Will she be required to pay the boarding fees? (e) Deedee signs the breeding contract and mails it to Chamberlain, but it does not arrive for a week. A day before he receives Deedee's contract, Chamberlain decides to increase his breeding fee. Is Chamberlain legally bound to honor the breeding fee he promised Deedee?

Consideration

Consideration is also required for a valid contract. Consideration is an exchange of something of value—usually money—but conceivably anything of value to

Figure 9-2
Questions That Arise in Contract Formation

QUESTIONS THAT ARISE IN CONTRACT FORMATION

Offer
Is the offer definite enough?
Does the offeror intend to enter into a bargain?
Has the offer terminated?

Acceptance
What kind of acceptance is required?
What happens if the purported acceptance differs from the offer?

Consideration
Have the parties exchanged something of value?
Have the parties given up something of value?

the parties. The original purpose of consideration seems to have stemmed out of the refusal to enforce promises of gifts when the person receiving the gifts did nothing in return. A gift can be distinguished from a contract because it involves no consideration—only one party receives something of value. With a contract, both sides receive something of value and give up something of value. If a grandfather promises to give his grandson $10,000 when he reaches 21, no contract is created because the grandson is unilaterally receiving something of value but is not giving up something of value in exchange. If, on the other hand, the grandfather promises to give the grandson $10,000 when he turns 21 if he does not smoke or drink until that time and the grandson agrees, a contract is created. In this case, the grandson will receive the benefit of money in exchange for suffering the detriment of abstaining from smoking or drinking. In return, the grandfather enjoys the benefit of having a grandson who neither smokes or drinks in exchange for giving up some of his money.

Generally, the courts do not review the adequacy of consideration even when parties make what appear to be poor bargains. The philosophy is that people should have the freedom to create whatever contracts they want, even if they are bad ones, and that, by the same token, they should not be allowed to get out of bargains they enter into simply because with hindsight they discover their mistake. The courts will intervene, however, when parties enter into a sham or "illusory" transaction by attempting to transform what is obviously a gift (a gratuitous promise) into a contract by creating nominal consideration. If a mother agrees to give her daughter land for the exchange of $1 and the daughter agrees, no enforceable contract has been created. The nominal consideration of $1 does not convert a gratuitous promise into a contract.

Consideration is a legal abstraction that is rarely of practical significance except when it serves as a strategy for finding a reason to avoid enforcement of a contract. Nevertheless, many form contracts require a recital of consideration to satisfy the consideration requirement. When custom dictates such a recital of consideration, adhering to standard practice is probably wise. The formation of option contracts is one area where consideration may be important.

Putting It Into Practice 9.5:

Deedee agrees to sell Chamberlain a mare for $1,000,000 in exchange for buying one of his mares for $1,000,000. They both know that these mares are actually worth closer to $500,000, but they want others in the industry to know about their deal and to rely on these inflated prices in making their own deals. Aside from the fact that they are perpetrating a fraud on the horse industry, have Deedee and Chamberlain formed an enforceable contract or is this a sham transaction?

NET NEWS

For more information about offers, acceptance, and consideration, go to *http://profs.lp.findlaw.com/contracts/index.html*. To see sample contract forms, go to *www.lectlaw.com/formb.htm* and *http://techdeals.lp.findlaw.com*.

"One of My Favorite Cases in School Was the 'What Is a Chicken?' Case."

"Is there anything we should know before meeting with Ms. Yuen?" inquired Mr. Johnson. Martha's words about archaic and endless rules were still reverberating in his mind and he was feeling uneasy about dealing with issues that seemed so nebulous.

"Not at all," Martha assured him. "Ms. Yuen is going to ask you a lot of questions about your business so she has a clear idea about what you do, what your concerns are, and what the trade practices are that are unique to your line of work."

"What do you mean by 'trade practice'? " followed up Mr. Johnson.

"Conduct and terminology that is standard to your trade. Let me give you an example. One of my favorite cases in contract law was the 'What is a chicken?' case. It involved two companies that got into a dispute about what was meant by *chicken*. The buyer said that term referred to a young chicken while the seller had a much broader interpretation of the term. In resolving this conflict, one of the factors the court considered was the standard usage of that term in the industry."

"All right. I think I understand what you're saying. So we just need to tell Ms. Yuen what it is we do and she'll make sure we don't get in trouble doing it."

"I think that's a fair assessment," smiled Martha. "And you couldn't be in better hands. Ms. Yuen just recently was offered a partnership in the firm, which means the partners are very pleased with what she's been doing. She also has one of the best paralegals in the firm working for her—Neal Honyaktewa. Neal used to work for a sole practitioner until one of the partners came up against him in a case and was so impressed that he talked him into working for us. In fact, Neal was recently accepted into law school and will be leaving us when the fall semester begins. One of his greatest attributes is his uncanny eye for detail. He'll no doubt assist Ms. Yuen in drafting and reviewing any contracts. Consider yourselves lucky to have him helping you."

CONTRACT INTERPRETATION

Even when parties believe they have reached a contractual agreement, they may discover at a later time that they did not have the "meeting of minds" they had thought. If they cannot resolve their conflict, a third party (often a court) must intervene. The question then becomes a matter of interpreting the words of their agreement. A general rule of contract law is that statements should be given an objective interpretation, that is, they should be given the interpretation that a reasonable person standing in the shoes of those who reached the agreement would give them. This interpretation is based on the reasonable person knowing everything that those who reached this agreement knew when they entered into the agreement. So, for example, if the parties had special knowledge because of their trade, as they did in *Frigaliment Importing*, the interpretation must acknowledge this special knowledge.

extrinsic evidence evidence outside the contract

Traditionally, **extrinsic evidence** (evidence outside the contract itself) was not admissible to interpret the contract. But modern courts are more liberal about allowing extrinsic evidence to show what the parties intended. A related question is whether parties can admit an alleged earlier oral or written agreement or contemporaneous oral agreement (called **parol evidence**) that was not included in the written contract but that was intended to be part of the contract. Under the parol evidence rule, if the parties intended their written contract to be their final and complete expression of their agreement, parol evidence is not allowed to add to, vary, or contradict the terms of their writing.

parol evidence earlier oral or written agreement or contemporaneous oral agreement that was not included in a written contract but that was intended to be part of it

Suppose, for example, that Carl agrees to sell Gustav 1,000 bales of hay by August 1, an agreement which they commit to writing. Before signing the contract, Carl informs Gustav that he may not be able to deliver on August 1 if he is unable to bale the hay because of heavy rains. Gustav indicates that he will still accept the hay even if

For some hints about writing contracts, go to *www.nolo.com* and find your way to *www.nolo.com.encyclopedia/articles/sb/ smallbiz_contracts.html.*

it is delivered after August 1, but neither he nor Carl changes the delivery date. Carl's concern about heavy rains is warranted and he is unable to deliver the hay until August 10, at which point Gustav refuses to accept it, pointing to the agreed upon delivery date of August 1. Under the parol evidence rule, Carl cannot introduce evidence of their verbal agreement unless he can show that they did not intend their written agreement to be their final and complete agreement. If they had entered into this oral agreement *after* signing the written contract, the parol evidence rule would not apply because the modification is subsequent to rather than before or contemporaneous with the written agreement. The UCC takes a more liberal approach and allows the admission of parol evidence unless the matter covered in the parol agreement "certainly would have been included" in the written agreement (UCC Sec. 2-202, comment 3).

▰▰▰ *Putting It Into Practice 9.6:*

Deedee agrees to breed one of her mares to TeraZon but wants to make sure the mare is bred in February and March so she will have a foal in January or February. All registered horses are considered to be a year older the first day of January, and so young horses that are being shown that are born at the beginning of the year have a competitive advantage over those that are born later in the year. Because Deedee plans to show the offspring of the mare she is breeding, the mare's conception date is very important to her.

Chamberlain agrees verbally to Deedee's request, but neither he nor Deedee remembers to put this provision in the written contract. Chamberlain later decides to keep TeraZon on the show circuit until May so that the stallion is not available for breeding until then. Deedee wants Chamberlain to refund her money because she does not want to breed the mare at this late date, but Chamberlain refuses. Will evidence of their oral agreement be admissible if Deedee sues Chamberlain for breach of contract?

Cite as: 190 F.Supp. 116

United States District Court S.D. New York.
FRIGALIMENT IMPORTING CO., Ltd., Plaintiff,
v.
B.N.S. INTERNATIONAL SALES CORP., Defendant.
Dec. 27, 1960.

FRIENDLY, Circuit Judge.

The issue is, what is chicken? Plaintiff says 'chicken' means a young chicken, suitable for broiling and frying. Defendant says 'chicken' means any bird of that genus that meets contract specifications on weight and quality, including what it calls 'stewing chicken' and plaintiff pejoratively terms 'fowl'. Dictionaries give both meanings, as well as some others not relevant here. To support its, plaintiff sends a number of volleys over the net; defendant essays to return them and adds a few serves of its own. Assuming that both parties were acting in good faith, the case nicely illustrates Holmes' remark 'that the making of a contract depends not on the agreement of two minds in one intention, but on the agreement of two sets of external signs—not on the parties' having meant the same thing but on their having said the same thing.' . . . I have concluded that plaintiff has not sustained its burden of persuasion that the contract used 'chicken' in the narrower sense.

The action is for breach of the warranty that goods sold shall correspond to the description, New York Personal Property Law, McKinney's Consol. Laws, c. 41, § 95. Two contracts are in suit. In the first, dated May 2, 1957, defendant, a New York sales corporation, confirmed the sale to plaintiff, a Swiss corporation, of

'US Fresh Frozen Chicken, Grade A, Government Inspected, Eviscerated 2 1/2-3 lbs. and 1 1/2-2 lbs. each all chicken individually wrapped in cryovac, packed in secured fiber cartons or wooden boxes, suitable for export

75,000 lbs. 2 1/2-3 lbs........ @$33.00
25,000 lbs. 1 1/2-2 lbs........ @$36.50
per 100 lbs. FAS New York
scheduled May 10, 1957 pursuant to instructions from Penson & Co., New York.' [footnote omitted]

The second contract, also dated May 2, 1957, was identical save that only 50,000 lbs. of the heavier 'chicken' were called for, the price of the smaller birds was $37 per 100 lbs., and shipment was scheduled for May 30. The initial shipment under the first contract was short but the balance was shipped on May 17. When the initial shipment arrived in Switzerland, plaintiff found, on May 28, that the 2 1/2-3 lbs. birds were not young chicken suitable for broiling and frying but stewing chicken or 'fowl'; indeed, many of the cartons and bags plainly so indicated. Protests ensued. Nevertheless, shipment under the second contract was made on May 29, the 2 1/2-3 lbs. birds again being stewing chicken. Defendant stopped the transportation of these at Rotterdam.

This action followed. Plaintiff says that, notwithstanding that its acceptance was in Switzerland, New York law controls under the principle of Rubin v. Irving Trust Co., . . .; defendant does not dispute this, and relies on New York decisions. I shall follow the apparent agreement of the parties as to the applicable law.

Since the word 'chicken' standing alone is ambiguous, I turn first to see whether the contract itself offers any aid to its interpretation. Plaintiff says the 1 1/2-2 lbs. birds necessarily had to be young chicken since the older birds do not come in that size, hence the 2 1/2-3 lbs. birds must likewise be young. This is unpersua-

sive—a contract for 'apples' of two different sizes could be filled with different kinds of apples even though only one species came in both sizes. Defendant notes that the contract called not simply for chicken but for 'US Fresh Frozen Chicken, Grade A, Government Inspected.' It says the contract thereby incorporated by reference the Department of Agriculture's regulations, which favor its interpretation; I shall return to this after reviewing plaintiff's other contentions.

The first hinges on an exchange of cablegrams which preceded execution of the formal contracts. The negotiations leading up to the contracts were conducted in New York between defendant's secretary, Ernest R. Bauer, and a Mr. Stovicek, who was in New York for the Czechoslovak government at the World Trade Fair. A few days after meeting Bauer at the fair, Stovicek telephoned and inquired whether defendant would be interested in exporting poultry to Switzerland. Bauer then met with Stovicek, who showed him a cable from plaintiff dated April 26, 1957, announcing that they 'are buyer' of 25,000 lbs. of chicken 2 1/2-3 lbs. weight, Cryovac packed, grade A Government inspected, at a price up to 33 cents per pound, for shipment on May 10, to be confirmed by the following morning, and were interested in further offerings. After testing the market for price, Bauer accepted, and Stovicek sent a confirmation that evening. Plaintiff stresses that, although these and subsequent cables between plaintiff and defendant, which laid the basis for the additional quantities under the first and for all of the second contract, were predominantly in German, they used the English word 'chicken'; it claims this was done because it understood 'chicken' meant young chicken whereas the German word, 'Huhn,' included both 'Brathuhn' (broilers) and 'Suppenhuhn' (stewing chicken), and that defendant, whose officers were thoroughly conversant with German, should have realized this. Whatever force this argument might otherwise have is largely drained away by Bauer's testimony that he asked Stovicek what kind of chickens were wanted, received the answer 'any kind of chickens,' and then, in German, asked whether the cable meant 'Huhn' and received an affirmative response. Plaintiff attacks this as contrary to what Bauer testified on his deposition in March, 1959, and also on the ground that Stovicek had no authority to interpret the meaning of the cable. The first contention would be persuasive if sustained by the record, since Bauer was free at the trial from the threat of contradiction by Stovicek as he was not at the time of the deposition; however, review of the deposition does not convince me of the claimed inconsistency. As to the second contention, it may well be that Stovicek lacked authority to commit plaintiff for prices or delivery dates other than those specified in the cable; but plaintiff cannot at the same time rely on its cable to Stovicek as its dictionary to the meaning of the contract and repudiate the interpretation given the dictionary by the man in whose hands it was put . . . Plaintiff's reliance on the fact that the contract forms contain the words 'through the intermediary of:', with the blank not filled, as negating agency, is wholly unpersuasive; the purpose of this clause was to permit filling in the name of an intermediary to whom a commission would be payable, not to blot out what had been the fact.

Plaintiff's next contention is that there was a definite trade usage that 'chicken' meant 'young chicken.' Defendant showed that it was only beginning in the poultry trade in 1957, thereby bringing itself within the principle that 'when one of the parties is not a member of the trade or other circle, his acceptance of the standard must be made to appear' by proving either that he had actual knowledge of the usage or that the usage is 'so generally known in the community that his actual individual knowledge of it may be inferred. . . .' Here there was no proof of actual knowledge of the alleged usage; indeed, it is quite plain that defendant's belief was to the contrary. In order to meet the alternative requirement, the law of New York demands a showing that 'the usage is of so long continuance, so well established, so notorious, so universal and so reasonable in itself, as that the presumption is violent that the parties contracted with reference to it, and made it a part of their agreement.' . . .

Plaintiff endeavored to establish such a usage by the testimony of three witnesses and certain other evidence. Strasser, resident buyer in New York for a large chain of Swiss cooperatives, testified that 'on chicken I would definitely understand a broiler.' However, the force of this testimony was considerably weakened by the fact that in his own transactions the witness, a careful businessman, protected himself by using 'broiler' when that was what he wanted and 'fowl' when he wished older birds. Indeed, there are some indications, dating back to a remark of Lord Mansfield, Edie v. East India Co., 2 Burr. 1216, 1222 (1761), that no credit should be given 'witnesses to usage, who could not adduce instances in verification.' . . . While Wigmore thinks this goes too far, a witness' consistent failure to rely on the alleged usage deprives his opinion testimony of much of its effect. Niesielowski, an officer of one of the companies that had furnished the stewing chicken to defendant, testified that 'chicken' meant 'the male species of the poultry

industry. That could be a broiler, a fryer or a roaster', but not a stewing chicken; however, he also testified that upon receiving defendant's inquiry for 'chickens', he asked whether the desire was for 'fowl or frying chickens' and, in fact, supplied fowl, although taking the precaution of asking defendant, a day or two after plaintiff's acceptance of the contracts in suit, to change its confirmation of its order from 'chickens,' as defendant had originally prepared it, to 'stewing chickens.' Dates, an employee of Urner-Barry Company, which publishes a daily market report on the poultry trade, gave it as his view that the trade meaning of 'chicken' was 'broilers and fryers.' In addition to this opinion testimony, plaintiff relied on the fact that the Urner-Barry service, the Journal of Commerce, and Weinberg Bros. & Co. of Chicago, a large supplier of poultry, published quotations in a manner which, in one way or another, distinguish between 'chicken,' comprising broilers, fryers and certain other categories, and 'fowl,' which, Bauer acknowledged, included stewing chickens. This material would be impressive if there were nothing to the contrary. However, there was, as will now be seen.

Defendant's witness Weininger, who operates a chicken eviscerating plant in New Jersey, testified 'Chicken is everything except a goose, a duck, and a turkey. Everything is a chicken, but then you have to say, you have to specify which category you want or that you are talking about.' Its witness Fox said that Hin the trade 'chicken' would encompass all the various classifications. Sadina, who conducts a food inspection service, testified that he chicken. The specifications approved by the General Services Administration include fowl as well as broilers and 'Young chickens' and 'Mature chickens,' under the general heading 'Total chickens.' and the Department of Agriculture's daily and weekly price reports avoid use of the word 'chicken' without specification.

Defendant advances several other points which it claims affirmatively support its construction. Primary among these is the regulation of the Department of Agriculture, 7 C.F.R. § 70.300-70.370, entitled, 'Grading and Inspection of Poultry and Edible Products Thereof.' and in particular 70.301 which recited:

"Chickens. The following are the various classes of chickens:
(a) Broiler or fryer . . .
(b) Roaster . . .
(c) Capon . . .
(d) Stag . . .
(e) Hen or stewing chicken or fowl . . .
(f) Cock or old rooster . . .

Defendant argues, as previously noted, that the contract incorporated these regulations by reference. Plaintiff answers that the contract provision related simply to grade and Government inspection and did not incorporate the Government definition of "chicken" and also that the definition in the Regulations is ignored in the trade. However, the latter contention was contradicted by Weininger and Sadina and there is force in defendant's argument that the contract made the regulations a dictionary, particularly since the reference to Government grading was already in plaintiff's initial cable to Stovicek.

Defendant makes a further argument based on the impossibility of its obtaining broilers and fryers at the 33cent price offered by plaintiff for the 2 1/2–3 lbs. birds. There is no substantial dispute that, in late April, 1957, the price for 2 1/2–3 lbs. broilers was between 35 and 37 cents per pound, and that when defendant entered into the contracts, it was well aware of this and intended to fill them by supplying fowl in these weights. It claims that plaintiff must likewise have known the market since plaintiff had reserved shipping space on April 23, three days before plaintiff's cable to Stovicek, or, at least, that Stovicek was chargeable with such knowledge. It is scarcely an answer to say, as plaintiff does in its brief, that the 33 cent price offered by the 2 1/2–3 lbs. "chickens" was closer to the prevailing 35 cent price for broilers than to the 30 cents at which defendant procured fowl. Plaintiff must have expected defendant to make some profit—certainly it could not have expected defendant deliberately to incur a loss.

Finally, defendant relies on conduct by the plaintiff after the first shipment had been received. On May 28, plaintiff sent two cables complaining that the larger birds in the first shipment constituted "fowl." Defendant answered with a cable refusing to recognize plaintiff's objection and announcing, "We have today ready for shipment 50,000 lbs. chicken 2 1/2–3 lb. Broilers 1 1/2–2 lbs.," these being the goods procured for shipment under the second contract, and asked immediate answer "whether we are to ship this merchandise and whether you will accept the merchandise." ' After several other cable exchanges, plaintiff replied on May 29 'Confirm again that merchandise is to be shipped since resold by us if not enough pursuant to contract chickens are shipped the missing quantity is to be shipped within ten days stop we resold to our customers pursuant to your contract chickens grade A you have to deliver us said merchandise we again state

that we shall make you fully responsible for all resulting costs.' [FN2] Defendant argues that if plaintiff was sincere in thinking it was entitled to young chickens, plaintiff would not have allowed the shipment under the second contract to go forward, since the distinction between broilers and chickens drawn in defendant's cablegram must have made it clear that the larger birds would not be broilers. However, plaintiff answers that the cables show plaintiff was insisting on delivery of young chickens and that defendant shipped old ones at its peril. Defendant's point would be highly relevant on another disputed issue—whether if liability were established, the measure of damages should be the difference in market value of broilers and stewing chicken in New York or the larger difference in Europe, but I cannot give it weight on the issue of interpretation. Defendant points out also that plaintiff proceeded to deliver some of the larger birds in Europe, describing them as 'poulets'; defendant argues that it was only when plaintiff's customers complained about this that plaintiff developed the idea that 'chicken' meant 'young chicken.' There is little force in this in view of plaintiff's immediate and consistent protests.

When all the evidence is reviewed, it is clear that defendant believed it could comply with the contracts by delivering stewing chicken in the 2 1/2–3 lbs. size. Defendant's subjective intent would not be significant if this did not coincide with an objective meaning of 'chicken.' Here it did coincide with one of the dictionary meanings, with the definition in the Department of Agriculture Regulations to which the contract made at least oblique reference, with at least some usage in the trade, with the realities of the market, and with what plaintiff's spokesman had said. Plaintiff asserts it to be equally plain that plaintiff's own subjective intent was to obtain broilers and fryers; the only evidence against this is the material as to market prices and this may not have been sufficiently brought home. In any event it is unnecessary to determine that issue. For plaintiff has the burden of showing that 'chicken' was used in the narrower rather than in the broader sense, and this it has not sustained.

This opinion constitutes the Court's findings of fact and conclusions of law. Judgment shall be entered dismissing the complaint with costs.

FN2. These cables were in German; 'chicken', 'broilers' and, on some occasions, 'fowl,' were in English.

Figure 9-3
Timeline for Frigaliment

TIMELINE FOR *FRIGALIMENT*	
DATE	**TRANSACTION**
April 23	P reserves shipping space; at this time price of 2 1/2–3 lb. chicken is 35–37 cents per lb.
April 26	P sends cable indicating intent to buy 2 1/2–3 lb. chickens on May 10 at 33 cents per lb.
April ?	D accepts P's offer
April ?	Supplier of chickens to D asks D to clarify whether "frying chickens" or "fowl" are desired
May 2	D confirms sale to P for two contracts (one due May 10 and the other due May 30)
May 10	First shipment of chickens is sent
May 17	Balance of chickens under first contract is sent
May 28	P protests that chickens are "stewing chickens" (also called "fowl")
May 28	D fails to respond to P's objections and asks whether P will accept shipment
May 29	P responds to D's telegram, and D ships chickens

Putting It Into Practice 9.7:

(a) Summarize the most significant facts in this case. (b) How does the plaintiff-buyer define *chicken* differently than the defendant-seller? (c) Does the court agree with the plaintiff's contention that, according to trade usage, the term *chicken* means "young chicken"? (d) What objective evidence supports the defendant's subjective interpretation of the term *chicken*? (e) Why does the court find for the defendant?

ALTERNATIVES TO PERFORMANCE

discharged   extinguish a legal duty

Ideally, a contract is **discharged** by both parties performing as agreed to under the terms of the contract. But in some instances, performance is impossible or impracticable or the parties may decide to end their agreement before performance is complete. If a party performs most but not all of his required duties under the contract,

substantially performed
performance of most but not all of the required duties under a contract

he is said to have **substantially performed** but is liable for any damages resulting from his incomplete performance. The other party is not relieved of her obligations under the contract. If a party commits a **material breach,** however, the other party is relieved of her contractual obligations.

material breach   failure to perform under the terms of a contract to such an extent that the non-breaching party can terminate the contract as well as sue for damages

Distinguishing between a minor breach, in which case the non-breaching party can sue the breaching party for damages but cannot terminate the contract, and a material breach, in which case the non-breaching party can terminate the contract as well as sue for damages, is not easy. Each case depends on such factors as the extent to which the breaching party has already performed, the degree of hardship imposed on the breaching party, and the extent to which the non-breaching party can be compensated. If a contract has a "time-is-of-the-essence" provision, indicating that time of performance is a material term in the contract, even a slight delay in performance will be considered a material breach.

repudiates   indicate by word or conduct an intent to refuse any further performance

A party who **repudiates** a contract (indicates by word or conduct an intent to refuse any further performance), excuses the other party from any further performance. The non-repudiating party can treat the repudiation as a material

Figure 9-4
Rules of Contract Interpretation

RULES OF CONTRACT INTERPRETATION

Contracts are interpreted using an objective standard.

Extrinsic evidence can sometimes be admitted to show what the parties intended.

Evidence of a parol agreement cannot be admitted if this agreement adds to, varies, or contradicts the terms of the parties' written agreement if that agreement was intended to be the parties' complete and final agreement (parol evidence rule).

UCC is more liberal than parol evidence rule and admits evidence of parol agreements unless the matter covered in the parol agreement "certainly would have been included" in the written agreement.

Evidence of a subsequent agreement that modifies a written contract can be introduced as evidence. (Parol evidence rules do not apply to subsequent agreements.)

breach of contract and can bring an immediate action for the entire value of the promised performance.

Under the UCC, the "perfect tender rule" allows a buyer who receives non-conforming goods to either accept the goods, reject them, or accept them in part and reject them in part. This rule can be deviated from if the parties agree in advance to overlook the lack of conformity or if the seller notifies the buyer, before the time for performance is over, that he intends to rectify the situation (UCC Sec. 2-601). If the buyer accepts substandard goods, she can then sue the seller for the difference between the value of the goods as promised and the value of the goods as received (UCC Sec. 2-714).

A party can also claim the defense of impossibility of performance because a party has died or become too ill to carry on his responsibilities under the contract or because an object that was to be sold has been stolen or destroyed. If a race horse dies, for example, before being transported to the buyer, the seller can claim impossibility as a defense. For this defense to apply, the party must show that the contract cannot be performed and not merely that the party cannot perform it.

Even if a contract is not impossible to perform, it may be commercially impracticable to perform. In this case, a change in economic circumstances has made it too costly for one of the parties to perform. If this change in circumstances could have been foreseen, however, the courts will generally not grant relief.

Putting It Into Practice 9.8:

(a) TeraZon contracts an infection that renders him sterile. Is Chamberlain in breach of his contract because he is no longer able to breed Deedee's mare? (b) Deedee agrees to breed one of her mares to TeraZon, but insists on including a provision in the contract that the mare must be bred beginning in February. Chamberlain keeps TeraZon on the show circuit until May. When he tells Deedee she can now have her mare bred, she tells him that she wants her money back. Is she entitled to this? (c) Suppose Deedee buys a colt from Chamberlain that she intends to use as a stallion, but six months later discovers that only one testicle has descended, making it difficult or impossible to use him as a stallion. His value as a gelding is substantially less than it would be as a stallion. Chamberlain was not aware and could not in all likelihood have been aware of the colt's condition when he sold him. What are Deedee's options?

Figure 9-5
Factors to Consider in Deciding Whether Breach Is Material

FACTORS TO CONSIDER IN DECIDING WHETHER BREACH IS MATERIAL

Repudiation by one party
Degree to which breaching party has already performed
Degree of hardship imposed on the non-breaching party
Extent to which the non-breaching party can be compensated
Time-is-of-the-essence provision

Consequences of Material Breach

Breaching party must pay damages
Non-breaching party is relieved of contractual obligations
Under UCC "perfect tender rule," party can reject non-conforming goods or accept them and sue for difference in value of goods as promised and value as received

Defenses to Material Breach

Impossibility
Commercial impracticability

liquidated damages clause
clause that fixes the amount of damages in the event of a breach

"Difficulty of Performance Is Not a Legally Recognized Defense."

A call from the receptionist alerted Martha that Ms. Yuen was ready to meet with the Johnsons. She escorted them to her office, introduced them to Kim Yuen and Neal Honyaktewa, and politely excused herself. Kim immediately perceived that her first order of business was to relax the Johnsons, who were obviously ill at ease. When she observed Mr. Johnson sit back in his chair, she knew she had been successful. She then focused on their motivation for drawing up a contractual agreement for their customers and quickly ascertained that they were still traumatized by having come so close to losing their business. Having gleaned the details about having been sued by the disgruntled client, she set about assuring them that they could prepare a contract that would protect them to some extent if, for some reason, they were not able to perform in the future.

"In that situation, you were potentially liable for more than simply the cost of securing a substitute caterer. Because you provide a unique catering service, your client faced a virtually impossible task of replacing you at the last minute. Unfortunately for you, as a result of the fiasco their party turned into, they not only lost any future business with their client but they also suffered what appears to be a serious blemish to their reputation. While you certainly weren't at fault for not being able to fulfill your contractual obligations, you had no legal defense to raise. Difficulty of performance is not a legally recognized defense," explained Kim.

"So how could we have changed this by having a contract?" questioned Mr. Johnson, puzzled by how a piece of paper could protect them if they had no legal defense.

"For one thing, we can include what is called a **liquidated damages clause** in the contract. This will allow you to establish up front what the damages will be in the event you should ever find it necessary again to breach a contract with a customer. In essence, such a provision allows you to limit the damages the other party can recover."

"And this is legal?" queried Mrs. Johnson.

"As long as it's done correctly," assured Kim. "We don't like to give advice that's illegal," she added smiling.

"Of course, I know that. What a silly question," said Mrs. Johnson, somewhat flustered.

"No, I understand your concern. It sounds too good to be true. Let me assure you that you can't use this provision to avoid paying damages, but you can agree in advance what your damages will be."

NET NEWS

Contracts can now be prepared electronically. To read about new laws pertaining to electronic contracting, go to *www.nolo.com* and find your way to *www.nolo.com.encyclopedia/articles/ilaw/esignatures.html* and click on "New Law Makes E-Signatures Valid" and to *http://library.lp.findlaw.com/contracts_general_1.html* and click on "California is First State in Nation to Adopt Electronic Contracting Law."

DAMAGES

Compensatory damages damages that compensate the non-breaching party for its losses

When one of the parties breaches its contract, the primary goal of contract law is to restore the non-breaching party to the position it would have been in had the contract been performed. In essence, damages are designed to give the non-breaching party the "benefit of its bargain." As such, **Compensatory damages** are designed to compensate the non-breaching party for its losses. These damages can come in the form of payment for the cost of replacement or the difference between the contract price and market price when the sale of goods is involved. They can also come in the form of payment for the cost of completion, as when a construction project is not completed. Damages are recoverable only if they are reasonably foreseeable and if their amount is reasonably certain of computation. In other words, speculative damages cannot be recovered.

To better understand Compensatory damages, consider Brian, who has agreed to buy Samantha's car for $5,000 and then shows up with only $3,000. If Samantha takes the $3,000, she can then sue Brian for the $2,000 difference between what she received and what she was promised, thereby restoring her to the position she would have been in had Brian performed as promised. If Brian reneges on the deal and Samantha sells the car to someone else for $3,000, she can sue Brian for the $2,000, the difference between the price of the sale and the contract price. She can also recover **incidental damages,** the expenses she incurs in finding another buyer. In commercial transactions, typical incidental damages include the cost of shipping, storing, and insuring goods; the costs incurred while purchasing substitute goods; and the cost of advertising for a resale.

incidental damages expenses incurred

cover process of finding a substitute good

Suppose, on the other hand, that Samantha is the one who decides not to sell the car and that Brian has to find another car. (Under the UCC, this process of finding a substitute good is called **cover.**) If Brian has to pay $7,000 to find a car comparable to the one Samantha promised to sell him, he can recover the cost of the substitute car ($7,000) minus the contract price ($5,000) or $2,000. If Brian decides not to look for another car, he can still recover the difference between the contract price and the market price.

consequential damages damages resulting from a buyer's particular circumstances

The non-breaching party can also recover **consequential damages** in some cases. These are damages that result from a buyer's particular circumstances—ones that go beyond the damages that arise naturally out of a breach of contract. These damages can be recovered only if the seller has reason to know that the consequential damages were the probable result of the breach. A common example of consequential damages is lost profits. Suppose Beatrice, for example, contracts to buy welding equipment from Sherry to facilitate the construction of her artwork and Sherry subsequently refuses to sell it. This forces Beatrice to complete her work by hand and prevents her from selling her work at a prestigious auction. She is able to sell her artwork at a later time, but for a substantially reduced price. If Beatrice had made it clear to Sherry why she needed the welder, she could sue Sherry for the difference between the profits she earned after Sherry's breach and the profits she would have earned if Sherry had sold her the welder as promised.

mitigated reduce or avoid by reasonable efforts

A non-breaching party is not allowed to recover for damages that could have been **mitigated,** that is, reduced or avoided by reasonable efforts. As mentioned previously, under the UCC, a buyer has a right to cover if the seller fails to deliver goods. If the buyer fails to cover, she cannot recover consequential damages that could have been avoided by covering. If a seller is in the process of manufacturing goods when the buyer repudiates its contract, the seller cannot run up its damages by continuing production, unless to do so would facilitate resale and thereby reduce the damages. If an employee is wrongfully terminated, he has a duty to mitigate his damages by seeking another comparable job.

To facilitate the litigation of damages, attorneys sometimes add a *liquidated damages clause*, which fixes the amount of damages in the event of a breach. These clauses must bear a reasonable relationship to the actual loss and are not enforceable if they are penalty clauses. They are used with contracts in which the damages that would result from a breach are impracticable or extremely difficult to estimate. If a court finds a liquidating damage clause to be invalid, the non-breaching party is entitled only to the actual damages it can prove.

specific performance court order that a party perform its contractual obligations; used when monetary damages are inappropriate because no comparable substitute is possible

An alternative to monetary damages is **specific performance.** This remedy is appropriate when no comparable substitute is possible. If Susan agrees to sell Bonnie an original painting by a famous artist and then refuses to make the sale, Bonnie can seek specific performance, asking the court the require Susan to sell her the painting. In this case, Bonnie would not be adequately compensated by monetary damages because it is the specific (and unique) painting in which she is interested. This remedy is appropriate only when money is an inadequate remedy and cannot be used to enforce service contracts. Bonnie could not, for example, use specific performance to enforce Susan's agreement to paint her portrait.

Rescission destroy a contract

Reformation correct a contract so that it more accurately reflects the intent of the parties

Courts also have the option of rescinding or reforming contracts. **Rescission** destroys the contract and puts the parties back in the position they were in before they entered into an agreement. **Reformation** occurs when the court corrects a contract so that is more accurately reflects the intent of the parties.

Putting It Into Practice 9.9:

(a) Deedee agrees to buy a mare from Chamberlain for $50,000. After signing the contract, Deedee is told that the mare is not doing as well as expected on the show circuit and that she is probably not worth what Deedee promised to pay. She breaches her contract with Chamberlain, who is then forced to sell the mare again. This time the best price he can get is $40,000. What can Chamberlain recover from Deedee if he sues her for his damages? (b) Deedee wants to buy the mare because of her unique bloodlines. Chamberlain, not she, reneges on the deal. What can Deedee ask a court to do if Chamberlain refuses to sell her the mare and she knows there is no other mare with comparable bloodlines? (c) What could Deedee have done in advance to protect herself in the event of this breach of contract occurring? (d) Suppose instead that Deedee could purchase another mare with comparable bloodlines but that she would have to pay more money. What does the UCC require her to do and what can she recover in damages? (e) Suppose that Deedee's plan was to breed the mare to her best stallion because they would have produced a foal with a very popular combination of bloodlines that would have likely brought a very high price. Now she will have to breed using another mare having less prestigious bloodlines, and the foal is not likely to be worth nearly as much. Assume that the price of foals depends not only on their bloodlines but on their conformation (how well they are built). Will Deedee be able to recover consequential damages?

Figure 9-6
Possible Remedies for Breach of Contract

POSSIBLE REMEDIES FOR BREACH OF CONTRACT

Compensatory damages

Compensation for losses

Incidental damages

Compensation for expenses incurred

Consequential damages

Compensation for damages unique to parties' circumstances

Specific performance

Remedy when monetary damages are inadequate

Rescission

Destruction of contract

Reformation

EQUITABLE PRINCIPLES

equitable   based on fairness

Some of the traditional rules of contract law can be unduly harsh and can result in unfair outcomes. To mitigate this harshness, modern courts have created **equitable** doctrines that create more just results. Historically, courts of equity were created so that the courts had the power to create a fair resolution when monetary damages were insufficient. Suppose some citizens of a community do not want to see a historic building destroyed as a result of new construction and will not be satisfied if a court awards them monetary damages. What they want is an equitable remedy—to have the construction project halted. To do this, a court can be asked to issue an **injunction,** a court order requiring that a party do something or stop doing something.

injunction   court order requiring a party to perform a certain act or to stop a particular action

Another equitable remedy courts use involves the creation of a **quasi-contract,** even if no actual contract was formed. Modern courts have devised this concept for situations in which people have been "unjustly enriched" by the mistakes of others. To illustrate, suppose that Enrique observes someone paving the dirt road leading up to his house, knowing that he did not make arrangements for this paving but realizing that it will certainly make it easier for him to access his home when it rains or snows. If the paving company had actually contracted with Enrique's neighbor, should Enrique be required to pay the company even though he had never contracted with this company? Courts will allow the paving company to recover from Enrique if it can show that it had conferred a benefit on Enrique with the expectation that it would be paid, that Enrique knew or had reason to know of the paving company's expectation, and that Enrique would be unjustly enriched if he were allowed to retain the benefit of the paving without paying for it.

quasi-contract   equitable remedy fashioned by the courts when a defendant receives a benefit for which the plaintiff expects to be paid and the defendant would be unjustly enriched if he were allowed to retain the benefit without paying

Another situation in which the courts apply their equitable powers occurs when a party relies on another's promise to that party's detriment. Even though no contract was formed, justice demands that the party be compensated. Suppose Barbara is promised a franchise in a cosmetics chain for $20,000. To raise the money, Barbara sells her home and works extra hours at her job. When she pulls together the $20,000, she goes back to the representatives of the franchisor, who inform her that the price has now escalated to $30,000 and that she will need to get training before she can be given the responsibility of running her own business. Undeterred, Barbara relocates to another city, works as a trainee at the franchise and raises the $30,000. Nevertheless, the company refuses to give her the franchise. Although Barbara was never guaranteed a franchise, she relied on representations made to her during her contract negotiations with the franchisor and she incurred significant expense and hardship in making the sacrifices necessary to secure the franchise. She is in a position to ask for compensation based on the doctrine of **promissory estoppel.** Under this doctrine, a promise will be legally enforceable, at least to the extent of the plaintiff's reliance on that promise, if the defendant induced that reliance and should reasonably have expected that reliance. The plaintiff must prove that the defendant made a promise with the intent of inducing the plaintiff to act, the plaintiff must act, and the court must believe that to not enforce the promise would be unjust.

promissory estoppel
doctrine that allows for the enforcement of a promise to the extent the plaintiff relied on a defendant's promise, if the defendant induced that reliance and should reasonably have expected such reliance

Putting It Into Practice 9.10:

(a) Marlene's mare accidentally gets loose and goes on Chamberlain's property, which is adjoining Marlene's property, while the mare is in season. Chamberlain's stallion impregnates her. Chamberlain wants Marlene to pay him his $10,000 breeding fee. Is a court likely to find a quasi-contract even though he and Marlene never formed a contract? (b) Suppose instead that Chamberlain had promised Marlene a breeding to his stallion for a special $5,000 fee, that Marlene sold her other two horses to raise the money, and that when she called a few months later to tell Chamberlain she had the money and wanted to breed her mare, he said he had changed his mind and that she would have to pay the full amount of $10,000. Is a court likely to grant Marlene equitable relief?

Figure 9-7
Equitable Relief

EQUITABLE RELIEF

Quasi-Contract

Plaintiff conferred a benefit on Defendant with the expectation that it would be paid

Defendant knew or had reason to know of the expectation and Defendant would be unjustly enriched if he were allowed to retain the benefit without paying for it

Promissory Estoppel

Defendant made a promise with the intent of inducing Plaintiff to act

Plaintiff acted

Not enforcing the promise would be unjust

NET NEWS

To better understand the principles of equity, go to *www.law.cornell.edu/topics/equity.html.*

Figure 9-8
Possible Defenses to a Contract

POSSIBLE DEFENSES TO A CONTRACT

Lack of Contractual Capacity
Mental illness
Voluntary intoxication
Minor

Illegal Contract
Prohibited by statute
Violates public policy
Adhesion contract
Exculpatory clause

No Meeting of the Minds
Fraud
Duress
Undue influence
Mutual mistake of fact

Statute of Frauds

Warranty
Express warranty
Implied warranty of merchantability
Implied warranty of fitness for a particular purpose

exculpatory clause   clause that releases a party from being liable as a result of his own actions

"By the same token," continued Kim, "we can include an **exculpatory clause** in your contract absolving you of liability for lost profits. Like the liquidated damages provision, they must be done appropriately to be enforceable, but it's another example of how we can protect you from re-experiencing what you went through with this other lawsuit."

"Thank you," said Mr. Johnson after a few seconds. "I believe I understand what you're suggesting. So what must we do to have this contract prepared?"

"What Neal and I need to do is pick your brains for awhile to make sure we're very clear on what your business entails, what kinds of customs and practices are common, and what terminology you use. We will then draft a contract that is unique to you. Now this doesn't mean we'll be starting from scratch. We'll use bits and pieces of other contracts we have written previously, but we'll customize it to meet your particular needs, concerns, and practices."

"Yes, Martha explained to us about trade practices and the court that had trouble figuring out what was meant by the term *chicken*," related Mr. Johnson with great seriousness.

Kim was not sure how to relate to Mr. Johnson's comment about the chicken, but Neal broke into a wide grin. "Oh, yes, the famous 'What is a chicken?' case. I remember reading that in my contracts class."

"I guess I skipped class that day," said Kim good humoredly. "At any rate, let's get started finding out what makes your business tick."

NET NEWS

An online version of Emanuel's law school outlines (used by law students everywhere) for contract law is available at *http://lawschool.lexis.com/emanuel/contracts/index.html.* Other Web sites that have outlines of contract law are *www.freeadvice.com/law/518us.htm* and *www.wld.com/conbus/weal/wcontral.htm.* Articles and books about contract law can be found at *http://smallbiz.findlaw.com/legal/contracts/index.html.* An overview of contract law can be found at *www.paralegals.org/Reporter/home.html.* Click on "Spring 1997" and then on "Basic Contract Law."

DEFENSES

Parties to a contract can subsequently argue that the contract was invalid because:

- ◆ one or both of the parties lacked the capacity to create a contract;
- ◆ the contract was illegal;
- ◆ the parties failed to have a "meeting of the minds" because of fraud, duress, undue influence, or mistake;
- ◆ the contract had to be in writing; or
- ◆ the product that was the subject of the contract was defective and in violation of the seller's warranties.

Lack of Capacity to Contract

A party that is intoxicated, mentally ill, or underage may lack the capacity to enter into a contract. Voluntary intoxication is generally viewed with disfavor by the courts as a defense but can be successful if the party raising it can show that his intoxication (by either alcohol or drugs) prevented him from understanding the nature, purpose, and effect of what he was doing. This same criterion is applied to the mentally ill: only someone whose mental capacity is so impaired that he does not know the nature, purpose, and effect of what he was doing can claim lack of capacity to contract. Under this "cognitive test," which is still used by the majority of courts, an individual with psychological or emotional problems cannot claim a lack of mental capacity to contract. The Restatement of Contracts articulates a more liberal rule, allowing for the defense to be raised when someone is "unable to act in a reasonable manner, and the other party has reason to know of his condition" (Restatement (Second) of Contracts Sec. 15). In many states, any contracts entered into by someone who has been adjudicated insane are **void,** rather than simply **voidable.** A void contract is invalid on its face, whereas a voidable contract will be deemed invalid by a court based on evidence of its defectiveness.

A contract entered into by a minor (an age determined by statute) is voidable at the option of the minor. As a result, the contract can be enforced against the adult party but not against the minor. Even if the minor **disaffirms** a contract (takes back his contractual obligations), however, he may still retain the benefits of that contract. He does have to return any goods that he still retains at the time of disaffirmance, although he does not have to repair or replace any damaged goods. In most states, minors must, however, pay the reasonable value of any goods or services that are considered "necessaries," such as food, clothing, and shelter. Based on these rules, you can see why adults should avoid entering into contracts with minors.

Illegal Contracts

Illegal contracts are void. A contract is illegal because it is prohibited by statute (e.g., a gambling contract) or because it violates public policy. An **Adhesion contract** is one type of contract that violates public policy. An Adhesion contract is one in which the contracting parties have very unequal bargaining positions and the party in the inferior bargaining position is forced to adhere to the other's terms on a "take-it-or-leave-it" basis, without being allowed to negotiate the terms. If, for example, a severe housing shortage exists and a landlord insists that a potential tenant must agree to waive her right to having the premises maintained in a habitable condition, any ensuing contract would be considered an Adhesion contract. If a court found such a contract to be grossly unfair, it could declare it to be unconscionable and

---

◆ **LOCAL LINKS** ◆

In your state are contracts entered into by those adjudicated insane considered void?

void   contract that is invalid on its face

voidable   contract that will be deemed invalid by a court based on evidence of its defectiveness

disaffirms   take back one's contractual obligations

◆ **LOCAL LINKS** ◆

What are the rules in your state when a minor disaffirms a contract?

Adhesion contract   contract in which the contracting parties have unequal bargaining positions and the party in the inferior bargaining position is forced to adhere to the other's terms without being allowed to negotiate the terms

refuse to enforce it. Adhesion contracts are most likely to be found in the fine print of pre-printed forms used in residential leases, insurance policies, and loan agreements. In an effort to protect the weaker parties (i.e., the consumers) in these situations, modern courts that find contracts to be Adhesion contracts bind the parties only to those provisions that are not unfairly surprising.

Exculpatory clauses can also be unconscionable in certain circumstances. An exculpatory clause that relieves a party from liability resulting from his own intentional wrongs or gross negligence is likely to be considered in violation of public policy and therefore unenforceable. Exculpatory clauses that relieve parties of liability for negligence are more problematic, but courts generally strike down such clauses if the general interest of the public is involved. For that reason, a hospital admission form that waives any claims for medical malpractice against either the hospital or its doctors would be considered unconscionable and therefore void. But a sky diver who signs a form releasing the company sponsoring a tournament from liability for any injuries the sky divers might sustain would probably be upheld as long as the exculpatory clause was easily visible. Sky diving is an inherently dangerous sport and those who engage in it do so by choice. Provisions relieving a party from liability for lost profits or damage to property caused by a party's negligence are often upheld as long as the injured party had a choice in agreeing to these provisions and was not unfairly surprised.

BONUS POINTERS:

BAD FAITH

Bad faith is an intentional tort that occurs when an insurance carrier (insurer) unreasonably delays payment on a policy, acts unconscionably toward an insured (person who is paying insurance premiums), or engages in unfair claims practices. Historically, some courts have viewed insurance contracts as Adhesion contracts and held that certain policy provisions could not necessarily be utilized against an insured and that the insured was not presumed to understand all the terms of the insurance contract. Courts later developed a rule of law requiring contracts to be interpreted in favor of the non-drafter (the insured) so that any "ambiguities" would be construed against the carrier and in favor of the insured.

The modern-day "reasonable expectation" doctrine protects the insured's reasonable expectation that coverage will be provided and not defeated by provisions that would be unanticipated by the ordinary insured and that were never negotiated between the insured and the carrier. The court will reform the contract to the reasonable expectation of the insured even though a detailed review of the contract itself does not support those expectations.

In their efforts to curb the sometimes misused discretion of insurance carriers, courts have looked for remedies outside of those found in contract law because such remedies impose a relatively small penalty on overreaching carriers. A carrier found in breach of contract is liable only for the amount owed to the insured plus attorney fees and court costs. Because insurance companies know that, at the worst, they will have to pay only a minor penalty for their indiscretions, they can afford to be rather cavalier in their actions toward their insured. The tort of bad faith has evolved as a means of providing relief to insureds.

The damages that can be recovered in a bad faith claim go beyond the compensatory and consequential damages of contract law. They include recovery for the legal fees incurred by the insured in pursuing a claim against the insurer, any emotional distress suffered by the insured, and any other monetary loss or damage to the insured's credit or reputation. If the insurance carrier's conduct is egregious enough, punitive damages may be warranted. The amount of punitive damages is based on the financial condition of the insurer and the degree of its misconduct rather than the impact of its misconduct on the insured. Because the insurance business is often very lucrative, a plaintiff asking for relatively small actual damages may seek punitive damages in the millions of dollars range.

fraudulently intentionally misrepresenting a material fact; also called intentional misrepresentation

duress acting involuntarily

undue influence one of the parties to a relationship based on trust and dependency misusing that trust to influence the actions of the other

mutual mistake mistake by both parties to a contract; also called a *bilateral mistake*

unilateral mistake mistake by one party to a contract

No Meeting of the Minds

Courts will not enforce agreements where there was no "meeting of the minds." This lack of consensus can occur if one of the parties has acted **fraudulently,** if a party acted under **duress** or as a result of **undue influence,** or if one or both of the parties acted as a result of a mistake.

A party who acts fraudulently acts with the intent to deceive another regarding a material fact and that person justifiably relies on the misrepresentation to his detriment. The real estate agent who sells the proverbial swampland in Florida by intentionally misrepresenting it as a buyer's paradise commits fraud. (Intentional misrepresentation is discussed further in Chapter 11.) An individual acts under duress if she enters into an agreement by force rather than voluntarily. Undue influence occurs when a confidential relationship based on dependency and trust exists between two parties, such as between a caretaker and an aging patient, and one party misuses that trust to influence the actions of the dependent party. The classic example of undue influence occurs when a caretaker urges a dying, elderly patient to rewrite her will naming the caretaker as the sole or primary beneficiary. (Undue influence is discussed more fully in Chapter 11.)

When both parties to a contract have a different idea about what is included in a contract, they do not have a "meeting of the minds" and either can rescind the contract. This is a case of **mutual mistake** of fact, also called a *bilateral mistake.* When only one of the parties is mistaken (**unilateral mistake**), both parties will be bound by the contract unless the other knew or should have known of the mistake or the mistake is based on a mathematical error. These rules apply only to mistakes of fact, not to errors in judgment regarding the value or quality of a good or service being contracted for. If Barnabas agrees to buy a violin from Serena believing it to be worth $10,000, and Serena knows that its market value is actually closer to $7,500, their contract is enforceable even though Barnabas is mistaken about the value of the violin. If, on the other hand, they decide to have the violin appraised and discover to their mutual surprise that the violin is actually a very rare Stradivarius worth $500,000, some courts would classify this as a mutual mistake of fact and allow the contract to be rescinded.

Writing Requirements

Contracts are not necessarily required to be in writing and, in fact, an oral contract may be perfectly valid. All states, however, have a statute of frauds that lists those contracts that are required to be in writing. Those contracts include contracts involving land, contracts that cannot be performed within one year, and contracts for the sale of goods valued at $500 or more. The purpose of a statute of frauds is to prevent a party from fraudulently claiming that a contract was made and to ensure that evidence is available to clarify any significant or complicated matters. The writing need not be a formal contract. A check or memo is sufficient as long as it fully expresses the terms of the agreement.

Warranties

A defense based on warranty is a hybrid one, containing characteristics of both tort law and contract law. Originally, a warranty action was deemed a form of misrepresentation and was therefore considered a tort. But because most warranties arise under the common law in situations involving a contract of sale, contract law was also applicable. Today this amalgamated form of law is made even more complicated by the UCC's efforts to deal with warranties on a statutory basis.

In deciding whether to apply contract law or tort law, a court must consider the nature of the defect in the product and the type of loss for which the plaintiff seeks compensation. In a tort claim, a plaintiff is alleging she was exposed by means of a hazardous product to an unreasonable risk of injury. In a contract case, however, the plaintiff is alleging that the product failed to perform in accordance with expectations one would have for a product of a particular quality and fit for ordinary use. Tort law, then, is reserved for defects that result in unreasonably dangerous products. Contract remedies are more appropriate when the defect involves only the quality of the product and presents no unreasonable danger to people or property.

The type of loss—personal injury, property loss, or economic damage—also determines whether the plaintiff will select a contract or tort claim. A majority of jurisdictions restrict contract liability to recovery for commercial or economic loss and tort liability to recovery for damage to persons or property, but this distinction has been challenged by some modern courts. Some have reasoned that if the plaintiff's only loss is an economic one, the parties are best left to their commercial remedies, but if the plaintiff's economic loss is accompanied by some physical damage to a person or other property, the party's interests are best protected via tort liability.

There are two types of warranties: express and implied. With an **express warranty**, a seller expressly represents that the goods possess certain qualities. A description of a windshield by a manufacturer as being "shatterproof" is an example of an express warranty. If the purchaser can later show that the product does not possess such qualities (if, for example, the windshield shatters after being hit by a stone), she may sue for breach of warranty.

An express warranty can be made in one of three ways: (1) an "affirmation of fact or promise" regarding the goods; (2) a description of the goods; and (3) use of a sample or model of the goods (UCC Sec. 2-313). A seller might describe goods as being water-resistant, for example, or might use a model to demonstrate how the product works, thus suggesting to consumers the product they buy is similar in nature. A plaintiff whose damages are solely economic, such as lost profits, can recover the difference between what the product would have been worth had it been as it was warranted and what it was in fact worth with its defect (UCC Sec. 2-714(2)). The buyer can also recover incidental and consequential damages (UCC Sec. 2-715).

A seller also makes certain implied warranties by virtue of offering a product for sale. The two most common types of implied warranties are the **warranty of merchantability** and the **warranty of fitness for a particular purpose.**

A warranty of merchantability is implied in a contract for the sale of goods if the seller is a merchant in the regular business of selling the kind of goods in question. According to UCC Sec. 2-314, for goods to be merchantable they must meet these criteria among others.

- ◆ be "fit for the ordinary purposes for which such goods are used"
- ◆ be "within the variations permitted by the agreement, of even kind, quality and quantity within each unit and among all units involved"

express warranty warranty in which the seller expressly represents that the goods possess certain qualities

warranty of merchantability warranty that is implied when the seller is a merchant in the regular business of selling the kind of goods in question

warranty of fitness for a particular purpose warranty created when a seller who knows that a buyer wants goods for a particular purpose makes a recommendation on which the buyer relies

◆ be "adequately contained, packaged, and labeled as the agreement may require"

◆ "conform to the promises or affirmations of fact made on the container or label, if any"

The courts have consistently held that retailers impliedly warrant the merchantability of their products. A few courts, however, have created what is known as the "sealed container" doctrine, which absolves retailers who sell sealed containers of any liability.

An implied warranty of fitness for a particular purpose is created when a seller who knows that a buyer wants goods for a particular (noncustomary) purpose makes a recommendation on which the buyer relies (UCC Sec. 315). Suppose, for example, a consumer asks for advice from a salesman at a hardware store regarding what type of lumber he should purchase for a particular construction project. If the type of lumber he purchases turns out to be unsuitable for such use, the consumer can sue the hardware store on the basis of breach of implied warranty.

A direct purchaser, that is, someone who buys directly from the defendant, can recover the same damages for breach of implied warranty as can be recovered for breach of express warranty. But with a remote purchaser, that is, someone who buys a product from a dealer rather than the manufacturer, what can be recovered is less clear. Remote purchasers can recover for personal injury damages and some states allow recovery for property damage alone. But a remote purchaser probably cannot recover for purely economic damages, such as lost profits. According to the majority position, such a purchaser should sue the immediate seller to recover for economic damages.

disclaim   deny a warranty

Under the UCC, a seller can **disclaim** both express and implied warranties. To disclaim a warranty of merchantability, the UCC requires that the seller use language that is conspicuous and that specifically mentions merchantability (UCC Sec. 2-316). Alternatively, an implied warranty of merchantability is disclaimed if the product is sold "as is" or if the buyer has an opportunity to examine the goods but refuses to do so. Federal law precludes any manufacturer that provides consumers with a written warranty from disclaiming any implied warranty. Any written warranty provided by a manufacturer must therefore include the implied warranty of merchantability.

Sellers sometimes try to limit the remedies available to plaintiffs for breach of implied warranty by providing that they (sellers) will not be liable for consequential damages. "[L]imitation of consequential damages for injury to the person in the case of consumer goods is *prima facie* unconscionable" (UCC Sec. 2-719(3)). Therefore, provisions limiting the seller's liability for repair or replacement of goods will not be enforced in cases involving personal injuries resulting from defects in products designed for personal use. Limitation of damages is not unconscionable, however, when the loss is commercial, that is, involving intangible economic loss (UCC Sec. 2-719(3)).

Putting It Into Practice 9.11:

(a) Deedee attends an auction at which Chamberlain is selling many of his prize horses. Before the auction begins, she offers to buy one of his mares for $50,000 and Chamberlain accepts. Have they formed an enforceable contract? (b) Deedee is a bidder at the auction at which Chamberlain serves cocktails. After Deedee becomes visually intoxicated, she successfully bids on a gelding for which she pays $40,000. After she sobers up the next day, she calls

Chamberlain to tell him that, despite the written contract she had signed, she really did not want the gelding and that she never would have bought him had she not been drunk. Can Chamberlain enforce the contract? (c) Suppose that Deedee purposefully bought the gelding with the intent of showing him in jumping classes, that she had told Chamberlain of her intent, and that he assured her that the gelding would make an excellent jumper. The gelding appeared to be in good shape when she bought him, but when she got him home she discovered that he was lame. Her veterinarian suspects that the horse had been given a pain killer before the auction so that he would appear to be sound, but he says he cannot prove this. What possible causes of action does Deedee have against Chamberlain? What are the possible results if she is successful? Assume that the contract she signed indicated that she bought the horse "as is." (d) Deedee's niece, Mindy, is staying at Deedee's ranch while Deedee is away. While visiting, Mindy makes arrangements with one of Chamberlain's trainers to take riding lessons. She takes four lessons before Deedee discovers what she is doing. Deedee refuses to pay Chamberlain's trainer for the riding lessons because she never consented to them and Mindy, who is 17, tells the trainer she has changed her mind and does not want to take lessons any more. Can Chamberlain's trainer enforce the written agreement he had with Mindy or at least get paid for the lessons he has given her? (e) Deedee offers riding lessons to some of her clients. She requires them to sign a contract, which includes a provision (in boldface and capital letters) that reads "TRAINER IS NOT LIABLE FOR ANY DAMAGES TO PERSONAL PROPERTY OR FOR ANY INJURIES SUSTAINED BY CLIENTS DURING RIDING LESSONS, DEMONSTRATIONS . . ." During one lesson, one of Deedee's students is injured when her horse bucks her off. Deedee later discovers that the groom who saddled the horse failed to make sure the saddle was cinched tightly before the student mounted. Deedee believes that the horse probably started bucking when she felt the saddle move, but Deedee is confident that she cannot be sued for negligence because of the provision in her contract absolving her of liability. Is she correct?

"So, Neal, is there anything you can think of that we haven't covered?" asked Kim.

"Just one thing," responded Neal, as he turned to address the Johnsons. "I think it's important you know that we prepare our contracts using plain English. We do our best to avoid legalisms—the party of the first part heretofore agrees to provide the party of the second part—and any kind of language that muddies rather than clarifies what is being said."

"Good point," agreed Kim. "We don't think that either our clients or the parties they are dealing with are well-served by signing contracts that neither of them understands. In years past, that kind of formalized, obtuse language was something that clients expected and lawyers were only too glad to deliver. But all that has changed with the plain English movement. Now our goal is to make our writing as clear as possible."

NET NEWS

For more information about warranties, go to *www.nolo.com/encyclopedia/faqs/ctim/ctim13.html.*

Figure 9-9
Warranties

WARRANTIES

EXPRESS WARRANTY

Creation

Affirmation of fact or promise

Description of the goods

Use of sample or model

Recovery

Difference between value of product as warranted and value with defect

Incidental damages

Consequential damages

IMPLIED WARRANTY

Creation of Implied Warranty of Merchantability

Goods are merchantable if:

Fit for the ordinary purposes for which they are used

Of even kind, quality, and quantity

Adequately contained, packaged, and labeled

Conforming to promises made on the container or label

Recovery

Direct purchaser

Difference between value of product as warranted and value with defect

Incidental damages

Consequential damages

Remote purchaser

Can recover for pure economic loss by suing immediate seller

DISCLAIMER OF IMPLIED WARRANTIES

Using conspicuous language

Specifically mentioning merchantability

Selling goods "as is"

Buyer has an opportunity to examine and refuses to do so

Written warranty by manufacturer must include implied warranty

of merchantability

RECESS

....

SUMMARY – PART A

Contract formation is controlled by the common law and the Uniform Commercial Code. The UCC has been successful in standardizing the law governing commercial transactions. It has also served to simply, clarify, and modernize the law and promote the expansion of commerce. Article 2 of the UCC deals with the sale of goods only and does not apply to real estate transactions, sales of services, and employment contracts. Certain provisions of the UCC apply only to merchants.

A valid contract contains an offer, acceptance, and consideration. For an offer to be valid, the offeror must intend to enter into a bargain and the terms of the offer must be definite, although under the UCC a contract can still be formed even if the offer is indefinite because it is lacking certain terms. Requirements and output contracts are enforceable even though they lack quantity terms. An offer creates a power of acceptance by an offeree. The power of acceptance ends when the offer expires, when the offeree rejects the offer or makes a counteroffer, when the offeror revokes the offer, or by operation of law. Bilateral contracts are formed when an offer is to be accepted by a promise and a unilateral contract is formed when an offer is to be accepted by performance. Under the common law "mailbox rule," if an offer is accepted by a communicated promise using the mail, the acceptance is effective as soon as it is sent. Under the "mirror image rule," an acceptance must be a mirror image of the offer. Anticipating the "battle-of-the-forms" problem that occurs when parties use pre-printed forms, the UCC allows an acceptance that contains terms that are additional to or different from those in the offer as long as the acceptance is not conditioned on agreement to additional or different terms. The exchange of consideration is what distinguishes a contract from a gift. Generally, the courts do not get involved in looking at the adequacy of consideration even when parties make what appear to be poor bargains. As a practical matter, consideration is usually considered only when parties are seeking a way to avoid enforcing a contract.

When parties who believe they have formed a contract later discover they did not have a "meeting of the minds," the courts must determine what their agreement was. To do this, courts use an objective standard. Although traditionally courts did not consider extrinsic evidence in interpreting contractual terms, modern courts are more willing to do so. Under the parol evidence rule, if the parties intended their written contract to be the final and complete expression of their agreement, parol evidence will not be allowed to add to, vary, or contradict the terms of their writing. The UCC, on the other hand, allows the admission of parol evidence unless the matter covered in an earlier oral or written agreement or contemporaneous oral agreement would certainly have been included in the contract.

In some instances, parties are unable to complete their contractual duties because of a change in circumstances that makes it impossible or impractical for them to perform. If they have substantially performed, the other party must still meet its contractual obligations; but if they commit a material breach, the other party is relieved of its contractual obligations. Distinguishing between a minor breach and a material breach is not easy, but if a contract contains a "time-is-of-the-essence provision," even a minor delay will be considered a material breach. A non-breaching party can treat a repudiation as a material breach. Under the "perfect tender rule" of the UCC, a buyer who receives non-conforming goods can either accept the goods, reject them, or accept them in part and reject them in part.

When a party breaches a contract, contract law serves to restore the non-breaching party to the position it would have been in had the contract been performed. The non-breaching party can recover compensatory, consequential, and incidental damages, but also has a duty to mitigate its damages. Damages are recoverable only if they are reasonably foreseeable and their amount can be computed with reasonable certainty. Parties to contracts can expedite the litigation of damages by including a liquidated damages clause if it is appropriate. Courts can grant specific performance when monetary damages are inappropriate because no comparable substitute is available to compensate the non-breaching party. Courts also have the option of rescinding and reforming contracts.

To mitigate the harshness of the common law rules, modern courts have created equitable concepts, such as quasi-contracts and the doctrine of promissory estoppel, that permit more just results. Both of these concepts apply to situations where no contract has been formed. The promissory estoppel doctrine requires that the plaintiff prove that the defendant made a promise with the intent of inducing the plaintiff to act, the plaintiff acted, and not enforcing the promise would be unjust. A quasi-contract is formed when one party confers a benefit on another with the expectation of being paid, the party receiving the benefit knows or has reason to know of the other party's expectation and would be unjustly enriched if it were allowed to retain the benefit without paying for it.

Parties that want to rescind a contract can argue that it was invalid because one or both of the parties was under age, mentally ill, or intoxicated at the time they entered into the contract. The latter two defenses are viable only if the mentally ill or intoxicated party was unable to understand the nature, purpose, and effect of what he was doing. A contract entered into by a minor is voidable at the option of the minor, although the minor can enforce a contract against an adult. Illegal contracts that are prohibited by law or that violate public policy are void. Adhesion contracts violate public policy, as do some types of exculpatory clauses. Courts will not enforce contracts where there was no "meeting of the minds" due to duress, undue influence, fraud, or mutual mistake. If a unilateral mistake is involved, the contract will be enforced unless one party knew or should have known of the other party's mistake or the mistake involved a mathematical error. State statutes of fraud require contracts involving land, contracts that cannot be performed within one year, and contracts for the sale of goods valued at $500 or more to be in writing. Breach of warranty is a hybrid of contract and tort law. With an express warranty, a buyer whose damages are solely economic can recover the difference between what the product would have been worth had it been as it was warranted and what it was, in fact, worth with its defect, as well as incidental and consequential damages.

Direct purchasers can recover the same damages for breach of an implied warranty of merchantability and a warranty of fitness for a particular purpose, but what remote purchasers can recover is less clear. An implied warranty of merchantability can be disclaimed if a seller uses language that is conspicuous and that specifically mentions merchantability, if the product is sold "as is," or if the buyer has an opportunity to examine the goods and refuses to do so. Generally, sellers cannot limit the remedies available to buyers for breach of implied warranty unless the loss is a commercial one.

KEY TERMS

Adhesion contract	Exculpatory clause	Offeror	Undue influence
Bilateral contract	Express warranty	Option contract	Unilateral contract
Boilerplate	Extrinsic evidence	Output contract	Unilateral mistake
Compensatory damages	Fraudulently	Parol evidence	Void
Consequential damages	Incidental damages	Promissory estoppel	Voidable
Consideration	Injunction	Quasi-contract	Warranty of fitness for a
Cover	Liquidated damages clause	Reformation	particular purpose
Disaffirms	Material breach	Repudiates	Warranty of
Discharged	Merchant firm offer	Requirements contract	merchantability
Disclaim	Mitigated	Rescission	
Duress	Mutual mistake	Specific performance	
Equitable	Offeree	Substantially performed	

REVIEW QUESTIONS – PART A

1. What is the purpose of the UCC?
   a. What does Article 2 cover? What does it not cover?
   b. Why is it important to know if a party is a merchant for purposes of analyzing a contract under the UCC?
2. How is a contract defined differently by the Restatement than the UCC?
3. What are the three elements of a valid contract?
4. What are the requirements of a valid offer?
   a. How definite does an offer have to be?
   b. What is missing in requirements and output contracts?
5. What ends the power of acceptance?
6. When does the time for acceptance of an offer end?
7. What is the difference between a unilateral and a Bilateral contract?
   a. When can a unilateral contract be revoked?
   b. When can a Bilateral contract be revoked?
8. What is the "mailbox rule" and what is its purpose?
9. What is the "mirror image rule"?
   a. How does the UCC change this rule?
   b. How does this resolve the "battle-of-the-forms" problem?
10. What is the purpose of requiring consideration for contract formation?
    a. What is an "illusory" transaction?
    b. What is the practical legal significance of consideration?
11. What is the consequence of committing a material breach?
    a. What is the consequence of substantially performing?
    b. What factors are considered in determining whether a breach is minor or material?
    c. What option does a non-breaching party have if the other party repudiates its contract?
12. What is the "perfect tender rule"? Under what conditions can this rule be deviated from?
13. Under what conditions can a party claim impossibility or commercial impracticability as a justification for not performing?
14. What is the purpose of compensatory damages? What is required before they can be awarded?
15. When are consequential damages appropriate?
16. What are incidental damages? When are they awarded?
17. What is the duty of mitigation?
18. What is the "cover" requirement of the UCC? What can a buyer recover after meeting this requirement?
19. What is a liquidated damages clause? Under what conditions is it enforceable? What is the consequence to the non-breaching party if this clause is found to be invalid?
20. Under what circumstances is specific performance an appropriate remedy? When is it not?
21. What are the consequences of a court rescinding a contract? Of reforming it?
22. Explain how the concepts of quasi-contract and promissory estoppel mitigate the harshness of the common law rules.
23. Under what conditions can an individual claim lack of mental capacity to enter into a contract based on intoxication or mental illness?
24. What are the possible consequences of contracting with a minor?
25. Give an example of the following.
    a. a void contract
    b. a voidable contract
    c. an Adhesion contract
    d. an exculpatory clause
26. When might the following be raised as a defense?
    a. fraud
    b. duress
    c. undue influence
    d. mistake
27. Under what circumstances is a contract required to be in writing?
28. When is breach of warranty a contract-law based claim? When is it a tort-law based claim?
29. Give an example of an express warranty.
    a. How are express warranties created?
    b. What can a buyer recover based on breach of express warranty?
30. What are the two implied warranties of merchantability?
    a. What is the difference between the two?
    b. What can a buyer recover based on breach of an implied warranty?

PRACTICE EXAM – PART A

MULTIPLE CHOICE

1. The UCC
   a. is designed to standardize the law governing commercial transactions
   b. is geared toward promoting commerce
   c. has simplified and modernized contract law
   d. all of the above

2. Article 2 of the UCC pertains to
   a. real estate transactions
   b. secured transactions
   c. the sale of goods
   d. the sale of services

3. When analyzing a contract under the UCC
   a. it is not necessary to know whether the party is a merchant
   b. you must know whether a sale of goods is involved
   c. you should remember that the UCC tends to restrict commerce
   d. the distinction between sales and service is not relevant

4. The Restatement defines a contract
   a. as an exchange of enforceable promises
   b. an enforceable agreement
   c. a legal obligation resulting from parties' agreement
   d. none of the above

5. The terms of an offer are considered definite if it includes
   a. the price
   b. the quantity
   c. the subject matter of the proposed bargain
   d. all of the above

6. Under the UCC
   a. a contract may not be formed if it lacks definiteness
   b. if a term for price is missing, it becomes a reasonable price
   c. a contract is formed even if the offer lacks terms regarding quantity
   d. a contract is formed no matter how many terms are missing

7. The power of acceptance ends
   a. only by operation of law
   b. if the offeree rejects the offer but not if the offeree makes a counteroffer
   c. if the offeror revokes the offer
   d. none of the above

8. The time for acceptance of an offer ends when
   a. the offer indicates it ends
   b. after a reasonable time if the offer does not indicate a specific time

   c. in accordance with business custom if the offer does not indicate a specific time
   d. all of the above

9. If I tell you I will pay you $500 if you will paint the exterior of my house
   a. I am seeking a unilateral contract
   b. I am seeking a Bilateral contract
   c. you can accept by promising to paint my house
   d. you cannot accept because the offer is too indefinite

10. If I want to revoke the offer to have you paint my house, I can revoke by
    a. simply sending you a letter telling you I've changed my mind even if you do not receive the letter until after you have already painted the house
    b. telling you I've changed my mind even if you have begun painting the house (under the traditional view)
    c. telling you I've changed my mind even if you have begun painting the house (under the modern view)
    d. I cannot revoke

11. Under the mailbox rule
    a. an acceptance is effective as soon as it is sent
    b. an acceptance is effective even if it is lost in the mail
    c. the creation of long-distance contracts is facilitated
    d. all of the above

12. Under the UCC
    a. an acceptance must be a mirror image of the offer
    b. new terms in an acceptance become part of the contract even if they materially alter the contract
    c. new terms become part of the contract unless the original offer limits acceptance to its terms
    d. none of the above

13. If a father promises to give his son $15,000 if he lives to be 21
    a. he has given his son a gift
    b. he has created a contract with his son
    c. he has given him consideration
    d. none of the above

14. The purpose of consideration
    a. is to make sure people enter into good bargains
    b. is to distinguish gifts from contracts
    c. is a very important aspect of contractual formation except when option contracts are involved
    d. all of the above

15. Consideration is an important aspect of
    a. an option contract
    b. an illusory transaction
    c. any contract and its recital must be precisely worded
    d. all contracts because it must be adequate for a court to uphold the contract

16. When courts interpret a contract
    a. they never use extrinsic evidence
    b. they are not allowed to use parol evidence
    c. any consider special knowledge the parties have because of their trade
    d. of the above

17. Under the parol evidence rule, if the parties agree that a contract is their final and complete agreement
    a. they cannot introduce evidence of a contemporaneous oral agreement that alters their final agreement
    b. they cannot introduce evidence of a subsequent oral agreement that modifies their final agreement
    c. they cannot introduce evidence of a subsequent written agreement that modifies their final agreement
    d. all of the above

18. Determining whether a material breach has been committed
    a. is relatively easy
    b. depends on degree of hardship imposed on the non-breaching party
    c. has no relationship to whether the non-breaching party can be compensated
    d. all of the above

19. The perfect tender rule
    a. can be deviated from if the parties agree in advance to overlook the lack of conformity
    b. can never be deviated from
    c. cannot be deviated from by the seller notifying the buyer that he intends to rectify the situation
    d. none of the above

20. A party can claim impossibility if
    a. a change in economic circumstances makes it too costly to perform
    b. the subject of the contract has been lost or destroyed
    c. the party cannot perform its duties
    d. all of the above

21. Compensatory damages
    a. are designed to restore the breaching party to the position it would have been had the contract been performed
    b. give the non-breaching party the benefit of its bargain

    c. can be speculative
    d. are not necessarily reasonably foreseeable

22. Incidental damages include
    a. the cost of shipping, storing, and insuring goods
    b. the loss of profits
    c. the cost of replacement
    d. all of the above

23. Consequential damages
    a. are those that arise naturally out of a breach of contract
    b. include such expenses as those incurred in advertising for a resale
    c. can be recovered if the seller has reason to know that these damages would be the probable result of a breach
    d. all of the above

24. A liquidated damages clause
    a. fixes the amount of damages in the event of a breach
    b. is a type of penalty clause
    c. need not bear any relationship to the actual loss
    d. are used when the damages that would result from a breach are fairly easy to estimate

25. Specific performance
    a. is an ideal remedy when a service contract is involved
    b. can be awarded in addition to monetary damages
    c. is an appropriate remedy if a unique parcel of land is involved in a breach of contract case
    d. all of the above

*26. A bad faith claim allows for recovery of
    a. punitive damages if the conduct is egregious enough
    b. damages resulting from emotional distress
    c. legal fees incurred by the insured in pursuing a claim against the insurer
    d. all of the above

27. A court may find the creation of a quasi-contract when
    a. one of the parties has been unjustly enriched
    b. a party has conferred a benefit on another with the expectation of being paid
    c. when a party receiving a benefit had reason to know the other party expected to be paid
    d. all of the above

28. Relief based on promissory estoppel is justified
    a. only when an actual contract has been formed
    b. when the plaintiff relies on the defendant's promises to the plaintiff's detriment
    c. even if the defendant had no intention of inducing the plaintiff to rely on promises made
    d. all of the above

29. A person lacks the capacity to enter into a contract
    a. if he is suffering from any kind of mental illness
    b. if he is intoxicated
    c. if he is too drunk or mentally ill to understand the nature, purpose, and effect of what he is doing
    d. all of the above

30. A minor
    a. can disaffirm a contract at his option
    b. can retain the benefits of a contract even if he disaffirms it
    c. does not have to repair or replace any damaged goods if he opts to disaffirm his contract
    d. all of the above

31. Illegal contracts
    a. include any contract that has an exculpatory clause
    b. may violate public policy because they are unconscionable
    c. are voidable
    d. all of the above

32. Adhesion contracts
    a. violate public policy
    b. are most often found in the fine print of insurance contracts, loan agreements, and residential leases
    c. involve parties of unequal bargaining position
    d. all of the above

33. An exculpatory clause is most likely permissible if it
    a. relieves a party from liability resulting from his own intentional wrongs
    b. relieves a party from liability for negligence and the general interest of the public is involved
    c. relieves a party from liability for lost profits resulting from negligence
    d. none of the above

34. Fraud occurs when
    a. there is a false representation regarding a material fact
    b. a party acts involuntarily
    c. there is a confidential relationship
    d. one party misuses the trust and dependency of another

35. Mistake is a valid defense when
    a. there is a mutual mistake of fact
    b. there is a unilateral mistake
    c. there is a mutual mistake regarding value or quality of a product
    d. all of the above

36. Statutes of fraud
    a. apply to all sales of goods
    b. ensure that evidence is available to clarify any significant or complicated matters
    c. apply to all contracts that can be performed in a year
    d. require the creation of formal written contracts

37. Breach of warranty
    a. is based on tort law when the losses are purely economic
    b. is based on tort law when a defect involves only the quality of the product
    c. is based on contract law when a product failed to perform in accordance with the expectations one would have for a product fit for ordinary use
    d. is based on contract law when the plaintiff was exposed to an unreasonable risk of injury

38. An express warranty can be created
    a. using a model
    b. by an affirmation or promise
    c. using a description of the good
    d. all of the above

39. A remote purchaser who is suing on the basis of breach of implied warranty
    a. cannot recover for personal injury damages
    b. cannot recover for property damages alone
    c. can recover for purely economic damages
    d. should sue the immediate seller to recover for economic damages

40. An implied warranty of merchantability can be disclaimed
    a. by using conspicuous language that specifically mentions merchantability
    b. unless the product is sold "as is"
    c. unless the buyer has an opportunity to examine the product and refuses to do so
    d. if the manufacturer disclaims the implied warranty in its written warranty

FILL IN THE BLANK

41. The _____ was drafted by preeminent legal scholars as an attempt to standardize the law governing commercial transactions.

42. A person who makes an offer is called an _____, while the person who accepts the offer is called an _____.

43. The term for quantity is missing in both _____ _____ contracts (contracts in which the buyer agrees to buy all that he requires of a product from the seller) and _____ contracts (contracts in which the seller agrees to sell all that he produces of a product to a particular buyer).

44. Under the UCC, a _____ is someone who "holds himself out as having knowledge or skill peculiar to the practices or goods involved" in the contract.

45. The power of acceptance is terminated when the person who makes the offer _____ it, or the person to whom the offer is made _____ it or makes a _____.

46. If an offer is to be accepted by a promise, it is a _____ contract, but if an offer is to be accepted by performance, it is a _____ contract.

47. An offeree can keep an offer open for a specified time period by giving the offeror _____ (something of value). Doing this results in a separate contract between the offeror and offferee called an _____. Under the UCC a merchant can create an offer that is irrevocable for a reasonable time period called a _____; this can done without giving _____.

48. Under the _____ rule, an offer is effective as soon as it is dispatched, and under the _____ rule, the acceptance has to mirror the offer.

49. The _____ problem occurs when merchants use pre-printed forms with Boilerplate language that result in an offer and acceptance having details that do not match.

50. A gift can be distinguished from a contract because it involves no _____.

51. Courts will intervene when parties enter into an _____ transaction by attempting to transform (a gratuitous promise into a contract by creating nominal consideration.

52. Generally, _____ evidence (earlier or written agreement or contemporaneous oral agreement) is not allowed to add to, vary, or contradict the terms of a written contract.

53. A party who _____ is liable for any damages resulting from his incomplete performance, but the other party is not relieved of her contractual obligations. If a party commits a _____, however, the other party is relieved of her contractual obligations.

54. A party who _____ a contract (indicates by word or conduct an intent to refuse any further performance), excuses the other party from any further performance.

55. Under the _____ rule, a buyer who receives non-conforming goods can either accept the goods, reject them, or accept them in part and reject them in part.

56. If Boris agrees to buy a ring from Stanislav for $1000 and then reneges on the deal, Stanislav can recover $100 in _____ damages if he sells the ring to someone else for $900. He can also recover $10 in _____ damages based on his advertising expenses he incurred in selling the ring a second time.

57. If Stanislav reneges on his deal after agreeing to sell Boris his ring for $1000, Boris is required under the UCC to _____ (find a substitute ring). If he does, he can recover the difference between the _____ price and the _____ price.

58. A non-breaching party can sometimes recover _____ damages (those that result from a buyer's particular circumstances), such as lost profits.

59. A non-breaching party cannot recover for damages that could have been _____ (avoided by reasonable efforts).

60. Parties that want to expedite the litigation of damages in the event of a breach can include a _____ clause in their contract. This provision will be invalid if the court interprets it as a _____ clause.

61. _____ is an appropriate remedy when no comparable substitute is available.

62. A court has the option of _____ (destroying) a contract and putting the parties back into the position they were in before entering into an agreement, or of _____ a contract to more accurately reflect the parties' intent.

*63. The intentional tort of _____ can be used when an insurer treats an insured in an unconscionable manner.

64. Even when parties have not formed a contract, courts may use their equitable powers to provide relief using such concepts as _____ and _____.

65. A contract entered into by someone who is legally insane is _____ (invalid on its face), whereas a contract entered into by a minor is _____ (its defect must be shown).

66. A minor who _____ a contract (takes back his contractual obligations) may still retain the benefits of that contract although he does have to pay for such _____ as food, clothing, and shelter.

67. One type of illegal contract is an _____ contract, in which the contracting parties have unequal bargaining positions and the party in the inferior bargaining position is forced to adhere to the other's terms on a "take-it-or-leave-it" basis.
68. An _____ clause (one that releases a party from being liable as a result of his own actions) can be unconscionable in certain circumstances.
69. The courts will not enforce contracts where there was no _____ (consensus). This lack of consensus can occur if there is _____ (deceit regarding a material fact), _____ (acting involuntarily), or _____ (when one party misuses the trust of another to influence that person's actions.)
70. Parties can rescind a contract that is based on _____ mistake, but usually cannot rescind one that is based on _____ mistake.

71. A state statute that lists those contracts that must be in writing is called a _____.
72. Breach of warranty is based on both _____ law and _____ law.
73. A manufacturer's description of a windshield as being "shatterproof" is an example of an _____ warranty. A _____ is a type of warranty that is implied when a seller is a merchant in the regular business of selling the kind of goods in question. An implied warranty of _____ is created when a seller who knows that a buyer wants goods for a particular purpose makes a recommendation on which the buyer relies.
74. Under the _____ doctrine, retailers of products that are sealed are absolved of liability for damages resulting from those products.
75. A seller can _____ a warranty of merchantability by using conspicuous language that specifically mentions merchantability.

TRUE OR FALSE

____ 76. In deciding whether the UCC applies to a combination of sales and services, courts determine which aspect is predominant and apply the UCC only if service prevails.
____ 77. Under the UCC, merchants are expected to be familiar with normal business practices in their trade.
____ 78. A statement that is an invitation to negotiate or to deal is still an offer.
____ 79. In deciding whether an offer has been made, the courts look not only at the words of the parties, but the circumstances surrounding their statements.
____ 80. An advertisement is usually considered an offer.
____ 81. An offer creates a power of acceptance by an offeree.
____ 82. Under the UCC, a contract may be formed even if it lacks definiteness for a lack of terms.
____ 83. In the majority of states, a revocation is effective when it is sent out.
____ 84. An offer is terminated when circumstances make it impossible for the offeree to accept.
____ 85. With a unilateral contract, an offeror's obligation under the contract is discharged if the offeree does not notify the offeror within a reasonable time that she has completed performance.

____ 86. Under the mirror image rule, an acceptance that is not a mirror image of the offer becomes a counteroffer and the offer expires.
____ 87. The mirror image rule has been adopted by the UCC.
____ 88. Consideration must involve an exchange of money even if the exchange is nominal.
____ 89. With contracts, both sides must receive something of value and give up something of value.
____ 90. Adequacy of consideration is a major concern of the courts.
____ 91. Consideration is a legal abstraction that is rarely of practical significance.
____ 92. Courts interpret contracts using a subjective standard.
____ 93. Modern courts refuse to consider extrinsic evidence when deciding what contracting parties meant.
____ 94. Like the common law, the UCC prohibits the admission of parol evidence.
____ 95. In the case of a minor breach, the non-breaching party can terminate the contract as well as sue for damages.
____ 96. If a contract has a "time-is-of-the-essence" provision, even a slight delay in performance will be considered a material breach.

____ 97. A non-repudiating party can bring an immediate action for the entire value of the promised performance when the other party repudiates its contract.

____ 98. Under the UCC, if a buyer accepts substandard goods, she cannot sue for damages.

____ 99. To claim the defense of impossibility, a party must show that the contract cannot be performed and not simply that the party cannot perform it.

____100. Commercial impracticability is not an excuse for non-performance if the change in economic circumstances was foreseeable.

____101. Damages are recoverable only if they are reasonably foreseeable and can be computed with reasonable certainty.

____102. Under the UCC, a buyer can recover all of her damages for breach of contract even if she fails to cover.

____103. A seller who is in the process of manufacturing goods when a buyer repudiates has no obligation to stop production to reduce its damages.

____104. Liquidated damages clauses are used when the damages that would result from a breach are impracticable to estimate.

____105. If a court finds a liquidating damage clause to be invalid, the non-breaching party is not even entitled to the actual damages it can prove.

____*106. Bad faith has evolved as a means of providing insureds with relief that goes beyond the relatively minor damages provided by contract law when insurance carriers refuse to honor their contractual obligations.

____107. The concept of a quasi-contract and the doctrine of promissory estoppel are applicable even though no contract has been formed.

____108. Under the "cognitive test," an individual with psychological or emotional problems cannot necessarily claim a lack of mental capacity to contract.

____109. The Restatement of Contracts has adopted a more restrictive test than the majority rule for determining when an individual is too incapacitated mentally to enter into a contract.

____110. Minors who decide to disaffirm a contract do not have to pay the reasonable value of any goods or services they receive even if they are considered "necessaries," such as food, clothing, and shelter.

____111. A court that finds a contract to be an Adhesion contract will bind a consumer only to those provisions that are not unfairly surprising.

____112. Exculpatory clauses that relieve parties of liability for lost profits or damage to property caused by a party's negligence are often upheld even if the injured party had no choice in agreeing to these provisions and was surprised by their existence.

____113. Fraud occurs when one person intends to deceive another if the other person does not rely on that misrepresentation.

____114. Undue influence occurs when a confidential relationship exists between two parties and one of the parties misuses that trust to influence the actions of the other.

____115. Both parties are bound by a contract where one party has made a mistake even if one party knew or should have known of the mistake or the mistake is based on a mathematical error.

____116. Pursuant to most statutes of fraud, oral agreements are not valid.

____117. A check or memo meets the statute of fraud requirements as long as it fully expresses the terms of the agreement.

____118. In breach of warranty cases, a majority of jurisdictions restrict contract liability to recovery for commercial or economic loss and tort liability to recovery for damage to persons or property.

____119. With breach of express warranty, a buyer whose damages are solely economic can recover the difference between what the product would have been worth had it been as it was warranted and what it was, in fact, worth with its defect, but cannot recover incidental and consequential damages.

____120. A warranty of fitness for a particular purpose means that a product is fit for the ordinary purposes for which such goods are used.

____121. Sellers can disclaim express warranties, but cannot disclaim implied warranties.

____122. Any written warranty provided by a manufacturer must include the implied warranty of merchantability.

____123. Sellers are allowed to limit the consequential damages buyers can recover even if personal injury is involved.

* Questions taken from Bonus Pointers.

PART B

> ### *"This Would Be a Wonderful Opportunity For You To Consider Creating a Business Organization that Would Protect You Better Than the One You Have Now."*
>
> When Terrell Johnson was sure they had provided Kim and Neal with all the information they needed, he broached another subject. "Ms. Yuen, I'd like to talk to you about another matter. Our son, Mike, as you may know, is going to be receiving a lot of money from his lawsuit. He insists that he wants his mother and me to have half of whatever he ends up getting. We haven't been able to talk him out of doing this, so we've decided we would like to use that money to open up a small restaurant. His fiancee, Carmela, is quite a cook and would like to go to chef school some day. With us owning a restaurant, she'd have a place to work when she was ready and we'd be able to expand our catering business. If we did it right, we thought it would be a good way to invest Mike's money."
>
> "Of course, we haven't quite figured out how to combine South American and French cooking," laughed Mrs. Johnson.
>
> "Oh, that can't be any stranger than Chinese and Mexican food. Last week I went to the opening of Señor Lee's. You just haven't lived until you've eaten sweet and sour tortillas while listening to mariachi music and sitting at the feet of a statue of Buddha," said Kim, obviously enjoying her recollection of this experience.
>
> "I see," responded Mr. Johnson, wondering how his careful explanation had prompted this dialogue between his wife and Ms. Yuen.
>
> Seeing immediately that her attempt to interject a little humor had fallen flat with Terrell, Kim came right to the point. "This would be a wonderful opportunity for you to consider creating a business organization that would protect you better than the one you have now. As it stands now, you are personally liable for any debts or obligations you might incur through your business. You'd be better served by a form of business that would protect your personal assets. Also, if Mike were to invest his money in your restaurant rather than give it to you directly, you'd be spared getting hit with gift taxes."
>
> "We're very interested in hearing about this, Ms. Yuen, especially in light of our most recent experiences. Please tell us more," replied Mr. Johnson politely.

sole proprietorships business owned by one individual who owns all of the assets, who is solely responsible for all of the business's debts, and who is the sole decision-maker

general partnership business in which two or more persons own all of the assets of the business and share in the decision-making, losses, and profits

general partners partners who are personally liable for any business debts and obligations and are liable for the torts and misconduct of other partners

limited partnership business managed by general partners who are liable for all debts and obligations of the business, and that is invested in by limited partners

limited partners partner who neither manages nor controls the business and whose liability is limited by the amount of his investment

OVERVIEW OF BUSINESS ORGANIZATIONS

Businesses can be formed in several ways.

Sole Proprietorship

A **sole proprietorship** is a business owned by one individual who owns all of the assets, who is solely responsible for all of the business's debts, and who is the sole decision-maker. The vast majority of businesses in the United States are sole proprietorships.

General Partnership

A **general partnership** is a business in which two or more persons own all of the assets of the business and share in the decision-making, losses, and profits. **General partners** are personally liable for any business debts and obligations and are liable for the torts and misconduct of other partners.

Limited Partnership

A **limited partnership** is a business managed by general partners who are liable for all debts and obligations of the business, and invested in by **limited partners,** who neither manage nor control the business and whose liability is limited by the amount of their investment. General partnerships are easily created by agreement, but limited partnerships are created only by strictly conforming to applicable state statutes.

NET NEWS

To read more about S corporations, go to *www.paralegals.org/Reporter/home.html,* click on "Spring 1997," and look for the article entitled "What's New with Sub S Corporations."

Corporation

corporation business created by those who organize it, owned by shareholders, and managed by a board of directors

shareholders owners of a corporation who are not personally liable for the debts and obligations of the corporation and whose losses are limited to the amount of their investment

S corporation corporation that avoids the double taxation imposed on other corporations

C corporations typical corporation; term used to distinguish a corporation from an S corporation

professional corporations corporation organized by professionals that allows them to retain the tax benefits of a business corporation

close corporations small corporation owned by family members and friends in which the shareholders actively manage the business

nonprofit (not-for-profit) corporations corporation formed for charitable purposes rather than with the intent of earning a profit that is distributed to its shareholders

A **corporation** is a business created by those who organize it and owned by **shareholders** who are not personally liable for the debts and obligations of the corporation and whose losses are limited to the amount of money they invest in the corporation. The corporation is managed by a board of directors, which appoints officers to carry out the policies and goals established by the directors. A corporation is considered a legal entity and, as a "person," is subject to taxation. Because the shareholders must also pay taxes on whatever distributions they receive, they are subject to double taxation.

To avoid this double taxation, some businesses create an **S corporation** (named after the original subchapter of the Internal Revenue Code that provides for this tax relief). An S corporation does not pay taxes and all income the corporation earns is passed on to its shareholders. Only certain corporations are eligible for S status and all shareholders (who can number no more than 75) must agree to elect S status. Typical corporations are referred to as **C corporations** to distinguish them from S corporations.

Professionals such as doctors, attorneys, and accountants, often form **professional corporations,** which are unique in that all shares must be held by these licensed professionals (as defined by state statute.) Professional corporations allow their members to retain certain benefits of a corporation, such as fringe benefits plans. These professionals remain personally liable, however, for their own negligence and the negligence of those working for them.

Small corporations owned by family members and friends and in which the shareholders actively manage the business may qualify to be **close corporations.** Shareholders are usually allowed to operate the corporation without adhering to all of the formalities required of larger corporations. Only certain types of corporations qualify as close corporations.

Corporations that are formed for charitable purposes, rather than with the intent of earning a profit that is distributed to its shareholders, are called **nonprofit (not-for-profit) corporations.** These corporations are usually formed for religious, educational, health, or scientific purposes or for the mutual benefit of its members (e.g., homeowners' associations or professional associations). Creation of a nonprofit corporation requires compliance with state statutes. Earning the federal tax-exempt status that such entities may qualify for requires applying with the Internal Revenue Service.

Nonprofit corporations are allowed to compensate their directors, officers, and employees, but if this compensation becomes extravagant and little is spent on accomplishing its designated purpose, the corporation can be dissolved by the state and lose its tax-exempt status. Such corporations will not be penalized if they are prudent in their investments and earn a profit as long as they do not distribute their income or profits to their directors, officers, or members. Because some organizations that distribute grants require that companies applying for these grants be nonprofit organizations, companies seeking grant monies benefit from having a nonprofit status. Attracting wealthy donors is often easier for nonprofit corporations because, in many cases, donors who make contributions to such corporations can claim these contributions as deductions.

Limited Liability Corporations (LLCs)

limited liability corporations (LLCs) hybrid business organization that combines the best features of a corporation with the best features of a partnership

A **limited liability corporation** (**LLC**) is a relatively new business structure that combines the best characteristics of a partnership with the best characteristics of a corporation. Like the shareholders in a corporation, the owners of an LLC have limited liability. Like a partnership, an LLC is not taxed; all income is passed to the owners, who are taxed on this income. Creation of an LLC requires strict adherence to state statutes. LLCs are not yet recognized in all states.

limited liability partnership (LLP) similar to an LLC except that its members are not necessarily protected from all potential personal liability

Another new business structure that combines elements of partnerships and corporations is a **limited liability partnership.** In such partnerships, the partners are not liable for the torts or misconduct of the other partners. In some states, partners are not liable for the contractual obligations taken on by the partnership or the other partners; in other states, partners remain liable for these contractual obligations. These partnerships are most often formed with professional (e.g., medical, legal, and accounting) practices with branch offices so that partners in one office are not liable for the acts of other partners in their office or in branch offices. With the advent of LLPs, fewer professional corporations are likely to be formed.

◆ **LOCAL LINKS** ◆

Are LLCs recognized in your state?

Putting It Into Practice 9.12:

Identify the kind of business organization that is indicated in each of the following examples. (a) Alonzo owns a restaurant. A customer is injured when a waitress accidentally pours scalding coffee on him. The customer sues and a judgment is obtained against the restaurant. Alonzo must pay the judgment from his own personal savings. (b) Same scenario as in (a), except that the judgment is paid from the restaurant's monies and not Alonzo's. (c) Same facts as in (b), except that Alonzo owns and operates the restaurant with other family members. The restaurant must pay taxes on the income it receives. (d) Same facts as (d), except that the restaurant does not pay taxes on the income it receives. (e) Alonzo's restaurant is a small health-food restaurant and is part of a larger organization whose primary purpose is to teach the public about good nutrition. This organization is the recipient of several major grants.

Having given the Johnsons an overview of the different types of organizations, Kim explained how their lack of formal agreement implicitly resulted in them having a general partnership. "As it stands now, if either you or one of your employees does something negligent or does anything that results in your business breaching a contract, you are personally liable. This means that if someone gets a judgment against you, they can seize your personal assets. If the judgment were large enough, it could put you into bankruptcy." The somber looks on the Johnsons' faces assured Kim she had made her point.

NET NEWS

For information about forming a small business, go to the Web site for the Small Business Association at *www.sba.gov* or to *http://sbinformation.about.com/msub7.htm*, which provides state-specific information about starting a small business.

Figure 9-10
Common Forms of Businesses

COMMON FORMS OF BUSINESSES

Sole proprietorship

Owner solely liable for business debts and obligations
and sole decision-maker

General partnership

Owners share decision-making and are personally liable
for business debts and obligations

Limited partnership

General partners are personally liable for business debts and obligations
Limited partners are liable only to the extent of their investment

C corporation

Owned by shareholders and managed by board of directors who appoint
officers to carry out goals and policies

No personal liability

Double taxation

S corporations

Special kind of corporation that avoids double taxation

Professional corporation

Special kind of corporation used by professional groups

Close corporation

Special kind of corporation used when operation is less formal and is usually managed by family or friends

Nonprofit corporation

Special kind of corporation used when primary purpose is
charitable rather than profit-making

Limited liability company

Hybrid of corporation and partnership

Limited liability partnership

Hybrid of corporation and partnership

PARTNERSHIPS

General Partnerships

◆ LOCAL LINKS ◆

Has your state adopted the
UPA or RUPA?

joint ventures   a coming
together of two or more people or
entities to carry out a single
enterprise for profit; a joint
venture terminates when the
enterprise is complete

Partnerships are governed by either the Uniform Partnership Act (UPA) or the Revised Uniform Partnership Act (RUPA), depending on which set of uniform laws the state has adopted. (Louisiana has created its own case law regarding partnerships.) These model codes are similar but define partnerships somewhat differently and have different rules pertaining to the breakup of partnerships.

Both UPA and RUPA define a partnership as "an association of two or more persons to carry on as co-owners of a business for profit." Partnerships can be distinguished from **joint ventures,** which are a coming together of two or more people or entities to carry out a single purpose for profit. Joint ventures terminate when that purpose is accomplished, whereas the business of a partnership is ongoing. The primary advantages of partnerships are that they are easily formed, they allow for

---

NET NEWS

For more information about forming partnerships, go to *www.law.com*, click on "Business," and then on "Business Legal Resources." Scroll down to the topic of your choice. You can find forms for partnerships and joint ventures at *www.lectlaw.com/formb.htm*. Also try *www.siccode.com/forms.php3*.

---

shared management and decision-making, they provide those going into business with additional sources of capital, and they permit the sharing of losses as well as profits. Unless partners decide otherwise, they have equal rights in the management of their business, decision-making is by majority vote, and they share both profits and losses equally. Of course, partners can alter any of these assumptions by agreement. They can, for example, agree not to share losses and profits in proportion to their initial contribution to the partnership and they can agree that one of the partners will be the managing partner.

The primary disadvantage of a general partnership is that each partner has unlimited personal liability for the debts and obligations of the partnership. This means that a partner's personal assets can be seized to satisfy debts and obligations of the partnership. In fact, each partner is jointly and severally liable, which means that a creditor can choose to collect a judgment from all of the partners or can choose the one with the greatest wealth. Furthermore, because each partner has the authority to bind the partnership, a partner can be held personally liable for acts incurred by another partner of which she knew nothing.

Limited Partnerships

Limited partnerships address the concerns of wealthy business partners who may be willing to invest in a business but who do not want to incur unlimited personal liability. As long as limited partners do not manage or control the business or allow their name to be used in the business name, they will not be liable for any amount beyond their original contribution to the business. This lack of control, however, is one of the greatest disadvantages of a limited partnership. While they have a right to be informed about what is going on in the business, limited partners forego any right to participate in its operation. Therefore, limited partners are fully dependent on the skills and business acumen of the general partners.

Limited partnerships are more difficult to form than general partnerships. Although anyone forming a general partnership is advised to use a formal partnership agreement that spells out the terms relating to the operation, management, and control of the partnership, a general partnership can be formed by a simple oral agreement. Limited partnerships, which are governed by either the Uniform Limited Partnership Act (ULPA) or the Revised Uniform Limited Partnership Act (RULPA), can be formed only after filing a **limited partnership certificate** with the secretary of state in which the partnership will operate.

The ULPA originally required 14 items to be included in this certificate, including an identification of each partner's contribution and each limited partner's share of the profits. The content of the certificate is considerably more streamlined under the RULPA, requiring only the following.

- ◆ name of the limited partnership
- ◆ name and business address of each general partner
- ◆ name and address of the **agent for service of process** (entity appointed to receive the summons and complaint in the event the partnership is sued)

◆ **LOCAL LINKS** ◆
Has your state adopted the ULPA or RULPA?

---

limited partnership certificate   document that must be filed with the secretary of state to create a limited partnership

agent for service of process entity appointed to receive the summons and complaint in the event the partnership is sued

Direct links to the home page for each state's secretary of state are available at the Web site for the National Association of Secretaries of State at *www.nass.org.*

dissolve change relationships of partners when one partner leaves or dies, generally resulting in termination of partnership

◆ latest date upon which the partnership is to **dissolve** (*Dissolution* refers to the change in the relationship of the partners when one of the partners leaves or dies, which generally results in a termination of the partnership.)

◆ any other matters the general partners decide to include

Putting It Into Practice 9.13:

Miguel and Sonja want to create a business they would like to call Colorado Capers. The purpose of the business is to organize outdoor experiences for tourists, including white-water rafting trips, hunting expeditions, and cross-country skiing trips. They do not have enough money to capitalize this venture on their own, but they are adamant about being the ones who run the business. They are thinking about forming either a general partnership or a limited partnership. (a) Which of these partnerships would better meet their needs? Why? (b) Why might they be ill-advised to form a partnership? (c) If they decide to go ahead, what must they do to create this form of business?

◆ **LOCAL LINKS** ◆

Can forms for a certificate of limited partnership be downloaded from your state's Secretary of State's Web page?

Figure 9-11
Differences Between General and Limited Partnerships

DIFFERENCES BETWEEN GENERAL AND LIMITED PARTNERSHIPS

Liability

General partners are personally liable for all business debts and obligations

Limited partners are liable only to the extent of their original contribution (as long as they do not manage or control the business)

Laws that Govern

General partnerships are governed by Uniform Partnership Act or Revised Uniform Partnership Act (except Louisiana)

Limited partnerships are governed by Uniform Limited Partnership Act or Revised Uniform Limited Partnership Act (except Louisiana)

Creation

General partnerships can be created informally by oral agreement or by formalized partnership agreement

Limited partnership must be created by filing limited partnership certificate with secretary of state

"So do you suggest we incorporate?" asked Mr. Johnson, anticipating Kim's advice and not wanting to dwell any further on the potential disasters of a partnership.

"At one time I would have said yes, but now that we have LLCs, I recommend this form of organization to most of my clients. With an LLC you'll have all the advantages of a corporation—most importantly, the protection from personal liability—but you can also retain the advantages of a partnership. For example, one of the downfalls of a corporation is that you get taxed twice. The corporation gets taxed when it receives income, and the shareholders—which would be you—get taxed when you receive your **dividends.** With an LLC you get taxed only once, just like a partnership. You can also distribute the profits and losses as you want. An LLC also allows for management by its members, a member, or a select group of members."

dividends　distribution of corporate profits

CORPORATIONS

Nature of a Corporation

A corporation is very much a creation of the state. Its existence begins when the state declares it exists and it dissolves when the state terminates its existence. A corporation is a unique business entity in that it is considered a person for purposes of the law. As such, a corporation continues to exist even if all of the shareholders die. It can be sued just like a natural person can be sued, even though a corporation is considered an artificial person. In fact, when the president of a corporation signs a contract, the artificial person of the corporation is bound by that contract, not the president herself. As persons, corporations enjoy certain First Amendment rights of speech and Fourth Amendment protections against unreasonable searches and seizures. Like individuals, corporations cannot be deprived of property without due process.

The primary advantage of a corporation is the limited liability protection it provides to its shareholders, directors, and officers. Because corporations can enter into contracts and borrow money in their own name, they—rather than their shareholders, directors and officers—are responsible for meeting these debts and obligations. The greatest disadvantage of incorporating is double taxation, which occurs because the money is taxed once when the corporation receives it and a second time when it is distributed to the shareholders. As we have seen, this double taxation can be avoided by forming a limited liability company or an S corporation.

ETHICAL ETIQUETTE

ATTORNEY-CLIENT PRIVILEGE FOR CORPORATIONS

The issue of attorney-client privilege becomes somewhat complicated when dealing with corporate clients. Because corporations are persons, the privilege applies to them; but because communications are obviously made by natural persons, not the artificial person of the corporation, the question is who within a corporation is actually protected by the privilege. Some jurisdictions use the "control group" test, which limits the privilege to communications between an attorney and the management responsible for dealing with the legal matter at hand. Others follow the "subject matter" test, which more broadly defines those covered by the privilege, extending it to all employees who communicate in confidence with the attorney as she is rendering legal services to the corporation.

As the holder of the privilege, only the corporation can waive that privilege. An employee does not have a right to object to a corporation's waiver. Decisions about waiving the privilege rest with the current board of directors; therefore, policy regarding waiver may change over time.

Incorporation Process

The incorporation process is very formalized and requires strict compliance with the corporation laws of the state in which the incorporation takes place. Businesses can choose to incorporate in any state. The flexibility of a state's incorporation laws is one of the factors taken into consideration when deciding where to incorporate. Delaware, known as the "Corporation Capital of the World," is renowned for its liberal corporation statutes and has induced many major corporations to incorporate there. When making this decision, a business that plans to do business in primarily one state needs to be aware of how that state regards **foreign corporations** (corporations formed in one state and doing business in another). A state may, for example, give special preference to **domestic corporations** (corporations operating in the state of their incorporation) when awarding contracts.

Great care must then be given to selecting the corporate name. This name must comply with state statutes, must be available, and must not be the same as (or deceptively similar to) another's name. Once an available name is found, it must be reserved. (Reservations often require a fee and must be in writing.) Corporations, as well as partnerships and sole proprietorships, can choose to operate under a **fictitious** (or **assumed**) **name** because of consumer-related issues or for a number of other reasons. Kentucky Fried Chicken, for example, has officially changed its name to KFC (because of negative consumer reaction to the term *fried*), but if it had operated as KFC while maintaining its corporate name as Kentucky Fried Chicken, Inc., it would have been operating under a fictitious name. Businesses that do this must file a **fictitious business name document** (also called a **dba statement** or "doing-business-as" statement) with the appropriate state or local agency. This document protects consumers by allowing them to determine who actually owns a business if they decide to file a lawsuit against that business.

The next step in incorporation is the preparation of and filing with the secretary of state the **articles of incorporation** (also called *certificate of incorporation*). Although there is considerable variation among the states, these articles commonly include the following.

- ◆ corporation's name and address
- ◆ name and address of the agent for service of process
- ◆ name and address of each incorporator
- ◆ broadly-stated purpose of the corporation
- ◆ number of **shares** the corporation is authorized to issue

The corporation is authorized to issue only the number of shares it has designated in its articles of incorporation. These articles should also describe the type of stock being issued. If there is to be only one class of stock, it is called **common stock**, but if one kind of stock possesses features that make it more desirable than common stock, such as guaranteed dividends, it is called **preferred stock.** The **par value** of the stock must also be established in the articles of incorporation. The par value refers to the minimum value for which a stock can be sold. If no par value is indicated, stock can be issued for any amount the directors decide is appropriate.

Once completed, the articles of incorporation must be filed with the appropriate state agency, usually the state's corporation commission or secretary of state, along with the required filing fee. During the corporation's formation, the **bylaws** (rules governing the operation and management of the corporation) must be drafted. The **corporate supplies** (including the minute book, in which the minutes of corporate meetings are recorded, and the stock certificate book, which contains the stock certificates that are to be issued to shareholders) must be

◆ **LOCAL LINKS** ◆

What agency in your state regulates corporations? What is the filing fee for incorporation? Can forms for articles (certificate) of incorporation be downloaded from the Web page of the agency in your state that regulates corporations?

foreign corporations corporation formed in one state and doing business in another

domestic corporations corporation operating in the state of its incorporation

fictitious (or **assumed**) **name** name adopted by a business that is not its true name

fictitious business name document (also called a **dba statement**) document filed with an appropriate state agency that protects consumers by allowing them to determine who actually owns a business

articles of incorporation documents that must be filed with the appropriate state agency to create a corporation

shares units in which the ownership interests of a corporation are divided

common stock stock that has no special features

preferred stock stock that has special features

par value minimum value for which a stock can be sold

bylaws rules governing the operation and management of the corporation

corporate supplies tools needed to operate a corporation, including minute book and stock certificate book

Often the best place to find forms pertaining to incorporation in your state is the home page for your secretary of state, which can be accessed at *www.nass.org*. Other sites that contain sample forms are *www.lectlaw.com/formb.htm* and *www.lawsmart.com*, where you select your state and "Business and Corporations," then click on "Free Legal Forms."

organizational meeting
initial meeting at which a corporation is launched

annual report report describing the performance of the corporation during the preceding year

bonds representations of a corporation's debt to investors

bondholder one who owns a bond

securities shares in the enterprise of the issuer or obligations of the issuer

privately held corporation corporation formed by family or friends in which shareholders agree not to sell shares to anyone "outside" of the corporation before offering them to existing shareholders

publicly held corporation corporation that sells its shares to the public at large

registration statement document that describes the security being offered, the nature of the issuer's business, the management of the issuer, and any pending litigation against the issuer

prospectus document that describes the investment so that investors can evaluate the potential risks involved in buying the security

ordered. Most states require that corporations hold an **organizational meeting,** the initial meeting at which the corporation is launched. At this meeting, the directors are elected (if they have not already been named in the article of incorporation), the officers are appointed, the bylaws are adopted, the value of stock is established, and other preliminary accounting, financing, and accounting decisions are made. Paralegals are often asked to prepare minutes of these meetings. Subsequently, each year thereafter that a corporation is in business, it must file an **annual report,** which describes the performance of the corporation during the preceding year.

Financing a Corporation

Corporations finance themselves in one of two ways. They issue shares (stocks) to shareholders: insiders in a corporation who, by virtue of their stock, own a percentage of the corporation. As such, they are entitled to vote on corporate issues and to receive dividends (distribution of corporate profits). Corporations also issue documents called **bonds,** which represent a corporation's debt to investors. Unlike a shareholder, a **bondholder** (one who owns a bond) is an outsider who has no right to vote and no right to dividends. A bondholder does, however, have a right to be paid back at a mutually agreeable time and under mutually agreeable terms. Stocks and bonds are both considered **securities**: shares in the enterprise of the issuer or obligations of the issuer.

If a corporation is a small, **privately held corporation,** it is formed by family or friends and the stock is not sold to the public. Typically, shareholders in these corporations agree not to sell shares of the corporation to anyone "outside" of the corporation before offering them to existing shareholders. A **publicly held corporation,** on the other hand, such as Westhinghouse or IBM, sells its shares to the public at large. The public sale of these stocks (and bonds) is regulated by state securities laws as well as the Federal Securities Act of 1933 and the Securities Exchange Act of 1934. Essentially, these laws are designed to protect investors from fraud and unfair business practices.

The federal agency that regulates securities is the Securities Exchange Commission (SEC). The SEC's primary function is to ensure that material information is disclosed to the public. Before a company can issue stock, for example, the SEC requires that it file a **registration statement,** which describes the security being offered, the nature of the issuer's business, the management of the issuer, and any pending litigation against the issuer. A financial statement is also provided. The primary component of the registration that is of value to potential investors is the **prospectus,** which, among other things, describes the investment so that investors can evaluate the potential risks involved in buying the security. The SEC also requires corporations to file quarterly and annual reports, both of which provide information about the status of the corporation's financial health. Certain securities, such as small offerings of securities that total less than $5 million, are exempt from these registration requirements.

The Web page for the SEC is at *www.sec.gov* where you will find EDGAR (Electronic Data Gathering, Analysis, and Retrieval system), the database for registration statements, annual reports, and other corporate reports. Be sure to click on "Information About EDGAR" before attempting to find any records.

Figure 9-12
Formation of a Corporation

FORMATION OF A CORPORATION

Decide where to incorporate
Determine availability of corporate name
Reserve corporate name
File articles of incorporation
Draft bylaws
Order corporate supplies
Conduct organizational meeting

Putting It Into Practice 9.14:

(a) Why might Miguel and Sonja want to incorporate rather than form a partnership? (Assume that they will control the corporation.) (b) What steps must they take if they want to incorporate? (c) What information will they need to decide about their stock before they can incorporate? (d) Once they have decided to incorporate, what else must they do? (e) Suppose that Sonja creates a sleeker, faster snow board that becomes so popular that Nike buys the patent from Sonja. What information should Miguel and Sonja look for before deciding whether to buy shares in Nike? Where would they find this information?

◆ **LOCAL LINKS** ◆

How much does it cost to form an LLC in your area? A corporation?

"It sounds like an LLC is the way for us to go, don't you think?" asked Mr. Johnson, turning to his wife to get her feedback.

"Yes, it does," agreed Mrs. Johnson, "as long as it's not too difficult to do."

"It's no more difficult than forming a corporation although it is more expensive," Kim assured them. "What we'll have to do is this. Neal and I will prepare the articles of organization—the LLC equivalent to a corporation's articles of incorporation—and then an operating agreement, which is a rough equivalent to a corporation's bylaws. The operating agreement will be very detailed so that each member will know what limitations and obligations will be imposed, how capital contributions will be made, how the profits and losses are to be distributed, how the LLC is to be dissolved, and any other terms and conditions you and the other members think are important."

"So as I understand it, we could invite people other than our family members to participate in this LLC? Our accountant, for example, is a close personal friend and might be interested in investing in our restaurant," clarified Mr. Johnson.

"You certainly can have investors, but I think your accountant, like an attorney, would have some ethical prohibitions against investing in a client's business," cautioned Kim.

"Actually, I don't know if Walter would even be interested," explained Mr. Johnson. "I was just using him as a for instance. I just wanted to make sure I understood what we were creating here."

NET NEWS

To read more about LLCs, go to *www.paralegals.org/Reporter/home.html*, click on "Summer 1996," and look for the article entitled "The Limited Liability Company."

◆ **LOCAL LINKS** ◆

Has your state adopted the UCLLA?

LLCS AND LLPS

Recall that members of an LLC or LLP can participate in the management of the company at the same time they are protected from personal liability and double taxation. Both can be formed only by complying with state statutory requirements. Although these statutory requirements vary tremendously, the Uniform Limited Liability Company Act (UCLLA), which borrows from both corporate and partnership law to standardize the law regarding LLCs, has been adopted by some states.

Although an LLC and LLP are very similar they do have some distinctions.

◆ An LLC provides full protection from personal liability for all tort-related and contract-related actions, whereas an LLP may expose its members to personal liability for contractual obligations. (In states having "partial shield" statutes, a partner in an LLP remains liable for the contractual debts and obligations incurred by another partner. In those states having "full shield" statutes, partners are not liable for these debts and obligations.)

◆ An LLP must involve at least two people, whereas some states permit one-member LLCs.

◆ An LLC may be allowed to operate on a nonprofit basis, whereas LLPs must operate on a for-profit basis.

◆ An LLC can be managed by appointed managers, whereas an LLP is usually managed by all of the partners.

◆ Most LLC statutes require written operating agreements, whereas an LLP's partnership agreement can be written or oral.

Because LLCs combine the best of corporations and partnerships, they have become an increasingly popular form of business organization. Some even predict that S corporations and limited partnerships will eventually become entities of the past and that even general partnerships will be adopted only by small, informal businesses that do not want to incur the expense of forming an LLC.

Putting It Into Practice 9.15:

Why might Miguel and Sonja prefer to form an LLC or LLP rather than a partnership or corporation? If their biggest concern is about potential liability, why might they be better off forming an LLC rather than an LLP?

E T H I C A L   E T I Q U E T T E

BUSINESS TRANSACTIONS WITH CLIENTS

In general, attorneys should avoid entering into business transactions with clients because of the potential conflict that may arise between the attorney's own interests and the client's interests. An attorney should not, for example, go into business with a client, form a corporation in which the attorney has an interest, and then continue representing the corporation. Both the *Model Rules* and the *Model Code* prevent attorneys from entering into business transactions with clients unless the client consents. This consent requires that the client be given full disclosure regarding the terms of the transaction. The transaction must be such that the client will not be adversely affected in any way by the attorney's financial, business, property, or personal interests. The attorney should also recommend and encourage the client to seek the advice of independent counsel, the client's consent should be obtained in writing, and the client should be given ample time to reflect on the wisdom of entering into the transaction and to consult with independent counsel.

Such conflicts may also arise with paralegals, but are not usually as problematic as they are for attorneys. A paralegal may, for example, be asked to buy stock in a client's company. Because clients rely on the legal advice of the attorney, they are in a more vulnerable position with an attorney than they are with a paralegal. Nevertheless, paralegals should be aware of this potential conflict and should notify their supervising attorney if they believe it may be necessary to get a client's consent.

In the process of discussing the transformation of their business, Terrell mentioned that when they bought the restaurant, they planned to sell the equipment they were currently using, some of which was quite expensive. This information prompted Kim to caution them to protect themselves in case the buyer defaulted. "Be sure to have whoever buys this equipment sign a security agreement and then follow up by filing a UCC-1 financing statement with the secretary of state's office." The blank looks and lack of response from the Johnsons confirmed to Kim that she needed to walk them through the purpose and mechanics of secured transactions.

security agreement
agreement that describes the collateral and that has been signed by the debtor

UCC-1 financing statement
(also called a *financing statement*) document that identifies the debtor, creditor, and the debtor's collateral

secured transactions
transaction in which the debt is secured by an asset that can be seized upon the debtor's default

attach seize property

security interest interest created when a debtor puts up collateral that the creditor can seize if the debtor defaults

perfecting means of protecting creditors from claims of third parties

SECURED TRANSACTIONS

Creditors often want assurance that they have something of value they can sell if a debtor should fail to pay what he owes to the creditor. For this reason, creditors may require that a debtor pledge something of value, such as equipment or a car, in addition to promising to pay the debt. The creditor can then seize this property and sell it if the debtor fails to repay the loan. This kind of transaction, called a **secured transaction**, is governed by Article 9 of the UCC.

To be able to **attach** (seize) property used as collateral by a debtor, the creditor must have an enforceable **security interest** in the property. A creditor can do this only if (1) the debtor has rights to the collateral, (2) the creditor gave something of value to the debtor, and (3) the creditor either possesses the collateral or a security agreement that describes the collateral and that has been signed by the debtor. If the debtor defaults, a creditor with an enforceable security interest in collateral can take this collateral from the debtor, unless another creditor has priority.

A creditor can obtain priority over other creditors by **perfecting** his security interest. One common way to perfect a security interest is to file a financing statement (often called a *UCC-1 financing statement*) with the secretary of state. This financing statement identifies the creditor, debtor, and collateral. It also provides a public record so that subsequent lenders can determine if the collateral is already subject to a prior creditor's claim. When the debt is paid, the secured party releases the security interest in the property by filing another form (UCC-3) that indicates the debt has been paid and that the creditor no longer has any interest in the secured property. Paralegals are often asked to conduct UCC-1 searches when clients are buying assets of another entity to ensure that these assets are free and clear of outstanding security interests.

Even creditors with perfected security interests must bow to a "buyer in the ordinary course of business," that is, an ordinary customer. This rule prevents creditors from going after consumers if a business fails to repay its loan. Nevertheless, by perfecting its security interest in collateral, a creditor has priority over general creditors and creditors with unperfected security interests.

Putting It Into Practice 9.16:

Miguel and Sonja must buy numerous sets of skis and snowboards when they open their business. The seller of this equipment wants to make sure he is protected in case Miguel and Sonja's business does not fare well and they are unable to pay their debt. How can he make sure he gets paid? What will he have to do if they do go out of business and renege on their debt?

Figure 9-13
*Elements of a Secured
Transaction*

ELEMENTS OF A SECURED TRANSACTION

Creditor Creates an Enforceable Security Interest

Debtor has rights to the collateral

Creditor gives something of value to debtor

Creditor possesses collateral or has debtor sign security agreement

Creditor Perfects Security Interest

Files financing statement

Gives creditor priority over general creditors and creditors with
unperfected security interests

Creditor Attaches Debtor's Collateral If Debtor Defaults

BONUS POINTERS:

BANKRUPTCY

Bankruptcy is one way individuals and businesses can deal with the problem of over-indebtedness. It provides relief to debtors and protects creditors by permitting the debtor's assets to be gathered and distributed equitably to creditors. Bankruptcy falls within the exclusive control of the federal courts and falls within Title 11 of the U.S. Code. Chapters 7, 11, and 13 are the chapters that cover individual and commercial bankruptcies.

Chapter 7, which is called the "Liquidation" chapter, involves the process of collecting a debtor's assets and distributing them to creditors. To apply for bankruptcy, an individual must not have declared bankruptcy within the previous six years. A trustee is appointed by the court to determine which creditors' claims are valid and to then distribute the debtor's non-exempt assets in accordance with the priorities established by law. Some debts, such as alimony and child support, are not dischargeable and some property is exempt from being included in the assets. When the process is complete, the bankrupt is no longer responsible for those debts that have been discharged.

Chapter 11, the "Reorganization" chapter, is geared toward saving businesses that are financially distressed. Under this approach, the debtor must propose a reorganization plan, which must be approved by certain creditors and stockholders and ultimately by the court. Approval allows the debtor to make a fresh start, subject to any requirements imposed by the court.

Chapter 13 ("Adjustment of Debts of an Individual with Regular Income") allows a debtor to defer payment of debts so that they can eventually be paid. (Some are paid in full.) This chapter applies to individuals and sole proprietorships who have a source of income that will allow them to pay their debts in the future. The debtor must devise a plan that can either be accepted or rejected by creditors and that must be approved by the court.

Paralegals who work in bankruptcy law are often allowed great latitude in the tasks they perform. Because bankruptcy is very form-driven, paralegals can do just about everything except sign papers and offer clients legal advice. Most paralegals work for law firms that represent creditors, debtors, or trustees, but a few work for bankruptcy judges. Their duties include those listed below.

- ◆ help clients fill out questionnaires regarding their assets and debts
- ◆ help clients assemble documents
- ◆ check UCC filings and real property records
- ◆ prepare inventories of debts and assets
- ◆ request documentation from creditors regarding claims
- ◆ draft bankruptcy petitions and status reports
- ◆ serve as liaison with trustee in bankruptcy
- ◆ attend bankruptcy proceedings

To read some articles about bankruptcy, go to *www.paralegals.org/Reporter.home.html*, click on "Fall 2000," and then click on "The Bankruptcy Petition Preparer" and "Basics of Bankruptcy." Then go to the "Paralegal Roles and Responsibilities" section, which has interviews with a paralegal who does bankruptcy work for a small firm and another who works for a bankruptcy trustee.

"Whether a Worker Is Classified as an Employee or an Independent Contractor Has Much Less to do With How the Parties View Themselves and Much More to do With the Nature of Their Relationship."

"Is there anything else I can help you with?" asked Kim, as a means of wrapping up her meeting with the Johnsons, having discussed the estimated fees for the serviced to be rendered.

"Actually, there is one more thing," responded Mr. Johnson. "Yesterday, one of our drivers was involved in a minor accident while en route to one of our customers. The accident appears to have been her fault—she was the one ticketed. We have always told our drivers that they are not our employees and that we're not responsible for anything they do while driving for us. Are we correct in this?"

"Well, I'm afraid it's not that simple, Mr. Johnson," explained Kim. "Whether a worker is classified as an employee or an **independent contractor** has much less to do with how the parties view themselves and much more to do with the nature of their relationship. For example, do these drivers work only for you and under your direct supervision, or do they work for a number of businesses? Do they have control over what they do and when they do it? How do you pay them? Do you provide the vehicles they use? You see, it's a lot more complicated than simply declaring somebody to be an independent contractor."

"Yes, I can see that," replied Mr. Johnson, his crestfallen expression communicating his concern.

"Does this mean we could be liable for any damages or injuries this driver caused?" asked Mrs. Johnson reluctantly.

"I'm afraid so," admitted Kim. "You'd have to give me more information before I could advise you. But as you can see, this is just one more reason we need to get this LLC formed as quickly as possible. It won't resolve this situation for you, but it will protect you in the future. I can also help you structure your relationship with your drivers so that they are actually independent contractors. The Arizona courts have given us fairly concrete guidance in how to do that."

independent contractor
someone who works as his own boss, at his own pace, in his own way, and under his own supervision

agents   anyone who acts for or represents another

principal   anyone who directs or gives another permission to act on his behalf

fiduciary duty   duty to act in good faith, with candor, and in the best interests of the principal

LAW OF AGENCY

Understanding the law of agency is essential if you want to understand how businesses operate. Because businesses usually have **agents,** such as employees, who act on their behalf, it is important to know when and to what extent these agents can bind or obligate the **principal** (business). An agent is anyone who acts for or represents another, and a principal is anyone who directs or gives another permission to act on the principal's behalf. Typically, legal disputes arise when a third party tries to hold a principal liable for the acts of the agent and the principal seeks to avoid liability by denying that the agent had authority to act on the principal's behalf.

Agents owe a **fiduciary duty** to the principal in that they have a duty to act in good faith, with candor, and in the best interests of the principal. As part of this duty, agents have a duty to (1) perform the duties required by the principal; (2) notify the principal about any important information; (3) be loyal to the principal (by acting for the sole benefit of the principal); and (4) keep an accounting of all monies spent and received. Agents who fail any of these duties are potentially liable for damages resulting from this failure. By the same token, principals have three primary duties to their agents. They must (1) compensate agents for their services; (2) reimburse agents for costs and expenses incurred on the principal's behalf; and (3) cooperate by doing nothing that hinders the agent in the performance of her duties.

Agency law permeates business relationships. As agents of partnerships, partners have the authority to bind the partnership and other partners by signing contracts, purchasing goods, and hiring employees. Directors and officers are agents of corporations and thus owe a fiduciary duty to the corporation, including their undivided loyalty to the company.

An agent may have **actual authority** (authority that is granted by the principal) to bind his principal or **apparent authority**. Actual authority can either be **express** (in that the principal has verbally or in writing told the agent what his duties are) or **implied** (in that these duties customarily flow out of the agent's performance of his express authority). A movie star who hires an agent to represent her expressly authorizes that agent to find suitable movies for her to work in. In exercising this express authority, the agent has the implied authority to talk with movie producers and casting agents and to read scripts. Apparent authority arises when a principal allows a third person to reasonably believe that the agent has the authority to act on the principal's behalf. Suppose that the movie star has allowed her agent in the past to notify producers when she is willing to accept a part. If the agent then contacts a producer with whom he has been in negotiations and confirms that the star is willing to play the lead role, the producer can certainly argue that he believed the agent had the apparent authority to act on the movie star's behalf. If the star subsequently tells the producer, who has publicly announced her acceptance of the role and hired other actors based on her acceptance, that she does not want the role, she will be precluded from arguing that her agent lacked the authority to accept the role on her behalf. Her conduct in the past reasonably led the producer to believe she had given her agent the authority to speak on her behalf.

A question that frequently arises in agency law is whether a principal is liable for the negligence of its agents. Under the doctrine of *respondeat superior* (discussed in Chapter Four), employers are vicariously liable for any negligent acts their employees commit. Employers are not vicariously liable, however, for the negligence of an independent contractor.

So what is the distinction between an employee and an independent contractor? An employee is usually viewed as someone under the control of the person who hires him; an independent contractor, although hired to produce certain results, is considered his own boss. An independent contractor works at his own pace, in his own way, and under his own supervision. The distinction is not always clear, however. In considering whether someone is an employee or an independent contractor, courts look at such factors as the amount of control the employer exercises over the individual's work, the nature of the work being done, the method of payment, and the length of employment. The mere fact that an employer refers to someone as an independent contractor is not dispositive in classifying the relationship. The nature of the relationship and not the label that is attached to the relationship determines its classification. Therefore, an employer cannot evade liability by simply casting the label of independent contractor on an employee.

In some instances, employers are liable even for the negligence of independent contractors. An employer who is negligent in dealing with an independent contractor (e.g., hiring someone the employer knows will not perform the work safely) will be liable if that contractor injures someone while doing work for the employer. Also, if the employer hires the contractor to do something involving an unusual risk

actual authority   authority granted by a principal to his agent

apparent authority   authority that arises when a principal allows a third person to reasonably believe that the agent has the authority to act on the principal's behalf

express authority   actual authority expressed orally or in writing

implied authority   actual authority that naturally flows out of an agent's exercise of his express authority

that is recognizable in advance, such as dynamiting, the employer will not be absolved of vicarious liability.

The question of whether a newspaper carrier is an employee or independent contractor is raised in *Santiago v. Phoenix Newspapers, Inc.* The court looks at a number of factors in rendering its decision, all of which would be considered by Ms. Yuen in creating an employer-independent contractor relationship between the Johnsons and their drivers. Notice that the language in the parties' contract does not determine the nature of their relationship.

◼ *Putting It Into Practice 9.17:*

Without telling Miguel, Sonja hires Makayla to transport their customers from the local airport to their office. On her first run from the airport with customers onboard, Makayla negligently causes an accident, resulting in injury to several of Miguel's and Sonja's clients. Because Sonja did not check out Makayla's driving record, she was unaware that Makayla had been involved in three accidents in the previous six months. Makayla has been in the transport business for a year and had clients for another business on her bus when she had the accident. If Colorado Capers is a general partnership, are Michael and Sonja liable for the injuries to their customers? Has Sonja violated her fiduciary duty to Miguel and the partnership?

Cite as: 164 Ariz. 505, 794 P.2d 138

Supreme Court of Arizona, In Banc.
No. CV-89-0042-PR.
William **SANTIAGO**, a single man, Plaintiff/Appellant,
July 3, 1990.
v.
PHOENIX NEWSPAPERS, INC., an Arizona corporation, Defendant/Appellee.
OPINION

SARAH D. GRANT, Chief Judge, Court of Appeals.

The appellant, William Santiago (Santiago), asks this court to review the court of appeals' decision affirming the trial court's entry of summary judgment in favor of Phoenix Newspapers, Inc. (PNI). We granted review to consider whether the trial court correctly found as a matter of law that PNI was not vicariously liable for the injuries Santiago sustained in a collision with a PNI delivery agent. . . .We have jurisdiction pursuant to Ariz. Const. art. 6, § 5(3) and A.R.S. § 12-120.24.

PROCEDURAL HISTORY

On April 20, 1986, a car driven by Frank Frausto (Frausto) collided with a motorcycle driven by Santiago. At the time Frausto was delivering the Sunday edition of the Arizona Republic on his route for PNI. Santiago filed a negligence action against Frausto and PNI, alleging that Frausto was PNI's agent. Both par-

ties moved for summary judgment. The court, finding no genuine issues of material fact, concluded that Frausto was an independent contractor. The court of appeals agreed, stating that "[p]arties have a perfect right, in their dealings with each other, to establish the independent contractor status in order to avoid the relationship of employer-employee, and it is clear from the undisputed facts that there was no employer-employee relationship created between PNI and Frausto." *Santiago v. Phoenix Newspapers, Inc.,* 162 Ariz. 86, 90, 781 P.2d 63, 67 (1988). Santiago seeks review of this ruling. [FN1]

FN1. The trial court granted PNI's motions for summary judgment on the issues of vicarious liability and negligence in hiring and supervising Frausto as its agent. Santiago does not seek review of the court's decision on the negligent hiring and supervising claim. Frausto is not a party to this petition.

FACTS

We view the facts most favorably to Santiago, as the party opposing the summary judgment . .

Frausto began delivering papers for PNI in August 1984 under a "Delivery Agent Agreement," prepared by PNI. The agreement provided that Frausto was an "independent contractor," retained to provide prompt delivery of its newspapers by the times specified in the contract. Although Frausto had the right to operate the business as he chose, he could engage others to deliver papers on his route for no more than 25% of the delivery days. He was free to pursue any other business activities, including delivering other publications, so long as those activities did not interfere with his performance of the PNI contract. Frausto was also required to provide PNI with satisfactory proof of liability insurance, a valid driver's license, and a favorable report from the Arizona Motor Vehicle Division.

The contract was for a period of six months, renewable at PNI's option. Either party could terminate the agreement prior to six months without cause with 28 days notice and for cause with no notice. Under the contract, cause for termination by PNI existed if complaints from home delivery subscribers exceeded an undefined "acceptable" level, or if Frausto failed to maintain "acceptable" subscriber relations or provide "satisfactory service," defined as banding and bagging newspapers to insure they were received in a dry and readable condition. PNI was also free to breach the agreement if it ceased publishing the paper, defined in the contract as "excusable non-compliance." There is no correlative definition of cause for termination by Frausto. Customers paid PNI directly and any complaints about delivery were funnelled through PNI to Frausto. Additionally, the contract required Frausto to allow a PNI employee to accompany him on his route "for the purposes of verifying distribution, subscriber service, or regular newspaper business."

Early each morning, Frausto drove to a PNI-specified distribution point to load the papers into his car. He then delivered the papers before a PNI- specified time to addresses on a delivery list provided and owned by PNI. He could deliver the papers to listed addresses only. When customers were added to and taken from this list by PNI, Frausto was required to incorporate these changes into his route. According to Frausto, the number of papers delivered fluctuated by as much as thirty papers. For these services, PNI paid Frausto a set amount each week. That amount did not vary when addresses within or beyond the contracted delivery area were added to or taken away by PNI from the delivery list. PNI provided Frausto with health and disability insurance, but did not withhold any taxes.

In ruling on the summary judgment motion, the court considered the affidavits of Frausto and David L. Miller, a delivery agent and former employee driver. Frausto stated in his affidavit that, despite the contractual nomenclature, he considered himself an employee and delivered the papers any way his supervisor directed him to. This included placing the paper in a particular spot if requested by a customer. If he did not comply with these requests, his supervisor would speak to him and he could be fired. Miller stated in his affidavit that he had been a service driver, later switched to being a delivery agent, and that, in his view, there was no significant difference between the level of supervision provided to those holding the two positions.

DISCUSSION

The court may grant summary judgment only if no dispute exists as to any material facts, if only one inference can be drawn from those facts, and if the moving party is entitled to judgment as a matter of law. . . Even when the facts are undisputed, summary disposition is unwarranted if different inferences may be drawn from those facts . . . If the inference in this case is clear that no master-servant relationship exists, the trial court was correct in granting summary judgment; if it is not clear, the case should have been presented to the jury to decide. . . . We apply the rule in this case by asking whether the courts below correctly decided that no inferences could be drawn from the material facts suggesting Frausto was acting as PNI's employee when the accident occurred.

Section 220 of the *Restatement (Second) of Agency*, adopted by Arizona, . . , defines a servant as "a person employed to perform services in the affairs of another and who with respect to the physical conduct in the performance of the services is subject to the other's control or right to control." The *Restatement* lists several additional factors, none of which is dispositive, in determining whether one acting for another is a servant or an independent contractor. We now review those factors, along with the cases considering them, for evidence of an employer-employee relationship which could preclude the entry of summary judgment.

As a prefatory note, we reject PNI's argument that the language of the employment contract is determinative. [FN2] Contract language does not determine the relationship of the parties, rather the "objective nature of the relationship, [is] determined upon an analysis of the totality of the facts and circumstances of each case." . . .

FN2. The agreement is drafted with the intent of designating delivery agents, such as Frausto, independent contractors. It specifically labels agents as independent contractors, and recites that [t]he Company is interested only in the results to be obtained by the Delivery Agent as described in this agreement, and the manner and means to be employed by the Delivery Agent are matters entirely within the authority and discretion of the Delivery Agent over which the Company has no jurisdiction.

The fundamental criterion is the extent of control the principal exercises or may exercise over the agent. . . . The liability must come from the fact that the employer exercises control over the actions of the person in his employment.") . . .

In determining whether an employer-employee relationship exists, the fact finder must evaluate a number of criteria. They include:

1. The extent of control exercised by the master over details of the work and the degree of supervision;
2. The distinct nature of the worker's business;
3. Specialization or skilled occupation;
4. Materials and place of work;
5. Duration of employment;
6. Method of payment;
7. Relationship of work done to the regular business of the employer;
8. Belief of the parties.

ANALYSIS OF RELATIONSHIP BETWEEN FRAUSTO AND PNI

1. *The extent of control exercised by the master over the details of the work*

Such control may be manifested in a variety of ways. A worker who must comply with another's instructions about when, where, and how to work is an employee. *See Restatement* § 220 comment h. In *Throop*, . . ., the plaintiff's husband was killed in a collision with a car driven by Hennen, a salesman for the defendant company. Plaintiff sought recovery against the company on a theory of vicarious liability. At the close of evidence, the trial court granted a directed verdict in favor of the company. On appeal, we examined the record for evidence of the company's control. Hennen was required to call on accounts in person and to present all inventory items, to submit written reports on these visits and to make collections. Although Hennen had these responsibilities for a seven-year period, he could sell anywhere in the country, visit prospects whenever he chose, use his own vehicle exclusively, and select all prospects himself,

visiting the office only a few times a year. Based on these facts, we agreed the trial court properly directed the verdict in the company's favor because no reasonable juror could find it had exercised sufficient control over Hennen to make him an employee.

Missing in *Throop* was the right to control the details of how Hennen made his sales. Where this right of control exists, the inference of the employer-employee relationship is strengthened. For example, an appellate court overturned the trial court's finding of no employer-employee relationship in *Gallaher v. Ricketts* . . The newspaper carrier in *Gallaher* provided his own transportation and was paid a commission for every dollar worth of papers delivered on his assigned route. The company conducted training programs, including tips on how to distribute the paper and stimulate sales, reimbursed him for some transportation expenses, and retained the right to terminate him at any time. The court concluded that these indices of control demonstrated that the carrier "was merely a cog in the wheel of the defendant's enterprise," and held that Ricketts was an employee. . .

A strong indication of control is an employer's power to give specific instructions with the expectation that they will be followed. . . In deciding whether a worker is an employee we look to the totality of the circumstances and the indicia of control . . .

In this case, PNI designated the time for pick-up and delivery, the area covered, the manner in which the papers were delivered, *i.e.*, bagged and banded, and the persons to whom delivery was made. Although PNI did little actual supervising, it had the authority under the contract to send a supervisor with Frausto on his route. Frausto claimed he did the job as he was told, without renegotiating the contract terms, adding customers and following specific customer requests relayed by PNI.

2. *The distinct nature of the worker's business*

Whether the worker's tasks are efforts to promote his own independent enterprise or to further his employer's business will aid the fact finder in ascertaining the existence of an employer-employee relationship. *Tanner v. USA Today*, 179 Ga.App. 722, 347 S.E.2d 690 (1986). The agent in *Tanner* contracted with USA Today to distribute papers. The agent in turn hired carriers to deliver the papers using his trucks. USA Today had no control over the choice of drivers, the trucks used, or the route taken. Under these circumstances, and despite USA Today's imposition of time parameters for delivery, the court found insufficient evidence to raise the issue of an employer-employee relationship.

A concomitant inquiry to this factor also considers whether the worker's job performance results in a profit or loss for the worker. Thus, where the worker purchases the product and then sells it at a profit or loss, the worker is more likely to be found an independent contractor. . . .

As far as the nature of the worker's business, Frausto had no delivery business distinct from that of his responsibilities to PNI. Unlike the drivers in *Tanner,* Frausto had an individual relationship and contract with the newspaper company. Furthermore, he did not purchase the papers and then sell them at a profit or loss. Payments were made directly to PNI and any complaints or requests for delivery changes went through PNI. If Frausto missed a customer, a PNI employee would deliver a paper.

3. *Specialization or skilled occupation*

The jury is more likely to find a master-servant relationship where the work does not require the services of one highly educated or skilled. *See Restatement* § 220 comment h. PNI argues that its agents must drive, follow directions, and be diligent in order to perform the job for which they are paid. However, these skills are required in differing degrees for virtually any job. Frausto's services were not specialized and required no particular training. In addition, an agreement that work cannot be delegated indicates a master-servant relationship. *Restatement* § 220 comment j. In this case, Frausto could delegate work but only up to twenty-five percent of the days.

4. *Materials and place of work*

If an employer supplies tools, and employment is over a specific area or over a fixed route, a master-servant relationship is indicated. *Restatement* § 220 comment h. In this case, PNI supplied the product but did not supply the bags, rubber bands, or transportation necessary to complete the deliveries satisfactorily. However, PNI did designate the route to be covered.

5. *Duration of employment*

Whether the employer seeks a worker's services as a one-time, discrete job or as part of a continuous working relationship may indicate that the employer-employee relationship exists. The shorter in time the relationship, the less likely the worker will subject himself to control over job details. *See Restatement* § 220 comment j. In addition, the employer's right to terminate may indicate control and therefore an employer-employee relationship. The "right to fire" is considered one of the most effective methods of control. . . [footnote omitted] In this case, the contract provided for a six-month term, renewable as long as the carrier performed satisfactorily.

Frausto could be terminated without cause in 28 days and with cause immediately. The definition of cause in the contract was defined only as a failure to provide "satisfactory" service. A jury could reasonably infer that an employer-employee relationship existed since PNI retained significant latitude to fire Frausto inasmuch as the "satisfactory service" provision provides no effective standards. In addition, the jury could also infer that PNI provided health insurance to encourage a long-term relationship and disability insurance to protect itself in case of injury to the carrier, both of which support the existence of an employer-employee relationship.

6. *Method of payment*

PNI paid Frausto each week, but argues that because Frausto was not paid by the hour, he was an independent contractor. Santiago responds that payment was not made by the "job" because Frausto's responsibilities changed without any adjustment to his pay or contract . .

7. *Relation of work done to the employer's regular business*

A court is more likely to find a worker an employee if the work is part of the employer's regular business. *Restatement* § 220 comment h. The court of appeals addressed this factor in *Anton.* . . . [footnote omitted] The contractor in that case, Perkins, entered into an agreement to harvest certain trees and deliver the lumber to Southwest. Southwest gave Perkins detailed specifications for the wood which Perkins passed on verbatim to his woodcutters. Perkins hired Anton as one of these woodcutters under a written contract. That contract required Anton to fell trees, cut them into logs, stack the logs into cords, and clean up the forest afterwards, all in accordance with the Southwest specifications. Perkins reserved to himself only the task of picking up and delivering the wood to Southwest. During the process, Perkins checked Anton's work, making sure he cut the logs correctly, selected the correct quality of wood, stacked the timber as directed, cleaned the forest sufficiently, and worked quickly.

The court noted that in reality the woodcutters conducted virtually every facet of Perkin's enterprise related to the Southwest contract. In deciding whether Anton was an employee for purposes of workers' compensation, the court considered whether the work performed was an *integral* part of the employer's *regular* business . . It found Anton was an employee because Perkins had not limited his attempt to contract to a particularly "well-defined incidental activity . . . ancillary to the central concerns of his business . . . but rather the ongoing basic employment activity" itself. . .

We find the Anton . . [analysis] particularly pat here. Home delivery is critical to the survival of a local daily paper; it may be its essential core. As one court explained:

> The delivery of newspapers within a reasonable time after publication is essential to the success of the newspaper business. For the greater portion of its income the paper depends on advertising, and the rates for advertising are governed by the paper's circulation. Circulation is a necessity for success. The delivery boys are just as much an integral part of the newspaper industry as are the typesetters and pressmen or the editorial staff. . .

PNI is hard-pressed to detach the business of delivering news from that of reporting and printing it, especially when it retains an individual relationship with each carrier. . .

8. *Belief of the parties*

As stated above, Frausto believed that he was an employee, despite contract language to the contrary. Even if he believed he was an independent contractor, that would not preclude a finding of vicarious liability. As the *Restatement* explains: It is not determinative that the parties believe or disbelieve that the relation of master and servant exists, except insofar as such belief indicates an assumption of control by the one and submission of control by the other." *Restatement* § 220 comment m. . . . [footnote omitted] In addition to the parties' belief, the finder of fact should look to the community's belief. "Community custom in thinking that a kind of service is rendered by servants . . . is of importance." *Restatement* § 220 comment

h. The fact that the community regards those doing such work as servants indicates the relation of master and servant. The newspaper's customers did not have individual contact or contracts with Frausto. All payments, complaints, and changes were made directly to PNI. From these facts, a jury could infer that the community regarded Frausto as PNI's employee.

Again, analyzing these factors in relation to the facts of this case a jury could determine that an employer-employee relationship existed between PNI and Frausto. [footnote omitted]

CONCLUSION AND DISPOSITION

Whether an employer-employee relationship exists may not be determined as a matter of law in either side's favor, because reasonable minds may disagree on the nature of the employment relationship. A jury could infer from these facts that Frausto was an employee because PNI involved itself with the details of delivery, received directly all customer complaints and changes so as to remove much of Frausto's independence, retained broad discretion to terminate, and relied heavily on Frausto's services for the survival of its business. The jury could also infer that Frausto was an independent contractor because he used his own car, was subject to little supervision, provided some of his own supplies, and could have someone else deliver for him within limits. Therefore, the trial court erred in finding as a matter of law that Frausto was an independent contractor. Summary judgment on the vicarious liability claim was inappropriate. The opinion of the court of appeals is vacated and the case is remanded to the superior court for proceedings consistent with this opinion.

▰▰ *Putting It Into Practice 9.18:*

(a) Why does Santiago want to sue PNI?

(b) What is the question before the court?

(c) Is the language of the employment contract determinative of the nature of the relationship between Frausto and PNI?

(d) What factors does the court consider in determining whether an employer-employee relationship exists?

(e) What factor is a strong indication of control, according to the court? What facts indicate that PNI had control over Frausto?

(f) Does the court find Frausto's business to be distinct from his responsibilities to PNI? What facts support this conclusion?

(g) Does the court find Frausto's job to be specialized?

(h) Did PNI supply the "tools" of the trade to Frausto? Was the route he was to take fixed?

(i) Which is more likely an indication of an employer-employee relationship: a one-time discrete job or a continuous working relationship? What effect does the right to terminate have on this classification?

(j) Is a court more likely to find a worker to be an employee if his work is part of the employer's regular business? Is the delivery of newspapers part of PNI's regular business?

(k) Did Frausto believe he was an employee? If he had believed that he was an independent contractor, would that have precluded a finding of vicarious liability?

ROLE OF THE PARALEGAL

Corporate law departments are a major employer of paralegals. In fact, about 20 percent of paralegals work for corporations.[1] In some corporations, the attorneys provide in-house legal advice and coordinate the work of outside counsel, who actually perform most of the legal services. In other corporations, attorneys delegate very little work to outside counsel. Corporate departments typically have many subdepartments that specialize in litigation, contracts, securities, employee benefits, mergers and acquisitions, and intellectual property. The wide variety of tasks a corporate paralegal may perform includes the following.

- reviewing and preparing legal documents
- conducting factual and legal research
- filing documents with government agencies
- serving as liaison between in-house attorneys and outside counsel
- communicating with shareholders
- scheduling and organizing corporate meetings
- drafting meeting notices, agendas, and minutes
- collecting and interpreting technical information for corporate reports to regulatory agencies
- drafting and reviewing contracts
- assisting with compliance with SEC regulations
- assisting in incorporating and dissolving corporations
- assisting with mergers and acquisitions

Job satisfaction seems to be high with paralegals in corporate law departments, perhaps because they tend to receive higher salaries and more benefits than paralegals in law firms. They also do not have the billing requirements of paralegals in law firms and are not usually expected to put in as much overtime. The opportunity for advancement is greater as well because corporate legal departments usually have several layers of paralegal positions and have many departments in which to work. On the other hand, corporate work lacks the excitement and fast pace characteristic of many law firms (although the pace can certainly become frenetic around tax time or at the annual meeting time).

NET NEWS

To read more about what it is like to be a corporate paralegal, go to *www.paralegals.org/Reporter/home.html*, click on "Summer 1996," and look for the article entitled "A Different Road to Success."

Such Is the Gift of Trust That is Every Attorney's Privilege and Responsibility to Carry.

The Johnsons stood in stunned silence before the elevator. Their minds were reeling from all the information they had been given, and they were apprehensive about the possibility of another lawsuit in their future. Despite the swirling chaos in their minds, they were both serenely confident that Ms. Yuen would guide and protect them through whatever lay before them. They trusted her implicitly and stood ready to rely on her judgment without any further evidence of her competency or credibility. In the relatively short time they had spent with her, a professional bond of trust and respect had been forged. They were willing to put the future of their business in her hands. Such is the gift of trust that is every attorney's privilege and responsibility to carry.

They were unaware that Martha was in the same elevator they stood waiting to enter and that, as she made her rapid descent to the street level, she was embarking on a legal adventure of her own.

■ TIM'S TECHNO TIPS

Bankruptcy Practice

Many law firms specialize in bankruptcy law. Some do complicated business and personal bankruptcies; others concentrate on personal and small business cases. Many general practitioners also do some straightforward Chapter 7 or 13 cases. Because bankruptcy is a matter of federal law and bankruptcy petitions are filed in federal bankruptcy courts, bankruptcy practice is relatively standard everywhere in the United States.

District courts, and their associated bankruptcy courts, have local rules of practice. It is imperative that you be familiar with any local nuances and requirements. Also keep in mind that the bankruptcy courts are bound by the precedent of the Circuit Court of Appeals for their location. Substantive law and interpretations of procedural law can vary in each of the federal circuits.

TECHNO TRIP

As with the other software packages we have discussed, and as is mentioned in Chapter 11 for real estate software, it is important for bankruptcy software to manipulate data so that information is entered only once and that the software "put" the information, be it personal, financial, addresses, and the like, where it should be on the forms to be generated. The software should also allow a basic template to be used so that the law firm's letterhead or logo appears.

To get the feel of how and what is needed in a bankruptcy case, go to *www.bestcase.com/download.htm.*

Download the demonstration version of the bankruptcy software. (It is 8.1MB, so it will take awhile.) After installing it, click on WINBFS.EXE to start the program. In the setup portion, where you put in the firm name, attorney's names, jurisdiction, and so on, you can move on to the next screen without inputting any information. If you feel adventurous, put in your personal data as a new client and review the forms the software prepares. The "help" file is quite extensive and can give you a better understanding of the program and what it can do.

SUMMARY – PART B

Businesses can take the form of sole proprietorships, general and limited partnerships, corporations, limited liability companies, and limited liability partnerships. Most businesses are sole proprietorships.

General partnerships are governed by some form of the UPA or RUPA (except in Louisiana). Unlike joint ventures, partnerships engage in an ongoing business for profit. General partners are jointly and severally liable for the debts and obligations of the partnership and can be held personally liable for the acts of another partner.

As long as limited partners do not participate in the management of the business they are not liable beyond the extent of their original contribution. Limited partnerships, which are governed by some form of the ULPA or RULPA (except in Louisiana), are formed by filing a limited partnership certificate with the secretary of state.

Corporations are owned by shareholders, who are not personally liable for debts and obligations of the corporation. One of the disadvantages of a corporation is that it is subject to double taxation, which can be avoided by forming an S corporation. Other special forms of corporations are close corporations, professional corporations, and nonprofit corporations. A corporation is an artificial person in that it can be sued, it is bound by the acts of its agents, and it has some of the rights that natural persons do. Incorporation is a highly formalized process that begins with the business's choice of where to incorporate. This decision is important because some states' incorporation laws are more flexible than other states and because some states treat foreign corporations differently than domestic corporations. Great care must be given to select a name that complies with state statutes and that is available. Businesses also have the choice of operating under fictitious names, but to do so must file a fictitious business name document (dba statement) with the appropriate state agency. Once a name is reserved, articles of incorporation must be filed with the appropriate state agency (usually the secretary of state). After the corporation is formed, bylaws must be drafted, corporate supplies must be ordered, and an organizational meeting must be held. A corporation can issue only the number of shares it designates in its articles of incorporation, which must describe the type of stock being issued and the par value of that stock. Corporations finance themselves by issuing shares and bonds. Shareholders are entitled to vote on corporate matters and to receive dividends. Bondholders are entitled to be paid back at a mutually agreeable time and under mutually agreeable terms. The sale of such securities as stocks and bonds by publicly held corporations are regulated by state securities laws and the federal Securities Exchange Commission to protect investors from fraud and unfair business practices. The SEC requires that certain publicly held corporations file registration statements, the most important component of which is the prospectus.

Two new business forms that combine the best attributes of partnerships are the limited liability company (LLC) and the limited liability partnership (LLP). Unlike partnerships, LLCs and LLPs allow their members to manage a company while still being protected from personal liability, and unlike corporations, they protect their members from double taxation. Both can be formed only by complying with state statutory requirements. Although very similar business forms, LLCs provide more protection from liability than LLPs do. LLCs are an increasingly popular form of organization that some believe will ultimately render limited partnerships and S corporations extinct.

A corporation is the holder of the attorney-client privilege. Only the board of directors can decide to waive that privilege. In deciding who is covered by this privilege, courts use either the "control group" or "subject matter" test. Attorneys are generally advised to avoid doing business with their clients. They may do so, however, if they obtain the client's consent in writing after encouraging them to get independent legal advice.

Secured transactions are governed by Article 9 of the UCC. Creditors who have an enforceable security interest in a debtor's collateral can attach that collateral if the debtor defaults. Creditors with a perfected security interest have priority over general creditors and those with unperfected security interests. One way to perfect a security interest is to file a UCC-1 financing statement.

Agency law is an important aspect of business relationships because agents, including directors and officers of corporations and partners in partnerships, have the authority to bind their principal. Agents' fiduciary duty to their principal includes performing the duties required by the principal, notifying the principal about any important information, being loyal to the principal, and accounting for all monies spent and received. Principals are required to compensate their agents for their services, to reimburse them for costs and expenses incurred, and to do nothing that hinders the agent's performance of her duties. Employers are vicariously liable for the negligence of their employees, but not of independent contractors unless they are negligent in dealing with the independent contractor or hire the contractor to do something involving an unusual risk. An independent contractor is his own boss, works at his own pace, in his own way, and under his own supervision. In deciding whether someone is an employee or independent contractor, courts look at the amount of control the employer exercises over the individual's work, the nature of the work being done, the method of payment, and the length of employment.

About 20 percent of paralegals are employed by corporations. Job satisfaction appears high among corporate paralegals. The pay and benefits received are usually superior to those received by paralegals in law firms, the opportunities for advancement are good, and they are not subject to the same billing practices that paralegals in law firms are.

KEY TERMS

Actual authority
Agents
Agent for service of
  process
Annual report
Apparent authority
Articles of incorporation
Attach
Bonds
Bondholder
Bylaws
C corporations
Close corporations
Common stock
Corporate supplies
Corporation

Dissolve
Dividends
Domestic corporations
Express authority
Fictitious business name
  document/dba
  statement
Fictitious name/assumed
  name
Fiduciary duty
Foreign corporations
General partners
General partnership
Implied authority
Independent contractor
Joint ventures

Limited liability
  corporations (LLCs)
Limited liability
  partnership (LLP)
Limited partners
Limited partnership
Limited partnership
  certificate
Nonprofit (not-for-profit)
  corporations
Organizational meeting
Par value
Perfecting
Preferred stock
Principal
Privately held corporation

Professional corporations
Prospectus
Publicly held corporation
Registration statement
S corporation
Secured transactions
Securities
Security agreement
Security interest
Shares
Shareholders
Sole proprietorships
Stock
UCC-1 financing
  statement

REVIEW QUESTIONS – PART B

1. Distinguish among each of the following.
   a. sole proprietorship
   b. general partnership
   c. limited partnership
   d. limited liability partnership

2. Distinguish among each of the following.
   a. C corporation
   b. S corporation
   c. close corporation
   d. professional corporation
   e. nonprofit corporation
   f. LLC

3. What is the difference between a partnership and a joint venture?

4. What is the difference between a general partnership and a limited partnership?
    a. How is each of these formed?
    b. What laws govern the formation and operation of each?
    c. What are the advantages and disadvantages of being a limited partner?

5. Give examples of how a corporation is a "person."

6. What are the advantages and disadvantages of forming a corporation?

7. Describe the incorporation process.

8. Why is the choice of where to incorporate an important one?

9. Distinguish between a foreign corporation and a domestic corporation. A publicly held corporation and a privately held corporation. Common stocks and preferred stocks. Stocks and bonds.

10. What is a fictitious name? What must a business do before it can use this name?

11. What is the purpose of each of the following?
    a. an organizational meeting
    b. corporate supplies
    c. bylaws

12. What is the purpose of the SEC and state securities laws?
    a. What is a registration statement?
    b. What is a prospectus?

13. What are the primary advantages of LLCs and LLPs?
    a. In what ways are these two forms slightly different?
    b. What do some believe will happen someday to limited partnerships and S corporations as a result of these business forms?

14. What is a secured transaction?
    a. What must a creditor do to obtain an enforceable security interest in a debtor's collateral?
    b. How can a creditor perfect that interest?
    c. What is the advantage of having a perfected security interest?

15. Which communications are protected by a corporation's attorney-client privilege?

16. What must an attorney do before entering into a business transaction with a client?

17. What duties does an agent owe a principal?
    a. What duties does a principal owe an agent?
    b. In business situations, how do conflicts with principals and agents generally arise?

18. In what ways are independent contractors treated differently than employees?
    a. How do the courts distinguish between employees and independent contractors?
    b. Under what conditions are employers liable for the negligence of independent contractors?

19. What advantages do corporate paralegals have over paralegals who work for law firms?

PRACTICE EXAM – PART B

MULTIPLE CHOICE

1. A limited partnership
    a. is managed by limited partners
    b. is invested in by general partners
    c. has general partners who are personally liable for all business debts and obligations
    d. none of the above

2. An S corporation
    a. does not pay taxes
    b. can be created only under special circumstances
    c. must be consented to by all the shareholders
    d. all of the above

3. Nonprofit corporations
    a. are often formed for educational, religious, or scientific purposes
    b. cannot compensate their officers or directors
    c. cannot make a profit
    d. all of the above

4. An LLP
    a. member remains liable for the misconduct of other partners
    b. member is never liable for contractual obligations taken on by other partners
    c. is most commonly formed by family members
    d. none of the above

5. In a partnership
    a. the general partners must share profits and losses equally
    b. decision-making must be by majority vote
    c. there is shared management
    d. all of the above

6. A general partner
    a. cannot be held personally liable for the acts of another partner
    b. is jointly and severally liable for the debts and obligations of the partnership

c. cannot have his personal assets seized to satisfy a judgment against the partnership

d. none of the above

7. A limited partner

  a. can still participate in the management of the business

  b. is dependent on the business acumen and skills of the general partners

  c. can allow his name to be used in the business name

  d. all of the above

8. A limited partnership certificate

  a. is more streamlined under the ULPA than under the RULPA

  b. is recommended but not necessary to form a limited partnership

  c. should include the name and address of each general partner

  d. must contain the names and addresses of the limited partners

9. A corporation

  a. is a person

  b. cannot be sued

  c. has no First or Fourth Amendment rights

  d. all of the above

10. The choice of where to incorporate

  a. is important because some states have more flexible incorporation laws than others

  b. is easy because Delaware is the only sensible place to incorporate

  c. is not significant because foreign and domestic corporations are treated equally

  d. none of the above

11. A business cannot use a corporate name

  a. that does not comply with state statutes

  b. that is not available

  c. that is deceptively similar to another's name

  d. all of the above

12. Articles of incorporation

  a. must be prepared and kept in the corporation's files but need not be filed with any state agency

  b. typically include a broadly stated purpose of the corporation and the name and address of each incorporator

  c. are prepared after the first organizational meeting

  d. never contain any information about corporate stock

13. A corporation

  a. can issue common stock but not preferred stock

  b. does not need to indicate in its articles of incorporation what kind of stock it intends to issue

  c. can issue only the number of shares it has designated in its articles of incorporation

  d. does not need to indicate the par value of stock in its articles of incorporation

14. An organizational meeting

  a. is something paralegals are not allowed to attend

  b. often involves the election of directors and the appointment of officers

  c. is a perfunctory, formal meeting at which little business of real substance is accomplished

  d. is not required by most corporations

15. A bondholder

  a. is an insider in a corporation

  b. has a right to be paid back

  c. has a right to vote

  d. all of the above

16. The SEC

  a. protects investors from unfair business practices

  b. requires that corporations selling stock to the public disclose certain material information

  c. requires that corporations file registration statements in certain circumstances

  d. all of the above

17. LLCs

  a. provide less protection to their members than LLPs as far as liability is concerned

  b. allow their members to participate in the management of the business

  c. are not as popular as limited partnerships

  d. can be formed on the basis of a handshake

18. LLPs

  a. are governed by the provisions in the Uniform Limited Liability Company Act

  b. can involve only one person

  c. cannot operate on a not-for-profit basis

  d. must be managed by appointed managers

19. To create an enforceable security interest

  a. a creditor must possess the collateral

  b. a creditor can have the debtor sign a security agreement

  c. a debtor need not have rights to the collateral

  d. a creditor can file a financing statement

20. A UCC-1 financing statement

  a. allows subsequent lenders to determine if collateral is equal in value to the debt owed

  b. must be filed with the secretary of state

  c. allows a creditor to perfect her security interest

  d. all of the above

21. Before entering into a business transaction with a client, an attorney
    a. is encouraged to get the client's consent but need not do so
    b. should recommend and encourage the client to consult with independent counsel
    c. may want to provide disclosure to the client
    d. all of the above
22. An agent has a duty to
    a. act in the best interests of the principal
    b. act for the sole benefit of the principal
    c. keep an accounting of all monies spent and received
    d. all of the above
23. A principal
    a. has duties to its agents
    b. must compensate its agents but need not necessarily reimburse them for their expenses
    c. does not violate the principal-agent relationship by doing things that interfere with the agent's performance of his duties
    d. none of the above
24. Employers are not liable
    a. for the acts of an independent contractor
    b. for the acts of an independent contractor even if they are negligent in hiring that contractor

c. for the acts of an independent contractor doing something involving an unusual risk
d. all of the above

25. An independent contractor
    a. is someone who acts under the control of the person who hires her
    b. works at her own pace
    c. is under the direct supervision of an employer
    d. none of the above
26. In deciding whether someone is an employee or an independent contractor, the courts
    a. focus on the belief of the parties
    b. do not look beyond the label used by the parties
    c. consider the method of payment and the length of employment
    d. all of the above
27. Corporate paralegals
    a. have the same billing requirements as paralegals in law firms
    b. usually have greater opportunity for advancement than paralegals in law firms
    c. receive lower pay and fewer benefits than paralegals in law firms
    d. all of the above

FILL IN THE BLANK

28. A _____ is a business owned by one individual who is solely responsible for all of the business's debts. A _____ is a business owned by two or more people who are personally liable for all business debts and obligations. A _____ is managed by _____ partners who are liable for all business debts and obligations, and invested in by _____ partners, whose liability is limited by the amount of their investment.
29. A corporation is owned by _____ and managed by a board of _____, who establish goals and policies that are carried out by _____.
30. To avoid double taxation, some companies form an _____, which is not taxed on its income.
31. Doctors, lawyers, and accountants often create _____, which allow them to retain certain tax benefits enjoyed by corporations.

32. A small corporation owned by family members and friends and in which the shareholders actively manage the business may qualify to be a _____.
33. Corporations that are formed for charitable purposes rather than for the primary purpose of making profits are called _____.
34. Two new business forms that combine the best of corporations and partnerships are _____ and _____.
35. In all states except Louisiana, general partnerships are governed by the statutes based either on the _____ or the _____. Limited partnerships are governed by either the _____ or the _____.
36. Partnerships are ongoing businesses for profit, but a _____ terminates when the enterprise is accomplished.
37. Limited partnerships are formed by filing a _____ with the secretary of state.

It should contain the name and address of the _____ (entity appointed to receive the summons and complaint if the partnership is sued) as well as the latest date upon which the partnership is to _____ (change in the relationship of the partners).

38. A corporation is a creation of the _____.

39. _____ corporations (corporations that are incorporated in one state and doing business in another) are sometimes treated differently than _____ corporations (corporations operating in the state of their incorporation) in the bidding process.

40. _____ is known as the "Corporation Capital of the World" because of its liberal corporation statutes.

41. A business that decides to use a _____ (assumed) name must file a _____ or _____ with the appropriate state agency.

42. Businesses who want to incorporate must file _____ with the appropriate state agency, usually the secretary of state.

43. Corporations can issue both _____ stock (when there is only one class of stock) and _____ stock (which has features that make it more desirable). The articles of incorporation must establish the _____ of this stock (minimum value for which the stock can be sold).

44. After a corporation is formed, the _____ (rules governing the operation and management of the corporation) must be drafted, the _____, which include the minute book and the stock certificate book, must be ordered, and an _____ must be held, at which paralegals are often asked to take minutes. Every year thereafter, the corporation must file an _____, which describes the performance of the corporation during the preceding year.

45. Corporations finance themselves by issuing _____, which allow people to own a percentage of the corporation) and _____, which represent a corporation's debt to investors. Both of these are considered _____, whose sale is regulated by state securities law and the _____ (federal agency) for corporations that are _____ in that they sell their stock to the public at large, as contrasted with _____

corporations, whose stock is not sold to the public and which are usually formed by family and friends.

46. Shareholders are entitled to receive _____ (distribution of corporate profits).

47. In some cases, corporations may be required by the SEC to file a _____, which describes the security being offered, the nature of the issuer's business, the management of the issuer, any pending litigation against the issuer. The primary component of this statement is the _____, which describes the investment so that investors can evaluate the potential risks involved in buying the security.

48. A _____ is a transaction in which a creditor receives a guarantee of repayment from the debtor in the form of collateral. These transactions are governed by article _____ of the UCC.

49. If a debtor defaults, a creditor can _____ (seize) the debtor's collateral if he has an enforceable _____ in that property. To create that interest, the creditor must either possess the collateral or must require the debtor to sign a _____, describing the collateral.

50. A creditor can obtain priority over other creditors by _____ her security interest. One common way to do that is by filing a _____ with the secretary of state. Even though a creditor has gone through this process, she does not have priority over a _____.

51. Under the _____ rule, a creditor with a perfected security interest does not have priority over a consumer.

52. Under the _____ test, the attorney-client privilege is limited to communications between an attorney and the management responsible for dealing with the legal matter. Under the _____ test, the privilege extends to all employees who communicate in confidence with an attorney who is in the process of rendering legal services to the corporation.

*53. Under Chapter _____ bankruptcy, a trustee is appointed by the court to gather the debtor's assets and distribute them to creditors. Under Chapter _____ bankruptcy, a debtor must come with a plan that could eventually result in full payment to creditors. Chapter ____ coordinates the reorganization of financially distressed businesses.

54. As an _____ of a partnership, a partner has the authority to sign contracts that will bind the partnership, which is the _____ (one who directs or gives another permission to act on its behalf). The partner owes a _____ duty to the partnership in that he has an obligation to act in good faith, with candor, and with fairness in all of his dealings with the partnership.

55. An employer is liable for the negligence of an employee, but is not generally liable for the negligence of an _____ (someone who acts as her own boss).

*Questions taken from Bonus Pointers

TRUE OR FALSE

____ 56. Most businesses in the United States are LLCs.

____ 57. General partnerships are easily created by agreement, but limited partnerships are created only by strictly conforming to applicable state statutes.

____ 58. Shareholders are not personally liable for the debts and obligations of the corporation.

____ 59. Corporations are not considered legal entities.

____ 60. Corporations are subject to double taxation.

____ 61. Typical corporations are referred to as C corporations to distinguish them from S corporations.

____ 62. The professionals in professional corporations are liable for their own negligence and the negligence of those who work for them.

____ 63. Close corporations must adhere to same formalities of a C corporation in their operation.

____ 64. Only certain types of corporations qualify as close corporations.

____ 65. Nonprofit corporations automatically qualify for tax-exempt status at the federal level.

____ 66. Having a nonprofit corporation may make it easier for a business to apply for grants and to receive gifts from wealthy donors.

____ 67. An LLC is taxed like a corporation and its members enjoy limited liability.

____ 68. An LLC and an LLP can be formed by informal agreement of its members.

____ 69. Unless partners decide otherwise, they have equal management rights and share profits and losses equally.

____ 70. A creditor can select only one general partner against which to collect a judgment against the partnership.

____ 71. A partner can be held personally liable for acts incurred by another partner of which she knew nothing.

____ 72. A limited partner's personal assets can be seized to satisfy the debts and obligations of the partnership.

____ 73. Lack of control is one of the biggest disadvantages of being a limited partner.

____ 74. General partnerships and limited partnerships are both easy to create and can arise out of a simple oral agreement.

____ 75. A corporation ceases to exist when all of its shareholders die.

____ 76. If the president of a corporation signs a contract, the corporation is bound by the contract.

____ 77. A corporation can be deprived of property without due process.

____ 78. Corporations cannot enter into contracts and borrow money in their own name.

____ 79. A corporation's income is taxed once when the corporation receives it and a second time when it is distributed to the shareholders.

____ 80. Businesses are limited in where they can incorporate.

____ 81. Incorporation is a very informal process, requiring only that creators of corporations comply substantially with the statutes governing this process.

____ 82. Once those wanting to incorporate have found an available name, they automatically have permission to use it.

____ 83. The purpose of requiring businesses using a fictitious name to file fictitious business name documents is to protect consumers if they decide to sue those businesses.

____ 84. If no par value is indicated in a corporation's articles of incorporation, stock can be issued for any amount the directors decide is appropriate.

____ 85. Paralegals are often asked to take minutes at a newly formed corporation's organizational meeting.

____ 86. At an organizational meeting, bylaws are adopted, the value of stock is established, and other preliminary accounting and financing decisions are made.

_____ 87. Both shareholders and bondholders have a right to dividends.

_____ 88. As insiders in a corporation, shareholders have a right to vote on corporate matters.

_____ 89. The Federal Securities Act of 1933 and the Securities Exchange Act of 1934 are designed to protect corporations from fraud.

_____ 90. LLCs and LLPs must comply with state statutory requirements.

_____ 91. An LLC is a hybrid of a corporation and a partnership, whereas an LLP has only the attributes of a partnership.

_____ 92. An LLP does not necessarily provide its members full protection from liability for all tort and contract-related actions.

_____ 93. Both LLCs and LLPs require written operating agreements.

_____ 94. Some believe that S corporations and limited partnerships will one day be rendered extinct because of LLCs.

_____ 95. A UCC-1 financing statement is a public record that identifies the creditor, debtor, and collateral in a secured transaction.

_____ 96. UCC-1 financing statements are filed when a secured party releases her security interest in the property.

_____ 97. Conducting a UCC-1 search allows a paralegal to determine if assets are free and clear of outstanding security interests.

_____ 98. Perfecting a security interest gives a creditor priority over general creditors, creditors with unperfected security interests, and buyers in the ordinary course of business.

_____ 99. A corporation is the holder of the attorney-client privilege.

_____ 100. An employee has a right to object to a corporation's waiver of the attorney-client privilege.

_____ 101. Both paralegals and attorneys are encouraged to enter into business transactions with their clients as a means of fostering good relations with their clients.

_____ *102. Bankruptcy is within the exclusive control of the state courts.

_____ *103. When the bankruptcy process is complete, the bankrupt is no longer responsible for those debts that have been discharged.

_____ 104. Agents who fail to notify their principal of important information are potentially liable for damages resulting from this failure.

_____ 105. Partners do not have the authority to purchase goods or hire employees on behalf of the corporation.

_____ 106. Directors and officers of a corporation owe their undivided loyalty to that corporation.

_____ 107. In deciding whether someone is an employee or independent contractor, courts consider the amount of control the employer exercises over the individual's work and the nature of the work being done.

_____ 108. The fact that an employer refers to someone as an independent contractor is usually dispositive in classifying the relationship.

_____ 109. Less than 10 percent of all paralegals work for corporations.

*Questions taken from Bonus Pointers

LEGAL LINGO

What's My Name?

1. I receive complaints and summonses on behalf of corporations.
2. I am a contract that begins with a promise and ends with performance.
3. I am the remedy when money will not do.
4. I am an investor who has limited liability.
5. I am a contract that is defective on its face.
6. I am what will happen to the contract in number 5.
7. I keep an offer open.
8. I am how a creditor gets priority over another creditor's security interest.
9. I am what a stock's initial minimum value is.
10. I am a corporation doing business in a state other than the state where I was incorporated.

11. I am the value exchanged to create a contract.
12. I am the duty an agent owes to a principal.
13. I describe the creditor, debtor, and debtor's collateral.
14. I am created when a manufacturer uses a model or sample to show what a product will do.
15. I am a previous oral agreement that changes or adds to a written contract.
16. I am prepared when a corporation does business under an assumed name.
17. I am a short-term business enterprise involving two or more people.
18. I am a hybrid of a corporation and a partnership.
19. I am a provision in a contract that limits the damages in the event of a breach.

20. I am a provision in a contract that waives liability for a party's negligent acts.
21. I am a special kind of stock.
22. I am the part of a registration statement that helps investors evaluate the risk involved in buying a security.
23. I am an agreement to buy everything a particular seller produces.
24. I am governed by Article 9 of the UCC.
25. I am a corporation that avoids double taxation.
26. I do this by buying substitute goods when the seller fails to deliver acceptable goods.
27. I am what a shareholder earns.
28. I am my own boss.
29. I am an equitable remedy that is appropriate when someone relies on another's promise to his detriment.
30. I am filed so that a corporation can be formed.

LEGAL LOGISTICS

1. Coral advertises her services as a healer. She does "readings" for people in which she listens to their physical, mental, and emotional issues and then suggests how they might deal with these issues. In some cases, she suggests they use some formulas she has prepared or she prepares a special formulation for that person. She does a reading for Lorenzo, who is suffering from various allergies. After taking Coral's specially designed formula, his allergies continue to worsen and eventually become so severe he goes to a medical doctor, who decides that Lorenzo is suffering from an allergic reaction to something in Coral's preparation. Lorenzo wants to recover the $1000 he has spent on Coral's formulas.

    a. Is their transaction governed by the UCC?
    b. Has Coral breached her contract with Lorenzo?
    c. Has she breached any implied warranties?
    d. To what damages might Lorenzo be entitled?
    e. Suppose that Lorenzo does not go to a medical doctor after taking the formulas even though his allergies are worse and that he eventually has an anaphylactic reaction (severe allergic reaction) requiring his hospitalization. Should Coral be required to pay his hospital bills?
    f. Coral will not refund Lorenzo's money and files a counterclaim against him for the remaining $1,000 he owes her for the formulas. Has Lorenzo breached his contract with Coral? What defense(s) might he raise? Do you think a court will find that he must pay the remaining $1,000?
    g. Suppose that Lorenzo read Coral's advertisement and shows up at her establishment requesting help. After discovering that Lorenzo is suffering from cancer, Coral refuses to work with him or to sell him any of her formulas because she does not, as a matter of policy, work with anyone with a potentially life-threatening disease. Lorenzo insists that she sell him a formula. Does he have a legal right to this formula?
    h. Suppose instead that Coral did not prepare the special formula that she promised Lorenzo and that, when he arrived to get this formula, Coral said she did not have time to prepare it but that she would give him one that was generally useful for allergies. She is willing to pay him the difference in price but he insists that she prepare his unique formula. Does he have a legally enforceable remedy in this case?
    i. Suppose that Coral does ultimately create the formula but that she does not deliver it to Lorenzo until he has already found an effective alternative and is healed. Does Coral have a legal right to be paid for her efforts?
    j. Suppose Coral makes the formula for Lorenzo and that before he uses it, he has it tested by a chemist, who says there is nothing in it but water. He sues Coral for breach of contract and fraud. In her defense, Coral says that she "charged" the water with spiritual qualities that no chemist would ever be able to detect. Coral sincerely believes in the powers of these formulas and brings in other healers who testify that this charging practice is common and report healings they have witnessed using this practice. Lorenzo argues that he believed that the formula he was buying had physical components in it. Has Coral committed fraud? Could Lorenzo argue mistake of fact? How should a court interpret the parties' usage of the term "formulas"? Do you think Coral and Lorenzo formed a contract?
    k. Coral has Lorenzo sign a written contract before she does a reading. The contract includes a clause in fine print that absolves her of any liability should he experience any adverse

physical reactions as a result of taking any formulas she prepares. Lorenzo is in a weakened condition when he meets with Coral, but is reluctant to sign anything he has not read carefully. She tells him that she will not treat him unless he signs it. Lorenzo is desperate to work with Coral, who has a widespread reputation as a powerful healer, and signs the contract. Will this contractual provision protect Coral from being sued by Lorenzo if his physical condition should worsen after he works with her?

l. After a lengthy consultation with Coral, Lorenzo finally admits that he has a problem with erectile dysfunction and that, because of this, he is afraid to marry his girlfriend. Coral says she will prepare a very expensive formula that she assures him is 100 percent effective in curing this problem, but that she will not begin its preparation until she has the $2000 fee. Lorenzo asks his girlfriend to marry him and she accepts. After months of planning their elaborate wedding, Lorenzo brings his hard-earned cash to Coral and asks her to prepare the formula. Coral tells Lorenzo that making this formula is a complicated and time-consuming process and that she no longer makes it. Despite Lorenzo's begging, she refuses to make it for him. As a result, he has to confess his problem to his fiancee, who cancels the wedding and breaks his heart. Does Lorenzo have any legal remedy?

2. Jessee reads an ad in the real estate section of the newspaper describing a guest ranch that he visited as a child. The ranch is for sale for $1 million. Wanting to make sure that he buys this ranch before anyone else does, he mails a letter immediately, telling the owner he will buy the ranch for the asking price.

   a. Has Jessee formed a valid contract?

   b. Suppose that Jessee calls Harold, the owner of the ranch, and offers him $900,000 for the ranch and that Harold, who thinks he can sell it to someone else for his asking price, wants to make sure that Jessee's offer remains open for another 30 days. What can Harold do to accomplish this?

   c. Suppose instead that Harold accepts Jessee's offer of $900,000 as long as Jessee pays the full amount in cash. Have they formed a valid contract?

   d. Suppose that Jessee agrees to Harold's requirement that he pay in cash and that he sends his written agreement to Harold. Before

receiving Jessee's letter, Harold accepts $1 million in cash from someone else. Have Jessee and Harold formed a contract?

   e. Suppose that Jessee changes his mind after he and Harold have signed a written contract. Can he ask a court to rescind the contract on the grounds that he (Jessee) is bipolar and that at the time he entered into his agreement with Harold he was not taking his medication?

   f. Suppose instead that Jessee and Harold both believe they know the legal boundaries of the ranch but that a survey proves them both wrong and that a lake that both believed to be on Harold's property is actually on state land. Will a court rescind their contract at Jessee's request?

   g. Suppose that Jessee discovers after signing the contract that the land is probably worth closer to $2 million. Can Harold get the contract rescinded on the grounds of inadequate consideration?

   h. Suppose that Harold is Jessee's elderly grandfather and that, in an effort to get Harold to bequeath him the ranch, Jessee agrees to live with Harold so that he can take care of things around the ranch. He also hires a nurse to tend to Harold when he gets sick. Harold asks Jessee what he can do to repay him for his kindness and Jessee mentions that he would very much like to live on the ranch after Harold dies. Harold agrees to sell Jessee the ranch for $1. Is this a valid contract?

   i. Suppose instead that Harold promised Jessee that, if he would give up his prestigious career in the city to come live with him on the ranch and take care of him, he would leave the ranch to him in his will. Jessee does give up his job and takes care of Harold and the ranch for the next two years. When Harold dies, Jessee discovers that he never changed his will and that the ranch will go to Harold's daughter, Jessica. What might Jessee argue to get a court to award him the ranch? On what basis might Jessee request specific performance rather than monetary damages?

   j. Suppose that Jessee eventually gets the ranch, which raises and sells cutting horses. He sells an expensive horse on credit and wants to make sure that he can get the horse back if the buyer fails to make payments. What should he do?

3. Kyland decides to buy a building where he can offer Tai Chi and meditation classes. What are the advantages and disadvantages of his buying a building on his own?

a. Suppose that Kyland discovers that he cannot afford to buy any building that meets his space and design needs and that he asks his friend, Chow Yun, to buy a building with him. They want to share in the costs of running the building but would like to retain control over their own classes. They want to keep their business relationship as simple as possible and decide to take care of any concerns about liability by buying insurance. What kind of business organization would probably meet their needs?

b. Suppose that neither Kyland nor Chow Yun has enough money to buy the building, but that one of their clients is very wealthy and would like to support them by providing them with enough capital to buy the building. The client wants to own part of their business but does not want to participate in any way in running the business. What kind of business would be best for them to form? What will they have to do to form this organization?

c. Kyland and Chow Yun want to get some research grants so they can study the effects of meditation and Tai Chi on physical and mental health. They also want to attract donors that will help fund their research. What kind of business organization should they form? What steps will they need to take to form this organization?

d. Kyland and Chow Yun hire an instructor, Shu-Lin, who teaches 40 hours each week. They give the instructor great leeway in teaching her classes, but tell her the kinds of meditation and the style of Tai Chi they want taught. They pay her a weekly salary and benefits. According to their contract, she is an independent contractor. After attending four weeks of Shu-Lin's meditation course, one of her students experiences a psychotic break. Although rare, this occasionally happens to students of meditation who are not prepared to handle the potentially powerful effects of meditation. Experienced instructors can usually see this coming on with a student and take steps to prevent it from happening. This is Shu-Lin's first experience with teaching meditation and she is totally unprepared for this occurrence. The student has to be hospitalized for a short time. Can she recover damages from Kyland and Chow Yun personally if they have formed a general partnership? Would your answer change if Chow Yun had hired and fired Shu-Lin while Kyland was on vacation so that Kyland knew nothing about Shu-Lin until he was served with a complaint by the injured student?

A TRIP TO THE MOVIES

Consider the movie *The Insider,* which we visited in Chapter 3.

1. Explain why Dr. Wigand and CBS did or did not create a contract when Wigand agreed to an on-the-air interview with Mike Wallace.

2. If they did not form a contract, discuss whether you think Wigand was entitled to some kind of equitable relief when CBS refused to air the interview.

3. Describe the agreement that Wigand signed with Brown & Williamson.
   a. Do you think this was a legally enforceable contract?
   b. What did Brown & Williamson threaten to do if Wigand testified?
   c. Do you think Wigand had any legal grounds for breaching this contract?
   d. What damages do you think the company was entitled to as a result of this breach?

4. How did Bergman find out the real motivation behind CBS's refusal to air the Wigand interview?

5. Suppose that Lowell Bergman asks Dr. Jeff Wigand to do an interview on "60 Minutes" with Mike Wallace and that Wigand agrees to do so. Have they formed a binding contract?
   a. Suppose Bergman says, "I have authority from CBS to pay you $10,000 if you will do an interview with Mike Wallace on '60 Minutes'." Is this a valid offer? What must Wigand do to accept? Is Bergman's offer binding on CBS?
   b. Suppose Wigand signs a written agreement to do the interview for $10,000 and mails the agreement to Lowell Bergman. After Wigand mails the agreement, Bergman calls to tell him that CBS has changed its mind and does not want to do the interview. What recourse does Wigand have?
   c. Suppose that, when Wigand signed the agreement, he wrote at the bottom of the agreement, "I agree to the terms of this contract as long as CBS promises to keep the whereabouts of myself and my family a secret." Have they formed a valid contract?
   d. Suppose that Bergman and Wigand agree verbally before Wigand signs the contract that

CBS will help Wigand and his family relocate. This agreement is not included in the written contract. Can Wigand enforce the verbal agreement? Would your answer be different if Bergman and Wigand agreed to this after Wigand signed the agreement?

6. Do you think that Brown & Williamson could be sued by consumers for fraud?

7. Was Brown & Williamson justified in being afraid of whistleblowers like Wigand? What effect do you think Wigand's testimony has had on subsequent litigation against tobacco companies?

INTERNET INQUIRIES

1. Go the Web page for the Securities Exchange Commission at www.sec.gov and read about the EDGAR database. Then click on "EDGAR Form Definitions" and find out what a 10-K is.
   a. Describe a 10-K.
   b. Conduct a search on EDGAR. Go to "EDGAR CIK" and enter "CBS Corp." You will be given a number. Use that number to do a search on the "EDGAR Archives."
      (1) When did Westinghouse buy CBS Corp?
      (2) What other companies does Westinghouse own?
      (3) Where was Westinghouse incorporated and when?
      (4) Give an example of litigation in which Westinghouse has been involved.

2. Go to *http://chss.montclair.edu/leclair/LS/ students/corporations.html,* which will link you to the secretary of state's home page for your state. This site also provides links to the agency that regulates businesses/corporations in your state as well as the agency that has UCC records, if these agencies are online in your state. Use these links to answer the following questions.
   a. Does the secretary of state in your state have a Web page? If so, what is the Web address?
   b. What information is available at that site?
   c. Pick a corporation you know exists in your state and find its corporate records. If your state does not have corporate records available online, go to the Web page for Arizona's Corporation Commission and use the corporation "Cortez Street, Inc." to answer the following questions. (Notice that Cortez Street, Inc. is doing business as the "Satisfied Frog"—a fictitious name.)
      (1) What is the name of the agency that records information about corporations in your state? What is this agency's web address? Keep track of the links you follow to find the corporate records for the corporation you have chosen and write a summary here of the steps you take.

      (2) Find out the following information about the corporation you have chosen.
   a. What is the complete name of the corporation?
   b. What are the names of the officers?
   c. What is the name and address of the statutory agent?
   d. When was the corporation formed?
   e. What information can you find about its stock?
   f. Can you find any information about the corporation's debts and liens?

3. Go to the Web page for your state's secretary of state's office and look for access to partnership records. (If these records are not available online, go to Arizona's secretary of state's page to get an idea about what information is available in some states.)
   a. Can these records be accessed online?
   b. What is the Web address for the secretary of state?
   c. If there is a subscription fee, what is that fee?
   d. What information about a limited partnership is available?

4. If UCC records are available online in your state, have your instructor give you the name of an individual or company you can use to answer the following questions. If they are not available, go to the Web page for Arizona's secretary of state and use the company name "Hearty Hen, Inc." to answer these questions.
   a. What is the Web address where you can access UCC records in your state?
   b. What is the debtor's name you used for your search?
   c. What is the name of the secured party?
   d. What is one item that was used for collateral?
   e. When will the filing expire, or has it been terminated?

5. Paralegals are sometimes asked to determine a company's assets prior to suit or prior to entering into a business transaction. One way to do this is to use companies like Dun & Bradstreet to assess a company's financial resources. Go to the home page for Dun & Bradstreet (*www.dnb.com/dnbhome.htm*).

Click on "Click Here to Run D&B Report" and then on "View Sample Reports." Scroll down to "Contract Customers" and click there and then go to "Comprehensive Report which will take you to the "Supplier Evaluation Sample Report" for Gorman Manufacturing.

a. Who is the CEO for Gorman Manufacturing?
b. What special event occurred in 199__ to the company?
c. What is its D&B rating?
   1. For what reason does the report indicate that this supplier should be looked into more carefully?

d. Have any suits, liens, or judgments been filed against this company?
e. What does this company do?
f. How many accounts does it have?
g. How many employees does it have?
h. Does it have any branch offices?
i. When was the company incorporated?
j. How old are its officers?
k. Does this company sometimes put accounts in collection even when the amount of debt is in dispute?

ENDNOTES

[1]"Are They Paying You What You're Worth? *Legal Assistant Today's* 1998-99 Salary Survey Results," *Legal Assistant Today,* January/February 1999, pp. 53–57.

10 Family Law

So It Was That Within a Week of Her Initial Conversation With George, Martha Found Herself Sitting in the Waiting Room of Esparanza & Ali.

Having decided mediation was the best route for her and George to resolve their differences, Martha set about finding an attorney to advise her about her legal rights and obligations. Because White and Treadwell did not have a **domestic relations** department, she asked some of her friends and colleagues for referrals. Ernesto surprised her by suggesting his wife's legal clinic, which focused on providing affordable legal services, especially in the area of family law. Martha knew Ernesto's wife was an attorney but she had no idea she and Ernesto were so idealogically different. As Ernesto described the clinic, he grumbled about the inordinate number of *pro bono* cases his wife and her partner, Nafisa, took on, but Martha could hear the pride in his voice. She knew first-hand of Ernesto's insistence on quality work, and she was sure his wife would be no less conscientious.

So it was that within a week of her initial conversation with George, Martha found herself sitting in the waiting room of Esparanza & Ali. The contrast with the genteel waiting area of White & Treadwell was striking. A little taken aback by the noise level and the unrestrained interactions among some of the clients, she couldn't help but overhear the conversation between two women sitting across from her.

"Actually, I'm not here to get a divorce," protested the younger woman in response to the motherly woman next to her. "An annulment," she finally volunteered reluctantly.

"Really," said the older woman, arching her eyebrows and sitting back expectantly, awaiting an explanation. When none was forthcoming, she folded her arms and looked across at Martha, sizing up her potential as a conversationalist. Not one to openly share her personal life, Martha averted her eyes and feigned interest in the *Good Housekeeping* magazine in her lap.

"Well, you'll never guess why I'm here," announced the older woman to no one in particular. Both Martha and the young girl looked up to see who was the target of this verbal missile. Having captured their interest, the woman waited a few more seconds to achieve the dramatic suspense she was seeking and then declared: "Bigamy." Pleased with the attentive stares focused on her, she went on. "Yep, I've been married to a bigamist all these years. Now ain't that somethin'?"

To read about cases in the news pertaining to family law issues, go to the current edition of the *Family Law Reporter,* which is available online at *http://subscript.bna.com/SAMPLES/flr.nsf/Highlights/Highlights?OpenDocument.*

To see each state's requirements for marriage, go to *www.law.cornell.edu/topics/Table_Marriage.htm.*

Figure 10-1
Requirements for Marriage

> # REQUIREMENTS FOR MARRIAGE
>
> Parties must be of age
> Parties must be legally capable of agreeing to marry
> Marriage must be entered into knowingly and voluntarily
> License must be obtained
> Some states require waiting period
> Many states require blood tests

domestic relations law
family law

ENTERING INTO MARRIAGE

From a legal perspective, marriage is viewed as a contract, albeit one with ramifications going far beyond the rights and obligations of other contracts. The sacred aspects of the marriage union are not lost on the courts, and family law treats marriage more as an institution than as a mere agreement. The states also have an interest in creating and preserving marriages, which is reflected in the statutory schemes that govern family relationships.

The requirements for marriage are relatively straightforward. Each person must be of age and must be legally capable of agreeing to marry. Marriage must be entered into knowingly and voluntarily. A marriage license must be obtained. Although the requirements for getting a license vary, individuals will be denied a license if (1) one or both of them lacks legal capacity; (2) they have a degree of kinship that is prohibited by state law; (3) one of them is already married; or (4) they are both the same sex. (Efforts have been made to challenge this prohibition.)

Some states require a waiting period between the issuance of the license and the marriage ceremony. This waiting period presumably encourages parties to consider the significance of what they are doing. Blood tests are typically required to alert the parties to being the carrier of a sexually transmitted disease and to having conflicting blood types that make it potentially dangerous for the health of any future children.

> ◆ **LOCAL LINKS** ◆
> What are the requirements for marriage in your state?

MARRIAGE CONTRACTS THAT ARE VOID OR VOIDABLE

In many states, a marriage contract is void if (1) one of the parties is already married (bigamy); (2) one of the parties is under age; (3) one of the parties lacks mental competence to enter into marriage; or (4) the parties have a forbidden kinship relationship (e.g., brother and sister).

Figure 10-2
Void and Voidable Marriages

> # VOID MARRIAGE
>
> Void on its face
> One of parties is already married
> One of parties is under age
> One of parties lacks mental competence
> Parties have a forbidden closeness of kinship
>
> # VOIDABLE MARRIAGE
>
> Requires proof of defect
> Marriage was entered into under fraudulent conditions
> Formal requirements for marriage were not honored

annulment   court order declaring that a marriage never existed

Such marriages are null and void on their face and can be **annulled** through a court order declaring that the marriage never existed. This order makes the voiding of the marriage official.

A marriage contract is voidable if it is entered into under fraudulent conditions or if the formal requirements for marriage are not honored. A marriage based on a voidable contract can also be annulled. A marriage in which a spouse purported to want children and then after marriage declared he was unwilling or unable to have children could be annulled. A marriage entered into on a dare or as a sham for getting a visa would also be subject to annulment. Note that a void marriage is null and void on its face, whereas a voidable marriage is not null and void until a court annuls it. In other words, a voidable marriage requires the parties to prove a defect in the marriage whereas a void marriage requires no proof because the defect speaks for itself.

What is the difference between an annulment and a divorce? An annulment declares that the marriage never actually existed whereas a divorce decree recognizes the existence of a marriage but then terminates it. As a result, an annulment means that the parties were never legally married so that generally no obligation exists to support the other spouse. If children are involved or if the parties have contributed to the relationship, however, the courts will use the same equitable grounds to resolve disputes as are used in divorce actions.

Putting It Into Practice 10.1:

Harry knows Sally will not have sexual relations with him unless they are married, so he arranges a sham wedding ceremony. After a few weeks, he admits to Sally that the "minister" was a friend of his and that he had manufactured the wedding license. Is the marriage void or voidable? What must Sally do to get it annulled?

Martha Silently Raised a Prayer of Gratitude that Her Situation, However Unpleasant, Did Not Begin to Compare with the Trauma This Woman Was Experiencing.

Martha's response was cut short when a paper airplane landed unceremoniously in her lap.

"I'm so sorry," apologized a harried young mother, balancing a baby on one hip as she retrieved the errant plane. Sternly commanding her four-year-old son to stay in the designated play area, she turned around and continued her apology. "He's really a good kid. It's my fault. I wasn't watching him close enough. I'm trying to get the last of this paperwork filled out before Danny comes out."

"Getting ready for a hearing?" asked Martha politely.

"Yeah. We've got an **order to show cause hearing** next week and Danny—he's a paralegal here—is helping me get everything together. I've just gotta convince the judge that I need more money from my ex—well, soon to be ex—husband. If I don't, I'm gonna lose the house."

Hearing the terror rising in her voice, Martha sought to say something comforting. "I'm sure the judge will be very understanding. Most judges do their best to find a fair solution, you know."

"Oh, I know," agreed the young woman emphatically. "I was in court just a few weeks ago getting a **TRO** against Troy— my husband—and the judge was really nice to me."

"I take it your husband was threatening you?" inquired Martha, surprising herself with her unabashed interest in this stranger's life.

"Actually, it makes Troy sound worse then he really is. He never hit me while we were married, but we got into a really bad fight and I guess he just kinda lost his head. But I sure wasn't gonna let him have another crack at me, so I called Danny and he and Ms. Esparanza got me before a judge right away."

"I'm sorry you've been having such a rough time of it," said Martha sympathetically.

"Thanks. I'd heard horror stories from some of my friends who'd gotten divorced and for a while I thought Troy and I'd be different. When we finally decided we couldn't stay together any more, we wrote up a **separation agreement.** I was sure that would take care of everything. Things did go pretty smoothly until Troy lost his job. Then the stress got to us and we both started saying things—you know, those terrible things you wish you could take back as soon as you said them." She sighed and unconsciously stroked her baby, who seemed mesmerized by her mother's lips. "Anyway, things are bound to get better. Troy got another job last week and even though he'll be making less money for awhile, at least he has a steady paycheck again."

Martha silently raised a prayer of gratitude that her situation, however unpleasant, did not begin to compare with the trauma this woman was experiencing. Before she formulated what she thought might be a reassuring statement, the young woman bolted out of her seat, rescuing a hapless plant from her son's inquisitive fingers.

PREMARITAL AGREEMENTS

antenuptial agreement   also known as a *prenuptial agreement;* agreement entered into in anticipation of marriage that specifies the obligations and rights of the parties during marriage and upon termination of the marriage

Most states encourage an equitable division of property acquired during the marriage when divorce occurs. To decrease this percentage, couples can enter into an **antenuptial** (also called *prenuptial*) **agreement.** Such an agreement is signed in anticipation of marriage and specifies the parties' rights and obligations during marriage as well upon termination of the marriage by death or divorce. People who gravitate toward these kinds of agreements often have children from a previous marriage and want to ensure those children have first claims on property acquired

order to show cause hearing   hearing at which the defendant must explain why the plaintiff's request for temporary relief is not justified

TRO *temporary restraining order*   temporary order by a court for a party to do something or to stop doing something

separation agreement   agreement regarding division of property, child support and custody, and other terms of the anticipated separation

To read more about antenuptial/prenuptial agreements, go to a financial Web site, Bankrate.com, at *www.bankrate.com/brm/prenup.asp* and to a Web site that offers legal advice to consumers and small businesses, MyCounsel.com, at *www.mycounsel.com/content/familylaw/marriage/prenuptial.htm1*.

before the second marriage. Or they may have substantial property of their own and may not want their spouse to have claims on that property.

At one time, courts viewed antenuptial/prenuptial agreements with disfavor because they were perceived as instruments that fostered divorce. Indeed, some states refuse to enforce any provisions defining rights in the event of divorce. Today, however, most states favor them as long as the parties fully disclose their financial assets prior to signing the contract (although a waiver of this disclosure may be possible). Any provisions that violate public policy are unenforceable. For example, parties cannot agree in advance to waive claims for child support because the rights of children cannot be contracted away. These contracts can be challenged on the same grounds as any contract: unconscionability, fraud, and duress.

> ◆ **LOCAL LINKS** ◆
> Are antenuptial/prenuptial agreements recognized in your state?

> ◆ **LOCAL LINKS** ◆
> Are separation and postnuptial agreements recognized in your state?

▰ *Putting It Into Practice 10.2:*

Delia is reluctant to marry Harvey. She is afraid he might be marrying her because of her trust and the sizable estate she will inherit upon her mother's death. Why might Harvey be wise to suggest preparing an antenuptial agreement?

POSTNUPTIAL AGREEMENTS

postnuptial agreement
agreement in reference to financial and related matters reached while the marriage is harmonious and separation is not being considered

Agreements can also be entered into during marriage and are then called **postnuptial agreements.** These agreements resolve financial and related issues while the marriage is harmonious and the couple is not considering separation. An agreement signed in anticipation of or after separating is called a *separation agreement.* It covers the division of property, child support and custody, and other terms of the parties' separation. As with antenuptial agreements, the courts increasingly favor recognition of postnuptial and separation agreements.

Figure 10-3
Types of Agreement Couples May Enter Into

TYPES OF AGREEMENTS COUPLES MAY ENTER INTO		
NAME	**TIME OF ENTRY**	**PURPOSE**
Antenuptial	Before marriage	Reach agreement in regard to financial and related matters during marriage and upon divorce
Postnuptial	During marriage while harmonious	Reach agreement in regard to financial and related matters upon divorce
Separation	During marriage	Reach agreement in regard to financial and related matters upon separation
Settlement	During divorce proceedings in anticipation of separation	Reach agreement in regard to financial and related matters upon divorce

INTERLOCUTORY RELIEF

Once a divorce action has been filed, a long period of time may ensue before a final divorce decree is obtained. In the interim, the parties are faced with answering such critical questions as "Who will assume the role of custodial parent?", "Who will retain possession of the marital residence?", and "Will temporary spousal support and/or child support be paid and, if so, how much?" These questions complicate an already tense, emotionally-charged relationship between the spouses; Often they are incapable of resolving these questions themselves and judicial intervention is required. Furthermore, the courts are sometimes needed to protect a spouse and/or children from an abusive spouse or to prevent a party from removing or hiding assets.

Interlocutory (temporary) **relief** (referred to as *relief pendente lite* or *nisi relief* in some jurisdictions) can be requested by either party by means of a pleading or motion. Many jurisdictions require that parties first seek a resolution through mediation. If no resolution is reached, a hearing is scheduled and a **show cause order** is filed. This order requires the defendant to appear at the hearing and explain, or "show cause," why the temporary relief requested by the plaintiff should not be granted. At this hearing, the judge makes an interim finding about how best to resolve the issues presented so that the parties can function until these questions are resolved permanently.

In preparation for an interlocutory hearing (sometimes called an *order to show cause hearing*), the parties must assimilate all the essential financial information the court will need to render its decision. Typically, the client must locate all the facts and corroborating details to present to the court. Often, however, a paralegal assists the client by helping to organize the materials and explaining their relevance and necessity.

In the event of domestic violence, a more immediate response is needed from the court to prevent harm to the endangered spouse and/or children. Once a claim for relief from domestic violence is filed, a hearing is typically scheduled within 10 days or less. If the threat of harm is immediate, the hearing may be conducted *ex parte* in that only one side is present to offer evidence. If the judge is convinced that the party requesting the hearing is in immediate danger, he may issue a *temporary restraining order (TRO)*, which temporarily orders a party to do something or to stop doing something until the court has time to consider a more permanent ruling on the matter. Violation of this TRO (sometimes called an **order of protection** or **protective order** in cases of domestic violence) can result in the offender's being incarcerated, fined, or both. In anticipation of potential conflict between divorcing couples, many courts issue a general mutual restraining order when a complaint to divorce is filed.

interlocutory relief
temporary relief; also known as *pendente lite* or *nisi* relief

show cause order order requiring a defendant to appear at a hearing and explain why (show cause) why the relief requested by the plaintiff is not justified

> ◆ **LOCAL LINKS** ◆
> What is interlocutory relief called in your state? What must a party do to qualify for interlocutory relief?

ex parte hearing at which only one side presents evidence

order of protection also known as a *protective order* or *temporary restraining order* issued in domestic violence cases

protective order same as order of protection

> ◆ **LOCAL LINKS** ◆
> What is the basic procedure for getting a TRO in your state?

Putting It Into Practice 10.3:

What is the difference between an order to show cause hearing and a hearing to get a TRO?

NET NEWS

To see the criteria and procedure for getting a TRO in California, go to the Justice Center at *www.hrh.servsite.com/jc,* click on "Free Information," and scroll down to "Temporary Restraining Orders." For information about TRO procedures in Oregon, go to the Web site for the Oregon Coalition Against Domestic and Sexual Violence at *www.ocadsv.com/temporary restraining.html.*

BONUS POINTERS: **DOMESTIC VIOLENCE**

TROs are often generated as a result of domestic violence, an issue that so pervasively affects every stratum and dimension of our society that it has become the focus of countless studies, commissions, and organizations. A survey conducted by the National Institute of Justice in July, 2000 entitled "The Extent, Nature and Consequences of Intimate Partner Violence" involved 8,000 female and 8,000 male respondents and revealed the following.

◆ 1.5 percent of the women and 0.9 percent of the men surveyed said they had been raped and/or physically assaulted by an intimate partner within the previous 12 months. This means that approximately 1.5 million women and 834,732 men are raped and/or physically assaulted by intimate partners annually. Because many are victimized more than once, it is estimated that about 4.9 million intimate partner rapes and physical assaults occur against women each year and about 2.9 million intimate partner physical assaults occur against men each year.

◆ 0.5 percent of women and 0.2 percent of men surveyed reported being stalked by an intimate partner within the previous 12 months, making stalking by intimates more prevalent than previously believed.

◆ The role of race in domestic violence remains unclear. Although Asian American women reported lower rates of intimate partner violence and African American and Native American women reported higher rates of intimate partner violence, these differences diminished when socio-demographic and relationship variables were controlled.

◆ Women experience more chronic and injurious physical assaults than men.

◆ Physical violence is often accompanied by emotional and controlling behavior. In fact, having a verbally abusive partner was the variable most likely to predict that a woman would be victimized by an intimate partner.

◆ Most intimate partner victimizations are not reported to the police. Only approximately one-fifth of rapes, one-fourth of physical assaults, and one-fourth of stalkings were reported by female respondents to the police. Male respondents reported even fewer such incidents. The majority indicated they did not call the police because they believed the police could not help them.

NET NEWS

For more information stemming from the National Institute of Justice survey, go to *www.ojp.usdoj.gov/vawo/statistics.htm.* For additional statistics about domestic violence, go to the American Bar Association site, *www.abanet.org/domviol/stats.html.* To read about some of the myths surrounding domestic violence, go to *www.abanet.org/domviol/myths.html.* Additional information about domestic violence can be found at the Web page for Violence Against Women Online Resources at *www.vaw.umn.edu/dv.asp.*

"I Prefer to Think of Him as Eccentric. But He's Definitely Not Your Run-of-the-Mill Kind of Guy."

Martha was reflecting on what it must be like to be a paralegal at the clinic when the receptionist called her name and ushered her back to a small office. Soon a young African American woman introduced herself as Letitia Moreland and explained that she would be conducting the initial interview. She made it clear she was a paralegal and began to outline what a paralegal's responsibilities entailed.

"No need to explain," interrupted Martha. "I'm a paralegal with White & Treadwell."

"Oh, all right," Letitia replied, looking a little perplexed.

"I'm here because we don't do any DR [domestic relations] work in our firm," added Martha in explanation, "but one of my supervising attorneys, Ernesto Esparanza, highly recommended you."

"I'll bet he did," grinned Letitia mischievously. "What's that wild man up to these days?"

Martha had never quite considered Ernesto in that light and wasn't sure how to respond. "Right now he's knee-deep in depositions for a products liability case."

"Well, you tell him he owes me a pool game. I never evened the score after the last time he whipped me." Letitia was looking intently at Martha's intake questionnaire and was completely unaware of Martha's look of incredulity. Turning to the business at hand, Letitia set about finding out what information Martha needed and getting the data her supervising attorney would need before talking with Martha

"All right. I see you've been divorced for, let's see, about six years. Your husband is living in the marital residence. Now that you have a job, you're no longer receiving **spousal maintenance** and you have **joint custody** of your two daughters. Is that correct?"

"Yes."

"I take it that everything was working well as far as child support was concerned until your ex-husband decided he wanted to get an advanced degree and asked you to assume full financial responsibility for your children?"

"Exactly. Let me add that this will be George's third advanced degree and that he's been working in his latest field—computer sciences—for only three years."

"Interesting," acknowledged Letitia. "Would you say he's unstable?"

"I prefer to think of him as eccentric," mused Martha. "But he's definitely not your run-of-the-mill kind of guy."

no-fault divorce   divorce in which the parties do not have to prove that one party unilaterally broke the marriage bond but only have to show that the marriage is irretrievably broken

spousal maintenance   also known as *spousal support* or *alimony*

joint custody   shared custody; parents can have joint legal and/or physical custody of children

covenant marriages   marriage in which a couple agrees to premarital counseling and must meet certain statutorily-defined conditions to get a divorce

GROUNDS FOR DISSOLUTION OF MARRIAGE

Traditionally, a spouse was required to provide evidence to the court that grounds for divorce, as specified by statute, existed. Such grounds included physical or mental cruelty, abandonment, adultery, drug abuse, or habitual drunkenness. The more modern concept of **no-fault divorce** requires only that one party has decided that they are no longer interested in remaining married, thus laying the groundwork for "irreconcilable differences." Under this approach, one spouse no longer need claim that the other spouse unilaterally broke the marriage bond.

As states have made it easier to establish the grounds for divorce, they have simultaneously imposed additional requirements on no-fault divorces. Some, for example, require a lengthy separation before a no-fault divorce will be granted. Other states require spouses to enter into court-monitored mediation before a no-fault divorce will be considered. Because getting a no-fault divorce can be more time-consuming than getting a fault-based divorce, some couples privately agree to grounds for divorce in order to divorce more quickly.

Alarmed by the current divorce rate, three states (Arkansas, Arizona, and Louisiana) have created **covenant marriages.** A couple that opts for a covenant marriage rather than a traditional marriage agrees to premarital counseling and vows to seek counseling if their marriage appears in trouble. To obtain a divorce, the couple must meet certain statutorily-defined conditions, such as, proving that one spouse committed adultery, sexually or physically abused a spouse or child, or abandoned the home for a year.

NET NEWS

To see the grounds for divorce as they vary from state to state, go to *www.abanet.org/family/familylaw/table4.html.* To find divorce laws in any state, go to *www.law.cornell.edu/topics/Table Divorce.htm,* then to "Statutes," and click on the state in which you are interested. Or you can go to *www.divorce-without-war.com,* where you can also find information about mediation services.

POTENTIAL CONFLICTS OF INTEREST IN FAMILY LAW

Potential conflicts of interest abound in family law. Commonly, parties entering into a divorce, with all of its concomitant issues, (i.e., alimony, child custody, child support, and property division) naively believe they can resolve all of their differences amicably and that they need an attorney only to help formalize their agreement. More times than not, they find to their chagrin that the same irreconcilable differences that led to their divorce also foil their civility when confronted with tangible, and often difficult, decisions. For this reason alone, attorneys are wise to strongly advise parties up front that they should have separate representation.

At the very least, attorneys are ethically bound to alert clients that they cannot represent both sides of a legal issue and that to do so would constitute a conflict of interest. Even if the divorce is uncontested, the property division issues appear relatively straightforward, and the parties opt to use one attorney to save money, the attorney must make it clear that if a conflict arises, he will not be able to continue representing both of them. In fact, he will probably have to withdraw from representing either of them (although in some instances, he may be able to represent one of them). In some states no ethical quandary exists because attorneys are clearly forbidden from representing both spouses even in an uncontested divorce.

With that in mind, an attorney can represent both the husband and wife in an uncontested divorce (assuming the ethical rules of the state permit this) if the parties have voluntarily resolved all issues, such as property division, alimony, child custody and support; the parties have agreed to joint representation and have been fully informed about the possible ramifications of such representation; and the attorney reasonably believes that joint representation will not adversely affect either of the parties.

Another situation that frequently occurs in the realm of domestic relations is that the attorney, who represented the couple in a previous matter, is subsequently asked to represent one of the spouses when they decide to dissolve the marriage. In these situations, the attorney must assess the degree to which the divorce proceeding is related to the previous litigation. If the previous matter was a bankruptcy, for example, the attorney could not represent either spouse in the divorce because he would have gleaned confidential information from both spouses in order to represent them in the bankruptcy. If he had represented them in a real estate transaction, the answer is less clear. If the attorney had not gained any confidential information from one spouse that could be used to the detriment of the other spouse, the subsequent representation in the divorce proceeding would probably be permissible.

Conflicts of interest can also arise in the preparation of prenuptial agreements. An attorney will find it difficult, if not impossible, to zealously represent the best interests of both parties simultaneously. If a court later determines that the parties were not fully informed about their rights and liabilities, it may decide not to enforce the agreement.

◆ **LOCAL LINKS** ◆

What does your state require before permitting parties to seek a no-fault divorce?

Putting It Into Practice 10.4:

Herberto and Angelina are very close to Angelina's brother, Julio, who is an attorney. When they decide to divorce, they ask Julio to represent them both. Their divorce is uncontested, they have one child, and own a small house. The couple has agreed to child support, child custody, and the division of their property. Should Julio represent them both?

DIVORCE PROCEDURES

To initiate a divorce proceeding, one of the parties must file a petition or complaint requesting the divorce and stating the reasons why a divorce should be granted. If the divorce is sought on a fault basis, the petitioner must indicate the grounds on which the alleged fault is based. Financial affidavits attesting to the financial assets and liabilities of the parties are usually required to accompany the petition.

Under most state statutes, the party filing the petition for divorce must have been a resident of the state for a specified period of time prior to initiating the

◆ **LOCAL LINKS** ◆

Are parties seeking divorce in your state required to engage in some form of alternative dispute resolution?
Are they required to attend parenting classes?

settlement agreement
agreement reached by parties who have initiated divorce proceedings; this agreement sets forth the rights and obligation of the parties

divorce. Alternatively, a court may have jurisdiction if the marriage was formalized there or if the grounds for divorce occurred while the parties were residing in that state (even if the time requirement is not met).

The opposing party has the option of either not contesting the divorce or of countersuing. After the petition is filed, the court will, upon request of either party, usually hold a hearing to temporarily resolve issues pertaining to child custody, child support, alimony, liability for various debts, and the protection of existing joint assets. Some courts require the parties to engage in mediation or some other form of alternative dispute resolution to resolve issues regarding property division, child support, and child custody. In addition, some states require parents to attend parenting classes to help them understand the impact of the divorce process on children.

If at some point the parties are able to resolve their differences, they can submit a **settlement agreement** to the court. This agreement sets forth the rights and obligations of the parties in relation to alimony, child custody, child support, and other issues related to divorce. Parties should do their best to hammer out a settlement agreement, which will then be formalized by the court into an order. Otherwise they must submit themselves to the vagaries of a trial and the discretion of a judge, who knows only what the evidence shows and nothing of the intimate details that shade a family's dynamics. In fact, one of the most devastating consequences of divorce is the parties' relinquishment of their autonomy. Major life decisions, in which no court would normally have a right to intervene, after divorce fall within the purview of the court's rulership. For example, because a court once resolved the issues pertaining to George and Martha's divorce, a court could now intervene in George's decision to pursue a new career—an intervention to which courts are not normally entitled.

Another unfortunate but common side-effect of divorce is the severe economic consequences often suffered. Maintaining two households is obviously more expensive than maintaining only one. A family's whose resources were stretched wafer-thin when it existed as a unit often snap when that unit is broken. Consequently, the standard of living, particularly for women and children, decreases significantly in the first year after divorce. In fact, one of the reasons the federal government has taken such an active role in enforcing child support payments is the adverse effect the lack of payment has had on divorced parents and on welfare programs, such as Aid for Dependent Children (AFDC).

NET NEWS

To learn about mediation in the context of divorce, go to *www.divorce-without-war.com* or *www.nolo.com/encyclopedia/div_ency.html* and click on "Divorce Mediation." For information about on-line mediation in divorce cases, go to *www.mediate-net.org* (University of Maryland experimental on-line mediation project relating to family law matters).

An online support center for individuals seeking divorce is located at *www.divorcesupport.com/home.shtml*. At this site, you can find links to state laws and guidelines, state-specific forms, guidelines for calculating child support, and a variety of professionals used in divorce cases.

FindForms.com has a number of state-specific forms used in divorce cases (*www.uslegalforms.com/findforms/divorce.htm*). A fee is charged to order these forms.

Figure 10-4
Divorce Process

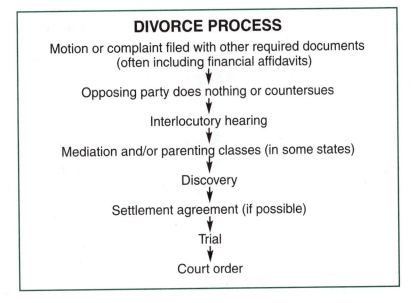

ALIMONY

Alimony (referred to as **spousal maintenance** or **spousal support** in some jurisdictions) is the payment of support made by a former spouse for the benefit of the other former spouse. Although alimony was traditionally paid by the husband to the wife, that is no longer true. Because alimony is based on the relative assets and financial requirements of each party, husbands have the same right to receive alimony as wives do. Furthermore, in light of many women's economic independence today, alimony is not awarded as often as it once was. When short-term maintenance is awarded, the goal is to provide the receiving spouse sufficient time and resources to gain financial independence.

Alimony can take a variety of forms. It can be permanent in that the obligation to pay alimony remains until either party dies or the receiving party remarries (or in some states, cohabits). It can be rehabilitative, assisting a former spouse while she is being educated or trained to obtain marketable skills that will make her self-supporting. It can also serve as restitution to reimburse a party who worked to put the former spouse through school. A woman who works to put her husband through medical school, for example, may be awarded restitutive alimony if she was never able to reap the rewards of her sacrifice because of their divorce. Alternatively, many courts take the value of the advanced degree into consideration when dividing the marital property.

The amount of alimony awarded is highly discretionary, although most states have guidelines for judges to follow. Generally, the amount awarded is based on the recipient's need and the paying spouse's ability to pay. Additional factors listed in the Uniform Marriage and Divorce Act follow.

◆ standard of living during marriage
◆ length of marriage

NET NEWS

To see the factors each state considers in awarding alimony, go to *www.abanet.org/family/familylaw/table1.html*.

For more information about alimony in general, go to *www.nolo.com/category/div home.html* and click on "Property Division and Alimony."

Figure 10-5
Types of Alimony

TYPES OF ALIMONY

Permanent
Obligation remains until either party dies or remarries
(or in some states, cohabits)

Rehabilitative
Assists spouse in attaining financial independence

Restitutive
Reimburses spouse for efforts during marriage

◆ LOCAL LINKS ◆
What factors do the courts in your state consider when awarding alimony?

- age, physical, and emotional condition of recipient
- legal obligations of spouse paying alimony to another family created by a previous divorce
- child-rearing responsibilities that make a return to the work-force impracticable

If the spouse paying alimony fails to make payments, the receiving spouse can petition the court asking that the offending spouse be found in contempt of court.

▰ *Putting It Into Practice 10.5:*

Hannah was married to Samuel for 30 years. During that time, Hannah never worked; she raised their five children and is currently raising one of their grandchildren, who is five. She has no interest in working or pursuing a career. Samuel is a highly successful marketing consultant. Do you think Hannah, who is 50-years-old, should be given alimony? Defend your response.

PROPERTY DIVISION

separate property   all property owned prior to marriage and all property acquired during marriage by gift, inheritance, or personal earnings

equitable distribution
dividing of property in accord with the principles of equity (fairness)

The majority of states are considered **separate property** states in that they classify all property owned prior to marriage and all property acquired during marriage by gift, inheritance, or personal earnings (without the contribution of the other spouse) as separate property. When property is divided at divorce, the courts in these states award separate property to the respective parties before deciding how to divide the marital property. Marital property is then divided in accordance with the doctrine of **equitable distribution.** The courts consider the following factors when dividing property equitably.

- income potential of each party
- contribution of each party in acquiring the property
- length of the marriage
- age and health of the parties
- needs of minor children and the custodial parent

community property
property acquired during marriage by personal earnings as well as property owned prior to marriage but contributed to marriage

In a minority of states (nine, at the date of this publication) that are considered **community property** states, property acquired by either spouse during marriage by personal earnings is considered marital property. Property that is gifted to or inherited by one spouse, remains separate property. During a divorce proceeding in these states, the court isolates all separate property and then divides the community property equally. This classification of property as separate or community property

commingled property having attributes of both marital and separate property

becomes more complicated when the property has been **commingled,** that is, when property has attributes of both separate property and marital property. If a wife has a savings account before she is married and she and her husband both make deposits to that account during their marriage, the savings account is commingled property. Courts vary in how they treat commingled property.

◆ **LOCAL LINKS** ◆

Do you live in a separate property or community property state?

Putting It Into Practice 10.6:

Assume that everything that Hannah and Samuel own is marital property. Argue on Hannah's behalf that she is entitled to half of the marital property even though she has never worked outside the home in their 30 years of marriage.

In either separate property or community property states, the situation will arise in which property cannot simply be divided between the parties. A house, for example, cannot be split in half. In such cases, courts routinely require that the property be sold and that the proceeds be equitably distributed. Alternatively, a court may order that a percentage of the appraised value of the house be given to the spouse not residing there. This payment may be in the form of cash or in something of comparable value.

To better understand the practical implications of dividing property, read the case of *Gastineau v. Gastineau.* Notice how the court must determine what the marital assets are, who contributed to the creation of those assets, and how those assets were dissipated before deciding how the assets should be equitably distributed.

Cite as: 151 Misc.2d 813, 573 N.Y.S.2d 819

Supreme Court, Suffolk County, New York.
Lisa **GASTINEAU,** Plaintiff,
v.
Marcus **GASTINEAU,** Defendant.
June 21, 1991.

H. PATRICK LEIS, III, Justice.

This action for divorce, equitable distribution and other ancillary relief was tried on February 25, 28, March 5, and 6, 1991. The Plaintiff, Lisa Gastineau, is represented by counsel. The Defendant, Marcus Gastineau appeared pro se. A written summation was received from Plaintiff's counsel on March 13, 1991 and from Marcus Gastineau on April 3, 1991.

FACTS

The parties were married in December of 1979. This action was commenced in September 1986. Consequently, this is a marriage of short duration. The Plaintiff is thirty-one years old and the Defendant is thirty-four. The parties have one child, Brittany, born on 11/6/82.

At the beginning of the trial the Plaintiff testified as to specific allegations of cruel and inhuman treatment allegedly committed by the Defendant. The Defendant

remained mute, neither admitting nor denying these allegations. The Court thereupon granted the Plaintiff a divorce based on cruel and inhuman treatment. . . .

The parties married just after Marc Gastineau had been drafted by the New York Jets to play professional football. The Plaintiff, at that time, was a sophomore at the University of Alabama. The Plaintiff never completed her college education, nor did she work during the course of the marriage.

In 1982, when Britanny was born, the parties purchased a house in Huntington, New York for $99,000.00. In addition to the purchase price, the Plaintiff and Defendant spent another $250,000.00 for landscaping and other renovations. This money came from the Defendant's earnings as a professional football player.

According to the uncontroverted testimony of the Plaintiff, in 1979 (the Defendant's first year in professional football) the Defendant earned a salary of $55,000.00.

In his second year, 1980, the Defendant's salary was approximately $75,000.00. In 1981 it was approximately $95,000.00 and in 1982 he earned approximately $250,000.00. The Defendant's tax returns (which were not available for the years 1979 through 1982) indicate that the Defendant earned $423,291.00 in 1983, $488,994.00 in 1984, $858,035.00 in 1985, $595,127.00 in 1986, $953,531.00 in 1987 and in 1988, his last year with the New York Jets, his contract salary was $775,000.00 plus $50,000.00 in bonuses. It must be noted that in most years the Defendant earned monies in excess of his contract salary as a result of promotions, advertisements and bonuses.

In 1985 the parties purchased a home in Scottsdale, Arizona for $550,000.00. During the course of the parties' marriage Plaintiff and Defendant acquired many luxury items including a power boat, a BMW, a Corvette, a Rolls Royce, a Porche, a Mercedes and two motorcycles. They continually had a housekeeper who not only cleaned the house but prepared the parties' meals. In addition, the parties frequently dined out at expensive restaurants. The Plaintiff testified that as a result of this life style she has become accustomed to buying only the most expensive clothes and going to the best of restaurants.

In 1988 the Defendant began an illicit relationship with Brigitte Nielsen. When Ms. Nielsen was diagnosed as having cancer the Defendant testified that he could no longer concentrate on playing football. At that time the Defendant was under contract with the New York Jets at a salary of $775,000.00. He left professional football in October 1988 (breaking his contract) after the sixth game of the 1988 season. The Defendant went to Arizona and remained with Ms. Nielsen while she underwent treatment for cancer.

Regardless of whether the Defendant wanted to be with his girl friend while she underwent treatment for cancer, he had a responsibility to support his wife and child. The Court cannot condone Mr. Gastineau's walking away from a lucrative football contract when the result is that his wife and child are deprived of adequate support.

According to the testimony adduced at trial, there are sixteen games per season in the NFL. Players are paid one-sixteenth of their contract salary at the end of each game. Based on the Defendant's salary for 1988 ($775,000.00), he received $48,437.00 per game. The Defendant played six games in the 1988 season and received approximately $290,622.00 plus $50,000.00 in bonuses. He was entitled to an additional $484,437.00 for the ten games remaining in the season. This Court finds that by walking away from his

1988-89 contract with the NFL the Defendant dissipated a marital asset in the amount of $484,437.00.

Whether or not the Defendant would have been offered a contract by the New York Jets for the 1989/90 football season if he had not broken his 1988/89 contract is pure speculation. In professional football there are no guarantees. Variables such as age, how an athlete plays, the ability of other players seeking to fill his position, as well as possible injuries sustained during the season, make it impossible to determine with certainty whether or not the Defendant would have been re-signed by the New York Jets had he finished the 1988/89 season. It must also be noted that there has been no testimony offered by the Plaintiff to establish that the Defendant would have been re-signed by the New York Jets for the 1989/90 season had he not broken his contract.

The speculative nature of the Defendant's future in professional football is highlighted by the fact that in 1989 he tried out for the San Diego Chargers, the LA Raiders and the Minnesota Vikings, without success. The New York Jets also refused to offer him a contract. In 1990 the Defendant did acquire a position with the British Colombia Lions in the Canadian Football League at a salary of $75,000.00. He was cut, however, less than half way through the season. The Defendant played five of the 18 scheduled games and was paid approximately $20,000.00. The Defendant's performance in the Canadian Football League lends credence to his claim that he no longer has the capacity to earn the monies that he once made as a professional football player. Under these circumstances the Court is limited to considering the dissipation of a marital asset valued at $484,437.00, to wit: the remaining amount of money that the Defendant was eligible to collect pursuant to his 1988/89 contract.

While Defendant admits that he has name recognition, he claims that his name has a negative rather than a positive connotation. The Defendant testified that because of his antics on the field (such as his victory dance after sacking a quarterback), the fact that he crossed picket lines during the NFL player's strike and because he walked away from his professional football career, his name has no value for promotions or endorsements. There has been no evidence presented to the contrary by the Plaintiff.

The Defendant testified that his chances of obtaining employment with a professional football team are almost nil. Although he is presently attempting to obtain a position at a Jack LaLanne Health Spa he could not provide details as to the potential salary. The Defendant has also attempted to enter professional boxing. No testimony has been elicited by the Plaintiff, however, as to the Defendant's financial potential as a professional boxer. Since the Defendant left professional football he has not worked or earned any money (except for the $20,000.00 that he earned when he played football in Canada). According to the Defendant, Ms. Nielsen paid for all of the Defendant's expenses during the period of time that they lived together.

* * * * * *

After the Defendant failed to appear for a number of court dates and also failed to comply with this Court's *pendente lite* order, the Court directed that the Defendant's NFL severance pay be sequestered pursuant to DRL § 243 and the Plaintiff be appointed receiver and sequestrator of said funds (which amounted to approximately $83,000.00 after deducting taxes).

According to Plaintiff the entire $83,000.00 (reflecting the Defendant's total net severance pay from the NFL) was spent by her as follows: Thirty-two thousand dollars ($32,000.00) was used to pay mortgage arrears on the Huntington house (which still has approximately $15,000.00 outstanding in arrears), $22,000.00 went to the Plaintiff's attorneys, $15,000.00 went to repay loans taken out by the Plaintiff to pay necessary expenses and the rest, approximately $14,000.00, went for landscaping, medical insurance, electricity, fuel oil, telephone bills, dental and doctor bills.

* * * * * *

PRIMARY MARITAL ASSETS

With all of the money that the Defendant earned throughout the course of his professional football career he has retained only three significant marital assets. (1) The Huntington house, which has been valued at approximately $429,000.00 and has an outstanding mortgage of $150,000.00. (2) A house located in the state of Arizona which was purchased for approximately $550,000.00 and has a $420,000.00 mortgage (which in all probability will be sold at foreclosure); (3) The Defendant's severance pay from the NFL of approximately $83,000.00.

It is clear that the Defendant has also dissipated a marital asset worth approximately $324,573.00 (to wit: $484,437.00 the Defendant was entitled to receive pursuant to his 1988/89 contract tax effected by 33%, reflecting approximate federal and state income tax). Although neither the Plaintiff nor the Defendant attempted to tax effect this dissipated marital asset, it is clear that the Defendant would not have actually received $484,437.00 had he finished the 1988/89 season. The Court therefore, on its own, has tax effected this amount by 33%, approximately what the Defendant would have

paid in federal and state taxes had he actually received the $484,437.00. In this regard the Court has considered the tax returns of the parties (which are in evidence) with reference to their tax consequences and takes judicial notice of the fact that compensation for service constitutes income . . . which is taxable . . .

* * * * * *

EQUITABLE DISTRIBUTION

It is a guiding principle of equitable distribution that parties are entitled to receive equitable awards which are proportionate to their contributions, whether direct or indirect, to the marriage . . . In this case, the Plaintiff testified that during the course of the marriage she supervised the renovations made on the Huntington house, traveled with the Defendant wherever he trained and, with the assistance of a full-time nanny, raised and cared for their child.

This is not a long term marriage, and there has been minimal testimony elicited concerning the Plaintiff's direct or indirect contributions to the Defendant's acquisition of marital assets. Although it was the Defendant's own athletic abilities and disciplined training which made it possible for him to obtain and retain his position as a professional football player, equity dictates, under the facts of this case, that the Plaintiff receive *one-third of the marital assets*. The Defendant's decision to voluntarily terminate his contract with the New York Jets, depriving Plaintiff and the parties' child of the standard of living to which they had become accustomed, his failure to obtain meaningful employment thereafter and the indirect contributions made by the Plaintiff during the course of the marriage warrant an award to the Plaintiff of one third of the parties' marital assets. The Court is also mindful of the fact that during the years of the Defendant's greatest productivity, the Plaintiff enjoyed the fruits of Defendant's labors to the fullest . . ., unlike the landmark *O'Brien* case (*O'Brien v. O'Brien*, 66 N.Y.2d 576, 498 N.Y.S.2d 743, 489 N.E.2d 712 (1985)), where a newly licensed professional discarded his wife after she provided years of contributions to the attainment of his medical license.

There are only two marital assets to be considered in granting Plaintiff her one-third distributive award, (1) the Huntington house, and (2) the $324,573.00 dissipated marital asset. The Arizona house has no equity.

The Huntington house is valued at $429,000.00. It has a $150,000.00 mortgage with $15,000.00 owed in back mortgage payments. It thus has an equity of $264,000.00. One third of the equity would entitle the Plaintiff to $87,120.00. When one adds $107,109.00

(1/3 of the $324,573.00 tax effected marital asset which was dissipated), the Plaintiff would be entitled to $194,229.00. This would encompass Plaintiff's 1/3 distributive award of the parties' sole remaining marital asset (the Huntington house) and her 1/3 share of the marital asset dissipated by the Defendant. If one adds this $194,229.00 to the arrears owed by the Defendant on the pendente lite order ($71,707.00) Plaintiff could be awarded the total equity ($264,000.00) in the Huntington house in full satisfaction of her one-third distributive award of the parties' marital assets and still have approximately $1,936.00 remaining as a credit. The Court awards Plaintiff the Huntington house and grants her a Judgment for $1,936.00 for the remaining arrears owed to her.

Neither side has offered proof as to the present value of the Arizona house or the extent of arrears on mortgage payments . . . It would appear however, that there is no equity remaining in the Arizona house. The Court awards the Arizona house to the Defendant. The Court directs that each party take whatever steps are required to effect the transfer of the deed to the real property awarded to the other party so as to convey title to said property in said other's name alone.

Putting It Into Practice 10.7:

(a) Why did the defendant walk away from his football career? (b) Why does the court not consider the defendant's future football career and his name recognition as marital assets? (c) What three marital assets does the court conclude exist? (d) Why does the court order that the defendant's severance pay be sequestered? (e) What does the court conclude is an equitable distribution of the parties' assets? (f) On what basis does the court arrive at that distribution?

Certain types of property interests merit special attention. Benefits from pension plans and employee benefit plans are subject to some division upon divorce. If one spouse acquired an interest in a pension or benefit plan during marriage, the other

Figure 10-6
Property Division Issues

PROPERTY DIVISION ISSUES

Property Classification
Is property marital property, separate property, or commingled?

Pensions and Benefits Plans
What is an equitable share for spouse who is not receiving this benefit?

Personal Injury Proceeds
What aspects are separate property and what aspects are marital property?

Advanced Degrees
Should a degree be part of the property to be divided or is it a factor to be considered when awarding alimony?

Debts
Which debts are considered joint debts?
What happens if the party responsible for payment of the debt does not pay?

NET NEWS

To see the factors that each state considers when dividing property, go to *www.abanet.org/family/familylaw/table5.html*. For ;more information about property division in general, go to *www.nolo.com/category/div home.html* and click on "Property Division and Alimony."

QDRO qualified domestic relations order that assigns some or all of a pension participant's benefits to a former spouse or child to satisfy family support or marital property obligations

spouse may have a right to a portion of the amount to be received under that plan. A court order that is considered a "qualified domestic relations order" (known as a **QDRO**, can assign some or all of a pension participant's benefits to a former spouse or child to satisfy family support or marital property obligations. Computation of that percentage is a dilemma for the courts. Because the divorce often occurs long before the benefits are received and because the spouse has not yet earned the maximum benefit possible, calculating what an equitable share of the benefit will be can be difficult.

In some states, professional degrees such as M.D., Ph.D., or J.D. may also be considered part of the property to be divided. When a degree is included in the marital property that is to be divided, it must be assigned a value, which requires expert testimony. Other states treat a degree as one of the factors to be considered in awarding alimony.

Some aspects of the proceeds from a personal injury claim are also considered marital property. The lost income (special damages) portion of a judgment is often considered marital property and is to be divided at divorce. The compensation for pain and suffering, on the other hand, is usually considered separate property and is not divisible at divorce.

The same tests that are applied to individual and marital property are also applied to individual and marital debts. Judges seek to distribute debt equitably between the parties, but several issues can arise. For example, is property purchased using a credit card a joint debt if the debt was incurred individually? The presumption is that even debts taken on individually are joint debts if they were incurred during marriage because the debt presumably benefited both parties. You may be surprised to know that if a spouse who is determined by the court to be responsible for paying a debt fails to honor that responsibility, the creditor can collect from the other spouse. The rationale is that the creditor is not a party to the distribution of debts and is therefore not constrained by any court order. To prevent this from happening (which, as you might expect, occurs quite regularly), divorce decrees should provide reimbursement to a spouse who pays a debt for which the other spouse was responsible.

◆ **LOCAL LINKS** ◆

What do the courts in your state consider when dividing property?

RECESS

SUMMARY– PART A

The marriage contract must be entered into knowingly and voluntarily by people of legal age who have obtained a marriage license. A blood test is often required and, in some states, a waiting period is required before a license will be granted. A void marriage can be annulled without proof, but a voidable marriage requires proof of a defect before it can be annulled.

Parties who have children from a previous marriage or substantial property of their own may want to sign an antenuptial agreement prior to marriage. Most states favor such agreements as long as they do not violate public policy and both parties make full disclosure of their financial assets. Courts increasingly favor postnuptial agreements and separation agreements as well.

In the time period between the filing of a divorce and the issuing of the final decree, questions may arise that require judicial intervention. This intervention can be sought through a motion or pleading requesting interlocutory relief (also referred to as *pendente lite* or *nisi* relief). If an interlocutory hearing (sometimes called an order to show cause hearing) is required, the judge will evaluate the evidence presented by both parties and render a decision that will temporarily resolve the matter. In matters involving domestic violence, a party who is in immediate danger may request an *ex parte* hearing and ask the court to issue a temporary restraining order (TRO), also known as a protective order or order of protection. Those who violate a TRO can be fined, incarcerated, or both.

Traditionally, parties had to establish statutory grounds for divorce. Under the terms of today's no-fault divorce, spouses need only claim irreconcilable differences. Some states, however, have added requirements, such as lengthy separations or mediation, to no-fault divorces. A divorce is initiated by the filing of a petition or complaint accompanied by financial affidavits. Courts have jurisdiction if one of the parties resides in the forum state (usually for a specified time), if the marriage was formalized in that state, or if the grounds for divorce occurred while the parties resided in that state. In some states, the parties are required to utilize some form of alternative dispute resolution to resolve their differences and in others they are required to attend parenting classes. If the parties are able to resolve their differences, they can submit a settlement agreement to the court; otherwise they must submit to the will of the court. One of the consequences of divorce is losing the right to make major life decisions without court intervention. Another is a decline in the standard of living, particularly for women and children.

Attorneys should generally advise spouses seeking divorce that they should have separate representation and in some states attorneys are absolutely forbidden from representing both spouses. In an uncontested divorce, an attorney can, in a state whose ethical rules permit it, represent both parties. Both parties must consent (after the ramifications of joint representation have been fully explained), they must first resolve all the relevant issues, and the attorney must reasonably believe such representation will not adversely affect either party. Attorneys who have represented a couple in previous litigation cannot represent one of the spouses in a subsequent divorce if the attorney gained confidential information from one spouse that could be used to the detriment of the other spouse.

Alimony is based on the relative assets and financial requirements of each party. In light of women's increased economic independence, alimony is more often awarded on a short-term rehabilitative basis than on a permanent basis, although it can be awarded for restitutive purposes. Most states have detailed guidelines judges must follow in awarding alimony.

In separate property states, property is divided in accord with the doctrine of equitable distribution. In the minority of states that are community property states, marital property is divided equally at divorce. In either separate property or community property states, property that cannot be divided is sold and the proceeds are equitably distributed or a percentage of the assessed value of the property is given to one spouse while the other spouse is paid in cash or something of comparable value. Dividing the benefits from pension plans can be problematic. In some states, professional degrees are considered marital property that must be divided or considered as one of the factors in determining alimony or division of property. Some aspects of the proceeds from personal injury claims are considered marital property and must be divided. Debt must be distributed equitably, but if the spouse who a court determines is responsible for a debt does not honor this responsibility, the creditor can collect from the other spouse.

KEY TERMS

Alimony

Annulment

Antenuptial agreement/prenuptial agreement

Commingled

Community property

Covenant marriage

Domestic relations law

Equitable distribution

Ex parte

Interlocutory relief/ *pendente lite/ nisi* relief

Joint custody

No-fault divorce

Order of protection/ protective order

Order to show cause hearing

Postnuptial agreement

Protective order

QDRO (qualified domestic relations order)

Separate property

Separation agreement

Settlement agreement

Show cause order

Spousal maintenance (support)

TRO temporary restraining order

REVIEW QUESTIONS – PART A

1. What are the typical requirements of getting married?
2. Under what conditions is the marriage contract void? Under what conditions is it voidable?
3. What is the difference between an annulment and a divorce? How is a marriage that is void treated differently than one that is voidable for purposes of getting an annulment?
4. Under what conditions will a court uphold antenuptial agreements and postnuptial agreements?
5. What is the difference between a postnuptial agreement and a separation agreement?
6. What kinds of interlocutory relief are available to parties who have initiated a divorce? Why might such relief be necessary?
7. What is an *ex parte* hearing and why might it be allowed? Under what circumstances might a judge order a TRO or order of protection? What are the consequences of violating these orders?
8. What must parties do to get a no-fault divorce? Why do some people choose a fault-based divorce?
9. What problems may arise when divorcing spouses are represented by the same attorney?
    a. Under what conditions is common representation allowed?
    b. When is an attorney who represented a couple prohibited from representing one of the spouses in a subsequent divorce?
10. Describe the procedures that parties are commonly required to follow to obtain a divorce.
    a. On what basis can a court have jurisdiction over a divorce proceeding?
    b. Why might parties benefit from entering into a settlement agreement?
11. What are the potential side-effects of divorce?
12. For what purposes is alimony awarded? How has alimony changed over time?
13. What is the difference between separate property and community property states?
    a. How do they divide property differently?
    b. What problems arise in dividing the benefits from pension plans and employee benefit plans?
    c. How are advanced degrees divided in some cases?
    d. What should debtors who are divorced know about the debts they incurred during marriage?

PRACTICE EXAM – PART A

MULTIPLE CHOICE

1. In all states, the requirements for marriage include:
    a. a blood test
    b. a license
    c. a waiting period
    d. requirements are different in every state
2. A marriage will be denied if
    a. either of the parties lacks legal capacity
    b. the parties have a degree of kinship prohibited by state law
    c. one of them is already married
    d. all of the above
3. A marriage is void
    a. if one of the parties is under age
    b. if it is entered into fraudulently
    c. if the formal requirements for marriage are not honored
    d. all of the above
4. With an annulment
    a. the courts recognize that marriage existed but then terminate its existence
    b. support obligations still exist
    c. no marriage ever existed
    d. child support is never required
5. Antenuptial agreements
    a. will not be enforced by some courts if they anticipate divorce
    b. set forth the terms of marriage but not of divorce
    c. are particularly relevant to young couples who have few financial assets
    d. allow parties to waive claims of child support
6. Interlocutory relief
    a. is also known as *pendente lite* relief
    b. can be provided *ex parte* in the case of TROs
    c. may be provided at an order to show cause hearing
    d. all of the above
7. An interlocutory hearing
    a. is always scheduled immediately after it is requested by a party
    b. requires the defendant to show cause why the temporary relief requested by the plaintiff should not be granted
    c. requires little preparation
    d. none of the above

8. A TRO
   a. will not be issued on an *ex parte* basis
   b. is also known as an order to show cause
   c. is appropriate when a judge believes immediate protection is called for
   d. is rarely used in cases of domestic violence

9. No-fault divorce
   a. requires that parties prove the grounds for their divorce, such as adultery, drunkenness, or cruelty
   b. is generally granted more often than fault-based divorce
   c. requires that parties prove they have irreconcilable differences
   d. none of the above

10. Attorneys
    a. can never in any state represent both spouses in a divorce
    b. may be able to represent both spouses in a divorce
    c. can never represent one spouse in a divorce if they have represented the couple in previous litigation
    d. can continue to represent both spouses in a divorce even if a conflict arises between them

11. Attorneys can represent both parties in a divorce
    a. if they reasonably believe joint representation will not adversely affect either party
    b. as long as the parties have already resolved some issues
    c. if the parties have been generally informed about the ramifications of joint representation
    d. all of the above

12. To initiate a divorce proceeding
    a. both parties must reside in the state in which the petition is filed
    b. the party initiating the divorce must establish the grounds of fault on which the divorce is based
    c. one of the parties must file a petition or complaint accompanied by financial affidavits
    d. all of the above

13. After a divorce has been initiated
    a. some states require parents to attend parenting classes
    b. some states require the parties to mediate issues pertaining to property division, child support, and child custody
    c. a hearing is often scheduled to provide interlocutory relief
    d. all of the above

14. Some of the consequences of divorce may include
    a. loss of autonomy regarding major life decisions
    b. a decline in the standard of living
    c. a strain on the welfare system
    d. all of the above

15. Alimony
    a. is based on the financial needs and assets of the parties
    b. is almost always paid by the ex-husband
    c. is usually paid on a permanent basis
    d. is not designed to reimburse former spouses who put their partners through school

16. Alimony can be
    a. permanent, in which case it continues even when the receiving spouse remarries
    b. rehabilitative in that it is designed to make the receiving spouse independent
    c. restitutive in that it compensates the receiving spouse for enduring a painful marriage
    d. all of the above

17. Alimony
    a. can be based on the age and physical condition of the receiving spouse but not on the length of marriage
    b. cannot be based on the standard of living during the marriage
    c. can be based on whether child-rearing makes a return to the work-force impracticable
    d. is not affected by the legal obligations of the spouse paying alimony to another family created by a previous divorce

18. Under the doctrine of equitable distribution, the factors to be considered when dividing property
    a. include the needs of minor children
    b. include the age but not the health of the parties
    c. include the contribution of each party to the marriage, but not the income potential of each party
    d. do not include the length of the marriage

19. Benefits from pension plans and employee benefits plans
    a. are not property that the other spouse is entitled to share
    b. are relatively easy to compute
    c. are difficult to evaluate because the spouse earning them has not accrued the maximum benefit at the time of the divorce
    d. none of the above

20. Property that is never considered marital property includes
    a. debts incurred by one or both spouses
    b. proceeds from personal injury claims
    c. professional degrees
    d. all of the above can be marital property

21. Debt that exists at the time of divorce
    a. is presumed to be joint debt even if it was incurred individually during the marriage
    b. and that is assigned by the court to one spouse to pay can be collected by the creditor from the other spouse if the spouse assigned the debt fails to pay
    c. is divided equitably between the parties
    d. all of the above

FILL IN THE BLANK

22. An _____ means that the marriage never existed.

23. People who own substantial property or who have children from a previous marriage may want to have their partner sign a(n) _____ before marriage. If they enter into a similar agreement after marriage, in which they address financial and related matters, it is called a _____, and if they enter into an agreement regarding the terms of their anticipated separation, it is called a _____ agreement.

24. Parties wanting judicial intervention to resolve questions in the time period between their filing for divorce and their obtaining a final divorce decree may seek _____ (also known as _____) relief.

25. A _____ order requires a party to explain to the court why the temporary relief requested by the other spouse should not be granted.

26. If the threat of harm to a spouse is imminent, a party may allow an _____ hearing at which only one side presents evidence. If the judge is convinced that the party is in danger, she may issue a _____, also known as _____.

27. After a divorce is initiated, parties who are able to resolve all the issues pertaining to their property and children can sign a _____, which sets forth the rights and obligations of the parties.

28. _____ (also called _____) is the payment of support made by a former spouse to benefit the other former spouse.

29. In _____ property states, all property acquired before marriage and all property acquired during marriage by gift, inheritance, or personal earnings is considered individual property. In these states, marital property is divided in accordance with the doctrine of _____ at divorce. In _____ property states, all property acquired during marriage by personal earnings and all property individually owned prior to marriage is considered marital property and is divided equitably at divorce. The classification of property becomes more difficult when it has been _____ (mixed together).

TRUE OR FALSE

____ 30. The marriage contract is no different than any other contract.

____ 31. Same-sex marriages are now allowed in most states.

____ 32. The purpose of requiring a waiting period before issuing a marriage license is to encourage the parties to reflect on the seriousness of what they are doing.

____ 33. The only reason for requiring a blood test for couples planning on marrying is so they will be aware of their partner's blood type in case they decide to have children.

____ 34. A voidable marriage is null and void on its face.

____ 35. Antenuptial and postnuptial agreements are generally disfavored by the courts.

____ 36. An antenuptial agreement will not be enforced if it violates public policy or was agreed to under duress.

____ 37. Many jurisdictions require parties to mediate their dispute before they can file for interlocutory relief.

____ 38. Paralegals often assist clients in preparing for interlocutory hearings.

____ 39. Violation of a TRO can result in a fine but not incarceration.

____ 40. Many courts issue mutual restraining orders when parties file a complaint to divorce.

____*41. Nearly 5 million intimate partner rapes and physical assaults occur against women each year.

____*42. Research shows that stalking by intimate partners is far less prevalent than once believed.

____*43. Most violence by intimate partners is reported to the police.

____*44. Having a verbally abusive partner is the strongest predictor that a woman will be victimized by an intimate partner.

____ 45. Under the no-fault divorce approach, parties do not need to claim that the other spouse unilaterally broke the marriage bond but those who enter into a covenant marriage must prove certain statutorily-defined conditions exist.

____ 46. Some states require couples to go through a court-monitored mediation before applying for a no-fault divorce.

____ 47. Attorneys cannot represent both parties in a divorce if a conflict between the parties arises.

____ 48. An attorney who represents a couple cannot ethically represent one of the spouses in a subsequent divorce if he gleaned confidential information from one spouse that could be used to the detriment of the other spouse.

____ 49. Attorneys find it easy to represent both parties drawing up an antenuptial agreement because conflicts of interest rarely occur.

____ 50. Jurisdiction may exist in the state where a marriage was formalized or where the grounds for divorce occurred.

____ 51. In most states, the party filing for divorce must be a resident of the state, but usually no specified time period of residency is required.

____ 52. A divorce decree entered where the court lacks jurisdiction to resolve issues pertaining to the marital assets should be registered with the court that has jurisdiction over the parties and those assets.

____ 53. Despite the equal rights movement, husbands do not have the same right to receive alimony as wives do.

____ 54. Most states provide little guidance to judges in their awarding of alimony.

____ 55. Modification of an award of alimony is allowed if the petitioner can prove that the original award was unprincipled.

____ 56. If the spouse paying alimony fails to make payments, the receiving spouse can ask a court to find the offending spouse in contempt of court.

____ 57. When courts have to split property that cannot be divided (such as a house), their only option is to sell the property and divide the proceeds equitably.

____ 58. A professional degree can either be considered as part of the marital property or as a factor to consider when awarding alimony.

____*59. Lost income from a personal injury claim is always considered separate property.

____*60. Debt incurred individually is presumed to be a joint debt when debts are being divided at the time of divorce.

____ 61. Divorce decrees should provide for reimbursement to a spouse who pays a debt for which the other spouse was responsible.

____ 62. A qualified domestic relations order (QDRO) allows a spouse to protect his stock investments and prevent the other spouse from receiving any benefits.

* Questions taken from Bonus Pointers

PART B

"In Light of This Situation with George, I'm Afraid I'm Going to Have to Dip Into the Trust Fund Just to Make Ends Meet."

"All right, Martha, let me make sure I understand what you're looking for," summarized Letitia. "You want to know how the courts would likely respond to your ex-husband's request to stop paying child support while he attends medical school. You'd like Ms. Esparanza to give you an idea about how to create a win-win situation for you and your ex regarding child support during this interim period. Additionally, you'd like to talk to her about George's request that you be responsible for selling the marital home, in which he's been residing since your divorce."

"Yes, but there is one thing I didn't mention yet. My parents created a trust in my name that I have always intended to use for the girls' college education. Now, in light of this situation with George, I'm afraid I'm going to have to dip into the trust fund just to make ends meet. George doesn't think there's anything wrong with my doing this, but I don't think I should be put in this position."

"And you'd like to get Ms. Esparanza's take on this," anticipated Letitia.

Martha nodded her head in concurrence as Letitia continued writing.

"All right. You've got a lot to get settled here, so let's get Ms. Esparanza in here right away." Letitia disappeared momentarily. When she reappeared, she signaled Martha to follow her.

"So nice to finally meet you, Martha. I'm Corazon Esparanza." Corazon came around from behind her desk and began shaking Martha's hand enthusiastically. "I've heard such wonderful things about you from Ernesto. He's so impressed with you, you know."

"Really," was all Martha could get out before Corazon continued her amiable monologue, working her way back toward her chair as she talked.

"Of course, you don't know. How could you? He'd never tell you such a thing. Just like he's probably never told you much about my work. Don't get me wrong: Ernesto is very proud of what I do, but he'd prefer I get a job in a 'real' firm doing 'important' legal work," explained Corazon, grinning as she accentuated her words with quotation marks in the air. Leaning forward, she continued in mock hushed tones, "Bet you don't know, though, that he's a done a ton of *pro bono* work for us here."

"No, I didn't" responded Martha, shaking her head. This Ernesto is turning out to be quite an enigma, she mused.

As if reading Martha's thoughts, Corazon said, "Yep, the 'rain maker' himself—a closet do-gooder." She laughed and then added in a bit more serious tone, "Don't put that man of mine in a box, Martha. He won't fit."

"I can see that," Martha agreed.

Glancing up at the clock, Corazon pulled herself up in her chair, looked down at the papers on her desk, and prepared herself to address Martha's questions. "I'd love to spend more time getting to know you, Martha, but you have a hectic schedule and so do I, so we'd best get to seeing what we can do to help you out of the pickle you're in." Corazon began by summarizing what she thought the issues were as Letitia had presented them to her. When she was sure she had a good grasp of the issues that needed to be resolved, she began by addressing the question of custody of Martha's girls.

CHILD CUSTODY

physical custody parent with whom a child lives

legal custody parent responsible for making decisions regarding a child's welfare

sole custody having both physical and legal custody

split custody arrangement in which one parent has legal and physical custody for part of the year and the other parent has custody for the remainder of the year; can also involve splitting the children between the parents

Issues relating to child custody, visitations, and child support are often the most contentious aspects of a divorce. Preserving the parent-child relationship, especially in light of the disintegration of the family unit, is a fundamental goal of the courts. After all, the role of parenting continues even after the role of spouse has been abandoned.

An examination of custody requires an understanding of basic terminology. Custody is both physical and legal. **Physical custody** refers to the parent with whom the child will live whereas **legal custody** refers to the parent(s) who will be responsible for making decisions relating to the child's well-being, such as educational and health-care related issues. A parent who has **sole custody** of a child has both physical and legal custody. Parents often have joint (or shared) legal custody, giving them both the right to make decisions regarding the child's welfare even though one parent has physical custody. Joint physical custody is also possible, requiring the child to live part of the time with each parent. If a parent has **split custody,** as is often the case when the parents live in different states, one parent has physical and legal custody for part of the year (e.g., during the school year), and the other parent assumes that custody for the remainder of the year. Split custody also refers to those unusual situations in which the court splits the children between the parents, awarding custody of some children to one parent and the remaining children to the other parent. In a family with a 4-year-old girl and a 14-year-old boy, for example, split custody may be the most appropriate solution because of the contrasting parenting needs of the two children.

Historically, children, especially those in their "tender years" (pre-teens), were more likely to be placed with the mother, who was presumably more nurturing.

With the equal rights movement, this presumption has disappeared. Theoretically, fathers now have an equal right to be awarded custody of their children, and several groups today support fathers in their quest for custody. Now that women are better able to find a place in the work world, judges can no longer assume that they are unable to join the workforce. As a result, the best interests of the child has become the guiding standard for judges. Many courts do a case-by-case evaluation of which parent can better meet the needs and interests of the child.

The question of whether a parent's sexual orientation should be a significant factor in awarding the custody of children is a controversial issue today. As recently as 1996, a Florida judge awarded custody of an 11-year-old girl to her father, who had recently served eight years in prison for killing his first wife when the girl's mother admitted to living with a female partner. The judge argued that the girl should be given the "option to live in a non-lesbian world."[1] Although courts are more open today about allowing gay and lesbian parents custody, their odds of being granted custody are best when the heterosexual parent is unfit or absent.

Joint custody has replaced sole custody as the preferred custody scheme in many states, although some states are still adverse to it. Allowing both parents input into the raising of their children may be ideal, but it is impractical when ongoing animosity between the parents stands in the way of their being able to work things out for the best interests of their children. If parties appear incapable of setting aside their personal differences at least in relationship to their children, courts are reluctant to grant joint custody. Experience teaches that such parents will probably return to the court to mediate issues they cannot resolve, creating additional legal expenses for the parents and ongoing disruption for the children.

The following factors are considered in awarding custody.

- preserving a child's connections with community, school, and extended family members
- keeping siblings together
- ability to care for child personally (without excessive reliance on child-care facilities)
- ability to meet special needs of child
- immoral conduct that would directly affect child
- physical and mental health of all involved
- wishes of child

joint custody allows both parents input into the raising of their children

◆ **LOCAL LINKS** ◆
Is joint custody encouraged in your state?

◆ **LOCAL LINKS** ◆
What factors do the courts in your jurisdiction consider when determining custody of a child?

Putting It Into Practice 10.8:

Alexis and Nate have petitioned for divorce. They have three children, ranging in age from three to 15. Both parents work, but Nate works out of his home office and has more flexible hours than Alexis, who has a demanding job as a litigation paralegal. Because of her work hours, she would have to have child care for the three-year-old and after school care for the seven-year-old. Nate, on the other hand, could care for both of these children himself and is willing to do so. The oldest child wants to stay with her mother but does not want to be separated from the other two children. How would you arrange custody if you were the judge? Consider the child custody guidelines in your state in making this determination.

NET NEWS

To see the factors that each state considers when determining custody of a child, go to *www.abanet.org/family/familylaw/table2.html.*

To read more about child custody in general, go to the World Wide Legal Information Association at *www.wwlia.org/us-cus.htm* and to *www.nolo.com/category/div_home.html.* Click on "Child Custody and Visitation."

Not too many years ago, parents could thwart a court's custody order by taking the child to another state and seeking a judicial determination of custody in that state. Because the rules for awarding custody varied significantly from state to state, parents had a good chance of changing the outcome of the custody decision by doing this. To discourage such child snatching, to avoid jurisdictional conflicts among states, and to prevent re-litigation of jurisdictional decisions, every state has passed some form of the Uniform Child Custody Jurisdiction Act (UCCJA). The UCCJA provides a uniform basis for jurisdiction, establishes cooperation among the states in the enforcement of custody orders, and ensures that litigation regarding custody occurs in the state having the closest connections to the child and his family.

Although the issue of jurisdiction may seem abstract, it can have a huge practical impact on parties' lives. Consider the case of a 14-year-old Wisconsin girl, Stephanie Ray, who had contracted AIDS from her mother (who had been infected through a blood transfusion) at birth. Stephanie's mother died of an AIDS-related illness when Stephanie was five; she lived with her father until she was removed from his custody because of alleged neglect and alcohol abuse on his part. After visiting her paternal aunt and uncle in Arizona several times and living with them for a total of four years, Stephanie decided she wanted to stay in Arizona. She did not want to return home to live with her foster mother (her father's former girlfriend) or go to the AIDS shelter she thought the judge might send her to until her father was able to regain custody. Although two Arizona attorneys fought vigorously to prevent Stephanie from having to comply with a Wisconsin court order to return to Wisconsin, they were unable to do anything more than delay her return for a few months. What was it that prevented both the juvenile court and court of appeals panel who heard the case on an emergency basis from intervening? Lack of jurisdiction.[2]

BONUS POINTERS:

CHILD ABUSE AND NEGLECT

Historically, the state has been reluctant to intervene with parents' raising of their children. But when evidence points to abuse or neglect, the state is not only justified, it is compelled to intervene. Normally, such intervention begins when someone reports suspicious behavior. Teachers, doctors, and others entrusted with the care of children are obligated by law to report suspected abuse. Such reports give the state the power to investigate, beginning with a request for compliance followed by court-ordered examinations of the child and evaluations of the family. During this process, the child may be appointed a guardian *ad litem* to represent her interests. If the court determines that the child is in danger, it can require the child to be placed in foster care.

If a court has clear and convincing evidence that a parent is unfit, it can order a termination of parental rights. Because of the harsh consequences of this determination, courts reserve this outcome for the most egregious circumstances.

Corazon listened carefully to Martha's explanation about how she believed that allowing George to continue having joint legal custody of the girls when he no longer wanted to pay child support would be unfair. She began by assuring Martha that she thoroughly understood and appreciated her reasoning. Then Corazon suggested diplomatically that, while Martha was certainly reasonable in wanting sole custody, she might want to reflect on whether this was in the best interest of the girls and whether this arrangement would foster a healthy relationship between George and the girls. Having planted the seed, she moved on to the subject of visitation.

"Do you think George and you can work out a new visitation plan?" asked Corazon.

"I don't anticipate that being a problem," Martha assured her. "We've never had any problems with that in the past and we're both aware we're going to have to be pretty flexible to accommodate his and the girls' school schedules. The fact that George will be coming here to Phoenix on a fairly regular basis to see his folks will make it easier for him and the girls to get together."

VISITATION

In most cases, the non-custodial parent is given visitation rights. A court has the option of awarding "reasonable" visitation rights, but because parties often have trouble reaching consensus about what is "reasonable," many courts spell out the times and arrangements for visitation. Court-ordered visitation plans establish the minimum rights of the non-custodial parent, but the parties can later agree to more liberal terms. Child custody agreements, whether by agreement or court order, should specify which party is to transport the child, the exact times of visitation, and the notice that is required if visiting privileges are going to be denied or are not going to be exercised.

Because a custodial parent's move to another state can adversely affect the visitation privileges of the non-custodial parent, the latter has a right to challenge the relocation. Generally speaking, courts will not interfere with a custodial parent's relocation unless the non-custodial parent can prove that the move is not in the child's best interest. The court must then consider the advantages of the move for the child and custodial parent, the motives for the relocation, and the degree to which the visitation rights of the non-custodial parent must be modified to preserve that parent's relationship with the child.

A parent who fails to honor the requirements of a court-ordered visitation plan by not having the children available, by convincing the children to avoid visitation, or by out-and-out refusing to allow visitation, exposes herself to potential penalties. The non-custodial parent can bring an action for contempt of court, which, if successful, can result in a fine or incarceration. In extreme cases, the judge may change the custody order.

If a court is convinced that visitation could result in physical or emotional harm to the child, it may decide to limit or place conditions on the visitation. A judge can, for example, require that the visitation be supervised by a third party or confined to a specific location. A court can also limit visitation rights if the non-custodial parent is mentally ill or a substance abuser or has a history of infrequent visitations. In extreme cases, the court may deny visitation.

NET NEWS

To learn about the visitation rights of third parties on a state-by-state basis, go to *www.abanet.org/family/familylaw/table6.html.*

For more information about visitation in general, go to *www.nolo.com/category/div home.html* and click on "Child Custody and Visitation." In some states, visitation is also considered for grandparents, step-parents, unwed fathers, and others.

◆ **LOCAL LINKS** ◆

Who is allowed visitation rights in your state?

Putting It Into Practice 10.9:

Your friend and her husband are contemplating visitation rights as part of their separation agreement. Your friend believes that a provision for "reasonable visitation rights" for her husband, who is to be the non-custodial parent, should be acceptable. Explain why she might want to consider more clearly defining visitation rights and what you would suggest she include in their agreement.

"If I Could Figure Out a Way for George to Go to Medical School Without Adversely Affecting Me and the Girls, I'd be the First One to Encourage Him to Do This."

"So, let's move on to the issue of child support. That seems to be the matter that's really bothering you," suggested Corazon.

"I think it's the area we're furthest apart on," concurred Martha.

"Let me ask you outright, Martha. Are you opposed to George's getting another degree?" Corazon had picked up on Martha's emphasis to her that this would be George's third advanced degree and wondered if Martha might resent George's latest foray into higher education.

"Not at all," Martha responded emphatically. "George is extremely bright and I think he should explore as many avenues of learning as he can. I just don't think he should do it at our children's expense."

"Okay. I needed to know where you stood on that before I could make any suggestions. Are you willing to make any compromises or are you adamant about his making child support payments?"

"Let me put it this way. If I could figure out a way for George to go to medical school without adversely affecting me and the girls, I'd be the first one to encourage him to do this. But I don't think it's right for us to have to move or to make really drastic changes in our lifestyle just so he can go to school again."

"That's fair. Then let me suggest something for you to consider. What about the possibility of promising George you will not sue him for the next four years—long enough for him to get through medical school—for his child support payments? During that time, you could use the money from your family trust to help support you and the girls and to send them to college. In return, at an agreed upon time, George would be required to make monthly payments until such time as he had fulfilled the child support obligations he would have had if he had not gone to medical school. In addition, he will have to agree to waive a statute of limitations defense."

"What about the interest on the money he wouldn't be paying for those four years?"

"You could certainly require him to pay that as well," agreed Corazon.

Martha was quiet for a bit and Corazon did nothing to interrupt her reflection. After awhile, Martha said quietly, "This is something I'll need to think about, but it does open up some possibilities for both of us. The main thing I'm concerned about is whether I can support myself and the girls with the money I'm making plus the money from the trust. Let's suppose I could make ends meet with these two sources of income. What do I do if something happens to me and I can't work or if one of the girls or myself should get hurt or ill? I mean, our insurance will only cover so much." In the back of her mind, Martha was remembering the strain Mike's injury had put on his family financially.

"Good questions," agreed Corazon. "You obviously need to consider all these contingencies in any agreement you work out. What I wanted to offer you, however, was a possible resolution for you to think about before going into mediation. You're clearly willing to support George as long as what he's doing doesn't harm you, so I thought my proposal might present one possible solution."

"I appreciate your suggestion and I think it has some merit. What I need to do, though, is sit down with some actual figures and see if there's any realistic way this could work."

"Absolutely." Corazon was beginning to understand why her husband had so much respect for Martha. She observed that Martha, unlike many of her clients, did not dwell on the past events in her marriage. Practical and matter-of-fact, when faced with a possible solution, she immediately began examining the ramifications.

CHILD SUPPORT

When one parent serves as the primary care-giver and therefore provides more than her share of support, she is entitled to contribution from the other spouse. Mothers and fathers have an equal duty of support; if the father has custody of the children, the mother may be ordered to provide child support. Unwed fathers have a legal obligation to support their children just as adoptive parents have an obligation to support their adopted children.

Child support is a right that belongs to the child, not the parent. Therefore, a parent cannot waive the right to receive child support and that right does not terminate with the receiving parent's remarriage. The right to child support continues until the child reaches the age of majority (usually 18) or graduates from secondary school or, in some states, college. The obligation for child support may continue indefinitely for children who are physically or mentally unable to care for themselves.

The amount of child support awarded by a court is based on the child's need and the parent's ability to pay. The child's resources do not necessarily reduce the parent's obligations to provide support, however. If a child is the beneficiary of a trust established by his grandparents, for example, the child support awarded by the court will probably not be diminished.

Federal laws dictate that every state must develop child support guidelines for the courts to follow. These guidelines are designed to promote fairness and uniformity in the awarding of child support so that parties will receive comparable awards regardless of which judge issues the award. Courts can deviate from these guidelines under certain statutorily-defined extenuating circumstances. The format for these guidelines varies tremendously. Some merely outline an acceptable range of support while others specify exact computations based on such factors as the parents' incomes and the number of dependent children. In some states, courts must consider any special medical or educational needs of a child, the standard of living the child would have enjoyed had no divorce occurred, and whether one of the parents provides health insurance for the child.

> **◆ LOCAL LINKS ◆**
>
> Describe the guidelines that exist in your state regarding child support. What factors for determining child support are laid out in these guidelines?

Putting It Into Practice 10.10:

Charles has several theories about child support. Which of these theories is correct?

(a) He should not have to pay child support because he never married the mother of his child (although he acknowledges that the child is his).

(b) He should not have to pay child support because the grandparents of his child have established a trust that will provide for the child's needs.

(c) He should not have to pay child support because the mother of his child has just gotten married.

(d) Even if he does owe child support, his obligations will cease as soon as his child gets a part-time job after school.

(e) If a court determines he has to pay child support, how much he will have to pay will depend on the whims of that judge.

BONUS POINTERS:

TAX LAW

Tax laws can have a significant effect on the economic impact of a divorce. In divorces involving large sums of money, tax professionals should be consulted to advise the parties about their best strategies, but in all cases, family law practitioners must be familiar with the tax consequences of the advice they offer.

Here are some examples of tax law that affect a divorcing couple.

◆ Alimony is deductible from the payor's income, whereas child support is not.
◆ Alimony is included in the income of the payee, but child support is not.
◆ IIf certain criteria are met, the custodial parent has a right to claim dependency exemptions and enjoy the resulting tax benefits.
◆ Transfers of property incident to a divorce are not treated as taxable events and, therefore, are the equivalent of gifts between spouses, no matter what the intent.

Tax law is a specialty in and of itself. Paralegals who work in this area perform a variety of tasks.

◆ compiling the data required to prepare tax returns
◆ locating missing information
◆ assisting in the valuation of assets
◆ correcting returns based on new information
◆ calculating tax liability
◆ compiling supporting data for returns

Paralegals also find a knowledge of tax law helpful if they work in corporate, real estate, probate, or employee benefits law.

If the non-custodial parent fails to pay child support, the custodial parent can file an action requesting that the court find the non-paying parent in contempt of court. Parents who are found to be in contempt of court can be fined, have their wages garnished (although federal law now requires that the payors' employer be served with a wage assignment to ensure payment), or even jailed, if the contemptuous conduct has been ongoing. In some states, the license (drivers, professional, liquor, etc.) of the parent failing to pay child support can be revoked. Please note that child support and visitation are two separate issues. Courts do not condone the custodial parent's punishment of a non-paying parent by denying that parent visitation of the children.

CHILD SUPPORT ENFORCEMENT

Despite these measures, enforcement of child support continues to be a problem. In an effort to reduce the costs of welfare by cutting back on the payments made to single-parent families, both state and federal governments have stepped up efforts to collect child support arrearages. Under the Federal Enforcement Initiative of 1974, arrears that are collected are to be credited to welfare payments that have been made. In fact, applicants for Aid to Dependent Children (AFDC) must agree to assign their rights to uncollected child support to the state and must promise to assist in the collections process. Amendments to this Initiative require employers to withhold child support from the paychecks of employees in arrears and require

---

NET NEWS

To see the factors that govern the determination of child support in each state, go to *www.abanet.org/family/familylaw/table3.html*. For online access to the actual text of child support guidelines and information about child support enforcement in every state, go to *www.supportguidelines.com/main/html*. This site also has links to online child support calculations and to Chapter 1 of the treatise Child Support Guidelines: Interpretation and Application. This treatise contains a history of child support guidelines and a discussion of the implementation of each jurisdiction's guidelines. Excellent links to a number of legal research resources as well as resources for lay people are also available at this site.

NET NEWS

For more information about child support in general, go to *www.nolo.com/category/div_home.html* and click on "Child Support." To read the 1997 Census Bureau Report on child support across the United States, which indicates that the percentage of child support payments that were collected increased from 1993 until 1997, go to *www.census.gov/hhes/www/chldsupt.html.*

To read more about URESA, RURESA, and UIFSA, go to the World Wide Legal Information Association Web site at *www.wwlia.org/us-uifsa.htm.*

◆ **LOCAL LINKS** ◆

Has your state adopted URESA, RURESA, or UIFSA?

---

arrears in excess of $1,000 to be deducted from state and federal income tax refunds. Since 1988, new orders for child support or orders modifying child support must be automatically deducted from paychecks even if the payor is not in arrears.

The Uniform Reciprocal Enforcement of Support Act (URESA), its revised version (RURESA), and the Uniform Interstate Family Support Act (UIFSA) were created to assist in interstate enforcement of child support orders. These Acts solve the problem of personal jurisdiction when a child support debtor lives in a different state than the recipient creditor. All allow a child support order issued in one state to be enforced in another. A major difference in these Acts is that under URESA and RURESA, an enforcing state can modify an original child support order, whereas under UIFSA it cannot. The recipient of child support can bring an action in her own state that can then be tried in the state of the debtor, thereby saving the creditor the expense of traveling to the debtor's state. Because of these Acts, debtors can no longer flee to another state to avoid paying child support.

BONUS POINTERS:

PATERNITY ACTIONS

The collection of child support may be prevented if the mother is unable to establish the paternity of the child. The mother can file a paternity action, which is a civil action designed to establish the identity of the child's father and to create a legal obligation on the part of the father to support the child.

Paternity actions can also be filed by state agencies seeking reimbursement for funds paid to the child because of the father's failure to support the child. In fact, one focus of the welfare reform movement has been the identification of unwed fathers. Some states now require mothers to identify the father of their children as a qualifying condition for receiving welfare. The state may then actively search for the alleged father, requiring him to submit to DNA tests and to pay child support if paternity is established. Courts have the power to order DNA tests and a putative (alleged) father who refuses to cooperate can be held in contempt of court. The results of properly administered DNA tests for which a proper foundation has been laid are admissible at trial. Although such tests cannot affirmatively establish paternity, they can exclude paternity or establish a probability of paternity.

On the other hand, paternity actions also arise as a result of fathers seeking to share custody and/or establish visitation rights. In these cases, a paternity action establishes the plaintiff as the legally recognized father of the child. In some states, such fathers can sign a putative fathers' registry, entitling them to notification before a court can make any determinations regarding adoption.

A minority of states have adopted the Uniform Parentage Act (UPA). This Act establishes the procedures to be followed in paternity actions; the conducting of DNA tests; the establishing of custody, visitation, and child support; and the enforcing and modifying of any judgments obtained.

NET NEWS

To read more about child support enforcement efforts, go to *www.paralegals.org/Reporter/home.html,* click on "Summer 1995," and look for the article entitled "Going After the Deadbeats: Paralegals in Child Support Enforcement."

Figure 10-7
Child Support

CHILD SUPPORT

Enforcement Efforts

Federal law requires every state to develop guidelines
URESA, RURESA, and UIFSA prevent parents from leaving state
to avoid paying child support

Federal Enforcement Initiative of 1974 requires applicants for
AFDC to assist in collection efforts and Amendments require
employers to withhold child support payments from
employees' paychecks

Consequences of Failure to Pay

Fines

Jail

Wages garnished

Revocation of license

"How long has it been since you reviewed your child support figures?" Corazon continued. "If it's been a few years, you may very well be entitled to additional support, which is obviously something you'll want to consider in your negotiations with George."

"Good point. I'll certainly take a look at the numbers. But let me ask you something else. If we did take this child support issue to the courts, what do you predict would happen?"

"I never predict anything when it comes to the courts," smiled Corazon. "But I can tell you that many courts would not be very sympathetic to George's request. Probably the Arizona courts are more likely than many to allow George to adjust his child support payments long enough to pursue his educational goals. They would, of course, carefully scrutinize his reasons for making this request to ensure he had no ulterior motives."

MODIFICATION

If, after a final divorce decree is entered, the circumstances of the parties' lives change significantly, a modification in the decree may be justified. The modification may be in the amount of alimony or child support paid, the visitation rights of the non-custodial parent, or the physical and/or legal custody of the children. Some states have statutes that impose time limits on the filing of petitions for modification. They may, for example, prohibit the filing of such a petition within two years after the date of the divorce decree or after the previous attempt at modification. Without such laws, some litigious parties will be relentless in their pursuit of yet another modification.

In deciding whether a modification is warranted, the court must decide whether the alleged change is significant. If the financial status of either parent changes significantly, for example, a modification of an alimony award may be warranted. In some states, "live-in-lover" laws justify a decrease or elimination of

◆ **LOCAL LINKS** ◆

Do you have some type of "live-in-lover" laws in your state?

alimony payments if the party receiving the alimony is cohabiting with someone of the opposite sex and having sexual relations. The rationale is that allowing someone to continue receiving alimony in addition to being supported by another person is unjust. These laws apply to alimony only, not child support.

Child custody and visitation rights can also be modified if a significant change has affected the welfare of the child. A change in custody is warranted under the following conditions.

◆ One of the parents has remarried and can now provide a more suitable home for the child.
◆ The child prefers to live with the other parent and has reached an age (defined by statute) where this preference is considered.
◆ The custodial parent frequently moves.
◆ The custodial parent is using drugs or is having sexual relations that adversely affect the child.
◆ The child is exposed to violence or the threat of violence.

Modification of a visitation plan is justified when one of the parents moves or the custodial parent alleges that the non-custodial parent poses a physical or emotional threat to the child.

Property division is generally not subject to modification. One exception involves the marital residence. Exclusive possession of the marital residence may be awarded to one party while still permitting the parties, if they so desire, to maintain joint ownership of the home. This arrangement permits both parties to benefit from the building of equity, but will often need to be changed when one of the parties remarries or all the children reach the age of majority.

The court must also explore the reason for the change. A payor who takes a lesser paying job simply because he does not want to work as many hours will probably not be allowed to reduce his alimony or child support payments. On the other hand, a payor who changes jobs or reduces his hours for medical reasons will more likely be seen as having a legitimate reason to decrease his payments. George's request to stop paying child support while pursuing another advanced degree would be viewed differently in different states. The case law in the forum state would serve as the basis for the judge's decision.

Any attempt at modification (as well as any defense of a modification petition) must begin with a review of the divorce decree and any separation agreement to determine the amount and type of payments owed. Such a review may reveal that the parties agreed to waive their right to seek modification for alimony. (They could not waive the right to modify child support.) If that is the case, a court will deny a subsequent request for modification, although some courts will allow it if some compelling reason exists for modification (e.g., a drastic change in a party's health due to serious illness or injury).

Depending on the procedural requirements of the state, modification is initiated by filing a motion, petition, complaint, or claim specifying the reasons for the modification. With alimony and child support issues, the court issuing the original divorce decree retains jurisdiction. When modification of custody or visitation is involved, however, the court where the custodial parent lives has jurisdiction. Interlocutory modification is usually possible to resolve critical issues during the interim before a final hearing can be scheduled. During the discovery process in which the parties seek to determine what, if any, significant changes have occurred in the parties' financial status, the production of documents is emphasized. The pertinent financial documents that must be collected and reviewed include tax returns, financial statements, bank statements, and credit applications. If child support is at issue, discovery also focuses on significant changes in the child's financial, educational, health, or emotional needs. Under federal law, child support orders must, upon request of a parent, be reviewed every 36 months to ensure that the payments continue to be in alignment with the statutory guidelines.

▰ *Putting It Into Practice 10.11:*

Terrence's ex-wife is planning on remarrying and moving out of state with their three children. On what grounds is Terrence entitled to ask for a modification of their divorce decree?

"One Minute She's Soothing Some Irate Client Who's Threatening to Hide All Her Assets and Leave the State and the Next She's Poring Over a Spreadsheet in Preparation for an Order to Show Cause Hearing."

"Excuse me for a moment," Corazon said as she answered her phone. After a few perfunctory "Uh-huh's," she turned to Letitia, who had been quietly taking notes while Corazon and Martha had been talking. "You need to take care of this. It's one of our clients. She's hysterical—something about her husband threatening to take the kids away from her. Says she won't talk to anybody but you."

"Oh, I know who it is. This woman's in constant turmoil about one thing or another. I think I can get it straightened out. I'm on the phone with her at least once a week," explained Letitia as she made her way to the door.

"Good luck," said Corazon sympathetically. Knowing that Martha would appreciate the value of a conscientious paralegal, Corazon began extolling Letitia's virtues. "I know it seems trite, but I really don't know what I'd do without that lady. She's amazing. One minute she's soothing some irate client who's threatening to hide all her assets and leave the state and the next she's poring over a spreadsheet in preparation for an order to show cause hearing. She does it all—and she does it with grace."

"From what I could see while I was in your waiting room, she also has to be able to work with a very diverse clientele," observed Martha admiringly.

"That she does. And what I love about Letitia is that she always makes time for everyone, no matter how much some of them must try her patience. I know they try mine," Corazon added laughingly.

ROLE OF THE PARALEGAL

Paralegals working in the area of family law have not only a wide range of duties but they must also be familiar with a number of areas of the law, including real estate, probate, and tax law. They often have a lot of client contact, not only because they sometimes serve as buffers between the attorney and client, but because clients often feel more comfortable talking with them than with the attorney. Because of the severe emotional stresses many DR clients are experiencing, they can be more demanding, unreasonable, and volatile than they would be under less trying circumstances. Dealing with this kind of ongoing reactivity can be draining for paralegals; not everyone has the temperament for this type of stress.

Family law paralegals perform many tasks, including the following.

- ◆ interviewing clients and potential witnesses
- ◆ drafting correspondence to clients and others associated with the case
- ◆ assisting with discovery, pretrial, and trial preparation
- ◆ drafting petitions, motions, stipulations, temporary orders, and decrees

- ◆ helping clients assemble and review financial records
- ◆ analyzing income and expenses of clients
- ◆ assisting clients in financial planning
- ◆ researching family law issues
- ◆ drafting separation and settlement agreements
- ◆ interacting with mediators, counselors, and other professionals who assist families
- ◆ working with financial advisors, brokers, accountants, and other financial experts
- ◆ retaining appraisers for real and personal property
- ◆ preparing financial affidavits
- ◆ preparing and recording documents for transfer of assets

"So You're the 'Woman'—"

Corazon's phone rang again. This time her secretary was notifying her that an overseas call had come in regarding an adoption for one of her clients.

"I apologize, Martha, but I really need to take this call. I have some clients who are adopting a baby from China and the agency over there is calling to finalize all the arrangements."

"No problem," said Martha graciously.

Corazon waited expectantly to make the connection but none was forthcoming. In a minute, her secretary came back on the line to confess that she had inadvertently disconnected them. While waiting for her to reconnect them, Corazon asked Martha who she was going to have conduct the mediation.

"I don't know at this point. Actually, I opted for mediation at the advice of my friend, Tim, who does quite a bit of mediation himself. I've asked him to recommend some possible mediators."

"Your friend wouldn't be Tim McFay, would he?" asked Corazon, her curiosity piqued.

"Yes, it is. But how would you know Tim?" Martha was stunned by this it's-a-small-world connection.

"Long story made short," began Corazon enthusiastically, sitting forward in her chair. "It was Tim who dragged me kicking and screaming into representing some of the inmates at the state prison. If you know Tim, you're no doubt aware of his passionate work on behalf of the prisoners and how fervent he is about keeping prisoners and their families together. It's a real problem, you know. So many families break apart when the mother or father ends up in prison. Anyway, Tim has been a very persuasive advocate on behalf of these people. And, of course, once I got involved I found it harder and harder to resist his pleas for help." Corazon was so enthralled with relating Tim's exploits she didn't immediately notice the look of incomprehension on Martha's face. A bit sheepishly, Corazon added, "I take it that you were unaware of Tim's work at the prison."

"I only recently discovered that he'd been in prison himself. Actually, it came as quite a shock to me," admitted Martha. "And I'm afraid I didn't take it very well."

"So you're the 'woman'—" began Corazon, who was abruptly cut off when her secretary came back on the line with the long distance connection.

ADOPTION

As you are probably aware, adoption is the legal process by which an individual assumes legal parental responsibilities for a child. This process can be handled by an agency, which assumes temporary responsibility for children born out of wedlock, and then screens individuals who are willing to accept responsibility for the care of these children. Adoptions can also take place through private agreements between the birth parents and the adoptive parents. Either process requires an investigation by an approval agency and a formal acceptance by the courts.

Before an adoption can be finalized, the birth parents must sign a document agreeing to terminate their parental rights. Absent a showing of fraud, the birth parents cannot later reclaim their parental rights once they have signed this document. To protect the privacy of all concerned, adoption records have historically been sealed. Because of many requests in recent years by adults who yearn to learn the identity of their birth parents, many states have devised systems whereby adopted children and their biological parents can notify a state agency that they want to be reunited. If contacted by both parties, the agency has a right to facilitate such a reunion. Adoption records can also be opened if there is a compelling medical reason to do so.

Adoption can also arise out of **surrogacy contracts.** In these contracts a woman agrees to conceive a child (usually through artificial insemination.) When the child is born, the woman delivers the child to the father and severs her parental rights so that the father's wife (who is incapable of bearing children) can adopt the child. Many courts have been loathe to enforce these agreements, seeing them as violating public policy.

surrogacy contracts   contract in which a woman agrees to conceive and bear a child and to then terminate her parental rights so that the father's wife can adopt the child

■ TIM'S TECHNO TIPS

Family Law Resources

Various sites can get you to a wealth of information on family law. The Hieros Gamos portal at *www.hg.com* has numerous links to family law as well as other areas of the law. In many cases, you end up at Cornell Law School's site at *www.law.cornell.edu.* (Another cross-connected site is *www.familylaw.org.*) Cornell's site has links to the family laws of each state. Because each site displays the information differently, you may find one portal to the same information more convenient and easier to use than the others. Some are broken down by areas such as marriage, divorce, juvenile law, and child support.

Many states have their own child support calculation programs that allow you to input the applicable financial data and to calculate the final child support amount (and often prepare the necessary forms). Child support calculators for most of the states can be found at *www.alllaw.com/calculators/childsupport.* Another source for child support calculators is *www.supportguidelines.com/main.html.* Be very careful in using these programs. Without a thorough knowledge of the state's family law, you may not be aware of vital information that should be considered. You may not know, for example, how much discretion the trial judge has in varying from the guidelines or what is and is not included in gross income for a particular state for child support determination.

Tables showing various comparisons between each state's family laws have been given in various "Net News" throughout this chapter. They can be found at *www.abanet.org/family/familylaw/tables.html.*

TECHNO TRIP

Go to *www.supportguidelines.com/main.html.* Review the states on that site that have child support calculators. Now go to *www.alllaw.com/calculators/childsupport.* How many more states are on the alllaw site?

Assume a mother has custody of two children and earns $2,500 per month. Child care is $400 per month. There are no extraordinary expenses. Further assume the father earns $3,500 per month and pays $200 per month for health insurance for the children. The father has visitation for a total of 82 days per year. Neither parent has children by a prior relationship. Select two states and input the above figures. Which state requires the most child support to be paid?

SUMMARY – PART B

Parents have the option of having sole or joint legal and physical custody of their children; split custody is another option for physical custody. Although judges at one time almost always determined that mothers should be the custodial parent of children in their "tender years," today the guiding standard is the best interests of the children. Joint custody is the preferred custody scheme in many states, although it is avoided when the parents appear to be unable to get past their own animosity to do what is best for the children. Judges are extremely reluctant to modify custody awards because they do not want to disrupt the stability of children's environment. To prevent child-snatching and the re-litigation of child custody issues, every state has passed some form of the Uniform Child Custody Jurisdiction Act (UCCJA).

In most cases, non-custodial parents are awarded visitation rights. Courts typically delineate the times and arrangements for these visitations to minimize potential conflict. Visitation plans must be modified when one of the parents relocates and visitation rights can be terminated or limited if the judge believes the child is in danger either physically or emotionally. Parents who refuse to honor a visitation plan can be found in contempt of court.

Primary care-givers of children have a right to contribution from the other spouse. The amount of this support depends on the child's need and the parent's ability to pay. Because this is a right that belongs to the child, it does not end with the custodial parent's remarriage and it continues until the child reaches the age of majority or graduates from high school or college. Every state has child support guidelines from which judges can deviate only under extenuating circumstances. The format for these guidelines varies tremendously. Parents who fail to pay child support and are found in contempt of court can be fined, have their wages garnished, be jailed, and, in some states, have a variety of licenses revoked. Because the collection of child support remains a problem despite these possible consequences, both state and federal agencies have increased their efforts to collect child support payments. URESA, RURESA, and UIFSA were all created to facilitate interstate enforcement of child support orders by eliminating the problem of jurisdiction that normally exists when the creditor and debtor live in different states. UIFSA differs from URESA and RURESA in that only one valid child support order can exist at any one time.

Modification of the provisions in divorce decrees is permitted although time limits are sometimes imposed on when petitions for modification can be filed. In assessing these petitions, courts must examine the reason for the request for modification and determine whether the change in the parties' lives prompting this request is significant. Under federal law, child support payments are, at a parent's request, to be reviewed every 36 months. When alimony and child support issues are involved, the court that issued the original decree retains jurisdiction, but when child custody and visitation issues are involved, the court where the custodial parent lives has jurisdiction. Modification of property division is not generally allowed except when it involves such things as the marital residence.

KEY TERMS

Joint custody	Physical custody	Sole custody	Surrogacy contracts
Legal custody	Split custody		

REVIEW QUESTIONS – PART B

1. What options do judges have in awarding child custody?
   a. How and for what reasons have the preferences for those options changed over the years?
   b. How have the states discouraged re-litigation of child custody issues?
2. What should be included in any agreement regarding visitation?
   a. Under what conditions might that agreement be modified?
   b. What are the consequences of failing to honor a visitation plan?
3. What are the consequences of the fact that child support is a right of the child?

   a. How do the child support guidelines vary from state to state?
   b. What have the states and federal government done to enforce the payment of child support?
   c. What is the purpose of URESA, RURESA, and UIFSA? Do they differ in any significant respects?
4. For what reasons and when are modifications to a divorce decree permitted?
   a. Describe the modification process.
   b. In what situation is modification to provisions regarding property division allowed?
5. What should a paralegal know before considering the realm of family law as a possible area of practice?

PRACTICE EXAM – PART B

MULTIPLE CHOICE

1. Children
   a. in their tender years are usually placed in the custody of their mother
   b. are placed with the parent who is best able to meet the needs of the children
   c. at all ages are allowed to choose the parent with whom they would prefer to live
   d. none of the above
2. Child custody decisions
   a. almost always ignore the wishes of the child
   b. have no connection to whether a parent will be providing personal child care or will be relying on a child-care facility
   c. are based on an attempt to keep siblings together whenever possible
   d. focus on any kind of perceived immoral behavior of a parent
3. The UCCJA
   a. promotes cooperation among the states in the enforcement of child custody orders
   b. has had little effect on child snatching
   c. allows for litigation of child custody issues even in states having only a remote connection to the child
   d. all of the above
4. An agreement regarding visitation rights
   a. should leave the exact times of visitation to the parties
   b. should spell out the exact times of visitation

   c. should not contain such details as the notification procedure when a visitation has to be cancelled
   d. are created by the courts and cannot be modified by the parties even if they agree to do so
5. When a custodial parent wants to relocate, the court
   a. will never intervene
   b. will intervene if the move is not in the best interests of the child
   c. is not allowed to consider the motives for the move
   d. may allow the move, but probably will not modify the visitation rights
6. A court can limit visitation
   a. by requiring that the visitation be supervised
   b. if the non-custodial parent is mentally ill or is abusing drugs
   c. by specifying that the visitation take place at a specific location
   d. all of the above
7. Child support
   a. is an obligation of the biological father
   b. is not an obligation of unwed fathers
   c. is an obligation of the non-custodial parent
   d. is not an obligation of adoptive parents
8. Child support terminates
   a. when the custodial parent remarries
   b. when the custodial parent waives it
   c. at the age of majority in all states
   d. none of the above

9. The Child Support Enforcement Amendments of 1984 are
   a. designed to promote fairness and uniformity in the awarding of child support
   b. cannot be deviated from even if extenuating circumstances exist
   c. guidelines having the same format in every state
   d. all of the above

*10. Some facts about tax laws that are relevant to family law are
   a. child support is deductible from the payor's income, but alimony is not
   b. child support is included in the income of the payee, but alimony is not
   c. transfers of property incident to divorce are the equivalent of gifts because they are not taxable events
   d. the custodial parent usually cannot claim dependency exemptions

*11. Paralegals who work in the area of tax law
   a. help prepare tax returns
   b. assist in the valuation of assets
   c. help calculate tax liability
   d. all of the above

12. Parents who fail to pay child support
   a. can have their wages garnished but cannot be jailed
   b. can have certain licenses revoked in some states
   c. can flee to another state to avoid paying the debt
   d. none of the above

13. UIFSA
   a. solves the problem of personal jurisdiction when the parent paying child support lives in a different state than the parent receiving child support
   b. allows any state to modify the original court order
   c. allows conflicting child support orders to be in existence at the same time
   d. all of the above

14. To reduce the cost of welfare payments to single-parent families
   a. the Federal Enforcement Initiative of 1974 requires that arrears that are collected must be credited to welfare payments already made
   b. those applying for Aid to Dependent Children must agree to assign their rights to uncollected child support payments to the state
   c. employers must now automatically deduct payments for child support from an employee's check even if that employee is not in arrears
   d. all of the above

15. Modification of a divorce decree
   a. is never allowed in the case of property division
   b. is justified if there has been a significant change in events that affect the welfare of the children
   c. is justified only when children are in imminent physical danger
   d. can only be done by the court that issued the original decree

FILL IN THE BLANK

16. Judges have to determine which parent has _____ custody (where the child will live) and _____ custody (which parent will make decisions affecting the child's welfare). They have the option of awarding _____ custody (one parent having total custody) or _____ custody, in which the parents share the custodial duties. When parents live in different states, judges are likely to award _____ custody.

17. The _____ promotes uniform jurisdiction in child custody cases and ensures litigation in the state having the closest connection to the child and his family.

18. The amount of child support that is paid is based on _____ and _____.

19. Child support is a right that belongs to the _____.

20. Three acts that are designed to prevent parents from fleeing to another state to avoid paying child support are _____, _____, and _____.

*21. A _____ action is a civil action brought to determine the identity of a child's father.

TRUE OR FALSE

____ 22. Sole custody is generally preferred over joint custody today.

____ 23. Judges are reluctant to award joint custody to parents who appear to be incapable of getting past their personal differences in order to work in the best interests of their children.

____ 24. Child custody awards can be easily modified.

____ *25. When evidence of child abuse or neglect exists, the state is compelled to become involved.

____ *26. A court can terminate parental rights when a preponderance of the evidence shows that the parent is unfit.

____ 27. Courts prefer to award "reasonable" visitation rights rather than specify the exact terms of the visitations.

____ 28. Non-custodial parents do not have a right to challenge a custodial parent's relocation.

____ 29. A custodial parent who continually thwarts the visitation rights of the non-custodial parent could conceivably lose custody.

____ 30. Child support will be diminished for any child who is the beneficiary of a trust.

____ 31. Child support payments may continue indefinitely for children who are physically or mentally unable to care for themselves.

____ 32. In all states, judges awarding child support consider not only the income of the parents and the number of dependent children but also the standard of living the children would have enjoyed had no divorce occurred.

____ 33. Because of the Uniform Reciprocal Enforcement of Support Act, the recipient of child support can bring an action in his state that can then be tried in the debtor's state.

____ *34. Mothers can bring paternity actions, but state agencies do not have the right to bring such actions.

____ *35. Some states require mothers to identify the father of a child before they can receive welfare.

____ *36. Men who refuse to take a court-ordered blood test can be found in contempt of court.

____ 37. Some states impose time limits on when a modification to a divorce decree can be filed.

____ 38. Under no circumstances will a court consider a petition for modification if the parties have previously agreed to waive their right to modification.

____ 39. The only relevant consideration for a court in reviewing a petition for modification is whether a significant change has occurred in the parties' lives.

____ 40. The laws in some states justify the elimination or reduction in alimony payments when the receiving spouse is cohabiting with someone of the opposite sex.

____ 41. Interlocutory modification of decrees is not generally allowed.

____ 42. Federal law requires that child support payments be reviewed every 36 months if one of the parents requests it.

____ 43. When modification of custody or visitation is at stake, the court that issued the original divorce decree has jurisdiction.

____ 44. Modification of child custody may be justified when one of the parents remarries.

____ 45. In many cases, the marital residence is awarded to one party while still allowing both parties to have joint ownership so that they can build equity.

____ 46. Family law is one of area of practice where paralegals have little client contact.

____ 47. Paralegals working in domestic relations must have a working knowledge of real estate, probate, and tax law as well as family law.

____ 48. Surrogacy contracts are usually favored by the courts.

*Questions taken from Bonus Pointers

LEGAL LINGO

Word Scramble

Unscramble the letters to form words using the clues provided.

1. LANUMNTEN
2. DREOROTWOHSESAUC

3. DINGMOCLEM
4. TILETANPUNI

1. court order declaring that a marriage never existed
2. hearing where defendants must explain why plaintiff's request is not justified
3. property having attributes of separate and marital property
4. agreement entered into before marriage

5. RUTOYRINLETCO
6. RAXPETE
7. NOILAMY
8. QUEBATILE
9. YUMMICONT

10. TOJIN
11. TINCOPTIER
12. TOFULAN

13. NEDEPTENTILE
14. MELTESTENT
15. GALEL

16. SERAU

5. temporary relief
6. one-sided hearing
7. spousal support
8. distribution of property in accordance with principles of fairness
9. property acquired during marriage as well as property owned prior to but contributed to during marriage
10. shared custody
11. order of _____; also known as TRO
12. divorce in which parties do not have to prove which one broke bonds of marriage
13. temporary relief
14. agreement reached by parties who have initiated divorce
15. custody giving parent right to make decisions affecting child's welfare
16. act relating to child support

LEGAL LOGISTICS

1. Charles is a long-standing client of your firm. A confirmed bachelor, he is, at the age of 50, considering marriage to a 30-year-old fifth grade school teacher. As a successful mortgage broker with substantial assets, he wonders if a prenuptial agreement might be wise, but his fiancee is insulted that he is even considering such a possibility. In his discussion with your supervising attorney, he also reveals that he is aware that his fiancee really wants children, but he believes that this passion of hers will diminish over time. What advice do you think the attorney should offer?

2. Mandy has been married for 10 years and has three children. Her husband was in a serious car accident a few years ago, suffered a head injury, and has been experiencing severe mood swings during which he sometimes becomes violent. Although he has threatened to strike Mandy and her children, he had never done so until last evening, when he hit Mandy. She is now frightened of what he might do and wants him to leave their home.
   a. How can she get him out of the house?
   b. Would she be better off trying to work out an agreement with him as far as any separation is concerned, or should she let a court resolve that for them?
   c. How will custody of the children be decided? She is concerned that her eight-year-old son will want to stay with his father and she is concerned for his safety.
   d. Is a court likely to give the father visitation rights?
   e. Will Mandy get alimony?
   f. Will she be able to keep the house?

   g. Where can she find out about child support? Show her how the calculations would be done. They live in California and her husband makes $50,000 a year; she does not work outside the home.

3. Carla has been divorced for five years. A year ago, her ex-husband moved out of state and has made only two child support payments in the last ten months.
   a. What are her options as far as getting him to pay past-due child support? What might she do to ensure he makes future payments?
   b. He wants the children to visit him during the holiday break, but Carla thinks he should be denied any visitation as long as he is not paying child support? Who will prevail?
   c. Carla is getting remarried. Will she be entitled to continuing spousal maintenance and child support?
   d. At this point, she and her ex-husband have split custody of the children. When he discovered she was marrying a man of a different race and that they were relocating to Europe, he announced that he wanted sole custody of the children or that, at the very least, he would petition the court to prevent her from taking the children out of the country. Is he likely to prevail?

4. Wilma and Henry have been married for five years and are now divorcing. How would the following property be classified in a separate property state? In a community property state?
   a. An Arabian show horse mare and her foal. Henry owned the horse prior to marriage and paid $50,000 for her. During their marriage, the couple paid for the mare's training, showing, and breeding.

b. 500 shares of stock that Wilma inherited

c. A lottery ticket that Wilma bought while they were separated that is now worth $100,000

d. Debts over $10,000 that Henry incurred using his own credit card

e. A $40,000 settlement that Wilma received as a result of being injured in a car accident

f. Wilma's Ph.D., which Henry helped make financially feasible by taking on a second job

g. Henry's retirement benefits, which he will be entitled to receive in another 10 years

A TRIP TO THE MOVIES

Remember the movie *Kramer v. Kramer* (mentioned in Chapter 8) in which the parents of Billy, a seven-year-old boy, become embroiled in a bitter custody battle when the mother returns to reclaim the son she left behind when she left the marriage to "find her voice."

1. What arguments could you make on the father's behalf that he should have custody of Billy? What arguments could you make on the mother's behalf? If you were the judge, how would you have resolved the custody issue? Explain your reasoning.

2. What kind of visitation arrangements do you think would be appropriate?

3. Suppose Ms. Kramer had filed for divorce rather than leaving. Do you think a judge would have been likely to award her alimony? Why or why not?

4. Suppose Mr. Kramer is granted custody of Billy and that Ms. Kramer subsequently remarries. Should she and her new husband then be awarded custody of Billy?

5. Suppose Ms. Kramer petitions the court for a custody modification because she and her new husband are planning on moving, but she cannot get a hearing scheduled for at least six months. What can she do if she is supposed to leave town within the month? Can she file a petition for modification in the state where she is moving?

6. Suppose Ms. Kramer is awarded custody of Billy. How much child support would Mr. Kramer have to pay if he earned $100,000 a year and Ms. Kramer earned $50,000 per year? (Do not consider insurance, child care, etc.) Go online to answer this question.

7. If Mr. Kramer remarried, moved to another state, and stopped paying child support, what could Ms. Kramer do?

8. Go online and find out what the grounds for divorce are in the state where the Kramers lived.

INTERNET INQUIRIES

1. A father of two dependent children earns $200,000 a year. The mother earns $25,000 a year. Medical insurance, paid by the father is $300 per month for the children only. The mother's child care expenses are $500 per month. The father has visitation for 2 days every other week, one 3 hour visitation mid-week, and 6 weeks summer visitation. In your state, how much would the father have to pay in child support?

   What other factors would be considered in your state?

2. Find out what the procedures are for getting a TRO in your state. Summarize them here.

3. Locate someone who does divorce mediation in your state. Summarize how you found this information, including the addresses of the Web sites you visited.

4. What agency is responsible for enforcing child support payments in your state? What is the Web address for this agency?
   Summarize the process for getting this agency's assistance in collecting child support arrears.

5. Go to the Internet and use the search terms "[your state] marriage records (or certificates)." Alternatively, you can go to *www.vitalcheck.com*. Follow the links until you find a page that explains the process for obtaining a marriage certificate in your state.

   a. Where are marriage records located in your state?

   b. What is the cost of obtaining a marriage certificate?

   c. What information must you provide before you can get a marriage certificate?

d. In your state, can you order marriage certificates by mail? In person? By fax? By telephone? Online?

e. Record the name, address, phone number, and fax number of the office in your state that provides marriage certificates.

6. Go to the Internet and use the search terms "[your state] divorce records (or decrees)." Follow the links until you find a page that explains the process for obtaining a divorce decree in your state.

a. Where are divorce records located in your state?

b. What is the cost of obtaining a divorce record?

c. What information must you provide before you can get a divorce record?

d. In your state, can you order a divorce record by mail? In person? By fax? By telephone? Online?

e. Record the name, address, phone number, and fax number of the office in your state that provides divorce records.

ENDNOTES

[1]Linda Gibson, National Law Journal, Feb. 12, 1996 at A9 "Mom's a Lesbian. Dad's a Killer. Judge: She's Unfit" Vol. 18, Number 24.

[2]To read the details of this case, see Tom Eigo *Arizona Attorney,* "Character, Courage, and Little Caution," Jan. 2001 at 31.

11 Real Estate and Probate Law

OBJECTIVES:

In this chapter you will learn:

- what is included in real property ownership
- the restrictions that can be imposed on land use, including licenses, easements, restrictive covenants and zoning
- what a nuisance claim is and why it is used in environmental cases
- the various forms of co-ownership of property
- the information available in a deed
- the importance of title searches and title insurance
- the various forms of estates conveyed by deeds
- the difference between a mortgage and a deed of trust
- the various types of liens that can encumber property
- the basic elements of a real estate contract
- the tasks a paralegal must perform before, during, and after a real estate closing
- the potential ethical questions that can arise in real estate closings

- the elements of intentional misrepresentation and how it arises in real estate sales
- to distinguish between various leasehold estates
- the rights and obligations of landlords and tenants
- how property is distributed when someone dies intestate
- the requirements of a valid will
- the elements of a basic will
- how to revoke a will
- the grounds for contesting a will
- the basic steps in probating an estate
- the purpose of a trust
- the various types of trusts that can be created
- the roles of the settlor, trustee, and beneficiary
- the tasks performed by paralegals in real estate and probate law

"So I Put Two and Two Together and Figured You to Be the 'Dream Lady.'"

"What do you mean 'that woman'?" pursued Martha as soon as Corazon got off the phone.

Corazon took a deep breath and then began. "First off, let me tell you something about myself. In my line of work, I tend to see people at their worst: failed relationships, bitter recriminations, and all that kind of stuff. So in my personal life I look for happy endings. I'm a big sucker for romance—saw *Pretty Woman* something like 15 times and cried every time—you know, that kind of thing. Anyway, just about all the female staff at the prison where Tim does volunteer work know me and they know I'm a compulsive matchmaker. Well, most of the single gals there have eyes for Tim, but none of them can seem to get anywhere with him. He'll kid with them and be nice, but nothing ever leads to anything. So they asked me to find out if he was involved with someone. I did, and he told me that he'd met someone whom he was really serious about—called her the 'woman of his dreams.' Huge disappointment to all the girls, but at least they knew," Corazon laughed. "Anyway, several months ago I talked with Tim over the phone and he seemed really depressed, so I asked him if anything was wrong. He claimed he was fine, but I knew better. Then I asked him how his 'dream lady' was and he said he didn't want to talk about it. So, I put two and two together and figured you to be the 'dream lady,'" concluded Corazon.

"I see," said Martha soberly, neither affirming nor denying Corazon's conclusion.

But Corazon could see from Martha's face that her assumption was accurate. When Martha said nothing, she continued, "All I can say is, Martha, that guy's a keeper. And if you throw him back in the ocean, there's going to be a real feeding frenzy," she added, hoping to bring a smile to Martha's face. When that did not work, she sighed and re-focused her attention on the remaining legal questions Martha had raised. "So back to the problem at hand. Does George have any interests in real estate that would be of value to you—that you could use as a negotiating tool?" inquired Corazon.

"Not that I know of." Grateful to get Tim's face out of her mind, Martha re-directed her thoughts and then remembered. "But you know, when we were first married we bought some silver mine claims. We used to go out and work our claims on the weekends—more for fun than profit, I can assure you. George always enjoyed that and it's possible he's actually invested in something that's paid off. He always used to say that investing in real estate was one of the wisest ways to invest your money if you knew what you were doing. Anyway, it's a good question. I'll ask him."

"Something you said reminded me, Martha, of a phone call I got yesterday from a lawyer I went to school with. She wanted to know if I knew of a paralegal who might be interested in assisting her with her work at the Attorney General's Office in reference to the Archaeological Resources Protection Act. She's working in conjunction with archaeologists and law enforcement officers to prosecute those who are unlawfully taking Indian artifacts and destroying or defacing cultural ruins. This is a very new area of law and she's having to learn as she goes. She's been given permission to hire a paralegal and she's looking for someone who's a quick learner, self-motivated, independent—all the things I've heard Ernesto say about you."

"Actually, that does sound interesting. I've been fascinated with Indian artifacts ever since George and I found some around an Indian ruin on some of that land we bought. Mind you though, I'm not in the market for a new job and I certainly couldn't afford to take a pay cut at this point in my life."

"Don't worry. I'm not *even* going to tell Ernesto about this. He'd kill me if you left White & Treadwell," Corazon assured Martha. "But if you're interested, I'll give you my friend's number and you can check it out."

BONUS POINTERS:　　**EMERGING LEGAL SPECIALTIES**

One of the exciting aspects of paralegal work is that new areas of the law appear all the time. For example, Internet specialists are a relatively new breed of paralegals who have expertise in conducting both legal and factual research on the Internet. They are also capable of designing and implementing Web sites for law firms. Other new legal specialties include animal law, natural resources law, and cyberlaw.

Other areas of legal specialization that are not new but that are experiencing exceptional growth in the last few years are environmental law and elder law (both discussed briefly in Bonus Pointers later in this chapter.) Another area of fast growth is employee benefits law. Paralegals who work in this field often work for law firms that specialize in implementing and ensuring compliance with employee benefit plans of corporate clients, or they may work with corporations, assisting in the drafting and maintenance of employee benefit plans. Work in this area requires excellent research and writing skills. An increasing number of paralegals are finding employment as immigration paralegals, who assist clients involved in deportation proceedings and help others determine their immigration status.

NET NEWS

Information about animal law can be found at *www.paralegals.org/Reporter/home.html*; click on "Fall 2000," and then go to the article entitled "Animal Law." A student-run law journal that addresses animal rights can be found at *www.lclark.edu/~alj/*. Information about archaeological resources protection work can be found at *http://forums.law.arizona.edu/library/Chiorazzi/tjafek/Arch.htm*; information about natural resources law can be found at *www.colorado.edu/law/NRLC/*; and the Web page for the Cyberlaw Association is at *www.cyberlawassociation.com*. Information about immigration law resources and statutes can be found at *www.immigration-usa.com/resource.html*.

REAL PROPERTY

real property   land and anything that is permanently attached to it

personal property (*chattel*) any movable good that is not land or permanently attached to it

tangible property   goods that can be seen and touched

Property is classified as either **personal property** or **real property,** often defined as land and anything that is permanently attached to it. Personal property (also called *chattel*) is any movable good that is not land or attached to it. It includes both **tangible property** (goods that can be seen and touched, such as vehicles, televisions, and clothes) and **intangible property** (goods that cannot be touched, but are represented by documents, such as stocks, bonds, bank accounts, and patents).

BONUS POINTERS:

INTELLECTUAL PROPERTY LAW

intangible property   goods that cannot be touched but that are represented by documents

One area of the law in which many paralegals are involved is intellectual property law, which deals with such intangible property as copyrights (which protect literary and artistic works), trademarks (the distinctive symbols and mottos that identify businesses), and patents (which protect inventions). Intellectual property law is becoming one of the more popular—and higher paying—legal specialties for paralegals. Paralegals in this area may work for a firm that specializes in intellectual property law, a firm that deals with this area of the law in addition to many others, or for a corporate legal department.

Among the tasks paralegals may perform in reference to clients who want to register for a copyright, trademark, or patent are the following.

- ◆ interviewing clients
- ◆ conducting research to determine if the copyright, trademark, or patent has already been applied for
- ◆ collecting the necessary data and drafting the documents required to apply for a copyright, trademark, or patent
- ◆ determining filing fees
- ◆ monitoring responses from government offices
- ◆ assisting in infringement (unlawful use of intellectual property) litigation
- ◆ drafting contracts or licensing agreements providing for another's authorized use of intellectual property
- ◆ monitoring others' use of intellectual property
- ◆ researching pertinent intellectual property laws

Real property[1] goes beyond the land and the buildings that are attached to it; it encompasses all of the ownership rights that are part of land ownership. Owning a piece of land means you own the plants that grow on it (other than those that are grown as a result of human labor, which are considered personal property) and the minerals, such as oil and gas, that are beneath its surface. You also own the air space above it, which can be valuable in an urban area because it provides building space as well as in a rural area where it may provide a scenic view. In this day of solar energy, air space is increasingly valued as a means of allowing the sun to reach solar panels.

NET NEWS

Recent case decisions in intellectual property can be found at the Intellectual Property Center at *www.ipcenter.com.*

NET NEWS

To read more about the prior appropriation doctrine, go to *http://profs.lp.findlaw.com/water/index.html.*

◆ **LOCAL LINKS** ◆

Does your state use the prior appropriation doctrine or the riparian rights approach?

fixture   property that begins as personal property and becomes so attached to real property that it becomes characterized as real property

Landowners also have limited ownership rights to the water on the surface or beneath the surface of their land—a right that is of vital interest to those areas of the country that experience water shortages. In the West, for example, the "prior appropriation doctrine" provides that those landowners who first use water from a natural source (such as a river, stream, or natural lake) have a superior right to those who begin using that water at a later date. Consequently, if the water available is insufficient to meet the needs to all landowners, those with first rights may have all of their water needs fulfilled while those later in time may get little or no water. Contrast this approach with the "riparian rights" allowed in states with more plentiful water resources, in which all landowners have equal ownership rights. Under this approach, landowners are prevented from doing anything that would violate others' water rights, such as building a dam that prevents water from flowing to other landowners, but otherwise have a right to use all the water they need. Many states have enacted laws detailing water rights, and in the West and other areas of the country where water shortages are common, water law is an important specialty of law practice.

Property can begin as personal property and end up becoming so much a part of real property that it is eventually characterized as real property; such property is called a **fixture.** A central air conditioning unit, for example, becomes a fixture once it is installed because it becomes part of the house. Knowing whether property is a fixture becomes important when the property is sold because anything that is a fixture is considered part of the real property and will be transferred along with the rest of the real property. This classification also becomes important when property is used as a security for a debt and the creditor is entitled to any fixtures because they are part of the real property. (See the discussion regarding secured transactions in Chapter 9.) In deciding whether property is a fixture, courts look to the intent of the parties, the property's degree of permanency, the character of the property, and its relative attachment to the property. A spa that is deliberately designed to fit into a deck, for example, would be considered a fixture. On the other hand, a satellite dish that is installed on the roof but that can be removed without damage to the roof would not be considered a fixture.

Putting It Into Practice 11.1:

Lacy is buying 100 acres of land in northeastern New Mexico. She plans to raise horses and have a small farming operation.

(a) What kinds of water rights does she most likely have? Why might that pose a potential problem?

(b) After the sale of the property, the sellers tell Lacy that they will be taking the 12-stall barn with them to their new location. Lacy insists that the barn is part of the real property she has just purchased. Is she correct?

(c) Suppose that, in the process of digging to build a new riding arena, Lacy discovers what appears to be silver. Does she have a right to mine this silver?

For a list of links to anything related to real estate, go to *www.katsuey.com* and click on "Real Estate." The real property statutes in most states are available at *www.law.cornell.edu/topics/state_statutes.html#property*.

Figure 11-1
What Is Included in Real Property?

WHAT IS INCLUDED IN REAL PROPERTY?

Buildings

Plants (except crops)

Minerals

Air Space

Water

(within limits of prior appropriation or riparian rights)

Fixtures

"I understand your ex has asked you to sell the marital home, which he's been living in. Is that correct?"

"Yes, it is. But let me tell you something up front that needs to get straightened out before I put it on the market," Martha began. "Our fence, which runs about 200 feet, is about one foot over on our neighbor's property. It's a chain-link fence we put up when we moved in. We didn't realize what we had done until our neighbors had their land surveyed. They agreed to let the fence stand until one of us sold our property. What do you suggest I do?"

"You'll certainly have to disclose to any potential purchasers that the fence is not on the property line and that it will have to be moved when the house is sold," explained Corazon.

USE OF REAL PROPERTY

Limits on the Use of Property

license permission to perform certain acts on another's land

A landowner can give another permission to perform an act(s) on her land; in doing so, the landowner gives that person a **license.** An owner who gives a neighbor permission to walk across his land so the neighbor can get to his own property has granted that neighbor a license. A license can be given verbally or in writing or can be implied from conduct. An implied license or one that is given without any consideration is revocable, but one that is given in return for payment of consideration is not revocable.

easement property interest in the land of another that entitles the owner of the easement to use that land for a specific purpose

A landowner can also give another the right to use her property for a specific purpose, and this is called an **easement.** Unlike a license, which is merely permission to perform an act, an easement is an actual property interest. Utility easements, for example, are given to utility companies so that they can install and repair transmission lines. Easements are commonly given to parties so they have

express easement easement created by a formal document

implied easement easement implied by conduct

prescriptive easement easement created when a party uses a landowner's property for a specified time without the owner's consent

easement by necessity easement created when a party is landlocked and needs easement to gain access to public streets

restrictive covenant provision in a deed that prohibits specific uses of land

deed document that describes the quality of the title transferred and any restrictions regarding the transfer of the property

covenants, conditions, and restrictions (CC&Rs) restrict what owners can do with their property

zoning government regulations designed to control land use

eminent domain power of government to take private property for public use

a right to travel across a landowner's property in order to gain access to a public street.

Easements can be **express** (through a formally prepared document) or **implied** (in certain circumstances). A **prescriptive easement** is obtained when a party uses a landowner's property for a specified period of time without the owner's permission. This use of the owner's property must be for a specific purpose on a continuous, uninterrupted basis for a long enough time (the required time period varies in each state) that a party gains a prescriptive easement. Easements can also be obtained by **necessity** in many states when landowners are landlocked in that they have no access to public streets except across private land. Such easements are usually very restricted and are obtained only by compliance with statutory procedures.

Owners can restrict the uses of real property by creating **restrictive covenants.** These are usually provisions in a **deed** that prohibit specific uses of the property. They might, for example, restrict the use of architectural designs or require a minimum square-footage of homes. In some communities designed specifically for senior citizens, for example, the builders include restrictive covenants that prohibit young children from living in the community. Most homeowners' associations have **covenants, conditions, and restrictions** (known as CC&Rs) that restrict what owners can do with their property. Some CC&Rs dictate what color paint can be used, what kinds of additions are permitted, what types of lawns can be put in, and so on. Some homeowners' associations enforce these restrictions with the zeal of an over-protective bodyguard, so potential purchasers are advised to thoroughly familiarize themselves with all the CC&Rs prior to making a decision to buy.

Prohibitions that might be allowed as restrictive covenants, such as the prohibition of children, would not be allowed as a **zoning** regulation, which is created by the government as a means of controlling land use, and cannot be discriminatory. The validity of zoning is contingent on its promotion of the public welfare. Any zoning that is unreasonable may be considered a "taking" of the property, in which case the property owner is entitled to receiving compensation or having the zoning voided. Although the government can exert its power of **eminent domain** in its taking of private property for public use (for the building of freeways or airports, for example), it must first establish that the property was needed for public use and must then adequately compensate the private landowner.

Zoning sets forth the types of structures and the uses for those structures that are allowed in each district within a city or county. Notice must be given and a public hearing must be held before a zoning regulation can be passed so that landowners have an opportunity to express their opposition.

◆ **LOCAL LINKS** ◆
Which agency is responsible for creating zoning regulations in your town or city?
In your county?

▰ *Putting It Into Practice 11.2:*

Luke is planning to buy some property in a residential area where he wants to build a teen center. He is concerned about whether the place has sufficient parking, but the seller assures him that the neighbor who owns the vacant lot to the south of the property has been letting him park the cars he restores for a hobby there for the past ten years. What should Luke find out before buying this property?

Figure 11-2
Limits on the Use of Land

LIMITS ON THE USE OF LAND

License
Verbal

Written

Implied

Easement
Express

Implied

Prescriptive

Necessity

Covenants

Zoning

---

nuisance   using one's land in
such a way as to interfere with
others' use and enjoyment of their
land; a nuisance is private if it
affects the plaintiff's use of her
land and public if it affects a use of
land that is common to the public

private nuisance   creates an
unreasonable interference with the
plaintiff's use and enjoyment of
her land

public nuisance   interferes
with a right that is common to the
public

◆ **LOCAL LINKS** ◆

Is nuisance a commonly
used cause of action in
your jurisdiction?

Unreasonable Use of Property

Although landowners have wide discretion in the use of their land, if they use it in such a way as to interfere with others' use and enjoyment of their land, they have committed the tort of **nuisance.** Landowners who refuse to clean up the trash and refuse in their yard, thereby creating not only an eyesore but foul odors for the neighborhood to contend with, can be sued for nuisance. A nuisance can be private in that it creates an unreasonable interference with the plaintiff's use and enjoyment of her land, or public in that it interferes with a right that is common to the public. Playing extremely loud music at 2:00 A.M. is a **private nuisance,** whereas maintaining a feedlot in close proximity to a residential neighborhood can be a **public nuisance.**

The claim of nuisance is enjoying a resurgence in environmental law. Most claims for money damages for pollution brought under state common law have a nuisance claim, arguing that hazardous waste contamination interferes with others' use and enjoyment of their land and causes substantial harm to their health. Public nuisance claims provide environmental plaintiffs with a cause of action that is both flexible and powerful. Even though the federal government has passed such statutes as the Comprehensive Environmental Response, Compensation, and Liability Act (CERCLA), which authorizes the Environmental Protection Agency (EPA) to clean up sites contaminated by toxic wastes, the nuisance claim is still widely used. Nuisance claims have no statute of limitations, they do not require the showing of physical harm to the land, and they often result in higher damage awards than do claims under CERCLA. *Wood v. Picillo* chronicles the evolution of nuisance law in the context of environmental concerns. Notice how the court acknowledges and conforms to changes in societal attitude and scientific knowledge.

Cite as: 443 A.2d 1244

Supreme Court of Rhode Island.
W. Edward **WOOD** et al.
v.
Warren V. **PICILLO** et al.
No. 80-419-Appeal.
April 9, 1982.

WEISBERGER, Justice.

This is an appeal from a judgment of the Superior Court entered after trial without the intervention of a jury. Finding that the defendants created a public and private nuisance in maintaining a hazardous waste dump site on their Coventry farm, the trial justice enjoined further chemical disposal operations at the defendants' property and ordered the defendants to finance cleanup and removal of the toxic wastes. The defendants now contend that the trial justice erred in finding the disposal operation to be a public and private nuisance. We strongly disagree. Accordingly, the judgment of the Superior Court is affirmed.[footnote omitted]

The testimony elicited during the extensive hearings conducted on this case revealed the following dramatic events. On September 30, 1977, an enormous explosion erupted into fifty-foot flames in a trench on defendants' Coventry property. Firefighters responded to the blaze but could not extinguish the flames. As the fire raged within the trench, additional explosions resounded. From the conflagration billowed clouds of thick black smoke that extended "as far as the eye could see on the Eastern horizon."

Not unexpectedly, the extraordinary blaze aroused the interest of various state officials. The state fire marshal declared the dump site a fire hazard and ordered defendants to cease disposal activity and to remove all flammable wastes. Personnel from the Department of Environmental Management (DEM) also investigated the dumping operation, conducting soil, water, chemical, and topographical analyses of defendants' property and adjacent areas. Despite the fire marshal's order and the ongoing official investigations, the dumping and burying of chemical wastes continued.

A general description of the Picillo property and adjacent lands is helpful in evaluating the evidence. According to the testimony of various witnesses, the Picillos owned acreage on Piggy Hill Lane in Coventry, Rhode Island. Piggy Hill Lane, which serves only the Picillos' property, is a winding dirt road running from Perry Hill Road. Near the entrance of the property defendants maintain pigs, and two houses are also located in this general area. A three to five-acre clearing in once-wooded land lies approximately 800 feet uphill from the two homes. It is this clearing that houses the chemical dump site. About 600 feet downhill to the north-northwest of the clearing is a marshy wetland. The wetland is part of the Quinabog River Basin; the wetland waters drain in a gradual southwesterly flow into the Quinabog River, Wickford Pond, the Roaring Brook, and Arnold Pond. These fish-inhabited waters are utilized both by the general public and by a commercial cranberry grower.

The dump site proper might best be described in the succinct expression of the trial justice as "a chemical nightmare." John Quinn, Jr., chief of the DEM's solid-waste management program, visited defendants' property on October 13, 1977 and testified to what he saw. Quinn stated that at one side of the clearing lay a huge trench which he estimated to be 200 feet long, 15 to 30 feet wide, and 15 to 20 feet deep. A viscous layer of pungent, varicolored liquid covered the trench bottom to a depth of six inches at its shallowest point. Along the periphery of the pit lay more than 100 fifty-five gallon drum-type and five-gallon pail-type containers. Some of the containers were upright and sealed, some tipped, and some partially buried; some were full, some partially full, and some empty. An official from the state fire marshal's office also visited the dump site. He testified that on October 15, 1977, he observed a truck marked "Combustible" offloading barrels of chemical wastes. The truck operator knocked the barrels off the truck's tailgate directly onto the earth below, and chemicals poured freely from the damaged barrels into the trench. In 1979 state officials discovered a second dump site when "sink holes" emitting chemical odors opened in the earth at some distance from the previously described pit.

Several witnesses testified at trial to the immediate and future effects of the chemical presence. Neighbors of the Picillos reported that in the year preceding the fire, tractor-trailer traffic to and from defendants' property greatly increased. According to the testimony many of the trucks bore "Flammable" warnings and the name of a chemical company. The neighbors also testified that on several occasions during the summer of 1977 pungent odors forced them to remain inside their homes. The odors were described variously as "sickening," "heavy," "sweet," "musky," "terrible," and like "plastic burning." One neighbor testified that the odors induced in her severe nausea and headaches, while another stated that on one occasion fumes from the Picillo property caused her to cough severely and to suffer a sore throat that lasted several days.

At trial expert witnesses developed a scientific connection between the neighbors' experiences and the Picillos' operations. Laboratory analyses of samples taken from the trench, monitoring wells, and adjacent waters revealed the presence of five chemicals: toluene, xylene, chloroform, III trichloroethane, and trichloroethylene.[FN2] Doctor Nelson Fausto, a professor of medical sciences in the pathology division of the Department of Biological and Medical Sciences at Brown University, described the toxic effects of the five discovered chemicals. Doctor Fausto testified that chloroform is a narcotic and an anesthetic that will induce vomiting, dizziness, and headaches in some persons exposed to it. Trichloroethane and trichloroethylene, according to Dr. Fausto, are similar to chloroform in chemical structure and in toxic effect. Toluene and xylene are also toxins, Dr. Fausto testified, that may cause irritation of the mucous membranes in the upper respiratory tract.

FN2. These were the only chemicals for which tests were conducted.

Doctor Fausto explained that the chemicals in question also exert chronic or long-term effects on animals and humans. According to the professor, chloroform, trichloroethane, and trichloroethylene are strong carcinogens that cause cirrhosis (cell death) of the liver and hepatoma (cancer of the liver). Doctor Fausto asserted that there is no safe level of human or animal exposure to these chemicals. Regarding toluene and xylene, Dr. Fausto testified that neither is as yet known to be carcinogenic, but both exert a toxic effect on bone marrow, causing anemia in susceptible persons. Additionally, Dr. Fausto stated, the presence of chloroform in areas where it might be heated presents further potential danger. Heated to sixty-eight degrees Fahrenheit, chloroform converts to phosgene gas, a nerve gas of the type utilized in World War I. Doctor Fausto stated that direct sunlight would provide sufficient heat to turn chloroform present in surface water into phosgene.

According to the experts, the chemicals present on defendants' property and in the marsh, left unchecked, would eventually threaten wildlife and humans well downstream from the dump site. Mr. Frank Stevenson, the principal sanitary engineer for the DEM, and Dr. William Kelly, an Associate Professor of civil and environmental engineering at the University of Rhode Island, testified as experts in soil mechanics and groundwater hydrology. The experts established that the soil at the dump site consisted of an unstratified composition of sand, gravel, and silt of varying sizes. The permeable nature of this soil would allow any liquid or chemical in or on it to percolate down to the water table and to travel with the groundwater in a northerly flow. The opinion of the experts was buttressed by the documented presence of toluene, xylene, chloroform, trichloroethane, and trichloroethylene in the northern marsh and in several monitoring wells.[FN3] The only possible source of the pollutants, according to Dr. Kelly, was the Picillo dump site.

FN3. The chemicals were detectable not only through laboratory processes but also by gross visual inspection. Experts reported a reddish discoloration and an oily surface in one section of the wetland, along with a pungent chemical odor. Doctor Kelly stated also that at one location chemicals seeped out of the ground as if from a spring.

Expert testimony further revealed that the chemicals had traveled and would continue to travel from the dump site into the marsh at the rate of about one foot per day. From the marsh, predicted the experts, the chemicals would flow in a southwesterly direction into the Quinabog River and its tributaries Moosup River and Roaring Brook, and Wickford Pond. These waters are inhabited by fish and used by humans for recreational and agricultural purposes.

On these and other facts the trial justice determined the dump site to be a public and private nuisance. He found also that the current danger to the public health and safety posed by the chemical presence would worsen unless effective remedial action was quickly taken. The trial judge thus permanently enjoined disposal operations on defendants' property and ordered that all chemicals and contaminated earth be removed to a licensed disposal facility. Because defendants had in the past displayed an unwillingness or inability to remedy the danger, the Superior Court justice authorized plaintiffs to effectuate cleanup of defendants' property at defendants' expense.

The defendants contend that the evidence adduced at trial was insufficient to support a finding of public and private nuisance. The defendants point to two alleged evidentiary inadequacies: (1) that plaintiffs failed to establish any significant injury to persons or to natural wildlife and (2) that plaintiffs failed to meet their obligation to show that defendants acted negligently in disposing chemical wastes on their property. We find both assertions to be without merit.

The essential element of an actionable nuisance is that persons have suffered harm or are threatened with injuries that they ought not have to bear. . . Distinguished from negligence liability, liability in nuisance is predicated upon unreasonable injury rather than upon unreasonable conduct. . . Thus, plaintiffs may recover in nuisance despite the otherwise nontortious nature of the conduct which creates the injury. . .

In his brief defendant has accurately stated that the injury produced by an actionable nuisance "must be real and not fanciful or imaginary * * *." . . The defendant next suggests that the injuries in the case at bar are of the insubstantial, unactionable type. It is this statement, however, rather than the purported injuries, that is fanciful. The testimony to which reference is made in this opinion clearly establishes that defendants' dumping operations have already caused substantial injury to defendants' neighbors and threaten to cause incalculable damage to the general public. The Picillos' neighbors have displayed physical symptoms of exposure to toxic chemicals and have been restricted in the reasonable use of their property. Moreover, expert testimony showed that the chemical presence on defendants' property threatens both aquatic wildlife and human beings with possible death, cancer, and liver disease. Thus, there was ample evidence at trial to support the finding of substantial injury implicit in the trial justice's finding of public and private nuisance.[FN4]

FN4. On appeal our review of the trial justice's findings is very limited. We must uphold the trial justice's factual findings unless they are clearly wrong or unless the trial justice overlooked or misconceived material evidence.

The defendants' remaining contention is that Rhode Island case law requires plaintiffs to prove negligence as an element of the nuisance case and that plaintiffs failed to do so.[footnote omitted] Generally, this court has not required plaintiffs to establish negligence in nuisance actions.[footnote omitted] . . . In one case, however, the Rhode Island Supreme Court refused to impose nuisance liability upon an oil refining company absent proof of negligence. See Rose v. Socony-Vacuum Corp., 54 R.I. 411, 421, 173 A. 627, 631-32 (1934). The defendant asserts that the Rose case is apposite to and controls the case at bar. We disagree.

The facts of Rose are somewhat similar to the facts of the present case. The plaintiff, Manuel Rose, owned a fifty-seven-acre farm in East Providence, Rhode Island, on which he maintained a piggery and hennery. Rose drew drinking water for his family and for the hens from a fresh-water well dug on the property, and the pigs drank from a stream that traversed the farm. The well and the stream were fed by waters that percolated from an underground source.

The defendant in Rose was the owner of a large oil refinery and several storage tanks situated directly across the street from the plaintiff's farm. The refinery and the storage tanks discharged and leaked petroleum, gasoline, and waste products into basins, streams, and ponds on the defendant's property. These substances, however, did not remain in their natural repositories. Rather, the oil products percolated through the soil into the groundwater and discharged into the plaintiff's well and stream. The pollutants contaminated the plaintiff's drinking water, killing 700 hens and 75 breeding sows. The plaintiff instituted suit against Socony-Vacuum, alleging private nuisance but not negligence.

The Superior Court sustained defendant's demurrer. On appeal, the Supreme Court framed the issue in the following terms:

"While the defendant could appropriate to its own use the percolating waters under its soil-providing that in so doing it was not actuated by an improper motive and was not negligent-can it, by the use to which it puts its land, deprive the plaintiffs of such waters by rendering them unfit for plaintiffs' use by contamination?" . . .

The court held that the defendant could with impunity contaminate the plaintiff's drinking water if the defendant polluted nonnegligently. . . The court reasoned that because "courses of subterranean waters are * * * indefinite and obscure," rights to them are less easily definable than riparian rights to surface streams. Suggesting that it might be unjust to subject landowners to liability for the unforeseeable consequences of legitimate land uses, the court looked to the teaching of other courts that had considered the issue. Examination of the cases disclosed a split of authority; jurisdictions with primarily agricultural economies imposed nuisance liability without proof of negligence, whereas jurisdictions with primarily industrial economies required a negligence showing. The Rose court determined that petroleum products were vital to the highly developed industrial economy of the local area, and held as a matter of policy that injury of the type occasioned by the defendant's percolating pollutants was, absent negligence, "damnum absque injuria." . . .

Since this court decided Rose v. Socony-Vacuum in 1934, the science of groundwater hydrology as well as societal concern for environmental protection has developed dramatically. As a matter of scientific fact the courses of subterranean waters are no longer obscure and mysterious. The testimony of the scientific experts in this case clearly illustrates the accuracy with which scientists can determine the paths of groundwater flow. Moreover, decades of unrestricted emptying of industrial effluent into the earth's atmosphere and waterways has rendered oceans, lakes, and rivers unfit for swimming and fishing, rain acidic, and air unhealthy. Concern for the preservation of an often precarious ecological balance, impelled by the spectre of "a silent spring," has today reached a zenith of intense significance. Thus, the scientific and policy considerations that impelled the Rose result are no longer valid. We now hold that negligence is not a necessary element of a nuisance case involving contamination of public or private waters by pollutants percolating through the soil and traveling underground routes.[footnote omitted]

For the reasons stated, the defendants' appeal is denied and dismissed. The judgment of the Superior Court is affirmed. The papers in the case may be remanded to the Superior Court.

Putting It Into Practice 11.3:

(a) What facts support a finding that the defendants' dump site constitutes a nuisance? (b) How does a negligence claim differ from a nuisance claim? (c) What facts support the plaintiffs' contention that they were injured by the chemical wastes harbored by the defendants? (d) On what basis does the court distinguish *Rose?* (e) Must negligence be shown in a case involving contamination of public or private waters by pollutants percolating through soil and traveling underground?

BONUS POINTERS:

ENVIRONMENTAL LAW

One of the fastest growing legal specialties for paralegals is environmental law. Paralegals can work for government agencies, such as the Environmental Protection Agency, helping with the enforcement and implementation of regulations or for the legal department of a large corporation, helping to ensure that the corporation is in compliance with all pertinent environmental regulations. They can also work for lobbyists representing groups having an interest in environmental issues or large real estate development companies who are concerned with complying with all relevant environmental regulations. The work may entail research of environmental rules and regulations, drafting opinions regarding potential environmental liability, reviewing corporate procedures to determine compliance with appropriate rules and regulations, monitoring the status of proposed rules and regulations, obtaining necessary permits, and assisting in litigation.

NET NEWS

To read more about environmental law issues, go to the Web site for the Center for International Environmental Law at *www.ciel.org.* A guide to electronic resources for environmental law can be found at the site for the American Society of International Law, *www.asil.org;* click on "Information and Resources," and then on "ASIL Guide to Electronic Resources for International Law."

Putting It Into Practice 11.4:

In which of the following circumstances might a nuisance exist? (a) An unusual number of children develop leukemia and other forms of cancer which their parents believe can be linked to their drinking water, allegedly contaminated by chemicals pouring into the water from a neighboring chemical plant. (b) A no-kill shelter for dogs and cats is built in a rural area, but eventually two housing developments are built around the shelter and the neighbors complain about the noise and smell. (c) Neighbors of an apartment complex complain to the landlord about his failure to control a drug-dealing operation, resulting in the neighbors' being confronted with drug dealers, prostitutes, and drug customers as well as the sounds of gunshots, fighting, and yelling, all of which has made them fear for their lives. (d) Jet noise from an airport is described as being comparable to the noise of a riveting machine; it interrupts residents' sleep, makes it difficult for them to converse on the phone, and causes their plaster to fall.

"So, do you both own the house"? Corazon continued.

"Yes. When we were married, we owned it as **joint tenants with right of survivorship.** When Arizona amended its community property laws to allow property to be held as **community property with right of survivorship,** we changed our title to that form. When we got divorced, we became **tenants in common.** Because George was to be responsible for maintaining the house, making repairs, and so on, we agreed that he would have a 60 percent ownership interest and I would have a 40 percent ownership interest. We agreed that it would be sold when our youngest child reached 18."

"And I take it your deed reflects that?" followed up Corazon. Martha nodded her affirmation. "Do you own the property free and clear?"

"Don't I wish," moaned Martha. "No, we have a pretty hefty debt secured by a **deed of trust.**"

"Is the loan assumable?" asked Corazon, knowing that if it were the house might be easier to sell. Corazaon wanted to have a clear understanding of the financing arrangements in regard to the house so that she could determine how much equity Martha and George had in it.

---

joint tenants with right of survivorship   co-ownership of property in which the parties have an equal, undivided interest in the property with a right of survivorship

community property with right of survivorship   new marital property interest recognized by statute in some community property states that allows a married couple to hold title to property as a community asset, but to retain the ease of transfer permitted by joint tenancy

tenants in common   co-ownership of property in which the parties have separate interests with no right of survivorship

deed of trust   type of security instrument in which the land is used as collateral in case the borrower defaults; the borrower agrees to convey title to the real property to a trustee, who holds the title in trust on behalf of the lender

---

NET NEWS

To read more about nuisance actions, zoning, easements, and licenses, go to *http://prairielaw.com*, click on "Article List," scroll down to "Residence," and look for the articles on these subjects. To read about CC&Rs, go to *www.nolo.com/encyclopedia/re_ency.hmtl* and look for the article entitled "Homeowners' Associations and CC&Rs."

SHARED OWNERSHIP OF PROPERTY

tenancy by the entirety
co-ownership of property by a married couple with right of survivorship

When parties own property together, they can own it in several ways: (1) joint tenants with right of survivorship; (2) tenants in common; (3) **tenants by the entirety;** or (4) as community property (with or without right of survivorship) as explained in Chapter 10.

With a joint tenancy form of co-ownership, the parties have equal and undivided interests in the property. This means that each owner has the right to own and use the entire piece of property. The owners also have a right of survivorship, which means that when one joint tenant dies, title to the property remains with the surviving joint tenants. So if, for example, A, B, and C are joint tenants and C dies, A and B will hold title to the property and C's heirs will have no interest in the property. This process continues until the survivor of the joint tenants owns all of the property. The survivorship aspect of a joint tenancy cannot be severed by a will, so that even if a joint tenant provides in her will that her property is to go to a designated individual, it will pass on to the other joint tenants. A joint tenancy can be severed, however, when the property, or an interest in the property, is sold.

Tenants in common hold separate interests in property (unlike the single ownership that joint tenants have); these interests can be equal or unequal shares in the land. In other words, both tenants can own one-half interest in a piece of land, or one tenant can own one-third and the other two-thirds of the land. Unlike a joint tenancy, no right of survivorship exists. Upon death of one of the tenants in common, the ownership interest of the deceased passes on to his heirs. Because most states prefer a tenancy in common, if a deed does not indicate how ownership is to be held, the ownership will be deemed a tenancy in common. Community property states, however, have different preferences when the property is owned by husband and wife and presume it is community property.

A tenancy by the entirety is a special type of joint tenancy reserved only for married couples. It is based on the common law principle that husbands and wives are one in reference to the ownership of land. As with a joint tenancy, when one spouse dies the other spouse takes title to the property exclusive of any heirs. Unlike a joint tenancy, neither spouse can transfer the property without the other's consent.

In all forms of co-ownership, the co-owners have a duty of reasonable care to the property. They are each responsible for their share of expenses, such as repairs and taxes. By the same token, they are entitled to a proportionate share of any incomes or rents produced by the property.

◆ **LOCAL LINKS** ◆
Do you live in a community property state? Does your state recognize community property with right of survivorship? Does your state recognize tenancies by the entirety?

Figure 11-3
Types of Co-Ownership

TYPES OF CO-OWNERSHIP

Joint Tenancy with Right of Survivorship
Joint tenants have equal, undivided interests in property
If one joint tenant dies, property goes to remaining joint tenants
until ultimately title is with last remaining survivor

Tenancy in Common
Tenants have separate interests in property that can be equal or unequal
If one tenant dies, property goes to that tenant's heirs
Preferred form of ownership except in community property states

Tenancy by the Entirety
Joint tenancy for a married couple

Community Property with Right of Survivorship
Ownership by married couple as community asset
Transfer on death of one spouse same as with joint tenancy

◆ **LOCAL LINKS** ◆
What agency records deeds
in your locale?

general warranty deed deed that warrants that the title to property is free from any encumbrances and that the seller guarantees to defend the buyer's good title forever

grantor seller (transferor) of real property

encumbrances restrictions on the use and sale of real property

mortgages type of security instrument in which the real property serves as collateral for the loan being made by the lender to the borrower

grantee buyer (transferee) of real property

limited (or **special warranty deed**) **warranty deed** deed that warrants only that the seller has done nothing to encumber title to the property, but provides no guarantees about the seller's predecessors

quitclaim deed transfers seller's interest in land and contains no warranties of title

habendum clause clause in a deed indicating what kind of estate is being conveyed

estate type of ownership interest

fee simple best form of ownership interest in which owner is entitled to the entire estate with unconditional rights to dispose of the property and to transfer it upon the owner's death

fee simple conditional ownership interest in which property reverts back to the grantor's ownership if certain conditions are not met

Putting It Into Practice 11.5:

If A, B, and C own property as joint tenants, and A and B both die, who owns the property? Who owns the property if A, B, and C are tenants in common?

DEEDS

Deeds are documents that describe the quality of the title transferred and any restrictions regarding the transfer of the property. A **general warranty deed** warrants the following.

◆ The **grantor** (seller) has possession of the land (or at least a right to possession).
◆ The grantor has a right to convey ownership of that land.
◆ The land is free from any **encumbrances** (restrictions, such as **mortgages,** liens, and easements that would limit the use of the land or be a debt on the land).
◆ The grantor promises to make any conveyances necessary in the future to vest the title intended to be conveyed now.
◆ The **grantee** (buyer) will be able to use the land without fear of being evicted or having third parties assert adverse claims.
◆ The grantor guarantees to defend the grantee's good title to the property forever so that if any of the covenants in the deed are breached, the buyer can sue the seller for damages.

A **limited** or **special warranty deed** warrants only that the seller has done nothing to encumber title to the property. It does not provide any guarantees about the seller's predecessors. Therefore, the seller is liable only for any defects in title caused by his own actions. A **quitclaim deed** transfers only the seller's interest in the land and not the land itself. It contains no warranties of title and conveys complete ownership of land only if the seller has complete ownership of the land.

A typical deed (shown in Figure 11-4) consists of the following.

◆ a caption showing where the deed was executed (sometimes called a venue statement)
◆ a preamble identifying the parties and the date the deed was executed
◆ a granting clause indicating that the land is being conveyed or granted and sometimes giving a recital of consideration
◆ a legal description of the land
◆ a **habendum clause** indicating what kind of **estate** is being transferred
◆ a warranty clause containing words of warranty
◆ an exception clause to indicate what encumbrances or conditions are not warranted
◆ an execution portion of the deed

Further exploration of the term *estate* is necessary to understand exactly what a deed is conveying. An estate refers to the ownership interest that a party has. The most common and best form of ownership is called a **fee simple,** which means that the owner is entitled to the entire estate with unconditional rights to dispose of the property and to transfer it upon the owner's death. A **fee simple conditional** occurs when the property reverts back to the grantor's ownership if certain conditions are not met. If a grantor donates property to a charity with the requirement that the property be used as a park, the charity's estate is a fee simple conditional. If the charity were to use the land to put up an office building, the land would revert back to

Figure 11-4
General Warranty Deed

This instrument was recorded
at the request of:

WHITE & TREADWELL
John Morgan, Esq.
2020 North Central Avenue, Suite 3200
Phoenix, Arizona 85005

The recording official is
directed to return this Deed
to the above person.

GENERAL WARRANTY DEED

County and State
Where Real Property
is Located: Maricopa County, Arizona
Escrow No. – TA 01-259
Tax Parcel No. – 211-66-098D
GRANTORS: Clancy D. Smith, a married man dealing with his sole and
separate property and Joanne Y. Smith, a single woman.

GRANTEE: Sharon L. Johnson, a married woman dealing with her sole and
separate property.

SUBJECT REAL PROPERTY (Legal Description)

An undivided one-half interest, as a tenant in common, of Parcel 18, WEST
VALLEY RANCH, according to the plat of record in the office of the County
Recorder of Maricopa County, Arizona, recorded in Book 494 of Maps, Page 133.

EXCEPT all mineral deposits and rights as reserved by the State of Arizona in
Deed recorded in Book 360 of Deeds, Page 10, Fee No. 19684, records of
Maricopa County, Arizona.

For consideration of Ten Dollars ($10.00), and other valuable consideration,
Grantors do hereby convey the Subject Real Property. We do warrant the title
against all persons whomsoever, subject to any matters set forth below.

[Subject to current taxes and assessments, reservations and all easements, rights of
way, covenants, conditions, restrictions, liens and encumbrances of record.] [MOST
WARRANTY DEEDS HAVE AN EXCEPTION CLAUSE SUCH AS THIS ONE]

Clancy D. Smith

_____
Joanne Y. Smith

STATE OF ARIZONA   )
)   ss.
County of Maricopa   )

The foregoing instrument was acknowledged before me this _____ day of July,
2001, by Clancy D. Smith.

My commission expires:

_____
Notary Public

STATE OF MICHIGAN   )
)   ss.
County of _____   )

The foregoing instrument was acknowledged before me this _____ day of July,
2001, by Joanne Y. Smith.

My commission expires:

_____
Notary Public

life estate ownership interest that lasts for the life of holder of the life estate or some other person and then reverts back to the grantor or a third person

estate for years ownership interest that lasts for a designated period of time

estate at will ownership interest that exists after an estate for years expires, but the grantee continues to live there and the grantor continues to accept payment

mortgagee lender or party holding a mortgage

mortgagor borrower or party occupying mortgaged land

trustor borrower or party occupying land serving as security for a deed of trust

trustee party that holds title to real property in trust for a lender

escrow company company that handles the details of property transfer and deed conveyance

title company company that issues title reports and title insurance policies

trustee's sale public auction at which land used as collateral for deed of trust is sold to pay a debt

promissory note promise by one party to pay another

lienholder party holding a lien

tax liens lien imposed by the government for failure to pay taxes in a timely manner

mechanic's liens (or construction liens) lien imposed by those who have provided labor or materials for the improvement of real property and who have not been paid

the grantor's ownership. Such an estate allows the grantor to have control over the property after its transfer and even after her death.

A **life estate** grants ownership that lasts for the life of the holder of the life estate or the life of some other person. After the named person dies, ownership reverts back to the grantor or passes on to a third party. An **estate for years** is created when the rights to property are transferred for a specified period of time. It turns into an **estate at will** if the estate for years expires and the grantee continues to live there with the grantor's permission. An estate at will can be terminated by either party at any time, although some statutory notice requirements may need to be fulfilled.

■ *Putting It Into Practice 11.6:*

Guillermo plans to buy some property so that he can build a goofy golf course. When he gets a copy of the deed to the current owner of the property, he notices that it is a special warranty deed whose habendum clause reads "To Michael Jones on the condition that the land be used for school purposes." What should be of concern to Guillermo?

Deeds will also indicate what kinds of encumbrances have been imposed on the property. Typical encumbrances are mortgages, deeds of trust, and liens (discussed previously in Chapter 2). A mortgage is a type of security instrument in which the real property serves as collateral for the loan being made by the **mortgagee** (lender) to the **mortgagor** (borrower). If the mortgagor should default on a loan payment, the mortgagee has the option of "accelerating" the full loan amount so that the entire amount of the loan (plus interests and penalties) is due immediately. If the mortgagor fails to cure this default, the mortgagee can then bring a court action to foreclose on the property and sell it at public auction.

With a deed of trust, the borrower (**trustor**) agrees to convey title of the real property to a **trustee** (usually an **escrow** or **title company**), who holds the title in trust on behalf of the lender. If the borrower defaults, the trustee can sell the land at a public auction, called a **trustee's sale**, and use the proceeds to pay the debt. The foreclosure procedure for deeds of trust is generally simpler, cheaper, and faster than those involving a mortgage because no court action is required.

Because most purchasers do not have sufficient cash to buy a home, most have to get a loan. Lenders require borrowers to sign a **promissory note** (promise by one party to pay another) and this note is secured by a mortgage or deed of trust. When a new purchaser assumes a loan (if the loan documents allow an assumption), she becomes responsible for paying the debt. If she fails to do so, the lender can sue the new owner as well as the original mortgagor.

A lien also encumbers land because it is a claim against property that secures a debt owed by the property owner. You may recall that a lien allows the **lienholder** (person holding the lien) to sue to get a court order forcing the sale of the property to satisfy an outstanding debt. **Tax liens** can be attached to private property by the federal, state, or local governments when a taxpayer fails to pay taxes in a timely manner. Tax liens can be imposed for failure to pay income taxes, inheritance taxes, business-related taxes, and real property taxes. The latter take priority over all other liens and can be enforced only against the real property that is the subject of the tax. **Mechanic's liens** (also called *construction liens*) allow those who have provided labor or materials for the improvement of real property and who have not been paid to place a lien on real property and ultimately foreclose on it. Those who are entitled to file mechanic's liens are specified by statute and generally include general contractors, subcontractors, laborers, and suppliers of materials.

NET NEWS

For more information about mortgages and liens, go to *http://prairirelaw.com*, click on "Article List," and scroll down to "Residence." Additional information about mortgages can be found by going to *www.nolo.com/encyclopedia/re_ency.html* and clicking on "Mortgage Basics FAQ," and by going to the Web site for American Mortgage Online at *http://amo-mortgage.com/library/info.htm*.

Figure 11-5
Overview of a Deed

OVERVIEW OF A DEED

Preamble

Caption

Granting Clause

Legal Description

Habendum Clause
Fee Simple
Fee Simple Conditional
Life Estate
Estate for Years
Estate at Will

Warranty Clause
General Warranty
Limited (special) Warranty
Quitclaim (no warranty)

Exception Clause
Easements
Mortgages
Deeds of Trust
Liens
Taxes
Assessment

Execution

Putting It Into Practice 11.7:

Minerva goes online and finds the recorded deed for some property she is interested in buying. She notices that a mortgage exists on the property and that a tax lien was recorded the year before. What are two conditions she should impose on any offer she makes?

"I Think Renegotiating the Distribution of the Proceeds of the Sale Could Go a Long Way Toward Resolving Your Conflict with George."

Having determined that Martha potentially had a substantial equity interest in the marital home, Corazon made her recommendation. "I would suggest that you and George sign a contract providing that, in light of your agreement to be responsible for selling the home, making the necessary repairs, painting, and anything else that needs to be done to prepare the house for sale, you be awarded 50 percent of the proceeds. If your estimate of the increase in the value of the house since you bought it is anywhere near accurate, you could get as much as $25,000. Now, of course, you'll need to get the house appraised to see if this figure's realistic, but I think renegotiating the distribution of the proceeds of the sale could go a long way toward resolving your conflict with George."

"That it could," agreed Martha wholeheartedly. "In fact, I may be able to sell it without investing much at all. I have a cousin who's always loved that house and it would be ideal for her because it's only five miles from where she works. She'd have to sell her house, but I think she could turn it over pretty fast. And if she and I make a deal, I won't be out the commission to a realtor." Martha brightened as she began to see some light around the once dark issue of finance.

"Sounds great," said Corazon encouragingly. "But make sure you have someone help you prepare your sales-purchase agreement or at least have an attorney review it before you sign it. And do a thorough **title search,** or have someone else do it, before you agree to anything with George. You don't want to find out later that he has some liens on the property."

"Absolutely," agreed Martha. "Actually, I began my work as a paralegal in the real estate area. I've prepared a few sales contracts and done some title searches. But I would certainly want to have any contracts I enter into reviewed by an attorney first and I will no doubt order a title search done by a reputable title company before I agree to anything with George."

title search　search of public records to determine if the title to real property is free from any encumbrances that would reduce the value of the property or threaten foreclosure against it

SALE OF REAL PROPERTY

Real Estate Contracts

A real estate contract has all the same requirements as any other contract. It should include the following.

- ◆ identities of the buyers and sellers
- ◆ consideration exchanged
- ◆ precise description of the real property being sold, any personal property to be included, and any property that is to be excluded
- ◆ purchase price of the property or an exact means of computing that price (e.g., price per square foot or per acre)
- ◆ method of payment
- ◆ quality of title seller is obligated to provide and buyer is willing to accept
- ◆ definite date buyer will take possession of the property
- ◆ closing date (date by which parties agree to perform all of their promises under the contract)
- ◆ list of documents parties will be expected to sign at closing
- ◆ all closing costs and who will be responsible for paying them
- ◆ warranty as to the condition the property will be in at the time of possession and who will bear the risk of any losses
- ◆ any warranties or representations the parties relied on in entering into the contract
- ◆ any contingencies on which the contract is conditioned
- ◆ rights and obligations of the parties in case of default
- ◆ any notice requirements

BONUS POINTERS:

LEGAL DESCRIPTIONS OF PROPERTY

A legal description of property is far more precise than a street address in that it sets forth the exact boundaries of the property, describing it with such specificity that it distinguishes it from all other pieces of real estate. A legal description can have one of three forms: (1) metes and bounds; (2) government survey; or (3) plat.

A metes and bounds legal description is the oldest of the three descriptions and, many believe, the most detailed. It outlines the boundaries of a property, beginning with a starting point, describing the direction and distance that boundary line travels from that point around the perimeters of the property, and returning to the starting point. An example of part of such a description follows.

Begin at the SW corner of Section 20, then north along section line 30 feet, then west 20 feet to the Point of Beginning, then due west a distance of 25 feet, then north 55 45′ west a distance of 64 feet . . .

The most widely used description is the government survey description, which is based on a grid system. The grid is organized according to meridians (running north-south) and base lines (running east-west) and is subdivided into townships (a six-mile square), which are then divided into sections (a one-mile square). An example of such a description follows.

The northwest quarter (NW1/4) of the northeast quarter (NE1/4) of the southwest quarter (SW1/4) of Section 23, Range 4 East, Township 6 North, of the Gila and Salt River Base and Meridan, Maricopa County, Arizona.

(The above property description is a 10 acre, rectangular-shaped parcel that is 660′ wide and 660′ long, one acre being 43,560 square feet.)

The plat method is the simplest of the three descriptions. It references a piece of property to its location on a plat map, which is recorded in the land records in the county in which the property is located. A plat map breaks down a large tract of land into blocks, which are referenced by number or letter. Each block is further broken down into lots, which are referenced by number. A plat description also includes the legal description for the entire tract, which may be a metes and bound or government survey description. An example of a plat description follows.

Lot 76, Block 2, of BLISS ACRE ESTATES, 4TH SECTION according to the plat thereof, recorded in the Plat Book 89, Page 24, of the Public Records of Maricopa County, Arizona.

---

title examination same as title search

title insurance insurance of someone with an interest in real property against any losses caused by encumbrances or defective title

foreclosure a legally permitted sale of real property from which proceeds are used to pay a debt

Title Searches and Title Insurance

Crucial to any transfer of real property is an assurance to the buyer that he is receiving good title to the property. Three things are done by real estate attorneys and their paralegals to determine if the title to property is clear: (1) requesting a general warranty deed from the seller; (2) conducting a title search (or **title examination**); and (3) making sure the buyer gets appropriate **title insurance.**

The buyer of real estate cannot rely solely on a warranty deed because the grantor of the deed may die, disappear, or be insolvent, and because other limitations restrict liability on a warranty deed. A prudent buyer always conducts a title search: a search of all public records to determine if the title is free from any encumbrances that would reduce the value of the property or threaten **foreclosure** against

---

NET NEWS

The U.S. Census Bureau provides detailed street grids at *http://tiger.census.gov.* If you want to try drawing a map based on a legal description, you can download a 30-day trial version of a map drawing program at "MapDraw Deed Plotter" at *www. informatik.com/mapdraw.html.*

To do a property records search in almost any state, go to *www.netronline.com/Property-Records-AO.htm.*

the property. (Foreclosure is a legally permitted sale of real property from which proceeds are used to pay a debt.) This search is extremely important because the law charges a buyer with the responsibility for learning about all title matters that could result from an inspection of the property itself or from an examination of public records. In other words, a purchaser generally cannot later claim ignorance of an encumbrance on the title of real property he has bought if that encumbrance could have been discovered through a search of public real property records.

Certainly, a thorough title search is essential to discover any encumbrances that have been imposed on real property by mortgagees, trustors, lienholders, and so on (assuming these people have properly recorded their interests). But a title search is only as good as the skill of the examiner who does it and the availability of information. Sometimes examiners make mistakes (and their malpractice insurance limits may be inadequate), and sometimes information is simply not available in public records. For example, title to property can be achieved through **adverse possession,** that is, taking possession of another's land without the owner's consent and retaining possession of that land for a period of time prescribed by statute. Adverse possession can occur when a neighbor puts his fence on his neighbor's yard and the neighbor (because of ignorance or indifference) does not object, or when a cattleman grazes his cattle on grasslands adjoining his own land. Because the titled owner may not be aware of this possession and no public records would be filed, a title search would not reveal it. In Martha's case, if the fence had been in place for the statutory time period, she and George might have been able to claim the land inside the fence by adverse possession if the neighboring landowner had not consented to the fence's placement on his land.

Title insurance is available to protect the insured in case a defect in legal title or an encumbrance that affects the title is later discovered. The American Land Title Association (ALTA) was created to meet the demands for uniform title insurance protection. Most title insurance companies belong to ALTA and use their standard form title insurance policies.

adverse possession taking possession of another's land without the owner's consent and retaining possession of that land for a period of time prescribed by statute

settlement statement a written statement showing where all the funds are being dispersed; also called a *closing statement*

Putting It Into Practice 11.8:

What are the possible consequences for a buyer who fails to do a thorough title search? Who fails to buy title insurance?

After discussing all the factors Martha should keep in mind in relation to selling the house, Corazon was satisfied that Martha knew how to protect her legal and financial interests. "Oh, and one more thing," she added before going on the next issue. "Remember to instruct the escrow agent to disburse 50 percent of the proceeds to you at the time of the closing. Ask to review the preliminary disbursal instructions prior to the closing so that you can catch any errors early on. And you'll want to make sure that the **settlement statement** is accurate, that the computation of taxes and interest are correct, and that any fees charged are correct."

"Thanks for the reminders," acknowledged Martha gratefully. "I know there's a lot that can get overlooked at a closing and I appreciate the heads-up."

NET NEWS

Online links to assessment offices nationwide can be found at *www.people.virginia.edu/~dev-pros/Realestate.html.* You can search by owner name or address to get the most recent assessed value.

Real Estate Closings

real estate closing transfer of documents and monies to complete a real estate transaction

A **real estate closing** refers to the transfer of documents and monies to complete a real estate transaction. The closing agent can be an escrow agent, title company, or law firm. Paralegals can be involved in real estate closings if they work for a lender's in-house counsel, a title company, a corporation, or a law firm that handles real estate transactions.

Real estate closings require meticulous attention to details and good organization skills. The tasks that must be performed prior to a closing include the following.

- ◆ ordering and reviewing surveys and title search
- ◆ drafting closing documentation
- ◆ keeping track of deadlines set forth in the contract and loan documents
- ◆ verifying all computations in the closing documents
- ◆ verifying that all obligations have been fulfilled by seller and buyer and that all loan requirements have been satisfied
- ◆ requesting satisfaction amounts on any encumbrances to be paid at the closing
- ◆ preparing all contracts and loan documents
- ◆ preparing packet of closing documents

If the paralegal serves as an assistant at closing, she will need to review all the documents with the parties, make sure they are properly executed, disburse the monies, and see that keys and other pertinent items are given to the buyer. Subsequent to the closing the paralegal must do the following.

- ◆ record all documents with the court
- ◆ obtain all satisfactions for any encumbrances
- ◆ order final title search and verify proper recording of all documents
- ◆ review final title insurance policy
- ◆ transmit recorded deed and title insurance policy to buyer and recorded loan documents to lender
- ◆ organize closing packages for buyer, seller, and lender

Putting It Into Practice 11.9:

What are some of the potential errors that could occur in a real estate closing?

NET NEWS

Real estate forms can be found at the following sites:

www.vandema.com/Forms.htm; *www.alllaw.com/forms/real_estate*; and *http://forms.lp.findlaw.com*; At *www.lectlaw.com*, click on "The Library's Rotunda," "Forms Room," "Business and General Forms," and scroll down almost to the bottom to "Real Estate Forms."

ETHICAL ETIQUETTE

REAL ESTATE CLOSINGS

Real estate closings raise the possibility of three different ethical violations. First is the question of whether paralegals should be allowed at real estate closings without the presence of a supervising attorney. Some states allow this; others do not. The concern is that the parties are likely to raise legal questions that a paralegal may be tempted to respond to, resulting in the unauthorized practice of law. In those states that do allow this practice, the tasks that the paralegal performs must be purely ministerial, an attorney must have supervised any work done prior to the closing, and an attorney must be available to answer any legal questions that arise during the closing.

Copious documents have to be signed and notarized at a real estate closing, so another potential dilemma that can occur is whether a paralegal who is a notary should ever agree to notarize a document if she is not present to witness the signing. The answer: a conscientious paralegal *should never* agree to notarize something she has not personally seen being signed. By notarizing a signature, a notary is swearing under the notarial oath that she has seen the person, has made reasonable efforts to assure that person's identity, and has seen that person sign the document. Therefore, if she has not actually seen what she is swearing under oath to have seen, she is committing perjury. Paralegals who are to serve as notaries should make it clear at the beginning of their employment that they refuse to notarize any document they have not actually seen signed.

A third ethical issue that frequently arises at real estate closings involves unrepresented parties who ask an attorney who represents only one of the parties to give them legal advice. In such situations, attorneys must clarify their position as advocates for their client and decline to provide any legal advice. Some courts have suggested that attorneys in this situation should explain the material terms of the closing documents so that the unrepresented party understands what he is signing. An alternative, and perhaps wiser approach, is to provide that party with a blank form and advise him to seek his own counsel who can explain the legal consequences of the agreement into which he is entering.

Putting It Into Practice 11.10:

Luis is supposed to meet his supervising attorney at a real estate closing. After waiting for 20 minutes and making several unreturned phone calls to the attorney, the parties decide to go forward with the closing without the attorney. Luis's firm represents one of the buyers, who asks Luis a few questions that Luis indicates he is unable to answer because he is not an attorney. He notices, however, that one of the other buyers, who does not have an attorney, is questioning the attorney for the seller in regard to some of the documents he is signing. After the parties leave, the attorney for the seller notices that the seller failed to sign one of the documents. He asks Luis, who served as a notary during the closing, if he would go ahead and notarize the document so that the attorney can send it to his client to sign. What ethical issues arose in this closing and how do you think they should be handled?

◆ LOCAL LINKS ◆

Are paralegals allowed to attend real estate closings without attorney supervision in your state?

latent defect   hidden defect

"It's a Latent Defect and Failing to Disclose That Information Could Be Considered Concealment."

"Just one more question about the sale of the house," added Martha.

"Ask away," encouraged Corazon.

"The basement of our house got flooded a few years ago when we had one of those infamous 100-year floods. We put in new carpet and painted the walls so you really can't tell there was ever any water damage. Am I right in assuming I should disclose what happened to a purchaser?"

"Is it possible this could happen again?"

"Not likely, but possible. The house is next to a ravine that, on very rare occasions, does flood."

"Then yes, I would say you do. It's a **latent defect** and failing to disclose that information could be considered concealment," opined Corazon.

ETHICAL ETIQUETTE

INTENTIONAL MISREPRESENTATION

Intentional misrepresentation (the equivalent to fraud or deceit under the common law) is committed when in the following circumstances.

◆ The defendant misrepresents something with the intent of inducing the plaintiff's reliance on the misrepresentation.

◆ The defendant knows that the representation is false or acts with reckless indifference to the truth.

◆ The plaintiff justifiably relies on the misrepresentation.

◆ The plaintiff suffers damages stemming from the reliance.

In short, a defendant commits misrepresentation by affirmatively making a false statement or by intentionally concealing a fact from the plaintiff. A seller of a house, for example, who deliberately paints the ceiling to conceal from the plaintiff-buyer that the roof is leaking commits misrepresentation.

Under the common law, mere failure to disclose a material fact was not considered misrepresentation. Until the 1950s, the doctrine of caveat emptor ("let the buyer beware") reigned and sellers of real estate had virtually no duty to disclose what they knew about the condition of their property to potential buyers. In the modern view, however, nondisclosure may be considered concealment under certain circumstances, especially when the defect is latent. A duty to disclose, for example, is frequently set forth in the so-called "termite" cases, in which the homeowner fails to tell the purchaser that the house has been infested with termites.

Liability may be imposed even if a defendant presents a half-truth, a statement that, although literally true, tends to be misleading. A statement such as "We have no termites in this house" is a half-truth if the termites have been long-standing residents up until a month before the statement was made. The courts are more likely to find misrepresentation if a non-disclosed fact is essential to the transaction. If a seller of land fails to disclose to a buyer that nothing can be grown on the land even though she is aware the buyer intends to use the land to grow crops, she is likely to be found liable for misrepresentation. Today, a small but rapidly growing number of states have enacted legislation or created regulations that require sellers of residential property to disclose certain aspects of the property's physical condition to potential purchasers.

intentional misrepresentation
affirmatively making a false statement or intentionally concealing a fact from the plaintiff

Putting It Into Practice 11.11:

Morana has had an ongoing problem with rats in her attic that have caused considerable damage to her heating and air-conditioning ducts. (a) Does she have a duty to disclose this to a buyer? (b) Would your answer change if the question were whether she should disclose the fact that her husband was brutally murdered in the house, which is why she wants to move? (c) What if she was aware that a convicted sex offender lives in the neighborhood and that the family interested in buying her home has two young children. Should she have to disclose what she knows about the sex offender?

"Any other questions you have about the sale of the house?" asked Corazon before moving on.

"Well, one thing I didn't mention is that George has a buddy of his renting the house temporarily on a month-to-month lease. I don't anticipate having any problems getting him to leave when the time comes, but is there anything I should be aware of?"

"As you probably know, a month-to-month tenancy requires a 30-day notice be given prior to the next rental date before you can ask him to leave. Also, you should get a letter from the tenant acknowledging that he has an oral month-to-month lease, what the agreed upon rent is, and the date the rent is due. This is to ensure that he doesn't later say he has a longer lease. If he won't sign the letter, you'll know there's a problem right away.

LEASING OF PROPERTY

lease document conveying a leasehold interest in real property; includes the right to possession but not ownership

leasehold estate (nonfreehold estate) uninheritable estate of limited duration; refers to a landlord-tenant relationship

tenancy for years (tenancy for a term) tenancy for a designated time period

periodic tenancy tenancy with no designated ending date; parties must give proper notice before terminating lease

tenancy at will tenancy with no designated ending date; parties need not give notice before terminating the lease

tenancy at sufferance tenancy created when a tenant stays on the land without the landlord's permission

◆ **LOCAL LINKS** ◆

Has your state adopted some form of URLTA?

abate pay less

constructive evicted tenant's moving out without paying rent for the remainder of the lease term because of landlord's failure to maintain habitable premises

security deposits money collected by the landlord in advance to defray cost of repairs when the tenant leaves

If the owner of land wants to rent her property to another, she can enter into a **lease** agreement with that individual. A **leasehold estate** (also known as a **nonfreehold** estate) is of limited duration and uninheritable; it refers to the landlord-tenant relationship. It can take one of four forms. A **tenancy for years** (also referred to as a *tenancy for a term*) continues for a designated period of time. A tenancy in years that lasts longer than a year is required to be in writing. A **periodic tenancy** has no definite ending date and will continue until one of the parties follows the steps mandated by statute to terminate the lease. Periodic tenancies are usually established for set periods (such as a week-to-week or month-to-month); at the end of each rental period the lease can be terminated with proper notice—a key legal requirement that must be strictly honored. As with a periodic tenancy, a **tenancy at will** has no designated ending date, but both parties retain the right to terminate the tenancy at any time without having to give notice. (Some state laws do require some form of notice.) Tenancies at will usually begin as tenancies in years and convert to tenancies at will when the tenancy period ends and the landlord agrees to allow the tenant to remain. A **tenancy at sufferance** is created when a tenant stays on the land without the landlord's permission, giving the landlord the choice of evicting the tenant or of "suffering" his presence. Although in common law no notice was required, most states require that some type of notice be given before terminating a tenancy at sufferance.

Leases are governed not only by contract law but by state statutes. Many states have adopted some version of the Uniform Residential Landlord and Tenant Act (URLTA). Most states require landlords to maintain premises in a habitable condition. This *implied warranty of inhabitability* exists even if not explicitly provided for in the lease. This warranty requires that (1) all reasonable repairs be made in a reasonably timely manner; (2) all common areas (e.g., elevators, stairways, and hallways) be kept clean and safe; (3) running water, reasonable amounts of hot water, and reasonable heat and cooling be supplied at all times; and (4) all electrical, plumbing, heating, ventilating, air-conditioning, and sanitary facilities be supplied and maintained.

A landlord cannot negate his statutory responsibilities by including a lease provision in which the tenant agrees to waive the right to a warranty of habitability.

If a landlord fails to maintain the premises in a habitable condition, the tenant has several options.

◆ She may terminate the lease after providing the landlord with written notice of the problem and giving the landlord reasonable time to correct that problem.

◆ He may make the necessary repairs or hire someone to make them and deduct the cost of repairs from the rent owed.

◆ She may **abate** the rent (pay less rent) based on the reduction in value of the premises.

◆ He may move out without paying rent for the rest of the lease term, in which case the tenant is considered to have been **constructively evicted**. This is permitted in only the most egregious of circumstances.

Other state statutes regulate the landlord-tenant relationship, such as those that pertain to the handling of **security deposits** (money collected in advance by the landlord to defray the cost of repairs needed when the tenant moves out). Some states have rent control statutes that restrict the amount of rent that can be charged. Most states have open housing laws that prohibit landlords from discriminating in reference to the tenants to whom they agree to rent.

◆ **LOCAL LINKS** ◆

Does your state have rent
control statutes?
Does your state have open
housing laws?

Tenants have obligations as well. They must keep the premises clean and safe, must use appliances in a reasonable manner, and must not negligently or willfully destroy property or allow their guests to do so. If a tenant fails to honor her obligations, the landlord may have grounds for entering the premises, correcting the problem, and charging any repairs to the tenant. If the tenant's breach is serious enough, the landlord may have grounds for terminating the lease. To do this, the landlord must comply with the statutory requirements regarding notice (when and how it is to be served), must file a complaint, and ask to be awarded a judgment allowing the tenant to be evicted and, in some cases, obtain past rent owed. Until a judgment is obtained, the landlord can do nothing to harass the tenant or to disrupt his services.

Putting It Into Practice 11.12:

Beth and Sandoval Ortiz have a month-to-month lease. For the most part, they enjoy their apartment and its surroundings, but they are angry with the landlord because, despite repeated promises to fix their toilets, he has not done so and they continue to overflow on a regular basis. What are the Ortiz's options? What is the landlord's option?

Figure 11-5
Landlord-Tenant Relationship

LANDLORD TENANT RELATIONSHIP

Types of Leasehold Estates
Tenancy for years
Periodic tenancy
Tenancy at will
Tenancy at sufferance

Landlord Obligations
Maintain premises in habitable condition

Tenant Obligations
Keep premises clean and safe
Use appliances reasonably
Do not destroy property or allow guests to destroy property

Landlord Rights
If tenant fails to honor his obligations, the landlord can:
enter the premises, correct the defect, and charge cost of repairs to tenant
terminate lease after providing proper notice and getting a judgment

Tenant Rights
If landlord fails to maintain premises in habitable condition, tenant can:
make repairs and deduct cost of repairs from rent
Terminate lease (after giving proper notice)
Abate rent
Constructive eviction

NET NEWS

For links to the landlord-tenant laws in most states, go to *http://cses.com/rental/ltlaw.htm*. Several articles at this site regarding landlord-tenant relationships are also available dealing with such issues as the types of tenancy, the implied warranty of habitability, tenants' duties, landlord-tenant disputes, and security deposits.

To find out more about what paralegals do in real estate law, go to *www.paralegals.org/Reporter*, click on "Summer 1997," and look for the article entitled "So You Want to Work in Real Estate." Also, click on "Spring 1999" and go to the section entitled "Paralegal Roles and Responsibilities" to read interviews with paralegals working in this field.

ROLE OF THE PARALEGAL

As you can probably deduce from this brief overview of real property law, paralegals who work in this area must be highly organized and detail-oriented. In addition to law firms, they can work in property management companies, title companies, realty companies, and construction companies. No matter where they work, they must be prepared to perform a wide variety of tasks.

- ◆ researching zoning regulations
- ◆ ordering and reviewing title searches
- ◆ drafting land sale contracts
- ◆ preparing deeds, notes, and loan documents
- ◆ reviewing real estate transfer documents
- ◆ providing lenders with required documents
- ◆ drafting preliminary title opinions
- ◆ collecting data necessary for closing
- ◆ preparing and organizing documents for closing
- ◆ assisting in obtaining financing
- ◆ recording documents
- ◆ assisting at closings and with foreclosures

RECESS

SUMMARY – PART A

Ownership of real property includes ownership of the land, the buildings and plants on it, the minerals beneath its surface, and the air space above it. It also includes limited rights to use of the water on it and beneath its surface. Fixtures are also included in real property; knowing whether property is classified as a fixture becomes important when the land on which the fixture is located is sold or when the land is used as security for a debt.

A landowner can grant a license to another verbally, in writing, or by implied conduct. She can also grant an easement, which is an actual property interest that can be granted expressly, by implication, or by necessity. An easement can also be obtained by prescription if it is used for a specified period of time without the owner's consent. Purchasers of land, particularly those in which a homeowners' association is involved, should look in the deed for any restrictive covenants that limit land use. Land use can also be regulated by the government through zoning. Zoning must promote the public welfare and must be reasonable; if it is unreasonable, it constitutes a "taking" for which the landowner may be entitled to compensation. Changes in zoning regulations require that notice of the change be given so that a public hearing be held at which the public can express its opposition. Landowners who use their land in such a way as to interfere with others' use and enjoyment of their land can be used for nuisance. Public nuisance is a commonly used tort action alternative to CERCLA claims made by environmental law plaintiffs.

Parties can own land as joint tenants with right of survivorship, by which they have equal, undivided interests in the land that go to the surviving joint tenants when one of them dies, or as tenants in common, by which they have separate interests in the land that pass to their heirs when one of them dies. Married couples can own property as tenants by the entirety, which has the same survivorship provisions as a joint tenancy. In all three cases, common owners must share in their responsibilities for the care of the land as well as the benefits they reap from the land.

Purchasers of property prefer buying property that has been conveyed by means of a general warranty deed because it provides so many more warranties than limited warranty or quitclaim deeds. In addition to spelling out warranties, a deed contains a legal description of the land and indicates the type of estate being conveyed, which can be a fee simple, a fee simple conditional, a life estate, an estate for years, or an estate at will. Deeds indicate the types of encumbrances imposed on a property, such as mortgages, deeds of trust, and liens. With both mortgages and deeds of trust, the land is used as collateral and can be sold at a public auction if the borrower defaults on the loan. Liens allow the lienholder to get a court order forcing the sale of the property to satisfy an outstanding debt. Tax liens are imposed by the government and mechanics' (construction) liens are imposed by those who provide materials or labor for the improvement of real property. In addition to demanding a general warranty deed, a buyer who wants to make sure she is receiving good title can have a title search done and can buy title insurance. A buyer cannot later claim ignorance of an encumbrance on the title of real property if that encumbrance could have been discovered by searching public records. Title insurance protects purchasers when information is not available in any public records, such as when someone is in adverse possession of property. Sellers have an ethical duty to avoid intentionally misrepresenting their property by affirmatively making false statements or by intentionally concealing a fact from the buyer, particularly when the undisclosed fact is material to the transaction.

Real estate closings can be conducted by an escrow agent, title company, or law firm. They involve an extraordinary amount of paperwork and require meticulous attention to detail. An ethical question exists as to whether paralegals should be allowed at real estate closings when a supervising attorney is not present. Two other ethical questions that arise at closings relate to dealing with unrepresented parties and notarizing signatures without personally witnessing them.

A leasehold (nonfreehold) estate can be a tenancy for years, a periodic tenancy, a tenancy at will, or a tenancy at sufferance. Leases are governed by contract law as well as state statutes, many of which are based on the Uniform Residential Landlord and Tenant Act (URLTA). An implied warranty of habitability in any lease requires that landlords must maintain their premises in a habitable condition. If a landlord fails to maintain the premises in a habitable condition, the tenant can terminate the lease (after providing written notice and giving the landlord reasonable time to correct that problem), make the necessary repairs (or hire someone to do them) and deduct the cost of repairs from the rent, abate the rent, or move out without paying rent. If a tenant fails to honor his obligations, the landlord may have grounds for terminating the lease, but to do so must comply with all notice requirements and other statutory procedures.

KEY TERMS

Abate
Adverse possession
Community property
    with right of
    survivorship
Constructive evicted
Covenants, conditions,
    and restrictions
    (CC&Rs)
Deed
Deed of trust
Easement
Easement by necessity
Eminent domain
Encumbrances
Escrow company
Estate
Estate at will
Estate for years
Express easement

Fee simple
Fee simple conditional
Fixture
Foreclosure
General warranty deed
Grantee
Grantor
Habendum clause
Implied easement
Implied warranty of
    habitability
Intangible property
Intentional
    misrepresentation
Joint tenants with right of
    survivorship
Latent defect
Lease
Leasehold estate
    (nonfreehold estate)

License
Lienholder
Life estate
Limited warranty deed/
    special warranty deed
Mechanic's
    liens/construction liens
Mortgages
Mortgagee
Mortgagor
Nuisance
Periodic tenancy
Personal property
    (chattel)
Prescriptive easement
Private nuisance
Promissory note
Public nuisance
Quitclaim deed
Real estate closing

Real property
Restrictive covenant
Security deposits
Settlement statement
Tangible property
Tax liens
Tenancy for years
    (tenancy for a term)
Tenancy at will
Tenancy at sufferance
Tenants by the entirety
Tenants in common
Title company
Title examination
Title insurance
Title search
Trustee
Trustee's sale
Trustor
Zoning

REVIEW QUESTIONS – PART A

1. What does ownership of real property include?
   a. Differentiate real property from personal property.
   b. What does personal property include?
2. What is the difference between the prior appropriation doctrine and the riparian rights approach to water rights?
3. What is a fixture?
   a. What factors are considered in determining whether property is a fixture?
   b. When is a property's classification as a fixture important?
4. What is the difference between an easement and a license?
   a. How is a license obtained?
   b. How is an easement obtained?
5. How does a restrictive covenant differ from a zoning regulation?
   a. Why should CC&Rs be reviewed carefully?
   b. What is required before a zoning change can occur?
   c. What is a "taking" and how does it relate to the concept of eminent domain?
6. What is a nuisance? For what reason is it being used frequently today?
7. Distinguish owning land as joint tenants with right of survivorship from owning it as tenants in common or tenants by the entirety.

8. Why is a general warranty deed preferable to a limited warranty or quitclaim deed?
9. Identify each of the following.
   a. fee simple
   b. fee simple conditional
   c. life estate
   d. estate for years
   e. estate at will
10. What types of encumbrances can be imposed on real property?
    a. What is the difference between a mortgage and a deed of trust?
    b. What are tax liens and mechanics' liens?
11. What are three things a purchaser can do to ensure she is receiving good title to real property?
    a. Why is conducting a thorough title search so important?
    b. How does title insurance protect a purchaser?
12. Describe the ethical duty of sellers in regard to their duty to disclose information to buyers.
13. What kinds of tasks might a paralegal perform in relation to a real estate closing?
14. Under what conditions might a paralegal be allowed to attend a real estate closing without an attorney's supervision?
15. What ethical question can arise in reference to the notarizing of signatures? What is the suggested response?

16. How should an attorney deal with unrepresented parties at a real estate closing?
17. Explain the difference between a tenancy for years, a periodic tenancy, a tenancy at sufferance, and a tenancy at will.
18. What does an implied warranty of habitability provide?

19. What options does a tenant have if a landlord fails to provide a habitable place?
20. What obligations does a tenant have? What must a landlord do to terminate a tenant's lease?

PRACTICE EXAM – PART A

MULTIPLE CHOICE

1. Ownership of real property includes
   a. ownership of any crops, which are also considered real property
   b. ownership of the oil and gas beneath the property's surface
   c. ownership of the air space above, although that is of little value
   d. ownership of any water to the exclusion of all others

2. The riparian rights approach
   a. is used primarily in the West
   b. can result in landowners with first rights to water getting their water needs fulfilled while those later in time getting little or no water
   c. provides equal ownership rights to everyone
   d. allows landowners upstream to build a dam that prevents those downstream from getting any water

3. In deciding whether property is a fixture
   a. the property's degree of permanency is important
   b. the intent of the parties is not considered
   c. the character of the property is not important
   d. the relative attachment of the property to the land is the only factor that is considered

4. A ranch owner who gives his neighbor permission to graze his cattle on his land creates
   a. an easement
   b. a license
   c. a covenant
   d. none of the above

5. Easements
   a. are often given to utility companies
   b. can be implied
   c. by necessity are usually very restricted
   d. all of the above

6. Zoning regulations
   a. need not promote the public welfare
   b. can be done in secret
   c. can be considered a taking
   d. are created by the government and cannot be voided simply because they are discriminatory

7. Eminent domain can be exerted by the government
   a. any time it needs private property
   b. only if it can show that private property is needed for public use
   c. and does not require any kind of compensation for the private landowner
   d. none of the above

8. A nuisance
   a. claim has a short statute of limitations
   b. can be both private and public
   c. is no longer used in the environmental area because of CERCLA
   d. all of the above

9. Tenants in common
   a. own property interests that go to the other tenants when one of them dies
   b. own separate, equal interests in the land
   c. are inferred in most non-community property states if a deed does not specify how the land is held
   d. all of the above

10. A tenancy by the entirety
    a. prohibits one spouse from transferring property without the other spouse's consent
    b. is based on the common law principle that a husband and wife are one for purposes of land ownership
    c. has a right of survivorship provision
    d. all of the above

*11. A legal description of land is in the form of
    a. metes and bound
    b. plat
    c. government survey
    d. all of the above

12. A deed that transfers only the seller's interest in the land and not the land itself is called a
    a. habendum deed
    b. quitclaim deed
    c. limited warranty deed
    d. general warranty deed

13. A limited warranty deed warrants
    a. that the grantee can use the land without fear of having adverse claims filed by third parties in the future
    b. that the land is free of any encumbrances
    c. only that the seller is liable for any defects in title caused by his own actions
    d. none of the above

14. A general warranty deed warrants that
    a. the grantee will be able to use the land without fear of being evicted
    b. the grantor has a right to convey ownership of that land
    c. the grantor promises to make any conveyances necessary in the future to vest the title intended to be conveyed now
    d. all of the above

15. A typical deed consists of
    a. a preamble and caption
    b. a habendum clause
    c. warranty and exception clauses
    d. all of the above

16. A type of land ownership that gives the grantor power over the land after it is transferred and even after her death is called
    a. an estate for years
    b. an estate at will
    c. a fee simple conditional
    d. a fee simple

17. With a mortgage
    a. the mortgagee has the option of accelerating the full loan amount if the mortgagor defaults on a loan payment
    b. no court action is required to foreclose on the property
    c. the property is held in trust by a title company
    d. all of the above

18. A real estate purchase contract
    a. must contain the exact purchase price of the property and not simply indicate how that price is to be computed
    b. should include the closing date, but need not list the date the buyer will take possession
    c. should include all the closing costs and who will be responsible for paying them
    d. should indicate the rights and obligations of the parties in case of default, but should not mention any contingencies on which the contract is conditioned

19. A buyer of real property
    a. cannot rely solely on a general warranty deed
    b. need not do a title search if he has a general warranty deed

c. need not get title insurance as long as he gets a general warranty deed
    d. can later sue the grantor for a defective title even if he could have discovered that defect through a search of public real property records

20. Even if a purchaser has a title search done, he may not be fully protected against defective title because
    a. someone may have gained adverse possession of the property
    b. the title examiner may have inadequate malpractice insurance
    c. the title examiner may have made a mistake
    d. all of the above

21. A closing agent
    a. must keep track of all deadlines set forth in the contract and loan documents
    b. verify all computations in the closing documents
    c. verify that all obligations have been fulfilled by seller and buyer
    d. all of the above

22. At the closing, a closing agent
    a. is supposed to review all documents with the parties and make sure they are properly executed
    b. is not responsible for disbursing any monies
    c. should have already recorded all documents with the court
    d. none of the above

23. A paralegal can attend a real estate closing without being supervised by an attorney
    a. under no condition
    b. even if she performs tasks that go beyond being merely ministerial
    c. as long as an attorney is available to answer the parties' legal questions
    d. in every state

24. Attorneys faced with an unrepresented party at a real estate closing
    a. cannot even explain the terms of the closing documents to that party
    b. should advise the party to get his own counsel
    c. must first clarify their role as an advocate and then can provide legal advice
    d. none of the above

25. An implied warranty of habitability
    a. has no requirements regarding the common areas
    b. does not require landlords to make repairs
    c. requires that reasonable amounts of heat and cooling be supplied
    d. requires landlords to maintain electrical and plumbing facilities, but says nothing about ventilating and air-conditioning facilities

26. If a landlord fails to maintain the premises in a habitable condition, the tenant
    a. can make the necessary repairs himself but cannot deduct the cost of repairs from his rent
    b. can abate the rent
    c. cannot simply move out without paying rent
    d. can immediately terminate his lease without notice

27. If a tenant fails to honor his obligations
    a. the landlord can enter the premises and correct the defect
    b. cannot terminate the lease
    c. can terminate the lease immediately without giving notice
    d. can disrupt the tenant's services

28. A seller of a house
    a. has no duty of disclosure to a buyer because of the principle of "caveat emptor"
    b. commits misrepresentation by making a false statement or acting with reckless indifference to the truth
    c. commits misrepresentation even if the buyer does not rely on the misrepresentation and suffers no damages
    d. can tell half-truths but cannot make affirmatively false statements

FILL IN THE BLANK

29. Under the _____ doctrine, landowners who use water from a natural source have a superior right to those who begin using that water at a later date. Under the _____ approach, all landowners have equal ownership rights.

30. Personal property that becomes so attached to real property that it is eventually characterized as real property is called a _____ . Personal property is also known as _____ , and includes both _____ property, such as cars and furniture, and _____ property, such as stocks and bonds.

*31.   Intellectual property deals with _____ (which protect literary and artistic works), _____ (the distinctive symbols and mottos that identify businesses), and _____(which protect inventions).

32. A landowner who gives another permission to use her land grants a _____ , but a landowner who gives another an actual property interest in his land creates an _____ . If the latter is obtained without the owner's consent because an individual uses the property without permission for a specified period of time, it is called a _____ .

33. _____ are provisions in a deed that restrict land use. The restrictions imposed by homeowners' associations are called _____ .

34. _____ is a regulation created by government to control land use; if such a regulation is unreasonable, it may constitute a _____ , for which the private landowner may be entitled to compensation.

35. The government can exert its power of _____ by taking private property for public use.

36. People who play extremely loud music at 3:00 A.M. commit the tort of _____ , whereas a company that pollutes the water of a whole town commits the tort of _____ .

37. When landowners have equal, undivided interests in land that pass to the other co-owners upon the death of one of them, they own the land as _____ . If they own it as a married couple and the land goes to the surviving spouse when the other spouse dies, they own the land as _____ (unless they live in a community property state that has adopted the new property interest called _____). Landowners who have separate interests in land that pass to their heirs when one of them dies own the land as _____ .

38. A _____ is a document that describes the quality of title being transferred and any restrictions regarding the transfer of the property.

39. A _____ deed warrants that the _____ (seller) has possession of the property and that the _____ (buyer) will be able to use the land without fear of being evicted or having third parties assert adverse claims. A _____ deed, on the other hand, warrants only that the seller has done nothing to restrict the title to the property, but does not guarantee anything about the seller's predecessors. A _____ deed contains no warranties of title and conveys complete ownership of land only if the seller has complete ownership of the land.

40. A landowner who has an unconditional right to dispose of property and to transfer it upon his death owns a _____ , but if the property reverts back to the grantor's ownership if certain conditions are not met, the landowner has a _____ . A _____ is an estate that lasts for the life of the tenant or the life of some other person, while an _____ is created when the rights to property are transferred for a specified period of time. Such an estate turns into an _____ if the grantee continues to live there after the estate expires and the grantor continues to accept payment.

41. A _____ is a type of security instrument in which real property is collateral for a loan being made by a _____ (lender) to a _____ (borrower).

42. A _____ is a type of security instrument in which the _____ (borrower) conveys title to the real property to a _____ , who holds the title in trust on behalf of the lender. If the borrower defaults, the trustee can sell the land at a public auction called a _____ and use the proceeds to pay the debt.

43. When a buyer borrows money to buy real property, the lender has him sign a _____ , which is a promise by the borrowed to pay the lender. If a new purchaser _____ a loan, he becomes responsible for paying the loan.

44. A lien allows a _____ (person holding a lien) to force the sale of property to satisfy an outstanding debt. _____ liens can be attached to private property by the government when a taxpayer fails to pay taxes in a timely manner and a _____ (or _____) lien can be attached by those who have provided labor or materials for the improvement of real property and who have not been paid.

45. Buyers should always conduct a _____ , a search of all public records to determine if a title is free from any encumbrances that would reduce the value of the property or threaten _____ (a legally permitted sale of real property from which proceeds are used to pay a debt).

46. An individual can take title to property by _____ if he takes possession of the land without the owner's consent and retains possession of it for a period of time prescribed by statute.

47. _____ protects the insured if a defect in legal title or an encumbrance that affects the title is later discovered.

48. A _____ involves the transfer of documents and monies to complete a real estate transaction.

49. A _____ estate, which refers to the landlord-tenant relationship, can be a _____ (which lasts for a designated period of time), a _____ , which has no designated ending date and can be ended when one of the parties gives proper notice, a _____ , which has no designated ending date and can terminate without notice being given, or a _____ , which occurs when a tenant stays on the land without the landlord's permission.

50. Most state statutes regarding landlord-tenant relations are based on the _____ Act, which includes an _____ requiring landlords to maintain their premises in a habitable condition.

51. If a landlord fails to maintain premises in a habitable condition, a tenant may (in the most egregious of circumstances) consider herself _____ and move out without paying rent.

52. State statutes often regulate the handling of _____ , which is money collected in advance by the landlord to defray the cost of repairs needed when the tenant moves out.

53. A seller commits _____ by affirmatively making false statements or by intentionally concealing facts from the buyer.

TRUE OR FALSE

____*54. Intellectual property law is becoming one of the more popular and higher paying legal specialties for paralegals.

____ 55. In the West, water law is an important specialty of legal practice.

____ 56. Fixtures are generally not transferred when real property is sold.

____ 57. A dishwasher is probably not a fixture.

____ 58. A license cannot be implied from conduct.

____ 59. A license for which consideration is received is not revocable.

____ 60. An easement by necessity is obtained by using a landowner's property on a continuous, uninterrupted basis for a specified period of time.

_____ 61. Easements require a formal document preparation.

_____ 62. Prescriptive easements are often given to landowners who are landlocked.

_____ 63. CC&Rs can be used to limit the types of lawns homeowners put in and the type of paint they use on the exterior of their house.

_____ 64. Changes in zoning regulations require that notice be given and that a public hearing be held.

_____ 65. Nuisance claims require a showing of physical harm to the land.

_____ 66. If A, B, and C own property as joint tenants and A dies, the land goes to B and C.

_____ 67. The survivorship aspect of a joint tenancy can be severed by a will and by selling the property.

_____ 68. Tenants by the entirety are reserved for married couples.

_____ 69. Those who own land together are responsible for their proportionate share of repairs and taxes.

_____ 70. With a general warranty deed, the grantor guarantees to defend the grantee's good title to the property forever so that if any of the covenants in the deed are breached, the grantee can sue the grantor for damages.

_____ 71. A typical deed indicates what encumbrances are not warranted, but usually does not contain a legal description of the land.

_____ 72. The most common and best form of land ownership is the life estate.

_____ 73. With a life estate, the property reverts back to the grantor's ownership if certain conditions are not met.

_____ 74. An estate at will can be terminated by either party at any time unless statutory notice requirements apply.

_____ 75. If the mortgagor defaults on a loan payment, the mortgagee has the option of making the entire amount of the loan (plus interests and penalties) due immediately.

_____ 76. Foreclosures for mortgages are simpler, easier, and faster than those for deeds of trust.

_____ 77. If a purchaser of real property assumes a loan and fails to make a payment, the lender can sue the new owner as well as the original mortgagor.

_____ 78. Real property tax liens take priority over all other tax liens.

_____ 79. Only general contractors and subcontractors have a right to file a mechanic's liens.

_____ 80. A purchaser who later discovers a defect in the title to his real property can still recover damages even if the grantor has died or is insolvent.

_____ 81. Under the law, a buyer is responsible for learning about all title matters that could result from an inspection of the property itself or from an examination of public records.

_____ 82. Adverse possession can occur when a neighbor puts his fence on his neighbor's yard even if the neighbor objects.

_____ 83. Most title insurance companies belong to ALTA and use their standard form title insurance policies.

_____ 84. Only title companies and escrow agents can conduct real estate closings.

_____ 85. Real estate closings require meticulous attention to detail and good organization skills.

_____ 86. Subsequent to a closing, a paralegal should obtain all satisfactions for any encumbrances and order a final title search.

_____ 87. The concern with paralegals attending real estate closings without attorney supervision is that they may be tempted to engage in acts that would constitute the unauthorized practice of law.

_____ 88. In some circumstances, paralegals can notarize signatures they have not personally witnessed being signed.

_____ 89. A tenancy in years that lasts longer than a year must be in writing.

_____ 90. Tenancies at will are usually established for set periods, such as month-to-month, and can be terminated at the end of each rental period with proper notice.

_____ 91. Periodic tenancies usually begin as tenancies in years and convert to periodic tenancies when the tenancy period ends and the landlord agrees to allow the tenant to remain.

_____ 92. Leases are governed not only by contract law but by state statutes, many of which are based on URLTA.

_____ 93. A landlord can negate her statutory responsibilities by including a lease provision in which the tenant agrees to waive the right to a warranty of habitability.

_____ 94. Very few states have open housing laws that prohibit landlords from discriminating in reference to the tenants to whom they agree to rent.

_____ 95. A tenant's only obligation is to keep the premises clean and safe.

____ 96. To terminate a tenant's lease, a landlord must comply with the statutory notice requirements but need not obtain a judgment.

____ 97. Under the common law, sellers had no duty to disclose facts to buyers. Under the modern view, non-disclosure can be considered misrepresentation, especially if the concealment relates to a latent defect.

____ 98. The courts are more likely to find misrepresentation when the undisclosed fact is essential to the transaction.

____ 99. Real estate paralegals must be highly organized and very detail-oriented.

____*100. Environmental law is one of the slowest growing areas of the law.

*Questions taken from Bonus Pointers

PART B

"George Isn't in Denial About Death, He's More in Denial About Life."

"One more thing—something I advise everyone to do when they get a divorce," continued Corazon. "Have you re-written your will since you got a divorce?"

"Yes, I redid mine as soon as the divorce was final. But you know, I'll be willing to bet George still hasn't redone his. I reminded him a couple of times, but I doubt he remembered to do it," said Martha frowning.

"Doesn't want to think about dying, huh?" surmised Corazon.

"Not really. George isn't in denial about death. He's more in denial about life. I mean, half the time I'm not sure he's in the same reality as the rest of us. It's hard to keep him focused on practical, everyday matters because he's usually off pondering some esoteric question. That's one thing I love about . . .," said Martha, catching herself before she finished her sentence.

"Tim?" Corazon nonchalantly filled in the blank. "I'd imagine he's very much in the here and now."

"I was going to say 'That's what I love about being single,' " finished Martha lamely. Wanting to forestall any further comments about Tim, she asked a question to which she already knew the answer. "So what happens to the girls if George has not prepared a new will?"

"If he dies **intestate,** all of his property will go to his children. You, of course, will receive nothing because any previous will in which you were provided for is revoked by law because of your divorce."

"Then I guess there's no real advantage to the girls in having him redo his will," concluded Martha.

"Not unless he should remarry. Then if he died intestate, his new wife would receive half of his property and your girls would split the other half," explained Corazon.

"And the only way to change that would be to get him to rewrite his will," said Martha, thinking out loud.

"Right," agreed Corazon. "And you'll have no way of knowing if he decides to change his will at any time. Probably a better way for you to provide for your girls in case of George's death is to have him purchase a life insurance policy naming the girls as the sole beneficiaries. This way they would be provided for in the event he was no longer able to pay child support."

"So maybe I should make that a condition of any settlement we reach as far as child support is concerned."

"Now you're thinking like a negotiator," grinned Corazon.

intestate   dying without a will

will   document expressing the decedent's will as to how his property should be distributed

intestate succession   manner in which a decedent's property will be distributed when no will applies

decedent   deceased person

DYING WITHOUT A WILL

A person who dies without a **will** is said to have died intestate and his property will be distributed in accordance with the laws of **intestate succession** applicable in his state. Although these laws vary, they are all controlled by the family relationships of the **decedent.** Note that personal property is distributed in accordance with the intestate succession laws of the state where the decedent was domiciled, whereas real property is distributed in accordance with the laws of the state where the real property is located.

All state intestacy statutes begin by giving all or a proportion of the estate to the surviving spouse and the remainder to any surviving children. If there is no

issue lineal descendants

descendants blood relative of decedent related in a descending lineal line (e.g., children and grandchildren)

per capita distribution of property based on giving equal shares to all those entitled to the estate

Figure 11-6
Per Capita Distribution

surviving spouse, the property will be distributed to the **issue** (lineal **descendants,** such as children and grandchildren) of the intestate. It can be distributed on a **per capita** basis or a **per stirpes** basis. With a *per capita* distribution, an equal share is given to each descendant with the same degree of relationship to the decedent. With a *per stirpes* distribution, the shares are based on the relationship of the descendant to the decedent. For example, suppose Hubert dies intestate with two surviving children, Albert and Bernice, and one child who predeceased him, Candace, who has two surviving children, Cory and Carla. Under the *per capita* approach, there would be a total of four heirs and so each would receive one-fourth of the estate.

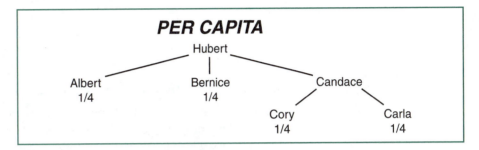

per stirpes distribution of property that depends on the relationship to the intestate of those entitled to the estate

Figure 11-7
Per Stirpes Distribution

Under the *per stirpes* approach, each of Hubert's children would be entitled to receive one-third of Hubert's estate, but because Candace is deceased, her children, Cory and Carla, would split their mother's share and each would receive one-sixth of Hubert's estate.

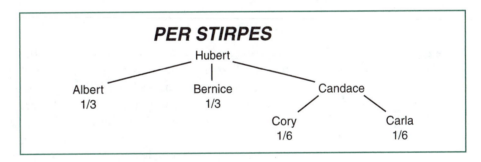

In most states and under the Uniform Probate Code (UPC), a uniform probate law that has been adopted in some form by a minority of the states, property is passed down in the following order.

1. First to the surviving spouse and children
2. If none, then to other lineal descendants (grandchildren and great-grandchildren)
3. If none, then to lineal **ascendants** (parents or grandparents)
4. If none, then to **collateral** relatives (those who have the same ancestors as the decedent but who did not descend from the decedent (e.g., brothers and sisters of the decedent)
5. If none, then other blood relatives of the decedent
6. If none, the property will **escheat** (pass to the state)

ascendants ancestor; blood relative of decedent related in an ascending lineal line (e.g., parents and grandparents)

collateral someone having the same ancestors as the decedent, but not descending from the decedent (e.g., brothers and sisters)

escheat pass to the state

In most states, relatives by marriage (other than the surviving spouse) receive nothing through intestate distribution. Adopted children are treated like natural children of the decedent. Illegitimate children are entitled to inherit from their mother, but receive nothing from their biological father unless they have been legitimized.

Figure 11-8
Typical Intestate Succession of Property

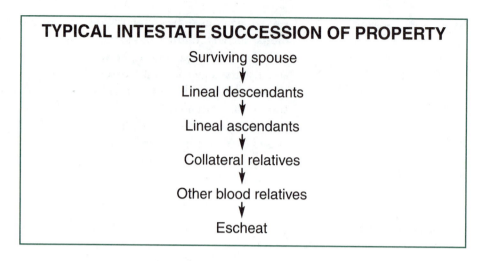

TYPICAL INTESTATE SUCCESSION OF PROPERTY

Surviving spouse
↓
Lineal descendants
↓
Lineal ascendants
↓
Collateral relatives
↓
Other blood relatives
↓
Escheat

◆ **LOCAL LINKS** ◆

Has your state adopted some form of the UPC? Does your state use a *per capita* or *per stirpes* distribution with intestate estates?

Putting It Into Practice 11.13:

Winona dies intestate. Her husband and their three children survive her. (a) To whom will her property go? (b) To whom would her property go if her husband had predeceased her? (c) Would your answer change if one of the children were adopted? (d) Suppose that two of Winona's children, Nina and Jeremiah, are alive but that her other child, Alexandra, died two years ago. Alexandra is survived by three children, Portia, Patrick, and Petra. What are two possible ways her property would be distributed?

WILLS

estate planning   process of arranging one's assets to most effectively protect oneself and one's family during and after life as well as facilitating the smooth transfer of property after death

Preparing a will is one of the more common forms of **estate planning,** which is the process of arranging one's assets to most effectively protect oneself and one's family during and after life as well as facilitating the smooth transfer of property after death. Thoughtful estate planning allows the family to receive the maximum benefit and enjoyment of their property and minimizes the income, gift, inheritance, and estate taxes they must pay. Other than wills, commonly used estate planning tools are trusts (discussed later in this chapter), co-ownership of property, life insurance, and the making of lifetime gifts (to avoid death taxes).

testator   person making a will

testatrix   female making a will (term used in some states)

beneficiaries   recipient of a benefit from a will or trust

A will provides one of the easiest ways of giving an individual a voice in how he wants his property distributed and avoiding the legal problems that can arise when someone dies intestate. On the other hand, probating a will can be an expensive and time-consuming process that may create problems the **testator** (person making a will; in some states a female testator is called a **testatrix**) never anticipated. To avoid these problems, a will must be carefully designed and well-drafted to meet the needs of the testator and his intended recipients (**beneficiaries**), persons who receive a benefit from a will or those receiving the benefits of a trust.

NET NEWS

To see South Dakota's version of the Uniform Probate Code, go to *www.law.cornell.edu/uniform/probate.html*. This same site shows the states that have adopted the UPC.

A gateway to estate planning can be found at *www.estateplanninglinks.com*. This site includes information about probate, different types of trusts, insurance, valuation of assets, and many more items of interest to those involved in estate planning. To read more about the estate planning process, go to *www.nolo.com/encyclopedia/ep_ency.html*.

testamentary capacity one's ability to know what one owns, what one desires to be done with what one owns, and the identity of family members and others for whom one has affection

To be valid a will must be (1) made by an adult (usually 18); (2) made by someone with **testamentary capacity** (i.e., knows what she owns, what she wants done with it, and who her family members and others for whom she has affection are; and (3) created voluntarily (by free will and choice).

holographic will will that is handwritten by the testator

A will can be formal (prepared on a word processor or typewriter), signed, and properly witnessed. It can also be **holographic** (handwritten by the testator with no witnesses) or **noncupative** (oral). Many states do not recognize such wills, especially noncupative ones.

noncupative oral will

◆ **LOCAL LINKS** ◆

Are holographic and noncuptaive wills recognized in your state?

Putting It Into Practice 11.14:

Sloan's wife puts him in an adult care facility when she is no longer able to care for him. Sloan, who has been diagnosed as suffering from Alzheimer's, asks one of his caregivers one day to give him a pad and pencil so he can prepare his last will and testament. Why might any will he prepares not be recognized by the courts?

◆ **LOCAL LINKS** ◆

What are the witness requirements in your state? Can testators create self-proving wills?

executor individual responsible for carrying out the directives in the will; a female executor is referred to as an *executrix* in some states

A typical will consists of the following components.

◆ a declaration clause declaring the age, capacity, and residence of the testator
◆ a debt clause providing for payments of all debts, expenses, and taxes
◆ an appointment clause appointing the **executor** (masculine) or *executrix* (feminine) or, as they are now known in many states, the personal representative (individual responsible for carrying out the directives in the will) and possibly describing the executor's powers

devise gift of real property

◆ a gift clause disposing of the testator's property through a **devise,** or gift of real property, or **bequest** (also called a *legacy*), or gift of personal property, to specified beneficiaries
◆ a residual clause disposing of any property remaining after the distribution designated in the gift clause
◆ an execution and signature clause

bequest gift of personal property; also called a *legacy*

Witness requirements, such as the number of witnesses and whether a witness can be a beneficiary, vary from state to state. Some states require that the witnesses sign in the presence of the testator and in the presence of one another and that they all be present when the testator signs the will. Many states allow testators to create **self-proving wills,** which are presumptively valid and dispense with the need to call in witnesses to prove their validity. This can be done by having the testator and witnesses sign a notarized affidavit swearing that the testator is of age, appears to be of sound mind, and was not acting under some outside influence.

self-proving wills will with a notarized affidavit signed by the testator and witnesses attesting that the testator is of age and sound mind and prepared the will voluntarily

If a testator executes a second will, the first will is revoked. Most subsequent wills contain a clause indicating that the testator "hereby revokes any prior wills and

---

NET NEWS

To read more about will preparation, go to *www.nolo.com/encyclopedia/ep_ency.html* and click on "Wills." To see sample wills and to read about the requirements for making a will, go to *www.lectlaw.com/formb.htm*. To see the wills of such famous people as John F. Kennedy, Jr., Linda McCartney, and Elvis Presley, go to *www.ca-probate.com/wills.htm*.

PARALEGAL SUPERVISION OF WILL EXECUTION

Although in many law firms, paralegals commonly witness the signing of wills, the issue of whether paralegals can supervise the execution of a will has not been addressed by most states. The concern is that paralegals will be put in a position of giving legal advice if they are asked to explain the legal implications of a document being signed.

Figure 11-9
Wills in a Nutshell

WILLS

Requirements of a Valid Will
Testator is an adult
Testator has testamentary capacity
Will is made voluntarily
Adheres to witness and signature requirements

Elements of a Typical Will
Declaration clause
Debt clause
Appointment clause
Gift clause
Residual clause
Execution and signature clause

How to Revoke a Will
Prepare a second will
Prepare a codicil
Destroy or partially destroy will
Revocation by law when family relationships
of testator change

Grounds for Contesting a Will
Testator was not of age
Testator was not of sound mind
Will was made under undue influence
Formalities of execution of will were not observed
Will was not signed

codicil addition to a will

codicils." A **codicil** (addition to a will), which has to be signed and witnessed like the will, serves to revoke any provisions in the original will with which it is inconsistent. In addition, most states provide for revocation or partial revocation by law when the family relationships of the testator change. In many states, for example, a divorce automatically revokes that portion of a will where any property is left to the former spouse. By the same token, marriage after a will has been executed often entitles the new spouse to at least an intestate share of the testator's property. Testators can deliberately revoke a will by destroying it (e.g., cutting, tearing, burning, or writing "Void" or "Cancelled" across the will). The interpretation of partial

◆ **LOCAL LINKS** ◆

In your state, what must a testator do to revoke a will? In your state does a partial destruction of a will invalidate the whole will?

undue influence   acting under another's direction rather than out of free will and choice

confidential relationship relationship based on trust and dependency

destruction varies. In some states, crossing out portions of a will serves to revoke those sections only; in other states, it serves as a revocation of the entire will.

The validity of a will can be contested by anyone having an interest in the testator's estate—a beneficiary named in the will or an omitted heir. A will can be set aside if the testator was not of age or of sound mind, if the will was not signed, or if the formalities of execution were not honored. One of the more common grounds for challenging a will is the allegation that the testator was under **undue influence.** In essence, the argument is that the testator did not make the will voluntarily but was acting under someone's direction. The most frequent scenario occurs when an elderly testator's caregiver, on whom the testator is dependent for his daily living needs, becomes the sole beneficiary of the testator's will to the exclusion of the testator's other relatives. A presumption of undue influences exists when (a) a **confidential relationship,** based on trust and dependency, exists between the testator and the major beneficiary; (b) the testator's weakened condition made a subversion of her free will easy; and (c) the influencer actively participated in preparing the will or unduly profited as a beneficiary under the will. The case of *Troyer v. Plackett* nicely illustrates the factors a court considers in determining whether undue influence exists.

Cite as: 48 Or.App. 497, 617 P.2d 305

Court of Appeals of Oregon.
In the Matter of the ESTATE of Grace SWENSON, Deceased.
Jane **TROYER,** and Urinda Laura Lee Russell, Respondents,
v.
Cora **PLACKETT,** Personal Representative of the Estate of Grace Swenson,
Appellant.
No. 128786; CA No. 16071.
Argued and Submitted July 23, 1980.
Decided Sept. 29, 1980.

WARDEN, Judge.

This is a proceeding to contest the will of Grace Swenson brought by Jane Troyer and Urinda Laura Lee "Betty" Russell, daughters of the deceased. They contend that decedent lacked testamentary capacity and that the will was the product of undue influence exerted by the sole beneficiary, Cora Plackett.

The will was admitted to probate on March 20, 1978. Contestants filed objections to probate on July 20, 1978. After a hearing on those objections on July 23, 24 and 25, 1979, the trial court, on September 24, 1979, issued a letter opinion finding that at the time of the execution of the will decedent lacked testamentary capacity and, further, that the will was the result of the undue influence of Cora Plackett. By order entered October 12, 1979, the court made formal findings in accordance with its letter opinion, sustained the objections to probate, declared the will null and void, decreed the order admitting the will to probate set aside and

revoked the appointment of Cora Plackett as personal representative of the estate of Grace Swenson. Cora Plackett appeals this order. Our review is de novo. We affirm the trial court, finding that the will of Grace Swenson dated July 21, 1977, was the product of undue influence of Cora Plackett.

We abstain from the usual lengthy recitation of the facts in this type of case. We will recite facts in our discussion of the issue of undue influence which control our decision.

In In Re Reddaway's Estate, 214 Or. 410, 419-20, 329 P.2d 886 (1958), the Supreme Court said:

"Definitions of undue influence couched in terms of the testator's freedom of will are subject to criticism in that they invite us to think in terms of coercion and duress, when the emphasis should be on the unfairness of the advantage which is reaped as the result of wrongful conduct. 'Undue influence does not negative consent by the donor. Equity acts because there is want of conscience on the part of the donee, not want of consent on the part of the donor.' . . . Said in another way, undue influence has a closer kinship to fraud than to duress. It has been characterized as a 'species of fraud.' "

The burden of proving undue influence is upon the contestants. . . A confidential relationship between the testator and a beneficiary, considered together with other suspicious circumstances, may require the beneficiary to carry the burden of proof and present evidence to overcome the adverse inference of undue influence. . . . Cora Plackett bore a confidential relationship to decedent. She was decedent's "friend"; she bathed decedent, gave her drugs, shopped for her, wrote her checks and transported her.

The factors to be considered in determining whether undue influence is exercised were set out by the Supreme Court in In Re Reddaway's Estate, supra, and reiterated by this court in Carlton v. Wolf, supra.

The first of these factors is procurement, that is, participation of the beneficiary in the preparation of the will. Cora Plackett, after learning that decedent intended to disinherit both her daughters and shortly after being told by decedent that decedent was thinking of leaving her entire estate to her, urged decedent to make a new will. She gave decedent the phone book, made the phone call to the attorney for her, talked to the attorney at the time of his first conference with the decedent and escorted the decedent to the attorney's office for purposes of execution of the will on July 21, 1977. (It is also at least interesting to note that Cora Plackett did not list that date in her diary as one of the days on which she worked for decedent.)

The second factor is independent advice. A beneficiary who participates in preparation of a will and occupies a confidential relationship to the testator has a duty to see that the testator receives independent, disinterested advice. . . Cora Plackett did not seek to have decedent call either Mr. Hammond or Mr. Herbrand, attorneys, each of whom had drawn a will for decedent within ten months immediately preceding the drawing of this will. Instead, she helped the decedent contact a lawyer unknown to decedent. The attorney chosen had been in the practice of law less than two years and he relied in part on misinformation provided him by either decedent or Cora Plackett. The record discloses that he acted as little more than a scrivener. No effort was made by Cora Plackett to communicate with either of decedent's daughters, with other relatives or friends of the decedent, with doctors or with representatives of

social agencies serving decedent to secure independent advice.

The third factor is secrecy and haste. No notice was given to the decedent's family members, close friends, or social service personnel. Decedent's true condition was kept from her daughter, Jane Troyer, when she made inquiry of her mother's condition on June 27, 1977, after a cousin, who had visited decedent for a week, phoned Jane telling her that her mother needed help, was being taken advantage of, and was on "dope." The services of an attorney who did not know decedent were sought, rather than those of attorneys to whom she was known. Cora Plackett urged the decedent to change her will and acted to assist her in changing her will within a week after Cora Plackett learned from decedent that decedent was considering making her her sole beneficiary.

The fourth factor is change in attitude toward others. Decedent had made two wills in the ten months prior to making this will. In September, 1976, she made a will leaving her entire estate to her two daughters to be shared equally. In February, 1977, by a second will, she left her entire estate to both daughters, with one receiving but $5 and the residue going to the other. Though Cora Plackett testified that she did not seek to have decedent leave her entire estate to her, the record is also entirely void of any effort by her to urge upon decedent any reconciliation with her daughter, Jane Troyer, from whom she had become estranged. Jane Troyer was a friend of Cora Plackett's sister and had engaged Cora Plackett's services for the decedent.

The fifth factor is a change in the decedent's plan of disposing of her property. The two prior wills left decedent's entire estate to her daughters. This will disinherited them and gave the estate to a virtual stranger.

The sixth factor is that of an unnatural or unjust gift. The decedent disowned her two daughters, the natural subject of her bounty, and gave her entire estate to an acquaintance of less than two months duration. Decedent's original contact with the lawyer who drew the will was made only 33 days after Cora Plackett entered her home.

The seventh and final factor is susceptibility to influence. Decedent was physically sick, suffering from numerous ailments and injuries. She was unable to walk without help. She could not drive an automobile. She was dependent upon drugs and frequently used alcohol to excess. She had recently lost her husband of 40 years. She mistakenly accused one of her daughters of stealing her property. Her susceptibility to being taken advantage of was amply demonstrated by her dealings with a husband and wife, realtors, who befriended her and then took advantage of her in a series of transactions.

There are substantial conflicts in the testimony in this case. It is apparent from the record and the trial judge's decision that he did not accept the testimony of Cora Plackett as credible. As we have often stated, we give substantial weight to the findings of the trier of fact who saw and observed the witnesses.

We are satisfied from this record that Cora Plackett, the beneficiary of the July 21, 1977 will of Grace Swenson, exerted undue influence in the making of that will. Because we decide the case favorably to contestants on this issue, we do not address the question of the decedent's testamentary capacity. The judgment of the trial court is affirmed.

Putting It Into Practice 11.15:

(a) Why is the will being contested? (b) Did Cora Plackett have a confidential relationship with the decedent? (c) What are the seven factors the court considers in determining whether there was undue influence? (d) How were these factors met in this case?

Putting It Into Practice 11.16:

Homero is deeply appreciative of the loving care he has received from his nurse, Santiago. In the final week of his life, he asks Santiago to help him rewrite his will. He does not want to hire an attorney, so he asks Santiago to help him find the part in the will that provides for his daughter, Mercedes. He then crosses out all references to bequests to Mercedes and, at the end of the will, indicates that he wants to leave all of his personal belongings to Santiago, who has shown him so much kindness in the last days of his life. On what grounds might Mercedes be able to challenge the validity of the altered will?

ETHICAL ETIQUETTE

ATTORNEY/PARALEGAL AS BENEFICIARY OF WILL

Attorneys and paralegals must not draft a will for a testator when they are to be a beneficiary under that will. Doing so meets the criteria for the presumption of undue influence. It also violates the *Model Rules of Professional Conduct* (Rule 1.8(c)), which provides that a lawyer shall not prepare any instrument that gives the lawyer (or anyone related to the lawyer, including a spouse, parent, child, or sibling) a substantial gift from a client. An exception is made if the client is related to the lawyer receiving the gift.

BONUS POINTERS:

LIVING WILLS

The term *living will* (or *medical directive*) is commonly used today, but the document is not really a will. Rather than indicating how a person wants to dispose of her property, a living will expresses a person's desires in reference to being taken off artificial life support when no reasonable prospect for recovery exists. State statutory requirements must be met to create a living will. Specific language and the signing by disinterested witnesses may, for example, be required. Durable powers of attorney are also common and allow individuals to delegate the power to another to make medical or financial decisions if they become too incapacitated to make these decisions for themselves.

To read more about powers of attorney, go to *www.nolo.com/encyclopedia/ep_ency.html* and click on "Healthcare Directives and Powers of Attorney."

To read about life insurance, go to *www.nolo.com/encyclopedia/ep_ency.html* and click on "Life Insurance."

"Life insurance," repeated Martha. "That's a great idea. That way we could avoid the whole **probate process,** too."

"Absolutely," confirmed Corazon. "Not that probate is necessarily all that messy with a simple estate, but with life insurance the court needn't get involved and you don't have to worry about someone contesting it. I think in your situation a good policy would provide nicely for the girls and you wouldn't have to worry about whether George followed through on his will. It might be wise, however, to have the policy in your name and pay the premiums yourself. That way, if George gets behind in his bills while at school, you won't have to worry about the policy being cancelled. You could also add the cost of the policy to what George will have to repay you when he gets back to work."

probate process   proceedings that allow title to the decedent's property to pass to those for whom it was intended

administrator   person appointed to administer an intestate estate; in some states, a female administrator is called an *administratrix*

personal representative (PR)   term used under the UPC to refer to those who administer both intestate and testate estates

PROBATE PROCEEDINGS

In the probate process, the validity of the decedent's will is determined, the decedent's assets are collected, debts are paid, and the estate is distributed. The party responsible for carrying out the administrative details of probating an estate is the executor (or personal representative), appointed by the decedent in her will. If the decedent dies intestate, the person appointed to administer the estate is called the **administrator** (*administratrix*) or **personal representative (PR)** (term used by the UPC regardless of whether the decedent died intestate or testate). If the personal representative appointed by the will is unwilling or unable to serve, the court must appoint a party in accordance with state statutes, which dictate who can be appointed and the order of preference for appointment. These people are responsible for seeing that all payments are made and that all properties are distributed.

Probate proceedings begin when someone (the prospective PR, heirs, or beneficiaries) files an application or petition with the appropriate court, usually the probate division or probate court located in the decedent's domicile. The purpose of this application or petition is either to have the will admitted to probate or to prove that the decedent died intestate. The applicant (petitioner) must serve notice on all interested parties and heirs so that a hearing can be held, at which anyone who wants to challenge the validity of the proceeding can present evidence.

After the will is either admitted to probate or intestacy has been established, the PR files an inventory with the court and sends it to the heirs and beneficiaries. This inventory discloses the extent of the estate and serves as a reference point for the initial accounting by the PR. The PR must also collect all debts owed the estate, obtain all property to which the decedent held title, and pay all debts owed by the decedent. Most states require that a notice of probate (often called a *notice to creditors*) be published to alert all creditors that they need to file a claim with the estate. The PR must then decide which claims will be allowed. Of course, any creditor whose claim is disallowed has the option of filing suit against the estate.

Once creditors' claims, taxes, and administrative expenses have been paid, the PR must distribute the remaining estate. If the decedent died intestate, the court will often hold a hearing to determine who the heirs are. A hearing may be necessary even if the decedent had a will if that will is ambiguous. The court's function is to ascertain the intent of the testator, and if that intent is not clear from

To read about the probate process, go to *www.nolo.com/encyclopedia/ep_ency.html* and click on "Probate."

◆ **LOCAL LINKS** ◆

Make note here of any steps in the probate process in your state that differ from what has been described.

the will itself, the court may have to turn to extrinsic evidence to clarify the testator's intent.

Once all the proceeds have been distributed, the personal representative may close the estate. In some states, this can be accomplished informally by filing a closing statement; in other states, a hearing is required. Once the estate is closed it cannot be reopened to re-litigate heirs' or creditors' claims, barring a showing of fraud or wrongdoing in the administration of the estate.

Many states require that the state's department of revenue be notified and a waiver of tax (or tax receipt) be obtained. The waiver shows that the estate owed no estate taxes while the receipt shows any taxes due were paid. It may be necessary to record the waiver/receipt in any county where the decedent owned an interest in real property to show clear title, that is, that no estate taxes were owed that could become a lien on the decedent's real property interests. If the estate is large enough, a federal estate return will also need to be filed. Many states levy a tax equal to a percentage of the imposed federal estate tax so that, if no federal estate tax is due, no state estate tax need be paid. In any event, final state and income tax returns must be filed.

Putting It Into Practice 11.17:

A friend tells you that she has been asked to be the personal representative of an estate. She is not sure what this entails. Explain to her what she will have to do as PR.

Figure 11-10
Probate Process

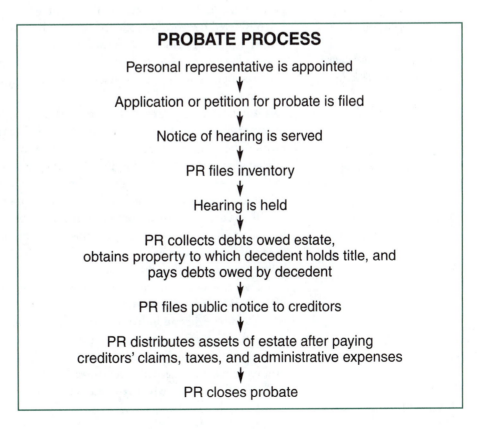

PROBATE PROCESS

Personal representative is appointed
↓
Application or petition for probate is filed
↓
Notice of hearing is served
↓
PR files inventory
↓
Hearing is held
↓
PR collects debts owed estate,
obtains property to which decedent holds title, and
pays debts owed by decedent
↓
PR files public notice to creditors
↓
PR distributes assets of estate after paying
creditors' claims, taxes, and administrative expenses
↓
PR closes probate

> ## *"My Dad Loves George, but Thinks He's—In His Words—a 'Flake.' He Wanted to Make Sure My Children and I Were Provided for in Case George Forgot to Come Home Sometime."*
>
> "All right. I guess the only thing we haven't discussed is your trust. What kind of trust do you have?" inquired Corazon.
>
> "After our first daughter was born, my parents created an irrevocable trust, naming First American Trust as the trustee and myself and any children I might have as beneficiaries. My Dad likes George, but thinks he's—in his words—a 'flake.' He wanted to make sure my children and I were provided for in case George forgot to come home sometime," offered Martha as explanation. "Anyway, they put almost $50,000 worth of stock in the trust. I receive income from the trust every three months, which I can use any way I choose, and when I die the trust **corpus** is to go to the girls, to be split evenly between them. I've been investing the money all along in a college fund for my children but, as I said earlier, I could use this money to augment my income."
>
> "You might want to talk to the trustee and ask if it would make sense to change the investment direction of the trust to an income generating basis. It appears that you've been focusing on growth, and since you'll be needing more cash for the next several years, it may be to your advantage to modify the trust's portfolio," suggested Corazon.

corpus body of the trust, including principal and accrued income

settlor person who creates a trust

trustee entity who manages and administers a trust

revocable trust that can be cancelled or changed under the express will of the settlor

irrevocable trust that cannot be cancelled or changed

legal title complete and absolute right of ownership

equitable title right of the beneficiary to profit or benefit from the trust property

TRUSTS

A trust is a property arrangement in which the **settlor** or **trustor** (person creating the trust) transfers real or personal property to a **trustee** (who manages and administers a trust), who holds legal title to the property for the benefit of one or more beneficiaries (who receive the benefit of a trust). If Sam conveys his ranch to Tina to hold in trust for the benefit of Barry, Sam is the settlor, Tina is the trustee, and Barry is the beneficiary of the trust. A trust can be **revocable** in that the settlor retains the right to revoke or change the trust at any time before his death. This power must be expressly stated in the document creating the trust or the trust will be considered **irrevocable** (one that cannot be revoked or changed by the settlor). Property placed in either a revocable or irrevocable trust is a nonprobate asset and is not subject to probate. Irrevocable trusts, if set up properly, are not subject to federal estate tax, but the trustor may be subject to gift tax on the property initially used to fund the trust.

When a trust is created by a settlor, **legal title** (a complete and absolute right of ownership) passes to the trustee, while **equitable title** (right of the beneficiary to profit or benefit from the trust property) passes to the beneficiary. This split of title is what separates a trust from a gift, where the legal title passes wholly from the seller to the buyer. A trust can be distinguished from a sale because with a trust, no consideration is required. It is a gratuitous transfer of property.

To make a valid trust, a settlor must own a transferable interest in property that he has a right to dispose of and he must have the ability to make a valid contract. (See contractual capacity discussed in Chapter 9.) Once a settlor creates a trust, he is no longer essential to that trust.

The trustee, on the other hand, is vital to the trust. He owes a fiduciary duty of honesty and loyalty to the beneficiary. Normally, the settlor selects a trustee, which can be either an individual or an institution, such as a bank, on the basis of that entity's integrity, experience, and ability. The courts reserve the right to appoint a trustee if the named trustee dies, refuses the position, proves to be incompetent, or a replacement is needed. The trustee's main duty is to carry out the terms and purpose of the trust, which are granted in the trust instrument. Typically, these powers are described in broad terms to give the trustee as much flexibility as possible and to allow him to resolve problems the settlor probably could not have foreseen. Common powers of trustees include the right to sell assets, to lease property, to lend or borrow money, to vote stock, to develop real property, to hire experts, and to carry on business. Trustees are bound to act in good faith and to use reasonable care, prudence, and diligence in managing the trust. The trustee is not allowed to profit personally from his role as trustee (other than any agreed upon fees he is to be paid for his services) and is obligated to act solely in the best interest of the beneficiary. The trustee also has a duty to protect the trust property from loss and damage, to judiciously invest the trust property, and to keep accurate records. The trustee is paid for her services in an amount designated by the trust; if no amount is indicated, she receives reasonable fees.

Many trusts have two kinds of beneficiaries: **income beneficiaries,** who receive the income generated by the trust for a set number of years or for the lives of the beneficiaries, and **remainder beneficiaries,** who receive the principal of the trust after the rights of the income beneficiaries have been met. When a **private trust** is created, the beneficiaries must be named or described in such a way that the trustee can identify them. With a **charitable trust,** however, the beneficiaries can be members of the general public or a general class of the public. Note that a private trust is created to benefit certain named or described beneficiaries while a charitable trust (also called *public trust*) is created to achieve a social benefit for the general public or class of the public. A charitable trust could be established, for example, to fund research for AIDS or to provide food and shelter to abused children or to fund a museum. Beneficiaries need not be humans. A charitable trust could be established to care for homeless dogs and cats, for example.

Two of the most common types of trusts are **living (*inter vivos*) trusts** and **testamentary trusts.** A living trust is a trust made while the settlor is alive (hence the name *inter vivos*—between living persons), whereas a testamentary trust takes effect when the settlor dies. Testamentary trusts are subject to federal estate taxes. Other than when they take effect, both trusts are similar and are designed to conserve property for the benefit of surviving beneficiaries, usually a spouse and/or children.

Many people are turning to living trusts today as a substitute for a will. With a living trust, they can transfer their entire estate to the trust, manage and control their property and receive income from it while they are alive, distribute the trust property to their beneficiaries (usually family) after they die, and spare their heirs the costs and delays of probate. It should be noted, however, that preparing a living trust can be more costly than preparing a will. You must pay for documentation and transfers to the trust at the time the trust is made rather than at death. Also, creditors do not have the shortened time limit in which they must present their claims as they do with a probated will. Because settlors often do not convey all of their estate to the trust, the need for probate usually arises anyway.

Putting It Into Practice 11.18:

What kind of trust does Martha appear to have? What kind of beneficiary is she? What kind of beneficiaries are her daughters?

Two other commonly used trusts are **spendthrift trusts** and **Totten trusts.** A spendthrift trust is created when the settlor anticipates that the beneficiary is likely to spend the money foolishly. To safeguard against the unwise or inexperienced spending habits of the beneficiary, the settlor provides that only a portion of the

---

income beneficiaries
beneficiary who receives income from the trust

remainder beneficiaries
beneficiary who receives the principal of the trust after the rights of the income beneficiaries have been met

private trust trust in which the beneficiaries are named or described in such a way that the trustee can identify them

charitable trust trust created for a social benefit; the beneficiaries can be members of the general public

living (*inter vivos*) trusts trust made while the settlor is still alive

testamentary trusts trust that goes into effect when the settlor dies

spendthrift trusts trust in which the settlor provides that only a portion of the trust funds will be allocated to the beneficiary at any one time to safeguard against the beneficiary's unwise or inexperienced spending habits

Totten trusts also called a *P.O.D.* (payable on death) account; a savings account in which the money is deposited in the depositor's name as trustee for the beneficiary

To read about the benefits of trusts, go to *www.nolo.com/encyclopedia/ep_ency.html* and click on "Living Trusts" and "Estate and Gift Taxes." To further contrast wills and living trusts, go to *www.lectlaw.com/formb.htm* and click on "Differences Between Wills and Living Trusts." This site also has samples of revocable and irrevocable trusts.

trust funds will be allocated to the beneficiary at any one time. The settlor also establishes that the beneficiary cannot assign anyone the right to receive future payments from the trust (as might happen if the beneficiary were to get into financial difficulties) and that creditors cannot reach the trust funds of the beneficiary by obtaining a court order. A spendthrift trust casts no limitations on any trust funds once they are received by the beneficiary; it guarantees only that the beneficiary will not lose the income before receiving it.

A Totten trust, also called a *P.O.D. (payable on death) account* is a savings account in which the money is deposited in the depositor's name as trustee for another person who is the beneficiary. A, the depositor, can create a Totten trust by establishing an account in the name of "A, in trust for B" or in the name of "A payable on death to B." This trust allows the depositor/trustee to withdraw monies while still alive and leave any remaining balance to the beneficiary upon the depositor's death.

Putting It Into Practice 11.19:

(a) Elroy has one-third interest in a restaurant. In his will, he gives his interest to his brother, Talbert, to hold and manage in trust for the benefit of his nephew, Michael. What kind of trust has Elroy created? Identify the settlor, trustee, and beneficiary. (b) In her will, Diane provides: "I give the National Diabetes Foundation $500,000 for the purpose of conducting research in reference to diabetes." What kind of trust has Diane created? (c) Eduardo, a single parent, age 45, owns property that he wants to transfer to his children, Jose and Eliana, now while he is alive, but he is concerned about how his children will handle the property. He would like to have a management company administer the property. What kind of trust should be create? (d) Marvin gives his book royalties to his financial advisor, Conrad, to hold in trust and to invest for the benefit of Marvin's only child, Margaret, and her children. Conrad is to pay Margaret income from the royalties for the remainder of her life. After her death, the royalties are to be given to her children. Marvin reserves the right to cancel the trust and recover his royalties if he is still alive. What kind of trust has Marvin created? Who holds legal title to the royalties? Who holds equitable title? Who are the beneficiaries under this trust and how do they differ?

Figure 11-11
Types of Trusts

TYPES OF TRUSTS

Revocable or irrevocable
Private or charitable
Inter vivos (living) or testamentary
Spendthrift
Totten (P.O.D. account)

To find out more about what it is like to work in the area of trusts and estates, go to *www.paralegals.org/Reporter* and click on "Summer 1998." Read the section entitled "Paralegal Roles and Responsibilities" and "Probate: An Overview."

Links to elder law resources can be found at the SeniorLaw Home Page at *www.seniorlaw.com/index.htm.*

ROLE OF THE PARALEGAL

Paralegals who work in the area of probate and estate planning may work in a law firm, but can also be employed by a bank or a probate court. They perform many tasks, including those listed below.

- ◆ interviewing clients
- ◆ drafting wills, trusts, and other documents
- ◆ obtaining information about insurance policies
- ◆ reviewing financial information submitted by clients and preparing summaries for attorney review
- ◆ performing investment analysis to provide information to an attorney
- ◆ locating heirs and notifying beneficiaries
- ◆ assisting in the valuation of assets
- ◆ getting information in reference to the assets and debts of the deceased, including inventorying contents of safety deposit boxes, bank accounts, and all real and personal property
- ◆ reviewing claims against an estate
- ◆ assisting with bookkeeping and accounting functions
- ◆ preparing and filing probate forms
- ◆ preparing estate tax returns
- ◆ assisting with litigation
- ◆ assisting in creating adult guardianships

Paralegals who practice in this area need to have effective interviewing skills, enabling them to get the information they need as well as allowing them to communicate effectively with clients experiencing grief and confusion. Because the probate process can be lengthy, explaining the process and where the client's case is in this process is an important facet of the paralegal's job. Paralegals who work in this area should also possess good mathematical skills because they are frequently involved in daily bookkeeping and accounting tasks.

BONUS POINTERS:

ELDER LAW

As the American population ages, one of the emerging specialties is elder law, which focuses on the special legal needs of seniors. In the first NALA Survey (1997) in which respondents were asked about elder law, twelve percent indicated they worked in this area at least part of the time. Elder law deals with such issues as estate and financial planning, social security, Medicare and Medicaid disputes, patients' rights, elder abuse, and guardianships.

The tasks paralegals in this area perform include the following.

- ◆ meeting with elderly clients to explain legal issues
- ◆ researching topics in elder law
- ◆ advocating for the elderly in meetings with administrative agencies
- ◆ communicating with social service agencies
- ◆ assisting with the appointment of guardians
- ◆ assisting with estate and financial planning

As Martha and Corazon were saying their good-byes, Corazon put her hand on Martha's shoulder and said, "Would you allow me just one little piece of non-legal advice?"

"Sure," said Martha agreeably.

"The happiest people I see in my practice are those who allow themselves to open up to new relationships. The saddest ones are those that shrivel up and won't let anyone touch them. Follow your heart, Martha, and I assure you, everything will work out just fine."

Martha was contemplating Corazon's comment on her drive home when she saw Mike waving at her. She turned her car around and pulled over to the curb so they could talk awhile. Mike came around to her door and embraced her warmly as she got out.

"Aren't you looking wonderful!" Martha exclaimed as she looked deeply into Mike's eyes. She saw an equanimity there she had never before seen. "You must have discovered something that really agrees with you because I haven't seen you looking this well since before the shooting."

"It's spelled C-A-R-M-E-L-A," said Mike, his eyes virtually sparkling as he said her name.

"Yes, I hear congratulations are in order," said Martha as she nudged him affectionately.

"Great! My folks spilled the beans. I wanted to be the one to tell you."

"Your folks are so delighted. I think your mom would have exploded if she hadn't been able to tell me," offered Martha as a means of offsetting Mike's disappointment.

"Yeah, I know. They really love Carmela," admitted Mike, his voice softening.

"Well, I'm very happy for you both. You've been through a lot—you deserve great happiness. So do you still plan to apply for medical school?" asked Martha as tactfully as she could, concerned about the effect his upcoming marriage might have on his career plans.

"Actually, I've been thinking about going into counseling or some aspect of psychology. The counselor I've been working with has really opened me up to some new ways of seeing the world and I think he's helped speed up my healing process."

"If he's responsible for the progress you've made since I last saw you, he's got my vote for counselor of the year!"

"Well, he's helped me a lot. But if you really want to know who's helped me the most, other than Carmela, I'd have to say it was Tim."

"Tim?" Martha was not aware Mike even knew Tim except as a passing acquaintance, and could not imagine what conceivable role he could have played in Mike's miraculous transformation. "How so?"

"Shortly after the trial was over, Tim came by to see me. He told me about being in prison and about some of the things that had happened to him there and how he'd seen some men shrivel up and virtually die in prison while others found a way to make changes in their lives.

"The story I remember best was about a volunteer who came in to work with Tim's substance abuse group. The guy's name was Regis. It turns out that Regis had been put in prison when he was in his early 20s. He got drunk one night and ran into another car, killing the driver—a young man about his age. It was Regis's fourth DUI and the court sentenced him to prison. Regis's family basically disowned him and he felt like his life was over. He was so depressed he tried to commit suicide twice. One day he was told that the mother of the young man he'd killed wanted to see him. Regis put her off and put her off. He didn't want to see the pain he'd caused and he knew of no way to express his deep remorse for what he'd done. But the woman was persistent and finally they came face to face. When she looked into his eyes for the first time, the woman started crying and Regis knew why their meeting was a mistake. But he was stunned when the woman took him in her arms and hugged him, telling him that she forgave him and that she knew that her son had forgiven him too.

"After that, Regis changed. He began to participate in programs offered by the prison, he went to counseling, and he started taking classes toward his GED. The woman, and eventually her husband, came to visit him every week, ultimately adopting him into their family. Regis decided that if his life mattered to the people whose only son he'd killed, it should matter to him. He went on to get a degree in counseling, and when he was released from prison, he devoted his life to working with alcoholics in and out of prison."

Tears welled up in Martha's eyes as she heard Mike tell about Regis. "What a moving story."

"Tim told me that Regis helped him see things differently, and that he decided when he was released he would use his experiences to help others in prison. I thought a lot about what Tim said and finally I decided to go and see the guys who shot me. I came to the conclusion that what was really tearing me up inside was all the anger I felt toward them. And the counselor explained how this anger could actually inhibit my healing."

"So have you gone to see them?" asked Martha, awed by the maturity and courage required to make that visit.

"Yes. At first they all refused to see me. Al still won't seem me. But Daniel and Max eventually agreed to meet with me."

"So how did it go?" prompted Martha in her eagerness to know the boys' reaction to Mike's visit.

"As well as could be expected, I guess. I did most of the talking; they mainly listened. After that, Daniel agreed to let me visit him and I've been going to see him every week."

"That's incredible, Mike. I had no idea you were doing that."

"What keeps me going back is the subtle changes I've begun to see in Daniel. He's made some overtures at healing the rift between him and his dad and he's started attending some Narcotics Anonymous meetings. He's got a long way to go, but at least he's taking some steps forward. Oh, and yesterday, I got a call from Max. He'd like to see me the next time I come to visit Daniel."

"That's encouraging."

"Yes, it is. And you know, Mrs. Fletcher, I feel such a sense of peace ever since I decided to meet with these guys."

"That's what I noticed about you immediately today. The last time I saw you, Mike, you looked so tired and, well, defeated. Now you look like someone at peace with the world."

"And I am." After a long pause Mike continued. "A few years ago a lady I was wheeling to radiation for her treatment told me that cancer was the best thing that had ever happened to her. I didn't understand her then, but I do now. Being shot was the most horrible but also the most transformative thing that has ever happened to me. If it hadn't been for that experience, I'm not sure I would be with Carmela today, and I know I wouldn't be the person I've become."

"I think you're right, Mike," agreed Martha soberly, silently assessing all the changes she had seen in Mike since the shooting. "You've achieved a depth of understanding and acceptance I can't say I've ever seen in a young man your age. I commend you," she said, bowing her head slightly in recognition of his accomplishment.

"Thanks, but I think Tim is the real hero. If it hadn't been for his being willing to reveal himself to me, I doubt that it ever would have occurred to me that helping Daniel, Max, and Al would help me. Tim does a lot of things behind the scenes—like volunteering at the prison—that change a lot of people's lives."

"Until today, I didn't know about his volunteer work," admitted Martha.

"I think there's a lot about him you don't know, Mrs. Fletcher," said Mike pointedly.

"As I am discovering by the minute," thought Martha to herself.

Martha gave Mike another congratulatory hug and promised to invite him and Carmela over for dinner very soon. Eagerly she headed for home and went directly to the phone.

"Hello, Tim? I think I'm ready for that first date. How about tonight? My treat!"

■ **TIM'S TECHNO TIPS**

Specialized Legal Software

Many companies create specialized programs for different areas of the law. We have previously looked at more general software packages for case management, timekeeping and billing, spreadsheets, and criminal case management. While some of these programs could be used by any practitioner, regardless of specialty, a non-litigation specialist will want a software program that generates the many forms she needs. As with general packages, it is very important that individual information be entered only once and that the program insert the appropriate information in each applicable form. These forms, often referred to as *templates,* should be easily modified to allow for permanent changes such as letterhead

and firm identification. The templates should provide for easy insertion of state or local data specific to the user's location. These changes should also be permanent, if desired by the user.

In a real estate practice, specialized legal software packages have some aspects of a spreadsheet in that data manipulation and financial calculations, such as for a settlement statement or for pro-rations, are necessary. Other areas of specialization that require financial data manipulation include domestic relations (for child support calculations), probate and estate planning (for annual reports, accountings, and gift and estate tax preparation, tax law, and bankruptcy.

TECHNO TRIP

Go to *www.reesa.com,* Reesa by Accu-Ware. Download the demonstration version of their closing software and review the various help files to get a feel for how the program operates. Attorneys and those working for attorneys are authorized to go to the forms section to pick up individual forms. Create a hypothetical closing: add names, addresses, purchase price, and so on, and view the completed documents. How much would they have to be modified to be useable in your state?

SUMMARY – PART B

The property of an intestate is distributed in accordance with state statutes, providing first for the surviving spouse and children, and, if none exist, then for other lineal descendants, followed by lineal ascendants, collateral relatives, and so on, until no relatives are found and the estate escheats.

Wills are one of the commonly used tools of estate planning. They allow testators to distribute their property to their beneficiaries as they see fit, although a poorly drafted will can be expensive and time-consuming to probate. To be a valid will, the testator must be of legal age and of sound mind and must prepare it voluntarily. Written wills are preferable because, in many states, holographic and noncupative wills are not recognized by the courts. In addition to declaration and debt clauses, most wills contain an appointment clause (appointing the executor) and a gift clause (designating the devises and bequests to be given the beneficiaries). Most states have not addressed the ethical question of whether a paralegal should be allowed to supervise the execution of a will. Testators can revoke a will by destroying it, by preparing a new will, or by preparing a codicil, which serves to revoke at least those provisions that conflict with the provisions of the original will. Most states provide for at least a partial revocation of a will when the family relationship of the testator changes. The validity of a will can be contested if the testator was not of age or of unsound mind, if the will was not signed, if the formalities of execution were not observed, or if the testator was under undue influence. An attorney or paralegal who is a beneficiary under a will should not prepare that will unless she is related to the client for whom the will is being prepared.

The probate process begins when the personal representative (or an heir or beneficiary) files an application or petition with the appropriate court and serves notice of a hearing on all interested parties. At the hearing, the will is either validated or the decedent is determined to have died intestate. The PR is appointed and must file an inventory with the court and send it to all heirs and beneficiaries. The PR is also responsible for collecting all debts owed the estate, obtaining all property to which the decedent held title, and paying all debts owed by the decedent. Most states require the PR to publish a notice in the newspaper to all creditors so they can file their claims against the estate. Once all the creditors' claims, taxes, and administrative expenses have been paid, the PR must distribute the remaining assets of the estate. Another hearing will be necessary if the decedent died intestate or if the will is ambiguous. Once all the assets have been distributed, the PR can close the estate, which precludes any future claims by creditors or heirs unless there is a showing of wrongdoing in the administration of the estate.

A trust is created when a settlor transfers real or personal property to a trustee, who holds legal title in the property in trust for one or more beneficiaries, who hold equitable title to the property. A trust can be revocable or irrevocable; neither is subject to probate. A trust can also be private, charitable, testamentary or *inter vivos* (living). A trustee owes a fiduciary duty to the beneficiary, his main duty being to carry out the terms and purpose of the trust. A trustee is not allowed to profit personally from his role as trustee, has a duty to act in good faith and use reasonable care in managing the trust, must act solely in the best interest of the beneficiary, must judiciously invest the property, must keep accurate records, and must avoid loss or damage to the trust property. Spendthrift trusts are designed to protect beneficiaries who are inexperienced or likely to be foolish in their spending. A savings account can be used to create a Totten trust when the depositor puts money in the account and provides that the money is to go to a named beneficiary when the depositor dies.

KEY TERMS

Administrator/
  adminstratrix
Ascendants
Beneficiaries
Bequest/legacy
Charitable trust
Codicil
Collateral
Confidential relationship
Corpus
Decedent

Descendants
Devise
Equitable title
Escheat
Estate planning
Executor/executrix
Holographic will
Income beneficiaries
Intestate
Intestate succession
Irrevocable

Issue
Legal title
Living (*inter vivos*) trusts
Noncupative will
Per capita
Per stirpes
Personal representative
  (PR)
Private trust
Probate process
Remainder beneficiaries

Revocable
Self-proving wills
Settlor/trustor
Spendthrift trusts
Testamentary capacity
Testamentary trusts
Testator/testatrix
Totten trusts
Trustee
Undue influence
Will

REVIEW QUESTIONS – PART B

1. How is property distributed when someone dies intestate? How does a *per capita* distribution differ from a *per stirpes* distribution?
2. What are the advantages of preparing a will? Why should it be carefully drafted?
3. What are the requirements of a valid will?
4. What are the elements of a typical will?
5. How can a will be revoked?
6. On what grounds can a will be contested?
7. Describe the process used to probate a will.
   a. Who must be notified that probate is proceeding?
   b. What is the consequence of closing probate?

8. Give an example of a trust. Identify the settlor, trustee, and beneficiary.
   a. What is the difference between legal and equitable title?
   b. How does a revocable trust differ from an irrevocable one?
   c. What is the difference between a private trust and a charitable trust?
   d. What is the difference between an *inter vivos* (living) trust and a testamentary trust?
9. What duties does the trustee owe to the beneficiary?
10. What is a spendthrift trust? How does it protect a beneficiary?
11. What is a Totten trust?

PRACTICE EXAM – PART B

MULTIPLE CHOICE

1. Most intestate statutes provide that
   a. lineal ascendants receive before lineal descendants
   b. collateral relatives receive before lineal descendants
   c. the surviving spouse receives all or part of the estate
   d. adopted children are treated differently than biological children
2. If Cecilia, whose husband predeceases her, has one child (who has no children) who survives her and three grandchildren from another child who has predeceased her, under a *per stirpes* distribution, Cecilia's three grandchildren will receive
   a. one-sixth share of the estate
   b. one-fourth share of the estate
   c. one-ninth share of the estate
   d. none of the above

3. The intestate succession laws of most states
   a. allow relatives by marriage to inherit an intestate's property
   b. do not allow illegitimate children to inherit from their father unless they have been legitimized
   c. treat adopted children differently than biological children
   d. all of the above
4. Estate planning
   a. does not include co-ownership of property
   b. includes the making of trusts, but not the making of gifts
   c. can minimize the paying of inheritance and estate taxes
   d. all of the above

5. A will
   a. is not necessarily easy and inexpensive to probate
   b. must be in writing to be valid
   c. does not have to be witnessed if it is a self-proving will
   d. none of the above

6. A will
   a. can be made by anyone of any age
   b. is valid even if there is evidence of undue influence
   c. is valid even if the testator lacks testamentary capacity
   d. none of the above

7. Typically, a will
   a. identifies the executor and specifies her powers
   b. describes the bequests and devises to be given
   c. provides for payment of debts, expenses, and taxes
   d. all of the above

8. Witnesses to a will
   a. must sign in the presence of the testator and the other witnesses
   b. must be present when the testator signs
   c. can never be beneficiaries
   d. none of the above

9. A will can be revoked
   a. by preparing a second will, but not by preparing a codicil
   b. when the testator divorces or remarries
   c. if the testator completely destroys it, but not if he merely writes "Cancelled" on it
   d. only by preparing a formal revocation

10. A will can be contested
    a. if the formalities of execution are not observed
    b. if the testator is of unsound mind or under undue influence
    c. if the will is not signed
    d. all of the above

11. Undue influence is presumed
    a. even if a confidential relationship does not exist
    b. when the testator is in a weakened condition and dependent on the influencer
    c. even though the influencer had nothing to do with preparing the will
    d. all of the above

12. The probate process
    a. takes place in the court where the decedent was domiciled
    b. can be initiated only by the personal representative
    c. is initiated when the personal representative files an inventory
    d. all of the above

13. The PR is responsible for
    a. collecting all the debts owed to the estate, but not for paying debts the estate owes
    b. obtaining property to which the decedent had title
    c. determining whether the will is valid
    d. all of the above

14. A court hearing is not needed to distribute an estate's assets if
    a. a decedent dies intestate
    b. a decedent dies with a valid will
    c. a decedent dies with a valid, unambiguous will
    d. none of the above

15. The closing of probate
    a. can be accomplished only by a formal hearing
    b. can be carried out by the PR filing a closing inventory
    c. precludes any future litigation by creditors or heirs even if there is evidence of wrongdoing in the administration of the estate
    d. none of the above

16. A revocable trust
    a. can be created implicitly
    b. must be probated
    c. is a nonprobate asset
    d. is not subject to probate or to federal estate tax

17. A trust
    a. requires a split in title to the property being transferred
    b. is created in exchange for consideration
    c. results in equitable title being transferred to the trustee
    d. all of the above

18. A trustee
    a. can profit from his role as trustee as long as he does not damage the beneficiary
    b. owes a fiduciary duty of honesty and loyalty to the beneficiary
    c. cannot be appointed by a court
    d. all of the above

19. A trustee is obligated to
    a. keep accurate records
    b. act solely in the best interest of the beneficiary
    c. protect the trust property from loss and damage
    d. all of the above

20. With a charitable trust
    a. the beneficiaries must be named or described so that the trustee can identify them
    b. the purpose is to provide some kind of social benefit
    c. the beneficiaries must be human
    d. all of the above

21. *Inter vivos* trusts
    a. allow settlors to manage their property while they are still alive
    b. must still be probated
    c. give creditors only a limited time during which to file their claims
    d. are no substitute for a will

22. A spendthrift trust
    a. puts limitations on trust funds when they are received by the beneficiary
    b. allows beneficiaries to assign another the right to receive future payments from the trust fund
    c. allocates portions of the trust funds a little at a time
    d. all of the above

FILL IN THE BLANK

23. A _____ (deceased person) who dies _____ (without a will) will have her property distributed in accordance with the applicable _____ laws. If there is no surviving spouse, the property will be distributed to the _____ (e.g., children and grandchildren) or _____ (e.g., parents and grandparents) or _____ relatives (e.g., brothers and sisters) on a _____ (equal share) or _____ (based on relationship to the deceased) basis. If no relatives can be found, the estate will _____ (go to the state).

24. A _____ (person making a will) or _____ (female making a will) is well advised to prepare a written will because _____ (handwritten) and _____ (oral) wills are often considered invalid.

25. The appointment clause of a will provides for the appointment of the _____ or _____ (female administrator of an estate), while the gift clause describes how the property will be disposed of by means of _____ (gifts of real property) and _____ (gifts of personal property).

26. Many states allow the creation of _____ wills by having the testator and witnesses sign a notarized affidavit attesting to the will's validity.

27. A _____ (addition to a will) revokes any provisions in the original will with which it is inconsistent.

28. _____ (writing a will under another's direction) occurs most frequently when a _____ relationship (one based on trust and dependency) exists between the testator and the influencer.

29. The _____ refers to proceedings in which the validity of the decedent's will is determined, the decedent's assets are collected, debts are paid, and the estate is distributed. The person responsible for attending to the administrative details of this process is called an _____ or _____ (referring to a female) or a _____ , which is used under the UPC to refer to those administering either testate or intestate estates.

30. The purpose of an _____ or _____ filed with the probate court is to determine the validity or invalidity of the will.

31. A trust is created when a _____ transfers real or personal property to a _____ , who has _____ title to the property and who manages and administers the property for the benefit of one or more _____ , who hold _____ title to the property.

32. A trust can be _____ in that the settlor expressly reserves his right to cancel the trust or _____ in that the settlor does not expressly reserve this right.

33. _____ receive the principal of a trust after the _____ have received the income generated by a trust.

34. With a _____ trust, the beneficiaries must be named or described in such a way that the trustee can identify them, but with a _____ trust, the beneficiaries can be members of the general public.

35. An _____ or _____ trust is created while the settlor is still alive, whereas a _____ trust takes effect when the settlor dies.

36. A _____ trust allows the settlor to safeguard against the beneficiary's anticipated unwise or inexperienced spending.

37. A _____ trust is a savings account in which the money is deposited in the depositor's name as trustee for the beneficiary; it is also called a _____ .

TRUE OR FALSE

____ 38. The intestate succession laws of the state where a decedent's personal property is located govern that property's distribution.

____ 39. Probating a will can be an expensive and time-consuming process.

____ 40. A testator must have testamentary capacity, thereby preventing people who are mentally ill from preparing a will.

____ 41. Witness requirements are standard in every state.

____ 42. A self-proving will is presumptively valid.

____ 43. In most states, a paralegal can handle the execution of a will without an attorney's supervision.

____ 44. A testator who executes a second will revokes the first will.

____ 45. Most states provide for the revocation or partial revocation of wills when the family relationships of the testator change.

____ 46. In some states, crossing out portions of a will serves to revoke those sections only.

____ 47. Only beneficiaries can contest the validity of a will.

____ 48. Lawyers and paralegals should not prepare wills in which they are beneficiaries unless they are related to the client for whom the will is being prepared.

____*49. A living will is a will prepared when the testator is facing some kind of major surgery.

____*50. A durable power of attorney delegates the power to another to make medical or financial decisions for the individual creating the power of attorney if that person becomes too incapacitated to make those decisions for herself.

____ 51. The PR is not required to alert potential creditors that an estate is being probated.

____ 52. If a will is ambiguous, the court's function is to determine the intent of the testator, either from the document itself or from extrinsic evidence.

____ 53. Irrevocable trusts are not subject to federal estate tax.

____ 54. A trust is a gratuitous transfer of property.

____ 55. A settlor is indispensable to a trust even after the trust has been created.

____ 56. The trustee's main duty is to carry out the terms and purpose of the trust, which are usually spelled out very specifically.

____57. Trustees are bound to use reasonable care, prudence, and diligence in managing the trust.

____ 58. With a testamentary trust, settlors can transfer their entire estate to the trust, manage and control their property, receive income from it while they are alive, and distribute the trust property to their beneficiaries after they die.

____ 59. Creditors can reach the funds of a spendthrift trust by obtaining a court order.

____ 60. A spendthrift trust casts no limitations on any trust funds once they are received by the beneficiary.

____ 61. A P.O.D. account allows a depositor to withdraw monies while still alive and leave any remaining balance to the beneficiary upon the depositor's death.

____*62. Elder law is a declining area of legal practice.

* Questions taken from Bonus Pointers

LEGAL LINGO

Across

4. children and grandchildren
5. company that handles the details of property transfer
7. seller of land
10. distribution based on relationship to deceased
12. restriction
13. interference with another's use of land
15. power of government to take property
16. type of savings account
17. reduce rent
19. ownership interest in property
22. person writing will
25. recipient of real property in a will
27. distribution of property based on equal shares
28. provision in deed that restricts use of property
30. oral will
32. type of trust designed to protect beneficiary
33. type of tenancy with right of survivorship
34. kind of title received by beneficiary
40. deceased person
42. type of estate planning tool

43. dying without a will
44. type of eviction
46. brothers and sisters of a decedent
48. model act pertaining to landlord-tenant relationship
49. _____ simple
50. beneficiary that receives principal of trust

Down

1. personal property that becomes real property
2. handwritten will
3. living trust
6. permission to use another's property for specific purpose
8. type of trust that can be changed
9. property ownership interest that allows party to use another's land for specific purpose
11. use of land without owner's consent

14. closing statement
18. abbreviation for administrator of estate
20. best kind of ownership interest in land
21. addition to will
23. creator of trust
24. model code relating to probate
26. property reverts back to state
29. trust involving savings account created by depositor
31. tenancy with no definite ending date
35. deed having no warranties
36. type of co-ownership for spouses
37. female administrator of estate
38. influence arising out of confidential relationship
39. ownership
41. document that indicates any restrictions regarding transfer of property
45. type of lien imposed by government
47. gift of personal property in will

LEGAL LOGISTICS

1. Bruce is planning to buy five acres of vacant land in the suburbs outside a large city. He wants to keep five horses and some cattle there to do some roping. His surrounding neighbors have one-acre lots and none has livestock. He plans to fence in the entire five acres. The adjoining acre is also vacant, and Bruce notes that there is a path going across it that serves as a short-cut to the state land where he plans to ride. He wants to know if he would be trespassing if he used this path.
   a. What should Bruce find out before he buys this property?
   b. Assume that Bruce's previous home was taken by the state to build a new freeway. What did the state have to do prior to taking his land?
   c. Suppose instead that Bruce has someone who is interested in buying his land in the city. He has corrals and fencing on that property that he plans on taking up and bringing to his new place. Does he have a right to do this if the buyer objects?
   d. A review of the deed on his house reveals that he has a mortgage and a judgment lien. What must happen before the buyer can get title to Bruce's property?
   e. Suppose Bruce has a life estate in his current property. What is the significance of this to the buyer?

2. Lonnie owns an apartment complex. Some of the tenants have repeatedly damaged the plumbing because of the things they flush down the toilets. Despite repeated admonitions to stop this, the tenants continue this behavior. In his frustration, Lonnie has refused to repair the heating system of some of these tenants. It is the middle of winter and the night temperatures are below freezing.
   a. Explain the tenants' options.
   b. What are Lonnie's options if his tenants keep ruining the plumbing?

   c. Suppose Lonnie wants to expand his holdings and buy the apartment complex next to his. Why should he do a title search before purchasing this complex?
   d. What information could he get from looking at the deed for this property?
   e. Why might he be well advised to buy title insurance?
   f. Why might his lender prefer a deed of trust to a mortgage as a security instrument?
   g. Is the seller of the complex obligated to disclose to Lonnie that he has been having ongoing problems with the plumbing?

3. Dixie left her husband over a year ago to live with her lesbian lover, Mattie. She developed pancreatic cancer and was cared for diligently by Mattie. A few weeks before she died, she made a holographic will. At the time she made the will she was heavily sedated and her writing is barely legible. In her will, she gave her home, which was her only real asset and which she owned in joint tenancy with her husband, to Mattie. She wanted to ensure that Mattie was well provided for after her death and reasoned that her husband could live with her children, all of whom had refused to speak to her after she moved in with Mattie.
   a. Will Mattie get Dixie's home?
   b. Is the will valid?
   c. Suppose Dixie's husband had predeceased her and that she dies intestate. How would her estate be distributed if she had three daughters and one son, who had predeceased her, if that son had two sons? Assume the estate is distributed on a *per stirpes* basis.
   d. Suppose Dixie has a substantial investment portfolio she wants go to Mattie rather than her children. Explain how she might achieve this and also minimize the taxes Mattie would have to pay.

A TRIP TO THE MOVIES

In the movie *Erin Brockovich,* the protagonist ultimately takes on Pacific Gas & Electric in a dramatic toxic tort case. The case begins as a real estate case.
1. Why does Ed Masry have this case?
2. What is unusual about the real estate records Brockovich is asked to file?
3. If this had been a typical real estate case in which the family had received an offer to buy from Pacific

Gas & Electric, what might a paralegal have been assigned to do initially?
4. Suppose the question arose in the toxic tort case about who actually owned the river. How could that question have been answered?
5. What would have had to be shown in this case to allege that Pacific Gas & Electric committed a nuisance?

INTERNET INQUIRIES

1. Go to *www.netronline.com/Property-Records-AO.htm* and find a link to the agency that records deeds in your locale.
   a. What is the Web address for that agency?
   b. What information must you have to find a deed?
   c. Using your name, your parents' names, or the names of someone you know who owns land, find a deed.
      (1) What kind of deed is on the property you find?
      (2) What kind of estate does this person have?
      (3) What kind of land description is used?
      (4) What kinds of encumbrances do you find?

2. Go to *www.people.virginia.edu/~dev-pros/Realestate.html* to find a link to the assessment office in your locale.
   a. Record the Web address for this office.
   b. What information do you need to find the most recent assessed value of a piece of property?
   c. Can you find any records of this person's real property?
      (1) If yes, what is the assessed value of this property?
      (2) Describe the process you used to find these records.
      (3) Are records for the assessment of commercial properties available online in your jurisdiction?

   d. Find out if any tax liens exist on this entity's personal or real property. Do you find any tax liens? Have these liens been released?

3. Go to *http://tiger.census.gov* and pull up a street map for your city or town or the town closest to you. How much detail is provided in this map?

4. Go to the following sites, find out what real estate forms are available, and make a list of those forms: *www.vandema.com/Forms.htm; www.alllaw.com/forms/real_estate;* and *http://forms.lp.findlaw.com;* At *www.lectlaw.com,* click on "Rotunda," "Forms Room," "Business and General Forms," and scroll down almost to the bottom to "Real Estate Forms."

5. You have been asked to find information for a client about the process she must go through to secure her Social Security benefits now that her husband has died. She wants to know how to find this information on the Internet. Summarize the steps you follow in accessing this information from the Web. Give the names of publications and other resources you find that might be of help to your client.

6. Go to *www.estateplanninglinks.com* and make a list of all the resources and information available there that you think might be helpful in assisting seniors in their estate planning.

ENDNOTES

[1]Property is called real property because under the common law, "real actions" were used when land was involved. These actions required a return of the thing itself.

Afterword by the Authors

We know—textbooks don't have "afterwords." But this is not a typical textbook, as you have probably already surmised. That said, we have a few remarks we would like to share in conclusion, and an afterword seems an appropriate place to do so.

First, please go back to Chapter 1 and review the list of tasks performed by paralegals in the criminal, domestic relations, environmental, and trusts and estates areas of practice. (You thought we forgot about it, didn't you?) Do you now recognize the terms and concepts presented in that list? Do you remember how strange those words seemed to you when you first saw them? You've come a long way since then, haven't you?

Most textbooks provide objectives, warning you of what to expect in a chapter, and summaries, reminding you of what you have read. We have done that. But we would also like to tell you what we hoped you got out of this book (to see if we have indeed accomplished what we set out to do). Here are some of things we hope you have gained.

- an appreciation for not only the specific tasks but also the challenges that face a paralegal
- an understanding of the realities of law practice, including the physical, mental, and emotional demands that will be placed on you as a paralegal
- an understanding of the realities of working with others, including clients, attorneys, other paralegals, legal secretaries, witnesses, and experts
- a basic level of fluency with common legal terms and concepts
- a sense of the broad range of tools and resources available to you on the Internet
- a clear picture of the processes that a cause of action must go through from that initial interview of the client to the ultimate collection of a judgment
- an appreciation of what lies ahead of you in your education in terms of the basic information and skills you will need to acquire if you are going to find employment as a paralegal

- a balanced perspective of the criminal justice system and its processes
- an awareness of ADR, tribal court, and administrative processes and how they contrast with the civil litigation process
- a conviction that you will do your best to master the procedural aspects of the law, focusing particularly on the details that paralegals are responsible for and a sense of pride in the career you have chosen

We suspect that you may have commented somewhere along the way that some of the experiences and dialogues the characters had were unrealistic. Please know that everything depicted in Martha's story line as well as others emerged from our own personal experiences, the experiences of those we know, or the experiences of those about whom we have heard or read. We do not pretend that all of the characters' experiences were typical and, in fact, some of them were manipulated to make a point, but they are, more often than not, realistic, and, in all cases, possible.

Some of you might also be asking whether the characters themselves were realistic. Again, we created these characters out of our experiences with students, paralegals, and attorneys we have known. We have done our best to take them out of the cardboard depictions that commonly inhabit textbooks and fleshed them out as three-dimensional characters with feelings, flaws, and opinions. In some instances, we imbued them with emotional qualities you might have been uncomfortable with or found inappropriate in a textbook. Although the appropriateness of demonstrating emotions in a professional setting is certainly debatable, it is no doubt part and parcel of being human. In our commitment to creating a textbook that reflected real people, real events, and real issues, we opted to preserve our characters' humanity.

You might be interested to know that these characters became very real to us as we worked with them. In a few instances, we actually changed the story line from what we had originally anticipated to accommodate the evolution of their personalities. For instructional purposes, we admit to painting some of them in the extreme. We hereby apologize to Ernesto, Marianne, and some of the other characters for casting them in such a negative light. However, they, along with Martha, who was occasionally depicted as more uninformed or naive than we know someone of her caliber to be, graciously consented to being used as instructional tools.

And now a word about ethics. We have introduced you to some of the most important ethical rules that govern the legal profession. But we encourage you to go beyond mere compliance with these rules and consider the following discussion about what it means to be a professional.

PROFESSIONALISM

The ethical canons and considerations are the legal profession's attempt to encapsulate the most critical rules of professionalism. As with any codified law, however, these rules tend to represent the bottom line for the profession. Mere adherence to them does not ensure that a member of the legal profession has attained a high standard of practice any more than an individual's adherence to the law of the state indicates that he is a model citizen. Professionalism requires more than avoiding a violation of the ethical code. It is a way of conducting oneself that brings honor to the profession, that enhances one's integrity, and that creates a sense of trust all with whom one comes into contact.

What kind of actions and behaviors does professional conduct entail? It means doing what one says she will do when she says she will do it. If a professional says she is going to call on a certain day, she does. If she promises to deliver something by a particular date, she does. If she commits to taking on a project, she completes it.

Legal professionals are civil at all times, no matter what the circumstances. They do not belittle or ridicule others and they do not harass their opponents. They co-operate as much as possible in scheduling meetings and court dates and are courteous about granting time extensions and continuances when circumstances dictate their necessity. They actively seek ways to ease the negotiation and litigation processes by trying to resolve matters as expeditiously and fairly as possible. At the very least, they do nothing to further antagonize their opposition. They advocate vigorously for their clients but remain impeccably honest with the court and their opponents. In short, they practice the Golden Rule of litigation and never do to another what they would not want done to them.

Being a professional does not imply being a workaholic. The law is often depicted as a "jealous mistress" and many a lawyer and paralegal have been seduced by its never-ending demands. The healthy professional, however, has a balanced life that denies neither family, friends, nor personal development. Such a person also contributes to the well-being of the community by doing pro-bono (volunteer legal work) and public interest work. She also supports the profession as a whole by serving on committees, attending professional meetings, and volunteering to organize and participate in workshops, conferences, and seminars.

As paralegals strive to shape their place in the legal community, they would be well-advised to avoid the traps into which lawyers have fallen. Seeds of discontent permeate the legal profession. They can be seen in the disproportionate number of lawyers leaving the profession for alternative careers as well as those experiencing problems with substance abuse, marital crises, emotional instability, and other problems reflecting the burnout and stress that have become characteristic of their profession. As paralegals mold their professional image, they must create a model that reflects balance and integrity as well as competence and skill.

We wish you well on your journey into paralegalism. We hope that you enjoyed our brief time together and we welcome your comments and suggestions. Please feel free to contact us at *linda.edwards@azbar.org*.

Appendix A: Answers

ANSWERS TO PUTTING IT INTO PRACTICE QUESTIONS

Chapter 1

1.1 Answers will vary.

1.2 In joining a professional organization as a student, you might meet people who can connect you with possible employment opportunities, who can mentor you, and who can write recommendations when you go job seeking, assuming they get to know you.

1.3 1. Paralegals should be able to type at least 40 words per minute with very good accuracy. Some firms require a typing speed of 70 words per minute. Skill in using voice recognition software may supplement your typing skills. Remember that many firms are on a network and may not have your voice recognition program or may be unwilling to pay for the network version.

2. Typing and keyboarding skills are very closely related. Many more keys and functions are, however, included on the keyboard than on a typewriter. Be sure to know what the keys you are looking at every day represent, but remember that different programs may use them in different ways.

3. You should be proficient in both WordPerfect and Word. They are the major word processing programs used in the legal profession with WordPerfect having a substantial, but declining lead over Word.

4. Knowledge of both the MacIntosh and PC would be an advantage. The vast majority of law offices use PCs.

5. Although there are many operating systems, most law firms use Windows. Most are at, at least, Windows 95. Many firms that use a server and network their computers use Windows NT.

6. Scanners have become an office staple. Many offices use single-sheet flatbed scanners if the workload is light. Firms engaged in heavy-duty litigation with voluminous documents often have sheet-fed scanners and sophisticated numbering and OCR software.

7. OCR (optical character recognition) is a commonplace feature in many law offices. Most OCR programs have similar features, but may be enabled differently. Xerox and Pagis have two commonly used OCR programs.

8. Both WordPerfect and Word have the capability to create a table of cases. You should know how to utilize this feature in both programs.

9. Both WordPerfect and Word have the capability to search a document for a word or phrase and, if directed, to replace the word or phrase with another word or phrase. You may set the parameters to either require or to ignore capitalization.

10. You should be familiar with all of the programs listed and be proficient in each, or in a major competitor's version of a similar program.

1.4 Answers will vary.

1.5 Answers will vary.

1.6 Answers will vary.

1.7 If no internship is offered, consider volunteering your services. Don't be afraid to make "cold calls," using the phone book as your guide. Better yet, attend meetings of paralegal organizations and ask for some suggestions. Take out a notice in a local newspaper and let people know you're looking for a learning opportunity.

1.8 Answers will vary.

1.9 Yes. Without adequate supervision she runs a high risk of committing a serious error and could be charged with the unauthorized practice of law.

1.10 She needs to work with this attorney to set reasonable parameters for their relationship. It is inappropriate for him to use her as his personal "slave," and she needs to tell him politely, but firmly, that his requests fall outside the scope of her professional responsibilities. By the same token, she should let him know how his public chastisements feel and discuss how he could convey his concerns (in private) without humiliating her. Finally, she needs to insist on clear instructions and keep asking questions until she gets them. If they cannot reach a consensus and he has a supervisor, she should discuss these matters with the supervising attorney and/or with her supervisor.

1.11 Slim to none. She needs to upgrade her computer skills, take a business class that will teach her the basics of office conduct, get a part-time job in a law office or do an internship, and ask her instructors to recommend classes, workshops, or training she could undertake to improve her ability to organize, take instruction, and attend to detail. If she is unwilling to follow such suggestions, she should consider another profession.

1.12 Answers will vary.

1.13 She has little hope of progressing in this job unless she learns to take the initiative in "going the extra mile," begins to speak up and participate in firm activities, and, in general, lets others know she is motivated and capable.

1.14 Answers will vary.

1.15 His request certainly violates the spirit of the prohibition of solicitation rule. If he had asked Martha to do this as an agent of the firm, he would have committed solicitation, so the only question is whether having her children, who are not agents of the firm, talk to the client is still solicitation.

Chapter 2

2.1 Yes. Even though Marianne has changed the names of the parties, others could possibly figure out whom she is referring to, especially if the facts are particularly unique.

2.2 The natural law theorists see God as the source of law, the positivists consider the state the source of law, the realists look to the courts, and the critical legal theorists point to the politicians.

2.3 The legislature creates laws and then delegates some of its power to an administrative agency, which is then responsible for carrying out those laws.

2.4 Business law is primarily substantive while litigation is primarily procedural.

2.5 Both. She can sue for damages and ask the state to prosecute on her behalf. She will have an easier time of proving her case in the civil system because the standard of proof is lower.

2.6 It might be counterproductive because they fail to avail themselves of an opportunity to get a sense of the kind of person the client is, what kind of witness he or she would be, and other types of information that could prove important if they decide to take the case. They also fail to put the client at ease and may lose valuable information the client may feel uncomfortable about disclosing. At a practical level, they lose an opportunity to foster a relationship that could lead to future business with this client or others the client might refer to them.

2.7 Lunch conferences should be avoided because the client may inadvertently waive the attorney-client privilege by discussing the matter in a location where others may overhear the conversation.

2.8 Who else did she see at the scene of the shooting? What did the gunman do after shooting Mike? Where was she when she saw the gunman? When did she first see the gunman? Why does she think the gunman shot Mike? How did the others at the scene react after the gunman fired the shots?

2.9 Marianne is missing the non-verbal cues the client is sending and she is doing nothing to assure the client that she is listening. Because she asks only prepared questions and is so intent on writing, she is probably missing some of what the client is telling her. Beyond that, she is making no effort to establish a rapport with the client. At the end she has not summarized what the client has said, thereby assuring the client that she has heard it correctly, she has failed to inform the client about what she can expect to happen, and she has no idea what the client's goals and expectations are.

2.10 They need to find out about Mike's medical and employment history and his insurance coverage. They also need to get a detailed account of his injuries, his prognosis for recovery, the types of rehab he should anticipate, and what types of long-term effects he is likely to suffer. Finally, they need to determine the financial status of each of the defendants.

2.11 Greta and all of the students who witnessed the shooting; the staff, faculty, and administrators at the school; Mike's treating physicians, the emergency room doctors, his therapists, and his social worker (if he has one); the officers and technicians who investigated the scene and who analyzed the physical evidence.

2.12 You need to learn what to pay attention to, how to stay focused, how to prevent your reactions to what is being said from allowing you to hear it accurately, how to convey your interest and non-judgment, and how to balance your need to get the requisite legal information with your efforts to hear empathically. In addition, you need to be aware of racial and gender-based perceptions and how to interpret non-verbal language.

2.13 The paralegal wants to find out if the witness will either validate or contradict the client's perception of the facts, to identify other possible witnesses and leads, and to assess the witness's credibility and his value as a witness.

2.14 This measure would make it more difficult for Ms. Sinclair to later deny or modify her statement regarding the anonymous phone call.

2.15 Answers will vary.

2.16 Answers will vary.

2.17 Answers will vary.

2.18 Answers will vary. If the Phoenix Library site is used, some of the resources available online are newspaper archives, information about various types of businesses, medical journals and pamphlets, magazine articles, federal government publications, references to encyclopedias, access to phone directories, and documents from a wide variety of sources.

2.19 The firm might want to obtain photos of Mike's injuries, showing the extent of his original injuries and documenting the progression of his healing. A video showing his rehabilitative process and the effects of his injuries on his everyday activities would also be helpful to show to the jury to impress upon them the impact of his injuries.

2.20 Physical evidence might include the weapons used, the bullets and expended cartridge casings, and the gunshot residue and pattern on Mike's clothing. Shoe prints might be found at the scene. This evidence would be in the custody of the police department. The crime lab report should be requested because it will show the nature of the evidence collected and the tests performed on that evidence.

2.21 Answers will vary.

2.22 (a) Yes. The restaurant owes a duty of care to its patrons to serve food that is not contaminated with insects. She can rely on the doctrine of *res ipsa loquitur* to help prove the restaurant was negligent. (b) No. Under the "eggshell skull" rule, the restaurant must take its plaintiff as it finds her. (c) Yes. This may be evidence of negligence per se.

2.23 He has committed battery and intentional infliction of emotional distress

2.24 She can still recover on the basis of strict liability because manufacturers are strictly liable for any defective products they sell. Fault need not be shown.

2.25 The file should include the notes from her interviews and John's interviews with Mike and any witnesses, a list of the names and telephone numbers of any potential witnesses, any medical records that have been received, the police report, the crime lab report, and Martha's to-do list. Her to-do list should include getting Mike to sign medical authorization forms, getting a copy of the police report, finding an expert witness, taking photos at the scene, doing financial checks on the movie company and the boys' parents, conducting conflicts checks, writing a letter to Mike, opening a file, finding a case, and researching the immunity statutes and the case law on foreseeability.

2.26 Answers will vary.

2.27 His chances are very high because of his failure to regularly communicate with his clients and to keep them abreast of the progress of their case. His failure to keep his clients regularly informed may constitute a breach of ethics and is the most common cause of client complaints against attorneys.

2.28 Yes. Ernesto's wife's interests in protecting the school district are adverse to Ernesto's interests in representing Mike against the school district.

Chapter 3

3.1 You must begin by filing a case in the district court. You must then appeal the decision to the court of appeals in the circuit in which the district court sits. Finally, you must file a writ of certiorari with the U.S. Supreme Court.

3.2 A principal purpose is to protect him or her from being terminated simply because he or she makes a decision that is unpopular with the people. This protection allows a judge to make a decisions without fear of reprisal. The disadvantages are that judges may become impervious to changes in society, which should arguably be reflected in changes in the law, and may be difficult to remove when they are no longer doing a good job.

3.3 She will find *Byers* in the *Louisiana Reporter* and in the *Southern Reporter* (2d)

3.4 She should look online in Westlaw or LEXIS or ask for the slip opinion, which is probably on reserve at the front desk of the law library. She should also check the advance sheets for the reporters.

3.5 Caption—Ronald A. Weirum et al., Plaintiffs and Appellants v. RKO General, Inc., Defendant and Appellant, Marsha L. Baime, Defendant and Appellant. Docket number—L.A. 30452. Headnotes 1-5 and 9-10 deal with negligence.

3.6 Volume 101 of the *Federal Reporter,* page 595; Volume 99 of the *South Eastern Reporter* (2d), page 104; Volume 94 of the *Colorado Reporter,* page 54 and volume 105 of the *Pacific Reporter,* page 67.

3.7 539 P.2d 36 (Cal. 1975)

3.8 Decedent's family brought a wrongful death action against the teenage drivers, the maker of the decedent's car, and RKO, the owner of the radio station. The jury returned a verdict against RKO. RKO is appealing the judgment that was entered and the order denying its motion for judgment notwithstanding the verdict.

3.9 A rock radio station that appealed to a largely teenage audience set up a contest encouraging its listeners to follow the movements of one of its well-known disc jockeys in their vehicles in order to win a cash prize and an on-the-air interview with the DJ. In the process of trying to outmaneuver each other to get to the DJ first, two of the teenage listeners raced down a freeway, forcing the decedent off the road and killing him.

3.10 Issue 1: Does a radio station owe a duty to third parties who are injured by listeners of the station who are responding to a giveaway contest in which contestants are directed to speed to a given location if they want to collect a prize?
   Holding (1) Yes
   Issue (2) Does the imposition of a duty violate the First Amendment?
   Holding (2) No.

3.11 1: It is reasonably foreseeable that teenage contestants will speed in their efforts to secure a prize and momentary fame and in doing so will create a danger to other motorists. The gravity and likelihood of the danger to others outweighed the utility of the conduct (having a contest) and so created an unreasonable risk of harm.
   2: The First Amendment does not protect the creation of undue risk of harm to others.

3.12 Those in the entertainment industry have a duty to anyone harmed by viewers who injure them if those who create the entertainment do so with the intent of inciting viewers to engage in activities that create a reasonably foreseeable danger to others.

3.13 Answer will have samples page from *Am.Jur.* and *C.J.S.*

The student should note differences in breadth of coverage. *C.J.S.* provides many more references to cases than does *Am.Jur.*

3.14 Answer will have sample page from *Prosser.*

3.15 Answer will have sample page from digest.

3.16 a. Yes b. Yes c. Yes d. Yes

3.17 a. Yes b. Sec. 11 c. *Bass v. New York*

3.18 The Reporter's Note shows the age of majority for each state.

3.19 Answers will vary.

3.20 Few are overturned because of all the restrictions imposed on the appellate courts. They are bound by statutes, constitutions, and the principle of *stare decisis;* they cannot review issues that are not properly before them; and they usually cannot review issues of fact. Therefore, even if they would like to overturn a decision, they may not be afforded the opportunity to do so.

3.21 The court states the issue as follows: "Thus, the essential question is whether, on the undisputed material facts, a reasonable jury could conclude that the school breached its duties to Hill." To restate the issue involving the essential facts, you could say: "Does a school breach its duty to a student who is killed by another student if it had earlier questioned and then released these same students after they were involved in an altercation?" (a) One of the rules used in the opinion is (on page 113) ". . . student discipline is a matter entrusted to schools and their governing boards' discretion, and judicial intervention is called for only to correct 'a manifest abuse of discretion.' " (b) The court applies this rule by examining the evidence in the record, especially the assistant principal's testimony at Fast's trial (page 114), to see if there is any evidence that the school abused its discretion by not disciplining the boys when they had their altercation. (c) The court concludes (on page 115) that "it is not possible to conclude that the school abused its discretion by not imposing discipline . . ."

3.22 In *Hill,* the question is whether the school abused its discretion by not disciplining the students and whether it should have known that Fast (the student who shot Hill) would harm Hill. The court concluded that the school had no reason to suspect that Fast would kill Hill. In Mike's case, however, the school was specifically alerted to the possibility that someone would be killed on campus and it made no investigation of that threat. Even though it did not who would be injured, the school was on notice that someone would be hurt. Dissimilarities to be emphasized are that the school knew about a threat and that the shooting took place during school hours on campus, where school officials had a responsibility to supervise the activities of those on campus. It is most important to establish that the school was aware of a death threat and that the assailants had "dangerous propensities." It is vital to find out what exactly the principal was told in the phone call and what kinds of problems the assailants might previously have had on campus and how the school officials responded to those problems.

3.23 Title 14 of the North Caroline Statutes

3.24 There is no indication of immunity. Public entity is defined as the "state and any political subdivisions of the state." One reference is to Schabel v. Deer Valley Unified Sch. Dist.

3.25 She should begin with a discussion of the relevant cases, articulate the rules that can be gleaned from these cases, and apply the rules to Mike's case. In applying the rules, counterarguments would have to be made and, in making both arguments and counterarguments, Martha would need to show in what ways the cited cases would apply to Mike's case and in what ways they could be distinguished. For each subissue she discussed, she would need to draw a conclusion about what she predicted the courts would do in Mike's case.

Chapter 4

4.1 Failure to investigate a claim can be dangerous for an attorney if it turns out that the client has no good faith basis upon which to make such a claim. The attorney could face discipline by the state bar and risk Rule 11 sanctions.

4.2 No. They are able to make a good faith argument for the extension of the law in this area.

4.3 (a) If he sues in a state that adheres to the doctrine of joint and several liability, he could. In those states that have abolished this doctrine, he could not, and in those states that have modified it, he may not be able to. (b) He will want to sue both the employees and employer. If he is able to prove that the faculty were negligent, he can probably recover from the school district (the deep pocket).

4.4 A firm might refuse to represent if the defendant had no insurance or had insufficient non-exempt assets from which the recovery could be collected.

4.5 Fee disputes are common because attorneys either fail to have a written attorney-client agreement or fail to spell out in sufficient detail what their expectations are in reference to fees. They do not indicate in advance what types of costs are likely to be incurred, when those costs will need to be paid, what the client must pay if he loses the suit, what the attorney has agreed to do and has indicated he will not do, how the fees will be calculated, and whether the attorney has liens on any judgment that is awarded.

4.6 Marianne should refuse to withdraw monies from the trust account and should remind the attorney that he cannot require her to do something that is clearly unethical (and illegal). Although paralegals are allowed to answer questions about fee agreements, they are not allowed to establish fee agreements with clients. Because Marianne does not know what the client and her attorney have agreed to, she should defer to the attorney if the client has any questions.

4.7 Answers will vary.

4.8 They probably would not for two reasons: they probably make too much money and their case (a contractual dispute) is not the type of case Legal Services typically accepts.

4.9 A demand letter is probably premature because John does not have sufficient facts yet to establish liability against the school and CODA and he does not yet know the full extent of Mike's medical costs this early in Mike's recovery. He should check into any statutory pre-filing requirements in reference to the school.

4.10 All of the factors are applicable except that one of the defendants (CODA) is an out-of-state defendant (although it is doing business in Arizona) and one of the defendants (school district) is a government agency.

4.11 It does not have jurisdiction because there is not complete diversity (some of the plaintiffs and defendants reside in Arizona) and no federal question exists. (Even though CODA may raise the First Amendment as a constitutional defense, no constitutional issues are being raised by the plaintiff and no federal statutes are being relied upon.)

4.12 Yes. CODA caused an act to occur in Arizona and Mike's suit arises out of that act.

4.13 No. All of the plaintiffs and all of the other defendants reside in Arizona and the events in dispute occurred in Arizona.

4.14 Factors include the following: if the procedural or substantive laws in federal court benefited Mike; if he could get to trial more quickly in federal court than in state court; if the federal court judges would be more likely to rule in his favor on important issues than the state court judges; if the federal jury pool would be preferable to the state jury pool; if he would feel more comfortable litigating in federal court than in state court.

4.15 The attorney's concerns are valid because if the complaint does not conform to the local rules, the court clerk may reject it. The types of things Marianne should check for are the requirements pertaining to margins, font and type size, line spacing, paper size, backing sheets, line spacing, limits on length, line numbering, etc.

4.16 YOUR FIRM
YOUR ATTORNEY, Esq.
State Bar No. XXXXX [If required]
FIRM'S ADDRESS
FIRM TELEPHONE NO.

Attorneys for Plaintiff Molly Running Deer

IN THE SUPERIOR COURT OF [YOUR COUNTY OR DISTRICT] COUNTY
[YOUR JURISDICTION]

Molly Running Deer, a single woman,)		
)		
)	NO. _____	
Plaintiff,)		
)	Complaint	
vs.)	(Tort—motor	
)	Vehicle) [IF REQUIRED]	
Stuart Thames and Jane Joe Thames,)		
Husband and wife,)		
)		
Defendants.)		
_____)		

4.17 Plaintiff, by and through counsel undersigned, for her complaint against the defendants, alleges as follows:

JURISDICTIONAL ALLEGATIONS

1. Plaintiff Molly Running Deer (hereinafter Molly) is an adult single woman residing in [YOUR JURISDICTION].

2. Defendant Stuart Thames (hereinafter Stuart) is a resident of [YOUR JURISDICTION if that is the case]; that Jane Doe Thames is, upon information and belief, the wife of Stuart and that the acts of Stuart as alleged herein were done on behalf of the marital community [IF REQUIRED BY YOUR STATE]; that the true name of Jane Doe Thames is unknown to Molly at this time and leave of this court is requested to substitute her true name when it becomes known.

3. That Stuart caused an act to occur in [YOUR JURISDICTION] out of which Molly's cause of action arises.

4. Molly's monetary claims against defendants exceed the jurisdictional prerequisites of this court [IF REQUIRED].

5. This case is not subject to mandatory arbitration as Molly's monetary claims exceed $50,000 [IF APPLICABLE, SUBSTITUTE YOUR ARBITRATION LIMIT IF THERE IS ONE].

GENERAL ALLEGATIONS

6. On or about 9:00 p.m. on January 18, 2000, Stuart, while under the influence of an intoxicating beverage, caused an accident to occur in which Molly was severely injured.

7. That approximately one hour after the accident, Stuart's blood alcohol level was 0.15%, above the presumptive level for driving while intoxicated.

8. That the seriousness of Molly's injuries required her to be taken from the accident scene by helicopter and flown to a hospital where immediate surgery was performed.

9. That in addition to a subdural hematoma, Molly sustained severe bruises and lacerations on her head and upper body.

10. That Molly has sustained special damages in the form of lost wages, lost employment advancement opportunities as well as medical

and related expenses; additional expenses are reasonably expected to accrue after the date of this complaint.

11. [ADD ADDITIONAL FACTS TO TELL THE STORY]

4.18 **Count One—Negligence**

1. That Stuart had a duty to drive his vehicle in a lawful and prudent manner.

2. That Stuart's failure to stop at a lawful stop signal, his driving while intoxicated and his failure to drive his vehicle in a reasonable and prudent manner were all breaches of the duty he owed to Molly.

3. That Molly has sustained damages as a direct result of Stuart's breach of his duty to her.

4.19 Wherefore Molly prays for judgment against Stuart and Jane Doe Thames as follows:

1. For general damages in an amount to be shown by the evidence but alleged to be not less than $250,000 [IN MANY JURISDICTIONS THE ACTUAL DAMAGES ALLEGED ARE NOT SPECIFIED].

2. For special damages in an amount to be shown by the evidence but alleged to be not less than $60,000 [IN MANY JURISDICTIONS THE ACTUAL DAMAGES ALLEGED ARE NOT SPECIFIED].

3. For future medical expenses in an amount to be shown by the evidence but alleged to be not less than $20,000 [IN MANY JURISDICTIONS THE ACTUAL DAMAGES ALLEGED ARE NOT SPECIFIED].

4. For punitive damages in an amount to be shown by the evidence [IN MANY JURISDICTIONS THE AMOUNT OF PUNITIVE DAMAGES CLAIMED CANNOT, BY LAW, BE SPECIFIED].

4.20 She needs to find out the addresses of the student defendants and give the process server any additional details that might be necessary to find their homes. If she does not know the procedures required to sue a county governmental agency, she will need to do the appropriate research. She will also need to find out the address of the agent for CODA that is authorized to receive service.

4.21 His file should include a copy of his complaint, her notes and John's notes from interviews they have conducted, her research notes, Mike's med-

ical records and bills, any correspondence John may have written, and any memos she, John, or Ernesto may have written to the file.

4.22 If the missed deadline resulted in the case as a whole or certain elements of a case being dismissed, the client's only resort might be a claim against the attorney. If a paralegal miscalculated or forgot the deadline, she could not be sued, but might be fired for incompetence.

4.23 It will be due on January 2, 2001.

4.24 He will want to talk with the producers of *Teenage Stalkers* and any others involved with the making of the movie who could shed some light on its message and purpose. He should also watch the movie as soon as possible and should investigate the contentions in Mike's complaint.

4.25 If CODA is a subsidiary of a larger parent company, it may want to bring the larger company into the suit. If Mike did not sue the producer and directors involved in the creation of *Teenage Stalkers,* it may want to file third-party complaint against them. If a private security company were responsible for the security on campus, the district could bring a third-party complaint against that company.

4.26 (a) Stuart can allege contributory or comparative negligence (depending on the system in his state). Molly can still recover in a contributory negligence system if she can show that Stuart had the last clear chance to avoid the accident and did not do so. In a comparative negligence system, her damages would be reduced in proportion to her own degree of negligence, but she could still recover (except in some states where she would barred if her negligence was greater than 50 percent). (b) No. Driving does fall within the scope of judicial duties. (c) No. Necessity does not allow the defendant to subject others to potentially serious injury or even death. (d) Her claim is barred by the statute of limitations unless she can show that she could not reasonably have discovered her injuries any earlier and that the statute should not begin to run until she was able to discover those injuries (assuming this argument is allowed in her state).

4.27 Answering paragraph 2, defendant admits being a resident of Pima County, and is without knowledge or information sufficient to form a belief as to the truth of the allegation that Stuart Thames caused the act or event out of which plaintiff's complaint arose.

4.28 If Ms. Running Deer in some way contributed to the accident, Stuart could bring a counterclaim against her for negligence. He could bring a third-party claim against the mechanic.

4.29 If Stuart were uninsured with few assets, his best bet would probably be to default. If he had enough assets from which to collect a judgment, he might be well advised after a default judgment was obtained to seek bankruptcy. If he were a successful surgeon, he would be better off defending the lawsuit, finding ways to protect his assets, and doing what was possible to delay the suit.

Chapter 5

5.1 The opposing party is unlikely to disclose evidence that is not specifically requested, and the party making the request may not be able to accurately frame questions that target evidence of which they are unaware but which may be extremely helpful to their case.

5.2 Parties do not have to expend the time and money they did under the traditional rules trying to ferret out evidence their opponents might have because most of it should be revealed in the disclosure statement. The traditional tools can then be used to follow up on certain leads or to clarify and augment the information originally disclosed.

5.3 Answers will vary.

5.4 He will depose Ms. Sinclair to get her statement on record in case she changes her story later. He will depose the witness to get his statement on record so he can read it into the record at trial if he is unable to get the student to appear at trial. He will be assessing what kind of witness Hendershott will make when he gets on the stand and evaluating how credible he appears to be.

5.5 No. If they do, they will be less likely to follow up on a deponent's answers and to pay attention to a deponent's mannerisms and behavior during questioning. Most attorneys prepare an outline of questions and then use the deponent's testimony to help them create additional questions.

5.6 Molly Running Deer would probably be deposed first, followed by either the witnesses to the accident or Molly's treating physician. The witnesses would be interviewed first. If their testimony appeared to be helpful to Stuart, they would be deposed, but if they harmed his case, they would not be deposed. Any other experts Molly intended to have testify would also need to be deposed.

5.7 The district may use an expert as to the standard of care in reference to school security; a physician who could testify about the extent and duration of Mike's injuries; a vocational consultant who could

testify regarding the effects of Mike's injuries on his vocational prospects (e.g., his potential as an athlete with a major college team and potentially as a professional football player); and an economics consultant who could testify about the financial implications of Mike's injuries.

5.8 She will have to send copies of notices of deposition to the attorneys representing all the parties in the case. She will also need to arrange for court reporters for each deposition and will need to schedule the conference room (or whatever room is to be used for the deposition) for those dates.

5.9 She might be overlooking some information that will lead to evidence neither she nor her attorney had considered.

5.10 They will need to wade through tons of documents looking for specific and sometimes minor pieces of information. They also need to be able to categorize all of this information and keep track of who provided it. Furthermore, they must remember the status of each discovery request.

5.11 She will need to prepare a subpoena *duces tecum* directed to the custodian of the records for the company.

5.12 Because CODA has published its views on the advocacy of violence, John will want to get admissions that he can introduce into court and then use a deposition to flesh out the details of its philosophy.

5.13 He will have to pay the costs incurred by Molly Running Deer in proving this fact.

5.14 Request for Admission No. 1
Admit that CODA advocates the violent overthrow of the U.S. government.

Interrogatory No. 1
In the event that you deny the foregoing request for admission, state each and every fact upon which such denial is based and state each and every respect in which you contend that CODA does not advocate the violent overthrow of the government.

5.15 He will have to disclose the following witnesses: Greta, the students who witnessed the attack on Mike, the police who investigated Mike's case, the medical personnel involved in Mike's treatment and rehabilitation, and any experts that have been used or are expected to be used.

5.16 He will have to disclose Mike's medical records and any records relating to his therapy, the police report, and possibly records prepared by experts, although they may be protected under the work product doctrine discussed later in the chapter.

5.17 Marianne is going to have to spend time locating all of the bills when it comes time to prepare a disclosure statement. Also, she is more likely to misplace bills than if she kept them in one place. Keeping an ongoing tally would make it easy for her to compute the damages whenever that information was needed.

5.18 Because much of litigation involves the preparation of motions, responses, and replies, those who are able to write well are more likely to persuade judges than those who write poorly.

5.19 The judge may not grant oral arguments, and even if she does, she is likely to be adversely affected by the poor quality of the response.

5.20 No. The judge must assume for purposes of a motion to dismiss that everything in Molly Running Deer's complaint is true and can be proved.

5.21 The motion itself would consist of two paragraphs stating what was being requested and the procedural basis for the motion. It would be accompanied by a memorandum of points and authorities that would open with a summary of the argument as to why the judge should grant the motion to dismiss, followed by a brief summary of the relevant facts, the basis of the argument, and the conclusion CODA wanted the judge the reach. The argument itself would summarize the conclusion and the main points leading to that conclusion, and would then be divided into subsections addressing each of those points.

5.22 Mike is guaranteed a minimum recovery and gains the support of Hendershott against the other defendants. Hendershott is guaranteed a maximum amount of damages he has to pay and does not have to spend as much money preparing his defense. The other defendants may end up paying more damages than their degree of liability indicates they should. They are less likely to be able to settle with Mike because he has less incentive to settle now that he has reached an agreement with Hendershott.

5.23 She can make sure he covers all the areas that need to be explored; she can suggest he follow up any of Mr. Washington's answers that still seem vague or unclear; and can observe the subtleties in Mr. Washington's demeanor that she can bring to John's attention after the deposition.

5.24 First, the attorney would establish the ground rules for the deposition. Then she would allow the witness to tell everything he saw and would follow up with questions that would clarify and augment the witness's testimony. She would probably ask the witness to make a drawing of the accident from his perspective and would then mark the drawing and introduce it as exhibit in the record.

5.25 Knew about Jorge's threat to Mike but said nothing to anyone because Mike had asked him to keep what he had told him about his relationship with Carmela confidential. Concedes that in hindsight he could have warned security or the administration without betraying Mike's trust.

5.26 No. He has already confessed.

5.27 Paralegals are often involved in the preparation of discovery requests as well as responses to discovery requests. They need to know how to write discovery requests that are unlikely to be objected to, and when to object to unreasonable requests.

5.28 First, John should send a letter to the attorney representing the school and request the logs. Then he should follow the letter with a phone call. If the attorney refuses to provide the information, he should file a motion to compel if he considers the potential information important to his case and if he cannot get the logs any other way. He should not file a motion for sanctions unless he is successful in his motion to compel and the school continues to refuse to produce the logs.

Chapter 6

6.1 CODA would argue that no facts existed to support Mike's claim that it had breached its duty to Mike. In other words, no evidence existed that the boys had shot Mike because of what they had seen in the movie, and that if the case went to trial, the judge would have no choice but to dismiss the claims against CODA.

6.2 With a trial of that length, several things can happen that might preclude the judge from hearing the case on the specified date. A previous trial could run over; the judge could have other obligations that arise out of other cases; some of the witnesses or attorneys could become ill; one of the defendants could declare bankruptcy. Any number of unforeseen events could occur.

6.3 They reduce the number of objections and clarify in advance what evidence will and will not be presented at trial to prevent surprises and promote a smooth presentation of witnesses and exhibits.

6.4 Gag orders restrict parties' freedom of speech.

6.5 Questions alluding to Carmela's pregnancy are not relevant to the case at hand and could raise questions in the jurors' minds that could prejudice them.

6.6 Even though they may not influence the jury's decision, these instructions could be grounds for appeal and could result in an appellate court ordering a new trial.

6.7 Exhibits might include Mike's medical records and the police report; photos/videos showing his injuries, recovery, and rehabilitation; articles demonstrating Mike's successes in football; awards/honors received demonstrating Mike's academic excellence. Demonstrative evidence might include charts showing the costs of Mike's medical treatment, graphs demonstrating the economic impact of his injuries, blowups of critical testimony.

6.8 A paralegal might gather and copy the materials to be included in the notebook, such as pleadings, minute entries, the pretrial statement, and other documents. He might also make lists of witnesses, exhibits, and demonstrative evidence to be introduced, as well as organize the notebook and prepare the appropriate tabs.

6.9 The friend of Hendershott's family will be removed by the judge. The movie producer can be removed using a challenge for cause. A peremptory challenge will be needed to remove the student unless the student demonstrates an inability or unwillingness to decide the case impartially.

6.10 In answering this question, consider whom you think the primary target should be: the boys, the school district, or CODA.

6.11 The weakest link in reference to the district is breach of duty. For CODA, the issue of duty is clearly debatable; Mike must prevail on this to get to the other elements.

6.12 Hendershott can give the most complete explanation of what happened to Mike and, in contrast to the other two boys, will be cooperative due to the Gallagher agreement. If he is a hostile witness, they can ask leading questions and better direct his testimony.

6.13 (a) hearsay; (b) not a dying declaration because the declarant is available; an admission of party; (c) excited utterance; (d) Admission of party; (e) not hearsay because used for impeachment.

6.14 The plaintiff is then prohibited from allowing the jury to consider that claim despite all the time and money she has invested in finding evidence to support that claim.

6.15 It will need to go after the weakest link in the chain of Mike's case (probably breach of duty) and show that Mike has failed to prove with a preponderance of the evidence that the school breached its duty. Alternatively, the school could argue that Mike contributed to his own injuries (comparative or contributory negligence).

6.16 No. Little would be gained at this point by granting such a motion and much could be lost if the court of appeals overturned the directed verdict.

6.17 Closing arguments allow attorneys to help jurors put all the pieces together and see more clearly how all the evidence relates. Studies show that most jurors do not change their minds after hearing closing arguments.

6.18 A majority vote is less likely to result in a hung jury and a general verdict is less likely to get overturned on appeal.

6.19 The judge had concluded that no reasonable person could have concluded that watching *Teenage Stalkers* was the cause of the boys' attack on Mike.

6.20 It is important so they can accurately compute the deadline by which any appeals must be filed. They might argue about the form of judgment and taxable costs. Mike will not have to pay CODA's attorneys' fees unless the judge determined that the lawsuit against CODA was frivolous, which is unlikely in light of the fact that the judge refused to grant CODA's motions for a directed verdict.

6.21 Stuart can file for bankruptcy or obtain a stay by filing a supersedeas bond.

6.22 He will find out what property and money Thames has by subpoenaing him to bring all relevant documents and then questioning him about those documents and other properties, income, and expenses not reflected in those documents.

6.23 She can obtain a judgment lien on real estate owned by Stuart, file a writ of execution to levy upon his tangible personal property, or garnish Stuart's bank accounts and wages. The latter is preferable because such debts are easily traced.

6.24 He can file for bankruptcy, move to another state or country, or convert his assets into exempt assets.

6.25 It will have to prove that some kind of reversible error was committed.

6.26 He can ask the judge to certify his ruling for an immediate appeal. Because the judge is unlikely to do this, he can use this ruling as a basis for appeal if he loses.

6.27 Appealing is a costly, time-consuming process and there is little chance of getting an appellate court to find reversible error.

Chapter 7

7.1 In situations (b) and (f) the defendant has an expectation of privacy.

7.2 The informant can assist the officer in establishing probable cause by providing information supporting the officer's belief that a crime has been committed. The informant can also assist in describing the area to be searched and the items to be seized.

7.3 In situations (e) and (f) the officers need a warrant. In (e) the friend does not have the authority to give consent and in (f) the officers are not lawfully present so they cannot rely on the "plain view" doctrine.

7.4 (a) The officer conducted a lawful *Terry* patdown search of the defendant and found no weapons but upon feeling a small lump in the defendant's jacket and examining, the officer thought it felt like a lump of crack cocaine in cellophane and reached inside the jacket and took it out. (b) Whether contraband detected through the sense of touch during a patdown search is admissible? (c) To check for weapons. (d) When the search goes beyond what is necessary to determine if the suspect is armed. (e) If the police are in a lawful position from which they see an object, if its incriminating nature is immediately apparent to them, and have a lawful right of access to the object, they may seize it without a warrant. (f) As long as the contraband is in open view and the police observe it from a lawful point of view, there has no invasion of privacy and therefore no search. (g) As long as officer is lawfully patting down outer clothing and feels something that is immediately apparent as contraband, there has been no invasion of privacy beyond that authorized by search for weapons. (h) It rejected both contentions. (i) Because the incriminating nature of the equipment was not immediately apparent and the officer's moving of the stereo was not justified without a warrant. (j) Because the incriminating nature of the contraband was not immediately apparent to the officer and his further search was not justified without a warrant.

7.5 Yes, because a reasonable person in the defendant's shoes would not have believed he was free to leave. (Based on facts in *Florida v. Royer*, 460 U.S. 491 (1983). He could be detained for as long as was reasonably necessary for the officers to confirm or dispel their belief that he was smuggling drugs.

7.6 Yes, if Joe was in the custody of the police. Because he was taken to the station house, he was most likely in their custody.

(a) Was Joe being interrogated?
(b) No. The officers' deception had no bearing on Joe's decision to waive his *Miranda* rights.

7.7 Because the attorney can explain the nature of the charges against him and make arguments to the judge regarding his bail.

7.8 Because at the preliminary hearing his attorney would have an opportunity to ask questions of the state's witnesses.

7.9 A defendant charged with a serious felony, such as child molestation, who has little or no evidence to prove his innocence (e.g., no witness to provide an alibi, nothing but his word against the child's) may opt for a lesser sentence rather than risk going to trial and receiving a harsher sentence.

7.10 Because they have an obligation to zealously represent their client and yet they must not allow their client to perpetrate a fraud on the court. Furthermore, the defendant has a right to a trial and competent counsel and if they either withdraw or disclose the perjury, the defendant will almost certainly be convicted.

7.11 Because without representation most defendants would not be able to manage the intricacies of the criminal justice system and would not be afforded a fair trial. The Court has made proving ineffective assistance of counsel difficult to discourage defendants from making this claim. Otherwise, most defendants who were convicted would bring these claims.

7.12 (a) knowing (b) purposeful (c) criminal negligence (d) reckless

7.13 (a) Yes, he is not justified in using deadly force to defend his property.
   (b) The question is whether the amount of force she used was reasonably necessary to protect herself.
   (c) As a defense to first degree murder but not to manslaughter.
   (d) That either he did not know what he was doing or that he did not know that what he was doing was wrong (when he killed her).
   (e) No.
   (f) No, duress is not a defense if the threat is against reputation.
      (1) No, because Bruce is a private citizen.
      (2) Yes, because then Bruce is acting on behalf of law enforcement.

7.14 The prosecution will not be allowed to introduce the confession against Toby but will be allowed to use that confession against David (who has no standing). The good–faith exception does not apply to Fifth Amendment cases.

7.15 With a determinate sentence the defendant knows the maximum amount of time he will receive (if any good-time credit programs exist, he may be able to reduce that time) and he is less subject to the politics within an institution. An inmate who knows how "to play" the system may prefer an indeterminate sentence. Conceivably, inmates receiving indeterminate sentences might serve less time than those with determinate sentences if they were able to convince prison officials they had changed.

7.16 If the judge found the existence of aggravating circumstances.

7.17 The proponent of the death penalty could argue that the only just punishment for someone who takes the life of another is death (an eye for eye) and that this is the only way the offender can pay back his "debt" to society (retribution). He might also argue that death is the only effective deterrent in that the death penalty will deter others who are contemplating killing another (general deterrence) and that it will most certainly deter the individual sentenced to death (special deterrence). By the same token, the death penalty is the most effective tool of incapacitation once it is carried out.

7.18 Sentencing the offender to probation, to make restitution to his victims, to a work furlough program, or to be monitored daily using an electronic device.

7.19 If he has gained no skills while in prison he may be less able to find suitable employment. If he has become hardened by his experiences in his prison, he may be more angry and therefore more dangerous. If he loses his family and friends, he may be less stable and more vulnerable to getting involved in criminal activities.

7.20 Personal answer

Chapter 8

8.1 Arbitration could be mandated by statute, court rules, or by a provision in the agreement they signed when they accepted the neurologist's services. No, the award would not be binding.

8.2 Arbitration would be a more informal process, requiring less time and money to resolve the dispute. Attorneys may be uncomfortable with the informality of the process and the lack of information they having going into the arbitration because of the limited discovery process.

8.3 If attorneys are involved, the mediator will probably be more directive in suggesting resolutions and in guiding the parties through the process.

8.4 Their intent is to give the parties an opportunity to come up with a resolution they can live with. Because many of these disputes are so emotionally charged, mediation also gives the parties a chance to vent their feelings and then helps them focus on the real issues that divide them.

8.5 Mediators should possess good "people" skills. They should listen well, communicate clearly, and be patient, caring, respectful, and tolerant.

8.6 No. Arbitrators make the ultimate decision; they do not help the parties be self-determining.

8.7 The Johnsons would probably be better served by arbitration than mediation. Their dispute appears to be factual in nature and fairly straightforward. If a myriad number of issues were involved or if emotional issues were also at stake, mediation might be useful. Without good reason to resort to mediation, med-arb does not appear to be the most useful approach to resolving their dispute.

8.8 It might be a viable option if both sides believed they were going to win at trial and because of that refused to settle. Many malpractice cases involve potentially large awards and the trials are usually long. The attorneys would have to decide whether a jury could be expected to understand the issues involved if the evidence were presented in a summary fashion.

8.9 A mini-trial may help the parties settle after the neutral tells them the strengths and weaknesses of their case.

8.10 Private judging and neutral expert fact finding would be helpful.

8.11 Answers will vary.

8.12 Both are interested in restoring the victim, offender, and community; compensation is viewed as being more important than punishment.

8.13 A quasi-legislative function is the making of rules that taxpayers are to follow when filing their income tax returns; a quasi-adjudicative function is a hearing for a disgruntled taxpayer who is unhappy with the results of a tax audit; an executive function is the prosecution of a citizen who fails to pay taxes.

8.14 The public must be given sufficient notice to attend hearings regarding the anticipated rules and is allowed to offer comments about those rules. (NEED TO CHANGE THIS IN PARA-LEGAL STUDIES BOOK; IT IS NOW 8.18.)

8.15 The ALJ has the latitude of deciding what evidence will be heard and how much weight to give the evidence in rendering his decision. The trial court judge cannot overrule an ALJ's decision unless the ALJ clearly abused his discretion—a difficult burden to meet. Furthermore, because most claimants simply cannot afford to appeal the decisions of ALJs, their discretion is largely unchecked by judicial review.

8.16 The process is more informal, requiring less familiarity with the intricacies of the rules of evidence, and it is not unusual for lay persons to represent themselves in administrative hearings. Often the stakes are less and it is not cost-effective for attorneys to be involved.

8.17 (a) The appellant was not given benefits because he quit his job without good cause. He left before his discharge date because his employer found a replacement for him after he had told his employer he was quitting. Appellant said that to go back under these conditions would have been demeaning. (b) The act allows compensation for a limited period to those who can work, are available for work, and are involuntarily unemployed through no fault of their own. It provides that an employee is ineligible for benefits if he leaves work voluntarily without good cause. (c) He contends that the Department's regulation conflicts with the purpose and intent of the Employment Security Act. (d) It finds that the regulation is consistent with the purpose of the Employment Security Act. (e) The employee has good cause for leaving if he can show that he would suffer substantial detriment by remaining or if he quits to accept other work.

8.18 It resolves the question of bias on the part of the ALJ, preserves the independence of the ALJ and thereby tends to attract better qualified individuals as ALJs, is cost- and workload-efficient, and provides for greater public confidence in the decisions rendered.

8.19 Probably not. Great time and expense are entailed in first exhausting their administrative remedies.

8.20 (a) *Federal Register;* (b) *List of Sections Affected;* (c) *United State Government Manual* or *Federal Regulatory Directory;* (d) *Code of Federal Regulations (CFR).*

8.21 A warrant probably would be needed, although most labs would probably give consent.

8.22 More and more administrative agencies are employing paralegals themselves and are allowing paralegals to practice before them.

Chapter 9

9.1 (a) Both Deedee and Chamberlain are merchants under the UCC's definition. Both deal in the goods (Arabian horses) that are the subject of the contract and both have a knowledge (expertise in Arabian bloodlines) that relates to the sale of these goods. (b) Breeding might be seen as a sale of goods (semen), thereby implicating the UCC. This is especially valid when artificial insemination is used because the transaction literally involves a transfer of semen from the stallion to the mare. On the other hand, breeding could be seen as a service that only incidentally involves a good, in which case the UCC would not apply.

9.2 Yes. This agreement is governed by the UCC, which allows for the creation of output contracts where the quantity term is not specified. Although they have not agreed to a time and place of payment, the UCC fills in these terms. The term of price has some parameters that at least establish some limitations and the term "foaling season" is a term of trade used by merchants in the Arabian horse business.

9.3 (a) Bilateral (b) He probably cannot accept her offer because a reasonable time has passed, especially since the foaling season is over and Deedee is likely to have made offers to others who produced fillies in which she was interested. (c) Under the common law, he could create an option contract; under the UCC, he could request a merchant firm offer. (d) Under the majority rule, Deedee revoked her offer when she called Chamberlain, but under the minority rule, her revocation was not effective until he received the message. If her revocation was not effective, Chamberlain could still accept her offer. (e) No. Chamberlain's offer to sell the horse for $15,000 was a counteroffer, which terminated Deedee's original offer. Chamberlain's proposal to sell the horse for $10,000 is a new offer, which Deedee has a right to reject.

9.4 (a) Unilateral (b) No. Antonio's acceptance was to be by performance and the offer was no longer open when someone else accepted it. (c) Under the common law, Antonio had an obligation to notify Deedee that he had completed the shoeing within the time she had allotted him, but one could argue that the shoeing itself was notification, especially for a horse trainer/breeder, who should be aware that a horse has been recently shod. (d) Under the common law, the new terms would not be a mirror image of Deedee's offer and would not be part of their final contract. Under the UCC, the terms do not "materially alter" the original agreement and because they are standard in the industry, they would become part of the contract. (e) Yes. Under the mailbox rule, Deedee's acceptance was effective as soon as she mailed the contract.

9.5   They have formed a valid contract.

9.6   Under the common law, the oral agreement will not be admissible because the agreed-upon term is an addition to the written contract. Under the UCC's more liberal provisions, the additional term may be admissible.

9.7   (a) Defendant-seller (a New York sales corporation) entered into negotiations with plaintiff-buyer (a Swiss corporation) regarding the purchase of chickens. When asked by defendant's representatives what kind of chickens it wanted, plaintiff's spokesperson replied, "Any kind of chicken," and when asked to clarify an ambiguous cable, plaintiff's spokesperson affirmed that the cable was intended to apply to the purchase of either broiler or stewing chickens. Two contracts were entered into via cablegrams. Plaintiff agreed to buy the chickens, believing them to be broiler chickens, while the defendant believed it was selling stewing chickens (also called *fowl*). Stewing chickens were worth 35 to 37 cents per pound at the time; plaintiff-buyer paid 33 cents per pound for the chickens it purchased. After receiving the first shipment of chickens, which was short, plaintiff-buyer sent two cables, complaining that the chickens were "fowl." Defendant-seller refused to recognize plaintiff-buyer's complaint and asked whether plaintiff would accept the shipment. Based on plaintiff-buyer's ambiguous response, defendant-seller shipped stewing chickens to complete the first order and to fill the second order. (b) The plaintiff defines *chicken* as a young chicken suitable for broiling or frying. Defendant defines *chicken* more broadly to include any bird that meets contract specifications, including stewing chickens. (c) No. The court finds conflicting usage in the trade. (d) Evidence includes the dictionary definition, the definition by the Department of Agriculture Regulations, some usage in the trade, the realities of the market, and what the plaintiff's spokesperson said. (e) The plaintiff failed to sustain the burden of proving its definition of *chicken*.

9.8   (a) No. He can claim impossibility as a defense. (b) Yes. Chamberlain has committed a material breach in light of the provision in their contract that the mare is to be bred beginning in February. (c) Under the UCC's "perfect tender rule," she can either take the colt back and get her money back or keep the colt and sue for damages based on the difference in the colt's value as a stallion and his value as a gelding. (A question exists in this case as to whether Deedee's actions are timely. In view of the fact that the defect in the colt was latent and could not reasonably have been discovered by either party until the colt reached a certain age, she has most likely acted in a reasonably timely manner.)

9.9   (a) He can recover $10,000 plus any incidental damages. (b) Deedee can ask the court for Specific performance (c) She could have put a liquidated damages clause in the contract. (d) She must cover. She can recover the difference between the substitute price and the contract price. (e) She may be able to recover consequential damages if she can prove what those damages were likely to have been. The problem is that no one has any way of knowing what the foal resulting from the more prestigious bloodlines would actually have been worth. Despite its fine bloodlines, it could be deformed, ill, or just badly conformed (put together).

9.10 (a) No. A quasi-contract would not be appropriate because even though Marlene received a benefit, there is no evidence that she knew or had reason to know that her mare was on Chamberlain's property being bred. (b) Promissory estoppel would be an appropriate doctrine for a court to use in this instance because Marlene relied, to her detriment, on Chamberlain's promise.

9.11 (a) No. The contract is for a sale of goods for more than $500. (b) Yes, he can unless Deedee can prove that she was so intoxicated she did not know the nature, purpose, and effect of what she was doing when she signed the contract. (c) She can sue him for fraud if she has evidence that he intentionally misrepresented the condition of the horse. If she is successful, she can rescind the contract. She can also sue for breach of implied warranty of merchantability (because an unsound horse is not fit for the ordinary purpose for which it is used, namely riding), and for breach of fitness for a particular purpose (because Chamberlain knew of her intent to use the horse as a jumper). Even though the horse was sold "as is," thereby disclaiming the warranty of merchantability, Deedee may still be able to recover if she can show that Chamberlain deliberately deceived her by drugging the horse. If successful, she can recover the difference between the value of the horse as a jumper and the value of the horse in his unsound condition, plus any incidental and consequential damages she can prove. (d) He cannot if Mindy is considered a minor in their state. She can disaffirm the contract and retain the benefit of the lessons she received without paying for them. (e) Probably not. The courts view such exculpatory clauses with disfavor even though the language in this case was conspicuous and the students took the riding lessons by choice. If a court were to determine that what the groom did was gross negligence, the exculpatory clause will not apply.

9.12 (a) Sole practitioner; general partnership; general partner in limited partnership (b) C corporation; LLC; LLP (c) C corporation; close corporation (d) S corporation; LLC; LLP (e) nonprofit corporation

9.13 (a) A limited partnership would be best because they could manage the business and the limited partners could not get involved without losing their status as limited partners. (b) If they form a partnership, they will each be personally liable for any business debts and obligations even if they are incurred without their knowledge. (c) They must file a limited partnership certificate with the secretary of state.

9.14 (a) They will be protected from personal liability. (b) They must decide whether they want to incorporate in Colorado and find out if the name "Colorado Capers" is available. If it is, they must reserve it. Then they must prepare and file articles of incorporation with the secretary of state. (c) They will need to decide what kinds of stock they want to have and what the par value of the stock will be. (d) They must draft by-laws, order corporate supplies, and have an organizational meeting. (e) They should get information about Nike, its financial status, how it is managed, what kind of litigation it is involved in, and other fac-

tors that relate to the stability and strength of the company as well as information about the stock being sold. They could find this information in the registration statement filed by Nike, particularly in the prospectus. They should also consult the annual and quarterly reports on file with the SEC. Most importantly, they should consult an attorney regarding this type of sophisticated transaction.

9.15 With an LLC or LLP, they will get the best of the corporate and partnership forms of business. They will limit their personal liability and will avoid double taxation. They will get more protection from potential liability using an LLC as opposed to an LLP.

9.16 He can get an enforceable security interest in the equipment by having Miguel and Sonja sign a security agreement and can then perfect that interest by filing a UCC-1 financing statement. If they go out of business, he will have to attach the equipment. If he has priority over other creditors, he can take the property back.

9.17 Miguel and Sonja are liable even though Makayla appears to be an independent contractor. (She has been in business for a year and had other clients on the bus at the time of the accident.) Because Sonja was negligent in not checking out Makayla's driving record, she is liable even if Maykala is an independent contractor. As an agent of the partnership, her act of hiring Makayla bound the partnership and she and Miguel and both are liable for Makayla's negligence. In not telling Miguel that she had hired Makayla, Sonja violated her fiduciary duty to both Miguel and the partnership.

9.18 (a) He was injured in a collision with Frausto, one of PNI's newspaper carriers, and wants to hold PNI liable.

(b) Is the relationship between PNI and Frausto that of employer-employee or employer-independent contractor?

(c) No.

(d) It considers extent of control exercised by the employer and the degree of supervision; distinct nature of the worker's business; degree of specialization of worker's occupation; materials provided by employer; duration of employment; method of payment; relationship of worker's work done to the regular business of the employer; belief of the parties.

(e) Employer's power to give specific instructions with the expectation that they will be followed. PNI selected the time and place for delivery, the area to be covered, and the manner in which papers were to be delivered. PNI also added customers and relayed customer requests to Frausto.

(f) No. He had no delivery business distinct from his work with PNI; he did not purchase papers and resell them; payments were made and complaints were directed to PNI; PNI delivered if he missed a customer.

(g) No.

(h) They provided the papers but not the bags, rubber bands, or transportation. Yes.

(i) A continuous working relationship. A right to terminate indicates control and thus an employer-employee relationship. Frausto could be terminated with cause at any time and without cause after 38 days; his contract was for six months; PNI provided health and disability insurance.

(j) Yes. Yes.

(k) Yes. No.

Chapter 10

10.1 The marriage is voidable. To annul it, Sally will have to prove fraud.

10.2 Harvey may be able to prove to Delia that his love is sincere if he is willing to sign a contract agreeing that he will receive none of her personal assets (the trust and estate) if they should decide to divorce.

10.3 A hearing to get a TRO is an emergency, *ex parte* hearing, whereas an order to show cause hearing must be scheduled in advance. Additionally, in some cases, the parties are required to mediate first, and both parties are present at the hearing to present evidence.

10.4 He can if the ethical rules of his state permit it and as long as he is reasonably certain neither will be adversely affected by his representing both of them and both of them have consented. Because the couple has already ironed out the terms of their divorce, they do not appear to have any conflicts, but Julio must make it clear that if a conflict should occur, he will probably not be able to represent either one of them.

10.5 Hannah is a likely candidate for alimony because she has devoted her life to creating a home for her husband and caring for her children. At her age, she will find it difficult to begin a career, especially if she has no interest in doing so. The fact that she is raising her young grandchild further justifies her need to stay home.

10.6 Hannah's contribution to the marriage has been of equal value to Samuel's, even though they were not assigned a monetary value at the time. By maintaining the home and raising their children, she allowed Samuel to devote all of his time and energies to his career. She also contributed directly to his success as a marketing consultant by entertaining his clients, colleagues, and employers as well as offering her opinions when he solicited her advice. She sacrificed any possibilities for establishing her own career so that she might dedicate herself to the building of his. Her contributions, while less tangible, are no less valuable than Samuel's.

10.7 (a) The woman with whom he was having an affair was diagnosed with cancer. (b) His future in football is too speculative and his name recognition has a negative connotation. (c) The three assets are the Huntington house, the Arizona house (which the court subsequently concludes has no equity), and the defendant's severance pay. (d) The defendant failed to appear for a number of court dates and failed to comply with the court's *pendente lite* order. (e) Plaintiff is to receive one-third of the marital assets. (f) Although the marital assets were acquired as a result of the defendant's skill and training, it was his decision to terminate his contract that subjected his wife and child to a reduction in standard of living. The court also looked at the plaintiff's contribution to the marriage and the fact that the defendant had failed to secure meaningful employment.

10.8 Answer is dependent on state guidelines.

10.9 Experience teaches that failure to clearly define the limits and parameters of visitation rights can lead to confusion and strife later on. Although the parties can later agree to more liberal arrangements or can make necessary modifications if they both agree, generally couples are better able to meet each other's expectations when those expectations are clearly defined. Their agreement should specify the exact times for visitation, who will be responsible for transporting the children, and what kind of notice will be required if visiting privileges have to be denied or cancelled for some reason.

10.10 None of Charles' theories is correct.

10.11 Terrence is entitled to ask for a modification of alimony (stopping any future payments if he were paying alimony), child custody, and visitation. He may be entitled to a modification of child support based on a change of his ex-wife's income and/or the costs associated with visitation.

Chapter 11

11.1 (a) Her water rights will probably be governed by the appropriation doctrine. Therefore, if the water supply becomes limited, she will not get any water until the water needs of those whose rights precede hers in time are satisfied. (b) The barn is usually a fixture and is included in the real property transfer. Some barns, however, are designed to be portable and care must be used not to immediately assume all farm structures are fixtures. (c) She has right to any ores she finds beneath the surface of her land unless mineral rights are not being transferred with the land, something that happens more often than not in areas known to have precious minerals.

11.2 Luke should find out how the property is zoned to find out if he has a right to build a teen center there. He should review the deed to see if there are any restrictive covenants that might preclude the building of the center. He should get more information about the neighbor's granting permission to use the vacant lot. He should find out if the neighbor has granted the seller some kind of license, and, if so, what type of license, and if he could get the same or better license for the necessary period of time. It would be better for Luke to have a recorded ownership interest in the lot. He should also find out what kind of encumbrances are on the property that might limit his right to build or if any easements are lacking that might obstruct his entry to or use of the property. If the zoning does not allow a teen center, he might want to see if a variance or other deviation from the base zoning could be had and, if so, what opposition the neighbors might have.

11.3 (a) The odors of chemicals were obvious, as was visual evidence of chemicals in a trench and chemicals flowing from barrels. Trucks from chemical companies were seen entering the property. Soil samples were tested and found to contain a number of toxic chemicals. Testimony showed that the chemicals were traveling from the dump site to waters inhabited by fish and used by humans. (b) Nuisance requires a showing of unreasonable injury rather than unreasonable conduct. (c) The neighbors showed signs of exposure to toxic chemicals and testimony showed that the chemicals found on the defendants' property threatened wildlife and human life with possible death, cancer, and liver disease. (d) The science of hydrology has grown since 1934 when *Rose* was decided and societal concern for environmental protection has grown considerably since that time, so that the scientific and societal considerations that governed *Rose* no longer apply. (e) No.

11.4 In all four instances, a nuisance could be found by the courts.

11.5 C owns it if they are joint tenants; A's and B's heirs and C own if they are tenants in common

11.6 A special warranty deed warrants only that the seller has done nothing to encumber the property, so Guillermo knows nothing about the seller's predecessors. He is buying a conditional estate, and when he does not use it for school purposes, the land will revert back to the grantor.

11.7 The first is that the seller pay the taxes owed and have the lien released. The second is that the seller pay off the mortgage with the sales proceeds (unless the loan is assumable).

11.8 He may discover later that he does not have good title to the property and that he has no legal recourse to get good title. Without title insurance, he may not be able to recover anything if a defect is later discovered.

11.9 Documentation could be missing, computations could be wrong, deadlines might not be complied with, copies of documents could be missing, the title search could be incomplete, the buyer or seller may have failed to fulfill an obligation, or documents could contain erroneous information.

11.10 Three ethical questions arose. (a) Luis was present at a real estate closing without his supervising attorney and was asked to give legal advice, which he correctly refused to do. Because another attorney was present to answer any questions the parties had, Luis has probably not committed an ethical violation by remaining. (b) Luis heard an attorney giving legal advice to an unrepresented party, which attorneys should not do, although some courts suggest attorneys in those situations can explain to unrepresented individuals what they are signing and why. (c) Luis was asked to notarize a signature he did not witness being made. He should refuse even though he was in the room while the party signed other documents because he cannot swear that he witnessed that particular document being signed.

11.11 Morana should disclose the rat problem if it is an ongoing problem that has required repairs or that could constitute a potential health problem. (b) Disclosure of brutal murders are required in some states and not in others. (c) Disclosure is probably not required because the neighbor's sex offender status is a matter of public record, which the buyers can research themselves. Some would argue, however, that when children's lives are at risk, the duty to disclose is higher and should not be premised on the buyer's diligence.

11.12 The Ortizes could terminate their lease (after giving proper notice) or could pay someone to fix the toilets (or fix it themselves) and deduct the cost of their repairs from their rent. The landlord could terminate their lease provided he gave whatever notice was required by statute and the termination was not considered illegal retaliation.

11.13 (a) Her husband will either get all of the property or he will get some of it and the children will share the remainder. (b) The three children will split it equally. (c) No. (d) Under a *per capita* distribution, there would be five heirs and each would receive one-fifth share. Under a *per stirpes* distribution, Portia, Patrick, and Petra would split their mother's one-third share (each receiving one-ninth share) and Jeremiah and Nina would each receive one-third share.

11.14 (a) The decedent's daughters believe she lacked testamentary capacity and was under undue influence when she prepared the will. (b) Yes. (c) These factors are whether the beneficiary participated in the preparation of the will; whether the testator received independent advice; whether the will was prepared with secrecy and in haste; whether the decedent had a change in attitude toward others; whether the will changed the decedent's plan for the disposal of her property; whether the will provided an unjust and unnatural gift; and whether the decedent was susceptible to influence. (d) Cora assisted the decedent in making arrangements

to have a will drawn up and had the will made up by an attorney who was unfamiliar with the decedent rather than the attorneys who had drawn up previous wills for the decedent. No notice of the change in will was given to family members. The new will disinherited the decedent's daughters and was a dramatic change from her previous will, in which she had left her entire estate to her two daughters. There was ample evidence of her susceptibility to influence, including the fact that the she was ill, weak, and recently widowed.

11.15 The will may not be valid because it is likely that Sloan lacks testamentary capacity and because it is holographic.

11.16 She might be able to do so on the grounds of undue influence if she can show that her father's decision to change his will was not of his own free will and was directed by Santiago. Also, Homero's crossing out of the provisions pertaining to Mercedes may have revoked only those portions or may have revoked the entire will, in which case Homero would be considered to have died intestate.

11.17 She will be responsible for opening probate by filing an application or petition with the court and for serving notice on all interested parties. She will then be required to file an inventory with the court and participate at a hearing held by the court in which the validity of the will is determined. She will need to collect all the debts owed by the estate, obtain any property to which the decedent held title, and pay any debts owed by the decedent. After all the administrative expenses, taxes, and creditors' claims were paid, she would then be responsible for distributing the remaining assets of the estate. Finally, she would have to close probate by filing a closing inventory or preparing for a court hearing.

11.18 Martha has a private, living trust. She is an income beneficiary and her children are remainder beneficiaries.

11.19 (a) Elroy is the settlor, Talbert is the trustee, and Michael is the beneficiary of this private, testamentary trust. (b) Charitable trust (c) *Inter vivos* spendthrift trust (d) Marvin has created a revocable *inter vivos* trust in which Conrad holds legal title and Margaret and her children have equitable title. Margaret is an income beneficiary and her children are remainder beneficiaries.

Chapter 1

ANSWERS TO PRACTICE EXAM A

Multiple Choice

1. B
2. A
3. D
4. B
5. D
6. C
7. C
8. B
9. D
10. C
11. C
12. D

Fill in the Blank

13. legal technician
14. lay advocate
15. freelance
16. law clinics
17. in-house; legal service clinic; public interest
18. National Association of Legal Assistants; Certified Legal Assistant
19. National Federation of Paralegal Associations; Paralegal Advanced Competency Exam
20. runner; process server

True False

21. T
22. F
23. T
24. F
25. F
26. F
27. T
28. T
*29. T
*30. T
*31. F
*32. F
*33. F
*34. F
*35. T
*36. F
*37. T
*38. T
39. F
40. T
41. F
42. F
43. T
44. T
45. T
46. T

ANSWERS TO PRACTICE EXAM B

Multiple Choice

1. D
2. D
3. A
4. D
5. B

Fill in the Blank

6. certification; licensure
7. CLA; PACE
8. law office administrator
9. associate; law clerk
10. private practice; sole proprietorship; partnership; professional corporation
11. limited liability
12. general; staff
13. tortfeasor
14. canons, disciplinary rules, ethical considerations

True False

15. F
16. F
17. T
18. T
*19. T
20. T
21. F
22. T
23. F
24. F
25. F
26. T
27. F
28. T
29. F
30. F
*31. T
*32. T
33. F

Questions with * are taken from Bonus Pointers

34. T
35. T
36. F
*37. T
*38. T
39. F
40. T
41. F
42. F
43. T
44. F
45. F
46. F

Chapter 2

ANSWERS TO PRACTICE EXAM A

Multiple Choice

1. C
2. B
3. D
4. D
5. A
6. C
7. D
8. C
9. B
10. A
11. D
12. C
13. A
14. D
15. B
16. D
17. B
18. A

Fill in the Blank

19. confidentiality
20. natural law; positivists; realists
21. critical legal
22. constitution
23. separation of powers
24. statute; ordinance
25. case law; substantive; procedural
26. trial; appellate
27. civil; criminal
28. prosecutor; restitution

29. preponderance of the evidence; beyond a
    reasonable doubt
30. attorney-client privilege
31. cause of action; judgment; judgment proof
32. statute of limitations
33. tort; liability
34. jury consultants

True False

35. T
36. T
37. F
38. T
39. T
40. F
41. F
42. T
43. T
44. F
45. F
46. T
47. F
48. T
49. F
50. F
51. T
52. T
53. F
54. F
55. T
56. F
57. F
58. T
59. T
60. T
61. F
62. F
63. T
64. T
65. F
66. T
67. T
68. F
69. F
70. F
71. F
72. F
73. T
*74. T

Questions with * are taken from Bonus Pointers

75. F
76. T
77. F
78. T
*79. T
*80. F
*81. F
*82. F

ANSWERS TO PRACTICE EXAM B

Multiple Choice

1. B
2. C
3. D
4. C
5. A
6. B
7. C
8. B
9. A
10. B
11. D
12. C
13. B
14. A
15. A
16. D
17. B
18. D
19. C
20. A
21. D

Fill in the Blank

22. impeach; recant
23. authenticate; chain of custody
24. subpoena
25. expert
26. admissible; standard; element
27. foreseeable
28. immunity; insolvent
29. Freedom of Information
30. pro bono
31. conflict of interest
32. negligence; objective
33. negligence *per se*
34. *res ipsa loquitur*

35. actual; proximate; foreseeability
36. eggshell skull
37. batter; assault; false imprisonment; trespass to land; trespass to chattels; conversion; intentional infliction of emotional distress
38. strictly liable
39. abnormally dangerous activity

True False

40. T
41. T
42. T
43. F
44. T
45. T
*46. F
*47. F
*48. T
*49. T
50. F
51. T
52. T
53. T
54. T
55. F
56. F
57. F
*58. T
*59. F
60. T
61. F
62. F
63. F
64. T
65. T
66. F
67. T
68. F
69. T
70. T
71. F
72. T
73. F
74. F
75. T
76. F
77. T
78. T
79. T

Questions with * are taken from Bonus Pointers

80. F
81. F
82. F
83. T
84. F
85. F
86. T
87. F
88. F
89. F
90. T
91. F
92. T
93. T
94. T
95. T
96. F
97. T
98. F
99. F
100. T
101. T
102. T

Chapter 3

ANSWERS TO PRACTICE EXAM A

Multiple Choice

1. A
2. C
3. C
4. A
5. B
6. D
7. A
8. B
9. A
10. B
11. C
*12. D
13. C
14. A
15. D
16. A
17. D

Fill in the Blank

18. district; circuit
19. bankruptcy; magistrates

20. writ of *certiorari*
21. appellant; brief; appellee; oral arguments
22. affirming; reversing; remand
23. *en banc*
24. general; limited
25. official; unofficial; headnotes
26. annotated
27. caption; citation; docket number; syllabus
28. headnotes; West numbering system
29. concurring
30. parallel citation
31. slip opinion; advance sheets
32. first impression
33. brief
34. procedural history
35. dispose
36. *per curiam;* memorandum
37. plurality
38. overturn
39. holding; *dicta*
40. black letter; public policy

True False

41. T
42. T
43. F
44. T
45. T
46. F
47. T
48. F
49. F
*50. T
51. F
52. F
53. F
54. T
55. T
56. F
57. F
58. T
59. F
60. F
61. F
62. T
63. F
64. T
65. T
66. F
67. T

68. T
69. F
70. T
71. F
72. T
73. T
74. T
75. T
76. F
77. F
78. T

ANSWERS TO PRACTICE EXAM B

Multiple Choice

1. C
2. B
3. A
4. D
5. D
6. C
7. C
8. B
9. C
10. A
11. D
12. B
13. A
14. D

Fill in the Blank

15. primary; secondary
16. binding; persuasive
17. hornbooks
18. *American Digest;* Decennials
19. pocket parts
20. Shepardizing; citator
21. law; fact
22. *stare decisis;* distinguish
23. conservative; liberal
24. issue, rule, application, conclusion
25. conclusory
26. internal; advocacy
27. slips; session
28. *United States Code Annotated; United States Code Service*
29. legislative intent
30. legislative history
*31. canons of construction

Questions with * are taken from Bonus Pointers

True False

32. T
33. F
34. F
35. T
36. F
37. T
38. F
39. T
40. F
41. T
42. F
43. F
44. T
45. T
46. T
47. F
48. F
49. T
50. F
51. T
52. F
53. T
54. T
55. F
56. T
57. F
58. T
59. T
60. F
61. F
62. T
63. F
64. T
65. T
66. F
67. T
68. F
69. T
70. F
71. F
72. F
73. T
74. T
75. F
76. F
77. F
78. T
79. T
80. T

81. F
82. F
83. F

Chapter 4

ANSWERS TO PRACTICE EXAM A

Multiple Choice

1. D
2. B
3. D
4. A
5. B
6. A
7. D
8. C
9. B
10. B
11. D
12. A
13. C
14. B
15. D

Fill in the Blank

16. discovery
17. prejudice
18. vicariously
19. joint; joint liability; deep pocket
20. contingency; hourly; fixed
21. retainer
22. arbitration
23. demand
24. motion
25. forum; jurisdiction; venue
26. subject matter; personal
27. limited; general
28. federal question; diversity of citizenship; jurisdictional amount
29. domicile
30. serve process; tag; long-arm; minimum contacts
31. bench
32. strike (notice)

True False

33. T
34. F
35. T
36. T
37. T
38. F
39. T
40. T
41. F
42. T
43. T
44. F
45. F
46. T
47. T
48. F
49. T
50. F
51. F
52. T
53. F
54. F
55. T
56. F
57. T
58. F
59. F
60. T
61. T
62. F
63. T
64. T
65. F
66. F
67. F
68. F
69. T
70. F
71. T
72. T
73. F
74. T
75. T
*76. F
77. T
78. F
79. T
80. F
81. F
82. T
83. T
84. T
85. T
86. T

Questions with * are taken from Bonus Pointers

ANSWERS TO PRACTICE EXAM B

Multiple Choice

1. B
2. D
3. A
4. C
5. A
6. B
7. C
8. A
9. C
10. A
11. B
12. C
13. D
14. B
15. C
16. A
17. D
18. C
19. D
20. B
21. A
22. C

Fill in the Blank

23. complaint
24. prayer for relief
25. caption; preamble
26. allegations; counts
27. general; special
28. compensatory; punitive; nominal; pre-existing
29. conforms
30. personal; abode
31. affidavit or return or proof of service
32. docket
33. default
34. stipulate
35. third-party claim; counterclaim; cross-claim
36. indispensable
37. affirmative defense
38. contributory negligence; comparative negligence
39. assumption of risk
40. immunity; governmental immunity; interspousal immunity; parent-child immunity; charitable immunity
41. statute of limitations
42. transactional
43. certificate or proof of service
44. removed
45. automatic stay; discharge in bankruptcy

True False

46. F
47. T
*48. T
*49. T
50. F
51. T
52. F
53. T
54. T
55. T
56. F
57. T
58. T
59. T
60. F
*61. T
*62. F
*63. T
*64. F
*65. T
66. F
67. F
68. F
69. F
70. T
71. T
72. F
73. F
74. T
75. T
76. F
77. T
78. F
79. T
80. T
81. T
82. F
83. F
*84. T
*85. T
86. F
87. F
88. F
89. T
90. T
91. T

Questions with * are taken from Bonus Pointers

92. F
93. F
94. T
95. F
96. F
97. T
98. F
99. T
100. F
101. T
102. F
103. T
104. F
105. T
106. F
107. F
108. F
109. T
110. F
111. T
112. T
113. T
114. F
115. T
116. F
117. F
118. T
119. T
120. F
121. T
122. T
123. F
124. T

(a) With what does 21 CFR 170 deal? How did you find this answer?
(b) Can you get the List of CFR Sections Affected online? If so, how?
(c) Can you read a federal regulation online on the same day that it is published? If so, how?

Chapter 5

ANSWERS TO PRACTICE EXAM A

Multiple Choice

1. A
2. C
3. B
4. C
5. D
6. D
7. D
8. A
9. B
10. A
11. C
12. C
13. B
14. D
15. D
16. A
17. B
18. D
19. B
20. C

Fill in the Blank

21. evidence
22. common law
23. requests for production of documents and things; subpoena *duces tecum*
24. requests for admission; interrogatories; depositions
25. independent medical examination
26. disclosure statements
27. pre-trial conference
28. transcript; deponent
29. custodian of records
30. expert; lay
31. notice of an I.M.E.
32. propounded

True False

33. T
34. T
35. F
36. T
37. F
38. T
39. F
40. T
41. T
42. F
43. F
44. T
45. T
46. T
47. F
48. F

Questions with * are taken from Bonus Pointers

49. T
50. F
51. T
52. F
53. F
54. T
55. F
56. F
57. F
58. T
59. T
60. F
61. F
62. F
63. T
64. T
65. T
66. F
67. T
68. T
69. F
70. F
71. T
72. F
73. T
74. F
75. F
76. F
77. T
78. T
79. F
80. T
81. T
82. F
83. F
84. F
85. T
86. T
87. T

ANSWERS TO PRACTICE EXAM B

Multiple Choice

1. D
2. D
3. C
4. D
5. A
6. D
7. A
8. C
*9. A
10. D
11. B
12. A
*13. C
14. B
15. B
16. D
17. D
18. A

Fill in the Blank

19. oral arguments; under advisement
20. memorandum of points and authorities
21. movant; respondent; response; reply; motion papers
22. hearing; chambers
23. minute entry
24. motion; memorandum
25. public defender
26. Gallagher agreement
27. work product
28. motion to compel; motion for sanctions

True False

29. F
30. F
31. T
32. T
*33. F
34. T
35. F
36. T
37. T
38. F
39. F
40. F
41. F
42. F
43. T
44. T
45. F
46. F
47. F
48. T
49. F
50. F
*51. T

*52.	T
*53.	T
*54.	T
55.	T
56.	F
57.	F
58.	F
59.	T
*60.	F
61.	F
62.	F
63.	T
64.	T
65.	T
66.	T
67.	T
68.	F
69.	F
70.	T

Chapter 6

ANSWERS TO PRACTICE EXAM A

Multiple Choice

1. B
2. D
3. D
4. C
5. A
6. D
7. B
8. A
9. D
10. C
11. C
12. D
13. B
14. D
15. A
16. C
17. D
18. B
19. A
20. C

Fill in the Blank

21. motion for summary judgment
22. affiant
23. trial setting; motion to set and certificate of readiness
24. pretrial conference; joint pretrial statement
25. speech; fair trial; gag order
26. motion *in limine*
27. jury instructions; charging; Uniform or patterned
28. authentic
29. demonstrative evidence
30. trial notebook
31. *voir dire*
32. challenges for cause; peremptory challenges
33. directed verdict
34. leading; cross-examination; direct; hostile
35. scope; redirect
36. under the rule
37. foundation
38. hearsay; objection; overrules; sustains
39. relevant
40. rests; directed verdict
41. preponderance of the evidence; clear and convincing evidence
42. affirmative
43. rebuttal
44. sandbagging
45. closing arguments

True False

46. T
47. F
48. F
49. T
50. T
51. F
52. F
53. T
54. T
55. T
56. F
57. T
58. T
59. T
60. F
61. F
62. F
63. T
64. T
65. F

66. T
67. F
68. F
69. F
70. T
71. T
*72. T
*73. T
*74. F
75. F
76. F
77. F
78. T
79. T
80. T
81. F
82. F
83. T
84. T
85. T
86. T
87. T
88. F
89. T
90. T
91. F
92. T
93. T
94. F
95. T
96. F
97. T
98. F
99. T
100. T
101. F
102. F
103. F
104. T

ANSWERS TO PRACTICE EXAM B

Multiple Choice

1. B
2. A
3. C
4. C
5. D
6. B
7. D
8. C
9. D
10. B
11. D
12. A
13. D
14. A
15. B
16. C
17. B
18. A
19. C

Fill in the Blank

20. general; special
21. hung jury
22. poll
23. motion for a new trial
24. motion for judgment notwithstanding the verdict
25. *remittitur; additur*
26. entry of judgment
27. lodge; form of judgment
28. taxable costs
29. statement of costs
30. judgment creditor; stay; supersedeas bond
31. execution; debtor's examination
32. subpoena *duces tecum*
33. judgment lien
34. writ of execution; levy
35. garnishment; writ of garnishment
36. incorporate
37. exempt
38. reversible; harmless
39. cross-appeal
40. interlocutory
41. certify
42. notice of appeal
43. briefs
44. at issue
45. panel
46. law clerks
47. concurring; dissenting
48. mandate

True False

49. F
50. F

Questions with * are taken from Bonus Pointers

51.	T
52.	T
53.	F
54.	F
55.	F
56.	T
57.	T
58.	F
59.	T
60.	F
61.	T
62.	T
63.	T
64.	F
65.	T
66.	T
67.	F
68.	F
69.	T
70.	T
71.	F
72.	F
73.	F
74.	F
75.	T
76.	F
77.	T
78.	T
79.	T
80.	T
81.	F
*82.	T
*83.	T
84.	F
85.	F
86.	F
87.	T
88.	T
89.	F
90.	F
91.	F
92.	T
93.	F
94.	F
95.	T
96.	T
97.	T
98.	F

Chapter 7

ANSWERS TO PRACTICE EXAM A

Multiple Choice

1. A
2. B
3. B
4. C
5. A
6. B
7. C
8. B
9. C
10. D
11. D
12. C
13. D
14. B
15. A
16. D
17. B
18. A
19. C
20. B
21. D
22. D
23. C
24. D
25. D
26. A
27. B
28. C
29. D
30. D
31. A
32. D
33. B
34. B

Fill in the Blank

35. arrest
36. expectation of privacy; curtilage
37. open field
38. plain view
39. search warrant
40. probable cause; arrest warrant
41. hot pursuit; exigent

Questions with * are taken from Bonus Pointers

42. suppressed
43. reasonable suspicion; stop; frisk
44. seized
45. *Miranda* warnings; custodial interrogation
46. initial appearance; bail; post bond; release the defendant on his own recognizance
47. grand jury proceeding; preliminary hearing; indictment; information
48. arraignment
49. plea bargain
50. indigent; assigned counsel; felony; misdemeanor
51. *pro se*
52. critical stage
53. lineup

True False

54. F
55. F
56. T
57. F
58. T
59. F
60. F
61. T
62. T
63. F
64. T
65. T
66. T
67. F
68. F
69. T
70. T
71. F
72. T
73. T
74. F
75. F
76. F
77. T
78. F
79. F
80. T
81. F
82. F
83. F
84. T
85. F
86. T

87. F
88. F
89. T
90. T
91. F
92. F
93. F
94. T
95. F
96. F
97. T

ANSWERS TO PRACTICE EXAM B

Multiple Choice

1. A
2. C
3. B
4. B
5. A
6. D
7. C
8. D
9. B
10. A
11. B
12. C
13. B
14. D
15. C
16. A
17. D
18. B
19. A
20. D
21. C
22. D
23. D
*24. A
25. B
26. C

Fill in the Blank

27. petty offense
28. capital crime
29. mens rea; actus reus; causation
30. purposefully; knowingly; recklessly; criminal negligence
31. infer

Questions with * are taken from Bonus Pointers

32. criminal negligence; knowing
33. attempt; solicitation; conspiracy; inchoate
34. property; persons; public order
35. M'Naughten; irresistible impulse; substantial capacity
36. entrapment
37. standing
38. case-in-chief
39. good faith exception
40. indeterminate; determinate; good time credits
41. presumptive
42. retribution; deterrence; incapacitation; rehabilitation
43. specific deterrence; general deterrence
44. probation; probation officer
45. restitution; work furlough
46. institutionalization
47. recidivate

True False

48. T
49. T
50. F
51. T
52. F
53. T
54. F
55. F
56. F
57. T
58. F
59. T
60. F
61. T
62. F
63. F
64. F
65. T
66. F
67. T
68. F
69. T
70. T
71. T
72. F
73. F
74. F
75. F
76. F

77. T
78. T
79. F
80. F
81. T
82. F
83. T
84. F
85. F
86. T
87. T
88. T
89. F
90. F
91. T
92. T
*93. T
*94. F
*95. F
*96. T
*97. F
*98. T
99. F
100. T
101. F
102. T
103. T
104. F
105. T
106. F
107. T
108. T
109. F
110. T
111. F
112. F
113. F
*114. F
115. T
116. F

Chapter 8

ANSWERS TO PRACTICE EXAM A

Multiple Choice

1. D
2. C
3. A
4. D

Questions with * are taken from Bonus Pointers

5. B
6. A
7. B
8. C
9. B
10. D
11. D
12. C
13. B
14. D
15. A
16. D
17. B

Fill in the Blank

18. mediation
19. arbitration; mini-trials
20. med-arb
21. summary jury trial
22. binding; non-binding; *de novo*
23. mandatory
24. court-annexed; private
25. community; transformative
26. med-arb
27. summary jury trial
28. mini-trials
29. private judging; neutral expert fact-finding
30. ombudsmen

True False

31. F
32. T
33. F
34. F
35. T
36. T
37. T
38. F
39. T
40. F
41. T
42. F
43. F
44. F
45. T
46. F
47. T
48. F

49. F
50. T
51. T
52. F
53. T
54. F
55. F
56. F
57. T
58. F
59. T
60. F
61. F
62. F
63. F
64. T
65. T
66. F
67. T
68. F
69. F
70. F
71. T
72. F
73. T
74. T
75. F
76. T
77. T
78. F
79. T
80. T
81. F
82. T
83. T
84. T
85. F
86. F
87. T
88. T
89. F

ANSWERS TO PRACTICE EXAM B

Multiple Choice

1. A
2. C
3. D
4. D

Questions with * are taken from Bonus Pointers

5. B
6. C
7. A
8. B
9. A
10. C
11. D
12. B
13. D
14. A
15. C

Fill in the Blank

16. Courts of Indian Offenses
17. administrative agency; administrative law
18. administrative law judges; administrative decision
19. exhausts his administrative remedies
20. centralized panel
21. enabling statute
22. Administrative Procedures Act
23. Federal Register; Code of Federal Regulations (CFR)
24. United States Government Manual; Federal Regulatory Directory
25. executive; warrant

True False

26. T
27. T
28. F
29. T
30. F
31. T
32. F
33. F
34. T
35. T
36. F
37. F
38. T
39. F
40. T
41. T
42. T
43. F
44. T
45. T
46. F
47. F

48. T
49. F
50. T
51. F
52. F
53. T
54. T
55. F
56. T
57. T
58. F
59. T
60. F
61. T
*62. F
*63. T
*64. T
*65. F

Chapter 9

ANSWERS TO PRACTICE EXAM A

Multiple Choice

1. D
2. C
3. B
4. A
5. D
6. B
7. C
8. D
9. A
10. B
11. D
12. C
13. A
14. B
15. A
16. C
17. A
18. B
19. A
20. B
21. B
22. A
23. C
24. A
25. C

Questions with * are taken from Bonus Pointers

*26. D
27. D
28. B
29. C
30. D
31. B
32. D
33. C
34. A
35. A
36. B
37. C
38. D
39. D
40. A

Fill in the Blank

41. Uniform Commercial Code (UCC)
42. offeror; offeree
43. requirements; output
44. merchant
45. revokes; rejects; counteroffer
46. bilateral; unilateral
47. consideration; option contract; firm merchant offer; consideration
48. mailbox; mirror image
49. battle of the forms
50. consideration
51. illusory
52. parol
53. substantially performs; material breach
54. repudiates
55. perfect tender
56. compensatory; incidental
57. cover; substitute; contract
58. consequential
59. mitigated
60. liquidated damages; penalty
61. specific performance
62. rescinding; reforming
*63. bad faith
64. quasi-contracts; promissory estoppel
65. void; voidable
66. disaffirms; necessaries
67. adhesion
68. exculpatory
69. meeting of the minds; fraud; duress; undue influence
70. mutual (bilateral); unilateral

71. Statute of Frauds
72. contract; tort
73. express; warranty of merchantability; fitness for a particular purpose
74. sealed container
75. disclaim

True False

76. F
77. T
78. F
79. T
80. F
81. T
82. T
83. F
84. T
85. T
86. T
87. F
88. F
89. T
90. F
91. T
92. F
93. F
94. F
95. F
96. T
97. T
98. F
99. T
100. T
101. T
102. F
103. F
104. T
105. F
*106. T
107. T
108. T
109. F
110. F
111. T
112. F
113. F
114. T
115. F
116. F
117. T

Questions with * are taken from Bonus Pointers

118. T
119. F
120. F
121. F
122. T
123. F

ANSWERS TO PRACTICE EXAM B

Multiple Choice

1. C
2. D
3. A
4. D
5. C
6. B
7. B
8. C
9. A
10. A
11. D
12. B
13. C
14. B
15. B
16. D
17. B
18. C
19. B
20. D
21. B
22. D
23. D
24. A
25. B
26. C
27. B

Fill in the Blank

28. sole proprietorship; general partnership; limited partnership; general; limited
29. shareholders; directors; officers
30. S corporation
31. professional corporation
32. close corporation
33. nonprofit (not-for-profit) corporations
34. limited liability companies (LLCs); limited liability partnerships (LLPs)
35. Uniform Partnership Act (UPA); Revised Uniform Partnership Act (RUPA); Uniform Limited Partnership Act (ULPA); Revised Uniform Limited Partnership Act (RULPA)
36. joint venture
37. limited partnership certificate; agent for service of process; dissolve
38. state
39. foreign; domestic
40. Delaware
41. fictitious; fictitious business name document; dba statement
42. articles of incorporation (certificate of incorporation)
43. common; preferred; par value
44. by-laws; corporate supplies; organizational meeting; annual report
45. shares (stocks); bonds; securities; Securities Exchange Commission (SEC); publicly-held; privately-held
46. dividends
47. registration statement; prospectus
48. secured transaction; 9
49. attach; security interest; security agreement
50. perfecting; financing statement (UCC-1 financing statement)
51. buyer in the ordinary course of business
52. control group; subject matter
*53. 7; 13; 11
54. agent; principal; fiduciary
55. independent contractor

True False

56. F
57. T
58. T
59. F
60. T
61. T
62. T
63. F
64. T
65. F
66. T
67. F
68. F
69. T
70. T
71. T
72. F
73. T
74. F

Questions with * are taken from Bonus Pointers

75. F
76. T
77. F
78. F
79. T
80. F
81. F
82. F
83. T
84. T
85. T
86. T
87. F
88. T
89. F
90. T
91. F
92. T
93. F
94. T
95. T
96. F
97. T
98. F
99. T
100. F
101. F
*102. F
*103. T
104. T
105. F
106. T
107. T
108. F
109. F

Chapter 10

ANSWERS TO PRACTICE EXAM A

Multiple Choice

1. B
2. D
3. A
4. C
5. A
6. D
7. B
8. C
9. C
10. B
11. A
12. C
13. D
14. D
15. A
16. B
17. C
18. A
19. C
20. D
21. D

Fill in the Blank

22. nnulment
23. antenuptial (prenuptial) agreement; postnuptial agreement; separation agreement
24. interlocutory; *pendente lite* or *nisi*
25. show cause
26. *ex parte;* temporary restraining order; protective order or order or protection
27. settlement agreement
28. alimony; spousal maintenance or support
29. separate; equitable distribution; community; commingled

True False

30. F
31. F
32. T
33. F
34. F
35. F
36. T
37. T
38. T
39. F
40. T
*41. T
*42. F
*43. F
*44. T
45. T
46. T
47. T
48. T
49. F
50. T

Questions with * are taken from Bonus Pointers

51. F
52. T
53. F
54. F
55. F
56. T
57. F
58. T
59. F
60. T
61. T
62. F

ANSWERS TO PRACTICE EXAM B

Multiple Choice

1. B
2. C
3. A
4. B
5. B
6. D
7. C
8. D
9. A
*10. C
*11. D
12. B
13. A
14. D
15. B

Fill in the Blank

16. physical; legal; sole; joint; split
17. Uniform Child Custody Jurisdiction Act (UCCJA)
18. needs of child; parent's ability to pay
19. child
20. URESA, RURESA, UIFSA
*21. paternity

True False

22. F
23. T
24. F
*25. T
*26. F
27. F

28. F
29. T
30. F
31. T
32. F
33. T
*34. F
*35. T
*36. T
37. T
38. F
39. F
40. T
41. F
42. T
43. F
44. T
45. T
46. F
47. T
48. F

Chapter 11

ANSWERS TO PRACTICE EXAM A

Multiple Choice

1. B
2. C
3. A
4. B
5. D
6. C
7. B
8. B
9. C
10. D
*11. D
12. B
13. C
14. D
15. D
16. C
17. A
18. C
19. A
20. D
21. D
22. A

Questions with * are taken from Bonus Pointers

23. C
24. B
25. C
26. B
27. A
28. B

Fill in the Blank

29. prior appropriation; riparian rights
30. fixture; chattel; tangible; intangible
*31. copyrights; trademarks; patents
32. license; easement; prescriptive easement
33. restrictive covenant; covenants, conditions, and restrictions (CC&Rs)
34. zoning; taking
35. eminent domain
36. private nuisance; public nuisance
37. joint tenants with right of survivorship; tenants by the entirety; community property with right of survivorship; tenants in common
38. deed
39. general warranty; grantor; grantee; limited (special); quitclaim
40. fee simple; fee simple conditional; life estate; estate for years; estate at will
41. mortgage; mortgagee; mortgagor
42. deed of trust; trustor; trustee; trustee's sale
43. promissory note; assumes
44. lienholder; tax; mechanics'; construction
45. title search (examination); foreclosure
46. adverse possession
47. title insurance
48. real estate closing
49. leasehold (nonfreehold); tenancy for years; periodic tenancy; tenancy at will; tenancy at sufferance
50. Uniform Residential Landlord and Tenant; implied warranty of habitability
51. constructively evicted
52. security deposits
53. intentional misrepresentation

True False

*54. T
55. T
56. F
57. F
58. F
59. T
60. F
61. F
62. F
63. T
64. T
65. F
66. T
67. F
68. T
69. T
70. T
71. F
72. F
73. F
74. T
75. T
76. F
77. T
78. T
79. F
80. F
81. T
82. F
83. T
84. F
85. T
86. T
87. T
88. F
89. T
90. F
91. F
92. T
93. F
94. F
95. F
96. F
97. T
98. T
99. T
*100. F

ANSWERS TO PRACTICE EXAM B

Multiple Choice

1. C
2. A
3. B
4. C
5. A
6. D

Questions with * are taken from Bonus Pointers

7. D
8. D
9. B
10. D
11. B
12. A
13. B
14. C
15. B
16. C
17. A
18. B
19. D
20. B
21. A
22. C

Fill in the Blank

23. decedent; intestate; intestate succession; issue or lineal descendants; ascendants; collateral; *per capita*; *per stirpes*; escheat
24. testator; testatrix; holographic; noncupative
25. executor; executrix; devise; bequest or legacy
26. self-proving
27. codicil
28. undue influence; confidential
29. probate process; administrator; administratrix; personal representative
30. application; petition
31. settlor; trustee; legal; beneficiaries; equitable
32. revocable; irrevocable
33. remainder beneficiaries; income beneficiaries

34. private; charitable
35. *inter vivos*; living; testamentary
36. spendthrift
37. Totten; payable on death (P.O.D.)

True False

38. F
39. T
40. F
41. F
42. T
43. F
44. T
45. T
46. T
47. F
48. T
*49. F
*50. T
51. F
52. T
53. T
54. T
55. F
56. F
57. T
58. F
59. F
60. T
61. T
*62. F

(Cite as: 102 Misc.2d 848, 427 N.Y.S.2d 370)

Family Court, Richmond County, New York.

In the **Matter** of **CHARLOTTE K.**, Age 15, A
Person Alleged to be a Juvenile
Delinquent, Respondent.

April 21, 1980.

In a delinquency proceeding charging respondent juvenile with possession of burglar's tools, the Richmond County Family Court, Daniel D. Leddy, Jr., J., held that girdle, into which respondent dropped shoplifted items, was not a "burglar's tool" within the meaning of statute prohibiting possession of burglar's tools.

Dismissed.

WEST HEADNOTES

Burglary k12
67k12

Her girdle, into which respondent dropped shoplifted items, was not a "burglar's tool" within the meaning of statute prohibiting possession of burglar's tools. Penal Law § 140.35.

Allen G. Schwartz, Corp. Counsel, New York City by Archibald H. Broomfield, Staten Island, for petitioner.

Charles Schinitsky, Legal Aid Society, Brooklyn by Rhoda Cohen, Staten Island, Law Guardian for Child.

DANIEL D. LEDDY, Jr., Judge.

Is a girdle a burglar's tool or is that stretching the plain meaning of Penal Law Sec. 140.35? This elastic issue of first impression arises out of a charge that the respondent shoplifted certain items from Macy's Department Store by dropping them into her girdle.

Basically, Corporation Counsel argues that respondent used her girdle as a Kangaroo does her pouch, thus adapting it beyond its maiden form.

The Law Guardian snaps back charging that with this artificial expansion of Sec. 140.35's meaning, the foundation of Corporation Counsel's argument plainly sags. The Law Guardian admits that respondent's tight security was an attempt to evade the store's own tight security. And yet, it was not a tool, instrument or other article adapted, designed or commonly used for committing or facilitating offenses involving larceny by physical taking. It was, instead, an article of clothing, which, being worn under all, was, after all, a place to hide all. It was no more a burglar's tool than a pocket, or maybe even a kangaroo's pouch.

The tools, instruments or other articles envisioned by Penal Law Sec. 140.35 are those used in taking an item and not in hiding it thereafter. They are the handy gadgets used to break in and pick up, and not the bags for carrying out. Such is the legislative intent of this section, as is evident from the Commission Staff Comments on the Revised Penal Law of 1965. Title I, Article 140, N Sec. 140.35, which reads in relevant part:

"The new section, by reference to instruments involving larceny . . . expands the crime to include possession of numerous other tools, such as those used for breaking into motor vehicles, stealing from public telephone boxes, tampering with gas and electric meters, and the like." (Emphasis added.)

The Court has decided this issue mindful of the heavy burden that a contrary decision would place upon retail merchants. Thus is avoided the real bind of having customers check not only their packages, but their girdles too, at the department store's door.

The Court must also wonder whether such a contrary decision would not create a spate of unreasonable bulges that would let loose the floodgates of stop and frisk cases, with the result of putting the squeeze on court resources already overextended in this era of trim governmental budgets.

Accordingly, the instant allegation of possession of burglar's tools is dismissed.

(Cite as: 165 Ariz. 38, 796 P.2d 470)

Supreme Court of Arizona, In Banc.

ALHAMBRA SCHOOL DISTRICT, Petitioner,

v.

SUPERIOR COURT of the State of Arizona, In and For the COUNTY OF MARICOPA,

Honorable Cecil Patterson, a Judge thereof, Respondent Judge,
Brenda NICHOLS, a minor, By and Through her father, Russell NICHOLS; Russell
Nichols, individually; and Louise Klein, Real Parties in Interest.

No. CV-89-0249-PR.

July 12, 1990.

Reconsideration Denied Sept. 18, 1990.

High school student who was injured while crossing in crosswalk brought personal injury action against school district. The Superior Court, Maricopa County, Cause No. CV 87-21073, Cecil Patterson, J., denied district's motion for summary judgment and district filed special action. The Court of Appeals, 161 Ariz. 568, 780 P.2d 401, vacated and remanded with directions. Student brought petition for review. The Supreme Court, Feldman, V.C.J., held that school district owed both statutory and common-law duty of care to student.

Vacated, reversed and remanded.

Cameron, J., filed dissenting opinion.

WEST HEADNOTES

[1] Negligence ⚷ **210**
272k210
    (Formerly 272k2)

In negligence action, plaintiff must establish that defendant has duty to conform to particular standard of conduct to protect plaintiff against unreasonable risks of harm.

[2] Negligence ⚷ **1692**
272k1692
    (Formerly 272k136(14))

In negligence action, question of duty is generally matter of law for court.

[3] Negligence ⚷ **210**
272k210
    (Formerly 272k2)

In negligence action, concept of duty should not be equated with specific details of conduct; rather, specific details of conduct involved bear on issue of whether defendant has breached duty owed.

[4] Schools ⚷ **89.8(1)**
345k89.8(1)
    (Formerly 345k89.8)

School district which applied for and established specially marked crosswalk where none previously existed owed common-law duty of care, for negligence purposes, to high school student who was struck by motor vehicle and injured as she was crossing in crosswalk, despite district's contention that crosswalk was established only for students of adjacent elementary school.

[5] Negligence ⚷ **222**
272k222
    (Formerly 272k56(3))

Relationship between plaintiff and defendant that gives rise to duty of care for negligence purposes may be created by statute.

[6] Schools ⚷ **89.8(1)**
345k89.8(1)
    (Formerly 345k89.8)

Where school district followed statutory procedure to establish marked crosswalk, district assumed statutory duty of care, for negligence purposes, to persons using crosswalk, not just to students of abutting school. A.R.S. § 28-797.

Teilborg, Sanders & Parks, P.C. by John C. Gemmill, Alison Lewis, Jean E. Huffington, Phoenix, for petitioner.

The Langerman Law Offices by Amy G. Langerman, Richard W. Langerman, and Langerman, Begam, Lewis and Marks by <u>Elliot G. Wolfe,</u> Phoenix, for real parties in interest.

OPINION

<u>FELDMAN,</u> Vice Chief Justice.

Brenda Nichols petitions this court to review a court of appeals' opinion holding that the school district owed her no duty of care and directing entry of summary judgment in favor of the district. See <u>Alhambra School District v. Superior Court, 161 Ariz. 568, 780 P.2d 401 (Ct.App.1989).</u>

The court of appeals accepted jurisdiction of a petition for special action to review the trial court's order denying summary judgment. We granted review to decide whether the court of appeals erred in finding that the school district had neither a common law nor statutory duty of care to protect foreseeable users of a school crosswalk from unreasonable risks of harm. We have jurisdiction pursuant to <u>Ariz. Const. art. 6, § 5(3),</u> and <u>A.R.S. § 12-120.24.</u>

FACTS AND PROCEDURAL HISTORY

Brenda Nichols (Brenda), a student at Alhambra High School, was struck by a motor vehicle and injured as she was crossing North 35th Avenue in a school crosswalk that abutted Cordova Elementary School (Cordova) in Phoenix's Alhambra School District (District). Cordova is located at North 35th Avenue and West Montebello Street. Pursuant to <u>A.R.S. § 28-797,</u> the Arizona School Crosswalk Statute, the City of Phoenix and the District agreed before the accident to establish a crosswalk across 35th Avenue. In its application for the abutting school crossing, the District stated:

In event of approval and subsequent establishment by markings and appropriate signs, the undersigned school authority agrees to administer all duties as prescribed in <u>Section 28-797 of the Arizona Revised Statutes,</u> and to operate the crossing in conformance to the Arizona School Crossing Manual as adopted by the Arizona Highway Commission July 7, 1965. [FN1]

> FN1. In 1974, the name of the Highway Commission was changed to the Arizona Department of Transportation (ADOT). ADOT issued a School Safety Program Guidelines manual in January 1983. All parties and the court presume

that the 1983 publication supersedes the manual referred to in the agreement.

The application was approved with the provision that "the portable signs will be in place within the roadway between 7:45 a.m. and 4:00 p.m. during all days the school is in session." In addition, although not required to do so, the District hired a crossing guard to supplement the marking and signing required by <u>A.R.S. § 28-797</u>—yellow striping, 15 m.p.h. speed limit, no passing zones, and portable school crossing signs. Generally, the school did not place the portable signs in the road until between 7:50 and 8:00 a.m., and the crossing guard did not arrive until 8:00 a.m.

Brenda attended Cordova until she graduated from the eighth grade in 1986. She then attended Alhambra High School, which is part of the Phoenix Union High School District. On October 16, 1986, she was walking to the home of a friend who was to give her a ride to Alhambra. She was crossing 35th Avenue from east to west when she was struck by a southbound car.

Brenda's parents brought a damage action on her behalf against the District, alleging it negligently failed to post signs or provide a guard at the crossing during a time when such action should have been taken. [FN2]

> FN2. Nothing in this record explains just how the District's failure to post signs or provide a guard fell below the standard of reasonable care or, if it did, how it caused the accident. The case was not decided on these issues, however. The issue addressed by the court of appeals was the question of duty, and that is the only issue addressed in this opinion.

The District moved for summary judgment on the ground that it owed no duty of care to Brenda, who was not a student at Cordova. For purposes of summary judgment, it was assumed that Brenda was struck in the crosswalk between 7:45 and 8:00 a.m., at a time when the portable 15 m.p.h. school zone signs should have been in place but were not, and before the crosswalk guard arrived. The trial court denied the motion, as well as the motion for reconsideration that followed.

The District then petitioned the court of appeals for special action relief. The court of appeals accepted jurisdiction and granted the requested relief, ordering the trial judge to grant summary judgment in favor of the District. [FN3] See <u>Alhambra School Dist., 161 Ariz. at 573, 780 P.2d at 406.</u> A majority of the court held that the District owed a duty of care only to Cordova students. Id. at 572, 780 P.2d at 405. Thus, according to the court, the District did not owe Brenda, a student at Alhambra, a duty of care even though Brenda was legally using a crosswalk established by the District.

FN3. In general, appellate courts in Arizona follow a policy of declining jurisdiction when special action relief is sought in such a case. United States v. Superior Court, 144 Ariz. 265, 269, 697 P.2d 658, 662 (1985). As we stated in United States, "in our view appeal after judgment usually is an adequate remedy if the trial court has erred on the law in denying motions to dismiss or for summary judgment." Id.

Because the court held no common law duty was owed to Brenda, it concluded that if any duty existed, it must have been created by statute pursuant to the crosswalk agreement and the manual issued by ADOT. Id. at 570, 780 P.2d at 403. The court believed the construction of A.R.S. § 28-797, entitled "School Crossings," [FN4] was at the crux of the appeal. The majority held that § 28-797 did not impose a duty of care on the District with respect to any persons other than students at Cordova because it believed "the term 'persons' as used in (C) was intended to mean only children inasmuch as 'the portable signs' to be placed by the District must use the word 'children' rather than 'persons.' " Id. at 572, 780 P.2d at 405. In the majority's view, because Brenda was not a student at Cordova, no relationship existed between Brenda and the District that gave the District power to "require" Brenda to use any designated crosswalk. Id. at 571, 780 P.2d at 404. Accordingly, the court remanded the case for entry of summary judgment in favor of the District. Id. at 573, 780 P.2d at 405.

FN4. The pertinent subsections of that statute are as follows:

A. The director, with respect to state highways, or the officer, board or commission of the appropriate jurisdiction, with respect to county highways or city or town streets, by and with the advice of the school district governing board or superintendent of schools, may mark or cause to be marked by the department or local authorities crosswalks in front of each school building or school grounds abutting thereon where children shall be required to cross the highway or street.

. . . . .

C. The sign manual shall provide for yellow marking of the school crossing, yellow marking of the center line of the roadway and the erection of portable signs indicating that vehicles must stop when persons are in the crossing. The manual shall also provide the type and wording of portable signs indicating that school is in session, and permanent signs providing warning of approach to school crossings. D. When such crossings are established school authorities shall place within the highway the portable signs indicating that school is in session, placed not to exceed three hundred feet each side of the school crossings, and "stop when children in crosswalk" signs at school crossings. School authorities shall maintain these signs when school is in session and shall cause them to be removed immediately thereafter.

E. No vehicle approaching the crosswalk shall proceed at a speed to exceed fifteen miles per hour between the portable signs placed on the highway indicating "school in session" and "stop when children in crosswalk."

. . . . .

G. When the school authorities place and maintain the required portable "school in session" signs and "stop when children in crosswalk" signs, all vehicles shall come to a complete stop at the school crossing when the crosswalk is occupied by any person.

A.R.S. § 28-797 (emphasis added).

DISCUSSION

A. Duty

1. Did the District Owe Brenda a Common Law Duty of Care?

[1][2] In a negligence action the plaintiff must establish that the defendant has a duty to conform to a particular standard of conduct to protect the plaintiff against unreasonable risks of harm. See Markowitz v. Arizona Parks Bd., 146 Ariz. 352, 354, 706 P.2d 364, 366 (1985); Ontiveros v. Borak, 136 Ariz. 500, 667 P.2d 200 (1983). As Chief Judge Cardozo stated in Palsgraf v. Long Island Railroad Co., 248 N.Y. 339, 162 N.E. 99, 100 (1928): "The risk reasonably to be perceived defines the duty to be obeyed." See also Schnyder v. Empire Metals, Inc., 136 Ariz. 428, 430, 666 P.2d 528, 530 (Ct.App.1983) ("The scope of the risk created by

one's conduct defines the group of potential plaintiffs to whom a duty is owed"). The question of duty is generally a matter of law for the court. Markowitz, 146 Ariz. at 354, 706 P.2d at 366; Beach v. City of Phoenix, 136 Ariz. 601, 667 P.2d 1316 (1983).

[3] As we have previously stated, the concept of duty should not be equated with specific details of conduct. Markowitz, 146 Ariz. at 355, 706 P.2d at 367; Coburn v. City of Tucson, 143 Ariz. 50, 52, 691 P.2d 1078, 1080 (1984). Duty refers to the relationship between individuals; it imposes a legal obligation on one party for the benefit of the other party. Id. The specific details of conduct involved do not determine the duty owed but bear on the issue of whether a defendant has breached a duty owed. Markowitz, 146 Ariz. at 355, 706 P.2d at 367.

[4] The District argues that Cordova students were the only intended beneficiaries of the school crossing and that it is only those students, and not other users of the crosswalk, with whom it had a relationship that could impose a duty of care. The District asks why it should be forced to take on the responsibility of protecting not only its students but any person using the crosswalk. The answer, of course, is that the District applied for and established a specially marked crosswalk, where none previously existed. Certainly, the finder of fact could conclude that foreseeable users of the crosswalk might rely on the safety precautions normally attending such crosswalks.

School crosswalks are not limited by statute to use by the students of the school but are available for use by the general public, because they are on public thoroughfares. At the time it applied for establishment of this crosswalk, the District was aware that the crosswalk would be open to the general public and that nothing limits the use of a school crossing solely to students. Furthermore, the District took no steps to attempt to limit the use of this crosswalk to students of the abutting school or to disclaim any responsibility it might have to other crosswalk users.

Although pedestrians are not absolutely required to use crosswalks to cross a street, [FN5] it is certainly foreseeable that pedestrians might conclude they are required to use a crosswalk where one exists, or at least that use of a marked crosswalk would be the prudent thing to do. [FN6] A pedestrian might reasonably rely on the added safety of a marked crosswalk—

particularly a school crosswalk, with its additional protections.

> FN5. Local authorities may pass an ordinance prohibiting pedestrians from crossing any roadway in a business district or any designated highways except in a crosswalk. See A.R.S. § 28-791(B). Phoenix has not passed such an ordinance. Phoenix does have an ordinance that states:
>
> Except in a crosswalk, no pedestrian shall cross a roadway at any place other than by a route at right angles to the curb or by the shortest route to the opposite curb. A pedestrian shall not cross a roadway where prohibited by appropriate signs, markings, devices or by law. Phoenix City Code, art. X, § 36-128 (1966).
>
> FN6. A.R.S. § 28-792 provides that the driver of a vehicle shall yield the right of way to a pedestrian crossing the roadway within a crosswalk. A.R.S. § 28-793 provides that every pedestrian crossing a roadway at any point other than within a crosswalk (marked or unmarked) must yield the right of way to all vehicles.

We conclude, therefore, that in creating the marked crosswalk where none previously existed, the District created a relationship with those who would use the crosswalk and thereby assumed a duty of reasonable care with respect to its operation. Markowitz; see also Palsgraf. The particular facts of the case—the age of the injured person, the time of the accident, the configuration of the street near the crosswalk, what school activities were going on at the time, what the District agreed to do with respect to operating the crosswalk, such as posting signs during school hours, etc.—are the circumstances under which the reasonableness of the District's conduct is to be judged. [FN7] We conclude that the District owed Brenda a common law duty of care.

> FN7. In other words, in this case, the conduct of the District in not posting the signs by 7:45 a.m. does not determine whether the District owed Brenda a duty of reasonable care, but is relevant to determine whether the District breached any duty that was owed.

2. Statutory

[5][6] The relationship that gives rise to a duty of care may also be created by statute. See Ontiveros, 136 Ariz. at 509, 667 P.2d at 209; see also PROSSER

AND KEETON ON THE LAW OF TORTS § 36, at 220 (5th ed. 1984); Restatement (Second) of Torts §§ 285-86 (hereafter Restatement). In this case, both the District and the court of appeals' opinion construed the statute involved, A.R.S. § 28-797, to limit the District's duty solely to the students of Cordova. Relying on A.R.S. § 28-797, the opinion reasoned that, because the portable signs mentioned in subsections (D) and (E) must read "Stop when children in crosswalk," and because subsection (G) requires all vehicles to stop for any person in the crosswalk when the signs are in place, the term "persons" as used in the statute really was intended to mean "children" who were "required" to use the crosswalk. 161 Ariz. at 572, 780 P.2d at 405.

This construction of the statute strains the language beyond the bursting point. The common meaning of "person" clearly is not "students of Cordova Elementary School." The legislature has not expressed its intention that "person" should be read to mean "student of Cordova Elementary School," or even "children." [FN8] Surely we are not to infer that because the sign says "children," drivers are free to run down any adult who may be using the crosswalk. The legislature's intention is clear in this case. If it had intended to limit the protection only to students of Cordova, it could easily have done so. Therefore we must give effect to the statute's unambiguous meaning. By following the statutory procedure to establish a marked crosswalk, the District assumed a duty of care to "persons" using the crosswalk, not just students of the abutting school. We conclude that the District owed a statutory duty of care to Brenda Nichols.

> FN8. Even if we agreed that "person" meant "child" or "children," under the statutory definition of these terms, the District would still owe Brenda a duty of care. A.R.S. § 1-215(4) defines "child" or "children" as persons under the age of eighteen years. Because Brenda was only fourteen at the time of the accident, she falls within this definition.

CONCLUSION

Because we conclude that the District owes a duty of care to all users of the crosswalk, we find that the court of appeals erred in directing summary judgment in favor of the District. The opinion granting summary judgment is vacated, the judgment is reversed, and the case is remanded to the trial court for further proceedings consistent with this opinion.

GORDON, C.J., and MOELLER and CORCORAN, JJ., concur.

CAMERON, Justice, dissenting.

I dissent for the reasons set forth in the majority opinion of the court of appeals. See Alhambra School District v. Superior Court, 161 Ariz. 568, 780 P.2d 401 (Ct.App.1989).

(Cite as: 122 Ariz. 472, 595 P.2d 1017)

Court of Appeals of Arizona, Division 1, Department B.

Antonio M. CHAVEZ, personal representative and father of Deceased, Regina

Chavez, Appellant and Cross-Appellee,

v.

TOLLESON ELEMENTARY SCHOOL DISTRICT and Ida Moriarity, Appellees and
Cross-Appellants.

No. 1 CA-CIV 3794.

March 22, 1979.
Rehearing Denied April 27, 1979.
Review Denied May 22, 1979.

Parents of ten-year-old student, who left elementary school grounds and was abducted and slain, sued school district and certain school personnel for wrongful death. The Superior Court, Maricopa County, Cause No. C-290188, Sandra D. O'Connor, J., entered judgment n. o. v. and plaintiffs appealed. The Court of Appeals, Froeb, J., held that: (1) duty of school personnel in supervising students was one of ordinary care so that plaintiffs were not required to produce evidence relating to specific standard of care; (2) judgment n. o. v. could not be granted on ground not raised in motion for directed verdict, and (3) school personnel could not reasonably have foreseen that student would leave grounds without permission and thereafter be abducted and slain; thus district and school personnel were not liable for student's death.

Affirmed.

WEST HEADNOTES

[1] Schools 🔑 **89.2**
345k89.2

Public school district is liable for negligence when it fails to exercise ordinary care under the circumstances.

[2] Schools 🔑 **89.11(1)**
345k89.11(1)
(Formerly 345k89.11)

[2] Schools 🔑 **147**
345k147

School district and classroom teacher owe duty of ordinary care toward student during time student is under their charge and that duty is breached when conduct creates unreasonable risk of harm to student. A.R.S. § 15-442 [A][14].

[3] Negligence 🔑 **1693**
272k1693
(Formerly 272k136(14))

Existence of duty toward plaintiff and standard of care owed by defendant are initially questions of law for decision by trial judge and so is issue of whether breach of duty has occurred.

[4] Negligence 🔑 **1694**
272k1694
(Formerly 272k136(14))

If reasonable men would differ as to breach of duty owed plaintiff, question becomes one for jury based upon evidence.

[5] Schools 🔑 **121**
345k121

[5] Schools 🔑 **147**
345k147

Elementary school personnel had duty to use ordinary care in supervising students; thus plaintiffs suing district for wrongful death of student, who left school grounds without permission and was abducted and slain, were not required to produce evidence relating to specific standard of care to be provided by school personnel.

[6] Judgment 🔑 **199(1)**
228k199(1)

Judgment n. o. v. could not be granted on ground not raised in motion for directed verdict.

[7] Negligence 🔑 **210**
272k210
(Formerly 272k2)

As to negligence, duty in given situation is commensurate with dangers involved and it is unreasonable risk of harm which subjects the actor to liability.

[8] Negligence ☞ 213
272k213
    (Formerly 272k10)

Foreseeability is not only involved in determination of proximate cause in negligence case, it is also one of the yardsticks by which duty is measured.

[9] Negligence ☞ 202
272k202
    (Formerly 272k1)

For actionable negligence to exist, there must be duty on part of defendant to protect plaintiff from injury of which he complains, defendant must fail to perform duty, injury to plaintiff must proximately result from such failure, and there must be actual loss or damage.

[10] Negligence ☞ 213
272k213
    (Formerly 272k10)

In law of negligence, question of foreseeability is related to duty rather than to failure to perform duty.

[11] Negligence ☞ 1692
272k1692
    (Formerly 272k136(16))

In first instance, foreseeability is always question of law for court; court must determine duty issue of whether obligation is recognized by law requiring defendant to conform to particular standard of conduct toward plaintiff including whether injury to particular plaintiff was foreseeable.

[12] Judgment ☞ 181(33)
228k181(33)

[12] Negligence ☞ 1694
272k1694
    (Formerly 272k136(16))

[12] Negligence ☞ 1720
272k1720
    (Formerly 272k139(6))

If injury to particular plaintiff was not foreseeable as matter of law, trial judge may dismiss, enter summary judgment, or direct verdict, but if injury is foreseeable and duty is found by trial court to exist, the court may or may not refer foreseeability question to jury by instruction on issue of negligence.

[13] Negligence ☞ 431
272k431
    (Formerly 272k62(1))

Not every danger of harm must be recognized by reasonable man and if harm which results is caused by intervention of factors or forces which form no part of recognizable risk, actor is ordinarily not liable.

[14] Schools ☞ 89.11(1)
345k89.11(1)
    (Formerly 345k89.11)

[14] Schools ☞ 147
345k147

School personnel could not reasonably have foreseen that ten-year-old student would leave elementary school grounds without permission and thereafter be abducted and slain; thus district and school personnel were not liable for death of child.

[15] Appeal and Error ☞ 854(2)
30k854(2)

Decision of trial court will be affirmed where result is legally correct, even though based upon incorrect reason.

Charles Christakis, Phoenix, for appellant and cross-appellee.

Robbins, Green, O'Grady & Abbuhl, P. A. by Michael J. O'Grady, Harriet C. Babbitt, Phoenix, for appellees Moriarity and Tolleson Elementary School District.

Jennings, Strouss & Salmon by William T. Birmingham, Jack E. McCall, Phoenix, for appellee and cross-appellant Moriarity.

Dix W. Price and James A. Ullman, P. C. by James A. Ullman, Phoenix, for amicus curiae.

OPINION

FROEB, Judge.

On the morning of September 17, 1973, ten year old Regina Chavez left the school grounds of Tolleson Elementary School, Unit Two, and was abducted and slain by John Cuffle. Her body was found some three months later in a field a few miles from the school. This wrongful death action, brought by her father Antonio M. Chavez (plaintiff), against the Tolleson Elementary School District and certain school personnel (defendants), is based upon negligence.

On the day this tragic event occurred, Tolleson Elementary School, Unit Two, had been in fall session about one week. Shortly after school began that day, a puppy walked through the open door of the fifth grade classroom and down the aisle, causing the pupils to whisper and giggle. The teacher, Ida Moriarity, inquired if the dog belonged to anyone in the class. Several children raised their hands, including Regina Chavez, who told the teacher that the dog belonged to a neighbor. Regina asked if she could take the puppy home. In response, the teacher sent Regina to the principal's office with the dog to get permission. The school office is located inside the school grounds some thirty feet from the classroom. On arrival at the office with the dog, Regina was instructed by the school secretary, Sally Pina, to place the dog outside the office along the breezeway and to return to her classroom. Regina did not argue with the secretary, and left the office with the puppy. She was observed leaving the office by the custodian, James Arnett, and subsequently by a student, Melissa Chavez, and a passerby, Petra Ledesma. The only other evidence pertaining to the disappearance of Regina was the tape-recorded statement of her abductor, John Cuffle (later convicted and sentenced for the crime). Cuffle stated he abducted Regina outside the school grounds about 10:30 A.M. and took her to a field some six miles from the school. Cuffle further stated that after the killing, he left the area and arrived home in Phoenix at 11:30 or 12:00 noon.

The trial of the case resulted in a jury verdict of $400,000 for plaintiff. After the trial, the defendants brought a motion for judgment notwithstanding the verdict, and, in the alternative, a motion for new trial. The trial court granted the former and denied the latter. Plaintiff thereafter filed motions to set aside the order granting judgment notwithstanding the verdict and for a new trial, which were denied.

Plaintiff appealed from the judgment N.O.V. and the orders denying his post-trial motions. Defendants filed a cross-appeal from the order denying their alternative motion for new trial.

The order of the trial court granting judgment notwithstanding the verdict stated: "The judgment notwithstanding the verdict is granted because plaintiffs failed to establish by the evidence the standard of care required by the school district and by the teacher, Ida Moriarity."

The plaintiff asserts basically three issues on appeal. First, the trial court erred in granting judgment N.O.V. on a ground not specifically raised on defendants' prior motion for directed verdict. Second, the plaintiff was not, in any event, required to establish by the evidence a specific standard of care required by the school district and by the teacher beyond that of ordinary care. Third, the plaintiff is entitled to a new trial on the ground of surprise, since the ruling on the judgment N.O.V. "changed the substantive law."

The defendants respond by asserting first, lack of proof of the standard of care was raised in the motion for directed verdict, however imprecisely; second, standard of care is part of the larger question of duty which was raised with precision on the motion for directed verdict and is again asserted on appeal to sustain the judgment N.O.V.; third, evidence to prove the standard of care owed by the school district and its personnel was required; and, fourth, the trial court did not premise the judgment N.O.V. on new substantive law so as to warrant a new trial on the basis of surprise.

[1] A public school district in Arizona is liable for negligence when it fails to exercise ordinary care under the circumstances. Morris v. Ortiz, 103 Ariz. 119, 437 P.2d 652 (1968) is the leading Arizona case on the subject. In this decision, Justice Struckmeyer pointed out, "Negligence is, of course, the failure to act as a reasonable and prudent person would act in like circumstances." 103 Ariz. at 121, 437 P.2d at 654. The well-settled standard of liability is based upon a duty owed to the plaintiff and a breach of the duty which is the proximate cause of the injury. Crouse v. Wilbur-Ellis Co., 77 Ariz. 359, 272 P.2d 352 (1954).

[2] There can be little question that a school district and a classroom teacher owe a duty of ordinary care toward a student during the time the student is under their charge. Beyond the common law declaration of that duty is a statutorily imposed duty arising out of A.R.S. s 15-442 A(14) which directs the board of trustees of a school district to "provide for adequate supervision over pupils in all instructional and noninstructional activities."

The duty is breached when conduct falls below the standard of ordinary care by creating an unreasonable risk of harm to the plaintiff. Prosser, Law of Torts, 4th Ed., s 31; Harper & James, The Law of Torts, Vol. 2, s 16.9; Restatement of Torts, Second, ss 282, 284; Downs v. Sulphur Springs Valley Electric Cooperative, Inc., 80 Ariz. 286, 279 P.2d 339 (1956); Powder Horn Nursery, Inc. v. Soil and Plant Laboratory, Inc., 119 Ariz. 78, 579 P.2d 582 (App.1978).

[3][4] The existence of a duty toward the plaintiff and the standard of care owed by the defendant are initially questions of law for decision by the trial judge. Rodriguez v. Besser Co., 115 Ariz. 454, 565 P.2d 1315 (App.1977); Barnum v. Rural Fire Protection Company, 24 Ariz.App. 233, 537 P.2d 618 (1975). The issue of whether a breach of the duty has occurred is also initially a question of law for decision by the trial judge. If reasonable men would differ as to the breach of a duty, the question becomes one for the jury based upon the evidence. Moore v. Maricopa County, 11 Ariz.App. 505, 466 P.2d 56 (1970).

STANDARD OF CARE

In their motion for judgment N.O.V., defendants argued that plaintiff failed to prove (1) a duty owed by the defendants to protect Regina Chavez; (2) a failure by the defendants to perform that duty; and (3) injury which was a proximate result of such failure. The motion emphasized the argument that "plaintiffs failed to present any evidence as to the specific duty owed by the educational institution in question or its professional employees." In support of the need for such evidence, defendants relied heavily upon the decision of the Arizona Supreme Court in Maricopa County v. Cowart, 106 Ariz. 69, 471 P.2d 265 (1970), a wrongful death case involving the standard of care owed by the Maricopa County Juvenile Home to its inmates. The court there held that "the standard required for the protection of juveniles placed in (the custody of the juvenile home) is that the institution exercises the skill and knowledge normally possessed by like institutions in similar communities handling juveniles." 106 Ariz. at 71, 471 P.2d at 267. The defendants argued to the trial court in this case that plaintiff had the burden of presenting evidence relating to a specific standard of care owed by personnel of a public elementary school to its students. In support of this argument, defendants contended that teachers must be certified personnel; they require professional training; they must follow prescribed statutory duties; and, therefore, the standard of care to which they must be held falls outside of the common knowledge of the general public and must be proven by evidence.

[5] We find that the facts of this case, unlike Cowart, do not require that a specific standard of care be proven in order to establish negligence. We hold that the duty of the school personnel in this case as to the supervision of students in their charge was one of ordinary care. Morris v. Ortiz, above. The standard is not one which requires specific proof in order to be correctly applied by a jury. The common knowledge and experience of a jury provides the guide to ordinary care in a public elementary school setting and suffices in the determination of whether particular conduct meets or falls below the standard. There is, however, an additional ground for rejecting defendants' argument.

In later motion proceedings, plaintiff argued that judgment N.O.V. on this ground was unavailable since it was never presented to the trial court in defendants' motion for directed verdict. Plaintiff is correct on this point, both as to the law and the facts.

Rules of Civil Procedure, Rule 50(b), reads in part:

Motion for judgment notwithstanding the verdict. Whenever a motion for a directed verdict made at the close of all the evidence is denied or for any reason is not granted, the court is deemed to have submitted the action to the jury subject to a later determination of the legal questions raised by the motion. Not later than 15 days after the entry of judgment, a party who has moved for a directed verdict may file a motion to have the verdict and any judgment entered thereon set aside and to have judgment entered in accordance with his motion for a directed verdict. . . .

[6] Arizona cases are clear that a judgment N.O.V. cannot be granted on a ground not raised in the motion for directed verdict. LaBonne v. First National Bank of Arizona, 75 Ariz. 184, 254 P.2d 435 (1953); Glowacki v. A. J. Bayless Markets, 76 Ariz. 295, 263 P.2d 799 (1953).

We have carefully reviewed the oral arguments and written trial memoranda submitted by defendants in support of their motion for directed verdict and find nothing relating to the claimed failure of plaintiff to present proof on the issue of a specific standard of care. The rule requiring the issue to be raised on the motion for directed verdict is based upon the premise that the claimed omission in proof might be cured by a reopening of plaintiff's case if the trial court finds merit to the motion. This is obviously not possible when the issue is raised for the first time after trial on a motion for judgment N.O.V. We turn, then, to an issue raised by defendants both in the motion for directed verdict and the motion for judgment N.O.V.

DUTY

"The risk reasonably to be perceived defines the duty to be obeyed. . . ." <u>Palsgraf v. Long Island R. Co., 248 N.Y. 339, 344, 162 N.E. 99, 100 (1928); Bryan v. Southern Pacific Co., 79 Ariz. 253, 286 P.2d 761 (1955); Rosendahl v. Tucson Medical Center, 93 Ariz. 368, 380 P.2d 1020 (1963); Tucker v. Collar, 79 Ariz. 141, 285 P.2d 178 (1955).</u>

In their motion for directed verdict, as well as in the motion for judgment N.O.V., defendants argued that the risk of harm which took the life of Regina Chavez was not reasonably foreseeable and, therefore, their duty of precaution did not encompass it.

[7][8] Duty in a given situation is commensurate with the dangers involved. Crouse v. Wilbur-Ellis Co., above; <u>Mountain States Telephone & Tel. Co. v. Kelton, 79 Ariz. 126, 285 P.2d 168 (1955).</u> It is the Unreasonable risk of harm which subjects the actor to liability. Tucker v. Collar. Foreseeability is not only involved in the determination of proximate cause, it is also one of the yardsticks by which duty is measured.

[9][10][11][12] The point is well made in <u>City of Scottsdale v. Kokaska, 17 Ariz.App. 120, 495 P.2d 1327 (1972):</u>

The first element (of actionable negligence) is the Duty issue; the second is the Negligence issue; the third element is the causal relation or Proximate cause issue; while the fourth element is the Damage issue. To which issue is the question of foreseeability directed? Edwards says that it is the test for the second issue Negligence. However, our Supreme Court has said that it is an element of the first issue Duty. For instance in <u>Mountain States Telephone & Telegraph Co. v. Kelton, 79 Ariz. 126, 285 P.2d 168 (1955),</u> the court said that the duty the defendants owed plaintiff included the duty to take reasonable precautions to prevent injuring the plaintiff and that the reasonable precautions must be measured by the risk of anticipated harm (foreseeable harm). See also, <u>Bryan v. Southern Pac. Co., 79 Ariz. 253, 286 P.2d 761 (1955); Matsumato v. Arizona Sand & Rock Co., 80 Ariz. 232, 295 P.2d 850 (1956).</u>

(T)hree aspects of foreseeability have developed in Arizona law: first, the determination by the court as a matter of law whether as a part of duty, the injury to the Plaintiff was foreseeable under the circumstances; second, as in Tucker v. Collar, supra, where the Supreme Court held that foreseeability was a proper question for the jury on the issue of negligence; and

third, where the court views foreseeability as an element of proximate or legal causation in intervening force superseding cause situations as in <u>Salt River Valley Water Users' Ass'n v. Cornum, 49 Ariz. 1, 63 P.2d 639 (1937).</u>

We analyze the cases as saying that in the first instance foreseeability is always a question of law for the court. The court must determine the duty issue of whether an obligation is recognized by the law requiring the defendant to conform to a particular standard of conduct toward the plaintiff. This includes the question of whether the injury to the particular plaintiff was foreseeable. If it is not foreseeable then the trial judge usually disposes of the matter by dismissal, summary judgment, or the directed verdict route. If it is foreseeable and the duty is found by the trial court to exist, the trial court may or may not refer the foreseeability question to the jury by instruction on the issue of negligence. This issue is usually presented to the jury, as in Tucker v. Collar, supra, where there is a Debatable question whether the injury to plaintiff was within the foreseeable scope of the risk or whether defendant was required to recognize the risk or take precautions against it.

17 Ariz.App. at 124-126, 495 P.2d at 1331-1333.

[13] Not every danger of harm must be recognized by a reasonable man. Morris v. Ortiz, above. <u>Restatement of Torts, Second, s 289,</u> states a general test as follows:

The actor is required to recognize that his conduct involves a risk of causing an invasion of another's interest if a reasonable man would do so while exercising

(a) such attention, perception of the circumstances, memory, knowledge of other pertinent matters, intelligence, and judgment as a reasonable man would have . . . .

Where the harm which in fact results is caused by the intervention of factors or forces which form no part of the recognizable risk, the actor is ordinarily not liable. <u>Restatement of Torts, Second, s 281,</u> Comment f. As earlier stated, the death of Regina Chavez was brought about by the felonious actions of John Cuffle after she had wandered from the school grounds. In scrutinizing the foreseeability of this event and determining if the conduct of school personnel created an unreasonable risk that it would occur, we may look again to Restatement of Torts, Second, in the area of "superceding cause" for guidance:

The act of a third person in committing an intentional tort or crime is a superceding cause of harm to another resulting therefrom, although the actor's negligent conduct created a situation which afforded an opportunity to the third person to commit such a tort or crime, unless the actor at the time of his negligent conduct realized or should have realized the likelihood that such a situation might be created, and that a third person might avail himself of the opportunity to commit such a tort or crime.

Restatement of Torts, Second, s 448. See also Salt River Valley Water Users' Ass'n v. Cornum, 49 Ariz. 1, 63 P.2d 639 (1937) for a discussion of foreseeability of the acts of third persons analyzed in the proximate cause setting.

[14] There are no facts in the record indicating that school personnel should have been aware of the potential of criminal conduct in the area of Tolleson Elementary School, Unit Two. To say that murder is a foreseeable potential creating an unreasonable risk of harm to each child leaving school grounds each day in the state of Arizona is untenable. The heinous criminal conduct involved here, while shocking, is clearly in the category of the unforeseeable. If it were otherwise, prevision would become paranoia and the routines of daily life would be burdened by intolerable fear and inaction. The intervention of the criminal conduct was foreign to any risk created by the school personnel. As a matter of law, we hold that the defendants could not reasonably have foreseen that Regina Chavez would leave the school grounds without permission and thereafter be abducted and slain.

THE JUDGMENT N.O.V.

As previously stated, plaintiff correctly argues that it was error for the trial court to grant judgment N.O.V.

on the ground that plaintiff failed to introduce proof relating to the standard of care. As pointed out above, the ruling of the trial court was based on this issue. Nevertheless, the issue of duty and its necessary component, foreseeability, was squarely before the trial court, both in the motion for directed verdict and the post-trial motion for judgment N.O.V.

[15] It has been held on numerous occasions that a decision of the trial court will be affirmed where the result is legally correct, even though based upon an incorrect reason. Santanello v. Cooper, 106 Ariz. 262, 475 P.2d 246 (1970); Matter of Estate of Beaman, 119 Ariz. 614, 583 P.2d 270 (App.1978); Tiffany Construction Co. v. Hancock & Kelley Construction Co.,24 Ariz.App. 504, 539 P.2d 978 (1975). We do so here upon such authority. The issue was squarely presented.

ALTERNATIVE MOTION FOR NEW TRIAL

Plaintiff moved for a new trial in accordance with Rules of Civil Procedure, Rule 59(a)(3) on the ground of surprise. Plaintiff argues that if the judgment N.O.V. is affirmed (on the ground that plaintiff failed to present evidence on the standard of care), this constitutes a change in substantive law entitling him to a new trial. Since we have not affirmed the judgment on this ground, but have affirmed it on another ground, and there is nothing which would warrant a new trial, the contention is rejected.

CROSS-APPEAL

Defendants' cross-appeal raises several issues, but we do not reach them in view of our decision affirming the judgment N.O.V.

Judgment N.O.V. affirmed.

JACOBSON, Acting P. J., Department B, and EUBANK, J., concur.

(Cite as: 191 Ariz. 110, 952 P.2d 754)

Court of Appeals of Arizona,

Division 2, Department B.

Kathy HILL, individually and on behalf of the Estate of Clint Hill,
Plaintiff/Appellant,

v.

SAFFORD UNIFIED SCHOOL DISTRICT; B.B. Andrews and Jane Doe Andrews, husband
and wife, Defendants/Appellees.

No. 2 CA-CV 96-0301.

Dec. 30, 1997.

Following fatal shooting of high school student by fellow student, after school hours and away from school premises, negligence and wrongful death action was brought against school district and teacher. Summary judgment for defendants was entered by the Superior Court, Graham County, Cause No. 14775, Dudley S. Welker, J., and plaintiff appealed. The Court of Appeals, Espinosa, J., held that: (1) school did not fail to meet its statutory duty or create unreasonable risk to student who was shot, when it failed to discipline student who later shot him, after the two students were involved in a verbal altercation at school, and (2) shooting was not foreseeable so as to impose duty on school to discipline students for disorderly conduct on way to and from school, when teacher saw students gathered after school, apparently anticipating a fight.

Affirmed.

WEST HEADNOTES

[1] Appeal and Error ☞ 893(1)
30k893(1)

On appeal from summary judgment, Court of Appeals determines de novo whether there are any genuine issues of material fact and whether the trial court erred in applying the law, and Court of Appeals will affirm the trial court's decision if it is correct for any reason, even if that reason was not considered by the trial court.

[2] Schools ☞ 63(3)
345k63(3)

[2] Schools ☞ 147
345k147

School teachers and administrators have both a statutory and common law duty not to subject students within their charge to a foreseeable and unreasonable risk of harm through acts, omissions, or school policy. A.R.S. § 15-341, subd. A, par. 17.

[3] Negligence ☞ 1694
272k1694
    (Formerly 272k136(14))

Ordinarily, it is a jury's function as fact finder to determine whether a risk of harm created by a defendant was foreseeable and unreasonable; however, in approaching the question of negligence or unreasonable risk, the courts set outer limits, and where reasonable persons could not differ, the court properly takes the issue from the jury.

[4] Schools ☞ 89.11(1)
345k89.11(1)

High school did not fail to meet its statutory duty or create unreasonable risk to student, who was later fatally shot by second student after school hours and away from school premises, when it failed to discipline second student following argument between the two students at school; school investigated the matter, briefly detained both boys, took their statements, and decided no further action was necessary. A.R.S. §§ 15-341, subd. A, pars. 13, 14, 15-843, subd. B.

[5] Schools ☞ 169
345k169

Student discipline is a matter entrusted to schools and their governing boards' discretion, and judicial intervention is called for only to correct a manifest abuse of discretion. A.R.S. § 15-341, subd. A, pars. 13, 14.

[6] Schools 🔑 89.11(1)

345k89.11(1)

Student's death as result of shooting by another student after school and away from school premises was not foreseeable so as to impose duty on school to discipline students for disorderly conduct on way to and from school; there was no evidence that teacher who saw students gathered after school, apparently anticipating a fight, or any school official was aware of any students bringing guns or weapons to school, or that there was on-going gang difficulty at the school, or that any school personnel knew that the after-school gathering had any gang relation, or that shooter was known to have dangerous propensities. A.R.S. § 15-341, subd. A, par. 14.

[7] Negligence 🔑 213

272k213

(Formerly 272k10)

General test for whether defendant's conduct has breached standard of care is whether foreseeable risk of injury resulted from defendant's conduct; foreseeability of harm defines and limits the scope of conduct necessary to fulfill a duty.

[8] Negligence 🔑 213

272k213

(Formerly 272k10)

"Reasonably foreseeable" event, for purposes of cause of action in negligence, is one that might reasonably be expected to occur now and then, and would be recognized as not highly unlikely if it did suggest itself to the actor's mind.

[9] Negligence 🔑 220

272k220

(Formerly 272k2)

Duty of care may include measures to protect others from criminal attacks, provided the attacks are reasonably foreseeable.

[10] Negligence 🔑 213

272k213

(Formerly 272k2)

Reckless or criminal nature of a tortfeasor's conduct does not place it beyond the scope of a duty of reasonable care if that duty entails foresight and prevention of precisely such a risk.

Zachar & Doughty by Christopher J. Zachar and Sean W. Doughty, Phoenix, for Plaintiff/Appellant.

Thomas & Elardo, P.C. by Neal B. Thomas, Phoenix, for Defendants/Appellees.

OPINION

ESPINOSA, Judge.

Following an argument at school, Safford High School student Scott Fast fatally shot Clint Hill, another student, after school at a location outside the city of Safford. Plaintiff/appellant Kathy Hill, individually and on behalf of Clint Hill's estate, brought an action against defendants/appellees Safford Unified School District ("the school") and B.B. Andrews, a teacher at the school, to recover damages for negligence and wrongful death. The trial court granted summary judgment in favor of appellees, finding no liability as a matter of law. Appellant contends that the trial court erred because the school knew or should have known that Fast had dangerous propensities, it was foreseeable that Fast would harm or cause injury to Hill, and the school failed to take any action to prevent the events that led to his death. We affirm.

FACTUAL BACKGROUND

The facts in this case are largely undisputed and we view them, and all reasonable inferences therefrom, in the light most favorable to the party appealing summary judgment. Rogers v. Retrum, 170 Ariz. 399, 825 P.2d 20 (App.1991). On Friday, September 17, 1993, Hill and a friend, Justin Grotte, had a verbal altercation at school with another student, Troy White, who was a member of a small gang in Safford that called itself the "Eight Ball Posse." The altercation took place during school hours, and school officials called Safford police after questioning Grotte and White. White was taken to the police station for further questioning, and the school suspended him for five days. On Monday, September 20, another verbal confrontation took place during school, this time between Fast, a friend of White and fellow "Eight Ball Posse" member, and Grotte, who was then joined by Hill. Teachers brought Hill and Fast to the school office. After speaking with each student, the associate principal felt the situation was "defused" and allowed the boys to return to class, taking no further disciplinary action.

After classes ended, a group of students began to gather across the street from the school, apparently anticipating a fight between Fast and Grotte. Andrews happened to be driving by and he yelled, "Break it up," and, "Take it somewhere else." [FN1] Police were called, but before they arrived, several vehicles loaded with students left the scene and drove to an area outside of town known as Clay Knolls. When police responded, they were informed the students may have gone to that location. Meanwhile at Clay Knolls, Fast produced a gun and, after pointing it at several other students, shot Hill in the chest. The police arrived at the scene shortly after the shooting. Fast apparently had obtained the gun from a schoolmate's vehicle during the lunch period that day. School administrators had heard rumors about the "Eight Ball Posse" and had once searched Fast's school locker after hearing a rumor that he had a gun on school premises, although no gun was found. There had been no other shootings or similar incidents at or near the school.

> FN1. Although we view the facts favorably towards the party opposing summary judgment, Hill's assertion that Andrews said "take the fight somewhere else" is not supported by admissible evidence. See Wallace v. Casa Grande Union High School District No. 82, 184 Ariz. 419, 909 P.2d 486 (App.1995); cf. Ariz.R.Civ.P. 56(e), 16 A.R.S.

STANDARDS OF REVIEW

[1] On appeal from a summary judgment, we determine de novo whether there are any genuine issues of material fact and whether the trial court erred in applying the law. Wallace v. Casa Grande Union High School District No. 82, 184 Ariz. 419, 909 P.2d 486 (App.1995). We will affirm the trial court's decision if it is correct for any reason, even if that reason was not considered by the trial court. Glaze v. Marcus, 151 Ariz. 538, 729 P.2d 342 (App.1986); Chavez v. Tolleson Elementary School District, 122 Ariz. 472, 595 P.2d 1017 (App.1979).

DUTY

[2] Appellant correctly points out that school teachers and administrators have both a statutory and common law duty not to subject students within their charge to a foreseeable and unreasonable risk of harm through acts, omissions, or school policy. See A.R.S. § 15-341(A)(17) (governing board shall provide for adequate supervision over pupils); Jesik v. Maricopa County Community College District, 125 Ariz. 543, 611 P.2d 547 (1980) (statute imposes duty of protection for students against torts). In a different context, our supreme court recently addressed the question of the common law duty of a premises owner to protect a guest from criminal attack. Martinez v. Woodmar IV Condominiums Homeowners Assoc., Inc., 189 Ariz. 206, 941 P.2d 218 (1997). The court acknowledged the special relationship principle set

forth in the Restatement (Second) of Torts § 315 (1965), which states there is no duty so to control the conduct of a third person as to prevent him from causing physical harm to another unless (a) a special relation exists between the [defendant] and the third person which imposes a duty upon the [defendant] to control the third person's conduct, or (b) a special relation exists between the [defendant] and the [plaintiff] which gives to the [plaintiff] a right of protection.

Id. at 207-08, 941 P.2d at 219-20. The teacher-student relationship is a special relation that creates a duty of due care. See Rogers; see also Fedie v. Travelodge International Inc., 162 Ariz. 263, 782 P.2d 739 (App.1989). Hence, the relationship between the school and Hill imposed an additional obligation on the school to take reasonable precautions for Hill's safety. That the school owed duties of supervision and care to Hill, however, is not dispositive of the question whether summary judgment was appropriate. The essence of those duties is to exercise reasonable care in light of foreseeable and unreasonable risks. See Martinez; Rogers. Thus, the essential question is whether, on the undisputed material facts, a reasonable jury could conclude the school breached its duties to Hill. See **757Orme School v. Reeves, 166 Ariz. 301, 802 P.2d 1000 (1990). *113 We conclude it could not.

ALLEGED BREACH OF DUTY

[3] Ordinarily, it is a jury's function as fact finder to determine whether a risk of harm created by a defendant was foreseeable and unreasonable. See Robertson v. Sixpence Inns of America, 163 Ariz. 539, 789 P.2d 1040 (1990). However, "in approaching the question of negligence or unreasonable risk, 'the courts set outer limits' " and where reasonable persons could not differ, the court properly takes the issue from the jury. Rogers, 170 Ariz. at 402, 825 P.2d at 23 quoting Harper, James & Gray, The Law of Torts § 15.3 at 355 (2d ed. 1986); see also Orme School; Flowers v. K-Mart Corp., 126 Ariz. 495, 616 P.2d 955 (App.1980); Morris v. Ortiz, 103 Ariz. 119, 437 P.2d 652 (1968). In reviewing a grant of summary judgment, "we look at whether sufficient evidence of foreseeability and possible prevention was presented to create a genuine issue of material fact." Martinez, 189 Ariz. at 211, 941 P.2d at 223; see Coburn v. City of Tucson, 143 Ariz. 50, 691 P.2d 1078 (1984) (summary judgment proper if insufficient evidence of breach of duty).

In its extensive minute entry, the trial court observed:

At the oral argument, this Judge repeatedly asked counsel for the Plaintiff what it was that the school district did, or what it was that the school district failed to do, that constituted the negligence for which it should be held liable. Essentially, the answer that the court was given was that they should have done something to keep Clint Hill from being killed, and because he was killed the district was liable. The Court does not believe that the responsibility of the school goes so far as to impose what is essentially strict liability for anything that might happen to a student.

We note that appellant's briefs on appeal display a similar generality, primarily maintaining that the school "knew or should have realized that Scott Fast might avail himself of the opportunity to commit a tort or crime towards Clint Hill," and "[it] failed to provide any security or disciplinary measures to protect [him]." To determine the propriety of the trial court's ruling, we differentiate and address two recurring claims underlying appellant's argument and the evidence with respect to each.

1. School's Obligation to Supervise and Discipline

[4] Appellant contends that the school created an unreasonable risk to Hill when it failed to properly supervise Fast on May 20 by not disciplining him pursuant to A.R.S. §§ 15-341(A)(13) and (A)(14), [FN2] which provide:

> FN2. Formerly A.R.S. § 15-341(A)(14) and (A)(15), respectively. 1995 Ariz.Sess.Laws, ch. 268, § 16.

A. The governing board shall:

* * *

13. Hold pupils to strict account for disorderly conduct on school property.

14. Discipline students for disorderly conduct on the way to and from school.

Appellant argues that this statute imposes liability on a school for the tortious conduct of a student whether committed on or off school premises, and that the school "should have perceived a risk to Clint Hill that Scott Fast would act irrationally because of his [gang] affiliation, and that irrational conduct may result in injury or death" to Hill. Although we agree with appellant that liability for supervisory omissions may not necessarily be circumscribed by school boundaries, Rogers, we cannot find that the school either failed to

meet its statutory duty or created an unreasonable risk of harm to Hill.

[5] Sections 15-341(A)(13) and (14) require schools to proscribe, judge and rectify student conduct. See also A.R.S. § 15-843(B). [FN3] Although not determinative on the question of negligence, this court has previously held that student discipline is a matter entrusted to schools and their governing boards' discretion, and judicial intervention is called for only to correct "a manifest abuse of discretion." Tucson Public Schools, District No. 1 of Pima County v. Green, 17 Ariz.App. 91, 94, 495 P.2d 861, 864 (1972); see also Kelly v. Martin, 16 Ariz.App. 7, 490 P.2d 836 (1971) (legislature delegated control of high school affairs to the school governing board, and courts possess only limited power to review the reasonableness of school disciplinary regulations and actions). Other courts have held that schools have wide discretion in disciplining students' behavior where the disciplinary policies and rules are reasonable and rationally related to the schools' purpose in providing public education. See Beshears v. Unified School District No. 305, 261 Kan. 555, 930 P.2d 1376 (1997); Bencic v. City of Malden, 32 Mass.App.Ct. 186, 587 N.E.2d 795 (1992). Indeed, the Supreme Court has noted that school districts, teachers, and administrators have a substantial interest in maintaining discipline in the classroom and on school grounds, and a school's authority to maintain security and order requires a certain degree of flexibility in school disciplinary procedures. New Jersey v. T.L.O., 469 U.S. 325, 105 S.Ct. 733, 83 L.Ed.2d 720 (1985).

> FN3. A.R.S. § 15-843(B) provides that "[t]he governing board of any school district shall, in consultation with the teachers and parents of the school district, prescribe rules for the discipline, suspension and expulsion of pupils."

After the September 20 verbal altercation between Hill and Fast was brought to the school's attention, it was within the school's discretion, based on its disciplinary guidelines, to decide whether and to what extent to punish either student. The school investigated the matter, briefly detained both boys, took their statements, and decided no further action was necessary. Although school officials had called police and disciplined a student on Friday, September 17, the circumstances and students involved in that incident were different. On that day, it was White, not Fast, who was involved in the altercation. White had made a threatening hand gesture as if to shoot Grotte and "was behaving erratically." Moreover, White had been in trouble before. The record reflects that on September 20 there was only a heated exchange of words between Hill and Fast, nothing more. After both boys were brought to the office, the assistant principal spoke with each of them individually. The only evidence in the record about those interviews and the school's knowledge of any potential danger to Hill is found in portions of the assistant principal's testimony at Fast's criminal trial:

> Q. As a result of the interviews you conducted with Scott [Fast] and Clint [Hill] the afternoon of Monday the 20th, did you feel it necessary to take any disciplinary action against either of the boys at that time?
>
> A. No, I did not. I visited like I say with Clint first and all he wanted was for Scott to stay out of his face and leave him alone.
>
> And likewise, when Mr. Bonefas and I visited with Scott, he made a similar remark, that he just wanted Clint to mind his own business and he would mind his.
>
> * * *
>
> Q. . . . was it your understanding after talking with Clint and Scott Fast that the threats that had been going on between them that caused them to come into the office were just that they wanted to fight each other?
>
> A. Those feelings existed and I was trying to find out why.
>
> Q. And you felt those had been defused at the time they left your office?
>
> A. Yes.
>
> * * *
>
> Q. Do you recall whether Fast at that time told you of any threats that Troy White had told him about being made involving an organization called the Eight Ball Posse?
>
> A. We had rumors about the Eight Ball Posse around the school but as far as it being a part of the conversation, this is on Friday?
>
> Q. No, this is on Monday.
>
> A. Monday Mr. Bonefas and I inquired about that and Scott at that time was not part of the conversation [sic]. It didn't relate to what we were talking about.

> Q. So your understanding of what happened on the 20th is Eight Ball Posse was not part of the issue that existed between Clint Hill and Scott Fast at that time?
>
> A. Yes, we asked Scott about it and his response to us was that was not a part of it.

From this, it is not possible to conclude that the school abused its discretion by not imposing discipline or that it should have anticipated that Fast would "act irrationally" and cause Hill injury or death. Nor is there any evidence that the school failed to follow any of its guidelines or policies. Thus, there is nothing to support the claim that the school violated the supervisory requirements of § 15-341(A)(13) and (17) and created an unreasonable risk of harm to Hill when it released both boys after questioning them and determining the problem did not require further action.

2. Foreseeability of Harm After School

[6][7][8][9][10] Appellant also argues that the school breached its duty to discipline students for disorderly conduct on the way to and from school pursuant to A.R.S. § 15-341(A)(14) because it was foreseeable "that the students would 'take the fight somewhere else' as suggested by Defendant Andrews." The general test for whether a defendant's conduct has breached the standard of care is whether a foreseeable risk of injury resulted from the defendant's conduct. Robertson. Foreseeability of harm defines and limits the scope of conduct necessary to fulfill a duty. Martinez. A reasonably foreseeable event is one that might "reasonably be expected to occur now and then, and would be recognized as not highly unlikely if it did suggest itself to the actor's mind." Tellez v. Saban, 188 Ariz. 165, 172, 933 P.2d 1233, 1240 (App.1996); see Fazzolari v. Portland School District No. 1J, 78 Or.App. 608, 717 P.2d 1210 (1986), aff'd, 303 Or. 1, 734 P.2d 1326 (1987). As our supreme court noted in Martinez, a defendant's duty of care "may include measures to protect others from criminal attacks, provided the attacks are reasonably foreseeable." 189 Ariz. at 211, 941 P.2d at 223. The reckless or criminal nature of a tortfeasor's conduct "does not place it beyond the scope of a duty of reasonable care if that duty entails foresight and prevention of precisely such a risk." Rogers, 170 Ariz. at 401-02, 825 P.2d at 22-23.

Appellant repeatedly asserts that Hill's death was "foreseeable" and "predictable." We find nothing in the record, however, to support that claim. There is no evidence Andrews or any school official was aware of any students bringing guns or weapons to school, or that any student had a weapon at the time Andrews drove by the group of students after school. Nor is there any evidence in the record to support appellant's claim of "on going gang difficulty at the school," or that Andrews or other school personnel knew that the after-school gathering had any gang relation. Indeed, when asked earlier that day whether the altercation with Hill involved the rumored "Eight Ball Posse," Fast told the assistant principal "that was not a part of it." There is also no evidence that Fast "was known to have dangerous propensities and violent tendencies," that Hill "reported threats by Scott Fast to school personnel," or that the school or Andrews was aware that Hill and Fast "confronted each other" at the gathering across the street from the school as appellant claims.

A number of cases have examined the question of foreseeability in the context of particular fact scenarios and lend support to a finding of insufficient indicia of foreseeability here. See Fedie (directed verdict for motel managers upheld where evidence insufficient to support conclusion they should have foreseen that visitor had dangerous propensities and might obtain room occupant's gun); Hebert v. Club 37 Bar, 145 Ariz. 351, 701 P.2d 847 (App.1984) (victim's shooting in parking lot unforeseeable when no reason for bar owners or bartender to believe intoxicated patron was dangerous or violent); Brownell v. Los Angeles Unified School Dist., 4 Cal.App.4th 787, 5 Cal.Rptr.2d 756 (1992) (although school knew of gang activity in area, no similar incidents or other circumstances to alert it to possibility of off-campus shooting that occurred); Danna v. Sewanhaka Central High School Dist., 662 N.Y.S.2d 71 (App.1997) (fight between students and resulting injury not reasonably foreseeable when neither student previously involved in or disciplined for fighting, and only prior dispute was verbal exchange a month before); see also Morris (directed verdict on negligent supervision action upheld where nothing to alert teacher that shop student who had been asked to stand on large piece of metal would instead leap onto its jagged edge and sustain injury); compare Martinez (sufficient evidence of foreseeability of harm to condominium guest where plaintiff introduced evidence that defendant knew gangs frequented its parking lot and conducted criminal activities there, and was warned of the need for 24-hour patrols); Robertson (motel manager who knew of just completed armed robbery on premises and failed to warn security guard could anticipate harm to him); Jesik (student's repeated requests for help and warnings

that another was threatening to immediately kill him provided notice to school which imposed specific duty of protection).

Despite appellant's urging, this case bears only superficial resemblance to Jesik. There, a student had "words" with a man who told him he was coming back to the school with a gun to kill him. The student immediately reported the threat to a school security guard and received "assurances of help and protection." Id. at 544, 611 P.2d at 548. When the man returned with a briefcase, the student pointed both him and the briefcase out to the security guard, who again assured him of protection. Although the guard spoke to the man, the guard then left the area and the man pulled a gun from the briefcase and shot the student. Summary judgment was reversed because there was evidence that school personnel "had specific and repeated notice of both the actor and the exact type of harm that did in fact occur." 125 Ariz. at 547, 611 P.2d at 551. We find no like evidence here to support a breach of the school's duty of supervision or to put it on notice that Fast posed a danger to Hill, either during or after school.

This case bears more similarities to Brownell where a gang mistook a high school student for a rival gang member and shot him in the street outside the school after class. Although the school frequently removed gang-related items from students, had occasionally confiscated weapons, and another student previously had been threatened by "some Crips," there had been no prior shootings and no indications of potential gang violence the day of the assault. Brownell alleged negligent supervision in the school's failure to protect him from gang-related after-school violence. The California court of appeals disagreed, acknowledging the school could be held liable for injuries suffered by a student off school premises and after school hours, but finding no evidence that school officials were aware of a pending gang confrontation or similar violence, or any evidence "reflecting not necessarily this identical type of assault but that 'the possibility of this type of harm was foreseeable.' " 4 Cal.App.4th at 797, 5 Cal.Rptr.2d at 762 (citation omitted), see also Danna (breach of school's supervisory duty requires that third party acts could reasonably have been anticipated). As our supreme court noted in Morris: "[T]he principle is too well established for quibbling 'that before liability may be imposed for an act [or failure to act], the prevision of a reasonable person must be able to recognize danger of harm to the plaintiff or one in plaintiff's situation.' " 103 Ariz. at 121, 437 P.2d at 654 (citation omitted).

Appellant points to no evidence indicating the school's alleged knowledge of any pending gang activity or Fast's propensity for violence, other than nonspecific rumors of the "Eight Ball Posse" and a past rumor that Fast had a gun in his locker, a rumor the school investigated and dispelled. Moreover, the only concrete action appellant suggests the school could have taken was to detain Fast and call police or his parents after his verbal altercation with Hill the day of the shooting. [FN4] Appellant does not explain, however, why such action would have been warranted, much less required, other than because the school had done so in a similar situation three days earlier, notwithstanding that the two incidents involved different students and circumstances. Nor does appellant contend that detaining Fast and/or calling police would have prevented the ensuing tragedy. In thisregard, the trial court commented:

> FN4. Although appellant also asserts Andrews could have called police, the record shows police were notified, apparently within minutes of the after-school gathering, but does not reveal whether they were alerted by school personnel, a policeman already in the area, or someone else.

This Judge cannot come up with anything that the school could have done to discipline Scott Fast that would have prevented him from hurting anyone. The power to discipline Scott Fast by detaining him would be through to [sic] the Juvenile Court, not the school district . . .

*   *   *

The school district did not have the power to lock Scott Fast up, and that is really the only way that this death could have been prevented.

In sum, the evidence here simply does not support appellant's assertions that the shooting was "foreseeable" and "probable." Rather, on the record before us, this is that rare case where it can be said "as a matter of law Defendant could not have taken reasonable measures that probably would have prevented the attack." Martinez, 189 Ariz. at 212, 941 P.2d at 224.

CONCLUSION

Although we agree with appellant that the school owed a duty of reasonable care to Hill, our review of the record and the applicable precedents leads us to conclude as a matter of law that the school did not breach that duty, nor did it violate its supervisory duties under A.R.S. § 15-341. In view of our resolution of these issues, we need not address the question whether Fast's criminal act was an intervening, superseding event, as appellees argued below and on appeal. Because Hill's death was not reasonably foreseeable and did not result from an unreasonable risk created by the school or Andrews, the trial court properly granted summary judgment for the appellees.

Affirmed.

PELANDER, P.J., and HOWARD, J., concur.

(Cite as: 128 F.3d 233)

United States Court of Appeals,

Fourth Circuit.

Vivian RICE, Guardian and next friend of Tamielle Horn; Marilyn Farmer, Co-personal representatives of the estate of Mildred Horn; Tiffani M. Horn, Co-personal representatives of the estate of Mildred Horn; Michael D. Saunders, Individually and next friend of Colin D. Saunders, a minor and personal representative of the estate of Janice Y. Saunders; Colin D. Saunders; Janice Y. Saunders,

Plaintiffs-Appellants,

v.

The PALADIN ENTERPRISES, INCORPORATED, a/k/a The Paladin Press, Defendant-

Appellee,

and

Peter C. Lund, Defendant.
David Crump, Professor of Constitutional Law and Recipient of Friend of the First Amendment" Award; National Victim Center; Stephanie Roper Foundation, Incorporated; Victims Rights Political Action Committee; The Horror Writers Association; The Thomas Jefferson Center for the Protection of Free Expression; American Civil Liberties Union Foundation; American Civil Liberties Union of the National Capitol Area; American Civil Liberties Union of Colorado; ABC, Incorporated; America Online, Incorporated; Association of American Publishers; The Baltimore Sun Company; E.W. Scripps Company; Freedom to Read Foundation; Magazine Publishers of America, Incorporated; McClatchy ewspapers, Incorporated; Media General, Inc.; Media Professional Insurance; National Association of Broadcasters; Newspapers Association of America; The New York Times; The Reporters Committee for Freedom of the Press; Society of Professional Journalists; The Washington Post, Amici Curiae.

No. 96-2412.

Argued May 7, 1997.
Decided Nov. 10, 1997.

Relatives and representatives of murder victims brought state law wrongful death action against publisher of "hit man" instruction book that assisted murderer in soliciting, preparing for, and committing murders. The United States District Court for the District of Maryland, Alexander Williams, Jr., J., 940 F.Supp. 836, granted summary judgment to publisher. Plaintiffs appealed. The Court of Appeals, Luttig, Circuit Judge, held that: (1) genuine issues existed as to whether publisher acted with requisite intent to render it liable under Maryland law for aiding and abetting murders, and (2) book was not entitled to protection under First Amendment's free speech clause as abstract advocacy.

Reversed and remanded.

WEST HEADNOTES

[1] Constitutional Law ⚷ **90.1(1)**
92k90.1(1)

Abstract advocacy of lawlessness is protected speech under First Amendment. U.S.C.A. Const.Amend. 1.

[2] Constitutional Law ⚷ **90(3)**
92k90(3)

While even speech advocating lawlessness has long enjoyed protections under First Amendment, it is equally well established that speech, which, in its effect, is tantamount to legitimately proscribable nonexpressive conduct, may itself be legitimately proscribed, punished, or regulated incidentally to constitutional enforcement of generally applicable statutes. U.S.C.A. Const.Amend. 1.

[3] **Constitutional Law** 🔑 91
92k91

Although agreements to engage in illegal conduct undoubtedly possess some element of association, State may ban such illegal agreements without trenching on any right of association protected by First Amendment; fact that such agreement necessarily takes form of words does not confer upon it, or upon underlying conduct, constitutional immunities that First Amendment extends to speech. U.S.C.A. Const.Amend. 1.

[4] **Constitutional Law** 🔑 90.1(1)
92k90.1(1)

First Amendment's free speech clause does not necessarily pose bar to liability for aiding and abetting crime, even when such aiding and abetting takes form of spoken or written word. U.S.C.A. Const.Amend. 1.

[5] **Constitutional Law** 🔑 90.1(1)
92k90.1(1)

Those speech acts which government may criminally prosecute with little or no concern for First Amendment's free speech clause, government may likewise subject to civil penalty or make subject to private causes of action, at least where government's interest in preventing particular conduct at issue is incontrovertibly compelling. U.S.C.A. Const.Amend. 1.

[6] **Constitutional Law** 🔑 90(3)
92k90(3)

In civil context, First Amendment's free speech clause may, at least in certain circumstances, superimpose upon speech-act doctrine heightened intent requirement in order that preeminent values underlying that constitutional provision not be imperiled. U.S.C.A. Const.Amend. 1.

[7] **Constitutional Law** 🔑 90.1(1)
92k90.1(1)

To prevent punishment or even chilling of entirely innocent, lawfully useful speech, First Amendment's free speech clause may in some contexts stand as bar to imposition of liability on basis of mere foreseeability or knowledge that information one imparts could be misused for impermissible purpose. U.S.C.A. Const.Amend. 1.

[8] **Constitutional Law** 🔑 90.1(1)
92k90.1(1)

Where speaker—individual or media—acts with purpose of assisting in commission of crime, First Amendment does not insulate that speaker from responsibility for his actions simply because he may have disseminated his message to wide audience; this is certainly so where not only speaker's dissemination or marketing strategy, but nature of speech itself, strongly suggest that audience both targeted and actually reached is, in actuality, very narrowly confined. U.S.C.A. Const.Amend. 1.

[9] **Constitutional Law** 🔑 90.1(1)
92k90.1(1)

First Amendment's free speech clause poses no bar to imposition of civil (or criminal) liability for speech acts which plaintiff (or prosecution) can establish were undertaken with specific, if not criminal, intent. U.S.C.A. Const.Amend. 1.

[10] **Federal Civil Procedure** 🔑 2515
170Ak2515

Genuine issues of material fact, precluding summary judgment for publisher of "hit man" instruction book in civil wrongful death action arising from triple murder which, according to publisher's own stipulation, was perpetrated with assistance of instructions in that book, existed as to whether publisher acted with requisite intent to render it liable under Maryland law for aiding and abetting murders.

[11] **Constitutional Law** 🔑 90.1(1)
92k90.1(1)

[11] **Torts** 🔑 21
379k21

First Amendment's free speech clause did not bar murder victims' survivors' civil aiding and abetting claims under Maryland law against publisher of "hit man" instruction manual that, according to publisher's own stipulations, was intended to assist criminals in perpetration of murders, and which, in fact, was relied upon by perpetrator of murders in question. U.S.C.A. Const.Amend. 1.

[12] **Torts** 🔑 21
379k21

Maryland recognizes civil cause of action for aiding and abetting.

[13] **Torts** 🔑 **21**

379k21

Generally, Maryland defines tort of aiding and abetting in same way that it defines crime of aiding and abetting; "aider" is one who assists, supports, or supplements efforts of another, and "abettor" is one who instigates, advises or encourages commission of crime.

[14] **Criminal Law** 🔑 **59(5)**

110k59(5)

To warrant aiding and abetting conviction under Maryland law, it is not essential that there be prearranged concert of action, although, in absence of such action, it is essential that defendant should in some way advocate or encourage commission of crime.

[15] **Criminal Law** 🔑 **59(5)**

110k59(5)

Criminal aiding and abetting may be predicated under Maryland law upon counseling or encouraging criminal act, even if there is no agreement between principal and aider or abettor; aiding and abetting does not always require conspiracy.

[16] **Criminal Law** 🔑 **59(5)**

110k59(5)

[16] **Torts** 🔑 **21**

379k21

Maryland law of aiding and abetting, as predicted by Court of Appeals, prescribes higher intent standard for imposition of criminal liability than it does for civil liability.

[17] **Federal Civil Procedure** 🔑 **2540**

170Ak2540

In ruling on defendant's motion for summary judgment, district court lacked authority to allow defendant to unilaterally alter parties' stipulation of fact.

[18] **Constitutional Law** 🔑 **90.1(1)**

92k90.1(1)

"Hit man" instruction book was not entitled to protection under First Amendment's free speech clause as abstract advocacy; book methodically and comprehensively prepared and steeled its audience to specific criminal conduct through exhaustively detailed instructions on planning, commission, and concealment of criminal conduct. U.S.C.A. Const.Amend. 1.

*235 ARGUED: <u>Rodney Alan Smolla</u>, Marshall-Wythe School of Law, College of William & Mary, Williamsburg, VA, for Appellants. <u>Thomas Buchan Kelley</u>, Faegre & Benson, L.L.P., Denver, CO, for Appellee. ON BRIEF: <u>John Marshall</u>, Moldawer & Marshall, Rockville, MD; Howard Siegel, Rockville, MD; <u>Thomas L. Heeney</u>, Heeney, Armstrong & Heeney, Rockville, MD, for Appellants. <u>Steven D. Zansberg</u>, Faegre & Benson, L.L.P., Denver, CO; <u>Lee Levine, Seth D. Berlin</u>, Levine, Pierson, Sullivan & Koch, L.L.P., Washington, DC, for Appellee. <u>David Crump</u>, University of Houston Law Center, Houston, TX, for Amicus Curiae Crump. <u>Neal Goldfarb</u>, D. Thomas Nelson, Russell Butler, Charles G. Brown, Ingersoll & Bloch, Washington, DC, for Amici Curiae National Victim Center, et al. <u>Douglas E. Winter</u>, Bryan Cave, L.L.P., Washington, DC, for Amicus Curiae Horror Writers Association. Robert M. O'Neil, <u>J. Joshua Wheeler</u>, The Thomas Jefferson Center for the Protection of Free Expression, Charlottesville, VA; Dwight H. Sullivan, American Civil Liberties Union Foundation of Maryland, Baltimore, MD; <u>Arthur Spitzer</u>, American Civil Liberties Union of the National Capital Area, Washington, DC; <u>Mark Silverstein</u>, American Civil Liberties Union of Colorado, Denver, CO, for Amici Curiae Thomas Jefferson Center, et al. <u>Bruce W. Sanford, Henry S. Hoberman</u>, Michael J. Lorenger, Baker & Hostetler, L.L.P., College Park, MD, for Amici Curiae ABC, et al.

Before <u>WILKINS</u>, <u>LUTTIG</u>, and <u>WILLIAMS</u>, Circuit Judges.

Reversed and remanded by published opinion. Judge <u>LUTTIG</u> wrote the opinion, in which Judges <u>WILKINS</u> and <u>WILLIAMS</u> joined.

OPINION

<u>LUTTIG</u>, Circuit Judge:

> To Those Who Think,
>
> To Those Who Do,
>
> To Those Who Succeed.

Success is nothing more than taking advantage of an opportunity.

A WOMAN RECENTLY ASKED HOW I could, in good conscience, write an instruction book on murder.

*236 "How can you live with yourself if someone uses what you write to go out and take a human life?" she whined.

I am afraid she was quite offended by my answer.

It is my opinion that the professional hit man fills a need in society and is, at times, the only alternative for "personal" justice. Moreover, if my advice and the proven methods in this book are followed, certainly no one will ever know.

[A]lmost every man harbors a fantasy of living the life of Mack Bolan or some other fictional hero who kills for fun and profit. They dream of living by their reflexes, of doing whatever is necessary without regard to moral or legal restrictions. But few have the courage or knowledge to make that dream a reality.

You might be like my friends—interested but unsure, standing on the sidelines afraid to play the game because you don't know the rules. [But] within the pages of this book you will learn one of the most successful methods of operation used by an independent contractor. You will follow the procedures of a man who works alone, without backing of organized crime or on a personal vendetta. Step by step you will be taken from research to equipment selection to job preparation to successful job completion. You will learn where to find employment, how much to charge, and what you can, and cannot, do with the money you earn.

But deny your urge to skip about, looking for the "good" parts. Start where any amateur who is serious about turning professional will start—at the beginning.

[And when] [y]ou've read all the suggested material, you [will have] honed your mind, body and reflexes into a precision piece of professional machinery. You [will have] assembled the necessary tools and learned to use them efficiently. Your knowledge of dealing death [will have] increased to the point where you have a choice of methods. Finally, you [will be] confident and competent enough to accept employment.

[When you go to commit the murder, you will need] several (at least four or five pairs) of flesh-tone, tight-fitting surgical gloves. If these are not available, rubber gloves can be purchased at a reasonable price in the prescription department of most drug stores in boxes of 100. You will wear the gloves when you assemble and disassemble your weapons as well as on the actual job. Because the metal gun parts cause the rubber to wear quickly, it is a good practice to change and dispose of worn gloves several times during each operation.

[The bag you take to the kill also] should contain a few pairs of cheap handcuffs, usually available at pawn shops or army surplus stores.

Dress, as well as disguises, should be coordinated according to the job setting.

Black, dark brown or olive green clothes do not stand out and will probably appear at first glance to be a mechanic or delivery driver's uniform. . . . And underneath, you can wear your street clothes for a quick change after the job is completed.

The kill is the easiest part of the job. People kill one another every day. It takes no great effort to pull a trigger or plunge a knife. It is being able to do so in a manner that will not link yourself or your employer to the crime that makes you a professional.

[If you decide to kill your victim with a knife,] [t]he knife . . . should have a six-inch blade with a serrated edge for making efficient, quiet kills.

The knife should have a double-edged blade. This double edge, combined with the serrated section and six-inch length, will insure a deep, ragged tear, and the wound will be difficult, if not impossible, to close without prompt medical attention.

Make your thrusts to a vital organ and twist the knife before you withdraw it. If you hit bone, you will have to file the blade to remove the marks left on the metal when it struck the victim's bone.

Using your six inch, serrated blade knife, stab deeply into the side of the victim's neck and push the knife forward in a forceful movement. This method will halfdecapitate the victim, cutting both his *237 main arteries and wind pipe, ensuring immediate death.

[You might also use an ice pick to murder your victim.] . . . An ice pick can . . . be driven into the victim's brain, through the ear, after he has been subdued. The wound hardly bleeds at all, and death is sometimes attributed to natural causes.

[If you plan to kill your victim with a gun,] you will learn [on the following pages] how to make, without need of special engineering ability or expensive machine shop tools, a silencer of the highest quality and effectiveness. The finished product attached to your 22 will be no louder than the noise made by a pellet gun. Because it is so inexpensive (mine cost less than twenty dollars to make), you can easily dispose of it after job use without any great loss. . . . Your first silencer will require possibly two days total to assemble . . . as you carefully follow the directions step by step. After you make a couple, it will become so easy, so routine, that you can whip one up in just a few hours.

The following items should be assembled before you begin [to build your silencer]:

—Drill rod, 7/32 inch (order from a machine shop if not obtainable locally)

—One foot of 1-1/2 inch (inside diameter) PVC tubing and two end caps

—One quart of fiberglass resin with hardener

—One yard thin fiberglass mat

[List continues]

[If you plan to kill your victim with a gun,][c]lose kills are by far preferred to shots fired over a long distance. You will need to know beyond any doubt that the desired result has been achieved.

When using a small caliber weapon like the 22, it is best to shoot from a distance of three to six feet. You will not want to be at pointblank range to avoid having the victim's blood splatter you or your clothing. At least three shots should be fired to ensure quick and sure death.

[If you plan to kill your victim from a distance,] use a rifle with a good scope and silencer and aim for the head—preferably the eye sockets if you are a sharpshooter. Many people have been shot repeatedly, even in the head, and survived to tell about it.

The rifle has a ridge on top that will easily accept a scope, even though it is not cut for one. Put the scope in place, tighten it down, then sight it in. After sighting in, scratch a mark behind each scope clamp to allow remounting of the scope without resighting each time.

Extra clips are a must for both the rifle and pistol and should be carried as a precautionary measure. Hollow-point bullets are recommended because they deform on impact, making them nontraceable. As an added precaution, you can fill the hollows with liquid poison to insure success of your operation. . . . [Details follow]

To test your guns and ammunition, set up a sheet of quarter-inch plywood at distances of two to seven yards maximum for your pistol, and twenty to sixty yards maximum for your rifle. Check for penetration of bullets at each range. Quarter-inch plywood is only a little stronger than the human skull.

If the serial number is on the barrel of the gun, grinding deeply enough to remove it may weaken the barrel to the point that the gun could explode in your face when fired. To make these numbers untraceable, [instructions follow].

[After shooting your victim] run a [specified tool] down the bore of the gun to change the ballistic markings. Do this even though you intend to discard the crime weapon. . . . If, for some reason, you just can't bear to part with your weapon . . . alter the [specified parts of the gun according to the directions that follow].

Although several shots fired in succession offer quick and relatively humane death to the victim, there are instances when other methods of extermination are called for. The employer may want you to gather certain information from the mark before you do away with him. At other times, the assignment may call for torture or disfigurement as a "lesson" for the survivors.

There is no end to the various ways of torturing a mark until he would tell you what you want to know, and die just to get it over. Sometimes all it takes is putting a knife to his throat. Not from behind with the blade across the throat the way they do in the movies, but from the front with the tip of the blade creasing the soft hollow of the throat, where the victim can see the gleaming steel and realizes what damage it would do if fully penetrated.

The only time I can think of that explosives might be in order is when several marks will be together in one place at the same time, and you might be able to get them all with one shot. Notice that I stressed the word might. Shrapnel doesn't always kill. So in the aftermath, it will be your responsibility to enter the area and make sure that the desired result was accomplished.

[If you plan to kill your victim with a fertilizer bomb,] purchase a fifty pound bag of regular garden fertilizer from your garden center [and follow these detailed instructions for constructing the bomb]. Extend the fuse and light. . . .

Arson is a good method for covering a kill or creating an "accident."

Don't ever use gasoline or other traceable materials to start your fire. [Specified substance] is your best starter because it burns away all traces.

[In order to dispose of a corpse,] you can simply cut off the head after burying the body. Take the head to some deserted location, place a stick of dynamite in the mouth, and blow the telltale dentition to smithereens! After this, authorities can't use the victim's dental records to identify his remains. As the body decomposes, fingerprints will disappear and no real evidence will be left from which to make positive identification. You can even clip off the fingertips and bury them separately.

[Or] you can always cut the body into sections and pack it into an ice chest for transport and disposal at various spots around the countryside.

If you choose to sink the corpse, you must first make several deep stabs into the body's lungs (from just under the rib cage) and belly. This is necessary because gases released during decomposition will bloat these organs, causing the body to rise to the surface of the water.

The corpse should be weighted with the standard concrete blocks, but it must be wrapped from head to toe with heavy chain as well, to keep the body from separating and floating in chunks to the surface. After the fishes and natural elements have done their work, the chain will drag the bones into the muddy sediment. . . .

If you bury the body, again deep stab wounds should be made to allow the gases to escape. A bloating corpse will push the earth up as it swells. Pour in lime to prevent the horrible odor of decomposition, and lye to make that decomposition more rapid.

[After you killed your first victim,] you felt absolutely nothing. And you are shocked by the nothingness. You had expected this moment to be a spectacular point in your life. You had wondered if you would feel compassion for the victim, immediate guilt, or even experience direct intervention by the hand of God. But you weren't even feeling sickened by the sight of the body.

After you have arrived home the events that took place take on a dreamlike quality. You don't dwell on them. You don't worry. You don't have nightmares. You don't fear ghosts. When thoughts of the hit go through your mind, it's almost as though you are recalling some show you saw on television.

By the time you collect the balance of your contract fee, the doubts and fears of discovery have faded. Those feelings have been replaced by cockiness, a feeling of superiority, a new independence and self-assurance.

[E]verything seems to have changed.

The people around you have suddenly become so aggravatingly ordinary. You start to view them as an irritating herd of pathetic sheep, doing as they are told, doing what is expected, following someone, anyone, blindly. You can't believe how dumb your friends have become, and your respect diminishes for people you once held in awe.

You too have become different. You recognize that you made some mistakes, but you know what they were, and they will never plague you again. Next time (and you know there will be a next time), there will be no hesitation, no fear.

Your experience in facing death head-on has taught you about life. You have the power and ability to stand alone. You no longer need a reason to kill.

The things you have learned about life are important. You may wish to pass on your observations to someone you care about. When the bullshit starts to flow, you may feel compelled to set the record straight and tell those morons how it really is. When someone starts to brag, in confidence, about something he's done, the intimacy of the moment, the shared confessions, may inspire you to do a little bragging of your own. Or you may want to overawe some new woman in your life with your masculinity and you feel the urge to shock her just a little by hinting at your true profession.

Start now in learning to control your ego. That means, above all, keeping your mouth shut! You are a man. Without a doubt, you have proved it. You have come face to face with death and emerged the victor through your cunning and expertise. You have dealt death as a professional. You don't need any second or third opinions to verify your manhood.

Then, some day, when you've done and seen it all; when there doesn't seem to be any challenge left or any new frontier left to conquer, you might just feel cocky enough to write a book about it. [FN1]

> FN1. The foregoing passages from Hit Man: A Technical Manual for Independent Contractors have been selected by the court as representative, both in substance and presentation, of the instructions in Hit Man. These are but a small fraction of the total number of instructions that appear in the 130-page manual. And the court has even felt it necessary to omit portions of these few illustrative passages in order to minimize the danger to the public from their repetition herein.

I.

On the night of March 3, 1993, readied by these instructions and steeled by these seductive adjurations from Hit Man: A Technical Manual for Independent Contractors, a copy of which was subsequently found in his apartment, James Perry brutally murdered Mildred Horn, her eight-year-old quadriplegic son

Trevor, and Trevor's nurse, Janice Saunders, by shooting Mildred Horn and Saunders through the eyes and by strangling Trevor Horn. Perry's despicable crime was not one of vengeance; he did not know any of his victims. Nor did he commit the murders in the course of another offense. Perry acted instead as a contract killer, a "hit man," hired by Mildred Horn's ex-husband, Lawrence Horn, to murder Horn's family so that Horn would receive the $2 million that his eight-year-old son had received in settlement for injuries that had previously left him paralyzed for life. At the time of the murders, this money was held in trust for the benefit of Trevor, and, under the terms of the trust instrument, the trust money was to be distributed tax-free to Lawrence in the event of Mildred's and Trevor's deaths.

In soliciting, preparing for, and committing these murders, Perry meticulously followed countless of Hit Man's 130 pages of detailed factual instructions on how to murder and to become a professional killer.

Perry, for example, followed many of the book's instructions on soliciting a client and arranging for a contract murder in his solicitation of and negotiation with Lawrence Horn. Cautioning against the placement of advertisements in military or gun magazines, as this might prompt "a personal visit from the FBI," Hit Man instructs that "as a beginner" one should solicit business "through a personal acquaintance whom you trust." Hit Man at 87. James Perry offered his services as a professional killer to Lawrence Horn through Thomas Turner, a "good friend" of Perry's, and Lawrence Horn's first cousin. Perry v. State, 344 Md. 204, 686 A.2d 274, 278 (1996), cert. denied, 520 U.S. 1146, 117 S.Ct. 1318, 137 L.Ed.2d 480 (1997).

Hit Man instructs to request "expense money" from the employer prior to committing the crime, advising the contract killer to get "all expense money up front." Hit Man at 92 (emphasis added). The manual goes on to explain that this amount should generally range from five hundred to five thousand dollars, "depending on the type of job and the job location," and that the advance should be paid in cash. Id. Prior to commission of the murders, Lawrence Horn paid James Perry three thousand five hundred dollars through a series of wire transfers using phony names. Perry, 686 A.2d at 280.

Hit Man instructs that the victim's personal residence is the "initial choice" location for a murder and "an ideal place to make a hit," depending on its "layout"

and "position." Hit Man at 81-82. James Perry murdered the Horns at their place of residence. Perry, 686 A.2d at 277.

Hit Man instructs its readers to use a rental car to reach the victim's location, Hit Man at 98, and to "steal an out-of-state tag" and use it to "replace the rental tag" on the car, explaining that "[s]tolen tags only show up on the police computer of the state in which they are stolen." Id. James Perry stole out-of-state tags and affixed them to his rental car before driving it to the Horns' residence on the night of the murders. Perry, 686 A.2d at 276.

Hit Man instructs the reader to establish a base at a motel in close proximity to the "jobsite" before committing the murders. Hit Man at 101. On the night that he killed Mildred and Trevor Horn and Janice Saunders, James Perry took a room at a Days Inn motel in Rockville, Maryland, a short drive from the Horns' residence. Perry, 686 A.2d at 276.

Hit Man instructs that one should "use a made-up [license] tag number" when registering at the motel or hotel. Hit Man at 102. James Perry gave a false license tag number when he registered at the Days Inn on the night of the murders. Perry, 686 A.2d at 276.

Hit Man instructs that a "beginner" should use an AR-7 rifle to kill his victims. Hit Man at 21. James Perry used an AR-7 rifle to slay Mildred Horn and Janice Saunders. Perry, 686 A.2d at 279.

Hit Man instructs its readers where to find the serial numbers on an AR-7 rifle, and instructs them that, prior to using the weapon, they should "completely drill[ ] out" these serial numbers so that the weapon cannot be traced. Hit Man at 23. James Perry drilled out the serial numbers of his weapon exactly as the book instructs. Perry, 686 A.2d at 280.

Hit Man instructs in "explicit detail" (replete with photographs) how to construct, "without [the] need of special engineering ability or machine shop tools," a homemade, "whisper-quiet" silencer from material available in any hardware store. Hit Man at 39-51. James Perry constructed such a homemade silencer and used it on the night that he murdered Mildred and Trevor Horn and Janice Saunders. J.A. at 24.

Perry also followed any number of Hit Man's instructions on how to commit the murder itself. The manual, for example, instructs its readers to kill their "mark" at close range, so that they will "know beyond any doubt that the desired result has been achieved." Hit Man at 24. The book also cautions, however, that the killer should not shoot the victim at point blank range, because "the victim's blood [will] splatter [the killer] or [his] clothing." Id. Ultimately, the book recommends that its readers "shoot [their victims] from a distance of three to six feet." Id. James Perry shot Mildred Horn and Janice Saunders from a distance of three feet. J.A. at 24.

Hit Man specifically instructs its audience of killers to shoot the victim through the eyes if possible:

> At least three shots should be fired to insure quick and sure death. . . . [A]im for the head—preferably the eye sockets if you are a sharpshooter.

Hit Man at 24. James Perry shot Mildred Horn and Janice Saunders two or three times and through the eyes. Perry, 686 A.2d at 277.

Finally, Perry followed many of Hit Man's instructions for concealing his murders. Hit Man instructs the killer to "[p]ick up those empty cartridges that were ejected when you fired your gun." Hit Man at 104. Although Perry fired his rifle numerous times during the murders, no spent cartridges were found in the area. Compare Perry, 686 A.2d at 277, with id. at 280.

Hit Man instructs the killer to disguise the contract murder as burglary by "mess[ing] the place up a bit and tak[ing] anything of value that you can carry concealed." Hit Man at 104. After killing Mildred and Trevor Horn and Janice Saunders, James Perry took a Gucci watch, as well as some credit cards and bank cards from Mildred Horn's wallet. Perry, 686 A.2d at 278. According to the police report, a few areas of the Horns' residence appeared "disturbed" or "slightly tossed," and "a rug and cocktail table in the living room had been moved." Id. at 277.

Hit Man instructs that, after murdering the victims, the killer should break down the AR-7 in order to make the weapon easier to conceal. Hit Man at 105. James Perry disassembled his weapon after the murders, in accordance with the instructions in Hit Man. Perry, 686 A.2d at 280.

Hit Man instructs killers to use specified tools to alter specified parts of the rifle. Hit Man at 25. The author explains that the described alterations will prevent the police laboratory from matching the bullets recovered from the victims' bodies to the murder weapon. James Perry altered his AR-7 in accordance with these instructions. Perry, 686 A.2d at 280.

Hit Man also instructs the killer to dispose of the murder weapon by scattering the disassembled pieces of the weapon along the road as he leaves the crime scene. Hit Man at 105. And, after killing Mildred and Trevor Horn and Janice Saunders, Perry scattered the pieces of his disassembled AR-7 rifle along Route 28 in Montgomery County. Perry, 686 A.2d at 280.

In this civil, state-law wrongful death action against defendant Paladin Enterprises—the publisher of Hit Man—the relatives and representatives of Mildred and Trevor Horn and Janice Saunders allege that Paladin aided and abetted Perry in the commission of his murders through its publication of Hit Man's killing instructions. For reasons that are here of no concern to the court, Paladin has stipulated to a set of facts which establish as a matter of law that the publisher is civilly liable for aiding and abetting James Perry in his triple murder, unless the First Amendment absolutely bars the imposition of liability upon a publisher for assisting in the commission of criminal acts. As the parties stipulate: "The parties agree that the sole issue to be decided by the Court . . . is whether the First Amendment is a complete defense, as a matter of law, to the civil action set forth in the plaintiffs' Complaint. All other issues of law and fact are specifically reserved for subsequent proceedings." J.A. at 58.

> Paladin, for example, has stipulated for purposes of summary judgment that Perry followed the above-enumerated instructions from Hit Man, as well as instructions from another Paladin publication, How to Make a Disposable Silencer, Vol. II, in planning, executing, and attempting to cover up the murders of Mildred and Trevor Horn and Janice Saunders. J.A. at 61. Paladin has stipulated not only that, in marketing Hit Man, Paladin "intended to attract and assist criminals and would-be criminals who desire information and instructions on how to commit crimes," J.A. at 59, but also that it "intended and had knowledge" that Hit Man actually "would be used, upon receipt, by criminals and would-be criminals to plan and execute the crime of murder for hire." J.A. at 59 (emphasis added). Indeed, the publisher has even stipulated that, through publishing and selling Hit Man, it assisted Perry in particular in the perpetration of the very murders for which the victims' families now attempt to hold Paladin civilly liable. J.A. at 61. [FN2]

FN2. The full fact stipulation of the parties reads as follows:

JOINT STATEMENT OF FACTS

The parties agree that the matters set forth below represent facts that the plaintiffs and/or defendants would be able to establish by affidavit or otherwise in the context of defendants' motion for summary judgment under F.R.C.P. 56. These facts are offered only for the purposes of this motion and the parties specifically reserve the right to contest all statements which follow at any subsequent proceeding in this case. The parties agree that the sole issue to be decided by the Court in this motion is whether the First Amendment is a complete defense, as a matter of law, to the civil action set forth in the plaintiffs' Complaint. All other issues of law and fact are specifically reserved for subsequent proceedings.

1. Prior to March 3, 1993, Lawrence Horn began plotting with James Perry of Detroit, Michigan, to have Perry murder his ex-wife, Mildred Horn, and his son, Trevor. 2. On or about January 24, 1992, James Perry responded to a catalogue solicitation by the defendant, Paladin, advertising Hit Man: A Technical Manual for Independent Contractors (hereinafter referred to as "Hit Man"), and How to Make a Disposable Silencer, Volume 2 (hereinafter referred to as "Silencers"). Perry ordered both publications. Hit Man and Silencers were mailed to him by the defendants shortly thereafter.

3. Defendants had no other known contact with Perry and no contacts with Lawrence Horn.

4. Defendants concede, for purposes of this motion, and for no other purposes, that:

a. defendants engaged in a marketing strategy intended to attract and assist criminals and would-be criminals who desire information and instructions on how to commit crimes; and

b. in publishing, marketing, advertising and distributing Hit Man and Silencers, defendants intended and had knowledge that their publications would be used, upon receipt, by criminals and would-be criminals to plan and execute the crime of murder for hire, in the manner set forth in the publications.

c. The conditional factual concessions made in this § 4 relate only to the defendants' state of mind, and do not preclude defendants from contending that defendants' published words, in and of themselves, were neither directed at causing imminent unlawful action nor likely to produce such action, for purposes of the doctrine of Brandenburg v. Ohio, 395 U.S. 444, 89 S.Ct. 1827, 23 L.Ed.2d 430 (1969). 5. Plaintiffs concede, for purposes of this motion and for no other purposes, that:

a. defendants' marketing strategy was and is intended to maximize sales of its publications to the public, including sales to (i) authors who desire information for the purpose of writing books about crime and criminals, (ii) law enforcement officers and agencies who desire information concerning the means and methods of committing crimes, (iii) persons who enjoy reading accounts of crimes and the means of committing them for purposes of entertainment, (iv) persons who fantasize about committing crimes but do not thereafter commit them, and (v) criminologists and others who study criminal methods and mentality.

b. in publishing, marketing, advertising and distributing Hit Man and Silencers, as well as other publications, defendants intended and had knowledge that their publications would be purchased by members of the general public, including those persons and for those purposes listed in § 5(a).

c. The conditional factual concessions made in this § 5 shall not preclude the plaintiffs from contending that such facts are irrelevant to any issue before this court. 6. On March 3, 1993, James Perry traveled from Detroit, Michigan to Montgomery County, Maryland and murdered Mildred Horn, Trevor Horn, and Janice Saunders, Trevor's private duty nurse. Perry followed a number of instructions outlined in Hit Man and Silencers (set forth in § 7 below) in planning, executing and attempting to get away with the murders described in the complaint.

7. Defendants concede, for the purpose of this motion and for no other purposes, that in publishing, distributing and selling Hit Man and Silencers to Perry, defendants assisted him in the subsequent perpetration of the murders which are the subject of this litigation, in the ways set forth in paragraphs 18 and 19 of the Rice complaint and paragraphs 20 and 21 of the Saunders complaint which are incorporated by reference and are filed herewith as exhibit "D".

8. Hit Man was first published in 1983 and Silencers was first published in 1983. Approximately 13,000 copies of Hit Man and an unknown but not disproportionate number of copies of Silencers have been sold nationally.

9. At all relevant times, defendants had no specific knowledge (1) that either Perry or Horn planned to commit a crime; (2) that Perry and Horn had entered into a conspiracy for the purpose of committing a crime; and (3) that Perry had been retained by Horn to murder Mildred Horn, Trevor Horn, or Janice Saunders. 10. The defendants' current catalogue, and publications Hit Man and Silencers are filed herewith by the parties as exhibits A, B and C, respectively.

11. The parties may file affidavits or supplement but not alter the foregoing stipulation. Plaintiffs reserve the right to challenge defendants' affidavits declarations with counter-affidavits or pursuant to F.R.C.P. 56.

J.A. at 58-62.

Notwithstanding Paladin's extraordinary stipulations that it not only knew that its instructions might be used by murderers, but that it actually intended to provide assistance to murderers and would-be murderers which would be used by them "upon receipt," and that it in fact assisted Perry in particular in the commission of the murders of Mildred and Trevor Horn and Janice Saunders, the district court granted Paladin's motion for summary judgment and dismissed plaintiffs' claims that Paladin aided and abetted Perry, holding that these claims were barred by the First Amendment as a matter of law.

Because long-established caselaw provides that speech—even speech by the press—that constitutes criminal aiding and abetting does not enjoy the protection of the First Amendment, and because we are convinced that such caselaw is both correct and equally applicable to speech that constitutes civil aiding and abetting of criminal conduct (at least where, as here, the defendant has the specific purpose of assisting and encouraging commission of such conduct and the alleged assistance and encouragement takes a form other than abstract advocacy), we hold, as urged by the Attorney General and the Department of Justice, that the First Amendment does not pose a bar to a finding that Paladin is civilly liable as an aider and abetter of Perry's triple contract murder. We also hold that the plaintiffs have stated against Paladin a civil aiding and abetting claim under Maryland law

sufficient to withstand Paladin's motion for summary judgment. For these reasons, which we fully explain below, the district court's grant of summary judgment in Paladin's favor is reversed and the case is remanded for trial.

II.
A.

[1] In the seminal case of Brandenburg v. Ohio, 395 U.S. 444, 89 S.Ct. 1827, 23 L.Ed.2d 430 (1969), the Supreme Court held that abstract advocacy of lawlessness is protected speech under the First Amendment. Although the Court provided little explanation for this holding in its brief per curiam opinion, it is evident the Court recognized from our own history that such a right to advocate lawlessness is, almost paradoxically, one of the ultimate safeguards of liberty. Even in a society of laws, one of the most indispensable freedoms is that to express in the most impassioned terms the most passionate disagreement with the laws themselves, the institutions of, and created by, law, and the individual officials with whom the laws and institutions are entrusted. Without the freedom to criticize that which constrains, there is no freedom at all.

[2][3] However, while even speech advocating lawlessness has long enjoyed protections under the First Amendment, it is equally well established that speech which, in its effect, is tantamount to legitimately proscribable nonexpressive conduct may itself be legitimately proscribed, punished, or regulated incidentally to the constitutional enforcement of generally applicable statutes. Cf. Cohen v. Cowles Media Co., 501 U.S. 663, 669, 111 S.Ct. 2513, 2518, 115 L.Ed.2d 586 (1991) (noting "well-established line of decisions holding that generally applicable laws do not offend the First Amendment simply because their enforcement against the press has incidental effects on its ability to gather and report the news"). As no less a First Amendment absolutist than Justice Black wrote for the Supreme Court almost fifty years ago in Giboney v. Empire Storage & Ice Co., in rejecting a First Amendment challenge to an injunction forbidding unionized distributors from picketing to force an illegal business arrangement:

> It rarely has been suggested that the constitutional freedom for speech and press extends its immunity to speech or writing used as an integral part of conduct in violation of a valid criminal statute. We reject the contention now. . . .

. . .

. . . It is true that the agreements and course of conduct here were as in most instances brought about through speaking or writing. But it has never been deemed an abridgment of freedom of speech or press to make a course of conduct illegal merely because the conduct was in part initiated, evidenced, or carried out by means of language, either spoken, written, or printed. Such an expansive interpretation of the constitutional guaranties of speech and press would make it practically impossible ever to enforce laws against agreements in restraint of trade as well as many other agreements and conspiracies deemed injurious to society.

336 U.S. 490, 498, 502, 69 S.Ct. 684, 688-89, 691, 93 L.Ed. 834 (1949) (citations omitted). And as the Court more recently reaffirmed:

Although agreements to engage in illegal conduct undoubtedly possess some element of association, the State may ban such illegal agreements without trenching on any right of association protected by the First Amendment. The fact that such an agreement necessarily takes the form of words does not confer upon it, or upon the underlying conduct, the constitutional immunities that the First Amendment extends to speech. [W]hile a solicitation to enter into an agreement arguably crosses the sometimes hazy line distinguishing conduct from pure speech, such a solicitation, even though it may have an impact in the political arena, remains in essence an invitation to engage in an illegal exchange for private profit, and may properly be prohibited.

Brown v. Hartlage, 456 U.S. 45, 55, 102 S.Ct. 1523, 1529-30, 71 L.Ed.2d 732 (1982); see also Osborne v. Ohio, 495 U.S. 103, 110, 110 S.Ct. 1691, 1696-97, 109 L.Ed.2d 98 (1990) (quoting Giboney, 336 U.S. at 498, 69 S.Ct. at 688-89); New York v. Ferber, 458 U.S. 747, 761-62, 102 S.Ct. 3348, 3356-57, 73 L.Ed.2d 1113 (1982) (same); Ohralik v. Ohio State Bar Ass'n, 436 U.S. 447, 456, 98 S.Ct. 1912, 1918-19, 56 L.Ed.2d 444 (1978) (quoting Giboney, 336 U.S. at 502, 69 S.Ct. at 690-91); National Organization for Women v. Operation Rescue, 37 F.3d 646, 656 (D.C.Cir.1994) ("That 'aiding and abetting' of an illegal act may be carried out through speech is no bar to its illegality."); United States v. Varani, 435 F.2d 758, 762 (6th Cir.1970) ("[S]peech is not protected by the First Amendment when it is the very vehicle of the crime itself."); Laurence H. Tribe, American Constitutional Law 837 (2d ed. 1988)

("[T]he law need not treat differently the crime of one man who sells a bomb to terrorists and that of another who publishes an instructional manual for terrorists on how to build their own bombs out of old Volkswagen parts.").

Were the First Amendment to bar or to limit government regulation of such "speech brigaded with action," Brandenburg, 395 U.S. at 456, 89 S.Ct. at 1834 (Douglas, J., concurring), the government would be powerless to protect the public from countless of even the most pernicious criminal acts and civil wrongs. See, e.g., Model Penal Code § 223.4 (extortion or blackmail); id. § 240.2 (threats and other improper influences in official and political matters); id. § 241 (perjury and various cognate crimes); id. § 5.02 and § 2.06(3)(a)(i) (criminal solicitation); 18 U.S.C. § 871 (threatening the life of the President); Model Penal Code § 5.03 (conspiracy); id. § 250.4 (harassment); id. § 224.1 (forgery); id. § 210.5(2) (successfully soliciting another to commit suicide); id. § 250.3 (false public alarms); and the like. As Professor Greenawalt succinctly summarized:

The reasons of ordinary penal policy for covering communicative efforts to carry out ordinary crimes are obvious, and the criminal law sensibly draws no distinction between communicative and other acts. Although assertions of fact generally fall within a principle of freedom of speech, what these sorts of factual statements contribute to the general understanding of listeners is minimal, and the justifications for free speech that apply to speakers do not reach communications that are simply means to get a crime successfully committed.

Greenawalt, Speech, Crime, and the Uses of Language at 85 (1989).

[4] In particular as it concerns the instant case, the speech-act doctrine has long been invoked to sustain convictions for aiding and abetting the commission of criminal offenses. Indeed, every court that has addressed the issue, including this court, has held that the First Amendment does not necessarily pose a bar to liability for aiding and abetting a crime, even when such aiding and abetting takes the form of the spoken or written word.

Thus, in a case indistinguishable in principle from that before us, the Ninth Circuit expressly held in United States v. Barnett, 667 F.2d 835 (9th Cir.1982), that the First Amendment does not provide publishers a defense as a matter of law to charges of aiding and abetting a crime through the publication and distribution of instructions on how to make illegal drugs. In rejecting the publisher's argument that there could be no probable cause to believe that a crime had been committed because its actions were shielded by the First Amendment, and thus a fortiori there was no probable cause to support the search pursuant to which the drug manufacturing instructions were found, the Court of Appeals explicitly foreclosed a First Amendment defense not only to the search itself, but also to a later prosecution:

To the extent . . . that Barnett appears to contend that he is immune from search or prosecution because he uses the printed word in encouraging and counseling others in the commission of a crime, we hold expressly that the first amendment does not provide a defense as a matter of law to such conduct.

Id. at 843 (emphasis in original); see also id. at 842 ("The first amendment does not provide a defense to a criminal charge simply because the actor uses words to carry out his illegal purpose. Crimes, including that of aiding and abetting, frequently involve the use of speech as part of the criminal transaction."). The Ninth Circuit derided as a "specious syllogism" with "no support in the law" the publisher's argument that the First Amendment protected his sale of the instruction manual simply because the First Amendment protects the written word. Id. at 842.

The principle of Barnett, that the provision of instructions that aid and abet another in the commission of a criminal offense is unprotected by the First Amendment, has been uniformly accepted, and the principle has been applied to the aiding and abetting of innumerable crimes.

Notably, then-Judge Kennedy, in express reliance upon Barnett, invoked the principle in United States v. Freeman to sustain convictions for the aiding and abetting of tax fraud. 761 F.2d 549, 552-53 (9th Cir.1985), cert. denied, 476 U.S. 1120, 106 S.Ct. 1982, 90 L.Ed.2d 664 (1986). In Freeman, the Ninth Circuit concluded that the defendant could be held criminally liable for counseling tax evasion at seminars held in protest of the tax laws, even though the speech that served as the predicate for the conviction "spr[ang] from the anterior motive to effect political or social change." 761 F.2d at 551. Said the court:

[T]he First Amendment is quite irrelevant if the intent of the actor and the objective meaning of the words used are so close in time and purpose to a substantive evil as to become part of the ultimate crime itself. In

those instances, where speech becomes an integral part of the crime, a First Amendment defense is foreclosed even if the prosecution rests on words alone.

Id. at 552 (citations omitted). Thus, the court held that a First Amendment instruction was required only for those counts as to which there was evidence that the speaker "directed his comments at the unfairness of the tax laws generally, without soliciting or counseling a violation of the law in an immediate sense [and] made statements that, at least arguably, were of abstract generality, remote from advice to commit a specific criminal act." Id. at 551-52. For those counts as to which the defendant, through his speech, directly assisted in the preparation and review of false tax returns, the court held that the defendant was not entitled to a First Amendment instruction at all. Id. at 552. See also United States v. Mendelsohn, 896 F.2d 1183, 1186 (9th Cir.1990) (holding Brandenburg inapplicable to a conviction for conspiring to transport and aiding and abetting the interstate transportation of wagering paraphernalia, where defendants disseminated a computer program that assisted others to record and analyze bets on sporting events; program was "too instrumental in and intertwined with the performance of criminal activity to retain first amendment protection").

Our own circuit, and every other circuit to address the issue, has likewise concluded that the First Amendment is generally inapplicable to charges of aiding and abetting violations of the tax laws. See, e.g., United States v. Kelley, 769 F.2d 215 (4th Cir.1985); United States v. Rowlee, 899 F.2d 1275 (2d Cir.1990), cert. denied, 498 U.S. 828, 111 S.Ct. 87, 112 L.Ed.2d 59 (1990); United States v. Moss, 604 F.2d 569 (8th Cir.1979), cert. denied, 444 U.S. 1071, 100 S.Ct. 1014, 62 L.Ed.2d 752 (1980); United States v. Buttorff, 572 F.2d 619, 623-24 (8th Cir.1978) (holding that tax evasion speeches were not subject to Brandenburg because, although they did not "incite the type of imminent lawless activity referred to in criminal syndicalism cases," they did "go beyond mere advocacy of tax reform"), cert. denied, 437 U.S. 906, 98 S.Ct. 3095, 57 L.Ed.2d 1136 (1978).

Thus, in Kelley, we held that a defendant who "participate[d]" in the preparation of false tax forms for others by telling listeners "what to do and how to prepare the forms" and by supplying forms and materials was not entitled to the protections of the First Amendment, 769 F.2d at 217, even though the defendant offered his advice in a meeting of a group concededly dedicated to the political belief "that the federal income tax is unconstitutional as applied to wages," id. at 216. We observed, as the Ninth Circuit did with respect to the claim made in Barnett, that,

[t]he claim of First Amendment protection of [Kelley's] speech is frivolous. His was no abstract criticism of income tax laws. His listeners were not urged to seek congressional action to exempt wages from income taxation. Instead, they were urged to file false returns, with every expectation that the advice would be heeded.

The cloak of the First Amendment envelops critical, but abstract, discussions of existing laws, but lends no protection to speech which urges the listeners to commit violations of current law. Brandenburg v. Ohio, 395 U.S. 444, 89 S.Ct. 1827, 23 L.Ed.2d 430; United States v. Buttorff, 572 F.2d 619 (8th Cir.1978). It was no theoretical discussion of non-compliance with laws; action was urged; the advice was heeded, and false forms were filed.

Kelley, 769 F.2d at 217. Analogously, we held in United States v. Fleschner, 98 F.3d 155 (4th Cir.1996), cert. denied, 521 U.S. 1106, 117 S.Ct. 2484, 138 L.Ed.2d 992 (1997), that defendants who instructed and advised meeting attendees to file unlawful tax returns were not entitled to a First Amendment jury instruction on the charge of conspiracy to defraud the United States of income tax revenue because "[t]he defendants' words and acts were not remote from the commission of the criminal acts." 98 F.3d at 158-59.

[5] Indeed, as the Department of Justice recently advised Congress, the law is now well established that the First Amendment, and Brandenburg's "imminence" requirement in particular, generally poses little obstacle to the punishment of speech that constitutes criminal aiding and abetting, because "culpability in such cases is premised, not on defendants' 'advocacy' of criminal conduct, but on defendants' successful efforts to assist others by detailing to them the means of accomplishing the crimes." Department of Justice, "Report on the Availability of Bombmaking Information, the Extent to Which Its Dissemination is Controlled by Federal Law, and the Extent to Which Such Dissemination May Be Subject to Regulation Consistent with the First Amendment to the United States Constitution" 37 (April 1997) (footnote omitted) [hereinafter "DOJ Report"]; see also id. ("[T]he question of whether criminal conduct is 'imminent' is relevant for constitutional purposes only where, as in Brandenburg itself, the government attempts to restrict advocacy, as

such."). [FN3] And, while there is considerably less authority on the subject, we assume that those speech acts which the government may criminally prosecute with little or no concern for the First Amendment, the government may likewise subject to civil penalty or make subject to private causes of action. Compare Garrison v. Louisiana, 379 U.S. 64, 85 S.Ct. 209, 13 L.Ed.2d 125 (1964) (applying the same "actual malice" standard to both criminal libel prosecutions and private defamation actions) with New York Times Co. v. Sullivan, 376 U.S. 254, 84 S.Ct. 710, 11 L.Ed.2d 686 (1964). Cf. Cohen, 501 U.S. 663, 111 S.Ct. 2513, 115 L.Ed.2d 586 (finding in civil promissory estoppel case that First Amendment does not bar liability for newspaper's publication of confidential source's name); Zacchini v. Scripps-Howard Broadcasting Co., 433 U.S. 562, 97 S.Ct. 2849, 53 L.Ed.2d 965 (1977) (First Amendment does not bar liability for common law tort of unlawful appropriation of "right to publicity" where television station broadcast "human cannonball" act in its entirety without plaintiff's authorization); Harper & Row, Publishers, Inc. v. Nation Enterprises, 471 U.S. 539, 105 S.Ct. 2218, 85 L.Ed.2d 588 (1985) (rejecting First Amendment defense to copyright infringement action against magazine for printing unauthorized presidential memoir excerpts). Even if this is not universally so, we believe it must be true at least where the government's interest in preventing the particular conduct at issue is incontrovertibly compelling.

FN3. Congress, in the Antiterrorism and Effective Death Penalty Act of 1996 ["the AEDPA"], Pub.L. No. 104-132, 110 Stat. 1214, 1297, required the Attorney General to conduct a study concerning, inter alia, the extent to which there is available public access to materials instructing on "how to make bombs, destructive devices, or weapons of mass destruction"; the application of then-existing federal laws to such materials; and the extent to which the First Amendment protects such materials and their private and commercial distribution. The statutory mandate to the Attorney General was prompted by legislation proposed by Senators Feinstein and Biden in the aftermath of the Oklahoma City bombing, which would criminalize the teaching or demonstration of the manufacture of explosive materials "if the person intends or knows that such explosive materials or information will likely be used for, or in furtherance of" specified criminal offenses. The AEDPA required the Attorney General to submit to the Congress a report on these subjects and to make that report available to the public. Recognizing that the exhaustive legal analysis set forth in that report was directly relevant to the issues pending before us, the parties jointly moved for, and we granted them, permission to file the report with the court. The decision we reach today, which, as noted, was urged upon us by Attorney General Reno and the Department of Justice, follows from the principal conclusion reached by the Attorney General and the Department in that report:

The First Amendment would impose substantial constraints on any attempt to proscribe indiscriminately the dissemination of bombmaking information. The government generally may not, except in rare circumstances, punish persons either for advocating lawless action or for disseminating truthful information—including information that would be dangerous if used—that such persons have obtained lawfully. However, the constitutional analysis is quite different where the government punishes speech that is an integral part of a transaction involving conduct the government otherwise is empowered to prohibit; such "speech acts"—for instance, many cases of inchoate crimes such as aiding and abetting and conspiracy—may be proscribed without much, if any, concern about the First Amendment, since it is merely incidental that such "conduct" takes the form of speech. DOJ Report at 2 (emphasis added).

B.

We can envision only two possible qualifications to these general rules, neither of which, for reasons that we discuss more extensively below, is of special moment in the context of the particular aiding and abetting case before us.

1.

[6][7][8] The first, which obviously would have practical import principally in the civil context, is that the First Amendment may, at least in certain circumstances, superimpose upon the speech-act doctrine a heightened intent requirement in order that preeminent values underlying that constitutional provision not be imperiled. See, e.g., New York Times, 376 U.S. 254, 84 S.Ct. 710, 11 L.Ed.2d 686; cf. United States v. Aguilar, 515 U.S. 593, 605, 115 S.Ct. 2357, 2365, 132 L.Ed.2d 520 (1995) (rejecting

defendant's First Amendment construction in part because "the statute here in question does not impose such a restriction [on the disclosure of wiretap authorizations] generally, but only upon those who disclose wiretap information 'in order to [ob]struct, impede, or prevent' a wiretap interception" (emphasis added)); Haig v. Agee, 453 U.S. 280, 308-09, 101 S.Ct. 2766, 2783, 69 L.Ed.2d 640 (1981) ("[The defendant's] disclosures, among other things, have the declared purpose of obstructing intelligence operations and the recruiting of intelligence personnel. They are clearly not protected by the Constitution." (emphasis added)); United States v. Featherston, 461 F.2d 1119, 1122 (5th Cir.1972) (rejecting First Amendment challenge to federal statute criminalizing the teaching or demonstration of the making of any explosive device after construing statute to require "intent or knowledge that the information disseminated would be used in the furtherance of a civil disorder"), cert. denied, 409 U.S. 991, 93 S.Ct. 339, 34 L.Ed.2d 258 (1972); National Mobilization Committee to End the War in Viet Nam v. Foran, 411 F.2d 934, 937 (7th Cir.1969). That is, in order to prevent the punishment or even the chilling of entirely innocent, lawfully useful speech, the First Amendment may in some contexts stand as a bar to the imposition of liability on the basis of mere foreseeability or knowledge that the information one imparts could be misused for an impermissible purpose. Where it is necessary, such a limitation would meet the quite legitimate, if not compelling, concern of those who publish, broadcast, or distribute to large, undifferentiated audiences, that the exposure to suit under lesser standards would be intolerable. See discussion infra, Part IV. At the same time, it would not relieve from liability those who would, for profit or other motive, intentionally assist and encourage crime and then shamelessly seek refuge in the sanctuary of the First Amendment. Like our sister circuits, at the very least where a speaker—individual or media—acts with the purpose of assisting in the commission of crime, we do not believe that the First Amendment insulates that speaker from responsibility for his actions simply because he may have disseminated his message to a wide audience. See, e.g., Barnett, 667 F.2d 835 (holding that drug manufacturing instructions mailed to countless customers with whom the defendant had no personal contact could give rise to aiding and abetting conviction); Mendelsohn, 896 F.2d 1183 (holding that First Amendment did not forbid prosecution of aiding and abetting interstate transportation of wagering paraphernalia where computer programs for recording and analyzing illegal wagers were distributed generally and widely to the public); Buttorff, 572 F.2d at 622-23 (affirming, despite First Amendment challenges, convictions for providing tax-evasion information at "large public gatherings" to participants whom the defendants did not personally meet); Kelley, 769 F.2d 215 (similar); Moss, 604 F.2d 569 (similar); Freeman, 761 F.2d 549 (similar). This is certainly so, we are satisfied, where not only the speaker's dissemination or marketing strategy, but the nature of the speech itself, strongly suggest that the audience both targeted and actually reached is, in actuality, very narrowly confined, as in the case before us. See discussion infra at 253-256. Were the First Amendment to offer protection even in these circumstances, one could publish, by traditional means or even on the internet, the necessary plans and instructions for assassinating the President, for poisoning a city's water supply, for blowing up a skyscraper or public building, or for similar acts of terror and mass destruction, with the specific, indeed even the admitted, purpose of assisting such crimes—all with impunity.

[9][10] We need not engage in an extended discussion of the existence or scope of an intent-based limitation today, however, because we are confident that the First Amendment poses no bar to the imposition of civil (or criminal) liability for speech acts which the plaintiff (or the prosecution) can establish were undertaken with specific, if not criminal, intent. See DOJ Report at 42-43 (advising that "the government may punish publication of dangerous instructional information where that publication is motivated by a desire to facilitate the unlawful [conduct as to which the instructions inform, or] [a]t the very least, publication with such an improper intent should not be constitutionally protected where it is foreseeable that the publication will be used for criminal purposes. . . ."). In fact, this conclusion would seem to follow a fortiori from the Supreme Court's holding in New York Times, 376 U.S. 254, 84 S.Ct. 710, 11 L.Ed.2d 686, allowing the imposition of civil tort liability on a media defendant for reputational injury caused by mere reckless disregard of the truth of its published statements. And, here, as previously noted, see also discussion infra at 252-53, Paladin has stipulated that it provided its assistance to Perry with both the knowledge and the intent that the book would immediately be used by criminals and would-be criminals in the solicitation, planning, and commission of murder and murder for hire, and even

absent the stipulations, a jury could reasonably find such specific intent, see discussion infra at 253-55. Thus, Paladin has stipulated to an intent, and a jury could otherwise reasonably find that Paladin acted with a kind and degree of intent, that would satisfy any heightened standard that might be required by the First Amendment prerequisite to the imposition of liability for aiding and abetting through speech conduct. [FN4]

> FN4. In addition to their aiding and abetting counts, which require that Paladin have acted knowingly or intentionally, the plaintiffs also brought claims sounding inter alia in negligence and strict liability. The district court did not address these claims and we do not do so herein. We leave to the district court on remand the task of addressing these counts in the first instance.

2.

[11] The second qualification is that the First Amendment might well (and presumably would) interpose the same or similar limitations upon the imposition of civil liability for abstract advocacy, without more, that it interposes upon the imposition of criminal punishment for such advocacy. In other words, the First Amendment might well circumscribe the power of the state to create and enforce a cause of action that would permit the imposition of civil liability, such as aiding and abetting civil liability, for speech that would constitute pure abstract advocacy, at least if that speech were not "directed to inciting or producing imminent lawless action, and . . . likely to incite or produce such action." Brandenburg, 395 U.S. at 447, 89 S.Ct. at 1829. The instances in which such advocacy might give rise to civil liability under state statute would seem rare, but they are not inconceivable. Cf. Schenck v. United States, 249 U.S. 47, 39 S.Ct. 247, 63 L.Ed. 470 (1919) (criminal conspiracy prosecution predicated upon subversive advocacy); Frohwerk v. United States, 249 U.S. 204, 39 S.Ct. 249, 63 L.Ed. 561 (1919) (same); Debs v. United States, 249 U.S. 211, 39 S.Ct. 252, 63 L.Ed. 566 (1919) (criminal attempt prosecution predicated upon such advocacy). Again, however, an exhaustive analysis of this likely limitation is not required in this case.

Here, it is alleged, and a jury could reasonably find, see discussion infra Part III.A, that Paladin aided and abetted the murders at issue through the quintessential speech act of providing step-by-step instructions for murder (replete with photographs, diagrams, and narration) so comprehensive and detailed that it is as if the instructor were literally present with the would-be murderer not only in the preparation and planning, but in the actual commission of, and follow-up to, the murder; there is not even a hint that the aid was provided in the form of speech that might constitute abstract advocacy. As the district court itself concluded, Hit Man "merely teaches what must be done to implement a professional hit." J.A. at 218. Moreover, although we do not believe such would be necessary, we are satisfied a jury could readily find that the provided instructions not only have no, or virtually no, noninstructional communicative value, but also that their only instructional communicative "value" is the indisputably illegitimate one of training persons how to murder and to engage in the business of murder for hire. See id.; see also id. at 221 ("This Court, quite candidly, personally finds Hit Man to be reprehensible and devoid of any significant redeeming social value").

Aid and assistance in the form of this kind of speech bears no resemblance to the "theoretical advocacy," Scales v. United States, 367 U.S. 203, 235, 81 S.Ct. 1469, 1489, 6 L.Ed.2d 782 (1961), the advocacy of "principles divorced from action," Yates v. United States, 354 U.S. 298, 320, 77 S.Ct. 1064, 1077, 1 L.Ed.2d 1356 (1957), overruled on other grounds, Burks v. United States, 437 U.S. 1, 98 S.Ct. 2141, 57 L.Ed.2d 1 (1978), the "doctrinal justification," id. at 321, 77 S.Ct. at 1078, "the mere abstract teaching [of] the moral propriety or even moral necessity for a resort to force and violence," Brandenburg, 395 U.S. at 448, 89 S.Ct. at 1830 (quoting Noto v. United States, 367 U.S. 290, 297-98, 81 S.Ct. 1517, 1520-22, 6 L.Ed.2d 836 (1961)), or any of the other forms of discourse critical of government, its policies, and its leaders, which have always animated, and to this day continue to animate, the First Amendment. Indeed, this detailed, focused instructional assistance to those contemplating or in the throes of planning murder is the antithesis of speech protected under Brandenburg. It is the teaching of the "techniques" of violence, Scales, 367 U.S. at 233, 81 S.Ct. at 1488, the "advocacy and teaching of concrete action," Yates, 354 U.S. at 320, 77 S.Ct. at 1077, the "prepar[ation] . . . for violent action and [the] steeling . . . to such action," Brandenburg, 395 U.S. at 448, 89 S.Ct. at 1830 (quoting Noto, 367 U.S. at 297-98, 81 S.Ct. at 1520-21). It is the instruction in the methods of terror of which Justice Douglas spoke in Dennis v. United States, when he said, "If this were a case where those who claimed protection under the First Amendment

were teaching the techniques of sabotage . . . I would have no doubts. The freedom to speak is not absolute; the teaching of methods of terror . . . should be beyond the pale. . . ." 341 U.S. 494, 581, 71 S.Ct. 857, 903, 95 L.Ed. 1137 (1951) (Douglas, J., dissenting). As such, the murder instructions in Hit Man are, collectively, a textbook example of the type of speech that the Supreme Court has quite purposely left unprotected, and the prosecution of which, criminally or civilly, has historically been thought subject to few, if any, First Amendment constraints. Accordingly, we hold that the First Amendment does not pose a bar to the plaintiffs' civil aiding and abetting cause of action against Paladin Press. If, as precedent uniformly confirms, the states have the power to regulate speech that aids and abets crime, then certainly they have the power to regulate the speech at issue here.

III.

The district court's contrary conclusion, reached in an initial and then an amended opinion, must be attributed ultimately, we believe, to that court's failure at the time of its initial ruling to realize that Maryland does recognize a civil cause of action for aiding and abetting. Once the court's error with respect to the existence in Maryland of a civil aiding and abetting cause of action was brought to the court's attention by the parties on motion for reconsideration, it appears that the court was simply unprepared to revisit its decision, issued only the week before, in order to address the above-discussed cases, which the district court itself had observed are "factually similar" to the case at hand, J.A. at 156, but which the court had distinguished on the ground that they involved criminal prosecutions for aiding and abetting and Maryland does not provide a civil cause of action for aiding and abetting. J.A. at 155 ("Plaintiffs are asking the Court to allow the Defendants to be subjected to civil liability for murder, based on a theory of civil aiding and abetting—a claim that does not exist under Maryland law." (emphases added)). Perhaps ironically, this unwillingness foreordained what was, as we explain below, the district court's second error in the interpretation of Maryland law—its holding, on reconsideration, that Maryland would not recognize aiding and abetting liability under the facts as stipulated by the parties to this litigation, or on the facts as they appear from the record.

Whatever doubts the district court may have harbored about its interpretation of Maryland aiding and abetting law were almost certainly eased because it concluded alternatively (albeit in dicta) that Hit Man is entitled to the protections of <u>Brandenburg</u> in any event because it is a mere instructional manual for, and not an incitement to, murder. However, in this conclusion the district court erred as well, misunderstanding the Supreme Court's decision in <u>Brandenburg</u> to protect not just abstract advocacy of lawlessness and the open criticism of government and its institutions, but also the teaching of the technical methods of criminal activity—in this case, the technical methods of murder.

A.

[12] In its initial memorandum opinion, the district court rejected the plaintiffs' principal argument, that the First Amendment does not bar the imposition of liability for the aiding and abetting of murder, on the ground that the State of Maryland does not recognize a civil cause of action for aiding and abetting:

> Plaintiffs argue that Hit Man is not protected by the First Amendment because the First Amendment does not protect communication aiding and abetting murder. This argument must fail, however, because Plaintiffs do not cite, nor has the Court located, any reported decision that suggests that Maryland recognizes the tort of aiding and abetting. A federal court sitting in diversity cannot create new causes of action. Therefore, the Court cannot create a cause of action for aiding and abetting under Maryland law. . . .

J.A. at 153-54 (footnote and citations omitted). In response to submissions by both parties filed the very next day informing the court that Maryland does recognize civil aiding and abetting, the district court was obliged to amend its memorandum opinion to acknowledge the overwhelming authority that Maryland does, in fact, recognize such a cause of action. However, rather than address then the numerous precedents holding that the First Amendment offers little protection against claims of aiding and abetting criminal conduct, which in its initial opinion the court had agreed were similar to the instant case, the district court thereafter merely added to its original memorandum opinion the single conclusory footnote sentence (together with the necessary conforming changes to the relevant paragraph from its initial opinion [FN5]) that, "[a]lthough Maryland appears to recognize aider and abetter tort liability, it has never been applied to

support liability in this context." J.A. at 205 n.2 (internal citation deleted). [FN6] In this holding, as with its original holding that Maryland did not recognize a cause of action for civil aiding and abetting, the district court erred.

FN5. Thus, in relevant part, the amended opinion reads as follows:

Plaintiffs argue that Hit Man is not protected by the First Amendment because the First Amendment does not protect communication aiding and abetting murder. This argument, the Court believes, fails, however, because of the absence of any reported decision suggesting that Maryland extends the tort of aiding and abetting to the circumstances of this case. A federal court sitting in diversity cannot create new causes of action. Therefore, the Court cannot apply a new theory or extend the tort of aiding and abetting under Maryland law. . . .

J.A. at 205-06 (footnote and citations omitted; emphases added). As evidence of the haste with which the revised analysis was undertaken, the amended opinion elsewhere still includes a statement of the district court's initial conclusion that Maryland does not provide a civil cause of action for aiding and abetting. See id. at 207 ("Plaintiffs are asking the Court to allow the Defendants to be subjected to civil liability for murder, based on a theory of civil aiding and abetting—a claim that does not exist under Maryland law.").

FN6. The issue of whether, under the stipulated facts, Paladin could be held liable for aiding and abetting under Maryland law was not even before the district court. In fact, the parties had expressly stipulated that "[t]he parties agree that the sole issue to be decided by the Court in this motion is whether the First Amendment is a complete defense, as a matter of law, to the civil action set forth in the plaintiffs' Complaint. All other issues of law and fact are specifically reserved for subsequent proceedings." J.A. 58-59.

[13][14][15] Maryland's highest court has held that a defendant may be liable in tort if he "by any means (words, signs, or motions) encourage[s], incite[s], aid[s] or abet[s] the act of the direct perpetrator of the tort." <u>Alleco Inc. v. Harry & Jeanette Weinberg Foundation, 340 Md. 176, 665 A.2d 1038, 1049 (1995)</u> (quoting <u>Duke v. Feldman, 245 Md. 454, 226 A.2d 345, 347 (1967)</u>). It further appears that

generally Maryland defines the tort of aiding and abetting in the same way that it defines the crime of aiding and abetting. The state defines "aider" as one who "assist[s], support[s] or supplement[s] the efforts of another," and defines "abettor" as "one who instigates, advises or encourages the commission of a crime." Anello v. State, 201 Md. 164, 93 A.2d 71, 72-73 (Md.1952). The Court of Appeals has explained that in order for a conviction to stand, "it is not essential that there be a prearranged concert of action, although, in the absence of such action, it is essential that [the defendant] should in some way advocate or encourage the commission of the crime." Id. And, recently, the court has reiterated that criminal aiding and abetting "may be predicated upon counseling or encouraging" a criminal act, even if there is no agreement between the principal and the aider or abettor, and also that "[i]t is well settled that aiding and abetting does not always require a conspiracy." Apostoledes v. State, 323 Md. 456, 593 A.2d 1117, 1121 (1991).

[16] The primary, and possibly only, difference between Maryland's civil and criminal laws of aiding and abetting is the intent requirement. As Judge Learned Hand explained in discussing generally the difference between civil and criminal aiding and abetting laws, the intent standard in the civil tort context requires only that the criminal conduct be the "natural consequence of [one's] original act," whereas criminal intent to aid and abet requires that the defendant have a "purposive attitude" toward the commission of the offense. United States v. Peoni, 100 F.2d 401, 402 (2d Cir.1938); see also Nye & Nissen v. United States, 336 U.S. 613, 619, 69 S.Ct. 766, 770, 93 L.Ed. 919 (1949) (adopting Judge Hand's view of the criminal intent requirement). We assume that Maryland prescribes a higher intent standard for the imposition of criminal liability than it does for civil liability.

Especially in light of the caselaw discussed above, we are satisfied not only that the Maryland courts would conclude that an aiding and abetting cause of action would lie in the circumstances of this case, but also that plaintiffs have, by way of stipulation and otherwise, established a genuine issue of material fact as to each element of that cause of action. Perhaps most importantly in this regard, we conclude that plaintiffs have more than met their burden of establishing a genuine issue of material fact as to Paladin's intent, even assuming that the First

Amendment erects a heightened standard from that required under Maryland state law.

Paladin itself has stipulated that "Perry followed a number of instructions outlined in Hit Man " in preparing for and in murdering Mildred and Trevor Horn and Janice Saunders. J.A. at 61. In fact, as noted, the publisher has actually stipulated that it assisted Perry in the "perpetration of the murders." Id.

Even without these express stipulations of assistance, however, a reasonable jury could conclude that Paladin assisted Perry in those murders, from the facts that Perry purchased and possessed Hit Man and that the methods and tactics he employed in his murders of Mildred and Trevor Horn and Janice Saunders so closely paralleled those prescribed in the book. As discussed above, see discussion supra Part I, Perry followed, in painstaking detail, countless of the book's instructions in soliciting, preparing for, and carrying out his murders. Without repeating these in detail here, Perry faithfully followed the book's instructions in making a home-made silencer, using a rental car with stolen out-of-state tags, murdering the victims in their own home, using an AR-7 rifle to shoot the victims in the eyes from point blank range, and concealing his involvement in the murders. The number and extent of these parallels to the instructions in Hit Man cannot be consigned, as a matter of law, to mere coincidence; the correspondence of techniques at least creates a jury issue as to whether the book provided substantial assistance, if it does not conclusively establish such assistance.

A jury likewise could reasonably find that Perry was encouraged in his murderous acts by Paladin's book. Hit Man does not merely detail how to commit murder and murder for hire; through powerful prose in the second person and imperative voice, it encourages its readers in their specific acts of murder. It reassures those contemplating the crime that they may proceed with their plans without fear of either personal failure or punishment. And at every point where the would-be murderer might yield either to reason or to reservations, Hit Man emboldens the killer, confirming not only that he should proceed, but that he must proceed, if he is to establish his manhood. See discussion infra at 261-262. The book is so effectively written that its protagonist seems actually to be present at the planning, commission, and cover-up of the murders the book inspires. Illustrative of the nature and duration of the criminal partnership established between Hit Man and its readers who murder is the following "dialogue" that takes place when the murderer returns from his first killing:

> I'm sure your emotions have run full scale over the past few days or weeks.
>
> There was a fleeting moment just before you pulled the trigger when you wondered if lightning would strike you then and there. And afterwards, a short burst of panic as you looked quickly around you to make sure no witnesses were lurking.
>
> But other than that, you felt absolutely nothing. And you are shocked by that nothingness. You had expected this moment to be a spectacular point in your life. . . .
>
> The first few seconds of nothingness give you an almost uncontrollable urge to laugh out loud. You break into a wide grin. Everything you have been taught about life and its value was a fallacy.

Hit Man at 107. As this and other cases reveal, the book is arrestingly effective in the accomplishment of its objectives of counseling others to murder and assisting them in its commission and cover-up.

Finally, and significantly, Paladin also has stipulated to an intent that readily satisfies that required under Maryland law or the First Amendment. Even if the First Amendment imposes a heightened intent-based limitation on the state's ability to apply the tort of aiding and abetting to speech, see discussion supra at II.B.1, we are confident that, at the very least, the aiding and abetting of a malum in se crime such as murder with the specific purpose of assisting and encouraging another or others in that crime would satisfy such a limitation. Paladin has stipulated not only that it had knowledge that its publication would be used upon receipt by murderers and other criminals in the commission of murder, but that it even intended that the book be so used. Thus, the publisher stipulated, "defendants intended and had knowledge that their publications would be used, upon receipt, by criminals and would-be criminals to plan and execute the crime of murder for hire." J.A. at 59. Paladin has even stipulated that it "engaged in a marketing strategy intended to attract and assist criminals and would-be criminals who desire information and instructions on how to commit crimes." Id. These stipulations are more than sufficient to foreclose an absolute First Amendment defense to plaintiffs' suit. See DOJ Report at 43 & 44-45 n.71 ("[W]e believe that the district court in Rice v. Paladin erred insofar as it

concluded that Brandenburg bars liability for dissemination of [instructions on murder] regardless of the publisher's intent. . . . [Defendant Paladin's] concession[s] would, for purposes of summary judgment, seem to foreclose a constitutional defense . . .").

[17] The district court was never required to consider the intent requirement under Maryland's law of aiding and abetting, much less whether the First Amendment imposes a heightened intent standard in the context of authorizing liability for speech acts, because of its mistaken conclusion that Maryland does not recognize a civil cause of action for aiding and abetting. In analogizing this case to the copycat cases (and seemingly in order to permit the analogy), however, the district court accepted Paladin's post hoc "clarification" that it meant by its stipulation only that it was reasonably foreseeable to the publisher that, once the book was published and publicly available, it would be used by murderers to plan and to commit murder. Thus, in accepting the defendants' belated clarification, the district court said:

Defendants conceded that they intended that their publications would be used by criminals to plan and execute murder as instructed in the manual. . . . However, Defendants clarify their concession by explaining that when they published, advertised and distributed both Hit Man and Silencers, they knew, and in that sense "intended," that the books would be purchased by all of the categories of readers previously described and used by them for the broad range of purposes previously described.

J.A. at 215-16 (citations omitted). Of course, the district court was without authority to allow Paladin to alter the parties' stipulation unilaterally, particularly given that Paladin was the party moving for summary judgment. If anything, the stipulation should have been, and in any event must now be, interpreted in the light most favorable to the plaintiffs.

Furthermore, even if the stipulation only established knowledge, summary judgment was yet inappropriate because a trier of fact could still conclude that Paladin acted with the requisite intent to support civil liability. Wholly apart from Paladin's stipulations, there are four bases upon which, collectively, if perhaps not individually, a reasonable jury could find that Paladin possessed the intent required under Maryland law, as well as the intent required under any heightened First Amendment standard. Compare DOJ Report, at 45 n.71 ("[E]ven assuming arguendo that the defendants' own construction of the 'intent' stipulation were correct, that still would not justify the grant of summary judgment, since it would leave unanswered the question whether Paladin also had the specific purpose of facilitating murder.").

First, the declared purpose of Hit Man itself is to facilitate murder. Consistent with its declared purpose, the book is subtitled "A Technical Manual for Independent Contractors," and it unabashedly describes itself as "an instruction book on murder," Hit Man at ix. A jury need not, but plainly could, conclude from such prominent and unequivocal statements of criminal purpose that the publisher who disseminated the book intended to assist in the achievement of that purpose.

Second, the book's extensive, decided, and pointed promotion of murder is highly probative of the publisher's intent, and may be considered as such, whether or not that promotion, standing alone, could serve as the basis for liability consistent with the First Amendment. See Wisconsin v. Mitchell, 508 U.S. 476, 489, 113 S.Ct. 2194, 2201, 124 L.Ed.2d 436 (1993) ("The First Amendment . . . does not prohibit the evidentiary use of speech to establish the elements of a crime or to prove motive or intent."); cf. Noto, 367 U.S. at 299, 81 S.Ct. at 1521-22. [FN7] After carefully and repeatedly reading Hit Man in its entirety, we are of the view that the book so overtly promotes murder in concrete, nonabstract terms that we regard as disturbingly disingenuous both Paladin's cavalier suggestion that the book is essentially a comic book whose "fantastical" promotion of murder no one could take seriously, and amici's reckless characterization of the book as "almost avuncular," see Br. of Amici at 8-9. The unique text of Hit Man alone, boldly proselytizing and glamorizing the crime of murder and the "profession" of murder as it dispassionately instructs on its commission, is more than sufficient to create a triable issue of fact as to Paladin's intent in publishing and selling the manual.

> FN7. Cf. DOJ Report at 30 & n.47 (citations omitted) ("Insofar as publication of [bombmaking] manuals were criminalized on account of those manuals' advocacy of unlawful conduct, such a prohibition almost certainly could not pass constitutional muster. The First Amendment would not, however, prohibit the evidentiary use of such advocacy to demonstrate a disseminator's intent in conveying bombmaking information. Therefore, insofar as criminal culpability for dissemination of

such information depends upon the distributors' intent—for example, upon whether a disseminator of bombmaking manuals had the conscious purpose of helping others to use the information to engage in unlawful conduct—the substance of the advocacy in such manuals could be used as material evidence of such intent.").

Third, Paladin's marketing strategy would more than support a finding of the requisite intent. Cf. Direct Sales v. United States, 319 U.S. 703, 712-13, 63 S.Ct. 1265, 1269-70, 87 L.Ed. 1674 (1943) (holding that jury may infer intent to assist a criminal operation based upon a drug distributor's marketing strategy). It is known through Paladin's stipulations that it "engaged in a marketing strategy intended to attract and assist criminals and would-be criminals who desire information and instructions on how to commit crimes." J.A. at 59. But an inference as to such a strategy would be permitted from Paladin's catalogue advertisement of Hit Man. The publisher markets the book as follows, invoking a disclaimer which, the district court's characterization notwithstanding, a jury could readily find to be transparent sarcasm designed to intrigue and entice:

Learn how a pro gets assignments, creates a false identity, makes a disposable silencer, leaves the scene without a trace, watches his mark unobserved and more. Feral reveals how to get in, do the job and get out without getting caught. For academic study only!

Paladin Press Catalog, Vol. 26, No. 2 at 41 (emphasis in original). See also infra note 10. From this statement by the publisher in its own promotional sales catalogue, a jury could conclude that Paladin marketed Hit Man directly and even primarily to murderers and would-be criminals, and, from this permissible conclusion, in turn conclude that Paladin possessed the requisite intent necessary to support liability.

Certainly, such a conclusion would be reasonable based upon this promotional description coupled with the singular character of Hit Man, which is so narrowly focused in its subject matter and presentation as to be effectively targeted exclusively to criminals. In other words, despite the fact that Paladin may technically offer the book for sale to all comers, we are satisfied that a jury could, based upon Hit Man's seemingly exclusive purpose to assist murderers in the commission of murder, reasonably conclude that Paladin essentially distributed Hit Man only to murderers and would-be murderers—that its conduct was not, at least in law, different from that of a publisher (or anyone else) who delivered *Hit Man* to a specific person or group of persons whom the publisher knew to be interested in murder. And even Paladin effectively concedes that it could be liable were such a finding permissibly made. Paladin's Memorandum in Support of Summary Judgment at 33 n.24.

A conclusion that Paladin directed *Hit Man* to a discrete group rather than to the public at large would be supported, even if not established, by the evidence that *Hit Man* is not generally available or sold to the public from the bookshelves of local bookstores, but, rather, is obtainable as a practical matter only by catalogue. Paladin Press is a mail order company, and for the most part does not sell books through retail outlets. In order to procure a copy of *Hit Man*, the prospective reader must first obtain a copy of Paladin's catalogue, typically by completing a request form reprinted in one of Paladin's advertisements in specialized magazines such as Soldier of Fortune. After obtaining that catalogue, the reader must scan the list of book titles and read the accompanying descriptions. Once the reader finds the book he desires, he must then complete and mail another form to order the book.

From the requirements of this process, together with the book's character, a jury need not, but could, permissibly find that *Hit Man* is not at all distributed to the general public and that, instead, it is available only to a limited, self-selected group of people interested in learning from and being trained by a self-described professional killer in various methods of killing for money, individuals who are then contemplating or highly susceptible to the commission of murder.

Finally, a jury could reasonably conclude that Paladin specifically intended to assist Perry and similar murderers by finding, contrary to Paladin's demurs, as would we, that *Hit Man*'s only genuine use is the unlawful one of facilitating such murders. [FN8] Cf._____ J.A. at 221 (observation by district court that *Hit Man* is "devoid of any significant redeeming social value"). Although before us Paladin attempts to hypothesize lawful purposes for *Hit Man*, and it would doubtless advance the same hypotheses before a jury, at some point hypotheses are so implausible as to be deserving of little or no weight. The likelihood that *Hit Man* actually is, or would be, used in the legitimate manners hypothesized by Paladin is sufficiently remote that a jury could quite reasonably reject them altogether as alternative uses for the book.

If there is a publication that could be found to have no other use than to facilitate unlawful conduct, then this would be it, so devoid is the book of any political, social, entertainment, or other legitimate discourse. Cf. Miller v. California, 413 U.S. 15, 93 S.Ct. 2607, 37 L.Ed.2d 419 (1973) (distinguishing obscene from nonobscene material in part on basis of "whether the work, taken as a whole, lacks serious literary, artistic, political, or scientific value"). Thus, for example, a jury would certainly not be unreasonable in dismissing (in fact, it arguably would be unreasonable in accepting) Paladin's contention that *Hit Man* has significant social value in that the book, in the course of instructing murderers how to murder, incidentally informs law enforcement on the techniques that the book's readers will likely employ in the commission of their murders. Likewise, a reasonable jury could simply refuse to accept Paladin's contention that this purely factual, instructional manual on murder has entertainment value to law-abiding citizens. And, just as a permissible inference as to Paladin's marketing strategy would be supportable by evidence as to the specialized process by which one acquires *Hit Man*, either of these conclusions as to the absence of lawful purpose could be reinforced by the same evidence.

> FN8. Paladin contends that plaintiffs have stipulated "that the defendant's book has substantial informational value unrelated to the facilitation of crime." Appellee's Br. at 29 (footnote omitted). But they have not; they have stipulated only that Paladin's "marketing strategy" was intended to reach audiences beyond criminals and would-be criminals. J.A. at 60.

In summary, a reasonable jury clearly could conclude from the stipulations of the parties, and, apart from the stipulations, from the text of *Hit Man* itself and the other facts of record, that Paladin aided and abetted in Perry's triple murder by providing detailed instructions on the techniques of murder and murder for hire with the specific intent of aiding and abetting the commission of these violent crimes.

B.

[18] Any argument that *Hit Man* is abstract advocacy entitling the book, and therefore Paladin, to heightened First Amendment protection under Brandenburg is, on its face, untenable. Although the district court erred in its alternative conclusion that the speech of *Hit Man* is protected advocacy, see discussion infra at III.B.2, even that court expressly found that "the book merely teaches what must be done to implement a professional

hit." J.A. at 217-18; id. at 218 n. 4 (discussing "instructive nature" of book). Indeed, Paladin's protests notwithstanding, this book constitutes the archetypal example of speech which, because it methodically and comprehensively prepares and steels its audience to specific criminal conduct through exhaustively detailed instructions on the planning, commission, and concealment of criminal conduct, finds no preserve in the First Amendment. To the extent that confirmation of this is even needed, given the book's content and declared purpose to be "an instruction book on murder," Hit Man at ix, that confirmation is found in the stark contrast between this assassination manual and the speech heretofore held to be deserving of constitutional protection.

1.

Through its stipulation that it intended Hit Man to be used by criminals and would-be criminals to commit murder for hire in accordance with the book's instructions, Paladin all but concedes that, through those instructions, Hit Man prepares and steels its readers to commit the crime of murder for hire. But even absent the publisher's stipulations, it is evident from even a casual examination of the book that the prose of Hit Man is at the other end of the continuum from the ideation at the core of the advocacy protected by the First Amendment.

The cover of Hit Man states that readers of the book will "[l]earn how a pro makes a living at this craft [of murder] without landing behind bars" and,

how he gets hit assignments, creates a false working identity, makes a disposable silencer, leaves the scene without a trace of evidence, watches his mark unobserved, and more . . . how to get in, do the job, and get out—without getting caught.

In the first pages of its text, Hit Man promises, consistent with its title as "A Technical Manual for Independent Contractors," that the book will prepare the reader, step by step, to commit murder for hire:

Within the pages of this book you will learn one of the most successful methods of operation used by an independent contractor. You will follow the procedures of a man who works alone, without backing of organized crime or on a personal vendetta. Step by step you will be taken from research to equipment selection to job preparation to successful job completion. You will learn where to find employment, how much to charge, and what you can, and cannot, do with the money you earn.

But deny your urge to skip about, looking for the "good" parts. Start where any amateur who is serious about turning professional will start—at the beginning.

Hit Man at x-xi (emphasis in original). And, faithful to these promises, in the successive chapters of the 130 pages that follow, Hit Man systematically and in meticulous detail instructs on the gruesome particulars of every possible aspect of murder and murder for hire. The manual instructs step-by-step on building and using fertilizer bombs, constructing silencers, picking locks, selecting and using poisons, sinking corpses, and torturing victims. It teaches would-be assassins how to arrive at, and conduct surveillance of, a potential victim's house, and it instructs on the use of a fake driver's license and registration at a motel, the placement of stolen out-of-state license plates on rental cars, and the deception of the postal service into delivering weapons to the murder scene. The book instructs the reader in murder methods, explaining in dispassionate and excruciatingly graphic detail how to shoot, stab, poison, and incinerate people, and in gory detail it expounds on which methods of murder will best ensure the death of the victims. The book schools the reader on how to escape the crime scene without detection, and how to foil police investigations by disassembling and discarding the murder weapon, altering the ballistics markings of that weapon, stealing and switching license plates, and disguising the reader's physical appearance. And it counsels on how to manipulate the legal system, if caught.

At the risk of belaboring the obvious, but in order to appreciate the encyclopedic character of Hit Man's instructions, one need only consider the following chapter-by-chapter synopsis.

Chapter One of Hit Man, entitled "The Beginning—Mental and Physical Preparation," starts by outlining the "essential" steps to becoming a professional killer. Hit Man at 9. The book urges the reader to read other books from publishers such as Paladin Press, but it cautions that "[b]ooks on subjects related to the professional hit man are hard to find [and that] there are[only] a few publishers out there who have the backbone to provide those . . . who take life seriously with the necessary educational materials." Hit Man at 9-10. The book goes on to recommend that one read articles in magazines such as Soldier of Fortune, and military newsletters in order to "[s]tay abreast of new trends and developments [in weapons and techniques of killing] as well as new gadgets and inventions as they become available." Hit Man at 9. It also encourages the reader to comb fictional accounts of murder, on the off chance that, for example, "the warped imagination of a fiction writer will point out an obvious but somehow never before realized method of pacification or body disposal." Id. at 10. It instructs its readers to study their local newspapers carefully "to see who in your area might be your next employer . . . or victim," and to use the classified advertisements, among other things, to find "new toys and pick them up from private owners to avoid registering your weapons." Id. The book provides in-depth advice on using a variety of publicly available reference materials to locate weapons and other "equipment," gather information about victims, and plan murders for hire. For example, the book instructs its readers to go to the auto tag department of the county courthouse and "[l]ook up the mark by last name or tag number for address," because books containing such information are often "left out for public use." Id. at 12. Similarly, the book instructs the readers in how to use the postal service to "track[ ] down the last known address of anyone you choose as a function of the Freedom of Information Act," id. at 14, and to send weapons safely to the location of a planned murder, id. at 13.

In addition, Hit Man instructs its readers to become familiar with local law enforcement techniques, for example by obtaining law enforcement handbooks, and it provides practical advice on how to obtain these books, either from "any college bookstore where law enforcement courses are taught," id. at 14, or by theft. The book also offers the readers practical tips on diet, fitness, combat training, ("Veterans with wartime experience and the ability to kill are first choice instructors." Id. at 17), and observational skills. Although much of the information in this chapter is not explicit in outlining the methods of terror, it is explicit in advising the would-be assassin where to turn for additional information beyond that found between the covers of the book.

Chapter Two of the book, entitled "Equipment— Selection and Purpose," imparts a wealth of information on the "basic equipment" the "beginner" will need as tools of his trade, id. at 21, and provides detailed instructions as to the equipment's use. For example, the book first instructs the reader to obtain, inter alia, an AR-7 rifle, hollowpoint bullets, disposable silencers, liquid poison, disposable rubber gloves, a double-edged knife with a six-inch blade, handcuffs, and a ski mask. See id. at 21-22. The book next provides precise instructions on how to kill, using

each of the various weapons. The manual recommends "close kills," and teaches that:

When using a small caliber weapon like the 22, it is best to shoot from a distance of three to six feet. You will not want to be at point-blank range to avoid having the victim's blood splatter you or your clothing. At least three shots should be fired to ensure quick and sure death.

You can judge when death has occurred by observing the wound. When the blood ceases to flow, the heart has stopped working. Check for pulse at both the wrist and throat as an added precaution.

Id. at 24. The book goes on to teach which weapons to avoid and why, explaining, for example, that,

[a]lthough revolvers are often depicted as being a favorite tool among hit men, they are not recommended by this pro. Revolvers cannot be effectively silenced. The open cylinder allows gases to escape, thus making noise. When fired, gas is forced around the cylinder in a 360 degree circle, thereby throwing powder all over the person who fires the gun.

An automatic, on the other hand, is tightly sealed so that when it is fired almost all the powder residue is forced into the silencer, where it is trapped. This prevents the powder from escaping and covering the person who fired the shot. . . . If a shell catcher is used, the powder residue will become trapped inside the catch bag.

Id. at 26. The manual further instructs how to kill efficiently at close-range with a knife:

The knife you carry should have a six-inch blade with a serrated section for making efficient, quiet kills. . . .

The knife should have a double-edged blade. This double edge, combined with the serrated section and six-inch length, will insure a deep, ragged tear, and the wound will be difficult, if not impossible, to close without prompt medical attention.

Make your thrusts to a vital organ and twist the knife before you withdraw it. If you hit bone, you will have to file the blade to remove the marks left on the metal when it struck the victim's bone.

Id. at 27-28. The book also instructs on alternatives to the close-range kill, including instructions such as the following:

If you must do your shooting from a distance, use a rifle with a good scope and silencer and aim for the head—preferably the eye sockets if you are a sharpshooter. Many people have been shot repeatedly, even in the head, and survived to tell about it.

Id. at 24. Finally, the chapter includes a host of other instructions on how to use basic tools, ranging from handcuffs, to lock picks, to surveillance equipment, in the commission of murder. For instance, the book teaches the need for a hit man to always wear gloves and it discusses glove choice, recommending surgical gloves because,

[l]eather gloves are not to be considered as a job tool. The leather has the same individual, distinct characteristics as the human fingerprint. If you have to use leather gloves, destroy them immediately after the job. If found in your possession, they can convict you as quickly as a set of your own fingerprints.

Id. at 27. The chapter continues in like vein.

Chapter Three, entitled "The Disposable Silencer—A Poor Man's Access to a Rich Man's Toy," teaches the reader, with step-by-step instructions and accompanying photographic illustration, how to construct a "whisper-quiet," "inexpensive," and "effective" disposable silencer that is "reusable for over four hundred rounds." Id. at 47, 51. These directions are designed to allow the "amateur" to construct disposable silencers, which, the book explains, are "one of the most important tools a professional will ever have." Id. at 38. As the book explains, these "same directions can be followed successfully to construct a silencer for any weapon, with only the size of the drill rod used for alignment changed. . . ." Id. at 39.

Hit Man's Chapter Four, entitled "More Than One Way To Kill a Rabbit—The Direct Hit is Not Your Only Alternative," includes discursive instructions on numerous additional methods of killing and torture. If "several marks will be together in one place at the same time," the book teaches, one can kill all of the "marks" with a fertilizer bomb, and it goes on to teach the reader, through step-by-step instructions, how to build such a bomb. Id. at 54-55. The chapter teaches the reader how to kill by arson, admonishing and instructing, "Don't ever use gasoline or other traceable materials to start your fire. [Specified substance] is your best starter because it burns away all traces." Id. at 56. In addition, the chapter includes instructions such as that, "[a] fire victim will have smoke present in his lungs. Therefore, if this is your choice of extermination, your mark should be unconscious, but breathing, when the fire is set. Make sure no scratches or bruises point to foul play." Id . Later in the chapter, Hit Man discusses poisons. After

teaching an elaborate method for obtaining hard-to-find poisons through impersonation, the manual explains how one can successfully use substances such as tetrodotoxin, oleander, nicotine, and jessamine to kill his victims. See id. at 58-63. The chapter's discussion of torture techniques provides explicit advice on how to inflict sufficient pain to ensure that "people will tell you anything you want to know, even when they are sure they are about to die." Id. at 64. In what is offered as a helpful example, the book illustrates from the author's own experience:

We [the book's author and his accomplice, referred to only as "the Indian"] subdued the [victim], stripped him to the waist and tied him into a wooden chair.

. . .

The Indian pulled an ice pick from his hip pocket.

. . .

. . . Suddenly he stopped and inserted the tip of the pick into the [victim's] upper arm about a quarter of an inch. When he withdrew the pick, there was a sickening little popping sound as blood spurted from the wound for a second, then stopped.

. . .

Several stabs later, the [victim] was quivering like a jellyfish, his body like a pin cushion, while the Indian was getting more and more excited and more and more into his work.

. . . With a malicious grin, [the Indian] pulled a pair of pliers from his other hip pocket and gave me a sly wink. Pointedly, methodically, he began with the [victim's] little finger on his left hand and crunched each knuckle slowly with the pliers. It seemed to take no effort at all on his part as the soft bone gave way under the force of the simple tool. He had only gotten to the third finger when the[victim] began to cry like a baby and spill his guts.

Id. at 65-66. The chapter concludes with instructions for disposing of human corpses without detection, providing directions for, inter alia, hiding the bodies in a river:

If you choose to sink the corpse, you must first make several deep stabs into the body's lungs (from just under the rib cage) and belly. This is necessary because gases released during decomposition will bloat these organs, causing the body to rise to the surface of the water.

The corpse should be weighted with the standard concrete blocks, but it must be wrapped from head to toe with heavy chain as well, to keep the body from separating and floating in chunks to the surface. After the fishes and natural elements have done their work, the chain will drag the bones into the muddy sediment.

Id. at 67. And the instructions we repeat here are but a few of the methods of inflicting torture and death taught in the chapter.

The next chapter, entitled "Homework and Surveillance—Mapping a Plan and Checking It for Accuracy," instructs on how to obtain information about the victim from the client. It explains the importance of finding out information such as whether the victim has a dog or other pet that might provide a warning of the impending assassination, the layout of the victim's residence, and whether the victim has roommates or neighbors. The chapter includes a lengthy "sample information sheet" that may be used in planning a first kill. Id. at 73-80.

Chapter Six, entitled "Opportunity Knocks—Finding Employment, What to Charge, What to Avoid," teaches readers how to find someone who will hire their services as professional killers. The chapter explains where to find potential employers, what to look for in such persons, and what to charge for each murder:

Prices vary according to the risk involved, social or political prominence of the victim, difficulty of the assignment, and other factors. A federal judge [Judge Wood, slain in Texas in 1978] recently brought a price of $250,000, for example. A county sheriff might bring $75,000 to $100,000.

. . .

. . . It is not recommended that you take any contract that pays less than $30,000, and that is working mighty cheap. To work for any amount less would be amateurish. . . .

There are two good reasons for setting a $30,000 minimum for your services. First, the risks involved are high. . . . A fee of $5,000 or even $10,000 will be of little consolation as you wait helplessly behind bars.

Second, because the risks are so high and employment opportunities are limited, the money you earn should be sufficient to carry you over until your next job comes along.

Id. at 90-91. The chapter also provides instructions on how to communicate with the employer after the hit,

explaining, for example, that it is best to develop a code for informing the employer that the contract has been fulfilled, such as calling the employer's residence and asking to speak with a fictitious individual, whose name signals to the employer that the victim is dead. See id. at 93-94.

In the following chapter, titled "Getting the Job Done Right—Why the Described Hit Went Down the Way It Did," Hit Man provides instructions for reaching the victim's location, transporting tools, preparing to commit the murder, and cleaning up the crime scene and escaping after the killing. Illustrative of the chapter's directions for preparing to commit the murder:

Wipe down your weapons as you assemble them. Even the inner parts of your guns must be wiped to remove any prints that were left behind during the last cleaning.

Wipe down each bullet and wear rubber gloves as you load the clip. Just in case you leave behind an empty cartridge, you don't want your fingerprint emblazoned on the casing.

Id. at 103. Similarly, the manual instructs on how best to discard the clothes worn to commit the killing:

The first thing you should do when you reach the car [after killing your victims] is change into another disguise and get out of those work clothes. Check them for bloodstains. If there are none, you can toss them into a charity collection box or trash can. If the victim's blood is on those clothes, they must be burned or buried.

Id. at 105. And it explains, with respect to sanitization of the rental car:

[S]top and wipe the car for prints and wear driving gloves as you return the car to the rental agency. . . . [W]ash the car and vacuum the interior immediately when you arrive at your destination [because] foreign soil from the [crime scene] is now imbedded in the car's interior[and its] air filter. . . .

Id. at 106. Chapter 8, entitled "Danger: Ego, Women, and Partners—Controlling Your Situation" instructs the reader on how, as a professional killer, to use money, women, and partners. This chapter of the book, for example, instructs the reader on how to use women while committing professional killings without getting caught. Thus, after explaining that the "deceitful, 'game-playing' natures" of women make them potentially better professional killers than men, the book goes on to say that,

[f]ortunately for the world, a woman usually makes only one man her target, and the nesting instinct quickly takes her off the street and ties her down to the little world of babies, laundry and housework she creates and protects for her own. Unfortunately, even a hit man cannot deny that what women have to offer is a basic necessity.

. . .

[Cautioning against marriage], if [your wife] knows too much, she could someday become [your] worst enemy on the face of the earth and may someday have to be eliminated in the name of self-preservation.

And if she knows too little, her suspicious, jealous nature could lead to more snooping and following and conjecture on her part than is healthy—for either of [you].

. . .

. . . Women are highly emotional, rarely rational creatures. Is ten minutes of pleasure worth your life at the hands (or tongue) of an irate spouse?

. . .

Ideally, a professional hit man will remain single. He will either purchase his sexual pleasures or participate in impersonal one-night-stands. His involvement with women will only be on a sexual level. He will not live with them, nor will he let them invade his privacy. . . . In most cases, they won't even know his real name.

. . .

As a man, I appreciate as much as anyone a good-looking body and a warm, willing smile on a woman. As a professional, however, that seems to have lost some of its thrill as I've moved on to bigger, more exciting and more dangerous prey.

Id. at 114-17. The chapter also advises the reader on how to enjoy the fruits of crime without getting caught, warning that,

Unless you have additional sources of income to justify large expenditures like a new home, paying off an old mortgage or a new sports car, don't spend any of your earnings on big items of this type. Big expenditures arouse suspicion, not only of your friends and family, but of the IRS and the authorities if you should ever come under investigation.

Id. at 113. The final chapter of Hit Man, entitled "Legally Illegal," includes various sections instructing the reader on how and where to purchase false

identification, how to make false identification, how to launder illegal money, and how to act in encounters with law enforcement officers. For example, the book instructs on how to "launder" "illegal money" through the use of a tax haven in the Cayman Islands:

The procedure is really quite simple: You form a corporation in [an offshore Island country] and put your illegal monies into that corporation. Then you form a legal U.S. corporation as your business and borrow the money you need to get going from the foreign corporation you have previously set up. . . .

Let's say your legal American corporation is a land development company, because you want to invest your laundered monies into real estate. . . .

[Instructions continue].

Id. at 124. The book concludes by offering advice on how to escape punishment by exploiting legal technicalities in the event that the reader is arrested by the police, including how to avoid jailhouse snitches and undercover agents.

As Hit Man instructs, it also steels its readers to the particular violence it explicates, instilling in them the resolve necessary to carry out the crimes it details, explains, and glorifies. Language such as that which is reprinted in the prologue to this opinion, and similar language uncanny in its directness and power, pervades the entire work:

You may threaten, bargain, torture or mutilate to get the information you want, and you must be prepared to use whatever method works.

. . .

You are working. This is your job and you are a professional.

. . .

. . . You have the power and ability to stand alone. You no longer need a reason to kill.

. . .

. . . You are a hardened criminal. You are capable of performing cold-blooded murder for a fee. . . . [Y]ou are not fit to be a part of organized society.

Id. at 66, 100, 111, 127 (second emphasis added). Speaking directly to the reader in the second person, like a parent to a child, Hit Man addresses itself to every potential obstacle to murder, removing each, seriatim, until nothing appears to the reader to stand between him and his execution of the ultimate criminal act. To those who are reluctant because of the value of human life, Hit Man admonishes that "[l]ife is not robust and precious and valuable" and that "[e]verything you have been taught about life and its value was a fallacy [,] [a] dirty rotten lie." Id. at 107. To those who fear guilt or remorse, the book reassures:

You made it! Your first job was a piece of cake! Taking all that money for the job was almost like robbery. Yet here you are, finally a real hit man with real hard cash in your pockets and that first notch on your pistol.

. . .

[After killing your first victim] [Y]ou felt absolutely nothing. And you are shocked by that nothingness. You had expected this moment to be a spectacular point in your life. You had wondered if you would feel compassion for the victim, immediate guilt, or even experience direct intervention by the hand of God. But you weren't even feeling sickened by the sight of the body.

Id. at 106-07. And the book allays the natural apprehension about the immediate aftermath of the murders it counsels:

After you have arrived home [after your kill], the events that took place take on a dreamlike quality. You don't dwell on them. You don't worry. You don't have nightmares. You don't fear ghosts. When thoughts of the hit go through your mind, it's almost as though you are recalling some show you saw on television.

By the time you collect the balance of your contract fee, the doubts and fears of discovery have faded. Those feelings have been replaced by cockiness, a feeling of superiority, a new independence and self-assurance.

Id. at 108. Those who fear their cold-bloodedness are assuaged with the reminders that "a hit man has a wide range of feelings" and that he "may be extremely compassionate towards the elderly or disabled" or "even . . . religious in his own way." Id. at 106. And for those who fear only that they will be caught, comes the ominous pledge that "the American Justice System is so bogged down in technicalities, overcrowded jails, plea bargaining and a host of other problems that even if charged with a serious crime, we [as killers] can rest assured that the law is on our side," see id. at 125, that a "true" "professional" "won't ever have to face [various] legal predicaments." Id. at 130.

Indeed, one finds in Hit Man little, if anything, even remotely characterizable as the abstract criticism that Brandenburg jealously protects. Hit Man's detailed, concrete instructions and adjurations to murder stand in stark contrast to the vague, rhetorical threats of politically or socially motivated violence that have historically been considered part and parcel of the impassioned criticism of laws, policies, and government indispensable in a free society and rightly protected under Brandenburg. The speech of Hit Man defies even comparison with the Klansman's chilling, but protected, statement in Brandenburg itself that, "[the Ku Klux Klan is] not a revengent organization, but if our President, our Congress, our Supreme Court, continues to suppress the white, Caucasian race, it's possible that there might have to be some revengeance taken," 395 U.S. at 446, 89 S.Ct. at 1829; the protestor's inciteful, but protected, chant in Hess v. Indiana, 414 U.S. 105, 108, 94 S.Ct. 326, 328-29, 38 L.Ed.2d 303 (1973) that "[w]e'll take the fucking street again"; the NAACP speaker's threat, rhetorical in its context, to boycott violators that "[i]f we catch any of you going in any of them racist stores, we're gonna break your damn neck," which was held to be protected in NAACP v. Claiborne Hardware Co., 458 U.S. 886, 902, 102 S.Ct. 3409, 3420, 73 L.Ed.2d 1215 (1982); or the draft protestor's crude, but protected, blustering in Watts that "[i]f they ever make me carry a rifle the first man I want to get in my sights is L.B.J.," Watts v. United States, 394 U.S. 705, 706, 89 S.Ct. 1399, 1401, 22 L.Ed.2d 664 (1969).

Plaintiffs observed in their submissions before the district court that,

Hit Man is not political manifesto, not revolutionary diatribe, not propaganda, advocacy, or protest, not an outpouring of conscience or credo.

. . .

It contains no discussion of ideas, no argument, no information about politics, religion, science, art, or culture . . . it offers no agenda for self-governance, no insight into the issues of the day. . . .

Appellant's Br. at 32; Memorandum of Points and Authorities in Support of Plaintiffs' Opposition to Defendant's Motion for Summary Judgment at 31-32. And, this is apt observation. Hit Man is none of this. Ideas simply are neither the focus nor the burden of the book. To the extent that there are any passages within Hit Man's pages that arguably are in the nature of ideas or abstract advocacy, those sentences are so very few in number and isolated as to be legally of no significance whatsoever. [FN9] Cf. _____ Kois v.

Wisconsin, 408 U.S. 229, 231, 92 S.Ct. 2245, 2246, 33 L.Ed.2d 312 (1972) ("A quotation from Voltaire in the flyleaf of a book will not constitutionally redeem an otherwise obscene publication."); see also Miller, 413 U.S. at 24, 93 S.Ct. at 2614-15; Penthouse International, Ltd. v. McAuliffe, 610 F.2d 1353 (5th Cir.1980), cert. dismissed, 447 U.S. 931, 100 S.Ct. 3031, 65 L.Ed.2d 1131 (1980). Hit Man is, pure and simple, a step-by-step murder manual, a training book for assassins. There is nothing even arguably tentative or recondite in the book's promotion of, and instruction in, murder. [FN10] To the contrary, the book directly and unmistakably urges concrete violations of the laws against murder and murder for hire and coldly instructs on the commission of these crimes. The Supreme Court has never protected as abstract advocacy speech so explicit in its palpable entreaties to violent crime.

> FN9. This circuit and others have repeatedly rejected Paladin's argument that speech can be punished under the speech act doctrine, without regard to the strictures of Brandenburg, only when that speech has no purpose or value other than to facilitate a specific wrongful act. See Appellee's Supp. Br. at 9. Thus, in Kelley, we found the defendant's concrete promotion of, and provision of instructions for, tax evasion unprotected by the First Amendment, even though the defendant offered his advice in a meeting of a group indisputably dedicated to the political belief that the federal income tax is unconstitutional as applied to wages. 769 F.2d at 216-17. And in Freeman, the Ninth Circuit upheld a similar conviction, even though the defendant's speech "spr[ang] from the anterior motive to effect political or social change." 761 F.2d at 551. See also Agee, 453 U.S. at 308-09, 101 S.Ct. at 2782-83 (holding that a former Central Intelligence Agency employee's disclosure of intelligence information was unprotected by the First Amendment even though the employee was "also engaged in criticism of the Government").

> FN10. The several brief "disclaimers" and "warnings" in Hit Man's advertisement description and on its cover, that the book's instructions are "for informational purposes only!" and "for academic study only!," and that "[n]either the author nor the publisher assumes responsibility for the use or misuse of the information contained in this book," are plainly insufficient in themselves to alter the objective understanding of the hundreds of thousands of words that follow, which, in

purely factual and technical terms, tutor the book's readers in the methods and techniques of killing. These "disclaimers" and "warnings" obviously were affixed in order to titillate, rather than "to dissuade readers from engaging in the activity [the book] describes," as the district court suggested they might be understood, J.A. at 219.

2.

In concluding that Hit Man is protected "advocacy," the district court appears to have misperceived the nature of the speech that the Supreme Court held in Brandenburg is protected under the First Amendment. In particular, the district court seems to have misunderstood the Court in Brandenburg as having distinguished between "advocating or teaching" lawlessness on the one hand, and "inciting or encouraging" lawlessness on the other, any and all of the former being entitled to First Amendment protection. The district court thus framed the issue before it as "whether Hit Man merely advocates or teaches murder or whether it incites or encourages murder." J.A. at 212. And, finding that Hit Man "merely teaches" in technical fashion the fundamentals of murder, it concluded that "[t]he book does not cross that line between permissible advocacy and impermissible incitation to crime or violence." Id. at 218.

The Court in Brandenburg, however, did not hold that "mere teaching" is protected; the Court never even used this phrase. And it certainly did not hold, as the district court apparently believed, that all teaching is protected. Rather, however inartfully it may have done so, the Court fairly clearly held only that the "mere abstract teaching" of principles, id. at 447-48, 89 S.Ct. at 1830 (quoting Noto, 367 U.S. at 297-98, 81 S.Ct. at 1520-21) (emphasis added), and "mere advocacy," 395 U.S. at 448-49, 89 S.Ct. at 1830-31 (emphasis added), are protected. In the final analysis, it appears the district court simply failed to fully appreciate the import of the qualification to the kind of "teaching" that the Supreme Court held to be protected in Brandenburg. See J.A. at 217 (defining "advocacy" as "mere teaching" rather than "mere abstract teaching" but citing to Brandenburg, 395 U.S. at 448, 89 S.Ct. at 1830 (quoting Noto, 367 U.S. at 297-98, 81 S.Ct. at 1520-21)). As the Supreme Court's approving quotation from its opinion in Noto confirms, it is not teaching simpliciter, but only "the mere abstract teaching . . . of the moral propriety or even moral necessity " for resort to lawlessness, or its equivalent, that is protected under the commands of Brandenburg. 367 U.S. at 297-98, 81 S.Ct. at 1520-21 (emphasis added). [FN11]

FN11. Even if the district court were correct in its holding that Hit Man is speech somehow deserving of the protections of Brandenburg, we would yet be constrained to reverse the court's judgment. Given Paladin's remarkable stipulations that it knew that its murder manual would be used by murderers, would-be murderers, and other criminals "upon receipt " to assist them in the planning, commission, and cover up of their crimes, that the publisher intended that the manual would be so used, and that Hit Man actually assisted Perry's commission of the crime of murder, we could not conclude as a matter of law that Hit Man is not directed to inciting and likely to incite imminent lawlessness.

Although we believe the district court's specific misreading of Brandenburg was plainly in error, we cannot fault the district court for its confusion over the opinion in that case. The short per curiam opinion in Brandenburg is, by any measure, elliptical.

In particular, the Court unmistakably draws the distinction discussed above, between "the mere abstract teaching . . . of the moral propriety or even moral necessity for a resort to force and violence" on one hand, 395 U.S. at 448, 89 S.Ct. at 1830, and the "prepar[ation] [of] a group for violent action and steeling it to such action" on the other. Id. And it then recites in the very next sentence that "[a] statute which fails to draw this distinction," id. (emphasis added)—a seeming reference to the distinction between "mere abstract teaching" and "preparing and steeling"—is unconstitutional under the First Amendment. In the succeeding paragraph and a later footnote, however, the Court distinguishes between "mere advocacy" and "incitement to imminent lawless action," a distinction which, as a matter of common sense and common parlance, appears different from the first distinction drawn, because "preparation and steeling" can occur without "incitement," and vice-versa. See id. at 448, 89 S.Ct. at 1830 ("Neither the indictment nor the trial judge's instructions to the jury in any way refined the statute's bald definition of the crime in terms of mere advocacy not distinguished from incitement to imminent lawless action." (footnote omitted)); id. at 449 n. 4, 89 S.Ct. at 1831 n. 4 ("Statutes affecting the right of assembly, like those touching on freedom of speech, must observe the established distinctions between mere advocacy and incitement to imminent lawless action. . . .").

It would have been natural, based upon its prior cases, for the Court actually to have contemplated and intended both distinctions, and to have developed the latter only, because the case before it turned exclusively on that distinction. It is more likely, however, that the Court did not focus at all on the seeming facial incongruity between the first and the latter two of these distinctions. The Court, therefore, may well have intended to equate the preparation and steeling of a group to violent action with speech that is directed to inciting imminent lawless action and likely to produce such action. In other words, the Court may well have meant to imply that one prepares and steels another or others for violent action only when he does so through speech that is "directed to inciting or producing imminent lawless action and . . . [that is] likely to incite or produce such action," id. at 447, 89 S.Ct. at 1829, and thus that preparation and steeling is not per se unprotected. Compare id. at 447-48, 89 S.Ct. at 1829-30 ("As we said in Noto. . . .") with Noto, 367 U.S. at 298, 81 S.Ct. at 1521 (describing preparation and steeling through "a call to violence"). Assuming that it did so mean to imply, however, we are confident it meant to do so only in the context of advocacy—speech that is part and parcel of political and social discourse—which was the only type of speech at issue in Brandenburg, Noto, and the other cases relied upon by the Court. See, e.g., 44 Liquormart v. Rhode Island, 517 U.S. 484,——, 116 S.Ct. 1495, 1505, 134 L.Ed.2d 711 (1996) (Stevens, J., for plurality) (describing Brandenburg as setting forth "test for suppressing political speech"). The Court even so defined its own holding: "These later decisions have fashioned the principle that the constitutional guarantees of free speech and free press do not permit a State to forbid or proscribe advocacy of the use of force or of law violation except where such advocacy is directed to inciting or producing imminent lawless action and is likely to incite or produce such action." 395 U.S. at 447, 89 S.Ct. at 1829 (footnote omitted; emphases added). For, as this case reveals, and as the Court itself has always seemed to recognize, one obviously can prepare, and even steel, another to violent action not only through the dissident "call to violence," but also through speech, such as instruction in the methods of terror or other crime, that does not even remotely resemble advocacy, in either form or purpose. And, of course, to understand the Court as addressing itself to speech other than advocacy would be to ascribe to it an intent to revolutionize the criminal law, in a several paragraph per curiam opinion, by subjecting prosecutions to the demands of Brandenburg's "imminence" and "likelihood" requirements whenever the predicate conduct takes, in whole or in part, the form of speech—an intent that no lower court has discerned and that, this late in the day, we would hesitate to impute to the Supreme Court.

Accordingly, we hold that plaintiffs have stated, sufficient to withstand summary judgment, a civil cause of action against Paladin Enterprises for aiding and abetting the murders of Mildred and Trevor Horn and Janice Saunders on the night of March 3, 1993, and that this cause of action is not barred by the First Amendment to the United States Constitution.

IV.

Paladin, joined by a spate of media amici, including many of the major networks, newspapers, and publishers, contends that any decision recognizing even a potential cause of action against Paladin will have far-reaching chilling effects on the rights of free speech and press. See Br. of Amici at 3, 22 ("Allowing this lawsuit to survive will disturb decades of First Amendment jurisprudence and jeopardize free speech from the periphery to the core. . . . No expression— music, video, books, even newspaper articles—would be safe from civil liability."). That the national media organizations would feel obliged to vigorously defend Paladin's assertion of a constitutional right to intentionally and knowingly assist murderers with technical information which Paladin admits it intended and knew would be used immediately in the commission of murder and other crimes against society is, to say the least, breathtaking. But be that as it may, it should be apparent from the foregoing that the indisputably important First Amendment values that Paladin and amici argue would be imperiled by a decision recognizing potential liability under the peculiar facts of this case will not even arguably be adversely affected by allowing plaintiffs' action against Paladin to proceed. In fact, neither the extensive briefing by the parties and the numerous amici in this case, nor the exhaustive research which the court itself has undertaken, has revealed even a single case that we regard as factually analogous to this case.

Paladin and amici insist that recognizing the existence of a cause of action against Paladin predicated on aiding and abetting will subject broadcasters and publishers to liability whenever someone imitates or "copies" conduct that is either described or depicted in their broadcasts, publications, or movies. This is simply not true. In the "copycat" context, it will presumably never be the case that the broadcaster or publisher actually intends, through its description or depiction, to assist another or others in the commission of violent crime; rather, the information for the dissemination of which liability is

sought to be imposed will actually have been misused vis-a-vis the use intended, not, as here, used precisely as intended. It would be difficult to overstate the significance of this difference insofar as the potential liability to which the media might be exposed by our decision herein is concerned.

And, perhaps most importantly, there will almost never be evidence proffered from which a jury even could reasonably conclude that the producer or publisher possessed the actual intent to assist criminal activity. In only the rarest case, as here where the publisher has stipulated in almost taunting defiance that it intended to assist murderers and other criminals, will there be evidence extraneous to the speech itself which would support a finding of the requisite intent; surely few will, as Paladin has, "stand up and proclaim to the world that because they are publishers they have a unique constitutional right to aid and abet murder." Appellant's Reply Br. at 20. Moreover, in contrast to the case before us, in virtually every "copycat" case, there will be lacking in the speech itself any basis for a permissible inference that the "speaker" intended to assist and facilitate the criminal conduct described or depicted. Of course, with few, if any, exceptions, the speech which gives rise to the copycat crime will not directly and affirmatively promote the criminal conduct, even if, in some circumstances, it incidentally glamorizes and thereby indirectly promotes such conduct.

Additionally, not only will a political, informational, educational, entertainment, or other wholly legitimate purpose for the description or depiction be demonstrably apparent; but the description or depiction of the criminality will be of such a character that an inference of impermissible intent on the part of the producer or publisher would be unwarranted as a matter of law. So, for example, for almost any broadcast, book, movie, or song that one can imagine, an inference of unlawful motive from the description or depiction of particular criminal conduct therein would almost never be reasonable, for not only will there be (and demonstrably so) a legitimate and lawful purpose for these communications, but the contexts in which the descriptions or depictions appear will themselves negate a purpose on the part of the producer or publisher to assist others in their undertaking of the described or depicted conduct. Compare Miller, 413 U.S. 15, 93 S.Ct. 2607.

Paladin contends that exposing it to liability under the circumstances presented here will necessarily expose broadcasters and publishers of the news, in particular, to liability when persons mimic activity either reported on or captured on film footage and disseminated in the form of broadcast news. Appellee's Br. at 26 n.17. This contention, as well, is categorically wrong. News reporting, we can assume, no matter how explicit it is in its description or depiction of criminal activity, could never serve as a basis for aiding and abetting liability consistent with the First Amendment. It will be self-evident in the context of news reporting, if nowhere else, that neither the intent of the reporter nor the purpose of the report is to facilitate repetition of the crime or other conduct reported upon, but, rather, merely to report on the particular event, and thereby to inform the public.

A decision that Paladin may be liable under the circumstances of this case is not even tantamount to a holding that all publishers of instructional manuals may be liable for the misconduct that ensues when one follows the instructions which appear in those manuals. Admittedly, a holding that Paladin is not entitled to an absolute defense to the plaintiffs' claims here may not bode well for those publishers, if any, of factually detailed instructional books, similar to Hit Man, which are devoted exclusively to teaching the techniques of violent activities that are criminal per se. But, in holding that a defense to liability may not inure to publishers for their dissemination of such manuals of criminal conduct, we do not address ourselves to the potential liability of a publisher for the criminal use of published instructions on activity that is either entirely lawful, or lawful or not depending upon the circumstances of its occurrence. Assuming, as we do, that liability could not be imposed in these circumstances on a finding of mere foreseeability or knowledge that the instructions might be misused for a criminal purpose, the chances that claims arising from the publication of instructional manuals like these can withstand motions for summary judgment directed to the issue of intent seem to us remote indeed, at least absent some substantial confirmation of specific intent like that that exists in this case.

Thus, while the "horribles" paraded before us by Paladin and amici have quite properly prompted us to examine and reexamine the established authorities on which plaintiffs' case firmly rests, we regard them ultimately as but anticipatory of cases wholly unlike the one we must decide today.

Paladin Press in this case has stipulated that it specifically targeted the market of murderers, would-be murderers, and other criminals for sale of its murder manual.

Paladin has stipulated both that it had knowledge and that it intended that Hit Man would immediately be used by criminals and would-be criminals in the solicitation, planning, and commission of murder and murder for hire. And Paladin has stipulated that, through publishing and selling Hit Man, it "assisted" Perry in particular in the perpetration of the brutal triple murders for which plaintiffs now seek to hold the publisher liable. Beyond these startling stipulations, it is alleged, and the record would support, that Paladin assisted Perry through the quintessential speech act of providing Perry with detailed factual instructions on how to prepare for, commit, and cover up his murders, instructions which themselves embody not so much as a hint of the theoretical advocacy of principles divorced from action that is the hallmark of protected speech. And it is alleged, and a jury could find, that Paladin's assistance assumed the form of speech with little, if any, purpose beyond the unlawful one of facilitating murder.

Paladin's astonishing stipulations, coupled with the extraordinary comprehensiveness, detail, and clarity of Hit Man's instructions for criminal activity and murder in particular, the boldness of its palpable exhortation to murder, the alarming power and effectiveness of its peculiar form of instruction, the notable absence from its text of the kind of ideas for the protection of which the First Amendment exists, and the book's evident lack of any even arguably legitimate purpose beyond the promotion and teaching of murder, render this case unique in the law. In at least these circumstances, we are confident that the First Amendment does not erect the absolute bar to the imposition of civil liability for which Paladin Press and amici contend. Indeed, to hold that the First Amendment forbids liability in such circumstances as a matter of law would fly in the face of all precedent of which we are aware, not only from the courts of appeals but from the Supreme Court of the United States itself. Hit Man is, we are convinced, the speech that even Justice Douglas, with his unrivaled devotion to the First Amendment, counseled without any equivocation "should be beyond the pale" under a Constitution that reserves to the people the ultimate and necessary authority to adjudge some conduct—and even some speech—fundamentally incompatible with the liberties they have secured unto themselves.

The judgment of the district court is hereby reversed, and the case remanded for trial.

It is so ordered.

(Cite as: 404 Mass. 624, 536 N.E.2d 1067)

Supreme Judicial Court of Massachusetts,

Middlesex.

William V. YAKUBOWICZ, administrator, [FN1]

FN1. Of the estate of Martin Yakubowicz.

v.

PARAMOUNT PICTURES CORPORATION et al. [FN2]

FN2. Saxon Theatre Corporation.

Argued Dec. 8, 1988.

Decided April 18, 1989.

Father whose son was killed by youth who had attended violent motion picture produced and distributed by defendants brought suit for wrongful death of son. The Superior Court, Middlesex County, J. Harold Flannery, J., granted defendants' motion for summary judgment, and appeal was taken. The Supreme Judicial Court, O'Connor, J., held that: (1) motion picture portraying violent adventures of juvenile gang, but which did not overtly advocate or encourage unlawful or violent activity on part of viewers, was protected by free speech clause of First Amendment and was not unprotected "incitement," and (2) motion picture producer was not liable, on the failure to warn theory, for fatal assault committed miles from theater.

Affirmed.

WEST HEADNOTES

[1] **Negligence**   ☞ **1692**
272k1692
    (Formerly 272k136(14))

Existence of duty of care, breach of which might support claim in negligence, is question of law for court.

[2] **Negligence**   ☞ **233**
272k233
    (Formerly 272k4)

In deciding whether the law should impose duty of reasonable care on defendant, Supreme Judicial Court looks to existing social values and customs, and to appropriate social policy.

[3] **Products Liability**   ☞ **62**
313Ak62

Motion picture producer and distributor owed duty of reasonable care to movie patron with respect to the producing, exhibiting, and advertising of picture.

[4] **Constitutional Law**   ☞ **90.1(6)**
92k90.1(6)

[4] **Products Liability**   ☞ **62**
313Ak62

Motion picture portraying the violent adventures of juvenile gang, but which did not overtly advocate or encourage unlawful or violent activity on part of viewers, did not fall within "incitement" exception to First Amendment; accordingly, negligence action against producer and distributor of picture for injuries resulting from violent assault by theater patron was barred on free speech grounds. U.S.C.A. Const.Amend. 1.

[5] **Products Liability**   ☞ **62**
313Ak62

[5] **Products Liability**   ☞ **88**
313Ak88

Producer of motion picture dealing with street gang violence was not liable on failure to warn theory for assault committed miles from theater by teenage boy who had seen picture; assault could not be attributed, as matter of law, to a failure to warn theater owner or public officials of dangers of film-related violence.

[6] Intoxicating Liquors 🗝 **299**
223k299

Theater owner did not owe nonpatron murdered several miles from theater any duty to protect against violent acts of teenage moviegoer who smuggled alcohol into theater and became drunk while watching show.

Elizabeth N. Mulvey, Boston, for plaintiff.

David W. Rosenberg, Boston, for Paramount Pictures Corp.

James S. Dittmar (Gordon P. Katz, Rhonda L. Russian, Boston, & Joseph H. Caffrey with him), for Saxon Theatre Corp.

Before HENNESSEY, C.J., and ABRAMS, NOLAN, LYNCH and O'CONNOR, JJ.

O'CONNOR, Justice.

The plaintiff, William Yakubowicz, administrator of the estate of his son, Martin Yakubowicz, appeals from an order of the Superior Court granting summary judgment to the defendants, Paramount Pictures Corporation (Paramount) and Saxon Theatre Corporation (Saxon), on a complaint seeking damages for wrongful death under G.L. c. 229, § 2 (1986 ed.). The complaint alleges that sixteen-year-old Martin Yakubowicz died from a knife wound intentionally inflicted on February 15, 1979, by Michael Barrett, who was returning from a theatre in Boston operated by Saxon, after viewing the motion picture, "The Warriors," which was produced and distributed by Paramount. The complaint alleges that both defendants knew of violence and threats of violence perpetrated by members of "gangs" attending showings of the film in Boston and in California, and that Martin Yakubowicz's death was causally related to the defendants' exhibition of the film to Michael Barrett.

Specifically, count one alleges that Paramount produced, distributed, and advertised "The Warriors" in such a way as to induce film viewers to commit violence in imitation of the violence in the film. Counts two and four allege that Paramount and Saxon caused the decedent's death by continuing to exhibit the film after learning of "an unprecedented series of lawless violent acts" at or near theatres showing the film. Count three charges Paramount with failure to warn exhibitors and public authorities of the danger of violence, and "failure to take reasonable steps to protect [persons] at or near the theatre." Count five

alleges that Michael Barrett consumed alcohol while viewing "The Warriors," and left the theatre in an intoxicated state, and charges Saxon with failing to exercise proper supervision and control over its patrons.

Both defendants moved for summary judgment, arguing that, as a matter of law, they owed no duty to the decedent, and that the First Amendment to the United States Constitution and art. 16 of the Declaration of Rights of the Massachusetts Constitution, as amended by art. 77 of the Amendments, bar liability for their exhibition of the film. The judge who ruled on the motions for summary judgment noted that the "decedent was neither a patron nor within the proximity of the Saxon Theatre at the time of the incident," and that Saxon did not supply Barrett with any alcoholic beverages. He concluded that there was no "special relationship" between the plaintiff's decedent and either defendant and that therefore the defendants owed no duty to the plaintiff's decedent. Accordingly, the judge granted the defendants' motion without reaching the constitutional question. We affirm the summary judgment order, although our reasoning differs from that of the judge.

"Rule 56(c) of the Massachusetts Rules of Civil Procedure, 365 Mass. 824 (1974), provides that summary judgment is appropriate 'if the pleadings, depositions, answers to interrogatories, and admissions on file, together with the affidavits, if any, show that there is no genuine issue as to any material fact and that the moving party is entitled to a judgment as a matter of law.' 'The party moving for summary judgment assumes the burden of affirmatively demonstrating that there is no genuine issue of material fact on every relevant issue, even if he would have no burden on an issue if the case were to go to trial.' Pederson v. Time, Inc., 404 Mass. 14, 17, 532 N.E.2d 1211 (1989). Attorney Gen. v. Bailey, 386 Mass. 367, 371, 436 N.E.2d 139, cert. denied sub nom. Bailey v. Bellotti, 459 U.S. 970, 103 S.Ct. 301, 74 L.Ed.2d 282 (1982)." Leavitt v. Mizner, 404 Mass. 81, 88, 533 N.E.2d 1334 (1989). Accordingly, we look at the materials available to the judge for summary judgment purposes in the light most favorable to the plaintiff to see whether, as a matter of law, they support a claim for wrongful death.

The materials submitted to the motion judge present the following facts. "The Warriors" is a motion picture produced, distributed, marketed, and advertised by

Paramount. The film includes numerous scenes of juvenile gang-related violence in which youths battle with knives, guns, and other weapons as they pursue one gang, the "Warriors," through the subways of New York City. Advertising for the film depicted menacing youths wielding baseball bats. The film opened at the Saxon Theatre on February 9, 1979. Paramount executives scheduled the film for release in Massachusetts during February school vacation week in order to maximize attendance by high school-aged patrons.

On February 12, 1979, two youths were killed near theatres showing "The Warriors" in Palm Springs and Oxnard, California. [FN3] Paramount officials were aware of claims that the Palm Springs killing was related to the viewing of the film, "The Warriors." On February 13, 1979, Frank Mancuso, a Paramount employee in charge of film distribution throughout the United States, distributed a telegram to his district and branch managers ordering them to advise each theatre showing "The Warriors" to hire security guards. The telegram stated that "there have been incidents of violence at theatres that might have been prevented with proper security and crowd control." Paramount offered to pay for the extra security. Saxon, in a letter to Paramount dated February 15, 1979, accepted the offer of reimbursement for extra security and also reported a problem of vandalism at showings of "The Warriors."

> FN3. The plaintiff states "[u]pon information and belief" that these youths were killed "by persons who just had seen" "The Warriors." The plaintiff's brief supports this statement by citing the transcript of a news report; however, this news report does not in fact state whether the assailants had seen the motion picture.

On the evening of February 15, 1979, Michael Barrett and two friends went to see "The Warriors" at the Saxon Theatre on Tremont Street in Boston. Before arriving at the theatre, Barrett and one of his friends purchased liquor. Barrett's friend hid liquor bottles in the pockets of his jacket, and also poured a bottle of whiskey into a half-empty soft drink container. On the way into the theatre, an employee stopped Barrett, who was carrying the container. Barrett said to the theatre employee, "Want to smell it? It's only Coke," and the employee let him into the theatre with the container. This violated a Saxon policy against admitting patrons carrying alcoholic beverages or bottles of any kind. Once inside the theatre, Barrett began drinking, in violation of Saxon's policy against

consuming alcohol on the premises. Saxon did not have a license for the sale or distribution of alcoholic beverages, and Saxon employees did not provide Barrett with any alcohol. Barrett and his friends sat through two showings of the movie. Barrett became so intoxicated that he vomited and passed out at the theatre during the second showing. After the movie, Barrett and his friends left the theatre and headed back to Dorchester by way of the Park Street subway station.

Another group of Dorchester teenagers, including Dino Troila, attended the same showing of "The Warriors" and also headed home by way of the Park Street station. There was a history of arguments and "tension" between this group and the group of youths that Barrett "hung out" with. While the teenagers were waiting for the train, the decedent came onto the platform. He had not been to see "The Warriors," but had been at work at a ski shop on Boylston Street. The decedent was friendly with Troila and got on the train with that group. Barrett and his friends boarded the same car.

As the train approached the Fields Corner subway station in Dorchester, Barrett's friend, Mark Rogers, approached Troila and tried to arrange a fight "one on one" between the decedent and Barrett. Barrett also began yelling at the decedent and challenging him to fight. Barrett referred to a fight that had occurred several months earlier between Barrett and some friends of the decedent. The decedent was not present at that earlier fight. Barrett said to the decedent, "I want you, I'm going to get you," purportedly in imitation of a scene from "The Warriors." The decedent repeatedly told Barrett that he did not want to fight.

Both groups left the subway at the Fields Corner station. As the decedent passed through the turnstyle area, Barrett, who was still drunk, jumped on him and began to fight. Troila and Rogers also became involved in the altercation. Barrett pulled a knife and stabbed the decedent in the chest. The decedent died the following morning.

On February 16, 1979, the day following the stabbing, Frank Mancuso, on behalf of Paramount, distributed a telegram offering to release theatre owners from their contractual obligations to show "The Warriors." The telegram stated: "It has come to our attention through newspaper and television reports that acts of violence and vandalism have occurred in and around theatres exhibiting THE WARRIORS. . . .

Please be advised that in the event you believe that the exhibition of this motion picture in your theatre poses a risk to persons or property, then Paramount will relieve you of your obligation to exhibit the picture. . . ." The telegram also stated that Paramount was cancelling all Paramount supported advertising for "The Warriors." This was the first time that Paramount ever took such action. Saxon received this telegram, but continued to exhibit "The Warriors" daily through April 5, 1979.

Counts one through four of the complaint allege, in essence, that Paramount was negligent in the way it produced, distributed, advertised, and exhibited the film, "The Warriors," and that Saxon was negligent in its continued exhibition of the film, and that the defendants' negligence proximately caused the death of the plaintiff's decedent.

[1][2][3] "There can be negligence only where there is a duty to be careful," Theriault v. Pierce, 307 Mass. 532, 533, 30 N.E.2d 682 (1940), and whether there is a duty to be careful is a question of law. Monadnock Display Fireworks, Inc. v. Andover, 388 Mass. 153, 156, 445 N.E.2d 1053 (1983). In determining whether the law ought to provide that a duty of care is owed by one person to another, we look to existing social values and customs, and to appropriate social policy. Schofield v. Merrill, 386 Mass. 244, 246-254, 435 N.E.2d 339 (1982). A basic principle of negligence law is that ordinarily everyone has a duty to refrain from affirmative acts that unreasonably expose others to a risk of harm. Thus, we have held that a keeper of a tavern owes to travelers on the highway a duty of care with respect to the furnishing of alcoholic beverages to his customers, Cimino v. Milford Keg, Inc., 385 Mass. 323, 327, 431 N.E.2d 920 (1982); Adamian v. Three Sons, Inc., 353 Mass. 498, 233 N.E.2d 18 (1968), and the proprietor of a liquor store owes a duty of care to the public which may be violated by selling liquor to minors, Michnik-Zilberman v. Gordon's Liquor, Inc., 390 Mass. 6, 10-12, 453 N.E.2d 430 (1983). In keeping with that principle, Paramount and Saxon owed a duty of reasonable care to members of the public including the plaintiff's decedent with respect to the producing, exhibiting, and advertising of movies.

[4] The next question is whether there is a genuine issue with respect to whether that duty was violated. With reference to counts one, two, and four of the plaintiff's complaint alleging negligence in the creation and exhibition of "The Warriors," we conclude that, as a matter of law, the defendants did not violate their duty of reasonable care. This conclusion follows from the First and Fourteenth Amendments to the United States Constitution and art. 16. "Motion pictures are a significant medium for the communication of ideas." Joseph Burstyn, Inc. v. Wilson, 343 U.S. 495, 501, 72 S.Ct. 777, 780, 96 L.Ed. 1098 (1952). They are protected by the First Amendment just like other forms of expression. Id. at 502, 72 S.Ct. at 780. It is immaterial for First Amendment purposes whether speech is suppressed under the criminal law or by "penalties" imposed by tort law. See New York Times Co. v. Sullivan, 376 U.S. 254, 277, 84 S.Ct. 710, 724, 11 L.Ed.2d 686 (1964) ("What a State may not constitutionally bring about by means of a criminal statute is likewise beyond the reach of its civil law of libel"). Although freedom of speech is not absolute, and liability may exist for tortious conduct in the form of speech, see Weirum v. RKO Gen., Inc., 15 Cal.3d 40, 123 Cal.Rptr. 468, 539 P.2d 36 (1975), the recognized exceptions to First Amendment protection are narrowly defined and, as we discuss below, do not reach "The Warriors." We conclude that the defendants could not properly be found to have violated their duty of reasonable care by exercising protected rights of free speech. [FN4]

FN4. In any event, the defendants cannot be liable for exercising those rights. See New York Times Co. v. Sullivan, supra 376 U.S. at 283, 84 S.Ct. at 727.

The plaintiff contends that "The Warriors" falls within the "incitement" exception to First Amendment protection. This exception applies to speech which advocates "the use of force or of law violation . . . where such advocacy is directed to inciting or producing imminent lawless action and is likely to incite or produce such action." Brandenburg v. Ohio, 395 U.S. 444, 447, 89 S.Ct. 1827, 1829, 23 L.Ed.2d 430 (1969). But speech does not lose its First Amendment protection merely because it has "a tendency to lead to violence." Hess v. Indiana, 414 U.S. 105, 109, 94 S.Ct. 326, 329, 38 L.Ed.2d 303 (1973).

A copy of the film has been made available as part of the record on summary judgment. The undisputed affidavit of Alfred F. LoPresti, a Paramount senior vice president, asserts that this copy is identical to the one exhibited to Barrett at the Saxon Theatre. We treat as a question of law whether this film constitutes "incitement" for First Amendment purposes.

DeFilippo v. National Broadcasting Co., 446 A.2d 1036, 1041 (R.I.1982). Although that determination is essentially a factual one, it is our responsibility to decide it incidental to our legal determination whether the movie is protected by the First Amendment. See Bose Corp. v. Consumers Union of U.S., Inc., 466 U.S. 485, 505-506, 104 S.Ct. 1949, 1962-63, 80 L.Ed.2d 502 (1984); New York Times Co. v. Sullivan, supra 376 U.S. at 285, 84 S.Ct. at 728.

Based on our viewing of the film, we conclude that nothing in it constitutes unprotected incitement. "The Warriors" is a work of fiction portraying the adventures of one New York City youth gang being pursued through territory controlled by hostile gangs. Although the film is rife with violent scenes, it does not at any point exhort, urge, entreat, solicit, or overtly advocate or encourage unlawful or violent activity on the part of viewers. It does not create the likelihood of inciting or producing "imminent lawless action" that would strip the film of First Amendment protection. Brandenburg v. Ohio, supra. The movie does not "purport to order or command anyone to any concrete action at any specific time, much less immediately." McCollum v. CBS, Inc., 202 Cal.App.3d 989, 1001, 249 Cal.Rptr. 187 (1988). See Olivia N. v. National Broadcasting Co., 126 Cal.App.3d 488, 496, 178 Cal.Rptr. 888 (1981), discussing Weirum v. RKO Gen., Inc., 15 Cal.3d 40, 123 Cal.Rptr. 468, 539 P.2d 36 (1975). Therefore, we hold that the defendant Paramount did not act unreasonably in producing, distributing, and exhibiting "The Warriors," because such expression is protected by the First Amendment. Accordingly, Saxon, too, did not act unreasonably in exhibiting "The Warriors." "[I]t is simply not acceptable to a free and democratic society . . . to limit and restrict . . . creativity in order to avoid the dissemination of ideas in artistic speech which may adversely affect emotionally troubled individuals." McCollum v. CBS, Inc., supra 202 Cal.App.3d at 1005-1006, 249 Cal.Rptr. 187. We thus conclude that summary judgment for the defendants is proper on counts one, two, and four.

[5] Count three of the complaint alleges that Paramount failed to take reasonable steps "to warn the exhibitors of the film and those responsible for the safety of the public" and "to take reasonable steps to protect [people] at or near the theatre." The judge correctly ordered summary judgment for Paramount on count three. A fatal assault occurring miles from the theatre as a matter of law could not be attributed to a failure to "protect [people] at or near the theatre" or a failure to warn Saxon or public officials of the dangers of film-related violence.

[6] Count five of the complaint rests on the assertion that Saxon failed to exercise proper supervision and control over its patrons in that it permitted Barrett "to consume excessive amounts of alcoholic beverages and other intoxicants while viewing "The Warriors," and that, while under the influence of these intoxicants Barrett killed the decedent. The judge properly entered summary judgment for Saxon on this count on the ground that Saxon did not owe the decedent a duty to protect him from acts resulting from Barrett's self-induced intoxication. The uncontradicted affidavit of one of the persons accompanying Barrett to the theatre states that, during the showing of the movie, Barrett drank liquor that he and his friends had smuggled into the theatre. The record also contains the uncontradicted affidavit of the former manager of the Saxon Theatre that, on the night in question, Saxon personnel neither sold nor distributed any alcoholic beverages or other intoxicants to theatre patrons. Thus, Saxon's situation was entirely different from the situation of the defendants in Cimino v. Milford Keg, Inc., supra; Adamian v. Three Sons, Inc., supra; and Michnik-Zilberman v. Gordon's Liquor, Inc., supra. We have never imposed tort liability on a defendant whose premises are simply used for the consumption of alcoholic beverages, even with the defendant's knowledge, where the defendant did not serve or supply the intoxicants. See Dhimos v. Cormier, 400 Mass. 504, 509 N.E.2d 1199 (1987); Langemann v. Davis, 398 Mass. 166, 495 N.E.2d 847 (1986).

Judgment affirmed.

Ronald A. WEIRUM et al., Plaintiffs and Appellants.

v.

RKO GENERAL, INC., Defendant and Appellant, Marsha L. Baime, Defendant and Appellant.

L.A. 30452.

Supreme Court of California.

Aug. 21, 1975.

An action was brought for wrongful death of plaintiff's decedent who was killed when his automobile was negligently forced off a highway by a listener to defendant's radio station which was conducting a contest rewarding the first contestant to locate a peripatetic disc jockey. The District Court, Ventura County, Marvin H. Lewis, J., entered judgment for plaintiffs against radio broadcaster and it appealed. The Supreme Court, Mosk, J., held that evidence supported jury finding of foreseeability of injury or death in that it was foreseeable that broadcaster's youthful listeners, finding the prize had eluded them at one location, would race to arrive first at the next site and in their haste disregard demands of highway safety; the court further held that broadcaster was not insulated from such liability on basis of deference due society's interest in the First Amendment; it was further held that broadcaster could not escape liability on basis that it had no duty to control conduct of third parties, in view of fact broadcaster's liability was grounded upon an affirmative act of misfeasance creating an undue risk of harm, and not upon mere nonfeasance.

Judgment and orders affirmed.

Opinion, Cal.App., 119 Cal.Rptr. 151 vacated.

1. **Negligence k136(2)** The determination of existence of a duty of due care is primarily a question of law.

2. **Negligence k2** Any number of considerations may justify imposition of a duty of due care in particular circumstances, including guidance of history, refined concepts of morals and justice, convenience of the rule, and social judgment as to where loss should fall.

3. **Negligence k2** While question of whether one owes a duty of due care to another must be decided on a case-by-case basis, every case is governed by rule of general application that all persons are required to use ordinary care to prevent others from being injured as the result of their conduct.

4. **Negligence k10** Foreseeability of risk is a primary consideration in establishing element of duty of due care.

5. **Negligence 136(16)** While existence of duty of due care is a question of law, foreseeability of risk of harm from an activity is a question of fact for the jury.

6. **Appeal and Error k1001(1), 1002** Review of implied jury finding of foreseeability of risk of harm was limited to a determination of whether there was any substantial evidence, contradicted or uncontradicted, supporting the finding.

7. **Automobiles k244(22)** Evidence, in action for wrongful death arising out of an automobile collision allegedly caused by negligence of defendant radio station in conducting a contest wherein contestants had to drive their automobiles and be the first to locate a peripatetic disc jockey, supported jury finding of foreseeability of injury or death in that it was foreseeable that broadcaster's youthful listeners, finding the prize had eluded them at one location, would race to arrive first at the next site and in their haste disregard demands of highway safety.

8. **Automobiles k197(1)** A radio broadcaster was not excused from liability for negligence in sponsoring a radio contest under which it was foreseeable that listeners, in order to win a prize, would race about in their automobiles to be first to arrive at a certain site wherein a disc jockey of the broadcaster would appear, on basis that harm, if any, to other persons would be inflicted by third parties acting negligently; such concept is valid, only to extent intervening concept cannot be anticipated.

9. **Negligence k10** If the likelihood that a third person may react in a particular manner is a hazard which makes the actor negligent, such reaction whether innocent or negligent does not prevent the actor from being liable for the harm caused thereby.

10. **Negligence k1** Liability for negligence is imposed only if the risk of harm resulting from the act

is deemed unreasonable—that is, if the gravity and likelihood of the danger outweigh the utility of the conduct involved.

11. **Constitutional Law k90.1(9)**   A radio broadcaster's liability for negligence in conducting a giveaway contest in such manner as to create a high risk of injury or death to motorists and pedestrians was not insulated from such liability on basis of deference due society's interest in the First Amendment. U.S.C.A. Const. Amend. I.

12. **Automobiles k197(1)**   Imposition of duty of due care upon a radio broadcaster in regard to conducting of a contest requiring listeners to move about in their automobiles and find a certain disc jockey would not be denied upon basis that it might lead to unwarranted extension of liability to other entrepreneurs.

13. **Automobiles k197(1)**   A radio broadcaster which sponsored a contest rewarding first contestant locating a peripatetic disc jockey, could not escape liability on basis that it had no duty to control conduct of third parties in manner in which they drove their automobiles, in view of fact broadcaster's liability was grounded upon an affirmative act of misfeasance creating an undue risk of harm, and not upon mere nonfeasance.

14. **Appeal and Error k882(12)**   Defendant could not attack substance of instruction requested by plaintiff where defendant himself proposed a similar instruction.

15. **Trial k312(1)**   A trial court possesses inherent right on its own motion to recall jurors for further instructions.

16. **Appeal and Error k1069.3**   Recalling of jury in a negligence action during third day of its deliberations for reading to it of an unintentionally omitted instruction would not be considered prejudicial on basis of overemphasis where prefatory remarks of trial judge minimized any such tendency and where defendant failed to request either additional cautionary instructions or a rereading of all related instructions.

Robert O. Angle, Hollister & Brace, and Richard C. Monk, Santa Barbara, for plaintiffs and appellants.

Stearns & Nelson, Stearns, Nelson & LeBerthon, Robert S. Stearns, Hollywood, Lascher & Radar, Edward L. Lascher and Wendy Cole Wilner, Ventura, for defendant and appellant.

Benton, Orr, Duval, Buckingham and James F. McGahan, Ventura, for defendant and respondents.

MOSK, Justice.

A rock radio station with an extensive teenage audience conducted a contest which rewarded the first contestant to locate a peripatetic disc jockey. Two minors driving in separate automobiles attempted to follow the disc jockey's automobile to its next stop. In the course of their pursuit, one of the minors negligently forced a car off the highway, killing its sole occupant. In a suit filed by the surviving wife and children of the descendent, the jury rendered a verdict against the radio station. We now must determine whether the station owed decedent a duty of due care.

The facts are not disputed. Radio station KHJ is a successful Los Angeles broadcaster with a large teenage following. At the time of the accident, KHJ commanded a 48 percent plurality of the teenage audience in the Los Angeles area. In contrast, its nearest rival during the same period was able to capture only 13 percent of the teenage listeners. In order to attract an even larger portion of the available audience and thus increase advertising revenue. KHJ inaugurated in July of 1970 a promotion entitled "The Super Summer Spectacular." The "spectacular," with a budget of approximately $40,000 for the month, was specifically designed to make the radio station "more exciting." Among the programs included in the "spectacular" was a contest broadcast on July 16, 1970, the date of the accident.

On that day, Donald Steele Revert, known professionally as "The Real Don Steele," a KHJ disc jockey and television personality, traveled in a conspicuous red automobile to a number of locations in the Los Angeles metropolitan area. Periodically, he apprised KHJ of his whereabouts and his intended destination, and the station broadcast the information to its listeners. The first person to physically locate Steele and fulfill a specified condition received a cash prize.[1] In addition, the winning contestant participated in a brief interview on the air with "The Real Don Steele." The following excerpts from the July 16 broadcast illustrate the tenor of the contest announcements:

---

1. The conditions varied from the giving of a correct response to a question to the possession of particular items of clothing.

"9:30 and The Real Don Steele is back on his feet again with some money and he is headed for the Valley. Thought I would give you a warning so that you can get your kids out of the street."

"The Real Don Steele is out driving on—could be in your neighborhood at any time and he's got bread to spread, so be on the lookout for him."

"The Real Don Steele is moving into Canoga Park—so be on the lookout for him. I'll tell you what will happen if you get to The Real Don Steele. He's got twenty-five dollars to give away if you can get it . . . and baby, all signed and sealed and delivered and wrapped up."

"10:54—The Real Don Steele is in the Valley near the intersection of Topanga and Roscoe Boulevard, right by the Loew's Holiday Theater—you know where that is at, and he's standing there with a little money he would like to give away to the first person to arrive and tell him what type car I helped Robert W. Morgan give away yesterday morning at KHJ. What was the make of the car. If you know that, split Intersection of Topanga and and Roscoe Boulevard—right nearby the Loew's Holiday Theater—you will find The Real Don Steele. Tell him and pick up the bread."

In Van Nuys, a 17-year-old Robert Sentner was listening to KHJ in his car while searching for "The Real Don Steele." Upon hearing that "The Real Don Steele" was proceeding to Canoga Park, he immediately drove to that vicinity. Meanwhile in Northridge, 19-year-old Marsha Baime heard and responded to the same information. Both of them arrived at the Holiday Theater in Canoga Park to find that someone had already claimed the prize. Without knowledge of the other, each decided to follow the Steele vehicle to its next stop and thus be the first to arrive when the next contest question or condition was announced.

For the next few miles the Sentner and Baime cars jockeyed for position closest to the Steele vehicle, reaching speeds up to 80 miles an hour.[2] About a mile and a half from the Westlake offramp the two teenagers heard the following broadcast:

"11:13—The Real Don Steele with bread is heading for Thousand Oaks to give it away. Keep

listening to KHJ . . . The Real Don Steele out on the highway—with bread to give away—be on the lookout, he may stop in Thousand Oaks and may stop along the way. . . . Looks like it may be a good stop Steele—drop some bread to those folks."

The Steele vehicle left the freeway at the Westlake offramp. Either Baime or Sentner, in attempting to follow, forced decedent's car onto the center divider, where it overturned. Baime stopped to report the accident. Sentner, after pausing momentarily to relate the tragedy to a passing peace officer, continued to pursue Steele, successfully located him and collected a cash prize.

Decedent's wife and children brought an action for wrongful death against Sentner. Baime, RKO General, Inc., as owner of KHJ, and the maker of decedent's car. Sentner settled prior to the commencement of trial for the limits of his insurance policy. The jury returned a verdict against Baime and KHJ in the amount of $300,000 and found in favor of the manufacturer of decedent's car. KHJ appeals from the ensuing judgment and from an order denying its motion for judgment notwithstanding the verdict. Baime did not appeal.[3]

[1–4] The primary question for our determination is whether defendant owed a duty to decedent arising out of its broadcast of the giveaway contest. The determination of duty is primarily a question of law. (Amaya v. Home Ice, Fuel & Supply Co., 1963 59 Cal.2d 295, 307, 29 Cal.Rptr. 33, 379 P.2d 513 overruled on other grounds in Dillon v. Legg 1968 68 Cal.2d 728, 748, 69 Cal.Rptr 72, 441 P.2d 912. It is the court's "expression of the sum total of those considerations of policy which lead the law to say that the particular plaintiff is entitled to protection." (Proser, Law of Torts (4th ed. 1971) pp. 325–326.) Any number of considerations may justify the imposition of duty in particular circumstances, including the guidance of history, our continually refined concepts of morals and justice, the convenience of the rule, and social judgment as to where the loss should fall. (Prosser, Palsgraf Revisited (1953) 52 Mich.1.Rev. 1, 15.) While the question whether one owes a duty to

---

2. It is not contended that the Steele vehicle at any time exceeded the speed limit.

3. Plaintiffs filed a cross-appeal from an order entered after judgment denying them certain costs against Baime and KHJ. They do not assert before this court that the order was erroneous, and we shall therefore affirm the order on the cross-appeal.

another must be decided on a case-by-case basis,[4] every case is governed by the rule of general application that all persons are required to use ordinary care to prevent others from being injured as the result of their conduct. (Hilyar v. Union Ice Co. (1955) 45 Cal.2d 30, 36, 286 P.2d 21.) However, foreseeability of the risk is a primary consideration in establishing the element of duty. (Dillon v. Legg, supra, 68 Cal.2d 728, 739, 69 Cal.Rptr. 72, 441 P.2d 912) Defendant asserts that the record here does not support a conclusion that a risk of harm to decedent was foreseeable.

[5,6] While duty is a question of law, foreseeability is a question of fact for the jury. (Wright v. Arcade School Dist. (1964) 230 Cal.App.2d 272, 277, 40 Cal.Rptr. 812.) The verdict in plaintiffs' favor here necessarily embraced a finding that decedent was exposed to a foreseeable risk of harm. It is elementary that our review of this finding is limited to the determination whether there is any substantial evidence, contradicted or uncontradicted, which will support the conclusion reached by the jury.

[7] We conclude that the record amply supports the finding of foreseeability. These tragic events unfolded in the middle of a Los Angeles summer, a time when young people were free from the constraints of school and responsive to relief from vacation tedium. Seeking to attract new listeners, KHJ devised an "exciting" promotion. Money and a small measure of momentary notoriety awaited the swiftest response. It was foreseeable that defendant's youthful listeners, finding the prize had eluded them at one location, would race to arrive first at the next site and in their

---

4. Defendant urges that we apply the factors enumerated in Connor v. Great Western Savings and Loan Association (1968) 69 Cal.2d 850, 865, 73 Cal.Rptr. 369, 447 P.2d 609, in determining whether it owed a duty to a decedent. In that case, however, the primary issue was whether a duty was to be imposed upon the defendant notwithstanding the absence of privity, and we therefore examined considerations appropriate to that contractual framework. For example, the first of the enumerated elements was the extent to which the transaction was intended to affect the plaintiff. Such a consideration manifestly failed to illuminate our inquiry in the present case. Generally speaking, standards relevant to the determination of duty in one particular situation may not be applied mechanically to other cases.

haste would disregard the demands of highway safety.

Indeed, "The Real Don Steele" testified that he had in the past noticed vehicles following him from location to location. He was further aware that the same contestants sometimes appeared at conservative stops. This knowledge is not rendered irrelevant, as defendant suggests, by the absence of any prior injury. Such an argument confuses foreseeability with hindsight, and amounts to a contention that the injuries of the first victim are not compensable. "The mere fact that a particular kind of an accident has not happened before does not . . . show that such accident is one which might not reasonably have been anticipated." (Ridley v. Grifall Trucking Co. (1955) 136 Cal.App.2d 682, 686, 289 P.2d 31, 34.) Thus, the fortuitous absence of prior injury does not justify relieving defendant from responsibility for the foreseeable consequences of its acts.

[8,9] It is of no consequence that the harm to decedent was inflicted by third parties acting negligently. Defendant invokes the maxim that an actor is entitled to assume that others will not act negligently. (Porter v. California Jockey Club, Inc. (1955) 134 Cal.App.2d 158, 160, 285 P.2d 60.) This concept is valid, however, only to the extent the intervening conduct was not to be anticipated. (Premo v. Grigg (1965) 237 Cal.App.2d 192, 195, 46 Cal.Rptr. 683.) If the likelihood that a third person may react in a particular manner is a hazard which makes the actor negligent, such reaction whether innocent or negligent does not prevent the actor from being liable for the harm caused thereby. (Richardson v. Ham (1955) 44 Cal.2d 772, 777, 285 P.2d 269. Here, reckless conduct by youthful contestants, stimulated by defendant's broadcast, constituted the hazard to which decedent was exposed.

[10] It is true, of course, that virtually every act involves some conceivable danger. Liability is imposed only if the risk of harm resulting from the act is deemed unreasonable—i.e., if the gravity and likelihood of the danger outweigh the utility of the conduct involved. (See Prosser, Law of Torts (4th ed. 1971) pp. 146–149.)

We need not belabor the grave danger inherent in the contest broadcast by defendant. The risk of a high speed automobile chase is the risk of death or serious injury. Obviously, neither the entertainment afforded by the contest nor its commercial rewards can justify the creation of such a grave risk. Defendant could have accomplished its objectives of entertaining its listeners and increasing advertising revenues by adopting a contest format which would have avoided danger to the motoring public.

[11] Defendant's contention that the giveaway contest must be afforded the deference due society's interest in the First Amendment is clearly without merit. The issue here is civil accountability for the foreseeable results of a broadcast which created an undue risk of harm to decedent. The First Amendment does not sanction the infliction of physical injury merely because achieved by word, rather than act.

[12] We are not persuaded that the imposition of a duty here will lead to unwarranted extensions of liability. Defendant is fearful that entrepreneurs will henceforth be burdened with an avalanche of obligations: an athletic department will owe a duty to an ardent sports fan injured while hastening to purchase one of a limited number of tickets; a department store will be liable to injuries incurred in response to a "while-they-last" sale. This argument, however, suffers from a myopic view of the facts presented here. The giveaway contest was no commonplace invitation to an attraction available on a limited basis. It was a competitive scramble in which the thrill of the chase to be the one and only victor was intensified by the live broadcasts which accompanied the pursuit. In the assertedly analogous situations described by defendant, any haste involved in the purchase of the commodity is an incidental and unavoidable result of the scarcity of the commodity itself. In such situations there is no attempt, as here, to generate a competitive pursuit on public streets, accelerated by repeated importuning by radio to be the very first to arrive at a particular destination. Manifestly the "spectacular" bears little resemblance to daily commercial activities.

[13] Defendant, relying upon the ruled stated in section 315 of the Restatment Second of Torts, urges that it owed no duty of care to decedent. The section provides that, absent a special relationship, an actor is under no duty to control the conduct of third parties. As explained hereinafter, this rule has no application if the plaintiff's complaint, as here, is grounded upon an affirmative act of defendant which created an undue risk of harm.

The ruled stated in section 315 is merely a refinement of the general principle embodied in section 314[5] that one is not obligated to act as a "good samaritan." (Rest.2d Torts, § 314, com. (a); James,

Scope of Duty in Negligence Cases (1953) 47 Nw.U.1. Rev. 778, 803.) This doctrine is rooted in the common law distinction between action and inaction, or misfeasance and nonfeasance. Misfeasance exists when the defendant is responsible for making the plaintiff's position worse, i.e., defendant has created a risk. Conversely, nonfeasance is found when the defendant has failed to aid plaintiff through beneficial intervention. As section 315 illustrates, liability for nonfeasance is largely limited to those circumstances in which some special relationship can be established. If, on the other hand, the act complained of is one of misfeasance, the question of duty is governed by the standards of ordinary care discussed above.

Here, there can be little doubt that we review an act of misfeasance to which section 315 is inapplicable. Liability is not predicated upon defendant's failure to intervene for the benefit of decedent but rather upon its creation of an unreasonable risk of harm to him. (See Shafer v. Keeley Ice Cream Co. (1925), 65 Utah 46, 234 P. 300.)[6] Defendant's reliance upon cases which involve the failure to prevent harm to another is therefore misplaced, e.g., Wright v. Arcade School Distr., supra, 230 Cal.App.2d 272, 40 Cal.Rptr. 812 (school district held free of a duty of care to children injured on their way to and from school).

---

5. Section 314 states: "The fact that the actor realizes or should realize that action on his part is necessary for another's aid or protection does not of itself impose upon him a duty to take such action."

---

6. In Shafer defendant entered a float in a commercial parade and as the float traveled down the street, employees threw candy to the crowd. Children running to collect the candy injured a spectator. The court distinguished cases in which the conduct of the person who immediately caused the accident was not set in motion by any act of the defendant on the ground that the defendant, in throwing the candy, induced the response of the children which resulted in the plaintiff's injuries.

Contrary to defendant's assertion, Shafer is not distinguishable because there the defendant had actual knowledge children were following the float and scrambling for candy. Such knowledge only obviated the need for a determination that the acts of the children were foreseeable. In the present case, as we have seen, the jury's determination that the accident was foreseeable is supported by the evidence.

Finally, we address the propriety of an allegedly erroneous and prejudicial instruction. The challenged instruction, though approved by the trial judge after submission by plaintiffs, was inadvertently omitted from the charge to the jury. Although plaintiffs immediately called the oversight to the judge's attention, the absence of a court reporter prevented verification of the omission until the morning of the jury's third day of deliberations. Thereupon, the judge recalled the jury, explained his inadvertent error, and read the instruction, which stated: "One who undertakes to direct the action of another has a duty to do so with due care."

[14] Defendant contends that the instruction was argumentative in that it focused exclusively on KHJ and no other defendant. We need not examine the merit of this assertion for defendant itself requested and received an instruction to substantially the same effect. That instruction began, "Every person who engages in a business activity which directs or influences the conduct of others and who, while so engaged exercises ordinary care. . . ."[7] It is well settled that a party cannot attack the substance of an instruction if he himself proposed similar instructions. (Smith v. Americania Motor Lodge (1974) 39 Cal.App.3d 1, 7, 113 Cal.Rptr. 771.) For the same reason, we reject defendant's contentions that there was no support in the record for the challenged instruction and that it was ambiguous.

Additionally, defendant claims that independent prejudice arose from the tardy and isolated manner in which the instruction was given. The jury, it is asserted, attached undue importance to the instruction because it was given by itself on the third day of deliberations. We do not agree.

[15, 16] The trial court possesses the inherent right on its own motion to recall the jurors for further instructions. (People v. Western (1965) 237 Cal.App.2d 232, 238, 46 Cal.Rptr. 699; People v. Hewitt (1936) 11 Cal.App.2d 197, 199, 53 P.2d 365.) In Davis v. Erickson (1960) 53 Cal.2d 860, 3 Cal.Rptr. 567, 350 P.2d 535, we stated if a court recalls the jury for the purpose of reading unintentionally omitted instructions the danger that the instruction will be overemphasized may be avoided if the court admonishes the jury not to attach any particular emphasis to the fact that it is reading certain instructions which had been inadvertently omitted in its first reading or by rereading all the instructions. Here the prefatory remarks of the trial judge minimized any tendency of the jury to be unduly impressed by the circumstances under which the instruction was given.

Moreover, defendant failed to request either additional cautionary instructions or a rereading of all related instructions. Under similar circumstances, it was held in Stoddard v. Rheem (1961) 192 Cal.App.2d 49, 13 Cal.Rptr. 496 that the defendant should not be permitted to stand silently by, giving the appearance of acquiescence in the manner in which an instruction was given and be later heard to complain, too late for curative measures to be taken.

The judgment and the orders appealed from are affirmed. Plaintiffs shall recover their costs on appeal. The parties shall bear their own costs on the cross-appeal.

WRIGHT, C. J., and McCOMB, TOBRINER, SULLIVAN, CLARK and RICHARDSON, JJ., concur.

---

7. The entire instruction read: "Every person who engages in a business activity which directs or influences the conduct of others and who, while so engaged, exercises ordinary care (in the manner in which said activity is conducted) has a right to assume that every other person will perform his duty and obey the law, and in the absence of reasonable cause for thinking otherwise or actual notice to the contrary, it is not negligence for such person to fail to anticipate an accident which can be occasioned only by a violation of law or duty by another person (or persons).

Glossary

abate pay less

abode service/substituted service to leave a copy of the summons and complaint at the defendant's usual place of residence with a person of suitable age and discretion who resides therein

actual authority authority granted by a principal to his agent

actual cause factual cause of the plaintiff's injuries

actus reus act

additur increase by a court in the amount of damages awarded by the jury

Adhesion contract contract in which the contracting parties have unequal bargaining positions and the party in the inferior bargaining position is forced to adhere to the other's terms without being allowed to negotiate the terms

adjudicatory hearing hearing before an administrative agency to resolve a dispute between an individual and an agency

administrative agency agency that creates and enforces rules on behalf of the legislative and executive branches of government

administrative decision decision that resolves a dispute between an individual and an agency regarding the application or interpretation of a rule or regulation

administrative law the law concerning the powers and procedures of administrative agencies

administrative law judges (ALJ) judge who resolves disputes between individuals and agencies regarding the application or interpretation of rules and regulations; also known as *hearing examiner* and *hearing officer*

Administrative Procedure Act act that sets forth the guidelines by which federal administrative agencies must operate

administrator person appointed to administer an intestate estate; in some states, a female administrator is called an *administratrix*

advance sheets pamphlet forms in which cases are first put together before they are bound

adverse possession taking possession of another's land without the owner's consent and retaining possession of that land for a period of time prescribed by statute

advocacy memorandum persuasive memo prepared for the court; also called a *points and authority memorandum*

affiant person signing an affidavit

affidavit of service/return of service/proof of service filed with the court, this serves as proof that delivery of a summons and complaint was actually made

affirmed when an appellate court leaves a trial court's decision unchanged

affirmative defense defense relying on factual issues not raised in the complaint

agent for service of process entity appointed to receive the summons and complaint in the event the partnership is sued

agents anyone who acts for or represents another

alimony payment of support made by a former spouse for the benefit of the other former spouse

allegations numbered paragraphs in which the plaintiff spells out his or her version of what happened to cause the dispute (2) statements in pleading (documents filed with court in which parties explain what the dispute is about) in which a party sets forth its version of what caused the dispute

alternative dispute resolution (ADR) approaches to dispute resolution that save individuals the time, expense, and psychological trauma of going to trial

amici friend of the court; a non-party who provides information to the court

annotated contains references to cases and other legal sources

annual report report describing the performance of the corporation during the preceding year

annulment court order declaring that a marriage never existed

antenuptial agreement also known as a *prenuptial agreement*; agreement entered into in anticipation of marriage that specifies the obligations and rights of the parties during marriage and upon termination of the marriage

apparent authority authority that arises when a principal allows a third person to reasonably believe that the agent has the authority to act on the principal's behalf

appeals a formal request in which a party asks a higher court to review the decision of a lower court and change it in some way

appellant person who files an appeal; sometimes known as the *petitioner*

appellate court court that reviews decisions made by lower courts

appellee person responding to an appeal; sometimes known as the *respondent*

arbitration allows parties to enjoy all the benefits of a trial without the inordinate expenditure of time and money

arbitrator the neutral third party who hears the evidence and renders a decision in an arbitration

arraignment hearing at which the judge informs the defendant of the charges being brought and the defendant enters a plea

arrest interfering with a suspect's freedom to the extent that the suspect is no longer free to go

arrest warrant court document authorizing the police to arrest a suspect

articles of incorporation documents that must be filed with the appropriate state agency to create a corporation

ascendants ancestor; blood relative of decedent related in an ascending lineal line (e.g., parents and grandparents)

assigned counsel private attorney paid by the state on a contractual basis to represent indigent defendants

associates an attorney with a firm who is being trained and evaluated to determine if he or she is partnership material and who, during that training period, receives a salary

assumption of risk doctrine that bars a plaintiff from recovery or reduces her recovery if the defendant can show that the plaintiff voluntarily consented to take a chance that harm would occur

attach seize property

attempt taking steps that go beyond mere preparation toward committing a crime

attorney-client privilege evidentiary rule that prohibits attorneys from testifying about communications made to them by their client and that prevents clients from having to testify about communications made to them by their attorney

authenticate verify evidence is in substantially the same condition as when it was collected

automatic stay an order by the bankruptcy court ordering plaintiffs to refrain from proceeding any further with their suits

bail the security given by the defendant to the court to guarantee his or her presence at trial in exchange for immediate release from custody

bankruptcy judges federal court judge who hears bankruptcy cases

bench all of the judges taken together

beneficiaries recipient of a benefit from a will or trust

bequest gift of personal property; also called a legacy

beyond a reasonable doubt standard of proof in criminal cases requiring that all reasonable doubt is removed from the jurors' minds

Bilateral contract offer that is to be accepted by a promise

binding final; non-appealable (2) law that the court is obligated to follow

binding arbitration arbitration in which the arbitrator's decision is final and non-appealable

binding authority authority that a court is required to follow

black letter law law that is standard and not subject to change

Boilerplate standardized language in a contract, often in fine print and difficult to understand

bond a document signed by the defendant and a bail bondsman requiring the bondsman to pay the court if the defendant fails to appear in court

bondholder one who owns a bond

bonds representations of a corporation's debt to investors

booked the administrative process involved in bringing a suspect into the jail or police facility

brief (v.) to prepare a written summary of a case (2) written argument explaining why a party believes the trial court's decision was or was not in error

bylaws rules governing the operation and management of the corporation

C corporations typical corporation; term used to distinguish a corporation from an S corporation

canons statements of general principles

canons of construction rules that guide courts in interpreting statutes

caption beginning of a court opinion where the parties and their relationship are identified (2) title page of a complaint

case brief a written summary of a case

case-in-chief the part of the prosecutor's case providing direct proof of the defendant's guilt

case law resolution of fact-specific disputes

case of first impression case pertaining to an issue that the court hearing the case has not considered before

causation link between the intent and the act

cause of action facts giving rise to a legal right to sue (2) lawsuit

centralized panel organization of ALJs so that they are detached from any particular agency

certificate of service statement at the end of a court paper reflecting that the paper was mailed (or hand-delivered), recording the date of mailing, and listing the names and addresses of each recipient

certification a voluntary process that recognizes those individuals who have met specified qualifications set forth by NALA, NFPA, and other state organizations

certify decision by a trial judge that a ruling can be appealed before the case is over

chain of custody proof of the location and condition of physical evidence from the time it is created until it appears in the courtroom

challenge for cause removal of a potential juror because the judge believes that the juror is likely to base a decision on personal beliefs or prejudices rather than on the evidence and the judge's instructions

chambers judge's private office

charging the jury process of giving jury instructions

charitable trust trust created for a social benefit; the beneficiaries can be members of the general public

circuit court second level of courts in the federal system; also formally known as the U.S. Court of Appeals

citation (also known as a *cite*) part of a court opinion that provides information identifying where the case can be located

cite checking checking the accuracy of legal citations

civil law law covering law suits brought by those who have suffered private wrongs for which they are seeking some form of compensation

clear and convincing evidence burden of proof that requires more proof than a preponderance of the evidence and less proof than beyond a reasonable doubt

close corporations small corporation owned by family members and friends in which the shareholders actively manage the business

closing arguments final arguments made by attorneys after the close of their presentation of evidence

codicil addition to a will

codified law laws that have been arranged according to subject matter; also referred to as codes

collateral someone having the same ancestors as the decedent, but not descending from the decedent (e.g., brothers and sisters)

commingled property having attributes of both marital and separate property

common law court-made law originating in England with the Norman Conquest. Prior to the Conquest, England had no centralized court system and disputes were resolved based on local custom. When William, Duke of Normandy, was crowned King of England, he appointed judges who "road the circuit," settling disputes in the name of the King. Although at first the judges decided each case as if it were the first of its kind, over time they realized they could be more efficient if they shared their decisions with each other. The resulting law became known as the common law.

common stock stock that has no special features

community property property acquired during marriage by personal earnings as well as property owned prior to marriage but contributed to marriage

community property with right of survivorship new marital property interest recognized by statute in some community property states that allows a married couple to hold title to property as a community asset, but to retain the ease of transfer permitted by joint tenancy

commuted reduction of a sentence by the governor or President

comparative negligence doctrine that reduces the amount of damages a plaintiff who contributed to her own injuries can recover

compensatory damages damages that compensate the non-breaching party for its losses

complaint a formal, written statement in which the plaintiff describes, in summary fashion, what the dispute is about and what the plaintiff wants the court to do

compulsory counterclaim claim that must be brought because it will be lost if it is not raised

conclusive presumption a presumption that could not be rebutted

conclusory writing coming to a conclusion without offering any explanation for how the conclusion was drawn

concurring opinions opinion written by a judge who has reached the same conclusion as the majority but for different or additional reasons

confidential relationship relationship based on trust and dependency

confidentiality the obligation to preserve the confidences and secrets of a client

conflict of interest conflict between the interests of one party and the interests of another party

conformed stamp copies of the complaint with the case number assigned by the court clerk when the complaint is filed

consequential damages damages resulting from a buyer's particular circumstances

conservative judicial philosophy requiring a strict interpretation of statutes and constitutions

consideration exchange of something of value

conspiracy agreement between two or more people to commit a crime

constitutional courts courts whose existence is derived from Article III of the U.S. Constitution; also known as *Article III* courts

constructive evicted tenant's moving out without paying rent for the remainder of the lease term because of landlord's failure to maintain habitable premises

contempt of court willful disobedience of a court order; an act that embarrasses the court or obstructs it in administering justice; contempt of court can result in a fine or incarceration

contingency fee agreement agreement in which an attorney provides services for no charge (except for payment of costs) in exchange for receiving a percentage of the client's recovery

contributory negligence doctrine that bars a plaintiff who contributed to her own injuries from recovering any damages

corporate supplies tools needed to operate a corporation, including minute book and stock certificate book

corporation business created by those who organize it, owned by shareholders, and managed by a board of directors

corpus body of the trust, including principal and accrued income

corpus delicti body of a crime

counsel emeritus an attorney who has retired but who is still associated with a firm

counterclaim claim that a defendant brings against the plaintiff

counts section of a complaint establishing the elements of a particular cause of action

court-annexed arbitration arbitration that takes place within the court system and that is governed by local rules

Courts of Indian Offenses courts organized by the Bureau of Indian Affairs to keep order on Indian reservations and educate the tribes in Anglo-American norms

covenant marriages marriage in which a couple agrees to premarital counseling and must meet certain statutorily-defined conditions to get a divorce

covenants, conditions, and restrictions (CC&Rs) restrict what owners can do with their property

cover process of finding a substitute good

criminalists forensic scientist who analyzes evidence and testifies regarding the results of that analysis

criminal law law covering wrongs done to an individual that result in harm to society as a whole

cross-appeal an appeal by the appellee

cross-claim claim that a defendant brings against another defendant in the same lawsuit

cross-examination examination by opposing counsel

curtilage land around a dwelling

custodial interrogation being questioned while in police custody, i.e., being significantly deprived of one's freedom

custodian of the records someone in an organization who knows about its filing system and records. The custodian is often deposed so that the attorney can find out how the entity keeps its records. Also, many records today are kept electronically rather than on paper, so trying to guess what records a company has is foolhardy

debtor's exam questioning of judgment debtor to determine what assets he or she has; also called a *post-judgment discovery*

decedent deceased person

declarations another term for *affidavit*, which is used to show what a witness's testimony would be

deed document that describes the quality of the title transferred and any restrictions regarding the transfer of the property

deed of trust type of security instrument in which the land is used as collateral in case the borrower defaults; the borrower agrees to convey title to the real property to a trustee, who holds the title in trust on behalf of the lender

deep pocket defendant who may or may not be the primary tortfeasor but who pays all or most of a judgment because of his or her financial status

default judgment judgment entered against the defendant if the defendant fails to appear and respond to the plaintiff's complaint within the time period allowed by the rules and the plaintiff takes steps to obtain a judgment by default

defendant party who is being sued

demand letter letter sent by the plaintiff's attorney to the defendant's attorney or insurance company demanding a specific sum of money in return for a release of plaintiff's claims

demonstrative evidence visual aids used to help the jury understand the facts

denied writs court refused to review the lower court's decision

deponent witness being deposed

deposition notices notification of a pending deposition

depositions taking and recording of oral testimony

descendants blood relative of decedent related in a descending lineal line (e.g., children and grandchildren)

determinate sentence a set sentence determined by the court

deterrence punishment based on the belief that people will not commit crimes if the pain of punishment exceeds the pleasure they derive from committing the crime

devise gift of real property

dicta plural of *dictum* (coming from the Latin phrase *obiter dictum*) gratuitous remarks by the court in a court opinion regarding issues that were not raised by any of the parties

digest(s) summarize (2) set of books arranging cases by subject matter; used to locate cases

directed verdict verdict directed by a judge for the defendant because of the plaintiff's failure to prove one or more elements of her cause of action, or a verdict for the plaintiff because the plaintiff has clearly proven all the elements of her case and the defendant has failed to prove a defense

direct examination examination by an attorney that calls the witness to testify

disaffirms take back one's contractual obligations

discharged extinguish a legal duty

discharge in bankruptcy court order by the bankruptcy court wiping out a judgment debtor's debts

disciplinary rules rules that are mandatory

disclaim deny a warranty

disclosure statement a document each party is required to prepare and serve on opposing parties shortly after a lawsuit commences. This document must contain certain categories of information about that party's case

discovery process by which parties can obtain almost any information pertinent to their dispute, under compulsion of a court order, if necessary (2) process by which parties can obtain information pertinent to their dispute

discretionary within the discretion of the court

dismissed with prejudice judicial dismissal of case that precludes the case from being brought again

disposition practical effect of a court's decision

dissenting opinions opinion written by a judge who disagrees with the majority's conclusion

dissolve change relationships of partners when one partner leaves or dies, generally resulting in termination of partnership

distinguishing differentiate

district court trial court of general jurisdiction at the federal level

diversity of citizenship jurisdiction authority of federal courts to hear civil cases between citizens of different states

dividends distribution of corporate profits

docket put on the office calendars

docket number number assigned by the court clerk to a case

domestic corporations corporation operating in the state of its incorporation

domestic relations law family law

domicile state in which a person is physically present or in which a corporation is incorporated or has as its principal place of business

duress acting involuntarily

easement property interest in the land of another that entitles the owner of the easement to use that land for a specific purpose

easement by necessity easement created when a party is landlocked and needs easement to gain access to public streets

element a specific factor that must be proved in order to win a lawsuit

eminent domain power of government to take private property for public use

enabling statute statute that creates an administrative agency by broadly defining its powers

en banc all of the appellate judges sitting together to hear a case

encumbrances restrictions on the use and sale of real property

entrapment law enforcement inducing someone to commit a crime

entry of judgment day that the judgment is formally entered

equitable based on fairness

equitable distribution dividing of property in accord with the principles of equity (fairness)

equitable title right of the beneficiary to profit or benefit from the trust property

escheat pass to the state

escrow company company that handles the details of property transfer and deed conveyance

estate type of ownership interest

estate at will ownership interest that exists after an estate for years expires, but the grantee continues to live there and the grantor continues to accept payment

estate for years ownership interest that lasts for a designated period of time

estate planning process of arranging one's assets to most effectively protect oneself and one's family during and after life as well as facilitating the smooth transfer of property after death

ethical considerations aspirational comments that assist in interpreting the disciplinary rules

evidence factual information about a dispute presented to a judge or jury

examined question

exclusionary rule prohibition against the prosecution introducing evidence that was obtained in violation of the defendant's constitutional rights

execution seizing of property to pay for a judgment

executor individual responsible for carrying out the directives of a will; a female executor is referred to as an *executrix* in some states

exhausted his administrative remedies conform to the prescribed review procedures set forth by the agency before resorting to a court of law

exigent circumstance emergency

ex parte hearing at which only one side presents evidence

ex parte communications communications with a judge outside the presence of opposing counsel

exculpatory clause clause that releases a party from being liable as a result of his own actions

executor individual responsible for carrying out the directives in the will; a female executor is referred to as an executrix in some states

expert witness witness who, because of experience or training, has acquired special knowledge in a particular field; expert witnesses are allowed to present their opinions at trial whereas lay witnesses are not

express authority actual authority expressed orally or in writing

express easement easement created by a formal document

express warranty warranty in which the seller expressly represents that the goods possess certain qualities

extrinsic evidence evidence outside the contract

federal question jurisdiction authority of federal courts to hear all civil cases arising out of the Constitution, laws, or treaties of the United States

Federal Rules of Civil Procedure procedural rules created by the U.S. Supreme Court that dictate the procedures followed in all federal courts

fee simple best form of ownership interest in which owner is entitled to the entire estate with unconditional rights to dispose of the property and to transfer it upon the owner's death

fee simple conditional ownership interest in which property reverts back to the grantor's ownership if certain conditions are not met

felony crime for which the authorized punishment is a prison sentence of a year or more

fictitious (or assumed) name name adopted by a business that is not its true name

fictitious business name document (also called a dba statement) document filed with an appropriate state agency that protects consumers by allowing them to determine who actually owns a business

fiduciary duty duty to act in good faith, with candor, and in the best interests of the principal

findings of fact and conclusions of law court paper listing each of the factual and legal findings on which a judge's decision is based

First Amendment first amendment to the U.S. Constitution; this amendment protects the freedom of speech, press, and the exercise of religion

fixture property that begins as personal property and becomes so attached to real property that it becomes characterized as real property

foreclosure a legally permitted sale of real property from which proceeds are used to pay a debt

foreign corporations corporation formed in one state and doing business in another

forensic used in court

foreseeable reasonably anticipated (2) something that a person of ordinary caution would expect to occur

form of judgment exact wording of a judgment

forum court in which a lawsuit is filed

foundation background information necessary to prove that a document or physical evidence is authentic

fraudulently intentionally misrepresenting a material fact; also called intentional misrepresentation

Freedom of Information Act federal act requiring federal agencies to make certain records available to the public

freelance paralegals a self-employed paralegal who works as an independent contractor for attorneys on special projects. They are sometimes referred to as *independent paralegals* or *contract paralegals*. Others use the terms *independent paralegal* or *legal technician* to refer to a paralegal who works directly with the public and is not supervised by an attorney

frisk pat-down search of a suspect's clothing if the officer has reasonable suspicion to believe the suspect has committed or is about to commit a crime

gag order court order prohibiting attorneys from discussing a case with the media

Gallagher agreement agreement in which the defendant agrees to guarantee the plaintiff a certain amount of money if the plaintiff loses or recovers less than a designated amount and the plaintiff agrees to refund part of the defendant's payment if the verdict against the defendant is greater than a stated amount

garnishment process by which someone who owes money to the judgment debtor is made to pay it to the judgment creditor

general counsel top legal counsel in a corporate legal office

general damages losses that would naturally be expected to occur in every case based on the same theory of liability

general deterrence preventing the general population from committing crimes

general jurisdiction power of a court to hear all types of civil and criminal cases

general partners partners who are personally liable for any business debts and obligations and are liable for the torts and misconduct of other partners

general partnership business in which two or more persons own all of the assets of the business and share in the decision-making, losses, and profits

general subject matter jurisdiction power of a court to hear all types of cases

general verdict finding for plaintiff or defendant

general verdict with interrogatories finding for plaintiff or defendant and answering of questions about specific facts

general warranty deed deed that warrants that the title to property is free from any encumbrances and that the seller guarantees to defend the buyer's good title forever

grand jury jury that listens to evidence presented by the prosecutor to decide if probable cause exists to bind the defendant over for trial

grantee buyer (transferee) of real property

grantor seller (transferor) of real property

guardian ad litem a person appointed by the court to represent a minor or someone who is incompetent to sue on his or her own behalf

habendum clause clause in a deed indicating what kind of estate is being conveyed

harmless error error by a trial judge that does not affect the outcome of a case

headnote short, numbered paragraph at the beginning of an opinion that summarize points of law discussed by the court

headnote short numbered paragraph preceding an opinion

hearing proceeding in which the judge listens to oral arguments and asks the attorneys questions

hearing examiners term also used in reference to administrative law judges

hearing officers term also used in reference to administrative law judges

hearsay secondhand information used to prove the truth of the matter asserted

hearsay rule rule that hearsay is inadmissible

holding answer to the question raised in the issue

holographic will will that is handwritten by the testator

hornbook books that are devoted to one area of law and that are designed for law students

hostile witness uncooperative witness

hot pursuit police pursuit of a suspect into a private home

hung jury jury unable to reach a verdict

immunity absolute defense derived from a defendant's status (e.g., government official) or relationship to the plaintiff (e.g., spouse of the plaintif0

impeached discredited

implied authority actual authority that naturally flows out of an agent's exercise of his express authority

implied easement easement implied by conduct

incapacitation punishment that incapacitates the offender and prevents him or her from committing future crimes

incidental damages expenses incurred

income beneficiaries beneficiary who receives income from the trust

independent contractor someone who works as his own boss, at his own pace, in his own way, and under his own supervision

independent medical examination (I.M.E.) discovery tool that allows a party to have an opposing party examined by a physician of choice (2) examination of a party by doctors selected by the opposing party

indeterminate sentence sentence that is given as a range of years; the actual length of time served is determined by the correctional institution

indicted grand jury's written accusation that a defendant has committed a crime

indigent lacking adequate financial resources to afford legal representation

indispensable party party without whose presence in a lawsuit a just result cannot be achieved

infer draw a conclusion based on given facts

information charging document issued by a prosecutor accusing the defendant of having committed a crime

initial appearance first appearance of a suspect before a judge at which the suspect is formally charged, counsel is appointed, and bail is set

injunction court order requiring a party to perform a certain act or to stop a particular action

insolvent lacking money or assets

intangible property goods that cannot be touched but that are represented by documents

intensive supervisory probation any probation program that involves close monitoring and more stringent conditions than ordinary probation

intentional misrepresentation affirmatively making a false statement or intentionally concealing a fact from the plaintiff

intentional, reckless, or negligent types of intent. An individual acts intentionally if she intends a particular result. She acts recklessly if she acts with wanton indifference to the consequences of her actions, ignoring a substantial and unjustifiable risk than harm will occur. She acts negligently is she fails to use the care that a reasonable person in those circumstances would use. Intentional conduct is more egregious than reckless conduct, which is more egregious than negligence

intentional torts tort in which the tortfeasor intends or has a desire to bring about a particular consequence

interlocutory appeals appeal taken before a case is over and judgment is entered

interlocutory relief temporary relief; also known as *pendente* lite or nisi relief

internal memorandum informative memo prepared for internal use within a law office; also called an *office memorandum*

interrogatories written questions submitted to opposing parties

intestate dying without a will

intestate succession manner in which a decedent's property will be distributed when no will applies

irrevocable trust that cannot be cancelled or changed

issue lineal descendants

issues of fact issue relating to a factual question in the dispute between parties

issues of law issue relating to the application or interpretation of the law

jointly liable liability of each defendant for the entire loss suffered by the plaintiff

joint and several liability rule by which each defendant, can be held responsible for paying for the entire harm to the plaintiff or some designated portion of the harm as long as the harm cannot be apportioned among the defendants

joint custody allows both parents input into the raising of their children

joint custody shared custody; parents can have joint legal and/or physical custody of children

joint tenants with right of survivorship co-ownership of property in which the parties have an equal, undivided interest in the property with a right of survivorship

joint tortfeasors two or more tortfeasors who act together to produce a single tort

joint ventures a coming together of two or more people or entities to carry out a single enterprise for profit; a joint venture terminates when the enterprise is complete

judgment formal decision by a court

judgment creditor party to whom money was awarded

judgment debtor defendant who loses a lawsuit

judgment lien security interest giving the lienholder the right to sell the property to pay off a judgment

judgment of non-suit termination of an action based on lack of evidence

judgment proof without assets to pay off a judgment

judicial notice agreement by a judge to take note of certain readily verifiable facts without requiring the parties to provide evidence

jurisdiction authority of a court to hear a case

jurisdictional amount amount in controversy in a diversity case; at this point that amount must be $75,000 or more

jurisprudence study of the law and legal philosophy

jury consultant expert in psychology or communications who assists attorneys in selecting jurors that fall within the ideal demographics for the case and sometimes helps assess jurors' reactions during the trial

jury instructions formal instructions to the jury on points of law they will be asked to apply

latent defect hidden defect

law clerk law school student working in a law office

law office administrator someone responsible for the hiring, recruitment, training, and supervision of paralegals and other non-attorney personnel. In some firms those who recruit, hire, train, and supervise paralegals are called *legal assistant managers* or *paralegal coordinators*

lay advocates a layperson who represents individuals at administrative hearings in administrative agencies that permit lay representation

leading questions question that tells the witness what the attorney expects the witness to answer

lease document conveying a leasehold interest in real property; includes the right to possession but not ownership

leasehold estate (nonfreehold estate) uninheritable estate of limited duration; refers to a landlord-tenant relationship

legal custody parent responsible for making decisions regarding a child's welfare

legal secretary secretary whose primary task is the typing of legal documents; this person may also serve as a receptionist in a smaller firm and may perform some of the same tasks as a paralegal, such as keeping track of deadlines, scheduling meetings, preparing subpoenas, and so on

legal technicians a layperson who provides legal services directly to the public. Some use this term to indicate an independent paralegal, that is, someone who is trained to be a paralegal but who works independently

legal title complete and absolute right of ownership

legislative courts specialized federal courts created by Congress

legislative history history behind a statute, including the events that took place before the statute's passage and during its consideration that reflect on its purpose

levy seize

liability responsibility for damages

liberal judicial philosophy allowing judges to go beyond a literal interpretation of statutes and constitutions so that they can protect minorities and the politically disadvantaged

license permission to perform certain acts on another's land

licensure mandatory regulation by the government in which a government agency grants individuals permission to engage in a profession

lien security interest giving the holder of the lien the right to sell the property to pay off a debt. In this case, the hospital would have a right to collect on the judgment Mike gets to pay off his parents' debt to the hospital

lienholder party holding a lien

life estate ownership interest that lasts for the life of holder of the life estate or some other person and then reverts back to the grantor or a third person

limited (or *special warranty deed*) *warranty deed* deed that warrants only that the seller has done nothing to encumber title to the property, but provides no guarantees about the seller's predecessors

limited jurisdiction power of the courts to hear only a narrow range of cases

limited liability corporations (LLCs) hybrid business organization that combines the best features of a corporation with the best features of a partnership

limited liability partnership (LLP) similar to an LLC except that its members are not necessarily protected from all potential personal liability

limited liability partnership partnership form of law practice that limits the liability of partners

limited partners partner who neither manages nor controls the business and whose liability is limited by the amount of his investment

limited partnership business managed by general partners who are liable for all debts and obligations of the business, and that is invested in by limited partners

limited partnership certificate document that must be filed with the secretary of state to create a limited partnership

limited subject matter jurisdiction power of a court to hear only a few specific categories of cases

lineup where a witness picks the suspect out of a group of people

liquidated damages clause clause that fixes the amount of damages in the event of a breach

living (*inter vivos*) trusts trust made while the settlor is still alive

lodge prepare and deliver a judgment

long-arm statute statute that authorizes suits against nonresidents in certain situations

magistrates judge who assists the district court judge by performing certain limited functions

malpractice failure to conform to the reasonable standard of care expected of a professional

mandate order by the court of appeals telling the trial court what to do next

mandatory arbitration arbitration that parties must try before being granted a conventional trial

material breach failure to perform under the terms of a contract to such an extent that the non-breaching party can terminate the contract as well as sue for damages

matter of law disputed legal question, which is usually left for a judge to resolve

mechanic's liens (or construction liens) lien imposed by those who have provided labor or materials for the improvement of real property and who have not been paid

med-arb combination of mediation and arbitration

mediation uses a neutral third party to faciliate communication between disputing parties

mediator a neutral third party who facilitates communication between distributing parties

memorandum document setting forth legal arguments and explaining issues of law

memorandum decision decision that identifies the court's decision or order but offers no explanation

memorandum of points and authorities written legal argument that accompanies a motion

mens rea intent

merchant firm offer merchant's creation of an offer that is irrevocable for a reasonable time period

mini-trial a voluntary proceeding where attorneys prepare as if they were going to trial but then present their cases in an abreviated fashion

minute entry formal communication of a judge's order to the parties; also known as a *minute order*

Miranda warnings warnings an officer must give a suspect who is in custodial interrogation

Mirandized to give Miranda warnings

misdemeanor crime for which the authorized sentence is less than a year in jail

mitigated reduce or avoid by reasonable efforts

Model Penal Code a set of uniform criminal laws proposed by the American Law Institute, parts of which have been adopted by most state's legislatures

mortgagee lender or party holding a mortgage

mortgages type of security instrument in which the real property serves as collateral for the loan being made by the lender to the borrower

mortgagor borrower or party occupying mortgaged land

motion for a new trial request to the court for a new trial (2) motion requesting that the judge grant a new trial based on alleged judicial error

motion for judgment notwithstanding the verdict request that the judge disregard the jury's verdict and enter a verdict in favor of the party who lost at trial

motion for sanctions motion asking the judge to punish a party

motion for summary judgment motion asking the judge to dismiss a case on the grounds that no genuine issues of material fact are raised in the complaint (2) request for judgment in favor of the moving party on the grounds that no genuine issue of fact is in dispute

motion *in limine* motion asking a judge to rule in advance on an admissibility of evidence

motion papers motions, responses, replies, and the accompanying memoranda

motions formal request for a judge to do something

motion to compel motion requesting a judge to order a party to respond to a discovery request

motion to dismiss motion requesting that a judge keep a claim or defense from going forward because it is lacking in merit

motion to set and certificate of readiness form that provides the court with the information necessary to schedule a block of time for a trial

movant party filing a motion

mutual mistake mistake by both parties to a contract; also called a *bilateral mistake*

narrative reports reports prepared by medical doctors

negligence conduct that creates unreasonable risk of harm for another

negligence *per se* presumed negligence; arises from the violation of a statute

neutral expert fact-finding presentation of evidence to a neutral who has expertise in the question at issue

no-fault divorce divorce in which the parties do not have to prove that one party unilaterally broke the marriage bond but only have to show that the marriage is irretrievably broken

nolo contendere plea of no contest to criminal charges

nominal damages damages that are awarded when no actual damages are proved, but a tort is shown to have been committed

non-binding arbitration arbitration in which the arbitrator's decision can be appealed

noncupative oral will

nonprofit (not-for-profit) corporations corporation formed for charitable purposes rather than with the intent of earning a profit that is distributed to its shareholders

notice of independent medical examination court paper directing the person to be examined to appear at a specified doctor's office at a designated date and time

nuisance using one's land in such a way as to interfere with others' use and enjoyment of their land; a nuisance is private if it affects the plaintiff's use of her land and public if it affects a use of land that is common to the public

objection formal challenge made by an attorney when opposing counsel is trying to introduce evidence

objective standard that considers what a reasonable person in the same situation as the defendant would have believed

objective standard standard in which the defendant's actions are compared to those of a hypothetical reasonable person

offeree person who receives an offer

offeror person who makes an offer

office memorandum informative memo prepared for internal use within a law office; also called an *internal memorandum*

official reporter set of books containing cases that are authorized by the court

ombudsman individual hired by an organization to hear disputes and complaints and recommend resolutions

option contract promise by an offeror to keep an offer open for a specified time period

oral arguments verbal presentations made by attorneys to a judge (2) period during which attorneys have an opportunity to explain their arguments and answer any questions the appellate court judges assigned to their case have

order of protection also known as a *protective order* or *temporary restraining order* issued in domestic violence cases

order to show cause hearing hearing at which the defendant must explain why the plaintiff's request for temporary relief is not justified

ordinance law created by city or county agencies

organizational meeting initial meeting at which a corporation is launched

output contract contract in which the seller agrees to sell all of his output to a particular buyer

overrules deny an objection

overturned to change the decision of a lower appellate court

panel group of appellate court judges assigned to a case

paralegal or legal assistants a paraprofessional who is qualified by education, training, or experience to do work of a legal nature under the supervision of an attorney. The terms *paralegal* and *legal assistant* are synonymous; we have chosen to use the word *paralegal* throughout this text for the sake of consistency

parallel cites cite containing reference to both the official and unofficial reporters

parole suspension of prison sentence to assist prisoners in reintegrating back into community

parol evidence earlier oral or written agreement or contemporaneous oral agreement that was not included in a written contract but that was intended to be part of it

par value minimum value for which a stock can be sold

partnership law practice that employs associates and that is managed by partners

per capita distribution of property based on giving equal shares to all those entitled to the estate

***per curiam* opinion** court opinion with no identified author

peremptory challenge removal of a potential juror for no cause

peremptory exception pleading that questions the sufficiency of law in a petition

perfecting means of protecting creditors from claims of third parties

periodic tenancy tenancy with no designated ending date; parties must give proper notice before terminating lease

personal jurisdiction authority of a court to render a decision that will be binding on a party

personal property (chattel) any movable good that is not land or permanently attached to it

personal representative (PR) term used under the UPC to refer to those who administer both intestate and testate estates

personal service locating a defendant and personally handing papers to that person

per stirpes distribution of property that depends on the relationship to the intestate of those entitled to the estate

persuasive authority authority that a court has the option of following or ignoring

petition formal written request to a court asking that something be done

physical custody parent with whom a child lives

plaintiff party who is suing

plea bargain agreement by the defendant to plead guilty in exchange for the prosecutor's dropping or reducing some charges or recommending a lesser sentence to the judge

plurality opinions opinions in which no majority exists

polled asking each juror whether he agreed with the verdict

posting a bond process of paying money and promising to appear later in court in exchange for immediate release from custody

postnuptial agreement agreement in reference to financial and related matters reached while the marriage is harmonious and separation is not being considered

prayer for relief a concluding section of the complaint stating specifically what the plaintiff wants the court to do

preamble introductory paragraph or phrase of a complaint

precedential extent to which a court is controlled by an earlier court's decision

pre-existing conditions condition that existed prior to the plaintiff's being injured by the defendant

preferred stock stock that has special features

preliminary hearing hearing at which the judge determines if the state has shown probable cause to bind the defendant over for trial

preponderance of the evidence evidence showing that it is more probable than not that a given fact occurred (2) standard of proof in civil cases requiring proof that it is more likely than not the defendant committed the wrong alleged by the plaintiff

prescriptive easement easement created when a party uses a landowner's property for a specified time without the owner's consent

presentence report report summarizing the defendant's criminal record, work history, family background, and other factors relevant to sentencing

presumptive sentencing set sentence that can be increased if the judge finds aggravating circumstances or decreased if the judge finds mitigating circumstances

pretrial conference (known as a *scheduling conference* in many jurisdictions) conference between the attorneys and the judge at which the judge specifies what the attorneys can and cannot present at trial (2) conference at which the judge discusses the case with the attorneys and issues a scheduling order, specifying, at least in a general way, what motions will be filed, what discovery will be taken, and setting firm deadlines for the completion of each task

pretrial order similar to a pretrial statement except signed by the judge rather than the attorneys

pretrial statement court paper setting forth the parameters of what the attorneys can and cannot present at trial

prima facie presentation of credible evidence to support each element of a cause of action

primary authority law generated by a government body, such as a cour t legislature, or administrative agency

principal anyone who directs or gives another permission to act on his behalf

private arbitration arbitration based on a contractual agreement

private judging the parties involved agree to have a neutral, usually, a retired judge, hear and decide their case

private nuisance creates an unreasonable interference with the plaintiff's use and enjoyment of her land

private practice law practice in which attorneys work for themselves or other attorneys

private trust trust in which the beneficiaries are named or described in such a way that the trustee can identify them

privately held corporation corporation formed by family or friends in which shareholders agree not to sell shares to anyone "outside" of the corporation before offering them to existing shareholders

probable cause belief based on facts that go beyond reasonable suspicion that a crime has been committed or is about to be committed

probate process proceedings that allow title to the decedent's property to pass to those for whom it was intended

probation release of an offender from custody in exchange for the offender agreeing to meet certain conditions

probation officer individual responsible for supervising offenders to ensure they fulfill the conditions of their probation

pro bono publico an attorney's representation of a client for no fee; means literally "for the good"

procedural law law setting forth the rules that must be followed when working within the legal system

process server an individual who personally serves subpoenas and summonses

professional corporations corporation organized by professionals that allows them to retain the tax benefits of a business corporation (2) corporate form of a law practice that limits non-professional liability of attorneys without limiting their liability for legal malpractice

promissory estoppel   doctrine that allows for the enforcement of a promise to the extent the plaintiff relied on a defendant's promise, if the defendant induced that reliance and should reasonably have expected such reliance

promissory note   promise by one party to pay another

proponent   party preparing interrogatories

propound   submit

pro se   without legal representation

prosecutor   attorney who presents the state's case against criminal defendants; also known as *district attorneys* and *state's attorneys* at the state level and *U.S. attorneys* at the federal level

prospectus   document that describes the investment so that investors can evaluate the potential risks involved in buying the security

Prosser on Torts   shorthand title for the popular treatise *Prosser and Keeton on the Law of Torts*

protective order   same as order of protection

proximate cause   legal cause of the plaintiff's injuries

public defender   attorney paid by the government to represent criminal defendants who qualify for representation because of their financial status

public interest law firms   law firm dedicated to dealing with issues in the public interest, such as environmental and civil rights issues

public nuisance   interferes with a right that is common to the public

public policy   questions of fairness and justice that courts use to guide their decisions

publicly held corporation   corporation that sells its shares to the public at large

punitive damages   damages that punish defendants who have acted with ill-will or in conscious disregard for the welfare of others

QDRO   qualified domestic relations order that assigns some or all of a pension participant's benefits to a former spouse or child to satisfy family support or marital property obligations

quasi-contract   equitable remedy fashioned by the courts when a defendant receives a benefit for which the plaintiff expects to be paid and the defendant would be unjustly enriched if he were allowed to retain the benefit without paying

quitclaim deed   transfers seller's interest in land and contains no warranties of title

released on their own recognance   a defendant's promise in writing to reappear in court at a later date

real estate closing   transfer of documents and monies to complete a real estate transaction

real property   land and anything that is permanently attached to it

rebuttable presumption   a presumption that can be overcome with the presentation of evidence

recidivate   return to prison

Reformation   correct a contract so that it more accurately reflects the intent of the parties

registration statement   document that describes the security being offered, the nature of the issuer's business, the management of the issuer, and any pending litigation against the issuer

rainmaker   attorney who attracts new clients to a firm

rationale   reasoning used by the court

real estate closing   transfer of documents and monies to complete a real estate transaction

reasonable suspicion   a belief based on specific, articulable facts that a person has committed or is about to commit a crime

rebuttal   opportunity for the plaintiff to present arguments that contradict arguments made by the defendant

rebuttable presumption   a presumption that can be overcome with the presentation of evidence

recant   deny having made a statement

recidivate   return to prison

redact   mark out

re-direct examination   examination to repair any damage done during cross-examination

rehabilitation   punishment designed to heal the offender; based on the assumption that people's actions are influenced by factors outside of themselves

released on their own recognizance   a defendant's promise in writing to reappear in court at a later date

relevant   evidence that logically leads to the conclusion that a fact is either more or less probable

remainder beneficiaries   beneficiary who receives the principal of the trust after the rights of the income beneficiaries have been met

remand   when an appellate court sends a case back to the trial court to either change its judgment or redo a trial

remanded   send back to the lower court

remittitur   request that a jury award be reduced by the judge on the grounds that it is unreasonable and excessive

remove   transfer to another court

reply   answer to a counterclaim (2) court paper rebutting the arguments made in the response

reply memorandum   memorandum filed in response to an opposing party's memorandum

reporter   set of books containing reported cases

repudiates   indicate by word or conduct an intent to refuse any further performance

request for admissions   discovery tool used to elicit admissions from opposing parties

request for production of documents   discovery tool used to get documents from opposing parties

requirements contract   contract in which a buyer agrees to buy all of a product that he needs from a particular seller

Rescission   destroy a contract

res ipsa loquitur   doctrine the plaintiff can turn to in proving negligence when it is difficult to obtain information about the defendant's conduct

respondent   party responding to a motion

response   court paper explaining why a judge should not rule as requested in the motion to which the response is responding

rest action taken when a party is finished putting on witnesses

restitution payment by an offender to his or her victim to compensate the victim for the harm caused and losses suffered

restrictive covenant provision in a deed that prohibits specific uses of land

retainer advance received by an attorney from which he or she must pay expenses and from which he or she can collect fees

retribution punishment based on revenge and on the notion that the offender owes a debt to society

reversed when an appellate court changes a trial court's decision

reversible error error by a trial judge that justifies reversal or modification of the trial court's decision

revocable trust that can be cancelled or changed under the express will of the settlor

runner an individual who hand-delivers documents to law firms, agencies, the courts, and other entities

S corporation corporation that avoids the double taxation imposed on other corporations

scope extent of subject matter covered during examination

search warrant court document authorizing the police to search and seize certain items

secondary source finding tool for the law

secured transactions transaction in which the debt is secured by an asset that can be seized upon the debtor's default

securities shares in the enterprise of the issuer or obligations of the issuer

security agreement agreement that describes the collateral and that has been signed by the debtor

security deposits money collected by the landlord in advance to defray cost of repairs when the tenant leaves

security interest interest created when a debtor puts up collateral that the creditor can seize if the debtor defaults

self-proving wills will with a notarized affidavit signed by the testator and witnesses attesting that the testator is of age and sound mind and prepared the will voluntarily

senior partners attorney in a law firm who receives shares of the firm's profits and who participates in the firm's management; a senior partner has seniority in the firm

separate property all property owned prior to marriage and all property acquired during marriage by gift, inheritance, or personal earnings

separation agreement agreement regarding division of property, child support and custody, and other terms of the anticipated separation

serve process physically hand a defendant a complaint and summons

session laws chronologically ordered volumes of laws

settlement agreement agreement reached by parties who have initiated divorce proceedings; this agreement sets forth the rights and obligation of the parties

settlement conference conference involving the judge and the attorneys representing all of the parties at which an attempt is made to resolve the dispute between the litigants

settlement statement a written statement showing where all the funds are being dispersed; also called a *closing* statement

settlor person who creates a trust

shareholders owners of a corporation who are not personally liable for the debts and obligations of the corporation and whose losses are limited to the amount of their investment

shares units in which the ownership interests of a corporation are divided

Shepardize check on the history of a case and how it has been treated by other courts by using a *Shepard's* citator

show cause order order requiring a defendant to appear at a hearing and explain why (show cause) why the relief requested by the plaintiff is not justified

slip laws laws that have recently been enacted and have been published in sheet form

slip opinions form in which a case is originally published

sole custody having both physical and legal custody

sole proprietorship law practice owned by one attorney, who receives the profits

sole proprietorships business owned by one individual who owns all of the assets, who is solely responsible for all of the business's debts, and who is the sole decision-maker

solicitation asking another person to commit a crime (2) inducement by an attorney or an agent of an attorney to hire that attorney

sovereign immunity governmental immunity from suit

special damages particular losses that a client has suffered

special relationship legal relationship between individuals that requires one individual to take steps toward protecting the other. For example, a parent has a duty to protect her child from certain types of harm.

special verdict written findings on particular issues of fact

specific deterrence preventing a specific offender from committing future crimes

specific performance court order that a party perform its contractual obligations; used when monetary damages are inappropriate because no comparable substitute is possible

spendthrift trusts trust in which the settlor provides that only a portion of the trust funds will be allocated to the beneficiary at any one time to safeguard against the beneficiary's unwise or inexperienced spending habits

split custody arrangement in which one parent has legal and physical custody for part of the year and the other parent has custody for the remainder of the year; can also involve splitting the children between the parents

spousal maintenance also known as *spousal support* or *alimony*

spousal maintenance same as alimony

spousal support same as alimony

staff attorneys attorney who reports to general counsel

standard of proof amount of evidence required by law to prevail in a lawsuit

standing a right to make an argument before the Court because one's own constitutional rights have been violated

stare decisis let the decision stand; the doctrine requiring courts to follow case precedent

statement of costs document prepared by the winner of a lawsuit itemizing the costs incurred in the suit

statute law created by a state or federal legislature

statute of limitations statute that requires suit be filled on a particular type of claim within a specified length of time after the claim arises

stay court order prohibiting the judgment creditor from collecting on the judgment

stipulate mutually agree to avoid the need to present arguments

stipulated mutually agree to avoid the need to present arguments

stop temporarily detain a suspect

strict liability imposition of liability without showing of intent or negligence

strike; notice disqualify a judge

subjective standard that considers the actual belief of the defendant

subjective standard standard in which the question is whether the tortfeasor herself believes she acted reasonably

subject matter jurisdiction power of a court to hear cases of a given type

subpoena written court order compelling a person to appear before the court or to produce evidence

substantially performed performance of most but not all of the required duties under a contract

substantive law law setting forth the rights and duties of individuals

summary jury trial only ADR approach that uses an actual jury

summons court order requiring the defendant to appear before the court and defend the suit

supersedeas bond promise by the judgment debtor to pay when the appeal is over, accompanied by some form of security

supplement to amend a disclosure statement to include additional information a party finds out after filing the original disclosure statement

supplemental and amending petition formal request to court modifying the original petition

suppress prevent from being presented as evidence

surrogacy contracts contract in which a woman agrees to conceive and bear a child and to then terminate her parental rights so that the father's wife can adopt the child

sustains uphold an objection

syllabus brief synopsis of an opinion

taking the matter under advisement judge's decision to make a decision regarding the matter before him or her at a later date

tangible property goods that can be seen and touched

taxable court costs expenses related to a lawsuit

tax liens lien imposed by the government for failure to pay taxes in a timely manner

tenancy at sufferance tenancy created when a tenant stays on the land without the landlord's permission

tenancy at will tenancy with no designated ending date; parties need not give notice before terminating the lease

tenancy by the entirety co-ownership of property by a married couple with right of survivorship

tenancy for years (tenancy for a term) tenancy for a designated time period

tenants in common co-ownership of property in which the parties have separate interests with no right of survivorship

testamentary capacity one's ability to know what one owns, what one desires to be done with what one owns, and the identity of family members and others for whom one has affection

testamentary trusts trust that goes into effect when the settlor dies

testator person making a will

testatrix female making a will (term used in some states)

third party an individual or entity not a party to the lawsuit

third-party claim claim against someone who is not already a plaintiff or defendant in the suit

third-party defendant party defending against a third-party claim

third-party plaintiff party bringing a third-party claim

title company company that issues title reports and title insurance policies

title examination same as title search

title insurance insurance of someone with an interest in real property against any losses caused by encumbrances or defective title

title search search of public records to determine if the title to real property is free from any encumbrances that would reduce the value of the property or threaten foreclosure against it

tortfeasors person who has committed a tort, which is a private wrong resulting in injury to one or more persons

tort law also known as *personal injury law,* tort law involves the compensation of those who have been victims of private wrongs

Totten trusts also called a P.O.D. (payable on death) account; a savings account in which the money is deposited in the depositor's name as trustee for the beneficiary

transactional causes of action that arise out of the same factual setting

transcript typed or printed booklet in which the questions and answers are reproduced, word for word

transformative mediation less directive form of mediation in which parties are encouraged to speak freely until finished; no expectation of settlement exists

treatise volume devoted to one area of law, which is usually examined in depth

trial court first level of the court system in which trials are heard

trial *de novo* may be requested if either party is dissatisfied with the arbitrators awarded

trial notebook indexed compilation of the most important documents and resources that an attorney needs to access during trial

trial setting minute entry specifying a date, time, and place for trial

tribal court advocate a non-attorney who is allowed to represent individuals before the tribal court

TRO *temporary restraining order* temporary order by a court for a party to do something or to stop doing something

trustee party that holds title to real property in trust for a lender (2) entity who manages and administers a trust

trustee's sale public auction at which land used as collateral for deed of trust is sold to pay a debt

trustor borrower or party occupying land serving as security for a deed of trust

UCC-1 financing statement (also called a *financing statement*) document that identifies the debtor, creditor, and the debtor's collateral

under advisement judge's declaration that he will issue a decision later, after having time to consider a matter; sometimes referred to as under submission

under the rule court order that witnesses leave the courtroom and not discuss the case with anyone; also called *sequestering of witnesses*

undue influence one of the parties to a relationship based on trust and dependency misusing that trust to influence the actions of the other (2) acting under another's direction rather than out of free will and choice

uniform or **patterned instructions** recommended jury instructions that have been used successfully in previous trials

unilateral contract offer that is to be accepted by performance

unilateral mistake mistake by one party to a contract

unofficial reporter set of books containing cases that are published by private companies

venue limitation on place of suit based on convenience

vicarious liability liability for the torts of another. Employers, for example, are vicariously liable for the torts of their employees

void contract that is invalid on its face

voidable contract that will be deemed invalid by a court based on evidence of its defectiveness

voir dire questioning of prospective jurors

voluntary arbitration arbitration that parties use by choice as a means of attempting to resolve their dispute

warranty of fitness for a particular purpose warranty created when a seller who knows that a buyer wants goods for a particular purpose makes a recommendation on which the buyer relies

warranty of merchantability warranty that is implied when the seller is a merchant in the regular business of selling the kind of goods in question

Westlaw; LEXIS/NEXIS two of the most commonly used online databases for legal research

West numbering system numbering system used by West by which legal issues are organized alphabetically by topic and numerically by subtopic

will document expressing the decedent's will as to how his property should be distributed

work furlough program that allows offenders to work during the day and serve time on the weekends or evenings only

work product documents prepared by an attorney in anticipation of litigation or for trial; such documents are protected from being discovered by opposing counsel

writ of certiorari written request asking an appellate court to review a lower court's decision

writ of execution court order directing the sheriff to seize property and sell it at public auction

writ of garnishment court order directing person who owes money to the judgment debtor to pay it to the judgment creditor

zoning government regulations designed to control land use

Index

AAA. *See* American Arbitration
  Association
AAfPE. *See* American Association for
  Paralegal Education
Abate, 662
Abode service, 245
Acceptance, 530–531
Accessibility of legal services, 214–215
Actual authority, 576
Actual cause, 93
Actus reus, 435, 437–438
Additur, 378
Adhesion contract, 546
Adjudicatory hearings, 504–505
Administrative agencies, 500–503
  examples, 501
  functions, 500
  limitations, 502–503
  power, 501–502
  process, 507–508
Administrative decisions, 500
Administrative law, 4, 500
  investigative action, 512
  paralegal role, 513–514
  publication, 511
  research, 509–511
Administrative law judges, 504
Administrative Procedure Act, 502
Administrator, law office, 30
Admission, requests for, 276, 296–298
Admission to the bar, 458
Adoption, 630–631
ADR. *See* Alternative Dispute
  Resolution
Advance sheets, 125
Adverse possession, 658
Advocacy memorandum, 187
Affiant, 338
Affidavit of service, 245
Affirmative defenses, 253
Agency law, 575–577
Agent for service of process, 566
Alimony, 607–608
ALJ. *See* Administrative law judges
Allegations, 134, 232
A.L.R. *See American Law Reports* (A.L.R.)

Alternative dispute resolution
  advantages, 488–489
  arbitration (*See* Arbitration)
  disadvantages, 488–489
  med-arb (*See* Med-arb)
  mediation (*See* Mediation)
  mini-trial (*See* Mini-trial)
  quality control, 490
  summary jury trial (*See* Summary jury
    trial)
"Ambulance chasing," 39
American Arbitration Association, 476
American Association for Paralegal
    Education, formation of, 16
American Digest System, 158, 161
American Jurisprudence, 155
American Law Reports (A.L.R.), 167,
    170
American Lawyer, 20
Amici, 141
Amicus Attorney, 263
Analysis, legal, 177–179
Annulled, 599
Antenuptial agreement, 600–601
APA. *See* Administrative Procedure Act
Apparent authority, 576
Appeals
  application, 388
  briefs, submission of, 389, 390
  certify, 389
  cross-appeal, 389
  grounds for reversal, 388–389
  harmless error, 388
  interlocutory appeals, 389
  mandate, issuance of, 392
  notice of appeal, filing, 389
  panel, assignment to, 391
  process, 389, 391–392
  reversible error, 388
Appellate court
  adherence to statutes and constitutions,
    176
  constraints, 176
  distinguishing cases, 176
  issues of fact, 175
  issues of law, 175

  limitations, 175–177
  stare decisis, 176
Arbitration
  application, 475
  arbitrator, 475
  binding, 475
  court-annexed, 476
  definition, 213, 475
  forms, 475–476
  mandatory, 475
  non-binding, 475
  paralegal role, 477–478
  private, 476
  process, 477
  trial *de novo,* 476
  voluntary, 475
Arbitrator, 475
Arraignment, 421–422
Arrest and search warrants, 407–410
Arson, 439
Articles of incorporation, 569
Ascendants, 673
Assault, 95, 438
Assigned counsel, 425
Associates, 33
Associations, paralegal, 14–15
Assumption of risk, 254
Attach, 573
Attempt, 437
Attorney-client privilege, 60–61, 568
Authentication of evidence, 89
Auto-Cite, 166
Automatic stay, 261

Bad faith, 547
Bail, setting of, 419
Bankruptcy, 4, 260, 386–387, 574
Bates v. State Bar of Arizona, 39
Battery, 95
Bench, 224
Beneficiaries, 674
Beyond a reasonable doubt, 57
Bilateral contract, 529
Bilateral mistake, 548
Billing software, 263
Binding, 475